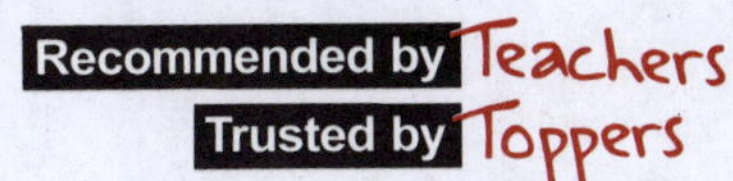

English Language & Literature

CBSE Class 10

Reading, Writing, Grammar & Literature | Review Exercises | Sample Papers & Board Papers

Authors
Parneet Kaur
Neha Vats

ARIHANT PRAKASHAN

(School Division Series)

卐 ADMINISTRATIVE & PRODUCTION OFFICES

Regd. Office

'Ramchhaya' 4577/15, Agarwal Road, Darya Ganj, New Delhi -110002
Tele: 011- 47630600, 43518550; Fax: 011- 23280316

卐 *Head Office*

Kalindi, TP Nagar, Meerut (UP) - 250002, Tel: 0121-7156203, 7156204

卐 SALES & SUPPORT OFFICES

Agra, Ahmedabad, Bengaluru, Bareilly, Chennai, Delhi, Guwahati, Hyderabad, Jaipur, Jhansi, Kolkata, Lucknow, Nagpur & Pune.

PO No. : TXT-59-T064291-04-25

Published By Arihant Publications (India) Ltd.

For further information about the books published by Arihant, log on to www.arihantbooks.com or e-mail at info@arihantbooks.com

Follow us on   

卐 PRICE ₹595.00

PRODUCTION TEAM

Publishing Managers	*Cover Designer*	*Inner Designer*
Mahendra Singh Rawat & Keshav Mohan	Rakesh Rawat	Ankit Tyagi
Project Head	*Page Layouting*	*Proof Readers*
Manju	Lalit Chaprana	Harsh Agarwal, Naina Rajya

Index *cum* Study Planner

One Book- Endless Features
to Help you Succeed

Chapter Summary

In each chapter of the Prose, Poetry & Supplementary, Summary of the chapter & Explanation is given in simple and easy to understand language. It will help the students to understand theme of the chapter easily.

CHAPTER 1

A Letter to God

by G L Fuentes

CHAPTER SUMMARY The following chapter 'A Letter to God' has been written by G L Fuentes. This chapter discusses the firm faith of a farmer called Lencho in God. When Lencho's crops are destroyed in the hailstorm and his whole family faces the prospect of going hungry, Lencho writes a letter to God asking for help. The story presents how Lencho is helped by the Postmaster who does not want to break Lencho's faith in God.

Word Meaning

In each chapter of the Prose, Poetry and Supplementary, difficult words are given along with their meaning. This will help students to understand difficult words easily.

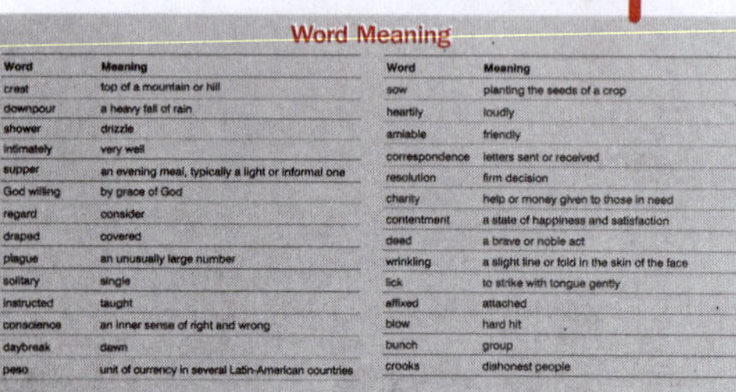

Word Meaning

Word	Meaning	Word	Meaning
crest	top of a mountain or hill	sow	planting the seeds of a crop
downpour	a heavy fall of rain	heartily	loudly
shower	drizzle	amiable	friendly
intimately	very well	correspondence	letters sent or received
supper	an evening meal, typically a light or informal one	resolution	firm decision
God willing	by grace of God	charity	help or money given to those in need
regard	consider	contentment	a state of happiness and satisfaction
draped	covered	deed	a brave or noble act
plague	an unusually large number	wrinkling	a slight line or fold in the skin of the face
solitary	single	lick	to strike with tongue gently
instructed	taught	affixed	attached
conscience	an inner sense of right and wrong	blow	hard hit
daybreak	dawn	bunch	group
peso	unit of currency in several Latin-American countries	crooks	dishonest people

Format of a Formal Letter

You are Nehal Kumar, Head of the Computer Club in Sunshine School, Noida. Digital literacy refers to someone's ability to use digital technology to find, evaluate, create and communicate information. You believe that digital literacy and navigating the digital world responsibly is crucial in today's technology-dependent age.

Write a letter to the Editor of a national daily, in about 120 words, stressing the need for promoting digital literacy among individuals of all age groups. Discuss the benefits and challenges of digital technology, and propose initiatives to empower people with digital skills. **CBSE Additional SQP 2023-24**

Sender's address: Sunshine School
Noida

Date: 31st September, 20XX

Receiver's address: The Editor
The Times
New Delhi

Subject of the letter: **Subject** Digital Literacy is the Need of the Hour

Salutation: Sir/Ma'am

Body of the letter:

Through the columns of your esteemed newspaper, I would like to highlight the crucial importance of digital literacy in today's technology-dependent age. As the Head of the Computer Club at my school, I firmly believe that digital literacy is a skill that can help every individual find a place in a rapidly changing world.

Digital literacy refers to someone's ability to use digital technology to find, evaluate, create and communicate information. In the time wherein technology and the internet have made the world smaller than ever, digital literacy and being skilled in the digital world responsibly is crucial. With various challenges like cyber security, misinformation, and online privacy, digital literacy is essential to help people use the digital world safely and responsibly. It helps in enhancing communication, creating access to resources, and equipping everyone to participate in a digital society.

To promote digital literacy, initiatives such as community workshops for a variety of age groups, and collaborations between educational institutions and technology companies can be established. By focusing on digital literacy, we can empower individuals to successfully utilise the full potential of technology.

Complementary Close: Thanking You

Sender's Name, Signature and Designation: Yours truly
Nehal Kumar
(Head of the Computer Club, Sunshine School, Noida)

Formats in Writing Section

In Writing section standard format has been given. This will help students to learn proper format of each writing task.

One Book- Endless Features

to Help you Succeed

Here, we have covered questions of CBSE Textbook (Intext & Exercise) with their detailed answer in simple and easy language.

Assessment Exercise

At the end of the chapter, there are unsolved questions for practice and assessment of students. By practising these questions, students can assess their preparation level for the chapter.

Review Exercise

Each chapter cover all types of questions like Extract Based Questions, Short Answer & Long Answer Type Questions.

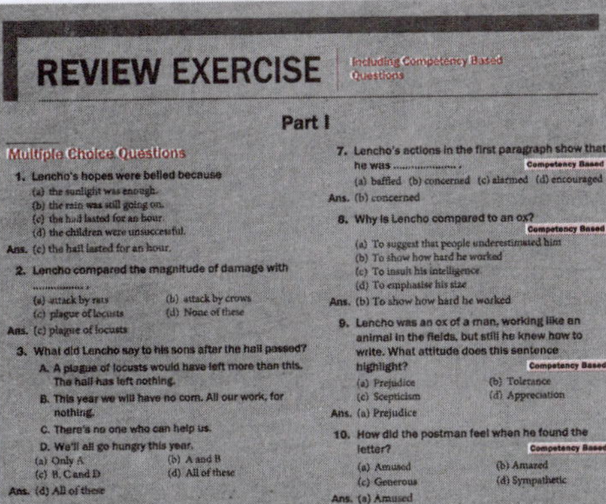

REVIEW EXERCISE | Including Competency Based Questions

Part I

Multiple Choice Questions

1. Lencho's hopes were belied because
   (a) the sunlight was enough.
   (b) the rain was still going on.
   (c) the hail lasted for an hour.
   (d) the children were unsuccessful.

Ans. (c) the hail lasted for an hour.

2. Lencho compared the magnitude of damage with ……………… .
   (a) attack by rats (b) attack by crows
   (c) plague of locusts (d) None of these

Ans. (c) plague of locusts

3. What did Lencho say to his sons after the hail passed?
   A. A plague of locusts would have left more than this. The hail has left nothing.
   B. This year we will have no corn. All our work, for nothing.
   C. There's no one who can help us.
   D. We'll all go hungry this year.
   (a) Only A (b) A and B
   (c) B, C and D (d) All of these

Ans. (d) All of these

7. Lencho's actions in the first paragraph show that he was ……………… . Competency Based
   (a) baffled (b) concerned (c) alarmed (d) encouraged

Ans. (b) concerned

8. Why is Lencho compared to an ox? Competency Based
   (a) To suggest that people underestimated him
   (b) To show how hard he worked
   (c) To insult his intelligence
   (d) To emphasise his size

Ans. (b) To show how hard he worked

9. Lencho was an ox of a man, working like an animal in the fields, but still he knew how to write. What attitude does this sentence highlight? Competency Based
   (a) Prejudice (b) Tolerance
   (c) Scepticism (d) Appreciation

Ans. (a) Prejudice

10. How did the postman feel when he found the letter? Competency Based
    (a) Amused (b) Amazed
    (c) Generous (d) Sympathetic

Ans. (a) Amused

Latest Course *Structure*

Section-wise Weightage

Sections			Weightage
A	Reading Skills	40 (Periods)*	20 Marks
B	Writing Skills with Grammar	40 (Periods)*	20 Marks
C	Literature Textbooks and Supplementary Reading Text	50 (Periods)*	40 Marks

Section A

Reading Skills

20 Marks

Reading Comprehension through Unseen Passage

i. Discursive passage of 400-450 words. *(10 marks)*

ii. Case-based passage (with visual input- statistical data, chart etc.) of 200-250 words. *(10 marks)*

(Total length of two passages to be 600-700 words)

Multiple Choice Questions / Objective Type Questions, and Short Answer Questions (to be answered in 30-40 words) will be asked to assess comprehension, interpretation, analysis, inference, evaluation and vocabulary.

Section B

II. Grammar

10 Marks

- Determiners
- Tenses
- Modals
- Subject – verb concord
- Reported speech
  - Commands and Requests
  - Statements
  - Questions

3. The courses at the secondary level seek to cement high professional grasp of grammatical items and levels of accuracy. Accurate use of spelling, punctuation and grammar in context will be assessed through Gap Filling/ Editing/Transformation exercises. Ten out of 12 questions will be attempted.

III Writing Skills **10 Marks**

4. Writing a Formal letter base on a given situation in 100-120 words. One out of two questions is to be answered. *5 marks*
5. Writing an Analytical Paragraph (100-120 words) on a given Map/Chart/Graph/Cue/s. One out of two questions is to be answered. *5 marks*

Section C **40 Marks**

Language through Literature

IV. Reference to the Context **(5+5 = 10 Marks)**

6. One extract out of two from Drama / Prose.
7. One extract out of two from poetry.
   Multiple Choice Questions / Objective Type Questions Very Short Answer Questions (one word/ One sentence), Short Answer Questions (to be answered in 30-40 words) will be asked to assess inference, analysis, interpretation, evaluation and vocabulary.

V. Short & Long Answer Questions **30 Marks**

8. Four out of Five Short Answer Type Questions to be answered in 40-50 words from the book FIRST FLIGHT to assess interpretation, analysis, inference and evaluation. . 4x3=12 marks
9. Two out of Three Short Answer Type Questions to be answered in 40-50 words each from FOOTPRINTS WITHOUT FEET to assess interpretation, analysis, inference and evaluation.
   2x3=6 marks
10 One out of two Long Answer Type Questions from FIRST FLIGHT to be answered in about 100-120 words each to assess creativity, imagination and extrapolation beyond the text and across the text. This can be a passage-based question taken from a situation/plot from the text. 6 marks
11. One out of two Long Answer Type Questions from FOOTPRINTS WITHOUT FEET, on theme or plot involving interpretation, extrapolation beyond the text and inference or character sketch to be answered in about 100-120 words. 6 marks

Prescribed Books: Published by NCERT, New Delhi

FIRST FLIGHT

A. Prose

1. A Letter to God
2. Nelson Mandela - Long Walk to Freedom
3. Two Stories About Flying
4. From the Diary of Anne Frank
5. Glimpses of India
6. Mijbil the Otter
7. Madam Rides the Bus
8. The Sermon at Benares
9. The Proposal (Play)

B. Poems

1. Dust of Snow
2. Fire and Ice
3. A Tiger in the Zoo
4. How to Tell Wild Animals
5. The Ball Poem
6. Amanda!
7. The Trees
8. Fog
9. The Tale of Custard the Dragon
10. For Anne Gregory

2. FOOTPRINTS WITHOUT FEET

1. A Triumph of Surgery
2. The Thief's Story
3. The Midnight Visitor
4. A Question of Trust
5. Footprints Without Feet
6. The Making of a Scientist
7. The Necklace
8. Bholi
9. The Book that Saved the Earth

Reading Comprehension

Let's REVISE Reading comprehension is the ability of deriving meaning from the given data which can be a paragraph, essay, poetry, charts, posters, diagrams, etc. The main objective of reading a passage is to gain an overall understanding of what is described in the text.

For Class X, CBSE includes two types of texts for evaluating comprehension skills. These passages are

(i) **Discursive Passage** (400–450 words) A discursive passage includes the opinions of a person which are generally argumentative, persuasive and interpretative. It allows students to arrive at a conclusion through reasoning and understanding rather than intuition.

(ii) **Case Based Factual Passage** (200–250 words) A case based factual passage is composed of information in a direct manner about a particular subject. It also contains visual and verbal inputs such as graphs, charts, pie-charts, etc. Such a passage focuses completely on details or facts.

Steps to Attempt Reading Comprehension Questions

- Read each and every line of the passage carefully. Reading the passage twice helps in better understanding of the passage and makes it easier for the students to find answers.
- If the title of the passage is given, read it first as it gives the central idea of the passage.
- Underline the difficult words while reading the passage.
- Always give emphasis on the beginning and end as these parts often hold the most important information of the passage.
- While answering, be sure that you've clearly understood the question. The answer must be relevant to the question.

SOLVED EXAMPLES

Discursive Passage

Read the following passages carefully given below.

PASSAGE 1

1. Fossil fuels (oil, coal and natural gas) are our most traditional sources for power generation. The energy that's produced from any source other than fossil fuels is termed as alternative energy. Between the two sources, using alternative energy has a lower environmental impact.

2. We now know that alternative energy sources are the sources we use to supplement or even replace traditional energy sources used for power generation. You could almost say the same thing about renewable energy sources. But there is one subtle difference between the two. All renewable energy sources fall under the category of alternative energy sources, but it doesn't work the other way around.

3. That's because renewable energy sources are derived from naturally replenished sources or processes of Earth, such as the Sun, wind and water. We refer to these resources as renewable or sustainable since, unlike fossil fuels, this naturally occurring continual renewal makes them inexhaustible. However, alternative energy sources are exhaustible, and therefore not renewable. That's the difference.

4. The equipment necessary to harness energy from alternative sources used to be so expensive that it wasn't practical for consumer use. However, thanks to increase demand, more experienced energy developers, competitive supply chains, improved renewable technologies and enhanced energy efficiency capabilities, that's no longer the case.
5. When it comes to energy efficiency, the leader of the renewable energy pack is wind energy. Behind wind comes geothermal energy, hydropower, nuclear energy, and then solar power. Wind power serves both individuals and entire communities. It is versatile, and can be produced from small - scale windmills or wind turbines on residential properties. It can also be produced from large - scale offshore wind farms in the ocean.
6. We generate geothermal power by tapping into underground reservoirs of hot water and steam. Geothermal electricity can directly heat and cool buildings. Generated from the energy of moving water, hydroelectricity (also know as hydropower) is produced when water behind a dam causes turbine blades to move as it flows through as intake. The turbine blades then rotate a generator to produce electricity that is sent to power homes.
7. Nuclear energy is created in the form of heat through the fission process of atoms. The initial fission process creates energy and triggers a chain reaction that repeats the process and generates more energy. In nuclear power plants, the heat, that fission produces creates steam. The stem then rotates a turbine, which leads to the production of electricity.
8. Solar power most commonly refers to the use of solar cells to create energy. On a small scale, you may see a few solar panels on a house roof used to produce energy for just that one home. On a larger scale, you may see a solar farm used as a power plant to produce electricity for its consumers. **CBSE 2024**

Questions

Based on your understanding of the passage, answer the following questions.

1. Which of the following statements best describes the difference between renewable energy sources and alternate energy sources?

(a) Alternative energy sources are more expensive than renewable energy sources.
(b) Renewable energy sources are inexhaustible whereas alternate energy sources could be exhaustible.
(c) Alternative energy sources are as renewable as renewable energy sources.
(d) Renewable energy sources are exhaustible but alternative energy sources are inexhaustible.

2. What is the tone of the writer in the given lines from paragraph 4? **Competency Based**
Rationalise your response-in about 40 words.
"However, thanks to increased demand, more experienced energy developers, competitive supply chains, improved renewable technologies, and enhanced energy efficiency capabilities, that's no longer the case."

3. Complete the sentence appropriately.
In the past, alternative energy sources were not used much by the consumers because ....

4. The passage includes some words that are opposite of each other. From the sets (a) - (e) below, identify two sets of antonyms.

(a) Generate and produce
(b) Exhaustible and inexhaustible
(c) Subtle and versatile
(d) Power and energy
(e) Sustainable and exhaustible

5. Who is the leader of renewable energy pack and why?

6. Based on the reading of the passage, examine, in about 40 words, the difference between geothermal electricity and hydroelectricity.

7. What is the message conveyed by the passage?

(a) Only those energy sources should be used which are renewable.
(b) Wind energy is a renewable as well as inexhaustible source of energy.
(c) There are plenty of renewable energy sources that can be used to replace traditional energy sources.
(d) Alternative energy sources are the emerging energy trends and are still evolving.

8. State whether the following statement is True or False with reference to the given extract.
Hydroelectricity as a renewable energy source is used for residential as well as commercial purposes.

Answers

1. (b) Renewable energy sources are inexhaustible whereas alternate energy sources could be exhaustible.
2. The tone of the writer in the given lines is optimistic and informative. The writer here tells us how due to increased demands, there has been an increase in more experienced energy developers and competitive supply chains. This has improved renewable technologies along with enhanced energy efficiency and affordability. This suggests a hope and progress for better and more viable energy alternatives.

3. the equipment required to harness energy from alternative fuels were not as accessible or cost-effective as traditional energy sources.
4. (b) Exhaustible and inexhaustible

   (e) Sustainable and exhaustible
5. Wind energy is the leader of the renewable energy pack due to its energy efficiency. It can serve both individuals and entire communities, and can be produced using different scales of equipment, from small-scale windmills or wind turbines on residential properties to large-scale offshore wind farms in the ocean.
6. Geothermal electricity is generated by tapping into underground reservoirs of hot water and steam, which can directly heat and cool buildings. In other words, it harnesses heat from the Earth's interior.

   Hydroelectricity, on the other hand, is generated using the energy of moving water, typically from a dam, to rotate a turbine and produce electricity. Geothermal energy relies on subsurface heat, while hydroelectricity depends on water flow above ground.
7. (c) There are plenty of renewable energy sources that can be used to replace traditional energy sources.
8. False. According to the last paragraph, solar energy is a renewable energy source used for residential as well as commercial purposes.

PASSAGE 2

1. The invention of the safety bicycle in the late nineteenth century transformed the world of cycling. While early versions of bicycles had been used in Europe since the seventeenth century, it was the safety bicycle with its lightweight hollow steel frame and equal-sized wheels that revolutionised the cycling experience.
2. This resulted in enhanced mobility for both men and women, allowing them to explore the countryside freely and travel between towns. Bicycles symbolised freedom, particularly for women, granting them self-reliable transportation and the ability to participate in recreational activities, like bicycle racing. The rise of bicycles also brought a shift in fashion, with more functional and relaxed clothing tailored specifically for cycling.
3. Bicyclists also became a political force. They played a significant role in the development of road maps, guiding riders along the best routes. They campaigned for better infrastructure to enhance their riding experiences.
4. Today, advances in technology, wearables and complex data analysis have transformed sports science, particularly in endurance sports, like cycling. Cyclists can now gather vast amounts of data simply by using mobile apps to track their activities.

   This data not only encompasses exercise details, like its volume or intensity, but also external factors like the impact of weather on the physiological response of the athlete. Furthermore, technology has made it very easy to monitor performance-influencing data outside of training, such as heart rate or sleep quality, through various wearables and cost-effective mobile apps.
5. However, just because we are able to monitor so much information does not mean that it is useful for improving the sports performance of our athletes.

   In this sense, we believe that we must be critical while adopting any new technologies or trends in training. The first thing we should know is whether there is scientific support for the use of that new gadget or wearable. For example, core temperature is of great importance in the mechanisms that produce fatigue and exhaustion in endurance sports. A few years ago, a device came on the market that estimated this measurement in a non-invasive way and we saw many top cyclists and runners wearing it. However, a study later showed it is an invalid device for measuring one's temperature.
6. Innovation in cycling has evolved from the invention of safety bicycles to technological advancements in sports science. Maximising the potential benefits of these developments requires critical thinking to enhance the training and performance of modern cyclists. **CBSE Additional SQP 2023 Modified**

Questions

Based on your understanding of the passage, answer the following questions.

1. It can be said the world of cycling has seen massive changes. Elaborate
2. Complete the following with the correct option from the two given.

   The passage is about ....
   (a) What were the primary societal changes brought about by the rise of bicycles?
   (b) How did the invention of the safety bicycle contribute to the development of wearable technology?
3. Imagine you are a sports scientist tasked with developing a new technological tool to aid cyclists in their training.

   Provide a brief description, within 40 words, of its specific features and why you chose to include them. **Competency Based**

4. Below are statements from cyclists. Identify two statements that could be said by a cyclist in the late nineteenth century.

1. "I like having a personal coach on my wrist. It just told me how many calories I have burned so far!"
2. "It's quite a struggle riding up these steep hills on my heavy steel-framed bicycle."
3. "I feel so liberated whenever I hop on my bicycle. I didn't have freedom like this before!"
4. "Ugh, there is so much traffic ahead. And I feel so pressured to meet my performance targets every time I hop on a bike."

5. State whether the following statement is True or False.

Cyclists were able to improve the accuracy of maps.

6. Which of these is opposite to 'invalid' as used in paragraph 5?

(a) Ethical (b) Accurate
(c) Authentic (d) Trustworthy

7. List any two points that indicate that bicycles can be seen as a symbol of empowerment.

8. In which sentence does the author express uncertainty about the use of new technologies in training? **Competency Based**

(a) '...advances in technology have transformed sports science.' (Paragraph 4)
(b) 'This data not only encompasses exercise details but also external factors like weather.' (Paragraph 4)
(c) '...just because we can monitor so much information does not mean it is useful.' (Paragraph 5)
(d) 'Maximising the potential benefits of these developments requires critical thinking.' (Paragraph 6)

Answers

1. It can be said that the world of cycling has been massive changes. This is so because of the development of safety bicycle with its lightweight hollow steel frame or equal-sized wheels of advances in technology, wearables and complex data analysis.
2. (b) How did the invention of the safety bicycle contribute to the development of wearable technology?
3. As a sports scientist tasked with developing a new technological tool to aid cyclists in their training, I would try to develop a tool that not only tracks their activities including exercise details like its volume or intensity but also records their physiological responses like heart rate and temperature accurately.
4. (2) "It's quite a struggle riding up these steep hills on my heavy steel-framed bicycle."
   (3) "I feel so liberated whenever I hop on my bicycle. I didn't have freedom like this before!"
5. True
6. (b) Accurate
7. Bicycles can be seen as symbols of empowerment because it enhanced mobility for both men and women, allowing them to explore the countryside freely and travel between towns. It symbolised freedom, particularly for women, granting them self-reliable transportation and the ability to participate in recreational activities.
8. (c) "...just because we can monitor so much information does not mean it is useful." (Paragraph 5)

Case Based Factual Passages

Read the following passages carefully given below.

PASSAGE 1

10m "Scouts and Guides Around the World"

1. Many young people aged between 6 and 25 belong to the Scout movement. It is a worldwide organisation, which was set up to help young people achieve their full potential as they grow up.
2. The organisation was established in 1907, by a British general called Robert Baden-Powell. While in the army, he wrote a publication about scouting (which means searching and keeping watch) and how to survive in the wild, called 'Aids to Scouting'.
   He realised how popular this was, and the result was another book, 'Scouting for Boys', which had a less emphasis on the military. To test his ideas, he held a week-long camp for 21 boys from various schools in London, Poole and Bournemouth. This took place in August 1907, on Brownsea Island, in Southern England. These boys had the chance to enjoy outdoors, which became another of the movement's objectives.
3. The Scout Movement quickly got established in Europe. It, then, spread throughout the world, starting in Chile in 1909. To begin with, the focus was on boys aged 11 to 18. However, as the movement grew, it was clear that younger boys, older boys and girls all wanted to be involved too. Baden-Powell's sister set up the Girl Guides in 1910, and in 1914 she started Rosebuds, later renamed Brownies, for younger girls. The movement's intention to help young people play useful roles in society applies equally to girls and boys. By 2010, there were 32 million scouts, and by 2006, there were 10 million guides around the world, from a total of 216 different countries.

4. 2007 marked 100 years of the Scout Movement, and events took place around the world to celebrate this centenary. To mark the occasion, a colourful badge was produced for scouts to sew onto their uniforms or bags. The design included the official scout emblem, as well as the phrase, 'one world one promise', and images of doves and the globe.
5. 2007 was also the 150th anniversary of Baden - Powell's birth. To honour both occasions, a flame was lit at Baden - Powell's grave in Nyeri. This is the place in Kenya where he spent the last few years of his life. The flame was then carried through several countries until it reached the UK.

Country	Membership	Population Participation	Scouting Introduced	Guiding introduced
India	41500000	0.3%	1909	1911
Indonesia	17100000	7.2%	1912	1912
Philippines	21500000	2.2%	1910	1918
Thailand	1300000	1.9%	1911	1957
United States	7500000	2.4%	1910	1912

CBSE 2024

Questions

Based on your understanding of the passage, answer the following questions.

1. Infer one reason for the following, based on the information given in paragraph 4.
   'Colourful badge was sewn onto the uniform and bags of the Scouts'.
2. From paragraph 1, we can infer that Scout Movement was set up ....
3. Complete the following analogy correctly with a word/phrase from paragraph 4.
   10 years : Decade : : 100 years : ....
4. After reading the passage, bring a contrast between the books 'Aids to Scouting' and 'Scouting for Boys'.
5. What does the writer mean by the following phrase?
   'One world one promise'.
6. According to the chart, which country took maximum time to introduce 'Guiding' after 'Scouting'? Choose your answer from the options given below.
   (a) India (b) Indonesia
   (b) Thailand (d) Philippines
7. List two reasons why a flame was lit at Baden-Powell's grave in 2007.
   (a) .... (b) ....
8. Fill in the blank by selecting the correct option.
   The establishment of Scout movement from 1907 to 2006 showed .... results.
   (a) uniform
   (b) encouraging
   (c) inconsistent
   (d) disappointing

Answers

1. One reason for the colorful badges to be sewn on to the uniform could be to commemorate and celebrate the 100th anniversary of the Scout Movement. The colourful badge was a symbolic way to mark this significant milestone.
2. to help young people aged between 6 and 25 achieve their full potential as they grow up
3. Century
4. 'Aids to Scouting' written by Robert Baden-Powell during his time in the army, focused on scouting in the context of war, specifically on searching and keeping watch, as well as survival in the wild. In contrast, 'Scouting for Boys' had less emphasis on the military aspect. Instead, it was geared more towards the broader idea of scouting, encapsulating outdoor activities. Further, it became the foundation for the Scout movement.
5. The phrase 'one world one promise' signifies unity and shared commitment among the worldwide Scout community. Regardless of their different cultures, countries or backgrounds, all Scouts share the same promise, which is to do their best, to do their duty to God and the country, help other people, and to obey the Scout Law.
6. (b) Thailand
7. (1) To honour the 100th anniversary of the Scout Movement.
   (2) To mark the 150th anniversary of Baden-Powell's birth.
8. (b) encouraging

PASSAGE 2

1. India is a country of many languages. The Constitution recognises 22 languages officially, but over 121 unique languages have been identified in the country.
2. To preserve and encourage the literary function of language, the government introduced 'classical languages' in 2004. According to the Ministry of Culture, a classical language is one that is at least 1,500 years old and has ancient, valuable literature recorded in it. Further, such a language is original and not derived from another language. Based on these guidelines, six languages have been classified as classical languages—Tamil, Sanskrit, Kannada, Telugu, Malayalam and Odia.
3. The following graph shows the percentage of Indian people whose mother tongue is a classical language. This is as per data collected by the census of 2011. The census was not conducted in 2021 due to the pandemic.

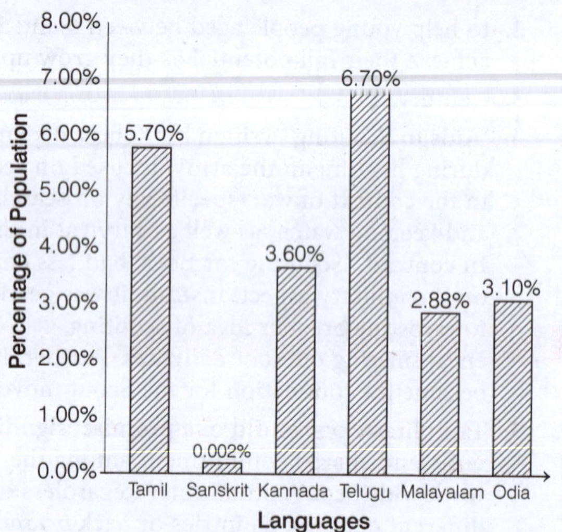

4. According to the graph, around 6.7% of the Indian population are native speakers of Telugu, whereas Sanskrit has been identified as a mother tongue by only 0.002% of the population, which is around 24,821 people. Malayalam has the second lowest number of native speakers, making up about 2.9% of Indians.
5. The 2011 census data also noted that a majority of the native speakers reside in the area that their mother tongue originated from. For example, 93% of Kannada speakers live in Karnataka. Similarly, 93% of Malayalam speakers live in Kerala.
6. Balancing preservation of culture and inclusivity is a delicate equation for a heterogeneous country like India. With growing awareness, concepts like 'classical languages' may help us achieve harmony.

CBSE Additional SQP 2023 Modified

Questions

Based on your understanding of the passage, answer the following questions.

1. Which of these pieces of information can be confirmed by reading the passage?

I. The number of people in India who speak Tamil.

II. Where the majority of native Sanskrit speakers live.

III. The reason Malayalam is considered a classical language.

IV. When the idea of classical languages was introduced in India.

(a) Only I (b) Only IV

(c) I and II (d) III and IV

2. Select the option that is true for the assertion and reason given below.

Assertion (A) Sanskrit can be called a dead language.

Reason (R) Sanskrit is spoken by 0.02% of the Indian population.

(a) Both the (A) and (R) are true, and (R) is the correct explanation of (A).

(b) Both the (A) and (R) are true, but (R) is not the correct explanation of (A).

(c) (A) is true, but (R) is false.

(d) (A) is false, but (R) is true.

3. Imagine that a committee was formed to ensure that classical languages have more native speakers by the time the next census is conducted. In 40 words, answer the following questions to help the committee achieve its objective. **Competency Based**

(i) Which classical language needs its attention most urgently and why?

(ii) Which classical language would be THIRD on its priority?

4. State an example from the passage that shows that India is a 'heterogeneous country'. Answer in one sentence. **Competency Based**

5. Fill in the blanks with the appropriate option from those given in brackets.

Based on the passage, the .... (functional/historical) value of a language is of utmost importance while .... (preserving/categorising) it as a classical language.

6. Why has the writer stated the following line in the passage? Give a reason.

The census was not conducted in 2021 due to the pandemic.

7. Complete the following suitably.

A classical language needs to be ....

8. Complete the sentence based on information from the passage.

If Tamil originated from Tamil Nadu, we can infer that .... of the native Tamil speakers would be living in Tamil Nadu.

9. Which of these hypothetical situations would help India achieve harmony?

Justify your answer in about 40 words.

(i) If the majority of Indians who speak a classical language are settled abroad.

(ii) If more languages from remote and tribal areas of India are identified as classical languages.

(iii) If the percentage of Indians who are native Telugu speakers increases to more than 10 percent.

Answers

1. (d) III and IV
2. (a) Both the (A) and (R) are true, and (R) is the correct explanation of (A).
3. (i) As a committee that would ensure that classical languages have more native speakers by the time the next census is conducted, my first focus would be Sanskrit as it is the mother tongue of only 0.002% of the population, which is around 24,821 people. If this number reduces, Sanskrit would become a dead language.

   (ii) The third language on the priority list would be Odia with only 3.10% spakers.
4. The fact that over 121 unique languages have been identified in the country highlights the fact that India is a 'heterogeneous country'.
5. historical, categorising
6. By stating that the census was not conducted in 2021 due to the pandemic, the author of the given passage wants to state that the data is old and the numbers might have changed.
7. atleast 1500 years old and should have ancient and valuable literature recorded in it.
8. majority
9. (ii) India can move on the path of achieving harmony if more languages from remote and tribal areas of India are identified as classical languages. Most of the divides in the country are a result of lack of acknowledgment of the languages and cultures present in the nation. Thus, if we start recognising them, we can ensure harmony.

REVIEW EXERCISE

Including Discursive and Case-Based Factual Passage

Discursive Passages

Read the following passages carefully given below.

PASSAGE 1

1. Creativity is our most precious resource and the most inexhaustible one. As anyone who has ever spent any time with children knows, every single human being is born creative; every human being is innately endowed with the ability to combine data and perceptions, materials and ideas and devise new ways of thinking and doing. What fosters creativity? More than anything else the presence of other creative people, contrary to that creativity is the province of great individual geniuses. In fact creativity is a social process. Our biggest creative breakthrough comes when people learn from, compete with, and collaborate with other people.
2. Cities are centres of creativity. With their diverse populations, dense social networks and public spaces, people can meet spontaneously and spark or catalyse new ideas. With their infrastructure for finance, organisation and trade, they allow the idea to swiftly reach its destination.
3. A study tracking the decline of unconventional thinking ability as children age, states that while 98 percent of 3 to 5 years olds exhibited creative thinking, this dwindled to 10 percent among 13 to 15 years olds and a mere 2 percent among 25 years olds. Thus, adulthood witnesses the erosion of innate creativity. There is a variance in creative vitality across cities. Although all cities harbour creative individuals by default, some are saturated with leaders, institutions and people that inhibit creativity.

4. Creativity (or the lack of it) follows the same general contours of the great socio-economic divide - our rising inequality - that plagues us. According to estimates, roughly one-third people are able to do work which engages our creative faculties to some extent, whether as artists, musicians, writers, techies, innovators, entrepreneurs, doctors, lawyers, journalists or educators. That leaves a group termed "the other 66 percent", in which their creativity is subjugated, ignored or wasted.

5. Creativity itself is not in danger. It is flourishing all around us - in science and technology, arts and culture, in our rapidly revitalising cities. But we still have a long way to go if we want to build a truly creative society that supports and rewards creativity of each one of us.

(Created for academic usage/410 words)

CBSE 2025

Questions

Based on your understanding of the passage, answer the following questions.

1. The central idea of this passage is that.
   (a) social interaction is necessary to nurture creativity.
   (b) creativity and ideas are gradually declining in all societies.
   (c) the creativity divide is widening in societies in line with socio-economic trends.
   (d) more people should work in jobs that engage their creative faculties.

2. Select the option that is true for the assertion and reason given below.
   Assertion (A) Creativity is the province of great individual genius is not true.
   Reason (R) Creativity is a social process.
   (a) Both the (A) and (R) are true, and (R) is the correct explanation of (A).
   (b) Both the (A) and (R) are true, but (R) is not the correct explanation of (A).
   (c) (A) is true, but (R) is false.
   (d) (A) is false, but (R) is true.

3. Identify the word in paragraph 1 which means something that cannot be used-up or depleted.

4. What important trends does a study tracking the decline in creative thinking ability in children reveal? Answer in about 40 words.

5. Read the given prompt and select the correct option in the bracket to fill in the blank.
   Our biggest creative breakthrough comes when people learn from, compete with, and collaborate with other people.
   Creativity is thus a .... (economic, industrial, social) process.

6. According to the passage, where does creativity thrive apart from arts and culture?

7. Complete the following with a suitable reason.
   About thirty-three percent citizens engage their creative faculties in tasks that use......... .

8. In the context of the last paragraph, explain how does the passage view the future of creativity in society.

PASSAGE 2

1. With the growing focus on sustainable living, the importance of kitchen gardens in urban regions has garnered greater acknowledgement. One significance of kitchen gardens in urban areas is their role in promoting food security. Rapid urbanisation has led to increased distances between food production centres and urban settlements, resulting in longer food supply chains and a decrease in the freshness and nutritional value of food.

2. By having a kitchen garden, urban dwellers can grow their own fresh produce at home, making good use of empty tins, old utensils, and clay flower pots, ensuring a constant supply of nutritious food for themselves and their families. This activity not only saves money and time but can also provide a healthy, practical, and environmentally friendly hobby for the whole family.

3. Not only do kitchen gardens contribute to food security, but they also play a crucial role in environmental sustainability. Traditional agricultural practices often involve the use of synthetic fertilisers, pesticides, and intensive irrigation methods, which may have adverse effects on the environment. However, kitchen gardens promote organic farming, reducing the use of harmful chemicals and preserving soil health.

4. In addition to fostering a sustainable environment, kitchen gardens provide numerous health benefits to urban dwellers. The availability of fresh and organic produce from the garden ensures a higher intake of essential nutrients, vitamins, and minerals, promoting better overall health and well-being.

5. Furthermore, kitchen gardens have proven to be an effective tool for education and community development. They provide an opportunity for individuals to reconnect with nature and learn about the basics of agriculture. Besides providing fruits and vegetables, gardening provides an aesthetic and therapeutic exercise that helps relieve stress.
The physical activity involved in tending to a garden helps individuals stay active, reducing the risk of obesity and related health issues.

6. By involving children in gardening activities, they can develop an appreciation for the environment and learn essential life skills. Moreover, kitchen gardens can also serve as a platform for community engagement, fostering social interactions and promoting a sense of belonging among urban residents.
7. Despite the numerous benefits of kitchen gardens, establishing and maintaining one in urban areas can be challenging. Limited space, lack of sunlight, and soil quality issues are common obstacles that urban gardeners face. However, innovative solutions such as vertical gardening, hydroponics, and rooftop gardens have emerged to overcome these challenges.
8. It is imperative to provide support and resources to encourage urban gardening initiatives as this can transform urban areas into sustainable havens where residents not only live but thrive in harmony with nature. **CBSE 2025**

Questions

Based on your understanding of the passage, answer the following questions.

1. What does the writer's use of phrases like 'in urban regions kitchen gardens have garnered great acknowledgement' suggest about kitchen gardening today?
   (a) It has reduced inflation.
   (b) It is an expensive hobby.
   (c) It provides nutritious food.
   (d) It does not minimise adverse effects on the environment.
   Paragraph (1)

2. Complete the following with a suitable explanation.
Growing a kitchen garden is cost effective because .... Paragraph (2)

3. Identify two differences between the methods adopted in traditional farming and kitchen gardens. Paragraph (3)

4. Substitute the underlined word with the correct word from Paragraph (4).
The local residents' <u>nurturing</u> of their surrounding flora and fauna helps to create awareness about civic responsibilities.

5. Tending to a kitchen garden has many health benefits. Explain in about 40 words. Paragraphs (4) and (5)

6. Select the option that best reflects the concept that kitchen gardening is an effective educational tool for children.
   (a) It contributes to effective community development.
   (b) It helps develop sensitivity and appreciation for nature.
   Paragraph (5)

7. What hurdles do kitchen gardeners face? Mention any two. Paragraph (7)

8. State whether the following statement is True or False.
Kitchen gardening should be practised by everyone living in the cities.

PASSAGE 3

1. Water is one of the most essential resources on Earth, yet it is often taken for granted. Despite its abundance, the reality is that only a small fraction of the world's water is fresh and available for human use. With increasing populations, climate change, and industrial demands, the pressure on our water resources is growing. This makes water conservation not just a collective responsibility but a crucial individual duty. Each person's effort towards conserving water can significantly impact the preservation of this vital resource for future generations.
2. One of the primary reasons individual water conservation efforts are so important is the cumulative effect of small actions which may seem trivial on their own. However, when multiplied by millions of people, these actions can lead to substantial water savings. For example, a single dripping tap can waste over 15 litres of water a day. Imagine the water saved if every household in a city repaired just one leaky faucet. This highlights the power of collective individual actions in reducing water waste.
3. Moreover, personal efforts towards water conservation often lead to greater awareness and education. When individuals take steps to conserve water, they become more conscious of their water usage and the importance of this resource. This awareness can then spread within communities, inspiring others to adopt similar practices. For instance, a family that installs water-saving devices in their home may encourage neighbours and friends to do the same, creating a ripple effect. This grassroots approach to conservation can be particularly effective in areas where larger-scale initiatives may be slow to implement or lacking in support.
4. In addition to daily habits, individuals can also make a difference through more significant lifestyle choices. For instance, opting for drought-resistant plants in gardens and supporting water-efficient agriculture can

all contribute to water conservation. Agriculture, especially livestock farming, is one of the largest consumers of water globally. By supporting sustainable farming practices, individuals can indirectly reduce the water footprint of their food.

5. Critics might argue that individual efforts are negligible compared to the large-scale water consumption by industries and agriculture. However, this perspective overlooks the potential for individual actions to drive systemic change. When people collectively make water-conscious choices, they send a powerful message to businesses and policymakers about the importance of conservation.
6. Each person's commitment to saving water, no matter how small, contributes to a larger culture of sustainability. By making conscious choices and spreading awareness, individuals can help ensure that future generations have access to the clean, fresh water they need to thrive. Water conservation is not just the responsibility of governments and industries; it is a shared duty that begins with each of us.

Created for Academic Usage / 441 words

CBSE SQP 2024

Questions

Based on your understanding of the passage, answer the following questions.

1. In paragraph 1, what does the phrase 'each person's effort towards conserving water can significantly impact the preservation of this vital resource emphasise?

2. Complete the following with the correct option from the two given.
Water is often taken for granted, despite its essential nature because .... (Paragraph 1)

(a) it is abundant and always easily accessible, making people less aware of its usage
(b) its importance is not always recognised, leading people to overlook its value

3. Support the writer's idea that small individual actions towards water conservation are not trivial. (Paragraph 2)

4. Select the option that best reflects the concept of a 'ripple effect' in the context of student life at school. (Paragraph 3)

(a) A student's act of volunteering at a local charity leads to the school administration organising a large-scale fundraising event.
(b) A student who consistently follows good study practices inspires classmates to improve their own study routines, creating a culture of academic excellence in the class. (Paragraph 3)

5. State whether the following statement is True or False. (Paragraph 3)
Grassroot efforts like personal efforts are more effective in water conservation.

6. The writer mentions 'sustainable farming practices' in paragraph 4. Which of the following is a sustainable farming practice?

(a) Using chemical fertilisers and pesticides extensively to increase crop yields.
(b) Clearing large areas of natural vegetation to expand farmland for organic farming.
(c) Implementing crop rotation and using organic compost to maintain soil health.
(d) Relying solely on monoculture farming to maximise production efficiency.

7. List any two points that a powerful message sent to businesses and policy makers about the importance of water conservation might include. (Paragraph 5)

8. Fill in the blank with the correct option from those given. (Paragraph 6)
In the phrase 'culture of sustainability,' the word 'culture' refers to ....

(a) a set of beliefs and practices shared by a group
(b) the artistic and traditional practices specific to a community's heritage.
(c) the lifestyle habits and choices that are popular among the urbane
(d) the techniques and methods used in development efforts

PASSAGE 4

1. The words probiotics, prebiotics, and postbiotics may sound like variations of the same thing, but what a difference a prefix makes. The first is a category of health-promoting microbes. The latter two groups are types of beneficial molecules. But all three biotics are critical for supporting the community of microscopic organisms that live in the gastrointestinal tract, known as the gut microbiome. With both beneficial and harmful bacteria living in the human body, these diet-related factors — the biotics — help tip the balance in the positive direction. It is important to understand their differences, as you'll see, because each of these factors serves a distinct purpose, even as they work together.
2. Despite their importance for the gut microbiome, the health benefits of these 'biotics', which are persent in

certain foods or result from their metabolism, extend beyond the digestive tract. A growing body of scientific evidence has linked prebiotics, probiotics, and postbiotics, with improvements in metabolic diseases — including obesity and cholesterol abnormalities — depressive symptoms and poor sleep quality, among many other conditions.

3. Besides promoting general gut health, consuming food rich in probiotics can improve irritable bowel syndrome and antibiotic-related diarrhea, prevent traveller's diarrhea, produce vitamins and increase nutrient absorption, and decrease the risk of common infections. In fact, when consumed regularly, probiotics have been found to reduce the occurrence of upper respiratory tract infections (like the common cold).
4. Many different types of beneficial bacteria are considered probiotics. The most common ones include *Lactobacillus and Bifidobacterium*, of which there are dozens of strains. "You have to match what it is you're concerned about with the probiotic you should use," says Gregor Reid. Many different types of beneficial bacteria are considered probiotics.
5. Some foods, such as yogurt, kefir, kimchee, and fermented soybeans and kombucha naturally contain probiotics. But here's where things get complicated : not all fermented foods or yogurts contain probiotics, Reid says. As a consumer, a good starting point is to look for the phrase "contains live and active cultures" on the label; it's even better if specific strains of bacteria are listed, because then you'll know you're getting the right stuff.
6. Simply put, prebiotics are sources of food for the those beneficial microbes — the probiotics. They are typically a form of carbohydrate or fiber that we don't have the enzymes to digest. As a result, they move through the digestive tract to the intestine, where beneficial bacteria (probiotics) can feast on them.
7. When you consume foods that are rich in probiotics and prebiotics, the microbes in your gut consume the undigestible prebiotic fiber and produce bioactive compounds called postbiotics. They are ultimately the endgame that we want — they affect how our gut operates and keeps the good bacteria there and the bad bacteria out. **CBSE 2024**

Questions

Based on your understanding of the passage, answer the following questions.

1. Which of the following statements best describes the author's attitude towards probiotics?
   (a) Probiotics, prebiotics and postbiotics are variations of the same theing, with just a difference of a prefix.
   (b) All fermented foods or yogurts naturally contain probiotics.
   (c) All three biotics are equally important to support microscopic organisms that live in the gut microbiome.
   (d) Only probiotics are important as they can improve irritable bowel syndrome and antibiotic-related diarrhea.
2. According to the writer, health benefits of all the 'biotics' extend beyond the digestive tract. Rationalise your response in about 40 words. **Competency Based**
3. Complete the sentence appropriately.
   To get the right probiotic and to match it with your body's requirement, it is important to see the label for ....
4. The passage include some words that are opposites of each other. From the sets (a) – (e) below, identify two sets of antonyms.
   (a) Increase and decrease (b) Probiotic and postbiotic
   (c) Beneficial and harmful (d) Feast and fermented
   (e) Consuming and digestive
5. Complete the sentence appropriately.
   The author wants to stress the fact that there is not just one type of beneficial bacteria considered as probiotic, in fact, some probiotics have ....
6. Based on the reading of the passage, examine in about 40 words, the importance of prebiotics for the human gut and how they are related to probiotics. **Competency Based**
7. As a consumer, if you want to pick a probiotic product, what is the most important thing to keep in mind?
   Pick the best answer.
   (a) Any fermented product that contains probiotics.
   (b) Checking the label for specific strains of bacteria.
   (c) All products under 'probiotics' section in a grocery store are safe to pick.
   (d) Checking the label which clearly says 'probiotics' is sufficient.

8. "Despite their importance for the gut microbiome, the health benefits of these 'biotics', which are present in certain foods or result from their metabolism, extend beyond the digestive tract." As per this statement from the passage, how relevant are the 'biotics' for humans? Pick the best answer.

(a) Their relevance has been proven by scientific evidence.

(b) Not very relevant as more study is needed.

(c) Their relevance cannot be generalised for everyone.

(d) Only probiotics are relevant for humans.

PASSAGE 5

1. As a high school student, studying poetry can be a rollercoaster ride. This journey is punctuated by moments of profound appreciation for simpler pieces and intermittent frustration with more complex works. Let's be real here - some poems are just plain confusing and no amount of re-reading seems to help decipher the intended meaning. The puzzlement that results from such instances can be both vexing and demotivating.
If solving a riddle is what was intended, then playing Sudoku is a better option. One is led to ponder if obscurity was the goal.
2. Conversely, some pieces resonate with the reader's soul. Stirring feelings of warmth, happiness and connection to the world. Often, these compositions centre on themes that are universally understood, such as love, nature, or faith. Being able to actually understand what the poet is trying to say can feel like a little victory and is a welcome relief after grappling with more perplexing poetry.
3. Then there are poems that are emotionally charged; the ones that make the reader curl up in a ball and cry or jump up and down with joy. One is left in awe of the poet's ability to convey emotion through words. Let's not forget the downright weird poems.
These are the ones that defy categorisation and leave the reader to their own devices in attempting to interpret meaning. The author's use of figurative language and unconventional imagery can create a sense of bewilderment that is either intriguing or off-putting. Regardless, the reader can appreciate the uniqueness of the work.
4. Despite the wide range of emotions and reactions that come with studying poetry, it can be a rewarding pursuit. Not only does reading poetry allow one to appreciate the artistic beauty of the written word but also enables one to develop crucial critical thinking and analytical skills.
The process of unlocking a poem's meaning can feel like cracking a code or solving a puzzle but the sense of accomplishment derived from mastering a challenging piece can be deeply gratifying.
Finally, impressing an English teacher with a well-analysed poem can be a source of pride and validation.
5. Overall, studying poetry is like a box of mixed chocolates, you never know what you're going to get. But whether it's complex, emotional, simple, or just downright weird, there's always something to be gained from the experience.
So, let's applaud all the poets out there, for making us laugh, cry, scratch our heads and occasionally feel like a genius. **CBSE Additional SQP 2023**

Questions

Based on your understanding of the passage, answer the questions.

1. What is the tone of the writer in the given lines from paragraph 1? Rationalise your response in about 40 words. **Competency Based**

If solving a riddle is what was intended, then playing Sudoku is a better option. One is led to ponder if obscurity was the goal.

2. Complete the sentence appropriately.

We can say that the author's tone becomes more neutral and objective when discussing weird poems, compared to other types of poetry because ....

(a) the author acknowledges that weird poems can be off putting and also appreciates the uniqueness and the challenge they present to the users.

(b) the author promotes that weird poems need to become the norm and also points out its usefulness in challenging social norms.

3. Based on the reading of the passage, examine, in about 40 words, how studying poetry can be like exploring a new city.

4. Which of the following statements best describes the author's attitude towards studying poetry?

(a) Recognises the challenges of studying poetry but also acknowledges the rewards it offers.

(b) Feels that poetry is too obscure and abstract for the average person to appreciate.

5. State whether the given statement is True or False.
The author's use of vivid imagery in the paragraph 3, such as "curl up in a ball and cry" and "jump up and down with joy", greatly affects the reader.

6. The passage includes some words that are opposites of each other. From the sets (a)-(e) below, identify two sets of antonyms.

(a) Intriguing and off-putting
(b) Deciphering and interpreting
(c) Appreciate and applaud
(d) Simple and challenging
(e) Emotions and feelings

7. State whether the following lines display an example of a simple/complex/emotionally charged/downright weird, poem.

The Sun rises in the East,
A new day begins, a fresh start. Birds chirp, nature wakes up,
A peaceful feeling in my heart.

8. What is the message conveyed by Hina's experience, in the following case?

Hina spends hours trying to analyse a poem for her assignment and finally feels a sense of accomplishment and pride, once she understands

(a) only those with natural talent for poetry should engage with it.
(b) persistence makes studying poetry a rewarding pursuit.
(c) study of poetry is guaranteed to impress others.
(d) the efforts of studying poetry is inversely proportional to the rewards gained.

PASSAGE 6

1. Mankind's fascination with gold is as old as civilisation itself. The ancient Egyptians held gold in high esteem. Gold had religious significance for them and King Tutankhamen was buried in a solid gold coffin 3300 years ago. The wandering Israelites worshipped a golden calf and the legendary King Midas asked that whatever he touched be turned into gold.
2. Not only is gold beautiful, but it is virtually indestructible. It will not rust or corrode. Gold coins and products fabricated from the metal have survived undamaged for centuries. Gold is extremely easy to work with. One ounce, which is about the size of a cube of sugar, can be beaten into a sheet nearly 100 square feet in size and becomes so thin that light can pass through it. An ounce of gold can also be stretched into a wire 50 miles long. Gold conducts electricity better than any other substance except copper and silver and it is particularly important in modern electronic industry.
3. People have always longed to possess gold. Unfortunately, this longing has also brought out the worst in human character. The Spanish conquerors robbed palaces, temples and graves and killed thousands of people in their ruthless search for gold. Even today, the economy of South Africa's gold mines depend largely on the employment of black labourers who are paid about 40 pounds a month, plus boarding and lodging. They work in conditions that can only be described as cruel. About 400 miners die in South Africa each year.
4. Much of the gold's value lies in its scarcity. Only about 80,000 tons have been mined in the history of the world. All of it can be stored in a vault 60 feet square, or a super tanker. Great Britain was the first country to adopt the gold standard, when the Master of the Mint, Sir Issac Newton, established a fixed price for gold in 1717. The discovery of gold in the last half of the nineteenth century in California, (1848) and later in Australia and South Africa changed everything. Before the discovery, there wasn't enough gold around for all the trading nations to link their currencies to the precious metal.
5. An out-of-work prospector named George Harrison launched South Africa into the gold age in 1886 when he discovered the metal in a farm near what is now Johannesburg. Harrison was given a 12 pounds reward by the farmer. He then disappeared and was eaten by a lion.
6. One of the biggest gold mining areas in the Soviet Union is the Kolyma River region, once infamous for its prison camp. The camp has gone, but in a way nothing has changed. Many ex-prisoners have stayed on to work in the mines and are supervised by ex-guards.
7. Despite the current rush to buy gold, 75 percent of the metal goes into making jewellery. Italy is the biggest consumer of gold for this purpose, and many Italian jewellers even tear up their wooden floors and burn them to recover the tiny flecks of gold. Historically, the desire to hoard gold at home has been primarily an occupation of the working and peasant classes, who have had no faith in paper money. George Bernard Shaw defended their instincts eloquently, "You have to choose between trusting the natural stability of the honesty and intelligence of the members of the government," he said "and with due respect to these gentlemen, I advise to vote for gold." **CBSE 2023 Modified**

Questions

Based on your understanding of the passage, answer the following questions.

1. When was King Tutankhamen buried?
2. Complete the following with the phrase from paragraph 1.

Opinion	Reason
	King Tutankhamen was buried in a solid gold coffin 3300 years ago.

3. Based on your reading of the text, list 2 reasons why the writer says that,
   Not only is gold beautiful but it is virtually indestructible.
   ....
   ....
4. Select the option that displays what the writer projects, with reference to the following.
   The wandering Israelites worshipped a golden calf ....
   (a) importance of religion
   (b) importance of the metal
5. State whether the given statement is True or False.
   Egyptians held gold in low esteem.
6. Who launched South Africa into the gold age?
   (a) Issac Newton (b) George Harrison
   (c) George Bernard Shaw (d) A farmer
7. Supply one point to justify the following.
   The desire to hoard gold at home has been primarily an occupation of the working and peasant classes.
8. According to the passage, which of the following statements is not true?
   (a) Gold is the best conductor of electricity.
   (b) Apart from gold, copper and silver are good conductors of electricity.
   (c) Gold can be easily beaten, hence it is easy to work with.
   (d) Gold plays an important role in the modern electronics industry.

PASSAGE 7

1. If you're like most kids, you may love snow. Not only can it get you out of school, but it's also fun to play with. Who doesn't love to sled and build snowmen? Snow can also be dangerous, too you may have heard your parents talk about how difficult it can be to drive in snow. Car accidents aren't the only dangers created by snow. If you're ever skiing in the mountains, you'll want to be aware of avalanches. An avalanche is a sudden flow of snow down a slope, such as a mountain. The amount of snow in an avalanche will vary based on many things, but it can be such a huge pile that it can bury the bottom of a slope in dozens of feet of snow.
2. Avalanches can be caused by many things. Some of them are natural. For example, new snow or rain can cause built up snow to loosen and fall down the side of a mountain Earthquakes and the movement of animals have also been known to cause avalanches. Artificial triggers can also cause avalanches. For example, snowmobiles, skiers, gunshots and explosives have all been known to cause avalanches. Avalanches usually occur during the winter and spring, when snowfall is greatest. As they are dangerous to any living beings in their path, avalanches have destroyed forests, roads railroads and even entire town.
3. Warning signs exist that allow experts to predict-and often prevent - avalanches from occurring. When over a foot of fresh snow falls experts known to be on the lookout for avalanches. Explosives can be used in places with massive snow build-up to trigger smaller avalanches that don't pose a danger to persons or property. When deadly avalanches do occur, the moving snow can quickly reach over 80 miles per hour. Skiers caught in such avalanches can be buried under dozens of feet of snow. While it's possible dig out of such avalanches, not all are able to escape.
4. If you get tossed about by an avalanche and find yourself buried under many feet of snow, you might not have a true sense of which way is up and which way out, only to find that they were upside down and digging themselves farther under the snow rather than to the top. Experts suggest that people caught in an avalanche try to 'swim' to the top of the moving snow to stay close to the surface. Once the avalanche stops, do your best to dig around you to create a space for air, so you can breathe easier. Then, do your best to figure out which way is up and dig in that direction to reach the surface and signal rescuers. **CBSE 2023**

Questions

Based on your understanding to the passage, answer the following questions.

1. Mention two reasons which destroyed the natural scenery.
2. Complete the sentence by choosing an appropriate option.

Avalanche can be caused by ....

(a) new snow or rain

(b) heavy winds

3. Comment on warning signs exist which allow experts to predict avalanches in two sentences.

4. The writer will agree with which of the given statements (Paragraph 4)?

(a) People caught in the Avalanche can try to swim to the top.

(b) Put on an oxygen Mask.

5. Select the option that corresponds to the following relation below. **Competency Based**

You may not have an idea of which way is up and which way is down.

(a) The crowd will gather at Gate No.1 and disperse from Gate No.2.

(b) Due to the torrential rain, there was a heavy flooding.

(c) The guest felt uneasy and uncomfortable watching the child's performance.

(d) The more the effort, the bigger the gain.

6. State whether the given statement is True or False. Plastic waste triggers an avalanche.

7. Where can explosives be used?

8. Select the most suitable title for the above passage.

(a) Avalanches (b) Adventure with Snow

(c) Ice Games (d) Calamity

PASSAGE 8

1. Organic food is very popular these days. It can also be very expensive. Some organic food costs twice as much as non-organic food. Parents of young children and even some pet owners, will pay high prices for organic food if they think it is healthier. But many others think organic food is just a waste of money.
2. There is one main difference between organic and non-organic food. Organic farms do not use agricultural chemicals such as pesticides that stop insects from damaging crops. In many countries, foods that claim to be organic must have special labels that guarantee they're grown organically.
3. Some people think organic also means 'locally grown' and originally it was indeed true. But over a period of time organic farming has become a big business, with many organic foods now being grown by large agricultural companies that sell their products far from where they're grown. Processed food made with organic ingredients has also become more popular. At first, only small companies produced these products. But as demand overtook supply, big food companies that had been selling non-organic products for many years also began selling organic products.
4. Is organic food safer and more nutritious? This is an important part of the debate. Many farmers and consumers believe it is safer and more nutritious. They think agricultural chemicals can cause serious illnesses such as cancer but there isn't much evidence proving this is true. However, recent studies have shown that eating organically-grown produce reduces your chances of developing heart diseases. Many doctors think it is more important to stop dangerous bacteria from contaminating foods. These bacteria can contaminate both organic and non-organic fruits and vegetables, and doctors recommend washing produce carefully before eating it. Meat, fish and chicken can also become contaminated so washing your hands before handling these foods is also very important. **CBSE 2023**

Questions

Based on your understanding of the passage, answer the following questions.

1. Based on your reading of the text, list one benefit of eating organic food.

2. Select the option that displays what the writer projects with reference to the following.

Is organic food safer and more nutritious? This is an important part of the debate.

(a) Denial

(b) Confirmation

3. The writer contrasts organic food to non-organic food. State one point of comparison between the two.

4. The writer says that people believe that it is safer and more nutritious to eat organic food. Select the reason for his skeptical view. **Competency Based**

(a) The price decides the popularity.

(b) There is no confirmed evidence.

5. State whether the given statement is True or False. Some people think organic also means 'locally grown'.

6. People are willing to pay high prices for organic food because

(a) it is not easily available.

(b) it helps in weight loss.

(c) it is produced by small companies.

(d) it does not contain agricultural chemicals.

7. What connect does the writer draw between contamination of food and washing hands?

8. Complete the following with a phrase from paragraph 3.

Opinion	Reason
Big food companies have started selling organic food products.	

(a) Because demand overtook supply
(b) Because organic foods were healthy
(c) Because of the profit it brought
(d) Because it was in vogue

PASSAGE 9

1. Floods are not new to India and this subcontinent, but in recent years the problem of flooding has received much greater attention, perhaps largely because it has led to greater damage now than it did in the past. Even though information on the impending occurrence of floods is now more accurate and certainly more timely, often there is very little time or support infrastructure in place by which damage can be minimised. This is particularly true in the case of flash floods resulting from sudden and excessive heavy rain.
2. In the case of India, flooding is very much related to the seasonal nature of our rainfall. The monsoons are spread over a short period during the year and often bring a concentrated volume of rain, which cannot be absorbed by the Earth and finds an outlet only in the form of streams that join up with our major river systems. Flooding due to heavy rain is confined not only to the main rivers of the country, but also affects smaller tributaries and streams. Once these streams spill over their banks they could cause excessive harm, mainly because those living near the banks of these streams, particularly in mountain areas, do not have easy recourse to moving away quickly.
3. One major factor that could lead to a higher severity of flooding in the future is the danger of climate change. While the evidence of the nature of impacts, resulting from climate change on precipitation and flooding at the regional level, is not entirely clear, it could happen that the Indian subcontinent witnesses and suffers the effects of a significantly changed pattern of monsoons. One set of scientists has estimated that the monsoons could be shorter in duration but far more intensive; in other words, much greater precipitation would take place in a much shorter period of time, thereby increasing the danger of floods. Climate change is the result of human actions through the increased concentration of greenhouse gases in the atmosphere, of which carbon dioxide is the most prominent.
4. At the local level also human actions have heightened the danger of floods through the cutting of trees in the mountains as well as in the plains. In case of India, the ecological damage through deforestation of the Himalayas has led to large-scale erosion of the mountain slopes and high levels of siltation. These lead to the deposition of silt on the riverbeds in the plains and hence, spillover of water whenever the volume in the river reaches a certain level. With siltation on the riverbeds, flooding occurs even at very shallow water levels. The vulnerability of the population has increased substantially because of population pressures. An example is the stubborn and perhaps helpless settling of slum dwellers on the banks of the River Yamuna in Delhi, who become victims of flooding. What is a mere trickle most of the year, bursts its banks during the monsoons, as has been the case in recent years.
5. Flood forecasting is critical to minimising the damage from floods. It is for this reason that the Central Water Commission has set up a network of forecasting stations, which cover the most important flood-prone interstate rivers in the country. These stations produce forecasts that are used to alert the public and to mobilise various official agencies so that they take both preventive as well as relief measures, whenever required. However, even in cases where forecasts have been timely and generally accurate, people have often been reluctant to move away, because in most cases they lack the means and physical options for moving away from a danger zone to one that is relatively safe. In the case of flash floods, forecasts are difficult to make and often the time available for relief is very short. **CBSE 2023**

Questions

Based on your understanding of the passage, answer the following questions.

1. Complete the following with a phrase from paragraph 3.

Opinion	Reason
Some scientists estimate that shorter duration of monsoon season leads to more intensive rainfall.	

2. Specify the option that displays what the writer projects with reference to the following statement.

One major factor that could lead to higher severity of flooding in the future is the danger of climate change. **Competency Based**

(a) Helplessness
(b) Speculative

3. The writer claims that flood forecasting is critical to minimising the damage from floods. State one reason for the claim.

4. The writer says that forecasts are difficult to make and time available is very short. Select the reason for it.

(a) Flash floods (b) Cyclonic rain

5. State whether the given statement is True or False. The worst hit people are slum dwellers.

6. The problem of floods has been considered more important recently because

(a) floods have led to much greater damage now than in the past.

(b) floods are resulting in increased relocation.

(c) floods occur only during the monsoon season.

(d) of problems of frequent Tornadoes and Cyclones in the subcontinent.

7. Based on your reading of the text, list two reasons why the writer says that in spite of timely forecasting people have suffered. **Competency Based**

8. Which of the following statement(s) is/are false?

The vulnerability of the population has increased substantially because of population pressures symbolised by.

I. People are superstitious.

II. Difficult to evacuate flood-affected areas.

Select the correct option.

(a) Only I (b) Only II

(c) Both I and II (d) None of these

PASSAGE 10

1. If they go unaddressed, life's annoyances can affect your well-being. Scientific studies have found that people who rate high on tests for anger are at an increased risk for high blood pressure and heart disease. To process anger in a healthy way, Todd Kashdan, a psychology professor at George Mason University in Virginia, recommends you attempt to understand why you feel upset. Without pinpointing why you're angry, he says, "You can't get a foothold to figure out what your body is mobilising to do."

2. When harnessed properly, anger can be a motivator. Frustration can drive us to choose a novel path while problem-solving or to become focused and committed—taking up a new cause, for example. Frustration may also be useful in negotiations. But watch, how you express it–raising your voice during a debate may be helpful, but the same tactic could potentially undermine collaborative work.

3. Vexation has limits. Kashdan recommends thinking of anger as a speedometer, where 10 kilometres per hour is irritation and 100 kilometres per hour is blind rage. Speed limits are a measure of effectiveness–momentary annoyance during a negotiation might be useful, but rage seldom is. If you use anger as a tool too often, people will learn to avoid you. While others may offer small amounts of time and effort to keep your temper from erupting, you'll miss out on their best contributions.

4. If you get into a disagreement with someone, pause for a moment and try to understand that person's point of view, then look for a mutually beneficial solution. Once you become angry, your thinking gets too narrow. To bring anger down a notch, psychologists recommend practising deep breathing. Focus on inhaling and exhaling and picture your breath travelling to your diaphragm. Create a playlist of music to help relax when you feel agitated. Different genres work for different people.

5. Keep disagreements from turning into fights by improving your communication skills. Avoid cutting others off or using accusatory adverbs like 'always' and 'never'. "Unhealthy anger, the inability to cool down when upset, can be a symptom of mental health disorders such as depression," says Darin Dougherty of the Harvard Medical School. Speak to your doctor if this feels familiar–medication and cognitive behavioural therapy help.

6. After anger runs its course, let go. Experts offer three steps for decompressing after you've been hurt–make sense of the wrongdoing with a loved one or a therapist; avoid dwelling after you've processed the issue; and, finally move on—find humour in the situation or leave the environment if it has become toxic. **CBSE 2024 C**

Questions

Based on your understanding of the passage, answer the following questions.

1. Complete the following statement.
According to the passage, it is important to understand the reason for your anger because ....

2. According to the author, which of the following is an effective way to bring down anger?

(a) Practicing deep breathing

(b) Playing a musical instrument for others

(c) Travelling to different places

(d) Going for a physical workout

3. Select the option that displays what the writer projects, with reference to the following.

If you get into a disagreement with someone, pause for a moment and try to understand that person's point of view. (Paragraph 4)

(a) Denial (b) Conviction
(c) Reflection (d) Compassion

4. Select the option which is closest in meaning to 'undermine'. (Paragraph 2)

(a) Collective (b) Emphasise
(c) Unilateral (d) Weaken

5. Explain this statement from paragraph 2. "Frustration can drive us to choose a novel path while problem-solving."

6. How can communication skills help in anger management?

7. Complete the sentence appropriately. If your anger remains uncontrolled,

(a) decisions will get delayed resulting in losses.
(b) you will not receive the best contributions.
(c) there can be momentary annoyance during a negotiation.
(d) people will respond equally aggressively.

8. How can you unwind after letting go of your anger? Give two suggestions from the text.

PASSAGE 11

Sifting through the Sands of Time

1. When you're on the beach, you're stepping on ancient mountains, skeletons of marine animals, even tiny diamonds. Sand provides a mineral treasure-trove, a record of geology's Earth-changing processes.

2. Sand- as children we play on it and as adults we relax on it.

It is something we complain about when it gets in our food and praise when it's moulded into castles. But we don't often look at it. If we did, we would discover an account of a geological past and a history of marine life that goes back thousands and, in some cases, millions of years.

3. Sand covers not just sea-shores, but also ocean beds, deserts and mountains. It is one of the most common substances on Earth. And it is a major element in man-made items too-concrete is largely sand, while glass is made of little else.

4. What exactly is sand? Well, it is larger than fine dust and smaller than shingle. Depending on its age and origin, a particular sand can consist of tiny pebbles or porous granules. Its grain may have the shape of stars or spirals, their edges jagged or smooth. They have come from the erosion of rocks, or from the skeletons of marine organisms which accumulate on the bottom of the oceans, or even from volcanic eruptions.

5. Colour is another clue to sand's origins. If it is a dazzling white, its grains may be derived from nearby coral outcrops, from crystalline quartz rocks or from gypsum. On Pacific islands jet black sands form from volcanic minerals.

6. Usually, the older the granules, the finer they are and the smoother the edges. The fine, white beaches, for instance, are recycled from sandstone several hundred million years old. Perhaps they will be stone once more, in another few hundred million.

7. Sand is an irreplaceable industrial ingredient whose uses are legion but it has one vital function you might never even notice. Sand cushions our land from the sea's impact and geologists say it often does a better job of protecting our shores than the most advanced coastal technology. **CBSE 2022 Term II Modified**

Questions

Based on your understanding of the passage, answer the following questions.

1. List the different shapes of sand.

2. Complete the sentence appropriately.
Two man-made materials that contain sand are ....

(a) watch and brick (b) concrete and glass

3. How is sand both a pain and a pleasure?

4. The passage includes some words that are opposites of each other. From the sets (a)-(e) below, identify two sets of antonyms.

(a) Irreplaceable and vital (b) Jagged and smooth
(c) Accumulate and derive (d) Ancient and advanced
(e) Tiny and fine

5. Select whether the given statement is True and False.

In comparison to recent granules, the older granules are smooth around the edges.

6. What is the origin of white sand?

(a) Coral outcrops (b) Crystalline quartz rocks
(c) Volcanic eruptions (d) Both (a) and (b)

7. How is sand a 'treasure-trove'? Answer in about 40 words.

8. Where, according to the passage, can beaches made of jet black sand be found?

(a) Pacific islands
(b) On very old island
(c) On any island
(d) On any beach

PASSAGE 12

1. The upcoming United Nations Summit of the Future, scheduled for 22nd-23rd September, 2024, comes at a pivotal moment for global governance. The world is grappling with a declining faith in multilateralism, following the COVID-19 pandemic and ongoing conflicts like those in Ukraine and Gaza. The summit's highlight, the 'Pact for the Future,' is envisioned as a blueprint for UN reform and a reinvigoration of global cooperation. However, many sceptics are unsure if this summit can address the longstanding structural issues plaguing the UN, particularly the outdated power dynamics within the Security Council.
2. Despite these challenges, the summit presents a unique opportunity for global collaboration and could serve as a catalyst for much needed reforms in the UN system. Including civil society and private sector actors in the discussions could inject fresh energy into the multilateral process. However, the success of the summit hinges on member states' willingness to move beyond superficial agreements and make meaningful, concrete commitments. While the 'Pact for the Future' may not lead to immediate transformative change, it could serve as a foundation for reinvigorating global governance and signalling that multilateralism, though weakened, remains crucial.
3. Multilateral institutions, such as the UN, IMF, World Bank, and WHO, play a significant role in global peacekeeping, economic stabilisation, health management, and climate change mitigation. These institutions are vital for conflict resolution, as demonstrated by UN peacekeeping missions in conflict zones. The IMF and World Bank have historically supported global economies during crises, such as the 2008 financial crisis and the COVID-19 pandemic. The WHO, particularly through initiatives like COVAX, has been central to managing global health crises.
4. However, the relevance of these multilateral institutions is being challenged. Shifting global power dynamics, the rise of sovereignty prioritisation, and institutional decision making paralysis are weakening their influence. Emerging economies, particularly the BRICS nations, are creating alternative forums for engagement, further undermining traditional institutions. Moreover, public trust in multilateral bodies has waned due to financial constraints, perceived elitism, and imbalances in representation.
5. Reform strategies for multilateral institutions include updating voting structures to reflect modern global realities, embracing digital technologies for inclusive decision-making, forming adaptive coalitions, enhancing transparency, and involving more stakeholders in governance processes. Though the challenges are immense, reforming these institutions is vital for addressing complex, interconnected global issues like climate change, public health, and economic instability. The UN Summit of the Future could serve as the first step toward revitalising these global institutions for the 21st century.

Questions

Based on your understanding of the passage, answer the following questions.

1. In paragraph 1, what does the phrase "a reinvigoration of global cooperation" emphasise?

2. Complete the following with the correct option from the two given.

The disastrous global events such as the COVID-19 pandemic and ongoing conflicts like those in Ukraine and Gaza have caused ....

(a) the global population's loss of faith in multilateralism
(b) the global population to look for alternative solutions

3. Support the writer's idea that challenges to multilateralism must be resolved to revitalise the faith of the people in global institutions.

4. Select the option that best reflects the concept of a 'ripple effect' in the context of economic instability.

(a) The inability of global institutions to deal with Covid-19 has caused inefficacy in their ability to combat challenges such as climate change.
(b) The inability of global institutions to deal with Covid-19 has caused the people to lose faith in their ability to combat challenges like public health and economic instability.

5. State whether the following statement is True or False.

The UN Summit of the Future could serve as the first step towards the goal of becoming AI free within the 21st century.

6. Which of the following lists multilateral organisations involved in global peacekeeping?

(a) COVAX, IMF and World Bank
(b) USA, World Bank, WHO
(c) IMF, UAE and WHO
(d) IMF, World Bank and WHO

7. List any two ways in which multilateral organisations have helped global economies in times of global crises.

8. Fill in the blank with the correct option from those given.

In the phrase 'member states' willingness to move beyond superficial agreements' the word 'hinges' refers to ....

(a) a jointed or flexible device on which a door, lid, or other swinging part turns
(b) a flexible ligamentous joint
(c) a small piece of thin gummed paper used in fastening a postage stamp in an album
(d) to be contingent on a single consideration or point

PASSAGE 13

1. Nature is our mother, our first teacher. The greatest lesson that she teaches us is to maintain an equilibrium in life. We learn to maintain composure through our joys, sorrows and fears. In fact, there are a thousand lessons that nature can teach us, provided we look for them.
2. With time, a sapling grows into a full-grown tree; something so tiny and delicate develops into a strong tree capable of supporting others. No matter how tall it grows, how much it may flourish or how many animals and birds it may support, its roots are firmly buried from where it once rose. That's a lesson to keep ourselves grounded, respect and embrace our roots and give something back to those humble beginnings that nurtured us into who we are.
3. Then there is the message of peaceful coexistence. 'I am because we are'. Nature provides every creature a chance to exist. However, the existence of one creature or being depends on the existence of the other. The tiger eats the antelope; without the antelope, the tiger wouldn't survive. Likewise, without tigers, the over-abundance of antelopes would cause them to starve to death.
4. I wonder if you have noticed that when birds or squirrels see a predator, they give out an alarm call to their fellow creatures, of the lurking danger. They put themselves in danger to save the lives of others. Many animals, like the salmon, usually die after they spawn, but this doesn't stop them. One life extinguished for the betterment of others is a small price to pay.
5. The snow melts in the warmth of spring to give birth to fresh green leaves. In autumn these leaves age into shades of gold only to be buried in the cold grave of winter. Change is inevitable; the sooner we embrace this, the better it is for us. We must also understand that even in pain there is growth. If you cut a hole in the tree, it will grow around it. No matter what may come in its way, a river will continue to flow. Similarly, no matter what grief may break your heart, nature teaches us that life goes on.
6. Keep in mind life isn't about making lists and trying to be one step ahead of others. Life is to live. Take a break-stop being a workaholic and smell the roses, do whatever makes you feel happy and most of all spend some time with nature to pick up invaluable lessons. **CBSE SQP 2021 Term I Modified**

Questions

Based on your understanding of the passage, answer the following questions.

1. What qualities do the birds and squirrels display when they warn others of possible danger? Answer in one word.

2. Choose the option that best conveys the message in 'I am because we are'.

(a) Everyone is dependent on each other.
(b) Humans are dependent on animals.

3. Complete the sentence appropriately.

According to the author, the greatest lesson being taught by nature is ....

4. The passage includes some words that are opposite of each other. From the sets (a) - (d) below, identify two sets of antonyms.

(a) Sorrows and fears
(b) Tiny and delicate
(c) Warmth and cold
(d) Stop and continue

5. Complete the sentence appropriately.

When they see a predator, birds give ....

6. Which of the following qualities from Paragraph 3 does the author wants us to imbibe?

(a) Accepting
(b) Resilient
(c) Perceptive
(d) All of the above

7. What does the writer advise in Paragraph 6? Answer in about 40 words.

8. Select the option that shows the correct relationship between (1) and (2).

(1) The changing of seasons show that nothing lasts forever.
(2) Humans are dependent on other creatures for survival.

(a) (2) is a contradiction of (1)
(b) (2) is independent of (1)
(c) (2) is an example of (1)
(d) (2) is the cause of (1)

PASSAGE 14

(Related to the Natural Disaster Led Assaults on a Hydropower Station in Gangtok)

Hydropower projects harness the energy of flowing water to generate electricity, making them one of the most widely used renewable energy sources worldwide. By using turbines and dams, hydropower stations convert the kinetic energy of water into mechanical energy, which is then transformed into electrical energy. Hydropower is seen as a cleaner alternative to fossil fuels, as it produces no direct emissions and utilises a renewable resource. However, while it offers numerous benefits, the development of hydropower projects presents both opportunities and challenges, particularly regarding environmental and social impacts.

One of the primary advantages of hydropower is its ability to generate large amounts of electricity with minimal environmental pollution. Unlike coal or gas plants, hydropower does not emit greenhouse gases or air pollutants. Additionally, once a hydropower station is built, the energy produced is often more cost effective over the long-term, given that water is a free resource and there are typically lower maintenance costs compared to fossil fuel plants. Moreover, hydropower stations can provide flexible energy solutions, as water flow can be adjusted to meet fluctuating energy demands, ensuring grid stability.

However, the construction and operation of hydropower projects have significant environmental and social consequences. Large scale dams often lead to the flooding of vast areas, resulting in the displacement of local communities and the destruction of natural habitats. Ecosystems that depend on natural river flows can be severely impacted, leading to loss of biodiversity, changes in water quality, and disruptions to aquatic life. Fish populations, in particular, can be harmed as dams block their migration routes, affecting their breeding cycles.

Additionally, the construction of dams alters the natural flow of rivers, impacting downstream water availability and sediment transport. This can lead to changes in agricultural practices, water supply for towns and cities, and even coastal erosion. In some cases, dams may also increase the risk of landslides and earthquakes in regions prone to geological instability.

The social costs of hydropower are also significant. In many instances, communities are displaced to make way for dam construction, leading to the loss of homes, agricultural land, and livelihoods. The resettlement of these communities is often fraught with challenges, as people struggle to rebuild their lives in new, unfamiliar locations. In many cases, the compensation provided is inadequate, resulting in long-term social and economic issues.

In conclusion, while hydropower projects offer a promising source of clean energy, their environmental and social impacts must be carefully considered. Thorough environmental impact assessments, sustainable planning, and transparent public engagement are essential to ensuring that the benefits of hydropower are realised without causing irreparable harm to ecosystems and communities.

Questions

Based on your understanding of the passage, answer the following questions.

1. In Paragraph 1, what does the phrase "Hydropower is seen as a cleaner alternative to fossil fuels" emphasise?
2. Complete the following with the correct option from the two given.

   Hydropower stations can provide flexible energy solutions, ...

   (a) as water flow can be adjusted to meet fluctuating energy demands, ensuring grid stability
   (b) as ecosystems that depend on natural river flows can be severely impacted
3. Support the writer's idea that Hydropower is seen as a cleaner alternative to fossil fuels.
4. Select the option that best reflects the challenges of hydropower generations.

   (a) Hydropower generation has unlimited water resources available year-round.
   (b) Hydropower generation can lead to ecological disruptions and displacement of communities.
5. State whether the following statement is True or False.

   The construction of dams alters the natural flow of rivers, impacting downstream water availability and sediment transport.
6. Which of the following states the possible risks associated with dam constructions?

   (a) Dam construction always leads to increased biodiversity in surrounding areas.
   (b) Dams have no impact on local water quality or ecosystems.
   (c) Dam construction provides permanent solutions to all flooding issues.
   (d) Dam construction can cause earthquakes, landslides and coastal erosion.

7. What are the key advantages of hydropower compared to fossil fuel energy sources, as outlined in the passage?

8. Fill in the blank with the correct option from those given.

   In the phrase 'fraught with challenges,' the word 'fraught' refers to ....

   (a) causing or characterised by emotional distress or tension
   (b) worked into shape by artistry or effort
   (c) something made from raw materials by hand or by machinery
   (d) to produce for the first time through the use of the imagination

PASSAGE 15

The rapid development of generative AI models, such as ChatGPT and Google's Gemini, is placing enormous energy demands on tech companies. These AI models require vast amounts of digital data to operate, leading to a surge in energy consumption. It is estimated that by the end of this decade, AI's energy needs could account for nine percent of all U.S. electricity, compared to four percent today. This sharp increase is driven in part by the competitive race among tech giants to dominate the AI space. However, the growing reliance on fossil fuels to meet these energy demands could jeopardise the sustainability goals of tech companies, many of which have pledged to become carbon neutral.

In response, tech companies are exploring renewable energy options to address these challenges. One promising solution is geothermal energy, which taps into the Earth's natural heat. Geothermal energy has been largely overlooked in the past, but advancements in technology are enabling its broader adoption. For instance, Facebook owner Meta recently partnered with Sage Geosystems, a geothermal startup, to develop a plant capable of producing 150 megawatts of carbon free energy, enough to power 70,000 homes. This collaboration represents a significant step forward in the use of geothermal energy for tech companies' growing energy demands.

Geothermal energy production is not new, but historically, it has been limited to areas with volcanic activity or hot springs. However, modern geothermal companies, like Sage Geosystems, are developing new methods to access hot rock found deep underground in a wider range of locations. By injecting water into these rocks, they can create heated reservoirs capable of producing electricity. This approach generates significantly fewer carbon emissions than traditional fossil fuel plants. Despite its potential, geothermal energy still faces challenges, such as high operational costs and scalability issues. While tech companies are investing in geothermal as a cleaner alternative, it remains to be seen whether it can meet the energy demands of AI driven innovations.

The rising energy needs of AI are straining the tech industry's sustainability efforts. AI models require significantly more electricity than standard searches or data processing, and the power demand is expected to increase dramatically with the growth of AI technologies like image and video models. Although geothermal energy could help mitigate this demand, it will take time to fully develop its capacity. For now, tech companies must balance their clean energy goals with the immediate need for reliable power sources, including fossil fuels.

Questions

Based on your understanding of passage, answer the following questions.

1. In paragraph 1, what does the phrase "the growing reliance on fossil fuels to meet these energy demands could jeopardise the sustainability goals of tech companies" emphasise?

2. Complete the following with the correct option from the two given.

   By injecting water into these rocks, ...

   (a) perform standard searches or data processing
   (b) they can create heated reservoirs capable of producing electricity

3. Support the writer's idea that the rising energy needs of AI are straining the tech industry's sustainability efforts.

4. Select the option that best reflects the attempts of tech giants to meet the energy demands of AI driven innovations.

   (a) Tech giants are reducing their energy consumption by eliminating AI projects.
   (b) Tech giants are partnering with geothermal startups to produce carbon-free energy.

5. State whether the following statement is True or False.

   Tech giants are solely relying on fossil fuels to meet AI energy demands.

6. Which of the following options states the effect of AI on the natural environment?

   (a) AI significantly reduces energy consumption in all industries.

(b) AI has no impact on natural resource management.
(c) AI promotes the restoration of ecosystems by reducing industrial activity.
(d) AI can lead to increased energy consumption and environmental degradation due to high computational demands.

7. What advancements are modern geothermal companies making to expand geothermal energy production, and what challenges do they face in becoming a viable alternative to fossil fuels?

8. Fill in the blank with the correct option from those given.

In the phrase 'enough to power 70,000 homes', the word 'power' refers to ....

(a) ability to act or produce an effect
(b) possession of control, authority, or influence over others
(c) the number of times as indicated by an exponent that a number occurs as a factor in a product
(d) a source or means of supplying energy

PASSAGE 16

1. Education for Sustainable Development (ESD) is now high on the international agenda and ESD is seen as a way to encourage greater sustainable consumption and production, (to counter the effects of climate change, address threats to biodiversity and provide more effective disaster risk reduction. Education for Sustainable Development is seen by UN as a lifelong process from early childhood to higher and adult education and goes beyond formal education. As values, lifestyles and attitudes are established from an early age, the role of education is of particular importance for children! (ESD has often been associated with curriculum projects linked with recycling, energy and water conservation; pollution reduction and sustainable consumption all developed to contribute towards achieving a more sustainable future.

2. Research from developmental psychology, longitudinal studies, social-cultural analysis, and neuroscience have all shown that it is in the early years that children have the greatest capacity to learn, and it is in these years that many of our fundamental attitudes and values are first put into place. Children are already investigating issues related to recycling, energy conservation, waste disposal and changes in their local environment. ESD in Early Childhood Care and Education (ECCE) is of great significance. The development of ESD and ECCE requires more than just curriculum development. It provides the possibility of a transformational reconstruction.

3. UNICEF reports show that children under the age of eight represent the highest percentage of affected population in today's global emergencies.
A UNESCO survey has shown that the ministries of education, environment and sustainable development in 97 UN member states identify poverty as the highest priority area to be addressed in achieving sustainable development. In fact, reductions in poverty and inequality are widely recognised as the priority in efforts to create a more sustainable world. At a global level, millions of children start school carrying the handicap that comes with the experience of malnutrition, ill-health and poverty. Yet, equitable access to high-quality pre-school programmes remain a problem in both rich and poor countries.
Sustainable development projects that enable rapid progress in maternal health, child nutrition and survival already exist, even in some of the world's poorest countries. Linking health and education agenda has been recognised as extremely important.

CBSE 2025

Based on your understanding of the passage, answer the following questions.

1. Complete the following with a suitable explanation with reference to Paragraph (1).
ESD is now high on the international agenda because ....

2. Based on the given passage, how does UN view ESD as a lifelong process? What are the critical areas of emphasis? (Paragraph 1)

3. List two curriculum projects that ESD (Education for Sustainable Development) has been linked with (Paragraph 1)

4. Complete the following suitably.
Many of our fundamental attitudes and values are put into plan in the early years as .... (Paragraph 2)

5. Substitute the underlined word with the correct word from Paragraph 2.

ESD in Early Childhood Care and Education provides the possibility of <u>transformational</u> reconstruction.

(a) positive change
(b) power to reform
(c) negative impact
(d) creative

6. What do UNICEF reports reveal about the vulnerability of children under the age of eight during global emergencies? (Paragraph 3)

(a) UNICEF reports highlight the resilience of children under the age of eight during global emergencies.

(b) UNICEF reports indicate that children under the age of eight are rarely affected by global emergencies.

(c) UNICEF reports show that children under the age of eight represent the highest percentage of affected population in global emergencies.

(d) UNICEF reports suggest that children under the age of eight are primarily responsible for responding to global emergencies.

7. What remains a problem in both rich and poor countries? What has been recognised as crucial? (Paragraph 3)

8. Complete the sentence with the correct response.
The writer's tone in the passage is ....

Case Based Factual Passages

Read the following passages carefully given below.

PASSAGE 1

1. In today's contemporary online shopping landscape, a perfect storm of choice engulfs consumers. Research consistently indicates that individuals presented with a limited selection tend to make more confident and efficient decisions compared to those confronted with overwhelming choices.
2. Consequently, assisting consumers in navigating the vast expanse of options available online has evolved into a thriving industry on a global scale. Many brands and retailers now employ marketing strategies revolving around the aspects given in the table below

Aspect	Description
Industry	Helping consumers decide what to buy online.
Marketing tools	Selecting, differentiation and discovery.
Data utilisation	Digital advertising, cataloging people by gender, income level, personal interests and more.
Retail Assistance	Algorithms, influencers and ad tech.
Challenge	Choice fatigue due to the overwhelming volume of consumer choices.
Solution	Lifestyle influencers on Instagram providing aspirational content and product recommendations.

3. For a relatively new breed of consumer product startups, a different approach emerges entirely. Rather than attempting to navigate the existing sea of products, these companies claim to revolutionise conventional consumer choices. Some brands offer limited, functional, mid-priced products, instilling customer confidence and breaking the cycle of consumerism.
4. The global product abundance could be more equitable. Unfortunately, creators often prioritise wealthier consumers.
5. For startups promising accessible simplicity, their very structure may eventually lead them back to an overwhelming array of choices. Most of these companies rely on hundreds of millions of dollars in venture capital funding, and their inventors typically expect rapid growth.

(Adapted for academic usage)

CBSE 2025

Questions

Based on your understanding of the passage, answer the following questions.

1. What does the use of the phrase 'a perfect storm of choice', by the writer, in Paragraph 1, tell us about their feelings?
   (a) The consumers are elated
   (b) The consumers are confused
   (c) The consumers are confident
   (d) The consumers are decisive
2. Identify the word in Paragraph 2, that indicates that the writer feels assisting consumers has become a profitable industry.
3. Based on the aspects mentioned in the table, mention the marketing approach that is primarily concerned with understanding consumers based on various factors.
4. Complete the following analogy approximately, based on your understanding of the table.

   Cataloging people by gender, income level, personal interests, etc. is to data utilisation as algorithms, influencers, and ad tech are to ....
5. Which aspect in the table pertains to presenting consumers with carefully selected choices to assist decision-making?
   (a) Challenge (b) Data utilisation
   (c) Marketing trends (d) Retail assistance
6. Based on your understanding, fill the blank with the appropriate option from those given in bracket.

   The solution to combat choice fatigue to .... (follow/employ/recommend) lifestyle influencers on Instagram who provide self-improving content and product references.
7. Complete the sentence suitably.

   The different approach to revolutionise consumer choices is to ....
8. Complete the following with a suitable reason.

   The writer believes that the global product abundance cannot be equitable because ....
9. In the context of the last paragraph though the startups promise simplicity of access, what are the drawbacks of such a structure?

PASSAGE 2

1. Silk is a natural protein fibre, some forms of which can be woven into textiles. Silk has a long history in India. It is known as *Resham* in Eastern and Northern India, and *Pattu* in the Southern parts of India. India is the second largest producer of silk in the world after China.
2. Silk is renowned for its luxurious qualities with a natural soft and smooth texture that feels comfortable on the skin. One of its unique qualities is to absorb and release moisture, regulating the body temperature, and keeping the wearer cool and dry.
3. Silk is one of the strongest natural fibres, but it loses up to 20% of its strength when wet. Its elasticity is moderate to poor: if elongated even a small amount, it remains stretched. It can be weakened if exposed to too much sunlight. It may also be attacked by insects, especially if left dirty.
4. The process of silk production is known as sericulture. Silk is produced by several insects; but, generally, only the silk of moth caterpillars has been used for textile manufacturing. To produce 1 kg of silk, 104 kg of mulberry leaves must be eaten by 3000 silkworms.
5. So what makes silk so costly? Firstly, cultivation of silk is a labour-intensive work. Secondly, the silk fabric is carefully derived from the larva of the silkworms which spin silk threads around themselves to make cocoons from natural sources. This makes the production limited due to factors like - climate, availability of quality mulberry leaves and time required by silkworms to complete their lifecycle. Thirdly, the intensive work can only be carried out with specialised knowledge and expertise by skilled artisans and craftsmanship. Lastly, superior quality silk fabrics are made from long and uniform silk fibres giving them a smooth and lustrous appearance. Thus, production requires careful selection, adding to the cost.

   In 2021, Karnataka was the highest producer of raw silk at 8483 metric tonnes followed by Andhra Pradesh at 5520 metric tonnes with Assam close behind at 5038 metric tonnes. At the other end of the spectrum there was Chhattisgarh (248 metric tonnes), Nagaland (230 metric tonnes) and UP trailed behind at 179 metric tonnes. **CBSE 2025**

Questions

Based on your understanding of the passage, answer the following questions.

1. Silk is a popular fabric in India.
   Support the above statement in 40 words with evidence from the text.
2. Select the option that is true for the Assertion and reason given below.
   Assertion (A) Silk feels comfortable to the skin.
   Reason (R) It made of natural protein fibre.
   (a) Both the (A) and (R) are true, and (R) is the correct explanation of (A).
   (b) Both the (A) and (R) are true, but (R) is not the correct explanation of (A).
   (c) (A) is true, but (R) is false.
   (d) (A) is false, but (R) is true.
3. Justify the following statement.
   Though one of the strongest natural fibres, silk remains stretched.
4. According to the passage, in what way is sunlight harmful to silk?
5. "To produce 1 kg of silk, 104 kg of mulberry leaves must be eaten by 3000 silkworms."
   State any one inference that can be drawn from the above statement.
6. Complete the following with one suitable reason from the text.
   Silk production work can be carried out by skilled artisans because ....
7. Based on the given text, which state was the smallest producer of silk.
8. Complete the sentence suitably.
   To carry out silk production requires careful selection because ....
9. Give one reason to support why production of silk is limited.

PASSAGE 3

1. A thorough study conducted across several villages of North-West India unveiled fascinating insights into the mural* landscape. It revealed that a significant majority, comprising around 80%, of these vibrant artworks are meticulously crafted by the villagers themselves. Approximately 15% of the murals stem from collaborative endeavours between villagers and local or visiting artists.
2. Surprisingly, a small fraction, about 5%, of the murals are the result of sponsored initiatives, often commissioned by governmental or non-governmental organisations. These murals convey social messages ranging from education and environmental conservation to public health awareness.
3. Among the locally crafted murals, nearly 55% depict scenes from mythology and folklore, celebrating the rich cultural heritage of the region. About 26 % of these murals showcase daily life in the villages, capturing moments of joy, struggle, and victory. The remaining 19% feature abstract or contemporary themes, reflecting evolving artistic expressions in rural settings.
4. Further analysis reveals that among the locally crafted murals, nearly 63% are found on the walls of community centres, temples, and other public spaces. Around 27 % adorn the exterior walls of residential houses. The remaining 10% are scattered across schools, health centres, and other institutional buildings, serving as educational tools and sources of inspiration for the younger generation.
5. To delve deeper, comparisons across various parameters such as demographic patterns, subject matter, techniques, community engagement, and impact are crucial. Analysing these facets not only provides a comprehensive understanding of mural creation in North-West Indian villages but also unveils avenues for cultural preservation, community development, and creative expression.

* a large painting or artwork that is typically created directly on a wall or ceiling

Created for academic usage/252 words **CBSE SQP 2024**

Questions

Based on your understanding of the passage, answer the following questions.

1. What does the use of the phrase 'fascinating insights' by the writer, in Paragraph 1, tell us about their feelings?
   (a) The writer is expressing surprise.
   (b) The writer is conveying boredom and frustration.
   (c) The writer is indicating interest and enthusiasm.
   (d) The writer is showing disappointment.
2. Select the option that is true for the Assertion and Reason given below.
   Assertion (A) The murals in North-West Indian villages are meticulously crafted.
   Reason (R) The murals are the result of collaborative endeavours.

(a) Both the (A) and (R) are true, and (R) is the correct explanation of (A).

(b) Both (A) and (R) are true, but (R) is not the correct explanation of (A).

(c) (A) is true, but (R) is false.

(d) (A) is false, but (R) is true.

3. Identify the word that indicates that the writer anticipated a higher percentage of sponsored initiative murals.

4. How do the murals in North-West Indian villages contribute to community engagement and awareness?

5. Read the given prompt and select the correct option in the brackets to fill in the blank.

In Hari's village, a mural depicting sustainable farming practices is showcased on the Panchayat office wall. The percentage of mural type that this would be counted in is (26% / 19% / 55%).

6. What does the highest percentage of different mural themes suggest about the artistic preferences and cultural priorities in North-West Indian villages?

7. Complete the sentence suitably.

The significant presence of murals on the exterior walls of residential houses highlight ....

8. Complete the following with a suitable reason.

The most likely reason the writer believes that a mural can serve as an 'educational tool' is because it can ....

9. In the context of the last paragraph, describe the significance of comparing various parameters such as demographic patterns, subject matter, techniques, community engagement, and impact in understanding the mural landscape in North-West Indian villages.

PASSAGE 4

1. Monsoon is the most delightful season—dark clouds adding drama to the skies, air fragrant with the unmatched scent of wet Earth getting drenched in the rains.

2. This one is for nostalgia. Though recently a neighbouring small town called Mawsynram has overtaken it, Cherrapunji is forever etched in our memories as the wettest place on Earth. It may be officially the second wettest place, but that's still a lot of rain to revel in! The best part about Sohra, as it is locally called, is that unlike other hill stations in the North-East, the roads are in good condition and driving in the rain is not a hazard. There are several waterfalls and viewpoints, including the milky white Nohkalikai Falls, which at 340 metres, is among the tallest waterfalls in the country.

3. Kochi in Kerala is the city that welcomes the monsoon into the country and is at its greenest this time of the year.
A nice breeze makes the walk around the old Fort Kochi area more enjoyable. Slow boat rides on the backwaters become more magical when rain starts to fall on the placid waters.

4. Gopalpur-on-Sea in Odisha, boasts of miles and miles of picturesque and unexplored beaches. One may sit on the golden sand and watch the casuarinas sway in the cool monsoon breeze. **CBSE 2024 C**

Places in India with Highest Annual Rainfall (calculated in approximation)

S. No.	Place	State	Rainfall	
			in mm	in inches
1.	Mawsynram	Meghalaya	11,871	467.4
2.	Cherrapunji	Meghalaya	11,777	463.7
3.	Agumbe	Karnataka	7,083	278.5
4.	Mahe	Puducherry	6,990	275.2
5.	Tuticorin	Tamil Nadu	6,492	255
6.	Amboli	Maharashtra	6,250	246
7.	Mahabaleshwar	Maharashtra	6,117	240.9

Questions

Based on your understanding of the passage, answer the following questions.

1. Complete the following analogy correctly with a word/phrase from Paragraph 1.
Golden : Sand : : .... : Land

2. Based on the information given in the table, fill in the blanks.
.... is the wettest place in India and .... officially stands next to it.

3. Infer the reason for the opinion provided below.

Opinion	Reason
Driving in the rain is not a hazard in Sohra	

4. How can the beauty of Kochi be enjoyed during the monsoon? (Any two)

5. Based on the text, which of the following options sums up the theme of the text?
(a) Nostalgic about the places he has visited in India.
(b) Boastful about the picturesque beaches of Odisha.
(c) Appreciative of monsoon as a delightful season.
(d) Critical of the hill stations situated in the North-East.

6. In the line - 'It boasts of miles and miles of picturesque and unexplored beaches, what does 'picturesque' most nearly mean?
(a) Placid (b) Attractive (c) Boastful (d) Serene

7. Fill in the blanks by selecting the correct option.
Nohkalikai Falls, which at 340 metres, is located in ...., which is the other name of ....
(a) Mawsynram, Cherrapunji (b) Cherrapunji, Sohra
(c) Sohra, Mawsynram (d) Mawsynram, Sohra

8. Replace the word 'reminiscence' with one word similar in meaning in the following sentence from Paragraph 2.
A wave of reminiscence swept over me when I saw my childhood home.

PASSAGE 5

1. After more than two years of halted travel. India's tourism and hospitality industry is now cautiously hopeful. Tourism constituted almost 3% of India's GDP and generated around 100 million jobs in 2019. But the sector was severely hit in India — like in other countries — in the past two years.
2. Indians are now travelling with a vengeance — 'revenge travel', as the phenomenon is called. And many, experts say, now prefer to travel within the country instead of flying to more expensive destinations abroad. The industy is also benefiting from new trends borne of the pandemic such as micro-holidays and workcations.
3. According to a survey, 51 percent of Indian travellers believed that international travel remained an important means of expanding their horizons and connecting with other cultures. Over two years, the survey said, Indian travellers are now dreaming about their next international trip and more than 70 percent of Indians are excited about being able to travel internationally.
4. There has also been an increase in the number of students going abroad to study. The increasing desire to study overseas is credited to the pent-up demand from the pandemic's two-year duration. This has got further pronounced because of growing aspirations and affordability among the middle-class students from Tier II and Tier III cities. The table below shows foreign travel by Indians for different purposes from 2019 to 2022.

Purpose	2019	2020	2021	2022
Business	14.7 L	2.6 L	1.2 L	4.6 L
Job	25.2 L	7.1 L	8.3 L	21.4 L
Residency	89.5 L	28.9 L	34.6 L	72.5 L
Education	5.8 L	2.6 L	4.4 L	6.5 L
Tourists	63.8 L	13.1 L	12.8 L	30.8 L
Visit	42.1 L	10.1 L	15.1 L	40.9 L
Medical	1,448	390	545	1,253
Pilgrimage	8.8 L	1.1 L	4,139	4.6 L
Others	2.6 L	54,775	58,767	1.6 L
Total	2.5 Crore	66.2 L	77.2 L	1.8 crore

Questions

Based on your understanding of the passage, answer the following questions.

1. Which of the following is the main takeaway from the study mentioned in the passage?
   (a) International travel remains an important means of expanding the horizons and connecting with other cultures.
   (b) Though travel, both domestic and international, has picked up, it has yet to reach its previous levels.
   (c) Indians are excited about being able to travel internationally.
   (d) The study needs to include experts from Tourism Department to offer any recommendations for further research.

2. Select the option that is true for the Assertion and Reason given below.
   Assertion (A) Tourism forms the largest GDP of the nation.
   Reason (R) Revenge travel promotes travelling within the country.
   (a) Both the (A) and (R) are true, and (R) is the correct explanation of (A).
   (b) Both the (A) and (R) are true, but (R) is not the correct explanation of (A).
   (c) (A) is true, but (R) is false.
   (d) (A) is false, but (R) is true.

3. Justify the following in about 40 words.
   After being cooped up inside their houses for more than two years, Indians are now excited about being able to travel internationally.

4. Based on the given table, for which 'purpose' did Indian foreign travel increase in 2022 as compared to 2019?

5. Fill in the blanks with the appropriate option from those given in brackets, based on your understanding of Paragraph 1.
   The statement that, "Tourism constituted almost 3% of India's GDP and generated around 100 million jobs in 2019", is a/an .... (fact/opinion) because it is a/an .... (subjective judgement/objective detail).

6. "The industry is also benefiting from new trends borne of the pandemic such a micro-holidays and workcations." Which 'industry' is being talked about here?

7. Complete the following appropriately.
   As per the given table, maximum number of Indians undertake foreign travel in 2019 for ...... and in 2022 for ....

8. Complete the following analogy appropriately, based on your understanding of Paragraphs 1 and 2.
   We can say that the situation when people were travelling with a vengeance is comparable to people going out to dine in hordes, because ....

9. Why are students today choosing to go abroad to study? (Answer in about 40 words.)

PASSAGE 6

1. Reduction in green areas has caused various environmental problems. People squeezed between concrete structures are looking for various ways to meet their longing for green. One of the ways to do so, is vertical gardens and green walls. Vertical gardening is a unique method of gardening where plants are grown in a vertical position or upward, rather than in the traditional method of planting them on the ground.
2. The purpose of vertical gardens and green walls, which arises from the studies of different disciplines (landscape architects, architects, engineers, etc.) is to close the cold image of concrete and increase the visual value. In these systems, nature and structures are integrated and thus, urban areas and the desired environment have become intertwined.
3. Vertical garden case studies often show that though functionality should be in the foreground, when vertical gardens are planned, they are generally made as aesthetic elements in the city's underpasses and city squares and decorative elements in residences, without seeking functionality.
4. Experts support that the visual quality and evaluation of landscape architecture is determined based on the satisfaction of the users. Hence, a survey questionnaire was prepared for residents of varied age groups from of a metropolitan city. The given Table 1, displays these responses.

Table 1 - Total number of participants : 400

No.	Survey statements	Strongly agree	Agree	Neutral	Disagree	Strongly disagree
Vertical gardens						
1	Improve quality of life of people in urban areas	191	138	43	9	19
2	Reduce noise pollution	128	164	77	25	6
3	Increase air quality—indoors and outdoors	172	147	51	28	2
4	Reduce energy and water consumption	58	47	125	68	2
5	Positively impact global warming	114	144	106	30	6
6	Have a relaxing and calming effect	161	177	44	7	11
7	Cost too much	86	107	152	42	13
8	Make plants look beautiful	195	139	44	6	16
9	Add naturalness to the environs	135	173	55	25	12
10	Are among the determining factor to visiting a place	59	133	141	54	13
11	Are inconvenient indoors	9	84	123	126	48
12	Can be applied in every place	71	132	97	77	23
13	Have a functional feature	81	207	100	10	2
14	Distract drivers	34	101	106	131	28
15	Funds are best used for social issues	57	72	100	130	41

5. The study acknowledged that vertical gardening has the potential to transform urban spaces into green, sustainable areas and further research should explore the impact of vertical gardening on the environment and human well-being.

Adapted for academic usage - 2019 case-study -Investigating the vertical garden applications in Turkey 225 words approx.

CBSE SQP 2023

Questions

Based on your understanding of the passage, answer the following questions.

1. Which of the following is the main takeaway from the study mentioned in the passage?

(a) Vertical gardening has minimal impact on the environment or human well-being.
(b) Vertical gardening is a sustainable practice that can transform urban spaces into green areas.
(c) The impact of vertical gardening on the environment and human well-being has already been thoroughly explored.
(d) The study needs to include experts from horticultural firms to offer any recommendations for further research.

2. Select the option that is true for the assertion and reason given below.

Assertion (A) Vertical gardens are a way to reduce environmental problems.

Reason (R) Vertical gardens add a visual value to the surrounding.

(a) Both the (A) and (R) are true, and (R) is the correct explanation of (A).

(b) Both the (A) and (R) are True, but (R) is not the correct explanation of (A).

(c) (A) is true, but (R) is false.

(d) (A) is false, but (R) is true.

3. Justify the following, in about 40 words. **Competency Based**

While the survey results suggest that vertical gardens may be effective in improving the quality of life in urban areas, further research and evaluation may be necessary to fully understand their effectiveness and potential drawbacks.

4. Based on the survey results, which two concerns should a city government, looking to install vertical gardens, address? **Competency Based**

5. Fill the blanks with the appropriate option from those given in brackets, based on your understanding of paragraph 2. **Competency Based**

The statement that, urban spaces have become more closely connected with the desired natural surroundings through the incorporation of nature and structures in vertical gardens and green walls, is a .... (fact/opinion) because it is a .... (subjective judgement/objective detail).

6. In Table 1, the Statement 3, "Vertical gardens increase air quality - indoors and outdoors," received the most neutral responses from participants, with 51 respondents indicating a neutral stance. State any one inference that can be drawn from this.

7. What does the given figure indicate?

It indicates ....

8. Complete the following analogy appropriately, based on your understanding of paragraphs 1 and 2.

We can say that the situation of people living in concrete structures is comparable with a fish living in a fishbowl and the need for vertical gardens to the need for decorations in the fishbowl because ....

9. Infer one benefit and one drawback of vertical gardening, in comparison to other solutions, such as community gardens or parks. (Answer in about 40 words)

PASSAGE 7

1. Starting Monday, the country's low-cost Mars Mission with the red planet for an extended period will enter the 'blackout' phase snapping communication with the satellite. From 8th to 22nd June the Sun will block Mars from the Earth snapping communication with the satellite.

2. A senior Indian Space Research Organisation official said. "This will be for the first time that there will be a communication break for such a long period of about 15 days. During this period, there will be no communication with the satellite", he added.

3. Expressing confidence about regaining control over the satellite once the 'blackout' phase is over, he said, "the scenario has been tested and the line of communication will be established." The spacecraft's life has been extended for another six months in March due to surplus fuel.

4. Stating that the spacecraft has been 'configured' for the blackout, the ISRO official said, "we are not sending any commands to the spacecraft now, till 8th June few hours of signals will be sent by the spacecraft that will be for about two to three hours per day". In May next year, the mission will have to go through a similar phase once again, if there is another extension of mission life when the Earth will come between the Sun and Mars.

5. Scripting space history, India on 24th September last successfully placed its low-cost Mars spacecraft in orbit around the red planet in its very first attempt, breaking into an elite club of three countries. **CBSE 2023**

Questions

Based on your understanding of the passage, answer the following questions.

1. The communication with the satellite will break for approximately .... days.

(a) 10 (b) 15 (c) 20 (d) 25

2. Read the following sentences. **Competency Based**

1. The 'blackout' was a sudden development.
2. Because of this, the officials are very nervous about the success of the spacecraft.

Codes

(a) Both 1 and 2 are true (b) Both 1 and 2 are false

(c) 1 is true and 2 is false (d) 1 is false and 2 is true

3. Substitute the word 'nonpareil' with one word similar in meaning in the following sentence from Paragraph 5.
India managed to get into the nonpareil club of Mars spacecraft in orbit.

4. Complete the following analogy correctly with a word/phase from Paragraph 2.
Aroma : Cooking : : .... : Space satellite
(**Clue** Just like Aroma is integral to cooking, similarly is/are integral to Space Research.)

5. Choose the appropriate option to fill in the blank.
From Paragraphs 1 and 2, we can infer that there will be ....
1. no communication with the people
2. 'blackout' phase
3. satellite will get no communication
4. Moon will block the Earth
5. the communication break will be for 15 days.

6. Why is the 'blackout' phase significant? **Competency Based**

7. Select the correct option to complete the following sentence.
The ISRO officials are .... about their control over the spacecraft after the 'blackout' phase.

8. Complete the sentence appropriately.
According to the ISRO official till 8th July, when Sun will block Mars, ... signal/signals per day will be sent to the spacecraft.

9. The spacecraft's life was extended by six months. Substantiate.

PASSAGE 8

1. Increasing of traffic congestion every year is causing increasing of air pollution, wasting of time and productivity and diverse respiratory diseases. Moreover, the cost of solving or reducing traffic congestion is enormous. However, neglecting the traffic jam problem would increase the social problems among citizens.
2. The number of vehicles has increased considerably in the city in the past five years. Due to this increase, the city roads witness frequent traffic congestions, but above all, the vehicles emitting pollutants are affecting the environment adversely.
3. The capital's vehicular population saw an addition of more than five lakh vehicles last year, registering an increase of over 4% according to the Delhi Economic Survey 2020-21.
4. In spite of largest road network, through metro and bus services, the transport system is not being able to keep pace with the growing demand, as a result of which, more and more people use their private vehicles, leading to increased congestion on the roads, still people in India prefer road travel over air and other means of travel.
5. Citizens of Delhi/NCR have, time and again, pondered over the possibilities of how to reduce the traffic congestion in the city, especially during the peak hours. People should use public transport, the government must increase the facilities of public transport, people should avoid the unnecessary collection of vehicles and should use carpool and vehicle sharing.
6. What is required is proper implementation of corrective measures by citizens to get an organised traffic management system. **CBSE 2023**

Questions

Based on your understanding of the passage, answer the following questions.

1. Select the appropriate option to complete the following sentence. The reasons for increased traffic congestion are ....
1. use of private vehicles
2. increase in demand for cars
3. inability to keep pace with population control
4. travelling by public transport
5. emission of pollutants

Codes
(a) 4 and 5 (b) 1 and 5
(c) 1 and 2 (d) 1 and 3

2. Select the appropriate option which states the methods of reducing traffic congestion.
1. Start car pooling
2. Add electric buses
3. Increase in public modes of transport
4. Increase car collection points
5. Increase taxation

Codes
(a) 1, 4 and 5 (b) 3 and 5
(c) 2, 3 and 4 (d) 1 and 3

3. Substitute the underlined word with one word similar in meaning in the following sentence.
Citizens of Delhi/NCR have time and time again have pondered over the possibilities of how to reduce traffic congestion. **Competency Based**

4. Give the reasons for increase in vehicular congestion.

5. Fill in the blank by selecting the correct option.
There are .... (beneficial/adverse) consequences of increasing vehicular congestion.

6. Infer one reason for the following based on information in paragraph 1.
Reducing traffic congestion in not easy.

7. Complete the following analogy correctly with a word/phase from paragraph 5.
Organised : Chaotic : : Lowest : ....
(**Clue** Just as organised is an antonym of chaotic lowest is an antonym of ....)

8. Complete the following sentence.
Use of public transport will reduce ....

9. Analyse the status of traffic between the years 2019-2022.

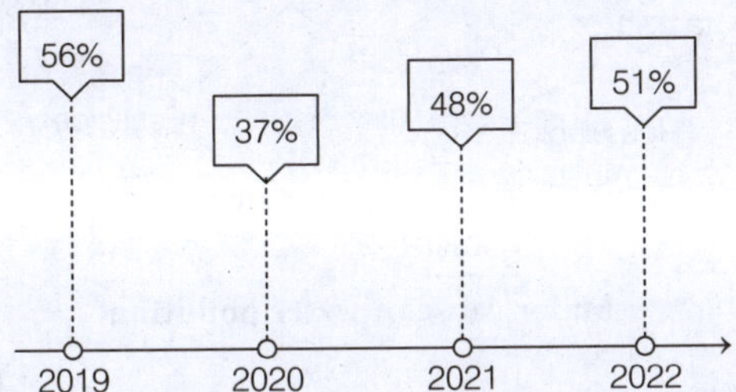

What is required to get an organised traffic management system?

PASSAGE 9

1. According to a new study, a vast blanket of pollution stretching across South Asia is cutting down sunlight by 10 per cent over India, damaging agriculture, modifying rainfall patterns and putting hundreds of thousands of people at risk.

2. It is said, "Acids in the haze may, by falling as acid rain, have the potential to damage crops and trees. Ash falling on leaves can aggravate the impact of reduced sunlight on the Earth's surface. The pollution that is forming the haze could be leading to several hundreds of thousands of premature deaths as a result of higher levels of respiratory diseases."

3. "The haze had cut down sunlight over India by 10 percent (so far) -- a huge amount! As a repercussion, the North-West of India is drying up," Prof. V. Ramanathan said when asked specifically about the impact of the haze over India. He said, "We are still in an early stage of the understanding of the impact of the haze."

4. Prof. V. Ramanathan was asked whether the current droughts in most parts of India after over a decade of good monsoons was owing to the haze. He said, "It was too early to reach a conclusion. If the droughts persist for about four to five years, then we would start suspecting that it may be because of the haze India, China and Indonesia are the worst affected owing to their population density, economic growth and depleting forest cover." **CBSE 2023**

Questions

Based on your understanding of the passage, answer the following questions.

1. The pollution spreading across South Asia is affecting India by ....
Choose the correct option from the ones given below.

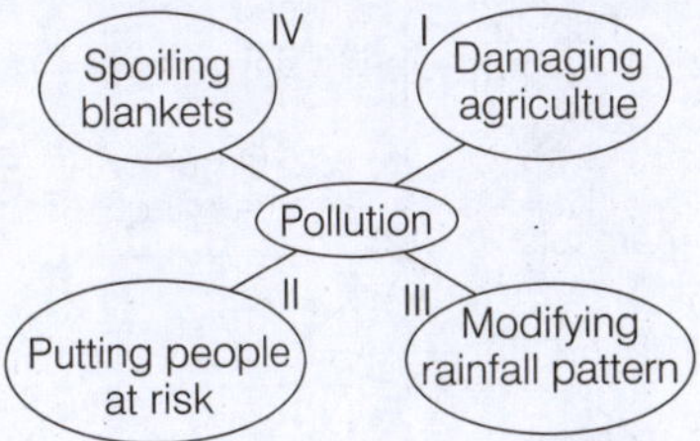

Codes

(a) I, II and III
(b) I, III and IV
(c) II, III and IV
(d) I, II and IV

2. Select the option that titles paragraphs 1-4 appropriately with reference to information in the text. **Competency Based**

(a) 1. Impact of Pollution in South Asia
2. Effects of Acid Rain
3. Understanding Consequences of Haze
4. Debate over Droughts

(b) 1. Impact of Droughts
2. Understanding Acid Rain
3. Effect of Haze
4. Debate over Pollution

(c) 1. Impact of Pollution in South Asia
2. Effects of Acid Rain
3. Debate over Droughts
4. Understanding Haze

(d) 1. Impact of Haze
2. Understanding Acid Rain
3. Debate over Pollution
4. Effect of Haze

3. Substitute the word 'repercussion' with one word similar in meaning in the following sentence from paragraph 3. **Competency Based**
The haze has cut down sunlight over India ... As a repercussion, the North-West of India is drying up.

4. Infer one reason for the following based on the information in paragraph 1.
In India, rainfall patterns are changing.

5. Fill in the blank by selecting the correct option.
Ash falling on leaves can .... (worsen/diminish) the impact of reduced sunlight on the Earth's surface.

6. List any two countries which are affected due to depleting forest cover.
7. Complete the following analogy correctly with a word/phrase from paragraph 2.
   Possibility : .... : : Suspecting : Doubting
8. Complete the following sentence appropriately.
   There has .... droughts were caused by the haze.
9. From the following pie chart, identify one reason each which does and does not contribute to weather disruption.

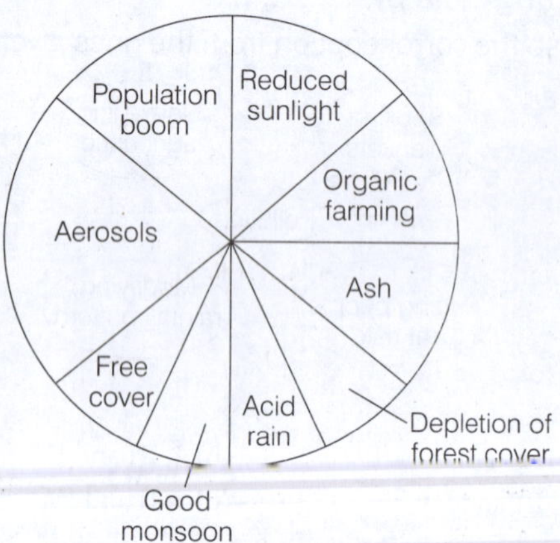

PASSAGE 10

1. Unsafe water kills more people each year than do war and all other forms of violence combined. Meanwhile, our drinkable water sources are finite: less than 1 percent of the Earth's fresh water is actually accessible to us. Without action, the challenges will only increase by 2050, when global demand for freshwater is expected to be one-third greater than it is now.
2. Water is uniquely vulnerable to pollution. Known as a 'Universal solvent', water is able to dissolve more substances than any other liquid on Earth. Water pollution is the release of substances into subsurface groundwater or into lakes, streams, rivers, estuaries and oceans to the point where the substances interfere with beneficial use of the water or with the natural functioning of ecosystems. In addition to the release of substances, such as chemicals, trash, or microorganisms, water pollution may also include the release of energy, in the form of radioactivity or heat, into bodies of water. The key causatives of water pollution in India are urbanisation, deforestation, industrial effluents and agricultural run-offs with the use of insecticides and pesticides. The other causes are social and religious offerings in water bodies and the use of detergents and fertilisers.
3. Water pollution can have disastrous consequences on the ecosystem. Further more, toxic chemicals can travel through the food chain and get into our bodies, causing diseases and death.
4. There is no single or simple answer to stop the water pollution crisis. However, there are many solutions to prevent water pollution, both in our daily lives and within industries. They are wastewater treatment, reducing plastic waste and water conservation. In addition to this, we must have water-efficient toilets, stormwater management and ozone waste water treatment.

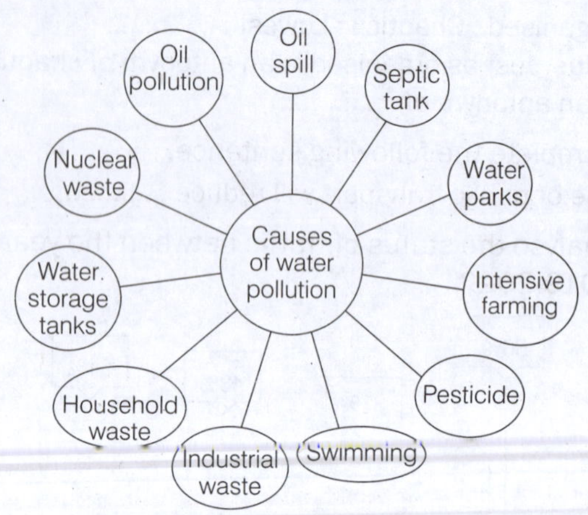

Major cause of water pollution

CBSE 2023

Questions

Based on your understanding of the passage, answer the questions given below.

1. Select the appropriate option to fill in the blank.
   Water is uniquely vulnerable to ....
   (a) season
   (b) pollution
   (c) water bodies
   (d) extreme weather conditions
2. Select the option that is true for the Assertion and Reason given below.
   Assertion (A) Less than 1 percent of the Earth's fresh water is actually accessible to us.
   Reason (R) As the world population grows, the demand for water increases.
   (a) Both the (A) and (R) are true, and (R) is the correct explanation of (A).
   (b) Both the (A) and (R) are true, but (R) is not the correct explanation of (A).
   (c) (A) is true, but (R) is false.
   (d) (A) is false, but (R) is true.
3. Substitute the word causative with one word similar in meaning in the following sentence.
   The key causative of water pollution in India must be addressed.

4. Complete the following analogy correctly with a word/phrase from paragraph 2.
Vulnerable : Resilient : : Artificial : ....
(**Clue** Just as resilient is the opposite of vulnerable, similarly the opposite of artificial is ....)

5. Select the correct option to complete the following sentence.
Water pollution can have disastrous consequences on ....
(a) the ecosystem (b) weather conditions

6. From the chart, identify two causes of water pollution in our homes.

7. Fill in the blank by selecting the correct option.
One of the solutions of preventing water pollution is ....

8. According to the writer, water pollution is defined as .... (Paragraph 2)

9. List one way in which religious rituals impact water bodies.

PASSAGE 11

Hindi Diwas is celebrated annually on 14th September marking the adoption of Hindi as one of India's official languages in 1949. Hindi, written in Devanagari script, is the most widely spoken language in India and one of the 22 scheduled languages.

Significance of Hindi Language

Hindi is culturally and politically significant in India. It is the language of major literary works and Bollywood, India's largest film industry.

Spoken by over 40% of the population, Hindi serves as a lingua franca, aiding communication across diverse linguistic regions.

Celebrations

Educational Institutions Activities like poetry recitations, essay writing and debates are organised to promote Hindi.

Government Offices Seminars, discussions, and workshops are held to promote the use of Hindi in official communication.

Media and Cultural Organisations Special programmes like Hindi films, interviews, and literary festivals are featured.

Debates Around Hindi

Support Hindi unifies a linguistically diverse country. It preserves India's literary and cultural heritage. Hindi enhances administrative efficiency.

Criticism Regional languages may feel marginalised. Some states resist the imposition of Hindi, fearing linguistic dominance. Educational disparities may arise for non-Hindi speaking regions.

Conclusion

Hindi Diwas celebrates the language's cultural importance and role in national unity while recognising the need to respect linguistic diversity.

Questions

Based on your understanding of the passage, answer the following questions.

1. What does the use of the phrase 'lingua franca' mean?
   (a) A language used for communication between groups of people who speak different languages.
   (b) A language used for communication between groups of people who speak the same language.

2. Select the option that is true for the Assertion and Reason given below.
   Assertion (A) The promotion of Hindi as a dominant language in India may marginalise regional languages.
   Reason (R) Many states resist Hindi's imposition due to concerns about linguistic dominance and the potential for educational disparities in non-Hindi speaking regions.
   (a) Both the (A) and (R) are true, and (R) is the correct explanation of (A).
   (b) Both the (A) and (R) are true, but (R) is not the correct explanation of (A).
   (c) (A) is true, but (R) is false.
   (d) (A) is false, but (R) is true.

3. Identify the word that indicates that the non-Hindi speaking people are not in favour of the Hindi language.

4. Why is Hindi Diwas celebrated and why?

5. What are some activities organised during Hindi Diwas celebrations?

6. What are the criticisms surrounding the promotion of Hindi?

7. Complete the sentence suitably.
   Hindi unifies a linguistically diverse country by ....

8. Complete the following with a suitable reason.
   Hindi Diwas celebrates linguistic diversity in India by ....

9. What role does Hindi play in India's linguistic landscape, and what are the various ways Hindi Diwas is celebrated to honour this language?

PASSAGE 12

1. Research from the Publishers Association has shown that films based on books take 44% more at the box office revenue in the UK and 53% more worldwide than original screenplays. The report explores what impact a book has when adapted for film and TV.
2. The report reads "Published material is the basis of 52% of top UK films in the last 10 years and accounts for an even higher share of revenue from these leading performers, at 61% of UK box office gross and 65% of worldwide gross." The Hollywood adaptation of 'My Cousin Rachel' was shown to have a significant impact on the sales of the Daphne Du Maurier thriller. The sales of the book in 2017 alone accounted for 23% of all sales since 1992.
3. The research suggests that adapted films tend to perform better, because films can 'leverage the popularity' of well-known books through an existing audience. Films adapted from books also tend to have a richer, more fully-developed story to draw on. In terms of TV adaptation, it was revealed that a quarter of dramas were based on literary sources and attracted a 56% larger share of the audience than those based on original scripts. Fourteen of the 35 high end series produced in the UK in the period between January and September 2017 were based on books, compared to seven based on true stories or historical events and five based on pre-existing films or TV stories.
4. In the case of the 2016 BBC broadcast of 'The Night Manager', research revealed that while the novel was in circulation for over 25 years, 82% of the copies it sold were in 2016 and 2017. Sales of the paperback edition remained strong in 2017 even after the series went off the air.
5. In conclusion, the report states that "there is a strong two-way relationship between publishing and the wider creative economy, wherein a successful adaptation often has spill-over effects and gives a substantial boost to the sales of the original book." **CBSE SQP 2021 Term I Modified**

Questions

Based on your understanding of the passage, answer the following questions.

1. Select the option that gives the correct meaning of the following statement.
The sales of the book in 2017 alone accounted for 23% of all sales since 1992.
(a) There were 23% higher sales in 2017 than previous years.
(b) A major chunk of sales happened in 2017.
(c) The sales were limited to 23% in 2017.
(d) There were very few books sold in the previous years.

2. Select the option that is true for the Assertion and Reason given below.
Assertion (A) The writing economy is intertwined with the creative world in a complex manner.
Reason (R) Adaptation has become the new norm in the creative world.
(a) Both the (A) and (R) are true, and (R) is the correct explanation of (A).
(b) Both the (A) and (R) are true, but (R) is not the correct explanation of (A).
(c) Both the (A) and (R) are true, but (R) is not the correct explanation of (A).
(d) (A) is false, but (R) is true.

3. What was the result shown by the research from the Publishers Association? **Competency Based**

4. How did the making of the novel 'The Night Manager' into a TV series affect the book?

5. What did the research reveal about dramas?

6. The maximum TV serials in UK in the year 2017 were based on what?

7. Complete the sentence appropriately.
According to the research, the films based on books have greater success because ....

8. Complete the sentence appropriately.
The purpose of the research by Publishers Association was to study the ....

9. Mention the two things that the given sentence refers to. **Competency Based**
Films adapted from books also tend to have a richer, more fully-developed story to draw on.

PASSAGE 13

1. India's population is expected to grow by 25%, with reference to 2011, to 1.52 billion by 2036, according to the final report of the technical group on population projections dated July 2020. The group was constituted by the National Commission on Population (NCP) under the Ministry of Health and Family Welfare with the mandate to provide population projections for the period 2011 to 2036.
2. India's population growth rate is expected to decline to its lowest since the Independence in the 2011-2021 decade, with a decadal growth rate of 12.5%. It will decline further to 8.4% in the 2021-2031 decade, as per the report, which the wire has seen. According to these

projections, India will overtake China as the world's most populous country around 2031 – almost a decade later than the United Nations projection of 2022. India's population is projected to increase to 1.52 billion by 2036.

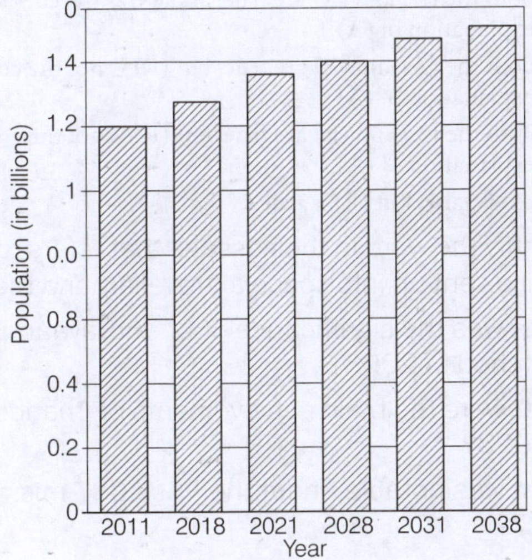

Source Report of the technical group on population projections

3. The projections have been delayed quite significantly. "Ideally, they should have come by 2016. But there were delays in setting up the committee and then more delays at the governments end even after we submitted the report. We had submitted our report in November 2019," said a member of the committee wishing to remain anonymous. This was confirmed by two other members as well.
4. India's population was 1.21 billion as per the census of 2011 and the projections now estimate that the population will grow by 311 million by 2036.
5. The report projects that as much as 70% of this increase will be in urban areas. India's urban population will increase from 377 million in 2011 to 594 million in 2036 – a growth of 57%. So, while 31% of Indians were living in urban India in 2011,that will grow to 39% by 2036.
6. Consequently, the proportion of the rural population will decline from 69% to 61% as the urban population is projected to increase more than twice the projected increase in the rural population.

Questions

Based on your understanding of the passage, answer the following questions.

1. The purpose of the above report was to give

(a) population projections for 2036

(b) population projections for 2011

(c) population projections for 2011-2036

(d) population projections for 2031

2. Select the option that is true for the Assertion and Reason given below.

Assertion (A) The Indian population growth had become a serious concern in the recent decade.

Reason (R) India became the world's most populous country a decade earlier.

(a) Both the (A) and (R) are true, and (R) is the correct explanation of (A).

(b) Both the (A) and (R) are true, but (R) is not the correct explanation of (A).

(c) Both the (A) and (R) are true, but (R) is not the correct explanation of (A).

(d) (A) is false, but (R) is true.

3. "It will decline further to 8.4% in the 2021-2031 decade..." What does this statement mean?

4. What does the research in the above passage mention about rural population? **Competency Based**

5. According to the passage, how much delay from the UN's projection can be seen in India becoming the most populated country in the world? **Competency Based**

6. Why did the projections come in July of 2020?

7. Complete the sentence appropriately.

The number by which the population of India is estimated to grow by 2036 is ....

8. Fill in the blank with the appropriate option.

This passage contains the decadal .... (growth/decline) rate for the decade 2011-2021, which is 12.5%.

9. Infer two facts about India on the basis of your reading of the passage.

PASSAGE 14

Top 5 ISRO Missions that Changed the Face of Space Exploration

1. **Aryabhata** (1975)

   Launch Date 19th April, 1975

   Significance India's first satellite, launched from the Soviet Union, designed for X-ray astronomy, solar physics and aeronomy.

   Impact Initiated India's space journey, despite technical issues, and provided valuable lessons in satellite technology.

2. **Mangalyaan** (Mars Orbiter Mission) (2013)

   Launch Date 5th November, 2013

Significance India's first mission to Mars, achieved orbit on the first attempt with a budget of $74 million.

Impact Demonstrated ISRO's efficiency and cost-effectiveness in interplanetary missions, providing valuable Martian atmospheric data.

3. **Chandrayaan Missions** (2008, 2019, 2023)

   Chandrayaan-1 (2008) Detected water molecules on the Moon, revolutionising lunar science.

   Chandrayaan-2 (2019) Advanced exploration of the Moon's South pole; orbiter provided critical data.

   Chandrayaan-3 (2023) Achieved a successful soft landing near the Moon's South pole.

4. **Aditya-L1** (2023)

   Launch Date 2nd September, 2023

   Significance India's first solar mission to study the Sun's outer layers.

   Impact Aimed to improve understanding of solar activities and their impact on space weather.

5. **PSLV and Its C37 Mission** (2017)

   Launch Date 15th February, 2017

   Significance PSLV-C37 set a world record by deploying 104 satellites in a single mission.

   Impact Showcased ISRO's advanced technology and versatility, boosting its global reputation.

Questions

Based on your understanding of the passage, answer the following questions.

1. Which of the following options does not mean the same as 'versatile'?

(a) Adaptable (b) Amateur (c) Flexible (d) Resourceful

2. Select the option that is true for the Assertion and Reason given below.

Assertion (A) Aryabhata, the satellite, marked an exciting phase of Indian space exploration.

Reason (R) Aryabhata was significant for being India's first satellite, marking the beginning of the country's space journey.

(a) Both the (A) and (R) are true, and (R) is the correct explanation of (A).

(b) Both the (A) and (R) are true, but (R) is not the correct explanation of (A).

(c) Both the (A) and (R) are true, but (R) is not the correct explanation of (A).

(d) (A) is false, but (R) is true.

3. Identify the word in the passage that refers to 'a device sent up into space to travel around the Earth'.

4. What was the significance of Chandrayaan-1, launched in 2008?

5. What were the main achievements of Chandrayaan-3 in 2023?

6. What was notable about the PSLV-C37 mission in 2017?

7. Complete the sentence suitably.

Aryabhata, launched on 19th April, 1975, was India's first satellite, designed ....

8. Complete the following with a suitable reason.

Mangalyaan, launched on 5th November, 2013, was India's first mission to Mars, achieving ....

9. How have ISRO's key missions, such as Aryabhata, Mangalyaan, and Chandrayaan, transformed India's space exploration landscape?

PASSAGE 15

1. **Coverage and Significance**
   - Oceans cover 71% of Earth's surface and hold 97% of the planet's water.
   - Vital for regulating weather, climate, coastlines, food supply, and producing oxygen.
   - Historical importance in trade and cultural exchange.

2. **World Oceans Day**

   Date 8th June, designated by the UN General Assembly (Resolution 63/111, 5th December, 2008).

   Purpose Raise awareness about the ocean's role and promote its protection.

   2024 Theme 'Awaken New Depths' aims to highlight the need for deeper commitment to ocean preservation.

3. **Challenges to Ocean Health**

   Climate Change and Global Warming Ocean temperatures have risen by 1.45°C on average, with some areas exceeding 2°C. Leads to coral bleaching and negative impacts on marine ecosystems.

Ocean Acidification Ocean absorbs 25-30% of CO_2 emissions, causing a 30% increase in acidity since pre-industrial times. Projected to rise by 170% by 2100, affecting marine species and coastal ecosystems.

Rising Sea Levels Contributing 40% of global sea level rise, with a 9 cm increase over the past three decades. Causes flooding, erosion and contamination of agricultural lands.

Plastics and Ocean Debris Over 80% of marine pollution comes from land-based sources; 8 million tons of plastic enter the ocean annually. Creates large garbage patches, harming marine life.

Other Pollutions Includes oil spills, noise pollution, and runoff from agriculture and industry.

Overfishing and Commercial Whaling Drives species to extinction, affecting food security and ecological balance.

Shipping and Transport Contributes to pollution through waste disposal and emissions.

4. **Solutions and Actions**

Marine Protected Areas (MPAs) Protect endangered species and local ecosystems.

Reducing Pollution Adopt renewable energy, enforce waste disposal regulations, and ban single-use plastics.

Changing Consumption Habits Promote sustainable fishing and plant-based diets.

Sustainable Energy Invest in clean technologies and lower emissions in maritime transport.

Research and Awareness Enhance scientific research and public education on ocean issues.

Protecting the ocean requires global cooperation, sustainable practices, and increased awareness to ensure its health and vitality for future generations.

Questions

Based on your understanding of the passage, answer the following questions.

1. Which of the following options does not mean the same as 'erosion'?

(a) Corrosion (b) Disintegration
(c) Breakdown (d) Construction

2. Select the option that is true for the Assertion and Reason given below.

Assertion (A) Implementing Marine Protected Areas (MPAs) is crucial for the conservation of endangered species and ecosystems.

Reason (R) Establishing MPAs helps reduce human impact on marine environments, while adopting renewable energy and sustainable practices further protects ocean health and biodiversity.

(a) Both the (A) and (R) are true, and (R) is the correct explanation of (A).
(b) Both the (A) and (R) are true, but (R) is not the correct explanation of (A).
(c) Both the (A) and (R) are true, but (R) is not the correct explanation of (A).
(d) (A) is false, but (R) is true.

3. Identify the word that refers to "an amount of a substance that is produced and sent out into the air that is harmful to the environment."

4. What percentage of the Earth's surface is covered by oceans and why are they significant?

5. What is the purpose of World Oceans Day and when is it celebrated?

6. What challenges do oceans face due to climate change?

7. Complete the sentence suitably.

The ocean absorbs 25-30% of CO_2 emissions, leading to a 30% increase ....

8. Complete the following with a suitable reason.

Rising sea levels contribute 40% of global sea level rise and have resulted in ....

9. What are some key solutions and actions to protect the ocean and why is global cooperation important?

PASSAGE 16

1. Electric Vehicles (EV) market is growing rapidly all over the world. In India also the EV market has gained significant momentum. It has grown more after the implementation of FAME (Faster Adoption and Manufacture of Hybrid and Electric Vehicles) scheme in 2015 by Ministry of Heavy Industry and Public Enterprises.
2. Electric vehicles are solutions to be independent and free from imported energy resources. Electric cars can bring a major change to India in becoming self-sustainable. EV could also be the alternative to decrease carbon dioxide gas. Carbon dioxide from automobiles is one of the causes of air pollution.
3. An EV can be used for flexible load, for standardising the grid with substantial share of fluctuating renewable energy generation. EV emits 30-80% less greenhouse gas when compared with Internal Combustion Engine (ICE) vehicle. EVs do not consume any energy when it is stationary as compared to ICE vehicles where fuel in consumed when it is idle. EV is recognised as promising alternatives to vehicles and will potentially replace ICE vehicles in the near future.
4. The electric vehicles have low emissions, high efficiency and smooth operation. The energy consumption and emissions for plug in hybrid electric vehicles found that compared to gasoline vehicles there

is 37.5% less energy consumption and 35% less greenhouse gas emissions.

The government have started financial policies to encourage EV adoption; however, decision makers have to plar a long-term perspective to get them implemented efficiently. **CBSE 2025**

Questions

Based on your understanding of the passage, answer the following questions.

1. What does the phrase 'gained significant momentum' in paragraph 1. tell us about the impact of EV market?
   (a) It is momentarily important
   (b) It has developed very quickly
   (c) It has gained profit
   (d) It has to develop a significant market
2. Select the option that is true for the Assertion and Reason given below.
   Assertion (A) Electric vehicles can bring a major change to India.
   Reason (R) It can bring India to becoming self-sustainable.
   (a) Both (A) and (R) are true, and (R) is the correct explanation of (A).
   (b) Both (A) and (R) are true, but (R). is not the correct explanation of (A).
   (c) (A) is true, but (R) is false.
   (d) (A) is false, but (R) is true.
3. Give two benefits of using electric vehicles over Internal Combustion Engine vehicles.
4. With reference to the passage, the word 'idle' in paragraph 3 most nearly means ....
5. How do electric vehicles contribute to diminishing a country's reliance on imported energy?
6. Read the given prompt and select the correct option in the brackets to fill in the blank.
   EV could be the alternative to .... (enhance / reduce) the carbon dioxide gas emission.
7. Give evidence from the passage to show that government is encouraging the use of Electric Vehicles.
8. Complete the sentence suitably.
   The result of the implementation of FAME (Faster Adoption and Manufacture of Electric vehicles) is ....
9. Complete the following with a suitable reason.
   The long-term perspective by decision-makers is to ensure ....

ANSWERS (REVIEW EXERCISE)

Discursive Passages

Passage 1

1. (b) creativity and ideas are gradually declining in all societies.
2. (a) Both the (A) and (R) are true, and (R) is the correct explanation of (A).
3. Inexhaustible
4. A study reveals that while 98% of children aged 3 to 5 display creative thinking, this drops to 10% by ages 13 to 15 and just 2% by age 25. This indicates a significant decline in creativity as individuals grow older.
5. social
6. According to the passage, apart from arts and culture, creativity thrives in science and technology too.
7. imagination, problem-solving, innovation and artistic or intellectual expression.
8. The passage views creativity as thriving in various fields but acknowledges that society has yet to fully support and reward individual creativity. While progress is evident, achieving a truly creative society requires further efforts to nurture and encourage creative potential.

Passage 2

1. (c) It provides nutritious food.
2. because as it reduces grocery expenses, reuses household waste for planting, and provides fresh produce at minimal cost
3. **Use of Chemicals** Traditional farming relies on synthetic fertilisers and pesticides, while kitchen gardens promote organic farming with minimal or no chemicals.

   Resource Consumption Traditional farming requires large-scale irrigation and land, whereas kitchen gardens use limited space and household water efficiently.
4. dweller
5. Tending to a kitchen garden promotes better health by providing fresh, organic produce rich in essential nutrients. It encourages physical activity, reducing obesity risks, and acts as a therapeutic exercise to relieve stress. Additionally, it reconnects individuals with nature and supports overall well-being.
6. (b) It helps develop sensitivity and appreciation for nature.

7. Kitchen gardeners face following hurdles
   (i) Limited space
   (ii) Lack of sunlight and soil quality issues
8. True

Passage 3

1. The given phrase emphasises that personal responsibility is critical in preserving water resources for generations to come. It means that small individual actions can come together as a collaborative effort to make a substantial impact on conserving water.
2. (b) its importance is not always recognised, leading people to overlook its value
3. The writer's idea that small actions can make a difference is supported by the fact that while individual actions may be minor, when collaborated, they can accumulate into substantial water saving. This is an indication of how individual efforts which are often looked at as insignificant, play an essential role in achieving conservation goals. This further highlights the significance of collaborative widespread participation in water-saving practices.
4. (b) In the context of student life at school, the ripple effect is reflected by a student who consistently follows disciplined study practices. This inspires the classmates to improve their study routines, creating a culture of academic excellence in the class.
5. True
6. (c) Implementing crop rotation and using organic compost to maintain soil health.
7. The passage sends a powerful message to businesses and policymakers about
   (i) Stressing the need to implement water-efficient technologies and methods which reduce their overall water consumption.
   (ii) The necessity of policymakers to create and enforce strict regulatory guidelines that help promote water conservation and address water management issues effectively.
8. (a) a set of beliefs and practices shared by a group

Passage 4

1. (a) Probiotics, prebiotics and postbiotics are variations of the same thing, with just a difference of a prefix.
2. According to the given passage, beside maintaining our digestive tract, 'biotics' also maintain our gut health while improving symptoms of depression. It also improves sleep quality and reduces the occurrence of respiratory tract diseases. Further, it helps in the absorption of other nutrients and decreases the risk of common infections.
3. the phrase 'contains live and active cultures'
4. (a) increase and decrease
   (c) beneficial and harmful
5. diverse strains or species, each with its own unique health benefits and functions
6. According to the given passage, prebiotics are a form of a carbohydrate or fibre which we cannot digest because we do not have the enzyme that does so. As a result, food containing prebiotics pass through the digestive tract into the intestine where beneficial bacteria or probiotics eat them. This digestion of prebiotics takes place due to the probiotics which in turn produces bioactive compounds called postbiotics. Thus, good bacteria remains inside while bad bacteria is excreted. This helps in improving gut health and reducing digestive tract problems.
7. (b) Checking that label for specific strains of bacteria
8. (a) Their relevance has been proven by scientific evidence.

Passage 5

1. The statement 'if solving a riddle is what was intended, then playing Sudoku is a better option" suggests that the writer is not impressed with the level of complexity in some poetry. Additionally, the phrase 'led to ponder if obscurity was the goal' implies that the writer believes some poets may intentionally make their work difficult to understand, which can be frustrating for readers. The author is of the opinion that poetry shouldn't be needlessly complex. Thus, the author's tone is sarcastic.
2. (a) the author acknowledges that weird poems can be off-putting and also appreciates their uniqueness and the challenge they present to readers.
3. Just as exploring a new city requires an open mind and a willingness to embrace the unexpected, studying poetry requires an openness to different styles and approaches, and a willingness to be challenged and surprised by what you find.
4. (a) Recognises the challenges of studying poetry but also acknowledges the rewards it offers.
5. True
6. (a) Intriguing and off-putting
   (d) Simple and challenging
7. The given lines display an example of a simple poem in terms of language structure and content. The poem is simple in a sense that it describes a natural scene, which is easy to comprehend and has a peaceful effect on the reader.
8. (b) persistence makes studying poetry a rewarding pursuit.

Passage 6

1. King Tutankhamen was buried 3300 years ago.
2. Egyptians held gold in high esteem with its religious significance.
3. The writer says that gold is not only beautiful but also virtually indestructible because of the following reasons

(i) Gold doesn't rust or corrode.

(ii) Gold can survive undamaged for centuries.

4. (b) importance of the metal
5. False
6. (b) George Harrison
7. The desire to hoard gold at home has been primarily an occupation of the working and peasant classes because they have no faith in paper money.
8. (a) Gold is the best conductor of electricity.

Passage 7

1. Two reasons which destroyed the natural scenery include earthquakes and avalanches.
2. (a) new snow or rain
3. Warning signs that allow experts to predict and often prevent avalanches from occurring include a fresh snowfall over a foot, which allows experts to be on the lookout for any sign of avalanches.
4. (a) People caught in the Avalanche can try to swim to the top.
5. (a) The crowd will gather at Gate No.1 and disperse from Gate No. 2.
6. False
7. Explosives can be used in places where there had been massive snow build-ups to trigger smaller avalanches. Such avalanches do not pose a threat to people or property.
8. (a) Avalanches

Passage 8

1. According to the given passage, organic foods are safer and more nutritious. Recent studies have shown that eating organically-grown produce reduces your chances of developing heart diseases.
2. (b) Confirmation
3. There is only one major difference between organic and non-organic foods. Organic farms do not use agricultural chemicals such as pesticides that stop insects from damaging crops.
4. (b) There is no confirmed evidence.
5. True
6. (d) it does not contains agricultural chemicals.
7. The writer states that contamination of food happens through dangerous bacteria which can be prevented by washing hands before consuming any produce.
8. (a) Because demand overtook supply

Passage 9

1. There is an adverse impact of climate change on monsoon patterns in India.
2. (b) Speculative
3. Flood forecasting is critical to minimising the damage from floods as it alerts the public regarding the disaster and mobilise various official agencies so that they take both preventive as well as relief measures, whenever required.
4. (a) Flash floods
5. True
6. (a) floods have led to much greater damage now than in the past.
7. Following are the two reasons because of which people have suffered from floods even after timely forecasting.

   (i) The flash floods are a sudden phenomena for which support structures are not available.

   (ii) People of lower social rungs lack the means and physical options to move from a danger zone to one that is relatively safe.
8. (b) Only II

Passage 10

1. it would help us process anger in a healthy way and help you figure out what your body is mobilising to do
2. (a) Practicing deep breathing
3. (c) Reflection
4. (d) Weaken
5. The given expression points out how the inability to process anger in a positive way can be detrimental to us. When anger or frustration is controlled and processed properly, it can help us take a better path. When this controlled frustration is combined with problem solving, we can become focused and committed to the new and better path.
6. Communication skills can greatly help in anger management as it teaches us to pause for a moment and try to understand that person's point of view. It keeps disagreements from turning into fights by avoiding the use of accusatory adverbs like 'always' and 'never'. Thus, it leads us to look for a mutually beneficial solution.
7. (b) you will not receive the best contributions.
8. You can unwind after letting go of your anger by trying to make sense of the wrongdoing with a loved one or a therapist or by finding humour in the situation or leaving the environment if it has become toxic.

Passage 11

1. The different shapes of sand include stars or spirals, with their edges smooth or jagged.
2. (b) concrete and glass
3. Sand is a pain when it gets in food and it is a pleasure when it is moulded into castles as children play and adults relax on it.
4. (b) Jagged and smooth (d) Ancient and advanced
5. True

6. (d) Both (a) and (b)
7. Sand contains many skeletons of marine life, as well as microscopic diamonds. It is also a source of minerals. A study including sand can help us keep a record of Earth's changing process. All of these make sand a 'treasure trove'.
8. (a) Pacific islands

Passage 12

1. In paragraph 1, the phrase 'a reinvigoration of global cooperation' emphasises that global cooperation has been sidelined in the past. The phrase suggests that there is a need to renew the spirit of global cooperation to fulfill the goals of the summit.
2. (a) the global population's loss of faith in multilateralism.
3. Revitalising faith in global institutions requires addressing challenges to multilateralism, as these obstacles undermine trust and cooperation. By fostering inclusive dialogue and effective solutions, we can strengthen international collaboration, ensuring that global governance reflects the needs and aspirations of all people.
4. (b) The inability of global institutions to deal with Covid-19 has caused the people to lose faith in their ability to combat challenges like public health and economic instability.
5. False
6. (d) IMF, World Bank and WHO
7. Multilateral organisations have helped global economies in times of crises in the following ways
   (i) The IMF and World Bank have historically supported global economies during crises, such as the 2008 financial crisis and the COVID 19 pandemic.
   (ii) The WHO, particularly through initiatives like COVAX, has been central to managing global health crises.
8. (d) to be contingent on a single consideration or point

Passage 13

1. Selflessness
2. (a) Everyone is dependent on each other.
3. to keep ourselves grounded, to respect and embrace our roots, and to give something back to those that nurtured us into who we are
4. (c) Warmth and cold (d) Stop and continue
5. out an alarm call to their fellow creatures of the lurking danger
6. (d) All of these
7. In the sixth paragraph, the writer advises us to have free time for ourselves, do whatever makes us feel happy, and spend time with nature to learn the most valuable lessons of life.
8. (b) 2 is independent of 1

Passage 14

1. The given phrase emphasises hydropower's role as a more environment friendly energy source compared to fossil fuels, highlighting its potential to reduce carbon emissions and promote sustainability.
2. (a) as water flow can be adjusted to meet fluctuating energy demands, ensuring grid stability
3. Hydropower is recognised as a cleaner alternative to fossil fuels because it generates electricity with minimal greenhouse gas emissions and significantly reduces air pollution. By harnessing renewable water resources, hydropower contributes to sustainable energy goals and helps combat climate change, promoting a healthier environment for future generations.
4. (b) Hydropower generation can lead to ecological disruptions and displacement of communities.
5. True
6. (d) Dam construction can cause earthquakes, landslides and coastal erosion.
7. Hydropower generates electricity with minimal environmental pollution, emits no greenhouse gases, is cost-effective over time and offers flexible energy solutions by adjusting water flow to meet varying demands, ensuring grid stability.
8. (a) causing or characterised by emotional distress or tension

Passage 15

1. The given phrase emphasises that increasing dependence on fossil fuels for energy threatens the sustainability objectives of tech companies, potentially undermining their commitment to environmental responsibility and long-term viability.
2. (b) they can create heated reservoirs capable of producing electricity
3. The increasing energy demands of artificial intelligence are putting significant pressure on the tech industry's sustainability initiatives. As AI applications expand, they require more power, often sourced from fossil fuels, which conflicts with efforts to reduce carbon footprints and achieve environmental goals. This challenges the industry's commitment to sustainability.
4. (b) Tech giants are partnering with geothermal startups to produce carbon-free energy.
5. False
6. (d) AI can lead to increased energy consumption and environmental degradation due to high computational demands.
7. Modern geothermal companies are developing techniques to access hot rock deeper underground, regions, creating heated reservoirs by injecting water. Despite generating lower carbon emissions, challenges

include high operational costs and scalability, raising concerns about meeting the energy demands of AI-driven innovations.

8. (d) a source or means of supplying energy

Passage 16

1. it encourages greater sustainable consumption and production, counters the effects of climate change, addresses threats to biodiversity, and provides more effective disaster risk reduction.
2. The UN views ESD as a lifelong process that extends from early childhood to higher and adult education, going beyond formal education. The critical areas of emphasis include fostering values, lifestyles, and attitudes from an early age to promote sustainability.
3. Two curriculum projects that ESD has been linked with are
   (i) Recycling
   (ii) Energy and water conservation
4. research from psychology, social-cultural analysis, and neuroscience shows that young children have the greatest capacity to learn during this stage.
5. (d) creative
6. (c) UNICEF reports show that children under the age of eight represent the highest percentage of affected population in global emergencies.
7. A problem in both rich and poor countries is equitable access to high-quality preschool programs. It has been recognised as crucial is linking health and education agendas to ensure sustainable development.
8. informative and persuasive

Case Based Factual Passages

Passage 1

1. (b) The consumers are confused
2. Thriving
3. Data utilisation
4. retail assistance
5. (d) Retail assistance
6. employ
7. offer limited, functional, mid-priced products that instill confidence and break consumerism
8. creators often prioritise wealthier consumers
9. The drawbacks of such a structure include
   - Overwhelming array of choices despite the promise of simplicity
   - Dependence on venture capital funding
   - Pressure for rapid growth, which may compromise consumer benefits

Passage 2

1. Silk is a popular fabric in India as it has a long history and is known as Resham in the North and Pattu in the South. India is the second-largest producer of silk, with Karnataka, Andhra Pradesh, and Assam leading production.
2. (a) Both the (A) and (R) are true, and (R) is the correct explanation of (A).
3. Silk is a strong natural fibre, but it has moderate to poor elasticity, meaning it does not fully regain its shape after stretching. It also loses upto 20% of its strength when wet, making it more prone to deformation over time.
4. Sunlight can weaken silk fibres if exposed for too long, reducing their strength and durability. This prolonged exposure can also cause the fabric to lose its natural luster and become brittle.
5. silk production is highly resource-intensive, requiring a large quantity of mulberry leaves and silkworms for a small amount of silk.
6. it involves delicate handling and precise techniques to extract and weave silk fibres
7. Uttar Pradesh
8. only high-quality silkworms and mulberry leaves can ensure fine silk production
9. Silk production is limited because it requires a long and labour-intensive process, as well as a large number of silkworms and mulberry leaves.

Passage 3

1. (c) The writer is indicating interest and enthusiasm.
2. (c) (A) is true, but (R) is false.
3. Surprisingly
4. The murals in North-West Indian villages contribute to community engagement and awareness as they not only beautify the village but also serve as educational visual platforms for conveying crucial social messages and are sources of inspiration.
5. 19% (category that features abstract or contemporary themes.)
6. The highest percentage of 55% is an indicator of deep-rooted connection of people with folklore and mythology, which showcases a desire to celebrate and preserve traditional narratives.
7. the integration of artistic skills into everyday life
8. convey and spread information through vivid visual representation, making people comprehend complex social issues easily.
9. The significance of comparing various parameters impacts on holistic understanding of mural creation and ads to identify trends and charts of various themes used in these paintings. It helps us understand the involvement of the community in these projects and evaluate the impact of murals on cultural preservation.

Passage 4

1. Wet
2. Mawsynram, Cherrapunji
3. The roads are in good condition.
4. The beauty of Kochi be enjoyed during the monsoon by either taking a walk around the old Fort Kochi or by enjoying a slow boat rides on the backwaters.
5. (c) Appreciative of monsoon as a delightful season.
6. (b) Attractive
7. (b) Cherrapunji, Sohra
8. nostalgia

Passage 5

1. (c) Indians are excited to travel internationally.
2. (d) (A) is false, but (R) is true.
3. It is true to say that after being cooped up inside their houses for more than 2 years, Indians are excited to travel internationally as they believe that international travel will help them expand their horizons and connect with other cultures. Further, the pent demand of students from Tier II and Tier III cities to grow and the new working trends had allowed Indians to take up international vacations.
4. As per the given data, travel for education increased from 5.8 L people in 2019 to 6.5 L in 2022.
5. fact, objective detail
6. The industry talked about in the given sentence includes service sector industries.
7. residency, emigration
8. of the increase in the number of people who aspire to travel internationally
9. Due to the increasing affordability and aspiration of middle-class children from Tier II and Tier III cities, more and more students decide to go abroad to study as it brings them better opportunities. Further, it allows them to grow and expand their horizons.

Passage 6

1. (b) Vertical gardening is a sustainable practice that can transform urban spaces into green areas.
2. (b) Both the (A) and (R) are true, but (R) is not the correct explanation of (A).
3. The given sentence is true because the majority of participants agreed that vertical gardens can improve the quality of life, increase air quality, and have a relaxing and calming effect. However, the survey does not provide information on the long-term effectiveness of vertical gardens or their potential impact on other aspects of urban life, such as traffic or community engagement.
4. A city government looking to install vertical gardens should consider addressing these two concerns
   (i) Cost of installation and maintenance should be reasonable.
   (ii) Areas of installation should be where driver distraction is less of an issue.
5. opinion, subjective judgement
6. It can be inferred that the participants did not have a strong opinion or preference regarding the effect of vertical gardens on air quality, which resulted in a neutral response.
7. intertwined
8. a fish needs decorations, such as plants or rocks, to simulate a natural environment and improve its quality of life. Similarly, people living in urban areas need green spaces such as vertical gardens to improve their physical and mental well-being.
9. A benefit of vertical gardening is that they can be installed in small spaces, making them ideal for urban cities with limited space. A drawback of vertical gardening is that the cost of installation and maintenance of a vertical garden may be higher than for other types of green spaces.

Passage 7

1. (b) 15
2. (b) Both 1 and 2 are false
3. elite
4. Communication
5. 2, 3 and 5
6. The blackout phase is significant because there will be a communication break for 15 days.
7. confident
8. signals
9. The spacecraft's life was extended by six months because of the extra fuel that needed to be burned.

Passage 8

1. (c) 1 and 2
2. (d) 1 and 3
3. contemplated
4. The rise in number of vehicles in the city and increased use of private cars are the reasons for increase in vehicular congestion.
5. adverse
6. Reducing traffic congestion is not easy because the cost of solving or reducing traffic congestion is enormous.
7. The antonym of lowest is 'highest' but the word is not mentioned in paragraph 5 of the passage. However, the nearest word that can be taken as the answer is 'peak'.
8. traffic congestion
9. To get an organised traffic manangement system, a proper implementation of corrective measures by citizens is essential.

Passage 9

1. (a) I, II and III
2. (a) 1. Impact of Pollution in South Asia
   2. Effects of Acid Rain
   3. Understanding Consequences of Haze
   4. Debate over Droughts

3. Consequence
4. India's rainfall patterns are changing because of the vast blanket of pollution.
5. worsen
6. India and China
7. Potential
8. not been enough time to determine that
9. **Does** Depletion of forest cover
   Does not Organic farming

Passage 10

1. (b) pollution
2. (b) Both (A) and (R) are true, but (R) is not the correct explanation of (A).
3. contributory   4. Natural   5. the ecosystem
6. Household waste and water storage tanks are the causes of water pollution in our homes.
7. water conservation and reducing plastic waste
8. the release of substances into subsurface groundwater or into lakes, streams, rivers, estuaries and oceans to the point where the substances interfere with beneficial use of the water or with the natural functioning of ecosystems.
9. Religious rituals contribute to water pollution as religious activities like immersion of flour, oil, soap, ash, detergents, floral offerings and mass bathing affect the water quality of the water body.

Passage 11

1. (a) A language used for communication between groups of people who speak different languages.
2. (a) Both the (A) and (R) are true, and (R) is the correct explanation of (A).
3. The word that indicates that the non-Hindi speaking people are not in favour of the Hindi language is 'imposition'.
4. Hindi Diwas is celebrated on 14th September to mark the adoption of Hindi as one of India's official languages in 1949.
5. The activities organised during Hindi Diwas celebrations include poetry recitations, essay writing, debates in educational institutions, and seminars and workshops in government offices to promote the use of Hindi.
6. Critics argue that promoting Hindi may marginalise regional languages, create linguistic dominance, and lead to educational disparities for non-Hindi speaking regions.
7. serving as a common means of communication, and promoting cultural exchange through literature and media.
8. promoting awareness and appreciation of various languages, and encouraging respectful dialogue about the importance of maintaining linguistic heritage alongside Hindi.
9. Hindi serves as a vital unifying force in India, representing cultural heritage. Hindi Diwas celebrations include poetry recitations, essay contests in schools, and seminars in government offices, all aimed at promoting Hindi's significance and encouraging its use across diverse communities.

Passage 12

1. (b) A major chunk of salses happened in 2017.
2. (a) Both (A) and (R) are true, and (R) is the correct explanation of (A).
3. The resarch of the Publishers Association showed that adapted films took 44% more at the box office revenue in the UK and 53% more worldwide than original screenplays.
4. The making of the TV series "The Night Manager' in 2016 increased the sale of the book so much so that 82% of the copies were sold in 2016 and 2017.
5. The research revealed that a quarter of dramas were based on literary sources and attracted 56% larger share of the audience.
6. The maximum TV serials in UK in the year 2017 were based on books.
7. the films get the advantage of the fame of the books
8. connection between books and films
9. The given sentence "Films adapted from books also tend to have a richer, more fully-developed story to draw on" means that the plot and the story-line of such films are better, and the setting and costumes are adapted from the book.

Passage 13

1. (c) population projections for 2011-2036
2. (b) Both the (A) and (R) are true, but (R) is not the correct explanation of (A).
3. The given statement means that India's population growth rate is expected to decline drastically.
4. The research in the given passage suggests that the rural population will decline in comparison to the growth of the urban population.
5. A delay of a decade from the UN's projection can be seen in India becoming the most populated country in the world.
6. The projections came in July of 2020 due to delays which are a result of delay in the setting up of the committee by the government.
7. 311 million   8. growth
9. According to the passage, India will become the most populous country in the world by 2031. The nation's population growth rate is expected to decline to its lowest since the Independence in the 2011-2021 decade.

Passage 14

1. (b) Amateur
2. (a) Both the (A) and (R) are true, and (R) is the correct explanation of (A).
3. The word in the passage that refers to 'a device sent up into space to travel around the Earth' is 'satellite'.
4. Chandrayaan-1, launched in 2008, was significant for detecting water molecules on the Moon, revolutionising lunar science and enhancing our understanding of the lunar environment.
5. Chandrayaan-3, achieved a successful soft landing near the Moon's South pole in 2023, marking a major milestone in India's lunar exploration efforts.
6. PSLV-C37, launched on 15th February, 2017, set a world record by deploying 104 satellites in a single mission, showcasing ISRO's advanced technology and versatility.
7. for X-ray astronomy, solar physics and aeronomy
8. orbit on the first attempt with a budget of 74 million dollars
9. ISRO's missions, including Aryabhata's groundbreaking satellite launch, Mangalyaan's successful Mars orbit and Chandrayaan's lunar discoveries, have significantly advanced India's space capabilities. These missions showcased technological innovation, cost-effectiveness and scientific contributions, positioning India as a formidable player in global space exploration and inspiring future endeavours in astrophysics and planetary science.

Passage 15

1. (d) Construction
2. (a) Both the (A) and (R) are true, and (R) is the correct explanation of (A).
3. The word that refers to 'an amount of a substance that is produced and sent out into the air that is harmful to the environment' is emissions.
4. Oceans cover 71% of Earth's surface and hold 97% of the planet's water playing a vital role in regulating weather, climate, and food supply.
5. World Oceans Day, celebrated on 8th June, aims to raise awareness about the importance of ocean's and promote its protection for future generations.
6. Climate change has raised ocean temperatures by an average of 1.45°C, causing coral bleaching and adversely affecting marine ecosystems, which threatens biodiversity and fisheries.
7. in acidity since pre-industrial times
8. a 9cm increase over the past three decades
9. The key solutions to protect the ocean include establishing Marine Protected Areas (MPAs), reducing pollution through renewable energy and regulations, promoting sustainable fishing and plant-based diets, investing in clean technologies, and enhancing research and public awareness. Global cooperation is crucial to ensure these practices are effectively implemented, safeguarding ocean health for future generations.

Passage 16

1. (b) It has developed very quickly
2. (a) Both the (A) and (R) are true, and (R) is the correct explanation of (A).
3. Two benefits of using EV over internal combustion engine vehicles are
   (i) EVs emit 30-80% less greenhouse gases compared to ICE vehicles.
   (ii) EVs do not consume fuel when stationary, unlike ICE vehicles that continue to burn fuel even when idle.
4. not in use/stationary
5. EVs reduce the dependence on fossil fuels, which are majorly imported. They utilise renewable energy sources such as solar and wind power, promoting energy independence.
6. reduce
7. Evidence from the passage showing the government is encouraging the use of EVs are
   - The government introduced financial policies to promote EV adoption.
   - The FAME scheme was implemented in 2015 to support the faster adoption of hybrid and electric vehicles.
8. the significant growth of EV market leading to increased adoption and manufacturing of electric vehicles.
9. the efficient implementation of EV policies for sustainable development and widespread EV adoption.

ASSESSMENT EXERCISE

Discursive Passage

Passage 1

1. Even international students whose first language is English can find themselves struggling to understand an alien academic culture. The problems are very familiar. Students' first problem is often with listening skills. They may feel nervous about this and it is certainly a steep learning curve. They need a structured listening experience, for instance how to pick out the main ideas. They also need help with academic reading—how to approach an article or book, how to skim, read and make notes.
2. However, while a student's confidence in listening skills grows, it is in the area of academic writing where more serious cultural differences become apparent. Much of British education is based on essay writing, but this may be a demanding task for students from other cultures. Suddenly, they are faced with the need to express their own ideas, develop their opinions and evaluate different issues, all in polished English. For some, the concept of originating this kind of written discourse can prove problematic and they may find themselves scoring low marks because of plagiarism or reproducing someone else's ideas. In Britain, plagiarism is regarded as academic theft, though this is not always the case in other countries. Students are expected to do research in a library before tackling an assignment and simply regurgitating lecture notes is also not acceptable.
3. The best way to overcome these hurdles is to be prepared. The first step is to take a test to assess the English language skills needed to cope with the issues of academic culture.
4. If an accredited test indicates that a student's language skills are not sufficient to embark on a university degree, the next step is to consider pre-sessional courses, generally at the university where the student will take a degree. These can last from three weeks to an academic year, so it is wise for students to be realistic about their needs. It is generally accepted that approximately 200 hours of study are needed to improve on one bad score on some tests. Some of the 'new' universities that formed from polytechnics in 1992 are experimenting with new styles of pre-sessional and foundation courses. Elspeth Jones, Director of the Centre for Language Study at Leeds Metropolitan University explains, "Our courses are monthly and so students from parts of the world with a different academic year can enrol at any time."
5. She feels that language training in new universities is generally more flexible than in older institutions. "Universities like ours can take students with lower language test grades and can put them through a programme that will bring them up to the required standard, though we cannot guarantee how long it will take."

Based on your understanding of the passage, answer the following questions.

1. Based on your reading of the text, list any 1 benefit of pre-sessional courses.

2. Complete the sentence appropriately.

Elspeth Jones feels that language training in older institutions is .... that in new universities.

(a) easier than (b) more effective than

3. Why is essay writing a demanding task? Answer in about 40 words.

4. Select the option that corresponds to the following relation below.

Even international students whose first language is English can find themselves struggling to understand an alien academic culture. (Paragraph 1)

(a) Even when she knew she could do it, she lost her motivation.

(b) Even medical practitioners who know the dos and don'ts find it difficult to fight and abstain from alcohol addiction.

5. Complete the sentence appropriately.

The British education is primarily based on ....

6. Which of the following will be the most appropriate title for the passage?

(a) Overcoming Language Hurdles

(b) Language Training

(c) British English-Ways to Cope

(d) Emergence of New Kinds of Courses

7. What, according to the author, causes international students to score low marks? Answer in about 40 words. State any one reason.

8. The passage includes some words that mean the same. From the sets (a)-(e) below, identify two sets of synonyms:

(a) Assess and evaluate (b) Opinions and discourse

(c) Overcome and cope (d) Tackling and regurgitating

(e) Originate and embark

Passage 2

Let the writer would-be beware! Anyone fool enough to embark on a career as a writer – whether it be an academic treatise, a novel or even an article – should first read this!

People think that writing as a profession is glamorous; that it is just about sitting down and churning out words on a page, or more likely these days on a computer screen. If only it were! So what exactly does writing a book entail? Being a writer is about managing a galaxy of contradictory feelings: relation, despair, hope, frustration, satisfaction and depression – and not all separately! Of course, it also involves carrying out detailed research: first to establish whether there is a market for the planned publication and second into the content of the book. Sometimes, however, instinct takes the place of market research and the contents are dictated by experience and knowledge.

Once the publication has been embarked upon, there is a long period of turmoil as the text takes shape. A first draft is rarely the final text of the book. Nearly all books are the result of countless hours of altering and reordering chunks of text and deleting the embarrassing bits. While some people might think that with new technology the checking and editing process is speeded up, the experienced writer would hardly agree. So a passage, endlessly reworked may end up nothing remotely like the original and completely out of place when compared with the rest of the text.

After the trauma of self-editing, it is time to show the text to other people for appraisal. At this stage, it is not wise to send it off to a literary agent or direct to publishers, as it may need further fine-tuning. Once an agent has been approached and has rejected a draft publication, it is difficult to go and ask for the revamped text to be considered again.

Although it is tempting to send the draft to every possible agent at one time, it is probably unwise. Some agents may reject the publication, but others may proffer some invaluable advice. The lucky few taken on by publishers or agents, then have their books subjected to a number of readers, whose job it is to vet a book: deciding whether it is worth publishing and whether the text as it stands is acceptable or not. After a book has finally been accepted by a publisher, one of the greatest difficulties for the writer lies in taking on board the publisher's alterations to the text. Whilst the overall story and the thrust of the book may be acceptable, it will have to conform to an in-house style, as regards language, spelling or punctuation, etc. More seriously, the integrity of the text may be challenged and this may require radical redrafting which is unpalatable to the author. A book's creation period is complex and unnerving, but the publisher's reworkings and text amputations can also be a tortuous process.

For many writers, the most painful period comes when the text has been accepted and the writer is waiting for it to be put together for the printer. By this stage, it is not uncommon for the writer to be thoroughly sick of the text. But does that mean abandon writing? Nonsense! Once smitten, it is not easy to escape the compulsion to create and write, despite the roller-coaster ride of contradictory emotions.

Based on your understanding of the passage, answer the following questions.

1. Why is it suggested that one should not send the final draft to literary agents?

2. Below are some words that could describe the process of writing. Identify two words which are appropriate for the subject.

(a) Bothersome (b) Arduous
(c) Unnerving (d) Flustering

3. While some people might think that with new technology the checking and editing process is speeded up, the experienced writer would hardly agree. Why?

4. In which sentence does the author express that the published books is different from its first draft?

(a) "Nearly all books are the result of countless hours of altering and reordering chunks of text..."
(b) "A first draft is rarely the final text of the book."

5. State whether the following statement is True or False.
Writing involves carrying out detailed research.

6. Select the option that shows the correct relationship between (1) and (2).

(1) The purpose of the passage is just to indicate the tiring process of getting a work published, not scare people off.
(2) The author states that it is not easy to give up writing despite the many troubles faced in getting a piece published.

Codes

(a) (2) is a contradiction of (1) (b) (2) is independent of (1)
(c) (2) is an example of (1) (d) (2) is the cause of (1)

7. One should to show the text to other people for appraisal before sending to a literary agent. Why?

8. Fill in the blank with the correct option.
The writer does not believe that writing as a profession is glamorous because ....

(a) writers are unkempt
(b) writing requires a lot of revision
(c) writers often get sick of editing
(d) writing does not satisfy any urge

Passage 3

1. A youngster quit Facebook in December after spending over three years on the social networking site.
With that one act, he bid a silent adieu to more than 300 contacts that he had added to his account during the period. Like almost everyone from his 'friend's circle', the 20-year-old was a regular on the service; visiting it every day to post photos and status updates but last week a new feature on Facebook called timeline forced him to reconsider the pros and cons of being on the networking site.
2. Everyone has some skeletons in their closet and I am just not comfortable with Facebook digging up and displaying all the facets of my life on a 'bulletin board', says this youngster who joined the network in July 2007 while he was in Class 11.
3. Facebook, you see, had compressed the time he spent on the site and arranged it in chronological order. While he initially liked the new neatly organised scrapbook-like feature he wasn't happy to reveal posts from the past that until recently were hidden under layers and layers of recent updates. Just clicking on a date on the timeline could transport his friends back in time and enable them to view every embarrassing comment link or photo he had posted on his profile.

4. "I think it's a recipe for disaster," he says. "In 2007, I had some wall posts which seemed appropriate at the time but now after a lapse of four years, I have moved on and don't want them to be openly displayed for all to see.

5. He is not alone. Many users, worried about how the Facebook activity could possibly affect their offline lives, are choosing to commit 'Facebook suicide.' While some have privacy concerns others feel that the site meant to bring them closer to their friends actually does the opposite- it reduces their friendship to something superficial.

6. Poking and liking are not enough to keep a friendship going, says a business analyst. Having quit Facebook three years ago, she prefers meeting her 'real' friends face-to-face, instead of reading their trite posts online. 'On Facebook, people hype everyday issues including what they ate and where they went on a daily basis,' says this analyst who continues to use Twitter.

7. "Facebook has become a time sink and it could not justify the time I spent on it," he says, "I spend more time calling up friends or relatives over the phone now......I also go out and meet people whenever possible and have a good offline life. I do not regret the change." Today, Facebook has 800 million users of which 37 million are Indians. The site has become an online identity for most, and many of those who decided to quit cannot overcome the withdrawal symptoms and return. Facebook, fully aware of its addictive powers, facilitates this return by allowing users to 'deactivate' their accounts but continues to store information on its servers so that they can return from their 'break', whenever they wish.

Based on your understanding of the passage, answer the following questions.

1. Why does the writer say Facebook is 'A recipe for disaster'?

2. In which sentence does the author express that the youngster left Facebook?
(a) "Everyone has some skeletons in their closet and..."
(b) "With that one act, he bid a silent adieu to..."

3. In paragraph 7, the author says 'allowing users to 'deactivate' their accounts but continues to store information on its servers so that they can return from their 'break', whenever they wish.' State the reason for doing so by Facebook.

4. Select the option that depicts what the writer projects, with reference to the following.
"Everyone has some skeletons in their closet and I am just not comfortable with Facebook digging up and displaying all the facets of my life on a bulletin board."
(a) Danger (b) Caution

5. Which of the following is the synonym of 'organised' from the passage?
(a) Adieu (b) Compressed
(c) Arranged (d) Regular

6. Complete the following sentence by providing a reason for the following opinion.
Many users, worried about how their activity on Facebook could affect their personal lives. This is because they ....
(a) are bored (b) want privacy
(c) want peace (d) have health concerns

7. Why are people leaving social media site Facebook?

8. The author says, "The site has become an online identity for most and many of those who decided to quit cannot overcome the withdrawal symptoms and return." What, according to the author, is an advantage with a disadvantage in Facebook?
(a) Its updates are in chronological order.
(b) Hype is created on Facebook.
(c) It facilitates the return of users.
(d) All of the above

Passage 4

We are often insensitive to the poetry of living life wisely. We are caught in the prose of what we want rather than what is truly wise. It is said, "God has given us two ears and one mouth, to listen more and talk less". Have we learnt the art of wise listening? We go to listen to lectures. Why? Have you asked this question to yourself? We collect more words, more concepts and they become our memory bank. Next time you listen to some other lecture, your memory bank becomes a kind of obstacle without your knowing it, for you have invested in what you know. Hence our knowledge of the past becomes our block. Is it not?

Are you reading this article more to confirm what you know or are you searching for something new? Listening or reading to find out something is very different from confirming what you know already. If you are listening more to confirm rather than to find out, then your listening has no significance, is it not? How can one's listening be anchored in 'finding out' rather than as confirmation of what one knows?

Try this out next time. When you listen to a lecture, be sensitive to the beginning and ending of any concept that is spoken and get the whole picture. See the 'newness' of what the speaker is saying; see what is it that you can practise from what the speaker is saying, can you be alert to be 'open' to what the speaker is saying and not allow your knowledge to interfere in your understanding? Try this out and then you will learn how to find out.

To find out something, one has to be open and fluid. If you have observed a river, how it flows, you will notice sometimes on the backwaters of the river, there are small ponds. Water stagnates in a pond, there are no fishes. But the river water is fresh, vibrant and flowing. If you become like a pond, you become stagnant to what you know, to your positionality, to your opinion, to your dogmas and so will end up missing the quality of freshness of the flowing river.

Our listening, when it is caught in our opinion, in our dogmas, in our likes and dislikes, we miss the freshness and openness of listening. When you are listening, learn to be open and flowing. Give space to the speaker, give space to your doubts, giving inner space, in being open. And from that openness when one listens, there is a different quality of understanding. Next time your boss is talking to you, don't be caught in your disagreement, give space to your preferences and give space to what he is saying, then you can intuit what he is saying.

Next time your spouse scolds you, just be open, don't get lost in what you want, give space for your spouse to say and from that openness listen to your spouse's scolding. You will understand better and not be bitter. Once you are bitter, you get isolated and in that isolation, you can't connect to your spouse. Isolation creates conflict and when in conflict, you get filled with frustration and your inner cup is filled with restlessness. Learn to empty your inner cup.

Swami Sukhabodhananda 'The Speaking Tree'

Based on your understanding of the passage, answer the following questions.

1. State the situations wherein one gets bitter.
2. Select the option that would fill the blank appropriately.

   The art of wise listening implies that ....
   (a) we must concentrate on what is being said
   (b) we must keep silent while someone is speaking
3. How can one's listening be anchored in 'finding out' rather than as confirmation of what one knows? Answer in about 40 words.
4. Complete the sentence appropriately.

   According to the passage, 'We are caught in the prose of what we want'. Such a person can be characterised as ....
   (a) selfless (b) selfish (c) perfect (d) angry
5. State whether the following statement is True or False.

   By the phrase 'Learn to empty your inner cup', the author means to talk.
6. The passage includes some words that are opposites of each other. From the sets (a)-(a) below, identify two sets of antonyms.
   (a) Poetry and prose (b) Obstacle and invested
   (c) Stagnates and flows (d) Preferences and doubts
   (e) Isolation and confirmation
7. When and how does listening become useless? Answer in 40 words.
8. What according to the author is 'truly wise'?
   (a) To live life wisely (b) To keep an open mind
   (c) To resolve conflicts (d) All of these

Passage 5

The art of living is learnt easily by those who are positive and optimistic. From humble and simple people to great leaders in history, science or literature, we can learn a lot about the art of living, by having a peep into their lives. The daily routines of these great men not only reveal their different, maybe unique life styles, but also help us learn certain habits and practices they followed. Here are some; read, enjoy and follow in their footsteps as it suits you.

A private workplace always helps. Jane Austen asked that a certain squeaky hinge should never be oiled so that she always had a warning whenever someone was approaching the room where she wrote. William Faulkner, lacking a lock on his study door, detached the doorknob and brought it into the room with him. Mark Twain's family knew better than to breach his study door—they would blow a horn to draw him out. Graham Greene went even further, renting a secret office; only his wife knew the address and the telephone number. After all, everyone of us needs a workplace where we can work on our creation uninterruptedly. Equally we need our private space too!

A daily walk has always been a source of inspiration. For many artists, a regular stroll was essentially a creative inspiration. Charles Dickens famously took three hour walks every afternoon and what he observed on them fed directly into his writing. Nineteenth century composer Erik Satie did the same on his long hikes from Paris to the working-class suburb where he lived, stopping under street lamps to jot down ideas that came on his journey; it's rumored that when those lamps were turned off during the war years, his music declined too. Many great people had limited social life too.

The routines of these thinkers are difficult. Perhaps it is because they are so unattainable. The very idea that you can organise your time as you like is out of reach for most of us, so I'll close with a toast to all those who worked with difficulties. Like Francine Prose, who began writing when the school bus picked up her children and stopped when it brought them back; or TS Eliot, who found it much easier to write once he had a day job in a bank than he had as a starving poet.

Being forced to follow someone else's routine may irritate, but it makes it easier to stay on the path. Whenever we break that trail ourselves or take an easy path of least resistance, perhaps what's most important is that we keep walking.

Based on your understanding of the passage, answer the following questions.

1. Which style did the famous composer Erik Satie follow?
2. What was specific about Austen's workspace?
   (a) She wanted a noisy door near her room.
   (b) She did not want a certain squeaky thing to be oiled.
3. How can we learn the art of living? Answer in 40 words.
4. Complete the following sentence appropriately.

   Francine Prose used to write when ....
5. Complete the sentence appropriately.

   The family of Mark Twain used to blow a horn instead of knocking at the door ....
6. The passage includes some words that mean the same. From the sets (a)-(e) below, identify two sets of synonyms.
   (a) Squeaking and warning
   (b) Detached and uninterrupted
   (c) Positive and optimistic
   (d) Resistance and difficulties
   (e) Humble and simple

7. State reasons that justify Graham Greene's decision to have a secret workspace. Answer in more than 40 words.
8. According to the passage, what is central to attaining success?
(a) Concentration
(b) Isolation
(c) Routine
(d) Practical skills

Passage 6

Ask anyone who has organised traditional Indian wedding what the most painstaking task of all is and the chances are the answer would be the entire process of sending out invitations. First one has to make a thousand calls to collect the addresses, write each of them on the card and then courier or post them. In addition to this, there is that special lot that needs to be delivered personally no matter how much time is wasted braving long hours in traffic jam.

It is a little wonder that e-invites or e-vites as they are popularly called, are catching on with the young and techie these days. They save paper, time and money and can be personalised to suit the couple. It is also environment friendly. The people can also be non-traditional in the sense that they can send light, amusing messages in the e-vites retaining the main purpose but this liberty can be taken with just a handful of people who would understand.

Paper invites, especially the designer ones, are expensive and can cost even ₹ 10,000 per card. For a Delhi's industrialist's wedding in Dubai, iPad Air Tabs were sent out as special invites and each reportedly cost ₹ 30,000. Excess, however doesn't always impress, no matter, how expensive or exotic the invitation. It eventually lands up in trash!

E-invites have their pros. They are not easy only to create and cheap to make but also make the process of inviting guests faster. There are no reports of cards getting lost on the way. However a few cons cannot be overlooked. They make a wedding feel less formal, can land up in scam and guests may still keep waiting for a physical invite and not send RSVPs. Some couples choose a middle path- send a save-the-date via e-mail followed by a physical invite.

There are many websites and apps that allow people to create their e-vites. Paperless post, offers around 390 free designs. It also lets you use the same design for digital as well as physical invites. Users can play around with fonts and colours of the text as well as the texture and shade of the envelope. And of course, the content is personalised. On Desievite.com, one can make e-invites in ten Indian languages apart from English. This site which is located in the US, has e-invites for a number of Indian festivals and religious events like Satyanarayan puja and Kali puja.

Based on your understanding of the passage, answer the following questions.

1. Complete the sentence given below appropriately.
The author of the passage states that excess doesn't always impress because ....
2. Why is the process of sending out invitations called painstaking?
(a) Because it is long and tedious
(b) Because it is useless and time taking
3. What can be the cons of e-vites?
4. Why are e-vites non-traditional?
(a) They do not involve face-to-face meeting.
(b) They are shared without a personal message.
5. State whether the following statement is True or False.
E-vites are better than traditional invites because they are hassle free.
6. Select the option that shows the correct relationship between (1) and (2).
(1) Desievite.com can make e-invites in ten Indian languages apart from English.
(2) Desievite.com has assimilated the Indian culture.
Codes
(a) (2) is a contradiction of (1)
(b) (2) is independent of (1)
(c) (2) is an example of (1)
(d) (2) is the cause of (1)
7. Analyse how the content of e-vites can be personalised.
8. Which of these means the same as 'enduring' as used in paragraph 5?
(a) Painstaking
(b) Baring
(c) Overlooked
(d) Liberty

Case Based Factual Passage

Passage 1

1. There was a time when human interference was minimum, the number of wild animals was quite high and there was no problem of their protection or conservation.
2. Due to the irrational use of natural and biotic resources of the Earth in the past, most of the wildlife has been destroyed beyond retrieval. According to an estimate, in India about 200 species of wild animals and birds have become extinct and another 2500 are on the verge of extinction. Some of them are black buck, chinkara, wolf, swamp deer, nilgai, Indian gazelle, antelope, tiger, rhinoceros, gir lion, crocodile, flamingo, pelican, bustard, white crane, grey heron, mountain quail, etc.
3. In India, the government and NGOs are taking keen interest in protection of wildlife. The Wildlife Protection Act, 1972, has several provisions for the conservation of wildlife. As many as 165 game sanctuaries and 21 national parks have been deployed to protect the natural habitat and wild animals. Apart from this, Wildlife Conservation Week is also celebrated from 1st to 7th October every year. But still there is a long way to go in this direction.
4. Preservation of wildlife does not mean a blanket protection to all faunal and floral species; rather it implies a proper, judicious control over the multiplication of plants and animals which interact together to provide a proper environment to man whose very existence is in peril today.

5. It is our urgent duty to protect the natural splendour of ecosystems and to evolve a system of co-existence with every living creature upon the Earth.

*Based on IUCN Red List Data

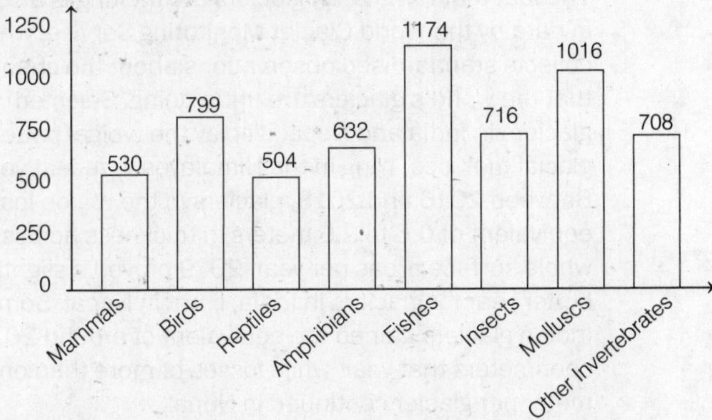

Based on your understanding of the passage, answer the following questions.

1. Select the correct option to complete the sentence.

Judicious control over the multiplication of plants and animals which provide

(a) natural splendour of ecosystem

(b) proper environment to man

(c) blanket protection

(d) happy and comfortable living

2. Select the option that is true for the Assertion and Reason given below.

Assertion (A) Preservation means judicious control over the expansion of all flora and fauna.

Reason (R) Preservation ensures that the flora and fauna interact with each other to provide proper environment to man.

(a) Both the (A) and (R) are true, and (R) is the correct explanation of (A).

(b) Both the (A) and (R) are true, but (R) is not the correct explanation of (A).

(c) (A) is true, but (R) is false.

(d) (A) is false, but (R) is true.

3. Infer one reason for the following, based on the information in the passage in about 40 words.

The number of wild animals was quite high and there was no problem of their protection or conservation.

4. On the basis of the passage, explain whether human interference with wildlife and the number of wild animals are directly or inversely proportional?

5. Fill in the blanks with the correct option from those given in brackets.

Most of the wildlife has been .... (destroyed/desertion) .. beyond .... (retrieval/revived) .. due to the irrational use of natural resources on the Earth.

6. List one reason why the Government makes certain recommendations for protection of wild animals.

7. Complete the following analogy correctly with a word/phrase from the passage.

Flowers : Garden : : .... : Sanctuaries

(**Clue** Just like flowers are in a garden, similarly .... are in the sanctuaries.)

8. List any two examples of Government and NGOs trying to protect the wildlife.

9. According to the graph, which is the most vulnerable animal species and the least vulnerable from the graph.

1. Birds 2. Insects 3.Fishes 4. Reptiles
5. Insects 6. Mammals 7. Molluscs

Passage 2

1. Playing video games provides entertainment and many social and psychological rewards. However, video game addiction also needs to be considered. Researchers have noted that the number of hours spent playing video games is not necessarily a core indicator of addiction. Instead, several factors such as how fun or challenging a game is, or being able to play with friends are also important determinants to understanding whether a game is addictive or just engaging.

2. A study investigated the reasons for smartphone game addiction. This was done by analysing the reviews of games. Reviews were collected from games across different categories in an app store. A total of 25,200 reviews were collected containing references to the game being addictive. These reviews were analysed and the number of times different factors were mentioned for terming a game as addictive was recorded.

Table 1: Frequency of factors associated with smartphone gaming addiction, as seen in the reviews of the games.

Types of Games	Factor 1 'Challenging'	Factor 2 'Friends'	Factor 3 'Fun'
Action	456	256	110
Board	420	697	120
Card	417	512	190
Word	812	23	123

4. It was seen that 22.37% of the total reviews in the study that described a game as 'addictive', also described it as 'challenging'. This was the most common factor associated with addictive games, out of all the 9 factors. This was followed by 15.7% of the reviews mentioning the factor of 'friends'. Although it is a cliche, the ubiquity of the internet has made the world a global village. Friends can now play and interact as a group, build virtual relationships within the game and attain social recognition from others, without even meeting in person. All of these factors can be highly engaging to players and for some, these could become addictive.

Based on your understanding of the passage, answer the following questions.

1. A developer of a crossword puzzle app is seeking advice to make improvements to the app. Based on the data provided, which of these ideas is BEST to recommend to the developer? Justify in 40 words/
   A. Make the puzzles tougher to solve.
   B. Allow players to team up or compete with other players.
   C. Create more levels in the game for players to win prizes.
   D. Change the colour and design to make it look more appealing.
2. Select the option that is true for the Assertion and Reason given below.

   Assertion (A) Most addictive games are challenging.

   Reason (R) Challenges is a factor that is most commonly associated with games.

   (a) Both the (A) and (R) are true, and (R) is the correct explanation of (A).
   (b) Both the (A) and (R) are true but (R) is not the correct explanation of (A).
   (c) (A) is true, but (R) is false.
   (d) (A) is false, but (R) is true.
3. The study mentioned in the passage used game reviews to understand what makes a game addictive. State why game reviews were analysed for the purpose of the study.
4. Based on the passage, state any two reasons why we need to study video games.
5. Based on paragraph 1, it can be said that the level of .... and .... in a video game determine how addictive it can be. Which of these can go in the blanks to complete the sentence correctly?
   1. variety
   2. violence
   3. difficulty
   4. popularity
   5. enjoyment
6. Layla spends two hours a day playing games on her phone. According to the passage, is this information sufficient to say she is addicted to video games? Why/Why not? Answer in one sentence.
7. Complete the following analogy correctly with a word from paragraph 1.

   Flourishes: Grows : .... (Determinants/Indicators) : Factors
8. Complete the sentence based on information from the passage.

   .... has converted the world into a global village.
9. Suggest a title for the passage. Write appropriate reason for your answer.

Passage 3

Glacial calving high up in the Himalayas caused a flash flood in the Indian state of Uttarakhand that killed dozens and washed away new dams and bridges. Calving - the breaking away of large chucks of ice from a glacier - is not typical in winter, but it is likely that global warming has played a role in the disaster. As The New York Times reports, glaciers in the region are shrinking fast, elevating the risk of floods and landslides. The Indian Government ignored warnings about the region's environmental instability when it went ahead with the now destroyed hydroelectric developments.

The fact that Himalayan glaciers are melting is also seen in data by the World Glacier Monitoring Service, which collects standardised observations about the changes that the world's glaciers are undergoing. Selected glaciers in India and Nepal display the typical patterns of glacial melt occurring in the Himalayas in recent years. Between 2016 and 2018, glaciers in the region lost the equivalent of 0.5 to 2.5 meters in thickness across their whole surface areas per year. 2019 proved a slightly better year for glaciers in India, if not in Nepal. Some Indian glaciers gained the equivalent of around 20-50 centimeters that year, while losses of more than one meter per glacier continued in Nepal.

Glacial melt does not only increase the risk of disasters through calving, increasing the risk that large ice chucks hit rivers of meltwater and cause flood surges. Meltwater from retreating glaciers can also form lakes or be stored inside the glacier, which carries the risk of spontaneous bursts as well. Additionally, the melting of glaciers poses threats to biodiversity and freshwater supply while also contributing to rising sea levels.

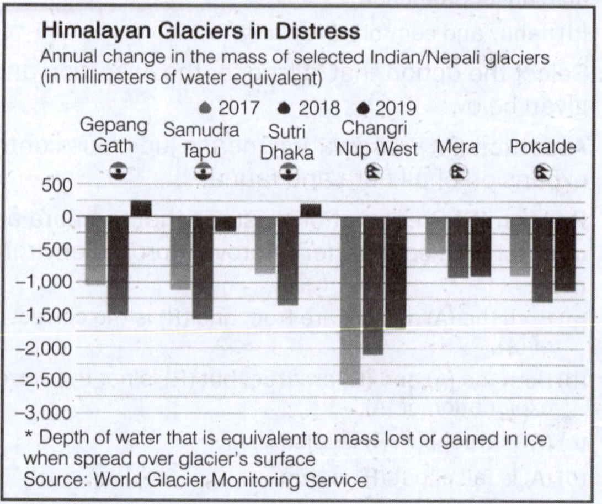

Based on your understanding of the passage, answer the following questions.

1. Which of the following shows the condition of glaciers in Nepal?

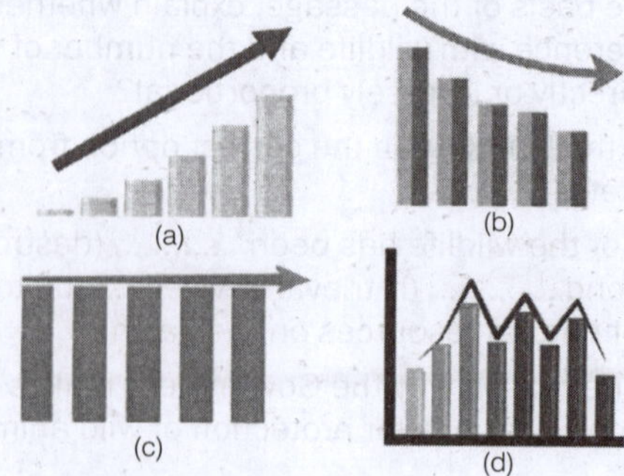

2. Select the option that is true for the assertion and reason given below.

Assertion (A) Glacial melting is not as disastrous as climate change.

Reason (R) Glacial melting causes surges in floods.

(a) Both the (A) and (R) are true, and (R) is the correct explanation of (A).

(b) Both the (A) and (R) are true, but (R) is not the correct explanation of (A).

(c) (A) is true, but (R) is false.

(d) (A) is false, but (R) is true.

3. Does the author blame the Indian authorities for Uttarakhand floods? State the reason for your answer.
4. Based on the given data, draw an inference of the loss of glaciers in India and China.
5. Fill the blank with the appropriate option from those given in bracket, based on your understanding of the passage.

.... (Melting of glaciers/Global warming) can be stated as the reason for a flash flood in the Indian state of Uttarakhand.

6. What are the risks associated with melting of glaciers?
7. Complete the sentence appropriately.

An appropriate title for the passage would be ....

8. According to the passage, glacial calving was a phenomenon common in ....
9. Justify the following in 40 words.

There is a immediate need for controlling the causes of global warming.

Passage 4

India's media and entertainment industry is rising rapidly and the nation is expected to soon reach the top-10 worldwide. The overall media and entertainment industry, segmented into television, print media , digital media, films, animation and VFX, out-of-home, gaming and radio and music, is expected to be valued at INR 3,224.24 Bn by 2025, growing at a CAGR of ~10% during 2020-2025 timeframe.

In both 2018 and 2019, the television segment accounted for the largest share of the market. The digital media segment involving over-the-top (OTT) services, however, is on the verge of disruption and is likely to surpass the print and film segments in terms of consumer revenue by 2025.

Although the OTT market is at a nascent stage, in the country its services have found widespread acceptance. On-demand, OTT content can be downloaded directly and accessed by users on connected devices such as smart TVs, PCs, laptops, smartphones and gaming consoles via the internet. OTT platforms are not cost-free and enable users to subscribe by paying monthly or yearly subscription fees to a specific OTT platform.

The Indian video OTT market in 2019 was estimated at INR 42.5 Bn and is projected to cross INR 237.86 Bn by 2025, growing during the forecast period at a CAGR of 33.10 per cent. Premium, original content, with a range of OTT channels vying for the attention of customers, is one of the key growth drivers and differentiators in the OTT industry.

Market Share of OTT Platforms in India

For the period Q2 (Apr-Jun) 2020

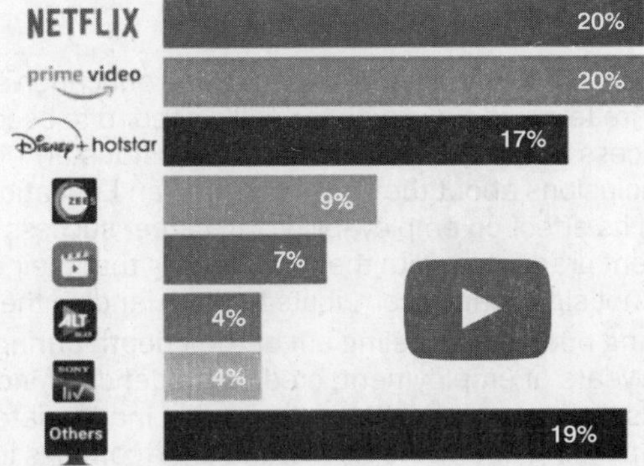

There were about 170 million video OTT-streaming users in India in 2019 and the user base is projected to grow at a rate of about 26.40% by 2025. Industry participants invest heavily in the acquisition or creation of new goods and services and also concentrate on enhancing the experience of consumers.

The market share of OTT Platforms in India is largely dominated by three global players Netflix, Amazon Prime Video and Disney+ Hotstar. While Netflix and Prime Video enjoy supremacy with 20 percent each, Disney+ Hotstar takes up 17 per cent market share.

Based on your understanding of the passage, answer the following questions.

1. What are OTT platforms?
2. Select the option that is true for the assertion and reason given below.

Assertion (A) The OTT markets developed in India even before 2019.

Reason (R) The three OTT giants are- Netflix, Amazon Prime and Disney + Hotstar.

(a) Both the (A) and (R) are true, and (R) is the correct explanation of (A).

(b) Both the (A) and (R) are true, but (R) is not the correct explanation of (A).

(c) (A) is true, but (R) is false.

(d) (A) is false, but (R) is true.

3. Which sectors comprise the Indian media and entertainment industry?

1. Television	2. Print media
3. Digital media	4. Animation and VFX
5. Gaming	

4. India's media and entertainment industry is expected to soon reach the top-10 worldwide. Substantiate.
5. Which industry will grow exponentially by 2025?
6. Why is the popularity of the OTT platforms increasing?
7. Identify the word which indicates good content and good technical usage in the media industry.

8. Complete the sentence with reference to the figure.
   The popularity of OTT platforms like Netflix and Amazon Prime has ....
9. How has the popularity of OTT platforms changed the media market industry?

Passage 5

Graduates in India feel let down by the education system's failure to equip them with the skills needed to become a success at work. A recent study from Hindustan Times drew conclusions about the state of the Indian Education System and its effect on employability and career success amongst recent graduates, with the youth feeling that their education did not significantly contribute to them landing their first jobs.

Young people are feeling out of their depth during the first few years of employment, crediting a deficit of industry links, lack of practical experience and inadequate career counselling at universities for the shortcomings in employability following graduation.

Aimed at assessing the efficacy of India's education system, the survey connected with 1,680 young professionals, men and women aged between 21 and 27. Those surveyed have been employed for three years or less, pursuing new-age careers – digital entertainment, advertising and media, retail, e-commerce, social media and start-ups – in the six base metro areas: Mumbai, Delhi, Kolkata, Bengaluru, Hyderabad and Chennai.

Only 26 per cent of those surveyed felt their education contributed highly to their interpersonal management skills – a key trait needed for interviews and employment. A problem with the relevance and timeliness of university curricula was also highlighted with respondents saying their college and university syllabus are not updated regularly.

An overwhelming majority of graduates felt that they lacked the necessary practical experience and blamed the deficiency on inadequate industry-academia linkages. A historical focus on rote learning still prevalent in much of India's Educational System can lead to graduates attaining good grades but failing to pick up the skills needed for innovation or out-of-the-box thinking that is so vital in today's workplace. Where some may lack in skills, however, they make up for in character with 26 per cent feeling they secured jobs through the sheer power of their personalities.

A case was also made for self-development and taking it upon oneself to bridge the gap inadequate education has left, with 24 per cent of respondents believing personal initiatives to improve their skills paid off when it came to landing a job.

Despite the negative outcome of the survey, founder of global learning company XSEED Ashish Rajpal told Hindustan Times the future isn't all bleak if the system can be overhauled at primary school level. By encouraging children at a young age to engage with the world around them, they learn more practical real world experience and bolster their communication skills and confidence to boot.

Based on your understanding of the passage, answer the questions given below.

1. Select the option that displays one of the skills relevant to the present day employment.
   (a) Innovation (b) Communication
   (c) Collaboration (d) All of these
2. Select the option that is true for the Assertion and Reason given below.
   Assertion (A) There are job in the Indian market but not suitable candidates.
   Reason (R) The lack of employable employees is a result of the rote-learning learning methodology of the country's education system.
   (a) Both the (A) and (R) are true, and (R) is the correct explanation of (A).
   (b) Both the (A) and (R) are true, but (R) is not the correct explanation of (A).
   (c) (A) is true, but (R) is false.
   (d) (A) is false, but (R) is true.
3. Do you think the researchers of the study aimed to highlight the changes required in the Indian Education System by pointing out the problems youth face in getting jobs?
4. Self Development was also promoted to bridge the gap inadequate education has left. Give a reason for such a claim.
5. Complete the sentence appropriately.
   According to the passage, professional education should be introduced at .... (primary/high school level)

6. Why does Ashish Rajpal find a solution in primary school level?

7. Complete the given sentence.

   Indian youngsters find that the education system ....

8. Complete the given sentence appropriately with one/two words.

   Apart from education, ... plays an important role in employability.

9. Based on the reading of the text, state a point to challenge the given statement.

   By focusing on industry links, practical experience and career counselling, individuals will be wasting their resources and fall back in their studies.

PASSAGE 6

Social media marketing is now the modern and innovative way of doing business specifically in service marketing, as marketers move from one strategy to another to another, looking for the right innovative strategy to improve their brand health. Social media capabilities are the birth of platforms such as YouTube, Facebook, Twitter, WhatsApp and Pinterest. This has become the new and attractive way as the world has become a global entity and wide coverage of information disseminations shared through social media.

The modern-day consumers especially millennials are increasingly using online tools, for example, blogs, 'Facebook' and YouTube to share their opinions about products and services they consume. The rise in Internet accessibility and availability of smartphones has led to the new form of what is known as Electronic Word Of Mouth (EWOM). Social media has become the new growth strategy for any company that wishes to realise growth and have a mark in this new and uptight market.

The start of the century introduced new technology innovations and social media platforms, which are to name a few Twitter, Facebook, YouTube and Pinterest, provide users with a variety of communication tools at their disposal. This innovation has embodied most of what we have come to define as social media since 2000 and it is not showing any signs of slowing down.

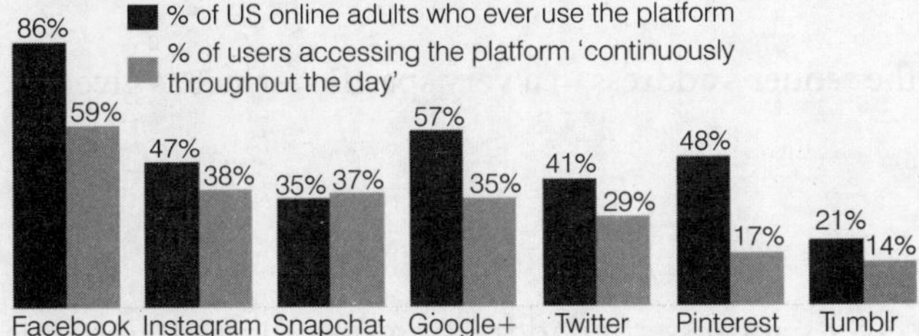

Published on MarketingCharts.com in April 2018 | Data Source: Reuters / Ipsos
Based on a survey of 2,237 adults ages 18+ who were interviewed online in English

Based on your understanding of the passage, answer the questions given below.

1. In which of the following sentences the word 'company' is not used as used in the passage?
   (a) Good company on the road is the shortest cut.
   (b) The company has a complex organisational structure.
   (c) Which company do you work for?
   (d) The company is in default on its loan agreement.

2. Select the option that is true for the Assertion and Reason given below.

   Assertion (A) Instagram comes after Facebook in the social media marketing survey.

   Reason (R) Instagram has more feature than Facebook.

   (a) Both the (A) and (R) are true, and (R) is the correct explanation of (A).
   (b) Both the (A) and (R) are true, but (R) is not the correct explanation of (A).
   (c) (A) is true, but (R) is false.
   (d) (A) is false, but (R) is true.

3. With reference to the figure, write a conclusion about social media marketing?

4. The modern-day consumers especially millennials are increasingly using online tools. How does it impact marketing?

5. What can be assumed by that there are people who access social media platform throughout the day?
   1. That some people are idle.
   2. That some people are dependent on them for decision making.
   3. That for some people social media is an important factor.
   4. That some people believe social media is always be correct.

6. What had been the result of social media capabilities?

7. Complete the sentence appropriately.

   .... provide users with a variety of communication tools at their disposal.

8. Fill in the blank appropriately.

   By stating that 'marketers move from one strategy to another to', the author wants to ....

9. Do you think you would recommend social media marketing to any brand as a marketing tool? Give reason for your answer.

Formal Letters

CHAPTER 1

Letters are the most common and the most convenient method of expressing our thoughts and opinions. They are an important mode of communication. There are two types of letters

1. **Formal Letters** These letters are written in formal, simple and polite language. They follow a certain format and are written for official purposes to authorities, companies, institutes, etc.
2. **Informal Letters** These letters are written to parents, friends and relatives. They are written in everyday and conversational language. They are mainly used for personal communication.

Types of Formal Letters

In CBSE Class X, questions on only formal letters of certain types are asked. The types of formal letters from which questions are asked are

1. Complaint letters
2. Enquiry letters
3. Letters for placing an order
4. Letters to the editor, etc.
5. Situation based letter

Parts of a Formal Letter

An effective formal letter is one which has the following parts

1. Sender's Address

It is the complete address of the person who has written the letter. It is written at the top left hand corner of the page with each part of the address written in a separate line.

Example 2554/20, Adarsh Nagar
Delhi - 110085

2. Date

It is the date on which the letter is written. It is written just after the sender's address in a very specific format as given below.

20th January, 20XX

3. Receiver's Post and Address

As official letters are addressed to an authority, we write the receiver's address after addressing the official. It contains the receiver's designation, organisation and full address in the format given below.

Example The Editor
The Times of India
Daryaganj
Delhi–110002

4. Subject

It expresses the main theme or objective of the letter clearly. It must be brief and to-the-point.

Example Subject Complaint regarding defective computer accessory

5. Salutation

It is the greeting to the person to whom the letter is addressed. In official letters, we use

Sir/Madam or Respected Sir/Madam

Note When writing the salutation, we have to keep in mind the gender of the receiver, if specified in the question; otherwise, write both.

6. Body of the Letter

It contains all the information that the writer wants to convey. The body includes three main parts :

(i) **Introductory Paragraph/Sentence** It states the purpose of writing the letter. It also gives an introduction of the writer of the letter, if required.

(ii) **Informative Paragraph** It gives details of the problem, its causes, effects, possible solutions, etc.

(iii) **Concluding Paragraph/Sentence** It states the writer's hopes, comments, requests, suggestions, etc.

7. Complimentary Closing

It's a courteous way of ending the letter. It is done in the following format

Thanking you
Yours sincerely/faithfully

Note
- The first letter of the second word (here 's', 'f', 't') is never written in capital.
- Do not use Your's instead of Yours.

8. Sender's Signature, Name and Designation

After the complimentary close, you must sign off the letter by mentioning your name and designation along with your signature.

Ajay Mehta
Citizen of the nation

Points to be Kept in Mind

- Do not use commas in any address, salutation and the complimentary close.
- The subject line should match with what is asked in the question.
- Get right to the purpose of the letter in polite and formal language. Do not give unnecessary details.
- Be clear, concise and to-the-point. Stick to the word limit of 100–120 words.
- Use simple language so that the letter is easy to understand. Do not use long sentences.
- Review your finished letter for clarity from the reader's viewpoint and to remove any grammatical errors.

Format of a Formal Letter

You are Nehal Kumar, Head of the Computer Club in Sunshine School, Noida. Digital literacy refers to someone's ability to use digital technology to find, evaluate, create and communicate information. You believe that digital literacy and navigating the digital world responsibly is crucial in today's technology-dependent age.

Write a letter to the Editor of a national daily, in about 120 words, stressing the need for promoting digital literacy among individuals of all age groups. Discuss the benefits and challenges of digital technology, and propose initiatives to empower people with digital skills. **CBSE Additional SQP 2023**

Sender's address	Sunshine School Noida
Date	31st September, 20XX
Receiver's address	The Editor The Times New Delhi
Subject of the letter	**Subject** Digital Literacy is the Need of the Hour
Salutation	Sir/Ma'am
Body of the letter	Through the columns of your esteemed newspaper, I would like to highlight the crucial importance of digital literacy in today's technology-dependent age. As the Head of the Computer Club at my school, I firmly believe that digital literacy is a skill that can help every individual find a place in a rapidly changing world. Digital literacy refers to someone's ability to use digital technology to find, evaluate, create and communicate information. In the time wherein technology and the internet have made the world smaller than ever, digital literacy and being skilled in the digital world responsibly is crucial. With various challenges like cyber security, misinformation and online privacy, digital literacy is essential to help people use the digital world safely and responsibly. It helps in enhancing communication, creating access to resources and equipping everyone to participate in a digital society. To promote digital literacy, initiatives such as community workshops for a variety of age groups, and collaborations between educational institutions and technology companies can be established. By focusing on digital literacy, we can empower individuals to successfully utilise the full potential of technology.
Complementary Close	Thanking You
Sender's Name, Signature and Designation	Yours truly Nehal Kumar (Head of the Computer Club, Sunshine School, Noida)

SOLVED EXAMPLES

Complaint Letters

Letters of complaint are written to address any type of wrongdoing, grievance or inconvenience arising out of a product, service, etc. The purpose of such a letter is to raise a concern and seek a productive outcome.

The letter includes the following

In case of a product/service

(i) Details of the faulty product/service

(ii) Nature of the complaint (replacement of product or refund)

(iii) Payment information (Bill, cash memo etc.)

In case of grievances

(i) Details of the grievance

(ii) Nature of complaint (social problem, personal grievance)

(iii) Date and place of the wrongdoing (if applicable)

(iv) Compensation or corrective action required

Any other details necessary for resolving the complaint

Scoring Corner

- The beginning of the body of the letter is very specific for letters of complaint
- This is with reference to Receipt no. .... (for product)
- This is to inform you that I am .... I have written this letter to bring to your notice .... (service/public facility)

1. You are Nirmal Pillai, a concerned citizen from Aluva, Kochi. Compose a letter in about 120 words, to the Project Head of the E-Waste Management Cell at Electronics Vatika, New Delhi, highlighting the adverse effects of e-waste* pollution. Suggest measures for addressing its management through community engagement and government initiatives.

*** Discarded electronic devices such as smartphones, computers and televisions, which are no longer in use or have reached the end of their lifecycle.** **CBSE SQP 2024**

Ans. 68, Vardhman Homes
Aluva, Kochi

5th September, 20XX

The Project Head
E-Waste Management Cell
Electronics Vatika, New Delhi

Subject Urgent action needed to address e-waste pollution and management

Sir/Madam

This is to draw your attention towards the spreading menace of e-waste in the community. E-waste is generated by discarded or damaged electronic products and various gadgets and hence, should be separated from everyday waste.

The adverse effects of such electronic waste includes leaching of hazardous material into soil and water, which is harmful for both human and animal health. It also adversely affects the health of plants and ceases their proper growth. E-waste leads to contamination of ecosystems by releasing hazardous chemicals. They are usually toxic in nature and unfit for human exposure.

Therefore, it is necessary to build a collaborative effort in order to manage the drastic amount of e-waste effectively. This could be done by organising e-waste collection drives and recycling events frequently. This will ensure proper disposal of such waste. Awareness campaigns can be conducted in schools, colleges, offices and community centres where e-waste management techniques should be discussed.

The government can further testify this by establishing e-waste collection centres in both urban and rural areas. Strict penalties can be enforced for illegal dumping of e-waste. There is an urgent need to address this issue, so that environmental risk can be minimised. I hope that you look into this matter and take necessary actions as soon as possible.

Thanking you

Yours sincerely
Nirmala Pillai
(A concerned resident)

2. You are Chhavi Pathak of Ranchi, Bihar. Write a letter in about 120 words addressing the Secretary of the City Municipal Authority. Detail the problem of overgrown trees and shrubs in the neighbourhood and request the delegation of personnel for regular pruning. **CBSE SQP 2024**

Ans. 341, Vinaykapur
Ranchi

5th September, 20XX

The Secretary
City Municipal Authority
Ranchi

Subject Request for pruning overgrown trees and shrubs in the neighbourhood

Dear Sir/Madam

This is to draw your attention towards overgrown trees and shrubs in my neighbourhood. The trees have grown beyond their height and the shrubs are unkempt which causes problems for both plants itself and the residents. The overgrown trees and shrubs reduce visibility of roads as they block the area with their height. It also poses a risk to motor commuters because of falling branches. It also blocks direct sunlight in homes and invites insects which further cause diseases. Moreover, this creates an unpleasant site which diminishes the aesthetic value of locality.

Kindly allocate the personnel for regular pruning of these trees and shrubs. This proactive measure will not only enhance the aesthetic beauty of our locality but also ensure the safety and convenience of residents and the pedestrians.

There is an urgent need to look into this matter. I would be grateful if you take the necessary measures as soon as possible.

Thanking you

Yours sincerely

Chhavi Pathak

(A concerned citizen)

3. You are pained to see that in your city, there is no proper arrangement for cleaning of drains. There are heaps of accumulated garbage and stagnant water. Write a letter to the Municipal Commissioner of your city complaining about the same as there is a fear of outbreak of disease. You are Alka/Ashish. (Word limit 100-120) CBSE 2023

Ans. 3/4, Anand Nagar
New Delhi

21st April, 20XX

The Municipal Commissioner
Municipal Corporation
Delhi–110 006

Subject Complaint about lack of cleanliness and hygiene in Anand Nagar

Sir/Ma'am

This is to inform you that I, Alka/Ashish, am a resident of Anand Nagar, Delhi. On behalf of the residents of Shiv Nagar, I have written this letter to draw your kind attention towards the prevailing unsanitary and unhygienic conditions of our locality.

In recent years, Anand Nagar has become a place identified because of its dirt and ding. The sewage is not cleaned and the drains are always overflowing. Garbage is littered at almost all corners and stagnant water can be found accumulated at various places. This is not to say that no sweepers come to the place. The sweepers come but they do not conduct their duties properly. They keep on piling the garbage at corners day by day without removing it. Moreover, the rubbish collection van does not come regularly. It has created a terrible smell and has made the life of residents miserable. Besides, mosquitoes, flies and other disease carriers breed in these garbage dumps and pose a serious health hazard.

I, therefore, request you to look into the matter. Garbage should be collected daily or atleast on alternate days so as to prevent the accumulation of waste.

Kindly do the needful at the earliest.

Thanking you

Yours sincerely

Alka/Ashish

(Resident, Anand Nagar)

4. You have purchased a computer for personal use. After using it for about a month, you have started having problems in it, like its CPU is not working properly, screen is flickering, etc. Write a letter to the manager of the complaint cell of Abott Computers Pvt. Ltd. about the faulty computer in about 100-120 words. Sign yourself as Dev/Devika of Janakpuri, Delhi. CBSE 2023

Ans. 101, Janakpuri
Delhi
27th February, 20XX

The Manager
Abott Computers Pvt. Ltd.
Delhi

Subject Complaint regarding computer purchased

Sir/Ma'am

This is with reference to receipt number ABC/789 dated 25th January, 20XX. I had bought a HP XYZ computer from your store. However, much to my dismay, the computer has started malfunctioning in not even a month since its purchase. For about a month (exactly 27 days), the computer worked perfectly. Now, it has started giving trouble. The CPU does not get easily switched on and even if it somehow switches on, it shuts down automatically. Further, the screen flickers and most of the images appear hazy.

Abott Computers Pvt Ltd is one of the best computer stores in our locality. With such trustworthiness, I expect the store to replace my system as I believe the system is faulty.

Hoping for an immediate replacement of the faulty computer.

Thanking you

Yours sincerely

Dev/Devika

(Customer)

5. You are the Principal of Adarsh Public School, Nagal, Punjab. You organised a trip to Nainital and Shimla for the students of Class X of your school for ten days where you had some bad experience because of improper arrangemets. Write a letter to the Director of Mount Travels and Tourism, Nagal, Punjab complaining about the same. Sign yourself as Anita Chaudhary. (100-120 words) Competency Based

Ans. Adarsh Public School

Nagal

Punjab

23rd June, 20XX

The Director

Mount Travels and Tourism

Nagal

Punjab

Subject Improper tour arrangements

Sir/Ma'am

This is with reference to the trip to Nainital and Shimla organised by your organisation for the students of Adarsh Public School. I, Principal of the school, have written this letter to express my displeasure at inferior arrangements made during our tour which took place between 10th June, 20XX and 19th June, 20XX.

The arrangements made by your agency were improper. We had to face several issues like

- Problems during check-in at the hotel as the staff did not have prior knowledge about our stay. So, we had to wait for them to make arrangements which, in turn, disturbed our itinerary.
- The hotel chosen by your agency had not maintained proper sanitation and hygiene, and the food also tasted stale.
- The transportation services, i.e. the buses were inadequate and could not cater to all students on the trip.

Evidently, we felt cheated by your organisation. As it is, I am expecting a refund of at least half of the amount paid for the tour!

I am enclosing a copy of the bill for your reference. Hoping for an early redressal.

Thanking you

Yours sincerely

Anita Chaudhary

(Principal)

Adarsh Public School

Encl: Copy of the bill

6. You are Raashi/Rahul of Simargargh, Himachal Pradesh. Write a letter in about 100-200 words to the Municipal Commissioner of the city drawing attention to the unattended condition of the public parks in your town. They are poorly maintained with the garbage strewn and pools of stagnant water. Give suggestions on how the parks can be maintained. CBSE 2025

Ans. 4221, Simargarh

Himachal Pradesh

5th March, 20XX

The Municipal Commissioner

Municipal Corporation

Simargarh, Himachal Pradesh

Subject Urgent need for maintenance of public parks

Dear Sir/Madam

I wish to bring to your attention the neglected condition of public parks in Simargarh. These parks, meant for recreation, are poorly maintained. Garbage is strewn all around, benches are broken, and pools of stagnant water have become breeding grounds for mosquitoes, posing a health risk.

To improve the situation, regular cleaning schedules should be implemented. Dustbins must be installed and emptied frequently. Proper drainage should be ensured to prevent waterlogging. Planting more trees and flowers will enhance the parks' beauty, and installing play equipment will attract children.

I sincerely request you to take prompt action to restore the parks for the well-being of residents.

Yours sincerely

Raashi/Rahul

7. You are Vinay Khosla, the Purchase Executive at Haven Book Store in Secunderabad, Andhra Pradesh. You had a telephonic discussion with a Sales Executive from Prakashan Book House, the wholesalers. The conversation pertained to the delivery of books, stationery, and art materials for your store. Despite the conversation, there has been no response from the Prakashan Book House, and attempts to contact them through the provided phone number have been unsuccessful.

Write a complaint letter, in about 120 words, to the proprietor of Prakashan Book House, 60, Haveli Market Street, Hyderabad, A.P.

CBSE Additional SQP 2023

Ans. The Haven Book Store
231, Gulmarg Bazaar
Secunderabad, A.P.

16th November, 20XX

The Proprietor M/s Prakashan Book House (Wholesalers)
60, Haveli Market Street
Hyderabad, A.P.

Subject Unresolved issue with follow-up of delivery details

Sir/Ma'am

This is with reference to our previous conversation *via.* telephone on 14th November, 20XX regarding an order to be placed with your store for books, stationery and art materials. I had a telephonic conversation with one of your Sales Executives, Khushi Sodhi, regarding the delivery schedule where we were told that we would be informed about the delivery soon.

However, we have not received any updates or communication from your end. Attempts to contact your office using the listed telephone number have been unsuccessful as the calls are not going through. This lack of communication and the absence of follow-up from your end have caused significant disruptions in our planned operations' schedule.

Therefore, I kindly request your prompt attention to this matter. Given the importance of our business relationship, we hope to resolve this issue amicably. Please feel free to reach out to me.

Hoping for an early response.

Thanking you

Yours sincerely
Vinay Khosla
(Purchase Executive, Haven Book Store)

Letters of Inquiry

A letter of inquiry is written when we want to get some specific information from someone. It could be about a product, a service, a course, etc. It is also written in response to advertisements.

The letter includes the following

- A brief introduction about yourself and/or your organisation.
- Details of the product or service required.
- Clearly mention the details you want to know.
- If there is a time limit within which you need the information, specify it in the letter.

Scoring Corner

Always start the body of your letter with – "This is with reference to a poster/advertisement dated ...."

1. You are Shivam/Shivani of C-12, Janakpuri, Indore. You wish to make a pilgrimage to Badrinath, Kedarnath and Haridwar with your family of six. Write a letter to R.K. Travels, enquiring about the schedule of their conducted tour by Deluxe buses to these places. Ask about the charges, boarding and lodging arrangements and the total time needed for the tour.

Competency Based, CBSE 2023

Ans. C-12, Janakpuri
Indore

25th January, 20XX

The Manager
R.K. Travels
Indore

Subject Enquiry about conducted tours

Sir/Ma'am

This is with reference to the poster regarding the tours conducted by your agency to Badrinath, Kedarnath and Haridwar. I wish to be a part of this tour with my family of six members. For the same, I would like to know a few things like your terms for conducted tours to the places mentioned above along with the tour dates and the overall charge per person. Also, provide me the breakup of the fare which should include lodging/boarding charges food and transport facilities. I would also like to know the duration of journey and halting.

With this information, I would be able to make an efficient decision. Kindly send me these details along with a proposed itinerary by post to the address mentioned above.

Hoping for an early response.

Thanking you

Yours faithfully
Shivam

2. You are Ankit/Ankita of Mahavir Public School, Delhi. You have seen an advertisement in 'The Times of India' regarding the starting of new batches of 'Astronomy Club' by the National Science Centre. You wish to join the club. Write a letter to the Director, enquiring about the venue, duration, fee-strucure, activities etc. CBSE 2023

Ans. Mahavir Public School
Delhi

5th February, 20XX

The Director
National Science Centre
Delhi

Subject Enquiry regarding new batch

Sir/Ma'am

With reference to your advertisement in 'The Times of India' dated 3rd February, 20XX related to new batches of 'Astronomy Club', I would like to join a batch starting from the coming fortnight.

For the same, I request you to send me some details regarding the batch that I want to join. The details that I need are

- Duration of the course
- Fee structure and transportation
- Venue where the classes will be held
- Various projects and activities covered in the class

I will be grateful to you if you send the details at the earliest so that I can make necessary arrangements for joining the classes.

Thanking you

Yours sincerely
Ankit

3. You are Kamal/Kanishka living at G-50, Kirti Nagar. Write a letter to the Principal I.T.I Pusa in about 100-120 words, enquiring about the diploma courses available in the institution, the duration of the course, the fee-structure, placement services and the admission process. CBSE 2023

Ans. G-50, Kirti Nagar
Delhi

10th November, 20XX

The Principal
I.T.I Pusa

Subject Enquiry about diploma courses

Sir/Ma'am

This is with reference to the advertisement in 'The Hindu' dated 9th November, 20XX, regarding the diploma courses offered by your institution. I have completed my schooling with extremely good grades and am interested in pursuing a diploma course in your institution. I would be grateful if you could provide me with the following details for admissions to the graduation diploma in IT.

- Details for Admission
- Eligibility Criteria
- Fee Structure
- Hostel Facility
- Prospects for Placement
- Scholarships Available (if any)

I would appreciate an early response from your end so as to enable me to decide my future course of action. I am sending along a self-addressed and duly stamped envelope so that you can send me a prospectus regarding this course at the earliest.

Hoping for an early response.

Thanking you

Yours sincerely
Kamal

4. You are Samina Zaveri, Class X, Vadodara, Gujarat. You come across the following information on a local library's notice board. CBSE SQP 2022 Term II

> **Create Your Own Board Game Competition!**
> Create an educational board game, and send it to us at Teen-Toggle Games Pvt. Ltd, 307, Satija building, Colaba, Mumbai by July 2022. The top 10 winning board games will be featured on our international portal. Attractive scholarships for the winners!

You wish to participate but require more information. Write a letter to Teen-Toggle Games Pvt. Ltd. in about 120 words enquiring about rules, scholarship details and deadlines. Also enquire about specifications for solo or group entries.

Ans. H-124, Skyhigh Apartments
Sayaji Path, Vadodara
Gujarat – 390020

12th January, 20XX

Teen-Toggle Games Pvt. Ltd.
307, Satija building
Colaba, Mumbai

Subject Enquiry regarding the Board Games Competition

Sir/Ma'am

This is with reference to a poster from your company on Shiksha Library's notice board today regarding creation of an educational board game. Board games have piqued my interest ever since I was young and thus, I wish to participate in the competition that your company is organising.

I had a few queries regarding the same like the rules, the deadline for the competition and if it is a strictly solo or group competition. The information contained in the poster was slightly vague. Hence, I would like to request you to explain the process of the competition. Also, please update me with details regarding the scholarship.

I request a swift and detailed response.

Thanking you

Yours sincerely
Samina Zaveri

5. You are Anuradha/Ashish, residing at 45, Westwood Street, Nainital. After being inspired by a billboard advertisement for a seaside report promoting relaxation and rejuvenation, you are interested in plannig a family getaway.

Let the waves of the water drench you with the ultimate bliss of being alive! Book a stay with us and experience the best holiday ever!

Write a letter (110-120 words) to the Resort manager requesting details about the costs, room options, nearby attractions and available activities. Please include any additional necessary information for planning the trip **CBSE 2025**

Ans. 45, Westwood Street
Nainital-263001

5th March, 20XX

The Manager
Ocean Bliss Resort
Goa

Subject Inquiry about accommodation and facilities

Dear Sir/Madam

I recently came across your advertisement promoting a relaxing seaside experience and am interested in planning a family getaway to your resort. Kindly provide details regarding room options, availability, and pricing. Additionally, I would like to know about any special packages, meal inclusions, and extra charges.

Could you also share information about nearby attractions and activities such as water sports, sightseeing, and cultural events? Details on transportation services and any seasonal discounts would also be helpful for our planning.

I look forward to your prompt response to finalise our arrangements.

Yours sincerely
Anuradha/Ashish

Letter for Placing an Order

These are business letters which include placing or cancelling an order for products/services from another company or organisation. They are written in a very well formatted and formal manner.

While placing an order, the writer has to be very careful about giving accurate information. Any inaccuracies may result in delayed/wrong deliveries with serious financial implications.

Such letters should give

- specifications (with quantities) of the products/services to be supplied.
- reference number of the quotation/price list against which the order has been placed.
- payment terms/credit terms (as applicable)
- required date of delivery
- mode of transport of goods (if required)
- all taxes/delivery charges
- any other terms and conditions

Scoring Corner

Always start the letter for placing an order with – "This is with reference to the advertisement dated ...." This is with reference to our previous correspondence ....

1. You are Niharika, Incharge of the Neighbourhood Library for children. Write a letter to Manautal Publishers placing an order for books 2 sets each of Panchatantra and Amar Chitra Katha in about 120 words. Mention mode of payment, library discount and date of delivery. **CBSE 2022 Term II**

Ans. Neighbourhood Library
Mumbai
29th March, 20XX

The Manager
Manautal Publishers
Mumbai

Subject Placing the order of books

Sir/Ma'am

This is with reference to your advertisement in 'Deccan Herald' dated 27th March, 20XX regarding Hindi books. The Neighbourhood Library wants to refill and update the library before the reopening of the schools for the new session. For the same, we would like to order the following books :

Book Name	No. of Sets
Panchatantra (Hindi)	2 sets
Amar Chitra Katha (Hindi)	2 sets

You are requested to send these items, duly packed, within a period of one week of receiving this letter. Payment shall be made through online mode-GooglePay, NEFT or Bank Transfer, once the shipping is confirmed. We expect a reasonable discount of at least 15% on the total amount.

Hoping for an early confirmation.

Thanking you

Yours sincerely
Niharika
(Incharge)
(Neighbourhood Library)

2. You are Vikram/Vanya, Librarian, B.S. Public School, Delhi. Write a letter to the Manager of Amar Publication House, Mumbai, placing an order for 4 sets of Social Studies books for grades 6-8 published by NCERT in not more than 120 words. Mention school discount, mode of payment and date of delivery. CBSE 2022 Term II

Ans. B.S. Public School
Delhi

1st March, 20XX

The Manager
Amar Publication House,
Mumbai

Subject Placing the order of books

Sir/Ma'am

This is with reference to your advertisement in 'The Hindu' dated 27th February, 20XX regarding the sale of NCERT books. B.S. Public School wants to order Social Studies textbooks for Classes 6-8, published by NCERT. The list of the books with the quantity required is as follows

Subject	Class	No. of Sets
Social Studies	6	4
Social Studies	7	4
Social Studies	8	4

You are requested to send these items, duly packed, within a period of one week of receiving this letter. Payment shall be made through online mode-GooglePay, NEFT or Bank Transfer, once the shipping is confirmed. We expect a reasonable discount of at least 15% on the total amount.

Hoping for an early confirmation.

Thanking you

Yours sincerely
Vanya
(Librarian B.S. Public School)

3. You are Vaibhavi Sinha, examination incharge, Goodway Public School, Aurobindo Road, Indore. You require 4 reams of white paper, 2 packets of carbon paper, one dozen registers, blue and red ball point pens (50 each). Place an order with Sunrise Stationery Mart, 12 Mall Road, Indore mentioning terms of payment, discount asked by you and delivery date. (100-120 words) CBSE 2020

Ans. Goodway Public School
Aurobindo Road
Indore

5th March, 20XX

Sunrise Stationery Mart
12, Mall Road
Indore

Subject Placing an order for stationery

Sir/Ma'am

This is with reference to our previous correspondence dated 4th March, 20XX. We have written this letter to inform you that we would like to place the bulk order of stationery items for the academic session 20XX-XX. The particulars of the products and the quantity to be supplied are given below.

S. No.	Product	Quantity
1.	White paper	04 reams
2.	Carbon paper	02 packets
3.	Registers	01 dozen
4.	Blue ballpoint pens	50 units
5.	Red ballpoint pens	50 units

Please send us fresh supplies by 4th July. Any delivery after that would be returned. Also, please send the bill at the time of delivery. As always, we will first check the supplies and then, transfer the payment digitally.

We hope that we will get additional discount as discussed.

Thanking you

Yours sincerely
Vaibhavi Sinha
(Examination Incharge)
Goodway Public School

4. As the Head of the Music Department of your school, write a letter to Mysore Music Associations, placing an order for some instruments such as flute, casio, sitar, harmonium, etc. You are Nandini/Namit Verma of Army School, Safdarjung, Enclave, Delhi. (100-120 words) Competency Based

Ans. Army School
Safdarjung Enclave
Delhi

12th April, 20XX

The Proprietor
Mysore Music Associations
Delhi

Subject Order for musical instruments

Sir/Ma'am

With reference to our previous correspondence dated 10th April, 20XX, we are glad to inform you that our school's management has decided to order musical instruments from your company. The prices mentioned in your quotation no. 12/49/17/82 dated 8th April, 20XX have been approved. The list of the instruments required is given below.

S. No.	Name of Instruments	Quantity
1.	Flutes	20
2.	Casio	5
3.	Sitar	3
4.	Harmonium	5
5.	Drums	2

Kindly ensure that the delivery is made within 15 days between 10 am and 2 pm. We are sure that proper packing of the instruments will be taken care of. Any damage caused during transportation will be your responsibility.

The payment will be made only after the quality of the instruments has been checked and approved by the school management.

For any enquiry, feel free to contact the undersigned.

Thanking you

Yours sincerely
Nandini/Namit Verma
(Head – Department of Music)
Mobile no. 97604XXXXX

5. You are Sonakshi, the Secretary of the Music Club in your school. Place an order for microphones, amplifiers and speakers from the local music shop for an upcoming music competition being hosted by your school. Write the letter in 100-120 words mentioning a date by when the equipment should be delivered. Competency Based

Ans. Basant Public School
Nashik

20th March, 20XX

The Proprietor
Music Maestro Instruments
Nashik

Subject Order microphones, amplifiers and speakers

Sir/Ma'am

This is with reference to the previous correspondence regarding our order of musical instruments. We are delighted to inform you that we are going ahead with our order with the agreed upon discount. The details of the order are as given below.

S. No.	Instruments	Quantity
1.	Wireless Microphones	5 sets
2.	Wired Microphones	5 sets
3.	Amplifiers	8 sets
4.	Speaker	10 sets

The given order is required by us for the upcoming music competition which will be held on 10th April, 20XX. The order should reach us within two weeks from now that is 4th April, 20XX. Please go through the order and confirm at the earliest along with the charges.

Yours sincerely
Radha Joshi
Principal

6. Recently, India created history by successfully touching down on the South pole of the moon with its third lunar mission Chandrayaan-3. You are organising a stargazing event to enhance the interest of students in astronomy. You wish to buy telescopes as well as stands to use at the event. Place an order with the local shop for scientific equipment. Write a

letter in 100-120 words mentioning a date by when the equipment should be delivered.

Ans. XYZ School
New Delhi-110085

24th March, 20XX

The Proprietor
Stargazers Emporium
Chandni Chowk

Subject Order for telescope and stand

Sir/Ma'am

This is with reference to your poster advertisement at APJ Space Centre, We, XYZ school, would like to place an order for telescopes and stands. The equipments are needed as we are organising a stargazing event to spark students' interest in astronomy. The event will be held on 15th April, 20XX.

Thus, we would like to purchase telescopes that are suitable for beginners and easy to use. Additionally, I require sturdy and adjustable stands to support the telescopes.

S. No.	Instruments	Quantity
1.	10*70 telescope	10
2.	Compatible telescope stand	10

Please ensure that the telescope is of good quality and easy to use for beginners. Additionally, the stand should be stable and adjustable to accommodate different viewing angles. We would like to request that the equipment be delivered by 5th April, 20XX. Payment will be done upon delivery and quality checking of the equipment.

For any enquiry, feel free to contact the undersigned.

Thanking you

Yours sincerely
ABC
[Ph. No. - 8076 XXXXXX]

Letters to the Editor

These are the letters written to the Editor of a newspaper, magazine or any other regularly printed publication. Their purpose is to highlight a social issue or a problem. An ideal letter to the Editor should

- grab/catch the reader's attention.
- explain the topic/issue of the letter at the start.
- explain why the issue is important.
- state the writer's opinion about what should be done.
- be brief.
- express writer's hope for the resolution of the problem.

Scoring Corner

A letter to the Editor always starts with "Through the columns of your esteemed newspaper, I would like to draw the attention of ...."

1. The household water supply in your locality is muddy and not fit for drinking. Despite several complaint letters to the civic authorities, the problem is still unresolved. Write a letter to the editor of a local daily, in about 120 words, expressing your concern at the situation and suggesting measures to resolve the problem and drawing attention of the concern authorities. You are Somil/Soumya of 769, Silver Apartments Ajitha Vihar Karampeeth. CBSE 2024

Ans. 768, Silver Apartments,
Ajitha Vihar, Karampeeth

5th March, 20XX

The Editor
The Times of India
New Delhi

Subject Muddy household water supply

Sir/Ma'am

Through the columns of your esteemed newspaper, I wish to bring the attention of the concerned authorities towards the alarming issue of polluted water supply in our locality.

Our area has been receiving dirty and contaminated water for the last two weeks. This polluted water is unfit for consumption and poses a serious threat to our health and well-being.

As a result, we have to buy 10-20 water bottles every day to beat the rising temperatures and for other day-to-day chores. The condition is dismal as even after previous complaints no action has been taken to resolve the situation.

I believe that the concerned authorities take immediate action to address this issue. There is a need to investigate the source of pollution and monitor water quality regularly.

Thanking you

Yours sincerely
Somil/Soumya

2. As Armaan Khan, the School Literary Captain of Ujjwal Academy, Old City, Kilanderabad, you believe that languages can help bridge regional divides and promote unity.
Write a letter to the Editor of a National Daily, in about 120 words, suggesting the introduction of an Online Regional Language Learning Programme managed and run by Student Councils and Language Clubs in the city. The programme aims to help residents who have recently relocated to a new region in picking up the local language organically. Share the importance and credibility of such a programme and suggest a feasible way to execute it along with possible activities. **CBSE SQP 2023**

Ans. Ujjwal Academy
Old City, Kilanderabad

12th March, 20XX

The Editor
India Samachar
Jamnagar, Kilanderabad

Subject Introduction of online regional language learning programmes

Sir/Ma'am

Through the columns of your esteemed newspaper, I would like to bring the kind attention of the citizens of the nation towards the need of introduction of an Online Regional Language Learning Programme in our city. As someone who believes that languages can help bridge regional divides and promote unity, I believe that the regional language learning programme can help the recently relocated residents (of all ages) establish a healthy rapport with the local residents and promote mutual understanding.

This online programme, organised and run by Student Councils and Language Clubs, can help these residents pick up the local language organically. This initiative may be conducted only on weekends for three months, making it feasible for participants to attend without hindering their work or studies. Activities such as language exchange programmes, cultural events and group discussions on the virtual platform can be undertaken to make this programme more engaging.

I hope that we all come together as a community to support this programme for its potential, to bring people together, promote language proficiency and foster a sense of brotherhood.

Thanking you

Yours faithfully
Armaan Khan
(School Literary Captain)

3. As Sharmila Sahani, a conscientious resident of 25/22, Rajpur, Fatehbad, you have recently come across numerous newspaper articles featuring tragic incidents where lives have been lost due to reckless driving and not following the traffic rules. Write a letter to the editor of a national daily, shedding light to this issue and give suggestions on what can be done. **Competency Based**

Ans. Sharmila Sahani
25/22, Rajpur
Fatehabad

19th February, 20XX

The Editor
Hindustan Times
New Delhi

Subject Rising concerns over reckless driving and traffic violations

Sir/Madam

Through the columns of your esteemed newspaper,

I wish to draw attention to the alarming increase in reckless driving and non-adherence to traffic rules. Recent reports of fatal accidents due to overspeeding, signal violations, and drunk driving are deeply concerning. Lives are being lost due to negligence, and urgent action is needed.

Strict enforcement of traffic rules, installation of more speed cameras, and harsher penalties for offenders can help curb this issue. Additionally, awareness campaigns should be launched in schools and colleges to educate young drivers about responsible driving. The government must also improve road infrastructure and ensure proper lighting and signage.

I hope this issue receives the attention it deserves, leading to safer roads for all.

Yours sincerely
Sharmila Sahani

4. You are Rohit/Rohini of A-15, Pitampura, Delhi. You observed that the subways in Delhi are seldom used by pedestrians who are always trying to cut across traffic. You have decided to write a letter to the Editor of 'Hindustan Times' highlighting the dire need of creating awareness about it. Based on the points given along with your own ideas write a letter.

– infrastructure unutilised
– pedestrians prone to accidents
– accumulation of stagnant water/garbage in subways
– need for improvement and regular cleanliness under proper supervision. **CBSE 2023**

Ans. A-45, Pitampura
Delhi

5th June, 20XX

The Editor
The Hindustan Times
New Delhi

Subject Importance of subways

Sir/Ma'am

Through the columns of your esteemed daily, I would like to draw the attention of the citizens of Delhi towards the ignorance regarding the use of the various subways present in the capital.

It is not unknown to us that the traffic jams are a grave concern in Delhi, especially for pedestrians who find it difficult to cross the roads safely. To tackle the issue, subways were constructed to provide easy and safe way to cross roads. However, these subways are barely used. People ignore the subways and prefer to cross the roads in the raging traffic inspite of knowing that their act makes them prone to road accidents. Look at the news and you will find many cases wherein accidents have happened because of such daredevilry. This doesn't mean that the subways are completely unused. Some people who prefer to use subways, do so when they are clean which is a rarity. Most of our subways are littered with garbage or filled with dirty stagnant water, making them unusable.

Hence, it is time for us to not only become aware of how these subways are of utmost importance for our safety, but also to make sure that the subways are properly maintained under proper supervision. If we maintain our infrastructures and use them appropriately, our nation will grow and develop efficiently.

Thanking you
Yours sincerely
Rohini
(A Concerned Citizen)

5. When you think about your city, you feel proud of its historical monuments, places of cultural interest. Shopping centres and beautiful parks. Write a letter in 100-120 words to the Editor of a National Daily expressing your views on your city. Also suggest ways to increase footfall to these places like the government's recent initiative of free entry to all historical monuments on the occasion 75th Independence Day.

You are Sangeeta /Sanjay, 45 Vijay Nagar, Delhi. (Word limit 100-125 words) **CBSE 2023**

Ans. 45, Vijay Nagar
Delhi

17th January, 20XX

The Editor
The Times
New Delhi

Subject Delhi - My city

Sir/Ma'am

Through the columns of your esteemed daily, I wish to draw the attention of the readers towards Delhi, the city of great historical importance. The capital of the country is a treat for all its residents and tourists with its grandeur and amalgamation of various cultures. With innumerable monuments reflecting the various phases of Indian history, museums, the Parliament House, Rashtrapati Bhawan, Metro, Delhi Haat, the shopping malls and beautiful parks, it is not wrong to say that we all are proud of Delhi and the experiences that it, offers. Delhi truly represents Emperor Shah Jahans belief written on Diwan-e-Khas at Red Fort, "If there be Paradise upon Earth, It is here."

As the capital has so much to offer, the government is making sure that more and more people come to Delhi and experience its historical grandeur. An important initiative taken by the government under the 75th Independence day celebration was opening up the monuments with free entry. Such initiatives along with great social media posts about the great history of Delhi is sure to increase the glory it enjoys.

I hope the government keeps up it's efforts to make Delhi one of the main tourist destinations for all.

Thanking you
Yours sincerely
Sangeeta
(A Concerned Citizen)

6. You are Anita/Anil of Panday Park. You recently worked on a school project on the powerful impact of media in promoting national integration. Write a letter to the Editor of The Hindu, sharing your views on the role of media. **CBSE 2023**

Ans. 29, Panday Park
New Delhi

30th January, 20XX

The Editor
The Hindu
New Delhi

Subject Role of media

Sir/Ma'am

Through the columns of your esteemed paper, I would like to draw the attention of media persons to the role that they can play in promoting national integration.

We know that India is a country where diversity is visible in every aspect and it is important for the people of India to stay united for the progress of the country. National integration is what aims to bind the people of India together and also provide them an environment that is conducive to their staying together. In promoting national integration, media plays a very important role. Media is what keeps people in different parts of the country abreast with what is happening in the other parts and therefore, acts as the most powerful means of communication. It is the role of media to present accurate information to the people of the country so that they can distinguish between the right and the wrong. With the help of media, the realities of the Indian political and social scene can be known and people can work for the betterment in all fields. It is the media that can help to remove social vices and maintain the required unity as well as integrity by helping people overcome communism and regionalism.

I hope that the media people play a responsible role in advocating national integration.

Thanking you

Yours faithfully
Anil
(A Concerned Citizen)

Situation Based Letters

Situation based letters are written to authorities to inform them of something or to give suggestions. These letter generally include

- an explanation of the situation
- your course of action
- suggestions (if applicable)

Scoring Corner

Always start a situation base letter with your introduction.

This is inform you that I am ......

1. As Geetanjali/Girish of 83, Star Apartments, Virbagh, You have noticed that a lot of senior citizens in your society are leading lonely lives. Write a letter in about 120 words, the President of RWA of your society, requesting him to organise more community get-togethers and celebrations to bring cheer to their lonely lives. CBSE 2024

Ans. 83, Star Apartments
Virbagh

20th March, 20XX

The President
Residents Welfare Association
Virbagh

Subject Increasing loneliness of the elderly

Respected Sir/Ma'am

This is to inform you that I am Geetanjali/ Girish, a resident of Star Apartments. I am writing this letter to you to address a matter of concern that has been weighing on the minds of many residents here. It has come to our attention that an increasing number of our senior citizens are experiencing feelings of loneliness and isolation. As a community, it is our duty to ensure that all members, especially our beloved elders, feel included and valued.

In light of this, I humbly request that the Resident Welfare Association (RWA) consider organising more frequent community get-togethers and celebrations. These events would not only provide opportunities for social interaction but also bring joy and cheer into the lives of our seniors. By fostering a sense of belonging and camaraderie, we can work together to alleviate the loneliness that some of our elderly residents are experiencing.

Thank you for your attention to this matter. I look forward to seeing our community come together in support of our senior citizens.

Thanking you

Yours sincerely
Geetanjali/Girish

2. As Vaishali Nathani of 214, Indrayani Apartments, Vaishali Street, Daipur, you believe that forming Ecology clubs and appointing Eco-minders in your city can aid in the preservation and conservation of nature.

Write a letter to the MLA of your city area, in about 120 words, suggesting the need to form such clubs. Share their importance and implications. Recommend the involvement of resident volunteers for implementation of Eco-club activities that nurture and protect the local ecosystem. CBSE SQP 2023

Ans. 214, Indrayani Apartments
Vaishali Street, Daipur

21st February, 20XX

The MLA
Janta House
Rajajipura, Daipur

Subject Suggestion regarding the need to form ecology clubs

Sir/Ma'am

This is inform you that I am Vaishali Nathani, a citizen of Daipur. I have written this letter to express my concern about the environmental degradation in our city and to suggest a solution that I believe could help in preserving and conserving nature. I believe that forming Ecology clubs and appointing Eco-minders in our city can aid in this endeavour.

Ecology clubs can be run by resident volunteers who may undertake activities such as making bird-houses, planting native trees, water harvesting and creating compost piles to nurture and protect the local ecosystem. By involving the residents in these activities, we can raise awareness about the importance of preserving nature and instil a sense of responsibility towards it.

Some of the implications of forming Ecology clubs are reduction of pollution levels, increase in biodiversity and promotion of sustainable practices. This initiative will enhance the quality of life of the residents by providing them with a green and healthy environment.

You are requested to kindly consider this suggestion to ensure better preservation and conservation of nature.

Thanking you

Yours sincerely
Vaishali Nathani
(A Concerned Citizen)

3. Food wastage is fast assuming a serious dimension. A staggering 1×3 billion tonnes of food is being wasted per annum globally. According to reports from UNEP (United Nations Environmental Programme), 811 million people go hungry every day. You are Sofia/Sohail, a resident of 242, Lajpat Nagar, Vayunagar. On behalf of the residents of your locality, write a letter to the Secretary, RWA of your area, requesting him/her to install a community fridge where people can contribute their excess food which can be accessed by the underprivileged. Write your letter in about 120 words.

Ans. 242, Lajpat Nagar
Vayunagar

12th October, 20XX

Resident Welfare Association
Vayunagar

Subject Request to install a community fridge

Sir/Ma'am

This is to inform you that I am Sofia/Sohail, a resident of Vayunagar. I have written this letter to request you to install a community fridge where people can contribute their excess food which can be accessed by the underprivileged.

In the world wherein approximately 811 million people suffer from hunger, nearly 1.3 billion tonnes of food is wasted annually. These staggering numbers show that the idea of food wastage in any situation is a critical issue that needs our urgent attention. While the problem can be tackled at a large scale with the efforts of the authorities, on a small scale, we can do our bit as a community too.

In this light, I propose the installation of a community fridge in our locality. This fridge would allow residents to contribute excess food, which can then be accessed by those in need, particularly the underprivileged members of our community. This initiative will not only help reduce waste but also foster a spirit of sharing and compassion among residents.

Thank you for considering this proposal. I look forward to your positive response.

Yours sincerely
Sofia/Sohail

4. You are Rakesh Mehta, Secretary of Rainbow Apartments, Marathalli, Bangalore. A major pipeline supplying water to your apartment complex burst recently. Repairs are expected to be time consuming and the available water is insufficient to meet the requirements of residents and staff within the premises. Write a letter to the Area Development Officer, Marathalli Area, Bangalore, in not more than 120 words, requesting him to complete the repair work at the earliest, drawing attention to the difficulties faced by the people and the challenges of procuring water from outside. **CBSE Additional SQP 2022**

Ans. Rainbow Apartments
Marathalli Bangalore

23rd March, 20XX

Area Development Officer
Marathalli Area
Bangalore

Subject Requesting timely completion of pipeline repair work

Sir/Ma'am

This is to inform you that I am Akshat from B-35 of the housing complex. I am writing this letter with reference to the ongoing repair work of the water supply lines in our area that burst earlier this week. We were informed that the repair work will be a lengthy and time-consuming process.

While we have provisions for water in our overhead water storage tanks, the stored water will be insufficient to meet everyone's daily needs, especially since it is the peak of summer. Additionally, the surrounding area has also been dug up for repairs, making the tanker drivers reluctant to come inside the apartment premises to deliver water. Besides, procuring water through them is very expensive.

The quality of water from alternate sources is also poor. Therefore, I sincerely request you to address this problem at the earliest and ensure the completion of the repair work.

Thanking you

Yours faithfully

Rakesh Mehta

5. You are Aritrika/Gaurav – a resident of Kasba, Kolkata, West Bengal. Vikas Sinha is the watchman of Shalimar Apartments, the building in which you stay. He has been guarding your building for the past eight years. Recently, he has been diagnosed with a serious aliment and is unable to afford the treatment.

Write a letter in 100-120 words to the secretary of the building requesting him to collect donations from the residents of the building to help Vikas. Mention why you feel helping him is essential. **Competency Based**

Ans. 34, Shalimar Apartments
Kasba, Kolkata
West Bengal

24th October, 20XX

Secretary
Shalimar Apartments
Kasba, Kolkata
West Bengal

Subject Request for acquiring funds to help our watchman in getting treatment for his illness

Sir/Ma'am

This is inform you that I am Aritrika, a resident of Shalimar Apartment complex. I am writing this letter to request your help in acquiring funds for our watchman. With great sorrow, we have got to know that our watchman, who has provided great service for 8 years, is unwell. He has been suffering from Stage 2 liver tumor which requires immediate treatment. However, due to lack of funds, he is not able to get proper medications and is also coming to duty every day. Hence, the children of the society have decided to collect funds for him.

We all know that the watchman had been loyal and extremely vigilant in his duty. Now, it is time for us to help him and save him from this illness. Therefore, we request you to call for donation from each and every apartment so that Shambu, our watchman can be saved.

I hope that you will help us. Hoping for early and favourable response.

Thanking you

Yours faithfully

Aritrika/Gaurav
(A Resident)

6. Your university lecturer gave you an assignment. You won't be able to submit your assignment on time. Write to your lecturer asking for an extension. In the letter describe the situation, explain why your assignment will be late. And say when you will be able to hand in your assignment. Competency Based

Ans. Lilavati hostel
Delhi

14th October, 20XX

Mr. Ajay Thakur
ABC University
Delhi

Subject Extension of submission date of the assignment

Sir/Ma'am

This is to inform you that I am Rohan Khanna, a student from the Business Studies department in your university. I am writing this letter to seek your permission for an extension to submit my assignment that I am supposed to hand over before 24th October, 20XX.

Right after you gave us the task on 7th October, I started working on mine. However, I suddenly caught a severe seasonal flu. I took advice from a doctor, and he prescribed some medicines and complete bed rest. I avoided attending classes and visiting the library to avoid spreading the flu virus.

Fortunately, I am doing better now and hope to get over the flu in a couple of days but I am afraid I will not be able to submit my assignment on time due to my illness.

I, therefore, request an extension to hand over my work to you. I am quite positive that I can submit my assignment before 28th October, 20XX.

I would be indebted if you permit to present my assignment before 28th May instead of the 20th of October.

Thanking you

Yours faithfully
XYZ

7. Recently you read in the news that the Union Cabinet has approved the establishment of the International Big Cat Alliance (IBCA). Compose a letter in about 120 words to the Director of the local zoo of your city talking about your favourite big cats. Enquire about how it will impact the big cats* at the zoo. Also suggest measures to address the mental well-being of the big cats in the zoo. Competency Based

***Big cats include animals like tiger, lion, leopard, snow leopard, puma, jaguar and cheetah.**

Ans. 61, Pratap Enclave
Bengaluru

2nd August, 20XX

The Director
Bannerghatta Zoo
Karnataka

Subject Discussion regarding the establishment of IBCA

Respected Sir/Ma'am

This is in reference to the Union Cabinet's approval of the International Big Cat Alliance (IBCA). This initiative is a significant step towards protecting and conserving these magnificent creatures. As a passionate admirer of big cats, I am particularly interested in understanding how this development will impact the big cats at our local zoo.

I have always been captivated by the grace and power of tigers, lions and leopards. Their presence in our zoo has been a source of great joy and education for many.

I would like to know how the IBCA's establishment will benefit our zoo's big cat population. Will there be increased opportunities for research, conservation efforts or international collaboration?

Moreover, I believe that the mental well-being of big cats in captivity is crucial. Could you share the zoo's current practices to ensure their psychological well-being? Perhaps measures like providing enrichment activities, social interactions and adequate space could be further enhanced to improve their quality of life.

Thank you for your time and attention to this important matter.

Thanking you

Yours faithfully
XYZ

ASSESSMENT EXERCISE

Complaint Letter

1. Due to India's hosting of the G20 Summit, the residents of Delhi have been facing many traffic-related issues. Major public roads are closed off without any forewarning, causing schedule delays, panic and fighting. You have personally witnessed many incidents of road rage issues due to this. Compose a letter of complaint in about 120 words, to the Chief Traffic Inspector, asking him to solve this issue.
2. Recently you travelled in a State Transport luxury bus from Chennai to Thiruvalluvar. To your shock, the air-conditioning in the bus was not working properly. The quality of the maintenance of the bus was also not up to the required standards of a luxury bus. Throughout the journey you spent the time in unbearable heat. Write a letter to the General Manager (Maintenance) of the State Transport for taking action in this matter in 100-120 words. You are Hema/Ganesh, 25, Officers Quarters, Egmore, Chennai.
3. You are Ravi/Renu of Ravidas Chowk, Sadar Bazar, Moradabad. You had bought a copy of the Social Science textbook of Class X, UP Board, from a nearby bookshop. After reading the book, you find that there is overlapping of print on a few pages. Also, some pages are missing due to defective binding. Write a letter of complaint to the publishers M/s Sarojini Publishers, Bareilly, asking for a free replacement in 100-120 words.
4. You are Ashwini/Aradhana, of 1/169, Civil Lines, Agra. You have recently purchased a new washing machine from the showroom of M/s Vikki Sales Corporation. However, the performance of the machine leaves much to be desired. Write a letter complaining about the poor performance to the Customer Service incharge of the company mentioning clearly the problems observed in 100-120 words. Also state the action you want to be taken from their side.
5. Write a letter to the Superintendent of Police of the district complaining about the unauthorised construction of a block of three shops adjacent to the public park in your area in 100-120 words. You are Suresh/ Sarojini, President of the Residents' Welfare Association of your area.
6. You are Pooja/Prateek, a resident of Hoysala Nagar Colony, Bengaluru, Karnataka. Last month, you enrolled for a month-long computer course at Hyderabad School of Computer Sciences. You were granted accommodation in the school's hostel for the duration of the course. However, when you contacted the hostel for confirmation, you found out that your name was not registered in the list.

   Write a letter in 100-120 words to the Head of School complaining about the issue. Mention how this impacts your travel plan and request for corrective action to be taken at the earliest. **Competency Based**

Letters of Inquiry

1. You are Sujata/Sudhir, Secretary of the Student Council, Nav Vihar Public School, Mumbai. You are planning an excursion to Jim Corbett National Park for students. Write a letter to the Director, Tourism Department, Jim Corbett National Park enquiring about a package for 100 students which would include transportation, sightseeing, boarding and lodging for 4 nights. **CBSE 2022 Term II**
2. You are Rita/Rahul and you came across the following information on your local club notice-board.

   Better Living

   How to tackle stress, build concentration and remain fit and healthy – Yoga, a way of life – Join free yoga camp for students.

   You wish to enrol but require more information. Write a letter to the Yoga Institute, M. G. Road, Pune enquiring details of timing, batch size, eligibility, etc. for joining the course. **CBSE 2022 Term II**
3. You are Salim/Sarika, Administrative Officer of M/s Sanjeev Security Agencies, Saharanpur. You are opening your new office in the city for which you require suitable office furniture for an office with two rooms and a hall. Draft an enquiry letter to M/s Office Suppliers, Saharanpur, asking for a quotation for the items required. Specify the number required for each item and ask for credit in payment. (100-120 words)
4. You are Sayan, a resident of Rajendra Apartments, Chennai. You have recently settled down in Tamil Nadu and would like to learn Tamil. Write a letter in 100-120 words applying for a 2-month basic language course at 'Language Learners Centre'. Enquire about the fees and the weekly schedule of classes. **Competency Based**
5. You are Pranab, a member of the Student Council at your school. Your school is organising a mock United Nations session for various schools in your district. In 100-120 words, write a letter to your local stationery shop giving a bulk order for notebooks and pens.

6. You are Sangeeta, a student of Class X. You recently came across a learning app on the internet that offers practise questions to prepare students for the board exams. In 100-120 words, write a letter to the operations officer of the app enquiring about their pricing and the duration of the free trial period. **Competency Based**

Letters for Placing an Order

1. You are Narendra Sharma/Nitin Sharma, Head, Fitness Group of Gold Gym, 234, Ram Vihar, Delhi. You wish to purchase certain herbal medicines and wellness products. Write a letter to the Store Manager, M/s East India, 54, Preet Vihar, Delhi placing an order for the specific products required by you.
2. You are Nalini/Vishal Hostel warden, Zenith Public School, Kosikalan. Write a letter to the Sales fans, Bharat Electronics and Domestic Appliances Limited, New Delhi, placing an order for a few fans, microwave ovens, geysers and tube-lights that you wish to purchase for the hostel. Also ask for the discount permissible on the purchase.
3. You are Sales Manager of DBM School, Gwalior. You need educational toys and play equipment for kindergarten students. Write a letter to the Manager, Kwality Toys, Kirti Nagar, Delhi in 100–120 words placing an order. You are Neeraj.
4. You are Neha Singh, Computer Incharge of DIPS.
Your school wishes to buy 20 computers and computer accessories from Apple Inc., Nehru Place, New Delhi, Draft a letter placing order giving all the specifications of the product and its quality.
5. You are Neeraj/Neeraja Shekhar, Principal, Vasant Public School, Pune. Your school has just started an Art Lab. Write a letter to the Manager of Art ItsyBItsy House, Pune, placing an order for DIY art supplies for the school. Ask for a discount on the catalogue prices. (120-150 words)
6. You are Pranab, a member of the Student Council at your school. Your school is organising a mock United Nations session for various schools in your district.
In 100-120 words, write a letter to your local stationery shop giving a bulk order for notebooks and pens. **Competency Based**

Letters to the Editor

1. You are Sonu/Sonali, living in 43 B, Dilshad Garden, Delhi. You happen to see a news item in the newspaper about the popularity of Indian handicrafts abroad. However, you are unhappy about the lack of recognition given to the artisans by the government. This is leading to the dying of traditional forms of art and craft. Write a letter to the Editor of 'The Times of India' in about 100-120 words about the difficulties faced by the artisans and suggest ways to revive and popularise Indian indigenous products. You may use the information given below

Indian Handicrafts Sought After

New Delhi Indian handicrafts are in great demand in the US, Europe and the Gulf countries. However, the artisans feel their products are not given the required publicity. Further, the products are bought from them at very low prices by the middle men and sold later at much higher prices abroad. The artisans hope that the government would do something in this regard.

2. You are Amit/Amita. Write a letter to the Editor of the local daily newspaper expressing your anguish over the problems faced by the people due to free sale of liquor everywhere.
3. The tourism industry can bring valuable income to the country. Write a letter to the Editor of a popular daily on how the government and the public can boost the development of this industry in 100-120 words. You are Rama/Ram, 4 Rani Road, Ranchi. **CBSE 2015**
4. There is a flood of advertisements on television channels these days. Useless commodities and superstitious beliefs are promoted through glamorous and exaggerated presentations. Write a letter to the Editor, 'New Indian Express', about the negative influence which such advertisements have on the minds of the people. You are Radha/Ramesh of Mayur Vihar, Lucknow (100-120 words). **CBSE 2015**
5. You are Polly Chawla, a resident of Worli Park, Mumbai. You recently saw a documentary about the youth of the nation titled, 'A Country in Good Hands'.
Write a letter of appreciation to the Editor of the Youth Times, in not more than 120 words, drawing her attention to the good that the youngsters around you are doing. Suggest ways in which they can further contribute to the betterment of society. **CBSE Additional SQP 2022**

6. As a regular commuter by bus from Noida to Delhi, you have been witnessing rash driving by the bus drivers daily without an exception. Write a letter to the Editor, 'The Times of India' in 120-150 words drawing the attention of the General Manager, Delhi Transport Corporation to this problem. You are Priti/Prakash, 15 Udyog Vihar, Noida. (120-150 words) **Delhi 2013**

Clues

- Creates a sense of panic among the pedestrians and commuters
- Leads to accidents
- Drivers should be fined heavily
- Strict enforcement of traffic rules
- Time to time training must be encouraged

Situation Based Letters

1. You have been offered a job, asking you to start next week. You want the job very much but, because of a previous commitment, you want to delay the start for another two weeks. Write to the Manager, accepting the job, but explaining your situation and asking for the change to your start date. You are Harishit/Harshita.
2. You are studying for a qualification, and you would like some time off from your work to complete it. Write a letter to your manager explaining your situation. You are Ambika.
3. You recently went shopping at the local supermarket. When you got home and noticed your bill, you found that you had been charged for items you did not purchase. Write a letter to the Supermarket Manager explaining what has happened. Tell the manager how you feel about the error and what you would like him/her to do about it.
4. You are Anuradha/Ashish, residing at 45, Westwood street, Nainital, After being inspired by a billboard advertisement for a seaside resort promoting relaxation and rejuvenation, you are interested in planning a family getaway.

   > Let the waves of the water drench you with the ultimate bliss of being alive! Book a stay with us and experience the best holiday ever!

   Write a letter (100-120) words) to the Resort manager requesting details about the costs, room options, nearby attractions and available activities. Please include any additional necessary information for planning the trip.
5. You have been invited to attend an admissions interview for a prestigious college. Unfortunately, you cannot come at the proposed time due to a previous appointment. Write a letter to the Admissions Tutor explaining your situation.
6. Indian Chess Prodigy, D. Gukesh has been making waves as he won the FIDE Candidates tournament in 2024, becoming the youngest ever challenger in the history of the World Chess Championship. You recently noticed some children of your society talking about Gukesh's achievement and discussing his chess games. You realise that the children did not have a proper space or the necessary equipment to play chess. Write a letter to the President of the RWA in about 100-120 words, requesting him to create a chess playground furnished with chess sets for the children to play.

CHAPTER 2

Analytical Paragraph

An analytical paragraph is a written text based on the analysis of a data which can be an extract, a chart, a poster, a map, a table or a graph. It basically explains your thesis or arguments regarding a subject with evidence from the given data. In other words, an analytical paragraph does not just describe the data but also points out some specific parts from it to justify your statement.

Elements of an Analytical Paragraph

- **Claim or Topic Statement** Make a clear statement or give a title to your paragraph about what you have concluded or found from the given data.
- **Evidence** Use the figures or the textual information to justify your argument.
- **Explanation** Explain your analysis and understanding of the data in detail.
- **Conclusion** End the paragraph with rewriting your argument in a new way.

Points to be Kept in Mind

For writing an analytical paragraph, the following points need to be kept in mind

- Read the data carefully.
- Understand the topic on which analytical paragraph is to be written.
- Carefully study the trends, figures and information given for analysis.
- Use the trends as an evidence to support your statement.
- Give a clear introduction and conclusion.
- Try to avoid repetition of information.
- Use simple language so that it is easy to understand.
- Do not divide the paragraph into various parts. Remember to present your information in one paragraph.
- Reread your paragraph to check for any grammatical error.

SOLVED EXAMPLES

1. The chart below displays details regarding online activity for four age groups in six categories. Write an analytical paragraph for the table provided in about 100 words.

Activity %	Age Teens	Age 20s	Age 30s	Age 40s
News	76	71	72	78
Downloads	85	35	35	25
Buying a product	44	67	67	69
Online games	88	36	36	28
Searching for a product	0	81	81	85
Searching for people	6	22	22	21

Ans. The advent of technology and faster internet service has changed the way we do things. From watching news, buying a product, searching for a product, service or information to playing games, everything has become dependent on the internet. A recent study trying to understand the use of internet and facilities used by different age groups found that while internet has been extensively used, different age groups use it for different purposes. The data found that teens use internet majorly for playing online games. Further, they are also highly interested in downloading certain things using internet. However, they show zero interest in searching a product online. In the 20's age group, the zero interest zone of the teens (searching for people) is the zone of highest interest. In the 30's, we see that the online games and downloads decrease among individuals but they are highly interested in searching and buying an online product. The 40's age group bring to our notice that searching and buying an online product along with watching news are the high interest zones. Hence, internet caters to people of all age groups.

2. The maps given below show the changes that have taken place in Meadowside Village and Fonton, a neighbouring town, since 1990. Analyse the changes that had taken place over the years and write an analytical paragraph in 100-120 words. **Competency Based**

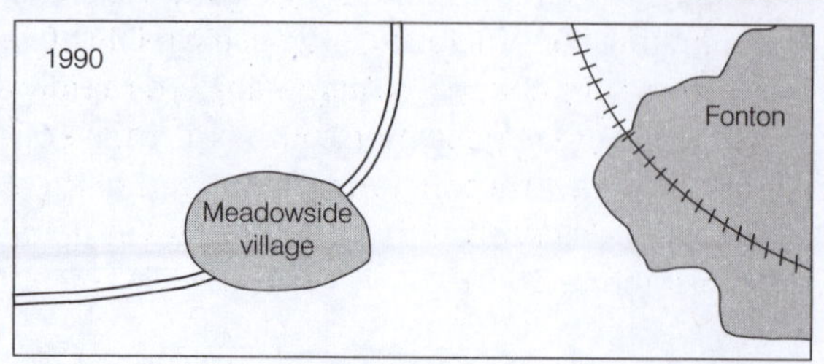

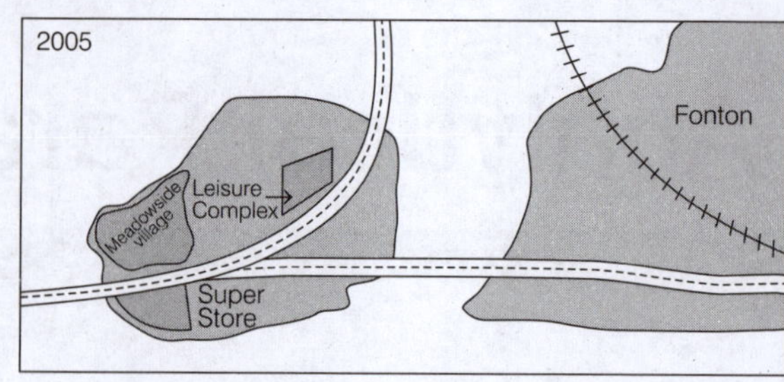

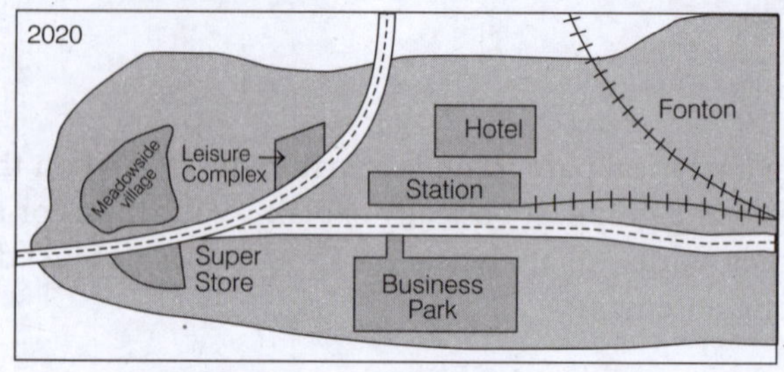

Ans. The Growth and Development of the Region

The given maps illustrate how the Meadowside Village and Fonton, its neighbouring town, have changed and developed over the span of 30 years. It depicts the map of both the locations for the years 1990, 2005 and 2020, respectively. It is pretty evident from the maps that both the village and the town increased its size, after finally merging together. In 1990, the village and town were separate entities with different infrastructures, housing and facilities. There were no roads or rails to connect the village with the town. While there was a railway line going through Fonton and a road from Meadowside village, they went in completely different directions. By 2005, both the locations not only grew in size but were also connected by another road that extended to the West. The growth and development of the region was unstoppable. Soon, the village and the town merged into a new area, housing many luxurious facilities. With further development, in 2020, the region had a new railway line and platform in between Meadowside village and Fonton. The new area even has a hotel and a business park that vouches for the great development of the region.

3. The chart below displays data about the annual consumption of petroleum products across the years 1997-2021. Write a paragraph in 100-120 words analysing the given data. **Competency Based**

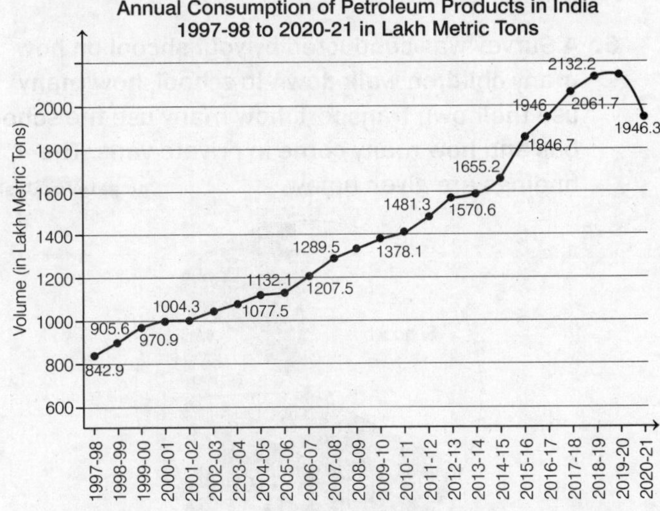

Source (edited): 'Petroleum Planning & Analysis Cell (PPAC)' - www.factly.in

Ans. As Asia's third largest economy, it is not surprising that the demand for fuel in India has been increasing and has reached the highest level in the past 24 years. This increasing consumption was proved by a recent survey. The data presented by the survey shows that fuel consumption from 1997 has increased over the years and has recorded the highest in the period 2019-2020. The volume of fuel consumption in 1997-98 was 842.9 lakh metric tonnes and it kept on rising gradually. Compared to the previous years, the period between 2008 and 2009 witnessed a fuel consumption of 1289.5 lakh metric tonnes. Simultaneously, the fuel consumption rate in 2019-2020 recorded the highest at 2132.2 lakh metric tonnes. However, in the year 2020-2021, the fuel consumption rate has fallen to 1946.3 lakh metric tonnes. Hence, we can say that with awareness, people are carefully using fuel leading to a reduction in its consumption.

4. Study the bar graphs given below and write an analytical report in 100-120 words on the effects of pollution on the migration of exotic birds that visit our country every year. Do you think pollution affects the native bird population too? Could there be reasons other than pollution that have a bearing on migration of birds? Suggest some practical solutions to stop the declining number of migratory birds visiting India. **Competency Based**

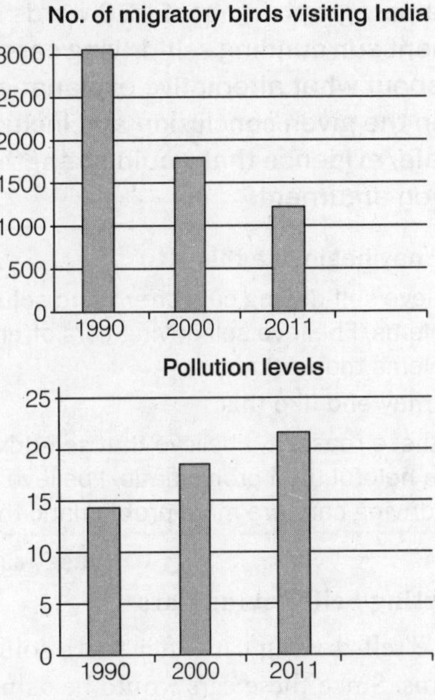

Ans. Citizen, scientists and bird watcher groups have been warning about a direct correlation between the declining number of migratory birds in India and air pollution. Their warnings were proved when a data published by a reputed firm indicated that the number of birds has steadily declined by more than 50% between 1990 and 2010 with the rising levels of pollution. When pollution was lowest in 1990, the number of migratory birds visiting India was the highest and the vice versa is true for 2010. Those migrating to escape the harsh winter get roasted in our hot climes made hotter by exhaust emissions, stubble burning, chemical fertilisers, vehicular gases, aerosols and HFCs. A large number of birds die due to unbearable heat, outbreaks of disease or separation from their flocks due to pollution. Thus, we need to urgently control pollution if we want to see the exquisite migratory birds visiting the nation.

5. Read the excerpt given below.

Speeding towards the Unknown

Self-driving cars are designed for travel without a human operator. Instead of a driver, the car will use a combination of sensors, cameras, radar and artificial intelligence to travel between destinations. They are going to revolutionise the transport industry by enhancing the efficiency and accessibility of vehicles. However, this change is happening too rapidly and self-driving cars pose more problems than solutions. There are several concerns with regard to the safety of such vehicles as well as their potential impact on employment.

Write a paragraph in about 120 words analysing the argument surrounding self-driving cars. You can think about what alternative explanations might weaken the given conclusion and include rationale/evidence that would strengthen/counter the given argument.

> **You may begin like this**
> I believe self-driving cars offer more solutions than problems/I believe self-driving cars offer more problems than solutions.
> **You may end like this**
> For these reasons, I believe that self-driving cars are more helpful than problematic/I believe that self-driving cars are more problematic than helpful.

CBSE Additional SQP 2023

Ans. Supporting Self-driving Cars

I believe self-driving cars offer more solutions than problems. Since these cars would be using the latest technology and advanced sensors and radars, they would be able to greatly reduce road accidents caused due to human error. Additionally, since people would not be actively engaged in driving, they could use their commute time for other activities and enhance their efficiency and productivity. Self-driving cars also solve the problem of commuting for non-drivers. With a self-driving car, anyone can have access to a vehicle irrespective of their skill. However, technology does also malfunction at times, which is why clear safety protocols and guidelines would need to be put in place before these cars can be on the roads. Thus, with proper regulations and planning, I believe self-driving cars can be more helpful than problematic.

Opposing Self-driving Cars

I believe self-driving cars offer more problems than solutions. While there are potential benefits associated with self-driving vehicles such as reduced road accidents, there are more significant concerns. One of the main worries is the safety of self-driving cars. As the cars heavily rely on complex sensors, there is a fear that they may fail in certain scenarios. Another aspect of this safety is that like any electronic device, a car could be hacked into and tampered with, leading to accidents. Additionally, the widespread adoption of self-driving cars may lead to job loss for millions of professional drivers, causing economic and social challenges. Moreover, the infrastructure required to support self-driving cars, such as advanced road systems may not be readily available in many regions. Therefore, I believe self-driving cars are more problematic than helpful.

6. A Survey was conducted by your shcool on how many children walk down to school, how many use their own transport, how many use the school bus and how many come in private vans. The findings are given below. **Competency Based**

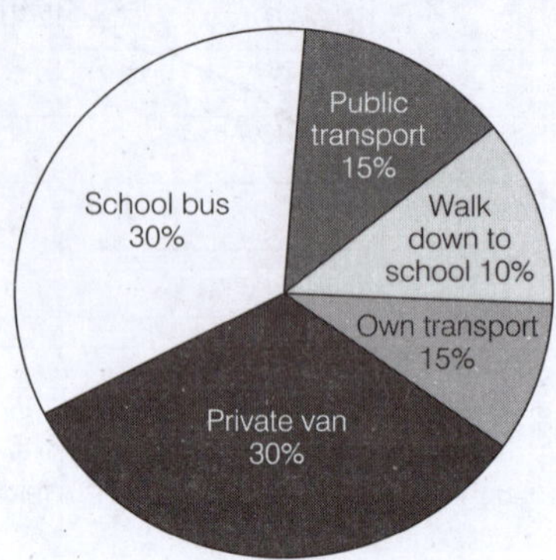

Based on the pie-chart given above write a paragraph analysing the information on 'Preference of Private vans to school buses'. Think of reasons for this preference by some parents in it more convenient and safer. (100-120 words).

Ans. Commuting to and from school is an activity that is a major consideration for many parents whenever a student has to join school. With plethora of commuting options available today, a research was conducted to find the preference of parents in this regard. The data revealed by the survey shows that today most parents prefer private vans and school buses. Almost 30% of students commute using private vans and an equal number uses school buses simply because they provide transportation of students in a safe and sound manner. There are parents who also consider dropping and picking children on their own by either their vehicles or by walking with 15% preferring vehicles and 10% walk. There are also parents (15%) who allow their children to commute though public transport. Hence, people have different preferences for travelling to school.

REVIEW EXERCISE

Including Competency Based Questions

1. **Read the product details on a label for a school bag.**

> **ECO-FRIENDLY SCHOOL BAG**
> - Made from recycled materials
> - Ergonomic* design with padded shoulder straps and breathable mesh back panel
> - Spacious main compartment with multiple pockets and organisers
> - Reflective strips for visibility and safety
> - Water-resistant fabric
> - Available in various vibrant colours and patterns

Now, analyse why this school bag would be a beneficial purchase. Write the analytical paragraph in 120 words, considering factors such as its eco-friendliness, comfort features, functionality, safety aspects, and design options.

*** Design that is intended to maximise comfort, efficiency, and safety for the user.** **CBSE SQP 2024**

Ans. The Eco-friendly school bag stands out as an excellent consumption choice for various reasons. Firstly, its use of recycled materials highlights and reinsures a commitment to environmental sustainability, making it an eco-conscious option. Additionally, the ergonomic design, featuring padded shoulder straps and a breathable mesh back panel, ensures maximum comfort for children during long school days.

The spacious main compartment with multiple pockets helps organise textbooks, notebooks, and other essentials, promoting efficiency and ease. Moreover, reflective strips that are included in the design enhance visibility and safety during low light conditions. The fabric is water-resistant. This further protects belongings from unexpected rain, making the bag durable and reliable. The bag is available in various vibrant colours and patterns, and not only meets functional needs but also allows for personal expression of style, making it a versatile choice for students.

2. **Read the given details of a playground intended for your resident area.**

> - A central climbing structure inspired by traditional Indian architecture, such as a miniature fort, with multiple levels and slides.
> - Swings adorned with colourful Indian patterns, along with monkey bars and a zip line.
> - A water play feature inspired by Indian fountains or rivers.
> - Shaded seating areas with benches and swings, resembling traditional chaupals or gazebos.
> - Trees, shrubs and flower beds.
> - Ample open space

Analyse the details and write an analytical paragraph in about 120 words about the suitability of this playground.

Focus on factors such as safety, inclusivity, fun features, suitability for different age groups, and overall experience. **CBSE SQP 2024**

Ans. The playground design proposed for the resident area embodies an intelligent collaboration of traditional Indian aesthetics and modern play elements. The central climbing structure, like a miniature fort, offers multifaceted play experiences, encouraging physical activity and imaginative exploration. The swings are to be decorated with vibrant Indian patterns coupled with monkey bars and a zip line, adding cultural flair as well as a sense of excitement to the playground. Additionally, the incorporation of a water play feature is inspired by Indian fountains or rivers. This not only provides sensory stimulation but also offers a refreshing respite from the heat. Shaded seating areas, resembling traditional chaupals or gazebos, provide comfortable spaces for parents and caregivers to supervise and socialise. Furthermore, the presence of ample greenery such as trees, shrubs and flower beds, along with ample open space, enhances the overall aesthetic appeal and promotes environmental sustainability. This playground prioritises safety, inclusivity, cultural enrichment and environmental consciousness, ensuring an engaging and enriching experience for residents of all ages.

3. The data given below represents the percentage of some of the electronic devices used in India. Summarise and analyse the data in about 120 words. Give all necessary details and compare the segments where relevant. **CBSE 2024**

S. No.	Devices	Percentage
1.	Television	86%
2.	Electronic toys	40%
3.	Mobile phones	96%
4.	Laptops	38%
5.	Refrigerators	69%
6.	Kitchen appliances	84%

Ans. The given data illustrates the percentage of some of the electronic devices in India. Among these, mobile phones stand out with an impressive 96% usage rate, indicating the widespread adoption and reliance on these devices across the country. Televisions also hold a significant presence, with 86% usage, reflecting their status as a common household item for entertainment and information. However, the usage rates of other electronic devices vary. Refrigerators and kitchen appliances show relatively high usage rates of 69% and 84%, respectively, underscoring their importance in modern households. In contrast, electronic toys and laptops have lower usage rates at 40% and 38%, suggesting they may not be as widely accessible or prioritised. Overall, this data provides insights into the penetration and popularity of various electronic devices in India, reflecting evolving consumer preferences and technological advancements.

4. Based on the following extract, write an analytical paragraph in about 120 words. **CBSE 2024**

"One of the biggest changes in our lives over the past decade is the ability to order items online and have them delivered to our doorstep. The prevalence of this raises an important question of how it affects our environment. Though buyers conserve fuel and reduce emissions from their vehicles, it is replaced by additional mileage of truck routes. Also a large amount of wastage is generated from packaging such as cardboard boxes, bubble wraps, plastic bags etc."

You may begin like this :
As a responsible citizen, I believe .....
You may end like this :
For these reasons, I believe, we need to limit the wastage associated with online shopping.

Ans. As a responsible citizen, I believe it's imperative to critically examine the environmental consequences of our actions. With the convenience of online shopping comes a significant ecological footprint that cannot be ignored. While it may seem like a convenient solution, the environmental impact is substantial. As we order items online, we contribute to increased fuel consumption and emissions from delivery trucks. Additionally, the excessive packaging materials, including cardboard boxes and plastic wraps, further exacerbate the issue by generating significant amounts of waste. For these reasons, I believe it is crucial to acknowledge and address the environmental implications of online shopping. We must work towards implementing sustainable practices to minimise wastage and mitigate the environmental harm associated with this increasingly prevalent mode of commerce. For these reasons, I believe, we need to limit the wastage associated with online shopping.

5. Tsering, of Class X, is contesting for the post of the Junior School Captain, in the upcoming student council elections. Given below is her character traits' graphic, shared in the public domain, by the school counsellor, for the awareness of student voters, at school. **CBSE SQP 2023**

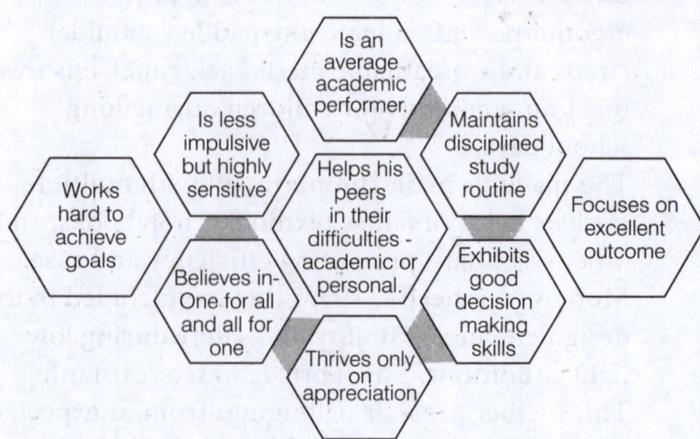

All Tsering's peers have been asked to write a paragraph in about 120 words, analysing these traits, to either support or oppose her candidature. As one of her peers, write this analytical paragraph, by selecting some of the traits that support your analysis.

> **You may begin like this**
> As a responsible student voter, I believe Tsering possesses / does not possess the necessary traits to be a School Captain.
> **You may end like this.**
> For these reasons, I believe she has / does not have the potential to be a good School Captain and I support/oppose her candidature.

Ans. Supporting Tsering's Candidature

As a responsible student voter, I believe Tsering possesses the necessary traits to be an excellent School Captain. Her disciplined study routine and hard work ethic indicate her ability to prioritise and manage her time effectively. Tsering is less impulsive but is sensitive and focuses on the excellent outcome of the tasks assigned to her, demonstrating good decision-making skills. Additionally, her willingness to help peers in academic and personal difficulties highlights her empathetic and caring nature. Furthermore, Tsering believes in the "One for all and all for one" policy, which is pivotal in fostering a sense of community and promoting inclusivity in the school. While she may be an average academic performer, her positive attitude and desire for appreciation will motivate her in her pursuit of excellence. For these reasons, I believe she has the potential to be a good School Captain and I support her candidature.

Opposing Tsering's Candidature

As a responsible student voter, I have reservations about Tsering's candidature for the School Captain's position. While she maintains a disciplined study routine, her average academic performance suggests a lack of academic discipline. Additionally, her quest for appreciation may cause her to prioritise recognition over the well-being of the school community. Moreover, Tsering's sensitivity, while admirable, may hinder her ability to make tough decisions and exercise effective leadership skills. While her willingness to help peers is commendable, it may also distract her from her responsibilities as the School Captain. Finally, Tsering's focus on the excellent outcome of tasks assigned to her may cause her to overlook the process and teamwork required to achieve those outcomes which are crucial for the school's smooth functioning. For these reasons, I believe she does not have the potential to be a good School Captain and I oppose her candidature.

6. As the Captain of the school's Cultural Club, you have been asked to study the given itinerary provided by a tour-organising vendor.

A 3N/2D Educational Tour for the Senior School Students.

Jabalpur and Ranha National Park (Vandhya Pradesh)

- Tour Travel and sightseeing by bus.
- Accommodation on quad sharing basis.
- One staff complimentary for every 20 students.
- Bottled mineral water throughout the tour.
- Dance Party on 22nd November.
- Insurance policy of ₹ 20,000/- per head.
- Provision of Tour Manager's assistance to all places.

Day	Estimated time of departure from	Estimated time of arrival	Sight-seeing Destination/Activity	Time spent at the destination
22nd Nov, 2023	8:49 am (Nagpur Junction)-8 hrs : 30 min	5:23 pm	Reporting at the hotel	
23rd Nov, 2023	9:00 am (hotel)	10:00 am	Bhawarlal Garden	1 hr
	11:00 pm (garden)	11:40 am	Bhedaghat Bhuandhar Falls	1 hr
	12:40 am (falls)	1:00 pm	Lunch (nearby restaurant)	1 hr
	2:00 pm (restaurant)	2:15 pm	Marble Rocks Cable car tour	1 hr : 30 mins
	3:45 pm (marble rocks)	4:45 pm	Rani Durgavati Museum	1 hr : 30 mins
	6:15 pm (museum)	7:00 pm	Back to the hotel	
24th Nov, 2023	5:30 am (hotel)-170 kms - 4hrs drive	9:30 am	Ranha Tiger Reserve	7 hrs
	4:30 am (Tiger Reserve)	9:00 am	Back to the hotel	
25th Nov, 2023	7:54 am (Jabalpur Railway Station)-8 hrs : 45 min	4:21 pm	Nagpur Railway Junction	

Analyse this itinerary to either approve or reject the tour proposal, while focusing on the students' safety, interest and physical wellness. Write this analytical paragraph in about 120 words, by selecting features that support your analysis. CBSE SQP 2023

You may begin like this
A thorough analysis of the itinerary provided by the tour organising vendor reveals that the tourproposal should be accepted/rejected.
You may end like this
Therefore, the tour proposal for the educational trip should be approved/rejected.

Ans. Accepting the Proposal

A thorough analysis of the itinerary provided by the tour organising vendor reveals that the tour proposal should be accepted. It is well-planned and includes an array of educational activities for the students. The inclusion of visit to Bhawartal Garden, Bhedaghat Dhuandhar Falls, Marble Rocks Cable car tour and Rani Durgavati Museum offers an opportunity for the students to learn about nature, history and art. The tour to Kanha Tiger Reserve adds an element of adventure and allows students to connect with wildlife. The provision of bottled mineral water, insurance policy and tour manager's assistance ensures the safety and well-being of the students. Inclusion of a DJ party adds to the entertainment, enjoyment and enthusiasm quotient of the tour. The complimentary staff provided for every twenty students further adds to the security of the students. Therefore, the tour proposal for the educational trip should be approved.

Rejecting the Proposal

A thorough analysis of the itinerary provided by the tour organising vendor reveals that the tour proposal should be rejected. While the tour includes various educational activities, we have concerns about the safety and well-being of the students. The tour includes a long journey of nearly nine hours from Nagpur Junction to Jabalpur and vice versa. Also, it mentions an early morning departure at 5:30 am to the Kanha Tiger Reserve and late evening arrival back to the hotel, on the last day. Long hours of travel and the hectic schedule may lead to physical exhaustion and hamper the learning experience of the students. Additionally, the inclusion of a DJ party may not be suitable for an educational tour. The tour organising vendor has not provided details on the quality of the hotel and the quad-sharing basis may not be comfortable for all students. Hence, considering the well-being of the students, the tour proposal for the educational trip, should be rejected.

7. Students at Rainbow School are divided into two houses — Blue or Red. The data in the table below shows the performance of these houses in different categories (out of a total score of 100).

	Blue House	Red House
Academics	91	79
Sports	75	90
Arts	82	85
Others	organised a successful Inter School Sports Tournament	organised a successful School-wide Recycling Campaign
	organised a Donation Campaign to encourage school	organised a successful Inter School Cultural Festival
	students to donate toys to the local orphange	

The school's Principal has decided that Blue House should win the Best House Trophy at the end of the year. As school captain, the Principal has asked for your input on this decision.

Analyse this data to either support or oppose the Principal's decision. Write this analytical paragraph in about 120 words with supporting details to justify your opinion. **CBSE Additional SQP 2023**

> **You may begin like this**
> A thorough analysis of the data provided indicates that Blue House should win the Best House Trophy/Red House should win the Best House Trophy.
> **You may end like this**
> Therefore, the Best House Trophy must go to Blue House/Red House.

Ans. Supporting the Principal's Decision

A thorough analysis of the data provided indicates that Blue House should win the Best House Trophy. Looking at the academic performance, Blue House scored significantly higher with a score of 91 compared to Red House's score of 79. This demonstrates their dedication and commitment to their studies. In terms of sports, although Red House scored higher with a score of 90 compared to Blue House's score of 75, Blue House showcased their versatility by excelling in other areas. They organised a successful Interschool Sports Tournament, showcasing their leadership skills. Additionally, Blue House demonstrated their involvement in the community by organising a toy donation campaign. While Red House excelled in arts and organised a successful Inter-School Cultural Festival, the overall performance of Blue House across various categories outweighs these achievements. Therefore, the Best House Trophy must go to Blue House.

Opposing the Principal's Decision

A thorough analysis of the data provided indicates that Red House should win the Best House Trophy. Although Blue House performed exceptionally well in academics with a score of 91 compared to Red House's score of 79, Red House did better in other areas. In sports, Red House scored significantly higher with a score of 90 compared to Blue House's score of 75, demonstrating their athletic skills and teamwork. Red House scored slightly higher than Blue House in the category of Arts. Based on the average scores across the categories, Red House (84.6) scored higher than Blue House (82.6). Moreover, Red House organised a successful inter-school cultural festival, showcasing their creativity and leadership skills. Therefore, considering their overall performance and accomplishments, the Best House Trophy must go to Red House.

8. The given bar graph shows the increasing use of skin care products by men and women over the period of three months. Write an analytical paragraph elaborating the given information in about 100 words. **CBSE 2023**

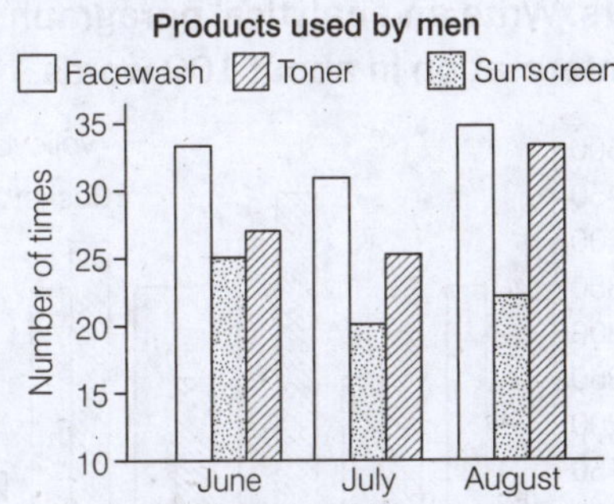

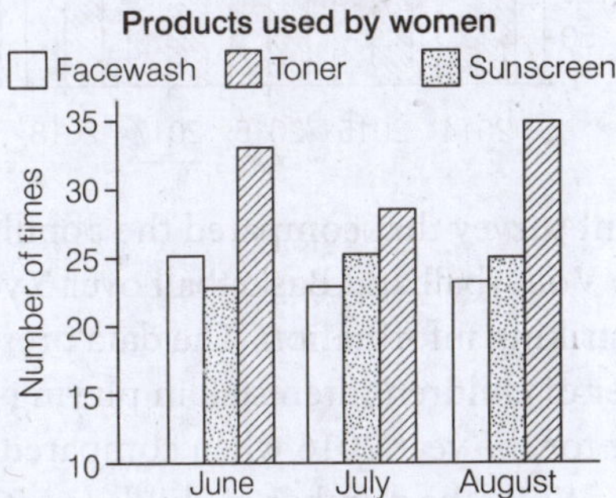

Ans. With an increasing focus on beauty and appearence, the scope of the beauty market has increased with more and more men and women using skin are and beautification products. A survey conducted recently showing the usage of skin care products by men and women over the time of three months found that the products most commonly used include facewash, toner and sunscreen. The data for men shows that the most used product by men is facewash. In the month of June, facewash was used around 33 times, in July 30 times and in August 35 times. The toner was used around 27 times, 20 times and around 33 times in the months of June, July and August respectively. The sunscreen was used 29 times in the month of June, 25 times in July and 32 times in August. The data for women shows that the most used product is sunscreen. In the month of June, facewash was used 25 times, in July 22 times and in August 24 times. The toner was used 22 times in the month of June, in July 25 times and in August 27 times. The Sunscreen being the most used product was used 34 times in June, 29 times in July and 35 times in August. To conclude the given information, the usage of facewash by man saw a rise in the month of August and reached its peak and usage of sunscreen by women saw its rise in the month of August too, reaching its peak of 35 times of usage.

9. The given bar graph shows the preferences of children in a school in playing different games over the span of six years. Write an analytical paragraph about the given information in about 100 words. **CBSE 2023**

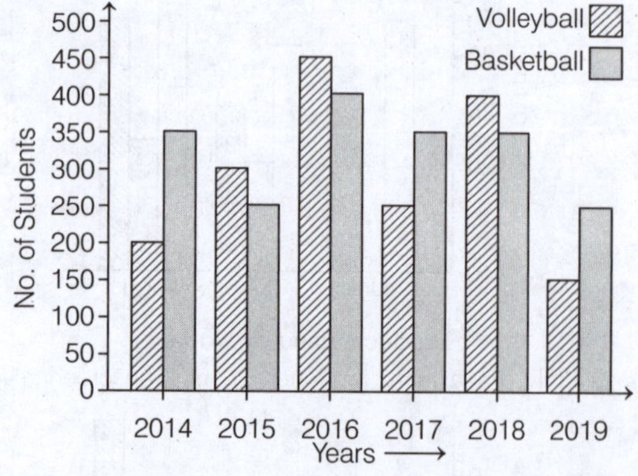

Ans. A recent survey that compared the popularity of the two sports, Volleyball and Basketball over 5 years found some striking information. The data presents that the number of children interested in playing Volleyball is greater for the year 2016 when compared to 2019 results. While the number of children interested in Basketball remains almost same with minor fluctuation over the 5 years. The data for both the sports, however, shows a fluctuation. For Volleyball, 200 children were interested in 2014, 300 in 2015, peaking at 450 in 2016, reducing to 250 in 2017, again rising to 400 in 2018, falling to the lowest 150 in 2019. For Basketball, the data shows that 350 children were interested in 2014, 250 in 2015, peaking at 400 in 2016, 350 in 2017, 350 in 2018 and falling to 250 in 2019. The data is important to understand the social implication of professional sports and their popularity on young children.

10. In an exclusive survey conduct by a leading daily, student of Class X expressed their job preferences.
On the basis of the information given in the pie chart, write a paragraph analysing the careers they want to pursue after school. (words limit 100-120 words.) **CBSE 2023**

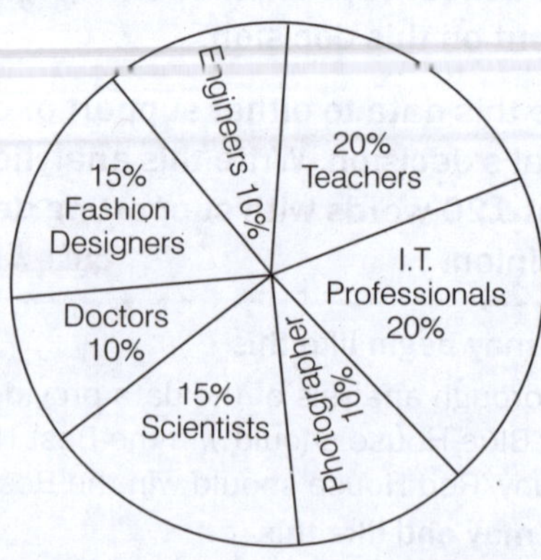

Ans. In the modern world, where career opportunities are expanding, students are still unaware of the changing job markets and the new job opportunities available in the market. This statement has aptly been justified by a survey conducted on students of Class X.
The data reveals that students are looking out to make their careers in the set traditional fields such as teaching, medicine, fashion, etc. The study found that most number of students (20%) wanted to be teachers and 20% wanted to be IT professionals. 15% of the students wanted to be scientists and an equal percentage of students wanted to become fashion designers. 10% of students wanted to be engineers, 10% doctors and 10% photographers.
Hence, with this immense focus on traditional careers, children need to be made aware of the different career opportunities coming up in the market.

11. Given below is a graph comparing the consumption of health care supplements amongst men and women between the age of 25-35 from the year 2018-2022 in terms of their sales. Write an analytical paragraph in about 100-120 words using the details given. **CBSE 2023**

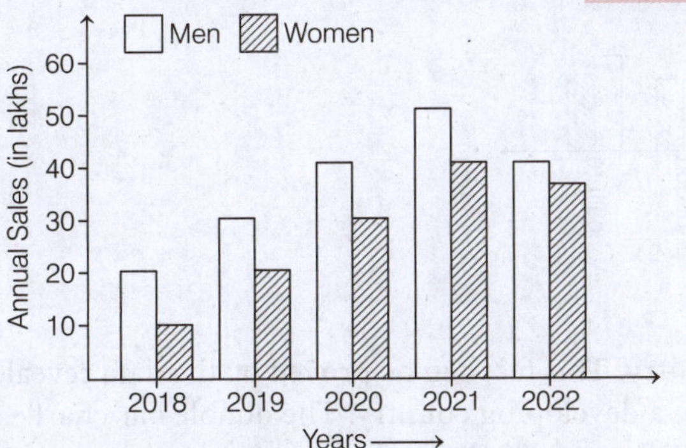

Ans. The devastating pandemic of 2020 had great socio-economic implications on our society. One such implication is the increase in the consumption of health supplements by both men and women. A recent study regarding the supplements taken by men and women found that while men were already taking health supplements more than women, it has now almost doubled. Looking at the sales of health supplements for both men and women, the study gathers that the pandemic had made people aware of their dietary lacks and the need to supplement the lack. Accordingly, while sales of supplements were about 20-30 lakhs for men and 10-20 lakhs for women, it increased exponentially in 2020 growing to 30-40 lakh for both the genders. The sales peaked in 2021 with 50 lakhs sales for men and 40 lakhs for women. The year, 2022 however, saw a minor reduction in these sales with sales reducing to 10 lakhs for men and 5 lakhs for women. Hence, it is suffice to say that people have realised the need to make sure that their health is at an optimum state even if that necessitates the use of health supplements.

12. Global weather has been undergoing a drastic change and global warming is responsible for creating arctic melt downs. Use the given pie-chart to write a paragraph analysing the reasons for climate change in about 100-120 words. **CBSE 2023**

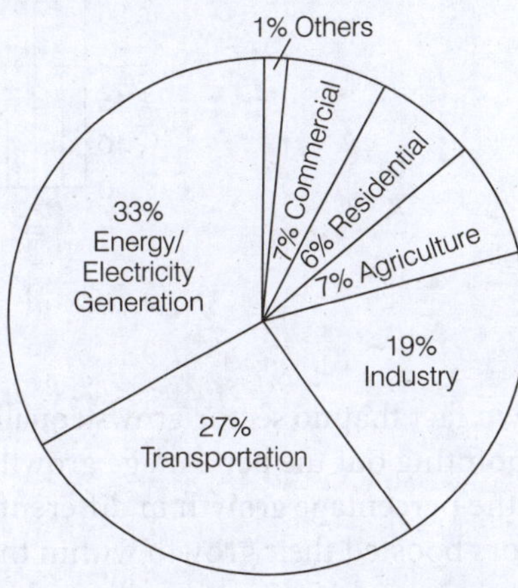

Ans. Global weather has been undergoing a drastic change and global warming is leading to the Arctic meltdown. This is primarily a result of the greenhouse effect caused by too much carbon dioxide in the atmosphere which acts as a blanket, trapping heat and warming the planet. The reasons for the increase in the carbon dioxide levels in the atmosphere are numerous. According to the data revealed by a recent study, most of the emissions are a result of Energy/Electricity Generation which accounts for 33% of the change in the climate. It is followed by transportation which accounts for 27% of the change and industry which accounts for 19% of the global warming. Commercial, residential, agricultural and other factors are responsible for 7%, 6%, 7% and 1% change in climate, respectively. The impact of global warming on our planet is extremely serious and if this problem is not tackled on an urgent basis, it will lead to melting of polar ice caps. This will lead to an increase in sea level drowning coastlines which would slowly submerge continents. Our generation needs to take up the task of healing the Earth which has suffered because of human actions.

13. Write an analytical paragraph based on the double bar graph showing the percentage growth in different sectors in a developing country from the year 2012 to 2022. **CBSE 2023**

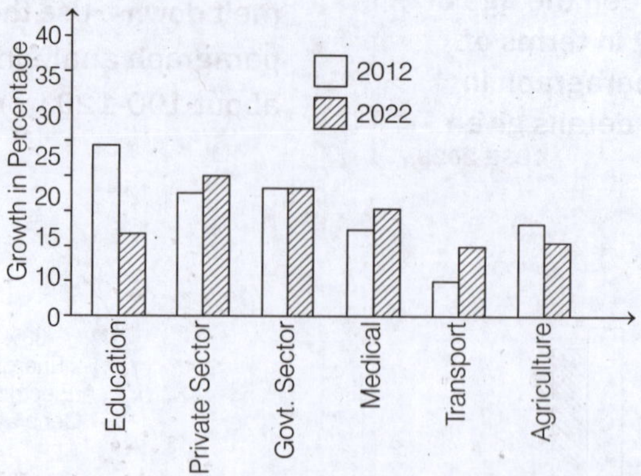

Ans. It is a known fact that no sector grows equally in a developing country. This fact can be proved by the data revealed by a firm pointing out the percentage growth of different sectors in a developing country. The double bar chart illustrates the percentage growth in different sectors in the years 2012 and 2022. It is evident from the data that most of the sectors boosted their growth within these two years. Private sector jumped from around 15% to 20%; Medicine, jumped from around 10% to 15% followed by Transport, which grew by a solid 5%. Besides, the sector which has remained unchanged is the government sector with a fixed contribution of between 15% and 20%. Moreover, there are sectors which have plummeted in their growth namely-education, from 25% to around 10% and the agriculture sector which experienced a growth percentage fall of not more than 2 to 3%. Overall, it can be said that not all the sectors have grown equally. While some have faced a slump in their contribution by a major or minor per cent, others have skyrocketed in their fields.

14. Study the concept chart from the self-help magazine section of a monthly publication. **CBSE SQP 2022 Term II**

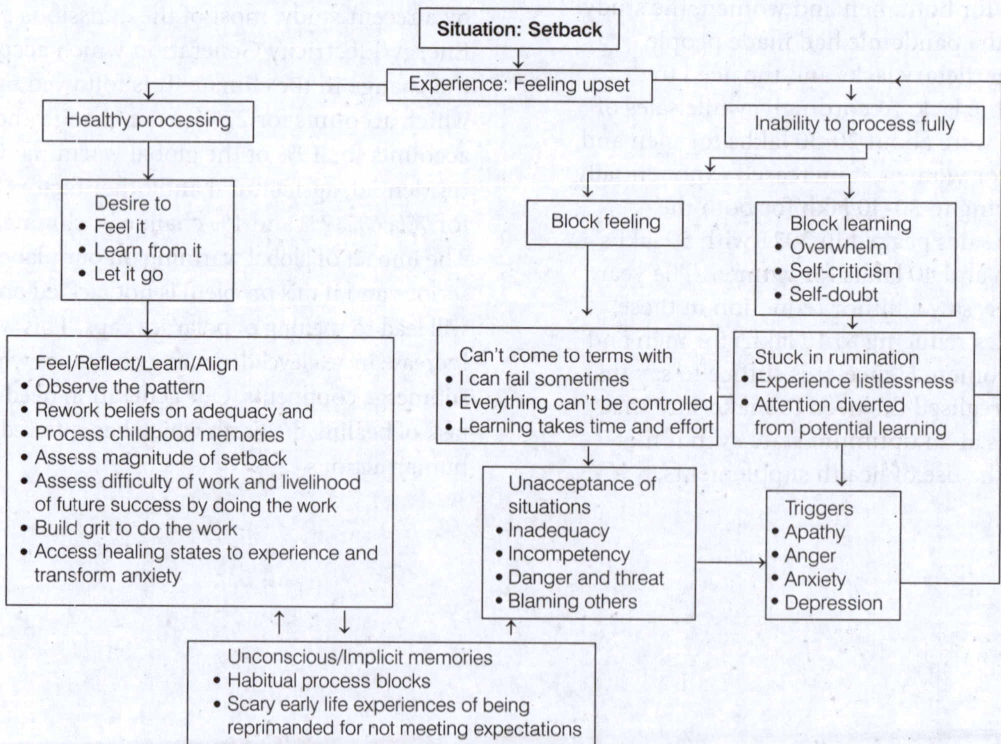

Write a paragraph in not more than 120 words, analysing the listed responses to the situation when one faces setbacks.

Ans. All of us in life have faced a setback and have had different reactions to it. Understanding these reactions is crucial to understanding human psychology. A recent data printed by a named publication presents a chart suggesting the possibilities of facing a setback in life. Accordingly, a person deals with a setback in either of the following two ways

(a) Keeps a healthy stance towards the setback and processes it in a healthy manner.

(b) Fails to process the experience.

If a person processes this setback in a healthy manner, they reflect upon it and try to learn from it. They do so by observing the pattern and assessing the situation and by learning the magnitude of the problem. They also transform any kind of anxiety they might have into productivity. This process, however, is not fool proof. It has certain issues like remembering implicit memories, their growth being blocked due to habitual process, etc. An alternative approach to handling a setback is to avoid addressing it. This leads to a blocking of feelings and learning process, which further leads self-doubt and self-criticism, eventually triggering a sense of failure and several mental issues including apathy, anger, anxiety and depression. Additionally, it may cause people to despair and become un-accepting of the situation and they may end up blaming others. Hence, an individual can face a tough situation in either of the given ways. However, only the first way is more productive and beneficial for an individual.

15. Gurmeet Kaur is an aspiring candidate for a public-funded engineering college in the suburbs. She belongs to a nearby village, has minimal technological skills and exposure, has the required cut-off percentage and is looking for a complete or partial scholarship.

Write a paragraph in about 100-120 words, analysing her SWOT notes to support your stand on whether she should join/not join the college.

Strength	Weakness
• Strong Curriculum • Quality faculty • Vibrant Activity Clubs • Green location • Close proximity to residential areas	• Lake of diversity • Students' behavioural problems • No hostel facility • Slow repair and maintenance work • Undertilisation of IT Services • Lack of Targeted advertisements to out-state students

Opportunities	Threat
• Practice based research • Partnership with professional organisation • Strong alumni • Acclaimed Student Exchange Programme with European countries	• Lace of Publicity in areas of excellence • Public perception towards funded colleges • Declining students' interest towards technical subjects • Low employee morale due to budget cuts

Ans. In favour

The given information illustrates the options Gurmeet would weigh in order to take the right decision about her admission in a public-funded engineering college. With availability of a strong curriculum, quality faculty and vibrant Activity Clubs, she will be assured of an enriching educational journey. Though hostel facilities are unavailable, she may take up accommodation in the suburbs or choose to travel daily from her village. Good opportunities of practice-based research, partnership with professional companies and international students exchange programmes will enhance her professional and interpersonal skills. Hard work, responsible behaviour and prudent decision-making could help Gurmeet thrive in the college even though it has a rigid and conventional culture. The strengths and opportunities work in favour of Gurmeet. Taking this opportunity will allow her to mend the incorrect public perception towards public-funded colleges and students' outlook towards technical subjects.

Against

The given information indicates Gurmeet's dilemma about seeking admission in a public-funded college. Though equipped with a strong curriculum, engaging activity clubs and an able faculty, the college lacks diversity and good conduct among the students, giving rise to concerns of a safe environment for a novice like Gurmeet. Underutilisation of IT services will be further detrimental to the progress of Gurmeet's educational journey and add to extra costs related to research work. If she does not qualify for a complete or partial scholarship, arrangement of own accommodation and additional expenses of the student exchange programme will increase her expenditure, too. Such a college environment may dampen her endeavouring spirit. The weakness and threats outweigh the strengths, in the case of Gurmeet. So, it is recommended that Gurmeet does not apply for admission to the said college.

16. A survey was conducted in the National Capital in over twenty schools about the different activities that interest the children in the age group of 13 years to 15 years. Write a paragraph in not more than 120 words, analysing the following information. CBSE 2022 Term II

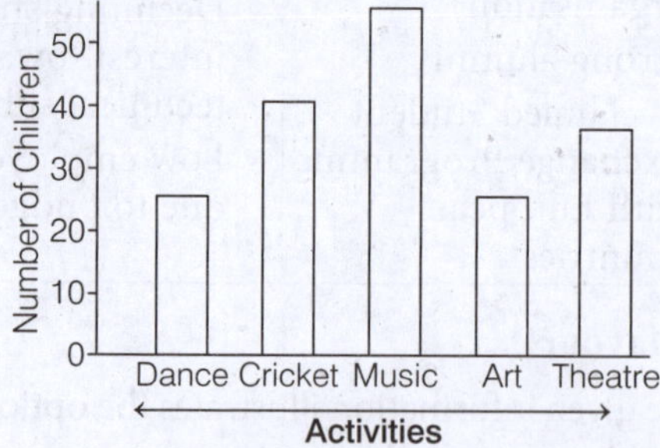

Ans. In a survey conducted in the National Capital across twenty schools on the areas of interest of the children in the age group 13 to 15 years, some interesting data was found. It was amazing to know that cricket was not the most popular sport. Surprisingly, music related activities were most sought after with 60% of the children showing a general inclination towards it. Cricket turned out to be the second most popular activity with interest shown by 40% of the students. Theatre occupied the interests of 35% of the respondents while Art and Dance each seem to have captured the interest of 25% of the children. The given data again proves the simple fact that each child is unique and has different choices and preferences.

17. School authorities and parents have realised the benefits of encouraging their children to play and participate in sports. The age-old myth that academics is the only foundation for a successful career has been replaced. Write a paragraph in not more than 120 words analysing the given information. CBSE 2022 Term II

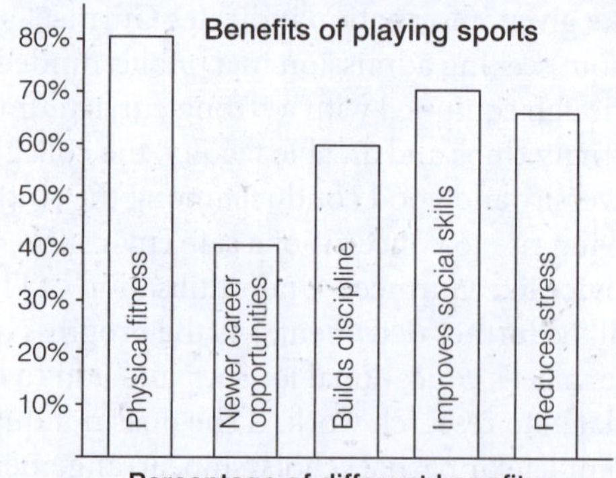

Ans. It is believed that a healthy body harbours a healthy mind. Sports and games had been accepted a long time ago as something essential for the proper growth and development of our body especially children. Gone are the days when the age old myth that academics is the only foundation for a successful career was widely accepted and practised. The myth has been replaced for the better simply because school authorities as well as parents have realised the benefits of encouraging their children to play and participate in sports. Such a change has been a result of the various studies that indicated the innumerable benefits that sports has on children. The studies found that while it is majorly responsible for ensuring physical fitness, it has many social and mental benefits. Sports and games boost discipline, reduce stress and improve social skills. Further, in the present world, sports offer many new career opportunities. Hence, sports is an important part of holistic schooling.

18. A survey was conducted to find out the main reasons for land degradation in the world. The pie chart below shows the main reasons why agricultural land becomes less productive. On the basis of the pie chart, evaluate the causes of worldwide land degradation and write an analytical paragraph based on it, in 120 words. CBSE 2024

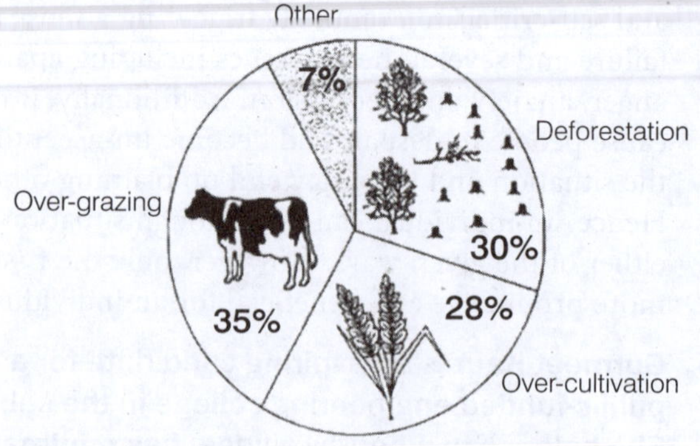

Ans. Land degradation is a critical global issue, significantly impacting agricultural productivity and environmental sustainability. A recent survey analysed the main reasons for this decline, revealing that deforestation, overgrazing and overcultivation comprise the largest segments of the contributing factors. Deforestation accounts for a substantial proportion, as trees play a vital role in maintaining soil health and preventing erosion. Overgrazing follows closely, as excessive livestock impact vegetation cover, leading to soil compaction and degradation. Additionally, improper agricultural methods, such as over cultivation and excessive chemical use, diminish soil fertility and harmful runoff. Ultimately, these interconnected issues necessitate immediate attention and a collaborative approach towards sustainable practices, reforestation initiatives, and effective land management strategies to mitigate land degradation and ensure food security for future generations.

19. Read the given details of different activities that interest children in the age group of 14-17 years.

- Dance, music, art
- Outdoor sports like cricket, hockey, basketball, soccer, tennis
- Computer games
- Net surfing
- Social media

Analyse the details and write an analytical paragrapgh in about 120 words about the suitability of the given activities. Focus on factors like interest, physical, mental and emotional development, personality development and suitability. **CBSE 2025**

Ans. Adolescents aged 14-17 engage in a variety of activities that contribute to their overall development. Creative pursuits like dance, music, and art enhance self-expression, emotional well-being, and cognitive abilities. Outdoor sports such as cricket, hockey, basketball, soccer, and tennis promote physical fitness, teamwork, and discipline, fostering both mental and emotional resilience. Computer games can improve problem-solving skills and hand-eye coordination but may lead to excessive screen time if not regulated. Net surfing and social media provide access to information and social interaction, aiding personality development. However, they can also pose risks like distraction and reduced physical activity. Balancing these activities is essential for holistic growth, ensuring that adolescents develop their interests while maintaining their physical, mental, and emotional well-being.

20. Today, many projects in India are being initiated and implemented with the aim of transforming India into a digitally empowered society and economy.

- Digital India Programme
- IT- Jobs
- E-governance
- E-Kranti Electronic Delivery of Services
- Broadband for all-Urban and Rural
- Information for all

CBSE 2025

Ans. India is rapidly advancing towards becoming a digitally empowered society and economy through various initiatives. The Digital India Programme is at the forefront of this transformation, aiming to improve IT infrastructure and increase digital literacy. One of the key aspects of this program is the creation of IT jobs, which has significantly boosted employment opportunities in the technology sector.

E-Governance has made government services more accessible and efficient, reducing paperwork and increasing transparency. The E-Kranti initiative focuses on delivering electronic services in areas like healthcare, education, and financial inclusion. Another crucial step is ensuring broadband connectivity for all, both in urban and rural areas, bridging the digital divide.

Additionally, the initiative Information for All ensures that citizens have easy access to government data and services, promoting transparency and inclusivity. These digital initiatives have strengthened India's economy and improved the quality of life for its citizens. With continuous advancements, India is moving towards a more connected and digitally empowered future.

21. There has been a visible impact of solar energy in the Indian energy scenario during the last few years. Solar energy-based decentralised and distributed applications have benefitted millions of people in Indian villages by meeting their cooking, lighting and other energy needs in an environment-friendly manner. On the basis of the bar graph given below, write an analytical paragraph on Solar Energy in India in 100-120 words.

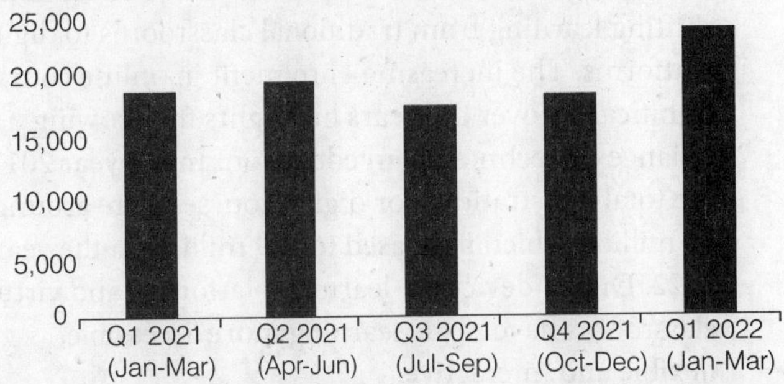

Ans. In recent years, solar energy has significantly shaped India's energy landscape, with a consistent increase in solar energy generation. The data reflects a growing trend, where solar generation rose from about 16,000 million units in the first quarter of 2021 to about 18,000 million units in the second quarter. Although there was a slight decline to 15,000 million units in the third quarter, the overall trajectory remained positive, culminating in a robust increase to 22,000 million units in the first quarter of 2022. This impressive growth indicates the successful implementation of solar energy initiatives, particularly in rural areas where decentralised applications have enhanced access to cooking, lighting and other essential energy needs, highlighting solar energy's role in promoting sustainable and environmentally friendly practices throughout India.

22. The effects of technology on education have been profound and multifaceted, influencing both teaching and learning in various ways. The data below shows the rising enrolment in online courses over the years. Analyse the data and write an analytical paragraph in about 120 words, about how technology has transformend teaching and learning by shifting from classrooms to digital devices. Discuss benefits such as access to information and challenges like digital divide. **CBSE 2025**

S.No.	Year	Total no. of enrolments in millions
1.	2017	26
2.	2018	43
3.	2019	59
4.	2020	76
5.	2021	143
6.	2022	189

Ans. Technology has significantly transformed education, shifting learning from traditional classrooms to digital platforms. The increasing enrolment in online courses significantly over the years highlights the growing reliance on technology in education. In the year 2017, the total registrations for digital courses were around 26 million which increased to 189 million in the year 2022. Digital devices, e-learning platforms, and virtual classrooms have made learning more accessible, flexible and interactive.

Students can now access quality education from anywhere, benefiting from resources like video lectures, e-books and online assessments. However, challenges such as the digital divide remain, as not all students have equal access to the internet and devices. While technology has revolutionised education by making learning more engaging and convenient, efforts must be made to bridge the digital gap and ensure equal learning opportunities for all.

23. Below is the map of the city of Siliguri. City planners have decided to build a new shopping mall for the area and two sites S1 and S2 have been proposed for the same. Analyse the map and write an analytical paragraph on which site is suitable in 100-120 words.

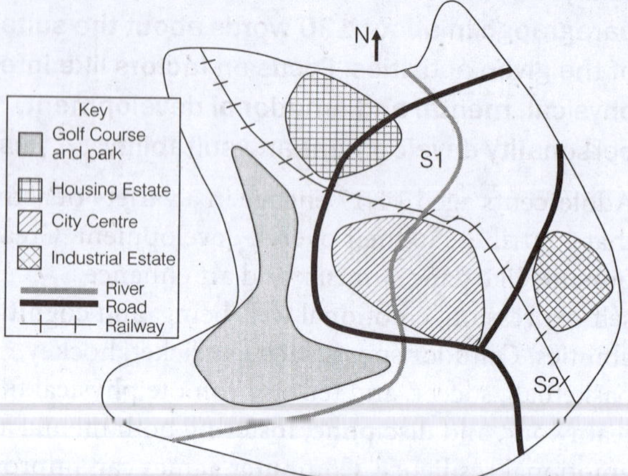

Ans. The map illustrates the plans for two possible sites for a shopping mall in the city of Siliguri. It can be seen that the two sites under consideration are in the North and the South-East parts of the town. The first possible site for the shopping mall, S1, is just North of the city center, above the railway line, which runs from the South-East of the city to the North-West. If the mall is built here, it will be next to a large housing estate, thus providing an easy access for those living on the estate and in the city center. It will also be next to the river that runs through the town which can become one of the main extractions of the mall. The site in the South-East, S2, is again just by the railway line and fairly close to the city center but it is near an industrial estate rather than housing which can be its biggest negative aspect. There is a main road that runs through the city and is close to both sites, thus providing good road access to either location. Given all the factors including the closeness to the golf course and park, S1 is more suitable as a location for the mall.

24. Look at the following newspaper cutout about the Chandrayaan-3. Analyse the details and write an analytical paragraph in 120 words about the mission as well as its impact on India.

Chandrayaan-3
Mission India's third lunar exploration mission.
Objective To demonstrate end-to-end capability in safe landing and roving on the lunar surface.
Launch 14th July, 2023, from Satish Dhawan Space Centre.
Components Lander (Vikram), Rover (Pragyan), Propulsion Module.
Landing Successfully landed near the Moon's South pole on 23rd August, 2023, making India the fourth country to do so.
Scientific Goals Conduct in-situ chemical analysis of the lunar surface and study the lunar environment.
Achievements India became the first country to land on the Moon's South pole.
Significance A major milestone in India's space programme and a testament to its scientific capabilities.

Ans. Chandrayaan-3, India's third lunar exploration mission, successfully demonstrated the country's capability in achieving a safe landing and roving on the lunar surface. Launched in July 2023, the mission consisted of a lander, a rover and a propulsion module. The successful landing near the Moon's South pole in August 2023 made India the fourth country to accomplish this feat, marking a significant milestone in the nation's space programme.

The mission's scientific goals include conducting in-situ chemical analysis of the lunar surface and studying the lunar environment, contributing to our understanding of the Moon's formation and evolution. Chandrayaan-3's achievements have not only enhanced India's reputation as a global space power but have also inspired a new generation of scientists and engineers. The mission's success serves as a testament to India's scientific capabilities and its commitment to space exploration.

25. Read the given details about pros and cons of Artificial Intelligence AI. With the help of the cues and your own ideas, write an analytical paragraph in about 120 words on 'AI- Benefits and Drawbacks'. **CBSE 2025**

- AI is possessed by machines
- Impacted our lives in many ways
- AI- Google Maps
- Knowledge at our fingertips
- Cannot wholly replicate humans
- Increase in cyber crimes

Ans. Artificial Intelligence (AI) has become an integral part of our daily lives, impacting various fields such as education, healthcare, and transportation. AI-powered tools like Google Maps help us navigate efficiently, while search engines provide knowledge at our fingertips. AI enhances automation, improves decision-making, and increases productivity.

However, AI cannot wholly replicate human emotions, creativity, and decision-making abilities. While it improves efficiency, it also raises concerns like job loss and ethical dilemmas. Additionally, AI has led to an increase in cybercrime, as hackers exploit its capabilities for fraudulent activities.

In conclusion, AI offers numerous benefits, but it must be used responsibly to minimise its drawbacks. A balance between human intelligence and AI is necessary for a safer future.

26. Read the statement given below. Many students do not participate in classroom discussions, whereas some students contribute valuable points. The curriculum should allot some marks for participation so that students are motivated to share in discussions.

Write a paragraph in about 120 words analysing the given argument. You can think about what alternative explanations might weaken the given conclusion and include rationale/evidence that would strengthen/ counter the given argument. **Competency Based**

Ans. Group discussion as a classroom learning tool is an effective part of academic studies in schools. However, we often see difference in active participation of students. Some students are found to actively participate in classroom discussion whereas some remain absent or least interested in it. Those who participate in these discussions are often the top scorers who we all find to do well in academics and hope that they will have a successful future. However, those who do not participate, need to be incorporated in the discussion so that they may develop the skills required for success.

For the same, the curriculum should be such that it encourages discussion. Further, some marks should be allotted for participation so that all students feel encouraged to actively engage in fruitful discussions. With a complete participation, all students come to know various viewpoints which opens them up towards vast knowledge. Moreover, students will feel confident about themselves and their growth in positive learning.

27. Stress and pressure sometimes has an adverse effect on young adults. 'Budding Minds' conducted a survey to show how the mental health of young people has been affected. 4,324 young people took part in the survey which shows stress and competition has impacted performance and mental health. Write an analytical paragraph in about 100 words on how the mental health of young people has been impacted in the modern world. **Competency Based**

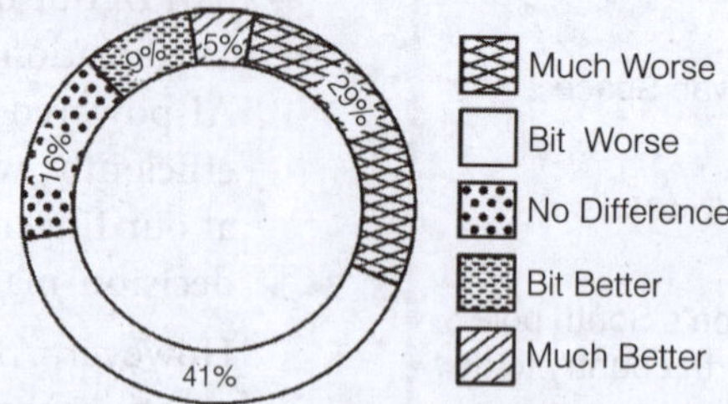

Ans. In the world where everyone is in a rat-race to succeed, stress and pressure have become friends of each and every individual. Everyone is suffering from stress, anxiety and depression which has negatively affected the young adults of today. In an attempt to understand how stress impacts young adults, 'Budding Minds' conducted a survey wherein 4,324 young people participated to find exactly how stress impacts our performance and mental health. The data revealed that mental health of 29% of young people has worsened while 16% of the people show no difference in their mental health. The data also reveals that sometimes stress and pressure brings positive impacts too. 9% of people have developed a better mental health. 5% people have become much better and have developed a positive mental health. Thus, stress and pressure usually deteriorates mental health but if utilised positively it can be useful in promoting mental health. In a nutshell mental health is as important as the physical health so it must be highly taken care of and should be protected by following various exercises.

28. Read the following excerpt from an international wildlife magazine. Write an analytical paragraph in 120 words analysing the importance of wildlife conservation.

A rare and elusive bear - the Tibetan brown bear (Ursus arctos pruinosus) - has been sighted in Sikkim, making it the first confirmed record of the animal being sighted in India according to sources in the Sikkim forest and environment department.

The Tibetan brown bear is characterised by its yellowish scarf-like collar that broadens from the shoulders to the chest, very different from the more commonly found Himalayan black bear in appearance. An omnivore, it usually inhabits high-altitude alpine forests and meadows 4,000 metres and above from sea level.

Ans. The sighting of a Tibetan brown bear in Sikkim marks a significant milestone for wildlife conservation in India. This rare and elusive species, characterised by its distinctive yellowish collar, has rarely been documented in the country. The discovery not only highlights the biodiversity of Sikkim's ecosystems but also underscores the importance of conservation efforts to protect endangered species. As an omnivore inhabiting high-altitude alpine forests, the Tibetan brown bear plays a vital role in maintaining the ecological balance of its habitat. Protecting this species and its habitat is crucial for preserving the region's biodiversity and ensuring the long-term health of our planet's ecosystems.

ASSESSMENT EXERCISE

1. The plans shown below includes the layout of the university sports center and how it will look after redevelopment. Write an analytical paragraph in 100-120 words focusing on how it will accommodate more students.

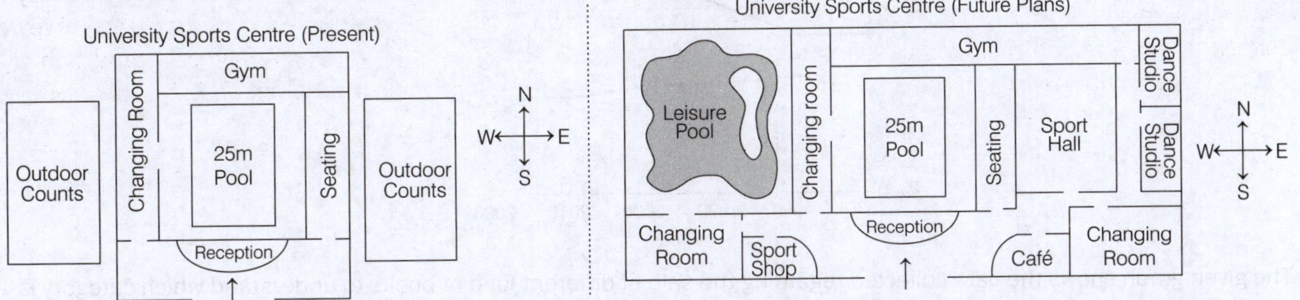

2. The following table gives information about some of the world's most studied languages. Summarise the information by analysing and reporting the main features in a paragraph and make comparisons wherever relevant, in 100-120 words.

Language	Number of People Learning the Language	Number of Native Speakers (Language as Mother Tongue)	Number of Countries where the Language is Spoken
English	1.5 billion	527 million	101
French	82 million	118 million	51
Chinese	30 million	1.39 billion	33
Spanish	14.5 million	389 million	31
Italian	8 million	67 million	29
Japanese	3 million	123 million	25

3. Wildlife protection is the need of the hour. The given graph depicts the percentage of the different animals found on our planet and their population statistics. Analyse the given data and write an analytical paragraph on 100-120 words pointing to the threat to the wildlife due to human activity.

Competency Based

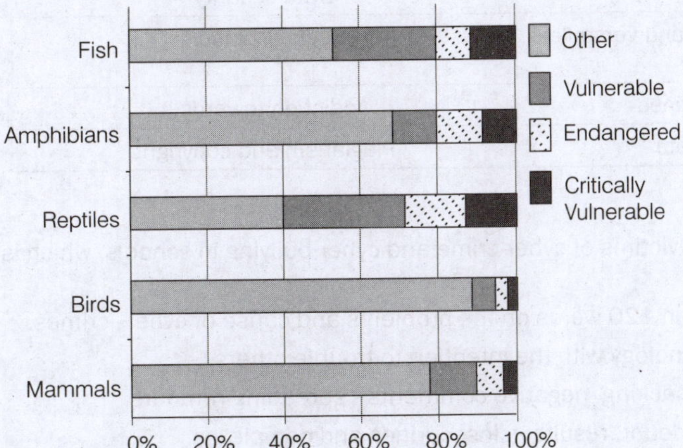

4. The given graph shows the average number of UK commuters travelling each day by car, bus or train between 1970 and 2020. Write an analytical paragraph based on the graph in 100-120 words. **Competency Based**

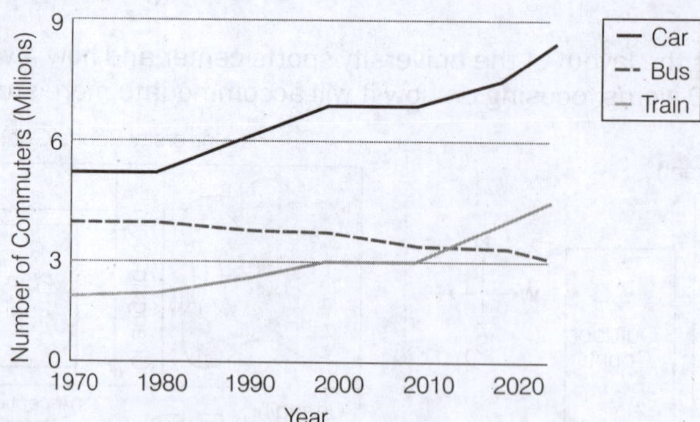

5. The given graph shows the data collected regarding the sale of different kind of books to understand which category is popular amongst teenagers. Using this data, write an analytical paragraph in 100-120 words.

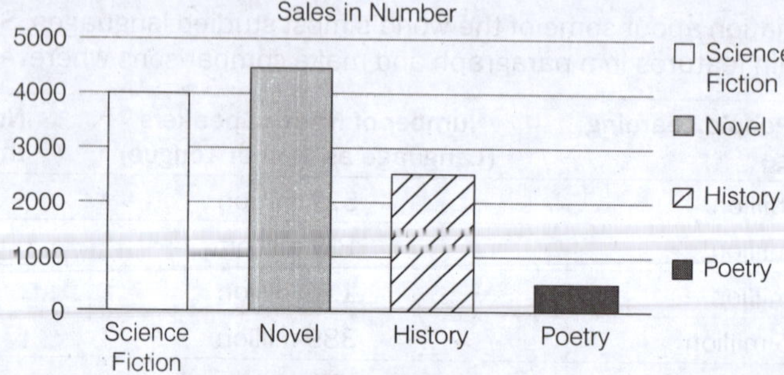

6. The Pros and Cons of using the internet in everyday life are numerous. The internet is like a double-edged sword. Based on the information provided in the table below, write an analytical paragraph on the topic 'Advantages and Disadvantages of the Internet' in not less than 120 words.

	Pros	**Cons**
1.	Connectivity	Data security
2.	Communication speed and versatile working	Social isolation
3.	Learning re-defined	Addiction towards it
4.	Transfer of data	Plagiarism and copyright

7. Read the following details.

Students today are becoming victims of cyber-crime and cyber bullying in schools, which is affecting the mental health of students.

Write as analytical paragraph in 120 words on the problems and cause of cyber-crimes.

- Misuse of Information Technology with the intention to trouble others.
- It comes in various forms-hacking, negative comments- spreading rumours.
- Impact- spoils image, self-doubt, results in insecurities and complexes.
- Causes- desire of power, seeking entertainment, escapism, inadequate regulations.

8. Read the statement given below.

Newspapers should go online completely and we should do away with printed copies. Printing newspapers wastes ink and paper in a digital age where most people get information from the internet. **Competency Based**

Write a paragraph in about 120 words analysing the given argument. You can think about what alternative explanations might weaken the given conclusion and include rationale/evidence that would strengthen /counter the given argument.

9. The increase in the number of news channels is indicative of their growing popularity in terms of viewership.

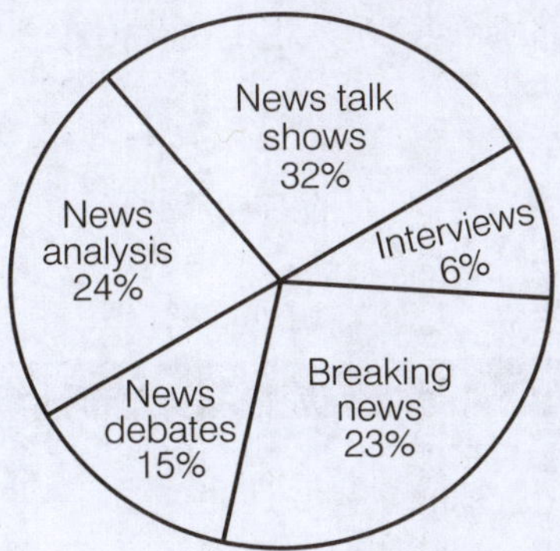

Write a paragraph analysing their above given pie chart on what viewers like watching in news channels (100-120 words)

Competency Based

10. Internet provides every information one seeks at the click of a button. As a result, children today are living in a comfort zone. According to research, this will result in long-term consequences which will affect their brain. Based on the following chart, write an analytical paragraph in not more than 120 words on activities to improve brain power. **CBSE 2022 Term II**

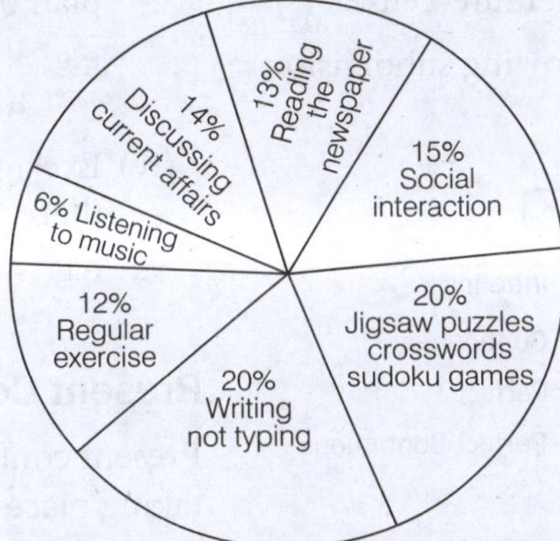

Activities to Stimulate Brain Power

Tenses

CHAPTER 1

Tense is defined as the form of verb that tells the relation between time and action. It denotes the time when the action is completed or the state of being.

Tenses are divided into three types

- Present Tense
- Past Tense
- Future Tense

These forms are further classified into the following subdivision

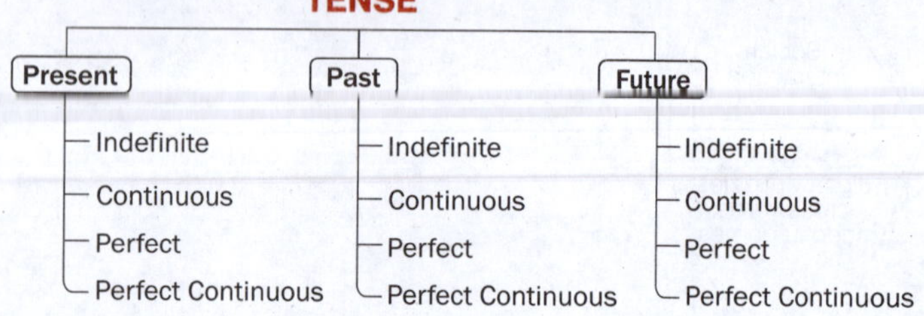

1.1 Present Tense

Present Indefinite (Or Simple) Tense

Present indefinite tense denotes an action that takes place in the present time.

Structure

Sentence Type	Structure	Example
Affirmative	Subject + V1 + (s/es) + Object	He looks for her.
Negative	Subject + do/does + not + V1 + Object	He does not look for her.
Interrogative	Do/Does + Subject + V1+ Object?	Does he look for her?

Note It **V1** First form of the verb/base form
V2 Second form of the verb/past form
V3 Third form of the verb/past participle

This form of the present tense is used in the following ways

(i) To express habitual action, or custom.

e.g.
- She goes for a walk in the evening.
- I wash clothes on Sundays.

(ii) To talk about a universal truth.

e.g.
- Budapest is the capital of Hungary.
- The Moon is Earth's natural satellite.

(iii) To indicate a future event which is part of a plan or arrangement.

e.g.
- The carnival starts next week.
- It starts in December.

(iv) Exclamatory sentences that begin with here or there.

e.g.
- Here he comes!
- There she does it again!

Present Continuous Tense

Present continuous tense denotes an action that is taking place at the time of speaking.

Structure

Sentence Type	Structure	Example
Affirmative	Subject + be verb (is, am, are) + V1 + ing + Object	Aryan is practising for the play.
Negative	Subject + be verb (is, am, are) + not + V1 + ing + Object	Aryan is not practising for the play.
Interrogative	be verb (is, am, are) + Subject + V1 + ing + Object?	Is Aryan practising for the play?

This form of the present tense is used in the following ways

(i) To indicate an action that is not happening at the time of speaking but is in progress.

e.g.
- Jin is studying in a university.
- I am working as an illustrator.

(ii) To denote an action that has been pre-arranged to take place in the near future.

e.g.
- I am playing a match in the evening.
- Kiara is going to the event tomorrow.

(iii) To express possibility or determination.

e.g. • They are going to buy a mansion.
• You are going to get indigestion.

(iv) To denote persistent and undesirable habit, especially with adverbs like always, continually, constantly, etc.

e.g. • She is always running late.
• They are continually moving around.

Present Perfect Tense

Present perfect tense describes an action that has just been completed.

Structure

Sentence Type	Structure	Example
Affirmative	Subject + has/have + V3 + Object	She has asked me to go with her.
Negative	Subject + has/have + not + V3 + Object	She has not asked me to go with her.
Interrogative	Has/Have + Subject + V3 + Object?	Has she asked me to go with her?

This form of the present tense is used in the following ways

(i) To describe an action that started sometime in the past and has continued to the present.

e.g. • I haven't gone to the garden in a while.
• She has studied in this school for twelve years.

(ii) To describe past events, the effect of which still exists.

e.g. • She has completed her homework so we are going to the market now.
• She is joining us on the trip as her parents have approved of it.

(iii) To describe an action whose time is not given or definite.

e.g. • She has been to Manchester.
• Have you played volleyball?

Present Perfect Continuous Tense

Present perfect continuous tense expresses an action that began at some time in the past and is still continuing.

Structure

Sentence Type	Structure	Example
Affirmative	Subject + has/have + been V1 + ing + Object	They have been helping the poor for many years.
Negative	Subject + has/have + not + been + V1 + ing + Object	They have not been helping the poor for many years.
Interrogative	Has/Have + Subject + been + V1 + ing + Object?	Have they been helping the poor for many years?

1.2 Past Tense

Past Indefinite (or Simple Past) Tense

Simple past tense indicates an action that was completed in the past.

Structure

Sentence Type	Structure	Example
Affirmative	Subject + V2 + Object	She ran back home.
Negative	Subject + did + not + V1 + Object	She did not run back home.
Interrogative	Did + Subject + V1 + Object?	Did she run back home?

This form of the past tense is used in the following ways

(i) It is often used in recounts and narratives.

e.g. • We went to watch the game yesterday.
• I heard this story a few days ago.

(ii) To indicate past habits or repeated events that are over now.

e.g. • I used to play video games every Sunday.
• She always wore plain clothes.

(iii) To indicate another action that happened in the middle of a longer action.

e.g. • The train went away while we were waiting for her.
• He reached the office after the manager had gone.

Past Continuous Tense

Past continuous tense indicates an action that was happening at some time in the past in which the time of action may or may not be indicated.

Structure

Sentence Type	Structure	Example
Affirmative	Subject + be verb (was, were) + V1 + ing + Object	It was raining yesterday.
Negative	Subject + be verb (was, were) + not + V1 + ing + Object	They were not playing carrom the whole afternoon.
Interrogative	Be verb (was, were) + Subject + V1 + ing + Object?	Were they playing carrom the whole afternoon?

This form of the past tense is used in the following ways

(i) To express an action that was going on during a given period or at a period of time in the past.

e.g. • While Anjali was watching the movie, Rohan was completing his homework.

• They were waiting for the doctor, when the fire broke out.

Past Perfect Tense

Past perfect tense denotes an action that was already completed before a certain point of time in the past.

Structure

Sentence Type	Structure	Example
Affirmative	Subject + had + V3 + Object	We had decided to move away.
Negative	Subject + had + not + V3 + Object	We had not decided to move away.
Interrogative	Had + Subject + V3 + Object?	Had we decided to move away?

This form of the past tense is used in the following ways

(i) To indicate an action completed before another past event.

e.g. • The wedding had finished before he reached the venue.

• The movie started after the director had arrived.

(ii) To indicate desires in the past that have not been fulfilled.

e.g. • I wish we had enjoyed our youth.

• We had wished to climb the Everest.

Past Perfect Continuous Tense

Past perfect continuous tense indicates an action that began in the past and continued up to a certain point of time in the past.

Structure

Sentence Type	Structure	Example
Affirmative	Subject + had + been + V1 + ing + Object	I had been waiting for an hour before she came.
Negative	Subject + had + not + been + V1 + ing + Object	He had not been working as a waiter before he completed his studies.
Interrogative	Had + Subject + been + V1 + ing + Object?	Had he been working as a waiter before he completed his studies?

This form of the tense is used in the following way

(i) To denote an action that is the cause of another action in the past.

e.g. • David was drowsy as he had been making the presentation the whole night.

• She was upset because she had been looking forward to the reunion.

1.3 Future Tense

Future Indefinite (or Simple Future) Tense

Simple future tense expresses an action that will take place at some time in the future.

Structure

Sentence Type	Structure	Example
Affirmative	Subject + will/shall + V1 + Object	She will join us for the trip.
Negative	Subject + will/shall + not + V1 + Object	She will not join us for the trip.
Interrogative	Will/Shall + subject + V1 + Object?	Will she join us for the trip?

This form of the future tense is used in the following ways

(i) To express a warning, order, request, advice or proposal.

e.g. • You will have to complete this task by next week.

• Shall we start the meeting?

Future Continuous Tense

Future continuous tense denotes an action that will be in progress at a point of time in the future.

Structure

Sentence Type	Structure	Example
Affirmative	Subject + will/shall + be + V1 + ing + Object	She will be going for a walk later.
Negative	Subject + will/shall + not + be + V1 + ing + Object	We shall not be coming on time tomorrow.
Interrogative	Will/Shall + Subject + be + V1 + ing + Object?	Shall we be coming on time tomorrow?

This form of the future tense is used in the following ways

(i) To indicate an action that will occur in a continuous course.

e.g. • She will be going on a trip tomorrow.
• I shall be staying with my grandparents.

(ii) To compare present and future events.

e.g. • She might be living an exhausting life now, but she will definitely be happy in the future.
• At this time next year, we shall be moving to Sikkim.

Future Perfect Tense

Future perfect tense denotes an action that will be completed at some point in the future.

Structure

Sentence Type	Structure	Example
Affirmative	Subject + will/shall + have + V1 + Object	She will have reached home by evening.
Negative	Subject + will/shall + not + have + V1 + Object	She will not have reached home by evening.
Interrogative	Will/Shall + Subject + have + V1 + Object?	Will she have reached home by evening?

Future Perfect Continuous Tense

Future perfect continuous tense denotes an action that will be in progress over a period of time or another event in the future.

Structure

Sentence Type	Structure	Example
Affirmative	Subject + will/shall + have + been + V1 + ing + Object	I shall have been working in this country for 20 years in 2025.
Negative	Subject + will/shall + not + have + been + V1 + ing + Object	I shall not have been working in this company for one year in 2024.
Interrogative	Will/Shall + Subject + have + been + V1 + ing + Object?	Shall I have been working in this company for one year in 2024?

Let Us Revise!

Types of Present Tense	Structure	Examples
Indefinite or Simple	Subject + V1 (+ s/es) + Object	He sings like a veteran artist.
Continuous	Subject + be verb (is, am, are) + V1 + ing + Object	He is singing like a veteran artist.
Perfect	Subject + has/have + V3 + Object	He has sung like a veteran artist.
Perfect Continuous	Subject + has/have + been + V1 + ing + Object	He has been singing like a veteran artist.

Types of Past Tense	Structure	Examples
Indefinite or Simple	Subject + V2 + Object	He sang like a veteran artist.
Continuous	Subject + be verb (was, were) + V1 + ing + Object	He was singing like a veteran artist.
Perfect	Subject + had + V3 + Object	He had sung like a veteran artist.
Perfect Continuous	Subject + had + been + V1 + ing + Object	He had been singing like a veteran artist.

Types of Future Tense	Structure	Examples
Indefinite or Simple	Subject +will/shall + V1 + Object	He will sing like a veteran artist.
Continuous	Subject +will/shall + be + V1 + ing + Object	He will be singing like a veteran artist.
Perfect	Subject +will/shall + have + V1 + ing + Object	He will have sung like a veteran artist.
Perfect Continuous	Subject + will/shall + have + been + V1 + ing + Object	He will have been singing like a veteran artist.

REVIEW EXERCISE

Objective and Subjective Questions

Objective Type Questions

I. Directions (Q. Nos. 1-12) Choose the correct tenses from the options to fill in the blanks.

1. The opportunity to volunteer at the local food bank made me .... the challenges faced by underprivileged communities. CBSE 2024

(a) realising (b) to realise
(c) realised (d) realise

2. Summer is an ideal time to take a hike, especially if you .... the opportunity to explore one of our country's many state and national parks. CBSE 2024

(a) are having (b) will have
(c) have (d) has

3. When he .... is not known. CBSE 2023

(a) will arrive (b) has arrived
(c) will have arrived (d) arrived

4. I just heard the journalist report that several highways in Uttrakhand .... blocked due to landslides as incessant rain batters the hill state.

(a) has been (b) have been
(c) were being (d) will have been

5. When a satellite .... (launch), the rocket begins by going slowly upwards.

(a) is launched (b) are launched
(c) have been launched (d) were launched

6. The students .... to participate in the workshop and submit a report at the end of the day to the English teacher. CBSE 2023

(a) were ask (b) had been asked
(c) will have asked (d) were asked

7. Since he woke up he .... CBSE 2023

(a) has been study (b) has been studying
(c) had studied (d) is studying

8. People who do not recycle items like bottles and cans .... the world's resources. CBSE 2024 C

(a) will waste (b) have wasted
(c) waste (d) are wasting

9. Several new species of plants have recently .... (discovers). CBSE 2024 C

(a) discovered (b) been discovered
(c) being discovered (d) have discovered

10. Reena always .... the truth. CBSE 2023

(a) speak (b) speaks (c) will speak (d) speaking

11. Good news, everyone! CBSE SQP 2024

Our school's robotics team has successfully .... a place in the semi-finals.

(a) securing (b) secured
(c) will secure (d) had secured

12. Anyas .... (eat) all the chocolates kept in the tray. CBSE 2023

(a) ate (b) eating
(c) have eaten (d) eaten

II. Directions (Q. Nos. 1-14) Choose the correct tenses from the options to fill in the blanks.

1. Although the world .... progress in achieving gender parity in education, girls still make up a higher percentage of out-of-school children than boys.

(a) is making (b) makes
(c) was made (d) has made

2. Globally, no country .... fully .... gender equality.

(a) is; attaining (b) has; attained
(c) is; attained (d) have; attained

3. She always .... every person. CBSE Additional SQP 2023-24

(a) trust (b) trusts
(c) trusting (d) have trusted

4. Girish, along with his father, ... every official meeting.

(a) attend (b) are attending
(c) have attended (d) attends

5. Are you looking for more books to read? Due to popular demand, we .... back our 'Buy One Get One Free' offer next weekend! CBSE Additional SQP 2023-24

(a) brings (b) brought
(c) will bring (d) were bringing

6. Dear Mr. Patel CBSE SQP 2024

We are pleased to inform you that your proposal for the upcoming project .... by the board of directors.

(a) had endorsed (b) will have been endorsed
(c) has been endorsed (d) have endorsed

7. She had already begun eating her dinner by the time I .... there. **CBSE Additional SQP 2023-24**
(a) reached (b) had reached
(c) was reaching (d) had been reaching

8. The experience of nursing an injured bird left me .... grateful for knowing the importance of being kind and compassionate to all creatures.
(a) feeling (b) having felt
(c) felt (d) feels

9. I feel certain that Soham .... in his new business because he works so hard all the time. **CBSE 2024 C**
(a) is succeeding (b) has succeeded
(c) will succeed (d) will be succeeding

10. Congratulations Change Makers!
The regional competition awards have been announced and our school music club .... the first prize. **CBSE Additional SQP 2023**
(a) had been won (b) will win
(c) was winning (d) has won

11. I am taking driving lessons now. I .... my driving test by november. **SQP (Term 1) 2021**
(a) will take
(b) would pass
(c) will have taken
(d) will be taking

12. The dog .... under the chair before the children arrived. **CBSE SQP (Term 1) 2021**
(a) has been hiding (b) was hid
(c) have hid (d) had hidden

13. At this time tomorrow, we .... our project details to ma'am. **CBSE SQP 2020**
(a) are presenting
(b) shall be presenting
(c) have been presenting
(d) will have presenting

14. Complete the given sentences by filling in the blank with the correct option.
After she .... her homework, Anaisha finally relaxed and watched a movie with her friends. **CBSE 2025**
(a) finished (b) had finished
(c) hare finished (d) will finish

15. Complete the given sentence about the reaction of some students, by selecting the correct option.
Since morning the group of students .... excited about the forthcoming cultural fest. **CBSE 2025**
(a) are (b) was
(c) has been (d) were

16. When they began to play it .... to rain. **CBSE 2025**
(a) start (b) started
(c) starts (d) having started

17. The information given here .... to all the products in this section. **CBSE 2025**
(a) apply (b) applied
(c) is applied (d) applies

III. Directions (Q. Nos. 1-5) Select the option that identifies the error and supplies the correction for the following line.

1. I can run fast when I was young. **CBSE 2023**

Options	Error	Correction
(a)	was	is
(b)	run	ran
(c)	can	could
(d)	when	whence

2. Whoever drove a motor vehicle without a safety belt or carries passengers without seat belts will be fined.

Options	Error	Correction
(a)	drove	drives
(b)	or	nor
(c)	without	within
(d)	fined	celebrated

3. The winning athletes were felicitation by the State Government and the city council.

Options	Error	Correction
(a)	winning	win
(b)	were	was
(c)	felicitation	felicitated
(d)	and	but

4. Facebook, with more than 1 billion users is celebrated its 10th birthday this year.

Options	Error	Correction
(a)	with	for
(b)	is	are
(c)	than	then
(d)	celebrated	celebrating

5. Select the option that identifies the error and supplies the correction for the line given below. **CBSE 2025**
He usually ate breakfast before he goes to school.

Options	Error	Correction
(a)	usually	always
(b)	ate	eats
(c)	before	after
(d)	goes	went

IV. Complete the following passages by choosing the correct answer from the following options.

1. In acupuncture, no drug is injected into the body, so it ....(i) no adverse effects. The stimulation of acupuncture points ....(ii) so far by very thin, sharp sliver needles. The prick .... (iii) almost painless. But now techniques like the use of laser beams (without using needles) .... (iii) in which there is no prick, no pain.

(i) (a) has (b) have (c) is (d) was

(ii) (a) is being done (b) was done (c) has been done (d) had done

(iii) (a) has been (b) is (c) is done (d) was

(iv) (a) will be using (b) are being used (c) were being used (d) has used

2. The development of cataract .... (i) a complex process. However, the following factors can be attributed to its formation. Cataract generally .... (ii) in old age but sometimes, children .... (iii) with cataract because of hereditary defect. This ....(iv) due to the various environmental factors.

(i) (a) is (b) has been (c) was (d) is being

(ii) (a) developed (b) is developed (c) develops (d) develop

(iii) (a) were born (b) have been born (c) are being born (d) are born

(iv) (a) are (b) is (c) has been (d) is being

Subjective Type Questions

I. Directions (Q. Nos. 1-15) Fill in the blanks using the correct form of the word given in the blanks.

1. The names of the applicants were .... (list) in the report and submitted to the manager. **CBSE 2023**
2. Last week it .... (rain) heavily and my house was flooded with water.
3. The students with the help of their teacher .... (create) a beautiful poster. **CBSE 2023**
4. Subject : Request for permission to participate in the Meet.

   Dear Sir

   I would like to request for permission to participate in the forthcoming inter-school cultural meet.

   I .... (interest) in taking part in the dance drama.
5. The school .... (organise) an educational tour to Kashmir in the summer break.
6. The teacher .... (complete) the preparations for the function before the term ended.
7. He was a renowned business person. He .... (purchase) a house in the city last year. **CBSE 2025**
8. Research .... (find) that individuals who live in low-income neighbourhoods are much more likely to develop problems with obesity, diabetes and hypertension than those who live in more affluent neighbourhoods.
9. The teachers .... (discover) that the students who did poorly in subjects such as Maths or Art could still do very well in other subjects.
10. Last year, I went to see the same monument but I was not .... (cycle) like last time.
11. He .... (go) to the gym everyday.
12. We .... (complete) the course by next year. **CBSE Additional SQP 2023-24**
13. I .... (spend) my whole day watching a series on Netflix.
14. By the time Neha comes home, I .... (wash) all the clothes.
15. I always rode a bicycle to school when I .... (be) young.

II. Directions (Q. Nos. 1-10) Fill in the blanks using the correct form of the word given in the blanks.

1. I .... (finish) my work so I can go shopping with you.
2. .... (do) this even make any sense to you?
3. When we met in Chicago, he .... (stay) in his Uncle's house for 5 years.
4. She ...... (be) always .... (fight) with others in those days.
5. He .... (marry) to her for ten years now.
6. The mother, on seeing his son's muddy clothes, ... (shout) at him and warned him that she .... (tell) his father about it.
7. Karina .... (finish) recording the song before Giselle came to the studio.
8. How many cups of coffee .... (drink) daily? You ....(look) dehydrated.
9. When he .... (walk) on the roadside yesterday, he .... (see) a pair of dogs roaming around a muddy pit.
10. I .... (apologise) for leaving the meeting early. I .... (feel) unwell yesterday.

III. Directions (Q. Nos. 1-9) Identify the errors in the given sentences and supply the corrections.

1. The campaign's focus is on reduce sugan intake among children by promoting healthier snacks. **CBSE 2024**

Error	Correction

2. Latex was a natural polymer found beneath the bark of a mature rubber tree. CBSE 2023

Use the given format for you response.

Error	Correction

3. Water was vital to human health and fitness.

Error	Correction

4. The children were exciting when they saw the leopard.

Use the given format for you response.

Error	Correction

5. The dog has eaten his food before the trainer arrived. CBSE 2023

Use the given format for you response.

Error	Correction

6. When I was a child, my grandmother often repetition the story of her childhood days.

Use the given format for your response.

Error	Correction

7. The Commissioner invitation the residents to share their problems regarding the sanitation issues.

Use the given format for your response.

Error	Correction

8. Mobile phones has become an integral part of life. CBSE 2025

Error	Correction

9. I missed the last bus that I usually catch and have to stay back at the bus stop last night.

Use the given format for your response.

Error	Correction

10. The company aimed at increasing authority in areas frequently visited by the clients. CBSE 2023-24

Use the given format for your response.

Error	Correction

IV. Fill in the blanks with correct forms of tense to complete the passage.

1. A recent survey (i) .... (publish) in Global Heart, a reputed medical journal, showed alcohol use (ii) .... (go) up from 16.1% to 25.6% among urban dwellers in Delhi in the past 20 years. The increase in alcohol use in rural areas in the corresponding period (iii) ...... (be) nearly four times– from 8% to 33.2% – the survey found. It can be concluded from the survey that the use of alcohol in rural areas (iv) .... (increase) more rapidly.

2. The association between humans and the house sparrow (i) .... (date) back to several centuries and no other bird (ii) .... (associate) with humans on a daily basis like the house sparrow. It (iii) .... (be) a bird that evokes fond memories of childhood and adds freshness to households through its presence. Unfortunately, the house sparrow
(iv) .... (become) a disappearing species.

ANSWERS

Objective Type Questions

I. 1. (d) realise
2. (c) have
3. (a) will arrive
4. (b) have been
5. (a) is launched
6. (d) were asked
7. (b) has been studying
8. (c) waste
9. (b) been discovered
10. (b) speaks
11. (b) secured
12. (a) ate

II. 1. (a) is making
2. (b) has, attained
3. (b) trusts
4. (d) attends
5. (c) will bring
6. (c) has been endorsed
7. (a) reached
8. (a) feeling
9. (c) will succeed
10. (d) has won
11. (c) will have taken
12. (d) had hidden
13. (b) shall be presenting
14. (b) had finished
15. (c) has been
16. (b) started
17. (d) applies

III. 1. (c) error – can, correction – could
2. (a) error – drove, correction – drives
3. (c) error – felicitation, correction – felicitated
4. (d) error – celebrated, correction – celebrating
5. (b) error – ate, correction – eats

IV. 1. (i) (a) has (ii) (b) was done
(iii) (b) is (iv) (b) are being used
2. (i) (a) is (ii) (c) develops
(iii) (d) are born (iv) (b) is

Subjective Type Questions

I. 1. listed
2. rained
3. created
4. am interested
5. is organising
6. had completed
7. purchased
8. has found
9. discovered
10. cycling
11. goes
12. will complete
13. spent
14. shall have washed
15. was

II. 1. have finished
2. Does
3. had been staying
4. was, fighting
5. has been married
6. shouts, will tell
7. had finished
8. do you drink, look
9. was walking, saw
10. apologise, was feeling

III. 1. Error – reduce, correction – reducing
2. Error – was, correction – is
3. Error – was, correction – is
4. Error – exciting, correction – excited
5. Error – has, correction – had
6. Error – repetition, correction – repeated
7. Error – invitation, correction – invites
8. Error – has; correction – have
9. Error – have correction – had
10. Error – aimed, correction – aims

IV. 1. (i) published (ii) has gone
(iii) is (iv) is increasing
2. (i) dates (ii) has been associated
(iii) is (iv) has become

Modals

Modals or Modal Auxiliary Verbs are used with the main verb to give us more information about the action. It tells us about the mood or attitude of the speaker and never changes its form.

The main purpose of these verbs is that it tells us whether a sentence expresses a possibility, ability, a wish, a necessity, willingness, promise, request, etc.

There are 9 modal auxiliaries in total

Can, Could, Shall, Should, Will, Would, May, Might, Must

2.1 Functions of Modals

Will

(i) To show promise, willingness or determination

e.g. • Ravi will buy me an iphone. *(promise)*

• I will look after your child. *(willingness)*

• We will pass this examination with flying colours. *(determination)*

(ii) To express request, characteristic or habit

e.g. • Will you pass me the remote? *(request)*

• He will be late as always. *(characteristic/habit)*

Would (Past Form of 'Will')

(i) It expresses the past form of 'will'

e.g. • He asked if I would be able to teach him Physics.

• Would you like some juice?

(ii) To express past habit

e.g. • He would walk his dog in the evening.

• My mother would crochet every Sunday.

(iii) To make a request

e.g. • Would you let me borrow the class notes?

• Would you practise volleyball with me?

(iv) To express a wish

e.g. I wish it would rain.

(v) To express an imaginary condition

e.g. • I would have travelled the world if I were rich.

• She would be a writer if she followed her dreams.

Shall

(i) To ask for suggestion, or advice

e.g. • Shall we start the presentation? *(suggestion)*

• What shall we do with this issue? *(advice)*

(ii) To indicate command, and assurance

e.g. • She shall stay inside the house. *(command)*

• You shall be fine. *(assurance)*

Should (Past Form of 'Shall')

(i) To express duty or obligation

e.g. • Students should follow the school's rules and regulations. *(obligation)*

• I should call my sister as it is her birthday today. *(duty)*

(ii) To ask for an opinion

e.g. • Should we ask him to go with us?

• Should I make a flowchart instead?

(iii) To give or take advice or suggestion

e.g. • You should respect your parents. *(advice)*

• Should we buy the flowers now? *(suggestion)*

(iv) After 'lest' when someone expresses fear

e.g. • Study well lest you should fail the exam.

• You should leave early lest you should miss the seminar.

Can

(i) To express an ability, capability, capacity or power

e.g. • She can solve the problem really fast. *(ability/capability)*

• Charlie can give Mr. Wonka some of his recipes. *(power)*

• Can you understand the spanish verbs? *(capacity)*

(ii) To show possibility

e.g. • Any person can achieve success.

• We can go to Lodhi garden next year.

(iii) To take or give permission

e.g. • Can you pass me the salt?

• You can sit here.

Could (Past Form of 'Can')

(i) To express ability/talent in the past

e.g. • She could lift 10 kgs in her teenage years.
• David could paly football when he was four.

(ii) To express polite request

e.g. • Could I have some milk?
• Could you explain once more?

May

(i) To show possibility or probability

e.g. • Virat may be waiting for us.
• Chelsea may win the championship.

(ii) To give or take permission

e.g. • May I borrow your pen?
• Yes, you may borrow it.

(iii) To wish or pray

e.g. • May you live long! (wish)
• May we prosper! (pray)

(iv) To show a purpose

e.g. • They are practising hard so that they may win.
• He goes home every week so that he may look after his parents

Might (Past Form of 'May')

(i) To express less possibility

e.g. • Rani might win lottery this time.
• He might be coming home.

(ii) For permission

e.g. • Might I ask for more data on this topic?
• Might we use the gym for our practice?

(iii) To express a guess

e.g. • Anil might be having a meeting
• It might rain tonight.

Note : 'May' and 'might' can be used interchangeably to express possibility. However, we usually use 'might' when something is less likely and 'may' when it is more likely to happen.

Must

(i) To express necessity or obligation

e.g. • Everyone must follow the traffic rules. (*obligation*)
• You must reach the school by 9 a.m. (*necessity*)

(ii) To indicate assumption or conclusion

e.g. • He must by here for his little brother. (*assumption*)
• Naruto must not be more than a year old when it happened. (*conclusion*)

(iii) In case of prohibition

e.g. • You must not talk like that.
• I must not disappoint my parents.

2.2 Semi Modals

Some verbs can be used as main verbs as well as modals. Such verbs are called Semi Modals. There are 5 semi modals- Ought to, Need/Need to, Dare and Used to.

Function of Semi Modals

Ought to

(i) To express moral obligation or duty

e.g. • Every citizen ought to respect the nation.
• You ought to love your parents.

(ii) To express possibility

e.g. • This bicycle ought to get out of stock soon.
• Sunaina ought to receive a scholarship.

Need/Need to

As a modal auxiliary, it is used in negative terms, it indicates absence of obligation. It expresses the speaker's authority or advice and is used for the present and the future.

e.g. • You needn't worry about me.
• Need I go there?

Dare

As a modal auxiliary, **dare** refers to being bold and courageous.

e.g. • Dare you disobey me?
• Don't you dare ruin the moment for me.

While the verb 'dare' is used as a modal the form 'dare + object + to' functions as main verb.

As a semi-modal, dare is more aften followed by 'not' to form a negative statement.

Used to

(i) A discontinued habit or a past situation which is not true in the present.

e.g. • We used to practice karate daily.
• There used to be a shopping mall here.

REVIEW EXERCISE

Objective and Subjective Questions

Objective Type Questions

I. Directions (Q. Nos. 1-20) Choose the modals from the options to fill in the blanks.

1. She is highly creative and likes to work at her own place. I doubt whether she .... cope with the stress of a corporate job. Competency Based

(a) could have to (b) will be able to
(c) may not have to (d) must not be able to

2. Residents are requested to segregate the wet from the dry waste.Residents .... adhere to civic norms. CBSE 2023

(a) can (b) ought to
(c) will be (d) might

3. It was so dark that I fell down the stairs last night. I .... fixed the light. CBSE 2024 C

(a) must have (b) would have
(c) could have (d) should have

4. Schools .... instruct students to wear full sleeved shirts during monsoon time.

(a) ought (b) would (c) might (d) ought to

5. The advertisement read, '............... we dress your day? Make you special. Pick the perfect look.'

(a) must (b) can (c) will (d) ought to

6. Students .... walk silently in the corridor during class hours. CBSE 2023

(a) should (b) may (c) must (d) would

7. Keep the environment clean. Do not litter. You .... follow the rules. CBSE 2023

(a) should (b) may (c) must (d) will

8. Where were you? You .... be in the class at the right time. CBSE 2023

(a) shall (b) should (c) will (d) would

9. One .... read the newspaper every day. CBSE 2023

(a) should (b) would (c) can (d) may

10. We .... not really change a man's mind and heart with money.

(a) can (b) could (c) may (d) might

11. Welcome to our website? You .... enjoy 10 percent off on your first purchase with code WELCOME. Click here to start shopping! CBSE 2025

(a) may (b) will
(c) should (d) might

12. If I were attending the workshop, I .... stay on till the end of the second session as well.

(a) would (b) may
(c) can (d) should

13. As a true patriot, I .... lay down my life for my motherland.

(a) might (b) could
(c) will (d) should

14. Drivers .... wear helmets for their safety. CBSE 2023

(a) must (b) can't
(c) don't (d) ought

15. The report read, "There .... heavy rainfall due to Western disturbances over the Arabian Sea." CBSE 2023

(a) should be (b) must be
(c) ought to be (d) will be

16. The report read, "There .... traffic diversion due to the student parade on the main street."

(a) cannot be (b) should be
(c) must be (d) will be

17. Children .... volunteer for an hour a week to spend time with the elderly.

(a) must (b) used to (c) ought to (d) will

18. People .... stay indoors as a severe storm is expected this evening. CBSE 2023

(a) ought to (b) must (c) will (d) would

19. You .... wear a seat belt.

(a) may (b) must (c) might (d) can

20. There .... be an accident at any time on this bridge. CBSE 2023

(a) will (b) must (c) could (d) shall

II. Directions (Q. Nos. 1-5) Select the options that identify the errors and supply the corrections for the following lines.

1. I can't never forget my childhood friend Bella. CBSE 2023

Options	Error	Correction
(a)	can't	can
(b)	forget	forgotten
(c)	my	mine
(d)	friend	friends

2. You don't run here. It is not allowed. **CBSE 2023**

Options	Error	Correction
(a)	you	your
(b)	don't	shouldn't
(c)	run	ran
(d)	allowed	allow

3. We should have to finish our assignment by this evening.

Options	Error	Correction
(a)	should	might
(b)	have to	to
(c)	our	us
(d)	by	in

4. I ought to call him at once.

Options	Error	Correction
(a)	ought to	should
(b)	call	to call
(c)	him	his
(d)	at	by

5. Rama can dance for three hours everyday when he was twenty.

Options	Error	Correction
(a)	can	could
(b)	for	on
(c)	everyday	every day
(d)	when	if

III. Choose the correct answers from the following options to complete the paragraph.

1. OTT platforms .... (i) be the best upgrade for movies and series lovers. Thanks to streaming platforms, fans of new films and web series .... (ii) gain access to them much sooner than TV. You .... (iii) access international level content from anywhere around the world. Additionally, it has provided a platform for creators to reclaim their status in the entertainment industry, which .... (iv) otherwise have been overshadowed by mainstream entertainment.

(i) (a) should (b) might (c) need to (d) has to
(ii) (a) can (b) could (c) may (d) might
(iii) (a) might (b) should (c) will (d) can
(iv) (a) may (b) might (c) shall (d) will

2. One of the biggest problems in the world today is global warming. Many scientists are being alarmed due to the rising average temperature globally. This ....(i) pose a great threat to the existence of human existence. Thus, we ....(ii) find a way to solve this problem as global citizens. Everyone .... (iii) contribute in saving our only home. It .... (iv) be our priority right now.

(i) (a) can (b) could (c) might (d) may
(ii) (a) are (b) must (c) have (d) need
(iii) (a) should (b) ought to (c) must (d) shall
(iv) (a) must (b) shall (c) could (d) should

Subjective Questions

I. 1. Fill in the blank by using the correct form of the word in the bracket for the given portion of the letter. **CBSE 2023**

Subject : Complaint about Poor Service.

Dear Sir,

I .... (will) like to draw your attention to the poor service provided by your technical team.

2. Fill in the blank using the correct form of the word in the bracket for the given portion of the letter.

Subject: Request for arrangement of extra class

Dear Madam,

On behalf of the students of Class X, I would like to state that the students of our class .... (will) require extra classes for Physics subject.

3. Fill in the blank by using the correct form of the word in the bracket for the given portion of the poster.

Water is an Essential Commodity to all Living Beings.

.... (Shall) we be wasting it without any thoughts?

4. Fill in the blank by using the correct form of the word in the bracket for the given portion of the headline from a food blog.

Various ranges of your favourites all in a place! .... (would) you miss this chance when it's right in front of you?

5. Fill the blank to complete the cautionary declaration, given below.

The traffic police .... penalise the law breakers strictly.

II. Directions (Q.Nos. 1–20) Fill in the blanks using appropriate modals to complete the sentences.

1. Caution! You .... not enter.
Only employees are allowed beyond this point.
2. She .... not be able to attend the online classes today.

3. He .... study for the entrance exam.
4. You .... apologise for your immature behaviour towards the guests.
5. If Reena left home two hours ago, she .... be reaching the destination anytime soon.
6. Punjab .... be quite hot in summer.
7. Since it is confidential, you .... not disclose this to anyone.
8. You .... have checked for the keys before going out.
9. Where .... they have gone at this hour?
10. I wish you .... take more care of yourself.
11. .... I book the seats in advance so that we don't have to wait in line?
12. If you improve your social skills, you .... advance in your current job.
13. Neha .... not be able to handle this situation.
14. Roshan .... play karate when he was twelve.
15. I .... go for jogging at 6 am in the morning.
16. Don't you .... make fun of the poor.
17. .... you help me open this door?
18. You don't .... attend the extra classes if you don't want to.
19. I .... always remember you. It is my promise to you.
20. You .... ask for another chance after everything you've done?

III. Identify the errors in the given sentences and supply the corrections.

1. Do you know that slouching should cause many problems? **CBSE 2023**
   Use the given format for you response.

Error	Correction

2. That needn't be Dad's jacket. It's too small. **CBSE SQP 2024**
   Use the given format for your response.

Error	Correction

3. I might not go there if I don't have to.
   Use the given format for your response.

Error	Correction

4. Should you please pass me the water bottle?
   Use the given format for your response.

Error	Correction

5. This delightful recipe must keep your hunger pangs at bay with its balanced spices and oriental flavour. **CBSE Additional SQP 2023-24**

Error	Correction

6. Note- Passengers will not reach the airport late in order to avoid a fine equivalent to 5% of the basic fare. **CBSE Additional SQP 2023-24**

Error	Correction

7. Sanya exclaims, "Look! My keys are in the refrigerator. I will have absent-mindedly put them here while putting away the groceries."
   Use the given format for your response.

Error	Correction

IV. Fill in the blanks using suitable modals to complete the passage.

1. A person with a fragile ego .... (i) take anything you say personally. They not only have a hard time ahead, but .... (ii) also feel insulted. They can get hurt and in return they .... (iii) hurt others. They are called sadists who .... (ii) certainly mar others' reputation.

2. If I .... (i) stop one heart from breaking,
   I .... (ii) not live in vain;
   If I .... (iii) ease one life the aching,
   Or cool one pain,
   Or help one fainting robin
   Unto his nest again,
   I .... (iv) not live in vain.

ANSWERS

Objective Type Questions

I. 1. (b) will be able to — 2. (b) ought to
3. (d) should have — 4. (d) ought to
5. (b) can — 6. (a) should
7. (c) must — 8. (b) should
9. (a) should — 10. (a) can
11. (b) will — 12. (a) would
13. (d) should — 14. (a) must
15. (d) will be — 16. (d) will be
17. (c) ought to — 18. (b) must
19. (b) must — 20. (c) could

II. 1. (a) error – can't, correction – can
2. (b) error – don't, correction – shouldn't
3. (a) error – should, correction – might
4. (a) error – ought to, correction – should
5. (a) error – can, correction – could

III. 1. (i) (b) might
(ii) (a) can
(iii) (d) can
(iv) (a) may
2. (i) (b) could
(ii) (b) must
(iii) (b) ought to
(iv) (d) should

Subjective Type Questions

I. 1. Would — 2. would
3. should — 4. would
5. must

II. 1. may — 2. would
3. needs to — 4. must
5. would — 6. can
7. must — 8. should
9. could — 10. would
11. Should — 12. will/shall
13. will — 14. could
15. shall — 16. dare
17. could — 18. need to
19. will — 20. dare

III. 1. Error – should, correction – can
2. Error – needn't, correction – cannot
3. Error – might, correction – would
4. Error – should, correction – could
5. Error – must, correction – will
6. Error – will, correction – should
7. Error – will, correction – must

IV. 1. (i) would — (ii) may
(iii) might — (iv) could
2. (i) can — (ii) shall
(iii) can — (iv) shall

Determiners

Determiners are words that can be used with nouns to determine or to modify their meaning. Determiners function like adjectives. They are also called 'fixing words'.

e.g. • I saw **an** old man on my way here.
• **Fewer** people attended the meeting.

3.1 Classification of Determiners

Determiners can be classified into

1. Articles
2. Demonstrative Adjectives
3. Quantifiers
4. Possessives Adjectives
5. Distributive Adjectives

Articles — A, An, The

Indefinite Articles

The words 'A' and 'An' are Indefinite Articles. They do not refer to any specific or unique noun. They make the noun general and are used only with singular nouns.

e.g. • Can you please buy **an** apple for me?
• I have left the key under **a** plant.

Use of Indefinite Article 'A' and 'An'

1. The article **'A'** is used with words that start with a consonant sound.

e.g. • I found **a** bag in the garden.
• He wants to become **a** veterinarian.

However, in some cases, the article 'A' is used before words that start with a vowel letter. This is so because the words begin with a consonant sound. For example,

- He is **a** European.
(European starts with the sound of 'y')
- Please give me **a** one hundred-rupee note.
(One- rupee note starts with the sound of 'w')
- I want to go to **a** university.
(University starts with the sound of 'y')

2. The article **'An'** is used with words that start with a vowel sound.

e.g. • My mother gave me **an** egg to eat.
• I should carry **an** umbrella as it is going to rain.

However, in some cases, the article 'An' is used before words that start with a consonant letter. This is so because the consonant letter is silent and the word starts with a vowel sound.

e.g. • Vishal will be late by **an** hour.
• My father is **an** honest man.

In these sentences, the sound of 'h' is silent. The words start with the sound of 'o'.

Definite Article

'The' is called the Definite Article. It is used to denote a specific noun, or a noun that has already been referred to.

e.g. • I found my sister's pet puppy in **the** neighbour's garden.
• **The** United Nations is an organisation that aims to maintain global peace.

Use of Definite Article : The

'The' is used before singular countable nouns, plural countable nouns and uncountable nouns.

'The' is used

I. While talking about a particular person or thing or one already referred to (that is, when it is clear from the context who/what **is** being mentioned).

e.g. This is **the** pen which you were looking for.

II. Before some proper names that denote physical features.

(i) *Oceans and seas* e.g. **the** Pacific ocean, **the** Arabian Sea

(ii) *Rivers* e.g. **the** Yamuna, **the** Ganga

(iii) *Canals* e.g. **the** Panama Canal

(iv) *Deserts* e.g. **the** Thar Desert, **the** Sahara Desert, **the** Mojave Desert.

(v) *Group of islands* e.g. **the** West Indies, **the** Netherlands, **the** Canary.

(vi) *Mountain ranges* e.g. **the** Himalayas, **the** Satpura Ranges, **the** Andes.

(vii) *A few names of countries, which include words like States, Republic or Kingdom*

e.g. **the** People's Republic of China, **the** United Kingdom, **the** USA, **the** Republic of Korea, **the** Hague, etc.

III. Before the names of religious or mythological books.

e.g. Vedas, **the** Puranas, **the** Mahabharata, **the** Bible, **the** Geeta.

IV. Before the names of things which are unique.

e.g. Sun, **the** Moon, **the** Indian Ocean

V. Before a proper noun, when it is qualified by an adjective or a defining adjectival clause.

e.g. Akbar **the** Great

The Mr. Verma whom you met last night is my boss.

VI. With superlative degrees.

e.g. She is **the** most talented student in our class.

VII. With ordinals.

e.g. Dr. Rajendra Prasad was **the** first President of independent India.

VIII. Before musical instruments.

e.g. I want to learn how to play **the** guitar.

IX. Before an adjective when the noun is understood.

e.g. **The** youth are the future pillars of a nation.

X. As an adverb with comparatives.

e.g. **The** more work we have, **the** lazier we become.

Omission of Article 'The'

- Before material, abstract and proper nouns used in a general sense.

  e.g.
  - Childhood is **the** best stage in life. (*not The childhood....*)
  - Iron is **the** most useful metal. (*not The iron....*)
  - Kuala Lumpur is **the** capital of Malaysia. (*not The Kuala....*)
- Before plural countable nouns used in a general sense.

  e.g. Students should be studious.
- Before names of people.

  e.g. Romila is absent today.
- Before names of continents, countries, cities, etc.

  e.g. Germany is one of **the** leading manufacturers of semi-conductors.
- Before names of individual mountains.

  e.g. Mount K2 is located in **the** Karakoram Range.
- Before names of meals used in a general sense.

  e.g. Have breakfast.
- Before languages and words like school, college, university, church, hospital.

  e.g.
  - I know how to write in Spanish.
  - I'm attending college now.
- Before names of relations, like father, mother, etc.

  e.g. Mother went to the market.

Demonstrative Adjectives (This, That, These, Those)

I. **This** (in case of plural, **these**)

It refers to person(s) or thing(s) that is near the speaker.

e.g.
- **This** matter is a serious one.
- **These** book are mine.

II. **That** (in case of plural, **those**)

(a) It refers to person(s) or thing(s) that is far from the speaker.

e.g.
- **That** house belongs to my uncle.
- **Those** bricks are quite in expensive.

(b) It is used to avoid the repetition of the preceding noun(s).

e.g.
- **That** painting is better than mine.
- **Those** devices are more developed than ours.

Quantifiers

A quantifier is a word or phrase which is used before a noun to indicate the amount or quantity. Types of quantifiers are as follows

(i) **Definite**	One, two, hundred, ..., first, second, both, etc.
(ii) **Indefinite**	Some, many, much, enough, few, a few, all, little, a little, several, most, etc.
(iii) **Difference**	Another, other.
(iv) **Comparative**	More, less, fewer.

Quantifiers can be used in affirmative sentences, questions, requests or commands with both countable and uncountable nouns.

e.g. (a) **Many** students are participating in the sports festival.

(b) I have **a few** questions to ask the teacher.

Uses of Quantifiers

I. **Use of few/a few/the few and little/a little/the little**

(a) **Few** and **a few**

Few emphasises the lack of something.

e.g. Five minutes are left till the ceremony starts.

A few emphasises that something still remains.

e.g. There are still **a few** copies left. You can take one of them.

The few means 'not much but all that is'.

e.g. There are refreshments for **the few** who stayed behind.

(b) **Little and a little**

Little emphasises the lack of something.

e.g. She is short-tempered so she has **little** patience towards bullying.

A little emphasises that something still remains.

e.g. There is **a little** sugar to add to your black coffee.

The little means 'not much but all that is'.

e.g. The cat has knocked down **the little** milk that was in the jug.

Note Few/a few/the few and little/a little/the little are used similarly except for one difference. Few/a few/the few is used with countable nouns while little/a little/the little is used with uncountable nouns.

II. **Use of much and many**

(a) We use **much** with singular uncountable nouns and **many** with plural nouns.

e.g. • I haven't got **much** work left to do.
• **Many** books are on sale today.

III. **Use of more, less and fewer** (Comparative determiners)

(a) We use **more** or **less** before singular uncountable nouns by adding 'than' after it, or for an additional or lesser quantity of something.

e.g. • I have **more** energy in the morning than evening.
• She requires **less** effort in completing the work.

(b) We use **fewer** before plural countable nouns to refer to a group of things smaller than another.

e.g. He would need **fewer** photos this time.

IV. **Use of each and every** (Distributive determiners)

We use **each** when the number in the group is limited or definite and **every** is used when the number is indefinite or unknown. Both of these are followed by countable nouns and singular verbs.

e.g. • **Each** child in the orphanage is learning how to write.
• **Every** book in this collection is fascinating and well written.

V. **Use of most, several and all**

(a) We usually use **most** with plural uncountable nouns.

e.g. I feel anxious **most** of the time.

(b) We usually use **several** with plural nouns, but it refers to a number which is not very large. (i.e., less than **most**)

e.g. There are **several** posters made for this festival.

(c) **All** requires a plural verb when used with a countable noun, but requires a singular verb with an uncountable noun.

e.g. • **All** family members are going to Varanasi.
• **All** but one has not submitted his or her report.

VI. **Use of another and other**

We use **another** only with singular countable nouns, whereas **other** can be used with singular countable, plural countable or uncountable nouns.

e.g. • Can I get **another** plate, please?
• He has never hung out with **other** people besides his chosen friends.

VII. **Use of either and neither**

(a) We use **either** to refer to two things, people, situations, etc. It may mean one or the other of two or each of the two.

e.g. She is free **either** in the late afternoon or evening

(b) We use **neither** with only singular countable nouns and a singular verb. **Neither** is the negative of **either**.

e.g. **Neither** Newton nor Max knew that they could invent wonders.

Possessives

(My, Your, His, Her, Its, Our and Their)

Possessive determiners or possessive adjectives tell us who owns something.

There are 7 Possessive Adjectives-my, your, their, his, her, its and our. They come in front of any other adjectives.

e.g. • I have **her** number.
• **My** house is that way.

REVIEW EXERCISE

Objective and Subjective Questions

Objective Type Questions

I. Directions (Q. Nos. 1-25) Choose the correct determiners to fill in the blanks.

1. The cash prize will be awarded to .... student who scores the highest in English across all sections. Competency Based

(a) a (b) no determiner needed
(c) the (d) this

2. .... educated mind can teach many. CBSE 2023

(a) The (b) A (c) An (d) This

3. The number of people attending this evening's annual function is .... than that of the previous year's. CBSE 2023

(a) fewer (b) few (c) less (d) much

4. It was .... historic day for the organisation when .... honour was bestowed upon its employees. CBSE SQP 2020

(a) a; an (b) an; the (c) the; a (d) an; a

5. It sent shivers down .... fibre of my being.

(a) Each (b) All (c) Every (d) This

6. I went out to the balcony to get .... fresh air.

(a) some (b) few (c) a few (d) all

7. She could do .... more poses.

(a) few (b) a few (c) little (d) a little

8. The facilities in our department are not .... satisfying.

(a) this (b) many (c) either (d) neither

9. He is asked to take part in .... the activities.

(a) one (b) many (c) much (d) all

10. You can take away as .... blankets as you want.

(a) many (b) much (c) neither (d) either

11. There is .... sugar in the container.

(a) little (b) a little (c) the little (d) much

12. Could you spare .... moment for me?

(a) some (b) little (c) a (d) many

13. .... of the students in the class is asked to bring A4 papers.

(a) Every (b) Each
(c) Neither (d) Either

14. Have you completed .... M.Sc.?

(a) a (b) an
(c) the (d) your

15. She found a great .... sheets of paper on the table.

(a) many (b) a few (c) the few (d) two

16. He has been elected as the .... president of the company.

(a) one (b) that (c) first (d) much

17. Could I have .... cup of coffee?

(a) other (b) another (c) that (d) this

18. Remember to take .... books from the desk.

(a) those (b) these (c) your (d) a

19. There isn't .... money in my wallet.

(a) many (b) much (c) some (d) more

20. He does .... work than his junior.

(a) the few (b) few (c) less (d) many

21. In our country, ... universities offer a range of courses. That's why foreign students prefer Indian universities. CBSE 2025

(a) more (b) each (c) many (d) few

22. .... deadline for this project is next week.

(a) A (b) The (c) Many (d) Fewer

23. .... people have been asked to attend the wedding than was anticipated.

(a) Fewer (b) The few
(c) Much (d) More

24. Attention all prefects, please be informed that the deadline for submitting your registrations for participation in the Art Exhibition has been extended. .... should be communicated to all students of Class IX-X. CBSE SQP 2024

(a) That (b) These (c) This (d) Those

25. With this, she has lost .... chance she had to win the competition.

(a) the little (b) a little (c) a few (d) the few

II. Directions (Q. Nos. 1 and 2) Fill in the blanks using appropriate determiners by choosing from the following options.

1. Medicine remains a dream career for ....(i).... and ....(ii).... of the aspirants go abroad to train as doctors. While the majority go to countries like ....(iii).... US for postgraduate training, some go to places such as China, Russia and Ukraine. Here are two experiences, one in the East and the ....(iv).... in the West.

(i) (a) much (b) many (c) all (d) none

(ii) (a) some (b) many
(c) few (d) much

(iii) (a) a (b) an
(c) the (d) no determiner required

(iv) (a) other (b) one
(c) some (d) another

2. Refugees are often forced to flee ....(i).... homes due to human violence: war, terrorism, and persecution. However, climate can also play ....(ii).... role. ....(iii).... severe drought forced this woman and her clan to move over 240 kilometers (150 miles) in order to find ....(iv).... water.

(i) (a) the (b) their
(c) no determiner required (d) his

(ii) (a) a (b) the
(c) some (d) a few

(iii) (a) a (b) an
(c) the (d) no determiner required

(iv) (a) much (b) many
(c) a few (d) no determiner required

Subjective Questions

I. Directions (Q. Nos. 1–25) Fill in the blanks using suitable determiners.

1. He got the scholarship among the .... applicants.
2. As I was absent from school, there are too .... assignments to do.
3. .... effort is required to achieve success in life.
4. Not .... stray dogs bite.
5. That child has never shown................ interest in creative art.
6. There was .... ado about nothing.
7. .... of the employees were asked to take on extra work.
8. The student showed .... interest in talking to me.
9. There are many inventions of science .... have benifited human beings in many ways. CBSE 2025
10. It is not easy to do .... tasks simultaneously.
11. There isn't .... work left to do.
12. This pen is mine but .... one is yours.
13. .... lights went out all of a sudden.
14. He is the .... in the family to have achieve this level of success.
15. .... of the answers is correct.
16. Would you like to meet .... son?
17. When they reached the venue, they already had .... guests.
18. Shillong is .... Switzerland of India.
19. Why are you staying in .... kind of place?
20. Could you please get me .... box from the table?
21. The employee who manipulated .... data should be fired.
22. Look at .... bracelet. My mother gave it to me.
23. I have .... money but more than I did a few years back.
24. Please do say .... words about yourself.
25. There was .... book fair near our school.

II. Directions (Q. Nos. 1 and 2) Fill in the blanks using appropriate determiners.

1. With ......(i)...... emergence of big data, companies have shifted ......(ii)...... focus to drive automation and data-driven decision-making across their organisations. While ......(iii)...... intention is usually, if not always, to improve business outcomes, companies are experiencing unforeseen consequences in ......(iv)...... of their AI applications, particularly due to poor upfront research design and biased datasets.
2. I saw some birds sitting on ......(i)...... roof of a green house. ......(ii)...... of them were sitting in one line while others were pecking at ......(iii)...... grains that had been scattered on the roof. Surprisingly, ...(iv)...... of them moved when a boy walked towards them. I felt either they were tamed or they had not seen the boy.

ANSWERS

Objective Type Questions

I. 1. (c) the
2. (c) An
3. (a) fewer
4. (a) a, an
5. (c) every
6. (a) some
7. (a) few
8. (a) much
9. (d) all
10. (a) many
11. (b) a little
12. (c) a
13. (b) each
14. (d) your
15. (a) many
16. (c) first
17. (b) another
18. (a) those
19. (b) much
20. (c) less
21. (c) many
22. (b) the
23. (a) fewer
24. (c) This
25. (a) the little

II. 1. (i) (b) many
(ii) (a) some
(iii) (c) the
(iv) (a) other
2. (i) (b) their
(ii) (a) a
(iii) (a) a
(iv) (d) No determiner required

Subjective Type Questions

I. 1. many
2. many
3. Much
4. all
5. any
6. much
7. Most
8. little
9. which
10. many
11. much
12. that
13. The
14. first
15. None
16. my
17. some
18. the
19. this
20. the
21. the
22. this
23. little
24. a few
25. a

II. 1. (i) the
(ii) their
(iii) the
(iv) some
2. (i) the
(ii) Some
(iii) the
(iv) None

CHAPTER 4

Subject-Verb Concord

Subject–Verb Concord refers to a set of rules that defines a grammatically correct and meaningful sentence. Following these rules ensures that the subject and the verb present in the sentence agree with each other.

e.g. • **Ridhi** and **Sanvika** teach underprivileged kids.
• **Rajni** works at a paper company.

In the above sentences, for plural subjects 'Ridhi and Sanvika', the plural verb 'teach' is used and for singular subject 'Rajni', the singular verb 'works' is used.

Subject and Verb in Person and Number

(i) If the subject is singular, it takes a singular verb and if the subject is plural, it takes a plural verb.

e.g. • He **is** practicing his handwriting. (Singular)
• We **are** going for a walk. (Plural)

(ii) When two or more singular subjects are joined together using 'and' a plural verb is used.

e.g. Harry and Harsh **are** playing Chess.

(iii) When two subjects together express one idea, singular verb is used.

e.g. Time and tide **waits** for no one. (Time and tide refer to the passing of time)

(iv) Nouns that appear plural but are treated as singular use a singular verb. These include nouns like glasses (spectacles), pants, trousers, shoes, people, police, scissors always take a plural verb. Also, descriptive nouns, like the rich, the blind, the guilty, etc. are always plural.

e.g. • News about the pandemic **is** spreading fast.
• Police **are** inspecting the area.

Note it But when used with 'a pair of', they are singular.
• A pair of trousers **is** what I need right now.

(v) Everybody, somebody, nobody, anybody and anyone take a singular verb.

e.g. Everybody **looks** tired today.

(vi) If two subjects are joined by 'either-or' or 'neither-nor', 'neither', the verb agrees with the subject nearest to it.

e.g. • Either the captain or the teammates **are** asked to meet the manager.
• Neither the members nor the speaker **was** able to answer the question.

(vii) The title of a book, play, story or a musical composition, even if plural, takes a singular verb.

e.g. • 'The Chronicles of Narnia' **revolves** around the journey of four siblings.
• 'Wild flowers' **is** a good song composition.

(viii) Sentences that start with 'here' or 'there' either take singular or plural verbs according to the subjects nearest to them.

e.g. • There **is a** book lying on the table.
• Here **are** some of the files that you asked for.

(ix) If subjects are joined by 'together with', 'as well as' 'with', 'along with', 'in addition to', the verb must agree with the first subject, irrespective of whether it is singular or plural.

e.g. • My mother, along with my siblings, **was** going on a trip.
• The volunteers, as well as the president, **are** on their way to the affected areas.

(x) Two nouns qualified by each or every, even though connected by 'and', require a singular verb.

e.g. • Every child and every parent **is** present in the hall.
• The chair and every table **was** brought out of the classroom.

(xi) None is singular but takes the verb according to the sense involved in the sentence.

e.g. • None of them **were** asked to attend the seminar.
• He was looking for a pen but none **was** found.

(xii) When the plural noun is a proper name for some single object or a collective unit, it must be followed by a singular verb.

e.g. • Science and technology **is** the backbone of the society.
• The United Nations **functions** all over the world.

(xiii) Uncountable nouns like advice, stationery, weather, progress, etc. are singular and take a singular verb.

e.g. • Today's weather **is** quite pleasant.
• Advice **is** not welcomed unless asked.

(xiv) A collective noun takes a singular verb when the collection is thought of as one whole. It takes a plural verb when the stress is on the individuals.

e.g. • The jury **is** announcing the final verdict Today.
• The jury **have** been arguing for an hour now.

(xv) A singular verb is used when a plural noun denotes some specific quantity or amount.

e.g. • Two kilometers **is** not a large distance.
• She asked for three hundred rupees which **is** a small sum for him.

REVIEW EXERCISE

Objective and Subjective Questions

Objective Type Questions

I. Directions (Q. Nos. 1-25) Answer the following questions by choosing the correct answer from the given options.

1. Neither she nor I ....this project.
(a) know (b) knows
(c) known (d) Both (a) and (b)

2. Age and experience .... wisdom to man.
(a) bring (b) brings
(c) brought (d) None of these

3. A bunch of keys .... been found in the car park.
(a) has (b) have
(c) had (d) None of these

4. The boys............... gone to school.
(a) has (b) have (c) are (d) is

5. The group of friends .... excited at the prospect of their upcoming adventure. CBSE SQP 2024
(a) are (b) has (c) is (d) were

6. NO NEWS .... GOOD NEWS.
(a) HAS (b) HAD (c) IS (d) ARE

7. The treasurer and secretary .... left from the bank. CBSE 2023
(a) have (b) has (c) are (d) is

8. Each of the boys .... rewarded. CBSE 2023
(a) are being (b) have been
(c) was (d) were

9. Two-thirds of the students .... present at the inaugural function. CBSE 2023
(a) is (b) being (c) was (d) were

10. Economics .... difficult for the students of grade nine.
(a) is (b) are (c) has (d) were

11. His brother along with his friends .... leaving for the stadium.
(a) are (b) has (c) is (d) were

12. Reena always .... the truth. CBSE 2023
(a) speak (b) speaks
(c) will speak (d) speaking

13. Bread and butter .... my favourite breakfast.
(a) is (b) am
(c) are (d) has been

14. Let's meet another day since neither Kavi nor Samantha .... free today as they have tennis practice.
(a) were (b) are (c) be (d) is

15. The weight of the mangoes ....
(a) vary (b) were varied
(c) varies (d) is vary

16. The children along with the dog.............running around in the playground.
(a) were (b) has (c) had (d) have

17. The police ....told to be careful since the criminal was dangerous.
(a) were (b) was (c) have (d) had

18. The news .... too good to be true.
(a) are (b) were (c) has (d) was

19. Pride and Prejudice .... a classic.
(a) is (b) has (c) are (d) were

20. Some of the students .... passed the examination with flying colours.
(a) have (b) has (c) was (d) is

21. The jury .... deciding the fate of the accused.
(a) is (b) are
(c) were (d) has been

22. **His family members .... going to USA next week.**

(a) is (b) are (c) were (d) are

23. **Either of the two boys .... lies.**

(a) tell (b) is telling
(c) were telling (d) are telling

24. **The orphanage .... good care of the children.**

(a) takes (b) are taking
(c) were taking (d) have been taking

25. **The Board of Directors .... dissatisfied with the President's final decision.**

(a) was (b) were (c) am (d) is

II. Directions (Q. Nos. 1-6) Select the option that identifies the error and supplies the correction for the following questions.

1. **The children cheers loudly when their captain scored the winning goal.** CBSE 2023

Options	Error	Correction
(a)	cheers	cheered
(b)	when	by
(c)	scored	scoring
(d)	winning	winner

2. **Yesterday, two man were rescued from a deep sewer by a policeman.**

Options	Error	Correction
(a)	man	men
(b)	rescued	rescue
(c)	from	for
(d)	by	in

3. **Place the garment on the ironing board, smoothening out as many wrinkle as possible.** CBSE 2025

Options	Error	Correction
(a)	on	in
(b)	many	any
(c)	wrinkle	wrinkles
(d)	possible	impossible

4. **Nearly all the sports practised nowadays is competitive.** CBSE 2023

Options	Error	Correction
(a)	Nearly	Really
(b)	practised	practiced
(c)	is	are
(d)	competitive	comparable

5. **Breaking and entering are against the law.**

Options	Error	Correction
(a)	Breaking	Broken
(b)	and	or
(c)	are	is
(d)	law	laws

6. **Every person are expected to submit their feedback to our customer service representative at the event.**

Options	Error	Correction
(a)	are	is
(b)	their	your
(c)	feedback	feedbacks
(d)	the	a

III. Fill in the blanks by choosing suitable options from the given options.

1. Finding a job where you can learn new skills .... a lot of effort. I have been looking for six months now. Six months .... a long time. Not even one company that I applied to .... responded. The HRs nor my friend who works there .... replied to my texts.

(i) (a) takes (b) take
(c) have taken (d) were taking

(ii) (a) are (b) was (c) is (d) were

(iii) (a) have (b) has (c) has to (d) have to

(iv) (a) has (b) have (c) has to (d) have to

2. A photograph of some children .... kept on the desk. Outside, there .... people and a cat on the street. However, neither the people nor the cat .... to take notice of each other. Sitting on the roof of a building .... a big crow.

(i) (a) are (b) is (c) have been (d) were

(ii) (a) are (b) is (c) has been (d) was

(iii) (a) seem (b) seems
(c) were seen (d) have seemed

(iv) (a) is (b) are (c) are being (d) has been

Subjective Type Questions

I. Directions (Q. Nos. 1-25) Fill in the blanks by using appropriate forms of the verbs.

1. Dear Sir

This is with reference to committee's letter of recommendation that .... (highlight) the nominations for 'Safe Residential Area' award for this current year. CBSE Additional SQP 2023-24

2. Every boy and each girl .... asked to wear red or white for Christmas party.
3. The board of directors .... anxious for the result.
4. The Committee .... divided on their views.
5. The principal, together with the teachers and staff members .... participating in the sports' events.
6. In the depths of the enchanted forest, where time .... (stand) still and mythical creatures roamed freely, a young adventurer embarked on a quest.
7. Each of the students .... given a black ribbon to commemorate the black day.
8. One of the bundles of paper .... (be) missing from the stock again, today! (Additional Paper)
9. Five hundred rupees .... a small change for rich people like them.
10. I, as well as you, ... take responsibility for his children.
11. One of the world's biggest experiments .... a nightmare.
12. Everybody .... asked to leave the place as soon as possible.
13. The girl with the flowers .... my sister's bestfriend.
14. There .... plum cakes on the table.
15. Soup and salad .... too light for lunch.
16. Diabetes .... becoming a major problem in modern day society as many people .... being affected by it.
17. Neither John nor his friends .... silent even after being told to.
18. Two hours .... not enough to finish his paperwork.
19. The team .... trying on their new uniforms.
20. A writer or an editor .... doing the final checking of the content.
21. The quality of these goods .... well known.
22. More students than one .... attended the class.
23. Each boy and each girl .... to attend the function.
24. No nook or corner .... left unturned.
25. My friend and benefactor .... come.

II. Directions (Q. Nos. 1-6) Identify the errors and supply the corrections for the given sentence.

1. Identify the error on a shop and supply the correction. **CBSE 2023**

World Wide Travels Pvt. Ltd. Beaspur, Sewana For travel informations, contact the twenty four help-desk

Use the given format for your response.

Error	Correction

2. Identify the error in the given sentence.
The ship Titanic and her fate continues to fascinate the imagination of the people. **CBSE 2023**
Use the given format for your response.

Error	Correction

3. Identify the error in the given sentence.
There is hurdles to jump in life.
Use the given format for your response.

Error	Correction

4. Identify the error in the given sentence.
Twelve years are the maximum sentence for that offense.
Use the given format for your response.

Error	Correction

5. Spend a night under the stars in a traditional camp, where you can experience the warmth of our hospitable and savour the delicious local cuisine.

Error	Correction

6. The board invite online applications from eligible candidates for the post of a senior English teacher.

Error	Correction

III. Fill in the blanks with most appropriate word.

1. The most important thing we've learned,
so far as children ....(i) (be)concerned,
............(ii) (be) to never, NEVER, NEVER let
them near your television set -
or better still, just don't install
the idiotic thing at all.
we've watched them gaping at the screen.
They loll and slop and lounge about,
and ...... (iii) (stare) until their eyes ...... (iv) (pop) out.

2. How useful this website and many other free ones .... (i) for studying English! This website .... (ii) founded in 2020. It .... (iii) helped a number of students in learning English effectively. One of my friends ....(iv) recommending it to everyone. That's how I came across the website.

ANSWERS

Objective Type Questions

I. 1. (a) know
2. (b) brings
3. (a) has
4. (b) have
5. (c) is
6. (c) IS
7. (b) has
8. (c) was
9. (d) were
10. (a) is
11. (c) is
12. (b) speaks
13. (a) is
14. (d) is
15. (c) varies
16. (a) were
17. (b) was
18. (d) was
19. (a) is
20. (a) have
21. (a) is
22. (b) are
23. (b) is telling
24. (a) takes
25. (a) was

II. 1. (a) error – cheers, correction – cheered
2. (a) error – man, correction – men
3. (c) error – wrinkle, correction – wrinkles
4. (c) error – is, correction – are
5. (c) error – are, correction – is
6. (a) error – are, correction – is

III. 1. (i) (a) takes
(ii) (c) is
(iii) (b) has
(iv) (a) has
2. (i) (b) is
(ii) (a) are
(iii) (b) seems
(iv) (a) is

Subjective Type Questions

I. 1. highlights
2. is
3. is
4. are
5. is
6. stands
7. is
8. was
9. is
10. will
11. becomes
12. is
13. is
14. are
15. is
16. is, are
17. are
18. is
19. are
20. is
21. is
22. have
23. is
24. is
25. has

II. 1. Error – informations, correction – information
2. Error continues, correction – continue
3. Error – is, correction – are
4. Error – are, correction – is
5. Error – hospitable, correction – hospitality
6. Error – invite, Correction – invites

III. 1. (i) are
(ii) is
(iii) stare
(iv) pop
2. (i) are
(ii) was
(iii) has
(iv) was

Reported Speech

CHAPTER 5

The act of reporting the words of a speaker is called narration. There are basically two ways in which the words of the speaker can be conveyed in writing.

(i) Direct speech/ narration

(ii) Indirect speech/ narration

5.1 Direct Speech (Direct Narration)

When the speaker states the exact words without making any changes to it, it is known as Direct Speech.

e.g. She said, "I have my art class in the evening."

In a sentence in Direct Speech

- the exact words of the speaker is stated in double quotation marks (" ")
- the direct speech of the speaker is separated from the introductory phrase using a comma (,)
- the exact words of the speaker start with a capital letter
- the punctuation mark of the exact words of a speaker like question mark (?), full stop (.) and exclamation mark (!) come before the closing quotation mark.

5.2 Indirect Speech (Indirect Narration)

When the speaker states the word in one's own words by making necessary changes to it , it is called Indirect Speech.

e.g. She said that she had her art class in the evening.

In a sentence in Indirect Speech

- the comma and the double quotation marks are removed
- the conjunction 'that' is used to join the introductory phrase and the speech
- the punctuation marks like the question mark (?) and exclamation mark (!) are replaced by a full stop (.).
- the tenses, pronouns and possessive adjectives along with words indicating nearness of time and position are also changed.

Reporting Verb and Reporting Speech

Reporting Verb

The verb that is not part of the speech (statement) which is inside the quotation marks is called the Reporting verb. It is the verb that is placed before the statement.

Reported Speech

The words spoken by the speaker and written in quotation marks ("......") are collectively called the Reported Speech.

e.g. He says, "I bought this watch last month."

In the above sentence, 'says' is the Reporting verb and 'I bought this watch last month' is the Reporting speech.

5.3 General Rules for Changing Direct Speech into Indirect Speech

(i) The commas and the quotation marks are removed in indirect speech.

(ii) The conjunction 'that' is generally to join the two parts of the introductory part and the exact words of the speaker.

e.g. • Mother says, "We are going to watch a movie." (Direct form)

• Mother says that we are going to watch a movie. (Indirect form)

Beside these changes, we change the tense, pronouns, modals, and time and place expressions. These are discussed below

Change in Tense

When we convert a sentence from direct to indirect speech, the tense of the speech may or may not change depending on the reporting verb.

(i) If the reporting verb is in Present, the tense of the verbs in the introductory phrase and exact words of the speaker does not change.

e.g. • Sarika says, "I prefer tea to coffee."

• Sarika says that she prefers tea to coffee.

(ii) If the reporting verb is in Past Tense, the tense of the speech in double quotation marks undergoes a change as given in the table.

Present Tense (Statement)

Rules of Conversion	Direct Speech	Indirect Speech
Simple Present to Simple Past	She said, "I want to see her."	She said that she wanted to see her.
Present Continuous to Past Continuous	He said, "I am going tomorrow."	He said that he was going the next day.
Present Perfect to Past Perfect	Mohan said, "He has fallen asleep."	Mohan said that he had fallen asleep.
Present Perfect Continuous to Past Perfect Continuous	Ritu said, "I have been practising Judo."	Ritu said that she had been practising Judo.

Past Tense (Statement)

Rules of Conversion	Direct Speech	Indirect Speech
Simple Past to Past Perfect	She said, "I wanted to see her."	She said that she had wanted to see her.
Past Continuous to Past Perfect Continuous	He said, "I was going to school."	He said that he had been going to school.

Note Statements in Past Perfect Tense and Perfect Continuous Tense forms do not undergo any change while transforming from direct speech into indirect speech.

Future Tense (Statement)

Rules of Conversion	Direct Speech	Indirect Speech
Simple Future will/shall changes into would/should	She said, "I shall want to see her."	She said that she should want to see her.
Future Continuous will/shall be changes into would/should be	He said, "I shall be going tomorrow."	He said that he should be going the next day.
Future Perfect will/shall have changes into would/should have	Mohan said, "He will have fallen asleep."	Mohan said that he would have fallen asleep.
Future Perfect Continuous will/shall have been changes into would/should have been	Ritu said, "She will have been practising judo."	Ritu said that she would have been practising judo.

Changes in Pronoun

(i) The pronoun in the indirect speech remains unchanged if the speaker is in first person.

e.g. • I said, "I took the other path today." (Direct speech)

• I said that I had taken the other path that day. (Indirect speech)

(ii) The pronoun in the indirect speech is changed to second person if the speaker is in second person.

e.g. • You said to me, "I am going to borrow your laptop." (Direct speech)

• You told me that you were going to borrow my laptop. (Indirect speech)

(iii) The pronoun in the indirect speech is changed to third person in accordance with the gender of the speaker, if the speaker is in third person.

e.g. • He said, "I am taking out my dog for a walk." (Direct speech)

• He said that he was taking out his dog for a walk. (Indirect speech)

Change in Modals

Modal verbs are changed in the following manner

- May – might
- Can – could
- Must – had to
- Ought to – ought to

Change in Time and Place Expressions

The words that indicate time or position also undergoes a change when we convert a direct speech into indirect speech.

Time Indicators

Direct Speech	Indirect Speech
Now	Then
Ago	Before
Today	That day
Tonight	That night
Yesterday	The previous day/the day before
Tomorrow	The next day/ the following day
In an hour	An hour later
Hither	Thither

Place Indicators

Direct Speech	Indirect Speech
Here	There
This	That
These	Those

Rules for Changing Interrogative Sentences into Indirect Speech

Interrogative sentences are of two types (i) Yes-No type questions or verbal questions (ii) Wh-type questions

(i) Yes-No Type Questions

When the reported speech is a yes-no type question

- the conjunction 'if' or 'whether' is used
- the interrogative sentence (or question) is converted into an assertive sentence
- the reporting verb is changed from 'says' and 'said' to 'asks' and 'asked' respectively.

Direct Speech	Indirect Speech
He said, "Is he coming back home?"	He asked if he was coming back home.
She said to me, "Could you pass me the salt?"	She asked me if I could pass her the salt.

(ii) Wh-Type Questions

No conjunction is used as the Wh-word itself works as a conjunction to join the reporting verb with the reported speech.

All other changes are made in the same manner as the yes-no type questions.

Direct Speech	Indirect Speech
He said, "Why do I feel so tired?"	He asked why he felt so tired.
Ronan says, "Who is he looking for?"	Ronan asks who he is looking for.

Rules for Changing Imperative Sentences into Indirect Speech

If the direct speech contains a request or a command, the reporting verb changes to told, requested, ordered, commanded, suggested, advised, etc according to the intent of the spoken words. Other changes are done according to the rules already mentioned.

Rules	Direct Speech	Indirect Speech
Use conjunction 'to' instead of 'that'.	• He said to Himadri, "Do not run around."	He ordered Himadri not to run around.
	• Mother says, "Bring me my bag, please."	Mother requested to bring her bag.
	• The doctor said, "Take some vitamin tablets daily."	The doctor advised to take some vitamin tablets daily.
In sentences beginning with 'Let', the reporting verb is changed to 'proposed' or 'suggested'.	• She says, "Let us discuss something important."	She suggests that we should discuss something important.

Rules for Changing Exclamatory Sentences into Indirect Speech

Changing of exclamatory sentences into indirect speech take place in following changes

1. The reporting verb 'said/ said to' is changed to 'exclaimed'.
2. The exclamatory word (interjection) is replaced by 'exclaimed with joy/ sorrow/ regret/ surprise/ contempt, etc.' Other changes are done according to the rules already mentioned.

Direct Speech	Indirect Speech
He said, "Alas! My father is no more."	He exclaimed with sorrow that his father was no more.
She said, "What a beautiful flower!"	She exclaimed with joy that the flower was beautiful.

REVIEW EXERCISE

Objective and Subjective Questions

Objective Type Questions

I. Directions (Q.Nos. 1-20) Choose the correct indirect forms of the following sentences.

1. The father said, "I bought a watch." (Change the speech) CBSE 2023

(a) The father said that I bought a watch.
(b) The father said that he bought a watch.
(c) The father said that he had bought a watch.
(d) The father said that he has bought a watch.

2. She said to me, "You may leave tomorrow."

(a) She said that she might leave the next day.
(b) She told me that you might leave tomorrow.
(c) She asked me if I should leave the next day.
(d) She told me that I might leave the next day.

3. Reema said, "She is studying now."

(a) Reema said that she was studying then.
(b) Reema informed that Rita was studying then.
(c) Reema said she had been busy in studying.
(d) Reema informed that she is busy in studying.

4. The lawyer said, "The law always believes in the evidence."

(a) The lawyer said that the law always believed in the evidence.
(b) The lawyer said that the law should always believe in the evidence.
(c) The lawyer said that the law always believes in the evidence.
(d) The lawyer said that the law has always believed in the evidence.

5. Ranjan said, "You cannot park here!"

(a) Ranjan said that I may not park here.
(b) Ranjan said to me that I was unable to park there.
(c) Ranjan exclaimed that I couldn't park there.
(d) Ranjan forbade me to park there.

6. Julia said, "I cannot attend your wedding."

(a) Julia said that she might not attend our wedding.
(b) Julia said that she could not attend our wedding.
(c) Julia said that she cannot attend our wedding.
(d) Julia said that she wished she could attend our wedding.

7. He said to me, "Welcome to my state."

(a) He said that he welcomed me to my state.
(b) He welcomes me to his state.
(c) He welcomed me to his state.
(d) I was welcomed to his state.

8. Father said to Meera, "I bought a heater."

(a) Father told Meera that he had bought a heater.
(b) Father said to Meera that he bought a heater.
(c) Father said Meera that he had brought a heater
(d) Father told Meera that he did buy a heater.

9. Passenger said to the clerk, "Please give me a ticket to Sikkim."

(a) Passenger asked the clerk to give her a ticket to Sikkim.
(b) Passenger told the clerk to give her a ticket to Sikkim.
(c) Passenger requested the clerk to give her a ticket to Sikkim.
(d) Passenger ordered the clerk to give her a ticket to Sikkim.

10. Rashid said, "Fine. I have got a certificate of improvement from the school."

(a) Rashid said that it was fine and he had got a certificate of improvement from the school.
(b) Rashid said that it was fine and he have got a certificate of improvement from the school.
(c) Rashid said fine and that he has got a certificate of improvement from the school.
(d) Rashid said that fine and he has a certificate of improvement from the school.

11. Father said to him, "How are you getting on with your studies?"

(a) Father said to him how he was getting on with his studies.
(b) Father told him how was he getting on with his studies.
(c) Father asked him how he was getting on with his studies.
(d) Father asked him whether he was getting on with his studies.

12. Chief Guest said to her, "Who inspired you to learn classical dance?"

(a) Chief Guest asked her who inspired her to learn classical dance.
(b) Chief Guest told her who had inspired her to learn classical dance.
(c) Chief Guest asked her who had inspired her to learn classical dance.
(d) Chief Guest told her who inspired her to learn classical dance.

13. Anish said, "Bill Gates is a billionaire."
(a) Anish said that Bill Gates was a billionaire.
(b) Anish said Bill Gates is a billionaire.
(c) Anish said that Bill Gates is a billionaire.
(d) Anish said that Bill Gates has been a billionaire.

14. He said to me, "Were you studying yesterday?"
(a) He asked me if I were studying the day before.
(b) He asked me whether I had been studying yesterday.
(c) He asked me if I was been studying yesterday.
(d) He asked me if I had been studying the previous day.

15. I said, "Yes, I can read and write."
(a) I said that I could read and write.
(b) I said yes and I could read and write.
(c) I said yes and that I could read and write.
(d) I said I can read and write.

16. She said, "The man met with an accident in the afternoon."
(a) She said the man met with an accident in the afternoon.
(b) She said that the man had met with an accident in the afternoon.
(c) She had said the man meet with an accident in the afternoon.
(d) She said the man was met with an accident in the afternoon.

17. He said to me, "Where is mother?"
(a) He asked me where is mother.
(b) He asked me where mother was.
(c) He asked me where mother is.
(d) He said where was mother.

18. Elsa said to Anna, "Go away."
(a) Elsa ordered Anna to go away.
(b) Elsa said Anna to go away.
(c) Elsa ordered Anna go away.
(d) Elsa said to Anna go away.

19. Anju said, "Alas ! I have failed."
(a) Anju exclaimed in sorrow that she failed.
(b) Anju exclaimed sadly that she had failed.
(c) Anju exclaimed in sorrow that I failed.
(d) Anju exclaimed that she failed.

20. She said to me, "I don't believe you."
(a) She said to me that she didn't believe you.
(b) She said I don't believe you.
(c) She said she don't believe me.
(d) She told me that she didn't believe me.

II. Directions (Q.Nos. 1–10) Fill in the blanks by choosing the correct option.

1. Read the conversation below and choose option that best presents the designer's words to Rachel. **Competency Based**

Ross Hey Rachel! What did the interior designer say about the new design?

Rachel The designer informed me that he would have the design ready by the following week.

(a) The designer said, "I will have the design ready by next week."
(b) The designer said, "I would have had the design ready by next week."
(c) The designer said, "I would have the design ready by the following week."
(d) The designer said, "I will be having the design ready by the following week."

2. Read the dialogue between Shabnam and her mentor, Sara, regarding her summer internship programme. **CBSE 2023**

Sara Why did you choose to participate in this internship programme?

Shabnam Ah! I am convinced this programme has the potential to enhance my abilities.

Select the correct option to complete the reporting of the above dialogue.

Sara asked Shabnam .... in that internship programme.

Shabnam sighed and exclaimed that she was convinced that programme had the potential to enhance her abilities.

(a) why to choose to participate
(b) to choose participation
(c) why she had chosen to participate
(d) with her choice in participating

3. Select the correct option to complete the narration of the dialogue between Shyam and Shivam.

Shyam Have you seen this actor's latest film?

Shivam Yes, I have. The actor has done a marvellous job.

Shyam met his friend Shivam and they began talking. Shyam asked Shivam whether he had seen the actor's latest film. Shivam affirmed and said ....

(a) that the actor has done a marvellous job
(b) that the actor had done a marvellous job
(c) that the actor has been doing a marvellous job
(d) that the actor could have done a marvellous job

4. Select the correct option to complete the narration of a dialogue between Raj and his wife. **CBSE 2023**

Raj I have invited my friends for dinner.

Wife I'll invite my friends too.

Raj told his wife that he had invited his friends for dinner. The wife added that ....

(a) she will invite her friends too
(b) she would invite her friends too

(c) she can invite her friends too
(d) she could invite her friends too

5. Select the correct option to complete the narration of the dialogue between a passerby and a farmer. **CBSE 2023**

Passerby Can you tell me the way to Rampur?
Farmer Drive for four kms and then turn right.
The passerby asked the farmer if he could tell him the way to Rampur. The farmer replied that ....

(a) he may drive for four kms and then turn right
(b) he should drive for four kms and then turn right
(c) he might drive for four kms and then turn right
(d) he had to drive for four kms and then turn right

6. Select the correct option to complete the narration of the dialogue between Ajay and his friend.

Friend Ajay, did you buy a zoom lens with your camera?
Ajay No, I did not. I ran out of money.
Ajay's friend asked Ajay whether he had bought a zoom lens with his camera. Ajay replied that he had not because ....

(a) he was running out of money
(b) he has ran out of money
(c) he have run out of money
(d) he had run out of money

7. Read the dialogue between Ankita and her mentor, Sharwari, about the cultural exchange programme.

Ankita Are we going to get some time off for sightseeing?
Sharwari Oh yes! All the students will get two days for sightseeing.
Select the correct option to complete the reporting of the above dialogue. **CBSE 2025**
Ankita asked Sharwari if they were going to get some time off for sightseeing, to which sharwari replied in the affermative .... two days for sightseeing.

(a) that all the students should get
(b) that all the students would get
(c) that all the students ought to get
(d) that all students must be getting

8. Select the correct option to complete the narration of the dialogue between the Postmaster and Rama. **CBSE 2023**

Postmaster Rama, who do you want to send the parcel to?
Rama I want to send it to my uncle.
The postmaster asked Rama whom did she want to send the parcel to, to which Rama replied ....

(a) that she wish to send to her uncle
(b) that she want to send to her uncle
(c) that she wanted to send to her uncle
(d) that she may send to her uncle

9. Select the correct option to complete the narration of the dialogue between the Postmaster and Rama. **CBSE 2023**

Postmaster Rama, show me a document to verify your identity.
Rama Sure, I will show you my driving licence.
The postmaster asked Rama to show him a document to verify her identity to which Rama affirmed and said ....

(a) that was her driving licence.
(b) this was her driving licence.
(c) this is her driving licence.
(d) that she would show him her driving licence.

10. Select the correct option to complete the narration of the dialogue between Tony and Sarita. **CBSE 2023**

Tony Why did you call me?
Sarita Will you go to the museum with me?
Tony asked Sarita why she had called him to which Sarita replied that she wanted to know whether Tony ....

(a) would go to the museum with me
(b) would go to the museum with her
(c) would go to the museum with him
(d) will go to the museum with me

III. Directions (Q.Nos. 1–3) Read the dialogues given below and fill in the blanks by choosing the correct options.

1. Julie : David, are you leaving for work? I can drop you on my way to office.

David Yes, let's go together.
Julie When does your work start?
David It starts at 9 am.
Julie asked David .... (i) and offered to drop him on her way to office. David replied that he was and suggested .... (ii) . Then Julie asked David..................(iii) he told her that it starts at 9 a.m.

(i) (a) whether he is leaving for work
(b) if he was leaving for work
(c) whether he left for work
(d) whether he had been leaving for work

(ii) (a) to go together
(b) that let's go together
(c) to let go together
(d) that they go together

(iii) (a) when his work had started
(b) when his work started
(c) when his work starts
(d) when did his work start

2. **Teacher : Did you brush your hair this morning?**
Asha Yes, I did, but the wind blew it over while I was coming to school.
Teacher Wear a hairband tomorrow.
The teacher asked Asha .... (i) Asha replied that she had, but the wind .... (ii) while she had been coming to school. The teacher instructed her .... (iii)

(i) (a) whether she brushed her hair this morning
(b) whether she brushed her hair that morning
(c) whether she had brushed her hair this morning
(d) whether she had brushed her hair that morning

(ii) (a) blew it over
(b) had blown it over
(c) blows it over
(d) blown it over

(iii) (a) that she wears a hairband tomorrow
(b) to wear a hairband tomorrow
(c) to wear a hairband the next day
(d) that she wears a hairband the next day

3. **Rohan : When is the fancy dress competition at your school?**
Seema It is after two weeks.
Rohan Are you taking part in it?
Seema Yes, I am taking part as a caterpillar.
Rohan Why have you chosen that?
Seema So that I can reach late.
Rohan asked Seema .... (i) Seema replied .... (ii) Rohan enquired .... (iii) Seema said that she was taking part as a caterpillar. Rohan asked why she had chosen that. Seema answered so that she could reach late.

(i) (a) when the fancy dress competition in her school was
(b) when the fancy dress competition in the school is
(c) when the fancy dress competition in her school had been
(d) when the fancy dress competition in your school was

(ii) (a) after two weeks
(b) that it was after two weeks
(c) that it was later two weeks
(d) after two weeks had gone

(iii) (a) that she was taking part in it
(b) if she took part in it
(c) if she had been taking part in it
(d) whether she was taking part in it

Subjective Type

I. Directions (Q.Nos. 1–15) Answer the following questions by reporting the given statements.

1. Abhilash and Neha had a conversation about the inauguration of Neha's Dance Academy. Report Abhilash's question.
Is your best friend helping you in this venture? **CBSE 2023**

2. Samar shared some information with Sameer about his recent visit to a wildlife sanctuary. Report Sameer's question.
Did you spot a tiger during the safari?

3. Sameer and Arun had a conversation about the importance of planting trees. Report Arun's question.
What is the importance of planting trees? **CBSE 2024 C**

4. Bela shared some information about her visit to her grandmother with Malini. Report Malini's question.
Is your grandmother feeling better now? **CBSE 2023**

5. Sunil shared some information with Sunita about the story he was reading. Report Sunita's question.
What was the theme of the story?

6. Samiksha shared some information with Sameer regarding the annual blood donation camp. Report Sameer's question:
How did you feel when you were donating blood?

7. Raman shared some information with Seema. Report Seema's question.
Can you solve the sum?

8. Kabir shared some information with Sahil about his travel plans. Report Kabir's plans.
I will go to Tripura tomorrow.

9. Rhea asked the following question to her colleage, Deepak. **CBSE SQP 2024**
Have you finished the magazine content to be submitted tomorrow?
Report Rhea's question correctly.

10. Rakhi shared some information with Ramesh about her school camping trip. Report Ramesh's question.
What challenge did you face on your trek?

11. Maria shared some information with Mathew about her flight to Kanpur. Report Mathew's question.
Were you nervous on your first flight?

12. Ragini shared some information with Jayanti about the new library set up in her colony. Report Jayanti's question.
Can anyone become a member of the library? **CBSE 2023**

13. Rashid shared some information about the piano with Tanu. Report Tanu's question.
Who could have broken the piano? **CBSE 2023**

14. Rachita shared some information with Reena about the trek in the mountains. Report Reena's question.
Was the trek difficult?

15. Kriva and Manish had a conversation about the engagement of Kriva's brother. Report Manish's question. How far is the engagement venue from your house? **CBSE 2025**

II. Directions (Q. Nos. 1- 10) Read the conversations and fill in the blanks using the proper form of speech.

1. Report the dialogue between a vendor and his customer, by completing the sentence. **CBSE SQP 2024**

   Vendor We missed your usual visit Sir!
   Customer I know, I had to travel for work.
   The vendor expressed that the customer's regular visits were missed, reaching out to the customer. The customer acknowledged this clarified that ....

2. Report the following dialogue between a doctor and his patient, by completing the sentence. **CBSE SQP 2024**

   Doctor Do you still have any pain in your lower back?
   Patient No, there is no pain in the lower back, but I feel a numbing sensation in my left leg.
   The doctor asked the patient if he still had any pain in his lower back. The patient answered in the negative and explained that ....

3. Report the dialogue between a vendor and his customer, by completing the sentence. **CBSE SQP 2023**

   Vendor It is nice to see you, Sir!
   Customer Yes, indeed! Unlike last month, I have been away for quite some time this month.
   The vendor greeted his customer respectfully and mentioned that he was pleased to see him.
   The customer answered in the affirmative and explained that ....

4. Read the conversation between a nurse and a patient.
   Complete the sentence by reporting the reply correctly.
   Nurse Has the wound started to heal ?
   Patient No, it is still bleeding.
   The nurse while trying to find out how the patient was feeling asked whether the wound had started to heal to which the patient replied .... **CBSE 2023**

5. Given below is the conversation between Sunil and a police officer. Complete the sentence by reporting it correctly. **CBSE 2024 C**

   Sunil Where is my car, sir? I parked it here.
   Police Officer The car has been towed away as you parked it in the 'No Parking Zone'
   Sunil asked the police where his care was that he had parked there. The police replied that the car towed away as ....

6. Report the dialogue between an employer and Raman. Complete the sentence using reported speech. **CBSE 2024 C**

   Employer Can you manage the post of a Public Relations executive?
   Raman I am sure I will be able to do the job completely.
   The employer asked Raman .... Raman assured him that he would be able to do the job complety.

7. Report the dialogue between two friends Seema and Anu, by completing the sentence.
   Seema What brings you here?
   Anu I am going to Dr. Sen's house.
   In response to the question about what brought Anu there, Anu says .... **CBSE 2023**

8. Read the conversation between a tourist and a guide. Complete the sentence by reporting the reply correctly.
   Tourist Where is the exhibit section of the fort?
   Guide In the far corner, on the second floor.
   The tourist asked the guide where the exhibit section of the fort was to which the guide replied ....

9. Read Sana's reply to her team leader, regarding the preparation of an important presentation. **CBSE SQP 2024**

   I'm sorry, I forgot ma'am, I'll have the presentation ready for you very soon today.
   Report Sana's reply by completing the following sentence correctly.
   Sana apologised for having forgotten and said ....

10. Read the conversation between a driver and his passenger.
    Complete the sentence by reporting the passenger's reply correctly.
    Driver Do the bus timings suit you?
    Passenger Yes, if I catch the 9 a.m. one, I reach office on time.
    The driver was trying to figure out whether the bus timings were convenient to the passenger. The passenger clarified that .... **CBSE 2023**

11. Report the dialogue between two friends by completing the sentence.

Ankita Will you help me plan my itinerary?

Tanu Yes, indeed! Where are you going?

Ankita asked Tanu if .... Tanu enthusiastically replied in the affirmative and asked where she was going. **CBSE 2025**

12. Report the dialogue between the residents and city planner, by completing the sentence.

City planner "The new park is a result of several months of research and planning."

Residents "We don't know who is more excited–we or our children!"

The city planner said that new park .... of several months of research and planning. The residents expressed their excitement, stating that they were unsure who was more excited they or their children. **CBSE 2025**

13. Report the dialogue between a teacher and a student, by completing the sentence.

Teacher Did everyone understand the new assignment?

Student Yes, we all got it, thank you!

The teacher asked if everyone had understood the new assigment, to which the students .... expressing their gratitude. **CBSE SQP 2024**

14. Read the conversation about social media, between a teacher and a student. How do you think social media influences our perception of reality?

Jagrit I believe it distorts our perception of reality by only showing the highlight reels of people's lives.

Report the student's response by completing the following.

The students remarked .... by only showing the highlight reels of people's lives.

Report the students' response by completing the following.

The student remarked .... by only showing the highlight reels of people's lives. **CBSE SQP 2024**

ANSWERS

Objective Type Questions

I. 1. (c) The father said that he had bought a watch.
2. (d) She told me that I might leave the next day.
3. (a) Reema said that she was studying then.
4. (c) The lawyer said that the law always believes in the evidence.
5. (d) Ranjan forbade me to park there.
6. (b) Julia said that she could not attend our wedding.
7. (c) He welcomed me to his state.
8. (a) Father told Meera that he had bought a heater.
9. (c) Passenger requested the clerk to give her a ticket to Sikkim.
10. (a) Rashid said that it was fine and he had got a certificate of improvement from the school.
11. (c) Father asked him how he was getting on with his studies.
12. (c) Chief Guest asked her who had inspired her to learn classical dance.
13. (c) Anish said that Bill Gates is a billionaire.
14. (d) He asked me if I had been studying the previous day.
15. (a) I said that I could read and write.
16. (b) She said that the man had met with an accident in the afternoon.
17. (b) He asked me where mother was.
18. (a) Elsa ordered Anna to go away.
19. (b) Anju exclaimed sadly that she had failed.
20. (d) She told me that she didn't believe me.

II. 1. (a) The designer said, "I will have the design ready by next week."
2. (c) why she had chosen to participate
3. (b) that the actor had done a marvellous job.
4. (b) she would invite her friends too
5. (b) He should drive for four kms and then turn right.
6. (d) he had run out of money
7. (b) that all the students would get
8. (c) that she wanted to send to her uncle.
9. (d) that she would show him her driving licence.
10. (b) would go to the museum with her

III. 1. (i) (b) if he was leaving for work
(ii) (a) to go together
(iii) (b) when his work started
2. (i) (d) whether she had brushed her hair that morning
(ii) (b) had blown it over
(iii) (c) to wear a hairband the next day

3. (i) (a) When the fancy dress competition in her school was
   (ii) (b) that it was after two weeks
   (iii) (d) whether she was taking part in it

Subjective Type Questions

I. 1. Abhilash asked Neha if her best friend was helping her in that venture.
2. Sameer asked Samar if he had spotted a tiger during the safari.
3. Sameer asked Arun what the importance of planting trees was.
4. Bela asked Malini if her grandmother was feeling better then.
5. Sunita asked Sunil what the theme of the story had been.
6. Sameer asked Samiksha how she had felt when she had been donating blood.
7. Seema asked Raman if he could solve the sum.
8. Kabir said that he would go to Tripura the following day.
9. Rhea asked Deepak if he had finished the magazine content to be submitted the next day.
10. Ramesh asked Rakhi what challenge she had faced on her trek.
11. Mathew asked Maria whether she had been nervous on her first flight.
12. Jayanti asked Ragini if anyone could become a member of the library.
13. Tanu asked Rashid who could have broken the piano.
14. Reena asked Rachita whether the trek had been difficult.
15. Gargi asked Ankita how the weather had been there.

II. 1. He had to travel for work.
2. There was no pain in his lower back but he felt a number sensation in his left leg.
3. he had been away for quite some time that month.
4. that it had not and it was still bleeding.
5. as he had parked it in the 'No Parking Zone'.
6. if he could manage the post of a Public Relations Manager.
7. that she is going to Dr. Sen's house.
8. that it was in the far corner and on the second floor.
9. that she would have the presentation ready for her very soon that day.
10. it was if he caught the 9 a.m. one as he reached office on time.
11. she would help her plan her itinerary
12. was a result of
13. responded by
14. that he believed social media distorts their perception of reality.

Integrated Exercise

Type I : Gap Filling

I. Directions (Q.Nos. 1–26) Fill in the blanks by choosing the most appropriate options.

1. Why do you look so stressed? Is everything alright? CBSE 2023

Mithu No! I just got some bad news. ....

(a) Aditya is in a car accident.
(b) Aditya has been in a car accident.
(c) Aditya had been in a car accident.
(d) Aditya will have been in a car accident.

2. Congratulations Change Makers!

The regional competition awards have been announced and our school music club .... the first prize. CBSE 2023

(a) had been won (b) will win
(c) was winning (d) has won

3. The river runs through your veins

The trees and mountains .... your name

The moon and stars watch over

You're guiding your way back home

To dream the night away. CBSE Additional SQP 2023

(a) will call (b) call
(c) had called (d) calls

4. .... we cut trees and destroy natural habitat? stop! before it is too late.

(a) might (b) may
(c) must (d) could

5. Is your child sitting at home you .... send your child to school.

(a) will (b) might
(c) should (d) must

6. Need a gift? You .... find one for every occasion.

(a) ought to
(b) would
(c) need
(d) will

7. When I was ten years old, I .... speak three languages. CBSE 2023

(a) would (b) could
(c) ought to (d) will

8. The hospital board clearly mentioned that you .... smoke in the hospital as it is a health hazard for all.

(a) cannot (b) must not
(c) need not (d) might not

9. There's never .... petrol left after Rahul uses the car. CBSE SQP 2021 Term 1

(a) much (b) little
(c) many (d) a little

10. You .... consult the Thesaurus if you need groups of synonyms for those words. CBSE SQP 2020-21

(a) had to (b) need to
(c) used to (d) might

11. Everybody .... keen to participate in the upcoming nukkad natak.

(a) are (b) has
(c) is (d) were

12. The good news is that.............. volunteers dropped out this month than the last two.

(a) fewer (b) less
(c) few (d) a little

13. The Komodo dragon .... follow its prey till it eventually dies due to its venomous bite.

(a) must (b) will (c) could (d) may

14. Sanju .... hear the speaker because the crowd was cheering so loudly.

(a) must not (b) would not
(c) could not (d) should not

15. When I .... out in the morning, my little sister was sleeping.

(a) went (b) had gone
(c) go (d) have gone

16. He .... meet me if he comes tomorrow.

(a) would not (b) will not
(c) should not (d) shall not

17. The government ....outline its country specific solution to the same problem that is, allocation of resources.

(a) must (b) ought to
(c) will (d) shall

18. You .... keep your promise.

(a) will (b) ought to
(c) shall (d) may

19. We had .... computers a year ago.

(a) a few (b) few
(c) fewer (d) little

20. I would have really appreciated even .... help from my close friends.

(a) little (b) a little
(c) some (d) a few

21. Author and publisher, Mrs. Baruah, ... in town to inaugurate the Book Fair.

(a) is (b) are
(c) have (d) were

22. The team members together with the captain .... to greet the principal.

(a) has come
(b) have come
(c) was coming
(d) had been coming

23. None of the experiments .... been a success so far.

(a) have (b) has (c) was (d) were

24. The military .... to overthrow the government. However, it turned out to be a futile effort.

(a) have attempted (b) attempted
(c) has attempted (d) had attempted

25. .... people connect happiness to achievement of certain goals.

(a) The
(b) Many
(c) A
(d) No determiner required

26. Once you start looking inwards, you .... to treat yourself as you would treat a valued friend.

(a) will have (b) shall have
(c) would have (d) should have

27. Choose an appropriate answer to complete the conversation given below. **Competency Based**

Kartika How old are you?
Ron I am turning twenty in the coming week.
Kartika For how many years have you been playing the guitar?
Ron ....

(a) Next week, when I turn twenty, I have played the guitar for twelve years.
(b) Next week, when I turn twenty, I am going to play the guitar for twelve years.
(c) Next week, when I turn twenty, I will have been playing the guitar for twelve years.
(d) Next week, when I turn twenty, I was going to play the guitar for twelve years.

28. Select the option to complete the reporting of the above dialogue. **CBSE 2024**

Adam asked Emma .... in journalism.
Emma passionately expressed that she couldn't resist her love for storytelling and her desire to expose the truth.

(a) why did she opt for a career
(b) why had she opted for a career
(c) why she opted for a carrer
(d) why she had opted for a career

29. Choose the option below to meaningfully complete the conversation. **Competency Based**

Sanith I .... get tickets for the football match last week.
Sonil You .... told me. I had extra tickets since my sisters backed out at the last minute.

(a) did not, need to have (b) might not, could have
(c) could not, should have (d) would not, ought to have

30. Select the correct option to fill in the blank in the given conversation. **CBSE 2024 C**

Mother What were you doing at the bank yesterday?
Son I .... ask my bank manager for a loan, and luckily, I managed to get it.

(a) had to (b) need to
(c) used to (d) ought to

II. Directions (Q. Nos. 1–30) Fill in the blanks using appropriate answers.

1. Dear Sir,
This is to inform you that our school has .... (decide) to place an order with your company for computers. **CBSE 2024 C**

2. Due to the irrational use of natural and biotic resources of the Earth in the past, most of the wildlife .... (destroy) beyond retrieval.

3. .... (determiner) story, to engage the interest of the readers, must include mystery and adventure.

4. The Chennai region .... (top) for the second consecutive year with 96.18% of students clearing the CBSE exam in 2010.

5. Children ....(love) picnics and outings with their parents.

6. ....(can) you give me a glass of water? I'm thirsty.
7. I .... (will) like to talk about the great scientists on this auspicious day.
8. Do .... (any/some) of you like pasta? I am thinking of ordering two plates.
9. One .... (ought to/must) help the old and needy people.
10. Would you have .... (a/an/the) one-rupee coin?
11. One day while entering through the gates of the palace, one of the guards .... (stop) him from entering further.
12. Two-thirds of the art supply .... (use) for the week.
13. When I went to his house, he .... (leave) for work.
14. Haldirams and co .... (be) a famous sweet shop chain in India.
15. You didn't eat ....,(much/more) did you?
16. How .... (many/much) kilograms of rice would you need?
17. Very .... (few) people are as talented as Sam.
18. .... (Either/Neither) of the two boys has taken the book. Both of them were present there when the book got missing.
19. "Where did you go for the holidays – Andaman or Goa?" "We went to ....(both/all). Four days in Andaman and a week in Goa."
20. .... (Can) you bring me those papers that I left on the table?
21. She .... (live) in Delhi for the past few months as she got transferred to the Delhi head office.
22. The quality of the books .... (degrade) over the course of five years.
23. It had started to rain just before the guests .... (arrive) the venue.
24. .... (Every/Any) one has paid for his ticket.
25. It will take .... (a little/few) time, but everyone will eventually learn how to use the new technology.
26. You have .... (few) minutes to consider my offer before I change my mind.
27. The news .... (be) not updated on time.
28. A parent ....(may/can) make his or her child feel special by encouraging and giving them support in their interested areas.
29. The headmaster and the secretary .... (has) decided to hold a conference in the meeting room.
30. A notice is a type of social .... (conversation/communication) used to notify or present information to a specific set of people. **CBSE 2025**

III. Directions (Q. Nos. 1–5) Fill in the blanks by choosing the right answers from the given options.

1. According to the findings of a sample survey .... (i) average Keralite now spends 90 minutes watching cable television and 80 minutes reading books. However, TV is not the only culprit; the survey, ... (ii) by the Kerala Library Council to mark the 50th anniversary of the library movement in the state .... (iii) that lack of interest and high price of books (g) is equally responsible for people running away from serious reading.

   (i) (a) a (b) the (c) an (d) all
   (ii) (a) was conducted (b) conduct (c) conducted (d) have conducted
   (iii) (a) is indicated (b) indicating (c) indicated (d) indicates

2. Aung San Suu Kyi .... (i) a figurehead for Myanmar's struggle for democracy since 1988. In 1988 when she returned home to care for her dying mother, Myanmar was in political chaos after .... (ii) new military junta took power. A nationwide uprising against the Generals started and Suu Kyi .... (iii) for freedom and democracy. Suu Kyi was kept under house arrest for the best part of two decades till 13th November, 2010. She was awarded the Nobel Prize.

   (i) (a) has been (b) had been (c) was (d) is become
   (ii) (a) the (b) some (c) a (d) many
   (iii) (a) is campaigned (b) campaigning (c) campaigned (d) was campaigning

3. Twenty years ago, kids in school ....(i) about the internet. ....(ii) internet is a vast resource for many types of information. It is like a giant bulletin that the whole world .... (iii).

   (i) (a) never heard (b) never hear (c) never been heard (d) had never heard
   (ii) (a) An (b) A (c) The (d) No article required
   (iii) (a) uses (b) has been using (c) have been using (d) use

4. As years pass by, the weather changes .... more noticeable. During the summers, the temperatures in various places are rising. Heatwaves have become quite common ....(ii) days. Many people have suffered heatstroke due to this tremendous heat. Doctors are suggesting that people ....(iii) not leave their homes between 9:00 A.M to 3 P.M. and if at all people have to go out, they must wear light coloured clothes.

(i) (a) becomes (b) are becoming
(c) were becoming (d) become

(ii) (a) the (b) these (c) those (d) some

(iii) (a) should (b) must
(c) ought to (d) would

5. British scientists ....(i) what they claim is a super broccoli, which can protect people against heat diseases and cancers, a statement of the Institute of Food Research and John Innes Centre in Norwich .... (ii). The new strain, Beneforte, looks like normal broccoli, but it .... (iii) three times as much of a health boosting nutrient called glucoraphanin.

(i) (a) have developed (b) has developed
(c) has been developing (d) have been developing

(ii) (a) say (b) said (c) says (d) has said

(iii) (a) contains (b) contained
(c) contain (d) containing

6. Choose the correct options to fill in the blanks to complete the note about the Wangala festival of Meghalaya. **CBSE SQP 2020**

The Wangala ....(i)......... festival for the Garo in Meghalaya, Assam and Nagaland. It is a post-harvest festival ......(ii)........ the end of the agricultural year. It is popularly known as 'The Hundred Drums' festival. During the signature dance, the leading warrior ....(iii)......... with synchronised dance steps and specific hand-head movements.

(i) (a) is important (b) are an important
(c) was the important (d) is an important

(ii) (a) being celebrated for marking
(b) celebrated to mark
(c) celebrated to marking
(d) being celebrated for mark

(iii) (a) leads the youngsters
(b) is lead the youngsters
(c) was leading the youngsters
(d) had leads the youngsters

7. Choose the correct options to fill in the blanks to complete Venu's narration. **CBSE SQP 2020**

Venu : Suppandi, what are you doing standing all alone here?

Suppandi : Uncle, I'm trying to win a Nobel Prize.

Venu : How will standing in my rice field help you win a Nobel?

Suppandi : because, that's how it's won. I've heard that the people who have won Nobel prizes were all outstanding in various fields.

Venu : Oh!

I saw Supanddi standing in the field. When I ....(i)....... doing there, he ....(ii)........ he was trying to win a Nobel prize. I was confused and enquired how standing in the rice field would help him do so. He stumped me by saying that he ......(iii)....... won Nobel prizes had all been out-standing in their fields!

(i) (a) exclaimed what he was
(b) told him what he was
(c) asked him what he was
(d) says to him about what

(ii) (a) ordered that (b) refused that
(c) questioned that (d) replied that

(iii) (a) has heard that people who has
(b) was hearing that people who were
(c) had heard that people who had
(d) did hear that people who had

IV. Directions (Q.Nos. 1–5) Fill in the blanks using appropriate answers.

1. In acupuncture, no drug is injected into .... (i) (a/an/the) body, so it has no adverse effects. The stimulation of acupuncture points .... (ii) (be) done so far by very thin, sharp sliver needles. The prick is almost painless. But now techniques like the use of laser beams (without using needles) .... (iii) (be)used in which there is no prick, no pain.

2. Enzymes which initiate and control almost ....(i) (every/all) chemical reaction in our bodies, ... (ii) (activate) in the sprouting process. Enzymes spark the entire digestive system to synthesize the nutrients in our food into blood. They are .... (iii) (a/an/the) key to longevity.

3. Sprouts .... (i) (enjoy) more when they are fresh. Mix sprouts with other foods and dressing, according to your taste and enjoy eating them. But eat them you .... (ii) (must/can), everyday! You will soon realise that making sprouts a part of your diet has a dramatic effect on your health. With this live food, all the cells of your body .... (iii) (become) active and agile.

4. The bee and the wasp .... (i) (make) a special kind of shelter. It is called the hive where a colony of bees or wasps .... (ii) (live) comfortably. A hive made by bees is called .... (iii) (a/an/the) beehive and beehive that stores honey is called honeycomb.

5. .... (i) (most/many) red fruits and vegetables contain antioxidants, which offer protection against ultraviolet rays and cancer, and helps to prevent urinary tract infections and diseases related to the circulatory system. Green vegetables along with being appealing .... (ii) (possess) excellent antioxidant properties that protect the eyes by keeping the retina in good condition and reduce .... (iii) (a/an/the) risk of cancerous tumours.

Type II : Editing

I. Directions (Q.Nos. 1–25) Select the options that identify the errors and supply the correction for the following lines. **CBSE 2024**

1. The study examine the association among exposure to sunlight and Vitamin D levels in the body.

Options	Error	Correction
(a)	examines	examine
(b)	to	for
(c)	among	between
(d)	levels	level

2. Your e-mail address can only be recorded if you choose to send a message. It will not be used for any other purpose, and will not be discolsed without your consent. **CBSE 2024**

Options	Error	Correction
(a)	can	will
(b)	choose	chooses
(c)	purpose	purposes
(d)	for	of

3. He usually ate breakfast before he goes to school. **CBSE 2025**

Options	Error	Correction
(a)	usually	always
(b)	ate	eats
(c)	before	after
(d)	goes	went

4. World leaders can work to establish peace of the world so that human and economic resources could be used to meet the pressing demands of mankind.

Options	Error	Correction
(a)	can	should
(b)	of	in
(c)	could	can
(d)	demands	demand

5. The finance minister announces that the taxes will be increasing from the beginning of the next financial year.

Options	Error	Correction
(a)	that	which
(b)	taxes	tax
(c)	will	would
(d)	increasing	increased

6. Nearly most shop was closed for the public holiday. **CBSE SQP 2024**

Options	Error	Correction
(a)	most	every
(b)	shop	shops
(c)	was	were
(d)	the	that

7. Thousands of years ago, great masters of Ayurveda notably Susruta and Charaka discussed in detail a uses of spices for culinary and medicinal purposes.

Options	Error	Correction
(a)	Thousands	Thousand
(b)	and	or
(c)	a	the
(d)	medicinal	medicine

8. Demonetisation refer to an economic policy where a certain currency unit leases to be used as a legal tender.

Options	Error	Correction
(a)	refer	refers
(b)	an	the
(c)	used	use
(d)	a	the

9. English is a West Germanic Language that is first spoken in the early medieval England.

Options	Error	Correction
(a)	a	the
(b)	Germanic	Germany
(c)	is	was
(d)	the	an

10. **How must one gain proficiency in any language?**

Options	Error	Correction
(a)	must	can
(b)	one	first
(c)	proficiency	proficient
(d)	any	all

11. **Hunger or thirst are the basic condition for living which is a reminder that the body should be fed with food or water.**

Options	Error	Correction
(a)	hunger	hungry
(b)	or	and
(c)	are	is
(d)	the	a

12. **Alan Turing was the first person to conduct substantial research in a field that he called Machine Intelligence.**

Options	Error	Correction
(a)	was	is
(b)	to	in
(c)	conduct	eonducting
(d)	a	the

13. **OTT television, usually called online television, Internet television or streaming television, remain the most popular OTT content.**

Options	Error	Correction
(a)	usually	as usual
(b)	or	and
(c)	remain	remains
(d)	the	a

14. **Malaria, caused by the bite of a female Anopheles mosquito will become dangerous if care was not taken.**

Options	Error	Correction
(a)	caused	cause
(b)	a	the
(c)	will become	becomes
(d)	was	is

15. **Crime and Punishment are rather a thrilling and interesting book.**

Options	Error	Correction
(a)	are	is
(b)	rather	much
(c)	a	the
(d)	book	books

16. **Every day, I am waking up late.**

Options	Error	Correction
(a)	every	each
(b)	day	days
(c)	am waking	wake
(d)	up	on

17. **If I will get a better job, I will buy a car.**

Options	Error	Correction
(a)	If	When
(b)	I will	I
(c)	better	good
(d)	will	would

18. **Shouldn't it be great if there were an offline grammar checker?**

Options	Error	Correction
(a)	Shouldn't	Wouldn't
(b)	if	that
(c)	there	their
(d)	were	is

19. **I made him cookies but he didn't eat none.**

Options	Error	Correction
(a)	him	his
(b)	but	and
(c)	didn't	did not have
(d)	none	any

20. **The new Democratic Party is increasing their popularity.**

Options	Error	Correction
(a)	is	are
(b)	their	its
(c)	increasing	increased
(d)	The new	New

21. **I will like to have a better job by the end of this month.**

Options	Error	Correction
(a)	will	would
(b)	have	do
(c)	by	till
(d)	the end	end

22. **I was not really enjoy telling the bad news to my family.**

Options	Error	Correction
(a)	was	did
(b)	enjoy	enjoyed
(c)	telling	tell
(d)	the bad news	bad news

23. **Did you know that animals have not the same rights around the world?**

Options	Error	Correction
(a)	know	knew
(b)	have not	do not have
(c)	the same	same
(d)	around	in

24. **I have been living here since I am born.**

Options	Error	Correction
(a)	have	had
(b)	living	lived
(c)	since	when
(d)	am	was

25. **I often wonder how many opportunities I would had had if I had finished university.**

Options	Error	Correction
(a)	wonder	wondered
(b)	how many	the many
(c)	would	will
(d)	had had	have had

II. **Directions (Q.Nos. 1–25) Identify the errors in the given sentences and use the given format for your responses.**

1. The campaign's focus is on reduce sugar intake among children by promoting healthier snacks. **CBSE 2024**

Error	Correction

2. The relationships of the country's inflation rate and GDP growth was analysis. **CBSE 2024**

Error	Correction

3. I come across this beautiful painting in an antique store last week. **CBSE 2024 C**

Error	Correction

4. The company continues to strives tirelessly to meet customer demands. **CBSE SQP 2024**

5. I was boring, so I thought it would be fun to go on a trip and visit the island.

Error	Correction

6. Mobile phones has become an integral part of life. **CBSE 2025**

Error	Correction

7. I read the book that you recommended, but I had not understand it.

Error	Correction

8. We all saw it when the cat catched the yarn ball.

Error	Correction

9. Can you make a few tea for the guests?

Error	Correction

10. A tagline is a concise, powerful description that represent a company.

Error	Correction

11. Unique is a overused word in the English language, but its uses is insurmountable.

Error	Correction

12. A sale for every seasons! Time is running out on these great discounts.

Error	Correction

13. In the mid-19th century the German chemist Justus von Liebig commented that the wealth of a nation can be gauged by the amount of sulfuric acid it produced.

Error	Correction

14. Empowered women contributes to the health and productivity of entire families and communities, improving prospects for the next generation.

Error	Correction

15. Many of this manifestations will not change unless you work hard.

Error	Correction

16. The language model of ChatGPT will answer questions and assist you with tasks, such as composing emails, essays, and code.

Error	Correction

17. Classical mechanics are the study of the motion of bodies under the action of physical forces.

Error	Correction

18. Onomatopoeia is a literary technique in which a writer use words that sound or look like the sound they make.

Error	Correction

19. Since there grandfather is retiring next week, they are throwing a party today.

Error	Correction

20. There are less books here than we thought.

Error	Correction

21. Rosie watched the movie and cries out loud.

Error	Correction

22. I can finish this task by today evening as the deadline is at midnight.

Error	Correction

23. There are plenty of fish in the sea.

Error	Correction

24. Everybody is in holiday mood as vacation starts tomorrow.

Error	Correction

25. The boys did much acts of mischief.

Error	Correction

Type III : Transformation of Sentences

I. Directions (1–22) Do as per the instructions given below.

1. Which option displays the correct change of the following to reported speech? **CBSE SQP 2021 Term 1**

Sunita asked Venkat, "How much is the rent for your flat?"

(a) Sunita asked Venkat how much was his rent for flat.
(b) Sunita asked Venkat how much the rent for his flat was.
(c) Sunita enquires from Venkat that how much rent he pays.
(d) Sunita told Venkat how much the rent for his flat was.

2. Which option displays the correct change of the following to reported speech? **SQP 2021-22 Term 1**

She said, "I told Damanjit to send you an e-mail three days ago."

(a) She told that Damanjit had mailed you three days then.
(b) She informed me that Damanjit has mailed me three days before.
(c) She says that she has told Damanjit to send me an e-mail three days then.
(d) She said that she had told Damanjit to send an e-mail to me three days before.

3. She hadn't got a wink of sleep since last night. (into simple present tense)

(a) She didn't get a wink of sleep since last night.
(b) She doesn't get a wink of sleep since last night.
(c) She hasn't got a wink of sleep since last night.
(d) She haven't got a wink of sleep since last night.

4. He asked me where I had gone during my winter vacation. (into direct speech)

(a) He said to me, "Where have you gone during your winter vacation?"

(b) He said to me, "Where did you go during your winter vacation?"

(c) He told me, "Where have you gone during my winter vacation?"

(d) He asked me, "Where did you go during my winter vacation?"

5. She has done a lot for me. (into present continuous tense)

(a) She has been doing a lot for me.

(b) She is doing a lot for me.

(c) She has doing a lot for me.

(d) She be doing a lot for me.

6. Taro said, "He didn't offer me any help." (into indirect speech)

(a) Taro said that he didn't offer him any help.

(b) Taro said he didn't offer him any help.

(c) Taro said that he had not offered him any help.

(d) Taro said that he had not been offering him any help.

7. I can run two miles in an hour. (into simple past tense)

(a) I could run two miles in an hour.

(b) I ran two miles in an hour.

(c) I can ran two miles in an hour.

(d) I could ran two miles in an hour.

8. She said,"I was working hard to support my family." (into indirect speech)

(a) She said that she was working hard to support her family.

(b) She told that she was working hard to support her family.

(c) She said that she had been working hard to support her family.

(d) She told that she has been working hard to support her family.

9. I had been waiting for her. (into simple present tense)

(a) I have been waiting for her.

(b) I am waiting for her.

(c) I wait for her.

(d) I waited for her.

10. I am leaving for Chennai tomorrow. (into simple future tense)

(a) I will leave for Chennai tomorrow.

(b) I shall leave for Chennai tomorrow.

(c) I will be leaving for Chennai tomorrow.

(d) I shall left for Chennai tomorrow.

11. She commanded him to wear a helmet. (into direct speech)

(a) She said to him, "Will you wear a helmet."

(b) She told him, "Wear a helmet."

(c) She commanded him, "Wear a helmet."

(d) She said to him,"Wear a helmet."

12. Ankita said to me, "Did you go to the book fair last week?"

(a) Ankita asked me if I had gone to the book fair the previous week.

(b) Ankita told me if I went to the book fair the previous week.

(c) Ankita asked me whether I went to the book fair the previous week.

(d) Ankita asked me if I went to the book fair last week.

13. He is learning German. (into past perfect continuous tense)

(a) He has been learning German.

(b) He had been learning German.

(c) He has being learning German.

(d) He was being learned German.

14. He had had a difficult time in his last school. (into simple past tense)

(a) He was had a difficult time in his last school.

(b) He have a difficult time in his last school.

(c) He had a difficult time in his last school.

(d) He was having a difficult time in his last school.

15. Why had you resigned from the company? (into future perfect tense)

(a) Why will you resign from the company?

(b) Why will you have resigned from the company?

(c) Why shall you resign from the company?

(d) Why shall you have resigned from the company?

16. She said to him, "Where are you going?" (into indirect speech)

(a) She told him where he was going.

(b) She asked him where he was going.

(c) She asked him where you were going.

(d) She asked him where I was going.

17. He asked me where I had kept the chocolates. (into direct speech)

(a) He said to me, "Where have you kept the chocolates?"

(b) He told to me, "Where you kept the chocolates?"

(c) He told me, "Where had been keeping the chocolates?"

(d) He said to me, "Where did you keep the chocolates?"

18. I wasn't lucky enough. (into past perfect continuous tense)

(a) I had not been lucky enough.

(b) I had not being lucky enough.

(c) I had not been luckily enough.

(d) I had not being luckily enough.

19. What were you watching last Saturday? (into present perfect tense)
(a) What have you watched last Saturday?
(b) What had you watched last Saturday?
(c) What were have you been watched last Saturday?
(d) What had been watched last Saturday?

20. She said to me, "Could you give me a glass of water, please?" (into indirect speech)
(a) She told me if I could give her a glass of water.
(b) She requested me to give her a glass of water.
(c) She said to me if I could give her a glass of water.
(d) She asked me to give her a glass of water pleadingly.

21. Ruel said, "I was searching for the TV remote." (into indirect speech)
(a) Ruel said that he had been searching for the TV remote.
(b) Ruel said that he was searching for the TV remote.
(c) Ruel said he have been searching for the TV remote.
(d) Ruel said that he had searched for the TV remote.

22. Mother exclaimed with sorrow that she had broken her favourite vase. (into direct speech)
(a) Mother said, "Alas! My favourite vase was broken."
(b) Mother said, "Alas! My favourite vase had broken."
(c) Mother said, "Alas! My favourite vase was being broken."
(d) Mother said, "Alas! My favourite vase had been broken."

II. Directions (Q.Nos. 1–20) Transform the sentences per the instructions.

1. The taxi driver said, "He opened the door and jumped out before I could say a word." (into Indirect speech)
2. The clock struck four and the students ran out. (into simple present tense)
3. Janis was barely able to stand straight. (into past perfect tense)
4. He drove into the wall with his car. (into Past perfect continuous tense)
5. She told me that she had been practising fencing. (into Direct speech)
6. "Why did they send you away?" said Alankar to me. (into Indirect speech)
7. Ramesh said to me, "Follow the traffic rules."
8. Were you able to send him away? (into present perfect tense)
9. Would you bea little patient? (into simple future tense)
10. Emily exclaimed with sorrow that she had such a bad luck. (into Direct speech)
11. He said, "Good-bye, my friends!" (into indirect speech)
12. She said to me, "Can I stay here?" (into indirect speech)
13. He asked if I had been living there. (into present continuous tense)
14. She had already eaten when I had reached the restaurant. (into Simple present tense)
15. The passenger said to the clerk, "When will the train arrive?" (into Indirect speech)
16. The speaker had risen from his seat when she reached the venue. (into Simple future tense)
17. She will have been working in this company for four years. (Into Present perfect continuous tense)
18. Akansha said to me, "You won't have to come for practice tomorrow." (into Indirect speech)
19. Samir said to her, "Close the door when you leave." (into Indirect speech)
20. She wished him that he might lead a peaceful life. (into Direct speech)

III. Directions (Q.Nos. 1 -5) Read the conversation given below and complete the paragraph that follows by choosing the correct answers from the given options.

1. Sherlock Do you know Lohan was hit by a car yesterday?
Watson Oh no! When did it happen?
Sherlock He was hit by the car on his way back from school.
Watson Is he badly hurt?
Sherlock asked Watson (i) .... Watson was shocked and wanted to know when (ii).............. Sherlock replied that (iii) .... on his way back from school. Watson enquired if he was badly hurt.

(i) (a) If he knows that Lohan was hit by a car yesterday
(b) If he knew that Lohan was hit by a car yesterday
(c) If he knows that Lohan has been hit by a car the previous day
(d) If he knew that Lohan had been hit by a car the previous day

(ii) (a) It happened (b) It had happened
(c) Happened it had (d) Had it happened

(iii) (a) He had been hit by the car
(b) He was hit by the car
(c) He was being hit by the car
(d) He has been hit by the car

2. Pinky Why do you look so worried?
Sonia My exam is approaching.
Pinky When will it start?

Sonia It starts from next week.

Pinky asked Sonia (i) .... Sonia replied that (ii) .... Pinky further asked when it would start. Sonia told Pinky that (iii) ....

(i) (a) If she was looking so worried
(b) Why she looks so worried
(c) Why she looked so worried
(d) Whether she was so worried

(ii) (a) Her exam was approaching
(b) Her exam had been approaching
(c) My exam had been approaching
(d) My exam was approaching

(iii) (a) It starts from the following week
(b) It started from the following week
(c) It starts from following week
(d) It started from following week

3. Staff May I help you?

Customer Can you tell me where can I find the sneakers section?

Staff Yes, please come this way.

Customer Thank you.

The staff asked the customer (i) .... The customer replied to his question by asking (ii) .... The staff replied in the affirmative and (iii) .... The customer thanked the staff.

(i) (a) If he can help him
(b) Whether he could help him
(c) If he may help him
(d) Whether he might help him

(ii) (a) If he could tell him where he could find the sneakers section
(b) If he could tell him where he can find the sneakers section
(c) Whether he could tell him where he can find the sneakers section
(d) Whether he can tell him where he could find the sneakers section

(iii) (a) Asked him to come that way
(b) Told him to come that way
(c) Asked him to come this way
(d) Told him to come this way

4. David Do you like sports?

Megha I have been fond of it since my childhood days.

David Which is your favourite one?

Megha Football is my favourite.

David asked Megha (i) .... Megha replied that she (ii) .... since her childhood days. David asked her (iii) .... Megha replied that football was her favourite.

(i) (a) If she liked sports (b) If she had liked sports
(c) Did she like sports (d) Had she liked sports

(ii) (a) Have been fond of it (b) Had been fond of it
(c) Had fond of it (d) Was fond of it

(iii) (a) Which was her favourite one
(b) Which her favourite one was
(c) Which had been her favourite one
(d) Which is her favourite one

5. Uncle How did you spend your winter vacation?

Niece I really enjoyed the vacation.

Uncle Did you go anywhere?

Niece Yes, we travelled to a desolate island.

Uncle asked his niece (i) .... Niece replied that (ii) .... Uncle then asked if she had gone anywhere. Niece replied in the affirmative. She told him that (iii) ....

(i) (a) How she spent her winter vacation
(b) How she had spent her winter vacation
(c) How had she spent your winter vacation
(d) How she had spent their winter vacation

(ii) (a) she had really enjoyed the vacation
(b) she really enjoyed the vacation
(c) she very much had enjoyed the vacation
(d) she really enjoyed her vacation

(iii) (a) she travelled to a desolate island
(b) they travelled to a desolate island
(c) they had travelled to a desolate island
(d) she had travelled to a desolate island

V. Directions (Q.Nos. 1–5) Read the conversation given below and complete the paragraph that follows.

1. Sangeeta Where are you going?

Me I am going to the metro station.

Sangeeta I am going that way too. Hop in the car!

Me Thanks a lot. It will save me time.

Sangeeta asked me (i) .... I replied that I was going to the metro station. Sangeeta said that she was going that way too and told me excitedly (ii) ....: I thanked her and told her that (iii) ....

2. Ricky I have been thinking about taking a cooking class.

Han I didn't know that you were interested in cooking.

Ricky Yes, I love cooking for friends and family, but I want to learn more.

Han There are tons of great cooking classes out there. I'm sure you'll find one that you love.

Ricky told Han that he had been thinking about taking a cooking class. Han told him that (i) .... Ricky replied in the affirmative. He told him that (ii) .... but he wanted to learn more. Han told Ricky that there were tons of great cooking classes out there and he was sure (iii) ....

3. **Percy** I can't believe I won the lottery!

   Elizabeth How do you feel about this?

   Percy I don't know what to say. I'm filled with excitement.

   Percy exclaimed with surprise (i) .... Elizabeth asked him (ii) .... Percy replied that he didn't know what to say and (iii) ....

4. **Patient** Good morning, Doctor!

   Doctor Good morning, how can I help you?

   Patient I am suffering from indigestion.

   Doctor Are you suffering from headache also?

   Patient Yes, I cannot sleep at night.

   Patient greeted the doctor good morning. The doctor replied the same and asked (i) .... The patient replied that (ii) .... The doctor further enquired (iii)................. The patient replied in the affirmative and told him that he could not sleep at night.

5. **Teacher** Why have you not done your homework?

   Student Sir, my sister was sick and I had to take her to the doctor.

   Teacher Wasn't there anybody else to take her to the doctor?

   Student No, Sir. My parents are out of station.

   The teacher asked the student (i) .... The student replied that (ii) .... and he had to take her to the doctor. The teacher enquired if (iii) .... The student replied in the negative and told him that his parents were out of station.

ANSWERS

Type I : Gap Filling

I. 1. (b) Aditya has been in a car accident.

2. (d) has won
3. (b) call
4. (c) must
5. (c) should
6. (d) will
7. (b) could
8. (b) must not
9. (a) much
10. (b) need to
11. (c) is
12. (a) fewer
13. (b) will
14. (c) could not
15. (a) went
16. (b) will not
17. (a) must
18. (b) ought to
19. (c) fewer
20. (b) a little
21. (a) is
22. (b) have come
23. (b) has
24. (d) had attempted
25. (b) many
26. (a) will have
27. (c) Next week, when I turn twenty, I will have been playing the guitar for twelve years.
28. (b) why had she opted for a career
29. (c) could not, should have
30. (a) had to

II. 1. decided

2. has been destroyed
3. A
4. has topped
5. love
6. could
7. would
8. any
9. ought to
10. a
11. stops
12. has been used
13. had left
14. is
15. much
16. many
17. few
18. Either
19. Both
20. could
21. has been living
22. has been degrading
23. arrived
24. every
25. a little
26. a few
27. is
28. can
29. have
30. communication

III. 1. (i) (c) an (ii) (c) conducted
(iii) (d) indicates

2. (i) (a) has been (ii) (c) a
(iii) (c) campaigned

3. (i) (d) had never heard
(ii) (c) the
(iii) (a) uses

4. (i) (b) are becoming (ii) (b) these
(iii) (a) should

5. (i) (a) have developed (ii) (c) says
(iii) (a) contains

6. (i) (d) is an important
(ii) (b) celebrated to mark
(iii) (a) leads the youngsters

7. (i) (c) asked him what he was
(ii) (d) replied that
(iii) (c) had heard that people who had

IV. 1. (i) the (ii) was
(iii) are being

2. (i) every (ii) are activated
(iii) the
3. (i) are enjoyed (ii) must
(iii) will become
4. (i) make (ii) live
(iii) a
5. (i) most (ii) possess
(iii) the

Type II : Editing

I. 1. (a) error – among, correction – between
2. (c) error – can, correction – will
3. (c) error – ate, correction – eats
4. (b) error – of, correction – in
5. (d) error – increasing, correction – increased
6. (a) error – most, correction – every
7. (c) error – a, correction – the
8. (c) error – used, correction – use
9. (b) error – Germanic, correction – Germany
10. (a) error – must, correction – can
11. (c) error – are, correction – is
12. (d) error – a, correction – the
13. (c) error – remain, correction – remains
14. (d) error – was, correction – is
15. (a) error – are, correction – is
16. (c) error – am waking, correction – wake
17. (b) error – I will, correction – I
18. (a) error – Shouldn't, correction – Wouldn't
19. (d) error – none, correction – any
20. (b) error – their, correction – its
21. (a) error – will, correction – would
22. (a) error – was, correction – did
23. (b) error – have not, correction – do not have
24. (d) error – am, correction – was
25. (d) error – had had, correction – have had

II. 1. Error – reduce, correction – reducing
2. Error – of, correction – between
3. Error – come, correction – came
4. Error – strives, correction – strive
5. Error – boring, correction – bored
6. Error – has, correction – have
7. Error – had, correction – could
8. Error – catched, correction – caught
9. Error – a few, correction – some
10. Error – represent, correction – represents
11. Error – a, correction – an
12. Error – every, correction – all
13. Error – can, correction – could
14. Error – contributes, correction – contribute
15. Error – this, correction – these
16. Error – will, correction – can
17. Error – are, correction – is
18. Error – use, correction – uses
19. Error – there, correction – their
20. Error – less, correction – fewer
21. Error – cries, correction – cried
22. Error – can, correction – must
23. Error – are, correction – is
24. Error – in holiday, correction – in a holiday
25. Error – much, correction – many

Type III : Transformation of Sentences

I. 1. (b) Sunita asked Venkat how much the rent for his flat was.
2. (d) She said that she had told Damanjit to send an e-mail to me three days before.
3. (c) She hasn't got a wink of sleep since last night.
4. (b) He said to me, "Where did you go during your winter vacation?"
5. (b) She is doing a lot for me.
6. (c) Taro said that he had not offered him any help.
7. (a) I could run two miles in an hour.
8. (c) She said that she had been working hard to support her family.
9. (c) I wait for her.
10. (b) I shall leave for Chennai tomorrow.
11. (d) She said to him,"Wear a helmet."
12. (a) Ankita asked me if I had gone to the book fair the previous week.
13. (b) He had been learning German.
14. (c) He had a difficult time in his last school.
15. (b) Why will you have resigned from the company?
16. (b) She asked him where he was going.
17. (d) He said to me, "Where did you keep the chocolates?"
18. (a) I had not been lucky enough.
19. (a) What have you watched last Saturday?
20. (b) She requested me to give her a glass of water.
21. (a) Ruel said that he had been searching for the TV remote.
22. (a) Mother said, "Alas! My favourite vase was broken."

II. 1. The taxi driver said that he had opened the door and had jumped out before he could say a word.
2. The clock strikes four and the children run out.
3. Janis had been barely able to stand straight.
4. He had been driving into the wall with his car.
5. She said to me, "I was practising fencing."
6. Alankarasked me why they sent me away.

7. Ramesh ordered me to follow the traffic rules.
8. Have you been able to send him away?
9. Will you be a little patient?
10. Emily said, "What bad luck!"
11. He bid his friends goodbye sadly.
12. She asked me if she could stay there.
13. He is asking if I have been living there.
14. She had already eaten when I reached the restaurant.
15. The passenger asked the clerk when the train would arrive.
16. The speaker will rise from his seat when she reaches the venue.
17. She has been working in this company for four years.
18. Akanshatold me that I would not have to come for practice the next day.
19. Samir commanded her to close the door when she left.
20. She said to him, "May you lead a peaceful life!"

III. 1. (i) (d) If he knew that Lohan had been hit by a car the previous day
(ii) (b) It had happened
(iii) (a) He had been hit by the car
2. (i) (c) Why she looked so worried
(ii) (a) Her exam was approaching
(iii) (b) It started from the following week
3. (i) (d) Whether he might help him
(ii) (a) If he could tell him where he could find the sneakers section
(iii) (b) Told him to come that way
4. (i) (a) If she liked sports
(ii) (b) Had been fond of it
(iii) (b) Which her favourite one was
5. (i) (b) How she had spent her winter vacation
(ii) (a) she had really enjoyed the vacation
(iii) (c) they had travelled to a desolate island

IV. 1. (i) Where I was going
(ii) To hop in the car
(iii) It would save me time
2. (i) He had not known that he had been interested in cooking
(ii) He loved cooking for friends and family
(iii) He would find one that he loved
3. (i) That he couldn't believe he had won the lottery
(ii) How he felt about that
(iii) He was filled with excitement
4. (i) How he could help him
(ii) He was suffering from indigestion
(iii) If he was suffering from headache also
5. (i) Why he had not done his homework
(ii) His sister had been sick
(iii) There had not been anybody else to take her to the doctor

Section C : Literature
Textbook : First Flight *(Prose)*

A Letter to God

by G L Fuentes

The following chapter 'A Letter to God' has been written by G L Fuentes. This chapter discusses the firm faith of a farmer called Lencho in God. When Lencho's crops are destroyed in the hailstorm and his whole family faces the prospect of going hungry, Lencho writes a letter to God asking for help. The story presents how Lencho is helped by the Postmaster who does not want to break Lencho's faith in God.

Lencho's Hope of Good Harvest

Lencho was a farmer who lived on the crest of a low hill with his family. His house was the only house in the entire valley. His field was full of ripe corn and easily visible from the house. Lencho was eagerly waiting for rain to have a good harvest so he could earn money for his family.

Lencho's Hope Turned into Despair

As Lencho had expected, it started raining at the time of supper (dinner). This made Lencho happy. He went outside to feel the rain on his body. The raindrops falling from the sky would make Lencho's crops better. As a result, Lencho would earn good money. Hence, the raindrops were like new coins for Lencho. However, suddenly strong winds began to blow and hailstones started to fall. The storm continued for an hour and the corn fields were completely destroyed.

This made Lencho sad. When the storm ended, Lencho went to his field with his sons. He told them that at least locusts (insects) would have left some crop that could be sold. Now, because of the storm, they have no crops to sell and earn money. As a result, they cannot buy food and would go hungry.

Lencho's Firm Belief in God

Though Lencho was a poor farmer and had lost all his crops, he had firm faith in God. He found his last hope in God and decided to write a letter to God for help. He asked God to send him a hundred pesos so that he could sow his field again and support his family until the new crops were harvested. He also wrote that if God would not help him, his family would die of hunger. Then, Lencho went to the post office and put his letter into the mailbox.

The Postmaster's Reaction to Lencho's Letter

In the post office, a postman found Lencho's letter and laughed after seeing the address on it. He took the letter to the postmaster who was a kind and friendly person. When the postmaster read the letter, he also laughed. However, soon he realised that the sender (Lencho) had true belief and faith in God. So, he decided to help the sender.

To help and keep the faith of Lencho in God, the postmaster requested his employees and friends to give some money for an act of charity. He also gave a part of his salary but he could collect only seventy pesos. He, then, put the money in an envelope and signed it as God.

Lencho Recieves the Money

Next Sunday, Lencho visited the post office where the postman gave him his letter. When Lencho saw the money, he wasn't surprised and became extremely happy. However, when he counted the money, his happiness turned to anger. It was seventy pesos while he had asked for hundred pesos.

Lencho Writes Another Letter

Lencho believed that God could not make such a mistake. So, he wrote a letter again. After writing his letter, Lencho again posted it. As soon as he left, the postmaster took out his letter and read it.

In that letter, Lencho had written that he had received only 70 pesos and asked God to send the remaining money. He also requested God not to send the money through post because the post office employees were a bunch of crooks, who might have stolen his money.

Word Meaning

Word	Meaning
crest	top of a mountain or hill
downpour	a heavy fall of rain
shower	drizzle
intimately	very well
supper	an evening meal, typically a light or informal one
God willing	by grace of God
regard	consider
draped	covered
plague	an unusually large number
solitary	single
instructed	taught
conscience	an inner sense of right and wrong
daybreak	dawn
peso	unit of currency in several Latin-American countries

Word	Meaning
sow	planting the seeds of a crop
heartily	loudly
amiable	friendly
correspondence	letters sent or received
resolution	firm decision
charity	help or money given to those in need
contentment	a state of happiness and satisfaction
deed	a brave or noble act
wrinkling	a slight line or fold in the skin of the face
lick	to strike with tongue gently
affixed	attached
blow	hard hit
bunch	group
crooks	dishonest people

NCERT FOLDER

NCERT Intext and Exercise Questions

ORAL COMPREHENSION CHECK 1 (NCERT PAGE 5)

Q.1 What did Lencho hope for?

Ans. Lencho hoped for a good rainfall so that his fields of ripe corn could provide him a good harvest.

Q.2 Why did Lencho say the raindrops were like 'new coins'?

Ans. Lencho said that the raindrops were like new coins because with rain, his fields of ripe corn would produce a good harvest. A good harvest would help him earn more money, bringing in prosperity to his family.

Q.3 How did the rain change? What happened to Lencho's fields?

Ans. The rain changed into a hail storm as a strong wind began to blow and huge hailstones began to fall. The hailstones completely destroyed Lencho's crops. They stripped his crops of flowers and leaves, leaving the fields barren and devoid of hope for a successful harvest.

Q.4 What were Lencho's feelings when the hail stopped? CBSE 2020

Ans. When the hail stopped, Lencho became sad and hopeless. All his flowering crops were destroyed due to the hailstones. He felt that no one could help his family and that they would face hunger.

CHECK 2 (NCERT PAGE 6)

Q.1 Who or what did Lencho have faith in? What did he do?

Ans. Lencho had faith in God. He believed that God sees everything and would help him.

Therefore, he wrote a letter to God asking him to send a hundred pesos so that he could sow his fields.

Q.2 Who read the letter? CBSE 2023

Ans. The postmaster read the letter.

Q.3 What did the postmaster do then? CBSE 2023

Ans. After reading Lencho's letter, the postmaster became serious and was impressed by Lencho's faith in God. He didn't want to break Lencho's faith. So, he decided to collect money from his employees and friends. He also gave a part of his salary and sent it to Lencho on behalf of God.

CHECK 3 (NCERT PAGE 7)

Q.1 Was Lencho surprised to find a letter for him with money in it?

Ans. No, Lencho was not surprised to find a letter with money in it. He completely believed that God would help him by sending the money.

Q.2 What made him angry?

The postmaster, experiencing the contentment of a man who had performed a good deed, handed the letter to Lencho. How did Lencho react when he counted the money? CBSE 2024 C

Ans. When Lencho counted the money in the envelope, he got angry. There were only seventy pesos in the envelope while he had asked for hundred pesos.

He believed that God could not have made a mistake or denied him what he asked for so the shortfall in the money made him angry and disillusioned.

THINKING ABOUT THE TEXT (NCERT PAGE 7-8)

Q.1 Who does Lencho have complete faith in? Which sentences in the story tell you this?

Ans. Lencho has complete faith in God. The sentences which show this are

- But in the hearts of all who lived in that solitary house in the middle of the valley, there was a single hope-help from God.
- All through the night, Lencho thought only of his one hope: the help of God, whose eyes, as he had been instructed, see everything, even what is deep in one's conscience.
- "God", he wrote, "If you don't help me, my family and I will go hungry this year."
- He wrote 'To God' on the envelope, put the letter inside and still troubled, went to town.
- God could not have made a mistake nor could he have denied Lencho what he had requested.
- It said, "God: of the money that I asked for, only seventy pesos reached me. Send me the rest, since I need it very much."

Q.2 Why does the postmaster send money to Lencho? Why does he sign the letter 'God'?

Ans. When the postmaster reads Lencho's letter, he realises the firm belief and faith that Lencho has in God. He does not want this faith to be broken and therefore, decides to send money to Lencho.

The postmaster signs the letter as 'God' so that Lencho believes that God has helped him and maintains his faith.

Q.3 Did Lencho try to find out who had sent the money to him? Why/why not?

Ans. No, Lencho did not try to find out who had sent the money to him. The reason was that he could not believe that it could be anybody other than God who would send him the money. His faith in God was so strong that he believed that only God could have sent money to him.

Q.4 Who does Lencho think has taken the rest of the money? What is the irony in the situation? (Remember that the irony of a situation is an unexpected aspect of it. An ironic situation is strange or amusing because it is the opposite of what is expected).

Ans. Lencho thinks that the post office employees have taken the rest of the money because he had asked for a hundred pesos from God. Howerer, in the letter there were only seventy pesos. He believes that God could not make such a mistake. So, he assumes that the post office employees must have stolen the money.

The irony in the situation is that Lencho suspected the people who helped him when he's in trouble. He tried to keep his faith alive in God while being blind to the goodness and godliness of his fellow humans.

Q.5 Are there people like Lencho in the real world? What kind of a person would you say he is? You may select appropriate words from the box to answer the question.

Greedy, Naive, Stupid, Ungraceful, Selfish, Comical, Unquestioning

Ans. Yes, there are people like Lencho in the real world. Such people have blind faith in God and believe that God will help them in bad situations.

Lencho is a simple and a hardworking farmer who has extreme faith in God. He is innocent and naive but not stupid. He has an unquestioning attitude for he is unable to realise that someone other than God would help him.

Q.6 There are two kinds of conflict in the story between humans and nature and between humans themselves. How are these conflicts illustrated?

Ans. The story illustrates various conflicts. One of the main conflicts is the one between humans and nature. In the beginning of the story, the hardworking farmer Lencho is completely sure that a good rainfall will lead to a fruitful harvest. However, nature had other plans. The kind rainfall that Lencho had expected, quickly transformed into an unforgiving hailstorm which completely destroyed his crops. Thus, nature stands against the hopes of the humans.

Another conflict emerges among the humans themselves because of their various modes of belief. While the post office employees understand that helping a fellow human is an act of charity, Lencho himself is naively dependent on God. He cannot consider that God is an absent figure and that the money he had received could be from another source. So, he accuses the post office employees of stealing the money that he believed had been sent by 'God'.

Thus, the story portrays Lencho against both nature and his fellow humans.

THINKING ABOUT LANGUAGE

(NCERT PAGE 8-9)

I. Look at the following sentence from the story.

Suddenly a strong wind began to blow and alongwith the rain very large hailstones began to fall.

'Hailstones' are small balls of ice that fall like rain. A storm in which hailstones fall is a 'hailstorm'. You know that a storm is bad weather with strong winds, rain, thunder and lightning.

There are different names in different parts of the world for storms, depending on their nature. Can you match the names in the box with their descriptions below and fill in the blanks? You may use a dictionary to help you.

gale, whirlwind, cyclone, hurricane, tornado, typhoon

Q.1 A violent tropical storm in which strong winds move in a circle ......c...... .

Ans. cyclone

Q.2 An extremely strong wind ......a...... .

Ans. gale

Q.3 A violent tropical storm with very strong wind ......p......

Ans. typhoon

Q.4 A violent storm whose centre is a cloud in the shape of a funnel ......n...... .

Ans. tornado

Q.5 A violent storm with very strong winds, especially in the Western Atlantic Ocean ......r...... .

Ans. hurricane

Q.6 **A very strong wind that moves very fast in a spinning movement and causes a lot of damage ......I...... .**

Ans. whirlwind

II. Notice how the word 'hope' is used in these sentences from the story:

(a) I hope it (the hailstorm) passes quickly.

(b) There was a single hope: help from God.

In the first example, 'hope' is a verb which means you wish for something to happen. In the second example, it is a noun meaning a chance for something to happen.

Match the sentences in column A with the meaning of 'hope' in column B.

	A		B
1.	Will you get the subjects you want to study in college? I hope so.	(a)	a feeling that something good will probably happen.
2.	I hope you don't mind by saying this but I don't like the way you are arguing.	(b)	thinking that this would happen (it may or may not have happened).
3.	This discovery will give new hope to HIV/AIDS sufferers.	(c)	stopped believing that this good thing would happen.
4.	We were hoping against hope that the judges would not notice our mistakes.	(d)	wanting something to happen (and thinking it quite possible).
5.	I called early in the hope of speaking to her before she went to school.	(e)	showing concern that what you say should not offend or disturb the other person: a way of being polite.
6.	Just when everybody had given up hope, the fishermen came back, seven days after the cyclone.	(f)	wishing for something to happen, although this is very unlikely.

Ans. 1. (b) 2. (e) 3. (a)
4. (f) 5. (d) 6. (c)

III. Relative Clauses

Look at these sentences

(a) All morning Lencho - *who knew his fields intimately* - looked at the sky.

(b) The woman, *who was preparing supper,* replied, "Yes, God willing."

The italicised parts of the sentences give us more information about Lencho and the woman. We call them relative clauses. Notice that they begin with a relative pronoun 'who'. Other common relative pronouns are whom, whose, and which.

The relative clauses in (a) and (b) above are called non-defining, because we already know the identity of the person they describe. Lencho is a particular person, and there is a particular woman he speaks to. We don't need the information in the relative clause to pick these people out from a larger set.

A non-defining relative clause usually has a comma in front of it and a comma after it (some writers use a dash (—) instead, as in the story). If the relative clause comes at the end, we just put a full stop.

Join the sentences given below using *who, whom, whose, which*, as suggested.

(i) I often go to Mumbai. Mumbai is the commercial capital of India. (*which*)

Ans. I often go to Mumbai, *which* is the commercial capital of India.

(ii) My mother is going to host a TV show on cooking. She cooks very well. (*who*)

Ans. My Mother, *who* cooks very well, is going to host a TV show on cooking.

(iii) These sportspersons are going to meet the President. Their performance has been excellent. (*whose*)

Ans. These sportspersons, *whose* performance has been excellent, are going to meet the President.

(iv) Lencho prayed to God. His eyes see into our minds. (whose)

Ans. Lencho prayed to God, *whose* eyes see into our minds.

(v) This man cheated me. I trusted him. (*whom*)

Ans. This man, *whom* I trusted, cheated me.

Sometimes the relative pronoun in a relative clause remains 'hidden'. For example, look at the first sentence of the story.

(a) The house — the only one in the entire valley — sat on the crest of a low hill. We can rewrite this sentence as:

(b) The house — which was the only one in the entire valley — sat on the crest of a low hill.

In (a), the relative pronoun which and the verb was are not present.

IV. Using Negatives for Emphasis

We know that sentences with words such as no, not or nothing show the absence of something, or contradict something. For example

(a) This year we will have no corn. (Corn will be absent)

(b) The hail has left nothing. (Absence of a crop)

(c) These aren't raindrops falling from the sky, they are new coins. (Contradicts the common idea of what the drops of water falling from the sky are)

But sometimes negative words are used just to emphasise an idea. Look at these sentences from the story

(d) Lencho...had done nothing else but see the sky towards the North-East. (He had done only this)

(e) The man went out for no other reason than to have the pleasure of feeling the rain on his body. (He had only this reason)

(f) Lencho showed not the slightest surprise on seeing the money. (He showed no surprise at all)

Now look back at example (c). Notice that the contradiction in fact serves to emphasise the value or usefulness of the rain to the farmer.

Find sentences in the story with negative words, which express the following ideas emphatically.

(a) The trees lost all their leaves.

(b) The letter was addressed to God himself.

(c) The postman saw this address for the first time in his career.

Ans. (a) Not a leaf remained on the trees.

(b) It was nothing less than a letter to God.

(c) Never in his career as a postman had he seen that address.

V. Metaphors

The word metaphor comes from a Greek word meaning 'transfer'. Metaphors compare two things or ideas–a quality or feature of one thing is transferred to another thing. Some common metaphors are

- the leg of the table: The leg supports our body. So, the object that supports a table is described as a leg.
- the heart of the city: The heart is an important organ in the centre of our body. So, this word is used to describe the central area of a city.

In pairs, find metaphors from the story to complete the table below. Try to say what qualities are being compared. One has been done for you.

Object	Metaphor	Quality or Feature Compared
Cloud	Huge mountains of clouds	The mass or 'hugeness' of mountains
Raindrops		
Hailstones		
Locusts		
		An epidemic (a disease) that spreads very rapidly and leaves many people dead
	An ox of a man	

Ans.

Object	Metaphor	Quality or Feature Compared
Cloud	Huge mountains of clouds	The mass or 'hugeness' of mountains
Raindrops	Coins	Money that a good crop will bring
Hailstones	Frozen pearls	Frozen water that looks like pearls
Locusts	A plague of locusts	An epidemic (a disease) that spreads very rapidly and leaves many people dead
Lencho	An ox of a man	Strong and hard-working

REVIEW EXERCISE

Including Competency Based Questions

Part I

Multiple Choice Questions

1. Lencho's hopes were belied because

(a) the sunlight was enough.
(b) the rain was still going on.
(c) the hail lasted for an hour.
(d) the children were unsuccessful.

Ans. (c) the hail lasted for an hour.

2. Lencho compared the magnitude of damage with ....

(a) attack by rats (b) attack by crows
(c) plague of locusts (d) None of these

Ans. (c) plague of locusts

3. What did Lencho say to his sons after the hail passed?

A. A plague of locusts would have left more than this. The hail has left nothing.

B. This year we will have no corn. All our work, for nothing.

C. There's no one who can help us.

D. We'll all go hungry this year.

(a) Only A (b) A and B
(c) B, C and D (d) All of these

Ans. (d) All of these

4. Why are locusts mentioned in the text? Competency Based

(a) To show how unpredictable farming can be
(b) To compare this event to a past experience
(c) To suggest that God was playing a role in the events
(d) To indicate how much damage was done to the crops

Ans. (d) To indicate how much damage was done to the crops

5. Lencho is .... when he says, "that's what they say: no one dies of hunger." CBSE SQP 2021 Term 1

(a) doubtful (b) stressed (c) confused (d) dismissive

Ans. (d) dismissive

6. What was the family's attitude the night after the hailstorm? Competency Based

(a) Frustrated (b) Optimistic
(c) Confident (d) Furious

Ans. (b) Optimistic

7. Lencho's actions in the first paragraph show that he was .... Competency Based

(a) baffled (b) concerned
(c) alarmed (d) encouraged

Ans. (b) concerned

8. Why is Lencho compared to an ox? Competency Based

(a) To suggest that people underestimated him
(b) To show how hard he worked
(c) To insult his intelligence
(d) To emphasise his size

Ans. (b) To show how hard he worked

9. Lencho was an ox of a man, working like an animal in the fields, but still he knew how to write. What attitude does this sentence highlight? Competency Based

(a) Prejudice (b) Tolerance
(c) Scepticism (d) Appreciation

Ans. (a) Prejudice

10. How did the postman feel when he found the letter? Competency Based

(a) Amused (b) Amazed
(c) Generous (d) Sympathetic

Ans. (a) Amused

11. Why did the postman laugh heartily?

(a) On seeing a letter addressed to God
(b) On seeing Lencho's condition
(c) He heard a joke
(d) All of the above

Ans. (a) On seeing a letter address to God

12. Why did the postmaster turn serious on seeing the letter addressed to God?

(a) Because he realised that Lencho was asking for money.
(b) Because he realised that Lencho need Government's help.
(c) Because he realised that Lencho had immense faith in God.
(d) Because Lencho had an important task to do.

Ans. (c) Because he realised that Lencho had immense faith in God.

13. **Lencho's response to the first letter shows that his faith in God can be best described as ....** Competency Based

(a) shaken (b) evolving
(c) absolute (d) newly discovered

Ans. (c) absolute

14. **Why did Lencho become angry when he counted the money?**

(a) He received forty pesos less than what he had demanded from God.
(b) He received seventy pesos less than what he had demand from God.
(c) He received thirty pesos less than what he had demanded from God.
(d) He received hundred pesos less than what he had demanded from God.

Ans. (c) He received thirty pesos less than what he had demanded from God.

15. **Why did Lencho ask God not to send the money through mail?**

(a) Because he did not want to come to post office.
(b) Because he thought the post office employees had stolen it.
(c) Because post office was far away.
(d) None of the above

Ans. (b) Because he thought the post office employees had stolen it.

16. **What type of conflict does the chapter highlight?**

(a) Conflict between nature and humans
(b) Conflict among humans
(c) Conflict among God and humans
(d) Both (a) and (b)

Ans. (d) Both (a) and (b)

17. **What is the irony in the story?**

(a) Lencho was sad after the hailstorm even though he was the one waiting for a shower.
(b) Postmaster laughed at Lencho but arranged money for him.
(c) Lencho blamed the post office employees who in fact helped him.
(d) There is no irony.

Ans. (c) Lencho blamed the post office employees who in fact helped him.

18. **The story 'A Letter to God' is all about**

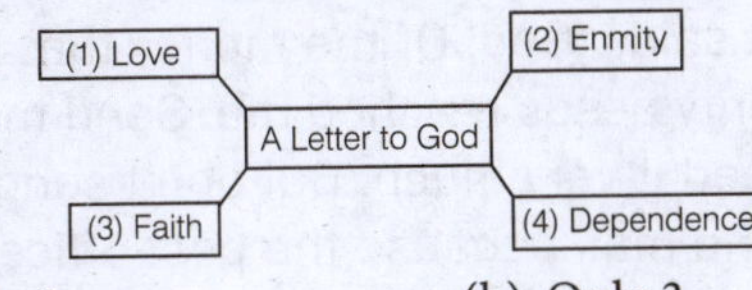

(a) Only 1 (b) Only 3
(c) 2, 3 and 4 (d) 1, 2 and 3

Ans. (b) Only 3

19. **What would you do if you were in the place of Lencho?**

1. You would blame God for everything happened
2. You would write a letter to God like Lencho
3. You would ask others for help
4. You would lose all hopes of regrowing your field ever

(a) Only 4 (b) Only 2 (c) 2 and 3 (d) 1 and 3

Ans. (a) Only 4

20. **After reading the second letter the postmaster is most likely to have been ....** Competency Based

(a) alarmed (b) offended
(c) distressed (d) bewildered

Ans. (b) offended

Extract Based Questions

1. **Read the following extract carefully and answer the questions that follow.**

The house-the only one in the entire valley-sat on the crest of a low hill. From this height one could see the river and the field of ripe corn dotted with the flowers that always promised a good harvest. The only thing the Earth needed was a good downpour or at least a shower. Throughout the morning Lencho who knew his fields intimately-had done nothing but see the sky towards the North-East. CBSE Question Bank 2021 Modified

(i) Read (a) - (c) and choose what Lencho is NOT likely to think while looking at his field?

(a) Just a downpour, God. And everything will be Perfect.
(b) All set for the grand harvest. I'm going to be rich
(c) I wish we have enough food to eat after this harvest.

Ans. (c) I wish we have enough food to eat after this harvest.

(ii) What do you understand by the phrase "the field of ripe corn dotted with the flowers"?

Ans. The given phrase means that the field of corn was completely covered by good and ripe harvest as well as flowers.

(iii) Fill in the blank with the correct word from the bracket.

Lencho's house was a .... (solitary/picturesque) house.

Ans. solitary

(iv) Why was Lencho hoping for rain while looking at the sky towards the North-East? Competency Based

Ans. Lencho was hoping for rain because his fields needed a good rain in order to produce a fruitful harvest. This would in turn earn him a good livelihood.

2. Read the following extract carefully and answer the questions that follow.

With a satisfied expression he regarded the field of ripe corn with its flowers, draped in a curtain of rain. But suddenly a strong wind began to blow and along with the rain very large hailstones began to fall. These truly did resemble new silver coins. The boys, exposing themselves to the rain, ran out to collect the frozen pearls.

"It's really getting bad now," exclaimed the man. "I hope it passes quickly." It did not pass quickly. For an hour the hail rained on the house, the garden, the hillside, the cornfield, on the whole valley. The field was white, as it covered with salt.

(i) Which of the following is a reason why the field was white?

(a) It was a cotton field
(b) It was drowned with ocean water
(c) It was covered with hailstones
(d) All of the above

Ans. (c) It was covered with hailstones

(ii) What can be said about Lencho on reading the words 'I hope it passes quickly'?

Ans. On reading the above text, it can be said that Lencho is an extremely faithful and optimistic man. Even though it starts to rain, which is soon accompanied by hailstones, he doesn't lose hope that nothing will go wrong with his cornfield. He has faith that no one will die of hunger because God will help them.

(iii) Fill in the blank with the correct word from the bracket.

Lencho is feeling .... (satisfied/hopeful) in the above extract.

Ans. hopeful

(iv) What does the author refer to as 'new silver coins'?

Ans. The author refers to the hailstones as new silver coins.

3. Read the following extract carefully and answer the questions that follow.

The following Sunday Lencho came a bit earlier than usual to ask if there was a letter for him. It was the postman himself who handed the letter to him while the postmaster, experiencing the contentment of a man who has performed a good deed, looked on from his office. Lencho showed not the slightest surprise on seeing the money; such was his confidence – but he became angry when he counted the money. God could not have made a mistake, nor could he have denied Lencho what he had requested.

(i) What was the belief of Lencho?

(a) God couldn't make a mistake in sending the money.
(b) God couldn't deny what he had requested.
(c) Money was stolen.
(d) Both (a) and (b)

Ans. (d) Both (a) and (b)

(ii) Who handed the letter to Lencho? What was the postmaster feeling while doing so?

Ans. The postman handed the letter to Lencho. While doing so, the postmaster was feeling both nervous and excited as he wanted to see Lencho's reaction upon receiving the money.

(iii) Read the given sentences and choose the correct statement(s). **Competency Based**

(A) Postmaster felt content on seeing Lencho receiving the money.

(B) Lencho became angry on seeing the money.

Ans. Both of the given statements are true.

(iv) Why did Lencho go a bit early to the post office the following Sunday?

Ans. Lencho went a bit early to the post office the following Sunday in order to receive the answer of his letter to God.

4. Read the following extract carefully and answer the questions that follow.

Lencho showed not the slightest surprise on seeing the money, such was his confidence - but he became angry when he counted the money. God could not have made a mistake, nor could he have denied Lencho what he had requested.

Immediately, Lencho went up to the window to ask for paper and ink. On the public writing table, he started to write, with much wrinkling of his brow, caused by the effort he had to make to express his ideas. When he finished, he went to the window to buy a stamp which he licked and then affixed to the envelope with a blow of his fist. The moment the letter fell into the mailbox the postmaster went to open it. It said, "God, Of the money that I asked for, only seventy pesos reached me. Send me the rest, since I need it very much. But don't send it to me through the mail because the post office employees are a bunch of crooks. Lencho."

CBSE Additional SQP 2022-23

(i) **Why was Lencho not surprised when he received the money?**

(a) Because he knew the post office employees were kind
(b) Because he knew his hard work would pay off
(c) Because he had been lucky in the past
(d) Because he had faith in a higher power

Ans. (d) Because he had faith in a higher power

(ii) **How did the postmaster most likely feel when he read Lencho's second letter?**

Ans. The postmaster would most likely feel a combination of confusion, worry, sympathy and frustration. He may also be offended at Lencho's claims that the employees of the post office were a bunch of crooks.

(iii) **Fill in the blank appropriately.**

The postmaster rushed to open Lencho's second letter. This tells us that the postmaster was .... to know the contents of the letter.

Ans. curious and eager

(iv) **Why did Lencho wrinkle his brow when writing the letter?**

(a) He was not able to put his thoughts into words.
(b) He was not sure that God would respond again.
(c) He was not comfortable writing in front of the others.
(d) He was not able to calculate how many pesos were missing.

Ans. (a) He was not able to put his thoughts into words.

5. Read the following extract carefully and answer the questions that follow.

When he finished, he went to the window to buy a stamp which he licked and then affixed to the envelope with a blow of his fist. The moment the letter fell into the mailbox the postmaster went to open it. It said: "God: Of the money that I asked for, only seventy pesos reached me. Send me the rest, since I need it very much. But don't send it to me through the mail because the post office employees are a bunch of crooks. Lencho."

CBSE Question Bank 2021 Modified

(i) **What was the most likely response that the postmaster expected in Lencho's second letter?**

(1) Sorrowful
(2) Gratitude
(3) Disappointment
(4) Elation
(5) Shock

Ans. 3 and 5

(ii) **Why did the postmaster rush to open the letter sent by Lencho?** **Competency Based**

Ans. The postmaster rushed to open the letter to read Lencho's response which he expected to be full of gratitude.

(iii) **Read (a) - (c) and pick the most suitable quote for this extract.**

(a) "It is easier to fool people than to convince them that they have been fooled." – Mark Twain
(b) "Real knowledge is to know the extent of one's ignorance."- Confucius
(c) "True generosity means accepting ingratitude." - Coco Chanel

Ans. (c) "True generosity means accepting ingratitude."- Coco Chanel

(iv) **How much money did Lencho receive?**

Ans. Lencho received only seventy pesos.

6. Read the following extract carefully and answer the questions that follow.

The moment the letter fell into the mailbox the postmaster went to open it. It said : "God : of the money that I asked for, only seventy pesos reached me. Send me the rest, since I need it very much. But don't send it to me through the mail because the post office employees are a bunch of crooks. Lencho."

CBSE 2021 Term 1 Modified

(i) **Fill in the blank with the correct word from the bracket.**

Lencho wrote the second letter as he was .... (hopeful/curious)

Ans. hopeful

(ii) **How can Lencho's tone be described in the second letter he wrote to God? Why?**

Ans. In the second Letter to God, Lencho's tone is haughty and demanding because he believes that he is owed the money he has demanded.

(iii) **The postmaster opened the letter expecting it to**

(A) be full of thanks to God
(B) show his happiness
(C) be full of anguish for getting less money
(D) be accusing God of being miserly

(a) (C) and (D)
(b) (A) and (B)
(c) (A) and (D)
(d) (D) and (B)

Ans. (b) (A) and (B)

(iv) **'The post office employees are a bunch of crooks'. The above statement is ....**

Ans. ironic

Part II

Short Answer Type Questions

1. Who was Lencho? What were his main problems?

Ans. Lencho was a hardworking farmer who lived on the top of a low hill with his family.

Lencho's main problems were rainfall and locusts. If rain had turned into hail or had not fallen when required, his crop would have failed. Further, if a plague of locusts had attacked his crops, he would have not been able to earn enough to feed his family.

2. What did Lencho hope for and why? **CBSE 2023**

Ans. Lencho hoped for good rainfall. He knew his fields very well and understood that his field of ripe corn needed a good rainfall to yield a good harvest.

3. What are the raindrops compared to and why? **CBSE 2023**

Ans. Raindrops are compared to coins. Lencho compares raindrops to coins because he knew that the raindrops would certainly be helpful in giving him rich harvest. Naturally, it would make him earn more money.

4. "The field was white, as if covered with salt." This is how the field is described after the hailstorm. The melting hailstones could have been easily seen as sugar cubes. Do you think comparing it with sugar would have been more appropriate? Why/ Why not?

Ans. No, comparing it with sugar would not be considered appropriate. This is because sugar signifies sweetness and happiness. It is often considered a metaphor for good things. Salt, on the other hand, signifies spoiling of things and can be used as a metaphor for bad things. In the story, the hailstorm had brought a lot of trouble and loss to Lencho's family. So, it is more appropriate to use salt rather than sugar.

5. Why did the night after the rains turn sorrowful for Lencho? **CBSE 2023**

Ans. The night after the rainfall turned sorrowful for Lencho because the rainfall he had hoped for, had turned into a hailstorm and completely destroyed his ripe crops. Because of this destruction, his family faced the prospect of going hungry that year.

6. People get support from family and friends during bad times. How does Lencho's family behave after the harvest is ruined? **CBSE Question Bank 2021**

Ans. After his entire crop was ruined in the hailstorm, Lencho's family members were despairing for the loss of their livelihood. However, they did not lose courage. In fact, they solaced him and asked him not to lose hope. They reminded him that in God's world, no one died of hunger. Lencho's entire family had faith in God's help.

7. "Lencho was an ox of a man, working like an animal in the fields, but still he knew how to write." What does this line tell us about the norm amongst such farmers then?

Ans. The given line indicates the general norm amongst people that farmers are hard working and diligent but they are uneducated. However, Lencho was literate, and could read and write.

8. What does Lencho's letter reveal about the socio-economic conditions of his community?

Ans. Lencho's letter highlights the struggles of rural communities, where farmers like him depend on successful harvests for survival. The devastation of the hailstorm highlights the vulnerability of agricultural livelihoods and the precariousness of economic stability.

9. In what way would writing a letter to God help Lencho tide over his crisis? **CBSE 2023**

Ans. Lencho had great faith in God and believed that God would definitely help him. In such a situation, writing a letter would allow him to directly ask God for help. This would ensure that Lencho received the proper help that he would need.

10. The postmaster had mixed emotions while opening the letter. Explain. **CBSE 2023**

Ans. It is true that the postmaster had mixed emotions on reading the letter written by Lencho to God. He laughed at the unusualness of the letter as no one had ever written such a letter addressed to God. At the same time, he realised that Lencho has great belief in God and so, he found the letter to be serious too.

11. Why and how did the postmaster help Lencho?

Or **Why does the postmaster send money to Lencho? Why does he sign the letter 'God'?** **DIKSHA**

Or **Who read the letter sent by Lencho? What did he do then?** **CBSE 2023**

Ans. The postmaster helped Lencho because he did not want Lencho's faith in God to be broken. He did so by collecting money from the post office employees and his friends. The postmaster himself also gave part of his salary. Then, he sent the collected money to Lencho through a letter and signed it in the name of God. It appeared that God had sent the money to Lencho.

12. Did the letter reach God? Why did the postmaster send a reply to Lencho?

Ans. The letter did not reach God in reality. It was the postmaster who took on the duty of God and collected as much money as he could to send to Lencho.
The postmaster replied to Lencho because he realised the firm belief and faith of Lencho in God. He did not want Lencho's faith in God to be broken and hence, wrote a letter from God to Lencho.

13. How much money did Lencho need? How much did he get? **Diksha**

Ans. Lencho needed one hundred pesos to sow a new crop and support his family till the next harvest. However, Lencho got only seventy pesos in the letter, which was less than what he had requested from God.

14. Why did Lencho call the post office employees crooks?

Ans. Lencho called the post office employees a bunch of crooks because he thought that they had taken some part of the money that God had sent him. He had asked for 100 pesos but received only 70 pesos.
He believed that God would not send him less money and thought that the post office employees had taken 30 pesos from his envelope.

15. Do you think that Lencho was right to call the post office employees a 'bunch of crooks'? Why or why not? **Competency Based**

Ans. I think Lencho was not right in calling the post office employees a 'bunch of crooks'. The reason is that the post office employees did not steal money from the letter. In fact, they contributed whatever they could and then, sent the money to Lencho.

16. Lencho waited eagerly for a reply to his letter to God. Do you think the postmaster was also very keen to know Lencho's reaction upon receiving the 'reply'? **CBSE Question Bank 2021**

Ans. Yes, I think that the postmaster was also keen to know Lencho's reaction as he thought that Lencho would have been ecstatic and surprised to see the money he had asked from God. He expected Lencho to be full of happiness and gratitude.

17. What, according to you, would have been the likely reaction of Lencho's wife upon knowing about him writing an actual letter to God? **CBSE Question Bank 2021**

Ans. According to me, if Lencho's wife got to know about the letter she would not have supported his idea. She would have preferred praying to God as a way to seek help. The woman would not have had such blind faith as to think that she could send a mail to God. She would have considered the letter to be a foolish act.

18. Explain how the description of the devastation caused by the hailstorm reflects the sadness within Lencho, in A Letter to God?
Refer to the given lines, from the text -
Not a leaf remained on the trees. The corn was totally destroyed. The flowers were gone from the plants. Lencho's soul was filled with sadness. **CBSE SQP 2023**

Ans. The description of the devastation caused by the hailstorm reflects the sadness within Lencho. Lencho's statements "not a leaf remained on the trees" and "the flowers were gone from the plants" suggests a sense of emptiness and loss. These statements reflect Lencho's feelings of despair and disappointment. The emptiness of the landscape thus serves as a powerful metaphor for Lencho's inner state of mind, emphasising his disappointment and hopelessness.

19. Lencho did not bother exploring any other means to resolve his situation but just turned to God. Do you feel that his approach was justified? Why/Why not? **CBSE Additional SQP 2023**

Ans. Lencho's approach cannot be justified as we know that even God helps those who help themselves. Seeking help from someone is understood but not putting in any effort and depending on others or hoping for one's luck to work is something one cannot practically believe in.

20. Why do you think Lencho from 'A Letter to God' is able to predict the forthcoming rainfall even before the clouds appear? Answer in 20-30 words.

Or **Was Lencho's prediction of the weather accurate? Give reasons for your answer.** **Competency Based**

Ans. Lencho is able to predict the forthcoming rainfall as he is a farmer. His profession requires him to be knowledgeable about weather and is conscious of the weather cycle as his harvest depends on it. Hence, he can understand the signs of good rainfall.

21. Explain the irony in the chapter, 'A Letter to God'. **CBSE 2024**

Ans. The irony in 'A Letter to God' lies in the protagonist's/Lencho's unwavering faith in God for financial assistance, only for his prayers to be answered by human actions. His belief that God would send him money is met, not through a miracle but by the post office workers who collected some money to send to him. The irony intensifies when Lencho, upon receiving less money than he asked for, blames the post office workers of stealing. He never doubted divine benevolence but failed to recognise the human compassion that answered his prayers.

22. Faith is like a ray of hope in a distressful situation. Discuss 'A Letter to God' with reference to Lencho's unflinching faith in God. CBSE 2025

Or **What role does faith play in Lencho and the postmaster's actions throughout the story?**

Ans. Faith serves as Lencho's guiding force, driving him to seek help from God in times of need. Despite adversity, he maintains unwavering faith in divine intervention, believing God will provide for him and his family. The postmaster's decision to respond to Lencho's letter reflects a belief in the power of faith and the importance of compassion. Despite his initial amusement, he recognises the sincerity of Lencho's plea and takes action to help him, demonstrating kindness and empathy.

23. What does the postmaster's reaction to Lencho's letter reveal about his character? CBSE SQP 2024

Ans. The postmaster's reaction to Lencho's letter reveals that the postmaster is deeply moved by Lencho's faith. This prompts a compassionate response rather than dismissal or mockery. This also highlights that he respects Lencho's belief system, despite its naivety, indicating a high regard for individual faith and personal convictions.

Long Answer Type Questions

1. The people at the post-office contribute to put together whatever they can manage, for Lencho.

(i) What do you think was the main reason behind their help? Would you have done the same if you were one of the employees?

(ii) As an employee, write about your perspective and reason(s) for contributing to the fund. The fact that you don't want to say 'no' to a cause initiated by your boss, can also be an equally compelling reason! CBSE Question Bank 2021

Ans. (i) The main reason behind helping Lencho is to keep his faith in God intact as well as to perform an act of charity. Yes, I would have done the same if I were one of the employees.

(ii) As an employee, the request of donation would have not been readily accepted by the people of the post office. However, at the same time, saying no to a cause initiated by the boss would also not have been correct. This would have been an equally compelling reason to agree to donate. Yet, I would have been driven to donate primarily by the true spirit of humanity which is to help others in time of need.

2. Lencho, the protagonist of 'A Letter to God', is portrayed as a hardworking and devout man who faces adversity with resilience and unwavering faith. Comment.

Ans. Lencho, the protagonist of 'A Letter to God', is portrayed as a hardworking and devout man who faces adversity with resilience and unwavering faith. Lencho is depicted as a diligent and industrious farmer deeply connected to his land. He works tirelessly in his fields, demonstrating a strong work ethic and a commitment to providing for his family through agriculture. As a family man, we see his concern for his family's well-being in his willingness to seek help from God to ensure their survival. He is motivated by his needs and the desire to provide for his loved ones, demonstrating a selfless and caring nature.

Lencho's faith in God is central to his character. He believes wholeheartedly in the power of prayer and seeks divine assistance when faced with challenges. His decision to write a letter to God requesting financial help reflects his profound faith and trust in a higher power. While Lencho is deeply religious and trusts God's providence, he is also pragmatic. He takes practical steps to address his challenges, such as writing a letter and seeking financial assistance, rather than passively resigning himself to fate.

Despite his hardships, Lencho remains humble and grounded. He does not harbour bitterness towards God or others for his misfortunes but accepts his circumstances. He refuses to give in to despair or hopelessness, instead of choosing to maintain hope for the future and continue working towards a better outcome.

Thus, Lencho emerges as a multifaceted character who embodies faith, resilience, generosity, practicality, and humility. His portrayal highlights the complexities of human nature and the capacity for hope and perseverance in the face of adversity.

3. Read the given anecdote and analyse the similarities and differences with reference to 'A Letter to God'.

A very poor woman called-in a radio station asking for help from God. A non-believer, also listening to this radio program, decided to make fun of the woman. He got her address, called his secretary and ordered her to buy food and take it to the woman. However, the instruction was: "When the woman asks who sent the food, tell her that it's from the devil." When the secretary arrived at the woman's house, the woman was very happy and grateful for the help. The Secretary then asked her, "Don't you want to know who sent the food?"

The woman replied, "No, I don't even care because when God orders, even the devil obeys!"

CBSE Question Bank 2021

Ans. There are many similarities between this anecdote and the story presented in 'A Letter to God'. In both the stories, people show immense faith in God. Much like

Lencho, the old woman blindly believes in God and hopes that God will help her. She also believes in the presence of devil just like Lencho who believes that people at the post office are crooks. Further, the people around both the old woman and Lencho make fun of them. Nonetheless, these people are the ones that help the needy.

The anecdote and the story also have some differences. In the case of Lencho, he gets angry when he finds that the money he received was less. On the other hand, the old woman is happy to accept help from a non believer.

4. The postmaster was a representative of God. Evaluate this statement in the context of your understanding of 'A Letter to God'.

CBSE Question Bank 2021

Ans. The postmaster is rightly depicted as a representative of God because he managed to collect money for Lencho who was helpless at that time. As God can't be physically present everywhere to help his children, people believe that he relieves their sufferings through his representatives. Here, that representative is the postmaster who acts as the epitome of humanity.

When Lencho needed money, he had written a letter to god asking for 100 pesos. When the postmaster found the letter, he laughed but eventually decided on helping Lencho. He used his salary and collected little amount of money from the other employees and managed to put together 70 pesos. He, then, put them in an envelope addressing himself as God so that Lencho's faith in God would not be broken. When Lencho was in trouble, the postmaster helped him without looking for anything in return. So, in this way the postmaster was a representative of God.

5. "Humanity still exists", is what one gets to know after reading 'A Letter to God' in which firm faith in God of a poor farmer and helpfulness of the post office employees are aptly depicted? Write a paragraph on the human qualities in it, in about 120-150 words. Give the paragraph a suitable title.

Ans. **Existence of Humanity**

The story 'A Letter to God' written by GL Fuentes reinforces our faith in humanity. After reading the story, we come to know that there are people who help others without any self-interest.

In the story, the postmaster and other post office employees illustrate an example of humanity and kindness for others. They were really moved by Lencho's faith in God and decided to help him to keep his faith alive and firm. Even though it was not possible for them to collect hundred pesos, they managed to collect seventy pesos and kept them in an envelope for Lencho. They signed it as 'God' to further reinforce Lencho's faith in God.

This act shows us the true picture of humanity and motivates us to be noble and kind.

ASSESSMENT EXERCISE

Extract Based Questions

Read the following extract carefully and answer the questions that follow.

On the public writing-table, he started to write, with much wrinkling of his brow, caused by the effort he had to make to express his ideas. When he finished, he went to the window to buy a stamp which he licked and then affixed to the envelope with a blow of his fist.

The moment the letter fell into mailbox, the postmaster went to open it. It said, "God of the money that I asked for, only seventy pesos reached me. Send me the rest, since, I need it very much. But don't send it to me through the mail, because the post office employees are a 'bunch of crooks'. Lencho."

(i) Why were Lencho's brows 'wrinkling'?

(ii) Select the option that correctly captures the usage of the word 'affix' in the above extract.

(a) Meanwhile he sought to affix Great Britain and Austria from the alliance.

(b) That means that they're less likely to affix.

(c) In the car, they secure easily to a stand and affix for portable use.

(d) The boy scout needed help to affix his badge to his uniform.

(iii) In your own words, write the content of Lencho's second letter to God.

(iv) What can you say about the postmaster's emotions in the given extract?

Short Answer (SA) Type Questions

1. How did Lencho react after the hailstorm stopped?
2. Why did the post office employees find Lencho's letter funny?
3. How did the postmaster decide to resolve Lencho's problem?
4. After receiving Lencho's response letter to God, how would the postmaster's impression of Lencho may change?
5. How does Lencho's reaction to the incomplete amount demonstrate his character?

Long Answer (LA) Type Questions

1. What qualities are reflected in the characters of the post office employees?
2. Do you believe in the existence of God? Give reasons on the basis of the lesson 'A Letter to God'.
3. Assuming that Lencho's sons found out about the letter Lencho had sent to God through mail. Write a short dialogue on the basis of their reactions and have they confronted their father. **Competency Based**
4. Every person places their faith in different things. Some have complete faith in God while others have faith in their abilities and optimism. Write a blog in about 100-120 words on what and where you put your faith and belief in. **Competency Based**

Nelson Mandela: Long Walk to Freedom

by Nelson Rolihlahla Mandela

CHAPTER 2

CHAPTER SUMMARY The following chapter 'A Long Walk to Freedom' has been taken from the autobiography of Nelson Mandela by the same name. The chapter portrays the installation of the first democratic government of South Africa in 1994. The chapter tells us about Nelson Mandela's views about freedom. The reader gets information about Mandela's childhood, adolescence, 30 years of his prison and his journey as a freedom fighter.

Establishment of the First Democratic Government of South Africa

On 10th May, 1994, the first democratic, non-racial government of South Africa was established. The inauguration ceremony took place in a sandstone ampitheatre formed by the Union Buildings in Pretoria. The Union Buildings had been the seat of white power for many years. However, on 10th May, for the first time, leaders from all across the world came to South Africa.

Nelson Mandela had come to the ceremony with his daughter Zenani. First, Mr. de Klerk was sworn in as the second Deputy President and Thabo Mbeki as the first Deputy President. After them, Mandela took his oath as the President of a free South Africa. He pledged to obey and uphold the Constitution and to devote himself to the well-being of the Republic and its people.

Mandela Addressed the Guests

After taking oath, Mandela addressed his guests. He promised to create a society which all humanity would be proud of. He thanked the international leaders for joining the ceremony that represented a common victory of justice, peace and human dignity.

He promised that he would work hard to remove poverty, deprivation, sufferings, gender and other discrimination from the society. He also promised that the new society would bring hope, equality and freedom for all.

Display of the Military Power by South African Jets

After Mandela had taken the oath, South African jets displayed the military power. They also showed the loyalty of military to democracy. The highest military generals saluted him. He recounted that they would have arrested him some years before. Impala jets flew overhead leaving a smoke trail of black, red, green, blue and gold-the colours of the new South African flag. It was followed by the playing of two national anthems. The whites sang '*Nkosi Sikelel-i Africa*' and the blacks sang '*Die Stem*' the old anthem of the Republic which ended the ceremony.

Apartheid and South Africa

On the day of the inauguration, Nelson Mandela remembered the past wherein the whites had formed a system of racial dominance against the blacks. He recalled that the days after the Anglo-Boer War when he was born in the first decade of the twentieth century, the white had started dominating the Africans.

They created a system that was the basis of the one of the harshest and cruelest societies. Now, after more than 80 years, the system of racial differentiation or apartheid has been replaced. Today, rights and freedom of all the people are recognised.

Mandela Recalled the Sacrifices of Freedom Fighters

On the auspicious day, Mandela regretted the loss of thousands of people and remembered their sacrifices for the freedom from oppression. He thought of himself as the sum of all those African patriots who sacrificed their lives before him. He was pained that he couldn't thank them.

He recalled great freedom fighters like Oliver Tambos, Walter Sisulu, Chief Luthuli, Yusuf Dadoo, Bram Fischer, Robert Sobukwe, etc. who were the men of uncommon courage, wisdom and generosity. He considered that depths of oppression create heights of character. From these freedom fighters, Mandela learnt that courage is not lack of fear but victory over that fear. Mandela believed that the citizens are the real wealth of the country.

Man's Natural Goodness

Mandela believed that being white or black is not the token of one's goodness or superiority. No one is born hating other people due to colour or religion. Mandela stated that if people can learn to hate, then they can be taught to love because love comes naturally to human heart. He believed that the flame of humanity's goodness could never be extinguished.

Twin Obligations of Man

Mandela believed that every man had two obligations-one to his family and the other to his nation. He believed that in a civil and human society every man should be able to fulfill both of them. However, a black man born in South Africa, like him, could not fulfill both. In order to do something for his nation, Mandela was taken away from his family. Thus, he could never fulfill his obligations towards his family.

Mandela's Concept of Freedom

Mandela remembered that as a child, freedom for him meant being able to do what he wanted. He wanted to run in the fields, swim in the river that flowed, roast mealies and ride the bulls. As long as he obeyed his father and the rules of his tribe, he was free in every possible way. As a student, he wanted freedom just for himself to stay out at night, read what he wanted and go wherever he chose. Then, as a young man in Johannesburg, he wanted freedom to achieve his dreams, start a family, earn for himself, etc. As he grew up, he started realising that the freedom that he enjoyed as a child was just an illusion.

Mandela Joined African National Congress

Mandela realised that his complete community including him lacked freedom. He joined the African National Congress with a desire to gain freedom, respect and dignity for his community.

The desire for freedom for people as a whole changed his whole life. He transformed from a frightened young man to a bold person which turned him from a law abiding person to become a criminal. He realised that freedom is indivisible. Mandela said that the chains on any one of the people, were the chains on all of them. And the chains on all of his people were the chains on him.

Mandela's Realisation

Mandela realised that he could not enjoy his freedom when his community was not free. He also realised that just like oppressed, the oppressor is also not free.

The oppressed is a prisoner of hatred, prejudice and narrow-mindedness. Thus, both the oppressor and the oppressed alike are robbed of their humanity. Both of them must be liberated.

Word Meaning

Word	Meaning
apartheid	racial segregation or racial discrimination
autobiography	life story (biography) of a person written by that person himself or herself
amphitheatre	large open theatre
dignitaries	eminent persons
oppression	harsh and unfair treatment
jubilant	joyful, happy
dawned	began
besieged	surrounded by
decades	periods of ten years
supremacy	being superior
installation	placement
sworn	took an oath
confer	to give
outlaws	deprived of the benefit and protection of the law
rare privilege	uncommon right
possession	control
emancipation	freedom from restriction; liberation
bondage	slavery
discrimination	state of being treated differently
reign	rule
awe	respect and fear
spectacular array	attractive display
troop carriers	vehicles carrying soldiers
pinpoint precision	complete/ perfect order
bedecked	decorated
not unmindful	aware
chevron	a figure or pattern having the shape of a 'V'
trail	line
symbolised	was like a symbol, represented
despised	hated
overwhelmed	have a strong emotional effect
patched up	settled
erected	built
racial domination	control due to race
inhumane	cruel
overturned	abolished, invalidated and reversed

Word	Meaning
wrought	done, worked into shape by efforts
profound	deep and strong
brutality	cruelty
unintended	not thought of
comrades	fellow patriots
resilience	ability to deal with any hardship
defies	challenges
conquers	gets victory
grimmest	saddest, worst
pushed to our limits	pressurised
glimmer	glimpse, a dim perception
humanity	sympathy and kindness
extinguished	put out
obligations	duties
inclinations	natural tendencies, leanings
isolated	separated from others
inevitably	unavoidably
ripped	taken away
twilight existence	not being allowed to live freely
roast mealies	bake maize corns
abided	obeyed
illusion	a false idea or belief
transitory	not permanent
yearned	desired deeply
obstructed	hindered
curtailed	limited
dignity	respect
animated	gave life to
law-abiding	who obeys rules
virtuous	having high moral standards
oppressor	a cruel person who prevents other people from having any rights or freedoms
oppressed	a person who is subject to harsh and authoritarian treatment
bars	obstacles
prejudice	hatred, bias
narrow-mindedness	state of having intolerant beliefs

NCERT FOLDER

NCERT Intext and Exercise Questions

ORAL COMPREHENSION CHECK ❶ (NCERT PAGE 18)

Q.1 Where did the ceremonies take place? Can you name any public buildings in India that are made of sandstone?

Ans. The ceremonies took place in the sandstone amphitheatre formed by the Union Buildings in Pretoria. Some public buildings in India made of sandstone are the Rashtrapati Bhawan and the Red Fort in Delhi.

Q.2 Can you say how 10th May is an 'autumn day' in South Africa?

Ans. Since South Africa is in the Southern hemisphere, the month of May has the autumn season. Thus, literally, 10th May was an autumn day. Metaphorically, autumn indicates a rebirth. In the context of the Democratic Government of South Africa, the day indicates a rebirth of a just, peaceful and dignified society.

Q.3 At the beginning of his speech, Mandela mentions "an extraordinary human disaster." What does he mean by this? What is the "glorious ... human achievement" he speaks of at the end?

Ans. By mentioning 'an extraordinary human disaster', Mandela is referring to the practice of apartheid followed in South Africa. This meant that there was segregation based on colour due to which the blacks suffered a lot. They were not allowed to demand freedom and did not have any basic human right.

The 'glorious .... human achievement' that Mandela referred to in the end was that as South Africa had gained its freedom and a black person had become its President.

It was an achievement for the nation as earlier racial discrimination, oppression and torture was the basis of the nation. Now with the first non-racial democracy, each and every human was entitled to certain rights, freedoms and equality which were earlier denied.

Q.4 What does Mandela thank the international leaders for?

Ans. Mandela thanked the international leaders for their presence in the inaugural ceremony. Due to their presence, the event could be considered as a remarkable victory of the South African people for justice, peace and human dignity.

Q.5 What ideals does he set out for the future of South Africa?

Ans. Mandela set out certain ideals for the future of South Africa. He stated that all people would be free from poverty, deprivation, suffering and discrimination of all kinds. He envisions a society based on justice, peace and human dignity, where everyone would enjoy equal rights and privileges.

CHECK ❷ (NCERT PAGE 21)

Q.1 What do the military generals do? How has their attitude changed and why?

Ans. The military generals saluted Mandela to express their loyalty to democracy.

Their attitude has changed from what it used to be before the ceremony. Earlier, these generals had treated Mandela as a criminal and had arrested him. This attitude is changed due to the fact that Mandela was now the elected President of their country.

Q.2 Why were two National anthems sung?

Ans. Two National anthems, one of the blacks and the other of the whites, were sung to symbolise the transition from the old era of apartheid to the new era of democracy and inclusivity. This gesture represented reconciliation and unity among all South Africans, regardless of their past divisions.

Q.3 How does Mandela describe the systems of government in his country (i) in the first decade and (ii) in the final decade, of the twentieth century?

Ans. Mandela describes the systems of government in his country as follows

(i) In the first decade of the twentieth century, the white-skinned people of South Africa ended their own differences. They started a system of racial domination against the dark-skinned people of South Africa. The system they created formed the basis of one of the harshest and most inhumane societies the world had ever known.

(ii) In the final decade of the twentieth century, the previous system had been removed forever. It had been replaced by one that recognised the rights and freedoms of all people, regardless of the colour of their skin.

Q.4 What does courage mean to Mandela?

Ans. For Mandela, courage did not mean the absence of fear but the victory over it. According to him, brave men did not need to be fearless but they should be able to conquer fear, even in the face of adversity.

Q.5 What does he think is natural, to love or to hate?

Ans. He thinks love is natural whereas hate is not natural. The feeling of love comes to our heart spontaneously. In contrast, we have to learn how to hate as this feeling does not develop by itself.

CHECK® (NCERT PAGE 24)

Q.1 Which 'twin obligations' does Mandela mention?

***Or* What, according to Nelson Mandela, are a man's twin obligations?**

Ans. According to Nelson Mandela, every man has twin obligations. The first obligation is to look after his family, parents, wife and children. The second obligation is to serve his people, his community and his country.

Q.2 What did being free mean to Mandela as a boy and as a student? How does he contrast these 'transitory freedoms' with 'the basic and honourable freedoms'?

Ans. As a boy, for Mandela 'being free' did not have much meaning as he thought he was born free. He was free to do what he liked. He believed that as long as he obeyed his father and the rules of his tribe, he was free in every way.

As a student, Mandela realised that the freedoms that he enjoyed as a child were an illusion and he was actually not free. Then, he wanted the temporary freedom that existed only for his own self. He wanted freedom to stay out at night, read what he pleased and go wherever he wanted.

Then, as a young man, Mandela wanted basic and honourable freedom of achieving his potential, of earning money, of marrying and having a family.

However, very soon, he realised that these are 'transitory freedoms' and not true freedom. True freedom for Mandela, was the freedom of his community to live life with dignity and self-respect.

Q.3 Does Mandela think the oppressor is free? Why/ Why not?

Ans. Mandela does not think that the oppressor is free. He thinks that the oppressor is a prisoner of hatred. He is locked behind the bars of prejudice and narrow-mindedness.

THINKING ABOUT THE TEXT (NCERT PAGE 24)

Q.1 Why did such a large number of international leaders attend the inauguration? What did it signify the triumph of?

Ans. A large number of international leaders attended the inauguration to support the end of apartheid and establishment of a non-racial government of South Africa. It signified the triumph of the people over discrimination and oppression. It also signified the recognition of human equality.

Q.2 What does Mandela mean when he says he is "simply the sum of all those African patriots" who had gone before him?

Ans. When Mandela says he is 'simply the sum of all those African patriots', he means that he represents the ideals and the dreams for which the African patriots sacrified their lives. These patriots created a path of unity and cooperation which supported him in his journey to make South Africa free. In other words, as the new President of the nation, he represented the vision of all African freedom fighters.

Q.3 Would you agree that the 'depths of oppression' create 'heights of character'? How does Mandela illustrate this? Can you add your own examples to this argument?

Ans. Yes, I agree that the 'depths of oppression' create 'heights of character'. To illustrate this, Mandela gives the example of many patriots like Oliver Tambo, the Walter Sisulu, the Chief Luthuli, the Yusuf Dadoo, etc.

These freedom fighters emerged due to the extreme oppression faced by the blacks. They had extraordinary courage, wisdom and generosity.

We can also add our own examples to illustrate this. In our freedom struggle, the oppression of the Britishers produced courageous patriots such as Bhagat Singh, Lala Lajpat Rai and Mahatma Gandhi, among many others.

Q.4 How did Mandela's understanding of freedom change with age and experience?

Ans. Mandela's understanding of freedom changed a lot with age and experience. As a child, freedom for him meant doing things that he wanted to do because he was born free. For him, as long as he obeyed his father and followed the rules of his tribe, he was free in every way.

As he grew up, he realised that freedom that he enjoyed as a young boy was just an illusion. Infact, he did not have any freedom. Now, he developed a desire to gain freedom. When he was a student, the freedom was just for himself but soon he wanted freedom for his community.

Mandela slowly realised that not only his but the freedom of all blacks was also curtailed. With this understanding, he developed a hunger for the freedom of his people and started working for it.

Q.5 How did Mandela's 'hunger for freedom' change his life?

Ans. Mandela's hunger for freedom transformed his life by leading him to become a prominent anti-apartheid activist and ultimately the first black President of South Africa. His commitment to the liberation of his people propelled him to endure personal sacrifices, including imprisonment and separation from his family, in pursuit of justice and equality.

THINKING ABOUT LANGUAGE

(NCERT PAGE 24-26)

I. There are nouns in the text (*formation*, *government*) which are formed from the corresponding verbs (*form*, *govern*) by suffixing - (at) ion or *ment*. There may be change in the spelling of some verb - noun pairs : such as rebel, rebellion; constitute, constitution.

Q.1 Make a list of such pairs of nouns and verbs in the text.

Noun	Verb
rebellion	rebel
constitution	constitute

Ans.

Noun	Verb
rebellion	rebel
constitution	constitute
formation	form
government	govern
obligation	oblige
transformation	transform
discrimination	discriminate
deprivation	deprive
demonstration	demonstrate
oppression	oppress
imagination	imagine

Q.2 Read the paragraph below. Fill in the blanks with the noun forms of the verbs in brackets.

Martin Luther King's .... (contribute) to our history as an outstanding leader began when he came to the .... (assist) of Rosa Parks, a seamstress who refused to give up her seat on a bus to a white passenger. In those days, American Blacks were confined to positions of second class citizenship by restrictive laws and customs. To break these laws would mean .... (subjugate) and .... (humiliate) by the police and the legal system. Beatings, ... (imprison) and sometimes death awaited those who defied the system. Martin Luther King's tactics of protest involved non-violent .... (resist) to racial injustice.

Ans. Martin Luther King's **contribution** to our history as an outstanding leader began when he came to the **assistance** of Rosa Parks, a seamstress who refused to give up her seat on a bus to a white passenger. In those days, American Blacks were confined to positions of second class citizenship by restrictive laws and customs.

To break these laws would mean **subjugation** and **humiliation** by the police and the legal system. Beatings, **imprisonment** and sometimes death awaited those who defied the System. Martin Luther King's tactics of protest involved non-violent **resistance** to racial injustice.

II. Using the Definite Article with Names.

You know that the definite article 'the' is not normally used before proper nouns. Nor do proper nouns usually occur in the plural. (We do not say: *The Nelson Mandela or *Nelson Mandelas,) But now look at this sentence from the text.

......the decades of oppression and brutality .... produced the Oliver Tambos, the Walter Sisulus, ... of our time.

Used in this way with the and/or in the plural, a plural noun carries a special meaning. For example, what do you think the names above mean?

Choose the right answer.

(a) for example Oliver Tambo, Walter Sisulu, ...

(b) many other men like oliver Tambo, Walter Sisulu ..../many men of their type or kind, whose names may not be as well known.

Did you choose option (b)? Then you have the right answer!

Here are some more examples of 'the' used with proper names. Try to say what these sentences mean. (You may consult a dictionary if you wish. Look at the entry for 'the')

(i) Mr. Singh regularly invites the Amitabh Bachchan and the Shahrukh Khan to his parties.

(ii) Many people think that Madhuri Dixit is the Madhubala of our times.

(iii) History is not only the story of the Alexanders, the Napoleons and the Hitlers, but of ordinary people as well.

Ans. (i) This means that Mr. Singh regularly invites famous personalities as of the calibre of Amitabh Bachchan and Shahrukh Khan to his parties.

(ii) This means that Madhuri Dixit is compared to a landmark in acting in the form of legendary actress Madhubala.

(iii) This means that history is not only the story of the great fighters and leaders such as Alexander, Napoleon and Hitler, but also of ordinary people.

III. Idiomatic expression

Match the italicised phrases in Column A with the phrase nearest meaning in Column B.

(Hint: First look for the sentence in the text which the phrase in Column A occurs.)

	A		B
1.	I was *not unmindful of* the fact.	(i)	had not forgotten was aware of the fact
		(ii)	was not careful about the fact
		(iii)	forgot or was not aware of the fact
2.	When my comrades and I were *pushed to our limits*	(i)	pushed by the guards to the wall
		(ii)	took more than our share of beatings
		(iii)	felt that we could not endure the suffering any longer
3.	To reassure me and *keep me going*	(i)	make me go on walking
		(ii)	help me continue to live in hope in this very difficult situation
		(iii)	make me remain without complaining
4.	The basic and honourable freedoms of ... *earning my keep*...	(i)	earning enough money to live on
		(ii)	keeping what I earned
		(iii)	getting a good salary

Ans.

	A		B
1.	I was not unmindful of the fact	(i)	had not forgotten; was aware of the fact
2.	When my comrades and I were pushed to our limits	(iii)	felt that we could not endure the suffering any longer
3.	To reassure me and keep me going	(ii)	help me continue to live in hope in this very difficult situation
4.	The basic and honourable freedoms of … earning my keep…	(i)	earning enough money to live on

WRITING (NCERT PAGE 26-27)

I. Looking at Contrasts

Nelson Mandela's writing is marked by balance: many sentences have two parts in balance. Use the following phrases to complete the sentences given below.

(i) they can be taught to love.
(ii) I was born free.
(iii) but the triumph over it.
(iv) but he who conquers that fear.
(v) to create such heights of character.

(i) It requires such depths of oppression ....

(ii) Courage was not the absence of fear ....

(iii) The brave man is not he who does not feel afraid ....

(iv) If people can learn to hate ....

(v) I was not born with a hunger to be free ....

Ans. (i) to create such heights of character.

(ii) but the triumph over it.

(iii) but he who conquers that fear.

(iv) they can be taught to love.

(v) I was born free.

II. This text repeatedly contrasts the past with the present or the future. We can use coordinating clauses to contrast two views, for emphasis or effect. Given below are sentences carrying one part of the contrast. Find in the text the second part of the contrast and complete each item. Identify the words which signal the contrast. This has been done for you in the first item.

(i) For decades the Union Buildings had been the seat of white supremacy and now ....

(ii) Only moments before, the highest generals of the South African defence force and police .... saluted me and pledged their loyalty. ... not so many years before they would not have saluted ....

(iii) Although that day neither group knew the lyrics of the anthem ..., they would soon ....

(iv) My country is rich in the minerals and gems that lie beneath its soil, ...

(v) The Air Show was not only a display of pinpoint precision and military force, but ....

(vi) It was this desire for the freedom of my people .... that transformed .... into a bold one, that drove .... to become a criminal, that turned .... into a man without a home.

Ans. (i) For decades, the Union Buildings had been the seat of white supremacy and now, it was the site of a rainbow gathering of different colours and nations for the installation of South Africa's first democratic, non-racial government.

(ii) Only moments before, the highest generals of the South African defence force and police, their chests bedecked with ribbons and medals from days gone by, saluted me and pledged their loyalty.
I was not unmindful of the fact that not so many years before they would not have saluted but arrested me.

(iii) Although that day neither group knew the lyrics of the anthem they once despised, they would soon know the words by heart.

(iv) My country is rich in the minerals and gems that lie beneath its soil but I have always known that its greatest wealth is its people, finer and truer than the purest diamonds.

(v) The Air Show was not only a display of pinpoint precision and military force but a demonstration of the military's loyalty to democracy, to a new government that had been freely and fairly elected.

(vi) It was this desire for the freedom of my people that animated my life, that transformed a frightened young man into a bold one, that drove a law-abiding attorney to become a criminal, that turned a family-loving husband into a man without a home.

REVIEW EXERCISE

Including Competency Based Questions

Part I

Multiple Choice Questions

1. In the second paragraph of the text, the lovely sandstone amphitheatre is highlighted as what? Competency Based

(a) An unusual seat of government
(b) An important symbol of democracy
(c) A historic symbol of the struggle for freedom
(d) A symbol of contrast between the past and the present

Ans. (d) A symbol of contrast between the past and the present

2. It was a celebration of South Africa's first .... government.

(a) autocratic, racial
(b) democratic, non-racial
(c) democratic, racial
(d) monarch, non-racial

Ans. (b) democratic, non-racial

3. What do you understand by the term 'an extraordinary human disaster' as said by Nelson Mandela in his speech?

1. Racial discrimination
2. Policy of apartheid
3. Equal rights given
4. Racial domination by the Whites

Choose the correct codes.

(a) 1, 2 and 4
(b) 1, 2 and 3
(c) 2, 3 and 4
(d) 1, 3 and 4

Ans. (a) 1, 2 and 4

4. Mandela refers to liberty as 'newborn' because it CBSE SQP 2021 Term 1

(a) was dependent on others for growth and guidance
(b) had recently been attained with lots of struggle
(c) made people experience infant-like excitement
(d) arrived unexpectedly for everyone

Ans. (b) had recently been attained with lots of struggle

5. "We have achieved our political emancipation." What is the meaning of emancipation in the given statement?

(a) Freedom from restriction
(b) Enslavement
(c) Slavery
(d) Both (b) and (c)

Ans. (a) Freedom from restriction

6. What did Nelson Mandela pledge to liberate the people of South Africa from?

(a) Bondage of poverty and suffering
(b) Not having one's rightful benefits
(c) Discrimination based on gender
(d) All of the above

Ans. (d) All of the above

7. "The structure they created formed the basis of one of the harshest, most inhumane, societies the world has ever known."

Which structure is Mandela talking about?

(a) Racial domination against the black skinned
(b) Poverty and suffering
(c) Discrimination against the poor
(d) Oppression of women

Ans. (a) Racial domination against the black skinned

8. Which of these lines from 'A Long Walk to Freedom' hints at the end of apartheid in South Africa?

(a) I was not born with a hunger to be free. I was born free–free in every way that I could know
(b) ...I yearned for the basic and honourable freedoms of achieving my potential, of earning my keep,...
(c) Although that day neither group knew the lyrics of the anthem they once despised, they would soon know the words by heart
(d) ... the white-skinned peoples of South Africa patched up their differences and erected a system of racial domination against the dark-skinned peoples...

Ans. (c) Although that day neither group knew the lyrics of the anthem they once despised, they would soon know the words by heart.

9. Why does Mandela mentions various historical figures? **Competency Based**

(a) Show that black South African do not lack courage
(b) Acknowledge their efforts in the struggle against apartheid
(c) Illustrate that character is hardened by difficult circumstances
(d) Suggest that even apartheid had some positive consequences

Ans. (b) Acknowledge their efforts in the struggle against apartheid

10. No one is born hating another person ...but never extinguished. What quality of Mandela's does this paragraph show? **Competency Based**

(a) Resolve
(b) Fortitude
(c) Optimism
(d) Perseverance

Ans. (c) Optimism

11. Man's goodness is a flame that can be hidden but never extinguished. What does the author suggest in the above statement? **Competency Based**

(a) Goodness in humans is eternal
(b) Human goodness is slowly disappearing
(c) Most people think that goodness is weak
(d) Life experiences suppress people's goodness

Ans. (a) Goodness in humans is eternal

12. 'In life, every man has twin obligations'. **CBSE 2021 Term 1**

(a) First to his community and the second to his country
(b) First to his family and the second to his country
(c) First to his country and the second to his parents
(d) First to his community and the second to his family

Ans. (b) First to his family and the second to his country

13. Why was it impossible to fulfill the two main obligations in South Africa?

1. Because of the policy of Apartheid
2. Because they were born Black
3. Because they were born White
4. Because it was not allowed in South Africa

Choose the correct option.

(a) Both 2 and 3 (b) Only 3
(c) Both 1 and 2 (d) Only 4

Ans. (c) Both 1 and 2

14. When did Mandela find that he was prevented from fulfilling his obligations as a son, a brother, a father and a husband?

(a) In an attempt to serve his people
(b) In an attempt to serve his country
(c) In an attempt to serve his family
(d) In an attempt to serve his parents

Ans. (b) In an attempt to serve his country.

15. What lesson did Mandela learn about courage? **Competency Based**

(a) Anyone can show courage
(b) Courage is not found in the absence of fear
(c) Courage cannot be shown when one is afraid
(d) Courage can be found under any circumstance

Ans. (b) Courage is not found in the absence of fear

16. When is a man not truly free according to Nelson Mandela?

(a) When a man takes away someone else's freedom
(b) When a man takes away someone's family from them
(c) When a man does not show humanity
(d) When a man is narrow-minded

Ans. (a) When a man takes away someone else's freedom

17. Why did Mandela feel that oppressor must be liberated?

(a) Because an oppressor is also not free to do anything
(b) Because an oppressor is a prisoner of hatred
(c) Because an oppressor is locked behind the bars
(d) All of the above

Ans. (b) Because an oppressor is a prisoner of hatred

18. **Choose the statement which is not true in the context of the chapter 'Nelson Mandela: Long Walk to Freedom'.**

(a) Nelson Mandela was accompanied by his daughter, Zenani
(b) Mandela did not believe in freedom of his people
(c) Mandela joined African National Congress for the cause of National freedom
(d) He was grateful to all the freedom fighters of his country

Ans. (b) Mandela did not believe in freedom of his people

19. **What is Mandela's attitude towards his oppressors** Competency Based

(a) Magnanimous (b) Patronising
(c) Altruistic (d) Liberal

Ans. (a) Magnanimous

20. **What is the main purpose of the text?** Competency Based

(a) To pay tribute to the sacrifice of participants in the struggle
(b) To describe the conditions that used to exist in the past
(c) To reflect on the past in order to move forward
(d) To create a vision for the future

Ans. (c) To reflect on the past in order to move forward

Extract Based Questions

1. **Read the following extract carefully and answer the questions that follow.**

TENTH May dawned bright and clear. For the past few days I had been pleasantly besieged by dignitaries and world leaders who were coming to pay their respects before the inauguration. The inauguration would be the largest gathering ever of international leaders on South African soil. The ceremonies took place in the lovely sandstone amphitheatre formed by the Union Buildings in Pretoria. For decades this had been the seat of white supremacy, and now it was the site of a rainbow gathering of different colours and nations for the installation of South Africa's first democratic, non-racial government. CBSE 2024

(i) What do you infer from the following statement?

"The inauguration would be the largest gathering ever of international leaders on South African soil." Competency Based

Ans. From the given statement, it can be inferred that the inauguration ceremony is an extremely significant event, attracting the attention of world leaders. It indicates that the inauguration may be a turning point or important moment in the history of South Africa.

(ii) Explain in about 40 words the effective shift from white supremacy to a rainbow gathering.

Ans. The transition/shift from white supremacy to a rainbow gathering signifies the end of racial segregation and dominance by whites in South Africa. The 'rainbow gathering' signifies unity and inclusion and that all races, colours and nations are now equal and welcome. Thus, it is the start of democratic and non-racial government.

(iii) Which phrase would correctly substitute 'pleasantly besieged' in the given sentences from the extract?

Ans. The phrases that can substitute 'pleasantly besieged' are delightfully surrounded or agreeably inundated.

(iv) State True or False with reference to the given extract.

In the past the 'amphitheatre' had been a seat for theatrical performances

Ans. False. The 'amphitheatre' in the given extract does not refer to a place for theatrical performances in the past. Rather, it refers to the Union Buildings in Pretoria which had been the seat of white supremacy.

2. **Read the following extract carefully and answer the questions that follow.**

On that lovely autumn day, I was accompanied by my daughter Zenani. On the podium, Mr. de Klerk was first sworn in as second Deputy President. Then Thabo Mbeki was sworn in as first Deputy President. When it was my turn, I pledged to obey and uphold the Constitution and to devote myself to the wellbeing of the Republic and its people. To the assembled guests and the watching world, I said: "Today, all of us do, by our presence here... confer glory and hope to newborn liberty. Out of the experience of an extraordinary human disaster that lasted too long, must be born a society of which all humanity will be proud".

(i) What pledge did Nelson Mandela take?

(a) To obey and uphold the Constitution
(b) To devote himself to the well being of the Republic and its people
(c) To respect and protect humanity
(d) All of the above

Ans. (d) All of the above

(ii) What is the source of the above extract? What does the source depict?

Ans. The source of the given extract is the chapter 'Nelson Mandela: Long Walk to Freedom', an autobiography credited to South African President Nelson Mandela.

It depicts the battle for Black people's freedom in South Africa. It is a reflection on the past so that one can move forward.

(iii) Read the following types of writing (a)–(c) and identify which one correctly corresponds to the extract.

The given extract is taken from a (Blog/Speech)

Ans. Speech

(iv) Who took oath before Nelson Mandela?

Ans. Mr. Thabo Mbeki and Mr. de Klerk took oath before Nelson Mandela.

3. Read the following extract carefully and answer the questions that follow.

To the assembled guests and the watching world, I said : Today, all of us do, by our presence here ..... confer glory and hope to newborn liberty. Out of the experience of an extraordinary human disaster that lasted too long, must be born a society of which all humanity will be proud. We who were outlaws not so long ago, have today been given the rare privilege to be host to the nations of the world on our own soil. We thank all our distinguished international guests for having come to take possession with the people of our country of what is after all, a common victory for justice, for peace, for human dignity. **CBSE 2023**

(i) A society that .... was born out of human disaster.

(a) all humanity would be proud of
(b) was full of extraordinary human disasters
(c) was full of outlaws and fighters
(d) hosts nations on their soil

Ans. (a) all humanity would be proud of

(ii) What, according to Mandela, were the 'former outlaws' given the privilege of? **Competency Based**

Ans. According to Mandela, 'the former outlaws' were given the privilege of hosting the leaders of various nations on the inauguration of the first democratic non-racial government.

(iii) Fill in the blank with the correct word from the blank.

The speaker was overwhelmed with the sense of .... (gratitude/achievement)

Ans. gratitude

(iv) State whether the following statement is True or False.

The common victory was when South Africa did not become an independent nation.

Ans. False

4. Read the following extract carefully and answer the questions that follow.

"We, who were outlaws not so long ago, have today been given the rare privilege to be host to the nations if the world on our own soil. We thank all of our distinguished international guests for having come to take possession with the people of our country of what is, after all, a common victory for justice, for peace, for human dignity." **CBSE Question Bank 2021 Modified**

(i) How do you think the speaker feels? Choose the option that best fits his state of mind.

(a) (i) emotional (ii) elated (iii) unmindful
(b) (i) elated (ii) unmindful (iii) overwhelmed
(c) (i) overwhelmed (ii) elated (iii) honoured
(d) (i) elated (ii) honoured (iii) unmindful

Ans. (c) (i) overwhelmed (ii) elated (iii) honoured

(ii) Why did the speaker say that it was a 'rare privilege'?

Ans. The speaker said that it was a 'rare privilege' because for the first time leaders from all across the world had come together to celebrate the inauguration of a non-racial, democratic government.

(III) Which word from the extract means the same as the underlined word/phrase?

He was able to <u>organise</u> the event without any hindrance.

Ans. host

(iv) Complete the sentence appropriately.

The guests at the spectacular ceremony are being called distinguished because ....

Ans. they were eminent world leaders witnessing it

5. Read the following extract carefully and answer the questions that follow.

We have, at last, achieved our political emancipation. We pledge ourselves to liberate all our people from the continuing bondage of poverty, deprivation, suffering, gender and other discrimination.
Never, never, and never again shall it be that this beautiful land will again experience the oppression of one by another.
The sun shall never set on so glorious a human achievement.
Let freedom reign. God bless Africa!

(i) State any one inference about Nelson Mandela from the given context : **Competency Based**
"We have, at last, achieved our political emancipation".

Ans. From the given statement we can infer that Nelson Mandela acknowledges the attainment of political freedom after a prolonged struggle.

(ii) **State True or False.**

When Mandela says, 'God bless Africa', he intends to mean well-being and welfare of only black people in South Africa.

Ans. False. Mandela's invocation of 'God bless Africa' likely encompasses all people in South Africa, regardless of race, aiming for the well-being of the entire nation.

(iii) **"Nelson Mandela's speech is full of optism." Elaborate in about 40 words with reference to the extract.**

Ans. Mandela's speech is full of optimism as he celebrates the realisation of political emancipation, signaling hope and progress for the nation after enduring hardships. His words reflect confidence in a brighter future despite past challenges.

(iv) **Which phrase would correctly substitute 'so glorious', in the given sentence from the extract.** Competency Based

"The Sun shall never set on so glorious a human achievement."

Ans. "The Sun shall never set on such a magnificent human achievement."

6. Read the following extract carefully and answer the questions that follow.

But the decades of oppression and brutality had another unintended effect and that was that it produced the Oliver Tambos, the Walter Sisulus, the Chief Luthulis, the Yusuf Dadoo, the Bram Fischers, the Robert Sobukwes of our times – men of such extraordinary courage, wisdom and generosity that their like may never be known again. Perhaps it requires such depths of oppression to create such heights of character. My country is rich in the minerals and gems that lie beneath its soil, but I have always known that its greatest wealth is its people, finer and truer than the purest diamonds. It is from these comrades in the struggle that I learned the meaning of courage. Time and again, I have seen men and women risk and give their lives for an idea. CBSE SQP 2021 Term 1 Modified

(i) **What was the unintended effect of the long oppression? Choose the correct option.**

(a) It made the people indifferent to injustice.
(b) It made the people reject oppression.
(c) It influenced a generation to fight against injustice.
(d) It made people accept their oppression.

Ans. (c) It influenced a generation to fight against injustice.

(ii) **Complete the sentence appropriately.**
Men of such extraordinary courage refers to the people who ....

Ans. demonstrated utmost strength to oppose the system

(iii) **Who were the men of extraordinary courage, wisdom and generosity? How did they come to be known?** Competency Based

Ans. Oliver Tambos, Walter Sisulus, Chief Luthulis, Yusuf Dadoo, Bram Fischers and Robert Sobukwes were the men of extraordinary courage, wisdom and generosity. As a result of decades of oppression and brutality, these men were known.

(iv) **When Nelson Mandela says, "I have seen men and women risk and give their lives for an idea", what does he mean about them?** Competency Based

Ans. When Nelson Mandela says, "I have seen men and women risk and give their lives for an idea." He means that they are committed to the said idea.

7. Read the following extract carefully and answer the questions that follow.

It is from these comrades in the struggle that I learned the true meaning of courage. Time and again, I have seen men and women risk and give their lives for an idea. I have seen men stand up to attacks and torture without breaking, showing a strength and resilience that defies the imagination. I learned that courage was not the absence of fear, but the triumph over it. The brave man is not he who does not feel afraid, but he who conquers that fear. CBSE 2024 C

(i) **Elaborate in about 40 words with reference to the extract.**
What does courage mean to the speaker?

Ans. Courage, according to the speaker, means overcoming fear and demonstrating strength in the face of adversity. It is about standing firm and enduring challenges for a greater cause. The speaker admires those who risk their lives for their beliefs.

(ii) **State any one inference about Nelson Mandela from the given context. "Courage was not the absence of fear, but the triumph over it."**

(a) preserving (b) dogmatic (c) defiant (d) triumphant

Ans. defiant

(iii) **Which phrase would correctly substitute 'resilience' in the given sentence from the extract ? "... showing a strength and resilience that defies the imagination."**

(a) an ability to defeat the enemy
(b) an ability to keep calm and quiet
(c) an ability to deal with hardships
(d) an ability to conquer the fear

Ans. (c) an ability to deal with hardships

(iv) State True or False

All of the terms (A) - (D) can be applied to the following statement.

'The brave man is not he who does not feel afraid ...'

(a) One who has never faced fear
(b) One who gives up in face of hardship
(c) One who believes in submitting to fear
(d) One who realises that fear is part of life

Ans. False

Or

(i) What effects does the experience as described in the lines below have on the speaker?

Time again and again, I have seen men and women risk their lives for an idea. **CBSE 2025**

Ans. The experience deeply impacts the speaker, Nelson Mandela, by teaching him the true meaning of courage and resilience. Witnessing people risk their lives for freedom strengthens his determination to fight against injustice and reinforces his belief in the power of sacrifice and perseverance.

(ii) Select one inference about the idea of courage from the given context.

I learned that courage was not the absence of fear, but the triumph over it. **CBSE 2025**

(a) Being fearless (b) Absence of fear
(c) Feeding your fears (d) Ability to overcome fear

Ans. (d) Ability to overcome fear

(iii) Answer in about 40 words, with reference to the extract.

According to the author, what does true courage entail? How does this perspective differ from a common misconception about courage? **CBSE 2025**

Ans. According to the author, true courage is not the absence of fear but the ability to overcome it. Many believe courage means being fearless, but Mandela clarifies that even the bravest people feel fear; what sets them apart is their strength to face and conquer it.

(iv) Fill in the blank with the correct phrase from the bracket in the context of the given extract.

Men stood up to torture showing strength and resilience that is .... (imposible to understand/seeded in reality). **CBSE 2025**

Ans. impossible to understand.

8. Read the following extract carefully and answer the questions that follows.

"It was only when I began to learn that my boyhood freedom was an illusion, when I discovered as a young man that my freedom had already been taken from me, that I began to hunger for it. At first as a student
I wanted freedom only for myself, the transitory freedoms of being able to stay out at night, read what
I pleased and go where I chose. Later, as a young man in Johannesburg, I yearned for the basic and honourable freedoms..." **CBSE Question Bank 2021**

(i) Which word from the extract means the same as the underlined word/phrase.

I was living under the <u>belief</u> that this is possible.

Ans. illusion

(ii) The speaker says, 'at first as a student I wanted freedom only for myself.' What did the speaker mean by this statement?

Ans. The statement means that when the speaker was young he wanted only his freedom. He did not realise that freedom was denied to others as well.

(iii) A part of the extract has been paraphrased. Choose the option that includes the most appropriate solution to the blanks in the given paraphrase of the extract. **Competency Based**

The speaker's belief about freedom, since childhood proved false. It was not until the speaker grew up to be a young man when it (i) .... on him that he was (ii) .... of freedom. Then he began (iii) .... it.

(a) (i) desired (ii) dawned (iii) depriving
(b) (i) dawned (ii) deprived (iii) desiring
(c) (i) dawned (ii) arrived (iii) desiring
(d) (i) arrived (ii) deprived (iii) dawned

Ans. (b) (i) dawned (ii) deprived (iii) desiring

(iv) Why do you think the speaker mentioned some freedoms as 'transitory'?

Ans. The speaker mentioned some freedoms as 'transitory' because those freedoms are momentary and keep changing with time. It is just like how the speaker craved for different types of freedoms as a boy, a student and a young man.

Part II

Short Answer Type Questions

1. For the past few days I had been pleasantly besieged by dignitaries and world leaders who were coming to pay their respects before the inauguration. Why does Mandela use the words 'pleasantly besieged'? Competency Based

Ans. The use of 'pleasantly besieged' indicates that Mandela was completely surrounded by foreign dignitaries. All of his time on the inauguration day was taken up by the world leader for a great cause. As a result, he did not mind anything and was happy.

2. Why was the site called "a rainbow gathering of different colours and nations"?

Ans. The site was full of leaders and dignitaries from all around the world. These leaders, irrespective of their colour, race and religion had gathered to celebrate the victory over the apartheid regime and to support the cause of peace, justice and human dignity.

Hence, the site was called a rainbow gathering of different colours and nations.

3. What promise did Mandela make in the beginning of his oath-taking speech?

Ans. At the beginning of his oath-taking speech, Mandela promised to obey and uphold the Constitution and devote himself to the well-being of nation and its people. He also promised to make the nation free from poverty, deprivation, oppression and discrimination of all kinds.

4. What do you understand by 'Apartheid'? Describe the effect of the policy of apartheid on the people of South Africa.

Ans. 'Apartheid' is a political system that divides people according to their race. The policy of apartheid created a deep and lasting wound in South Africa and its people. This policy was full of terror, oppression and torture on the blacks of South Africa. The wound created by this policy of racial discrimination would take many years to recover.

5. What were the two ideas intended to be conveyed by the display of military force? Competency Based

Ans. The two ideas conveyed by the display of military force are

(i) to display military strength

(ii) to display loyalty to democracy and the government.

6. What intended effect was produced by decades of oppression?

Ans. The decades of torture and oppression created an unintended effect on the blacks. The black people who fought against the unjust policies of apartheid were produced out of the oppression. Those people had extraordinary courage, wisdom and generosity. Those people included many South African patriots such as Walter Sisulu, Oliver Tambo, Bram fischer, etc.

7. Mandela says that his country's greatest wealth is its people and not the purest diamonds. Justify his statement. CBSE Question Bank 2021

Ans. South Africa is rich in minerals and diamonds but its people is its greatest wealth. Mandela felt that people are finer and truer than those purest diamonds. This is because the people of South Africa have pure hearts and souls filled with kindness and compassion.

8. Did Mandela fulfill his twin obligations? Justify your answer. Competency Based

Ans. No, Mandela did not fulfill his twin obligations. We know this because he himself mentions that in order to fulfill his obligation to his people and country, he couldn't fulfill the obligation of his family. Mandela could not fulfill his responsibilities as a father, son, husband and so on.

9. Based on your reading of the lesson, what can you infer about Mandela as a father and as a leader? CBSE Question Bank 2021

Ans. **Mandela as a Father** He regretted being unable to devote himself to his family during the fight against apartheid and afterward. Fathers can make themselves felt through their absence; Mandela did, by walking away from power after his term as President was up.

Mandela as a Leader As a leader, Nelson Mandela demonstrated remarkable leadership qualities, including advocacy for peace, positive thinking, focus on goals and missions beyond himself. Mandela's visions led him to fight for a better mankind.

10. What did Mandela realise about his brothers and sisters?

Ans. As Nelson Mandela grew up, he realised that his brothers and sisters of his community including him and nation were not free. As a result, his hunger for freedom which he earlier wanted for himself became great. Now, he desired freedom of his entire community.

11. What did Mandela think of oppressor and oppressed?
State two ways in which the oppressor and the oppressed are similar, according to Mandela.

Or **Why did Mandela feel that liberation was important for both the oppresson and the oppressed.** CBSE 2025

Ans. Mandela always thought that both the oppressor and the oppressed are deprived of their humanity. According to him, the oppressor is a prisoner of hatred and he is locked behind the bars of prejudice and narrow mindedness. So, both of them need to be liberated. He always desired people to live with dignity and respect.

12. If you were in Mandela's position, would you have given preference to your family or your country? Why?

Ans. If I were in Nelson Mandela's position, I would also have given preference to my country. As Mandela rightly said, "My freedom is my people's freedom." Being a responsible citizen of my country, it is my first and foremost duty to be available for my country whenever the need arises. My family comes after my country.

13. Explain the given statement with reference to Nelson Mandela's dreams. "A winner is a dreamer who never gives up." CBSE Additional SQP 2023

Ans. It is true to say a winner is a dreamer who never gives up. Nelson Mandela had dared to dream and had fought for his dreams. He struggled till he achieved his goal. As a result, his people were liberated from poverty, deprivation, suffering, gender and other discrimination. They were not oppressed by another. The new government that stopped 'Apartheid' recognised the rights and freedoms of all peoples, regardless of the colour of their skin was formed.

14. How did Mandela's leadership style contribute to South Africa's transition to democracy?

Ans. Mandela's leadership style was characterised by inclusivity, empathy and resilience. His ability to inspire unity and reconciliation enabled South Africa to navigate a peaceful transition to democracy, earning him respect and admiration domestically and internationally.

Long Answer Type Questions

1. What do you think about the obligations which the author is talking about? Also describe his feelings for them.

Ans. In the chapter, the author has talked about two obligations for every man. The first obligation is towards his family, parents, wife and children. The second is towards his community and his country. Being a social person, one has to fulfill these obligations. However, being a black in South Africa, a man was not free to perform his obligations. He got punished if he tried to live as a human being.

When Mandela was a child, the author never thought of such an obligation. However, as he grew older and started thinking about them in his oppressive society, he realised that he could not fulfill them. In his attempt to fulfill his duty to his people, community and nation, he was taken away from his family and home. He had to live in secrecy and isolation. As a result, Mandela couldn't fulfill both of his twin obligations. However, he fought for his people so that they could enjoy their freedom of performing their personal as well as social duties.

2. Describe the value of freedom for human beings and how it is important for the growth of civilisation and humanism as described in the lesson 'Nelson Mandela : Long Walk to Freedom'.

Ans. The value of freedom is better known to that human being who has not enjoyed it. A person, who is bound within limits and not allowed to perform his duties freely, values freedom more than anyone else.

For instance, the value of freedom is known better to Mandela who remained behind bars for most of his life. Think about a bird or animal which is caged. It's instinct suggests living with full freedom but in the cage, it is not free and its condition is very pitiable.

Life becomes hell if we are deprived of freedom. There is no growth of civilisation as it grows only when one has freedom. Similarly, humanism grows in the atmosphere of freedom. If a man is free to do his duties, he can produce better results.
An oppressed person always commits mistakes and is unable to perform well, so freedom is important for the growth of civilisation.

3. Why was Nelson Mandela overwhelmed with a sense of history? How did he succeed in ending the apartheid regime in South Africa? CBSE 2020

Ans. On the day of the inauguration, Mandela was overwhelmed with a sense of history. After looking at the loyalty displayed by the armed force to the new non-racial government, Mandela remembered how the same officers used to imprison him. He remembered that in the first decade of the 20th century and before his birth, the white skinned people of South Africa came together and created a system of racial discrimination against the dark-skinned people of their own land. This system was one of the most inhumane and violent system that the world had ever seen.

When Nelson realised that the black people of his nation were not free, he joined African National Congress to work for their freedom. Freedom for him became freedom of the people of his community to live with respect and dignity. To get it, he became a bold criminal who had to spend 30 years in prison. To work for his country, he could not do anything for his family. In the fight for freedom, he fought along with many other courageous freedom fighters who even sacrificed their lives for the cause. As a result, after long years of struggle, the black African people became free and a non-racial government was set up in South Africa.

4. Freedom is inconsequential if it is behind bars of prejudice and narrow mindedness. How would you explain this statement? Support your answer with suitable examples from the real world.

Ans. This statement was given by Nelson Mandela on the inauguration day of South Africa. According to him, one who enjoys one's own freedom by taking other people's freedom is not free at all. The oppressor needs to be liberated from hate like those oppressed in order to enjoy his own freedom. For example

(i) **Discrimination in workplace** When a suitable candidate is denied a job or admission in an institution and a candidate with no actual qualifications is given that opportunity because of some reference or reservation, it is called discrimination and prejudice.

(ii) Religious discrimination and attack on minorities in Pakistan depicts that they are bound by the shackles of prejudice and narrow mindedness.

5. After having read the lesson on the oppression that communities faced in South Africa, you were deeply hurt. You could also relate to the struggles and hardships of millions of Indians who fought against the oppressive British rule.
Write a diary entry expressing your feelings about oppression faced by people in their homeland. You may begin like this **CBSE Question Bank 2021**

> 24th August, 20XX, Monday 9:00 pm
>
> Dear Diary,
>
> My heart is filled with sadness as I think of the oppressed who had to tolerate the inhuman attitude of the oppressors in their own land. ....

Ans. 24th August, 20XX, Monday 9:00 pm

Dear Diary,

My heart is filled with sadness as I think of the oppressed who had to tolerate the inhuman attitude of the oppressors in their own land. Indian farmers were forced by Britishers to grow indigo in place of rice in their fields. It fetched a handsome amount of money for Britishers but destroyed the fertile fields of the Indian farmers. The English looted the poor women's dignity. No female was safe in the British era. Tears roll down my eyes when I think of the physical and mental torture that our freedom fighters faced. Everyone knows how cruel General Dyer turned a meeting into a massacre! These wounds are deep-rooted in the hearts of every Indian which can never be healed.

6. Prejudice based on race and colour or any other reason causes profound hurt. Write about any one character from the chapters in First Flight who was subjected to such prejudice? Discuss the consequence of this prejudice for the character. **CBSE Question Bank 2021**

Ans. Prejudice based on race and colour or any other reason causes profound hurt to the person who is discriminated against.

In 'From the Diary of Anne Frank' lesson, Anne and her family were victims of holocaust. She was a German - born Jewish girl who was hiding with her family and friends for two years during the German occupation of the Netherlands in World War II. Her group was betrayed and transported to concentration camp systems. She and her sister got separated from their parents and the people in those camps had to bear discrimination of all kinds. They did not get enough food and the living conditions were miserable. She died of typhus in Bergen-Belsen. Her father was the only survivor from the family who later got back to the hiding place to find Anne's diary which he later got published under the name 'The Diary of a Young Girl'.

7. Mandela said, "People must learn to hate and if they can learn to hate, they can be taught to love." Discuss. **CBSE 2023**

Or **"No one is born hating another person because of the colour of his skin, or his background, or his religion." Do you agree? Elaborate on the basis of the chapter 'Nelson Mandela - Long Walk to Freedom'.** **CBSE 2023**

Ans. I completely agree with Mandela's statement that no one is born hating another person on the basis of the colour of skin, background or religion. Mandela had believed that people must learn to hate and if they can learn to hate, they can be taught to love. According to him, no human being is born feeling hatred and any hatred in the hearts of the people against black skin must have been taught.

Believing this, Mandela states that if hatred has been learned then, love can be learned much more easily as it comes spontaneously to all human beings. Mandela himself finds evidence for this in the white guard who showed pity on the prisoners including Mandela. Thus, the hope that love is present in everyone is reaffirmed in Mandela.

8. Comment on the reactions and feeling of Lencho and Nelson Mandela when they faced challenges in their lives. **CBSE 2025**

Ans. Lencho and Nelson Mandela faced hardships with strong beliefs, but their reactions were different. In 'A Letter to God', Lencho, a poor farmer, loses his crops to a hailstorm. Instead of giving up, he places complete faith in God and writes a letter asking for money. However, when he receives less money than he requested, he becomes disappointed and mistrusts the post office employees. In contrast, 'Nelson Mandela, in Long Walk to Freedom', endures years of oppression under apartheid but responds with resilience, patience, and forgiveness. He does not let anger consume him and instead fights for justice and reconciliation. While Lencho relies on faith, Mandela takes action, making his response transformative and inspiring for an entire nation.

ASSESSMENT EXERCISE

Extract Based Questions

Read the following extracts carefully and answer the questions that follow.

1. I knew that the oppressor must be liberated just as surely as the oppressed. A man who takes away another man's freedom is a prisoner of hatred; he is locked behind the bars of prejudice and narrow-mindedness. I am not truly free if I am taking away someone else's freedom, just as surely as I am not free when my freedom is taken from me. The oppressed and the oppressor alike are robbed of their humanity.

(i) Why did Mandela feel that oppressor must be liberated?

(ii) What has been robbed off from the oppressed and the oppressor alike? How? **Competency Based**

(iii) Select the option that correctly captures the usage of the word 'hatred' in the above extract.

(a) A man of hatred talks little and listens much.

(b) His hatred of revolutionary principles was fanatical.

(c) A handful of common hatred is worth a bushel of learning.

(d) She has a strong hatred of justice and fairness.

(iv) Complete the analogy by selecting the suitable word from the text.

Profligate : Exorbitant :: Extricate : ....

2. In life, every man has twin obligations—obligations to his family, to his parents, to his wife and children; and he has an obligation to his people, his community, his country. In a civil and humane society, each man is able to fulfill those obligations according to his own inclinations and abilities. But in a country like South Africa, it was almost impossible for a man of my birth and colour to fulfill both of those obligations. In South Africa, a man of colour who attempted to live as a human being was punished and isolated. In South Africa, a man who tried to fulfill his duty to his people was inevitably ripped from his family and his home and was forced to live a life apart, a twilight existence of secrecy and rebellion. I did not in the beginning choose to place my people above my family, but in attempting to serve my people, I found that I was prevented from fulfilling my obligations as a son, a brother, a father and a husband.

(i) Why was it impossible to fulfill these obligations in South Africa?

1. Because of the policy of apartheid.
2. Because they were born black.
3. Because they were born white.
4. Because it was not allowed in South Africa.

Choose the correct option.

(a) Both 2 and 3

(b) Only 3

(c) Both 1 and 2

(d) Only 4

(ii) What are the twin obligations mentioned in the above extract?

(iii) When did Mandela find that he was prevented from fulfilling my obligations as a son, a brother, a father and a husband?

(iv) Fill in the blanks with appropriate word from bracket.

Mandela could not .... (fulfill/deny) his private obligations.

Short Answer (SA) Type Questions

1. What did the military generals do on that day?

2. Why does Mandela address the freedom as 'newborn liberty'?

3. Why does Mandela say that the sacrifices of the African patriots cannot be repaid?

4. Discuss the pledge did Mandela take on the installation ceremony? **Competency Based**

Long Answer (LA) Type Questions

1. If you had been in place of Nelson Mandela, what would you have done? Answer in the form of a blog post.

2. What were the thoughts of Nelson Mandela on the auspicious day in the history of South Africa?

3. Do you think there is colour or caste prejudice in our own country? How can we uproot it? What is your stand on it? Should we discriminate on the basis of caste or colour? **Competency Based**

Two Stories About Flying

CHAPTER 3

I. His First Flight

by Liam O' Flaherty

The first story 'His First Flight' has been written by Liam O' Flaherty. The story is about a family of seagulls wherein young seagulls are being taught to fly by their parents. One of the young seagulls is afraid of falling down and hesitates to take the first step to fly. The story showcases how this seagull is made to fly with some help from his mother.

The Young Seagull's Fear of Flying

The young seagull was alone on his ledge. His two brothers and his sister had already learnt to fly. However, he was afraid to fly because of the height and depth of the sea. He thought that his wings will not support him. So, he ran back to his hole under the ledge.

Therefore, the young seagull failed to gather up the courage to fly. His father and mother tried to persuade him to fly. They scolded and even threatened him, that if he does not try to fly, they would let him die of hunger. However, the young seagull did not move.

Parents Leave the Young Seagull Alone

Twenty four hours passed and no body came near him. All day, the young seagull watched his parents teaching his brothers and sister how to fly. They were also teaching them how to skim the waves and how to dive for catching the fish. He had seen his elder brother catch the first herring (a fish) and his parents praise him. It seemed that his whole family was taunting the young seagull for his cowardice.

The Hungry Seagull

As time passed, the young seagull could not tolerate the hunger and the heat. He moved closer to the ledge and pretended to fall asleep but nobody took notice of him. His two brothers and his sister were sleeping, and his father was cleaning the feathers on his white back. Only his mother noticed him. She was standing high on the plateau with a fish. As the young seagull saw the food, he felt even hungrier.

The Mother's Trick

Realising his madness for food, his mother tried to tempt him with pieces of fish. Initially, she tore the fish in the manner the young seagull loved to eat. This sight maddened him. Then, the mother flew nearer to him which filled the young seagull with joy.

However, the mother stopped near the edge of the ledge. Out of excitement and hunger, the young seagull ran towards his mother and jumped towards the fish.

The Joy of Flight

Initially, the seagull was scared and screamed with fear when he was falling down. But soon, he felt his wings spread outwards and he began to fly. He could feel the air all over his body. Finally, he was flying upwards and was no longer afraid of flying.

The Family's Celebration

As he was flying, his parents, brothers and sister flew around him. When all the family members landed on the green sea, they called the young seagull to be with them. As the young seagull landed on the green sea, his legs sank into it. He tried to fly again but he was tired and weak with hunger. Finally, his feet sank into the sea, his belly touched it and he was floating on it. The family members praised him and offered him pieces of dog- fish as he had made his first flight.

Word Meaning

Word	Meaning
ledge	a narrow horizontal shelf
brink	edge
flap	to move wings up and down
muster up	gather
plunge	dive
desperate	a great need or desire
shrilly	sharply
upbraiding	rebuking
starve	die of hunger
skim	moving lightly over an area or surface
dive	quick and sudden downward movement
herring	a kind of fish
devour	eat at a great speed
cackle	a sharp sound
taunting	a remark made to make someone angry or upset
blazing	shining with great heat, burning
dozing	sleeping lightly
preening	smoothing feathers with beak
scraped	rubbed
maddened	made mad

Word	Meaning
whet	to increase interest in it
derisively	mockingly
plaintively	sorrowfully
leaned out	bent his body outward
tapping	beating lightly
halted	stopped
monstrous	very fearful
seized	caught
headlong	head downwards
soaring	flying upwards
dizzy	confused, spinning
swooped	pounced
curveting	moving with an action resembling a horse's leap
banking	flying with one wing higher than the other
commended	praised
ridges	wavy edges
cawed	to utter a cry
beckoning	signalling
fright	fear

NCERT FOLDER

NCERT Intext and Exercise Questions

THINKING ABOUT THE TEXT (NCERT PAGE 36)

Q.1 Why was the young Seagull afraid to fly? Do you think all young birds are afraid to make their first flight, or are some birds more timid than others? Do you think a human baby also finds it a challenge to take its first step? CBSE 2019

Ans. The young seagull was afraid to fly because he felt that his wings would not support him and he would fall from a great height.

Yes, when something is done for the first time, it is a bit challenging and fearful. All birds get afraid while taking their first flight. However, it is also a fact that some birds are more timid than others and consequently, take more time to fly.

Just like a bird, a human baby is also afraid of taking the first step and finds it challenging.

Q.2 "The sight of the food maddened him." What does this suggest? What compelled the young Seagull to finally fly?

Or **'The sight of food maddened him.' What does this suggest?** **CBSE 2020**

Ans. The given line suggests that the young seagull was hungry and when he saw food, his hunger increased.

It was his hunger that ultimately compelled him to fly. His hunger intensified when he saw his mother tearing up a piece of fish that lay at her feet. He cried to her, begging her to get some food. So, she flew towards him with a fish in her beak and stopped at some distance. Unable to control himself, the young Seagull dived for food. Naturally, his wings spread out and he began to fly.

Q.3 "They were beckoning to him, calling shrilly." Why did the seagull's father and mother threaten him and cajole him to fly?

Ans. Unlike his siblings, the poor seagull could not gather enough courage to take his first flight. Thus, his parents taunted him for being a coward.
They threatened and cajoled him so that he might take his first flight.

Q.4 Have you ever had a similar experience, where your parents encouraged you to do something that you were too scared to try?

Ans. Yes, I had a similar experience while learning to ride a bicycle in Class VI. In my initial attempts, I fell down every time and developed a fear of cycling which was difficult to overcome. My father encouraged me to overcome the fear and helped in learning cycling. He took me on a small hill near our village, made me sit and asked me to put my hands on the handle and feet on the pedals. When he pushed me, the cycle moved and I enjoyed it without fear, which developed my confidence. Thus, I overcame my fear of cycling and started riding a cycle regularly after a little practice.

Q.5 In the case of a bird flying, it seems a natural act, and a foregone conclusion that it should succeed. In the examples you have given in answer to the previous question, was your success guaranteed, or was it important for you to try, regardless of a possibility of failure?

Ans. In the example I have given as an answer to the previous question, it is evident that initially my success was not guaranteed. I was afraid of failure and did not even want to try cycling. However, I was encouraged and motivated to do so.

I had to try, regardless of the possibility of failure.
I had to put in efforts and hard work. With willingness and determination, my success became guaranteed as when someone is determined, success is assured.

REVIEW EXERCISE

Including Competency Based Questions

Part I

Multiple Choice Questions

1. Who was there on the ledge with the young seagull for the last twenty-four hours?

(a) His two brothers (b) His sister
(c) His parents (d) He was alone

Ans. (d) He was alone

2. What was the young seagull afraid of?

(a) To fly in the sky (b) To land in the sea
(c) To fly over the vast sea (d) To catch fish

Ans. (c) To fly over the vast sea

3. Where did the young seagull run to hide?

(a) Little hole under the ledge (b) On the brink of the cliff
(c) On a tree (d) In his mother's wings

Ans. (a) Little hole under the ledge

4. Young seagull's parents threatened .... if he didn't fly away.

(a) to never talk to him (b) to punish him
(c) to starve him (d) to abandon him

Ans. (c) to starve him

5. What were young seagull's parents teaching his brothers and sisters?

(a) To perfect the art of flying (b) To skim the waves
(c) To dive for fish (d) All of these

Ans. (d) All of these

6. He stood at the edge of the ledge on one leg and closed his eyes because ....

(a) he was feeling sleepy
(b) it was a natural habit of seagulls

(c) he wanted to get the attention of his family
(d) he was afraid of the his family

Ans. (c) he wanted to get the attention of his family

7. How is the young seagull feeling at the beginning of the story? **Competency Based**

(a) Agitated (b) Vengeful
(c) Despondent (d) Confounded

Ans. (d) Confounded

8. "He had in fact seen his older brother catch his first herring and devour it." How did 'he' feel? **CBSE 2021 Term 1**

1. Angry **2. Greedy**
3. Jealous **4. Hungry**

(a) 1 and 2 (b) 2 and 3
(c) 3 and 4 (d) 4 and 1

Ans. (c) 3 and 4

9. When did young seagull's mother scream derisively at the young seagull?

(a) When he denied for flying
(b) When he acted sleeping
(c) When he begged her for food
(d) None of the above

Ans. (c) When he begged her for food

10. But he kept calling plaintively, and after a minute or so he uttered a joyful scream. Why did 'he' feel joyful? **Competency Based**

(a) He thought that his mother was going to feed him.
(b) He thought that his mother was going to help him fly.
(c) He thought that his mother was going to console him.
(d) He thought that his mother was going to keep him company.

Ans. (b) He thought that his mother was going to help him fly.

11. 'He was not falling headlong now.' What does the word 'headlong' mean in context of the story 'His First Flight'?

(a) With the head first
(b) Diving downwards
(c) With the feet first
(d) Both (a) and (b)

Ans. (d) Both (a) and (b)

12. Which of the following is true about the young seagull?

1. He was not afraid to fly.
2. His family was upbraiding him.
3. The young seagull's wings were bigger than those if his brothers and sisters.
4. He did not like to eat fish.
5. The young seagull took his first flight out of hunger.

(a) 1, 2 and 4 (b) 3, 4 and 5
(c) 2, 3 and 5 (d) All of these

Ans. (c) 2, 3 and 5

13. How did the young seagull's family welcome his first flight?

(a) All of them were scolding him
(b) All of them were soaring and diving to express their joy
(c) All of them went away
(d) All of them threw fish scrapes towards him

Ans. (b) All of them were soaring and diving to express their joy

14. Which of these is true about the seagull and his mother? **Competency Based**

(a) They disrespected each other but pretended to love one another
(b) They mocked each other but helped one another when it was needed
(c) They had different thoughts about their family but cared for each other
(d) They felt differently about the goal but wanted to achieve the same result

Ans. (d) They felt differently about the goal but wanted to achieve the same result

15. The purpose of the treatment, given to the young seagull by his parents, was to .... **CBSE SQP 2021 Term 1**

(a) teach him a lesson about the importance of food
(b) inculcate obedience towards them
(c) let him overcome his fear
(d) improve his relationship with his siblings

Ans. (c) let him overcome his fear

16. Select the option that shows the correct relationship between the following statements. **Competency Based**

1. The young seagull overcomes his fear and learns to fly.
2. The fear of firsts vanishes when one takes the leap sometimes.

(a) 1 is supporting detail for 2.
(b) 1 and 2 are unrelated.
(c) 1 is true but 2 is false.
(d) 1 contradicts 2.

Ans. (a) 1 is supporting detail for 2.

17. How does the young seagull's attitude towards flying CHANGE in the story 'His First Flight'? **Competency Based**

(a) He questions it and then accepts it.
(b) He enjoys it and then finds it uninteresting.

(c) He is uncertain about it and then, finds it thrilling.
(d) He is curious about it and then, thinks it is overrated

Ans. (c) He is uncertain about it and then finds it thrilling.

18. Which word best describes the seagull family?

(a) Malicious (b) Relentless
(c) Callous (d) Belligerent

Ans. (b) Relentless

Extract Based Questions

1. Read the following extract carefully and answer the questions that follow.

The day before, all day long, he had watched his parents flying about with his brothers and sister, perfecting them in the art of flight, teaching them how to skim the waves and how to dive for fish. He had, in fact, seen his older brother catch his first herring and devour it, standing on a rock, while his parents circled around raising a proud cackle. And all the morning the whole family had walked about on the big plateau midway down the opposite cliff taunting him with his cowardice.

(i) Based on the given sentence, pick the option that corresponds to what human parents would say.
'while his parents circled around raising a proud cackle.' **Competency Based**

(a) Well done! (b) Oh no!
(c) Ready?! (d) Really!?

Ans. (a) Well done!

(ii) What was the true intention behind the merciless taunting of the young seagull's family at his inability to fly?

Ans. The true intention behind the merciless taunting of the young seagull's family was to force him to take that final step and fly. They taunted him because they knew that the young gull would not be able to survive and hunt for food if he didn't learn how to fly.

(iii) Which of the following feelings did the young gull not feel according to the given context?
"...all day long, he had watched his parents flying about with his brothers and sister..."

(1) sad (2) incompetent
(3) excluded (4) ungrateful
(5) inspired (6) jealous
(7) anxious

Ans. 4, 5, 6

(iv) Select the most appropriate option for the following.
Nibble : Savour : : Guzzle : ....

Ans. Devour

2. Read the following extract carefully and answer the questions that follow.

But he kept calling plaintively, and after a minute or so he uttered a joyful scream. His mother had picked up a piece of the fish and was flying across to him with it. He leaned out eagerly, tapping the rock with his feet, trying to get nearer to her as she flew across. But when she was just opposite to him, she halted, her wings motionless, the piece of fish in her beak almost within rach of his beak. He waited a moment in surprise, wondering why she did not come nearer, and then maddened by hunger, he dived at the fish. With a loud scream he fell outwards and downwards into space. Then a monstrous terror seized him and his heart stood still. He could hear nothing. But it only lasted a minute. **Competency Based**

(i) Fill in the blank with the correct word from the bracket.
The shift in emotion the seagull experiences from the beginning to the end of the extract is .... (from anxious to nervous/from mournful to petrified)

Ans. from mournful to petrified

(ii) Why was the young seagull fearful of flying? How did he finally fly? **Competency Based**

Ans. The young seagull was fearful of flying because he thought that his wings would not work and he would fall down from a great height into the deep sea. He finally flew because of his extreme hunger.

(iii) What of these factors were not responsible for the young seagull learning to fly?

(a) The continuous efforts of his mother and father
(b) The depth and vastness of the ocean beneath him
(c) The hunger and weakness that was maddening him
(d) The success of his siblings in diving and catching prey

Ans. (b) The depth and vastness of the ocean beneath him

(iv) Why did 'it' last only a minute?

Ans. The fear felt by the young seagull lasted only a minute because soon his wings stretched outwards and he started to fly.

3. Read the following extract carefully and answer the questions that follow.

He waited a moment in surprise, wondering why she did not come nearer and then, maddened by hunger, he dived at the fish. With a loud scream he fell outwards and downwards into space. Then a monstrous terror seized him and his heart stood still. He could hear nothing. But it only lasted a minute. The next moment he felt his wings spread outwards.

(i) Select the option that correctly captures the usage of the word 'dived' in the above extract.

(a) The snow dived all day in big white flakes.
(b) He slipped and dived, hurting his leg quite badly.
(c) She dived headfirst into the pool.
(d) She dived in love with him as soon as they met.

Ans. (c) She dived headfirst into the pool.

(ii) Why did his mother stop mid-way while giving him the fish?

Ans. His mother stopped mid-way while giving him the fish, to get him to fly out of hunger and starvation.

(iii) What lasted only a minute for the seagull?

1. Anger **2. Surprise** **3. Fear**
4. Happiness **5. Time**

Ans. 3. Fear

(iv) How had the seagull been feeling in the given extract?

Ans. The seagull had been feeling hungry.

4. Read the following extract carefully and answer the questions that follow.

With a loud scream he fell outwards and given downwards into space. Then a monstrous terror seized him and his heart stood still. He could hear nothing. But it only lasted a minute. The next moment he felt his wings spread outwards. The wind rushed against his breast feathers, then under his stomach, and against his wings. He could feel the tips of his wings cutting through the air. He was not falling headlong now. He was soaring gradually downwards and outwards. **CBSE SQP 2024**

(i) What effect does the experience, as described in the lines below, have on the baby seagull?

With a loud scream he fell outwards and downwards into space. Then a monstrous terror seized him and his heart stood still.

Choose the most suitable option.

(a) exhilarates (b) overwhelms
(c) energises (d) confuses

Ans. (b) overwhelms

(ii) How does the author's use of descriptive language enhance the narrative technique in the paragraph?

Ans. The author's use of descriptive language clearly portrays the intense emotional journey of the baby seagull. It hints at the physical sensations experienced by the baby seagull during its first flight. This adds to the sensory experience. Phrases such as 'monstrous terror' and 'wind rushed against his breast feathers' help the reader in understanding what the seagull experienced. This enhances the emotional impact of the narrative and makes it more real.

(iii) Fill in the blank with the correct word from the bracket.

The use of the word 'rushed' adds to a sense of .... (speed/relief), in the extract.

Ans. speed

(iv) How does the seagull's feelings towards the end of the extract contrast with the initial feeling of terror?

Ans. A sharp contrast between seagull's feelings of exhilaration at the end of the extract with the initial feelings of terror can be seen when it learns to fly and soar high. The new feeling is the feeling of empowerment and excitement.

5. Read the following extract carefully and answer the questions that follow.

He just felt a bit dizzy. Then he flapped his wings once and he soared upwards. "Ga, ga, ga, Ga, ga, ga, Gaw-col-ah," his mother swooped past him, her wings making a loud noise. He answered her with another scream. Then, his father flew over him screaming. He saw his two brothers and his sister flying around him curveting and banking and soaring and diving. Then he completely forgot that he had not always been able to fly and commended himself to dive and soar and curve, shrieking shrilly.

CBSE Question Bank 2021 Modified

(i) Choose the option that correctly sequences the movements of the young seagulls brothers and sister.

(a) The young seagull's brothers and sister flew by tilting their wings, rose high, made darting movements and plunged headfirst.
(b) The young seagull's brothers and sister flew by plunging headfirst, making darting movements, titled their wings and rose high.
(c) The young seagull's brothers and sister flew with darting movements, titled their wings, rose high and plunged headfirst.
(d) The young seagull's brothers and sister flew by rising high, plunging headfirst, making darting movements and tilting their wings.

Ans. (b) The young seagull's brothers and sister flew by plunging headfirst, making darting movements, titled their wings and rose high.

(ii) Read (a) - (c) and choose which statement implies "he completely forgot that he had not always been able to fly?"

(a) Great confidence the young seagull had in his skills.
(b) Naturalness of the act of flying for the young seagull.
(c) Satisfaction and joy of flying together as a family.

Ans. (b) Naturalness of the act of flying for the young seagull.

(iii) What is the reason behind this line - 'He just felt a bit dizzy'? Competency Based

Ans. Maddened by hunger, when the young seagull dived to catch the fish, he fell downwards into space. His heart stood still in terror and he couldn't hear anything; however, he was able to fly soon. His wings spread, cutting through the air and he wasn't falling thereafter. This flight made him feel a bit dizzy.

(iv) Why did the young seagull feel dizzy?

Ans. The young seagull felt dizzy because he was flying for the first time.

Part II

Short Answer Type Questions

1. Why was the young seagull afraid to fly with his family members? CBSE 2023

Ans. The young seagull was afraid to fly with his family members because it was his first flight. He was uncertain whether his wings would support him. He was afraid of his wings not working and plunging towards death.

2. Family played a vital role in the first flight of the young seagull. Give examples to substantiate the above statement. CBSE 2023

Ans. It is true that family played a vital role in the first flight of the young seagull. When the young seagull refuses to fly, his parents and siblings scold and even threatened him to get him to fly. Later, his mother, knowing that the young seagull was hungry, tricks him to flying.

3. Why did the young seagull pretend to fall asleep on the brink of the ledge? Competency Based

Ans. The young seagull pretended to fall asleep on the brink of the ledge because he wanted to draw the attention of his family who were ignoring him. He wanted his family to show some sympathy and provide him food as he was very hungry.

4. Describe the young seagull's first flight. CBSE 2023

Ans. As the young seagull fell from the ledge, he was filled with fear. However soon, his wings spread out and he found himself flying. Upon realising that he was finally flying, the young seagull was overjoyed. He screamed with joy as he was no longer afraid of flying.

5. The young seagull's mother was very clever. Do you agree? Justify your answer. Competency Based

Ans. The young seagull's mother was very clever. She knew that her child, the young seagull had been hungry for more than 24 hours. So, he could be lured to fly. Using this as her opportunity, she comes near the ledge with food. However, she stayed on the edge. As she had predicted, her child was hungry and to satisfy his hunger, he jumped from the cliff and started to fly.

6. Describe the young seagull's emotions when he flew over the sea.

Ans. When the young seagull flew over the sea, he felt terror at once but the next moment his fear of flying was gone. He spread his wings wide in the air. He flew over the sea screaming loudly with happiness in success of his first flight.

7. How did the young seagull and his family celebrate his first flight?

Ans. When the young seagull started flying, he was filled with joy and delight. His family came near him and were flying around him. They celebrated the young seagull's first flight. They screamed with joy and praised him. They even offered him pieces of fish to eat.

8. The Oxford Dictionary defines 'hangry' as 'bad-tempered or irritable as a result of hunger'.

To what extent can the young seagull's motivation to fly be attributed to being hungry? Support your stance with evidence from the text. CBSE Question Bank 2021

Ans. It is true to say that it was the young seagull's hunger that motivated him to fly. The young seagull had not eaten for 24 hours. Hence, he was very hungry. In such a situation, when he saw his mother tearing food, his hunger increased. Later, when his mother came near him with food, he jumped at the fish without considering that his mother stooped near the edge. Hence, he fell down and soon, started flying.

9. "The young seagull was alone on his ledge." How far do you think this condition was by his choice?

Ans. The young seagull was alone on his ledge. This condition was the result of the young seagull's choice of not taking his first flight. Even after receiving repetitive scolding from his parents, the young seagull could not muster up the courage to fly with his family.

10. If you were the family member of the young seagull, would you also decide not go near him? Elaborate with reason.

Ans. If I were the family member of the young seagull, I would have also decided not to go near him. Sometimes parents and elders have to take strict decision to make their children able to face the hardships of life. Like in this case, the continuous scolding and leaving the young seagull alone hungry on the ledge made him overcome his fear of flying and he could take a plunge.

11. The young seagull "failed to muster up courage to take that plunge". In what way can the reference to the 'plunge' here be both literal and metaphorical? Explain. **CBSE Question Bank 2021** **CBSE Additional SQP 2023-24**

Ans. The literal meaning of plunge is 'a sudden jump'. Metaphorically, 'plunge' can be understood as diving deep into something new. So, the term can be applied to the young seagull correctly in both the senses. Literally, he had to dive from the hill cliff and metaphorically, he dived into the new act of flying.

12. The 'fight or flight response', that is, to stay and face a situation or run from it- is an automatic reaction to an event perceived as stressful or harmful.
How would you evaluate the young seagull's response on finding himself off the ledge?

Ans. When the young seagull realised that he dived off the ledge, he was full of terror. His heart stopped breathing momentarily. But soon after he felt his wings opened outwards he could feel the wind on his chest feathers. He was no more falling headway down the sea.
He realised that his wings supported him and he could fly like his family. Therefore, his natural response of flight came forward.

13. Validate the given statement with reference to baby seagull's fear.
"Fear doesn't exist anywhere else other than one's mind." **Competency Based**

Ans. The little seagull could not take flight because he believed that his wings won't support his body.
He saw his family fly yet the fear remained with him. It overpowered any sense of assurance and stopped him from believing in himself and his wings. This fear of the baby seagull validates the given statement.

14. Describe the mood of 'His First Flight' towards the end of the chapter. Support the answer with an example from the text. **Competency Based**

Ans. Towards the ends of the lesson, the mood of the story is celebratory as the young seagull had finally started flying. Initially, the young seagull had not flown because he was afraid of falling into the sea. However, after some efforts from his mother, he had flown perfectly. As a result, there is a feeling of accomplishment and joy among the family.

15. Flying is a natural act in birds. Then why was the young seagull 'exhausted by the strange exercise'? Justify the given statement with reference to baby seagull's fear. **CBSE 2024**

Ans. The young seagull was 'exhausted by the strange exercise', despite flying being natural for birds, because it was his very first attempt at flying. Fuelled by his fear of falling and failing, the initial exertion felt overwhelming. His exhaustion steammed more from the mental and emotional energy spent overcoming his deep-rooted fear than from the physical act of flying itself.

Long Answer Type Questions

1. "They were beckoning to him, calling shrilly". Why did the seagull's parents threaten him and cajole him to fly? Compare it with your experiences when your parents encouraged you to do something for the first time? **Competency Based**

Ans. The young seagull's parents wanted him to fly just like his two brothers and sister. So, when he got too afraid to fly, the young seagull's parents scolded him and even threatened him to let him starve.
To motivate the young seagull to fly, his parents even taunted him. However, he could not muster up courage to do so. Finally, his mother tempted the young seagull with food. This trick was successful and the young seagull finally started to fly. The policy used by the young seagull's parents was to encourage the young seagull whom they loved and cared for.
The situation faced by the seagull is similar to many situations we face in our lives. We are also filled with fear while doing a thing for the first time like riding a bicycle, swimming or travelling alone, etc. In these circumstances, our family, especially parents, encourage or sometimes even pressurise us to move ahead.
Even though they know that it could be a failure, they give us a boost to excel. The result of such a behaviour can be seen in the young seagull.

2. His father and mother had come around calling to him shrilly, upbraiding him, threatening to let him starve on his ledge unless he flew away.
In the above line 'His First Flight' do you think the seagull's parents took the right approach to make him fly? In 100-120 words, justify your stance with two reasons. **Competency Based**

Ans. No, I believe that their approach was incorrect because they let their anger take the decision for how to teach the young seagull. This might have made him feel abandoned and unsupported. The parents should have accepted his fear instead of threatening him and let his siblings tease him for it. Rather, they taunted him for his cowardice and isolated him. This added to his fear which affected his confidence and discouraged him. He quietly hid inside the little hole under the ledge.
This made him feel that he would never be able to fly like his brothers and sister.

However, I also understand that the parents were worried about their child and wanted him to accept his natural trait. They did not know how to get the young seagull to fly. As a result, they had to depend on such means to get the young seagull to fly.

3. Was the young seagull same bird at the beginning and at the end of the lesson? Compare and contrast two kinds of the same seagull in the lesson.

Ans. No, the young seagull was not the same bird at the beginning and at the end of the lesson. In the beginning, the young seagull used to be all alone on his ledge. His two brothers and sister had flown away the day before. He had been afraid of flying with them. Whenever he tried to flap his wings, he was seized with fear. He felt certain that his wings would never support him. His father and mother flew around calling to him shrilly. They were constantly scolding and taunting him. They were threatening to let him starve on his ledge unless he flew away.

However, the young seagull was more confident and sure of his success in the end. He was maddened by hunger and dived towards the fish. After trials and errors, his wings spread outwards. Gradually he was flying, forgetting all his hesitations and fears. He could float on the ocean now. His success was welcomed by his family as he had conquered his fear of flying.

**4. A noted author, Richard Bach wrote - "For most gulls it was not flying that mattered, but eating. For this gull, though, it was not eating that mattered, but flight."
Evaluate this statement with respect to the young seagull.** **CBSE Question Bank 2021**

Ans. Richard Bach's statement holds true for the young seagull in the story. Unlike most gulls, who prioritise eating above all else, the young seagull's primary focus is on flight. While food is essential for survival, the young seagull's desire to fly surpasses his hunger. This is evident when he chooses to separate himself from his family on the ledge to practice flying rather than joining them in searching for food.

The young seagull's passion for flight is driven by a deep sense of curiosity, adventure and a longing for freedom. He finds joy and purpose in the act of flying itself, experiencing a sense of fulfillment. Food becomes secondary to him as he becomes consumed by his desire to master the art of flight.

5. Look at the image of Maslow's hierarchy of needs. **CBSE Question Bank 2021**

Abraham Maslow devised a theory of motivation that shows the basic needs at the bottom and more advanced needs as you move up. It includes the theory that fundamental needs must be met before an individual can be motivated to achieve higher order needs.

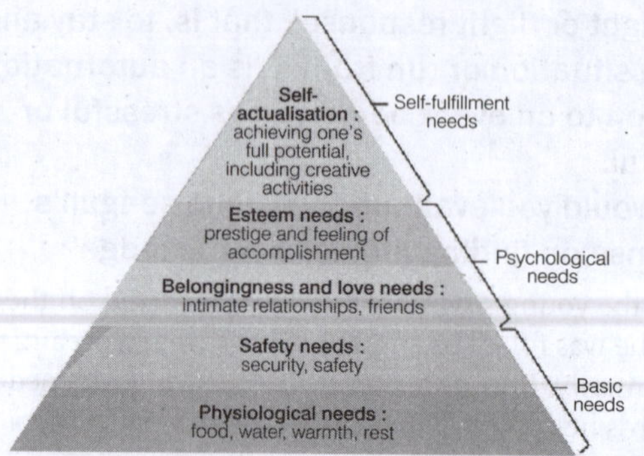

Where in this hierarchy of needs, would you locate the young seagull's first flight? Justify your response.

Ans. The young seagull's first flight would be located at the bottom of the pyramid under physiological needs.

Some German proverbs say- 'Wait is a hard word to the hungry' and 'A hungry belly has no ears'. A hungry living being cannot think of anything else except food. It is evident from the story that one can put even one's life to danger to satisfy one's hunger, a fundamental need according to Maslow's theory. Similarly, the seagull did not care about his life and forgot his fear while jumping off the ledge to take hold of the fish in his mother's beak to satisfy his hunger.

6. Look at the given image of different parenting styles and what they signify.

The Four Parenting Styles

	Sensitive & Responsive	Stern & Punitive
Demanding	Authoritative	Authoritarian
Doesn't enforce limits	Permissive	Uninvolved

Which of the given parenting styles would you attribute to the young seagull's parents?

Do you think there was a difference between the mother's and father's attitude?

Support your answer with reference to the text. **CBSE Question Bank 2021**

Ans. After reading the story 'His First Flight', it can be concluded that there was a difference between the mother's and father's attitude. The father displayed an 'Uninvolved' parenting style as he was not much concerned about the seagull's first flight. In contrast, the mother can be termed as 'Authoritative'. On one hand, she was adamant about making her child learn the art of flying and removing his fear of flying. On the other, the mother seemed worried about her hungry seagull and took a fish in her beak to give it to him. But, she knew that it was the right time to teach him. So, instead of spoon-feeding him, she played a trick on him. She halted just a few steps away from the seagull. The sight of food maddened the hungry seagull and he jumped towards her. Her trick worked like magic and the young seagull could take up his first step towards flying.

ASSESSMENT EXERCISE

Extract Based Questions

Read the following extracts carefully and answer the questions that follow.

1. The young Seagull was alone on his ledge. His two brothers and his sister had already flown away the day before. He had been afraid to fly with them. Somehow when he had taken a little run forward to the brink of the ledge and attempted to flap his wings he became afraid. The great expanse of sea stretched down beneath and it was such a long way down – miles down. He felt certain that his wings would never support him; so he bent his head and ran away back to the little hole under the ledge where he slept at night.

(i) (A) The young seagull was making excuses to not fly.
(B) The brothers and sisters of young seagull learnt to fly a day before.

(a) A is true B is false
(b) B is true A is false
(c) Both are true
(d) Both are false

(ii) Where did he run to hide?

(iii) The young seagull was ....

(iv) Pick out the word from the extract that means the same as the 'verge'.

2. He dropped his legs to stand on the green sea. His legs sank into it. He screamed with fright and attempted to rise again flapping his wings. But he was tired and weak with hunger and he could not rise, exhausted by the strange exercise. His feet sank into the green sea, and then his belly touched it and he sank no further. He was floating on it, and around him his family was screaming, praising him and their beaks were offering him scraps of dog-fish.

(i) Select the option that correctly captures the usage of the word 'fright' in the above extract.

(a) The rabbit looked fright as it ran.
(b) I am really fright about speaking in front of the class.
(c) She's fright to walk alone at night.
(d) The snake gave everyone a fright.

(ii) What was his family offering him? What is its purpose?

(iii) Why was his family praising him?

(a) He made his first flight.
(b) He ate scraps of dogfish.
(c) He conquered his fear.
(d) Both (a) and (c)

(iv) Complete the analogy by selecting the suitable word from the text.

Chuckling : Laughter :: Crumbs : ....

Short Answer (SA) Type Questions

1. Why did the young seagull fail to muster up his courage to fly?

2. What happened to the young seagull when his family left him alone on the ledge?

3. Do you sympathise with the young seagull? Give reasons in support of your view.

4. What significance does the green sea hold for the young seagull? **Competency Based**

Long Answer (LA) Type Questions

1. Do you think that the young seagull would have never tried to fly if the seagull family hadn't left him alone without food? Why or why not? **Competency Based**

2. The young seagull's family loved him. Justify.

II. The Black Aeroplane

by Frederick Forsyth

The second story 'Black Aeroplane' has been written by Frederick Forsyth. The story follows a reckless pilot who drives his old aeroplane into the storm clouds in an attempt to reach his family quickly. However, he gets lost in the storm clouds and fears for his life. Luckily, he is saved by the pilot of a mysterious black aeroplane, who directs him out of the storm.

The Narrator's Trip to England

The narrator was flying his old Dakota aeroplane over France back to England at night. The sky was clear and moon was shining. He was dreaming of his holiday and looking forward to be with his family.

It was 1:30 in the morning. When the narrator looked down, he saw the lights of Paris city in front of him. He called the Paris Control to get instructed about the way. Paris Control advised him to turn 12 degrees West.
The narrator switched to his last fuel tank and turned his airplane twelve degrees West towards England.

Appearance of Storm Clouds

When the narrator reached 150 km ahead of Paris, he suddenly saw huge storm clouds infront of him. He knew that it was not possible to fly up and over the clouds. He also did not have enough fuel to go around the clouds. First, he thought of going back to Paris. However, the thought of breakfast with his family, made him determined to fly through the clouds.

A Risky but Brave Decision

The narrator decided to take the risk and flew into the storm but everything went out of control. He was unable to see anything because everything outside the plane was black. The aeroplane jumped and twisted in the air, and the compass stopped working. He tried to contact the Paris Control for directions but his radio had also stopped working.

A Black Aeroplane Appears

When the narrator was lost in the storm, he saw another black aeroplane near him. It had no lights on its wings and its pilot's face was turned towards him. The pilot of the black aeroplane raised his hand and signalled the narrator to follow him. So, he followed the strange aeroplane.

Narrator Follows Black Aeroplane

The narrator followed the black aeroplane for about half an hour. Now, he only had the fuel to fly the plane for five or ten minutes. He felt frightened again. But suddenly, he saw two straight lines of lights ahead of him on the ground. They were the lights of an airport's runway. When he turned to look for the black aeroplane, he could not see it anywhere. He was able to land safely which brought him a lot of relief.

The Black Aeroplane Remains a Mystery

After landing, the narrator went to the control centre of the airport. He asked the woman in the control centre about the mysterious plane. He wanted to find out where the other plane was and wanted to thank its pilot for guiding him in the storm. However, the woman looked at him strangely and laughed. She told him that there was no other plane flying except his on such a stormy night. The narrator was surprised at this. He wondered who had helped him.

Word Meaning

Word	Meaning
countryside	a rural area
twisted	to rotate around a fixed point
dead	had stopped working
glad	relieved
radar	a machine used for locating objects at various distances

NCERT FOLDER

NCERT Intext and Exercise Questions

THINKING ABOUT THE TEXT (NCERT PAGE 40)

Q.1 'I'll take the risk'. What is the risk? Why does the narrator take it? CBSE 2023

Ans. The risk referred to here is the decision of the narrator to fly through the storm clouds. The narrator took the risk because he wanted to go home and have breakfast with his family in England the next day.

Q.2 Describe the narrator's experience as he flew the aeroplane into the storm.

Ans. The narrator had a very intense and frightening experience in the storm. As he entered the storm, his plane started jumping and twisting. He could not see anything outside the plane as it was totally dark. When he looked at the compass and other instruments, they had stopped functioning. It was a terrible experience full of danger and uncertainty.

Suddenly, he saw another black aeroplane by his side. The pilot of the plane signalled him to follow. The narrator followed it and soon landed safely.

Q.3 Why does the narrator say, "I landed and was not sorry to walk away from the old Dakota..."?

Ans. The narrator said this because he had a terrible experience of flying. He had entered a storm cloud in his old Dakota aeroplane. While in the cloud, the plane turned and twisted, and all its equipments had stopped working. So when he had landed safely, he was not sorry for leaving the plane. He was in fact relieved and happy for having survived the ordeal.

Q.4 What made the woman in the control centre look at the narrator strangely? Competency Based

Ans. The woman in the control centre looked at the narrator strangely because the narrator asked her about a black aeroplane. However, the airport's radar screen showed no plane except the narrator's plane in the sky during that stormy night.

Q.5 Who do you think helped the narrator to reach safely? Discuss this among yourselves and give reasons for your answer.

Ans. It is very difficult to identify the unknown pilot who helped the narrator to reach safely. However, one can think that perhaps it was the narrator himself who overcame his fear in the storm. This was so because no other plane was seen in the radar except the narrator's Dakota plane.

In that fearsome situation, he might have been imagining things. He himself was a skilled pilot; thus, he helped himself in landing safely.

It could also be a supernatural or divine entity that provided guidance to the narrator.

THINKING ABOUT LANGUAGE (NCERT PAGE 40)

I. Study the sentences given below.

(a) They looked like black mountains.

(b) Inside the clouds, everything was suddenly black.

(c) In the black clouds near me, I saw another aeroplane.

(d) The strange black aeroplane was there.

The word 'black' in sentences (a) and (c) refers to the darkest colour. But in (b) and (d) (here) it means without light/with no light.

'Black' has a variety of meanings in different contexts. For example:

(a) 'I prefer black tea' means 'I prefer tea without milk'.

(b) 'With increasing pollution the future of the world is *black*' means 'with increasing pollution the future of the world is very depressing/without hope'.

Now, try to guess the meanings of the word 'black' in the sentences given below. Check the meanings in the dictionary and find out whether you have guessed right.

Q.1 Go and have a bath, your hands and face are absolutely *black* ....

Ans. The meaning of 'black' in this sentence is that the face and hands are dark because of dust and dirt.

Q.2 The taxi-driver gave Ratan a black look as he crossed the road when the traffic light was green. ....

Ans. Here, 'black' refers to an angry look.

Q.3 The bombardment of Hiroshima is one of the *blackest* crimes against humanity. ....

Ans. Here, 'blackest' refers to the darkest and cruellest crime against humanity.

Q.4 Very few people enjoy Harold Pinter's *black* comedy ....

Ans. Here, 'black' refers to dark and gloomy comedy.

Q.5 **Sometimes shopkeepers store essential goods to create false scarcity and then sell these in *black*. ....**

Ans. The meaning of 'black' in this sentence is that the shopkeepers sell the described goods 'at a higher price'.

Q.6 **Villagers had beaten the criminal *black* and blue. ....**

Ans. Here, 'black' means that the criminal suffered excessive beating at the hands of the villagers and thus, was bruised.

II. ***Look at these sentences taken from the lesson you have just read :***

(a) I was flying my old Dakota aeroplane.

(b) The young seagull had been afraid to fly with them.

In the first sentence, the narrator was controlling an aircraft in the air. In the second sentence, the seagull was afraid to move through the air, using its wings.

Match the phrases given under Column A with their meanings given under Column B.

A	B
1. Fly a flag	(a) Move quickly/suddenly
2. Fly into rage	(b) Be successful
3. Fly along	(c) Display a flag on a long pole
4. Fly high	(d) Escape from a place
5. Fly the coop	(e) Become suddenly very angry

Ans. 1. (c), 2. (e), 3. (a), 4. (b), 5. (d)

REVIEW EXERCISE

Including Competency Based Questions

Part I

Multiple Choice Questions

1. What is an old Dakota?

(a) A town from where the pilot took off.
(b) A town where the pilot landed.
(c) The name of the plane the pilot had been flying.
(d) The other aeroplane.

Ans. (c) The name of the plane the pilot had been flying.

2. Why was the pilot of old Dakota happy while flying his plane?

(a) He was going to meet his family.
(b) He was alone up in the sky.
(c) He was going to have an English breakfast the following day.
(d) All of the above

Ans. (d) All of the above

3. How was the pilot feeling as he was approaching Paris? **Competency Based**

(a) Reckless (b) Reflective
(c) Optimistic (d) Whimsical

Ans. (c) Optimistic

4. "I should call Paris Control soon." Why did the pilot think of doing so?

(a) Because he was stuck in the storm.
(b) Because he wanted to know about the other pilot.
(c) Because he wanted the directions for England.
(d) Because he wanted to go to Paris.

Ans. (c) Because he wanted the directions for England.

5. Why was it impossible to see anything outside the aeroplane?

(a) As there were hailstorms outside.
(b) As there were dark clouds all around.
(c) It was night time.
(d) All of the above

Ans. (b) As there were dark clouds all around.

6. "I'll take the risk." Why did the pilot want to take the risk?

(a) To meet his family
(b) To have an English breakfast
(c) To prove his courage
(d) Both (a) and (b)

Ans. (d) Both (a) and (b)

7. I landed and was not sorry to walk away from the old Dakota near the control tower. What does this line indicates?

(a) The pilot's pride
(b) The pilot's relief
(c) The pilot's shame
(d) The pilot's confusion

Ans. (b) The pilot's relief

8. Why did the narrator desire to meet the pilot of the black aeroplane?

(a) To ask him what he was doing there

(b) To thank him

(c) To meet him and ask him to teach him flying

(d) To invite him to breakfast

Ans. (b) To thank him

9. Why was the pilot of the old Dakota shocked after hearing the woman's word?

(a) Because she told him that no other plane was flying that night.

(b) Because she told him that his plane was only plane seen on radar.

(c) Because she told him that no plane has landed on the airport.

(d) Both (a) and (b)

Ans. (d) Both (a) and (b)

10. What is the main theme of the story 'The Black Aeroplane'?

(a) The story oscillates or shifts between Miracle and Mystery.

(b) The pilot of the mysterious plane might be a figment of his own fertile imagination.

(c) Both (a) and (b)

(d) None of the above

Ans. (c) Both (a) and (b)

11. The Black Aeroplane is a/an .... story. CBSE 2021 Term I

(a) ghost (b) adventure (c) mystery (d) true

Ans. (c) mystery

12. Select the option that show the correct relationship between 1 and 2. Competency Based

1. The narrator might have been able to fly through the storm if he was in a new aeroplane.
2. Instruments in the narrator's aeroplane that were working well suddenly stopped functioning in the storm.

(a) 1 is the result of 2.

(b) 1 is the explanation for 2.

(c) 1 is an inference based on 2.

(d) 1 and 2 are independent of each other.

Ans. (c) 1 is an inference based on 2.

13. In the line given below from 'Black Aeroplane', when the writer refers to the clouds as black mountains, what is he referring to? They looked like black mountains standing in front of me across the sky.

(a) His hopelessness due to imminent death

(b) His despair for having to take a detour

(c) His excitement to fly over them

(d) His fear of their enormous size

Ans. (d) His fear of their enormous size

14. Choose the option that lists the set of statements that are not true about the other aeroplane according to 'The Black Aeroplane' story.

1. The other aeroplane was called the black aeroplane.
2. The other aeroplane had the narrator's mentor.
3. The other aeroplane was the narrator's inner conscience.
4. The other aeroplane helped the narrator through the storm clouds.
5. The other aeroplane was a ghost plane.
6. The narrator was aware of the mysterious nature of the other aeroplane.

(a) 4 and 5 (b) 1, 3 and 6 (c) 3 and 6 (d) 2, 5 and 6

Ans. (d) 2, 5 and 6

15. Choose the option that lists the set of statements that are not true for the pilot of old Dakota plane.

1. He was a pilot.
2. His plane had malfunctioned while flying.
3. He had entered a storm.
4. He was helped by a black aeroplane.
5. He was very adventurous and courageous.
6. He wanted to learn flying from the other pilot of the black aeroplane.

(a) 1 and 3 (b) 2 and 6 (c) 4 and 5 (d) Only 6

Ans. (b) 2 and 6

Extract Based Questions

1. The moon was coming up in the east, behind me, and stars were shining in the clear sky above me. There wasn't a cloud in the sky. I was happy to be alone high up above the sleeping countryside. I was flying my old Dakota aeroplane over France back to England. I was dreaming of my holiday and looking forward to being with my family. I looked at my watch: one thirty in the morning. CBSE 2025

(i) What time of the day is the above extract set in?

(a) Dawn (b) Afternoon

(c) Night (d) Dusk

Ans. (c) Dusk

(ii) State any one inference about the writer from the given context.

Ans. The writer was feeling nostalgic and excited about reuniting with his family, as indicated by the phrase, "I was looking forward to being with my family."

(iii) **Fill in the blank with the correct word from the brackets.**

The use of the phrase 'clear sky' along with adds to a sense of .... favourable/flavourful conditions.

Ans. favourable

(iv) **How does the serene atmosphere described by the narrator contribute to the mood and anticipation of his journey back to England? Elaborate in about 40 words, with reference to the extract.**

Ans. The serene atmosphere, with a clear sky, shining stars, and a peaceful countryside, creates a calm and dreamy mood. It reflects the narrator's joy and anticipation of returning home, making his journey feel more pleasant and memorable.

2. Read the following extract carefully and answer the questions that follow.

Inside the clouds, everything was suddenly black. It was impossible to see anything outside the aeroplane. The old aeroplane jumped and twisted in the air. I looked at the compass. I couldn't believe my eyes: the compass was turning round and round and round. It was dead. It would not work! The other instruments were suddenly dead, too. I tried the radio. "Paris Control? Paris Control? Can you hear me?" There was no answer. The radio was dead too. I had no radio, no compass, and I could not see where I was. I was lost in the storm. **CBSE 2023**

(i) **As soon as the pilot was inside the cloud ....**

(a) his ears got blocked (b) he choked with fear

(c) his vision was obstructed

(d) he was jumping up and down

Ans. (c) his vision was obstructed

(ii) **Why didn't the Paris air control reply to the pilot's call for help?**

Ans. The Paris air control didn't reply to the pilot's call for help because the pilot's call couldn't reach them. The storm had rendered all the instruments dead and the signal for help could not reach the Paris air control.

(iii) **Complete the sentence appropriately.**

The devices in the aeroplane had ....

Ans. stopped responding completely

(iv) **Why was the pilot unable to find a direction in the storm?**

Ans. The pilot was unable to find any direction in the storm because all of his instruments like the compass had stopped working. He couldn't estimate his position because everything outside the aeroplane was completely black due to the storm clouds.

3. Read the following extract carefully and answer the questions that follow.

Suddenly, I came out of the clouds and saw two long straight lines of lights in front of me. It was a runway! An airport! I was safe! I turned to look for my friend in the black aeroplane, but the sky was empty. There was nothing there. The black aeroplane was gone. I could not see it anywhere.

(i) **State True or False.**

All of the given statements are true according to the extract.

(a) He was struck in stormy clouds.

(b) He landed safely because of his courage.

(c) The black aeroplane was just an imaginary existence.

Ans. True

(ii) **Why is it fair that the narrator's tone, when he says 'I was safe?', is that of relief?**

Competency Based

Ans. The narrator was flying back to his home when he got caught in storm clouds. His radio was dead and so was the compass. He was saved by another plane in the storm which helped him come out of the clouds and land safely on the runway. Thus, the narrator rightly felt relief on being saved.

(iii) **The pilot was ....**

(a) relieved for landing safely at the airport

(b) scared how to reach the airport

(c) shocked to find the black plane missing

(d) sad to lose his friend in black aeroplane

Ans. (a) relieved for landing safely at the airport

(iv) **Why did the narrator turn back?**

Ans. The narrator turned back to see the black airplane.

4. Read the following extract carefully and answer the questions that follow.

I was safe! I turned to look for my friend in the black aeroplane, but the sky was empty. There was nothing there. The black aeroplane was gone. I could not see it anywhere. I landed and was not sorry to walk away from the old Dakota near the control tower. I went and asked a woman in the control centre where I was and who the other pilot was. I wanted to say 'Thank you'. She looked at me very strangely, and then laughed. "Another aeroplane? Up there in this storm? No other aeroplanes were flying tonight. Yours was the only one I could see on the radar." So, who helped me...

CBSE Question Bank 2021

(i) Which of the following is not true according to the given extract?

(a) The narrator was rather elated to get down from the old Dakota.

(b) The woman told him that she didn't pay much attention to the other aeroplane.

(c) The narrator wondered who could have helped him.

(d) The woman was inside the control centre.

Ans. (b) The woman told him that she didn't pay much attention to the other aeroplane.

(ii) What impression did the narrator leave on the woman in the control centre? Why?

Ans. The woman in the control centre must have thought the narrator to be a strange man who had the habit of dreaming things that are unreal. She could have also believed that the narrator was in shock because of his horrid experience inside the storm clouds.

(iii) Which phrase would correctly substitute 'walk away from', in the given sentence from the extract?

I landed and was not sorry to <u>walk away from</u> the old Dakota near the control tower.

Ans. I landed and was not sorry to <u>leave</u> the old Dakota near the control tower.

(iv) Why do you think the woman immediately knew that there had been no other planes on the radar, or in the sky?

Ans. The woman must have been aware of that information because of the fact that she was assigned to keep an eye on the radar and assist any passing aircrafts in course correction.

Part II

Short Answer Type Questions

1. Describe the narrator's feelings while he was flying his aeroplane back to England.

Ans. The narrator was feeling calm and content while flying his aeroplane back to England. It was the only aeroplane in the sky above the quiet countryside and he was happy for it. He was enjoying the sight of the moon and the stars in the clear night sky. The narrator was also excited because he knew that if he reached on time, he would be able to have a good breakfast with his family.

2. How would you describe the mood of the story, 'Black Aeroplane' as it begins? **CBSE Question Bank 2021**

Ans. The mood of the story in the beginning is very calm and happy. The pilot of the old Dakota plane is excited to meet his family and imagines having English breakfast with them.The stars are shining in the clear sky so he hopes to reach England before morning in his old Dakota plane.

3. Why did the narrator follow the pilot of another aeroplane?

Or What do you think prompted the narrator to act like 'an obedient child'?

Or I was very happy to go behind the strange aeroplane like an obedient child.

In 20-30 words, explain why the narrator said the above line in the story 'The Black Aeroplane'. **CBSE Question Bank 2021**

Ans. The narrator followed the pilot of another aeroplane because he had lost his way in the storm clouds. Its pilot signalled him to follow him. He thought he was trying to help him. So, he followed the black aeroplane like an obedient child, to get out of the clouds safely.

4. Why did the narrator want to meet the pilot of the black aeroplane?

Ans. The narrator wanted to meet the pilot of the black aeroplane because he wanted to thank its pilot. He had saved the narrator's life by guiding him out of the storm clouds. The narrator was able to land safely at an airport because of him.

5. What rational course of action should the pilot have taken when he saw the storm clouds? **Competency Based**

Ans. The only rational course of action that the pilot should have taken when he saw the storm clouds was to go back to Paris. He should have waited for the storm to pass and then, flew to England to be with his family.

6. Based on your reading, would you call the narrator a family man? Justify your stance.

Ans. It is evident from the story that the narrator took the risk to meet his family. He was excited to stay with them during the vacations. He was eager to join his family at the breakfast table. This shows him to be a family man.

7. Do you think that after his experience, the narrator would be able to truly enjoy the English breakfast he had yearned for? Why/Why not? **Competency Based**

Ans. After his experience with the storm, the narrator would not be able to truly enjoy the English breakfast he had yearned for. Even though he landed safely from that storm, he had certain questions and doubts about that black aeroplane and its pilot, whom he met up in the storm and who helped him pass through it.

8. As a reader, do you feel betrayed or let down in the way the story ends? Validate your opinion.

Ans. Yes, I feel betrayed in the way the story ends. The story ends without any information about the black aeroplane and its pilot. The author should have given a proper ending to the story. He should have given the details about the plane and its pilot; such as why there were no lights on the plane, why was it not on radar, etc. Readers are left to make assumptions about them.

9. James Lane Allen says, 'Adversity reveals character'. What do you learn about the narrator from the experience?
Mention any two traits supported by the textual evidence. **CBSE Question Bank 2021**

Ans. The statement 'Adversity reveals character' by James Lane Allen is very true. We can say so for the pilot too. He is revealed to be a bold, courageous and adventrous family man. He enters a huge storm cloud, despite knowing the risks to be with his family.

10. What is the message that the narrator wants to give to the readers through the lesson 'the Black Aeroplane?

Ans. The message that the narrator wanted to convey to his readers was to never lose hope in the most hopeless situation. The narrator was really in such a hopeless situation when he lost contact with Paris control and all his instruments were dead. It was the mysterious pilot who helped him and gave him hope that he could survive in such a situation.

Long Answer Type Questions

1. Why and when did the narrator say that 'everything' was going well, it was an easy flight? **CBSE 2020**

Ans. In the story 'The Black Aeroplane', the narrator was a pilot who was flying his own aeroplane Dakota over France to go to England. While flying, the atmosphere around him was very quiet. It was a clear night and the moon was coming in the East, and the stars were shining in the sky. The aeroplane enjoyed a smooth flight over a serene countryside.

Happy and calm, the narrator was dreaming of his holiday and looking forward to having English breakfast with his family. He contacted Paris control centre for directions and was asked to turn 12 degrees West. In total, the flight till now was easy and comfortable. No problems had yet been encountered and it was an enjoyable journey. At this time, the narrator said that everything was going well, it was an easy flight.

2. Do you agree that the story 'The Black Aeroplane' is a mystery story? Justify.

Ans. Yes, I agree that this is a mystery story. The narrator was flying his old Dakota plane on a clear night sky. The flying was easy in the quite sky. However, very suddenly and mysteriously he saw black storm clouds in the sky. He had limited fuel, so he could neither fly over the clouds nor go back to Paris.

So, he entered the storm clouds. Inside the storm clouds, everything was dark. The narrator could not see anything outside the plane. Again mysteriously, all the equipments of the plane had stopped working and the narrator was lost.

Suddenly, a mysterious black plane with no lights came. Its pilot guided him through the black clouds.

He took him out of a dangerous situation and led him to safety. After the narrator had landed, he wanted to thank the pilot for helping him. But he was surprised to know that only his aeroplane was seen on the radar.

Hence, 'The Black Aeroplane' is a mystery story.

3. Imagine that the narrator shared his story with friends and family once he got home. One of them, a spiritual leader, decided to incorporate the story as part of his weekly sermon to the congregation. Another friend, a psychologist, worked the story into his next lecture on survival instinct and crisis management.
Do you think the two interpretations of the story would be different? If so, how?
What insights might the narrator get about his mysterious experience, if he were to attend both the sessions? **CBSE Question Bank 2021**

Ans. Yes, I think the two interpretations of the story would be different. The spiritual leader would interpret the story in a way to tell his disciples that God takes care of his children even in extreme conditions. He would preach that God sent an angel to save the narrator. Thus, we should not lose hope and keep trusting God.

The psychologist friend would describe the incident in a totally different manner. He might say that God helps those who help themselves; the mysterious plane was the narrator's soul that drove him out of the storm.

If the narrator happens to listen to both of these workshops he would accept either of the two philosophies as true on the basis of his nature which is not specified in the story. If he is a religious person, he would accept the spiritual friend's opinion. But, he might like to go with the psychologist's interpretation if he is a man of logical thinking.

4. In a parallel world, the pilot of the black aeroplane narrates his adventure in a story titled 'The Old Dakota'. You come across an excerpt from the story, which responds to the ending questions of 'Black Aeroplane' and describes the black aeroplane pilot's decision to fly away after watching the Dakota land.
Compose the said excerpt of the story employing relevant details from 'Black Aeroplane'.

CBSE Question Bank 2021

Ans. Last night, I caught up in a black storm. I was struggling to find my way out. I was flying my latest well-equipped black aeroplane but the lights went off. Luckily, I did not lose connection with the control room. When I was trying to find out the right direction, I spotted an old Dakota plane flying amidst the black clouds which also seemed to be lost in the storm. I think the pilot was unable to contact the control room.

I felt like helping the pilot so I followed it. On coming closer, I waved at the pilot to follow me and he did so obediently. Almost half an hour later when the runway was visible, the Dakota plane landed at the airport whereas I continued forward towards my destination. I hope he landed safely!

5. Motivation plays an important role in taking risks in life and in succeeding. Do you agree? Discuss with reference to the pilot of the old Dakota and the young seagull. **CBSE 2023**

Ans. It is true to say that motivation plays an important role in taking risks in life and in succeeding. Every brave action is motivated by the need to accomplish something exceptional. One is encouraged to succeed by this desire to take chances.

The stories 'His First Flight' and 'The Black Aeroplane' emphasise that success requires taking risks.
Even though some choices seem risky, they must be made in order to fulfill one's goals successfully.
The inexperienced pilot and the young seagull make difficult choices but eventually succeed. The seagull made a risky choice because he unexpectedly fell off the ledge while attempting to get the fish from his mother's beak. He might have had a tragic ending if he hadn't found the courage to spread his wings.

The pilot made a risky choice by flying into stormy, dark clouds without sufficient information. The young seagull and the pilot shared a desire to succeed by taking chances. While the pilot's choice was influenced by his circumstances, the young seagull was driven or motivated by his hunger. He was forced to get home to spend time with his family and eat a hearty English breakfast. But once they both decided to succeed, there was no turning back.

6. The pilot in the black aeroplane was an illusion created by the narrator's own mind.
Justify the above opinion with reference to the story 'The Black Aeroplane'. In 100-120 words, mention two reasons why you think the narrator's mind may have played this trick. **Competency Based**

Ans. The story 'The Black Aeroplane' is a mystery story wherein a strange black aeroplane helps the author/narrator reach to safety. When the author goes out to find the pilot of the black aeroplane, he is surprised when he is told that there was no other aeroplane in the sky that night. Such a revelation makes us question about who helped the author.

In this regard, it is believed by many including me that there was no black pilot in reality. It was an illusion created by the author's mind so that the author could reach to safety. Such a claim is supported by the fact that the author was a skilled pilot who had undertaken a journey from Paris to England. He also thought that he would be able to come out of the storm safely. Hence, when his equipments stop working in the storm, his mind creates his illusion so that he could come out of the storm safely.

7. You have been asked to present an evaluation of the approaches of both, the Baby Seagull and the Pilot who was lost in the clouds, towards achieving their dreams of conquering the skies.
Write this presentation draft including your insights, comparing the approaches of both.
You may begin this way

One acknowledgement that both, the Seagull and the Pilot, wanted to .... however,..........

(Reference: Two Stories About Flying) **CBSE 2024**

Ans. One acknowledges that both the Seagull and the Pilot, wanted to move ahead in their dreams of conquering the skies but their approaches are very different. For the young Seagull, the dream to fly is its natural instinct.
It has the innate nature to fly and live its life to the fullest. However, it is scared for it feels that its wings won't work. Again its natural instinct called hunger came in to play. It was due to its hunger that it flew.

In contrast, the Pilot's decision to conquer the sky was driver by two things- his desire to visit his family and the confidence in his abilities that he would come out of the storm.

However, the fear of failure, in a situation wherein he could not see anything and the equipments malfunctioning, permeates his mind. Consequently, his subconscious comes into play and directs him into safety through the illusion of the black aeroplane.

Thus, while the dream and aspirations of the Seagull and the pilot coincide, they are successful in fulfilling them due to their different approaches.

ASSESSMENT EXERCISE

Extract Based Questions

Read the following extracts carefully and answer the questions that follow.

1. Paris was about 150 kilometers behind me when I saw the clouds. Storm clouds. They were huge. They looked like black mountains standing in front of me across the sky – I knew I could not fly up and over them, and I did not have enough fuel to fly around them to the North or South.

(i) Select the option that correctly captures the usage of the word 'storm' in the above extract.

(a) A sudden storm gave abundance of rain.

(b) The announcement provoked an immediate storm of protest.

(c) His speech was greeted with a storm of applause.

(d) The photos caused a storm when they were first published.

(ii) The author compares the clouds to ....

(iii) If you were in the author's position, how would you feel on seeing huge storm clouds?

1. Childish 2. Scared 3. Furious 4. Panicked

(iv) Why could the pilot not fly North or South to the clouds?

2. There was no answer. The radio was dead too. I had no radio, no compass, and I could not see where I was. I was lost in the storm. Then, in the black clouds quite near me, I saw another aeroplane. It had no lights on its wings, but I could see it flying next to me through the storm. I could see the pilots face turned towards me. I was very glad to see another person. He lifted one hand and waved.

"Follow me", he was saying. "Follow me."

'He knows that I am lost', I thought, 'He's trying to help me.'

(i) From where did the narrator expect an answer?

(ii) Why did the narrator not get any answer?

(iii) Why was the writer glad?

(a) To see another aeroplane in that storm

(b) He could connect to Paris Control Station

(c) He landed in England safely

(d) He returned to Paris

(iv) What was strange about the second plane?

Short Answer (SA) Type Questions

1. Where was the narrator going and why?

2. What problems did the pilot of the old Dakota plane face in the clouds?

3. How did the pilot of the black aeroplane help the narrator in the clouds?

Long Answer (LA) Type Questions

1. How had the narrator been rescued from the storm that night? Explain. What will be your reaction if you encounter such a situation?

2. 'God helps those who help themselves.' Do you think this statement is true with reference to 'The Black Aeroplane'? Elaborate. **Competency Based**

From the Diary of Anne Frank

by Anne Frank

CHAPTER SUMMARY

This chapter 'From the Diary of Anne Frank' is an extract from the diary of a 13 years old Jewish girl called Anne Frank. During the German occupation of the Netherlands, her family hid in her father's office in Amsterdam.

In the absence of a true friend, Anne wrote her experiences in a diary of Typhus. She died of Typhus in the concentration camps at Bergen Belsen. Her father, the sole survivor of the Holocaust, published this diary after her death in 1945.

Before you Read

Anne Frank or Anneliese Marie 'Anne Frank' was a Jewish girl born in Germany in 1929. Her family moved to Amsterdam during the Nazi occupation of Germany. As the Nazi occupation extended to the Netherlands, her family was trapped in Amsterdam. In July 1942, they went into hiding inside secret rooms in her father Otto Frank's office for two years. They were betrayed and transported to the concentration camp system where Anne and her sister died of typhus. When her father returned to his office, he found that Anne's diary was saved and published it.

The diary was given to Anne Frank for her thirteenth birthday and chronicles the events of her life from 12th June, 1942 until its final entry of 1st August, 1944. This book has been translated into several languages and is one of the most read books in the world. Several films, theatrical productions and even an opera have been based on this book. Since the diary provides an intimate examination of life under Nazi occupation, Anne Frank has become one of the most famous Holocaust victims.

Anne's Need to Write a Diary

Anne Frank, a thirteen years old girl, was gifted a diary by her father. She found writing to be a strange experience as she had never written a diary before. In her first entry, she expressed her desire to confide everything to the diary. She felt that paper had more patience than people. She thought that nobody would be interested in reading her diary.

Anne considered the diary to be a real friend with whom she could share all her secrets. She did not have any such friend. Even though Anne had a loving family and a number of friends, she could only talk to them about ordinary things. Therefore, she felt the need to write a diary. Anne made the diary her best friend and called it 'Kitty'.

Anne's Childhood and Family

Anne felt that a brief sketch of her family and life so far was necessary because it would help others understand what she was going to write in her diary. Anne called her father, Otto Frank the most adorable father. He was 36 years old when he married her mother Edith Hollander Frank, who was 25 years old.

She further wrote that her elder sister, Margot was born in 1926 and she herself was born on 12th June, 1929. Her family lived in Frankfurt till she was four. Then, her parents moved to Holland in 1933. At that time, Anne and her sister lived with their grandmother in Aachen. After their parents settled down in Holland, Margot went to Holland in December and Anne in February.

Anne's Schooling

Anne studied at the Montessori nursery school till she was six years old. At her farewell, she and her headmistress Mrs. Kuperus had tears in their eyes. Mrs. Kuperus gave her a heart breaking farewell.

The Death of Anne's Grandmother

Anne had great love for her grandmother. When her grandmother fell ill in the summer of 1941 and had an operation, Anne was very sad. Her grandmother died in January 1942. So, Anne lit a candle in her memory on her own birthday in June.

Anne's Views Towards School

After explaining about her life, Anne started her diary entry for 20th June, 1942. She started by writing about her day in the school when the teachers were going to tell the result.

All the students were afraid and they did not know who would enter the next class. Two boys, C.N. and Jacques had put their entire holiday savings on the bet of who would pass. Anne was frustrated at their continuous arguing so she would shout at them. However, they didn't shut down. Anne knew that she and her friend G.N. would go to the next class. She was only worried about Maths.
She always considered teachers to be the most unpredictable creatures on the Earth. So, she told her friends not to lose hope.

Anne's Relationship with the Teachers

Anne had nine teachers-seven men and two women. Anne was a good student and had a good relationship with all the teachers except Mr. Keesing, who taught her Maths. He was always annoyed by her talkative nature.

He used to give her extra homework as punishment. Once, he punished her by asking her to write an essay on the topic 'A Chatterbox'.

Completion of Extra Homework

After completing her homework, Anne started thinking about the essay 'A Chatterbox'.

Anne was unable to understand what she could write in the essay. Finally, she started writing to prove that talking was a necessity. She wrote three pages where she defined talking as a trait of a student and also mentioned that she had inherited this trait from her mother who was also very talkative.

More Punishments for Anne

Mr. Keesing read the essay in the class and laughed.
In another lesson when she talked, she was punished again. He gave her another essay as a punishment on the topic 'An Incorrigible Chatterbox'. Mr. Keesing did not complain for two lessons after she submitted the essay. However, during the third lesson, he caught Anne talking again.

So, he punished her again and asked her to write an essay on 'Quack, Quack, Quack, Said Mistress Chatterbox'. This made Anne woried as she did not have anything to write about on the topic.

Anne's Witty Homework

Anne wanted to write something interesting and different this time. So, with the help of her friend Sanne who was good at poetry, she wrote an essay in verse. The poem was about three baby ducklings of a father swan and a mother duck. The father swan bit the ducklings until they died because they quacked too much.

Anne was relieved when Mr. Keesing took the joke in the right way. He read the poem in the class as well as in other classes. Since then, Anne was allowed to talk and had not been assigned any extra homework. A change had come in Mr. Keesing's behaviour and he started cracking jokes in the class.

Word Meaning

Word	Meaning
musings	thoughts
listless	lacking energy or enthusiasm
brooding	thinking seriously
stiff-backed	with a hard cover
prompted	encouraged
confide	to tell someone a secret
liable	responsible
long awaited	expected for a long time
jot	write, put together
plunge	to go into
adorable	lovable
emigrated	went to settle
plunked down	put down forcefully
solemn	serious, grave
quaking	shaking because of fear
forthcoming	about to happen
outbursts	a sudden release of a strong emotion

Word	Meaning
staked	put on bet
pleading	requesting
glances	looks
dummies	persons of low intelligence
fogey	a dull, old-fashioned person
assigned	given
chatterbox	one who speaks too much
jotted	wrote
tucked	carried
ramble on	write at length
convincing	making agreeable
inherited traits	features taken from one's parents
proceeded	went ahead/forward
incorrigible	incurably bad, something that cannot be corrected
ingenuity	skill
quacked	talked
on the contrary	opposite to

NCERT FOLDER

NCERT Intext and Exercise Questions

ACTIVITY (NCERT PAGE 49)

Q.1 Do you keep a diary? Given below under 'A' are some terms we use to describe a written record of personal experience. Can you match them with their descriptions under 'B'? (You may look up the terms in a dictionary if you wish.)

	A	B
(i)	Journal	A book with a separate space or page for each day, in which you write down your thoughts and feelings or what has happened on that day.
(ii)	Diary	A full record of a journey, a period of time or an event, written every day.
(iii)	Log	A record of a person's own life and experiences (usually, a famous person).
(iv)	Memoir(s)	A written record of events with times and dates, usually official.

Ans.

	A	B
(i)	Journal	A full record of a journey, a period of time or an event, written every day.
(ii)	Diary	A book with a separate space or page for each day, in which you write down your thoughts and feelings or what has happened on that day.
(iii)	Log	A written record of events with times and dates, usually official.
(iv)	Memoir(s)	A record of person's own life and experiences usually, a famous person.

Q.2 Here are some entries from personal records. Use the definitions given in the previous question to decide which of the entries might be from a diary, a journal, a log or a memoir.

(i) I woke up very late today and promptly got a scolding from Mum! I can't help it – how can I miss the FIFA World Cup matches?

(ii) 10:30 AM Went to the office of the Director
01:00 PM Had lunch with Chairman
05:45 PM Received Rahul at the airport
09 : 30 PM Dinner at home

(iii) The ride to Ooty was uneventful. We rested for a while every 50 km or so and used the time to capture the magnificent landscape with my HandyCam. From Ooty we went on to Bangalore. What a contrast! The noise and pollution of this once-beautiful city really broke my heart.

(iv) This is how Raj Kapoor found me – all wet and ragged outside RK Studios. He was then looking for just someone like this for a small role in *'Mera Naam Joker'* and he cast me on the spot. The rest, as they say, is history!

Ans. (i) A diary (ii) A log (iii) A journal (iv) A memoir

ORAL COMPREHENSION CHECK❶ (NCERT PAGE 51)

Q.1 What makes writing in a diary a strange experience for Anne Frank?

Ans. Writing in a diary was a strange experience for Anne Frank as she had never written anything earlier. She also thought that nobody would be interested in reading the thoughts of a thirteen year old girl.

Q.2 Why does Anne want to keep a diary?

Ans. Anne wanted to keep a diary because she felt that she had no true and sincere friend with whom she could share her secrets. She believed that she could do so with her diary which would act as her best friend.

Q.3 Why did Anne think she could confide more in her diary than in people?

Ans. Anne thought that she could confide more in her diary than people because she felt that paper had more patience than people to listen to her thoughts. She believes her diary will listen without judgement or interruption, giving her a safe space to express herself freely and openly without fear of repercussions.

CHECK❷ (NCERT PAGE 51)

Q.1 Why does Anne provide a brief sketch of her life?

Ans. Anne provides a brief sketch of her life to provide context for her diary entries and to help her imaginary friend, whom she calls 'Kitty', understand her experiences and background. By sharing details about her family, upbringing, and significant events in her life, Anne lays the foundation for a deeper connection with her diary.

Q.2 What tells you that Anne loved her grandmother?

Or Describe Anne's love for her grandmother.

Ans. Anne's expression of love for her grandmother is evident in her recollection of her grandmother falling ill in the summer of 1941 and passing away in January 1942. Despite the lack of elaborate celebrations for her birthday during her grandmother's illness, Anne reflects on her love for her grandmother and the impact of her absence. Anne's continued thoughts of her grandmother and the inclusion of her candle in the birthday celebration in 1942 demonstrate the depth of Anne's affection and the significance of her grandmother in her life.

CHECK❸ (NCERT PAGE 54)

Q.1 Why was Mr. Keesing annoyed with Anne? What did he ask her to do?

Ans. Mr. Keesing, the Maths teacher was annoyed with Anne because she talked too much in the class.

Mr. Keesing gave her extra homework as a punishment. He asked her to write an essay on the topic 'A Chatterbox'.

Q.2 How did Anne justify her being a chatterbox in her essay?

Ans. Anne justified her being a chatterbox in her essay by explaining that talking was a student's trait and she would try to control it. However, being talkative was incurable as she had inherited this trait from her mother and no one could cure an inherited trait.

Q.3 Do you think Mr. Keesing was a strict teacher?

Ans. Yes, I think Mr. Keesing was a strict teacher but he was not rigid. He expected discipline and silence in his class while he was teaching. This can be seen in his reactions to Anne's talkative behaviour. He punished Anne by asking her to write an essay on 'A Chatterbox'. When Anne wrote a convincing essay, he received it with a good laugh/humour.

However, when Anne continued with her talking, he punished her again. This time the topic of the essay was 'An Incorrigible Chatterbox'. Even after this when she kept on talking, he asked her to write on the topic 'Quack Quack Quack, said Mistress Chatterbox" as a punishment. He was trying to play a joke on her. This time, Anne came up with a brilliant poem in response. Mr. Keesing was so impressed that he read this poem in the class, acknowledging its content. Therefore, in regard of these events, Mr. Keesing could not be labelled entirely as a strict teacher. He was fun-loving as well.

Q.4 What made Mr. Keesing allow Anne to talk in class?

Or How did Mr. Keesing's attitude towards Anne change? CBSE 2019

Ans. Anne wrote the essay on the topic 'Quack Quack Quack' said Mistress Chatterbox in the form of a poem. She wrote that a father swan had bit his ducklings to death for quacking too much. Mr. Keesing liked that essay and changed his attitude towards Anne. Since then, he allowed Anne to talk in class.

THINKING ABOUT THE TEXT

(NCERT PAGE 54-55)

Q.1 Was Anne right when she said that the world would not be interested in the musings of a 13 year old girl?

Ans. No, Anne was not right when she said that the world would not be interested in the musings of a thirteen year old girl.

The world became very much interested in her musings when her diary was published under the name 'The Diary of a Young Girl'. It became one of the world's most widely read and studied accounts of the Holocaust, providing valuable insights into the experiences of a young Jewish girl during World War II.

Q.2 There are some examples of diary or journal entries in the 'Before You Read' section. Compare these with what Anne writes in her diary. What language was the diary originally written in? In what way is Anne's diary different?

Ans. Anne's diary was essentially written as a diary of a young teenager and her life. Today, her diary resembles a memoir.

Anne's diary was initially written in Dutch language. Anne's diary is different because it was a lot more personal than other diaries. Her diary was her friend with whom she could share all her secrets. She had also named it Kitty. Further, Anne's diary contains introspective reflections personal experiences, and candid observations about life in hiding during the Holocaust. In contrast, other diary entries may delve less deeply into individual thoughts and emotions.

Q.3 Why does Anne need to give a brief sketch about her family? Does she treat 'Kitty' as an insider or an outsider?

Ans. Anne needed to give a brief sketch about her family to make the stories in her diary understandable for anyone who reads it. According to her, no one would understand her life if she had not given an overview of her life.

For Anne, her diary 'Kitty' was her friend with whom she could share all her secrets. She, therefore, thought of it as an insider.

Q.4 How does Anne feel about her father, her grandmother, Mrs. Kuperus and Mr. Keesing? What do these tell you about her?

Ans. Anne felt that her father, Otto Frank, was the most adorable father she had ever seen.

She loved her grandmother very much and after her death, thought a lot about her.

Anne was very attached to her teacher, Mrs. Kuperus and cried on separation from her.

Anne felt that his Maths teacher, Mr. Keesing was very strict and always annoyed with her for her talkative nature.

Anne's attachment with the people around her shows that she was very lovable and smart. She was also obedient and hardworking.

Q.5 What does Anne write in her first essay?

Ans. In her first essay, Anne wrote about her talkative nature. She tried to justify her trait as a characteristic of every student. She also stated that she would try to control it but was not sure she would be able to do so because she had inherited this trait from her mother and no one could cure an inherited trait.

Q.6 Anne says teachers are most unpredictable. Is Mr. Keesing unpredictable?

Ans. Yes, Mr. Keesing was unpredictable. In the beginning, he gave Anne unusual punishments. However, later he pardons her altogether.

His reactions to Anne's essays demonstrates his unpredictability. Instead of punishing Anne further, he reads her humorous poem to the class and other classes, appreciating her creativity and sense of humour. This unexpected response from Mr. Keesing contrasts with Anne's initial expectations, showing that he can be unpredictable in his reactions to students' behaviour.

Q.7 What do these statements tell you about Anne Frank as a person?

(i) We don't seem to be able to get any closer and that's the problem. Maybe it's my fault that we don't confide in each other.

(ii) I don't want to jot down the facts in this diary the way most people would, but I want the diary to be my friend.

(iii) Margot went to Holland in December and I followed in February, when I was plunked down on the table as a birthday present for Margot.

(iv) If you ask me, there are so many dummies that about a quarter of the class should be kept back, but teachers are the most unpredictable creatures on Earth.

(v) Anyone could ramble on and leave big spaces between the words, but the trick was to come up with convincing arguments to prove the necessity of talking.

Ans. (i) Anne was reserved due to which she was not able to make close friends.

(ii) Anne wanted to be different and original.

(iii) Anne has a good sense of humour. She knows how to narrate events in a family.

(iv) Anne was intelligent.

(v) Anne knew how to write convincingly and give acceptable arguments.

THINKING ABOUT LANGUAGE

(NCERT PAGE 55-56)

Q.1 **I. Look at the following words.**

headmistress	long-awaited	homework
notebook	stiff-backed	outbursts

These words are compound words. They are made up of two or more words.

Compound words can be:

- **nouns: headmistress, homework, notebook, outbursts**
- **adjectives: long-awaited, stiff-backed**
- **verbs: sleep-walk, baby-sit**

Match the compound words under 'A' with their meanings under 'B'. Use each in a sentence.

S.No.	A	B
1.	Heart-breaking	(a) Obeying and respecting the law.
2.	Homesick	(b) Think about pleasant things, forgetting about the present.
3.	Blockhead	(c) Something produced by a person, machine or organisation.
4.	Law-abiding	(d) Producing great sadness.
5.	Overdo	(e) An occasion when vehicles/ machines stop working.
6.	Daydream	(f) An informal word which means a very stupid person.
7.	Breakdown	(g) Missing home and family very much.
8.	Output	(h) Do something to an excessive degree.

Ans. 1. (d), 2. (g), 3. (f), 4. (a), 5. (h), 6. (b), 7. (e), 8. (c)

1 It was **heart-breaking** to know that I had failed the Maths exam this year.

2 I became **homesick** very soon after I started staying in the school hostel.

3 Tarun is a real **blockhead** as he couldn't even answer the questions of simple addition.

4 Sarvjeet is a **law-abiding** driver as he has never been fined by the police even after ten years of driving.

5 Please do not **overdo** your kindness towards me, as it will spoil me.

6 Ravinder will start to **daydream** if we keep him idle for long.

7 We had a power **breakdown** in our locality last night for 4 hours.

8 His daily **output** of work is much above the average.

II. Phrasal Verbs

A phrasal verb is a verb followed by a preposition or an adverb. Its meaning is often different from the meanings of its parts. Compare the meanings of the verbs get on and run away in (a) and (b) below. You can easily guess their meanings in (a) but in (b) they have special meanings.

(a) She got on at Agra when the bus stopped for breakfast.

Dev Anand ran away from home when he was a teenager.

(b) She's eager to get on in life. (succeed)

The visitors ran away with the match. (won easily) Some phrasal verbs have three parts: a verb followed by an adverb and a preposition.

(c) Our car ran out of petrol just outside the city limits.

(d) The government wants to reach out to the people with this new campaign.

1. The text you've just read has a number of phrasal verbs commonly used in English. Look up the following in a dictionary for their meanings (under the entry for the italicised word).

(i) plunge (right) in

(ii) kept back

(iii) ramble on

(iv) get along with

Ans.

(i) Plunge (right) in: To begin or undertake something eagerly or without hesitation.

(ii) Kept back: To prevent someone or something from progressing or advancing.

(iii) Ramble on: To talk or write at length in a wandering or unfocused way.

(iv) Get along with: To have a good relationship or rapport with someone.

Q.2 Now find the sentences in the lesson that have the phrasal verbs given below. Match them with their meanings. (You have already found out the meanings for some of them.) Are their meanings the same as that of their parts? (Note that two parts of a phrasal verb may occur separated in the text).

1.	Plunge in	(a)	Speak or write without focus
2.	Kept back	(b)	Stay indoors
3.	Move up	(c)	Make (them) remain quiet
4.	Ramble on	(d)	Have a good relationship with
5.	Get along with	(e)	Give an assignment (homework) to a person in authority (the teacher)
6.	Calm down	(f)	Compensate
7.	Stay in	(g)	Go straight to the topic
8.	Make up for	(h)	Go to the next grade
9.	Hand in	(i)	Not promoted

Ans.

	Phrasal Verb	Meaning Option	Whether its meaning is the same as its parts (Yes/No)
1.	Plunge in	(g)	No
2.	Kept back	(i)	Yes
3.	Move up	(h)	Yes
4.	Ramble on	(a)	No
5.	Get along with	(d)	No
6.	Calm down	(c)	Yes
7.	Stay in	(b)	Yes
8.	Make up for	(f)	No
9.	Hand in	(e)	No

Sentences from the text

(i) Plunge in - "Since no one would understand a word of my stories to Kitty if I were to plunge right in, I'd better provide a brief sketch of my life."

(ii) Kept back - "If you ask me, there are so many dummies that about a quarter of the class should be kept back, but teachers are the most unpredictable creatures on earth."

(iii) Move up - "The reason, of course, is the forthcoming meeting in which the teachers decide who'll move up to the next form and who'll be kept back."

(iv) Ramble on - "Anyone could ramble on and leave big spaces between the words, but the trick was to come up with convincing arguments to prove the necessity of talking."

(v) Get along with -"I get along pretty well with all my teachers."

(vi) Calm down - "Even G.'s pleading glances and my angry outbursts can't calm them down."

(vii) Stay in - "I finally stayed where I was, brooding."

(viii) Make up for - "This birthday celebration in 1942 was intended to make up for the other."

(ix) Hand in - "This time it was supposed to be on 'An Incorrigible Chatterbox'. I handed it in, and Mr. Keesing had nothing to complain about for two whole lessons."

III. Idioms

Idioms are groups of words with a fixed order, and a particular meaning, different from the meanings of each of their words put together. (Phrasal verbs can also be idioms; they are said to be 'idiomatic' when their meaning is unpredictable.) For example, do you know what it means to 'meet one's match' in English? It means to meet someone who is as good as oneself, or even better, in some skill or quality. Do you know what it means to 'let the cat out of the bag'? Can you guess?

1. Here are a few sentences from the text which have idiomatic expressions. Can you say what each means? (You might want to consult a dictionary first.)

(i) Our entire class is quaking in its boots.

(ii) Until then, we keep telling each other not to lose heart.

(iii) Mr. Keesing was annoyed with me for ages because I talked so much.

(iv) Mr. Keesing was trying to play a joke on me with this ridiculous subject, but I'd make sure the joke was on him.

Ans. (i) Our entire class is quaking in its boots: "Quaking in its boots" is an idiom that suggests intense fear or nervousness. So, in this context, the sentence means the whole class feels extremely scared or intimidated.

(ii) Until then, we keep telling each other not to lose heart: "Not to lose heart" means not to become discouraged or lose hope. So, in this context, the sentence implies that until a certain point in time, the speaker and others are encouraging each other to remain hopeful.

(iii) Mr. Keesing was annoyed with me for ages because I talked so much: "For ages" in this context means a long time. So, the sentence indicates that Mr. Keesing was annoyed with Anne for talking excessively or too frequently over an extended period.

(iv) Mr. Keesing was trying to play a joke on me with this ridiculous subject, but I'd make sure the joke was on him: "The joke was on him" is an idiom that means the prank or trick was turned back on the person who initiated it. This sentence suggests that despite Mr. Keesing's attempt to prank Anne, she would ensure that the joke or prank would ultimately affect Mr. Keesing instead.

2. Here are a few more idiomatic expressions in the text. Try to use them in sentences of your own.

(i) caught my eye (ii) he'd had enough

(iii) laugh ourselves silly (iv) can't bring myself to

Ans. (i) **Caught my eye** : The colourful painting caught my eye when I entered the art gallery.

(ii) **He'd had enough** : After waiting for hours at the airport, he'd had enough and decided to book a hotel room for the night.

(iii) **Laugh ourselves silly** : Whenever we watch a comedy show, we laugh ourselves silly.

(iv) **Can't bring myself to** : I know I should apologise, but I can't bring myself to admit I was wrong.

IV. Do you know how to use a dictionary to find out the meanings of idiomatic expressions? Take, for example, the expression caught my eye in the story. Where - under which word - would you look for it in the dictionary? Look for it under the first word. But if the first word is a 'grammatical' word like a, the, for, etc., then take the next word. That is, look for the first 'meaningful' word in the expression. In our example, it is the word caught.

But you won't find caught in the dictionary, because it is the past tense of catch. You'll find caught listed under catch. So you must look under catch for the expression caught my eye. Which other expressions with catch are listed in your dictionary?

Note that a dictionary entry usually first gives the meanings of the word itself, and then gives a list of idiomatic expressions using that word. For example, study this partial entry for the noun 'eye' from the Oxford Advanced Learner's Dictionary, 2005.

You have read the expression 'not to lose heart' in this text. Now find out the meanings of the following expressions using the word 'heart'. Use each of them in a sentence of your own.

1. break somebody's heart
2. close/dear to heart
3. from the (bottom of your) heart
4. have a heart
5. have a heart of stone
6. your heart goes out to somebody

Ans. 1. **Break somebody's heart** : to cause someone to feel sad.

Sentence Losing her beloved pet dog broke her heart into pieces.

2. **Close/dear to heart** : Something very important to you.

Sentence Preserving the environment is a cause dear to my heart.

3. **From the (bottom of your) heart** : Very sincere

Sentence His apology seemed sincere, as it came from the heart.

4. **Have a heart** : To be merciful or kind.

Sentence Please have a heart and forgive me for my mistake.

5. **Have a heart of stone** : To be kind or cruel.

Sentence Witnessing the suffering of others without feeling any empathy suggests that someone has a heart of stone.

6. **Your heart goes out to somebody** To feel sympathy for someone.

Sentence Watching the documentary about orphaned children, his heart went out to the less fortunate.

V. Contracted Forms

When we speak, we use 'contracted forms' or short forms such as these:

can't (for can not or cannot) I'd (for I would or I had) she's (for she is)

Notice that contracted forms are also written with an apostrophe to show a shortening of the spelling of not, would, or is as in the above example.

Writing a diary is like speaking to oneself. Plays (and often, novels) also have speech in written form. So we usually come across contracted forms in diaries, plays and novels.

1. Make a list of the contracted forms in the text. Rewrite them as full forms of two words.

For example : I've = I have

2. We have seen that some contracted forms can stand for two different full forms:

I'd = I had or I would

Find in the text the contracted forms that stand for two different full forms, and say what these are.

Ans. 1. I've - I have, Didn't - did not, Won't - will not, It's - it is / it has, I'd - I had / I would, Can't - cannot, I'm - I am, That's - that is, Who'll - who will, Don't - do not, Let's - let us, There's - there is, They're - they are, Haven't - have not

2. It's - it is / it has and I'd - I had / I would

REVIEW EXERCISE

Including Competency Based Questions

Part I

Multiple Choice Questions

1. Anne decided to write in her diary because .... Competency Based

(a) she had interesting ideas
(b) she wanted to share her thoughts
(c) she wanted to have the experience of writing in a diary
(d) she might want to understand her feelings in the future

Ans. (b) she wanted to share her thoughts

2. Why did Anne Frank finally decide to write in her diary? Competency Based

(a) She did not have anyone to talk to
(b) She felt burdened by her thoughts
(c) She wanted people to read her writing
(d) She wanted to know what it would feel like

Ans. (b) She felt burdened by her thoughts

3. "Paper has more patience than people." Which of the following is not true? CBSE 2021 Term I

(a) One can write anything on paper.
(b) People have good ears for listening.
(c) One can write one's diary even at night.
(d) One may express one's anger on paper.

Ans. (b) People have good ears for listening.

4. Anne agrees with the saying "Paper has more patience than people." This shows that her attitude towards people was

(a) Cynical (b) Cautious (c) Mocking (d) Thoughtful

Ans. (a) Cynical

5. Anne doesn't plan to let anyone else read her diary as CBSE Question Bank 2021 Modified

(a) she is secretive about her life.
(b) it's about her intimate feelings.
(c) she is unwilling to share it with anyone.
(d) she wants to cherish these moments herself.

Ans. (b) it's about her intimate feelings.

6. When and where was Anne Frank born?

(a) In Frankfurt in 1926
(b) Germany on 12th June, 1929
(c) In Aachen on 12th December, 1929
(d) In Germany in February 1926

Ans. (b) Germany on 12th June, 1929

7. With whom were Anne and her sister Margot sent to stay in Aachen?

(a) Their aunt (b) Their cousins
(c) Their grandmother (d) Alone

Ans. (c) Their grandmother

8. Why were Anne and her sister Margot sent to Aachen?

(a) Their parents emigrated to Holland.
(b) No one to look after them.
(c) They wanted to study there.
(d) Both (a) and (b)

Ans. (d) Both (a) and (b)

9. "... plunked down on the table as a birthday present for Margot." What tone is the writer trying to convey?

(a) Ironic (b) Cynical (c) Spiteful (d) Scornful

Ans. (a) Ironic

10. Why does Anne say the following line? Anyway, all we can do is wait.

(a) Because she believes that patience is a virtue
(b) Because she knows that she will succeed in due time
(c) To stop worrying about something that is not in her control
(d) To convince herself and her girlfriends that they will pass in math

Ans. (c) To stop worrying about something that is not in her control

11. Mr. Keesing was annoyed with Anne as CBSE 2021 Term I

(a) she was weak in maths.
(b) she had not done her home work.
(c) she was a naughty girl.
(d) she was very talkative.

Ans. (d) she was very talkative.

12. What was the trick in writing the essay assigned to Anne by Mr. Keesing?

(a) To make sure that the joke was on Mr. Keesing.
(b) To leave big spaces between the words.
(c) To come up with convincing arguments to prove the necessity of talking.
(d) To write against talking.

Ans. (c) To come up with convincing arguments to prove the necessity of talking.

13. Anne argued that .... CBSE 2023

(a) talking was a necessary trait for any student
(b) sleeping was a necessary trait for any student
(c) cleaning was a necessary trait for any student
(d) thinking was a necessary trait for any student

Ans. (a) talking was a necessary trait for any student

14. Pick the option with the list of words that best describe Mr. Keesing.

(a) Jovial and creative
(b) Strict and innovative
(c) Tolerant and strict
(d) Innovative and jovial

Ans. (b) strict and innovative

15. What was the subject on which Anne had to write?

(a) A Chatterbox
(b) An Incorrigible Chatterbox
(c) Quack, Quack, Quack, Said Mistress Chatterbox
(d) All of the above

Ans. (d) All of the above

16. Why did Mr. Keesing stop punishing Anne?

(a) She stopped talking in class
(b) Her arguments were very convincing
(c) He respected her efforts to convince him
(d) He believed that she was not worth the effort

Ans. (b) Her arguments were very convincing

17. Choose the option that lists the set of sentences that are not true according to 'The Diary of Anne Frank'.

1. Anne Frank was very talkative.
2. She was punished for her talkative nature.
3. She had inherited that trait from her mother.
4. Mr. Keesing was satisfied with her essay.
5. Anne was punished thrice.
6. She was failed by Mr. Keesing.

(a) Only 6 (b) 1 and 2
(c) 3 and 4 (d) Only 5

Ans. (a) Only 6

18. Why did Anne decide to start describing her life in a diary? Competency Based

(a) She was proud of her life.
(b) She wanted to help future readers.
(c) She thought it was how diaries were written.
(d) She thought it was the best topic for a diary.

Ans. (b) She wanted to help future readers

19. What word best describes Anne? Competency Based

(a) Flighty (b) Reflective
(c) Rebellious (d) Considerate

Ans. (b) Reflective

Extract Based Questions

1. Read the following extract carefully and answer the questions that follow. Writing in a diary is a really strange experience for someone like me. Not only because I've never written anything before, but also because it seems to me that later on neither I nor anyone else will be interested in the musings of a thirteen-year-old schoolgirl. Oh well, it doesn't matter. I feel like writing, and I have an even greater need to get all kinds of things off my chest.

'Paper has more patience than people.' I thought of this saying on one of those days when I was feeling a little depressed and was sitting at home with my chin in my hands, bored and listless, wondering whether to stay in or go out.

(i) Why did Anne Frank finally decide to write in her diary? Answer in about 40 words.

Ans. Anne believed that she does not have any close and true friends whom she can confide in. Though she had friends, she was never able to truly open up about her feelings with them. She had felt a need to get things off her chest and thought paper has more patience than people. So, she decided to write a diary.

(ii) What word best describes Anne?

(a) Rebellious (b) Reflective
(c) Flighty (d) Considerate

Ans. (b) Reflective

(iii) Anne agrees with the saying 'Paper has more patience than people.' What does this show us about her attitude towards people?

Ans. Anne believes that paper has more patience than people because it listens to her more patiently. This shows that she is a smart, reflective and judgemental girl who understands her surroundings very well.

(iv) If the diary were 'a real friend', which one of the following qualities would Anne expect it to have?

(a) Impatience (b) Good listener
(c) Confident (d) Energetic

Ans. (b) Good listener

2. Read the following extract carefully and answer the questions that follow.

"'Paper has more patience than people' I thought of this saying on one of those days when I was feeling a little depressed and was sitting at home with my chin in my hands, bored and listless, wondering whether to stay in or go out. I finally stayed where I was, brooding: Yes, paper does have more patience and since I'm not planning to let anyone else read this stiff- backed notebook grandly referred to as a 'diary', unless I should ever find a real friend, it probably won't make a bit of difference." **CBSE Question Bank 2021 Modified**

(i) If the diary were a 'real friend', what qualities would Anne expect it to have?
Pick the option that lists these correctly.

1. Optimistic	**2. Good listener**
3. Confident	**4. Energetic**
5. Non-judgemental	**6. Outgoing**
7. Ambitious	

(a) 1 and 4 (b) 5, 6 and 7
(c) 2, 3 and 5 (d) 3 and 7

Ans. (c) 2, 3 and 5

(ii) Anne believes that 'Paper has more patience than people'. What does that say about her personality?

Ans. Anne's belief that paper has more patience than people shows that she found people to be dismissive towards her thoughts and ideas. Such experiences must have made her secretive and shy, which is why she chose a diary to be her most trusted friend and secret confidante.

(iii) Fill in the blank with the correct option from the bracket.
She was .... (brooding/crying) over the matter and took a long time to decide.

Ans. brooding

(iv) What does the following line tell about Anne's perception of people?
"since I'm not planning to let anyone else read this... it probably won't make a bit of difference."

Ans. The given line shows that Anne was worried about the opinions of people towards her thoughts and words.

3. Read the following extract carefully and answer the questions that follow.

Let me put it more clearly, since no one will believe that a thirteen-year-old girl is completely alone in the world. And I'm not. I have loving parents and a sixteen-year-old sister and there are about thirty people I can call friends. I have a family, loving aunts and a good home. No, on the surface I seem to have everything, except my one true friend. All I think about when I'm with friends is having a good time.
I can't bring myself to talk about anything but ordinary everyday things. **CBSE SQP 2021 Term I Modified**

(i) Read (1) and (5) and choose the correct fillers. Why does Anne feel the following. **Competency Based**

...... no one will believe that a thirteen-year-old girl is completely alone in the world.

1. People knew she had a family.
2. People rejected the idea of loneliness.
3. She had several friends.
4. She had a cheerful personality.
5. Her life was comfortable.

Ans. Anne felt that no one will believe that a thirteen-year-old girl is completely alone in the world because people knew she had a family. She had several friends. She had a cheerful personality. Thus, (1), (3) and (4) are correct.

(ii) What do we get to know about Anne when she says the following? **Competency Based**
I can't bring myself to talk about anything but ordinary everyday things

Ans. When Anne says, "I can't bring myself to talk about anything but ordinary everyday things", it means she is unable to have a satisfying conversation.

(iii) Select the option which displays an example of 'having a good time'.

(a) He is out for a picnic with his friends and they are laughing and singing together.
(b) He is studying hard for the periodic test the following day to improve his scores.
(c) He is trying to convince his father to purchase the latest video games for him.

Ans. (a) "He is out for a picnic with his friends and they are laughing and singing together." is an example of 'having a good time'.

(iv) Anne's tone in the extract is ....

Ans. dissatisfied

Or **CBSE 2023**

(i) On the surface, it appears that Anne the thirteen year old girl ....

Ans. well loved by her friends and family

(ii) How can we infer that the speaker felt alone in the world?

(a) She had a family of many people.
(b) She had loving parents.
(c) She had thirty friends.
(d) She craves for a true friend.

Ans. (d) She craves for a true friend.

(iii) **Complete the sentence appropriately.**
Anne and her friends talked about ....

Ans. common everyday things

(iv) **Complete the analogy by selecting the suitable word from the text.**

Alone : Friends : : Nothing : ....

Ans. Anything

4. Read the following extract carefully and answer the questions that follow.

To enhance the image of this long–awaited friend in my imagination, I don't want to jot down the facts in this diary the way most people would do, but I want the diary to be my friend and I'm going to call this friend 'Kitty'.

(i) **Select the option that displays the reason why Anne Frank decided to maintain a diary.**

(a) She had no close friends.
(b) She was a good writer.
(c) She loved to express her thoughts.
(d) She wanted to be different.

Ans. (a) She had no close friends.

(ii) **Why did Anne call 'it/her' her long awaited friend? What would she write?**

Ans. Anne called her diary her long awaited friend because for a long time, she wanted to have a friend in which she could confide and 'Kitty', the diary, served this purpose. She would write her feelings and emotions in her diary.

(iii) **Complete the sentence appropriately.**
She wanted to write in her diary about ....

Ans. each and every detail of her life

(iv) **Who is the long-awaited friend mentioned in the extract?**

Ans. Her diary was the long-awaited friend mentioned in the extract.

5. Read the following extract and answer the questions that follow.

I started right away at the Montessori nursery school. I stayed there until I was six, at which time I started in the first form. In the sixth form my teacher was Mrs. Kuperus, the headmistress. At the end of the year we were both in tears as we said a heartbreaking farewell. In the summer of 1941 Grandma fell ill and had to have an operation, so my birthday passed with little celebration. **CBSE 2023**

(i) **Fill in the blank with the correct word from the bracket.**

The phrase 'right away' in this extract most nearly means .... (immediately/the correct way).

Ans. immediately

(ii) **What does the narrator mean by saying 'we were both in tears'?**

Ans. The narrator means that they cried as the narrator and Mrs. Kuperus bade a heart-breaking farewell at the end of the year.

(iii) **Select the option that correctly captures the application of the word 'form' as used in the extract.**

(a) Raghav was in good form while playing the match.
(b) Saheb was promoted to the next form after the annual exam.
(c) My brother did not know how to form a circle.
(d) Anne saw the form on the headmaster's desk.

Ans. (a) Raghav was in good form while playing the match.

(iv) **Complete the analogy by selecting a word from the text.**

Dawn : Dusk : : Mourning : ....

Ans. Celebration

6. Read the following extract carefully and answer the questions that follow.

Half the class is making bets. G.N. and I laugh ourselves silly at the two boys behind us, C.N. and Jacques, who have staked their entire holiday savings on their bet. From morning to night, it's "You're going to pass", "No, I'm not", "Yes, you are", "No, I'm not". Even G.'s pleading glances and my angry outbursts can't calm them down. If you ask me, there are so many dummies that about a quarter of the class should be kept back, but teachers are the most unpredictable creatures on Earth. I'm not so worried about my girlfriends and myself. We'll make it. The only subject I'm not sure about is maths. Anyway, all we can do is wait. Until then, we keep telling each other not to lose heart. **CBSE Additional SQP 2021**

(i) **How do Anne and her friend react to the boys behind them?**

Ans. Anne and her friend were irritated by the boys behind them. They also find them to be funny.

(ii) **Select the option that shows the correct relationship between (1) and (2).**

1. C. N. and Jacques keep making bets about passing.

2. Anne mentions that teachers are very unpredictable.

(a) 1 furthers the meaning of 2.
(b) 1 is false but 2 is true.
(c) 2 is a reason for 1.
(d) 2 is an effect of 1.

Ans. (c) 2 is a reason for 1.

(iii) Complete the sentence appropriately.

The girls (Anne and G.) and the two boys (C.N. and Jacques) are both ....

Ans. telling each other that they will be promoted

(iv) Why was the class making bets?

Ans. The class was making bets because they did not know who was going to the promoted to the next grade. The worry and anxiety to get their results made them bet with one another.

7. Read the following extract carefully and answer the questions that follow.

I wrote the three pages Mr. Keesing had assigned me and was satisfied. I argued that talking is a student's trait and that I would do my best to keep it under control, but that I would never be able to cure myself of the habit, since my mother talked as much as I did, if not more and that there's not much one can do about inherited traits. **CBSE 2023**

(i) Choose the option that lists the set of sentences that are not true according to the given extract.

(a) Anne Frank was very talkative.
(b) She had inherited that trait from her mother.
(c) Mr. Keesing was satisfied with her essay.
(d) None of the above

Ans. (d) None of the above

(ii) What was Anne's argument?

Ans. Anne's argument was that talking was necessary trait in any student. She also argued that she had inherited this trait from her mother who talked a lot as well. So, she argued that her talkative nature couldn't be cured.

(iii) Read the given statements and choose the correct answer. **Competency Based**

1. Anne was satisfied with her assignment.

2. Anne was talkative.

Ans. Both the statements are true.

(iv) What did Mr. Keesing ask Anne to write?

Ans. Mr. Keesing asked Anne to write an essay on 'A Chatterbox'.

8. Read the following extract carefully and answer the questions that follow.

Anyone could ramble on and leave big spaces between the words, but the trick was to come up with convincing arguments to prove the necessity of talking. I thought and thought, and suddenly I had an idea. I wrote the three pages Mr Keesing had assigned me and was satisfied. I argued that talking is a student's trait and that I would do my best to keep it under control, but that I would never be able to cure myself of the habit since my mother talked as much as I did if not but that I would never be able to cure myself of the habit since my mother talked as much as I did if not more, and that there's not much you can do about inherited traits. **CBSE 2024**

(i) State any one inference about Anne from the given context.

Ans. The given context suggests that Anne was a clever and reflective individual. She understood the importance of presenting logical arguments to validate her actions rather than merely offering excuses.

(ii) In about 40 words, elaborate on the justification Anne gives for her talkative nature.

Ans. Anne justifies her talkative nature by arguing that being talkative is a trait inherent among students — it's part of their character to be lively and expressive. Furthermore, she links her talkativeness to heredity, suggesting it's an inherited trait from her mother, implying that it's a natural aspect of her personality that is difficult to change.

(iii) Which one of the following best describes the tone of the given extract?

(a) Derogatory
(b) Persuasive
(c) Nostalgic
(d) Cautionary

Ans. (b) Persuasive

(iv) Which phrase would correctly substitute 'ramble on' in the given sentence from the extract?

Ans. The phrase 'ramble on' could be substituted with to speak at length in a confused or inconsequential way.

9. Read the following extract carefully and answer the questions that follow.

Mr. Keesing had a good laugh at my arguments, but when I proceeded to talk my way through the next lesson, he assigned me a second essay. This time it was supposed to be on 'An Incorrigible Chatterbox.' I handed it in and Mr. Keesing had nothing to complain about for two whole lessons. However, during the third lesson, he'd finally had enough. "Anne Frank, as a punishment for talking in class, write an essay entitled-'Quack, Quack, Quack, said Mistress Chatterbox." **CBSE Additional Paper 2023**

(i) How does Mr. Keesing's assignment of the essay "Quack, Quack, Quack, said Mistress Chatterbox" serve as both a punishment and a creative response to Anne Frank's talkative nature?

Ans. Mr. Keesing combines punishment and creativity as it playfully penalises Anne for her talkative behaviour. His punishment incorporates humour to address the issue and channels Anne's talkativeness into a creative outlet. It acts as a punishment as it aims to curb her chattiness while nurturing a more disciplined and imaginative approach to expression.

(ii) In the context of Mr. Keesing, the phrase, 'had a good laugh' implies ....

Ans. that Mr. Keesing found amusement in Anne Frank's arguments and did not take Anne's arguments too seriously

(iii) With reference to Anne Frank's approach to authority figures like Mr. Keesing, which option is the least likely? **Competency Based**

(a) Subtle resistance to authority
(b) Assertiveness and independence
(c) Enthusiasm for intellectual discourse
(d) Compliance with classroom norms

Ans. (d) Compliance with classroom norms

(iv) Select the correct option and give reason. For Anne, 'an Incorrigible Chatterbox can be taken as

(a) an article (b) an essay (c) a title

Ans. (b) an essay

Part II

Short Answer Type Questions

1. "Paper has more patience than people." What does the saying mean? **Competency Based**

Ans. The given saying means that one can write without any interruption. Paper does not stop you in between like people do. It does not judge you for your opinions and is always there for you whenever you want to talk about something.

2. Why does Anne think that 'paper' has more patience than people? **CBSE 2023**

Ans. Anne believes that paper has more patience than people because she thinks that she would have to monitor her thoughts if she were to talk to actual people. She would also be apprehensive about the reactions of her friends upon listening to her thoughts. But writing her thoughts on paper would eliminate all those worries and she would be free to write what she wanted to say, when she wanted to say it.

3. Anne wrote in her diary to get things off her chest. List any two reasons why getting things off one's chest is recommended by counsellors as therapeutic. **CBSE Question Bank 2021**

Ans. Getting things off the chest means to vent out your feelings if you are hurt or unhappy. The counsellors recommend it as therapeutic because it makes our mind and body feel light and relaxed. A relaxed mind and body is always good for physical and psychological health.

4. Who would Anne consider a real friend based on 'The Diary of Anne Frank'? Describe in 20-30 words. **Competency Based**

Ans. Anne would consider someone a real friend if she could share whatever is in her heart and confide in him or her without being judged for her various thoughts and ideas.

5. Kitty was a trusted friend to Anne. Elaborate. **CBSE SQP 2023**

Ans. Kitty was a trusted friend to Anne because Kitty was a diary. Anne used to write down all of her thoughts in Kitty. Kitty could never betray her secrets because Anne never planned to let anyone read her thoughts written in the diary.

6. What did Anne Frank write about her family in her diary?

Ans. Anne Frank wrote that she had a very lovely and caring family. Her parents and her elder sister loved her a lot. There were about thirty people whom she could call friends. She had loving aunts and a good home. However, she wanted to have a true friend with whom she could share her feelings and thoughts.

7. Why did Margot and Anne stay with their grandmother?

Ans. Margot and Anne stayed with their grandmother in Aachen when her parents migrated to Holland. The parents wanted to settle down before calling them. Anne was only four years old and Margot was seven years old at that time.

Both the girls were called there one-by-one-after a few months of staying with their grandmother.

8. Explain the emotion vested in Anne's statement, "...I was plunked down on the table as a birthday present for Margot." **CBSE Question Bank 2021**

Ans. Anne's statement showed the love between two sisters and the love showered upon them by their parents. Anne was shifted to Holland where her sister was. She presented her arrival in a humorous way.

9. "Anne finds it difficult to share her emotions with others." Justify this statement with two examples from the text. **Competency Based**

Ans. It is true to say that Anne found it difficult to share her emotions with her friends. She did not confide in her friends and told no one that she still loved her grandma. Further, she never told her friends about her feelings. As a result, no one knew how often she thought of her grandma and still loved her.

10. How was Anne feeling about her chance of moving to the next grade? Competency Based

Ans. About her change of moving to the next grade, Anne states that she was confident. She had performed well in all subjects and was only worried about maths. However, even then, she knew that she would pass.

11. Comment on the teacher-student relationship shared between Anne and Mr. Keesing. CBSE Question Bank 2021

Ans. The teacher-student relationship between Mr. Keesing and Anne was not amiable. He was annoyed with Anne's talking in class for which he punished her thrice. However, in the end, he praised her writing talent in front of the class and allowed her to talk.

12. Enumerate any two reasons that justify Mr. Keesing's displeasure at Anne's talking in class. Competency Based

Ans. The two reasons that justify Mr. Keesing's displeasure at Anne's talking in class are

(i) Mr. Keesing was an old-fashioned and strict Maths teacher. He wanted everyone to be attentive in class. Anne's talking would disturb everyone in the class.

(ii) Anne was not good at Maths and still used talk a lot instead of concentrating on the subject.

13. Describe your views about Mr. Keesing as a teacher.

Ans. Mr. Keesing, like most teachers, seemed to be a strict teacher. However, he actually believed in taking action with good intentions and for the development of children. He tried to control Anne's bad habit of talking too much. However, as soon as he was convinced that her habit did not affect her studies, he overlooked Anne's shortcoming.

14. Clarify why it is fair to say that Mr. Keesing was innovative with his punishments.

Ans. Mr. Keesing was innovative with his punishments because he punished Anne differently. Despite being a Maths teacher, he asked Anne to write essays on the topic of Chatterbox. He did this to make her understand the ill-effects of talking in the class and rectify herself.

15. 'Anne is a clever girl.' Do you agree? Justify your answer. Competency Based

Ans. I agree with the statement that Anne was a clever girl. We know of this because of the various humorous essays she had written as homework. Her responses to the three essays given as a punishment by Mr. Keesing for talking too much are smart and intelligent. They not only proved her point but also made everyone laugh.

16. How does Anne Frank's writing engage readers? Comment on any aspect with evidence from 'The Diary of Anne Frank' in 40-50 words. Competency Based

Or **Give two reasons to support the opinion that Anne's diary is interesting to readers.**

Ans. I think Anne Frank's writing engages readers because it is easy for readers to understand her story. For instance, before she starts her first entry, she gives a brief sketch of her life. This background information helps the reader to understand her context.

17. Anne says that she doesn't plan to let anyone else read her diary. What is ironical about this?

Ans. Anne believes that no one would be interested in reading a diary of a 13-year old teenager. In addition, she would not let anyone read her diary because she would share all her secrets with it.

These statements by Anne are ironical because after her death, her father Otto Frank published it and then, it was translated in many languages of the world. Today, it had become one of the most read books of all time.

18. How did Anne's handling of the essay assignments showcase her character traits?

Ans. Anne's handling of the essay assignments showcased her intelligence, creativity, and resilience. Despite initially facing punishment for talking in class, Anne turned the assignments into opportunities to showcase her wit and ingenuity, ultimately winning over her teacher and earning a more positive relationship with him.

Long Answer Type Questions

1. Anne wanted to write convincing arguments to prove the necessity of talking. What does this tell you about her? Did she possess a sense of humour?

Or **What do you think about Anne's talent for writing essays which she wrote convincingly, when punished by the teacher?** CBSE 2020

Ans. When Anne was given extra homework to write an essay on 'A Chatterbox', Anne thought that she had to write convincing arguments to prove the necessity of talking. This fact tells us that Anne was an intelligent and sensible girl with a good sense of humour. She thought about the essay and her arguments for a long time to get an idea. When she got it, she presented her essay. In her essay, Anne argued that talking was a student's trait. The only thing that she could do was to try to control it. She even justified that she could not cure it completely as she had inherited it from her mother.

Yes, Anne possesses a good sense of humour. Anne's sense of humour comes forward when in her third essay, she wrote a funny poem to express her trait of talking. Her poem consisted of a humorous story of how a father swan bit its ducklings to death because they quacked too much. Her poetry was received in the right way by Mr. Keesing and he never punished her after that.

2. 'From the Diary of Anne Frank' throws light on the teacher-student relationship, class atmosphere and discipline. Elucidate.

Ans. 'From the Diary of Anne Frank' clearly describes the teacher-student relationship, class atmosphere and discipline. Anne, who talks a lot in the class, gets punished by Mr. Keesing, her Maths teacher. He had been annoyed with her because of her talkative nature and asked her to write an essays on the subject, 'A Chatterbox'.

It was actually a blessing in disguise because he wanted her to focus on studies. He could not be blamed for the punishment as he did it for Anne's betterment. Thus, here the teacher-student relationship is very respectful. Such a relationship is about discipline and classroom manners. These are essential for every student as well as a teacher, otherwise both teaching and learning could be hampered.

This relationship is clearly shown in Mr. Keesing's and Anne Frank's actions. They both try to play a joke on each other but in a very humorous and healthy manner. Such a healthy relationship is needed in the classroom for effective teaching and learning.

3. Your teacher has organised a debate and you have been asked to speak on 'Consequences and Positive Reinforcements Have a Great Impact on Student Behaviour'. Write the debate script with three-four points to supplement your stand, either as a proposition speaker or as an opposition one.

CBSE Question Bank 2021

Ans. Debate - In favour

The desired behaviour of a student can be increased by positive reinforcements. Positive reinforcers include any actions, consequences, or rewards that are provided to a student when they do something successfully. They may include rewards and privileges that students like and enjoy. For example a student may earn physical rewards such as school supplies, healthy snacks. A pat on back from either the teacher or the Principal for a project can boost a student's confidence to make him/ her perform much better in next project.

Debate - Against

It may be true that positive reinforcement can improve the student's behaviour. However, sometimes it may have a negative effect on a student's thinking and performance. It can make the student arrogant and egoistic. The student might think of himself or herself superior to everyone and that he/ she does not need any further improvement. Therefore, it is important to keep a check if the child needs positive reinforcement every time or a negative reinforcement along with it.

4. How does Anne's writing style evolve throughout the diary entry, and what does it reveal about her character?

Ans. Anne's writing style evolves from an initial sense of uncertainty and self-consciousness to a more confident and expressive tone throughout the diary entry. Initially, she questions her diary's value and doubts whether anyone will be interested in her musings.

However, as she delves deeper into her thoughts and experiences, Anne's writing becomes more introspective and expressive. She displays keen observation, humour and resilience in adversity. This evolution in her writing style reveals Anne's growth from a young girl grappling with her identity and loneliness to a mature and insightful individual who uses her diary for self-expression and reflection.

5. Based on the excerpt, Anne Frank emerges as a complex and reflective character, grappling with the challenges of adolescence and the harsh realities of living in hiding during the Holocaust. Comment.

Ans. Anne's diary entries demonstrate that she was an introspective and reflective girl by nature. She reflects on her thoughts and feelings, pondering the significance of her experiences and the world around her. From the very beginning we know that Anne grapples with a desire for genuine connection and understanding. Despite having family and acquaintances, she longs for a true friend with whom she can share her innermost thoughts and feelings.

Anne's creativity and wit shine through in her interactions, particularly with her teacher, Mr. Keesing. She approaches challenges with creativity, finding humorous solutions to difficult situations. This displays her spirited defiance against authority. She refuses to be silenced or discouraged, using her intelligence and resourcefulness to overcome obstacles.

Through her diary entries, Anne navigates the complexities of adolescence, grappling with issues of identity, friendship and independence. Her writings reflect the universal experiences of growing up while also highlighting the unique challenges posed by the Holocaust. Further, Anne maintains a sense of optimism and resilience despite the challenging circumstances of her life in hiding. She finds moments of joy and humour amidst the darkness, refusing to succumb to despair.

Anne Frank is portrayed as a complex and spirited young girl who navigates the challenges of adolescence and the harsh realities of war with courage, humour and a profound sense of self-awareness.

6. Comment on Anne Frank's and Valli's journeys from innocence to self-awareness. CBSE 2024 C

Ans. The stories of both Anne Frank and Valli depict a transition from innocence to self-awareness. Anne Frank, a Jewish girl hiding from the Nazis during World War II, begins her journey with a youthful innocence, characterised by her dreams and aspirations. Anne Frank's journey from innocence to self-awareness is marked by her experiences. Her diary entries show a growing maturity and self-awareness, culminating in her philosophical reflections on the nature of good and evil. She matures into a sensitive thinker who thoughts are clear and deep. Hence, her arguments for any subject show great reflection and a a keen sense of humour.

Similarly, Valli, a cheerful girl of 8 years, starts as a naive girl who is fascinated by the outside world. She transforms into a mature and sensitive girl due to simple bus journey. Her journey to the city signifies her quest for independence and self-discovery. As she navigates through her experiences, she learns about the realities of life, including the challenges and responsibilities that come with adulthood. Valli's journey is a metaphor for the transition from childhood innocence to a more nuanced understanding of mystery of life and death.

Both Anne Frank and Valli experience a profound shift from innocence to self-awareness. Anne's journey is more introspective and philosophical, while Valli's is more symbolic and surreal. Both characters, however, illustrate how extreme circumstances can catalyse personal growth and a deeper understanding of oneself and the world.

ASSESSMENT EXERCISE

Extract Based Questions

Read the following extracts carefully and answer the questions that follow.

1. That evening, after I finished the rest of my homework, the note about the essay caught my eye. I began thinking about the subject while chewing the tip of my fountain pen. Anyone could ramble on and leave big spaces between the words, but the trick was to come up with convincing arguments to prove the necessity of talking. I thought and suddenly I had an idea. I wrote the three pages Mr Keesing had assigned me and was satisfied. I argued that talking is a student's trait and that I would do my best to keep it under control, but that I would never be able to cure myself of the habit since my mother talked as much as I did if not more and that there's not much you can do about inherited traits.

(i) Select the option that correctly captures the usage of the word 'trait' in the above extract.
(a) The penalty for trait was escalating.
(b) The feeling of trait settled into her bleak thoughts.
(c) Each success has some trait along the way.
(d) The personality trait was innate in the two men.

(ii) What was the subject on which she had to write? What were her original arguments?

(iii) What does the idiom 'caught my eye' means?

(iv) Complete the analogy by selecting the suitable word from the text.
Resolute : Reluctant :: Acquired : ....

2. My father, the most adorable father I've ever seen, didn't marry my mother until he was 36 and she was 25. My sister Margot, was born in Frankfurt in Germany in 1926. I was born on 12th June, 1929. I lived in Frankfurt until I was four. My father emigrated to Holland in 1933. My mother, Edith Hollander Frank, went with him to Holland in September, while Margot and I were sent to Aachen to stay with our grandmother. Margot went to Holland in December and I followed in February, when I was plunked down on the table as a birthday present for Margot.

(i) When and where was Margot Frank born?

(ii) What did Margot get for present? What does this tell about Anne's personality?

(iii) 1. Anne and her sister Margot were sent to stay with their grandmother in Aachen.
2. Anne hated her father very much.
(a) 1 is the cause 2 is the effect.
(b) 2 is the cause 1 is the effect.
(c) Both are contradictory.
(d) 1 is true 2 is false

(iv) What do you mean by the phrase 'plunked down'?

Short Answer (SA) Type Questions

1. What does Anne receive on her birthday? How is it useful for her?

2. How do most people use their diaries? How is Anne's diary different?

3. "Anne was not alone in the world." Do you agree? Give reason. Competency Based

4. Describe what made Mr. Keesing allow Anne to talk in class?

Long Answer (LA) Type Questions

1. Write the character sketch of Mr. Keesing, Anne's Maths teacher.

2. Anne finds a true friend in her diary? Justify your answer.

Glimpses of India

CHAPTER 5

I. A Baker from Goa

by Lucio Rodrigues

CHAPTER SUMMARY

The following Chapter 'A Baker from Goa' has been written by Lucio Rodrigues. In the chapter, the narrator presents a pen-portrait of a traditional Goan village baker or pader who still has an important place in the society. It illustrates that the old Portuguese traditions still exist within the state. The traditional cakes and breads baked during important occasions and festivals depict that baking is an important aspect of the Goan culture.

The Old Portuguese Days in Goa

The narrator's elders often remember the old days of Goa, the Portuguese and their famous loaves of bread. The Portuguese left Goa a long time ago but the traditional bakers and their furnaces (a machine for baking) still exist there. The mixers, moulders and the people who bake the loaves still exist carrying on their business of baking. The son carries on the family profession in the place of his father. The sound of the baker's bamboo in the morning can still be heard in some places. These bakers are still known as 'pader' in Goa.

The Baker and the Narrator's Childhood

The narrator recalls his childhood in Goa, when the baker used to be their friend, companion and guide. He came atleast twice a day. He came once in the morning while selling his bread and again in the evening after selling all the bread he had.

The baker used to arrive with a jingling sound of the bamboo stick that woke everyone up. As soon as the children heard the sound, they ran to meet the baker and get the bread-bangles which was sometimes made of sweet bread.

The Baker's Arrival

The baker used to carry the bread basket on his head along with a bamboo stick. His one hand supported the basket and the other hand banged the bamboo stick on the ground. As the baker came, he would greet the lady of the house and put his basket on the vertical bamboo stick.

The children would be pushed aside and the loaves would be delivered to the maid servant. However, the children still found a way to peep into the basket. The author remembers the sweet fragrance of the bread and how they did not even brush their teeth before eating anything. They did not trouble themselves with getting the mango leaf for the tooth brush. They believed that the hot tea would clean their teeth well.

Importance of Bread in Traditional Ceremonies

Marriages were incomplete without the sweet bread known as bol. Sandwiches were prepared by the lady of the house for her daughter's engagement. Cakes and bolinhas were essential for Christmas and other festivals. Therefore, the presence of the baker was essential for the Goan villages.

The Baker's Dress

The baker in Goa wore a special dress known as kabai. It was a single-piece long frock that reached down to his knees. During the narrator's childhood, bakers wore shirts and trousers, which were shorter than full-length and longer than half pants. Even today in Goa, if anyone in the streets is seen wearing half pants, he is referred to as a pader.

Baking : A Profitable Profession

The baker used to maintain his monthly accounts on a wall in pencil and collected his bills at the end of the month. In old days, baking was a profitable profession. A baker's family and servants were always happy and prosperous. Their plump bodies proved the fact that a baker and his family were never hungry.

Word Meaning

Word	Meaning
reminiscing nostalgically	thinking fondly of the past
vanished	to disappear
mixers	people who kneading the flour
moulders	people who give a particular shape to the bread
furnace	very hot enclosed chamber
extinguished	to end
thud	a dull and heavy sound

Word	Meaning
jingle	a light ringing sound
heralding	announcing
rebuke	disapproval or scolding
parapet	a low protective wall along the edge of a roof
fragrance	scent, smell
peculiar	particular, special
prosperous	marked success or economic well-being
plump physique	pleasantly fat body
open testimony	public statement about a character or quality

NCERT FOLDER

NCERT Intext and Exercise Questions

ORAL COMPREHENSION CHECK❶ (NCERT PAGE 64)

Q.1 What are the elders in Goa nostalgic about?

Ans. The elders in Goa are nostalgic about the good old Portuguese days. They remember the loaves of bread made by Portuguese bakers.

Q.2 Is bread-making still popular in Goa? How do you know?

Ans. Yes, bread-making is still popular in Goa.This is very clear from the narrator's statement that though the Portuguese have gone away, the traditional bakers and their furnaces still exist in Goa. The mixers, moulders and the people who bake the loaves still exist in Goa.

Q.3 What is the baker called?

Ans. The baker is called *pader* in Goa.

Q.4 When would the baker come everyday? Why did the children run to meet him?

Ans. The baker would come twice a day, once early in the morning and the second time when he returned after selling all his bread.

The children would run to meet him as they wanted bread-bangles, which they chose very carefully.

CHECK❷ (NCERT PAGE 65)

Q.1 Match the following. What is a must

(i) as marriage gifts?	– cakes and *bolinhas*
(ii) for a party or a feast?	– sweet bread called *bol*
(iii) for a daughter's engagement?	– bread
(iv) for Christmas?	– sandwiches

Ans. (i) as marriage gifts – sweet bread called *bol*
(ii) for a party or a feast – bread
(iii) for a daughter's engagement – sandwiches
(iv) for Christmas – cakes and *bolinhas*

Q.2 What did the bakers wear
(i) in the Portuguese days?
(ii) when the author was young?

Ans. (i) The bakers usually wore a special dress called *kabai*. It was a single-piece long frock reaching down to the knees.
(ii) When the author was young, he saw the bakers wearing a shirt and trousers. The trousers were shorter than full length and longer than half-pants.

Q.3 Who invites the comment – "he is dressed like a *pader*?" Why?

Ans. Any person who wears a half pant reaching just below the knees invites this comment. This is because the bakers, known as *pader*, used to dress like that.

Q.4 Where were the monthly accounts of the baker recorded?

Ans. The monthly accounts of the baker were recorded on some wall in the house with a pencil.

Q.5 What does a 'jackfruit-like appearance' mean?

Ans. It means having a plump and round physique, like a jackfruit. Such a physique was linked to the bakers because they never starved. Baking was a profitable profession. The baker and his family always looked happy and prosperous.

THINKING ABOUT THE TEXT (NCERT PAGE 66)

Q.1 Which of these statements are correct?
(i) The *pader* was an important person in the village in old times.
(ii) *Paders* still exist in Goan villages.
(iii) The *paders* went away with the Portuguese.
(iv) The *paders* continue to wear a single-piece long frock.
(v) Bread and cakes were an integral part of Goan life in the old days.
(vi) Traditional bread-baking is still a very profitable business.
(vii) *Paders* and their families starve in the present times.

Ans. (i) Correct (ii) Correct
(iii) Incorrect (iv) Incorrect
(v) Correct (vi) Correct
(vii) Incorrect

Q.2 Is bread an important part of Goan life? How do you know this?

Ans. Yes, bread is an important part of Goan life.
We know this as it is needed for marriage gifts, parties and feasts. Bread is needed by a mother for preparing sandwiches during her daughter's engagement. Cakes and bolinhas are essential for Christmas and other festivals.

Q.3 Tick the right answer. What is the tone of the author when he says the following?
(i) The thud and the jingle of the traditional baker's bamboo can still be heard in some places. (nostalgic, hopeful, sad)
(ii) Maybe the father is not alive but the son still carries on the family profession. (nostalgic, hopeful, sad)
(iii) I still recall the typical fragrance of those loaves. (nostalgic, hopeful, naughty)
(iv) The tiger never brushed his teeth. Hot tea could wash and clean up everything so nicely, after all. (naughty, angry, funny)
(v) Cakes and *bolinhas* are a must for Christmas as well as other festivals. (sad, hopeful, matter-of-fact)
(vi) The baker and his family never starved. They always looked happy and prosperous. (matter-of-fact, hopeful, sad)

Ans. (i) Nostalgic (ii) Hopeful
(iii) Nostalgic (iv) Funny
(v) Matter-of-fact (vi) Matter-of-fact

Q.4 In this extract, the author talks about traditional bread-baking during his childhood days. Complete the following table with the help of the clues on the left. Then write a paragraph about the author's childhood days.

Clues	Author's childhood days
the way bread was baked	
the way the pader sold bread	
what the pader wore	
when the pader was paid	
how the pader looked	

Ans.

Clues	Author's childhood days
The way bread was baked	Traditional methods use age-old furnaces.
The way the pader sold bread	The pader visited twice daily, once in the morning and again after emptying his basket. He carried bread in a basket on his head and used a bamboo staff to announce his arrival.

What the pader wore	In Portuguese days, the pader wore a single-piece long frock called the 'kabai'. Later, he wore shirts and trousers shorter than full-length but longer than half pants.
When the pader was paid	The pader collected his bills at the end of the month.
How the pader looked	The pader and his family looked happy and prosperous, with a plump physique indicating their well-being.

When the author was a child in Goa, bread-baking was very important. The pader, or baker, used old-fashioned methods to bake bread in special ovens. Every day, the pader came to the village twice. In the morning, he went with a basket of bread on his head and made a jingling sound with his bamboo stick to let everyone know he was there. The pader wore a long dress called the "kabai" or later, short trousers and a shirt. He collected money for the bread at the end of each month. The pader and his family always looked happy and well-fed, showing that bread-baking was a good job.

Q.5 Compare the piece from the text (on the left below) with the other piece on Goan bakers (on the right). What makes the two texts so different? Are the facts the same? Do both writers give you a picture of the baker?

Our elders are often heard reminiscing nostalgically about those good old Portuguese days, the Portuguese and their famous loaves of bread. Those eaters of loaves might have vanished but the makers are still there. We still have amongst us the mixers, the moulders and those who bake the loaves. Those age-old, time-tested furnaces still exist. The fire in the furnaces had not yet been extinguished. The thud and the jingle of the traditional baker's bamboo, heralding his arrival in the morning. can still be heard in some places. May be the father is not alive but the son still carries on the family profession.	After Goa's liberation, people used to say nostalgically that the Portuguese bread vanished with the paders. But the paders have managed to survive because they have perfected the art of door-to- door delivery service. The paders pick up the knowledge of bread-making from traditions in the family. The leavened, oven-baked bread is a gift of the Portuguese to India. *[Adapted from Nandakumar Kamat's The Unsung Lives of Goan Paders']*

Ans. The two texts provide different views on Goan bakers. The left/first text talks nostalgically about the past, remembering the old Portuguese days and the traditional methods of baking bread. It mentions how the old baker's routines and practices are still remembered and valued today. The right/second text focuses on how bakers have adapted and survived after Goa's liberation. It explains that even though Portuguese bread might have disappeared, the bakers, or paders, have continued their work by perfecting door-to-door delivery.

Both texts agree that bread-making is a significant part of Goan culture. They mention that traditional methods are still remembered and that paders remain important. The first (left) text provides a nostalgic picture of the baker's role and the old practices, while the second (right) text highlights how paders have adapted to modern changes and continued their tradition.

Yes, both texts provide a picture of the baker. The left text shows a nostalgic view, focusing on traditional baking methods and the baker's past role in the community. The right text describes how bakers have adapted to modern times and continue their work by improving delivery services.

Q.6 Now find a travel brochure about a place you have visited. Look at the description in the brochure. Then write your own account, adding details from your own experience, to give the reader a picture of the place, rather than an impersonal, factual description.

Ans. Manila is an incredible city bursting with history and energy. During my visit, I enjoyed exploring the enchanting old town of Intramuros, where cobblestone streets and ancient forts transport you back in time. The San Agustin Church is a timeless masterpiece, exuding an irresistible old-world allure. A leisurely stroll along Manila Bay treated me to awe-inspiring sunsets that painted the sky in breathtaking colours. The National Museum was a treasure trove of Filipino culture and heritage, offering a fascinating journey through the country's past. I couldn't resist exploring the local markets and savouring the mouthwatering street food, from crispy fish balls to luscious mangoes. Manila's vibrant pulse and warm-hearted locals left an indelible mark, seamlessly blending history with the city's lively spirit.

REVIEW EXERCISE
Including Competency Based Questions

Part I

Multiple Choice Questions

1. How is the traditional baker recognised?

(a) With the thud and jingle of the bamboo
(b) With his baking style
(c) With his clothing style
(d) None of the above

Ans. (a) With the thud and jingle of the bamboo

2. From where did the 'jhang-jhang' sound come?

(a) Basket of bread
(b) Musical instrument used by baker
(c) Noises of children
(d) Specially made bamboo staff of baker

Ans. (d) Specially made bamboo staff of baker

3. The author is .... when he says, "Loaves for the elders and the bangles for the children."

(a) despairing (b) proud
(c) nostalgic (d) regretful

Ans. (c) nostalgic

4. What word best describes the attitude of the children towards brushing their teeth? Competency Based

(a) Indifferent (b) Rebellious
(c) Contemptuous (d) Sarcastic

Ans. (b) Rebellious

5. What is the main idea expressed in the first paragraph? Competency Based

(a) Traditional bakers can still be found in Goa.
(b) Traditional bakers do not find customers in recent times.
(c) Traditional bakers make sure the business remains within the family.
(d) Traditional bakers are not a Goan tradition but a Portuguese one.

Ans. (a) Traditional bakers can still be found in Goa.

6. Who invites the comment – "he is dressed like a pader"?

(a) Anyone who wears a half pant which reached just below the knees
(b) Anyone who wears a long piece of frock till knees
(c) Anyone who wears a shirt and trousers
(d) Anyone who bakes bread

Ans. (a) Anyone who wears a half pant which reached just below the knees

7. "Even today, anyone who wears a half pant which reaches just below the knees invites the comment that he is dressed like a pader!" Which of these best describes the author's tone in the above lines? Competency Based

(a) Neutral (b) Playful
(c) Reflective (d) Welcoming

Ans. (b) Playful

8. Even today any person with a jackfruit-like physical appearance is easily compared to a baker. Competency Based
What does this statement indicate?

(a) How easily bakers can be identified
(b) Why bakers were often made fun of
(c) Why bakers were prosperous in Goan society
(d) How much of a part of Goan society the bakers are

Ans. (a) How easily bakers can be identified

9. Select the option which best describes the relationship between the following statements from the extract. Competency Based

(1) He, his family and his servants always looked happy and prosperous.

(2) Their plump physique was an open testimony to this.

(a) (2) gives a summary of (1)
(b) (2) explains the meaning of (1)
(c) (2) is an inference drawn from (1)
(d) (2) supports the point made in (1)

Ans. (d) (2) supports the point made in (1)

10. Choose the option that lists the set of sentences that are not true according to the story 'A Baker from Goa'.

(i) The loaves of bread loved by the narrator are Portuguese.

(ii) The loaves of bread are a special delicacy in Goa.

(iii) The baker is a celebrated personality of Goa.

(iv) **Baking as a profession is dead in Goa.**

(v) **The arrival of a baker is a special highlight of the day for the narrator.**

(vi) **The narrator misses the loaves of Portuguese bread sellers.**

(a) (i) and (ii)
(b) Only (iv)
(c) Only (vi)
(d) (iii) and (v)

Ans. (b) Only (iv)

11. What type of a text is 'A Baker from Goa'? **Competency Based**

(a) A factual essay on past practices.
(b) A diary entry about one's life events.
(c) A research article which analyses a concept.
(d) A historical account written based on personal knowledge.

Ans. (d) A historical account written based on personal knowledge.

12. Which of these best explains why the author chose 'A Baker from Goa' as the title for the text? **Competency Based**

(a) The author discusses his journey as a baker to describe the cuisines of Goa.
(b) The author details the adventures of a baker to explore the cultural issues of Goa.
(c) The author narrates the life of a baker to paint a vivid picture of Goa's cultural history.
(d) The author recounts his childhood memories of home-baking to show Goa's rich traditions.

Ans. (c) The author narrates the life of a baker to paint a vivid picture of Goa's cultural history.

Extract Based Questions

1. Read the following extract carefully and answer the questions that follow.

"Our elders are often heard reminiscing nostalgically about those good old Portuguese days, the Portuguese and their famous loaves of bread. Those eaters might have vanished but the makers are still there. We still have amongst us the mixers, the moulders and those who bake the loaves. Those age-old, time-tested furnaces still exist. The fire in these furnaces has not yet been extinguished. The thud and jingle of traditional baker's bamboo, heralding his arrival in the morning, can still be heard in some places." **CBSE Question Bank 2021 Modified**

(i) **Select the option that displays the reason why the narrator says that the furnaces were 'time-tested'.**

(a) They had been thoroughly tested each time, before being used
(b) They had proved the test of time and were working well
(c) They had been tested by modern day experts
(d) They had the power to withstand inexperienced usage.

Ans. (b) They had proved the test of time and were working well.

(ii) **"Those eaters might have vanished but the makers are still there."**

The tone of the narrator in the above statement is .... (critical and accusatory/ hopeful and nostalgic).

Ans. hopeful and nostalgic

(iii) **What does the 'fire in the furnaces has not yet been extinguished' imply?**

Ans. The 'fire in the furnace has yet not been extinguished' implies that the furnaces are still being used to bake the famous loaves of Portuguese bread.

(iv) **Why did the baker come in with 'a thud and a jingle'?**

Ans. The baker came with 'a thud and jingle' because he wanted to make people aware that he had come around to sell his breads.

2. Read the following extract carefully and answer the questions that follow.

We kids would be pushed aside with a mild rebuke and the loaves would be delivered to the servant. But we would not give up. We would climb a bench or the parapet and peep into the basket, somehow. I can still recall the typical fragrance of those loaves. Loaves for the elders and the bangles for the children.

(i) **Why were the children pushed aside?**

(a) Because they were making noise
(b) To deliver the bread to the servant
(c) To give them bread loaves
(d) So that bread seller could go inside the house

Ans. (b) To deliver the bread to the servant.

(ii) **What did the children do when they were pushed aside by the baker?**

Ans. When the children were pushed aside by the baker, they climbed a bench or the parapet to peep into the baker's basket.

(iii) **Fill in the blank with the correct option from the bracket.**

The basket had .... (bangles for children/bread for elders/bread bangles for children).

Ans. bread bangles for children

(iv) **Who are 'we' in the extract?**

Ans. 'We' in the extract refers to the narrator and his friends.

3. Read the following extract carefully and answer the questions that follow.

In our childhood we saw bakers wearing a shirt and trousers which were shorter than full-length ones and longer than half pants. Even today, anyone who wears a half pant which reaches just below the knees invites the comment that he is dressed like a Pader!

The baker usually collected his bills at the end of the month. Monthly accounts used to be recorded on some wall in pencil. Baking was indeed a profitable profession in the old days. The baker and his family never starved. He, his family and his servants always looked happy and prosperous. Their plump physique was an open testimony to this. Even today any person with a jackfruit-like physical appearance is easily compared to a baker.

Competency Based

(i) "Monthly accounts used to be recorded on some wall in pencil" Which of these best explains the author's purpose for using some wall in the above line?

(a) To convey that bakers were very organised in their job.
(b) To show that bakers were not very worried about their incomes.
(c) To indicate that bakers had more customers than they could service.
(d) To show that bakers were not too advanced in the systems they used.

Ans. (b) To show that bakers were not very worried about their incomes.

(ii) Why did the author choose 'A Baker from Goa' as the title of the text? **Competency Based**

Ans. The author chose 'A Baker from Goa' as the title of the text because he uses the life of a baker to trace the vivid history of the Goan villages that links them to the Portuguese people. Furthermore, the baker is also a perfect character to describe the beautiful culinary culture of the Goan villages.

(iii) "The author mainly focuses on the physical appearance of the baker in the above extract." Which of these lines best explains the author's purpose for using 'physical appearance' in the above line?

(a) The baker and his family never starved.
(b) The baker usually collected his bills at the end of the month.
(c) He, his family and his servants always looked happy and prosperous.

Ans. (a) The baker and his family never starved.

(iv) What is the meaning of the phrase 'open testimony'?

Ans. The phrase 'open testimony' means a public statement proving a specific point.

4. Read the following extract carefully and answer the questions that follow.

The baker usually collected his bills at the end of the month. Monthly accounts used to be recorded on some wall in pencil. Baking was indeed a profitable profession in the old days. The baker and his family never starved. He, his family and his servants always looked happy and prosperous. Their plump physique was an open testimony to this. Even today any person with a jackfruit- like physical appearance is easily compared to a baker.

(i) Why did the baker and his family never starve?

(a) Baking was a profitable profession
(b) They had enough of bread
(c) They used to be very rich
(d) Bakers used to have ancestral money

Ans. (a) Baking was a profitable profession.

(ii) "The monthly records were maintained on some walls in pencil". What does this show about the relationship between the baker and the Goan people? **Competency Based**

Ans. The baker and the Goan people shared a relationship based on trust and friendship as the baker did not require to remember the records of his sale.

(iii) Which word in the extract is same in meaning of 'build'?

(a) Construct
(b) Renovate
(c) Figure
(d) Physique

Ans. (d) 'Physique'

(iv) How can a baker be identified in Goa?

Ans. Any person with a jackfruit-like physical appearance or plump physique is easily identified as a baker.

Part II

Short Answer Type Questions

1. How did the baker make his entry?

Ans. The baker made his entry with the jingling sound of his especially made bamboo stick. His one hand supported the basket on his head and the other hand banged the bamboo on the ground. It was like a musical entry to get people's attention.

2. How does the author create a sense of nostalgia in the story? Competency Based

Or **'A Baker from Goa' is a nostalgic saga of childhood memories. Comment.** CBSE 2023

Ans. The author creates a sense of nostalgia in the story by describing several scenes of his childhood with a joyful tone. The passages describing the daily routine of the author with the routine arrival of the baker create a beautiful scene while making it clear that the author would love to go back to this simpler time which was full of joy.

3. 'The tiger never brushed his teeth'. Why does the author say so?

Ans. The author said so because when the baker used to bring bangles for children, they did not even care to brush their teeth or wash their mouths properly. At that moment, they did not feel it necessary to wash their mouths just like the tigers who never brush their teeth before meals.

4. The relationship between the writer's family and the baker was a very commercial one. Do you agree? Justify your response. Competency Based

Ans. No, it is not true to say that the relationship between the writer's family and the baker was a very commercial one. According to the narrator, the baker used to be their friend, companion and guide. He focuses on the baker being on an informal basis with them.

5. How did the baker become synonymous with celebrations and occasions in Goa? CBSE 2022 Term II

Or **Why was the baker's furnace essential in a traditional Goan village?** CBSE 2010, 2020

Or **How do we know that bakers were an integral part of Goan society?** CBSE Additional SQP 2023

How is the Goan baker still an important part of the life of a Goan village? CBSE 2023

Ans. The baker's furnace was essential in a traditional Goan Village because different kinds of breads were required for different occasions. Marriage gifts are meaningless without the sweet bread known as *bol*. The lady of the house must prepare sandwiches on the occasion of her daughter's engagement.

Cakes and bolinhas are essential for Christmas as well as other festivals.

6. What does the writer recall about his childhood in Goa? CBSE 2022 Term II

Ans. From his childhood in Goa, the author remembers when the baker would go door-to-door to sell his bread. He also mentions the importance of the baker in the cultural and social setup of Goa.

7. Describe any two aspects of the Goan lifestyle which show Portuguese influence. Support each aspect with evidence from the text. Competency Based

Ans. The following are the two aspects of Goan lifestyle which portray Portuguese influence

(i) The importance of the village baker in the rituals and culture of the Goan villages.

(ii) The prevalence of the short pants which were traditionally worn by the bakers, as well as the association it carries to being called a baker by the citizens of Goan villages.

8. Who are paders and why are they friends of children? CBSE 2023

Ans. Paders are the old Goan Portuguese bakers.

They are friends of the children because they bring bread bangles and loaves every morning. While the loaves are sold to households, the children enjoy freely munching on the delicious bread bangles.

Long Answer Type Questions

1. After reading the story 'A Baker from Goa', do you think our traditions, heritage, values and practices are the roots that nourish us? Why/Why not?

Ans. Yes, I think that our traditions, heritage, values and practices are the roots that nourish us. They shape our personality and provide us with emotional support. They make us mentally strong and enable us to face a difficult situation. They even impact our behavioural pattern towards the other people in the society. The story highlights the importance of the traditional practice of making breads at every occasion.

In Goa, every occasion is incomplete without bread. A marriage is incomplete if it does not include a sweet bread known as 'bol'. All festival and feasts are incomplete without cakes and bolinhas. Even today, the elders remember those famous breads baked by the Portuguese bakers. From childhood till their old age, they remember the Portuguese bread. This shows that bread is an important part of the Goan life even today. Thus, our traditional practices keep our heritage alive and also nourish us.

2. Why were the children fascinated by the baker? How did they show their eagerness to see him? CBSE 2020

Ans. The children, according to the narrator, were eager to see the Goan baker. They used to wake up as soon as they heard the jingling sound of the bakers's bamboo stick. Whenever the baker greeted the lady of the house, children would surround the baker who would rebuke them and hand over the loaves to a servant. Then, the children would climb over a chair to peep into the basket full of bread loaves.

These children didn't even brush their teeth before taking the bread bangles that they could choose carefully.
Their actions made it clear that they were fascinated by the baker and were always eager to see him.

3. "During our childhood in Goa, the baker used to be our friend, companion and guide." What does this statement tell us about the character of the baker? CBSE 2024

Ans. The given statement tells us that the baker was a very respected person in the Goan society. He would guide children about good behaviour. This happened when he mildly scolded them for peeping into his basket.
He taught children about giving respect to elders.
This was when he wished 'Good Morning' to the lady of the house. He was very informal with the children. So, the narrator considered him a friend and companion. He was not simply a vendor interested in selling what he made. Even though he scolded the children, he offered them bread bangles and sweet bread of their choice.

A party or feast lost its charm without bread. Cakes and bolinhas were a must for Christmas and other festivals. The presence of the baker's furnace in the village was absolutely essential. Thus, he was an important character in the Goan society of those days.

4. Justify the opinion that the traditional baker and his bread play a significant role in the cultural and social fabric of Goan society. CBSE Additional SQP 2023

Or **How does the author establish that the pader is an important part of Goan society?** Competency Based

Ans. It is true to say that the traditional baker or pader and his bread play a significant role in the cultural and social fabric of Goan society.

The author establishes this by linking the importance of baked goods to various cultural festivals and celebrations around the Goan villages. The author mentions that any wedding gift is incomplete without the sweet bread known as 'bol'. Further, it is necessary for the lady of the house to make sandwiches on the occasion of the daughter's engagement. The celebrations of festivals like Christmas are believed to be incomplete without cakes and 'bolinhas'. Thus, the baker is very important in a Goan village.

5. The narrator shares, "Baking was indeed a profitable profession in the old days."

(a) What do you feel has changed now? Why?

(b) State any one way, you feel, the paders can regain their lost glory. CBSE Question Bank 2021

Ans. (a) From the given text, one of the things that seems to have changed with time is the traditional dress of the baker. They are still an integral part of the Goan society and celebrations are incomplete without the presence of their baked breads and cakes.
However, their importance and presence has certainly diminished over time.

(b) One of the ways in which the paders could regain their lost glory is by revitalising their business fronts with new yet authentic branding. If these bakeries are marketed to be selling lost recipes of the famous Portuguese baking then the paders might have a chance at returning back to their glory days.

6. In the chapter, 'A Baker from Goa' the narrator talks about his childhood in Goa and his fond memories. Compare the childhood of Nelson Mandela with that of the narrator. CBSE Question Bank 2021

Ans. South Africa and India are two vastly different countries. As such, it is expected that the experiences of the people that reside in these different geographical locations would also be different. But childhood is a blissful time period no matter where one lives.
The innocence of childhood grants a specific innocence that makes children unaware of the harsh realities of their surroundings.

The experiences of both Nelson Mandela and Lucio Rodrigues were coloured by that same innocence.

Neither Rodrigues nor Mandela were aware of the changes taking place within their hometowns.
They had a happy, carefree childhood full of 'freedom'.
Rodrigues mentions the happy days of his youth where he would leave brushing his teeth in favour of eating the sweet bread-bangles brought by the Pader.
Mandela also mentions his happy childhood where he believed that as long as he followed the rules of his father and his tribe, he had all the freedom he liked.

ASSESSMENT EXERCISE

Extract Based Questions

Read the following extract and answer the questions that follow.

The thud and jingle of the traditional baker's bamboo, heralding his arrival in the morning, can still be heard in some places. Maybe the father is not alive but the son still carries on the family profession. These bakers are, even today, known as Pader in Goa. During our childhood in Goa, the baker used to be our friend, companion and guide. He used to come at least twice a day. Once, when he set out in the morning on his selling round, and then again, when he returned after emptying his huge basket. The jingling thud of his bamboo woke us up from sleep and we ran to meet and greet him. Why was it so? Was it for the love of the loaf? Not at all. The loaves were bought by some Paskine or Bastine.

(i) Which family profession is being talked about in the above extract?
   (a) Selling bamboo baskets
   (b) Baking
   (c) Selling goods in basket in streets
   (d) All of the above

(ii) Why did the children run to meet the baker? What does this depict about their relationship with the baker?

(iii) Read (a)–(c) and identify what does the given extract try to do.
   (a) Characterise the baker (b) Show how loved the baker was
   (c) Show how children reacted upon seeing the baker.

(iv) An onomatopoeia is a word that actually looks like the sound it makes (e.g. splash). Find an onomatopoeia word from the above extract.

Short Answer (SA) Type Questions

1. What did the baker do first once he reached a house?
2. How did the baker make his entry?
3. How did the baker ensure that he got his money for the bread supplied?

Long Answer (LA) Type Questions

1. The traditional practices in Goa show us how important they are in maintaining our roots. Do you think children should be taught these practices starting from their childhood? Why?
2. Instead of enjoying their childhood, children today are keen to enter adulthood. After reading about all the joys that the author Lucio Rodrigues experienced in his childhood, do you think such keenness on the children is desirable? **Competency Based**

II. Coorg

by Lokesh Abrol

CHAPTER SUMMARY The following chapter 'Coorg' written by Lokesh Abrol describes Coorg-a beautiful and heavenly place situated between Mysore and Mangalore. It is the home of evergreen forests, spices and coffee plantations. It is inhabited by a proud race of martial men, beautiful women and wild creatures.

A Heaven called Coorg

Coorg or Kodagu is the smallest district of Karnataka that lies between Mysore and the coastal town of Mangalore. It is a land of rolling hills that is inhabited by martial men, beautiful women and innumerable wild creatures.

Weather and Environment of Coorg

Coorg consists of evergreen forests which covers thirty percent of the district along with coffee and spice plantations. The heavy rainfall during monsoons keeps most of the tourists away. Hence, the best time to visit Coorg starts in September and continues till March. During this time, the weather is pleasant with some amount of rainfall and the smell of coffee all around. With coffee estates and colonial bungalows hidden in corners, the landscape seems like heaven on Earth.

The Origin of People of Coorg

The people of Coorg are possibly descendents of Greeks or Arabs. It is believed that Alexander's army moved South along the coast and settled there, when they were unable to return to their country. These people married among the locals and their culture can be seen in their martial traditions, marriages and religious rites which are different from the Hindu culture.

The theory of the Arab descent can be proved by their traditional clothes. The Kodavus wear a long black coat with an embroidered waist belt known as Kuppia. It resembles Kuffia worn by the Arabs and the Kurds.

Hospitality and Bravery of Kodavus

Coorgis or Kodavus are known for their hospitality. Also, there are many tales of bravery related to the people of Coorg. The Coorg Regiment is one of the most decorated regiments of the Indian Army.

The first Chief of the Indian-Army, General Cariappa was a Coorgi. Even today, Kodavus are the only people in India permitted to carry firearms without a licence.

River Kaveri and Wildlife in Coorg

The river Kaveri originates in the hills of Coorg. In the waters of the river, a large freshwater fish, Mahaseer can be found in abundance.

The land of Coorg is also home to a number of birds and animals including kingfishers, squirrels, langurs, elephants, slender loris, macaques, bees, butterflies, etc.

Tourism in Coorg

Coorg offers many adventurous activities such as river rafting, canoeing, rappelling, rock climbing, mountain biking and trekking. One can have a panoramic view of the entire Coorg by climbing the Brahmagiri hills. Other interesting places are the sixty-four acre Island Nisargadhama and the largest Tibetan settlement of Buddhist monks at Bylakuppe.

Fact File - How to Reach Coorg

To reach Coorg, one has to come to Madikeri, the district headquarters and the only gateway to Coorg. One can reach Coorg

- **By Air** One can take a flight to Mangalore (135 km) or Bangalore (260 km).
- **By Rail** By rail, one can travel to Mysore, Mangalore or Hassan.
- **By Road** There are two routes to Coorg from Bangalore. Both are almost the same distance (around 250-260 km). The route *via*. Mysore is the most frequented one. The other route is *via* Neelamangal, Kunigal, Chanrayanapatna.

Word Meaning

Word	Meaning
drifted	separated
martial	having to do with war
commences	begins
invigorating	make one feel strong, healthy and full of energy
tucked	hidden
canopies	roof like coverings that form shelters
prime	the best
fiercely	powerfully
descent	origin
mainstream	a tradition which most people follow
hospitality	generous and friendly treatment of visitors and guests
tales of valour	stories of courage and bravery, usually in war

Word	Meaning
most decorated	having received maximum number of awards for bravery in war
permitted	allowed
abound	exist in large numbers
scrubbed	to rub for purpose of clean
mahouts	the keepers of elephants
laidback	relaxed
rafting	travelling in a river in a raft
canoeing	travelling in a river in a canoe
rappelling	going down a cliff by sliding down a rope
trails	paths created by walking
panoramic view	a view of a wide area of land
misty	filled with fog
ochre	a moderate yellow-orange to orange colour

NCERT FOLDER

NCERT Intext and Exercise Questions

THINKING ABOUT THE TEXT

(NCERT PAGE 70-71)

Q.1 Where is Coorg?

Ans. Coorg or *Kodagu*, the smallest district of Karnataka, is situated in midway between Mysore and the coastal town of Mangalore.

Q.2 What is the story about the Kodagu people's descent?

Ans. One story about the descent of Kodagu is that they are descendants of Greeks or Arabs. It is believed that a section of Alexander's army moved South along the coast and settled here. These people married among the locals which influenced their clothing, martial practices and marriage rituals, and shows a difference from Hindu tradition.

Another theory is that they have Arabic origins as their traditional dress resembles the Arab Kuffia.

Q.3 What are some of the things you now know about

(i) the people of Coorg?

(ii) the main crop of Coorg?

(iii) the sports it offers to tourists?

(iv) the animals you are likely to see in Coorg?

(v) its distance from Bangalore and how to get there?

Ans. (i) The narrator has described the people of Coorg as a proud race of martial men and beautiful women. They are fiercely independent people and have descended from the Greeks or the Arabs. They are hospitable and courageous people.

They are the only people in India who are permitted to carry a gun without a licence.

(ii) Coffee is the main crop of Coorg.

(iii) It offers many adventure sports. These include river rafting, canoeing, rappelling, rock climbing, mountain biking and trekking.

(iv) The animals likely to be seen in Coorg are macaques, Malabar squirrels, langurs, slender loris, elephants, etc.

(v) The distance between Coorg and Bangalore is about 250-260 km. There are two routes from Bangalore that go to Coorg and both of them are of same distance.

Q.4 Here are six sentences with some words in italics. Find phrases from the text that have the same meaning. (Look in the paragraphs indicated)

(i) During monsoons it rains so heavily *that tourists do not visit Coorg*. (Para 2)

(ii) *Some people say that* Alexander's army moved South along the coast and settled there. (Para 3)

(iii) The Coorg people *are always ready to tell* stories of their son's and father's valour. (Para 4)

(iv) *Even people who normally lead an easy and slow life get smitten by* the high energy adventure sports of Coorg. (Para 6)

(v) The theory of the Arab origin *is supported by* the long coat with embroidered waist-belt they wear. (Para 3)

(vi) Macaques, Malabar squirrels *observe you carefully* from the tree canopy. (Para 7)

Ans. (i) to keep many visitors away

(ii) as one story goes

(iii) are more than willing to recount

(iv) the most laidback individuals become converts to

(v) draws support from

(vi) keep a watchful eye

THINKING ABOUT LANGUAGE

(NCERT PAGE 71-72)

Collocations

Certain words 'go together'. Such 'word friends' are called *collocations*. The collocation of a word is 'the company it keeps'. For example, look at the paired sentences and phrases below. Which is a common collocation and which one is odd? Strike out the odd sentence or phrase.

(a) 'How old are you?'
'How young are you?'

(b) A pleasant person
A pleasant pillow

Ans. (a) The odd sentence is 'How young are you?'

(b) The odd phrase is 'A pleasant pillow'.

Q.1 Here are some nouns from the text.

culture monks surprise experience weather tradition

Work with a partner and discuss which of the nouns can collocate with which of the adjectives given below. The first one has been done for you.

unique terrible unforgettable serious ancient wide sudden

(i) culture-unique culture, ancient culture

(ii) monks

....

(iii) surprise

....

(iv) experience

....

(v) weather

....

(vi) tradition

....

Ans. (ii) **monks** ancient monks, serious monks

(iii) **surprise** terrible surprise, unforgettable surprise

(iv) **experience** unique experience, terrible experience, unforgettable experience

(v) **weather** terrible weather, unique weather

(vi) **tradition** unique tradition, ancient tradition

Q.2 Complete the following phrases from the text. For each phrase, can you find at least one other word that would fit into the blank?

(i) Tales of ....

(ii) Coastal ....

(iii) A piece of ....

(iv) Evergreen ....

(v) .... **plantations**

(vi) .... **bridge**

(vii) Wild ....

Ans. (i) **Tales of** valour, bravery, adventure

(ii) **Coastal** town, belt, plains

(iii) **A piece of** heaven, cake, advice

(iv) **Evergreen** rainforests

(v) coffee, tea, banana **plantations**

(vi) rope, concrete, steel **bridge**

(vii) **Wild** creatures

REVIEW EXERCISE

Including Competency Based Questions

Part I

Multiple Choice Questions

1. The season of joy commences from September and continues till March. The given line suggests that

(a) September to March is the best time to visit Coorg
(b) September to March are the months of rainfall
(c) Coorg becomes even more beautiful between September and March
(d) Both (a) and (c)

Ans. (d) Both (a) and (c)

2. What is the 'season of joy' mentioned in the paragraph 2? Competency Based

(a) The season of rains
(b) The season of festivals
(c) The best season to visit
(d) The best season to grow coffee

Ans. (d) The best season to grow coffee

3. What was the embroidered waist-belt worn by Kodavus known as?

(a) Kuffia (b) Kuppia (c) Kurd (d) Waist-belt

Ans. (b) Kuppia

4. Who are the only people in India permitted to carry firearms without a license?

(a) Kodavus (b) Kurds
(c) Arabs (d) Greeks

Ans. (a) Kodavus

5. The climb to the .... hills brings one into a panoramic view of the entire misty landscape of Coorg.

(a) Brahmagiri
(b) Himalayan
(c) Nilgiri
(d) Parvati

Ans. (a) Brahmagiri

6. Which of the following destinations are mentioned in the lesson 'Coorg'? Choose the correct option.

1. Mangalore	**2. Mysore**
3. Karnataka	**4. Nisargadhama**
5. Bylakuppe	**6. Brahmagiri hills**

(a) 1, 3, 4 and 6 (b) 2, 3, 4 and 5
(c) 1, 2, 3 and 5 (d) All of these

Ans. (d) All of these

Extract Based Questions

1. Read the following extract carefully and answer the questions that follow.

Midway between Mysore and the coastal town of Mangalore sites a piece of heaven that must have drifted from the Kingdom of God. This land of rolling hills is inhabited by a proud race of martial men, beautiful women and wild creatures. Coorg or Kodagu, the smallest district of Karnataka, is home to evergreen rain forests, spices and coffee plantations. Evergreen rain forests cover thirty per cent of this district. During the monsoons, it pours enough to keep many visitors away. The season of joy commences from September and continues till March. The weather is perfect, with some showers thrown in for good measure. The air breathes of invigorating coffee. Coffee estates and colonial bungalows stand tucked under tree canopies in prime corners.

(i) Fill in the blank by choosing the correct phrase from the bracket.

The weather is perfect, with some showers thrown in for good measure. The given line suggests that .... (showers make the weather perfect/showers are not good for Coorg's weather).

Ans. Showers make the weather perfect

(ii) What does 'the air breathe of invigorating coffee' mean? Why?

Ans. The air in Coorg breathes of invigorating coffee means that the air smells of strong coffee. This is so because Coorg is home to many coffee plantations which lends the air, the beautiful smell of coffee.

(iii) The author says that from September to March, some showers thrown in for a good measure. This indicates that

1. the weather is pleasant
2. rainfall adds to the beauty
3. expect some rainfall during that time
4. rainfall is scarce
5. one can visit during the time

(a) 1, 4 and 5 (b) 1, 2, 3 and 5
(c) 2 and 3 (d) All of these

Ans. (a) 1, 4 and 5

(iv) Select the suitable word from the extract to complete the following analogy.

Pageants : Beauty : Army : ....

Ans. Martial

2. Read the following extract carefully answer the questions that follow.

These people married amongst the locals and their culture is apparent in the martial traditions, marriage and religious rites, which are distinct from the Hindu mainstream. The theory of Arab Origin draws support from the long, black coat with an embroidered waist-belt worn by the Kodavus, known as Kuppia, it resembles the Kuffia worn by the Arabs and the Kurds.

(i) What is so similar between Kodavus and Arabs?

(a) A traditional dress with embroidery
(b) A modern dress with stonework
(c) A long black coat with an embroidered waist-belt resembling the Kuffia
(d) A short coat with a simple waist-belt resembling the Kuffia

Ans. (c) A long black coat with an embroidered waist-belt resembling the Kuffia.

(ii) From the given options, identify the author's tone in the extract. Answer in one word.

Ans. Informative

(iii) Whom does 'these people' in the above extract refer to? To which country did 'these people' belong? **Competency Based**

Ans. 'These people' in the given extract refers to Alexander's army. These people originally belonged to Greece but later settled down in the Coorg region of India.

(iv) .... means 'related to war'.

Ans. Martial

3. Read the following extract carefully answer the questions that follow.

The river, Kaveri, obtains its water from the hills and forests of Coorg. Mahaseer — a large freshwater fish — abound in these waters. Kingfishers dive for their catch, while squirrels and langurs drop partially eaten fruit for the mischief of enjoying the splash and the ripple effect in the clear water. Elephants enjoy being bathed and scrubbed in the river by their mahouts.

(i) Why do you think squirrels drop partially eaten fruits into the river?

Ans. The squirrels drop partially eaten fruit in the river because they enjoy the splash and ripple effect created by the fruit hitting the water.

(ii) Which fish is found in abundance in the Kaveri waters? It is ....

Ans. Mahaseer

(iii) How does this passage describe Coorg's wealth of wildlife?

Ans. This passage mentions various wildlife creatures such as mahaseer, kingfishers, squirrels, langurs, and elephants. This description perfectly portrays the abundant wealth of wildlife present in Coorg.

(iv) Read the given statements and choose the statement that is true. **Competency Based**

1. Elephants enjoy being bathed and scrubbed in the river.

2. Their mahouts also enjoy bathing with them.

Ans. Statement 1 is true. Elephants enjoy being bathed and scrubbed in the river.

4. Read the following extract carefully answer the questions that follow.

The most laidback individuals become converts to the life of high-energy adventure with river rafting, canoeing, rappelling, rock climbing and mountain biking. Numerous walking trails in this region are a favourite with trekkers. Birds, bees and butterflies are there to give you company. Macaques, Malabar squirrels, langurs and slender loris keep a watchful eye from the tree canopy. I do, however, prefer to step aside for wild elephants.

(i) How does Coorg change the most laidback individuals?

(a) Into high energy adventurists
(b) Into trekkers
(c) Into hikers
(d) None of the above

Ans. (a) Into high-energy adventurists.

(ii) "...... keep a watchful eye from the tree canopy." Who keeps a watchful eye from the canopy? Why do you think they feel the need to do so? **Competency Based**

Ans. Macaques, Malabar squirrels, langurs and slender loris keep a watchful eye from the canopy.

I think they do so because they feel threatened due to the presence of humans amidst them and are taking safety measures.

(iii) Which high-energy adventure sports can be done in Coorg?

(a) River rafting
(b) Canoeing and mountain biking
(c) Rappelling and rock climbing

Ans. River rafting, canoeing, rappelling, rock climbing and mountain biking can be done in Coorg.

(iv) What are favourites with trekkers?

Ans. Numerous walking trails in Coorg are a favourite with trekkers.

Part II

Short Answer Type Questions

1. Coorg is known as 'the land of rolling hills.' Describe its picturesque beauty and biodiversity. **CBSE 2024 C**

Or **Why is Coorg called the land of rolling hills?** **CBSE 2020, 2022 Term II**

Ans. Coorg is called the land of rolling hills because it is situated on the gentle sloping hills that are covered with lush green rainforests. The hills on which it is located seem to be rolling down to a beautiful panoramic view which make it look like a piece of heaven on Earth.

2. Where is Coorg located? Write any two characteristics of the people of Coorg? **CBSE 2023**

Ans. Coorg is located midway between Mysore and the coastal town of Mangalore. The two main characteristics of the people of Coorg are that they are very hospitable and extremely brave.

3. Coorgis belong to a valorous and hospitable race. Comment on this statement with reference to the text. **CBSE Question Bank 2021**

Or **Valour and hospitality are inherent in the people of Coorg? Comment.** **CBSE 2023**

Or **"Coorgi homes have a tradition of hospitality and they are more than willing to recount numerous tales of valour related to their sons and fathers." Elaborate with reference to the chapter 'Glimpses of India'.** **CBSE 2024**

Ans. Coorgis are said to belong to a valourous and hospitable race as their homes have tradition of hospitality. There are innumerable tales of courage related to the people belonging to Coorg. In fact, the Coorg Regiment is one of the most decorated in the Indian Army, and the first Chief of the Indian Army, General Cariappa, was a Coorgi. Even now, Kodavus are the only people in India permitted to carry firearms without a licence.

4. What are the various stories regarding the origin of *Kodavu* people?

Or **What evidence is provided for the theory that the people of Coorg are from Arabia?** **Competency Based**

Ans. The two stories regarding the descent of Kodavu people are

(i) Kodavus are of Greek origin. A part of Alexander's army settled here and married among the locals. Their descendants are called Kodavus.

(ii) Kodavus are of Arab origin. They wear the same traditional dress Kuppia i.e. a long, black coat with embroidered waist belt, as the Kuffia of the Arabs and the Kurds.

5. Which time of the year would you recommend someone to visit Coorg? Justify your answer with details from the text. **Competency Based**

Ans. I would recommend people to visit Coorg during the months between September and March. The author mentions in the text that weather in Coorg during these months is pleasant and joyful. There are very light and refreshing showers, and the air smells of energising coffee.

6. Give an account of the river that originates from Coorg.

Ans. The river Kaveri originates from the hills of Coorg. Mahaseer, a large freshwater fish are found in abundance in its water. Kingfishers dive in this river for fish while elephants are bathed by their Mahout in the river. Further, wild animals such as squirrels and langurs drop half-eaten fruit for the mischief of enjoying the splash and ripple effect produced in the clear water.

7. "I do, however, prefer to step aside for wild elephants". What is the tone of the given line? What does the author want to indicate in this line? **Competency Based**

Ans. The tone of the given line is playful. The author wishes to indicate that although interactions with most of the animals of the jungle are okay, one should never mess with wild elephants because they are truly dangerous and unpredicatable creatures.

8. Describe any two tourist places of Coorg.

Ans. Two tourist places of Coorg are the Brahmagiri hills and Nisargadhama.

The climb of Brahmagiri hills brings in a panoramic view of the entire landscape of Coorg. A walk across a rope bridge leads to the sixty-four acre island of Nisargadhama. One can also meet Buddhist monks from India's largest Tibetan settlement, at nearby Bylakuppe.

9. Why does the author in 'Coorg' say that the visitors search for the heart and soul of India would be found in Coorg? **CBSE Question Bank 2021**

Ans. The author in 'Coorg' says that the visitors searching for the heart and soul of India would find it in Coorg because of its natural grandeur and different appearance of nature. Not only is the land of Coorg full of different species of flora and fauna but it also is a home to martial men and attractive women.

10. What attracts visitors to Coorg? **CBSE 2022 Term II**

Or **Mention any three surprises that awaits visitors in Coorg.** **CBSE 2025**

Ans. The beauty of Coorg attracts visitors. It includes the evergreen forests, the hills and the river Kaveri. Coorg also offers various adventure sports to indulge in. It is famous for its rainforests and spices and the aroma of coffee.

11. People visit Coorg only to rest and relax. Do you agree with the statement? Justify your answer. **Competency Based**

Ans. It is not true to say that people visit Coorg only to rest and relax. Coorg, according to the author, is a place which offers any high energy adventures sports such as trekking, river rafting, canoeing, etc. In fact, the author states that in Coorg, even the most laidback individuals become converts to the life of high energy adventure.

Long Answer Type Questions

1. The Coorgis are the descendants of the Greeks or the Arabs and are still able to maintain their traditional practices. Do you agree that following these practices today is important? Why or why not? **Competency Based**

Ans. After reading the text, I feel that it is important to follow the traditional practices. The reason is that it has kept the tradition of Coorgis known to the people even today. If the people of Coorg had not followed it, their tradition would have perished. Nobody would have remembered them today without their culture and traditional practices. According to the text, their traditions can be seen in the martial forms, religious rites and marriages. The Kodavus even wear the dress which resembles the dress of Arabs. Traditional practices also play a very important role in maintaining values amongst people.

They have an impact on shaping the behaviour of people. These practices bind us together in our social life. Just like the Kodavus who are bound to their ancestors even today, we are also bound to our ancestors because of the traditional values we have inherited from them.

2. How do Coorg's location, people and natural features add to diversity of India?

Ans. Coorg, the smallest district of Karnataka, is among the most beautiful regions of India. It's location, people and natural features add to the diversity of the nation. Coorg is called a piece of heaven that must have drifted from the kingdom of God. It has beautiful rolling hillsides that is filled with evergreen rainforests, spice and coffee plantations. It also includes a river, Kaveri along with many species of birds, insects and animals. Nature here exists in its original glory.

Further, Coorg's culture is distinct from the Hindu traditions. Its martial traditions, rituals and rites show a mixture of Arabic and Greek culture owing to Greek and Arabic descendance. In addition, the land is a home to many courageous men as well as religious Buddhist monks. Also, there are many other tourist destinations that add to its glory. All these features of Coorg together add to the diversity of the country.

3. Explain why the author describes Coorg as 'a piece of heaven that must have drifted from the kingdom of god'? **CBSE Additional SQP 2022**

Ans. The author describes Coorg as 'a piece of heaven that must have drifted from the kingdom of god' because of the natural beauty of the rolling hills as well as the hospitality of the people that live there. The coastal town of Coorg is home to evergreen forests, spices and coffee plantations. During the months of September till March, the land has a perfect atmosphere which is ornamented by the beautiful smell of coffee plants and light showers. To add to its beauty, coffee estates and colonial bungalow are enhanced by the tree canopies which are situated in the best corners of the place.

4. The people of Coorg have a tradition of courage and bravery. How has it been recognised in modern India? **CBSE 2023**

Ans. It is believed that the people of Coorg are descended from soldiers of the Greek army of Alexander the Great. Thus, the residents of Coorg have a culture of bravery and courage. This is recognised by the following facts in modern India

(i) The Coorg regiment is one of the most decorated regiment in the Indian army.

(ii) The first Chief of the Indian army was a Coorgi–General Cariappa.

(iii) Kodavus are the only people in India who are permitted to carry firearms without licence.

ASSESSMENT EXERCISE

Extract Based Questions

Read the following extract and answer the questions that follow.

Coorg, or Kodagu, the smallest district of Karnataka, is home to evergreen rainforests, spices and coffee plantations. Evergreen rainforests cover thirty per cent of this district. During the monsoons, it pours enough to keep many visitors away. The season of joy commences from September and continues till March. The weather is perfect, with some showers thrown in for good measure. The air breathes of invigorating coffee. Coffee estates and colonial bungalows stand tucked under tree canopies in prime corners.

(i) What do you understand by the term colonial bungalow?
 (a) The bungalows built in a colony
 (b) A large detached house with more than one storey
 (c) The residential unit for members of the British colonial community
 (d) A low house having only one storey

(ii) Which is the best time to visit Coorg? Why?

(iii) What can be inferred from the given line? "During the monsoons, it pours enough to keep many visitors away."

(iv) Choose the word from the extract to complete the following analogy.
 Take out : Tuck : : Tiring : ....

Short Answer (SA) Type Questions

1. Explain how Coorg is the soul of India.
2. Which sports attract the tourists most at Coorg? Why?
3. How can one reach Coorg?

Long Answer (LA) Type Question

1. The Kodavus are very far away from their origin, Greece or Arabia. Yet they carry on their unique values, customs and practices. Does this make you appreciate them? Why? **Competency Based**

III. Tea from Assam

by Arup Kumar Datta

This chapter 'Tea from Assam' has been written by Arup Kumar Dutta. It describes Assam which has the largest concentration of tea plantations in the world. The narrator has tried to explain the importance of tea in the country through a dialogue between two school students Rajveer and Pranjol

Pranjol and Rajvir Visit to Assam

Pranjol and Rajvir were classmates studying in the same school in Delhi. Pranjol belonged to Assam where his father was the Manager of a tea garden. He had invited Rajvir to visit his home during summer vacation. So, both of them were travelling to Assam by train. When the train had stopped on the way at a station, they bought tea from a vendor and started sipping it.

Popularity of Tea and Tea Gardens

While sipping tea, Rajvir told Pranjol that over 80 crore cups of tea are drunk everyday around the world. It is, thus, a very popular drink. As the train started moving, Rajvir looked out of the window. He was amazed to see the beautiful scenery outside. The soft rice fields gave way to tea bushes. Rajvir was fascinated by the vast stretch of the tea bushes.

On the other hand, Pranjol was reading his detective book. Pranjol was born and bought up in a tea plantation and thus, was not as excited. However, he told Rajvir that Assam had the largest concentration of tea plantations in the world.

Legends about the Discovery of Tea

Rajvir told Pranjol that there are many legends or stories about the discovery of tea. According to a legend, a Chinese emperor discovered tea when he was boiling water for drinking. When the water was put to boil, a few leaves of the twigs burning under the pot fell into the water. Thus, the boiled water got a delicious taste. It is believed that they were tea leaves.

Rajvir also told Pranjol about another legend from India which said that Bodhidharma, an ancient Buddhist monk, cut off his eyelids because he felt sleepy during meditations. Ten tea plantations grew out of his eyelids. It is believed that the leaves of these plants, when put in hot water and drunk, banished sleep.

Rajvir further told Pranjol that Tea was first drunk in China in 2700 BC and the words like 'tea', 'chai' and 'chini' are also Chinese. He also mentioned that tea first came to Europe in the sixteenth century and it was drunk more as medicine than as a beverage.

The Dhekiabari Tea Plantation

Rajvir and Pranjol reached the Mariani Junction where Pranjol's parents received them. In car, they went to Dhekiabari, the tea estate managed by Pranjol's father. On both the sides of the road, there were huge acres of tea bushes. Groups of tea-pluckers, with bamboo baskets on their backs and wearing plastic aprons, were plucking the newly sprouted leaves.

Looking at the tea-pluckers, Rajvir asked Pranjol's father whether it was the second flush or sprouting season. He also mentioned that this season lasts from May to July and yields the best tea. Rajvir's knowledge surprised Pranjol's father to which Rajvir told him that he expected to learn more during his visit.

Word Meaning

Word	Meaning
steaming	very hot
buried his nose in	started reading
ardent	keen
backdrop	scenery at the back
densely	thickly
dwarfing	making something appear small
sturdy	strongly and solidly built

Word	Meaning
billowing	a moving cloud or mass of smoke
legends	a story from the past that is believed by many people but cannot be proved to be true
ascetic	a person with incredible self discipline
banished	get rid of
veered	turned
pruned	cut

NCERT FOLDER

NCERT Intext and Exercise Questions

THINKING ABOUT LANGUAGE

(NCERT PAGE 74-75)

I.

Q.1 Look at these words: upkeep, downpour, undergo, dropout, walk-in. They are built up from a verb (keep, pour, go, drop, walk) and an adverb or a preposition (up, down, under, out, in). Use these words appropriately in the sentences below. You may consult a dictionary.

(i) A heavy .... has been forecast due to low pressure in the Bay of Bengal.

(ii) Rakesh will .... major surgery tomorrow morning.

(iii) My brother is responsible for the .... of our family property.

(iv) The ...... rate for this accountancy course is very high.

(v) She went to the enterprise company to attend a .... interview.

Ans. (i) downpour (ii) undergo (iii) upkeep (iv) dropout (v) walk-in

Q.2 Now fill in the blanks in the sentences given below by combining the verb given in brackets with one of the words from the box as appropriate.

over	by	through	out	up	down

(i) The Army attempted unsuccessfully to .... the government. (throw)

(ii) Scientists are on the brink of a major .... in cancer research. (break)

(iii) The State Government plans to build a .... for Bhubaneswar to speed up traffic on the main highway. (pass)

(iv) Gautama's .... on life changed when he realised that the world is full of sorrow. (look)

(v) Rakesh seemed unusually .... after the game. (cast)

Ans. (i) overthrow (ii) breakthrough (iii) bypass (iv) outlook (v) downcast

II. Notice how these -ing and -ed adjectives are used.

(a) Chess is an *interesting* game.
I am very *interested* in chess.

(b) Going *trekking* in the Himalayas this summer is an exciting idea.
We are very *excited* about the trek.

(c) Are all your school books *boring*?

He was *bored* as he had no friends there.

The -ing adjectives show the qualities that chess, trekking or these books have: they cause interest, excitement, or boredom in you. The –ed /-en adjectives show your mental state or your physical state: how you feel in response to ideas, events or things.

Q.1 Think of suitable -ing or -ed adjectives to answer the following questions. You may also use words from those given above. How would you describe

(i) a good detective serial on television?

(ii) a debate on your favourite topic 'Homework Should Be Banned'?

(iii) how you feel when you stay indoors due to incessant rain?

(iv) how you feel when you open a present?

(v) how you feel when you watch your favourite programme on television?

(vi) the look on your mother's face as you waited in a queue?

(vii) how you feel when tracking a tiger in a tiger reserve forest?

(viii) the story you have recently read, or a film you have seen?

Ans. (Sample answers are given. You may have a different answer.)

(i) Exciting (ii) Interesting
(iii) Bored (iv) Excited
(v) Interested (vi) Disappointed
(vii) Thrilled (viii) Entertaining

Q.2 Now use the adjectives in the exercise above, as appropriate, to write a paragraph about Coorg.

Ans. Coorg is a captivating destination in Karnataka, India, known for its enchanting coffee plantations and lush greenery. The area offers a perfect blend of natural beauty and cultural richness. The locals are friendly and always eager to share their stories and traditions. As I strolled through the plantations, I was thrilled by the stunning scenery and the fresh, invigorating air. The food was delightful, adding to my excitement with every meal. Coorg's rich history was fascinating, filled with tales of bravery and courage. Even though the long queues at famous tourist spots were frustrating at times, the entire experience was so engaging that I hardly noticed. Visiting Coorg was an unforgettable and enjoyable adventure.

REVIEW EXERCISE

Including Competency Based Questions

Part I

Multiple Choice Questions

1. Rajvir and Pranjol were going to Assam from ....

(a) Mumbai (b) Delhi (c) Pune (d) Ahmedabad

Ans. (b) Delhi

2. When Pranjol says, "You will see enough gardens to last you a lifetime!" he means that

(a) Rajvir would see many tea gardens in Assam that he would become bore at a point of time.

(b) Assam has many tea gardens that Rajvir wouldn't be able to see all of them during his lifetime.

(c) Rajvir would see enough tea gardens in Assam.

(d) Rajvir would see many tea gardens in Assam that he could experience their essence throughout his life.

Ans. (d) Rajvir would see many tea gardens in Assam that he could experience their essence throughout his life.

3. In Europe, tea was drunk as more of a .... than ....

(a) medicine, beverage (b) beverage, medicine

(c) sleep waver, medicine (d) sleep banisher, medicine

Ans. (a) medicine, beverage

4. The words like 'chai' and 'chini' are derived from ....

(a) India (b) China

(c) France (d) None of these

Ans. (b) China

5. Pranjol's and Rajvir's train stopped at

(a) Dhekiabari Junction (b) Dibrugarh Station

(c) Mariani Junction (d) None of these

Ans. (c) Mariani Junction

6. "You seem to have done your homework before coming," Pranjol's father said in surprise. Which homework is he talking about?

(a) Holiday homework (b) Tuition homework

(c) Knowledge about Assam (d) All of these

Ans. (c) Knowledge about Assam

7. The second sprouting of tea lasts from

(a) May to July (b) May to June

(c) June to July (d) July to August

Ans. (a) May to July

8. What word best describes Rajvir's attitude? Competency Based

(a) Enthusiastic

(b) Exhilarated

(c) Exuberant

(d) Fervent

Ans. (b) Exhilarated

9. What word best describes Pranjol's reaction to the stories about the origin of tea? Competency Based

(a) Amused (b) Sceptical

(c) Patronising (d) Fascinated

Ans. (d) Fascinated

10. At the end of the story, how is Pranjol's father most likely to feel about Rajvir? Competency Based

(a) Entertained (b) Impressed

(c) Satisfied (d) Thrilled

Ans. (b) Impressed

Extract Based Questions

1. Read the following extract carefully and answer the questions that follow.

"CHAI-GARAM... garam-chai," a vendor called out in a high-pitched voice.

He came up to their window and asked,"Chai, sa'ab?"

"Give us two cups," Pranjol said.

They sipped the steaming hot liquid. Almost everyone in their compartment was drinking tea too.

"Do you know that over 80 crore cups of tea are drunk every day throughout the world?" Rajvir said.

"Whew!" exclaimed Pranjol. "Tea really is very popular."

(i) How did Pranjol feel when he said, "Whew! Tea really is very popular."He feels .... (embarrassed/surprised)

Ans. surprised

(ii) Where were Rajvir and Pranjol going to? Why?

Ans. Rajvir and Pranjol were going to Assam. They were travelling to the Dhekiabari tea-garden which was managed by Pranjol's father. Pranjol was going back home and his friend Rajvir was there to visit the tea gardens.

(iii) Select the option that correctly captures the usage of the word 'exclaimed' in the above extract.

(a) Puja exclaimed Rupa to touch her things.

(b) The children exclaimed with wonder when they saw the elephant.

(c) The manager exclaimed the employee to do his work right.

Ans. (b) The children exclaimed with wonder when they saw the elephant.

(iv) Complete the analogy by selecting the suitable word from the text.

Venerate : Revere :: Drink : ....

Ans. Sipped

2. Read the following extract carefully and answer the questions that follow.

"Hey, a tea garden!" Rajvir cried excitedly.

Pranjol, who had been born and brought up on a plantation, didn't share Rajvir's excitement.

"Oh, this is tea country now," he said. "Assam has the largest concentration of plantations in the world. You will see enough gardens to last you a lifetime!"

"I have been reading as much as I could about tea," Rajvir said. "No one really knows who discovered tea but there are many legends." **CBSE Additional SQP 2023**

(i) How according to Rajvir does the world know about the discovery of tea?

(a) Historical places

(b) Traditional tales

(c) Authentic anecdotes

(d) Popular publications

Ans. (b) Traditional tales

(ii) What does Pranjol mean by saying that Assam has the largest concentration of plantations in the world?

Ans. By saying that Assam has the largest concentration of plantations in the world, Pranjol means that the tea cultivation is the highest in Assam.

(iii) Read (a)-(c) and select the reason why was Pranjol not as excited as Rajvir about the tea gardens.

(a) He disliked looking at tea gardens.

(b) He had worked in tea gardens himself.

(c) He had grown up in and around tea gardens.

Ans. (c) He had grown up in and around tea gardens.

(iv) Fill in the blank with one word only.

Pranjol's .... comes through clearly when he exclaims, "You will see enough gardens to last you a lifetime!"

Ans. frustration/irritation/exasperation

3. Read the following extract carefully and answer the questions that follow.

"Tell me another!" scoffed Pranjol.

"We have an Indian legend too. Bodhidharma, an ancient Buddhist ascetic, cut off his eyelids because he felt sleepy during meditations. Ten tea plants grew out of the eyelids. The leaves of these plants when put in hot water and drunk, banished sleep."

"Tea was first drunk in China," Rajvir added, "as far back as 2700 B.C.! In fact, words such as tea, chai and chini are from the Chinese. Tea came to Europe only in the sixteenth century and was drunk [more as medicine than as a beverage." **CBSE Question Bank 2021**

(i) What is the central idea of this extract?

(a) Tea as a popular beverage in Europe and how it spread

(b) Origin of tea in India and why it became popular in Europe

(c) Importance of India in popularising tea and influencing Europe

(d) Indian legend on tea and how it travelled from China to Europe

Ans. (d) Indian legend on tea and how it travelled from China to Europe.

(ii) What does the given extract mention about Bodhidharma?

Ans. The passage mentions that Bodhidharma was an ancient Buddhist ascetic, who cut off his eyelids because he felt sleepy during meditations. Ten tea plants grew out of the eyelids. The leaves of these plants, when put in hot water and drunk, banished sleep.

(iii) Based on this extract, how do you think Rajvir felt while narrating?

(a) Excited and agitated

(b) Nervous and enthusiastic

(c) Enthusiastic and passionate

Ans. (c) Enthusiastic and passionate

(iv) Why do you think Pranjol 'scoffed'?

Ans. Pranjol scoffed because he was amused and tickled at what Rajvir shared about tea.

4. Read the following extract carefully and answer the questions that follow.

Pranjol's father slowed down to allow a tractor, pulling a trailer-load of tea leaves, to pass. This is the second-flush or sprouting period, isn't it, Mr. Barua? Rajvir asked, "It lasts from May to July and yields the best tea." "You seem to have done your homework before coming", Pranjol's father said in surprise, "Yes, Mr. Barua", Rajvir admitted. "But I hope to learn much more while I'm here."

(i) Read (a)–(c) and select the options that correctly presents Mr. Barua's reaction in the extract.

(a) was surprised with Rajvir's knowledge of tea

(b) was angry with Pranjol

(c) was a busy businessman

Ans. (a) was surprised with Rajvir's knowledge of tea

(ii) Who was Mr. Barua and what was his relation with Pranjol?

Ans. Mr. Barua was Pranjol's father and the manager of a tea-garden in Upper Assam.

(iii) What is the sprouting period of tea?

(a) July to August (b) May to July

(c) June to July (d) May to June

Ans. (b) The sprouting period or the second-flush of tea lasts from May to July.

(iv) How did Rajvir want to spend his stay there?

Ans. Rajvir wanted to spend his time discovering the beauty of Assam. He wanted to learn more about the tea plantations of Assam.

Part II

Short Answer Type Questions

1. What did Rajvir see while looking outside from the train?

Ans. While looking outside from the window of the train, Rajvir saw greenary all around. First, he saw the green paddy (rice) fields which gave way to the tea bushes. Against the backdrop of densely wooded hills, he saw a sea of tea gardens that were pruned to the same height. The beautiful view amazed and fascinated him.

2. Rajvir was very fond of reading detective stories. Why did he not like to read then during his journey? CBSE 2020

Ans. Rajvir did not read detective stories during his journey because at that moment he wanted to keep looking at the beautiful scenery. It was green everywhere-soft paddy fields and then, came tea bushes. It was a magnificent view for Rajvir to see greenery as far as his eyes could see.

3. Pranjol buried his head in his detective book while Rajvir was eager to look at the beautiful scenery during the train journey. Why was there a difference in their attitude? CBSE Question Bank 2021

Or Why did Pranjol not share Rajvir's excitement at seeing the tea gardens? CBSE 2023

Or Pranjol seemed to have a different level of enthusiasm compared to Rajvir when they both saw the tree plantation. Justify. CBSE 2025

Ans. Pranjol buried his head in his detective book because he belonged to Assam and had travelled on the route and seen the green tea plantations many times. So, he was not eager to see the scene outside. In contrast, Rajvir was travelling to Assam for the first time. So, instead of reading a book, he was interested in looking at the beautiful scenery during the train journey.

4. What is the Indian legend about the discovery of tea? CBSE 2023

Ans. The Indian legend about the discovery of tea revolves around a Buddhist ascetic - Bodhidharma. He grew troubled by the fact that he felt sleepy during meditations. Therefore, he decided to cut-off his eyelids in an attempt to stop being sleepy. It is believed that ten tea plants grew out of those eyelids he cut off. The tea made from the leaves of these plants had the ability to banish sleep.

5. In what ways is China related to tea?

Ans. China is related to tea in many ways. According to a legend, tea was first discovered in China by a Chinese Emperor who always boiled water before drinking. One day, a few leaves of the tea twigs fell into the water and gave it a delicious flavour. It is believed that they were tea leaves. Further more, the words 'tea', 'chai' and 'chini' are from China.

6. 'This is a tea country now.' Explain this with reference to Assam.

Ans. Assam is known as 'tea country'. It has the world's largest concentration of tea plantations in the world. A large number of tea gardens can be found there. Everywhere in Assam, a sea of tea bushes can be seen as far as the eye could see. Most of the tea grown in Assam is supplied all over the world.

7. Why did Pranjol's father say that Rajvir had done his homework before visiting Assam?

Ans. Pranjol's father said that Rajvir had done his homework before visiting Assam because he told Pranjol's father many facts about the growing of tea and its popularity.

8. Rajvir did his study before his visit to the tea plantation. Is it good to do one's research before the start of a new venture or does it take away from the thrill of discovery? Elucidate your stance. CBSE Question Bank 2021

Ans. The fact that Rajvir did his study before his visit to the tea plantation and his knowledge about the land he was visiting shows that it is good to do research before starting a new venture.

By doing so, not only does one get an idea about the destination but one can also plan the journey accordingly. One can also identify places or activities of interest. It does not take one away from the thrill of discovery, instead it helps in planning a better holiday.

Long Answer Type Questions

1. What did Pranjol and Rajvir do during the journey? Why? CBSE 2023

Ans. During their journey to Dhekiabari, Pranjol was reading a detective book. In contrast, Rajiv was mesmerised with the views of the passing tea gardens. They had differing reactions because Pranjol was born in Assam and therefore, he was used to the sight of tea estates. Meanwhile, Rajvir had never seen tea gardens in his life. Therefore, he was completely engrossed in looking at the beautiful green views. Later, Pranjol and Rajvir drank tea and discussed the legends surrounding the discovery of tea. They were drawn to this topic due to the fact that everyone around them was drinking tea as well.

2. According to the text, Assam is said to be 'tea country'. Do you believe that Assam has some of the best tea plantations in the world that makes it a unique place?

Ans. Yes, I believe that Assam has some of the best tea plantations in the world that makes it a unique place. In India, some crops such as tea and coffee are grown in huge quantities. India is also home to many spices like haldi. While Assam is home to tea, Coorg is home to coffee.

One can see enough tea gardens in Assam. Between May and July is the best time to yield the best tea. On both sides of the roads of Assam, there are acres of tea-bushes, all neatly trimmed to the same height.

These plantations further use the traditional agricultural practices of India. Thus, these plantations make India a unique country which has traditional spices and beverage plants growing within it.

3. Inspired by the diversity in the chapter, 'Glimpses of India', you wrote an article for your school magazine on the topic, 'Diversity-the Uniqueness of India'. Write a paragraph, sharing two key opinions from the article. Competency Based

Ans. **'Diversity-the Uniqueness of India'**

by XYZ

India is a land of different cultures and traditions. No doubt, it's called the land of Unity in Diversity. Each and every culture in this land has its own uniqueness.

The geographical and cultural dissimilarities of each region makes every place distinct from the other. While on one hand, we have the beauty and bravery of Coorg which exemplifies martial bravery, beautiful women and magnificent landscapes full of flora and fauna.

On the other, Assam's geographical features make it appropriate for tea production. In the similar way stands the cultural heritage of Portuguese in Goa. Every region is identified by its own lifestyle which makes its diversity full of unique combinations.

4. The culture, lifestyle and traditions of a place are influenced by the people who lived or settled there at some point of time. Cultural assimilation adds flavour to the existing structure of a society. Summarise your opinion on the given idea.

Ans. The culture, lifestyle and traditions of a place are influenced by the people who lived or settled there at some point of time. Cultural assimilation or the amalgamation of another culture adds flavour to the existing structure of a society. This is especially true for the land of India. Starting from Goa to Coorg or Assam, this cultural assimilation is visible everywhere.

The Portuguese culture and its Baker has become an essential part of the Goan landscape.

The people of Coorg are of Greek or Arabic descent which brings its mark in the martial traditions, clothing, marriage and religious rites, which are distinct from the Hindu mainstream. Even the Assam Tea landscape derives its bounty due to the development of Tea in China.

5. Pranjol and Rajvir discuss their next vacation destination. They shortlist Coorg and Goa. Rajvir is keen on Coorg and tries to convince Pranjol. Develop a conversation between the two, based on your understanding of Glimpses of India.

You may begin like this

Rajvir Hey Pranjol! I think we should be visiting Coorg. It is a beautiful place with coffee plantations. I can smell the aroma already!

Pranjol I gave you the opportunity to explore a tea plantation last year, in Assam; I want to...

CBSE SQP 2022 Term II

Ans. **Rajvir** Hey Pranjol, let's visit Coorg for our next vacation.

It is a beautiful place between Mysore and Mangalore. It is home to evergreen rainforests and coffee plantations. You know how much I love coffee.

Pranjol I have already fulfilled one such wish when we visited the tea plantations in Assam last year. I don't want to visit forests this time; rather I am more interested in a beach. So, let's go to Goa specifically North Goa.

Rajvir Okay, but there is lot more to Coorg than just coffee. Due to the rainforests there, there is a substantial number of animal species that can be found there. The place also provides opportunity for various adventure sports like river rafting, canoeing, rock climbing, etc. Not just this, the place has a very rich history as it is believed that the people there are of Greek or Arabic descent, and are extremely polite and hospitable. Even the river Kaveri has its roots there, with a wide variety of aquatic life.

Pranjol That sounds interesting but I want to get away from the crowd and the hustle, and relax in some serene moments. And a few beaches in Goa would give me just that. Also, nothing calms like the ocean.

Rajvir Well, if you're looking for some calm then look no further than the Brahmagiri hills. We can climb it and at the end of that journey lies a beautiful landscape of Coorg. I read that the place even has the largest Tibetan settlement, near Bylakuppe. I am sure there will be much calm and spirituality in that place.

Pranjol I must say that you've done a great research about the place. And you've convinced me. Let's leave on this Friday.

ASSESSMENT EXERCISE

Extract Based Questions

Read the following extract carefully and answer the questions that follow.

It was a magnificent view. Against the backdrop of densely wooded hills a sea of tea bushes stretched as far as the eye could see. Dwarfing the tiny tea plants were tall sturdy shade-trees and amidst the orderly rows of bushes busily moved doll-like figures. In the distance was an ugly building with smoke billowing out of tall chimneys. "Hey, a tea garden!" Rajvir cried excitedly. Pranjol, who had been born and brought up on a plantation, didn't share Rajvir's excitement.

"Oh, this is tea country now," he said. "Assam has the largest concentration of plantations in the world. You will see enough gardens to last you a lifetime!" "I have been reading as much as I could about tea," Rajvir said. "No one really knows who discovered tea but there are many legends.

(i) According to the above extract, a legend is
  (a) an old story that is widely believed but cannot be proved to be true.
  (b) a famous or important person who is known for doing something.
  (c) a list that explains the symbols on a map.
  (d) an inscription or title on an object such as a coin.

(ii) Why do you think the building mentioned in the above extract is referred to as 'ugly'?
How does it connect to the discussion of environmentalism?

(iii) Select the option that correctly captures the usage of the word 'view' in the above extract.
  (a) He stood up to get a better view of the blackboard.
  (b) He has very strong views about politics.
  (c) I view life differently than I used to.

(iv) The figure of speech used in the phrase 'a sea of tea bushes' is ....

Short Answer (SA) Type Questions

1. Describe the Indian legend about tea.
2. Why is India called a country of tea?
3. What were people doing around the tea bushes?
4. What did Pranjol's father say in surprise that Rajvir had done his homework before coming there?

Long Answer (LA) Type Question

1. Rajvir was excited on seeing Assam from the train but Pranjol was not. What could be the reason for it? Is it appropriate for Pranjol to have no excitement? Justify your answer with reasons. **Competency Based**

Mijbil the Otter

by Gavin Maxwell

CHAPTER 

CHAPTER SUMMARY The chapter 'Mijbil the Otter' has been written by British naturalist Gavin Maxwell. The chapter, written in four parts, describes how the author's life changed after keeping an otter as a pet.

The chapter follows the author's travels to Iraq, the first few days with the otter Mijbil, the troubles in transporting Mijbil from Iraq to London and finally, the reactions of the Londoners to the previously unseen otter.

Part – I

Introduction

Gavin Maxwell lived in a cottage in Camusfearna in the West Highlands in Scotland. Maxwell decided to not keep a pet dog again as he was greatly saddened by the death of his pet dog Jonnie. However, he found life without a pet very lonely.

Choosing an Otter as Pet

Maxwell had travelled to Southern Iraq in 1956. By this time, he had decided to get another pet. He was convinced that an otter would find his home comfortable since Camusfearna was surrounded by water. After a discussion with his friend, he decided to get an otter from Iraq.

Maxwell's friend had advised him to get an otter from the Tiger marshes as the otters were commonly found there. These otters were also domesticated by the Arabs. So, Maxwell and his friend went to the Consulate-General in Basra to collect and answer their mail from Europe. There they found that while his friend's mail had already arrived, Maxwell's own mail was yet to arrive.

Maxwell's Mail Arrives

As Maxwell had not received his mail, he sent a message to England. He received no reply for three days. He couldn't use the telephone as the connection was out of order. On the second day, the place from where he could communicate (exchange) was closed for a religious holiday. On the third day too, there was no connection. So, Maxwell and his friends decided to meet after a week.

Finally, Maxwell's mail arrived after five days. When he went to his room to read it, he found two Arabs sitting on the floor with an otter in a bag. They handed him a note saying that the bag contained his otter.

Part - II

Mijbil the Otter

As Maxwell opened the bag, a new journey of his life had started. He became obsessed with otters. The source of his obsession was the creature that came out of the bag.

The otter that came out of the bag resembled a very small dragon. He was covered with symmetrical pointed scales and mud. Maxwell could not see the otter's velvet fur for a month because of the mud. However, the otter's true colours were exposed to Maxwell when all of the mud on the otter was removed.

Maxwell's Otter-New Species

Maxwell named the otter Mijbil. He later found that Mijbil's species was undiscovered by scientists. Therefore, the zoologists named him Lutrogale Perspicillata Maxwellia or 'Maxwell's otter'. For the first twenty four hours, Mijbil was neither unfriendly nor friendly. He slept on the floor far away from Maxwell's bed.

Mijbil Grows Friendly

On his second night, Mijbil climbed Maxwell's bed and slept between his knees. He soon started taking interest in his surroundings. Maxwell made a body belt for Mijbil and took him to the bathroom where the bathtub was filled.

Mijbil loved playing in the water. Maxwell discovered that otters cannot stand still while in the water and therefore, all the water must be spread out to wherever it could be. Two days later, he escaped from Maxwell's bedroom and went to the bathroom. Mijbil figured out how to turn the tap by himself to fill the bathtub with water. He would sometimes turn the tap in the opposite direction and then, make a sound in frustration when the water wouldn't flow.

Mijbil's Playtime

Mijbil soon started to follow the author without a lead and came whenever his name was called. He would spend hours playing with a rubber ball. He could dribble and throw the ball to a great height and distance. He was particularly capable at lying on his back and juggling things within his paws. His favourite toy was marbles and he would roll two or more on his flat belly without dropping it.

Part - III

Mijbil Goes to England

After spending some time in Basra, Maxwell decided to take Mijbil back to England, and then, to Camusfearna. Since the British Airline would not carry animals to London, he booked a flight to Paris, and then, from Paris to London on another airline. As told by the airline, the narrator prepared an 18 inches square box for Mijbil that could be kept at his feet during the flight. He put Mijbil inside the box an hour before he had to go to the airport so that he could get used to it.

Mijbil and the Box

When Maxwell returned from his meal, he found the box covered in blood. Upon opening the box, he found Mijbil had injured himself. He had torn the edge of the box to pieces.

While Maxwell made sure that the box had no sharp edges that could hurt Mijbil, he only had ten minutes to his flight and the airport was five miles away. So, he hurriedly put Mijbil in the box and took a taxi to the airport. The officials at the airport angrily took Maxwell to his flight because he was very late.

Luckily, Maxwell's seat was at the front. So, he covered the floor around his feet with newspapers. He gave the parcel of fish that was meant to be Mijbil's food to the airhostess to keep in a cool place.

Mijbil in the Flight

When he told the kind airhostess about the events of the past hour where Mijbil had hurt himself inside the box, she kindly suggested that he could keep his pet on his knee to comfort the scared animal. However, as soon as, Mijbil came out of the box, he disappeared down the aircraft. Thinking it to be a rat, the people in the aircraft were scared. As Maxwell tried to catch Mijbil, he got dirty as food fell on him.

So, the airhostess advised him to be seated and said that she would find the otter and bring it to him.

Very soon, the otter came near Maxwell and climbed on his knee. He hugged Maxwell's face and neck.

Part - IV

Mijbil Arrived in London

Maxwell and Mijbil stayed in London for a month.

In London, Mijbil used to spend his time playing with his toys, ping-pong balls, marbles, rubber fruit and a terrapin shell that Maxwell had brought back from the marshes. Mijbil invented a game where he would place a ball on the broken side of the narrator's suitcase and then, try to catch it before it rolled down the other side.

When Maxwell took him outside the house for walks, Mijbil developed some habits. On the way back from his walks, Mijbil would jump on the wall at the front of the primary school and run on it. Thus, he would distract the students and the staff of the school.

People could not Recognise an Otter

In London, many people had not seen an otter. So when they saw Mijbil, they made wild guesses about what he was. Otters belong to a group of animals called Mustellines, which also includes badger, mongoose, weasel, stoat and mink. The people of London would guess that Mijbil was a baby seal, squirrel, walrus, hippo, beaver, bear cub, leopard, and even a brontosaur! Maxwell particularly loved the interaction where a labourer stopped digging a hole, stared at him and Mijbil. He, then, asked Maxwell what Mijbil was.

Word Meaning

Word	Meaning
crossed my mind	come into my mind
ringed by	surrounded by
stone's throw	a very short distance
eminently	extremely
tamed	made calm or pet
cabled	sent a telegram
breakdown	fault
squirmed	twisted about
thraldom	being under the control of
fixation	a very strong attachment
spacious	wide and open
medievally-conceived	imagined in the middle-ages
dragon	an imaginary animal
symmetrical	well proportioned
pointed scales	sharp thin pieces of hard skin
mud armour	shield of mud
mole	an animal
at length	at last
christened	named
hostile	unfriendly
aloof and indifferent	keeping a distance
crook	bend
apathy	absence of interest
plunging	diving
slosh	splash of water
so to speak	as it were
static	fixed
provoking	causing anger on some other reaction
fumbling	trying to do something in a clumsy way
chitter	to make a twittering or chattering sound
lead	(here) a string
shuffling	to move things into different positions
flick	a light, quick movement
juggle	to keep several objects in motion in the air
dreaded the prospect	feared something that would happen in the future
transporting	taking

Word	Meaning
accustomed	get used to
appalling spectacle	a shocking scene
whipped off	quickly took off
blood spattered	covered in blood
whimpered	cried softly
shreds	small pieces
ricochetting	something that changes direction
infuriated	very angry
took her into my confidence	told her everything
retained	kept
in a flash	very quickly
squawks and shrieks	cries and high pitched sounds
portly	fat
curry	a dish
craning my neck	raising my neck
distressed chitter	unhappy sound
bounded on to	climbed up quickly
nuzzle	rub gently with nose
terrapin shell	shell of small turtle found in North America
native	one's place of birth
engrossed	busy
dash	run
ambush	to attack suddenly
crouching	keeping low
trot off	to leave
compulsive habits	habits that are impossible to control
upright	standing straight
frontage	front side
gallop	to walk or run in a particular manner
continuous barrage of conjectural question	questions full of guesses
affront	in an offensive manner
abreast	by side
spat	spit /speak in an angry manner
growled	to speak angrily

NCERT FOLDER

NCERT Intext and Exercise Questions

ORAL COMPREHENSION CHECK❶ (NCERT PAGE 84)

Q.1 What 'experiment' did Maxwell think Camusfearna would be suitable for? CBSE 2023

Ans. Maxwell thought Camusfearna would be suitable for the 'experiment' of keeping an otter as a pet. He thought so because Camusfearna was surrounded by water and since otters are marsh animals, they could live very well in water.

Q.2 Why does he go to Basra? How long does he wait there and why?

Ans. Maxwell went to Basra to collect and answer his mail from Europe. Maxwell waited there for five days as his mail had not arrived. During those five days, Maxwell faced many difficulties such as the telephone line not working properly or the office being shut because of a religious public holiday.

Q.3 How does he get the otter? Does he like it? Pick out the words that tell you this.

Or **How did Maxwell get the otter?**

Ans. Maxwell got the otter through his friend to whom he had expressed his desire to keep an otter as a pet. When the author got his mail after five days, he went to his room to read it. There, he found two Arabs waiting for him with an otter in a bag.

Yes, he liked the otter. The words that tell us this are "It is, in effect, a thraldom to otters, an otter fixation ....".

Q.4 Why was the otter named 'Maxwell's otter'?

Ans. The otter was named 'Maxwell's otter' because it was a species previously unknown to science. So, it was named by Zoologists as *Lutrogale Perspicillata Maxwelli* or Maxwell's otter.

Q.5 Tick the right answer. In the beginning, the otter was

(i) aloof and indifferent **(ii) friendly**

(iii) hostile

Ans. (i) aloof and indifferent

Q.6 What happened when Maxwell took Mijbil to the bathroom? What did it do two days after that?

Or **What happened when Maxwell took Mijbil to the bathroom? What does it tells us about Mijbil?** CBSE 2023

Ans. When Maxwell first took Mijbil to the bathroom, the otter went wild with joy in the water. It dived and rolled in it. It jumped up and down the length of the bathtub.
It sloshed and splashed the water.

Two days after that, Mijbil escaped from the author's bedroom and went to the bathroom. It turned the water taps with its paws in less than a minute to fill the bathtub with water. It tells us that Mij was a very intelligent creature who loved water.

CHECK❷ (NCERT PAGE 86-87)

Q.1 How was Mij to be transported to England?

Ans. For transporting Mij to England, the narrator booked a flight to Paris and then, from Paris to London. As instructed by the airline, Mij was put in an eighteen inch square box that was supposed to be placed on the floor near his feet.

Q.2 What did Mij do to the box?

Ans. Mij tore the lining of the box in his attempt to escape from it and in the process, he hurt himself.

Q.3 Why did Maxwell put the otter back in the box? How do you think he felt when he did this?

Ans. Maxwell put the otter back in the box as there was no other way to carry Mij to London.

Maxwell must have felt helpless and miserable to do this. He must be worried as well.

Q.4 Why does Maxwell say the airhostess was "the very queen of her kind"?

Or **Without the assistance of the airhostess, the narrator could not have transported Mijbil from Basra to London safely. Comment.** CBSE Question Bank 2021

Ans. Maxwell says that the airhostess was 'the queen of her kind' because she was very kind and helpful.
She understood the feelings of both the otter-Mijbil and the narrator, and suggested him to keep the pet on his knees.

Q.5 What happened when the box was opened? CBSE 2023

Ans. When the box was opened, Mijbil quickly ran out of the box and disappeared in the aircraft. It created a lot of chaos in the aircraft as people were scared and started screaming.

CHECK® (NCERT PAGE 88)

Q.1 What game had Mij invented?

Ans. Mij had invented a game of his own with the ping-pong ball. He found that if he placed the ball on the high end of a broken suitcase, it would run down the length of the suitcase. He would run around to the other end to catch it, then he would hide from it and take it by surprise. Further, he would grab it and run with it to the high end of the suitcase.

Q.2 What are 'compulsive habits'? What does Maxwell say are the compulsive habits of (i) school children (ii) Mij?

Or **Compare any one compulsive human habit with respect to the Otter's compulsive habit.** **CBSE Question Bank 2021**

Ans. Compulsive habits are usually strange acts or behaviour which a person does periodically without clear reason.

(i) According to Maxwell, the compulsive habits of school children are that on the way to school, they must place their feet squarely on the centre of each paving block. They must touch every seventh upright of the iron railings or pass to the outside of every second lamp post.

(ii) Maxwell says that the compulsive habits of Mijbil was that on his way back home, he would pull the author to a primary school wall opposite his house. Then, he would jump onto it and jump the full length. This distracted the pupils and staff of the school.

Q.3 What group of animals do otters belong to?

Ans. Otters belong to a comparatively small group of animals called Mustellines. The other animals of this group are badger, mongoose, weasel, stoat, mink, etc.

Q.4 What guesses did the Londoners make about what Mij was?

Ans. Londoners made the wildest possible guesses about Mij as otters are not found in England. Their guesses were a baby seal, a squirrel, a hippo, a brontosaur, etc.

THINKING ABOUT THE TEXT
(NCERT PAGE 88- 89)

Q.1 What things does Mij do which tell you that he is an intelligent, friendly and fun-loving animal who needs love? **CBSE 2020**

Ans. Mij does many things that tell us he is an intelligent, friendly and fun-loving animal. Initially, Mijbil was aloof and indifferent but later, he took keen interest in his surroundings. He would spend most of his time playing in water, with his toys, marbles, rubber balls, etc. Mijbil invented his own game out of ping-pong ball and a suitcase. He loved water and once he understood that on opening the tap water came out of it, he would get into the tub and play with water.

He had gradually formed a special attachment with Maxwell. He grew desperate when Maxwell packed him in a box and wanted to come out as soon as possible. Thus, Mijbil was an intelligent, friendly and fun-loving animal who needed love.

Q.2 What are some of the things we come to know about otters from this text?

Or **Peculiar behaviours are characteristics of Otters. Discuss with respect to 'Mijbil the Otter'.** **CBSE Question Bank 2021**

Ans. Some of the things we came to know about otter's from the text is that they belong to a comparatively small group of animals called Mustellines. This group of animals also includes the badger, mongoose, weasel, stoat, mink and others. They are found in large numbers in marshes. Arabs keep them as pets and domesticate them.

Otters love to spread water and splash in it. Maxwell's otter was of a race previously unknown to science. It was named by zoologists as *Lutrogale Perspicillata Maxwelli or Maxwell's otter.*

Q.3 Why is Mij's species now known to the world as Maxwell's otter?

Ans. Mij's species is now known to the world as Maxwell's otter because the species to which Mij belonged was first brought to Zoologist's notice by Gavin Maxwell. Hence, they named it *Lutrogale Perspicillata Maxwelli* or Maxwell's otter.

Q.4 Maxwell in the story speaks for the otter, Mij. He tells us what the otter feels and thinks on different occasions. Given below are some things the otter does. Complete the column on the right to say what Maxwell says about what Mij feels and thinks.

What Mij Does	How Mij Feels or Thinks
Plunges, rolls in the water and makes the water slosh and splash	
Screws the tap in the wrong way	
Nuzzles Maxwell's face and neck in the aeroplane	

Ans.

What Mij Does	How Mij Feels or Thinks
Plunges, rolls in the water and makes the water slosh and splash	He feels very happy and excited.
Screws the tap in the wrong way	He chitters with irritation and disappointment.
Nuzzles Maxwell's face and neck in the aeroplane	He feels much comfort and content after its distressed chitter.

Q.5 **Read the story and find the sentences where Maxwell describes his pet otter. Then choose and arrange your sentences to illustrate those statements below that you think are true. Maxwell's description**

(i) makes Mij seem almost human, like a small boy.

(ii) shows that he is often irritated with what Mij does.

(iii) shows that he is often surprised by what Mij does.

(iv) of Mij's antics is comical.

(v) shows that he observes the antics of Mij very carefully.

(vi) shows that he thinks Mij is a very ordinary otter.

(vii) shows that he thinks the otter is very unusual.

Ans. 1. (v) shows that he observes the antics of Mij very carefully. "I watched, amazed; in less than a minute he had turned the tap far enough to produce a trickle of water…"

2. (iii) shows that he is often surprised by what Mij does. "I was amazed to see him… fumbling at the chromium taps with his paws."

3. (i) makes Mij seem almost human, like a small boy. "He spent hours shuffling a rubber ball round the room like a four-footed soccer player…"

4. (iv) of Mij's antics is comical. "The woman stood up on her seat screaming out, 'A rat! A rat!'… I found my face covered in curry."

5. (vi) shows that he thinks Mij is a very ordinary otter. (This statement is not true based on the text. Maxwell describes Mijbil as quite unique and unusual.)

6. (vii) shows that he thinks the otter is very unusual. "Mijbil was, in fact, of a race previously unknown to science, and was at length christened by zoologists Lutrogale perspicillata maxwelli."

7. (ii) shows that he is often irritated with what Mij does. (This statement is not strongly supported in the text, as Maxwell's tone is more admiring and amused than irritated.)

THINKING ABOUT LANGUAGE

(NCERT PAGE 89-91)

I. Describing a Repeated Action in the Past

Q.1 **To talk about something that happened regularly in the past, but does not happen any longer, we use would or used to. Both would and used to can describe repeated actions in the past.**

(a) Mij would follow me without a lead and come to me when I called his name.

(b) He would play for hours with a selection of toys.

(c) On his way home... Mij would tug me to this wall.

(d) When I was five years old, I used to follow my brother all over the place.

(e) He used to tease me when Mother was not around.

Q.2 **To describe repeated states or situations in the past, however, we use only used to. (We cannot use would for states or situations in the past.) So we do not use would with verbs like be, have, believe, etc. Look at the following sentences.**

(a) When we were young, we used to believe there were ghosts in school. (Note: believe shows a state of mind.)

(b) Thirty years ago, more women used to be housewives than now. (Note: be here describes a situation.)

From the table below, make as many correct sentences as you can using would and/or used to, as appropriate. (Hint: First decide whether the words in italics show an action, or a state or situation, in the past.) Then add two or three sentences of your own to it.

Emperor Akbar		be fond of musical evenings
Every evening we	would	take long walks on the beach.
Fifty years ago, very few people		own cars.
Till the 1980s. Shanghai	used to	have very dirty streets.
My uncle		spend his holidays by the sea.

Ans. Would (for repeated actions in the past)

- Emperor Akbar would host grand musical evenings.
- Every evening, we would take long walks on the beach.
- My uncle would spend his holidays by the sea.

Used to (for repeated actions, states, or situations in the past)

- Emperor Akbar used to host musical evenings.
- Fifty years ago, very few people used to own cars.
- Till the 1980s, Shanghai used to have very dirty streets.
- When we were young, we used to believe there were ghosts in school.
- Thirty years ago, more women used to be housewives than now.

Additional Sentences

- I used to visit my grandparents every summer.
- In the past, people used to communicate by writing letters.
- As a child, I would play outside until it got dark.
- During my school days, I would stay up late studying for exams.

II. Noun Modifiers

1. **To describe or give more information about a noun (or to modify a noun), we use adjectives or adjectival phrases. Look at these examples from the text:**
   (a) An eminently suitable spot
   (c) Symmetrical pointed scales
   (b) His wide, flat belly
   (d) A ricocheting bullet

2. **Nouns can also be used as modifiers:**
   (a) The dinner party
   (b) A designer dress
   (c) The car keys

3. **We can use more than one noun as modifier. Proper nouns can also be used:**
   (a) The Christmas dinner party
   (b) A silk designer dress
   (c) The Maruti car keys

4. **In the examples below, there is an adjectival phrase in front of a noun modifier:**
   (a) The lovely Christmas party
   (b) A trendy silk designer dress
   (c) The frightfully expensive golden Maruti car keys

III. Noun Modifiers

Q.1 Look at these examples from the text, and say whether the modifiers (in italics) are nouns, proper nouns or adjective plus noun.

(i) An *otter* fixation (ii) The *iron* railings
(iii) The *Tigris* marshes (iv) The *London* streets
(v) *Soft velvet* fur
(vi) A *four- footed* soccer player

Ans. (i) Noun (ii) Noun
(iii) Proper noun (iv) Proper noun
(v) Adjective plus noun (vi) Adjective plus noun

Q.2 Given below are some nouns and a set of modifiers (in the box). Combine the nouns and modifiers to make as many appropriate phrases as you can. (*Hint*: The nouns and modifiers are all from the texts in this book.)

temple	girls	triangle	dresses	
person	thoughts	boys	roar	
gifts	scream	farewell	expression	
time	subject	landscape	handkerchief	
crossing	flight	chatterbox	profession	
physique	coffee	view	celebration	
college	rough	hundred	stone	ordinary
love	uncomfortable	white	slang	slack
bare	railroad	tremendous	family	marriage
plump	invigorating	panoramic	heartbreaking	birthday
incorrigible	ridiculous	loud	first	

Ans. (Note: only one combination of modifier and noun are given for each noun. There are many others.)

stone temple	plump girls	rough triangle	hundred dresses
ordinary person	ridiculous thoughts	rough boys	tremendous roar
marriage gifts	loud scream	heartbreaking farewell	uncomfortable expression
slack time	college subject	panoramic landscape	white handkerchief
railroad crossing	first flight	incorrigible chatterbox	family profession
plump physique	invigorating coffee	panoramic view	marriage celebration

IV. Read this sentence

He shook himself, and I half expected a cloud of dust. The author uses *cloud of dust* to give a picture of a large quantity of dust. Phrases like this indicate a particular quantity of something that is not usually countable. For example, a bit of land, a drop of blood, a pinch of salt, a piece of paper.

Q.1 Match the words on the left with a word on the right. Some words on the left can go with more than one word on the right.

(i) A portion of	—	blood
(ii) A pool of	—	cotton
(iii) Flakes of	—	stones
(iv) A huge heap of	—	gold
(v) A gust of	—	fried fish
(vi) Little drops of	—	snow
(vii) A piece of	—	water
(viii) A pot of	—	wind

Ans. (i) A portion of fried fish.
(ii) A pool of water, A pool of blood.
(iii) Flakes of snow.
(iv) A huge heap of stones, A huge heap of cotton.
(v) A gust of wind.
(vi) Little drops of blood, Little drops of water.
(vii) A piece of cotton, A piece of fried fish.
(viii) A pot of gold.

Q.2 Use *a bit of/a piece of/a bunch of/a lump of/a cloud of* with the italicised nouns in the following sentences. The first has been done for you as an example.

(i) My teacher gave me *some advice*.
(ii) Can you give me *some clay* please?
(iii) The *information* you gave was very useful.
(iv) Because of these factories, *smoke* hangs over the city.
(v) Two *stones* rubbed together can produce sparks of fire.
(vi) He gave me *some flowers* on my birthday.

Ans. (i) My teacher gave me a bit of advice.

(ii) Can you give me a lump of clay, please?

(iii) The piece of information you gave was very useful.

(iv) Because of these factories, a cloud of smoke hangs over the city.

(v) Two pieces of stone rubbed together can produce sparks of fire.

(vi) He gave me a bunch of flowers on my birthday.

V. WRITING

Q.1 Write a description of a person or an animal (such as a pet) that you know very well and love very much. Questions (4) and (5) in 'Thinking about the Text' will have given you some idea about how to do this. Mention some things the person or animal does, what you think the person or animal feels, etc.

Ans. Sample Answer

I have a meerkat named Mondu that I love very much. Mondu is very curious and playful. He often stands on his hind legs to look around, just like a little guard. Mondu loves to dig in the garden and finds the smallest insects. When happy, he makes a soft, chattering sound and runs around in circles. He feels excited and full of energy when he plays with his toys. Mondu also enjoys cuddling up with me at night, feeling safe and relaxed. His big, bright eyes always look so curious, and he brings so much joy into my life. Mondu is not just a pet but a dear friend and part of my family.

REVIEW EXERCISE

Including Competency Based Questions

Part I

Multiple Choice Questions

1. Camusfearna is most likely to be in the context of pets. Competency Based

(a) The place where the writer is staying.
(b) A type of otter people keep as pets.
(c) An otter owned by the writer's friend.
(d) A place where otters are easily found.

Ans. (b) A type of otter people keep as pets.

While (a) is factually correct, the use of most likely suggests a conjecture or assumption, in this light (b) is the correct answer.

2. What was the name of the author's pet dog in the chapter 'Mijbil the Otter'?

(a) Jennie (b) Jonnie (c) Jammie (d) Jinnie

Ans. (b) Jonnie

3. What could be the possible thoughts that Maxwell had when his pet dog died?

1. I miss my Jonnie very much.
2. I feel very lonely.
3. I will never have a pet again.
4. I want someone to play with.

(a) Only 4 (b) 1 and 2 (c) 1, 2 and 3 (d) All of these

Ans. (c) 1, 2 and 3

4. Early in the new year of 1956, Maxwell travelled to ....

(a) London (b) Southern Iraq
(c) India (d) Arabia

Ans. (b) Southern Iraq

5. What tone does the writer use to describe Mijbil's first encounter with water in a bathtub? Competency Based

(a) Indifference (b) Amazement
(c) Enthusiasm (d) Amusement

Ans. (b) Amazement

6. What is the writer most likely to be feeling when the otter arrived? Competency Based

(a) Relief (b) Surprise
(c) Sympathy (d) Amusement

Ans. (b) Surprise

7. Choose the correct scientific name given to otters by zoologist.

(a) Lutrogale Maxwelli
(b) Lutrogale Perspicillata
(c) Lutrogale Perspicillata Maxwelli
(d) Maxwelli Perspicillata Lutrogale

Ans. (c) Lutrogale Perspicillata Maxwelli

8. Why did the driver drive through the streets of Basra like a ricochetting bullet?

(a) Author was late for his flight
(b) Mijbil had hurt himself
(c) Someone was after the driver
(d) All of the above

Ans. (a) Author was late for his flight

9. Which of the following are the favourite toys of Mijbil? Choose the correct option.

1. Ping pong balls	**2. Marbles**
3. Bucket	**4. Rubber fruit**
5. Tap	**6. Terrapin shell**

(a) 1, 2, 4 and 6 (b) 2, 3, 4 and 5
(c) 1, 2, 3 and 5 (d) All of these

Ans. (a) Ping-pong balls, marbles, bucket, rubber fruit and terrapin shell.

10. How does the writer mainly feel about Londoners' reaction to seeing an otter? **Competency Based**

(a) Astonished (b) Perplexed
(c) Frustrated (d) Amused

Ans. (d) Amused

11. Based on the story, what word best describes Mijbil's feelings for the writer? **Competency Based**

(a) Affection (b) Gratitude
(c) Indifference (d) Bewilderment

Ans. (a) Affection

12. What is the main purpose of the story? **Competency Based**

(a) To draw attention to the difficulties in transporting pets
(b) To caution people wanting to keep otters as pets
(c) To highlight important events in the writer's life
(d) To recount a series of entertaining incidents

Ans. (d) To recount a series of entertaining incidents

Extract Based Questions

1. Read the following extract carefully and answer the questions that follow.

For the first twenty-four hours Mijbil was neither hostile nor friendly; he was simply aloof and indifferent, choosing to sleep on the floor as far from my bed as possible. The second night Mijbil came on to my bed in the small hours and remained asleep in the crook of my knees until the servant brought tea in the morning, and during the day he began to lose his apathy and take a keen, much too keen, interest in his surroundings. I made a body-belt for him and took him on a lead to the bathroom, where for half an hour he went wild with joy in the water, plunging and rolling in it, shooting up and down the length of the bathtub underwater, and making enough slosh and splash for a hippo.

CBSE Question Bank 2021 Modified

(i) Fill in the blank by choosing the correct option from the bracket.

Mijbil must have shifted his sleeping position for .... (safety/affection)

Ans. safety

(ii) What did Mijbil do on the second night? What is the significance of it?

Ans. On the second night, Mijbil came on to Maxwell's bed soon after midnight. He remained asleep between the knees of the author until morning. This action was significant because it showcased that Mijbil was losing his apathy and beginning to accept the presence of the author. It also shows that Mijbil was beginning to feel comfortable and safe in the author's presence.

(iii) The words 'slosh and splash' are examples of the onomatopoeic words that go together phonetically -resembling the sound that they describe. Choose the option that does not fit the given description.

(a) Hip hop (b) Bow wow
(c) Tick tock (d) Pitter patter

Ans. (a) Hip hop

(iv) Use the word 'apathy' from the given extract in a meaningful sentence.

Ans. The apathy of the manager towards her employees astounds me on a daily basis.

2. Read the following extract carefully and answer the questions that follow.

I made a body-belt for him and took him on a lead to the bathroom, where for half an hour he went wild with joy in the water, plunging and rolling in it, shooting up and down the length of the bathtub underwater, and making enough slosh and splash for a hippo. This,
I was to learn, is a characteristic of otters; every drop of water must be, so to speak, extended and spread about the place; a bowl must at once be overturned, or, if it will not be overturned, be sat in and sploshed in until it overflows. Water must be kept on the move and made to do things; when static it is wasted and provoking.

CBSE Additional SQP 2023

(i) Which of these best describes the narrator's tone in the extract?

(a) Tired and exhausted
(b) Fascinated and playful
(c) Doubtful and surprised
(d) Informative and objective

Ans. (b) Fascinated and playful

(ii) **What did the author learn about the behaviour of otters within a few days of keeping Mijbil?**

Ans. The author observed the behaviour of Mijbil and understood many facts about the otter. He learned that one of the main characteristics of otters is to play with every drop of water. Otters love to splash in water like hippos, and the sight of static water is provoking to them, The author, thus, learned that otters are playful creatures.

(iii) **Read (a)–(c) and select the reason for making a body belt for Mijbil.**

(a) Caution
(b) Necessity
(c) Desire

Ans. (a) Caution

(iv) **Why does the author compare Mijbil to a hippo?**

Ans. The author compares Mijbil to a hippo to show how much water a small creature like Mijbil can displace.

3. Read the following extract carefully and answer the questions that follow.

The days passed peacefully at Basra, but I dreaded the prospect of transporting Mij to England and to Camusfearna. The British airline to London would not fly animals, so I booked a flight to Paris on another airline and from there to London. The airline insisted that Mij should be packed into a box not more than eighteen inches square, to be carried on the floor at my feet. I had a box made and an hour before we started, I put Mij into the box so that he would become accustomed to it and left for a hurried meal.

(i) **Complete the sentence appropriately.**
The author was .... of carrying Mij to England.

Ans. fearful

(ii) **Why did the author book a flight to Paris even though he lived near London?**

Ans. The author booked a flight to Paris because he had to transport Mijbil to England but the airline with direct flight to London did not allow the transportation of animals. Therefore, he booked a flight in another airline and planned to travel to London from Paris.

(iii) **Select the option that correctly captures the usage of the word 'insisted' in the above extract.**

(a) She insisted the family business from her father.
(b) She insisted on seeing her lawyer.
(c) Baldness is insisted from the mother's side of the family.
(d) She insisted her father's deep blue eyes.

Ans. (b) She insisted on seeing her lawyer.

(iv) **Why did the author put Mij in a box?**

Ans. The author put Mij in a box so that he would become accustomed to it.

4. Read the following extract carefully and answer the questions that follow.

When I returned, there was an appalling spectacle. There was complete silence from the box, but from its airholes and chinks around the lid, blood had trickled and dried. I whipped off the lock and tore open the lid, and Mij, exhausted and blood-spattered, whimpered and caught at my leg. He had torn the lining of the box to shreds; when I removed the last of it so that there were no cutting edges left, it was just ten minutes until the time of the flight, and the airport was five miles distant. I put the miserable Mij back into the box, holding down the lid with my hand. I sat in the back of the car with the box beside me as the driver tore through the streets of Basra like a ricochetting bullet.

CBSE Question Bank 2021 Modified

(i) **Which of the following options does not state the possible reason for Maxwell's cutting the box edges off?**

(a) Mij could have injured himself further.
(b) It could have made the place untidy.
(c) Mij could have accidently swallowed the torn pieces.
(d) It could have obstructed the shutting of the lid.

Ans. (b) It could have made the place untidy.

(ii) **Why did the author put Mij back into the box?**

Ans. The author put Mij back into the box because he was getting late for the flight.

(iii) **Which of the following options correctly states Maxwell's likely feelings, in the situation below?**
"... I put the miserable Mij back into the box, holding down the lid with my hand."

(a) Anxious and insulted
(b) Disappointed and terrified
(c) Anxious and guilty

Ans. (c) Anxious and guilty

(iv) **What is the appalling spectacle as mentioned in the extract?**

Ans. The appalling spectacle was that Mij had shredded the lining of the box, and blood from its airholes and chinks had come out and dried. Also, there was complete silence from the box.

Part II

Short Answer Type Questions

1. Why did Maxwell get his mail after five days and what did he do to get it?

Ans. Maxwell got his mail after five days due to many delays in communication. Maxwell made many attempts to get his mail. On the first and third day, telephone lines were not working and on the second day, the exchange was closed due to a religious holiday.

2. What does Mijbil's behaviour suggest about the otter's adaptability to urban surroundings? CBSE Additional SQP 2023

Ans. Mijbil's behaviour suggests that as long as there is plenty of water to play with, an otter can easily adapt to urban surroundings. However, one still has to take certain precautions. The pet-parent of any otter would need to make sure to protect the otter from dangerous elements of an urban lifestyle such as running traffic.

3. What did the otter look like?

Ans. The otter looked like a small dragon belonging to the middle ages. It was covered with symmetrical pointed scales of mud. One could see from a soft velvet fur like that of a chocolate-brown mole from between the scale.

4. How does Mijbil's behaviour change when he's first brought home by the narrator in 'Mijbil the Otter'? Why do you think this change happens? Answer in 40-50 words. CBSE Question Bank 2021

Ans. When Mijbil is brought home by the narrator, he is indifferent towards the narrator and stays away from him. But by the second night, Mijbil goes to sleep near the author's knees. Soon, he shows curiosity towards his surroundings and begins to follow the narrator around. This change happens gradually because the otter becomes familiar with Maxwell.

5. What was the first characteristic of the otter discovered by the narrator?

Ans. The first characteristic of the otter discovered by the narrator was that the otter liked to play with water. When he was taken to the bathroom, for half an hour he played in the water with joy. He was plunging (falling steeply), jumping and rolling in the water.

6. "...every drop of water must be, so to speak, extended and spread about the place..." Describe Maxwell's observation regarding Mij with reference to the given quote. Competency Based

Ans. The given description of Mijbil as made by Maxwell highlights the love for water that an otter has. According to Maxwell, an otter loves to play in water. They spread and extend every drop of water that is surrounding them.

7. What happened to Mijbil in the box?

Ans. Mijbil had injured himself in the box. He was uncomfortable in the box and had tried to escape from it. To escape, he had torn the metal lining of the box into shreds. As a result, he hurt himself due to which he was covered in blood.

8. What would you say was the greatest obstacle faced by the narrator in transporting Mijbil to Camusfearna?

Ans. The greatest obstacle faced by the narrator in transporting Mijbil to Camusfearna was to make sure that Mij travelled safely in the flight. The narrator knew that Mijbil had to be packed in the box with specific dimensions. Mij did not like being packed and had hurt himself but he still had to be in the box.

9. Maxwell was justified in thinking very highly of the air hostess. Justify. Competency Based

Or **Why does the writer admire the air hostess?**

Ans. Maxwell was justified in thinking very highly of the airhostess because of her courtesy and a great concern towards the passengers. She made sure that even Mijbil was comfortable during the flight and thus, Maxwell calls her 'the very queen of her kind'.

10. Maxwell's fear of sending Mij to England was legitimate. Give a reason. CBSE Question Bank 2021

Ans. Maxwell's fear of sending Mij to England was legitimate because he knew that Mijbil would have to be kept in a box which will not be liked by his pet. Further, we know about it because, Mijbil ends up hurting himself in the box later.

11. There is not a dull moment when pets are around. Explain how this holds true in the case of 'Mijbil the Otter'. CBSE Question Bank 2021

Ans. The presence of pets inside a house means constant uproar and activity. This can be observed perfectly in the case of Mijbil the otter. Mijbil takes up every opportunity to play in the bathtub. He invented a game out of the broken suitcase of maxwell. Mijbil would spend hours juggling marbles on his belly or playing with a ball. Thus, it is true that there is not a single dull moment when pets are concerned.

12. What, according to the writer, is the 'real play' of the otter?

Ans. The real play of the otter, according to the writer, is lying on his back and juggling with small objects between his paws. Mijbil would roll two or more marbles up and down on his wide, fat belly without dropping even one to the floor.

13. Peculiar behaviours are a characteristic of Otters. Discuss with respect to 'Mijbil the Otter'. CBSE Question Bank 2021

Ans. It can be said that peculiar behaviours are a characteristic of otters by observing Mijbil the otter. Mijbil's playtime inside a bathtub resembled a hippo splashing water. He was a master at juggling objects within his paws while laying flat on his back. He also developed a peculiar compulsive habit while going on walks with Maxwell - he would always jump on the wall of the primary school and gallop the full length of it.

14. While staying in London, what was the pastime of Mij?

Ans. While staying in London, the pastime of Mij was to play for hours with his own selection of toys. His favourite toys were ping-pong balls, marbles, rubber fruit and a terrapin shell that Maxwell had bought from his native Marshes.

15. The writer suggests he still had a lot to learn about otters when he was bringing Mijbil to London. Justify the writer's claim with an example. Competency Based

Ans. The writer suggests he still had a lot to learn about otters when he was bringing Mijbil to London. This is so because he did not expect Mijbil to run away when he was taken out of the box. As a result, the writer was surprised when Mijbil did exactly that.

16. Mijbil was unhappy in the London flat. Do you agree with the statement? Justify your answer.

Ans. It is not true to say that Mijbil's behaviour in the flat indicated unhappiness. In fact, the author's description shows that Mijbil enjoyed his stay in London in the flat. Mijbil was playing happily in the flat with many different things.

17. Briefly describe any one event from the story 'Mijbil the Otter' that shows that otters are intelligent creatures? Competency Based

Ans. There are many incidents in the story that indicate that otters are intelligent creatures. Mijbil, himself invented and started playing new games with ping-pong balls. Mijbil also rolled balls of marbles on his belly. These activities showed that Mijbil was an intelligent animal.

18. Maxwell decides to keep an otter as a pet. Elucidate with reference to the fact that owning a pet is a life of commitment. CBSE 2024

Ans. The fact that Maxwell decided to keep an otter as a pet and how he takes care of his pet conveys the fact that when we decide to keep a pet, it is a commitment of lifetime. This is so because we are responsible for the well-being of that life and infact, keeping a pet at home is like bringing up and nurturing a child. Maxwell not only looks after his pet but also makes sure that he is comfortable while enjoying its life with him.

19. How does the ignorance about Mijbil as a creature in the urban environment of London reveal insights about people's perceptions and knowledge regarding animals? CBSE SQP 2024

Ans. The ignorance about Mijbil as a creature in the urban environment of London reveals limited understanding of diverse animal species. People may not recognise them outside of their natural habitat. This presents opportunities for education and awareness-building about wildlife conservation and responsible pet ownership. By learning about Mijbil's species and needs, people in London can gain a deeper appreciation for the diversity of life and understand the importance of respecting animals' natural behaviours and habitats.

20. The story, 'Mijbil the Otter', has it all- emotions, humour, certain surprising incidents and the freshness of a new and unique type of story. Explain how Maxwell has highlighted these in his story. CBSE 2025

Ans. In *Mijbil the Otter*, Maxwell beautifully blends emotions, humour, and surprises. His bond with Mijbil showcases deep affection, while Mijbil's playful antics add humour. Unexpected incidents, like Mijbil's escape on a plane, keep the story engaging. The unique pet choice adds freshness, making it captivating.

Long Answer Type Questions

1. The narrator developed a special bond with Mijbil and both became good campanions. In the light of the given statement, describe the relationship between the otter, Mijbil and Maxwell, the narrator.

Ans. The story 'Mijbil the Otter' describes an age old relationship that exists between man and an animal. In the story, the narrator, Maxwell gets an otter named Mijbil as a pet. Initially, Mijbil did not show any interest in his surrounding but slowly he became a part of it. He developed a unique and lovely relation with the narrator. The narrator took very good care of his pet. He made sure to keep his pet entertained and bought him many toys including marbles, rubber balls, fruits, etc. He even made sure to take Mijbil to play in water after realising his pet's fascination with water.

Maxwell was a keen observer of his pet's habits and traits. He encouraged Mijbil to do what he liked and also took him for a walk everyday. He was worried when he had to pack his pet in a box and was even more worried when he saw Mijbil covered in blood. Mijbil was happy with his owner. He would follow the narrator when he was called. Even when he was scared in the box and the aircraft, he found contentment with the narrator.

All this shows that both of them understood and loved each other.

2. Why do you think the otter was not friendly at first with the narrator? Can you relate this to human nature as well?

Or **Why do you think the otter was not friendly at first with the narrator? How did it behave at first? Why?**

Ans. At first, the otter was not friendly with the narrator as he had seen him for the first time. He was brought to a new place and new surroundings. He neither knew the narrator nor the place which made him stay aloof and indifferent. However, as soon as he started becoming comfortable with the surroundings, he became friendly and so it can be said that the otter almost behaved very close to the narrator.

This is very similar to human nature. Human beings first take time to understand others then only they become friendly with them. Unless they are comfortable in spending time with somebody, they try to stay away from that person.

3. "It is, in effect, a thraldom to otters, an otter fixation, that I have since found to be shared by most other people who have ever owned one." What does the narrator mean to convey in the above statement? Explain any two pieces of evidence from 'Mijbil the Otter' that support this statement in 100-200 words. CBSE Question Bank 2021

Or **What does the writer say is the effect of otters on their owners?** Competency Based

Ans. Through the given statement, the author means to convey that otters are very adorable creatures that are full of personality. Therefore, any pet-parent of an otter would love the creature very much. This opinion of the author is portrayed by various instances throughout the chapter. One such instance is when the author takes Mijbil to the bathroom for the first time. The curiosity and awe that the author feels while observing the actions of Mijbil in the bathtub portray his feelings.

Another such instance happens when the author leaves Mijbil inside the wooden box to be transported to London. When the distressed otter tears at the metal lining and ends up hurting himself, the author is greatly distressed. Even though the time of his flight to Paris was approaching very swiftly, he took his time to carefully remove all the torn parts which could've accidentally hurt Mijbil.

Thus, it is perfectly correct to say that the author was hopelessly caught in the 'otter fixation'.

4. In the name of rules and regulations, basic values are ignored but people like the airhostess in 'Mijbil the Otter' are a ray of hope. What virtues do we find in the airhostess?

Ans. It is true that in the name of rules and regulations, people forget and ignore their basic values. However, there are some people like the airhostess in the story 'Mijbil the Otter', who came as a ray of hope. The airhostess showed the value of being friendly. She could relate and empathise with the situation faced by the narrator.

She could understand the feeling of the narrator as well as the otter and even suggested the narrator to place the otter on his knees. This shows that apart from being professional, she was also a caring lady. She did not just want to do her job but also felt responsible in it as she helped Maxwell in finding Mijbil.

The airhostess did all that she could do for Maxwell and the otter. She was kindhearted, considerate and hardworking. Even when Mijbil created chaos in the aircraft, she was calm and had a charming smile.

Such an attitude makes a person respectable and successful in life.

5. Mijbil caused a sensation in London. Expound with reference to the chapter 'Mijbil the Otter'. CBSE Question Bank 2021

Ans. Mijbil's presence in London certainly did cause a sensation. One of the ways this happened was when the zoologists couldn't identify the species of Mijbil because it was an unknown species. Thus, Zoologists were presented with a sensational case of discovery. Another thing that caused a sensation in London was the fact no one had seen an otter and therefore, they could not recognise it. It led to a variety of humorous and incorrect guesses about what it could be. This made the people curious and they couldn't help but feel a sense of wonder. Therefore, Maxwell had great fun while he heard all the various wild guesses made by the Londoners. They called Mijbil a baby seal, a walrus, a hippo, and even a brontosaur.

ASSESSMENT EXERCISE

Extract Based Questions

Read the following extract carefully and answer the questions that follow.

When I casually mentioned this to a friend, he as casually replied that I had better get one in the Tigris marshes, for there they were as common as mosquitoes, and were often tamed by the Arabs. We were going to Basra to the Consulate-General to collect and answer our mail from Europe. At the Consulate-General we found that my friend's mail had arrived but that mine had not.

(i) What did the author find at the Consulate-General?

(a) That they were often tamed by Arabs

(b) That his friend's mail had not arrived

(c) That his mail had not arrived

(d) That they were as common as mosquitoes

(ii) Why did the author's friend advise him to get an otter from the Tigris marshes?

(iii) Read (a)-(c) and select why the narrator wanted the pet.

(a) To remove loneliness

(b) To get someone jealous

(c) To make a show

(iv) Complete the analogy by selecting the suitable word from the text.

Delight : Anger :: Wild : ....

Short Answer (SA) Type Questions

1. What happened when Mijbil was put inside the box?
2. Why were the people and staff near the school distracted?
3. How did the labourer react when he was digging a hole and saw Mijbil?

Long Answer (LA) Type Questions

1. The author and his pet Mij have been shown to be connected and friendly in the story. How do you think animals connect themselves to humans?
2. The author decided to keep an unusual pet rather than a common one. Also, there are many other people who keep some exceptional animals as their pets. Is it ethically correct to keep any animal as your pet? **Competency Based**
3. Ingenuity, originality and being inventive make one lovable, admirable and adorable. The author Gavin Maxwell and Mijbil, the otter, win our hearts for being original and inventive. Comment. **Competency Based**

Madam Rides the Bus

by Vallikkannan

CHAPTER 7

CHAPTER SUMMARY The given chapter 'Madam Rides the Bus' has been written by Vallikannan. This is a story about the first bus journey of an eight year old girl, Valli. The story has been written in four parts. Valli is a curious girl who develops a strong desire to travel on the bus. Therefore, she saves up money for the bus journey. The journey is a brief experience into the beauty as well as the harsh realities of life as Valli is introduced to the concept of death and the human limitations of knowledge about it.

Part - I

Valli and her Desire to Ride the Bus

Valliammai was an eight-year-old girl who was fondly called Valli. She was a curious girl and her time pass involved standing at the front door of her house, watching the happenings on the street. She had no playmates of her own age so, she just enjoyed looking out. For her, it was just as fun and enjoyable as the games that other children played.

Valli was most fascinated by the bus that travelled from her village to the nearest town. The sight of the bus with new passengers every hour filled Valli with joy and soon, she started to desire a bus ride. The desire to ride the bus turned into a longing as Valli saw the bus passing through her street everyday. If one of her friends got the chance to ride the bus and they described their experience, Valli would feel extremely jealous and shout "Proud!" which showed her disapproval.

Valli's Plan to Ride the Bus

For many days and months, Valli listened carefully to the conversations between her neighbours and the regular bus travellers. Sometimes, she would ask them questions to collect information about the bus and its journey.

In this manner, she gathered various small details about the bus journey. She found that the distance between her village and town was 6 miles, the fare of the bus was thirty paise for one side. She got to know that the bus took 45 minutes to reach the town. Further, she got to know that, if she stayed in her seat and paid another 30 paise, she could return home in the same bus. With all this information, Valli calculated the timings of her journey, planned and replanned her trip

Part - II

Valli's First Bus Journey

One day as the bus was about to leave the village stop, Valli stopped the bus and got on it. Valli acted like an adult lady while boarding the bus. The conductor, who was a jolly natured man, was amused by Valli's behaviour and started referring to her as 'Madam'. He showed her a seat at the front of the bus and as soon as Valli sat down, the bus started moving.

There were only six or seven passengers in the bus. It was a new bus with soft and luxurious seats. Its overhead bars were shining brightly and there was a clock just above the windshield.

Views Outside the Bus

Valli was curious to see everything in the bus and outside it. When she wanted to look outside, she couldn't see anything. This was so because a curtain (canvas) had covered her window. So, she stood up.

The bus passed along the banks of a canal. On one side of the narrow road, there were palm trees, grasslands, distant mountains and blue sky. On the other side of the bus, there was a deep ditch and beyond it, were acres of green fields. While she was enjoying the greenery, she heard an old man asking her to sit down on her seat.

Valli felt annoyed at the old man for thinking of her to be a child. She told him that she had paid full fare like others and then, asked the conductor to give her the ticket.

The conductor and the passengers were amused at an 8-year-old child acting like an adult. They laughed at her actions while the conductor handed her the ticket. He also explained to her that she needed to sit down or she would fall down and get hurt.

The Journey Continues

The bus stopped at one point and some new passengers got inside the bus. Valli took her seat in fear of losing it. An elderly woman sat beside her and asked Valli about her travelling alone in the bus. Valli found that lady ugly and unpleasant because she had big holes in her ear lobes, was wearing ugly earrings and was chewing betel nut. Valli got irritated with her questions and started to look out of the window.

Part - III

Valli's Elaborate Plans

Valli had to take great pains to save the sixty paise for the bus ride. She carefully saved her coins for months resisting her desire to buy peppermints, toys or riding merry-go round in the village fair. At last, she collected the money. Now, she had to slip out of the house without letting her mother know. Her mother napped every afternoon from one to four. Valli decided to take her first bus journey during this time period.

The Race with the Young Cow

The bus was moving smoothly, leaving all the obstacles behind. Suddenly, Valli saw a young cow running in the middle of the road, in front of the bus. The driver slowed down the bus and blew the horn but the cow got scared and ran even faster. Valli found it very amusing and laughed heartily while clapping her hands. Finally, the cow moved off the road.

The Halt at the Town

The bus, then, passed through the railway crossing and the train station. Then, it reached the nearest town to Valli's village. Valli stared at the shopping street and the big bright-looking shops. She was amazed by the glittering displays of clothes and the big crowds. All the passengers got off the bus except Valli. The conductor asked her to get down and explore the street and nearby sights but Valli refused because she was afraid. She informed him that she would be going back to the village in the same bus. After saying this, she gave the bus conductor another thirty paise for the ride back home. The conductor also offered her a cold drink but she refused it.

Part - IV

Valli's Return Journey

The bus started going towards the village and Valli saw the same beautiful sights again with same excitement. Then, her sight fell upon the dead cow which had been struck by some speeding vehicle.

The scene made her sad and she no longer wanted to look out of the window. She kept sadly thinking about the beautiful and lovable young cow which had lost all of its charm as it lay dead. She remembered the horrible sight of blood, the spread out legs and the lifeless eyes of the cow. The bus reached Valli's village at three forty. She bid a good bye to the conductor and the conductor warmly did the same. She got down the bus and ran towards her home.
As she entered her house, she saw her mother talking to one of her aunts. They were conversing about the everyday things and those that were beyond their knowledge and understanding. Valli agreed with them, smiled and went inside the house.

Word Meaning

Word	Meaning
crept	make way
overwhelming	(here) strong
wistfully	longingly
kindle	set alight (a fire) here, feelings
longings	wants
slang	a type of language consisting of words and phrases that are regarded as very informal
discreet	not likely to be seen or noticed by many people
jolly	happy and cheerful
slack	a time when there is not much work
gleaming	shining brightly
overhead	above someone's head
devoured	absorbed fully
canvas blind	curtain of thick cloth
peered	looked carefully
ditch	a pothole
startle	surprise
haughtily	proudly
chimed in	to break into a conversation or discussion
mimicking	copying the speech of someone
repulsive	causing strong dislike or disgust
curtly	sharply
drivel	talk in a very foolish or silly way
painstaking	diligent care and effort
thriftily	to spend money carefully

Word	Meaning
temptation	a strong urge or desire to have or do something
resolutely stifled	controlled with determination
excursion	a short trip, especially for pleasure
ventured out	went cautiously, courageously
hamlet	small village
gobbling up	hitting
pedestrian	a person travelling on foot
glee	joy
honked	sounded the horn
galloped	(of an animal) to run very fast
speck	a very small size
rattle	to make a rapid succession of short, sharp noises
traversed	travelled across or through
thoroughfare	a main road in a town
glittering	shining
gape	to look in surprise or wonder
merchandise	things for sale
shrugged	expressed indifference
spreadeagled	lying with arms and legs stretched out
haunted	returned repeatedly to the mind
dampening	reducing
chatterbox	talkative person
chit of a girl	immature girl
pokes her nose	take an interest in something that does not concern her

NCERT FOLDER

NCERT Intext and Exercise Questions

ORAL COMPREHENSION CHECK❶ (NCERT PAGE 97)

Q.1 What was Valli's favourite pastime?

Ans. Valli's favourite pastime was to stand at the front door of her house and enjoy the happenings on the street.

Q.2 What was the source of unending joy for Valli? What was her strongest desire?

Ans. The source of unending joy for Valli was the sight of the bus that travelled between her village and the nearest town. Valli's strongest desire was to ride a bus.

Q.3 What did Valli find out about the bus journey? How did she find out these details?

Or **How did Valli gather the details of the bus journey?** CBSE 2023

Ans. Valli found out that the town was six miles away from her village. The trip to town would take forty five minutes and the fare of one way was thirty paise.

Valli found out these details by listening carefully to the conversations between her neighbours and people who regularly rode the bus. She also asked a few questions to them.

Q.4 What do you think Valli was planning to do?

Ans. I think Valli was planning to go to the town and then, return back by the same bus.

CHECK❷ (NCERT PAGE 100)

Q.1 Why does the conductor call Valli 'madam'?

Ans. The conductor calls Valli 'madam' because she behaved like a mature woman. She declined his help and was very quick in her answers to the conductor's questions. The conductor was amused at her behaviour and to tease her, he called her 'madam'.

Q.2 Why does Valli stand up on the seat? What does she see now?

Ans. Valli stands up on the seat because she found her view blocked by the canvas that covered the lower part of the window. In order to have a better view, she stood up on the seat and looked over the canvas.

Valli could then see that the road was narrow. On one side of the road was a canal beyond which there were palm trees, grasslands, distant mountains and the blue sky. On the another side, she saw that there was a deep ditch and many acres of green fields.

Q.3 What does Valli tell the elderly man when he calls her a child?

Ans. Valli tells the elderly man that there was nobody in the bus who was a child. She told him that she had paid her fare of thirty paise like everybody else.

Q.4 Why didn't Valli want to make friends with the elderly woman?

Ans. Valli did not want to make friends with the elderly woman because she found the elderly woman to be quite ugly. She had big earholes and was wearing ugly earrings. Apart from this, she was chewing betel nut and it seemed that the juice of the betel would spill out of her mouth.

CHECK❸ (NCERT PAGE 103)

Q.1 How did Valli save up money for her first journey? Was it easy for her?

Ans. Valli saved up money for her first journey by not spending money on toys and eatables. She controlled herself from buying these things.

No, it was not easy for her at all. Even at the village fair, she resisted the temptation to be on the merry-go round. Thus, she was able to save sixty paise for her first bus journey.

Q.2 What did Valli see on her way that made her laugh?

Ans. Valli saw a young cow, running very fast in the middle of the road in front of the bus. The horn of the bus frightened the animal. The more the driver horned, the faster the cow ran in front of the bus. This all seemed very funny to Valli and she laughed heartily.

Q.3 Why didn't she get off the bus at the bus station?

Ans. Valli didn't get off the bus at the bus station because she wanted to return to her village in the same bus.

Q.4 Why didn't Valli want to go to the stall and have a drink? What does this tell you about her?

Or

What stopped Valli from going to the stall to have a drink? What do we learn about Valli from this? CBSE 2023

Ans. Valli didn't want to go to the stall and have a drink because she did not have the money to pay for it.

This tells us that she was well-mannered and had high self-esteem.

THINKING ABOUT THE TEXT (NCERT PAGE 105)

Q.1 What was Valli's deepest desire? Find the words and phrases in the story that tell you this.

Ans. Valli's deepest desire was to go on a bus ride.

The words and phrases in the story that tell us this are 'source of unending joy', 'stare wistfully' and 'kindle in her longings, dreams and hopes'.

Q.2 How did Valli plan her bus ride? What did she find out about the bus and how did she save up the fare?

Or **Valli's dream was to enjoy a ride on the bus to the nearest town. What preparations did she make to realise her dream?**

Ans. Valli planned her bus ride by listening carefully to conversations between her neighbours and people who regularly travel by the bus. She also asked a few questions to them.

She found out that the town was six miles from her village, the bus fare was thirty paise for one way and the bus trip took forty-five minutes. She also thought that if she stayed in the bus and came back by the same bus, it would cost her sixty paise.

She saved up the fare by controlling herself from buying toys, peppermints, etc. She did not even take a ride on the merry-go round at the village annual fare to save money. Finally, she was able to save sixty paise for her journey.

Q.3 What kind of a person is Valli? To answer this question, pick out the following sentences from the text and fill in the blanks. The words you fill in are the clues to your answer.

(i) "Stop the bus! Stop the bus!" And a tiny hand was raised ....

(ii) "Yes, I .... go to town," said Valli, still standing outside the bus.

(iii) "There's nobody here ....," she said haughtily. "I've paid my thirty paise like everyone else."

(iv) "Never mind," she said, "I can .... You don't have to help me". "I'm not a child, I tell you," she said, ...

(v) "You needn't bother about me. I .... ," Valli said, turning her face towards the window and staring out.

(vi) Then she turned to the conductor and said, "Well, sir, I hope ...."

Ans. (i) commandingly (ii) simply have to

(iii) who is a child (iv) get on by myself, irritably

(v) can take care of myself

(vi) to see you again

These sentences show that Valli is independent, assertive and self-reliant.

Q.4 Why does the conductor refer to Valli as 'madam'?

Ans. The conductor referred to Valli as 'madam' as she behaved like a grown up woman and did not think that she was a child. She also refused his help and told him that she could manage on her own. Therefore, to tease her, the conductor refers to her as 'madam'.

Q.5 Find the lines in the text which tell you that Valli was enjoying her ride on the bus.

Ans. The lines in the text which tell us that Valli was enjoying her ride on the bus are

(i) Oh, it was all so wonderful.

(ii) Suddenly, Valli clapped her hands with glee.

(iii) Somehow this was very funny to Valli. She laughed and laughed until there were tears in her eyes.

(iv) Valli wasn't bored in the slightest and greeted everything with the same excitement she'd felt the first time.

Q.6 Why does Valli refuse to look out of the window on her way back?

Ans. Valli refused to look out of the window on her way back as she saw the dead body of the cow who was running in front of the bus when she was going to town. This made her sad.

Q.7 What does Valli mean when she says,"I was just agreeing with you what you said about things happening without our knowledge"?

Ans. While saying this, Valli meant to hide the fact about her bus ride. She was also feeling happy and excited at making a successful attempt at her plan.

Q.8 The author describes the things that Valli sees from an eight-year-old's point of view. Can you find evidence from the text for his statement?

Ans. The evidence from the text for the statement that the author describes the things that Valli sees from an eight-year-old's point of view is as follows

(i) Sometimes, the bus seemed on the point of gobbling up another vehicle that was coming towards them or a pedestrian crossing the road.

(ii) Trees came running towards them but then stopped as the bus reached them and simply stood there helpless for a moment by the side of the road before rushing away in the other direction.

(iii) A young cow, tail high in the air, was running very fast, right in the middle of the road, right in front of the bus.

(iv) A speck of a train could be seen in the distance, growing bigger and bigger as it drew near.

WRITING

Write a page — about three paragraphs — on one of the following topics.

Q.1 Have you ever planned something entirely on your own, without taking grownups into your confidence? What did you plan, and how? Did you carry out your plan?

Ans. Yes, I once planned a surprise birthday party for a friend without telling any adults. I chose the theme, decorations and cake design. Then, I secretly contacted our friends to attend. I set up the venue by arranging balloons, streamers and a banner. I also organized games and picked out a playlist of our favorite songs. I managed everything on my own, even hiding the cake and gifts in a secret spot. The plan went smoothly, and my friend was thrilled with the surprise. It felt rewarding to see everything come together without adult help!

Q.2 Have you made a journey that was unforgettable in some way? What made it memorable?

Ans. Yes, I have made many journeys that have been unforgettable in some ways. The one that was most memorable was taken with my maternal family towards our old town in Bengal. The road trip, the songs and the fact that we all spend some time having fun without any serious discussion made it very memorable.

Q.3 Are you concerned about traffic and road safety? What are your concerns? How would you make road travel safer and more enjoyable?

Ans. Yes, I am very concerned about traffic and road safety. Many people get hurt or even lose their lives in accidents every year. I worry about how fast some cars go and how drivers sometimes do not pay attention. For example, I often see people using their phones while driving, which is dangerous. Also, I noticed that many drivers do not stop at red lights or do not watch for pedestrians at crosswalks. All these behaviours can lead to serious accidents and injuries.

We need better education for drivers and pedestrians to make road travel safer. Schools should teach children about road safety from a young age. For example, kids should learn to look both ways before crossing the street and to use pedestrian signals. Drivers should also attend classes on safe driving habits and avoiding distractions like texting. Further, stricter laws and penalties for speeding or reckless driving can help make the roads safer for everyone. Finally, I believe we can make road travel more enjoyable by improving the streets and making them more accessible. We can add more bike lanes and walking paths so that people have safe options besides cars. Parks or resting areas along busy roads can provide safe spots for families to stop and enjoy the outdoors. If we work together to make these changes, we can create a safer and more enjoyable environment for everyone who travels on the road.

REVIEW EXERCISE

Including Competency Based Questions

Multiple Choice Questions

1. What kind of person is Valli? Competency Based

(a) Innocent and honest
(b) Shrewd and rebellious
(c) Patient and meticulous
(d) Petulant and patronising

Ans. (c) Patient and meticulous

2. What is the main idea expressed in the first two paragraphs? Competency Based

(a) Valli was lonely
(b) Valli found ways to entertain herself
(c) Valli did not like to play with other children
(d) Valli did not have much to do during the day

Ans. (b) Valli found ways to entertain herself

3. "Valli would stare wistfully at the people who got on or off the bus." What is the meaning of 'wistfully'?

(a) Longingly
(b) Fearfully
(c) Carefully
(d) Willingly

Ans. (a) Longingly

4. Which word was used by Valli and her friends as a slang expression for disapproval?

(a) Okay! Okay!
(b) Yeah! Yeah!
(c) Proud! Proud!
(d) Oh okay!

Ans. (c) 'Proud! Proud!'

5. What was the next challenge for Valli once she'd saved enough money?

(i) Know about the timings of the bus

(ii) Buy a ticket

(iii) To sneak out of the house

Codes

(a) Only (i) (b) Only (iii) (c) Only (ii) (d) All of these

Ans. (b) Only (iii)

6. What was the timing of the afternoon nap taken by Valli's mother?

(a) 1 to 3 pm (b) 1 to 4 pm (c) 2 to 4 pm (d) 2 to 3 pm

Ans. (b) 1 to 4 pm

7. How did Valli act when she got on the bus? **Competency Based**

(a) She was very shy

(b) She was very obedient

(c) She tried to show confidence

(d) She showed her nervousness

Ans. (c) She tried to show confidence

8. From the following options, identify the conductor's intention behind calling Valli 'Madam'.

(a) Hatred (b) Envy (c) Joke (d) Sarcasm

Ans. (c) Joke

9. Select the correct option for (i) and (ii).

(i) Valli found the elderly woman repulsive.

(ii) The woman had large piercings in her ears, wore ugly earrings and chewing betel nut.

(a) (ii) is true (i) is false (b) (i) is true (ii) is false

(c) Both (i) and (ii) are false (d) (ii) is the cause for (i)

Ans. (d) (ii) is the cause for (i).

10. Valli's reaction to being mocked by the conductor changes from being **Competency Based**

(a) shy to resentful. (b) indifferent to hurt.

(c) confused to annoyed. (d) offended to accepting.

Ans. (d) offended to accepting.

11. What does it tell you about Valli when she refused to accept the conductor's treat?

(a) Responsible (b) Stubborn

(c) Rude (d) Disrespectful

Ans. (a) Responsible

12. What does the phrase 'a fixed stare from its lifeless eyes' from 'Madam Rides the Bus' mean?

(a) The animal was asleep (b) The animal was dead

(c) The animal was watching sky

(d) The animal was staring at Valli

Ans. (b) The animal was dead.

13. Valli's smile at the end can best be described as **Competency Based**

(a) nervous but optimistic

(b) shy and enthusiastic

(c) excited but confused

(d) smug and secretive

Ans. (d) smug and secretive

14. Valli's mother's reaction to seeing her suggests that she **Competency Based**

(a) was more interested in her conversation.

(b) knew Valli had done something naughty.

(c) liked Valli's spirit of adventure.

(d) had been looking for Valli.

Ans. (a) was more interested in her conversation.

15. Given below is the list of some adjectives. Choose the ones which can be associated with Valli based on the chapter 'Madam Rides the Bus'.

1. Intelligent **2. Cunning**

3. Mature **4. Responsible**

5. Cranky **6. Mannerless**

7. Curious **8. Active listener**

(a) 1, 3, 4, 7, 8 (b) 2, 3, 5, 6, 7

(c) 1, 2, 3, 4, 5, 6 (d) 2, 3, 4, 7, 8

Ans. (a) Valli was intelligent, mature, responsible, curious and active listener.

Extract Based Questions

1. Read the following extract carefully and answer the questions that follow.

But for Valli, standing at the front door was every bit as enjoyable as any of the elaborate games other children played. Watching the street gave her many new unusual experiences.

The most fascinating thing of all was the bus that travelled between her village and the nearest town. It passed through her street each hour, once going to the town and once coming back. The sight of the bus, filled each time with a new set of passengers, was a source of unending joy for Valli.

(i) What was the most interesting thing for Valli?

(a) The children playing elaborate games

(b) Watching the street

(c) The bus that travelled through her village

(d) All of the above

Ans. (c) The bus that travelled through her village

(ii) What did other children do on street?

Ans. Other children used to play elaborated games on the street.

(iii) How did Valli feel while standing at the doorway? For what specific reason did Valli stand at the doorway?

Ans. Watching the street gave Valli many new and strange experiences. She felt joyous standing at the doorway.

She would especially wait for the bus that travelled between her village and the nearest town. It was a source of immense joy for her.

(iv) How was Valli different from children of her age?

Ans. Valli was different from children of her age as she was not interested in playing any elaborate games.

2. Read the following extract carefully and answer the questions that follow.

"Day after day, she watched the bus and gradually a tiny wish crept into her head and grew there: she wanted to ride on that bus, even if it was just once. This wish became stronger, until it was an overwhelming desire. Valli would stare wistfully at the people who got on and off the bus when it stood at the street corner. Their faces would kindle in her longings, dreams and hopes. If one of her friends happened to ride the bus and tried to describe the sights of the town to her. Valli would be jealous to listen and would shout, in English: "Proud! Proud!"

(i) Fill in the blank with the correct expression. Valli would stare wistfully at the people as she .... (was inspired by the people travelling on the bus/had a strong desire to take a ride on the bus)

Ans. had a strong desire to take a ride on the bus

(ii) What does the line "gradually a tiny wish crept into her head and grew there" mean? What was the wish?

Ans. The line "gradually a tiny wish crept into her head and grew there" means that the wish developed in her head over a period of time. Valli wished to ride the bus.

(iii) Which of the following statements is not true as per the extract?

(a) As Valli watched the bus, her desire to ride the bus increased manifold.

(b) Valli thought that her friends who travelled by the bus and recounted the experience were too proud.

(c) Valli's wistful thought was to ride the bus, even if it was only once.

(d) Seeing passengers got on and off the bus made her long even more for the bus ride.

Ans. (b) Valli thought that her friends who travelled by the bus and recounted the experience were too proud.

(iv) 'Valli would be jealous to listen...' What does this line indicate?

Ans. 'Valli would be jealous to listen…' This indicates that Valli had a longing to ride the bus.

3. Read the following extract carefully and answer the questions that follow.

Over many days and months, Valli listened carefully to conversations between her neighbours and people who regularly used the bus and she also asked a few discreet questions here and there. This way she picked up various small details about the bus journey. The town was six miles from her village.

(i) How did Valli pick up small details about the bus journey?

(a) Listening to conversations of neighbours

(b) Asking a few discreet questions

(c) Both (a) and (b)

(d) None of these

Ans. (c) Both (a) and (b)

(ii) Choose the option that can describe Valli with reference to above extract.

(i) Curious	**(ii) Intelligent**
(iii) Active listener	**(iv) Irritating**
(v) Cautious	**(vi) Interrupting**

Ans. (i), (ii), (iii) and (v)

(iii) Complete the analogy by selecting the suitable word from the text.

Devoted : Loyal :: Diversified : ....

Ans. Various

(iv) What was Valli's overwhelming desire?

Ans. Valli's overwhelming desire was to travel by bus.

4. Read the following extract carefully and answer the questions that follow.

The bus slowed down to a crawl and the conductor, sticking his head out the door, said, "Hurry then! Tell whoever it is to come quickly." "It's me," shouted Valli. "I'm the one who has to get on." By now the bus had come to a stop and the conductor said, "Oh, really! You don't say so!" "Yes, I simply have to go to town," said Valli, still standing outside the bus, "and here's my money." She showed him some coins. "Okay, okay, but first you must get on the bus," said the conductor and he stretched out a hand to help her up. "Never mind," she said, "I can get on by myself. You don't have to help me." The conductor was a jolly sort, fond of joking. "Oh, please don't be angry with me, my fine madam," he said. "Here, have a seat right up there in front. Everybody move aside please – make way for madam."

Competency Based

(i) **"Hurry then! Tell whoever it is to come quickly." What is the conductor's assumption while saying this line?**

Ans. The given statement by the conductor shows that he thought that the child is trying to stop the bus for an adult family member.

(ii) **"The conductor was a jolly sort, fond of joking." Justify the statement with evidence from the text.**

Ans. The conductor was indeed a jolly person. This can be proved by following instances

(a) When he jokingly calls Valli a madam.

(b) When he makes everyone move aside to clear the way for Valli.

(iii) **Which of these can be said about Valli after reading the given extract?**

(a) She wants to change how adults view children.

(b) She wants to save money to seem responsible.

(c) She wants to be seen as an independent person.

(d) She wants to rebel against everyone who questions her.

Ans. (c) She wants to be seen as an independent person.

(iv) **What is the nature of the conductor when he calls Valli 'madam'?**

Ans. The conductor's nature is playful when he calls Valli 'madam'.

5. Read the following extract carefully and answer the questions that follow.

"Yes, I'm travelling alone," she answered curtly. And I've got a ticket too.'

'Yes she's on her way to town,' said the conductor. 'With a thirty paise ticket.'

'Oh, why don't you mind your own business,' said Valli. But she laughed all the same and the conductor laughed too.

But the old woman went on with her drivel. 'Is it proper for such a young person to travel alone? Do you know exactly where you're going in town? What's the street? What's the house number?

'You needn't bother about me. I can take care of myself,' Valli said, turning her face towards the window and staring out." **Question Bank 2021 Modified**

(i) **Valli told the conductor to mind his own business and laughed as well. This shows that Valli ...**

(a) was not really bothered about what the conductor said.

(b) didn't like the conductor speaking about her.

(c) disliked what the conductor said but was amused.

(d) was impressed with what the conductor said.

Ans. (a) was not really bothered about what the conductor said.

(ii) **The elderly woman in the bus keeps inquiring after Valli because Valli is a child. What assumptions could she have about children?** **Competency Based**

Ans. The elderly woman could have assumed that young children like Valli are incapable of taking care of themselves and that they are bound to act mischievously and get into trouble. She must have assumed that Valli ran away from home without telling her family about it. That is why she was worried about Valli.

(iii) **Complete the sentence appropriately. The old woman asked her questions because ....**

Ans. she was shocked to see an 8 year old girl travelling alone. Thus, she was worried for Valli.

(iv) **How do you think Valli felt when the old woman asked her questions?**

Ans. Valli felt upset and irritated when the old woman asked her questions.

6. Read the following extract carefully and answer the questions that follow.

Don't you want to have a look at the sights, now that you're here?" "All by myself? Oh, I'd be much too afraid." Greatly amused by the girl's way of speaking, the conductor said, "But you weren't afraid to come in the bus." "Nothing to be afraid of about that," she answered. "Well, then, why not go to that stall over there and have something to drink? Nothing to be afraid of about that either." "Oh, no, I couldn't do that." **CBSE 2023**

(i) **Why did the girl not want to look at the sights ?**

Ans. The girl did not look at the sights because she would be taking the same bus home and also wanted to be a responsible person since she was travelling alone.

(ii) **Why was the conductor amused with Valli's logic?**

Ans. The conductor was amused with Valli because her logic made no sense. She informed the conductor that she was not afraid to go on the bus trip six miles away from her village. But she was terribly afraid of stepping out of the bus and looking at the sights of the market.

(iii) **Select the option that correctly captures the application of the word 'sight' as used in the extract.**

(a) Rashid could not sight the tiger.

(b) Rashi lost his sight in the left eye.

(c) The General ordered the soldiers not to shoot at sight when they saw the enemy.

(d) Rashid was fascinated by the <u>sights</u> of the city as he went on a tour.

Ans. (d) Rashid was fascinated by the <u>sights</u> of the city as he went on a tour.

(iv) Complete the analogy using a word from the text.
Entertained : Amused : : Apprehensive : ....

Ans. Afraid

Part–II

Short Answer Type Questions

1. Why did Valli spend her time all alone and what became her favourite pastime?

Ans. Valli used to spend her time alone because she has no one of her age in her village/street.

Her favourite pastime was to see the things happening outside her home. She especially loved to see the bus that travelled between her village and the nearest town.

2. What was the most fascinating thing that Valli saw on the street?

Ans. The most fascinating thing that Valli saw on the street was the bus that travelled between her village and the nearest town. It passed through her street each hour, once going to the town and once coming back.

3. How did Valli save money to travel by bus? **CBSE 2023**

Ans. Valli saved the money to travel by bus by controlling every temptation to buy peppermints, toys, balloons and even a ride on the merry-go round at the village fair to save money for her bus journey.

4. "Her first journey – what careful, painstaking, elaborate plans she had to make for it!"
Why do you think Valli put in so much effort in planning for this journey? **Competency Based**

Ans. Valli must have put so much effort in planning for this journey because it was her strongest desire to ride the bus. The trip also required planning because she had to save the money for the trip herself. She also had to time the entire trip in a way that her mother would not be able to know anything about it.

5. Describe the bus in which Valli sat.

Ans. The bus in which Valli sat was new. Its outside was painted a gleaming white with some green stripes along the sides. Inside, the overhead bars shone like silver.

6. The passengers on the bus were friendly towards Valli. Do you agree? Justify your response. **Competency Based**

Ans. The passengers on the bus were very friendly towards Valli. The old man and the elderly woman chewing the betel nut on the bus were looking out for Valli's safety. That is why the old man advised her to sit down and the woman asked her various questions. The other passengers joined in on the good–natured laughter of the conductor, but they didn't make fun of Valli nor did they make her feel unwanted or scared.

7. Valli didn't like the way adults treated her during her bus journey. Describe how you would feel and react if you were to find yourself in a similar situation. **CBSE Question Bank 2021**

Ans. In a situation wherein adults are constantly ordering me during a journey, I would also react like Valli did because I would consider myself to be responsible enough to take the journey by myself. Just like Valli thought that she could take care of herself, I would also think the same and so, would dislike being interrupted by elders.

8. During her journey, Valli absorbed the natural beauty and clapped her hands in happiness on seeing a young cow running very fast. What does this reveal about Valli? **CBSE Question Bank 2021**

Ans. During her journey, Valli absorbed the natural beauty and clapped her hands in happiness on seeing a young cow running very fast. This shows that although Valli was a mature and a responsible girl, she was still a child at heart.

9. Why didn't Valli get off the bus when the bus stopped at the town?

Ans. When the nearest town was reached, everyone got off the bus except Valli because she wanted to return home in the same bus.

She only wanted to take a ride on a bus. So, she gave the conductor the fare to return home in the same bus.

10. The conductor was a generous man. Provide proof for the statement from the text. **Competency Based**

Ans. The conductor treated Valli with kindness while ensuring that she would not feel scared. He kept an eye on her throughout the journey to be assured of her safety and intervened everytime some stranger talked to Valli.

When the bus reached the town, the conductor offered to buy her a cold drink when she said she didn't have enough money. These actions show that the conductor was a kind and generous man.

11. How did Valli feel on seeing the dead cow on the road?

Or **What made Valli lose her excitement for the ride?**

Or **Why was Valli's excitement on the bus dampened on her return journey?** **Competency Based**

Ans. On seeing the dead cow on the road, Valli felt sad and she lost all her excitement for the ride. She thought that a lovable, beautiful creature just a little while ago had now suddenly lost its charm and its life. It looked so horrible and frightening. After that, she did not even look outside the bus.

12. Why did Valli smile to herself? Did her mother and aunt have any chance of knowing the secret of her smile? **Competency Based**

Ans. Valli smiled to herself when she realised that her mother and aunt would never know about her journey. They did not know anything about Valli's bus journey and had no chance of knowing Valli's secret.

13. Valli's unique maiden bus ride experience could be possible because she belonged to a small village. Do you agree? Why? Why not? (2 reasons) **CBSE SQP 2023**

Ans. Yes, I agree that Valli's unique maiden bus ride experience could be possible because she belonged to a small village. A bus ride in a city is not as interesting and adventurous as one in a village. Valli had been observing that bus for quite some time, which can only be possible in a village, not in a city where a large number of buses can be confusing.

14. What role does curiosity play in Valli's character throughout the story?

Ans. Curiosity drives Valli's actions throughout the story. Her desire to explore the world beyond her village motivates her to take the bus ride. She observes everything with excitement and wonder, always eager to learn more. However, her curiosity also leads her to confront complex realities like death.

15. Why didn't Valli appreciate the elders' care on her bus journey?

Ans. Valli didn't appreciate the elders' care on her bus journey because she felt independent and capable of caring for herself. She believed she was mature enough to handle the experience alone and found their concern or interference unnecessary. Valli wanted to prove she didn't need anyone's help or advice.

16. Assess the narrative's effectiveness in portraying the tension between the comfort of familiarity and the allure of the unfamiliar in'Madm Rides the Bus.' **CBSE SQP 2024**

Ans. Valli's longing to ride the bus showcases her yearning to break freefrom the confines of her everday life and explore the unknown. The familiar surroundings of her street represent safety and predictability, while the bus symbolises adventure and opportunity. This contrast creates a sense of tension as Valli grapples with her desire to step into a world of the unfamiliar.

Long Answer Type Questions

1. Age is not a barrier when it comes to doing something different and great. Which characteristics of Valli help her achieve the wonder of visiting the town at such a tender age?

Ans. In today's era, age is no more a barrier. Children are doing wonders at a very young age. Same goes with Valli. At an age of 8 years, Valli was able to pursue her dream all alone by travelling in the bus to town. She was no different from others, except that she had certain characteristics that made her fulfil her dreams. Valli was a very confident and a bold girl. She had a knowledge of proper planning and execution. She controlled her wishes to save money for the bus ride. Also, she was a very good observer and learner.

All these qualities made her realise the dream of visiting the town. Hence, one should always remember that there is no age to learn and experience new things.

2. Once we decide to achieve something, so many difficulties come in our way. With focused attention we can make that achievement. How did Valli succeed in fulfilling her desire of riding a bus?

Or **How did Valli fulfill her desire to ride a bus to the town and back?** **CBSE 2020**

Or **Valli was sensitive, but at the same time she was fearless and quite determined. Explain with reference to the text.** **CBSE 2022 Term II**

Or **Valli was an extraordinary girl who had self-confidence and courage to realise her ambition by planning and drawing on her spirit of adventure. Discuss in reference to the chapter 'Madam Rides the Bus'.** **CBSE 2023**

Ans. It is true that once we decide to achieve something, many difficulties come in our way to stop us from doing our best to achieve our goals. However, with focused attention and courage, we can make our achievement. The story 'Madam Rides the Bus' proves this fact to be true.

In the story, Valliammai or Valli, an eight year old girl develops a strong desire to take a ride on the bus that travelled from her street everyday. As a fearless, confident and bold girl, Valli not only gathered all knowledge about the journey but also meticulously planned her trip.

With extreme self-control, Valli saved the money she would require for a round trip in the bus. She was determined to fulfill her dream. She controlled her desire to buy peppermints, toys, balloons and even did not take a ride on the merry-go-round in the village fair. Then, she properly planned to take the journey quietly when her mother was taking her afternoon nap. Finally, she was able to fulfill her dream.

Her passion, self-dependence and self-respecting nature helped her to take the journey safely. Thus, it is true that with focussed attention, courage, determination and planning, one can achieve anything in life.

3. What kind of person is Valli? Illustrate your answer from the text that you have read.

Or **"Valli was a mature girl ahead of her age." Justify the statement with evidence from the text.** **CBSE 2020, 2022 Term II**

Ans. Valliammai or Valli was an eight-year-old curious girl who developed a strong desire to take a bus ride. In the story, Valli emerged as a clever, sensitive, self-respecting and fun loving girl. With determination and passion she worked towards fulfilling her desire.

Not only did she just gather all the information she would require for the bus journey but also sacrificed many things to achieve it. She controlled her simple desires of buying toys, balloons, etc to take a ride on the bus. During the bus journey, Valli proved to be mature, confident, bold and practical girl beyond her age. She was full of excitement and enthusiasm with which she enjoyed the scenes outside the bus.

Even the cow filled her with extreme joy. Valli was also a keen, observant, intelligent, and sensitive girl, she was friendly, polite as well as careful. She not only refuses to take a cold drink from a strange man but also shows her good manners while talking to the conductor.

Her nature is evident when she is saddened by the dead cow lying by the roadside. All these characteristics shows that Valli is different from other children of her age.

4. In such a fast moving world when we hear so many incidents happening with people, do you think Valli did right by not telling her mother about the bus journey?

Ans. No, I don't think that Valli did the right thing in travelling alone to the town without informing her mother. By doing this, she put herself in an unsafe position as she could have easily been a victim of child abuse if she came in contact with wrong people. In fact, she was lucky to return home safely. Children should always travel along with their parents or elders as they are easy targets for criminals. We hear a lot of instances of crimes committed against children these days like kidnapping, child abuse, molestation, etc.

Valli could have expressed her desire of travelling in the bus to her mother. I am sure that her mother would have fulfilled her wish by taking her on a bus ride. It might happen that her mother would not allow her that particular time. But being a caring mother, she would definitely take her on a bus ride. Travelling alone is never safe because one has no idea about the routes and might get lost. So, it is always better to inform parents before doing such acts.

5. Curiosity is the mother of learning. If one has an urge to know more about anything, one learns many things. Valli also has an urge to know more and more about things and her surroundings which makes her an intelligent, confident and mature girl. What traits of her character makes her so?

Or **The people and surroundings are a great book to learn from. Valli in the lesson 'Madam Rides the Bus' a lot from others. Mention the traits of her character which help her to learn from people and her surroundings.** **CBSE 2023**

Ans. Curiosity is the mother of learning. If one has an urge to know more about anything, one learns many things. In the story, 'Madam Rides the Bus', Valli also has the urge to know more and more about things and her surroundings. She is a curious eight year old girl who observes her surroundings and learns a lot from others.

She stands at the front door of her house and enjoys looking at the various activities around her house. When she develops a strong desire to ride in the bus, her curious nature helps her a lot. It allows her to listen to the conversations of other people who had travelled in the bus. She could even confidently ask questions so that she could gather as much information as she can regarding the bus journey.

While on her journey, Valli was friendly with the bus conductor and maturedly handled herself throughout the bus journey. Her curious nature makes her intelligent and confident.

6. As Valli, make a diary entry about your experience of riding the bus alone for the first time. **CBSE 2022 Term II**

Or **As Valli, make a diary entry sharing your joys and disappointments during the bus ride.** **CBSE 2022 Term II**

Ans. Thursday, 25th March, 20XX 8:45 p.m.

Dear Diary

Today, I am extremely happy because my wish to ride the bus came true. What a fascinating and exciting journey it was! I drank in all the beautiful sights from the window. The way the trees appeared to be rushing both in my direction and away from me at the same time was just beautiful. The bus passed the train station and as it approached the main street, I could see all the colourful stores and dazzling racks of clothing and other goods. A large crowd had gathered there. But a young cow was what truly made me laugh. With her tail up high in the air, it was moving extremely quickly in the middle of the road in front of the bus. I laughed nonstop at the sight. However, upon returning, I was disheartened to discover the same calf lying dead by the side of the road. It was a gloomy sight. It rooted me to my seat till the bus arrived in the village. I stepped inside my house a little happy, a little heartbroken and a lot wiser.

Valli

7. Valli was sensitive, but at the same time, she was fearless and quite determined. Think of another character from your textbook, who displayed similar traits.

Compare and contrast the lives of Valli and the other character, that you have chosen from the text of 'Two Stories about Flying'.

You may begin this way

The characters who are fearless and determined from two texts are Valli and ....

(Reference: Madam Rides the Bus and Two Stories about Flying) **CBSE 2024**

Ans. The characters who are fearless and determined from two texts are Valli from 'Madam Rides the Bus' and the young seagull from 'His First Flight' in 'Two Stories about Flying'. Both these characters exhibit remarkable courage and determination, overcoming their fears and embarking on ventures that mark significant milestones in their lives.

Valli, a young girl, is fascinated by the idea of riding the bus and exploring the world outside her village. Despite being only eight years old and without informing any adult, she plans her journey meticulously, saves money and takes the bus to town, all by herself.

On the other hand, the young seagull in 'His First Flight' is initially depicted as timid and fearful, hesitating to make his first flight off the ledge. Unlike Valli, who embarks on her journey out of a sense of adventure, the seagull is driven by a more basic instinct - the necessity to fly. Pressured by hunger and encouraged by his family, he ultimately overcomes his fear, takes the leap and discovers the exhilaration of flying.

Comparing the two, one can see both contrasts and similarities in their experiences.

8. Examine how both 'Madam Rides the Bus' and 'Tea from Assam' (Glimpses of India III), celebrate the power of exploration, with reference to Valli and Rajvir, respectively. **CBSE Additionally SQP 2023**

Ans. The chapters 'Madam Rides the Bus' and 'Tea from Assam' contain characters that have the power of imagination. Both Valli and Rajvir are not content with just knowing the places they are born in. They wish to travel, and see the beauty and wonder of the great world beyond their hometowns. The desire to ride the bus and see the sights on the journey empowers Valli to plan precisely and save up money. On the other hand, Rajvir makes sure to fulfill his desire of seeing the wonderful tea estates of Assam. He reads up about them in various books and his imagination was so fired up that he decided to accompany his college friend Pranjol to Assam.

Having an explorative spirit and a curious mind are wonderful qualities which help in the development of intellectual as well as physical capabilities of a human being. Journeys always teach new things to travellers. As such, Valli was introduced to the concept of death and the limitations of human understanding. Meanwhile Rajvir's explorative spirit inspired him to learn as much as he could on his visit to the Dhekiabari Tea estate, which was managed by Pranjol's father.

ASSESSMENT EXERCISE

Extract Based Questions

Read the given extract carefully and answer the questions that follow.

"Oh, please don't be angry with me, my fine madam," he said. "Here, have a seat right up there in front. Everybody move aside please - make way for madam." It was the slack time of day and there were only six or seven passengers on the bus. They were all looking at Valli and laughing with the conductor. Valli was overcome with shyness. Avoiding everyone's eyes, she walked quickly to an empty seat and sat down. "May we start now, madam?" the conductor asked, smiling. Then he blew his whistle twice and the bus moved forward with a roar.

(i) What do you understand by 'slack time of the day'?

(a) The time at which very few people travel, such as afternoon

(b) The time between morning and noon

(c) The time at which most people travel for their work

(d) The time at which Valli used to ride the bus

(ii) Why did Valli avoid everyone's eyes when she got on the bus?

(iii) Select the option that correctly captures the usage of the word 'slack' in the above extract.

(a) He slept deeply, refreshed by a little slack in the daily routine.

(b) I picked up the rod and wound in the slack.

(c) Slacking the outhaul allows you to adjust the sail.

(d) The workload can be evened out, instead of the shop having busy times and slack periods.

(iv) Choose a word from the extract to complete the following.

Overwhelm : Overcome : : Hesitation : ....

Short Answer (SA) Type Questions

1. What did the conductor advise Valli?
2. What did Valli do when the conductor asked her to get down the bus on reaching the town?
3. How did the bus passengers make Valli desirous for a bus ride?
4. How did Valli behave in the bus?
5. Why did Valli's aunt compare her with a grown up lady?

Long Answer (LA) Type Questions

1. On seeing the dead cow Valli felt very bad. Do you think there are people even today who feel bad for the animals? Why do you think such accidents happen?
2. Why do you think the old woman suggested Valli not to travel alone in the bus? Was she right in doing so?
3. Whenever we want to achieve something, difficulties always come in our way. What did Valli have to do to go and ride in a bus? **CBSE 2023**

The Sermon at Benares

by Betty Renshaw

CHAPTER

CHAPTER SUMMARY The following chapter 'The Sermon at Benares' has been taken from Betty Renshaw's book titled 'Values and Voices : A College Reader [1975]'. This chapter highlights the wisdom taught by Buddha in his first sermon at Benares. It was given after he attained enlightenment. In this sermon, Buddha talked about the incident related to the death of Kisa Gotami's only son. Through the story, he preaches that we must not be sad or sorrowful about the death of any of our near or dear ones. Nobody is free from death as all are subject to it. Only when we overcome grief we can get free from sorrows. Then we can get peace.

Gautama's Early life

Gautama Buddha (563 B.C.–483 B.C.) was born as a prince named Siddhartha Gautama in Northern India. When he was twelve years old, he was sent for schooling in the Hindu sacred scriptures. Four years later, he returned home and got married to a princess with whom he had a son. He lived a royal life for ten years, protected from all the sufferings of the world.

Gautama Feels Sufferings of the World

Gautama was 25 years old when he saw the sight of sufferings present in the world. One day, on his way to hunt, he saw a sick man, an aged man, a funeral procession and a monk begging for money or food. The sights had a deep impact on Gautama. He gave up on his royal life and went out to seek enlightenment about the sorrows he had witnessed (seen).

Gautama Seeks Enlightenment

Gautama travelled aimlessly for seven years and then, sat under a *peepal* tree until he attained enlightenment. He got enlightened after seven days and renamed the tree as 'Bodhi Tree' (Tree of Wisdom). He began to teach his new understandings and came to be known as the Buddha which means the 'Awakened' or the 'Enlightened'.

As Buddha, Gautama gave his first Sermon in Benares, the holiest of the dipping places on the river Ganges. The Sermon shows Buddha's wisdom about suffering.

The First Sermon of Buddha

Kisa Gotami's only son had died. She was so sad that she carried her dead son and went to her neighbours asking for medicines for her dead child. Eventually, she met a man who told her to go to Sakyamuni Buddha who could possibly have a solution for her problem. Kisa Gotami went to Buddha and asked him to cure his son. Buddha asked her to bring a handful of mustard seeds from a house where no one had lost a family member.

Kisa Gotami went from house to house in search of mustard seeds but she could not find any house where no one had ever died. Tired and hopeless she sat down at the wayside. As she saw the city lights shinning in darkness, she realised that human life is same for everyone. She realised that all humans beings will have to die and nobody can escape from it. The only person who can be immortal is the person who is not selfish at all.

Certainty of Death

Through the story, Buddha preached that our life is full of pain and sufferings. Everyone who is born has to die. It is not possible to avoid death. Everyone irrespective of the difference has to die because death is inevitable for all mortals. He further added that wise men understand the unavoidability of death. They do not lament, grieve or complain and are thus peaceful and away from sorrow. If one keeps on grieving, one will suffer both physically and mentally. Only those who move on are blessed.

Word Meaning

Word	Meaning
sacred	holy
scriptures	the holy writings of a religion
befitted	appropriate
heretofore	before now
shielded	protected
alms	money or food given to poor people
enlightenment	a state of high spiritual knowledge
chanced upon	came across by chance
wandered	moved in a leisurely or aimless way
vowed	a serious promise to do something
awakened	enlightened
sermon	a talk on a religious or moral subject
inscrutable	impossible to understand or interpret

Word	Meaning
repaired	went
procure	obtain
beloved	dearly loved
weary	feeling or showing extreme tiredness
flickered	shone unsteadily
extinguished	put out
valley of desolation	place filled with deep sorrow
mortals	those bound to die
earthen	made of baked or fired clay
kinsmen	near relatives
lamenting	expressing sorrow, regret or unhappiness about something
slaughter	the killing of animals for their meat
afflicted	affected

NCERT FOLDER

NCERT Intext and Exercise Questions

THINKING ABOUT THE TEXT

(NCERT PAGE 113)

Q.1 When her son dies, Kisa Gotami goes from house to house. What does she ask for? Does she get it? Why not?

Ans. When Kisa Gotami's son died, she went from house to house and asked for some medicine that would cure her child.

No, she did not get it because her child was dead and no medicine could have brought him back to life.

Q.2 Kisa Gotami again goes from house to house after she speaks with the Buddha. What does she ask for, the second time around? Does she get it? Why not?

Or **What does Kisa Gotami ask for when she goes from house to house after she speaks with Buddha? Does she get it? Why or why not?** **CBSE 2023**

Ans. The second time around Kisa Gotami asked for a handful of mustard seeds from a house in which no one has died. Kisa Gotami went from door to door, but couldn't find a single house where death had not taken a loved one away. Therefore, she could not get the mustard seeds.

Q.3 What does Kisa Gotami understand the second time that she failed to understand the first time? Was this what the Buddha wanted her to understand?

Or **What lesson did Kisa Gotami learn the second time that she had failed to learn the first time?** **CBSE 2020**

Ans. Kisa Gotami understood the second time that death is common to all. She understood that she was being selfish in her grief. There was no house where some beloved had not died. Yes, this was what the Buddha wanted her to understand.

Q.4 Why do you think Kisa Gotami understood this only the second time? In what way did the Buddha change her understanding?

Ans. Kisa Gotami understood this only the second time because she found that there was not a single house where a loved one had not died.

The Buddha changed her understanding by asking her to get a handful of mustard seeds from a house in which no one had ever died. When Kisa went to all the houses, she found she could not get the mustard seeds. Later, when she sat and thought about it, she realised that the fate of humans is such that they have to die. This shift in perspective helped her understand that she is not alone in her suffering, allowing her to aceept her loss and find peace.

Q.5 How do you usually understand the idea of 'selfishness'? Do you agree with Kisa Gotami that she was being 'selfish in her grief'?

Ans. I understand the idea of selfishness as being concerned only about one's own interests. I also understand it to mean showing complete disregard for others' interests.

Yes, I agree with Kisa Gotami that she was being 'selfish in her grief'. After her son's death, she was unable to see that death is something that strikes all living beings.

THINKING ABOUT LANGUAGE

(NCERT PAGE 114)

I. This text is written in an old-fashioned style, for it reports an incident more than two millennia old. Look for the following words and phrases in the text, and try to rephrase them in more current language, based on how you understand them.

- give thee medicine for thy child
- Pray tell me
- Kisa repaired to the Buddha
- there was no house but someone had died in it
- kinsmen
- Mark!

Ans.
- give you medicine for your child.
- Please tell me.
- Kisa went to the Buddha.
- there was no house in which no one had died in it.
- relatives.
- Listen!

II. You know that we can combine sentences using words like and, or, but, yet and then. But sometimes no such word seems appropriate. In such a case, we can use a semicolon (;) or a dash (—) to combine two clauses. She has no interest in music; I doubt she will become a singer like her mother.
The second clause here gives the speaker's opinion on the first clause.
Here is a sentence from the text that uses semicolons to combine clauses. Break up the sentence into three simple sentences. Can you then say which has a better rhythm when you read it, the single sentence using semicolons, or the three simple sentences?
For there is not any means by which those who have been born can avoid dying; after reaching old age there is death; of such a nature are living beings.

Ans. For there is not any means by which those who have been born can avoid dying. After reaching old age there is death. Of such a nature are living beings.

The single sentence using semicolons has a better rhythm when I read it. This is because the three parts of the sentence are connected to each other in their meanings.

The second clause gives further information on the first clause.

The third clause is directly related to both the first and the second. However, their meanings are better conveyed when they are joined by semicolons.

WRITING

Write a page (about three paragraphs) on one of the following topics. You can think about the ideas in the text that are relevant to these topics, and add your own ideas and experiences to them.

Q.1 Teaching someone to understand a new or difficult idea.

Ans. Teaching someone to comprehend a new or difficult concept is a delicate process that requires patience, empathy and a strategic approach. Whether the idea is rooted in mathematics, science, philosophy or an art form, the aim is to facilitate understanding by breaking down the complexities, engaging the learner and nurturing a continuous dialogue.

The first step in teaching a difficult idea is to strive for clarity. This involves simplifying the concept while preserving its essential components. Engagement is essential when teaching challenging material. To foster engagement, educators can incorporate interactive elements into the learning process. This might include hands-on activities, discussions, or problem-solving sessions that encourage active participation.

Creating a safe environment that encourages questioning is also critical to engagement. Students should feel comfortable admitting when they do not understand something. This can be achieved through open-ended questions, prompting discussion, and reassuring students that inquiry is a vital part of the learning process. Further, understanding the unique backgrounds, strengths, and learning styles of each student allows educators to tailor their approach accordingly.

Thus, teaching someone to understand a new or difficult idea is both an art and a science that requires clarity, engagement, and adaptability. Ultimately, the goal of teaching is not just to convey information but to empower individuals to think critically and engage with the world around them. Facilitating this understanding is one of the most rewarding aspects of education, shaping lifelong learners who can tackle complexity with confidence and curiosity.

Q.2 Helping each other to get over difficult times.

Ans. Helping each other through difficult times is a powerful reminder of the strength found in community and compassion. When individuals face challenges, whether emotional, financial or physical, the support of others can make all the difference. A kind word, a listening ear or a helping hand can alleviate burden from and provide comfort during moments of struggle. By offering empathy, understanding and practical assistance, we create an environment where people feel less isolated and more equipped to navigate hardships. Together, we can build resilience, foster hope and remind one another that no one has to face adversity alone. Through solidarity and mutual care, we pave the way for healing and growth.

Q.3 Thinking about oneself as unique, or as one among billions of others

Ans. There are billions of people worldwide, and each has their own story, experiences and feelings. However, we are all united too. Just like Kisa Gotami in the story of the Buddha, we often face our struggles and pain. At times, we may feel alone in our grief or challenges, thinking that no one else understands what we are going through. However, it is important to realise that many others share similar feelings. This understanding can help us feel less isolated and more connected to the world around us.

Recognising our uniqueness is also essential. Each person has talents, dreams, and perspectives. For example, some people may be great at art, while others excel in sports or academics. Celebrating our strengths helps us grow and contribute to society. Just like the Buddha taught Kisa Gotami about the nature of life and death, we can learn from each other's experiences. By sharing our stories and listening to others, we can better understand ourselves and the people around us.

REVIEW EXERCISE

Including Competency Based Questions

Part - I

Multiple Choice Questions

1. Prince Siddhartha lived for ten years as <u>befitted royalty</u>. What does the underlined phrase mean?

(a) Royal person

(b) Someone who lives by royal treasures

(c) Someone who lives as a king or a queen should

(d) None of the above

Ans. (c) Someone who lives as a king or a queen should

2. What could be the reason for shielding Prince Siddhartha from the sufferings of the world?

(a) To prevent him from becoming a great spiritual leader as foretold on his birth

(b) He was unable to accept the truth about the sufferings of the world

(c) He did not want to see the sufferings of the world

(d) None of the above

Ans. (a) To prevent him from becoming a great spiritual leader as foretold on his birth.

3. The Buddha did not see much suffering during his early years. Provide support for the statement from the text. Competency Based

(a) To illustrate a point

(b) To garner sympathy from the readers

(c) To provide an example of the Buddha's experiences

(d) To identify important turning points in the Buddha's life

Ans. (d) To identify important turning points in the Buddha's life

4. What is the main idea expressed in the first paragraph? Competency Based

(a) Who the Buddha was?

(b) What the Buddha's life was like?

(c) Why the Buddha became enlightened?

(d) How the Buddha became enlightened?

Ans. (d) How the Buddha became enlightened?

5. "She has lost her senses. The boy is dead." – Who is 'she' and 'the boy' in the given sentence?

(a) Kisa Gotami and her dead husband

(b) Kisa Gotami and Gautama Buddha

(c) Kisa Gotami and her dead son

(d) Kisa Gotami and a man from neighbourhood

Ans. (c) Kisa Gotami and her dead son

6. **Why did Kisa Gotami want to bring her dead child back to life? Choose the least possible reason.**
(a) She could not accept the truth that her only son was dead.
(b) She believed in rebirths.
(c) She believed that medicine could cure her son.
(d) She knew her son would not have died at such a young age.

Ans. (b) She believed in rebirths.

7. **"The mustard seed must be taken from a house where no one has lost a child, husband, parent or friend." Why did the Buddha lay this condition?** **Competency Based**
(a) He wanted to see how committed she was.
(b) He wanted to get rid of her as soon as possible.
(c) He needed specific materials to achieve a miracle.
(d) He wanted to show her that everyone must deal with death.

Ans. (d) He wanted to show her that everyone must deal with death.

8. **What does the metaphor of the ox show?** **Competency Based**
(a) The inevitability of death
(b) The helplessness of relatives
(c) The terrible nature of the world
(d) The wisdom in accepting one's faith

Ans. (a) The inevitability of death

9. **Why is Kisa Gotami mentioned in the sermon?** **Competency Based**
(a) To illustrate a point
(b) To garner sympathy from the readers
(c) To provide an example of the Buddha's experiences
(d) To identify important turning points in the Buddha's life

Ans. (a) To illustrate a point

10. **How does the sermon end?** **Competency Based**
(a) With a suggestion (b) On a note of warning
(c) With a piece of advice (d) In a tone of judgement

Ans. (c) With a piece of advice

11. **What does the sermon in the chapter 'The Sermon at Benares' reflect?**
(a) Buddha's wisdom (b) Buddha's enlightenment
(c) Story of Kisa Gotami (d) Death is common to all

Ans. (a) Buddha's wisdom

12. **What does the word 'enlightenment' mean in the context of the chapter 'The Sermon at Benares'?**
(a) A state of being innocent
(b) A state of high spiritual knowledge
(c) A state of deserted brain
(d) A state of begging alms

Ans. (b) A state of high spiritual knowledge

13. **Which of the following statement is not true in accordance with the chapter 'The Sermon at Benares'?**
(i) The real name of Gautama Budhha was Prince Devdatt.
(ii) The sight of a monk begging alms moved the prince towards the path of enlightenment.
(iii) Kisa Gotami was grieving for her dead husband.
(iv) It took Gautama Buddha ten years to gain enlightenment.
(v) Prince Siddhartha was married at the age of sixteen.
(vi) Prince Siddhartha was shielded from the sufferings of the world till twenty five years of his life.
(a) (i), (iv) and (v) (b) (i), (iii) and (iv)
(c) (ii), (v) and (vi) (d) (i), (ii) and (iii)

Ans. (b) Statements (i), (iii) and (iv)

14. **Which of the following are the teachings of Buddha as mentioned in the chapter 'The Sermon at Benares'?**
(i) The life of mortals in this world is troubled and brief and combined with pain.
(ii) There is no means by which those that have been born can avoid dying.
(iii) The fate of men is like city lights which flicker up and then extinguish again in darkness.
(iv) Not from weeping nor from grieving will anyone obtain peace of mind.
(a) Only (i) (b) (ii) and (iii)
(c) (i), (ii) and (iv) (d) None of these

Ans. (c) (i), (ii) and (iv)

15. **The tone of the text is mainly** **Competency Based**
(a) heartless (b) righteous (c) cautionary (d) patronising

Ans. (b) righteous

Extract Based Questions

1. **Read the following extract carefully and answer the questions that follow.**

At twelve, he was sent away for schooling in the Hindu sacred scriptures and years later he returned home to marry a princess. They had a son and lived for ten years as befitted royalty.

At about the age of twenty-five, the prince hereto fore shielded from the sufferings of the world, while going out on hunting, chanced upon a sick man, then an aged man, then a funeral procession, and finally a monk begging for alms. These sights so moved him that he at once became a beggar and went out into the world to seek enlightenment concerning the sorrows he had witnessed.

(i) What was the unintended effect of the sights Buddha saw?

(a) He felt dejected and sorrowful
(b) He renounced royalty
(c) He decided to become an ascetic
(d) He decided to consult a pandit

Ans. (b) He renounced royalty

(ii) Which phrase would correctly substitute 'chanced upon' in the given sentence from the extract?

"......... while going out on hunting, chanced upon a sick man, then ...." **Competency Based**

Ans. 'Ran into'

(iii) What did the sights Gautama witnessed at the age of twenty-five years drive him to?

Ans. The sights Gautama witnessed at the age of twenty-five years moved him to become an ascetic. He went out into the world to seek enlightenment concerning the sorrows he had witnessed. He wandered for seven years and finally sat down under a peepal tree, where he vowed to stay until enlightenment came.

(iv) Why was Prince Siddhartha send away at the age of twelve?

Ans. Prince Siddhartha was sent away at the age of twelve for schooling in sacred Hindu scriptures.

2. Read the following extract carefully and answer the questions that follow.

He wandered for seven years and finally sat down under a peepal tree, where he vowed to stay until enlightenment came. Enlightened after seven days, he renamed the tree the Bodhi Tree and began to teach and to share his new understandings. At that point he became known as the Buddha.

(i) What was the name of the peepal tree under which Buddha sat?

(a) Buddha tree
(b) Bodhi tree
(c) Enlightened tree
(d) No special name was given to the tree

Ans. (b) Bodhi tree

(ii) What did Siddhartha do while sitting under the tree?

Ans. Siddhartha vowed to achieve enlightenment while sitting under the peepal tree. He achieved enlightenment after seven days. After that, Siddhartha renamed the tree as 'Bodhi Tree'. He also began to teach and share his new understandings while sitting under the tree.

(iii) Buddha vowed to sit under a peepal tree until enlightenment came. Which of his qualities is evident from this act?

1. Determined **2. Distracted**
3. True to his word **4. Crafty**
5. Insouciant

Ans. 1 and 3

(iv) Complete the analogy by selecting the suitable word from the text.

Deceitful : Mendacious :: Pledged : ....

Ans. Vowed

3. Read the following extract carefully and answer the questions that follow.

The Buddha preached his first sermon at the city of Benares, most holy of the dipping places on the River Ganges; that sermon has been preserved and is given here. It reflects the Buddha's wisdom about one inscrutable kind of suffering.

(i) Read the given statements and choose the correct answer. **Competency Based**

1. Buddha preached his first sermon at Benares.

2. Buddha sat under Bodhi tree.

(a) 1 is true 2 is false
(b) 2 is true 1 is false
(c) Both are true
(d) Both are false

Ans. (c) Both are true

(ii) What does the sermon preached by Buddha reflect?

Ans. The sermon preached by Buddha reflects his wisdom about one unavoidable kind of suffering.

(iii) What was the topic of the first sermon of Buddha?

Ans. The topic of the first sermon was an inscrutable kind of suffering. Buddha wanted to teach that death is inevitable and that people must seek peace.

(iv) Find the exact word from the extract which means 'impossible to understand'.

Ans. 'Inscrutable' from the extract means 'impossible to understand'.

4. Read the following extract carefully and answer the questions that follow.

Poor Kisa Gotami now went from house to house, and the people pitied her and said, "Here is mustard-seed; take it!" But when she asked, "Did a son or daughter, a father or mother, die in your family?"

they answered her, "Alas! the living are few, but the dead are many. Do not remind us of our deepest grief." And there was no house but some beloved one had died in it. **CBSE Question Bank 2021**

(i) **The community's response to Kisa in the above extract was somewhat different from before. That was the case beacuse ....**

Ans. they were able to help Kisa in some way this time.

(ii) **What was the condition set by Buddha in front of Kisa Gotami? What is the significance of this request?** **Competency Based**

Ans. Buddha requested for a handful of mustard seeds because it is easy to procure and available in every household. The condition set by Buddha was to get the mustard seeds from a household where no one had lost a child, husband, parent, or friend to death. The purpose of this request was to make Kisa Gotami realise the universal nature of death.

(iii) **Pick the option that explains — '...the living are few, but the dead are many.'**

(a) It shows the high death rate and low birth rate in the city of Benares.
(b) It highlights the holy status of Benares where many Hindus go to die.
(c) It throws light on the numerous loved ones the villagers had lost over time.
(d) It reflects that many children who had died in the village for various reasons.

Ans. (c) It throws light on the numerous loved ones the villagers had lost over time.

(iv) **Why has Kisa Gotami been called poor?**

Ans. Kisa Gotami has been called poor because she was beset with an unfathomable grief - the death of her son. In her grief she was beginning to lose her grip on reality. Thus she was called poor Kisa Gotami.

5. Read the following extract carefully and answer the questions that follow.

"Not from weeping nor from grieving will anyone obtain peace of mind; on the contrary, his pain will be the greater and his body will suffer. He will make himself sick and pale, yet the dead are not saved by his lamentation. He who seeks peace should draw out the arrow of lamentation and complaint, and grief."

CBSE Question Bank 2021 Modified

(i) **What effect does weeping or grieving have on us?**

(a) Our body suffers
(b) Pain becomes greater
(c) Both (a) and (b)
(d) People become unwise

Ans. (c) Both (a) and (b)

(ii) **How can a person seek peace?**

Ans. The person can seek peace by not lamenting, complaining and grieving for the death of loved ones.

(iii) **Find the exact word from the text which means 'to express sadness about something'.**

Ans. 'Lamentation' from the extract means 'to express sadness about something.

(iv) **Read the following descriptions (a) - (c) and identify which one correctly corresponds to the extract.**

(a) A debate is a formal discussion on a particular topic, usually with two or more people presenting different viewpoints and arguments.
(b) A homily is a talk on a spiritual or moral subject.
(c) A hypothesis is a proposed explanation for a phenomenon.

Ans. (b) A homily is a talk on a spiritual or moral subject.

Part - II

Short Answer Type Questions

1. The Buddha did not see much suffering during his early years. Provide support for the statement from the text. **Competency Based**

Ans. It is evident from the text that Buddha didn't see much suffering during his early years. Buddha knew nothing of the sufferings of the world until the age of 25. He had been shielded from the sufferings of the world. Therefore, when he finally witnessed the sufferings of the world while he was out on a hunt, he was deeply affected.

2. What was the effect of observing the sufferings of the world on Buddha?

Or **"These sights so moved him that he at once went out into the world to seek enlightenment." What were the sights that moved him?** **CBSE 2022 Term II**

Ans. The sights of suffering sick man, old man, funeral process and a beggar had a deep impact on Buddha. He was so affected by the sufferings that he at once left his royal life in search of enlightenment and an understanding of the world around him.

3. Kisa Gotami was hopeful when she talked to the Buddha. Do you agree? Justify your response. **Competency Based**

Ans. Yes, Kisa Gotami was very hopeful when she talked to Buddha. She was delusional in her grief over the death of her son and hoped to revive him with some medicine. Therefore, when Buddha agreed to revive her son she was very hopeful.

4. Why did Kisa Gotami meet the Buddha? How did Buddha change her life? **CBSE 2023**

Ans. Kisa Gotami met the Buddha when her son had died and she was looking for medicine to revive her son. Buddha taught her that death is an inevitable reality of life which is shared by all humans. In this way, Buddha changed her life by teaching her the way to deal with grief.

5. What does Kisa Gotami understand from watching the lights? **Competency Based**

Or **How did Kisa Gotami realise that life and death is a process?**

Ans. Kisa Gotami sat down to watch the lights of the city as they flickered up and were extinguished again. Soon everything was covered in darkness as night fell. Then, Kisa Gotami understood that human life is exactly like those lights; they flicker up like bright lights but they must be extinguished at the end of the day. This is how Kisa Gotami understood the reality of the inevitability of death.

6. Why was Kisa Gotami sad? What did she do in her hour of grief?

Or **What did Kisa Gotami do after the death of her only son?** **CBSE 2023**

Ans. Kisa Gotami was sad over the death of her only son. In the hour of grief, she went house to house in order to find medicine for her son that could bring him to life. However, nobody could provide any medicine because his son was dead.

7. According to Kisa Gotami, what is the greatest grief of life? What should a wise person do when he or she is faced with such a situation?

Ans. According to Kisa Gotami, the greatest grief in life is the death of one's loved ones. Instead of lamenting on it, the wise should accept the truth of death. Weeping will only increase the pain and disturb the peace of mind of a person.

8. According to Buddha, who are wise men?

Ans. According to Buddha, wise men are those people who never complain or lament over their loss. They accept the truth and move on such people are calm and composed. They lead a blessed and peaceful life.

9. Elucidate any one quality that Siddhartha demonstrated when he gave up his status and family. Explain your choice. **CBSE Question Bank 2021**

Ans. Siddhartha demonstrated compassion, kindness and his determination in his decision to leave behind his family and princehood. He felt sympathetic towards others. He was disturbed to see people's sufferings and wanted to find out a solution to eradicate their sufferings and diseases.

10. Do you think being enlightened placed a far greater responsibility on the Buddha than being king would have? Justify your stance. **CBSE Question Bank 2021**

Ans. Yes, enlightenment placed far greater responsibilities than being a king would have on Buddha. As a king, he was more concerned with the physical well-being of only his countrymen but now he had an obligation to take care of the whole of humanity. As Buddha, he owed the responsibility of preaching and educating the people about the truth that he had realised.

11. What did Buddha say about death and suffering?

Or **Through the story of Kisa Gotami, what did the Buddha try to preach to the common man?** **CBSE 2023**

Or **Not from weeping nor from giving will anyone obtain peace of mind, on the contrary his pain will be greater and his body will suffer. Validate this preaching of the Buddha with reference to the story 'The Sermon at Benaras'.** **CBSE 2024 C**

Ans. Buddha said about death and suffering that they are part and parcel of life. None can avoid this truth. We have to meet our destined end one day. Whoever has come to the world, will die one day. In the hour of grief, we must remain calm and composed so that grief doesn't overcome us.

People who are wise, never complain or lament over their loss. They accept the truth and are blessed with it. So, wisdom lies in the fact that people should not get distressed with pain, suffering and death.

12. What is the significance of the Buddha's request for a handful of mustard seeds and the addition of a condition to it? **CBSE SQP Term II, 2022**

Ans. The Buddha's request of a handful of mustard seeds that seems extremely simple at first. However, it is the handful of mustard seeds that makes Kisa realise the universal nature and the inevitability of death. Hence, his request is very significant. The Buddha asked her to procure the seeds from a house where no one had lost a family member or a friend and at the end of her search Kisa is left empty handed.

This entire process ends her agony as she is finally able to deal with the loss of her son and understand that loss and death have not only affected her but also many other people.

13. How, according to Buddha, can one obtain peace of mind? **CBSE 2022 Term II**

Ans. According to Buddha, a person can get peace of mind only if they draw out the arrows of lamentation, complaint and grief. Buddha says that those who overcome all sorrows become free from disillusion, get peace of mind and are blessed.

14. Grief is often seen as a measure of love. Justify your response to Buddha's sermon. CBSE 2022 Term II

Ans. Buddha's sermon aims to make the person who is grief-stricken realise that grief and lamentation destroy peace of mind and grief can never help a person. Instead, only through the acceptance of loss and by letting go of the complaints can a grieving individual feel solace.

15. What is the main idea expressed in the sermon? Competency Based

Ans. The main idea expressed in the sermon is the reality of this world. Buddha says that the world is a valley of death, and death is common to all living creatures. Buddha teaches that since the life of mortals in this world is troubled and combined with pain, therefore we must not linger over the grief. We must seek peace by composing ourselves and drawing out the arrow of lamentation.

16. "As ripe fruits are in danger of falling early, so mortals, when born, are always in danger of death." With this statement of the Buddha, find out the moral values that Kisa Gotami learnt after the death of her child. CBSE 2023

Ans. Kisa Gotami learned the following values after the death of her child

Death and sorrow are the inevitable truths of life. Life is full of suffering, trials and tribulations, and each person must overcome them. Real wisdom is to accept the inevitability of death and continue to move ahead with the journey of life.

Long Answer Type Questions

1. Describe the journey of Siddhartha Gautama becoming the Buddha. CBSE 2020

Ans. Gautama Buddha was born in 563 BC in a royal family. His name was Siddhartha Gautama. At the age of twelve, he was sent away for schooling. He studied all the sacred Hindu scriptures. At the age of sixteen, he married a princess and later, they had a son. He lived a royal life for ten years and was shielded from the sufferings of the world.

However, when Siddhartha was twenty five, he saw a sick man, then an aged man and a funeral procession. Finally, he came across a monk begging for alms. This was his first encounter with the harsh realities of life. These sights made him so sad that he decided to renounce the worldly pleasures. He left his family and became a monk to seek spiritual knowledge.

Siddhartha Gautama wandered for seven years in search of wisdom and truth. Finally, he sat down under a big peepal tree to meditate. He vowed to stay there until he got enlightenment. After seven days, Gautama got enlightenment.

He came to be known as 'The Buddha' which means 'enlightened' or 'the awakened'. He began to teach and spread his message of wisdom and truth.

2. Life is full of trials and tribulations. Kisa Gotami also passes through a period of grief in her life. How does she behave in those circumstances?

Or **How did the Buddha make Kisa Gotami realise the reality of death?** CBSE 2020

Or **How does Buddha bring about a different perspective in Kisa Gotami's understanding of life?** CBSE 2022 Term II

Ans. After the death of Kisa Gotami's only child, she became very sad. She carried her dead child to her neighbours in order to get medicine to bring him to life. Her neighbours thought that she had gone insane as she was unable to accept the fact that her child is dead. It was then that someone suggested her to meet Gautama Buddha.

When she met Gautama Buddha, he asked her to collect mustard seeds from a house where no one had ever died. Kisa Gotami went from one house to another but was unable to find a single house in the town where no one had died. In this way, she realised that death is a part of life and anyone who is born is bound to die one day.

Thus, Buddha changed her understanding of death by this exercise. Buddha told her that only the wise do not grieve; instead they accept the reality. Mourning brings only pain and sufferings to the body. One who is composed obtains peace of mind and will be free from sorrow and be blessed. This gave her strength to overcome grief.

3. Through the story of Kisa Gotami what did the Buddha try to preach to the common man? CBSE 2020

Or **What lesson on death and suffering did the Buddha teach Gotami in the chapter, 'The Sermon at Benaras'?** CBSE 2018

Or **What does the Buddha say about the world?** CBSE 2023

Ans. The lesson that Buddha taught through the story was that death and suffering are part and parcel of life. No one can avoid this truth. One has to meet one's destined end one day. Whoever has come into this world will die one day. Thus, in the hour of grief for a loved one who has died, one must remain calm and composed. Then, one shouldn't occupy oneself with grief. Otherwise, they will feel the pain more.

People who are wise never complain or lament over their loss. They never try to bring back to life their loved ones who are dead, as Gotami wanted to do. They accept the truth and overcome their sorrow. People who overcome their sorrow will be blessed. So, wisdom is in the fact that people should not get distressed with pain, suffering or death.

4. Timely help and sympathy are a great help for those who are in grief. Gautama Buddha helped Kisa Gotami by his kind words and guidance in overcoming her grief. It is a big relief for grieving persons if support and care are extended to them. How are kindness and sympathy important in a peaceful and joyful life? CBSE 2023

Ans. Kindness and sympathy are very important for a joyful life. This can be explained through the example of Kisa Gotami. When Kisa Gotami's son died, she was distraught with grief. Thus, she could not understand the fact that death is inevitable. When she was walking around carrying the dead body of her son in the hope that someone would help her, no one helped her although everyone was sympathetic. This sympathy directed her to Buddha who understood the situation and treated Kisa Gotami with kindness and sympathy. This kindness allowed her to finally understand the truth about life and death. This acceptance would eventually open up the doors to mental peace and contentment. Thus, kindness and sympathy are two important aspects of a peaceful and joyful life.

ASSESSMENT EXERCISE

Extract Based Questions

Read the following extract carefully and answer the questions that follow.

Kisa Gotami became weary and hopeless, and sat down at the wayside watching the lights of the city, as they flickered up and were extinguished again. At last the darkness of the night reigned everywhere. And she considered the fate of men, that their lives flicker up and are extinguished again. And she thought to herself, "How selfish am I in my grief! Death is common to all; yet in this valley of desolation there is a path that leads him to immortality who has surrendered all selfishness."

(i) Select the option that correctly captures the usage of the word 'weary' in the above extract.

(a) Working on the new project was a weary change.

(b) The weary journey began late in the evening.

(c) She wearied great success in her new business.

(d) It is weary to hear some good news about him.

(ii) What lesson did she learn when she could not find a house where a beloved had never died?

(iii) Which path leads a man to immortality?

(iv) Find the word in the passage which is opposite in meaning to lively.

Short Answer (SA) Type Questions

1. What did Buddha do after he attained enlightenment? Why?
2. Why was the peepal tree later named as Bodhi Tree?
3. How did Buddha teach Kisa Gotami the truth of life?
4. Write in brief the teachings of Buddha as mentioned in lesson.
5. How did Kisa Gotami get to know about Buddha?
6. What did Siddhartha Gautama come across by chance when he was about twenty five years old?

Long Answer (LA) Type Questions

1. The teachings of a great person enable us to face even the most challenging problems in life. How does the lesson explain this statement?
2. A little help and guidance to those who are experiencing grief, may help them understand and overcome grief. It is a big relief for the grieving person if support and care are extended to them. Explain citing examples from the chapter 'The Sermon at Benares'. **Competency Based**

The Proposal (Play)

by Anton Chekov

CHAPTER SUMMARY This play titled 'The Proposal' has been written by the Russian dramatist Anton Chekov in 1888-89. It is a one act play about the tendency among rich families to use marriage as means to increase their wealth. In the story, Ivan Lomov, a rich man goes to his wealthy neighbour, Chubukov's house with a proposal to marry his daughter, Natalya. However, all three of them fight with each other over small issues. Even when the proposal is made, they continue with their quarrels.

Lomov at Chubukov's House

The play begins in a drawing room of Chubukov's house. Ivan Vassilevitch Lomov comes to meet Chubukov. Chubukov is extremely happy to meet him. He is surprised to see Lomov wearing a formal dress and asks him if he is going somewhere. Lomov informs him that he has come to meet him because he needs his help. Chubukov thinks that Lomov must have come to borrow money from him and states privately that he wouldn't give him any money. Finally, Lomov declares that he has come to ask for Natalya's hand for marriage.

Chubukov's Reaction to the Proposal

Chubukov gets very excited after hearing about the proposal. He hugs and kisses Lomov. He informs Lomov that he has been waiting for this proposal since a very long time. He even guarantees that Natalya would also agree to the proposal. He tells Lomov that Natalya is in love with him and goes to call her.

Lomov Thinks about Natalya and His Life

As Chubukov leaves, Lomov is left alone in the drawing room. He starts talking to himself. He considers that he must not allow himself to think about finding a real love otherwise he'll never get married. He finds Natalya Stepanovna to be a good housekeeper. She is well educated and not bad looking. He thinks that he needs to get married now because he is thirty-five years old and needs to live a quiet and peaceful life. He also thinks that he is always restless and cannot sleep properly. Infact, we (readers) find Lomov getting over excited and getting nervous while stating the proposal.

Natalya Meets Lomov

Natalya enters the drawing room and is surprised to see Lomov. She welcomes Lomov and starts talking about the work in the fields. Suddenly, she notices Lomov's dress and enquires if he is going to a ball.

Lomov is about to tell her the purpose of his visit. However, instead of talking about the proposal, Lomov tells her about the good relations between Lomovs and Chubukovs. He also mentions about Oxen Meadows that he has inherited from his aunt.

Argument over Oxen Meadows

After hearing Lomov claiming Oxen Meadows as his own, Natalya tells Lomov that the Oxen Meadows does not belong to him. They actually belong to Chubukov. As a result, an argument begins over the Oxen Meadows. Both of them constantly state that the Meadows are owned by them.

Lomov offers to show documents to prove his claims. He clarifies that the Oxen Meadows were once a subject of dispute between their families. His aunt's grandmother gave its free use to the peasants of Natalya's father's grandfather. The peasants used to make bricks for the grandmother. Since the peasants used the meadows for forty years, the Chubukovs started considering the land to be theirs, but now they belong to Lomov.

Argument Continues between Natalya and Lomov

Natalya does not agree and sticks to her point that those meadows belong to them. She insists that the land has been owned by them for nearly 300 years.

Both Lomov and Natalya insist that the land is not worth a lot of money but they want the land as a matter of principle. Lomov offers to make meadows as a present to Natalya. Natalya also says that she can make the meadows a present to Lomov. She reminded Lomov that they had always been good neighbours. They had even lent their threshing-machine to Lomov last year while postponing their own threshing till November. Meanwhile, Lomov gets offended because he believes that Natalya was calling him a land grabber. Natalya declares that she will send her mowers to the Oxen Meadows that very day.

Chubukov Joins the Argument

Chubukov enters the room and gets to know the reason for the argument. He supports Natalya and tells Lomov that Oxen Meadows are owned by them. The quarrel increases to such an extent that Lomov and Chubukov start abusing each other and their families. Chubukov asks Lomov not to talk to him so disrespectfully as he is twice of his age. Lomov calls Chubukov a land grabber and threatens to take Chubukov to the court.

He says that he was an honourable person unlike Chubukov's grandfather who had been tried for embezzlement (theft). This angers Chubukov who states that Lomov's grandfather was a drunkard and his younger aunt Nastasya Mihailovna ran away with an architect. He also calls Lomov a villain, a scarecrow and a monster who has the courage to propose. All this excites Lomov and his health deteriorates. Finally, Chubukov asks Lomov to leave his house and never come back again.

Natalya Gets to Know about the Proposal

As soon as Lomov leaves, Chubukov tells Natalya that Lomov had come to propose her for marriage. When Natalya hears this, she almost faints and starts crying. She blames Chubukov for irritating Lomov and asks him to bring Lomov back. Chubukov goes to get Lomov back.

Another Argument over Dogs

Lomov enters the house again. Natalya tells him that the Oxen Meadows belongs to Lomov and tries to shift the conversation towards the proposal. Then, they start talking about dogs. Lomov tells Natalya that his dog 'Guess' is the best dog. Natalya objects to Lomov's claims and calls her dog 'Squeezer' to be better than Guess. Lomov states that Natalya's dog Squeezer was overshot and that since his lower jaw was shorter than his upper jaw, he was a bad hunter. Natalya denies the claim while calling Lomov's dog Guess old and ugly.

Again, an argument begins. Both of them list the qualities of their dogs and claim their dog to be better than the other. Chubukov states that Lomov's dog had good points such as the fact that he was pure-bred with strong ribs. He also added that Squeezer was also defected because he was old and short in the muzzle. Again the argument grows to such an extent that they start abusing each other.

Chubukov Asks Lomov to Marry Natalya

While they are arguing, Lomov's condition worsens and he falls onto an arm chair. Both Natalya and Chubukov think that he has died and start crying. They think that Natalya's chance of getting married has gone. After sometime, Lomov comes to his senses. Chubukov tells Lomov that Natalya is ready for marriage and that they should get married soon.

He does not want to lose even a single moment and joins their hand. He asks them to kiss each other and blesses them. However, they start arguing about their dogs again while Chubukov calls everyone for Champagne.

Word Meaning

Word	Meaning
get up	dress
pardon	to excuse
to count on	to depend on
by jove	used to express surprise or emphasis
off my balance	excited
consent	to give permission for something
trembling	to shake slightly as you are afraid, nervous, excited, etc
egad	expressing surprise, anger or affirmation
palpitation (of the heart)	to beat quickly and strongly and often in a way that is not regular because of excitement, nervousness, etc
twitch	to make a slight, sudden movement that is not controlled or deliberate
lunatic	a crazy person
neglige	gown
shelling	removing shells
stacked	stored
regard	a feeling of respect and admiration for someone
meadow	a place for grazing cattle
marsh	a place with loose earth and water
wedged	to force into a narrow space, squeeze
perpetuity	the state of continuing for a long time
reckon	believed
dessiatins	a currency
implore	to make a very serious or emotional request to someone
make head or tail	understand
threshing	process of separating the grains from the plant
gypsie	a homeless person
impudent	failing to show proper respect and courtesy
carafe	a water container
mower	a person who cuts grass
clutch	to hold with the hand
hoarse	loud
restrain	to stop somebody from doing something
excruciating	very painful; causing great mental or physical pain
accustomed	habitual
agitating	disturbing, exciting or angering someone
pettifogger	one who argues about small issues
embezzlement	to steal the money of your employer
drunkard	a person who is drunk or who often gets drunk
hump-backed	having a hump at the back

Word	Meaning
guzzle	fat or drink (something) greedily
gambler	one who gambles
intriguer	cheater
malicious	having or showing a desire to cause harm
stagger	to move unsteadily from side to side
rascal	a cruel or dishonest man
scarecrow	a person who is very badly dressed, odd-looking or thin
impudence	quality of not showing respect for others
confounded	used for emphasis, especially to express anger or annoyance
wizen-faced	wrinkle-faced
frump	a colourless person
wail	to cry
hysterics	a wildey emotional and exaggerated reaction
fetch	to go after and bring back someone
heated	angry
lame	having an injured leg or foot that makes walking difficult or painful
twisted	forced out of its natural or proper shape
pedigree	the history of the family members in an animal's past especially when it is good or impressive
thoroughbred	of pure and unmixed breed
overshot	having the upper jaw extending the lower
worn-out	tired
pretend	assume
bursting	to break open or into pieces
rot	(here) rubbish
well-sprung	rounded
purebred (of an animal)	having parents that are of the same breed
muzzle	the usually long nose and mouth of an animal
neck and neck	very close (as in a race)
verst	a Russian unit of distance equal to 1.067 kilometres
worrying	(here) following
liable to	likely to
tracking	(here) hunting
partridge	a bird
milksop	a man who lacks courage
jesuit	one who cheats
damned	used to say that something is not important
bliss	complete happiness

NCERT FOLDER

NCERT Intext and Exercise Questions

THINKING ABOUT THE PLAY (NCERT PAGE 135)

Q.1 What does Chubukov at first suspect that Lomov has come for? Is he sincere when he later says "And I've always loved you, my angel, as if you were my own son"? Find reasons for your answer from the play.

Ans. At first, Chubukov suspected that Lomov had come to borrow money.

Chubukov was not sincere when he told Lomov that he had always loved him and that he was like his own son because he had decided to not give any money to Lomov.

If he truly meant what he said he would not have thought of not giving him money. He said so only because Lomov had asked for his daughter's hand in marriage.

Q.2 Chubukov says of Natalya: "... as if she won't consent! She's in love; egad, she's like a lovesick cat..." Would you agree? Find reasons for your answer.

Ans. Chubukov thought that Lomov was a good marriage prospect for his daughter. He had been waiting for this proposal. When Lomov expressed his doubt regarding Natalya's consent to the proposal, Chubukov immediately told him that she was in love with him. However, this was not true as Natalya did not seem to be in love with Lomov at any point in the play. It seemed like she was more attached to her land, Oxen Meadows and dogs than to Lomov. Infact, the way they kept getting into arguments about trivial matters suggests that neither Lomov nor Natalya was in love with the other.

Q.3 (i) Find all the words and expressions in the play that the characters use to speak about each other, and the accusations and insults they hurl at each other. (For example, Lomov in the end calls Chubukov an intriguer; but earlier, Chubukov has himself called Lomov a "malicious, doublefaced intriguer." Again, Lomov begins by describing Natalya as "an excellent housekeeper, not bad-looking, well-educated.")

(ii) Then think of five adjectives or adjectival expressions of your own to describe each character in the play.

(iii) Can you now imagine what these characters will quarrel about next?

Ans. (i) The words and expressions that have been used to describe each other by various characters of the play are

- Chubukov: intriguer, grabber, old rat;
- Natalya: a lovesick cat, an excellent housekeeper, not bad-looking, well-educated;
- Lomov: a good neighbour, impudent, pettifogger, malicious, double faced intriguer, rascal, blind hen, turnip ghost, a villain, scarecrow, stuffed sausage, etc.

(ii) Some of the adjectives or adjectival expressions that can be used to describe each character are excitable, impractical, nervous, formal, proud, silly, quarrelsome, money-minded, etc.

(iii) Do it yourself (Students can discuss amongst themselves the various subjects that these characters would most probably argue about)

THINKING ABOUT LANGUAGE (NCERT PAGE 137)

Q.1 I. This play has been translated into English from the Russian original. Are there any expressions or ways of speaking that strike you as more Russian than English? For example, would an adult man be addressed by an older man as my darling or my treasure in an English play?

Read through the play carefully, and find expressions that you think are not used in contemporary English, and contrast these with idiomatic modern English expressions that also occur in the play.

Ans. Following are the expressions from the play that are not used in contemporary English.

The following expressions are used by an old man (Chubukov) to address an adult man (Lomov)

(i) My darling (ii) My beauty
(iii) My angel (iv) My precious (v) My beloved

The following expressions are used as insults

(i) The scarecrow (ii) The stuffed sausage
(iii) The wizen-faced frump

The following expressions are used during normal conversations

(i) '... and so on...' (ii) '... and all that'
(iii) '... and all that sort of thing'

Following are the modern english expressions that occur in the play

(i) Madam (ii) My heart
(iii) I beg your pardon (iv) My dear fellow

Q.2 Look up the following phrases in a dictionary to find out their meaning, and then use each in a sentence of your own. (i) You may take it that (ii) He seems to be coming round (iii) My foot's gone to sleep.

Ans. (i) You may take it that- You should think that

You may take it that your hard work has truly paid off, earning you the well-deserved recognition and success you now enjoy.

(ii) He seems to be coming around- He seems to be recovering

He seems to be coming around after the horrible accident on New Year's Eve.

(iii) My foot's gone to sleep- When one cannot feel anything in one's legs

After sitting here for so long, my foot's gone to sleep.

II. Reported Speech You must have noticed that when we report someone's exact words, we have to make some changes in the sentence structure. In the following sentences fill in the blanks to list the changes that have occurred in the above pairs of sentences. One has been done for you.

1. To report a question, we use the reporting verb asked (as in Sentence Set 1).
2. To report a statement, we use the reporting verb ....
3. The adverb of place 'here' changes to ....
4. When the verb in direct speech is in the present tense, the verb in reported speech is in the.................. tense (as in Sentence Set 3).
5. If the verb in direct speech is in the present continuous tense, the verb in reported speech changes to .... tense. For example, ... changes to was getting.
6. When the sentence in direct speech contains a word denoting respect, we add the adverb .... in the reporting clause (as in Sentence Set 1).
7. The pronouns I, me, our and mine, which are used in the first person in direct speech, change according to the subject or object of the reporting verb such as.............. .... or........... in reported speech.

Ans. 2. declared 3. there
4. past 5. past continuous, is getting
6. respectfully 7. he/she, him/her, their, his/ hers

III. Here is an excerpt from an article the Times of India dated 27th August, 2006. Rewrite it, changing the sentences in direct speech into reported speech. Leave the other sentences unchanged.

"Why do you want to know my age? If people know I am so old, I won't get work!" laughs 90-year-old A. K. Hangal, one of Hindi cinema's most famous character actors. For his age, he is rather energetic. "What's the secret?" we ask. "My intake of everything is in small quantities. And I walk a lot," he replies. "I joined the industry when people retire. I was in my 40s. So I don't miss being called a star. I am still respected and given work, when actors of my age are living in poverty and without work. I don't have any complaints," he says, adding, "but yes, I have always been underpaid." Recipient of the Padma Bhushan, Hangal never hankered after money or materialistic gains. "No doubt I am content today, but money is important. I was a fool not to understand the value of money earlier," he regrets.

Ans. 90-year-old A. K. Hangal, one of Hindi cinema's most famous character actors, laughingly asked why they wanted to know his age. If people knew he was old, he would not get work. For his age, he is rather energetic. They asked him what the secret was. He replied that his intake of everything was in small quantities and he walked a lot. He said that he had joined the industry when people retire. He had been in his 40s. So, he did not miss being called a star. He was still respected and given work, when actors of his age were living in poverty and without work. He said that he did not have any complaints other than the fact that he had always been underpaid.

Recipient of Padma Bhushan, Hangal never hankered after money or materialistic gains. He said that there was no doubt that he was content at present but that money was important. He regretted that he had been a fool who had not understood the value of money sooner.

REVIEW EXERCISE

Including Competency Based Questions

Part I

Multiple Choice Questions

1. **'The proposal' ...perhaps continues! What is the main purpose of the text provided before the play?** Competency Based

   (a) To indicate the present-day relevance of the play.
   (b) To provide information about the writer
   (c) To describe the characters in detail
   (d) To explain the context of the play.

Ans. (d) To explain the context of the play.

2. **What was Lomov wearing when he entered the scene?**

   (a) Dress jacket and white gloves
   (b) Evening coat with hat
   (c) Waistcoat and trousers
   (d) Shirt and trousers

Ans. (a) Dress-jacket and white gloves

3. **What best describes Chubukov's initial response to Lomov's entry?** Competency Based

   (a) Optimistic (b) Pleased
   (c) Startled (d) Jubilant

Ans. (b) Pleased

4. **Chubukov thought that Lomov wanted to borrow money because he seemed** Competency Based

   (a) repentant (b) mortified (c) agitated (d) docile

Ans. (c) agitated

5. **Chubukov was blessing Lomov because he ....**

   (a) gave Oxen Meadows to Chubukov
   (b) gave his pet dog Guess to Natalya
   (c) asked Chubukov's daughter's hand in marriage
   (d) None of the above

Ans. (c) asked Chubukov's daughter's hand in marriage

6. **"If I give myself time to think, to hesitate, to talk a lot, to look for an ideal, or for real love, then i'll never get married." The given sentence shows that** Competency Based

   (a) Lomov regretted not having married earlier.
   (b) Lomov could not marry the woman he loved
   (c) Lomov's decision to marry Natalya was pragmatic
   (d) Lomov felt that Natalya was the most suitable bride for him.

Ans. (c) Lomov's decision to marry Natalya was pragmatic

7. **What was the first point of disagreement between Natalya and Lomov?**

   (a) Pet dog (b) Oxen Meadows
   (c) House (d) None of these

Ans. (b) Oxen Meadows

8. **"Dear one, why yell like that? You won't prove anything just by yelling." Who said this to whom in the play?**

   (a) Chubukov to Natalya (b) Chubukov to Lomov
   (c) Lomov to Natalya (d) Natalya to Lomov

Ans. (b) Chubukov to Lomov

9. **When does Natalya fall into the chair and demands to call Lomov back?**

   (a) When she gets to know that Lomov had come to propose her.
   (b) When she gets to know that Lomov suffers from excitement attacks.
   (c) When Natalya get to know that he has actually left the place.
   (d) None of the above

Ans. (a) When she gets to know that Lomov had come to propose her.

10. **After realising that Lomov had come to propose, Natalya's feelings changed from** Competency Based

    (a) contempt to fear (b) anger to remorse
    (c) frustration to love (d) distress to confusion

Ans. (b) anger to remorse

11. **After re-entering the scene, what reason did Lomov give Natalya for arguing over the ownership of the meadow?** Competency Based

    (a) It was the right thing to do
    (b) The meadow was valuable
    (c) He was proud of his family's heritage
    (d) He had documents that proved his ownership

Ans. (a) It was the right thing to do

12. **Natalya's pet dog Squeezer was a thoroughbred animal, the son of ....**

    (a) Harness and Chisles
    (b) Harness and Volchantesky
    (c) Chisles and Volchantesky
    (d) Chisles and cab-horse

Ans. (a) Harness and Chisles

13. What is the theme of the play?

(i) Human nature
(ii) Rich people
(iii) Physical weakness
(iv) Arguments and disputes
(v) Double faced people
(vi) Feelings for dogs

(a) (i), (iv), (v) and (vi) (b) (ii), (iii) and (iv)
(c) (i), (ii), (iii) and (v) (d) All of these

Ans. (d) All of these

14. Select the most appropriate option for (1) and (2).

1. Natalya and Lomov would not be a happily married couple.

2. Lomov does not Love Natalya.

(a) Both (1) and (2) are true
(b) (2) is the opposite of (1)
(c) (1) furthers the premise of (2)
(d) Both (1) and (2) are false

Ans. (a) Both (1) and (2) are true

15. What best describes the mood of the play?

Competency Based

(a) Foreboding (b) Tumultuous
(c) Melancholic (d) Suspenseful

Ans. (b) Tumultuous

Extract Based Questions

1. Read the following extract carefully and answer the questions that follow.

LOMOV It's cold... I'm trembling all over, just as if I'd got an examination before me. The great thing is, I must have my mind made up. If I give myself time to think, to hesitate, to talk a lot, to look for an ideal or for real love, then I'll never get married. Brr...It's cold! Natalya Stepanovna is an excellent housekeeper, not bad-looking, well-educated. What more do I want? But I'm getting a noise in my ears from excitement. (Drinks) And it's impossible for me not to marry. In the first place, I'm already 35- a critical age, so to speak. In the second place, I ought to lead a quiet and regular life. I suffer from palpitations, I'm excitable and always getting awfully upset; at this very moment my lips are trembling and there's a twitch in my right eyebrow.

CBSE Additional SQP 2023

(i) Which of the following is not a reason why Lomov thinks he must marry?

(a) He is already 35 years old.
(b) He suffers from palpitations.
(c) He is excitable and easily upset.
(d) He is in love with Natalya.

Ans. (d) He is in love with Natalya.

(ii) Why is it fair to say that Lomov's tone, when he says "What more do I want?", is uncertain and questioning? Answer in about 40 words.

Ans. It is fair to say that Lomov's tone when he says "What more do I want?" is uncertain and questioning because he is trying to convince himself that Natalya Stepanovna is a suitable match for him. However, he seems to be struggling with doubts and fears. His tone suggests that he is trying to reassure himself that he has made the right decision but he is not entirely convinced.

(iii) Read the following descriptions (a) – (c) and identify which one correctly corresponds to the extract.

(a) A debate is a formal discussion on a particular topic, usually with two or more people presenting different viewpoints and arguments.
(b) A soliloquy is a speech given by a character alone on stage, which reveals their innermost thoughts and feelings to the audience.
(c) An aside is a brief comment or remark made by a character directly to the audience, which is not intended to be heard by other characters on stage.

Ans. (b) A soliloquy is a speech given by a character alone on stage, which reveals their innermost thoughts and feelings to the audience.

(iv) If an actor were to enact this extract, what would he be required to focus on, while modulating his voice?

Ans. If an actor were to enact this extract while modulating his voice, he would be required to convey Lomov's nervousness and excitement.

2. Read the following extract carefully and answer the questions that follow.

LOMOV But you can see from the documents, honoured Natalya Stepanovna. Oxen Meadows, it's true, were once the subject of dispute, but now everybody knows that they are mine. There's nothing to argue about. You see, my aunt's grandmother gave the free use of these Meadows in perpetuity to the peasants of your father's grandfather, in return for which they were to make bricks for her. The peasants belonging to your father's grandfather had the free use of the Meadows for forty years, and had got into the habit of regarding them as their own, when it happened that...

NATALYA No, it isn't at all like that! Both grandfather and great grandfather reckoned that their land extended to Burnt Marsh – which means that Oxen Meadows were ours. I don't see what there is to argue about. It's simply silly!

CBSE 2023

(i) **Complete the sentence appropriately.**
The subject of the dispute was regarding ....

Ans. ownership of the Oxen Meadow

(ii) **According to Natalya, why did Oxen Meadows belong to them?**

Ans. According to Natalya, Oxen Meadows belonged to them because both her grandfather and great grandfather reckoned that their land extended to Burnt Marsh - which meant that the Oxen Meadows were theirs.

(iii) **Find the word from the extract which means 'continuance':**

(a) Dispute (b) Perpetuity
(c) Belonging (d) Reckoned

Ans. (b) Perpetuity

(iv) **Lomov's aunt's grandmother gave Oxen Meadows to Natalya's father's grandfather in lieu of ....**

Competency Based

Ans. Lomov's aunt's grandmother gave Oxen Meadows to Natalya's father's grandfather in lieu of their peasants making bricks for her.

3. Read the following extract carefully and answer the questions that follow.

"But, please, Stephen Stepanovitch, how can they be yours? Do be a reasonable man ! My aunt's grandmother gave the Meadows for the temporary and free use of your grandfather's peasants. The peasants used the land for forty years and got accustomed to it as if it was their own, when it happened that ....

(i) **Why did the peasants treat the land as their own?**

(a) They used the land for forty years
(b) They got accustomed to using the land
(c) Both (a) and (b)
(d) None of the above

Ans. (c) The peasants treated the land as their own because they used the land for forty years and got accustomed to using it as their own land.

(ii) **What light do these lines throw on the speaker's character?**

Ans. These lines tell that speaker is logical, rational and polite.

(iii) **Who is the speaker of the above lines? What light do these lines throw on the speaker's character? What reaction did his words get?**

Ans. Lomov is the speaker of the given lines. The given lines show his poor personality and a bad sense of talking that seems irrelevant with place and person. He is interrupted by Chubukov who refuted his claim by pointing out that Oxen Meadows' standing as disputed land was the only reason the peasants were permitted to use it at no cost.

(iv) **Why did his aunt's grandmother give the meadows? Answer in about 40 words.**

Ans. His aunt's grandmother gave the meadows for the temporary and free use of the peasants employed by Stephan Chubukov's grandfather in return for which they were to make bricks for her.

4. Read the following extract carefully and answer the questions that follow.

CHUBUKOV You may take it that I know whether I have the right or not. Because, young man, I'm not used to being spoken to in that tone of voice, and so on. I, young man, am twice your age and ask you to speak to me without agitating yourself and all that.

LOMOV No, you just think I'm a fool and want to have me on! You call my land yours, and then you want me to talk to you calmly and politely! Good neighbours don't behave like that, Stepan Stepanovitch! You're not a neighbour, you're a grabber!

CHUBUKOV What's that? What did you say?

NATALYA Papa, send the mowers out to the Meadows at once!

(i) **Select the option that displays the reason why Lomov called Chubukov 'a grabber'.**

(a) Chubukov called Oxen Meadows as Lomov's
(b) Chubukov called Oxen Meadows as theirs
(c) Chubukov called Oxen Meadows as Natalya's
(d) None of the above

Ans. (b) Lomov called Chubukov 'a grabber' because Chubukov called Oxen Meadows as theirs.

(ii) **How did Chubukov want Lomov to talk to him? Why?**

Ans. Chubukov wanted Lomov to speak to him without agitating himself because he was twice Lomov's age.

(iii) **Fill in the blank with the correct phrase from the bracket.**
Lomov used an .... (aggressive/frustrated) tone in these lines.

Ans. aggressive

(iv) **Where did the argument between Lomov and Chubukovs reach? Why? Answer in about 40 words.**

Ans. The argument between Lomov and Chubukovs reached to a point where they were calling names and abusing each other. This conflict was due to the fact that Chubukov demanded respect and Lomov thought that Chubukov took him for a fool and didn't behave like good neighbours.

5. **Read the following extract carefully and answer the questions that follow.**

LOMOV Never mind about my people! The Lomovs have all been honourable people, and not one has ever been tried for embezzlement, like your grandfather!

CHUBUKOV You Lomovs have had lunacy in your family, all of you!

NATALYA All, all, all!

CHUBUKOV Your grandfather was a drunkard, and your younger aunt, Nastasya Mihailovna, ran away with an architect, and so on...

LOMOV And your mother was hump-backed. [Clutches at his heart] Something pulling in my side... My head.... Help! Water!

CHUBUKOV Your father was a guzzling gambler!

CBSE Question Bank 2021 Modified

(i) Choose the option that correctly identifies the tone of the characters in the given extract.

(1) antagonistic (2) humourous
(3) contemptous (4) ironical

Ans. (1) and (3) The tones of the characters can be described as antagonistic and contemptous.

(ii) If according to Chubukov and Natalya, Lomovs are not 'honourable people', why do they still consider Lomov's proposal?

Ans. Chubukov and Natalya still consider Lomov's proposal because his status in society superseded everything.

(iii) Imagine you found the playwright's notes for each scene in the play and noticed that some of the words were missing. Choose the option that fills the missing words most appropriately.

A conversation that starts pleasantly quickly turns into a (i) .... argument. With (ii) .... of Oxen Meadows at the heart of the matter, Lomov and Natalya quarrel and are later joined by Chubukov. Thus, begins a (iii) .... of insults, accusations and name-calling. All (iv) .... disappears. Eventually, Lomov leaves clutching at his heart, his foot numb.

(a) (i) petty ; (ii) history ; (iii) series; (iv) politeness
(b) (i) vicious ; (ii) ownership ; (iii) circus ; (iv) civility

Ans. (b) (i) vicious ; (ii) ownership ; (iii) circus ; (iv) civility

(iv) The playwright's intention in the given extract is to ....

Ans. satirise the superficiality of the upper class in Russian society

6. **Read the following extract carefully and answer the questions that follow.**

NATALYA What proposal?

CHUBUKOV Why, he came here to propose to you.

NATALYA To propose? To me? Why didn't you tell me so before?

CHUBUKOV So, he dresses up in evening clothes. The stuffed sausage! The wizen-faced frump!

NATALYA To propose to me? Ah! [Falls into an easy-chair and wails] Bring him back! Back! Ah! Bring him here.

CHUBUKOV Bring whom here?

NATALYA Quick, quick! I'm ill! Fetch him!

CHUBUKOV What's that? What's the matter with you? [Clutches at his head] Oh, unhappy man that I am! I'll shoot myself! I'll hang myself! We've done for her!

NATALYA I'm dying! Fetch him!

(i) Who is being referred to as 'he'?

Ans. Lomov is being referred to as 'he' in the extract.

(ii) Why did he meet Chubukov?

(a) To tell them that Oxen Meadows was his
(b) To tell them that his dog was better than theirs
(c) To ask for Natalya's hand
(d) To tell them that he wanted a quiet and relaxed life

Ans. (c) To ask for Natalya's hand.

(iii) Why did Natalya ask Chubukov to bring Lomov back? What is Chubukov's response? Answer in about 40 words. **Competency Based**

Ans. Natalya asked Chubukov to bring Lomov back because he had come to propose to her and she was also longing for the proposal. Natalya's conflicting opinion irritates and infuriates Chubukov. He says that he'll shoot himself but as soon as Natalya starts yelling and threatening him with death, he goes to bring Lomov back.

(iv) How did Chubukov react when Natalya asked him to bring Lomov?

Ans. Chubukov was cursing himself as an unhappy man and wanted to shoot or hang himself.

7. **Read the following extract carefully and answer the questions that follow.**

LOMOV He is old, but I wouldn't take five Squeezers for him. Why, how can you? Guess is a dog; as for Squeezer, well, it's too funny to argue. Anybody you like has a dog as good as Squeezer... you may find them under every bush almost. Twenty-five roubles would be a handsome price to pay for him.

NATALYA There's some demon of contradiction in you today, Ivan Vassilevitch. First you pretend that the Meadows are yours; now, that Guess is better than Squeezer. I don't like people who don't say what they mean, because you know perfectly well that Squeezer is a hundred times better than your silly Guess. Why do you want to say he isn't?

LOMOV I see, Natalya Stepanovna, that you consider me either blind or a fool. You must realise that Squeezer is overshot! **CBSE 2023**

(i) To pay a 'handsome price' most nearly means

(a) to pay good looking money
(b) to pay for a good looking dog
(c) to pay a lot of money
(d) to pay less money

Ans. (c) to pay a lot of money

(ii) What is the demon of contradiction in what Lomov says?

Ans. Lomov argues that Guess is a purebred dog but Squeezer is so common that it would be hard to establish his true parentage. This is a stupid argument from Natalya's point of view because she had already stated that the Chubukovs had bought Squeezer for 85 roubles. This is why Natalya says that there is a demon of contradiction in Lomov.

(iii) Read (a) - (d) and choose the correct statement. Lomov argues that

1. Squeezer is more intelligent than Guess.
2. Natalya does not love animals.
3. Guess is a better dog than Squeezer.
4. Natalya disagrees with Lomov's opinion.

Ans. Statement 3 is correct. Guess is a better dog than Squeezer.

(iv) Fill in the blank with one word only. Lomov degrades Squeezer by commenting that dogs like him are very ....

Ans. common

Part – II

Short Answer Type Questions

1. How does Lomov come to Chubukov's house? For what does he come? How is he received?

Or **What was the objective of Lomov's visit to Chubukov's house?** **CBSE 2022 Term II**

Ans. Lomov came to Chubukov's house in the evening dress with gloves on.

Lomov came to propose Chubukov's daughter Natalya for marriage.

Lomov is treated with respect by Chubukov who felt happy on seeing him.

2. What about Lomov's appearance made Chubukov curious? **Competency Based**

Ans. Chubukov was curious about Lomov's appearance because he was wearing his formal evening dress with gloves. Such an attire is worn to formal events and balls. It is not worn to houses of near and dear ones or to visit people with whom you want to build a relationship.

3. Chubukov accepted Lomov's request without any resistance. Justify the statement using evidence from the story. **Competency Based**

Ans. Chubukov accepted Lomov's request of marrying his daughter Natalya without any resistance as he did not take even a second to cry out in excitement and happiness. He was so glad to hear the proposal that he couldn't even believe his own ears.

4. How does Chubukov react when Lomov asked for the hand of his daughter in marriage? **CBSE 2023**

Ans. When Lomov says that he has come to ask for the hand of his daughter in marriage, Chubukov gets excited with joy. He hugs and kisses Lomov, sheds a tear of joy and calls for God's blessing for Lomov and Natalya.

5. What were Lomov's reasons for choosing Natalya? **Competency Based**

Ans. Lomov had the following reasons for choosing Natalya Stepanovna for marriage.

(i) She was an excellent housekeeper.
(ii) She was good looking and well-educated.

6. Which two issues about himself convinced Lomov of his decision to get married? **CBSE SQP 2022 Term II**

Ans. Two issues about himself that convinced Lomov of his decision are

(i) Lomov is thirty-five years old and quite unhealthy. He often gets upset about little things and also suffers from palpitations.
(ii) Lomov wants to live a regular and settled life, quietly with a partner as he is expected by people to marry.

7. When Natalya comes to meet Lomov, she quotes her father's words – "and papa said", "Go; there's a merchant come for his goods." What do you think Chubukov meant? **CBSE Question Bank 2021**

Ans. When Natalya comes to meet Lomov, she quotes her father's words – 'and papa said', "Go; there's a merchant come for his goods." These words of Chubukov represents that Lomov had come to propose marriage with Natalya.

8. Why did Natalya feel surprised when Lomov paid her a visit to her house?

Ans. Natalya felt surprised when Lomov paid a visit to her house because Lomov was wearing an evening dress, jacket and white gloves. Usually one does not visit ones' neighbours in a formal dress.

9. "The Lomovs and the Chubukov's have always had the most friendly, and I might almost say the most affectionate, regard for each other." How would you evaluate Lomov and Chubukov's relationship as neighbours? CBSE Question Bank 2021

Ans. The statement "The Lomovs and the Chubukov's have always had the most friendly, and I might almost say the most affectionate, regard for each other" may seem true at first. Both Lomov and Chubukov have been neighbours for years and for this very reason, Lomov comes to Chubukov's house with a proposal of marrying Natalya. However, as one moves ahead, the relationship may not be as affectionate as it seems. They constantly quarrel with each other over trivial issues and do not trust each other even a bit. They insult each other, call each other names but still maintain a façade of a happy relationship.

10. Describe Oxen Meadows. How were they a source of quarrel between Lomov's and Natalya's family?

Ans. Oxen Meadows is a land wedged between Birchwoods and the Burnt Marsh. It becomes the source of quarrel between Lomov's and Natalya's family as both of them lay claim over it. Lomov tries to prove that the Oxen Meadows were given to Natalya's great grandfather's peasants for free use. Because of using it for 40 years, they had started thinking that the Meadows belonged to them while Chubukov's contest (contradict) Lomov's claims.

11. Justify the title of the play 'The Proposal' with reference to the characters and plot. CBSE 2024

Ans. The title of the play is 'The Proposal' is a very apt one because the whole play is about Lomov proposing Natalya. Right from the beginning to the end of the play, the story revolves round a marriage proposal and how it gets delayed to finally become successful. Lomov comes to Natalya's house to propose to her but even before he does it, they both start fighting. The proposal, however, is successful in the end with the prospect of the couple living a quarrelsome life.

12. What kind of a man is Lomov?

***Or* Write a brief character sketch of Lomov.** CBSE 2022 Term II

Ans. Lomov is a 35 years old comical character who came to propose Natalya. However, he is so nervous and excited that he continues quarrelling with Natalya over small things and fails to make the proposal. He has no confidence and no self-control.

13. What opinion of Chubukov do you form after reading 'The proposal'?

Ans. Chubukov is a rich landlord and a neighbour of Lomov. He is short tempered and rude in behaviour. He wants Lomov to be married to Natalya. However, he forgets the main proposal and joins the quarrel between Lomov and Natalya. Chubukov also becomes abusing and insulting. However, he grabs the opportunity as soon as it comes, and blesses the couple in the end.

14. How does Natalya react when she comes to know that Lomov had come to propose her? CBSE 2014

Ans. When Natalya comes to know that Lomov had come there to propose her, she was shocked. She cries, changes her stance and asks her father to bring Lomov back. When he proposed her, she became very happy as she also wanted to marry him.

15. Besides Oxen Meadows what is the other important cause of quarrel between Lomov and Natalya?

Ans. After the quarrel regarding the Oxen Meadows is over, Lomov and Natalya started another quarrel. This time, it is about their dogs, Squeezer and Guess. Natalya thinks that their Squeezer was a better dog than Lomov's dog, Guess. She further calls Guess old and worthless, thus, starting the quarrel.

16. To what end does the playwright employ Lomov's palpitations in the play? CBSE Question Bank 2021

Ans. The play 'The Proposal' as the name suggests is about Lomov proposing to Natalya for marriage. However, all the characters in the play engage in trivial arguments which delays the purpose of Lomov. His palpitations, then has been employed by the playwright to meet the purpose of proposal. It is only after Lomov gets unconscious due to his palpitations, that the proposal is made and accepted.

17. Natalya is obstinate and argumentative. Give two examples from the story highlighting her nature. CBSE 2024 C

Ans. In Anton Chekhov's play 'The Proposal', Natalya is portrayed as an argumentative and quarrelsome character. Here are two examples from the story that highlight her nature:

(i) **Land ownership** Natalya and Lomov argue over the ownership of a piece of land called Oxen Meadows. Natalya claims that the meadows are not worth much to her but she cannot stand unfairness.

(ii) **Dog superiority** Natalya and Lomov argue about the superiority of their dogs, Squeezer and Guess. Natalya insists that Squeezer is of the finest pedigree. Lomov refuses to accept that his dog, Guess, is worse than Squeezer.

In both the cases, Natalya didn't flinch from her point. Further she acted stubbornly when she learnt that Lomov had come to propose to her, wailed over the lost chance and forced her father to call him back showing her obstinate nature.

18. What is the significance of the characters' attitudes toward their dogs?

Ans. The argument over the superiority of their dogs, Squeezer and Guess, reflects their competitive natures and stubbornness. This debate reveals their inability to communicate effectively and foreshadows the humorous absurdity of their relationship, highlighting their pettiness and the play's comedic elements.

19. What role does Chubukov play in the relationship between Lomov and Natalya?

Ans. Chubukov acts as a mediator and father figure, expressing frustration with Lomov and Natalya. He oscillates between supporting his daughter and criticising Lomov, ultimately encouraging the proposal and attempting to resolve their conflicts.

20. How does the physical state of Lomov contribute to the scene's humour?

Ans. Lomov's exaggerated physical ailments, such as heart palpitations and numb feet, add comedic elements to the scene. His frequent complaints and near-collapse heighten the situation's absurdity, emphasising the ridiculousness of their arguments over trivial matters.

21. In what ways do Lomov and Natalya's characteristics complement each other?

Ans. Lomov's anxious demeanour complements Natalya's fiery personality, creating dynamic and humorous tension. Their contrasting traits drive the conflict and highlight their compatibility, as social expectations drive both characters. It ultimately makes them suitable partners despite their frequent quarrels.

22. How do misunderstandings drive the plot in 'The Proposal'?

Ans. Misunderstandings fuel the plot as Lomov and Natalya misinterpret each other's intentions and emotions. Their inability to communicate effectively leads to humorous conflicts, showcasing the characters' insecurities and revealing how poor communication can derail important moments. It ultimately highlights the absurdities in human relationships.

Long Answer Type Questions

1. Among neighbours we should have cordial relations and not lose our temper. How do Natalya and Lomov lose their temper on trivial issues?

Or **Forgiveness is the foundation of a cordial relationship. Do your agree? How is this message conveyed in the paly 'The Proposal'?** CBSE 2023

Or **The principle 'forgive and forget', helps a lot in maintaining cordial relations in society. Do you think Anton Chekov conveys this message in the play 'The Proposal'?** Competency Based

Ans. It is true that the principle 'forgive and forget' is the foundation of all the cordial relationships in our society. Any communication gap or misunderstanding develops bitter feeling which leads to enmity.

In such cases, one must sit together and resolve the issue calmly. One must learn to forgive another and forget the issue.

In the play 'The Proposal', Anton Chekhov conveys this message through two neighbours, Lomov and Chubukov as well as Chubukov's daughter Natalya. They started quarrelling over small issues. Initially, the argument was about the ownership of Oxen Meadows. Then, it was about their dogs. Their arguments slowly developed into fights and they started abusing each other.

This damaged their relationship. Because of their quarrel, important issues were left behind. It was only when Natalya came to know that Lomov had come to propose her that the argument was left behind. Natalya and Chubukov both asked for forgiveness and even forgot the initial argument. Hence, it is essential to remember the principle of 'forgive and forget' if people want to have a cordial relationship with their neighbours.

2. The proposal of the marriage was forgotten amidst the arguments over petty things. Which right approach should have been followed by Lomov and Natalya ? CBSE 2020

Ans. In the play 'A Marriage Proposal' by Anton Chekhov, the characters Lomov and Natalya are caught up in an absurd series of arguments over trivial matters, which overshadow the real purpose of their interaction-Lomov's proposal of marriage to Natalya. To avoid this confusion and focus on the true objective, here is the right approach they should have followed

- **Clear Communication** Lomov should have directly and calmly expressed his intention to propose to Natalya at the start of their conversation. This would have set a clear tone for the discussion, rather than getting bogged down by unrelated arguments.

- **Stay Focused on the Purpose** Both Lomov and Natalya should have kept their focus on the main topic: marriage. By avoiding unnecessary distractions like the quarrel over land ownership, the dogs, or petty misunderstandings, they could have had a more productive and sincere conversation.
- **Active Listening** Both characters should have listened to each other more carefully, instead of jumping to conclusions or interrupting each other. If they had genuinely tried to understand one another's feelings and perspectives, the conversation could have been more harmonious.
- **Patience and Empathy** Lomov should have been more patient and understanding of Natalya's emotions and behavior. Similarly, Natalya could have been more considerate of Lomov's nerves and anxieties about the proposal.
- **Respectful Discussion** Instead of fighting over small disagreements, they could have had a respectful discussion about their feelings, goals, and expectations regarding marriage. This would have helped them connect on a deeper level, beyond surface-level arguments.
- **Clarity of Intentions** Lomov should have been straightforward in his proposal, without letting minor irritations and tensions build up. Being clear and direct about his desires might have prevented the situation from escalating into absurd conflicts.

In essence, they should have prioritised mutual respect, clear communication, and focused on the serious matter of marriage, rather than letting trivial disputes undermine the opportunity for a meaningful and successful proposal.

3. The play 'The Proposal' highlights the social and practical necessities of marriage. Support this statement with reference to each character.

Competency Based

Ans. The play 'The Proposal' highlights the social and practical necessities of marriage in a subversively funny way. The decisions and behaviours of all of the three characters are influenced because of the question of marriage.

(i) **Stephen Stepanovitch Chubukov** He is a money minded and hypocritical man. His main concerns are upholding his false pride and getting his twenty-five year old daughter married. This 'burden' influences the way he behaves with his neighbours as well.
He cries over the fact that he is the father of a single daughter many times throughout the play. He is even ready to forgive and forget the bad behaviour of Lomov if it means that he can get Natalya married to him.

(ii) **Natalya Stepanovna** Natalya is a headstrong and quarrelsome girl. She has inherited her bad temper as well as her pride from her father. She would happily quarrel over trivial matters such as dogs, but she changes her tune entirely when she comes to know that Lomov had come to propose marriage to her. She even concedes that Oxen Meadows did in fact belong to Lomov just to make him happy and make sure that she can still get married.

(iii) **Ivan Vassilevitch Lomov** Ivan Lomov is very headstrong and quarrelsome exactly like Natalya and Chubukov. He had a desire to find true love but he gives up that desire to be socially practical, and therefore decides to marry Natalya. He finds the concept of marriage so necessary that he plans to marry a woman he doesn't even find beautiful because she is an "excellent housekeeper".

In these ways, Chekhov's play portrays that the institution of marriage is necessary both practically and socially.

4. Farce is a kind of comedy which includes situations and dialogues that are ridiculous, exaggerated and even absurd. Evaluate the play, The Proposal, as a farce.

CBSE SQP 2022 Term II

Ans. Farce can be defined as a comedy that contains highly exaggerated and improbable elements. In a farce, laughter, which is integral to all comedies, arises from the absurdity of the situation. A farce requires the use of comical language. It is also characterised by stylish and lavish clothes and physical appearance of extravagance.

The play 'The Proposal' presents the story of Lomov who proposes Natalya for marriage. His proposal leads to an argument that just keeps happening. At first, Natalya insults him and her father drives him out of the house, followed by a keenness in her to marry Lomov. However, when the marraige is agreed upon, it is again followed by an argument over the superiority of their hunting dogs. This shows the characters as quarrel loving. Even Natalya's father joins in their argument and sides with his daughter.

The constant arguing causes Lomov to faint from exhaustion, causing Natalya and her father to fear that he is dead. They began behaving crazily when minutes later he gains consciousness. What follows is a forceful agreement to marry each other and immediately after, they began quarrelling again.

The play is a situational humour through which the playwright is exposing the fakeness of the world. The entire action of the play is comically exaggerated, with the features of a farce. From Lomov's formal evening dress to his physical illness and the couple's fight on minor issues, everything is exaggerated to produce laughter.

5. Russian society emerges as an important character in the play, 'The Proposal'. Support your answer giving instances. **CBSE 2022 Term II**

Ans. The play 'The Proposal' throws light on the lifestyle of the landlords of Russia in the 19th Century. The farm labourers worked on their farms while the landlords led a comfortable life. The landlords were full of pride and quarreled over trivial issues.

Through the play, a lot can be learnt about the Russian society. For instance, according to the play, the Russians are very particular about their appearance and attire and thus, have particular dresses for special occasions. Further, the play portrays them as hypocrites. They show off sweet nature and at the very next moment they start fighting over trivial issues. In the play, Chubukov refers to Lomov as 'my angel', but soon after he fights with Lomov. They put up the pretence of being good neighbours but inside their heart, they feel no sense of camaraderie for each other.

Thus, the Russian society becomes an integral part of the play 'The Proposal'.

6. Natalya and her father Chubukov 'turn around' when Lomov puts his proposal in the open. As a reader, briefly describe what you think of Natalya and Chubukov from the play 'The Proposal'. **CBSE 2022 Term II**

Ans. In the play 'The Proposal', Chubukov and Natalya are the Russian father and daughter. Chubukov wanted to marry off Natalya and in his opinion, Lomov was a good match for his daughter. He is a wealthy landowner and Lomov's next-door neighbour. He is irritable and hasty in his actions. He wants Lomov and Natalya to marry. However, he loses sight of the primary issue and becomes involved in the argument between Lomov and Natalya. He merely adds to the blaze. He has a tendency to be aggressive and insulting. However, in the end, he blesses Natalya and Lomov.

Natalya is his daughter and a twenty-five-year-old lady. Lomov thinks she's a terrific man with nice looks. She, gets into pointless fights over Oxen Meadows and dogs. She even uses harsh language to degrade Lomov. However, common reason wins and she does not miss out on the chance to marry Lomov.

7. Compare and contrast what Anne from the poem 'Anne Gregory' would look for in a life partner as compared to Natalya from 'The Proposal'. Justify your answer with one example from each of the texts. **CBSE Additional SQP 2022**

Ans. It is true that both Anne from 'Anne Gregory' and Natalya from 'The Proposal' have very differing views on what they would look for in a life partner. They both are different girl with different natures, behaviours and situations. As a result, we find them expecting different things from their life partners.

Anne is looking for true love who would love her for her inner beauty and not her external beauty. She wants a partner who is sincere and not superficial. To get such a life partner, Anne would colour her hair such that she could find someone to love her for who she was rather than how she looked.

In contrast, Natalya is looking for social mobility and security, and not love. She does not seem to truly love or feel affection for Lomov, and seems to constantly argue with Lomov about who owns a piece of land or whose dog is better. However, she still agrees to marry him for economic reasons. She knows that she needs to get married according to the norms of her society.

8. Based on your understanding of the Play, 'The Proposal', what do you think of relationships?

Prepare a speech draft on relationships based on Natalya's and Anne Frank's characters.

You may begin this way

Good morning everyone

Relationships are the bond between two people based on mutual likes, understanding, need or love. I'd like to discuss relationships as portrayed in the two texts.....

You may end this way

To conclude, I'd like to say that.....

Thank you,

(Reference: The Proposal and From the Diary of Anne Frank) **CBSE 2024**

Ans. Good morning everyone

Relationships are the bond between two people based on mutual likes, understanding, need or love. Today, I'd like to delve into the nuances of relationships as portrayed in 'The Proposal' by Anton Chekhov, featuring Natalya, and 'From the Diary of Anne Frank', highlighting Anne Frank's perspective.

Natalya's relationship dynamics in 'The Proposal' humorously underscore the complexities and absurdities that sometimes drive our interactions. Her character, engaged in arguments over land and petty disputes, reflects how pride and misunderstanding can overshadow the essence of relationships, namely love and companionship.

On the flip side, Anne Frank, in her diary, offers a poignant view of relationships forged under the shadow of adversity. Her reflections showcase resilience, the capacity for love, understanding and hope even in the bleakest times.

The stark contrast between Natalya's and Anne's circumstances and their handling of relationships illuminate a spectrum of human connections. From Chekhov's satirical portrayal to Anne's heartfelt confessions, we discern that relationships, in any form, require a foundation of understanding, patience and sometimes, a willingness to look beyond our flaws.

To conclude, I'd like to say that whether it's in the comedic setting of a Russian estate or the concealed quarters of a wartime annex, relationships are our mirror, reflecting our best and worst, reminding us of our humanity.

Thank you

ASSESSMENT EXERCISE

Extract Based Questions

Read the given extract carefully and answer the questions that follow.

CHUBUKOV What a weight off my shoulders, ouf!

NATALYA But, still you will admit now that Guess is worse than Squeezer.

LOMOV Better!

NATALYA Worse!

CHUBUKOV Well, that's a way to start your family bliss! Have some champagne!

LOMOV He's better!

NATALYA Worse! Worse! Worse!

CHUBUKOV [trying to shout her down] Champagne! Champagne!

(i) Read (a)-(c) and choose the correct statement.

Based on the extract, Lomov and Natalya's closing lines can best be seen as

(a) a humorous and ironic take on typical marriage vows.

(b) a reflection of their affections for Guess and Squeezer.

(c) a sign of the prospective instability in their marital bliss.

(ii) The argument about the dogs reflected that both Lomov and Natalya loved their respective dogs very much. Do you agree? Why/ why not? **Competency Based**

(iii) Choose the option from the following that correctly uses the idiom 'weight off the shoulders'.

(a) I have a lot of weight off my shoulders and it hurts.

(b) Finally paying off my student loan is a great weight off my shoulders.

(c) She feels like she's carrying a weight off her shoulders.

(d) He helped the old man take the weight off his shoulders by helping him carry the heavy bags.

(iv) What does the liberal use of exclamation marks in the given extract indicate?

Short Answer (SA) Type Questions

1. What opinion did Lomov have about Chubukov?
2. What did Lomov tell about the relation of the Lomovs and Chubukovs in the past?
3. Why were Natalya and Lomov arguing over the Oxen Meadows?
4. What opinion do you form of Natalya after reading the play?
5. The quarrel over oxen Meadows is finally resolved. Explain. **CBSE 2023**
6. Why do you think Natalya Stepanovna asked her father to call Lomov back when she heard that he had come with a proposal?

Long Answer (LA) Type Questions

1. Do you think that forgiveness is better than arguing? Give reasons supporting your answer.
2. "The way Chubukov, Natalya and Lomov fought over petty issues is against the behaviour and mannerisms of neighbours." Comment. What would you have done to resolve the issue if you were in place of Chubukov?
3. Neighbour must have a cordial relationship which Lomov and Natalya do not have. Discuss with reference to their first fight. **Competency Based**

Section C : Literature
Textbook : First Flight *(Poetry)*

Dust of Snow

by Robert Frost

Introduction The following poem 'Dust of Snow' has been written by Robert Frost. This poem expresses the significance of small things in one's life. Through this poem, we get the message that we should hope for the best even in the worst situations. We must also remember that nature and its objects have the ability to make one happy and overcome hopelessness.

Stanzawise Explanation

Stanza 1

The way a crow
Shook down on me
The dust of snow
From a hemlock tree

Explanation In this stanza, the poet remembers a small incident that changed his mood. Once, the poet was in a depressed mood and was feeling hopeless. He was under a hemlock tree (It is not clear whether the poet was standing under or passing by the hemlock tree). Suddenly, a crow sitting on the tree shook it and some powdery snow from the tree fell on the poet.

Stanza 2

Has given my heart
A change of mood
And saved some part
Of a day I had rued

Explanation The powdery snow which fell on the poet changed his mood to happiness. Till now the poet had spent a part of his day in sadness. However, now he was feeling refreshed. This incident saved some part of the poet's day which he would have otherwise spent in sorrow and regret.

Poetic Devices Used in the Poem

Rhyme scheme abab

Symbolism Hemlock tree and crow are symbols that are generally associated with negative emotions and aspects. But the poet uses these symbols to bring about a positive change in him.

Alliteration is the repetition of the same constant sound in the nearby words.

- Has given my Heart
- And saved some part

Word Meaning

Word	Meaning
Stanza 1	
Shook	shake
Hemlock tree	a poisonous plant (tree) with small white flowers
Stanza 2	
Rued	held in regret

NCERT FOLDER

NCERT Exercise Questions

THINKING ABOUT THE POEM (NCERT PAGE 14)

Q.1 What is a 'dust of snow'? What does the poet say it has changed his mood? How has the poet's mood changed?

Ans. The 'dust of snow' means the fine particles of snow.

The sudden shower in the form of the dust of snow changed the poet's mood.

The poet's mood changed from the state of sadness to happiness. He felt refreshed and wanted to enjoy the rest of the day.

Q.2 How does Frost present nature in this poem? The following questions may help you to think of an answer.

(i) What are the birds that are usually named in poems? Do you think crow is often mentioned in poems? What images come to your mind when you think of a crow?

(ii) Again, what is 'a hemlock tree'? Why doesn't the poet write about more 'beautiful' tree such as a maple, or an oak, or a pine?

(iii) What do the 'crow' and 'hemlock' represent—joy or sorrow? What does the dust of snow that the crow shakes off a hemlock tree stand for?

Ans. Frost is often called the poet of nature. Unlike Wordsworth, he does not glorify nature but takes on an objective view. He describes the positive and negative aspects of nature. In the poem 'Dust of Snow', Frost presents a positive view of nature. His depressed and sad mood is changed in a happy one when a simple event happened with him. A crow shook down the dust of snow on him and changed his mood.

(i) Generally, poets take the birds which are known for their beauty and good qualities like peacock, swan, cuckoo, mynah, etc.

However, here Frost has taken a totally different approach as he chose a crow.

Crow is not often used in poems. Crow is black in colour and has a very harsh voice. It is believed to be a symbol of bad omen. Thinking of a crow brings very depressing and sorrowful pictures to our mind.

(ii) A hemlock tree is a poisonous plant with small white flowers.

The poet, Robert Frost, didn't choose to use beautiful trees like an oak, maple or pine tree. Instead, he chose the hemlock tree so that he could present his depressed mood and feelings.

(iii) The crow and hemlock tree represent sorrow and depression felt by the poet. The dust of snow that the crow shakes off from a hemlock tree is a sign of nature's blessing. It is a symbol of natural joy and energy. It means that the poet is passing through the sad and depressing moments, and is entering the time full of joy and optimism.

Q.3 Have there been times when you felt depressed and hopeless? Have you experienced a similar moment that changed your mood that day?

Ans. Yes, there have been number of times when I felt depressed and hopeless. Sometimes such moments were a result of my own actions and sometimes they were aroused by other people's behaviour and attitude.

Yes, I have experienced a similar moment that changed my mood. One day, I was very upset so I went out for a walk. I saw a small boy sitting in the park and enjoying with his friends. The sight and the joy that the boy was sharing with his friends changed my mood and I felt very happy for the rest of the day. I also joined him and enjoyed the company.

REVIEW EXERCISE

Including Competency Based Questions

Part – I

Multiple Choice Questions

1. Why does the poet call it 'dust of snow'?

(a) Snow particles were too tiny
(b) They came over him like dust
(c) They felt like dust
(d) They looked like dust

Ans. (a) Snow particles were too tiny

2. Which poetic device is used in the following line – 'and saved some part'?

(a) Simile
(b) Metaphor
(c) Hyperbole
(d) Alliteration

Ans. (d) Alliteration

3. The snow that fell from the hemlock tree changed the poet's mood. What could have been another outcome(s) of the falling of the snow on the poet?

(i) The poet could have gotten very angry.

(ii) The poet could have felt even more depressed because he would feel cold.

(iii) The poet could have killed the crow for ruining his clothes.

(iv) The poet could have cut off the hemlock tree.

(v) The poet could have removed the snow from his head and walked away.

(a) (i) and (iii) (b) (ii) and (iv)
(c) Only (iii) (d) (i), (ii) and (v)

Ans. (d) (i), (ii) and (v)

4. What is the conclusion of the poem 'Dust of Snow'?

(a) Hemlock tree and crow are the negativities in life
(b) Every small act in life can illuminate our soul and motivate us to do better
(c) Dust of snow can uplift the mood
(d) None of the above

Ans. (b) Every small act in the life can illuminate our soul and motivate us to do better.

5. What did poet realise when dust of snow fell on him?

(i) That he had wasted his time being in sorrow.

(ii) That he should utilise his remaining day in doing some useful tasks.

(a) Both (i) and (ii) are correct
(b) Only (i) is correct
(c) Only (ii) is correct
(d) Neither (i) nor (ii) is correct

Ans. (a) Both (i) and (ii) are correct

6. The prominence of a vowel sound throughout a line is called assonance, a literary device. Identify the line of the poem 'Dust of Snow' which uses assonance.

(a) Shook down on me (b) The dust of snow
(c) A change of mood (d) Of a day I had rued

Ans. (a) Shook down on me

7. Read the statement given below and answer the following question.

"And saved some part
Of a day I had rued."

What saved the poet's day?

(a) The hemlock tree
(b) The poet's changed mood
(c) The presence of crow
(d) The snow that fell on the poet

Ans. (d) The snow that fell on the poet

8. Read both the statements carefully and choose the correct alternative from the following.

(A) The poet's clothes became wet.

(B) The crow shook a branch of the hemlock tree that was covered in snow.

Codes

(a) (A) is right, (B) is false (b) (B) is right, (A) is false
(c) Both are true (d) Both are false

Ans. (b) (B) is right, (A) is false

9. In the poem 'Dust of Snow', which negative symbols have been used to create a positive effect? **CBSE SQP 2021 Term I**

(a) Hemlock tree; crow (b) Crow; snow
(c) Snow; hemlock tree (d) Crow; dust

Ans. (a) Hemlock tree; crow

10. "Has given my heart
A change of mood"
What is the poet's mood now? **CBSE 2021 Term I**

(a) Appreciative of nature (b) Thoughtful
(c) Happy (d) Cool

Ans. (c) Happy

11. "And saved some part
Of a day I had rued."
Based on the above lines, select the word that describes the poet's feelings at the end of the day. **CBSE Additional SQP 2022**

(a) Disappointed (b) Contented
(c) Ambitious (d) Regretful

Ans. (b) Contented

12. Of the many symbols the hemlock tree represents, choose the one that Frost drew upon, in all likelihood, for this poem.

(a) Longevity (b) Togetherness
(c) Healing (d) Protection

Ans. (c) Healing

Extract Based Questions

1. Read the following extract carefully and answer the questions that follow.

The way a crow
Shook down on me
The dust of snow
From a hemlock tree

(i) Select the correct option to complete the sentence, according to the extract.

Earlier, the poet was in a ...... (frustrated/gloomy) mood.

Ans. gloomy

(ii) Which tree did the crow shake?

Ans. The crow shook the Hemlock tree.

(iii) Choose the option showing the reason not corresponding with "... a crow /Shook down on me/The dust of snow". **Competency Based**

(a) The crow's landing on the branch of the tree.

(b) The shivering of the crow, due to the cold.

(c) The readjustment of position of the crow on the branch.

(d) The cawing of the crow hidden in the foliage.

Ans. (d) The cawing of the crow hidden in the foliage.

(iv) What is the significance of the crow and the hemlock tree in the given extract?

Ans. The presence of the crow and the hemlock tree in the extract sets the atmosphere of depression and sorrow. The poet feels depressed and sad. To represent these feelings, he had to use symbols of crow and hemlock tree which are generally associated with negativity and sadness.

2. Read the following extract carefully and answer the questions that follow.

Has given my heart
A change of mood
And saved some part
Of a day I had rued.

(i) What was the poet's mood?

(a) Happy (b) Sorrowful
(c) Celebratory (d) Nostalgic

Ans. (b) Sorrowful

(ii) Under/Near which tree was the poet standing?

Ans. Hemlock

(iii) Complete the following analogy on the basis of the above extract.

Pain: Lane :: Mood : ....

Ans. Rued

(iv) What was the effect of the fall of the dust of snow on the poet?

Ans. The fall of the dust of snow on the poet changed his mood.

3. Read the following extract carefully and answer the questions that follow.

The way a crow
Shook down on me
The dust of snow
From a hemlock tree
Has given my heart
A change of mood
And saved some part
Of a day I had rued.

(i) Fill the blank with one word.

.... is the poetic device used in the line 'And saved some part/of a day I had rued'.

Ans. Enjambment

(ii) Of the many symbols the hemlock tree represents, state the one that Frost drew upon in all likelihood, for this poem. **Competency Based**

Ans. The symbol of healing is one that Frost drew upon in all likelihood, for this poem.

(iii) To what is snow compared in the given extract?

(a) Hemlock tree (b) Dust
(c) The poet's heart (d) The poet's mood

Ans. (b) Dust

(iv) Comment on the poet's use of language in these lines. Answer in not more than 40 words.

Ans. The poet, Robert Frost, uses very simple, everyday and accessible language to invoke the strongest of emotions through the poem. The poet tells us that though his mood at the beginning was sorrowful and despairing, it has changed now to joy.

Part – II

Short Answer Type Questions

1. What does the poet Robert Frost want to convey through the poem 'Dust of Snow'?

Ans. Through the poem 'Dust of Snow', Robert Frost wants to convey a message that even little things can bring huge changes in our lives. An ordinary event also holds a capacity to bring about a major change in our mood. Further, joys and sorrow always go hand-in-hand and we must never lose hope. In addition, the poet highlights the healing capability of the natural world.

2. How has the poet observed 'nature' in the poem 'Dust of Snow'?

Ans. The poet observed that crows and hemlock trees are usually associated with bad omens or death and fear. However, Frost has presented them very beautifully. They bring cheer to him and are a source of joy. Thus, he conveys that everything around us in nature is beautiful. The only difference is a change in perspective.

3. What difference do you find between Robert Frost and other nature poets? **Competency Based**

Ans. All other nature poets are known for describing the well-known beautiful things in nature. They have described things like the nightingale, the cuckoo, the now-covered mountains, etc.

However, Robert Frost has described a crow and a hemlock tree. Such a choice shows that for Frost, every object in nature is beautiful. Such a unique thought makes him different from other poets.

4. The poem 'Dust of Snow' shows that human judgement can be misleading. How?

Ans. Robert Frost's poem 'Dust of Snow' shows how human judgement of certain issues can be misleading. There are certain objects, things that people associate with negativity. People overlook these objects when in search of happiness and positivity.

The poet tries to alter this mindset through this poem by showing how a crow, sitting on a hemlock tree (both negative symbols) shook dust of snow on him which instantly changed his mood.

5. Rationalise what you think the poet was probably doing when the dust of snow fell on him?

Ans. From the context and the depressed mood of the poem, we can make out that the poet was sad. He was taking a walk or was just standing near the hemlock tree, regretting something before the dust of snow fell on him.

6. What does the presence of a hemlock tree tell you about the setting of the poem? Competency Based

Ans. Hemlock tree is a poisonous tree. It is a negative symbol representing a bad omen. It is often used to indicate sadness, sorrow and despair. So, its presence shows that the poem is set in a scene where the poet is in a bad mood.

7. The dusting of snow on account of the crow helped make the poet's day better. How do you think the crow's droppings might have impacted the poet? CBSE Question Bank 2021

Ans. Although the dusting of snow refreshed the poet's mood and made him feel happier, his reaction would have been quite the opposite if the crow's droppings had fallen on him instead. His bad mood would have worsened and he would have been enraged.

8. The poem evokes a sense of black and white. Justify. CBSE Question Bank 2021

Ans. The poem does evoke a sense of black and white with its images. In the poem, there is a focus on two things- a crow and a snow covered hemlock tree. We know that the colours predominant in these two images are black of crow and white of snow. In addition, the poet's mood and consequently, the poem are also situated in blacks and whites. His mood at the start can be depicted to be covered in dark, sorrow and despair but in the end due to the falling of the snow, it is dissipated.

9. As a crow you feel highly injured by the incorrect perception humans have about your species. Imagine yourself to be a crow and write your opinion about this prejudice. Make a case for breaking stereotypes. CBSE Question Bank 2021

Ans. It's really bad. I don't know why people have such incorrect perceptions for me. I am just a black bird doing what my instincts tell me to do. I am just like any bird who can bring joys and sorrow to everyone. I am black in colour and have a coarse voice because God intended so, not because I did something wrong. I hope people understand how ignorant and hurtful these stereotypes are for all of us.

10. It is our attitude towards a situation that makes it positive or negative. Do you agree with it? Express your views with reference to the poem 'Dust of Snow'. CBSE 2024

Ans. I agree that our attitude significantly influences our perception of situations, as presented in the poem 'Dust of Snow.' The poem illustrates how a simple, seemingly insignificant moment-a crow shaking snow from a hemlock tree onto the narrator-alters his mood and outlook for the day. This encounter, though minor, shifts the narrator's perspective, turning his day positive.

It underscores how embracing moments, regardless of their simplicity, can change our outlook, highlighting the power of attitude in transforming our experiences from negative to positive.

11. Why do you think the speaker refers to snow dust as 'saved some part/Of a day I had rued'?

Ans. The speaker refers to the dust of snow as 'saved some part' because it has redeemed or salvaged a portion of the day that the speaker had previously regretted or felt distress about. The encounter with the dust of snow positively changes the speaker's emotions and offers a fresh perspective on the day's events.

12. How does the brevity of the poem contribute to its impact?

Ans. The poem's brevity contributes to its impact by focusing on a single transformative moment, making it concise yet powerful. The poem's simplicity and succinctness enhance the potency of the message, showing how a small, unexpected act of nature can significantly change one's emotional state.

13. What can we learn from 'Dust of Snow' about finding beauty in everyday experiences?

Ans. 'Dust of Snow' teaches us that finding beauty in everyday experiences can profoundly affect our outlook and emotions. Despite the presence of negativity represented by the crow and the hemlock tree, the simple and pure dust of snow falling on the speaker's head serves as a reminder to appreciate the small joys and simple pleasures that nature can offer, even during challenging times. It encourages us to find moments of solace and redemption in the seemingly ordinary occurrences of life.

14. Frost contrasts the dark and gloomy imagery of the crow and hemlock tree with the snow's light, refreshing dust. Comment.

Ans. Frost contrasts the dark and gloomy imagery of the crow and hemlock tree with the snow's light, refreshing dust. This contrast emphasises the theme of dualities in life-sorrow and joy, darkness and light-and how even the smallest positive element can counterbalance negativity.

15. The poem suggests that emotions are transient and subject to change. Do you agree? Justify your answer.

Ans. Yes, I agree with the statement that the poem suggests that emotions are transient and subject to change. The speaker's mood shifts from despondency (sadness) to a sense of upliftment and hope after encountering nature's dust of snow. It serves as a reminder that life's emotional landscape is ever-changing.

16. 'Dust of Snow' highlights the poet's positive attitude towards nature. Comment on how Robert Frost presents the power of nature in his poem. CBSE 2025

Ans. In 'Dust of Snow', Robert Frost illustrates the power of nature through a simple yet profound moment. The poem portrays how a small act, like snow falling from a tree, can change a person's mood and perspective. The snow, symbolising nature's subtle influence, has the power to lift the speaker's spirits, transforming a negative moment into one of renewal. Frost emphasises that even the smallest interactions with nature can have a profound, uplifting effect on human emotions, highlighting nature's quiet but powerful ability to influence and heal.

Long Answer Type Questions

1. What are possible themes of this poem? Cite evidence from the text to support your answer.

Ans. The poem 'Dust of Snow' revolves around various themes as discussed below

Nature's Influence One of the poem's prominent themes is nature's transformative power. The poem illustrates how a seemingly ordinary and insignificant event, such as the dust of snow falling on the speaker's head, can profoundly impact one's emotions and perspective. Nature, represented by the crow, hemlock tree and snow, catalyses change and renewal.

Redemption and Renewal The poem conveys a sense of redemption and renewal. The dust of snow falling on the speaker is portrayed as a positive and purifying force that interrupts the speaker's melancholy. It symbolises a small moment of grace that can unexpectedly lift one's spirits and offer a new outlook on life, even in the face of negativity and despair.

Contrast and Duality Frost contrasts the dark and gloomy imagery of the crow and hemlock tree with the snow's light, refreshing dust. This contrast emphasises the theme of dualities in life—sorrow and joy, darkness and light—and how even the smallest positive element can counterbalance negativity.

Appreciation of Simple Pleasures The poem highlights the importance of appreciating simple moments of beauty and joy. It encourages readers to find happiness and solace in the little things that can unexpectedly brighten their day.

Transient Nature of Emotions The poem suggests that emotions are transient and subject to change. The speaker's mood shifts from despondency (sadness) to a sense of upliftment and hope through encountering nature's dust of snow. It serves as a reminder that life's emotional landscape is ever-changing.

Acceptance of Imperfections The poem subtly reflects on the imperfections and burdens that everyone carries. By acknowledging these aspects of life, the poem suggests that finding moments of relief and redemption is possible.

2. Nature has the power to lift our mood even when we are highly despondent. Comment on the basis of your understanding of the poem 'Dust of Snow'.

Ans. The poem 'Dust of Snow' by Robert Frost is a poem which enlightens us on how small things of nature can refresh us and cheer us for the rest of the day. Frost has beautifully depicted a crow and a hemlock tree, which are associated with bad-omen and fear. However, they have been used by Frost to uplift his mood and make him feel positive. Frost's writing skill as a poet lies in the fact that he is able to effectively convey how such a trivial thing as the falling of dust of snow from the top of tree can have a refreshing effect on the mind of man.

So, every aspect of nature-be it a crow or a hemlock tree-can be a source of positivity and can be helpful in lifting a depressed mind. In other words, everything in the world is beautiful. Nature and its creations have the power to uplift our mood even when we are in a depressed state of mind. A small incident of dust of snow falling, by the action of a crow (who is considered a bad omen) takes away the sadness from the poet's mind and refreshes him for the rest of the day.

3. Small things in life make significant changes in our life. Elaborate with reference to the poem 'Dust of Snow'.

Ans. It is truly said that little things in life can make huge changes in our life. Even the small incidents can have a huge impact in our lives. The poem 'Dust of Snow' beautifully states this fact. In the poem, the poet's mood is transformed because of a small event. While he was passing by the hemlock tree, the dust of snow falls on him. Such an insignificant event changes his sad and depressed mood into a joyous one.

Just like the simple movement of the crow, the simple things that we do for others can make all the difference. Our random acts of kindness can brighten a person's day and sometimes change their future. Just like the poet, who had wasted some part of day in his sorrows, is enlightened by the event, we can also make ours as well as others life happier. Noticing and appreciating the things of less importance can cause us to have a spirit that is willing to change and therefore succeed.

4. Comment on use of symbols in this poem. What is the purpose to use those symbols? **Competency Based**

Ans. In the poem 'Dust of Snow', the poet has introduced three symbols, i.e. the hemlock tree, the crow and the dust of snow.

- Hemlock is a tree that contains poison so the hemlock tree is a symbol of death.
- Second, the crow is considered to be the ugliest bird and is associated with bad omen.
- Another symbol 'dust of snow' indicates natural joy and energy.

The poet uses two negative symbols to represent the negative aspect of mind. The falling of snow by the crow certainly improves his mood.

Perhaps, the poet is saying that even something that we generally associate with negativity can have a positive impact. So, we can say that Frost's use of symbols is very profound and meaningful.

5. Imagine that Frost is of present day and has been invited to write for an ezine - 'Teen Talk'.

He chooses to draw upon his experience with the crow and the dusting of snow to share his thoughts on 'Every cloud has a silver lining'. As Frost, express your thoughts for the magazine-zine.

CBSE Question Bank 2021

Ans. In today's pandemic-hit world, life has changed a lot. From taking precautions to staying home, a new normal has been established. Social life has almost come to a standstill. We now meet only those people who mean the most to us. It has made us spend quality time with our loved ones, with those folks who do not judge us, but only love us. So, there is lesser showing off and pretence and greater bonding. We have now started focussing on our basic requirements, leaving out the unnecessary aspects and the stress connected to them.

When I sat back and thought about being stuck at home, I realised that I wasn't really stuck. Instead, I had been liberated. Just like the snow had roused me from my thoughts, it took these difficult months for me to understand how life can indeed be less stressful. You simply need to understand your priorities. I now firmly believe that each cloud has a silver lining. One only needs to have a positive attitude to be able to enjoy the beauty of the silver lining.

6. In the poem, 'Dust of Snow', the crow symbolically transforms the narrator's mood, while in the story, 'His First Flight', the baby seagull undergoes a literal transformation as it learns to fly. Analyse how these avian characters play similar or different thematic roles in their respective poem and story.

CBSE Additional SQP 2023

Ans. The crow in the poem 'Dust of Snow' and the baby seagull in 'His First Flight', both serve as pivotal symbols of transformation and redemption, in their distinct ways. The crow's sudden interaction with the speaker in the poem brings about an unexpected change in the narrator's mood. The simple act of the crow shaking off snow onto the speaker becomes a metaphor for a transformative moment. It shifts the narrator from a state of sadness to a renewed appreciation for the beauty of nature.

On the other hand, the baby seagull's literal transformation through flight in the story signifies a rite of passage and growth. Through this literal transformation, the seagull not only learns to navigate the physical world but also gains a newfound sense of confidence and independence, contributing to the overall theme of self-discovery and growth in the narrative. The (Creatures that fly), while differing in their modes of impact, share the thematic role of catalysing positive change, whether through a change in perspective or the achievement of a significant milestone.

7. Imagine Robert Frost from 'A Dust of Snow' met with Lencho from 'A Letter to God' and discussed the various ways nature can influence a person's mood. Create this conversation in not more than 120 words. You may begin this way.

Lencho As a farmer, my livelihood depends on nature and sometimes nature can be cruel.

CBSE 2023

Ans. **Lencho** As a farmer, my livelihood depends on nature and sometimes nature can be cruel. Once, I was looking forward to the rain. In fact, I was hoping for it for my crops, and when it did start to rain, I was so satisfied. I even went outside in the rain to feel the rain on my skin and breathe in the sweet air. However, the weather very quickly changed and the rain turned into a hailstorm. As a result, all of my crops were destroyed.

Robert Frost I'm so sorry that happened to you. Nature can definitely be cruel but I've noticed that it can also be full of hope. I was once having a bad day when some dust of snow fell on me. It was so small and beautiful that it completely lifted my mood. I think the way nature influences our mood depends on a variety of factors. I felt hope because I saw the beauty in that moment. However, had I seen a hailstorm that destroyed a farm, I'm sure I would have felt hopeless too.

Lencho It's interesting you say that you found hope in nature. For me, I found hope and faith in God. And you're right, there are definitely a lot of factors that contribute to how nature can influence our mood. Once the hailstorm was over, my entire field was covered in a sheet of white. Anyone else seeing that may have felt it was beautiful and the view may have lifted their spirits. However, since that sheet of white meant that all my hard work had gone to waste and my family would go hungry, to me, it only represented sorrow.

Robert Frost Yes, we may not know whether nature can influence someone's mood in a good way or a bad way, but what we do know is that nature is powerful and capable of affecting our moods and feelings.

ASSESSMENT EXERCISE

Extract Based Questions

Read the following extract carefully and answer the questions that follow.

The way a crow
Shook down on me
The dust of snow
From a hemlock tree

(i) Select the appropriate option to complete the sentence, according to the extract.

The Hemlock tree here symbolises ....

(a) happiness (b) sorrow

(c) excitement (d) good omen

(ii) The poet has used a figure of speech in the following lines. Identify it.

"The way a crow
Shook down on me
The dust of snow
From a hemlock tree"

(iii) Comment on the tone of the extract. Answer in about 40 words.

(iv) What is the rhyme scheme of the extract?

Short Answer (SA) Type Questions

1. Did the snow change the speaker's mood for better or for worse? Support your answer with examples from the poem.

2. How was the poet's mood changed?

Long Answer (LA) Type Question

1. Do you think that judging other people with a prejudiced eye makes us impervious to any goodness in them? Discuss in context of 'crow and hemlock tree' in this poem. **Competency Based**

Fire and Ice

by Robert Frost

CHAPTER 2

Introduction The poem 'Fire and Ice' by Robert Frost expresses the idea that the world would end in either of the two ways, i.e., ice or fire. Fire here symbolises the intensity of human desires, cruelty, greed, etc. Ice symbolises indifference in human relationships, hatred for others, etc. The poet has the view that both fire and ice are equally competent in bringing the world to a complete end.

Stanzawise Explanation

Stanza 1

Some say the world will end in fire
Some say in ice.
From what I've tasted of desire
I hold with those who favour fire.

Explanation In these lines, the poet analyses the views of the people on the two possible causes for the end of the world. On one side, there are people who believe that the world will end because of fire. Here, fire represents the extreme desire, anger, greed, etc. present within human beings.

On the other side, there are people who favour ice. Here, ice represents the human emotions of hatred, intolerence, etc. From his experience, the poet believes that the world will end with fire. In other words, excess or too much of anything can destroy the world.

Stanza 2

But if it had to perish twice,
I think I know enough of hate
To say that for destruction ice
Is also great
And would suffice.

Explanation In these lines, the poet thinks that if the world had to end twice, ice would also be able to destroy it completely. For the poet, ice (hatred) is as powerful as fire (desire) and will be sufficient to bring an end of this world. Herein, the poet wants to highlight that hatred, discrimination, intolerance, etc. are long lasting. Hence, their existence will slowly but surely destroy the world.

Poetic Devices Used in the Poem

Alliteration Repetition of initial consonant sounds in the same line.

- Some say the world will end in fire
  Some say in ice.
- I hold with those who favour fire

Paradox A true statement but which seems untrue.

- But if it had to perish twice.

Symbolism

- Fire-a symbol for desire
- Ice-a symbol for hate

Word Meaning

Word	Meaning
Stanza 1	
Hold	to take side, favour
Favour	incline towards
Stanza 2	
Perish	die or destroy
Suffice	be sufficient

NCERT FOLDER

NCERT Exercise Questions

THINKING ABOUT THE POEM (NCERT PAGE 15)

Q.1 There are many ideas about how the world will 'end'. Do you think the world will end some day? Have you ever thought what would happen if the Sun gets so hot that it 'bursts' or grows colder and colder?

Ans. There are definitely many ideas about how the world will 'end'. I do believe that the world will end some day as anything that has a beginning is sure to have an end. This stands true for the world also.

If the Sun got so hot that it burst, the whole of the Earth would be destroyed immediately. No part of the Earth would be able to bear the heat of that intensity. However, even if the sun grew cold, everything will come to an end as without sunlight, life will end. Lack of warmth and chilly temperatures would effect the life of all creatures on this planet; thus, bringing an end to it.

Q.2 For Frost, what do 'fire' and 'ice' stand for? Here are some ideas

greed	avarice	cruelty	lust
conflict	fury	intolerance	rigidity
insensitivity	coldness	indifference	hatred

Ans. For Frost, 'fire' and 'ice' symbolise intense human emotions and attitudes that have the potential to lead to destruction. 'Fire' represents desires such as greed, avarice, lust, and fury, which can consume and ravage individuals and societies. On the other hand, 'ice' embodies qualities like coldness, indifference, insensitivity and hatred, which can freeze relationships and foster cruelty.

Both elements serve as metaphors for the darker aspects of human nature, highlighting the destructive consequences of unchecked desires and emotional coldness. Frost uses these symbols to explore the multifaceted nature of human emotions and their capacity to shape the world's fate.

Q.3 What is the rhyme scheme of the poem? How does it help in bringing out the contrasting ideas in the poem?

Ans. Robert Frost's 'Fire and Ice' rhyme scheme is ABAA BCBCB. This rhyme scheme contributes to the poem's structure and helps emphasise the contrasting ideas in each stanza. The consistent rhyme scheme creates a sense of rhythm and balance, drawing attention to the juxtaposition of 'fire' and 'ice' in each couplet. This structure highlights the poem's exploration of contrasting elements, as each stanza pairs a different aspect of desire (represented by fire) with a contrasting aspect of hatred (represented by ice). The rhyme scheme, thus, enhances the poem's thematic exploration by highlighting the duality and balance between these opposing forces, ultimately emphasising their equal potential for destruction.

REVIEW EXERCISE

Including Competency Based Questions

Part – I

Multiple Choice Questions

1. According to the poem 'Fire and Ice', some people say that the world will end in ice because humans are .... CBSE Additional SQP 2022

(a) greedy for wealth and power
(b) becoming spiteful towards each other
(c) passive towards the problem of climate change
(d) becoming increasingly unconcerned about security

Ans. (b) becoming spiteful towards each other

2. What is the rhyming scheme of the poem?

(a) abaa bcbcb (b) aaba bcbcb
(c) aaab bcbcb (d) abab bcbcb

Ans. (a) The rhyme scheme of the poem is abaa bcbcb.

3. Identify the poetic device used in the line 'Some say the world will end in fire'.

(a) Metaphor
(b) Personification
(c) Alliteration
(d) Oxymoron

Ans. (c) Alliteration

4. The poet, Robert Frost, deals with a very sublime subject in the poem 'Fire and Ice'. What is that subject?

(a) Love and hatred (b) Freedom
(c) End of the world (d) None of these

Ans. (a) Love and hatred

5. **Given below are two statements marked as Assertion (A) and Reason (R) on the basis of the poem. Read both the statements carefully and choose the correct alternative from the following.**
Assertion (A) According to the poet, the world will end in ice.
Reason (R) The poet suggests that the reason behind this destruction is the hatred in the world.

Codes

(a) Both (A) and (R) are true and (R) is the correct explanation of (A)
(b) Both (A) and (R) are true, but (R) is not the correct explanation of (A)
(c) (A) is true, but (R) is false
(d) (A) is false, but (R) is true

Ans. (a) Both (A) and (R) are true and (R) is the correct explanation of (A)

6. **What does Robert Frost confess in the poem 'Fire and Ice'?**
(a) He has written the poem quickly
(b) He himself has faced the consequences of desire
(c) He has done many injustices
(d) He wants the world to end

Ans. (b) He himself has faced the consequences of desire

7. **According to the poem 'Fire and Ice', 'Hate' born of cold reasoning, makes a man ....**
(a) strong person (b) a bitter human being
(c) a better individual (d) insensitive to feelings

Ans. (d) insensitive to feelings

8. **Why does the poet hold with those who favour fire?**
(a) Because love among people is increasing fast
(b) Because hatred among people is increasing fast
(c) Because the lust for material things is increasing quickly
(d) None of the above

Ans. (c) Because the lust for material things is increasing quickly

9. **Which option correctly replaces the underlined phrase in the give line from Fire and Ice?**
I <u>hold with</u> those who favour fire. CBSE SQP 2021 Term 1
(a) am as experienced as
(b) strongly disagree with
(c) have the same opinion as
(d) habitually avoid

Ans. (c) have the same opinion as

Extract Based Questions

1. **Read the following extract carefully and answer the questions that follow.**

Some say the world will end in fire
Some say in ice.
From what I've tasted of desire
I hold with those who favour fire.

(i) **According to the poet, what does fire refer to?**

Ans. According to the poet, fire refers to violent desires, passions and jealousy.

(ii) **Why does the poet hold with those who favour fire? Answer in about 40 words.** Competency Based

Ans. The poet agrees with those who believe that the world will be destroyed by fire and thus, connects it with desire. According to him, desire is powerful and would be a quick end. Moreover, the fact that he has had personal experience with desire leads him to conclude that the world will end in fire.

(iii) **Select the appropriate option to complete the sentence, according to the extract.**
The poetic device used in the above extract is .... (Anaphora/Oxymoron)

Ans. Anaphora

(iv) **What message does the poet want to convey through this poem?**

Ans. The poet wants to convey that life is transitory and death is inevitable.

2. **Read the following extract carefully and answer the questions that follow.**

But if it had to perish twice
I think I know enough of hate
To say that for destruction ice
Is also great
And would suffice.

CBSE Additional SQP 2023

(i) **Fill the blank with one word.**
When the speaker says that ice could also bring about the end of the world, he refers to ...., as the means for destruction.

Ans. hatred, indifference and intolerance

(ii) **What does the speaker's alignment with those who favour ice, suggest?**

Ans. The speaker's alignment with those who favour ice suggests that they have seen the destructive consequences of a lack of empathy and emotional connection.

(iii) Which of the following best describes the speaker's attitude towards destruction caused by ice?

1. Indifferent **2. Fearful**

3. Dismissive **4. Respectful**

(a) 1 and 2 (b) 2 and 3 (c) Only 1 (d) Only 4

Ans. (c) Only 1

(iv) Comment on the poet's use of language in these lines. Answer in about 40 words.

Ans. The language used in the lines by Robert Frost is simple and straightforward. The words and phrases are easy to understand and the poem is written in a conversational tone. Despite its simplicity, however, the poem carries a profound message about the destructive power of both fire and ice, and the inevitability of destruction. The use of simple language in this context makes the message more accessible to a wider audience and adds to the poem's overall impact.

Or **CBSE 2024 C**

(i) State whether the following statement is True or False.

Ice melts the hate and destructive forces present around us.

Ans. False

(ii) What is 'ice' symbolic of in the above extract?

Ans. In the given extract, ice is symbolic of qualities like coldness, indifference, insensitivity and hatred, which can freeze relationships and foster cruelty.

(iii) What does the poet mean by saying that 'ice would also suffice'?

Ans. By the given statement, poet means that ice can also bring in great destruction to our planet. Ice, or hatred, is also capable of destroying the world just as much as fire, or desire and passion.

(iv) The use of the word 'perish' corresponds best with

(a) disembark (b) revive

(c) replenish (d) disintegrate

Ans. disintegrate

3. Read the following extract carefully and answer the questions that follow.

Some say the world will end in fire,
Some say in ice.
From what I've tasted of desire
I hold with those who favour fire.
But if it had to perish twice,
I think I know enough of hate
To say that for destruction ice
Is also great
And would suffice.

CBSE Question Bank 2021 Modified

(i) Choose the correct statement about the given poem. **Competency Based**

(a) Fire and ice are images—they help the readers visualise the power of nature over man.

(b) Fire and ice are symbols—not of natural disasters, but of humanity's ability to create disasters of its own.

(c) Fire and ice are elements—not of Nature but man-made and possess the ability to create havoc for mankind.

(d) Fire and ice are agents—they change the thinking of mankind from negative to positive and bring harmony.

Ans. (b) Fire and ice are symbols—not of natural disasters, but of humanity's ability to create disasters of its own.

(ii) Classify the connotations for fire and ice, as suggested in the poem.

1. rage 2. violence

3. indifference 4. hate

5. greed

Ans. Fire-2, 5; Ice-1, 3, 4

(iii) Identify the most likely tone of the poet in the lines 'To say that for destruction ice/Is also great'.

Ans. Sarcastic

(iv) The poem is a .... put across by the poet.

Ans. powerful warning

Or

(i) Complete the analogy with reference to the text.

Wish : Desire : : Die : .... **CBSE 2023**

Ans. Perish

(ii) Complete the sentence appropriately.

It is clear that alliteration is the poetic device for the 'world will' because ....

Ans. the initial sounds of 'w' repeats in the closely connected words.

(iii) State whether the following statement is True or False.

The poet believes that both feelings like indifference and jealousy and violence and rage will end the world one day.

Can you justify your answer.

Ans. The given statement is true.
The poet believes that both feelings like indifference and jealousy, and violence and rage will end the world one day. Indifference and jealousy , and violence and rage leads to wars. This ultimately leads to loss of life and environmental degradation. Hence, slowly and gradually, our world will be destroyed.

(iv) **Select the appropriate option to complete the sentence, according to the extract.**

I .... those who favour ice.

(a) disbelieve
(b) support
(c) betray
(d) belittle

Ans. (b) support

Part – II

Short Answer Type Questions

1. How has Frost brought out the contrasting ideas in the poem?

Or **Briefly write about the ideas about how the world will end.**

Or **Write down the two different views about the end of the world.**

Ans. The poet has contrasted fire with ice. Fire is symbolic of man's desires, greed and lust. When a man wants to go after his desires caring about nothing else, world can be destroyed by this fire of desires. On the other hand, ice is symbolic of man's indifference and hatred or insensitivity. These feelings also give rise to conflicts and stop us from being kind to others.

2. How does Robert Frost caution the common man?

Ans. Robert Frost cautions the common man and says that he should not forget the bitter reality that everything in this world is transitory and death is inevitable. So, man should avoid being too desirous or too indifferent.

3. Why does the poet side with those who favour fire?

Or **Explain why the poet personally holds the conviction that the world will primarily end in fire.**

CBSE Additional SQP 2023

Ans. The poet takes side with those who believe that the world will be destroyed by fire. Frost connects fire with desire. According to the poet, desire is powerful and can bring a quick end. He states that he had personal experience with desire which lead him to conclude that the world will end due to fire.

4. Write the message that the poem 'Fire and Ice' conveys.

Ans. The message that the poet is trying to convey is that nothing in this world is eternal. The poet first concludes that the world must end in fire because of his personal experience with desire and passion the emotions represented by fire.

However, at the same time, ice or hatred can also bring total destruction of this world. We should thus, not forget this supreme reality and keep ourselves above all selfish matters.

5. To say that for destruction ice is also great for the poet, what does 'ice' stand for? How is it sufficient to bring destruction?

Ans. Ice symbolises hatred and indifference. While desire consumes, hatred can linger (stay) in one's mind and heart for a long time, leading to fury and cruelty.

One becomes hardhearted and insensitive to the feelings of others. This insensitivity and hatred, slowly and gradually leads to the destruction of the world.

6. 'But if it had to perish twice'. How will the world perish twice?

Ans. According to the poet, the world would definitely come to an end due to fire. However, he states that if the world could end two times, then ice would also be a great cause. Ice is symbolic of hatred. The poet feels that there is enough hatred in the world that is sufficient to destroy the world.

7. 'Fire and Ice' was first published in 1920. Briefly explain how the First World War might have influenced the theme of the poem.

CBSE Question Bank, 2021

Ans. The poem is written shortly after the end of the First World War and is greatly influenced by it. The war proved how men's technological, economic and intellectual progress led to self-destruction.

This is exactly what the theme of the poem 'Fire and Ice' is wherein the poet feels that the desire for conquest and the hatred against the people of another country can cause the destruction of the world.

8. The tone of the speaker contrasts with the seriousness of the subject matter. Justify.

Or **Compare the theme of the poem 'Fire and Ice' with the poet's tone.**

Competency Based

Ans. In the poem 'Fire and Ice', the speaker is presenting his personal opinion about the possibilities of the end of the world in a casual and conversational tone. In contrast to the serious matter which the poem presents, the use of the casual tone implicates the casualness with which humanity has been taking up wars and moving upon the way of self-destruction.

9. Fire and Ice projects a pessimistic outlook. Comment.

Ans. It is true that the poem 'Fire and Ice' projects a pessimistic outlook on the theme of the end of the world. According to the poet, the world will end anyhow.

There is no saving grace in the world. The unattainable dreams of humankind will in all cases lead to catastrophic destruction of the Earth.

10. Evaluate the line- "Some say the world will end in fire/Some say in ice"- in the context of volcanic eruptions, forest fires, meteor collisions, melting ice caps etc. **CBSE Question Bank, 2021**

Ans. The given lines essentially indicates two human follies- greed and hatred. However, literally it can refer to the various natural calamities which have to the power to destroy earth within a small time.

While these calamities may seem natural, it is human exploitation of the environment that has led to their increased occurrence.

The sheer number of eruptions, forest fires, meteor collisions, melting ice caps, etc. that we see today is as much a threat to mankind as are greed and hatred.

11. How might the poem be interpreted as a reflection on human relationships?

Ans. The poem can be interpreted as a reflection on human relationships by considering how the elements of fire and ice relate to emotional dynamics between individuals. Fire may represent intense passion or desire in relationships, leading to great connection or destructive conflict. Ice could symbolise emotional distance or apathy, resulting in relationships becoming cold and distant or emotional detachment.

12. Why do you think the poet chooses not to express personal preferences in the poem?

Ans. The poet does not express personal preferences in the poem to maintain objectivity and allow readers to interpret it. By not revealing his personal stance, Frost emphasises the universality of the themes presented. He wants readers to think critically and explore their perspectives on the destructive potential of human emotions and behaviours.

13. How do the poem's structure and short lines impact its impact?

Ans. The poem's structure, with short and compact lines, contributes to its impact by creating a sense of urgency and directness. The brevity of each line allows Frost to pack significant meaning into concise phrases, capturing readers' attention and making each word and idea count. The short lines enhance the poem's rhythm and flow are enhanced by the sharp lines, making it more memorable and thought-provoking.

Long Answer Type Questions

1. Discuss how extreme behaviour can hasten the end of the world with respect to 'Fire and Ice'. **CBSE 2013**

Ans. In the poem 'Fire and Ice', the poet highlights that extreme behaviours can lead to the end of the world. The poet points out the two different views regarding the end of the world and associates the extreme behaviours to it.

The first view is fire which symbolises deep emotions of desire, passion, etc. Desire, according to the poet, can become so intense that it can make people lose their calm. Fire of desires, if left uncontrolled, can lead to the destruction of humanity as well as the world.

The second view is ice which represents hatred, differentiation and insensitivity. Hatred, rigidity and icy reasoning give rise to contempt. It can end all positive human emotions such as human warmth, love, sympathy, kindness and consideration for others. This type of behaviour will only bring death to this world.

2. The poem 'Fire and Ice', carries with it very deep thematic ideas. Elaborate on these darkest traits of humanity. **Competency Based**

Ans. Frost presents the two of the darkest traits of humanity, i.e. the capacity to hate and the capacity to be consumed by lust or desire. Of the two, he suggests that the greater of the two evils is desire.

In giving desire the first position in regard to the destruction of the world, Frost is providing a powerful statement on the subject of greed and jealousy.
He emphasises that above all else, desire is the trait of humanity that is most likely to lead to its destruction. Desire represents the greatest problem that attributes to the cause of the war.

Frost, then, attributes hatred with the same capacity to do harm. However, he lessens the importance of hatred but still presents it as having the ability to lead to the destruction of the world if it were to happen for a second time.

3. Most of your classmates, like Frost, feel that man's greed and rage or hate, would lead the world to its destruction. You feel that the 'fire and ice' in Mankind can be addressed to create a harmonious world. Write a speech, for your classmates, expressing your belief/s with respect to the poem. **CBSE Question Bank 2021**

Ans. 'Some say the world will end in fire, some say in ice.' Today, we stand at the crossroads of these elemental forces within ourselves and our society.

Good morning to respected teachers and my dear friends. I'm here to speak on the topic of 'fire and ice'. In the tapestry of humanity, our actions are often coloured by the dual forces of fire and ice. The fire of passion and the ice of indifference can either lead to destruction or it can be used to bring about a constructive change.

To create a harmonious world, we must balance the flames of anger with the coolness of empathy and understanding. By recognising the destructive potentials of both extremes, we can direct and convert our passion into positive actions. By practicing empathy and kindness we can melt the icy barriers that divide us.

Let us build bridges that can withstand the heat of discord and endure the chill of indifference to create a happy community.

Thank you

4. Imagine that Nelson Mandela read 'Fire and Ice'. As Mandela, write a diary entry associating the impact of the troubled history of South Africa with the idea expressed in the poem.

You may begin like this.

10th May, 1994, Tuesday 10 p.m.

Today, when I am the President of South Africa, I can't help recalling Robert Frost's 'Fire and Ice'

CBSE Question Bank 2021

Ans. Tuesday, 10th May, 1994 10 p.m.

Dear Diary

Today, when I am the President of South Africa, I can't help recalling Robert Frost's 'Fire and Ice'.

My countrymen faced oppression and adversities caused by both desire and hatred. We have been the victims of such cruelty and torture that even thinking about it terrifies me . The people of South Africa spent fifty years in the struggle against discrimination based on the colour of skin.

Today, when we have gained freedom, it is like our world has gained life. Till now we were not alive because our freedom had been snatched away from us. I agree with Robert Frost's view that both Fire and Ice can destroy the world.

However, I feel that ice is stronger than fire, hatred can cause much more destruction as compared to greed. Yet,
I don't hope any destruction for anyone because I know that the world can be saved with love and peace.

Nelson

5. Both poems 'Dust of Snow' and 'Fire and Ice' use contrasting elements of nature to convey their respective messages about life and human emotions but they do it differently. Examine these differences. **CBSE SQP 2024**

Ans. Dust of Snow emphasises the potential for beauty and renewal in the smallest aspects of nature, whereas, Fire and Ice explores the darker aspects of human desire and hatred, highlighting the destructive forces shaping human existence. Dust of Snow employs imagery of lightness, purity and serenity through the snowfall and the hemlock tree.

In contrast, Fire and Ice utilises imagery of destruction and intensity highlighting the darker aspects of human emotions and relationships.

In Dust of Snow, the speaker's emotional response to nature is one of gratitude and appreciation. Conversely, Fire and Ice evokes a sense of fear and contemplation about the destructive forces inherent in human nature. Dust of Snow focuses on the idea of small, unexpected moments in nature leading to positive change and renewal in the individual. Fire and Ice suggests that these internal forces have the potential to shape not only individual lives but also the fate of humanity as a whole.

ASSESSMENT EXERCISE

Extract Based Questions

Read the following extract carefully and answer the questions that follow.

But if it had to perish twice,
I think I know enough of hate
To say that for destruction ice Is also great
And would suffice.

(i) How can 'Ice' bring an end to the world?
   (a) Ice symbolises hatred
   (b) Hatred can cause wars
   (c) Wars can bring total destruction
   (d) All of the above

(ii) The poet has used a figure of speech in the following lines. Identify it.
"To say that for destruction ice
Is also great"

(iii) What is the poet's world view here?

Select the option that applies the same rhyme scheme a the lines of the given extract.

(a) There was an Old Man in a boat,
Who said, 'I'm afloat, I'm afloat!'
When they said, 'No! you ain't!'
He was ready to faint,
That unhappy Old Man in a boat.

(b) "The people along the sand
All turn and look one way.
They turn their back on land.
They look at the sea all day.
To them it seems so grand.

(c) Helen, thy beauty is to me
Like those Nicean barks of yore,
That gently, o'er a perfumed sea,
The weary, way-worn wanderer bore
To his own native shore.

(d) In castle ruins
the tappings of a hand-drum
so clearly echo,
that in Komachi's dancing
even the moon seemed to smile.

Short Answer (SA) Type Questions

1. How would you describe the speaker's worldview? Is it pessimistic, realistic or just indifferent?
2. Do you think the extremes of fire and ice could exist in a person at the same time?

Long Answer (LA) Type Question

1. We've got a pretty good handle on what it means to 'taste' desire, but what do you think it means to 'know enough of hate'? Are there many kinds of hatred that can together destroy the world. Justify your answer. **Competency Based**

A Tiger in the Zoo *by Leslie Norris*

Introduction In this poem 'A Tiger in the Zoo', the poet tries to depict the poor condition of a caged tiger. He contrasts and compares the life of a caged tiger with a tiger living in his natural habitat, i.e. a jungle. Through the poem, the poet tries to convey that wild animals should be allowed to live freely in their natural habitat. Freedom is loved by all living beings not just humans.

Stanzawise Explanation

Stanza 1

He stalks in his vivid stripes
The few steps of his cage,
On pads of velvet quiet,
In his quiet rage.

Explanation In these lines, the poet is describing a tiger in a cage. The tiger with bright and clear stripes moves inside the cage. The cage is very small so the tiger can hardly take a few steps along its length. His paws are soft like velvet so no one can hear the sound of his footsteps.

Inspite of being the most powerful creature, he is imprisoned inside a cage. This situation has made the tiger angry. However, he is keeping quiet as he knows that he is helpless in the situation.

Stanza 2

He should be lurking in shadow,
Sliding through long grass
Near the water hole
Where plump deer pass.

Explanation In these lines, the poet is filled with sorrow for the caged tiger. He feels that a tiger should be free in his natural habitat.

He should be hiding in the shadows and quietly moving through the long grass near the water hole. He should be waiting for a fat and healthy deer to pass in the hopes of getting a heavy meal. The poet wants to convey that the actual life of a tiger is in a jungle and not in a cage.

Stanza 3

He should be snarling around houses
At the jungle's edge,
Baring his white fangs, his claws,
Terrorising the village!

Explanation In these lines, the poet explains what a tiger in his natural habitat should be doing. According to him, a tiger should be growling/roaring around the houses located at the jungle's edge. He should be showing his sharp white teeth and his claws to terrorise the villagers.

Stanza 4

But he's locked in a concrete cell,
His strength behind bars,
Stalking the length of his cage,
Ignoring visitors.

Explanation In these lines, the poet's focus returns to the angry tiger in the cage. The poet explains that unlike the tiger in the jungle, this tiger is not free. He is locked in the concrete cell.

His strength and power is of no use behind the bars of the cage. He is moving in his cage ignoring the visitors who are continuously visiting to have a look at him.

Stanza 5

He hears the last voice at night,
The patrolling cars,
And stares with his brilliant eyes
At the brilliant stars.

Explanation In these lines, the poet says that even at night the tiger is disturbed. He hears the last sound of the patrolling cars of the zoo officials. The tiger stares at the brilliant stars shining brightly in the sky with his brilliant eyes which hope for freedom.

Poetic Devices Used in the Poem

Repetition Repetition of words/phrases in the same line.

- velvet quiet, quiet rage
- brilliant eyes, brilliant stars

Alliteration Repetition of initial consonant sounds in the same line.

He stalks in his vivid stripes.

Metaphor Comparison of two ideas without using 'like' and 'as'.

Pads of velvet

Rhyme The rhyme scheme for first, second and fifth stanza is abcb and for third and fourth stanza is abcd.

Word Meaning

Word	Meaning
Stanza 1	
Stalks	stride, to move quietly and slowly in a threatening way
Vivid	bright and clear
Pads	the soft part under the foot of the tiger
Rage	anger
Stanza 2	
Lurking	hiding
Sliding	moving, walking with ease
Plump	fat
Stanza 3	
Snarling	growling or roaring
Baring	showing
Fangs	two long sharp teeth at the front of the mouths of some animals
Claws	Paw; nails
Terrorising	frightening or threatening
Stanza 4	
Concrete cell	a very small and unpleasant cage made of cement and stone
Stanza 5	
Patrolling	to go around an area at regular times to check that it is safe

NCERT FOLDER

NCERT Intext and Exercise Questions

THINKING ABOUT THE POEM

(NCERT PAGE 30)

Q.1 Read the poem again and work in pairs or groups to do the following tasks.

(i) Find the words that describe the movements and actions of the tiger in the cage and in the wild. Arrange them in two columns.

(ii) Find the words that describe the two places and arrange them in two columns.

Now try to share ideas about how the poet uses words and images to contrast the two situations.

Ans. (i)

In the Cage	In the Wild
• Stalks	• Lurking in shadow
• Few steps of his cage	• Sliding through long
• Quiet rage	• Grass
• Locked in concrete cell	• Snarling around
• Stalking the length of his	• Houses
• cage ignoring visitors	• Baring his white
• He hears the last voice	• Fangs his claws
• Stares at the brilliant stars	• Terrorising the villagers

(ii)

Cage	Wild
• Few steps of his cage	• Shadow
• Locked	• Long grass
• Concrete cell	• Water hole
• Behind bars	• Plump deer
• Visitors	• Houses at jungle's edge
• Patrolling cars	• Village

The poet contrasts the two situations through imagery and language. In the cage, words like 'concrete cell', 'bars', and 'length of his cage' evoke feelings of confinement and restriction. The tiger's actions within the cage, such as 'stalking' and 'ignoring visitors', suggest a sense of restlessness and frustration.

Q.2 Notice the use of a word repeated in lines such as these

(i) On pads of velvet quiet, In his quiet rage.

(ii) And stares with his brilliant eyes At the brilliant stars.

What do you think is the effect of this repetition?

Ans. This repetition is a poetic device used by the poet in order to increase the intensity of the tiger's rage and his helpless silence. 'Velvet quiet' refers to the quiet velvet paws of the tiger which cannot run. They can only walk around the limited space in the cage. The use of 'quiet rage' symbolises the anger and ferocity that is building up inside the tiger as it wants freedom, but the rage is quiet because he is locked in the cage and is helpless.

Similarly, the use of 'brilliant' for the tiger's eyes as well as the stars also brings out the magnificence of the poem. The tiger stares at the brilliant stars with his brilliant eyes dreaming about how beautiful his life could have been in the forest. The repetition thus, gives a wonderful effect to the poem.

Q.3 Read the following two poems one about a tiger and the other about a panther. Then discuss

Are zoos necessary for the protection or conservation of some species of animals?

Are they useful for educating the public?

Are there alternatives to zoos?

The Tiger

The tiger behind the bars of his cage growls,
The tiger behind the bars of his cage snarls,
The tiger behind the bars of his cage roars,
Then he thinks.
It would be nice not to be behind bars all
The time
Because they spoil my view
I wish I were wild, not on show.
But if I were wild, hunters might shoot me,
But if I were wild, food might poison me,
But if I were wild, water might drown me.
Then he stops thinking
And...
The tiger behind the bars of his cage growls,
The tiger behind the bars of his cage snarls,
The tiger behind the bars of his cage roars.

Peter Niblett

The Panther

His vision, from the constantly passing bars,
has grown so weary that it cannot hold
anything else. It seems to him there are
a thousand bars and behind the bars, no world.
As he paces in cramped circles, over and over,
the movement of his powerful soft strides
is like a ritual dance around a centre
in which a mighty will stands paralysed.
Only at times, the curtain of the pupils
lifts, quietly. An image enters in,
rushes down through the tensed, arrested muscles,
plunges into the heart and is gone. ***Rainer Maria Rilke***

Ans. Zoos are artificial habitats that can also develop into good scientific research centres.

Necessity of Zoos for Conservation Zoos can play a crucial role in protecting and conserving certain species, particularly those facing extinction or habitat loss. Zoos contribute to genetic diversity and species preservation through captive breeding programmes and conservation initiatives.

Educational Benefits Zoos serve as valuable educational resources, allowing the public to learn about diverse ecosystems and the importance of wildlife conservation. They enable people to engage with animals up close, fostering empathy and understanding.

However, zoos are not the perfect substitute for forests since animals are confined in small cages. As a result, their freedom to move around is restricted.

Yes, there are alternatives to zoos which are wild life sanctuaries, national parks or bio-reserves where animals live in an open but protected environment. They are able to roam around freely and are protected from hunters and poachers.

REVIEW EXERCISE

Including Competency Based Questions

Part - I

Multiple Choice Questions

1. How does the tiger scare the people?

(a) By growling
(b) Walking up and down
(c) Attacking people
(d) Baring his white teeth and claws

Ans. (d) Baring his white teeth and claws.

2. Why does the tiger 'snarl' in the poem?

(a) To show his anger (b) Because he is helpless
(c) To run away (d) Both (a) and (b)

Ans. (d) Both (a) and (b)

3. How does the tiger show his presence to the villagers as described in the poem 'A Tiger in the Zoo'?

(a) By baring teeth and claws (b) By sitting quietly
(c) By growling (d) Both (a) and (c)

Ans. (d) Both (a) and (c)

4. "He should be snarling around houses
At the jungle's edge,
Baring his white fangs, his claws,
Terrorising the village!"
From the given lines, the poet is suggesting that the ....

(a) tiger is a very proud animal
(b) tiger can get angry easily
(c) tiger should be in his natural habitat
(d) tiger can harm anyone

Ans. (c) tiger should be in his natural habitat

5. Name the poetic device used in the line "He stalks in his vivid stripes" from the poem 'A Tiger in the Zoo'.

(a) Metaphor (b) Alliteration
(c) Oxymoron (d) Personification

Ans. (b) Alliteration

6. Name the poetic device used in the line 'On pads of velvet quiet' from the poem 'A Tiger in the Zoo'.

(a) Metaphor (b) Assonance
(c) Oxymoron (d) Consonance

Ans. (a) Metaphor

7. Name the poetic device used in the line 'In his quiet rage' from the poem 'A Tiger in the Zoo'.

(a) Metaphor (b) Assonance
(c) Oxymoron (d) Consonance

Ans. (c) Oxymoron

8. Why should the tiger in the poem 'A Tiger in the Zoo' be lurking in shadow?

(a) Out of fear (b) Out of anger
(c) To hunt the deer (d) Both (a) and (b)

Ans. (c) To hunt the deer

9. Which line describes 'the tiger in a zoo' in the poem?

(a) Locked in concrete cell (b) Snarling around houses
(c) Shadow, long grass (d) Baring his white fangs

Ans. (a) Locked in concrete cell

10. What is the poet trying to say by 'ignoring visitors'?

(a) Tiger knows his power is restricted
(b) There is no use of showing rage
(c) He is less terrorising because of the cage
(d) All of the above

Ans. (d) All of the above

11. The phrase 'stalking the length of his cage' means

(a) the tiger can walk only till the length of the cage
(b) the tiger is measuring the length of the cage
(c) the tiger is staring at the cage
(d) None of the above

Ans. (a) the tiger can walk only till the length of the cage

12. In the poem 'A Tiger in the Zoo', what does the tiger's 'quiet rage', indicate? It indicates that the tiger's anger is CBSE SQP 2021 Term 1

(a) forgotten (b) provoked (c) suppressed (d) opposed

Ans. (c) suppressed

13. Which of these activities should the tiger be doing in the jungle? CBSE Additional SQP 2022

(a) Roar at visitors (b) Stare at people
(c) Wait for his prey (d) Drink clean water

Ans. (c) Wait for his prey

14. Why does the poet describe the cage as having 'few steps'?

(a) To draw attention to the stairs in the cage
(b) To show admiration for the size of the cage
(c) To convey the importance of protecting tigers
(d) To highlight the restriction on the tiger's freedom

Ans. (d) To highlight the restriction on the tiger's freedom

15. The contrast indicated in the given extract is between ....

(a) the tiger's reality and the tiger's ideal situation
(b) the luxury of a zoo and the simplicity of a jungle

(c) the tiger's actual feeling and how the tiger should feel
(d) the silence of the tiger in a zoo and his dominance in the jungle

Ans. (d) the silence of the tiger in a zoo and his dominance in the jungle

16. Select the option that describes the tiger in the lines below.

Lurking in shadow,
Sliding through long grass

1. sly 2. scared 3. dominant
4. light-footed 5. eye-catching

(a) 1 and 3 (b) 3 and 5 (c) 1, 3 and 4 (d) 2, 4 and 5

Ans. (c) 1, 3 and 4

Extract Based Questions

1. Read the following extract carefully and answer the questions that follow.

He stalks in his vivid stripes,
The few steps of his cage,
On pads of velvet quiet,
In his quiet rage.

CBSE 2024

(i) Explain the contrast created by words, 'stalks' and 'few steps of his cage'.

Ans. The word 'stalks' suggests a powerful, purposeful and potentially threatening movement, typically associated with predators in the wild, demonstrating their freedom and dominance. However, this powerful action is confined to the 'few steps of his cage,' creating a stark contrast that highlights the limitations imposed on the tiger, restricting its natural behaviours and freedom.

(ii) Which of the following best describes the tiger's feelings in the context?

(a) Anger (b) Conflicted
(c) Pessimism (d) Apprehension

Ans. (a) Anger

(iii) Comment in about 40 words on the poet's use of imagery in the above extract.

Ans. The poet's use of imagery in this extract vividly captures the tiger's condition and emotions. Describing the tiger's movement as stalking 'in vivid stripes' on 'pads of velvet quiet,' presents a clear, visual image of the tiger's majestic yet restrained presence. The juxtaposition of the tiger's silent, graceful movement against the backdrop of his 'quiet rage' effectively communicates the increasing anger and frustration of a magnificent creature trapped within the confines of a cage.

(iv) The poet mentions that the tiger walks a few steps on his velvet pads and in anger. Why is he angry?

Ans. The tiger is imprisoned in a cage. He cannot move around freely and even his strength is useless. His situation makes him angry but he remains quiet and walks softly because he is helpless in the situation.

Or **CBSE SQP 2024**

(i) What is the most likely reason the poet chooses to say 'vivid' stripes instead of just stating the colours of the stripes?

Ans. The use of the word 'vivid' stripes evokes a sense of intensity and liveliness in the appearance of the tiger. The word suggests that the stripes are not only distinct in colours but also vibrant and full of life. It conveys the idea that tigers' markings are not subdued but rather striking and attention-grabbing. This points to the magnificence of the animal.

(ii) Fill the blank with one word.

The tiger's stalking suggests a movement that is .... within the confines of its cage.

Ans. restless

(iii) How does the poet reinforce the contrast between the tiger's confined environment and its internal emotions?

Ans. The poet reinforces the contrast between the tiger's confined environment and its internal emotions by using the word 'quiet' twice in the given lines.

(iv) Select the option that applies the same rhyme scheme as the lines of the given extract.

(a) This bird so small and sweet, green,
Sings aloud in the morn,
Perched on a branch green, sweet,
Chirp, chirp, tweet, tweet.

(b) Perched on a branch
This bird so sweet and lean,
Sings aloud in a voice
Chirp, chirp, tweet, tweet.

(c) This bird sings without a care, sweet
Perched on a branch green,
A song with the world to share,
With its feelings so keen.

(d) This bird so small and
Sings aloud in the morn
Perched on a green branch
Singing its own melody

Ans. (a) This bird so small and sweet, green,
sings aloud in the morn,
Perched on a branch green, sweet,
Chirp, Chirp, tweet, tweet!

Or

(i) 'Quiet rage' refers to the tigers **CBSE 2023**

(a) helplessness
(b) he has not been able to hunt
(c) his prey has not come to the water hole
(d) he is not free

Ans. (a) helplessness

(ii) He is lurking in shadows because ....

Ans. he doesn't want to alert the deer of his presence

(iii) Complete the sentence appropriately.
It is clear that metaphor is the poetic device used for 'pads of velvet' because ....
(clue-explain how metaphor applies here).

Ans. the paws of the tiger are soft like velvet.

(iv) The tiger is stealthily waiting for the deer to come to the water hole. Which qualities of the tiger are mentioned in this line?

Ans. The given expression points out that the tiger is sly, graceful and light-footed. His natural instincts are strong and he is free to hunt its prey.

2. Read the following extract carefully and answer the questions that follow.

He should be lurking in shadow,
Sliding through long grass
Near the water hole
Where plump deer pass.

CBSE Question Bank 2021 Modified

(i) Complete the sentence appropriately.
According to the extract, the poet wishes for the tiger to be 'sliding' through the foliage as this would .... **Competency Based**

Ans. assist in keeping the prey unsuspecting of the predator's sound

(ii) Which fact does not connect with the significance of the water hole for the tiger?

(a) Many tigers chase prey into the water and holds the victim's head under water until it drowns.
(b) Prey feed in the water on water-lilies and often wander into the middle of the water hole, where they are vulnerable and easy for the tiger to kill.
(c) Prey that has quenched its thirst ensures consumption of hydrated meat for the tiger.
(d) Chasing the panicked prey from shallow to deep water where the tiger grabs it.

Ans. (c) Prey that has quenched its thirst ensures consumption of hydrated meat for the tiger.

(iii) Complete the sentence appropriately.
The word plump shows that deer is referred to as ....

Ans. healthy

(iv) What activity of the tiger is presented in the extract? Can you describe it?

Ans. The activity of the tiger presented in the extract is hunting.

3. Read the following extract carefully and answer the questions that follow.

He stalks in his vivid stripes
The few steps of his cage
On pads of velvet quiet
In his quiet rage.
He should be lurking in shadow
Sliding through long grass
Near the water hole
Where plump deer pass **CBSE 2023**

(i) 'He' is in a rage because he is

(a) hungry (b) tied (c) thirsty (d) in a cage

Ans. (d) in a cage

(ii) Complete the sentence with reference to the extract.
The above lines express the tiger's ....

Ans. anger

(iii) Complete the sentence with reference to the extract.
The contrast in the above extract is between life in the forest and life in the ....

Ans. zoo

(iv) Complete the sentence appropriately.
It is clear that metaphor is the poetic device used for 'pads of velvet' - because ....
(Clue : explain how metaphor is applied here.)

Ans. metaphor refers to a word or phrase applied to an object or action to which it is not literally applicable.

Or

(i) Complete the sentence appropriately.
The vivid stripes refer to .... **CBSE 2023**

Ans. the black stripes on the tiger's body

(ii) Which word from the extract is the opposite of 'loud'?

Ans. Quiet

(iii) The use of the phrase 'pads of velvet' means

(a) neck (b) tail (c) skin (d) paws

Ans. (d) paws

(iv) Why was the tiger lurking in shadow?

Ans. The tiger was lurking in the shadow to wait for a healthy deer to come near the water body. The tiger had to prey on the deer.

4. Read the following extract carefully and answer the questions that follow.

He should be snarling around houses
At the jungle's edge,
Baring his white fangs, his claws,
Terrorising the village!

(i) Why does the tiger 'snarl'?

Ans. The Tiger snarls because of his anger and helplessness.

(ii) How does the tiger show his presence?

Ans. The tiger shows his presence by baring teeth and claws and by growling.

(iii) Why does the poet think that the tiger should be 'snarling around houses'? Answer in about 40 words. **Competency Based**

Ans. The poet thinks that the tiger should be in the jungle, hiding in the shadow like the wild animal he is. He thinks that the tiger should move around quietly in the long grass near the water hole to prey on deer and should go around the outskirts of the jungle growling around houses and terrifying the villagers.

Select the option that applies the same rhyme scheme as the first four lines of the given extract.

(a) "I know the way to cure your groom
as I did mine, dad-nabbit.
Do what I did to my old Brad
and simply hide his teeth."

(b) It is an ancient Mariner,
And he stoppeth one of three.
'By thy long grey beard and glittering eye,
Now wherefore stopp'st thou me?

(c) As I walked out one evening,
Walking down Bristol Street,
The crowds upon the pavement
Were fields of harvest wheat.

(d) Hold fast to dreams
For if dreams die
Life is a broken-winged bird
That cannot fly.

Ans. (d)

5. Read the following extract carefully and answer the questions that follow.

But he's locked in a concrete cell,
His strength behind bars,
Stalking the length of his cage,
Ignoring visitors.
He hears the last voice at night,
The patrolling cars, ...

CBSE Question Bank 2021 Modified

(i) Which options correctly lists the reason for the tiger 'stalking the length of his cage'?

(a) Animals tend to cover large distances and burn a lot of their energy by hunting for prey in their natural habitat. Zoos deprive them of such stimulation and they are restless and bored.

(b) Animals are scared of visitors gazing at them in their unnatural surroundings. Zoos are places where animals are far removed from the privacy of their natural habitat.

(c) Animals dislike human noises in the city and react to them aggressively. Zoos are often located in cities or outskirts.

(d) Animals require human love and care and they miss it when in captivity. Zoos are places where they walk around mechanically to attract human attention.

Ans. (a) Animals tend to cover large distances and burn a lot of their energy by hunting for prey, in their natural habitat. Zoos deprive them of such stimulation and they are restless and bored.

(ii) What is the main contrasting idea as suggested by the extract?

Ans. Confinement and freedom is the main contrasting idea.

(iii) Why do you think the tiger is ignoring the visitors?

Ans. The tiger is ignoring the visitors because he knows that none would help him out of captivity.

(iv) What emotion is the tiger feeling in the extract?

Ans. Anger

6. Read the following extract carefully and answer the questions that follow.

He should be snarling around houses
At the jungle's edge,
Baring his white fangs, his claws,
Terrorising the village!
But he's locked in a concrete cell,
His strength behind bars,
Stalking the length of his cage,
Ignoring visitors.

CBSE Additional SQP 2023

(i) Fill in the blank with one word.

The speaker describes the tiger as 'stalking' up and down his cage to show how .... the tiger felt.

Ans. angry and restless

(ii) What could be a reason the speaker mentions the behaviour of the tiger at the jungle's 'edge' and not at its centre? Answer in about 40 words.

Ans. The author has described the tiger at the 'edge' of the jungle to show how a tiger would react and respond to the people encroaching his territory.

He would scare them. This is done to contrast how the tiger behaves towards people when caged.

(iii) Which of these explains the meaning of the phrase 'His strength behind bars'?

(a) The tiger's strength is in its ability to break free from the cage it is in.

(b) The tiger's strength is shown when he pushes against the bars of the cage.

(c) The tiger's strength is in his resilience and ability to adapt to a new environment.

(d) The tiger's strength is confined within the bars of the cage and this makes him less threatening.

Ans. (d) The tiger's strength is confined within the bars of the cage and this makes him less threatening.

(iv) What effect is produced by the usage of words such as 'snarling', 'terrorising' and 'claws'?

Ans. Through the use of the given words, the poet wishes to emphasise the fact that tigers are wild animals.

Or

(i) Fill in the blank with one word.
The tiger is reacting to his imprisonment in the zoo by .... visitors.

Ans. ignoring

(ii) We should protect the tigers as

(a) they are majestic to look at

(b) they attract visitors to the zoo

(c) they are ferocious

(d) they are part of our environment

Ans. (d) they are part of our environment

(iii) Why does the tiger terrorise the villagers?

Ans. The tiger terrorises the villagers as they have cleared his habitat.

(iv) Where should the strength of the tiger be used according to the poet?

Ans. The strength of the tiger should be used in the forest to hunt.

7. Read the following extract carefully and answer the questions that follow.

He hears the last voice at night,
The patrolling cars,
And stares with his brilliant eyes
At the brilliant stars.
He stalks in his vivid stripes
The few steps of his cage. **CBSE 2023**

(i) Whose is the last voice heard by the tiger?

Or **What do you think is the voice there?**

Ans. The last voice heard by the tiger is that of the patrolling cars of the guards of the zoo. The voices are there to ensure that everything is fine in the zoo at night.

(ii) Complete the sentence appropriately.
It is clear that 'Repetition' is the poetic device used for 'his brilliant eyes at the brilliant stars' because ....
(Clue: explain how repetition applies here)

Ans. the poet wants to bring into notice the tiger's desire for freedom. The tiger, with his shining eyes, keeps staring at the shining stars and desires to be free like them.

(iii) The main contrasting ideas in this extract are

(a) tiger and deer

(b) cruelty and sympathy

(c) confinement and freedom

(d) master and slave

Ans. (c) confinement and freedom

(iv) The use of word 'stalks' creates an image of

Ans. anger

Part - II

Short Answer Type Questions

1. Describe the tiger in the cage.

Ans. A tiger in the cage is imprisoned. He is not free. In the cage, the tiger can hardly move and his strength is useless. His situation makes him angry but he remains quiet as he is helpless in the situation.

2. Leslie Norris has described some of the activities of a tiger behind the bars of its cage. State some of them.

Ans. Some of the activities of the tiger behind the bars of its cage include stalking along the length of the cage, ignoring visitors, hearing patrolling cars and staring at the brilliant stars shining in the sky.

3. Why does the tiger express his rage quietly?

Ans. The tiger expresses his rage quietly because he can do nothing from behind the bars of his cage. He is helpless as he cannot use his strength to get out of the cage. He is no longer free as he was in the jungle.

4 Describe the tiger in the wild.

Ans. The tiger in the wild is majestic. He freely lies under the shade and hunts for prey. He moves near the water hole because food is in plenty there. Sometimes, he also growls and terrorises the villagers.

5. Where should the tiger have been according to the poet?

Ans. The poet thinks that the tiger should have been in the jungle, hiding in the shadow, quietly moving in the long grass near the water hole to prey on the deer. He should also be on the outskirts of the jungle growling around houses and terrifying the villagers.

6. Why should the tiger snarl around houses at the edge of the forest?

Ans. The tiger should snarl around houses at the edge of the forest for the following reasons

- First, the villagers will not disturb the peace of the forest.
- Second, villagers will not kill the animals for money or just for fun.

7. What is the tiger doing when it is seen in the cage the second time? Why is he ignoring the visitors?

Ans. The tiger is slowly and quietly moving along the length of the cage in a threatening manner.

He is ignoring the visitors because he considers them devoid of any feelings. None of them think of releasing him from his prison. Thus, he stops taking any notice of them.

8. Why do you think the tiger looks at the stars?

Ans. The tiger stares with hope at the brilliant stars shining in the sky as he feels very helpless in the cage. He hopes for the day when he would be able to run free in the wild. The brilliant stars, thus, provide him with some sort of comfort.

9. It is said that an animal's eyes have the power to speak a great language. Explain with reference to the tiger. **Competency Based**

Ans. In the poem, 'A Tiger in the Zoo', the tiger's eyes are very expressive. They depict anger with humans and a desire to live a free life in its natural habitat. While in the zoo, the tiger does not want to make eye contact with humans. When he looks at the stars, his eyes shine and sparkle expressing his sorrow and desire.

10. How does the poem point to the cruelty of animals in captivity?

***Or* In what ways does the contrast between the tiger's natural habitat and its confinement in a concrete cell enhance the poem's exploration of captivity and its consequences for wild animals?** **CBSE 2025**

Ans. The poem hints at the cruelty of animals in captivity by contrasting the life an animal lives in its natural habitat and zoo. The poet imagines how a tiger attacks a deer near the water hole, terrorises the villagers living on the outskirts and snarls at night. On the contrary, it shows how the same tiger is made to stay in a cramped space for the entertainment of humans.

11. The poet celebrates the strength of the tiger in this poem. Counter the statement. **CBSE Question Bank, 2021**

Ans. The poet acknowledges that the tiger is a powerful beast but its strength is no longer effective as it is in captivity. Now, the tiger strolls within the limits of the cell, hears the siren of the patrol vehicles and stares at the shining stars. It neither attacks the prey nor does it snarl and terrorise the village.

12. Do you think the tiger in the poem had lost its natural instinct due to captivity? Support your response with evidence from the poem. **CBSE Question Bank, 2021**

Ans. I believe that the tiger in the poem had lost its natural instinct due to captivity. His strength, courage and all other instincts are futile as they are never put in use while it is imprisoned in the four wall of concrete.

13. State any three disadvantages that the tiger faces inside a cage. **Competency Based**

Ans. In the poem, the poet has presented many disadvantages that a tiger faces inside a cage. They are

(i) **Loss of freedom** In the cage, the tiger does not have enough space to move about freely.

(ii) **Loss of natural instincts** By being imprisoned inside the cage, the tiger will slowly and gradually loose his natural instincts of hunting and terrorising.

(iii) **Loss of strength and peace** The tiger cannot use his strength inside the cage. In addition, the constant influx (coming) of people to see the tiger has stolen his peace.

14. How does Norris use the tiger as a symbol of both strength and vulnerability in the context of captivity? Provide specific examples from the poem to support your answer.

Ans. Norris shows the tiger as a strong animal, highlighting its majestic look and fierce nature. However, being in captivity makes it seem vulnerable, as seen in its small space and longing eyes. This contrast highlights the sadness of a wild animal losing its freedom, revealing the complicated nature of strength when it is trapped.

15. What is the significance of the title 'A Tiger in the Zoo'?

Ans. The title 'A Tiger in the Zoo' sets the poem's context, indicating that the focus will be on a tiger's life in captivity rather than its natural habitat. The title foreshadows the theme of confinement and serves as a reminder of the tiger's loss of freedom.

16. How does the poem convey the importance of preserving natural habitats for wild animals?

Ans. The poem conveys the importance of preserving natural habitats for wild animals by showing the stark contrast between the tiger's natural behaviour in the wild and its captivity in a zoo. It serves as a reminder that wild animals should be allowed to live freely in their natural environment, where they can exhibit their true nature and thrive as they are meant to be.

Long Answer Type Questions

1. Love for freedom is the natural instinct of every living being. Comment. CBSE 2014

Ans. It is true that love for freedom is the natural instinct of every living being in this universe. Freedom is liked by every living being. No one wants to live as a slave or in captivity. The tiger in this poem has been kept in a cage. He feels helpless and yearns for freedom. He could neither rest nor walk freely while in the cage.

He ignores visitors as he knows that none of them will help him to be a free being. How could he be happy living in the cramped space where there is no space to move, no open area, no prey to stalk and kill as is available in the natural habitat. His wistful stare at the shining stars in the sky reflects his desire to be free. We as human beings should ensure freedom of all other creatures as everyone yearns for freedom.

2. Is it right to confine wild animals into cages? Why or why not?

Ans. It is not right to confine wild animals into cages. Wild animals are meant to live in the wild. They are not meant to be caged and displayed in the zoos. We all know that the majestic species of tiger is on the verge of extinction. There used to be a time when they used to roam proudly and freely in the jungle. They are not meant to live a life in confinement. They also have the right to freedom like all other living beings.

Confinement leads to depression and misery. Moreover, their offsprings lose the hunting capabilities as they are not trained to hunt in the wild. As a result, they would not be able to feed themselves.

Furthermore, confining wild animals disturbs the whole ecological balance. We should, thus, let the animals run free in the wild. They belong to the forest and not in a cage.

3. Imagine that Man has been accused by the tiger of cruelty in an animal court. What would be the tiger's two major accusations and how would Man defend them? Present your answer in two paragraphs. CBSE Question Bank, 2021

Ans. **Tiger's Accusations** I am a mighty creature that can hunt anything that lives in the forest. I can even hunt and kill mankind! But, I choose not to. Then, why have I been wrongfully entrapped by humans to be put in a small cage and paraded around for their entertainment? Since I can think for myself and make decisions, I am a sentient being just like humans. Then, why have I been captured like a mute creature?

Man's defence We understand the pain caused by our actions to this magnificent creature but we need to teach our children about the wonders of the wild. That is why we resettled the tiger to the zoo. We make sure that it is provided with food of the best quality on a timely basis. But we have to keep it in an enclosure otherwise it would get free and harm the visitors which include children!

4. Examine the poem's sound devices, such as alliteration and assonance. How do these contribute to the poem's mood and enhance its thematic depth?

Ans. In 'Tiger in the Zoo', Norris uses sound devices like alliteration and assonance to create a rhythm that enhances the poem's emotional effect. The repetition of consonant sounds in phrases like 'tiger's eyes' and 'caged' adds a musical quality that highlights the tiger's grace and strength while also conveying a sense of confinement. Assonance, through repeated vowel sounds, creates a haunting effect that emphasises feelings of loneliness and longing. These sound devices draw the reader into the tiger's situation, intensifying the conflict between its wild nature and the harsh reality of captivity. Together, they deepen the theme of freedom versus confinement, making the reader feel the sadness of the tiger's lost vitality.

5. How does Leslie Norris use vivid imagery and metaphorical language in 'A Tiger in the Zoo', to effectively depict the confinement and oppression, experienced by the captive tiger? CBSE SQP 2023

Ans. Leslie Norris uses vivid imagery and metaphorical language in 'Tiger in the Zoo' to effectively depict the confinement and oppression experienced by the captive tiger.

The use of the words 'vivid stripes' and 'pads of velvet quiet' creates a powerful image of the tiger's physical beauty and grace that is restricted within the confines of the cage.

The metaphorical language used in 'quiet rage' and 'ignoring visitors' conveys the tiger's frustration and anger at being confined.

The contrast between the tiger's natural habitat and its captivity is highlighted through the description of its expected behaviour in the wild such as 'sliding through long grass' and 'snarling around houses' and its actual behaviour within the cage.

The last two lines, "He hears the last voice at night, the patrolling cars, and stares with his brilliant eyes at the brilliant stars", depicts the tiger's longing for freedom and its natural habitat. Finally, the poem explores the psychological impact of captivity on the tiger through the use of vivid imagery and metaphorical language.

6. Leslie Norris' 'A Tiger in the Zoo' reflects on the captivity of a majestic tiger within the confines of a zoo. Through vivid imagery and poignant language, the poem explores the themes of confinement, longing for freedom, and the inherent wildness of nature. Comment on the various themes present in the poem.

Ans. Leslie Norris' 'A Tiger in the Zoo' reflects on the captivity of a majestic tiger within the confines of a zoo. Through vivid imagery and poignant language, the poem explores the themes of confinement, longing for freedom, and the inherent wildness of nature.

Captivity The poem's primary theme revolves around the concept of captivity. The tiger, once a free and powerful creature in its natural habitat, is now confined to a concrete cage in a zoo. The poem delves into the tiger's emotions and experiences as it copes with the loss of freedom and the constraints of captivity.

Freedom vs. Confinement The poem contrasts the tiger's current state of confinement with its natural freedom in the wild. The vivid imagery of the tiger 'lurking in shadow' and 'sliding through long grass' in its natural habitat underscores the stark contrast between its past life and its present captivity.

Loss of Instincts Another theme explored in the poem is the loss of the tiger's instincts and behaviour due to captivity. In the wild, the tiger would "snarl around houses" and "terrorise the village", but in the zoo, it is reduced to pacing the length of its cage and ignoring visitors.

Human Exploitation The poem touches upon the ethical issue of human exploitation of wild animals for entertainment. The tiger's captivity in a concrete cell, behind bars, symbolises humans' dominance over nature and the commodification of wildlife for human amusement.

Isolation and Loneliness The poem conveys the isolation and loneliness the tiger experiences in captivity. Despite being surrounded by visitors and patrolling cars, the tiger remains detached from the outside world, longing for the vastness of its natural environment.

Empathy and Compassion The poet evokes empathy and compassion in readers as they witness the tiger's plight and the tragic consequences of its confinement. The reader is encouraged to empathise with the captive tiger and question the morality of keeping wild animals in zoos.

ASSESSMENT EXERCISE

Extract Based Questions

Read the following extract carefully and answer the questions that follow.

But he's locked in a concrete cell,
His strength behind bars.
Stalking the length of his cage,
Ignoring visitors.

(i) Study the following statements.
1. The tiger has been personified in the above lines.
2. The poet is happy to see the tiger in the cage.
3. The tiger likes visitors.

(a) 1 is right 2 is wrong (b) 2 is right 1 is wrong
(c) 3 is right 2 is wrong (d) 1 is wrong 3 is wrong

(ii) The poet has used a figure of speech in the following line. Identify it.
"His strength behind bars"

(iii) Where is the tiger? What is it feeling and why?

(iv) Select the option that applies the same rhyme scheme as the first four lines of the given extract.

(a) I was a cottage maiden
Hardened by sun and air,
Contented with my cottage mates,
Not mindful I was fair.

(b) As long as it takes to pass
A ship keeps raising its hull;
The wetter ground like glass
Reflects a standing gull

(c) They cannot look out far.
They cannot look in deep.
But when was that ever a bar
To any watch they keep?"

(d) Two golden-agers in a room
complained about mate's habits.
"It irritates and drives me mad,

Short Answer (SA) Type Questions

1. What should the tiger be doing if he were at the edge of the jungle?

2. Why does the tiger express his rage quietly?

Long Answer (LA) Type Question

1. Animals also understand the language of love and love their freedom. But in the name of conserving wildlife, they are being put in the zoos, which deprives them of their natural habitat. Comment with reference to 'A Tiger in the Zoo'. **Competency Based**

How to Tell Wild Animals

by Carolyn Wells

Introduction The following poem 'How to Tell Wild Animals' has been written by Carolyn Wells. This humorous poem suggests some of the dangerous ways to identify wild animals. The poet describes many ferocious and fearful animals including an Asiatic Lion, the Bengal tiger, the leopard, the bear, the hyena, the crocodile and the chameleon in a highly amusing manner. In addition to being entertaining, the poem is informative. It describes some of the unique features of the various animals with gentle humour.

Stanzawise Explanation

Stanza 1

If ever you should go by chance,
To jungles in the east;
And if there should to you advance
A large and tawny beast,
If he roars at you as you're dyin'
You'll know it is the Asian Lion ....

Explanation The poet describes the qualities of wild animals and tells how anyone can recognise them in a forest. In these lines, the poet says that if you go to the jungles of the East, you will see a large animal with brownish yellow skin. If he roars at you so loudly that you can die out of fear, you will come to know that you have encountered an Asian Lion.

Stanza 2

Or if some time when roaming round,
A noble wild beast greets you,
With black stripes on a yellow ground,
Just notice if he eats you.
This simple rule may help you learn
The Bengal Tiger to discern.

Explanation In these lines, the poet says that while roaming in the forest you may encounter a wild animal who is very impressive in size. This wild and noble animal has black stripes on his yellow body. If the animal attacks and eats you, you can identify that this animal is the Bengal Tiger.

Stanza 3

If strolling forth, a beast you view,
Whose hide with spots is peppered,
As soon as he has lept on you,
You'll know it is the Leopard.
'Twill do no good to roar with pain,
He'll only lep and lep again.

Explanation In these lines, the poet describes that while you are walking slowly and freely in the forest, you might see a wild animal, whose skin is covered with dark spots. If it jumps on you, you will come to know that it is the leopard. Even if you cry or shout in pain, there is no escape as the leopard will continue jumping on you.

Stanza 4

If when you're walking round your yard
You meet a creature there,
Who hugs you very, very hard,
Be sure it is a Bear.
If you have any doubts, I guess
He'll give you just one more caress.

Explanation In these lines, the poet says that while you are walking around in your yard, you may encounter a creature. If this animal hugs you very hard, you must be sure that you have encountered a bear. If you have any doubt in your minds, the bear will give you another tight hug. This hug may seem friendly but it can be fatal.

Stanza 5

Though to distinguish beasts of prey
A novice might nonplus,
The Crocodile you always may
Tell from the Hyena thus:
Hyenas come with merry smiles;
But if they weep they're Crocodiles.

Explanation In these lines, the poet says that it is very difficult for an inexperienced person to distinguish wild animals. They may not be able to distinguish between Hyena and a crocodile. A hyena behaves very weirdly as it always laughs while attacking its victim. A crocodile, on the other hand, weeps while eating its prey. The poet here warns that people should not wait for a hyena to laugh and a crocodile to weep. Both of these animals are dangerous so people should keep themselves safe and secure.

Stanza 6

The true Chameleon is small,
A lizard sort of things;
He hasn't any ears at all,
And not a single wing.
If there is nothing on the tree,
Tis the Chameleon you see.

Explanation In these lines, the poet describes a chameleon. He says that a chameleon resembles a small garden lizard. It doesn't have ears and wings. The poet adds that if you are unable to see a thing on the tree, you are seeing a chameleon as it changes its colour according to its surroundings to escape from its enemy.

Poetic Devices used in the Poem

Alliteration Repetition of initial consonant sounds in the same line.

- roaming round
- lep and lep again
- Who hugs you very very hard
- A novice might nonplus

Paradox A figure of speech in which a statement appears to contradict itself

- A noble wild beast greets you

Word Meaning

Word	Meaning
Stanza 1	
Advance	to move forward towards something, often in order to attack or threaten
Tawny	brownish-yellow in colour
Dyin	dying
Stanza 2	
Noble	here, very impressive in size
Beast	animal
Discern	see, identify
Stanza 3	
Strolling	to walk somewhere in a slow relaxed way
Forth	forward, away from a place
Hide (noun)	animal skin
Peppered	here, covered with spots
Lep (leap)	to jump high or a long way
Stanza 4	
Yard	a piece of land next to or around your house
Caress	a gentle, loving touch
Stanza 5	
Beasts of prey	an animal that hunts, kills or eats another animal
Novice	someone new to a job
Nonplus	be puzzled, confused, surprised
Hyena	a wild animal like a dog, that eats the meat of animals that are already dead and has a cry like a human laugh.
Stanza 6	
Chameleon	a small lizard that can change colour according to its surroundings
Tis	it is

NCERT FOLDER

NCERT Intext and Exercise Questions

THINKING ABOUT THE POEM
(NCERT PAGE 45)

Q.1 Does 'Dyin' really rhyme with 'lion'? Can you say it in such a way that it does?

Ans. No, 'Dyin' does not rhyme with 'lion'. However, we can say it in a manner that allows the words to rhyme. In poetry, elision, the omission of certain sounds or syllables, is often used to maintain the poem's rhythm. Here, elision plays a role in creating a rhyme between 'dyin' and 'lion'. By eliding the letter 'g' in 'dyin', the word might be pronounced as 'dyin', with the 'g' sound omitted, almost blending into the next word, thus simplifying the rhyme with 'lion.'

Q.2 How does the poet suggest that you identify the lion and the tiger? When can you do so according to him?

Ans. The poet says that while roaming in jungles of the East, we can identify the lion and the tiger in the following ways.

In the jungle, we can see a large animal with brownish yellow skin. If this animal roars at us so strongly that we can die out of fear, we can identify that it is an Asiatic Lion.

In the same forest, we can encounter a wild and noble animal which has black stripes on his yellow body. If this animal attacks and eats us, then we can identify that this animal is the Bengal Tiger.

Q.3 Do you think the words 'lept' and 'lep' in the third stanza are spelt correctly? Why does the poet spell them like this?

Ans. The words 'lept' and 'lep' in the third stanza are not spelt correctly. The poet has spelt them like this intentionally in order to maintain the rhythm of the poem. The correct spelling of the words, 'lept' is leapt and 'lep' is leap.

Q.4 Do you know what a 'bear hug' is? It's a friendly and strong hug-such as Bears are thought to give, as they attack you! Again, hyenas are thought to laugh and crocodiles to weep ('crocodile tears') as they swallow their victims. Are there similar expressions and popular ideas about wild animals in your own language(s)?

Ans. When the bear hugs the prey so tightly that the prey dies, it is known as a bear hug.

There are indeed similar expressions and popular ideas about wild animals in every language. For example, in Hindi, we say *Magarmach ke aansu aaana' (crocodile tears); Haathi ke daant dikhane ke aur, khane ke aur; Ab pachtaye hot kya jab chidiya chug gai khet; Girgit ke tarah rang badalna.*

Q.5 Look at the line 'A novice might nonplus', how would you write this 'correctly'? Why is the poet's 'incorrect' line better in the poem?

Ans. The line 'A novice might nonplus' can be written correctly as 'A novice might be nonplussed'. The poet's incorrect line is better in the poem as it maintains the rhyme scheme. By writing it incorrectly, 'nonplus' rhymes with 'thus'.

Q.6 Can you find other examples of poets taking liberties with language, either in English or in your own language? Can you find examples of humorous poems in your own language(s)?

Ans. One can find plenty of examples in poetry where poets take liberties with language. This is called 'poetic licence'.

Poets take such liberties in order to create proper rhyming and rhythm. For example, in the following lines, the word 'prest' is used instead of 'pressed' so that it may rhyme with 'breast'.

"A tree whose hungry mouth is prest
Against the earth's sweat flowing breast."

Q.7 Much of the humour in the poem arises from the way language is used, although the ideas are funny as well. If there are particular lines in the poem that you especially like, share these lines with the class, speaking briefly about what it is about the ideas or the language that you like or find funny.

Ans. The way the poet has used language and ideas in the poem is indeed humorous. The lines from the poem that appears to be funny are "A noble wild beast greets you." The idea that a wild beast is going to welcome you is quite funny. The language in the line, "He'll only lep and lep again" is also very humorous. The concept of 'lep' from the word 'leopard' generates the humour.

REVIEW EXERCISE

Including Competency Based Questions

Part - I

Multiple Choice Questions

1. What poetic device has been used in the following line?

'Twill do no good to roar with pain,
He'll only lep and lep again.

(a) Repetition (b) Alliteration
(c) Personification (d) Symbolism

Ans. (b) Alliteration

2. What will the bear do when he sees you?

(a) Gives you his food (b) Hugs you very hard
(c) Dances with you (d) Asks you to sing a song

Ans. (b) Hugs you very hard

3. Why does the bear hug you?

(a) As a gesture of friendship
(b) In order to kill
(c) It is his instinct
(d) Bears are friendly by nature

Ans. (b) In order to kill

4. How can a hyena and crocodile be told apart from one another?

(a) Hyena cries
(b) Crocodile laughs and hyena cries
(c) Hyena laughs and crocodile cries
(d) Crocodile and hyena cries

Ans. (c) Hyena laughs and crocodile cries

5. How can the chameleon be identified?

(a) No ears
(b) No wings
(c) Looks like a lizard
(d) All of the above

Ans. (d) All of the above

6. If there is nothing on the tree,
'Tis the chameleon you see. **Competency Based**

What does the poet imply about the chameleon in the above lines from 'How to Tell Wild Animals'?

(a) It moves swiftly
(b) It only lives on trees
(c) It has the ability to camouflage
(d) It does not have ears and wings

Ans. (c) It has the ability to camouflage

7. Which of the following beasts has not been mentioned in the poem?

(a) Snake (b) Chameleon
(c) Crocodile (d) Lion

Ans. (a) Snake

8. The rhyme scheme of the first stanza is

(a) abcabc (b) aabbcc (c) ababcc (d) aaabbb

Ans. (c) ababcc

9. Which literary device has been used in the line 'a noble wild beast greets you'?

(a) Metaphor (b) Anaphora
(c) Paradox (d) Dilemma

Ans. (c) Paradox

10. The tone of the poem is

(a) Satirical
(b) Ironical
(c) Humorous
(d) Pedantic

Ans. (c) Humorous

11. Which of these best describes the Bengal Tiger from 'How to Tell Wild Animals'? **Competency Based**

(a) It is loving and affectionate
(b) It is energetic and beautiful
(c) It is gigantic and leaps with grace
(d) It is hungry and craves human flesh

Ans. (d) It is hungry and craves human flesh

12. If when you're walking round your yard
You meet a creature there,
Who hugs you very, very hard,
Be sure it is a Bear,
If you have any doubts, I guess
He'll give you just one more caress.

Which of these best describes the poet's tone in the above lines from 'How to Tell Wild Animals'? **Competency Based**

(a) It is cautionary as that bear might attack anytime.
(b) It is humorous as he compares deadly attack to a hug.
(c) It is analytical as he compares the bear to other animals.
(d) It is full of wonder as he observes the bear in its natural habitat.

Ans. (b) It is humorous as he compares deadly attack to a hug.

Extract Based Questions

1. Read the following extract carefully and answer the questions that follow.

If ever you should go by chance
To jungles in the east;
And if there should to you advance
A large and tawny beast,
If he roars at you as you're dyin'
You'll know it is the Asian Lion ....

(i) How does the poet say an Asiatic Lion can be identified?

Ans. In a humorous manner, the poet says if a person goes to the jungles in the East and comes upon a large and brownish wild animal whose roar is scary enough to make them die, they should know it is an Asiatic Lion.

(ii) Fill in the blank with one word from the bracket.

If a person wishes to meet an Asiatic lion, they must go to the jungles of .... (North/East)

Ans. East

(iii) What happens when the lion roars?

Ans. When the lion roars, one's heart begins to beat fast as one is scared.

(iv) Select the option that applies the same rhyme scheme as the given extract.

(a) I think my missteps all have come
when swept away in ecstasy.
When bored my actions aren't so dumb;
I contemplate what costs might be
and calculate events to come.
I'm prey to hospitality.

(b) We pray the fickle flag of truce
Still float deceitfully and fair;
Our eyes must love its sweet abuse;
This hour we will not care,
Though just beyond to-morrow's gate,
Arrayed and strong, the battle wait.

(c) The foxes sleep without concern
then yawn and wake and take their turn
at foraging with time to burn;
and when they're done
from all their worries they adjourn.
and just have fun.

(d) The foxes sleep without concern
then yawn and wake and take their turn
At foraging with time to burn;
and when they're done
from all their worries they adjourn.
and just have fun

Ans. (b)

2. Read the following extract carefully and answer the questions that follow.

Or if some time when roaming round,
A noble wild beast greets you,
With black stripes on a yellow ground,
Just notice if he eats you.
This simple rule may help you learn
The Bengal Tiger to discern. **CBSE 2023**

(i) Complete the sentence appropriately.

The word 'discern' in line 6 of the extract means the same as ....

(Clue: explain contextual meaning here)

Ans. identify

(ii) In the given lines, what effect does the poet create?

'Just notice if he eats you
This simple rule may help you learn
The Bengal Tiger to discern'.

(a) Irony
(b) Terror
(c) Sympathy
(d) Criticism

Ans. (a) Irony

(iii) Select the appropriate option to complete the sentence.

The tone of the poet when telling how to identify a wild animal is both scary and ....

Ans. humorous

(iv) Identify the poetic device used and explain its usage in the given lines.

With black stripes on a yellow ground...
...Whose hide with spots is peppered

Ans. The given lines use the poetic device named imagery wherein the words create a picture in the minds of the reader. The given lines in its description of the two animals helps us visualise what the animal looks like.

3. Read the following extract and answer the questions that follow. **CBSE 2023**

If strolling forth, a beast you view,
Whose hide with spots is peppered,
As soon as he has leapt on you,
You'll know it's the leopard.
"Twill do no good to roar with pain, He'll only lep and lep again.

(i) One can find out that it is a leopard by the way it ....

(a) leaps
(b) eats
(c) looks
(d) roars

Ans. (a) leaps

(ii) **Which option lists the statement that is not true according to the extract?**

(a) The poet asks the reader to hide on seeing the leopard.
(b) The poet cautions the reader about a leopard when walking through its territory.
(c) The poet informs the reader that a leopard can launch repeated attacks.
(d) The poet tells the reader that a leopard attack can result in pain.

Ans. (a) The poet asks the reader to hide on seeing the leopard.

(iii) **Complete the sentence appropriately.**

It is clear that repetition is a poetic device used for 'lep and lep again' because ....

(Clue : explain how repetition is applied here.)

Ans. the word 'lep' has been repeated

(iv) **Compare the physical description of the Royal Bengal Tiger to that of leopard.**

Ans. The Royal Bengal Tiger has black spots on its yellow skin while the leopard's skin is filled with spots.

4. Read the following extract and answer the questions that follow.

If when you're walking round your yard
You meet a creature there, Who hugs you very, very hard, Be sure it is a Bear,
If you have any doubts, I guess
He'll give you just one more caress.

(i) **Why does a bear hug very hard?**

Ans. A bear hugs a person very hard to kill them.

(ii) **The poet has used some special qualities to describe the animals and create humour in the poem. Each of us also has some special qualities which make us quite different from others. Do you agree? Comment.** **Competency Based**

Ans. The poet has used the selected words and expressions to describe animals and to create humour. For instance, 'a bear's hug' and 'Hyena smiles' are mentioned to create this effect. Like these animals, each of us also has some special, defining qualities which make us different from others. These distinctive qualities give us a unique identification.

(iii) **Where can a bear be found?**

Ans. The bear can be found in forests.

4. Select the option that applies the same rhyme scheme as the given extract.

(a) The foxes sleep without a care,
their ears alert to what's out there
detecting sounds with time to spare
and then they play.
It's here and now, not when and where.
Let's live today!

(b) Whenever the moon and stars are set,
Whenever the wind is high,
All night long in the dark and wet,
A man goes riding by.
Late in the night when the fires are out,
Why does he gallop and gallop about?

(c) HERE in this sequester'd close
Bloom the hyacinth and rose,
Here beside the modest stock
Flaunts the flaring hollyhock;
Here, without a pang, one sees
Ranks, conditions, and degrees.

(d) Here be shadows large and long;
Here be spaces meet for song;
Grant, O garden-god, that I,
Now that none profane is nigh,-
Now that mood and moment please,-
Find the fair Pierides!

Ans. (b)

5. Read the following extract and answer the questions that follow.

Though to distinguish beasts of prey
A novice might nonplus,
The crocodiles you always may
Tell from the Hyena thus :
Hyenas come with merry smiles;
But if they weep they're crocodiles.

CBSE 2023

(i) **Select the appropriate option to complete the sentence, according to the extract.**

Crocodiles can be identified by their ....

Ans. tears

(ii) **What two different behavioural traits of animals are mentioned in the extract?**

Ans. The two behavioural traits mentioned in the extract are that crocodiles cry when it is eating its prey while hyena laughs.

(iii) **The poet uses 'A novice might nonplus' instead of the novice might get confused. How does this usage impact the poem?** **Competency Based**

(a) Adds an incorrect option
(b) It is associated with beasts
(c) It rhymes and adds humour
(d) It simplifies the meaning

Ans. (c) It rhymes and adds humour

(iv) **'Novice' in line 2 means the same as ....**

Ans. beginner

6. Read the following extract and answer the questions that follow.

The true Chameleon is small,
A lizard sort of things;
He hasn't any ears at all,
And not a single wing.
If there is nothing on the tree,
'Tis the Chameleon you see.

(i) Study the following statements.

1. A chameleon looks like a lizard.
2. A chameleon can easily camouflage.

(a) Only 1 is right
(b) Only 2 is right
(c) Both 1 and 2 are right
(d) Neither 1 nor 2 are right

Ans. (c) Both 1 and 2 are right

(ii) Why do chameleon change their colour?

(a) To look beautiful (b) To escape from enemies
(c) To attack insects (d) None of these

Ans. (b) To escape from enemies

(iii) Where do chameleons live?

Ans. Chameleons live inside jungles and on trees.

(iv) Why can't the chameleon be seen on the tree?

Ans. Chameleon can't be seen on the tree because it can change its skin colour; it has the ability to camouflage.

Part - II

Short Answer Type Questions

1. What does the Bengal tiger look like? What is so distinct about him?

Ans. The Bengal tiger is noble and majestic in stature. It has a yellow body covered with black stripes.

Its distinct feature is that its movements are so quick that it can attack and eat its prey in a moment.

2. How can you distinguish between a tiger and a leopard? CBSE 2011

Ans. A tiger has black stripes on its yellow body. On the other hand, a leopard does not have any stripes. It has spots peppered on its body.

Moreover, a tiger kills only when it is hungry, while a leopard can kill for the pleasure of killing by jumping on its prey continuously.

3. How does the poet describe the bear?

Ans. The poet describes the bear in a humorous way. He says that as soon as a bear sees a human being, it hugs him tightly.

It holds its prey tightly with both its hands and squeezes him to death. If he is still alive, it gives him another tight hug to kill him.

4. What is so weird about the hyena and the crocodile?

Ans. Some animals such as the hyena and the crocodile are famous for their weird behaviour. A laughing Hyena's voice resembles the laughter of a human being.

Moreover, a hyena laughs while attacking its prey while a crocodile weeps whent it is swallowing its victims.

5. Why does the poet use the term 'noble' and 'wild' for the tiger? CBSE 2020

Ans. In the poem 'How to tell wild Animals', the poet calls the Bengal tiger 'noble' as well as 'wild' because the tiger hunts only when he is hungry unlike other animals who may kill a prey for the pleasure of killing.

6. "If he roars at you as you're dyin'/ You'll know it is the Asian Lion..." Comment on the irony of the quote from the poem 'How to Tell Wild Animals'. CBSE Question Bank 2021

Ans. As per the given lines, the poet tells us that if the animal roars when you die, you can recognise the animal as an Asian Lion. This situation is ironical because if the animal attacks us and we die, we will not be alive to recognise the animal as an Asian Lion.

7. Hyperbole is a literary device used when the poet exaggerates an image to make it comical. State two instances from the poem 'How to Tell Wild Animals' where the literary device is used. CBSE Question Bank 2021

Ans. The two instances of hyperbole are

(i) The crocodile tears and the hyenas smile. Both these reference are exaggerations as we have never seen a crocodile cry or a hyena smile.

(ii) The identification of a chameleon is also expressed through hyperbole as the poet states is an individual sees nothing on a tree, there must be a chameleon on it. It is an exaggeration to say that chameleons become completely non-visible.

8. Which genre is most appropriate for the poem? Substantiate your choice with reference to the poem 'How to Tell Wild Animals'. CBSE Question Bank 2021

Ans. The poem 'How to Tell Wild Animals' is a humorous poem. It depicts the ways to identify different dangerous animals which may not be practical. However, when the poem is read, the approaches evoke fun and laughter.

9. What is the poet's purpose in using behavioural cues like roaring, smiling, or weeping in the poem 'How to Tell Wild Animals'? CBSE Additional SQP 2023

Ans. The purpose of using behavioural cues like roaring smiling, or weeping in the poem is to educate the reader humorously and playfully about identifying wild animals based on their behaviours.

By associating specific behaviours with certain animals, the poet makes the information more memorable and engaging. The use of these cues adds an entertaining element to the educational content, making it accessible and enjoyable for readers, and creating a memorable and lighthearted exploration of the animal kingdom.

10. What is the theme of Carolyn Wells' poem, and how does she use humour and clever wordplay to convey her message about playfully identifying various wild animals?

Ans. Carolyn Wells' poem is a playful and humorous exploration of identifying wild animals in the jungles of the East. The overarching theme revolves around the comical nature of human encounters with these creatures and the importance of correctly recognising them for one's safety. Wells employs clever wordplay and rhyme schemes to make the poem entertaining and informative. Through humorous descriptions and absurd scenarios, she gives readers memorable cues for identifying animals like the Asian Lion, Bengal Tiger, Leopard, and Crocodile. Using such a method ensures that the descriptions stick in the reader's mind while imparting a valuable message about animal identification in a fun and memorable way.

11. Every creature possesses a unique characteristic that defines it, and this trait is closely linked to its nature. This concept is beautifully illustrated in the poem 'How to Tell Wild Animals'. Elucidate. CBSE 2025

Ans. In 'How to Tell Wild Animals', Carolyn Wells humorously highlights the unique traits of various wild animals. Each creature is described through its distinctive features and behaviour, such as the lion's roar, the tiger's ferocity, and the leopard's quick attacks, making identification entertaining and vivid.

Long Answer Type Questions

1. "Humour is the best medicine for every ailment in life." Comment.

Ans. It is true that humour is the best medicine for any ailment in life as it is infectious. When humour is shared, it binds people together and increases happiness. Humour strengthens our immune system, boosts our energy, diminishes pain and protects us from the damaging effects of stress.

It is a priceless medicine for every ailment in life. The poet, in the poem 'How to Tell Wild Animals' creates humour by describing the various beasts of prey. The way the poet explains the things is very funny yet interesting.

The poet has depicted the wildlife very vividly and in a lively manner. While reading the poem, the readers enjoy the poet's work and it leaves them refreshed and happy.

2. The poem 'How To Tell Wild Animals' expresses the poet's love for wild animals. Discuss.

Ans. The poem 'How to Tell Wild Animals' describes various wild animals which live in forest. The poet has described the peculiarities, body colour and typical actions of particular animals. This shows us the poet's love for wildlife.

The Asian lion, the Bengal tiger, the leopard, the bear, the hyena, the crocodile and the chameleon all have been described in an amusing manner.

We come to know about the features of various animals through the poem. Thus, the poem is as informative as entertaining. By doing this, the poem calls upon us indirectly to be aware of the special marks of some animals. The knowledge about animals is a must as a safeguard against danger from anyone of the wild animals.

3. Briefly describe the themes present in the poem.

Ans. The themes present in the poem are

Nature and Wildlife Observation The poem encourages the reader to pay attention to the characteristics and behaviours of various wild animals, highlighting the importance of keen observation when encountering them in their natural habitats.

Animal Characteristics It humorously describes different wild animals' distinguishing features and behaviours, providing a lighthearted guide to identifying them. This theme emphasises the diversity of the animal kingdom.

Survival and Caution The poem playfully suggests that identifying these animals correctly can be a matter of life and death, implying the importance of caution and knowledge when encountering potentially dangerous wildlife.

Humour and Wordplay The poem is primarily a work of humour, using clever wordplay, puns and humorous scenarios to entertain the reader. Each stanza presents a comical situation related to encountering a specific animal, creating a light and enjoyable tone.

Cultural References Some descriptions may be seen as caricatures or stereotypes of how these animals are perceived in popular culture or folk tales. This reflects how humans often anthropomorphise (Giving human characteristics, emotions, or qualities to non-human entities, such as animals, objects, or even abstract concepts) and mythologise the animal kingdom.

4. The tiger in the poem 'A Tiger in the Zoo' presents a contrasting image with the tiger in the poem 'How to Tell Wild Animals'. Compare and contrast the two tigers with reference to the manner in which they have been presented in both poems. **CBSE Question Bank, 2021**

Ans. It is true that the tiger in the poem 'A Tiger in the Zoo' presents a contrasting image with the tiger in the poem 'How to Tell Wild Animals'. In the poem 'A Tiger in the Zoo', the tiger is cramped in the cage. He is angry and frustrated as his freedom, strength and courage is curbed. His natural instincts and his royal demeanor is lost in the zoo where he is made to act like a piece of entertainment.

However, the same tiger is seen in a different situation in the poem 'How to Tell Wild Animals'. In this poem, the poet depicts the tiger as an animal that roams in the jungle and belongs to a royal clan. The colour of its skin is yellowish with black stripes. In the poem, the poet highlights the cleverness and the strength possessed by a tiger in its natural habitat.

ASSESSMENT EXERCISE

Extract Based Questions

Read the following extract carefully and answer the questions that follow.

If when you're walking round your yard
You meet a creature there,
Who hugs you very, very hard,
Be sure it is a Bear.
If you have any doubts, I guess
He'll give you just one more caress.

(i) Complete the sentence, according to the extract.
The word that can be used to replace 'gentle loving touch' is ....

(ii) Where might a person meet a bear?

(a) In the forest (b) In the zoo
(c) In the museum (d) In their yard

(iii) How can you recognise a bear?

(iv) The poet has used a figure of speech in the following line. Identify it ....
'Who hugs you very-very hard'

Short Answer (SA) Type Questions

1. How does the poet create humour in the poem?
2. What is a bear hug? How does the bear behave upon meeting a human?

Long Answer (LA) Type Question

1. The poet has mentioned some of the wild animals of the forest. Name them. Also, write a short note on what you have learnt about these wild animals after reading the poem. **Competency Based**

The Ball Poem

CHAPTER 5

by John Berryman

Introduction 'The Ball Poem' by John Berryman describes the grief of a boy over the loss of his ball. With this loss, he senses his first responsibility in a materialistic world. Through this, the poet suggests that the people whom we love and our material possessions will not be with us forever. One has to understand the nature of loss and learn to cope up with it. The child has to learn that loss is a part of everyday life and still life goes on.

Stanzawise Explanation

Stanza 1

What is the boy now, who has lost his ball,
What, what is he to do? I saw it go
Merrily bouncing, down the street, and then
Merrily over - there it is in the water!
No use to say 'O there are other balls':

Explanation The poem starts with the poet looking at the boy who has lost his ball. The poet wants to know about him and his reaction after losing his ball. The poet himself saw the ball bouncing happily down the street and then, falling into the water. The poet says that there is no use to tell the boy that there are other balls as he would get many other balls. However, he would never be able to get the lost ball and the memories associated with it back.

Stanza 2

An ultimate shaking grief fixes the boy
As he stands rigid, trembling, staring down
All his young days into the harbour where
His ball went. I would not intrude on him;
A dime, another ball, is worthless.

Explanation In these lines, the poet describes the condition of the boy after losing his ball.

The boy feels very sad due to the loss of his ball. He is standing like a statue at one place. He is shivering and staring down the ball, which symbolises the memories of his young days. The boy is filled with sorrow and just keeps staring in the direction where his ball is going.

The poet says that he would not interfere in the boy's thoughts as he feels that through this experience, the boy will learn the meaning of loss.

According to the poet, it is not worth it to tell the boy that another ball can be bought. This is so because the poet knows that even though the boy can buy another ball, he would not get the memories attached with the lost ball back. The boy would never get the ball which was with him from his very childhood. Hence, the new ball would be worthless.

Stanza 3

.... Now
He senses first responsibility
In a world of possessions. People will take
Balls, balls will be lost always, little boy.
And no one buys a ball back. Money is external.

Explanation In these lines, the poet says that the boy is learning his first responsibility of taking care of his things and how to bear the loss of something in a world of possessions. The poet adds that balls will be lost many times. In other words, the poet wants to highlight that losses are a part of our lives.

Money is external as it can not buy memories nor can it replace the lost things.

Stanza 4

He is learning, well behind his desperate eyes,
This epistemology of loss, how to stand up
Knowing what every man must one day know
And most know many days, how to stand up.

Explanation In these lines, the poet suggests that from the loss of the ball, the boy is learning the meaning of loss. He is also learning how to stand up from the loss. The poet says that knowing that every man has to stand up after such losses, the boy too will learn how to stand up and leave the losses behind. He would have understood the true meaning and nature of loss.

Poetic Devices Used in the Poem

Repetition Repetition of words/phrases in the same line

- What, what
- Balls, balls

Alliteration Repetition of initial consonant sounds in the same line

- What, what
- Balls, balls
- buys a ball back

Metaphor Comparison between two different objects without the use of comparison words.
The lost ball here is a metaphor for the boy's childhood. With the loss of the ball, the boys's childhood is also lost.

Word Meaning

Word	Meaning
Stanza 1	
Merrily	happily
'O there are other balls'	the words suggest that the loss is not important enough to worry about
Stanza 2	
Ultimate	final
Shaking grief	sadness which greatly affects the boy;
Rigid	stiff, like a statue
Trembling	shivering
Harbour	a place where ships load and unload goods
Intrude on	(here) to enter a situation where one is not welcome
A dime	a ten cent coin (US)
Stanza 3	
Possessions	something that is owned or possessed
External	superficial, extrinsic
Stanza 4	
Desperate	hopeless
Epistemology of loss	understanding the nature of loss or what it means to lose something

NCERT FOLDER

NCERT Intext and Exercise Questions

THINKING ABOUT THE POEM

(NCERT PAGE 47)

In pairs, attempt the following questions

Q.1 Why does the poet say, "I would not intrude on him"? Why doesn't he offer him money to buy another ball? CBSE 2020

Ans. The poet says, "I would not intrude on him" because he knows that the boy is deeply absorbed in his emotional turmoil. The poet recognises the profound grief and sense of responsibility that the boy is experiencing, and he respects the boy's need for solitude and reflection during this moment of loss. Further, he does not want to interfere in the natural process of learning. He wants the boy to learn the meaning of loss on his own.

He also doesn't offer him money to buy another ball because that would be worthless.

In addition, money cannot fully compensate for the sentimental value of the lost ball, and the poet understands that this experience is a valuable lesson in coping with loss and growing up.

Q.2 " .... staring down
All his young days into the harbour where His ball went .... "
Do you think the boy has had the ball for a long time? Is it linked to the memories of days when he played with it?

Ans. Yes, the boy has had the ball for a long time. It is linked to the memories of days when the boy played with it.

When it bounced into the water, all his memories of the days of his childhood flashed in front of him. This led to a realisation that those moments would not come back, just like the ball.

He can buy new balls and can similarly create new moments, but those memories, which are gone, would not return.

Q.3 What does 'in the world of possessions' mean?

Ans. The phrase 'in the world of possessions' means that we are living in a world where everybody is worried about material possessions. Today's world encourages materialism and a sense of possession. Every one is in the race of possessing more and more.

Q.4 Do you think the boy has lost anything earlier? Pick out the words that suggest the answer.

Ans. No, it seems that the boy had not lost anything earlier.

The words that suggest so is 'And most know many days'. This phrase suggests a deeper understanding of loss beyond the immediate experience with the ball. 'An ultimate shaking grief' implies a profound, sorrow. 'Knowing what every man must one day know' and 'most know many days' suggest recognition of universal human experiences, indicating the boy may have encountered loss or hardship before. 'How to stand up' implies resilience learned from the challenges.

Q.5 What does the poet say the boy is learning from the loss of the ball? Try to explain this in your own words.

Ans. The poet says that the boy is learning to bear the loss of the ball. He is experiencing grief and learning to grow up in this world of possessions. He learns that there are so many things in life that are lost and cannot be brought back. He is sensing his first responsibility as he has lost the ball. The boy will learn how to stand up and leave the losses behind as he would have understood the true meaning and nature of loss.

Q.6 Have you ever lost something you liked very much? Write a paragraph describing how you felt then, and saying whether - and how - you got over your loss.

Ans. Yes, I've experienced losing something I cherished deeply. Losing the vintage pen my grandfather gave me was a deeply saddening experience. It held sentimental value, representing a cherished connection to him. When I realised it was missing, I felt a profound sense of loss and sadness for it everywhere, as if a part of my heritage had vanished. Initially, I searched for it everywhere, hoping to recover it, but I accepted its absence as time passed. While the pain lingered, I found solace in memories of my grandfather and the moments we shared. Eventually, I realised that while the physical pain was gone, the sentiment behind it remained intact. Over time, I learned to appreciate the memories it evoked and the lessons it imparted, allowing me to move forward while treasuring its significance in my heart.

REVIEW EXERCISE

Including Competency Based Questions

Part - I

Multiple Choice Questions

1. In 'The Ball Poem', the ball is a symbol of ....

(a) materialistic gains (b) boy's childhood
(c) the boy's nature (d) playing with toys

Ans. (b) boy's childhood

2. 'Balls, balls will be lost always, little boy.' What does the poet wish to convey in this line?

(a) Boys always lose their belongings
(b) Loss of things is fact of life
(c) It is okay to keep losing balls
(d) All of the above

Ans. (b) Loss of things is fact of life

3. Which of the following statement(s) is/are correct in reference to 'The Ball Poem'?

1. The boy finds his ball after a couple of hours.
2. The boy has many other balls to play with.
3. The poet brings the ball out of water and gives it to the boy.
4. The poet gives his ball to the boy.
5. The boy is very sorrowful to lose his ball.
6. The boy runs after his ball to save it, but fails.
7. The poet recognises himself as an adult, not a young boy.

(a) 1, 2, 3 and 4 (b) 1, 4, 5 and 6
(c) 5, 6 and 7 (d) 2, 3 and 7

Ans. (c) 5, 6 and 7

4. Identify the literary device used in "Merrily bouncing, down the street and then Merrily over— there it is in the water!"

(a) Metaphor (b) Simile
(c) Alliteration (d) Anaphora

Ans. (d) Anaphora

5. Identify the literary device used in 'And no one buys a ball back.'

(a) Metaphor (b) Simile
(c) Alliteration (d) Anaphora

Ans. (c) Alliteration

6. The phrase 'epistemology of loss' in 'The Ball Poem' means ....

(a) contrasting ideas (b) understanding the problem
(c) nature of loss (d) None of these

Ans. (c) nature of loss

7. What should we learn from 'The Ball Poem'?

(a) That we should be careful
(b) Things once lost cannot be found
(c) Life is very long
(d) Gain and loss are two sides of the same coin

Ans. (d) Gain and loss are two sides of the same coin

8. Literal and metaphorical meanings of 'The Ball Poem' are given below. Choose the correct option.

(i) **Literal meaning** It is a soulful picture of little boys growing up and learning to deal with the loss of the first in his possession.
(ii) **Metaphorical meaning** It is the story of mankind learning to deal with the loss of their loved things or people.

(a) Only (i) is correct
(b) Only (ii) is correct
(c) Both (i) and (ii) are correct
(d) Neither (i) nor (ii) is correct

Ans. (c) Both (i) and (ii) are correct

9. What is the tone of 'The Ball Poem' towards the end?

(a) Encouraging (b) Happy
(c) Depressing (d) Exciting

Ans. (a) Encouraging

10. What is the rhyming scheme of the stanza?

(a) abcbc (b) ababab
(c) abcba (d) No rhyming scheme

Ans. (d) No rhyming scheme

11. The loss of a possession should make one feel

(a) angry (b) responsible (c) sad (d) careless

Ans. (b) responsible

12. "No use to say 'O there are other balls" Which of these is the poet conveying in the above line from 'The Ball Poem'? Competency Based

(a) There are multiple choices in life.
(b) What is lost is often irreplaceable.
(c) Collecting things is a sign of greed.
(d) Grown ups can cope with loss easily.

Ans. (b) What is lost is often irreplaceable.

13. Which of these best describes the poet's tone in 'The Ball Poem'? Competency Based

(a) It is rational as he analyses the incident like an experienced adult.
(b) It is regretful as he is not able to console the boy even though he wants to.
(c) It is indifferent as he says that one must not console the boy who is crying.
(d) It is full of wonder as he observes the boy closely to discover the nature of loss.

Ans. (d) It is full of wonder as he observes the boy closely to discover the nature of loss.

14. Select the option that shows the correct relationship between (1) and (2) from 'The Ball Poem'.

1. **The poet chooses not to intrude on the boy.**
2. **The poet believes loss to be permanent and irreparable.** Competency Based

(a) 2 is the meaning of 1
(b) 2 is the opposite of 1
(c) 2 explains the reason for 1
(d) 2 is a fact and 1 is an opinion

Ans. (d) 2 is a fact and 1 is an opinion

15. Choose the option that correctly identifies what the narrator is feeling in the line given below.
"As he stands rigid, trembling, staring down" CBSE Additional SQP 2021

1. **Guilt** 2. **Shock**
3. **Shame** 4. **Fearlessness**
5. **Hopelessness**

(a) 1 and 3 (b) 2 and 5
(c) 2, 3 and 5 (d) 2, 4 and 5

Ans. (c) 2, 3 and 5

Extract Based Questions

1. Read the following extract carefully and answer the questions that follow.

What is the boy now, who has lost his ball,
What, what is he to do? I saw it go
Merrily bouncing, down the street, and then Merrily
over- there it is in the water!

CBSE Question Bank 2021 Modified

(i) Mention the situation that corresponds to the emotion behind the exclamation mark in the poem.

Ans. I don't know where I've placed my ID-card. Let me check the bag once more, Ah, finally!

(ii) The poem begins with a question. Based on your reading of the poem, state what the speaker is doing?

Ans. Based on the poem, it can be said that the poet is thinking to himself.

(iii) The extract suggests that the poet is ....
(a) an observing onlooker
(b) a parent recounting the incident
(c) the boy talking about himself
(d) imagining the incident

Ans. (a) an observing onlooker

(iv) What does the poet seem to have indicated the 'Merry bouncing of the ball' to?

Ans. The poet seems to have indicated the 'Merry bouncing of the ball' to contrast with the dejected feelings of the boy.

2. Read the following extract carefully and answer the questions that follow.

Merrily over — there it is in the water!
No use to say 'O there are other balls':
An ultimate shaking grief fixes the boy
As he stands rigid, trembling, staring down
All his young days into the harbour where
His ball went. I would not intrude on him;
A dime, another ball, is worthless.
.... Now
He senses first responsibility
In a world of possessions. People will take
Balls, balls will be lost always, little boy.
And no one buys a ball back.
Money is external.

CBSE Additional SQP 2023

(i) Complete the conversation with what the boy would most likely say. Answer in about 40 words.

"John Oh don't worry, there are plenty of other balls to play with".

Boy ....

Ans. No, there is none like that ball as that ball was special to me.

(ii) Which line first indicates that the ball is a metaphor for something else?
(a) Merrily over — there it is in the water!
(b) An ultimate shaking grief fixes the boy
(c) All his young days into the harbour where
(d) I would not intrude on him

Ans. (c) All his young days into the harbour where

(iii) Which literary device does the speaker use to describe the boy's sorrow? Why does the speaker use this device? Answer in about 40 words.

Competency Based

Ans. The speaker uses visual imagery to describe the boy's sorrow because it creates a clear picture of the depth of the boy's grief. The lines 'An ultimate shaking grief fixes the boy /As he stands rigid, trembling, staring down' paints a visual picture of the boy's grief and sorrow.

(iv) Based on the extract, what makes a possession valuable? Answer in about 40 words.

Ans. The line 'And no one buys a ball back. Money is external' indicates that the value of a possession is not determined by its cost or monetary value. Instead, the value of a possession is determined by the emotional attachment towards it, as seen in the way the boy values his ball.

3. Read the following extract carefully and answer the questions that follow.

An ultimate shaking grief fixes the boy
As he stands rigid, trembling, staring down
All his young days into the harbour where
His ball went. I would not intrude on him;

CBSE 2021

(i) Fill in the blank.

Why does the speaker choose not to intrude? This is so because the poet ....

Ans. feels that it's important that the boy learn an important life lesson, undisturbed

(ii) The boy is very young in this poem. As a mature, balanced grown-up, he might look back and think that his reaction of 'ultimate shaking grief' was
1. disproportionate to the loss
2. pretension to procure a new toy
3. according to his exposure and experience then
4. a reaction to the failure of retrieving the toy
5. justified and similar to what it would be currently

(a) 2 and 5 (b) 1 and 3 (c) 2 and 4 (d) 3 and 5

Ans. (d) 3 and 5

(iii) Why did the poet not interrupt the boy?

Ans. The poet did not interrupt the boy so that he could learn to cope with the loss.

(iv) How is the boy feeling on loss of his ball?

Ans. The boy is trembling and staring down at his ball.

Or **CBSE Additional SQP 2023**

(i) In the line, "ultimate shaking grief fixes the boy", what does the following tell us? Answer in a total of about 40 words

(a) 'ultimate' - This tells us ....

(b) 'fixes' – This tells us ....

Ans. (a) the extreme nature of this grief / overwhelming sorrow that the boy has experienced.
(b) that the grief becomes a central and unshakeable part of the boy's emotional state.

(ii) Complete the following with a correct option.

The use of 'rigid' and 'trembling' in the same line creates a powerful contrast between ....

(a) unchangeable circumstances and visible sobbing
(b) defence mechanism and submission to a situation
(c) emotional numbness and physical quivering
(d) strong beliefs and unexpected reality

Ans. (c) emotional numbness and physical quivering

(iii) State why the following statement is True or False.

The line 'All his young days into the harbour where/His ball went' refers to losing the ball as just a material loss.

Ans. False. The given line is not true because the loss of the ball signifies a moment of transition, a loss of innocence and a realisation of the complexities of life. All of these is far more than just a material loss.

(iv) Fill in the blank with an appropriate phrase from those given in the bracket.

The speaker chooses not to intrude on the boy. This choosing not to intrude, reflects a sensitivity to the boy's emotional state and a respect for the .... of the grieving process. (universal occurrence/passing over/personal nature)

Ans. personal nature

4. Read the following extract carefully and answer the questions that follow.

Now
he senses first responsibility
In a world of possessions.
People will take
Balls, balls will be lost always, little boy.
And no one buys a ball back. Money is external.

(i) What does the poet mean by 'money is external?

Ans. By the given phrase, the poet means that money is meant to be spent.

(ii) Which word can be used for the world described by the poet?

(a) Angry (b) Materialistic
(c) Selfish (d) All of these

Ans. (b) Materialistic

(iii) Comment on the poet's use of the phrase 'no one buys a ball back' in these lines. Competency Based

Ans. The given phrase means that no one can buy something that is lost forever. No one can buy the boy that ball which he had lost. Money is an external thing. It is a medium of possessing things but even money cannot compensate for the sense of loss suffered by a person.

(iv) What does the boy understand?

Ans. The boy understands to grow up and cope with loss.

5. Read the following extract carefully and answer the questions that follow.

Money is external.
He is learning, well behind his desperate eyes,
The epistemology of loss, how to stand up
Knowing what every man must one day know
And most know many days, how to stand up.

CBSE SQP 2021 Term I Modified

(i) The poet says money is external. What does it mean in this extract?

Ans. The poet says money is external. It means money buys only materialistic things and can be earned again, when lost.

(ii) What does the boy learn by losing the ball, according to the extract?

1. Loss is the unavoidable truth of life.
2. Material objects can be replaced.
3. Money buys happiness.
4. Losses in life can be prevented with care.
5. Life continues despite losses.

(a) 1, 2 and 5 (b) 2 and 4
(c) Only 1 (d) 3 and 5

Ans. (a) 1, 2 and 5

(iii) Which option lists who is speaking these lines?

(a) An observer (b) The boy's parent
(c) The ball salesman (d) A friend

Ans. (a) An observer

(iv) The boy is learning how to stand up .... This means that he is learning to be .... in the face of difficulties.

Ans. resilient

6. Read the following extract carefully and answer the questions that follow.

And no one buys a ball back. Money is external.
He is learning, well behind his desperate eyes,
The epistemology of loss, how to stand up
Knowing what every man must one day know
And most know many days, how to stand up.

(i) What is the boy learning?

1. The meaning of life
2. Meaning of responsibility
3. To cope up with loss
4. Meaning of happiness
5. To accept happiness

Select the correct option.

(a) Only 3 (b) 2 and 5
(c) 1 and 4 (d) 2, 4 and 5

Ans. (a) Only 3

(ii) Complete the following analogy on the basis of the above extract.

Cautious : Discreet :: Epistemology : ....

Ans. Assertion

(iii) What is the rhyming scheme of the stanza?

Ans. No rhyming scheme

(iv) How are the boy's eyes?

Ans. The boy's eyes have a desperate look.

Or

(i) When the poet says that 'no one buy a ball back', what does he refer to in the context of the poem? CBSE 2024

Ans. When the poet says that 'no one buys a ball back,' he is referring to the irrevocable nature of loss. In the context of the poem, it symbolises that certain things, once gone, cannot be retrieved or replaced, highlighting the permanence of some losses in life.

(ii) Complete the sentence with an appropriate option.

The lines from the poem tell us that the boy is experiencing ....

(a) distress (b) terror (c) realisation (d) elation

Ans. (c) realisation

(iii) What is the significance of the term 'desperate' used to describe the boy's eyes in the poem and how does it contribute to the overall mood and tone of the poem?

Ans. The term 'desperate' used to describe the boy's eyes signifies a deep sense of loss and an earnest desire to reclaim what has been lost, conveying a sense of helplessness and sadness. It contributes to the overall mood and tone of the poem by evoking a feeling of empathy from the reader, as it captures the profound impact of loss and the struggle to come to terms with it, adding depth to the emotional landscape portrayed in the poem.

(iv) Identify and discuss the poet's use of metaphor in the poem 'The Ball Poem'. Competency Based

Ans. The poet's use of metaphor in 'The Ball Poem' is pivotal, as the lost ball represents much more than a physical object; it symbolises the boy's first encounter with loss and grief. The ball, thus, becomes a metaphor for innocence, the carefree nature of childhood, and the things in life that are lost and cannot be replaced. This metaphor extends to teach a broader lesson about growing up and learning to handle loss, suggesting that such experiences are integral to personal development and understanding the value of what we hold dear.

Part - II

Short Answer Type Questions

1. What does John Berryman want to convey through this poem?

Or **Write the sum and substance of the poem 'The Ball Poem'.**

Or **Explain briefly the central idea of the poem.** CBSE 2023

Ans. The poet, John Berryman through the poem, wants to convey the importance of loss and responsibility in life. We all should learn our responsibility and how to cope up with the loss. The poet also wants us to learn that things will get lost from time to time and money simply cannot replace them all.

2. How does the boy feel at the loss of his ball?

Ans. The boy is very much troubled at the loss of his ball. He experiences grief at the loss of his much loved possession. Like a statue, he keeps staring at the ball with his desperate eyes. He finds it difficult to cope up with the loss.

3. 'Money is external'. What does the poet mean by this expression?

Or **Why does the poet say 'Money is external in the poem'?** CBSE 2023

Ans. The poet says that 'Money is external' to make the boy understand about his responsibility and that the loss is immaterial. By this phrase, the poet means that every loss cannot be replaced by money. Money cannot buy the memories associated with a thing and cannot replace the things that we love, for example the boy's lost ball.

4. A ball is an easily available, inexpensive thing. Then why is the boy so upset to lose it?

Ans. Yes, a ball is an inexpensive thing and easily available but the ball that the boy has lost is very valuable to him.

The boy was upset on losing his ball because it was his valued possession. It was a much loved possession which he had since his childhood. It had been with him for a long time and was linked to the memories of the days when he played with it. Now, the ball was lost forever for him. He could buy a new ball but the memories with the lost ball is lost forever.

5. Why did the poet not console the boy?

Ans. The poet did not console the boy for two reasons. One the boy was too shocked and grief sticken to listen to any consolation. The poet also wanted to make him understand that any loss is part of our life and money cannot buy the lost thing.
Moreover, the poet also observed that the boy was trying to somehow stand up or bear the loss on his own, which is much more effective.

6. Do you think the 'I' in the poem is the poet or an observer? Give a reason for your choice of response.

Ans. I think the 'I' in the poem is an observer who later on got inspired to write a poem on his observation about a child's grief who lost his favourite toy. I also feel that his decision was to be an observer so that the boy who had lost the ball could learn the lesson of moving on himself.

7. Explain how, 'Out of sight, out of mind' might apply to the boy, towards the end of the poem. **Competency Based**

Ans. The proverb 'Out of sight, out of mind' essentially means that if one thing is taken away from us, we forget about it and move on. This is what the boy needs to learn. The boy had lost his ball and will never be able to get it back. He is grief-stricken because of it but this grief will be only for some time as he will forget about the lost ball. The boy will get a new ball that will replace the lost ball.

8. A popular quote states: 'Responsibility is self-taught'. How does the poem address this thought? **Competency Based**

Ans. The quote 'Responsibility is self-taught' is central to the poem. The poet addresses this thought by becoming an observer to the situation of the boy. He could have gone to the boy and bought him a new ball. However, he wanted the boy to learn for himself that his irresponsibility cost him the ball. Until and unless, he comes to the realisation on his own, he would not learn anything about responsibility.

9. Suggest a suitable by-line for 'The Ball Poem' with a reason for your choice.

Ans. As the given poem talks about the understanding of responsibility and the need to move on, the by-line for the poem should be 'Understanding Responsibility and Moving On'.

10. What feelings do you think, might be experienced, at the loss of a mobile phone, for a youngster today? Explain how these would be different from those felt by the boy in the poem.

Ans. The loss of a mobile phone would elicit a similar response to that of the loss of the ball today. In the present world, mobile phones have become a necessity replacing almost every other thing including toys. So, the reaction at such a loss will be similar.

11. What does the poet mean by epistemology of loss in 'The Ball Poem'? **CBSE 2023**

Ans. The given phrase, 'epistemology of loss' means understanding the meaning and nature of loss. According to the poet, the epistemology of loss is the greatest lesson, the boy is learning. It teaches him to value and preserve his cherished things.
It also teaches him to recover from the loss and move on with his life. When we try to understand what it means to lose something, we are more careful about the further losses. Thus, it helps us to be self-reliant and stand up on our own feet.

12. He senses first responsibility in a world of possessions.
In the above lines from 'The Ball Poem' what does the poet mean when he says that the boy senses 'first responsibility' after losing the ball? Answer in 20-30 words. **Competency Based**

Ans. The given line and phrase indicate that this is the first time the boy has lost something. As a result, he understands the meaning and nature of loss. This first loss teaches him to value and preserve his cherished things. It also teaches him to recover from the loss and move on with his life. When we try to understand what it means to lose something, we are more careful to check the further losses. Thus, it helps us to be self-reliant and stand up on our own feet.

13. Examine the structure of the poem. How do the line breaks and stanza arrangements contribute to the overall meaning and impact of the poem?

Ans. The poem's uneven line breaks and stanza arrangements create a feeling of fragmentation, reflecting the boy's confusion after losing the ball. The short, abrupt lines highlight the harsh reality of loss, while the longer lines allow for more thought and reflection. This movement between short and long lines emphasises the boy's struggle to accept what he has lost.

14. What is the significance of the title 'The Ball Poem'?

Ans. The title 'The Ball Poem' is justly chosen to capture the poem's central metaphor and thematic essence. The ball serves as a symbolic representation of innocence, childhood joy and the transient nature of life's pleasures. Just as a ball is an ordinary object of play and enjoyment for children, it also symbolises loss and the harsh realities of growing up. Through the loss of the ball, the poem explores profound themes of impermanence, grief and the universal experience of learning to navigate the complexities of life. Thus, the title briefly reflects the tangible object at the heart of the poem and hints at its deeper layers of meaning and reflection on the human condition.

15. How does the poem explore the concept of responsibility in the face of loss?

Or **'The Ball Poem' deals with the undertones of loss and responsiblity. How is the poem very relatable to our lives and what important messages do we learn from it?** CBSE 2025

Ans. The poem explores the concept of responsibility by suggesting that the boy is learning about it through the experience of loss. Losing his ball teaches him that in a world of possessions, people will take things, and things will be lost, prompting him to recognise the need for responsibility in caring for his belongings.

16. What is the significance of the final line, 'How to stand up', in the context of the poem?

Ans. The final line, 'How to stand up', holds significance in the poem's context as it encapsulates the boy's central lesson from losing his ball. It symbolises resilience and the ability to confront and overcome challenges. By learning how to stand up in the face of loss, the boy gains a deeper understanding of responsibility and resilience, ultimately growing emotionally stronger from the experience.

17. Comment on the tone of the poem.

Ans. The tone of the poem is primarily sombre and reflective. It conveys a sense of sadness and nostalgia. The poet explores the profound emotions of loss, grief and the transition from childhood to adulthood. The language and imagery used in the poem evoke a sense of melancholy, emphasising the seriousness of the experience for the young boy who has lost his ball.

Long Answer Type Questions

1. Why is it important for everyone to experience loss and to stand up after it? CBSE 2014

Ans. Experiencing loss is a fundamental aspect of the human condition. It teaches resillience (courage), empathy and the profound strength found in hardships. It allows one to appreciate the changing nature of life and encourages personal growth. Standing up after loss is crucial as it signifies not only the physical strength to carry on but it is also a proof of the undefeatable human spirit. It signifies the transformative power of adversity, molding grief into strength. This journey of recovery encourages a deeper understanding of oneself, while also making the person emotionally strong.

Through the loss of ball, the boy learns real knowledge of the world. If he is able to bear the loss, he will be able to face the difficulties of life courageously. The boy must know how to stand up after a loss. It is essential for every human being to be able to move on or stand up after being knocked down. Here, the ball signifies losing something valuable that can not be bought or replaced. The poet wants us to understand that loss is inevitable and everyone must learn to cope up with the loss with patience and courage.

2. Why does the poet not offer money to the boy to buy another ball?

Ans. When a person is trying to overcome his grief on his own, he is busy making himself understand certain things. In such a situation, if someone intrudes or disturbs, the chain of thoughts is broken which irritates the person. Moreover, self-consolation, realisation and understanding is more effective and lasting than when it is done by an external agency or a person.

These facts are proven in the poem 'The Ball Poem'. In the poem, the poet states that neither will he interfere in the boy's sorrowful mood nor will he offer him any money.

He believes that the boy will learn the harsh reality of loss on his own. The boy will learn to cope up with loss and move on by his own understanding.

Further, he believes that the offer to buy another ball would be useless because he may get a new ball but he would not be able to get back the memories of his childhood that were attached to it. No other ball can take place of the old ball of the boy's childhood. So, the poet does not offer money to the boy to buy another ball.

3. 'The Ball Poem' by John Berryman is a concise yet emotionally powerful poem that explores the themes of loss, responsibility, and the inevitability of growing up. Comment.

Ans. 'The Ball Poem' by John Berryman is a concise yet emotionally powerful poem that explores the themes of loss, responsibility and the inevitability of growing up.

Loss and Impermanence The poem opens with the loss of the boy's ball, quickly emphasising the significance of this loss to the child. The bouncing ball is a metaphor for the transitory nature of childhood innocence and joy. The poem highlights how loss is an inevitable part of life and the boy's realisation that 'Balls will be lost always' underscores the impermanence of youth and happiness.

Responsibility As the boy watches his ball sink into the water, he experiences a sense of responsibility for the first time. The loss of his ball is a metaphor for growing up and facing the consequences of one's actions. This newfound responsibility is a part of the boy's journey, as he learns that life involves taking care of one's possessions and dealing with the consequences of one's actions.

Epistemology of Loss The poem suggests that the boy is learning the 'epistemology of loss', which refers to the philosophical study of knowledge and how we understand things. In this context, the boy is gaining a deeper understanding of the nature of loss and how it shapes one's perspective on life. The poem portrays the boy's painful realisation of the irreplaceability of what he has lost.

Transition to Adulthood The poem hints at the boy's transition from childhood to adulthood. He is learning a lesson that all people must eventually confront, and this process of growing up involves accepting the inevitability of loss and learning how to cope with it.

11. "Not from weeping nor from grieving will anyone obtain peace of mind". If you had to use the message of the given quote from the Buddha's sermon 'The Sermon at Benares' to help the boy cope with the loss of his ball and what it signifies 'The Ball Poem', what would you include in your advice? **CBSE SQP 2023**

Ans. The Buddha's words teach us to cope with the loss of irreplaceable things. They tell us that the loss of irreparable things brings griefs and sorrow but as wise people we must learn to stay calm and accept the loss while understanding that we might lose things we love, even people we once loved. The existence of some things in our lives is ephemeral. This acceptance helps us in living normally and forgetting about loss.

These words can help the boy in 'The Ball Poem' cope with the loss of the ball by making him understand that loss is a constant and important part of life. Only by learning to accept and adapt to it can we live a normal life. This notion might be too difficult for the boy to understand because he is too young. He is all alone in his loss. There is no one beside him to explain everything about the loss. So, he must learn from his experience painstakingly. For the same he may require time to cope since he can easily feel disheartened at such a young age.

ASSESSMENT EXERCISE

Extract Based Questions

Read the following extract carefully and answer the questions that follow.

What is the boy now, who has lost his ball,
What, what is he to do? I saw it go
Merrily bouncing, down the street, and then
Merrily over - there it is in the water!
No use to say 'O there are other balls':

(i) Complete the sentence appropriately.
It is clear that assonance is the poetic device used in the line "Merrily over - there it is in the water!" because .... (Clue: explain how assonance applies here)

(ii) What happened to the ball?
(a) Went across the field
(b) Lost in the crowd
(c) Was drowned in water
(d) Got disfigured

(iii) What is the ball symbolic of?

(iv) Complete the sentence, according to the extract.
The boy's ball in the above extract falls in the water and .... found.

Short Answer (SA) Type Questions

1. What is the central idea of the poem 'The Ball Poem'?
2. What does 'in the world of possessions' mean? Why is money 'external'?

Long Answer (LA) Type Question

1. The poem teaches us to learn, to accept and let go and not cling onto something that we can never have. Elaborate.

Amanda!

by Robert Klein

Introduction The following poem 'Amandal!' has been written by Robert Klein. 'Amanda!' is a poem about a teenager's psychology. The poem tells us about a little girl Amanda who is constantly and continuously being scolded and instructed, most probably by her mother. However, Amanda is lost in her own world. She is not paying attention to what her mother is saying. The poem, then, points that parents must give some freedom to growing children. Constant scolding may adversely affect a child's development.

Stanzawise Explanation

Stanza 1

Don't bite your nails, Amanda!
Don't hunch your shoulders, Amanda!
Stop that slouching and sit up straight,
Amanda!

Explanation In these lines, Amanda, a little girl is being scolded and instructed by her mother for her actions. Amanda is advised to stop biting her nails. She is also told to sit up straight without bending her shoulders.

The use of exclamation mark with Amanda in the last line of the stanza shows Amanda's mother's irritation and frustration. It is important to note here that the instructions are given for Amanda's benefit. The mother here, then, is giving instructions to teach good habits to Amanda and to correct her posture.

Stanza 2

(There is a languid, emerald sea,
where the sole inhabitant is me—
a mermaid, drifting blissfully.)

Explanation Amanda is lost in her world of imagination while her mother is instructing her. In her world, she imagines that she is a mermaid who lives alone in the beautiful green sea. As a mermaid, she would move in the soft waves of the sea. Amanda believes that as a mermaid, her life would be more peaceful and relaxing.

Stanza 3

Did you finish your homework, Amanda?
Did you tidy your room, Amanda?
I thought I told you to clean your shoes,
Amanda!

Explanation In these lines, Amanda is being inquired about her work. Amanda's mother is asking about whether she has finished her homework and whether she has cleaned her room. Amanda is also reminded that she was asked to clean her shoes.

Stanza 4

(I am an orphan, roaming the street.
I pattern soft dust with my hushed, bare feet.
The silence is golden, the freedom is sweet.)

Explanation Again, Amanda is not paying any attention to her mother. She is in her world of imagination. She imagines that she is an orphan child who is freely roaming around on the street. She has no shoes on her feet and is making patterns on the soft dust with her quiet and bare feet.

She is loving the silence and freedom to do anything in her world of imagination.

Stanza 5

Don't eat that chocolate, Amanda!
Remember your acne, Amanda!
Will you please look at me when I'm speaking to you, Amanda!

Explanation In these lines, Amanda is instructed by her mother to not eat chocolates. She is reminded that eating chocolates had previously caused her acne. However, as Amanda is lost in her own thoughts, she is not paying attention to her mother. So, her mother strictly asks her to listen to what is being told to her.

Stanza 6

(I am Rapunzel, I have not a care;
life in a tower is tranquil and rare;
I'll certainly never let down my bright hair!)

Explanation Amanda is still in her world of imagination. Now, she dreams of herself as Rapunzel (character of a German fairy tale who lived alone in a tower). As Rapunzel, she would not have to worry about anything, and her life would be calm and peaceful in the tower. She emphasizes that unlike Rapunzel, she would never let her hair down and permit anyone to come to her in the tower.

Stanza 7

Stop that sulking at once, Amanda!
You're always so moody, Amanda!
Anyone would think that I nagged at you, Amanda!

Explanation In these lines, Amanda is not reacting to her mother's instructions. It seems that she is annoyed due to constant instructions. Amanda's mother is asking her to stop being upset and moody. She said that her (Amanda) upset behaviour will show anyone that she is disturbed due to her mother's constant instructions.

Poetic Devices Used in the Poem

Alliteration Repetition of initial consonant sounds in the same line

- Stop that slouching and sit up straight.
- Stop that sulking at once, Amanda!

Allusion A reference to a statement, person, place, etc. from history, religion, literature or any other field

- Mermaid - To be free. (Taken from fairy tales)
- Rapunzel - Who lived alone on a tower for a long time. (Part of a German fairy tale)

Metaphor A device which compares two things or qualities which are unlike

- Languid, emerald sea – languid and emerald type qualities are assigned to the sea.
- Silence is golden
- Freedom is sweet

Repetition Repeating a word or phrase for emphasis

- Use of the word 'Amanda'

Brackets Generally used to indicate the thoughts that are not spoken out loud

- Stanza 2, 4 and 6 are the inner thoughts of Amanda.

Word Meaning

Word	Meaning
Stanza 1	
Hunch	raise shoulders and bend the upper portion of body in forward position
Slouching	sitting in a lazy, drooping way
Stanza 2	
Languid	reluctant to exert itself
Mermaid	an imaginary sea creature having a woman's head and body with a fish's tail instead of legs;
Drifting	a slow and steady movement
Stanza 3	
Tidy	arrange neatly and in order
Stanza 4	
Hushed	very quiet and still
Stanza 5	
Acne	common skin disease characterised by pimples, especially on face
Stanza 6	
Rapunzel	Rapunzel is the name of a girl in a German fairy tale who was made to live alone in a high tower and had very long, beautiful golden hair. She was held captive by a witch who used to come up to the tower by climbing her long hair
Tranquil	free from any trouble or anxiety, to be in a peaceful state of mind.
Stanza 7	
Sulking	to be upset about something
Nagged	to irritate someone by complaining about his or her habits again and again

NCERT FOLDER

NCERT Exercise Questions

THINKING ABOUT THE POEM (NCERT PAGE 62)

Q.1 How old do you think Amanda is? How do you know this?

Ans. Amanda is a little, 8-12 years old school going girl.

We know this because of the reference of a mermaid and Rapunzel. Further, the instructions given to her for doing homework, nail biting, correcting posture, etc. are generally given to children of this age group.

Q.2 Who do you think is speaking to her?

Ans. Any one of Amanda's elders or parents is speaking to her. From the instructions given to Amanda, one can say that it is most probably Amanda's mother or governess.

Q.3 Why are stanzas 2, 4 and 6 given in parenthesis?

Ans. Stanza 2, 4 and 6 are given in parenthesis because they reflect Amanda's inner thoughts. Amanda is lost in her dream world and is not listening to what her mother is asking/telling her.

Q.4 Who is the speaker in stanzas 2, 4 and 6? Do you think this speaker is listening to the speaker in stanzas 1, 3, 5 and 7?

Ans. The speaker in stanza 2, 4 and 6 is the child, Amanda.

No, Amanda is not listening to the speaker of stanza 1, 3, 5 and 7 as she is lost in the world of her imagination.

Q.5 What could Amanda do if she were a mermaid?

Ans. If Amanda were a mermaid, she could be the only resident of the beautiful green sea where she would float in the soft waves of the sea. There, she could relax and enjoy her freedom.

Q.6 Is Amanda an orphan? Why does she say so?

Ans. No, Amanda is not an orphan though she wishes to be one. She says so because she is upset at being scolded again and again by her mother. Thus, she thinks that if she had been an orphan, she would be free and her life would be peaceful.

Q.7 Do you know the story of Rapunzel? Why does she want to be Rapunzel?

Ans. Rapunzel was a beautiful golden haired princess who lived in a tower. She had very long hair by which she used to allow people to come into her tower.

Amanda believes that Rapunzel's life in the lonely tower would be very happy. So, she wanted to be Rapunzel and wished to live in such a tower, away from everyone. She even imagines that in order to live a happy life she would never allow anyone to come into her tower.

Q.8 What does the girl yearn for? What does this poem tell you about Amanda?

Ans. The girl Amanda yearns for freedom and peace in life.

According to the poem, Amanda feels that her freedom has been limited by her mother. As a result, she dreams of being a mermaid in a calm sea, an orphan with freedom, and Rapunzel in a tranquil tower. These dreams show that Amanda wants to escape the constant demands and criticisms of the adult speaking to her. She wishes for a life without rules and nagging, where she can be herself and enjoy her thoughts. The poem tells us that Amanda feels overwhelmed by the expectations placed on her. She uses her imagination to cope with stress and find happiness. Amanda is creative and seeks a sense of calm and independence, highlighting the conflict between her inner world and the pressures from the adults in her life.

Q.9 Read the last stanza. Do you think Amanda is sulking and moody?

Ans. No, Amanda is neither sulking nor is she acting moody. The speaker (her mother) of the last stanza thinks so because Amanda is not paying any attention to her instructions, rather she is lost in her own world.

REVIEW EXERCISE

Including Competency Based Questions

Part – I

Multiple Choice Questions

1. What does the poem 'Amanda' inform us about the speaker?

(a) Loves giving instructions
(b) Physical beauty is important
(c) Wants to control Amanda
(d) All of the above

Ans. (d) All of the above

2. Emerald sea means ....

(a) clear sea
(b) green sea
(c) sea filled with emeralds
(d) None of the above

Ans. (b) green sea

3. A transferred epithet is a literary device where the modifier or epithet is transferred from the noun it is meant to describe to another noun in the sentence. Based on the given definition of 'transferred epithet', choose the option that lists an example of transferred epithet. CBSE Question Bank 2021

(a) soft dust (b) hushed (bare) feet
(c) freedom (is) sweet (d) silence (is) golden

Ans. (b) hushed (bare) feet

4. Which option completes the popular adage given below? .... silence is gold. CBSE Question Bank 2021

(a) Precious are words for (b) Speech is silver
(c) Silver is the tongue (d) Ideas may be precious but

Ans. (b) Speech is silver

5. Will you please look at me when I'm speaking to you, Amanda!
Read the given lines and tell why is Amanda not looking at the speaker?

(a) Amanda is listening to music
(b) Amanda is playing
(c) Amanda is sleeping
(d) Amanda is lost in her own thoughts

Ans. (d) Amanda is lost in her own thoughts

6. What causes acne to Amanda according to the speaker?

(a) Biting nails (b) Cleaning the room
(c) Eating chocolates (d) Eating pizzas

Ans. (c) Eating chocolates

7. In the poem 'Amanda!', the speaker is so worried about acne. What does it show?

(a) This shows that importance is given to physical beauty.
(b) This shows her concern towards Amanda.
(c) This shows Amanda's carelessness.
(d) Both (a) and (b)

Ans. (a) This shows that importance is given to physical beauty.

8. What do the words tranquil and rare signify?

(a) Pleasant surrounding (b) Freedom and peace
(c) Music and excitement (d) Peace and no nagging

Ans. (d) Peace and no nagging

9. Why has the poet used bracketed lines in the poem 'Amanda'.

(a) To show they are important
(b) To show mother's words
(c) To show Amanda's imagination
(d) To show poet's words

Ans. (c) To show Amanda's imagination

10. Amanda wants to be Rapunzel because ....

(a) she wants to have long hair
(b) she wants a prince to save her
(c) she wants to lead a carefree life
(d) she wants to be a princess

Ans. (c) she wants to lead a carefree life

11. What all things did Amanda imagine while her mother was giving her instructions?

1. To be a mermaid
2. To be an orphan
3. To be Rapunzel

(a) Only 1 (b) 1 and 2
(c) 2 and 3 (d) All of these

Ans. (d) All of these

12. When Amanda's mother says, "Stop that sulking at once, Amanda!" She means that

(i) Amanda is annoyed by her mother's constant nagging.
(ii) Amanda is ignoring the instructions given by her mother.

(a) (i) is correct (ii) is incorrect
(b) (i) is incorrect (ii) is correct
(c) Both (i) and (ii) are correct
(d) Neither (i) nor (ii is correct

Ans. (c) Both (i) and (ii) are correct

Extract Based Questions

1. Read the following extract carefully and answer the questions that follow.

Don't bite your nails, Amanda!
Don't hunch your shoulders, Amanda!
Stop that slouching and sit up straight,
Amanda!

CBSE Question Bank 2021 Modified

(i) Complete the sentence appropriately.

The purpose of the speaker's words in the given extract is to ....

Ans. improve the listener's posture and habits

(ii) Select the option that fits with the following.

Slouching : Straight :: .... : ....

Ans. Lazy : Agile

(iii) Alliteration is a literary device used in the extract. Which of the following options does not include examples of this literary device?

(a) The moon and the shimmering stars watched over us.
(b) With that charming chat, Catherine choose comfort.
(c) Away ran the pathetic pooch pouting like a princess.
(d) Dee dee was driving down day after day.

Ans. (a) The moon and the shimmering stars watched over us.

(iv) What does the repetition of 'Amanda!' at the end of each line reflect?

Ans. The repetition of Amanda at the end of each line reflects the frustration of the speaker.

2. Read the following extract carefully and answer the questions that follow.

There is a languid, emerald sea,
where the sole inhabitant is me —
a mermaid, drifting blissfully.

(i) Complete the sentence with the appropriate option.

The poet has used .... in the following lines. Identify it and explain it.

"There is a languid, emerald sea,
where the sole inhabitant is me"

Ans. The poetic device used here is enjambment. Enjambment is the continuation of a sentence or clause across a line break. It encourages the reader to continue reading from one line to the next.

(ii) Why is this stanza given within brackets?

1. To show inner thoughts of mother
2. To show the day dreaming by Amanda
3. To show the contrast

Codes

(a) Only1
(b) 1 and 2
(c) Only 3
(d) Both 2 and 3

Ans. (d) Both 2 and 3

(iii) Comment on the imagery that the poet creates in these lines.

Ans. In the given lines, the poet employs vivid and evocative imagery. The word 'languid' suggests a slow, relaxed and almost dreamlike quality to the sea. This sets an unhurried mood. The use of 'emerald' as an adjective not only adds colour to the scene but also evokes a sense of richness and beauty. The next line 'where the sole inhabitant is me' creates a sense of solitude and isolation in the vastness of the rich emerald sea. Together, these lines paint an image of a serene and solitary encounter with nature.

(iv) Why does Amanda want to be sole inhabitant of sea?

Ans. Amanda wants to be away from this noisy and disturbing atmosphere and hence, wishes to be the sole in habitant of the sea.

3. Read the following extract carefully and answer the questions that follow.

Don't eat that chocolate, Amanda!
Remember your acne, Amanda!
Will you please look at me when I'm speaking
to you, Amanda!
(I am Rapunzel, I have not a care;
life in a tower is tranquil and rare)

(i) Why is Amanda not looking at the speaker?

Ans. Amanda is lost in her own thoughts which is why she is not looking at the speaker.

(ii) Fill the blank with one/two words.

The speaker suggests that .... causes acne.

Ans. eating chocolates

(iii) The speaker is so worried about acne. What does it show?

(a) This shows that importance is given to physical beauty.
(b) This shows her concern towards Amanda.
(c) This shows Amanda's carelessness.
(d) Both (a) and (b)

Ans. (a) This shows that importance is given to physical beauty.

(iv) What does this stanza inform us about the speaker?

Ans. The stanza informs us that the speaker, i.e. Amanda's mother, is controlling and restricting. She constantly nags Amanda and tries to direct her actions. She is also very concerned with physical beauty as she reminds Amanda to keep her skin acne-free.

Or

(i) What is the central idea of the poem as reflected in the lines above? Answer in about 40 words. **CBSE 2024**

Ans. Through the given lines, one can state that Amanda does not like being nagged by her mother for eating chocolates and other things. From this, we can say that the poet wants the convey an important message that children should never be restricted from their free thoughts and wishes. Constant nagging and instructions hamper their freedom and growth.

(ii) Complete the sentence with the appropriate option.

"Will you please look at me when I'm speaking to you, Amanda!" tells us that the mother's attitude is ....

(a) loving (b) relaxed
(c) authoritative (d) thoughtful

Ans. (c) authoritative

(iii) Identify any one poetic device used in the above extract.

Ans. The given lines uses the poetic device called allusion as it makes a reference to a princess named Rapunzel found in many fairy tales.

(iv) For what reason does Amanda imagine herself to be Rapunzel?

Ans. Amanda imagines herself to be Rapunzel so that she could live a free and peaceful life in a tower away from people.

4. Read the following extract carefully and answer the questions that follow.

I thought I told you to clean your shoes,
Amanda!
(I am an orphan, roaming the street.
I pattern soft dust with my hushed, bare feet.
The silence is golden; the freedom is sweet.)
Don't eat that chocolate, Amanda! (Amanda!)

CBSE Additional SQP 2023

(i) Which of the following best describes the symbolic meaning of the soft dust and hushed, bare feet in Amanda's orphan daydream?

(a) A sense of isolation and loneliness
(b) Freedom and independence
(c) Poverty and hardship
(d) Conformity and obedience

Ans. (b) Freedom and independence

(ii) What does the contrast between the speaker's commands and Amanda's daydream suggest about her imaginative escape? (Answer in 30-40 words)

Ans. The contrast between the speaker's commands and Amanda's daydream about her imaginative escape suggests the difference between their contrasting desires. In reality, Amanda is not given any freedom or peace. As a result, her imagination becomes her means of asserting her freedom, finding peace and resisting the limitations imposed by her reality. It serves as a coping mechanism and a form of rebellion against the constraints imposed on her.

(iii) Complete the following with the impact on the reader.

The lack of the special use of parentheses would have resulted in ....

Ans. reduced importance of Amanda's daydreams resulting in the reader not recognising the contrast between the external commands and her inner thoughts.

(iv) How does the line, "I thought I told you to clean your shoes, Amanda!" help us infer that Amanda's actions are being closely monitored and directed. **Competency Based**

Ans. The use of the given line suggests a reminder/ frustration on the part of the speaker, supporting the idea that Amanda's behaviour is under close scrutiny. This implies a relationship where Amanda is expected to adhere to specific instructions and fulfill assigned tasks, reinforcing a sense of external control and authority over her actions.

5. Read the following extract carefully and answer the questions that follow.

(I am an orphan, roaming the street.
I pattern soft dust with my hushed, bare feet. The
silence is golden, the freedom is sweet).

(i) What is the tone of the given lines?

1. Analytical **2. Despairing**
3. Peaceful **4. Nervous**
5. Serious

Select the correct option.

(a) Only 3 (b) 1 and 2
(c) 4 and 5 (d) None of these

Ans. (a) Only 3

(ii) Complete the following analogy on the basis of the above extract.

Lovely : Flowers :: .... : Dust

Ans. Soft

(iii) Why is Amanda imagining herself to be an orphan?

Ans. Amanda is imagining herself to be an orphan because she is irritated by the speaker's constant nagging and she wants some peace and quiet.

(iv) What is Amanda imagining in the above extract?

Ans. Amanda is imagining that she is an orphan who can freely roam around in bare feet.

6. Read the following extract carefully and answer the questions that follow.

(I am Rapunzel, I have not a care;
life in a tower is tranquil and rare;
I'll certainly never let down my bright hair!)

(i) Why are these lines bracketed?

Ans. The given lines are bracketed because they show Amanda's imagination which is away from the reality where her mother is scolding her.

(ii) What is Amanda doing?

Ans. Amanda is imagining herself as Rapunzel.

(iii) State whether the following statement is True or False.

Rapunzel does not have to worry about anything.

Ans. True

Select the option that applies the same rhyme scheme as the given extract.

(a) Children three that nestle near,
Eager eye and willing ear,
Pleased a simple tale to hear

(b) I know not how it falls on me,
This summer evening, hushed and lone;
Yet the faint wind comes soothingly

(c) Far or forgot to me is near;
Shadow and sunlight are the same;
The vanished gods to me appear;

(d) The Caterpillar on the Leaf
Repeats to thee thy Mothers grief
Kill not the Moth nor Butterfly

Ans. (a)

7. Read the following extract carefully and answer the questions that follow.

(I am Rapunzel, I have not a care;
life in a tower is tranquil and rare;
I'll certainly never let down my bright hair!)
Stop that sulking at once, Amanda!
You're always so moody, Amanda!
Anyone would think that I nagged at you, Amanda!

CBSE 2025

(i) Complete the following suitably.

Amanda sulked and became moody because.

Ans. She was constantly being scolded and nagged by an authoritative figure, likely a parent, which made her feel trapped and long for freedom.

(ii) What does the girl constantly yearn for? What do you pattern about Amanda from the poem?

Ans. Amanda constantly yearns for freedom, peace, and solitude. She imagines herself as Rapunzel, living in a tranquil and rare tower, free from any disturbances. From the poem, we can infer that Amanda feels constrained and unhappy due to constant instructions and reprimands.

(iii) What kind of picture is painted by the poet through the line "life in a tower is tranquil and rare"?

Ans. The poet paints a picture of solitude, peace, and exclusivity. The tower represents an escape from the chaotic and restrictive reality Amanda faces, where she can live freely without interference.

(iv) The tone of the speaker in the exclamation "Stop that sulking at once, Amanda!" is

1. uncertain **2. aggressive**
3. dominating **4. meek**

(a) 1, 2 and 4 (b) 2 and 3
(c) 2, 4 and 5 (d) 4 and 5

Ans. (b) 2 and 3

Part - II

Short Answer Type Questions

1. Justify the title of the poem 'Amanda'.

Ans. The title of the poem 'Amanda' is very appropriate. The poem is about a little girl, Amanda who is constantly scolded by her mother. Throughout the poem, the focus is on Amanda and her world of imagination. In this world, she lives a free and peaceful life without any interruptions.

2. Why does Amanda wish to be a mermaid, an orphan or Rapunzel?

Ans. Amanda wishes to be a mermaid, an orphan and Rapunzel to live a life of freedom. She is constantly scolded by her mother. So, she escapes into her own world of imagination wherein she lives a peaceful life, all alone. As a mermaid, she would be the sole resident of a beautiful sea and as an orphan, she would enjoy freedom. Finally, as Rapunzel, she would live a carefree life.

3. List the things about which Amanda's mother nag her.

Or Amanda was blamed for a number of things. Mention any two. **CBSE 2022 Term II**

Or Mention any two issues over which Amanda was nagged and scolded. **CBSE 2022 Term II**

Ans. Amanda's mother nags or scolds her about the following things

- Amanda is instructed to not eat chocolates and to clean her room as well as shoes.
- Amanda is also asked to finish her homework.

4. Why does Amanda seem moody most of the time?

Ans. Amanda seems moody most of the time because she is so involved in her world of imagination that she does not pay attention to her mother. Amanda often escapes from reality into her world of fantasy to get away from the continuous scoldings. Her day dreaming makes her look moody and uninterested.

5. Do you think it is Amanda's fault in the poem? Justify your answer.

Ans. No, Amanda is not at fault. In the poem, Amanda is constantly instructed and scolded by her mother. Her mother restricts her freedom. Therefore, Amanda desires the peace and freedom which is not granted to her. So, she escapes into her own world where she enjoys the calmness.

6. Does Amanda's mother have a nagging behaviour? Justify your answer.

Ans. Amanda's mother has a nagging behaviour. She is always instructing Amanda and finding faults within her.

Her mother constantly tell her the dos and don'ts. Such a nagging behaviour affects Amanda who feels that her freedom is restricted. Amanda's mother's responsibility to instill (develop) good manners in the child makes Amanda retreat (escape) into her imagination where she seeks peace and freedom.

7. Comment on the tone of the speaker when they say 'Will you please look at me when I'm speaking to you, Amanda!'. **CBSE SQP 2022 Term II**

Ans. The speaker is one of Amanda's parents, who is instructing and reprimanding their daughter for not behaving in a proper manner. In the given line, their tone is that of irritation and annoyance as they are telling their daughter to listen to what they are saying. This is happening as their daughter's mind seems distracted and irritated by the constant nagging.

8. What kind of an image does 'languid, emerald sea' evoke? **CBSE Question Bank 2021**

Ans. 'Languid, emerald sea' evokes an image of a calm and green sea. 'Languid means moving slowly with little energy, often in an attractive way. 'Emerald' is a green coloured gemstone that refers to the green colour of sea water.

9. Would you call Amanda a disrespectful child? Provide one reason to justify your opinion.

Ans. Yes, I would call Amanda a disrespectful child because she does not respond to her parent's repeated instructions. She is lost in her imagination and does not even look towards her mother when she is yelling at her.

10. The reader sympathises with the speaker in the poem. Support this opinion with a reason. **CBSE Question Bank 2021**

Ans. The speaker (probably Amanda's mother) is worried about Amanda as she is lost in her thoughts. Amanda does not pay attention to what her mother says and this makes the reader sympathise with her mother.

11. "Don't bite you nails Amanda!
Don't hunch your shoulders Amanda!"
What does this reflect about Amanda's mother and Amanda? **CBSE 2022 Term II**

Ans. The given lines reflect the constant nagging of Amanda's mother regarding basic ethics to not do certain things that kids of her age are accustomed to. Simultaneously, on the child's part, it reflects her imagination and creation of stories, and her wish to become a mermaid, orphan or Rapunzel to simply escape the nagging.

12. 'Amanda is alone but not lonely in the world she envisions.' Give instances from the poem to justify. **CBSE 2022 Term II**

Ans. Amanda feels that she is constantly being pressurised by her mother. So, she wants to be alone and enjoy being herself.

She wants to roam around in the streets alone and finds silence 'golden' and freedom 'sweet'. Hence, even when she envisions a world where she is alone, she is not lonely.

13. Why does Amanda wish to be a mermaid? **CBSE 2023**

Ans. Amanda wishes to be a mermaid to live a life of freedom. She is constantly scolded by her mother. So, she escapes into her own world of imagination wherein she lives a peaceful life, all alone. As a mermaid she would be the sole resident of a beautiful sea.

14. Amanda gets a list of instructions from her mother of dos and don'ts. What do these tell you about the relationship between Amanda and her mother? CBSE 2023

Or **Amanda's mother gives her a list of dos and dont's. What impact does this have on Amanda?** CBSE 2023

Ans. Amanda's mother's constant instructions like not to bite her nails or not to bend her back and shoulders, or not to hunch her shoulders but sit up straight deprive Amanda of her freedom of life in the open. Hence, their relationship appears a bit strained.

15. How does the repeated use of the name 'Amanda' influence the overall tone of the poem? CBSE Additional SQP 2023

Ans. The repeated use of the name 'Amanda' throughout the poem creates a sense of authority and control. The repetition conveys a commanding tone, as if someone in a position of authority, such as a parent, is speaking directly to Amanda. It also adds a sense of familiarity and intimacy to the tone. It suggests a close relationship between the speaker and Amanda, indicating that the instructions and restrictions come from a place of care and concern. Further, as the name 'Amanda' is repeated numerous times, followed by instructions or directions, it also creates a tone of frustration or annoyance.

16. What impression do you form about Amanda in the poem? CBSE 2023

Ans. The poem tells us that Amanda is a young, restless girl with a vivid imagination. Even as she is being scolded by her mother, Amanda's mind wanders to imaginary scenarios where she is a mermaid, an orphan or Rapunzel. We also get to know that she is not granted any freedom and has no peace in her life as she is frustrated with the constant instructions that she gets.

17. How does the tone of Amanda's imagination contrast with the tone of the commands she receives? Competency Based

Ans. The tone of Amanda's imagined scenarios is tranquil, blissful and carefree, providing a sense of escape and freedom. In contrast, the commands she receives from the adult figure are stern, critical and nagging, highlighting the oppressive nature of her reality and the desire for escape through fantasy.

18. What emotions do you think Amanda feels in response to the constant instructions and nagging?

Ans. Amanda likely feels frustration, resentment and a sense of suffocation in response to the constant instructions and nagging. She may also experience a desire for freedom, autonomy and escape from the oppressive control imposed by the adult figure in her life.

19. What does the adult's criticism of Amanda's habits and appearance suggest about their relationship?

Ans. The adult's criticism of Amanda's habits and appearance suggests a strained relationship marked by control and dissatisfaction. The nagging reflects a lack of acceptance and understanding, indicating a power dynamic where the adult seeks to impose their standards onto Amanda, potentially hindering mutual respect and communication in their relationship.

20. How does the poem illustrate the tension between Amanda's inner world and her external reality?

Ans. The poem illustrates the tension between Amanda's inner world and external reality by juxtaposing her imaginative escapades with the mundane demands of the adult figure. Amanda seeks refuge in fantastical realms to escape reality's oppressive nature, highlighting the stark contrast between her desires for freedom and tranquillity and the constraints of her everyday life.

21. How does the mother's nagging affect Amanda's self-esteem and sense of self? What long-term consequences might this have?

Ans. The mother's constant nagging eats away at (negatively impacts) Amanda's self-esteem, causing her to doubt her abilities. Such an ongoing pressure can create a long-term struggle with self-identity, and make her feel inadequate. The behaviour of Amanda's mother may cause her to lose confidence in her own abilities in the future.

22. How might the poem be interpreted regarding societal expectations placed on children and the desire for autonomy or self-expression? Competency Based

Ans. The poem can be interpreted as a commentary on the conflict between societal expectations and the desire for autonomy, assertion and self-expression. Through the repetitive commands directed at Amanda, the poem illustrates the pressures on young children to conform to societal norms and fulfil expected roles. Amanda's internal fantasies of freedom, embodied by the mermaid, the orphan and Rapunzel, symbolise her longing for autonomy and escape from these constraints. This juxtaposition highlights the universal struggle to balance societal obligations (especially for a girl child) with personal desires for individuality and self-expression.

Long Answer Type Questions

1. Discuss the importance of proper upbringing with reference to the poem 'Amanda' by Robert Klein.

Ans. Upbringing plays an essential role in personality development of a child. Whenever we wish to admire or criticise someone, we talk about the upbringing of that person. Robert Klein's poem 'Amanda' highlights the problems of 'proper' upbringing of a child. To instil good values and moral principles in a growing child is the foremost duty of the parents. However, the poem shows how a child feels upset because of constant instructions.

Amanda, the little girl in the poem, goes through such a situation. She is instructed and scolded for her habits. She gets no freedom and space for herself. As a result, she enters her world of imagination. This world proves to be her defence against her scolding mother. In her world, she seeks freedom and peace. She imagines herself as a mermaid who is the sole resident of a beautiful sea.

Then, she imagines herself as an orphan who is free to do anything. Finally, she wants to be Rapunzel and live a peaceful life in a tower. Therefore, elders/parents must maintain a balance. While instilling good manners, they should also give some freedom to their children.

2. How does Amanda tackle the nagging nature of her mother? Explain with examples from the poem. **Competency Based**

Ans. In the poem, 'Amanda', the little girl named Amanda often escapes into her own world. Her world of dreams give her the freedom and peace that she seeks in reality where she is constantly nagged by her elders.

Her mother continuously instructs and scolds her for her ill-manners and laziness. She is asked not to bite her nails, not to eat chocolates, to clean her room and so on.

As Amanda's mother is giving her instructions, she is lost in her daydreams. The persistance of Amanda's mother leave a harmful impression in her mind. Her retreat, then, is her way of tackling her mother. It is her shield and defence against the harsh realities that she goes through. In her reality, her freedom is restricted.

Her need for freedom and peace, finds expression in her dreams where she imagines a carefree and happy life as an orphan, mermaid and Rapunzel, without her mother. Amanda may seem moody and upset, to her mother, but is not really so. The nagging nature of her mother makes her escape into a world away from the realities of her life.

3. Escapism is one way to run away from harsh realities. Discuss in the context of the poem 'Amanda!'. **Competency Based**

Ans. It is true that escapism is one way to run away from harsh realities. By going through the whole poem, we come to know that Amanda's mother keeps instructing her all the time. Amanda's mother's intention may be to discipline the little girl and make her a mature person. But, children need love and a caring attitude in their elders.

Advice in the form of nagging leaves a very harmful impression in the child's mind. The reality becomes harsh for them and they try to escape these realities by indulging in their own fantasy world.

In this poem, Amanda's life is frustrating as she is forbidden to do anything without seeking permission. Continuous instructions of her mother and constant scoldings leave a very negative impact on a child's personality.

In such situation, Amanda adheres to a defence mechanism where she imagines herself to be free and without parents so that she is not nagged. She drifts into an imaginary situation to escape from the harsh realities of her life. It is the mother's behaviour that is forcing her to do so. Thus, parents need to understand that their child also requires a certain amount of freedom which must be given to them.

4. How does the poem use repetition, specifically in the repeated use of Amanda's name and the recurring commands directed towards her?

Ans. The poem employs repetition in the frequent use of Amanda's name and the recurring commands directed towards her. By repeatedly addressing her as 'Amanda' before issuing instructions or criticisms, the speaker emphasises Amanda's identity and the personal nature of the rebukes. This repetition highlights the speaker's authoritative tone and Amanda's consistent presence throughout the poem.

The repeated commands like 'Don't bite your nails, Amanda!' and 'Stop that sulking at once, Amanda!' reinforce the constraint and expectation placed upon Amanda by societal norms or parental figures.

The repetition creates a rhythmic quality that reinforces the persistent nature of these demands in Amanda's life.

5. What insights can be gained about Amanda's character based on her responses to the speaker's instructions, or lack thereof?

Ans. Amanda's character can be inferred through her responses or lack thereof to the speaker's instructions. Her compliance or defiance, as indicated by her actions or lack of action, provides insight into her temperament and attitude towards authority. If Amanda consistently follows the commands, she may be obedient or resigned to fulfilling others' expectations, even begrudgingly or resentfully. On the other hand, if she frequently disregards the instructions or displays signs of defiance, it hints at a rebellious or independent streak within her character. Her internal thoughts or emotions hinted through the fantastical imagery further illuminate her desires for escapism or freedom from the constraints imposed upon her.

6. **Discuss the shifting tone and mood of the poem. How does the poet create a sense of tension and frustration?**

Ans. The poem constantly shifts in tone and mood, turning from initial innocence to growing frustration on Amanda's part. The poet effectively uses imagery and language to create tension within the poem. For instance, peaceful descriptions of Amanda's daydreams clash with the harsh realities of her mother's demands. As Amanda struggles with her mother's expectations, the tone of her mother grows increasingly oppressive, suggesting a sense of suffocation.

Even the internal scenarios that were previously hopeful or whimsical become charged with frustration, revealing Amanda's internal struggle. The repetition of commands from her mother intensifies the feeling of being trapped. This contrast of Amanda's colourful imagination against her mother's restrictive control reflects the universal struggle between fantasy and reality. Ultimately, the poem captures the complexities of growing up, while showing how external pressures can negatively affect one's inner world and sense of self.

7. **How does the power dynamic between Amanda and her mother shift throughout the poem? Who holds more power, and how is it exercised?** **Competency Based**

Ans. Throughout the poem, the power dynamic between Amanda and her mother fluctuates significantly. Initially, the mother holds the dominant position, wielding authority through commands and expectations, attempting to mould Amanda into a socially acceptable figure. Her repetitive instructions-focused on behaviour and responsibilities-demonstrate her control and create an oppressive atmosphere.

However, as the poem progresses, Amanda's internal voice becomes stronger, revealing her desire for freedom and self-expression. This change suggests that while the mother exerts power through societal norms, Amanda's daydreams and fantasies provide her with a form of resistance. The power struggle becomes evident as Amanda's silence symbolises her defiance. Although her mother seems to have the upper hand, Amanda's imaginative escape reflects her inner strength. Ultimately, the poem illustrates a complex interplay of power, highlighting the tension between parental authority and the quest for personal identity.

8. **You have been asked to present an evaluation of he approaches of the mothers of both, the baby seagull and Amanda, towards helping their children. Write this presentation draft including your insights, in about 120 words, comparing the approaches of both parents.**

You may begin this way

One acknowledges that both parents, Amanda's mother and the baby seagull's mother both....however, ...

(Reference -Amanda! and His First Flight)

CBSE Additional SQP 2023-24

Ans. One acknowledges that both parents, Amanda's mother and the baby seagull's mother, wanted to help their child. However, their approaches were very different. The baby seagull's mother was a parent who wanted to better her child's life by pushing him out of his comfort zone and encouraging him to learn new skills. She believed that her son is capable of flying, even though he was afraid and tried to motivate him by showing him how much fun it could be.

Amanda's mother, on the contrary, is depicted as a strict and critical figure who is presented as always correcting Amanda's behaviour, from her posture and habits to her academic performance and personal hygiene. While her intentions may be good, her methods are shown to be ineffective and in some cases, harmful.

In comparison to Amanda's mother, the seagull's mother seems to be more attuned to her child's needs and abilities. She recognises that the baby seagull is capable of flying and wants to help him achieve his full potential. In contrast, Amanda's mother seems to be too focused on correcting her daughter's flaws and may not be paying enough attention to her strengths and abilities.

ASSESSMENT EXERCISE

Extract Based Questions

Read the following extract carefully and answer the questions that follow.

Don't eat that chocolate, Amanda!
Remember your acne, Amanda!
Will you please look at me when I'm speaking to you,
Amanda!

(i) What is the tone of the speaker in the above extract?
1. Demanding
2. Pleasing
3. Polite
4. Authoritative
5. Furious

(ii) The speaker wants Amanda to look at her to ensure
(a) Amanda obeys
(b) stops eating chocolate
(c) Amanda follows the instructions
(d) does not sleep

(iii) Why is Amanda not looking at the speaker?

(iv) Select the option that applies the same rhyme scheme as the given extract.

(a) But I am carried back against
My will into a childhood where
Autumn is bonfires, marbles, smoke;

(b) Yellow, and black, and hectic red,
Pestilence-stricken multitudes: O thou,
Who chariotest to their dark wintry

(c) The winged seeds, where they lie low,
Each like a corpse within its grave, until
Thine sister of the Spring shall blow

(d) To this urn let those repair
That are either true or fair;
For these dead birds sigh a prayer

Short Answer (SA) Type Questions

1. 'Anyone would think that I nagged at you'. Explain.
2. What idea does the reader form about Amanda?
3. Amanda's mother gives her a list of do's and don'ts. What impact does this have on Amanda?
4. List the things that Amanda's mother nags her for.

Long Answer (LA) Type Questions

1. Amanda loves to live in a dream world and does not appreciate any interference.
Her parent tries to bring her back to the real world. Therefore, there is always a conflict going on. Elaborate.
2. If you were in place of Amanda, what situations would you imagine? Briefly describe atleast 2 such situations?
Competency Based

The Trees

by Adrienne Rich

Introduction The poem 'The Trees' by Adrienne Rich shows the conflict between man and nature. With the growth and development of society, human beings have used nature for their own benefit and caused a lot of harm to natural environment. The poet wants to give the message that the presence of a few trees inside our homes does not give us the feeling of nature. Real nature is outside in the forests that we have destroyed. The poem tells us how the trees want to break free from the walls that humans have put around them and go out into the forest.

Symbolic Meaning of the Poem

On a deeper level of understanding, the poem embraces feminist themes. Adrienne Rich is a feminist who takes trees as an extended metaphor for women and their ability to give life. Thus, 'The Trees' may also be a remark on the tortured existence of women in our patriarchal (male dominated) society. Such an understanding is secondary as the images of a treeless forest and the mirror in the poem emphasise the theme of deforestation.

Stanzawise Explanation

Stanza 1

The trees inside are moving out into the forest,
the forest that was empty all these days
where no bird could sit
no insect hide
no sun bury its feet in shadow
the forest that was empty all these nights
will be full of trees by morning.

Explanation The poet starts the poem by saying that the trees in her house are moving outside into the forest which was empty for a long time. These trees are cut from the forests and kept into the houses to create a false impression of nature or for decoration. As the forests were empty, no bird could sit on the branches of the trees, no insect could hide themselves in the trees and the sunlight could not be covered by the shadow of the trees.

The poet says that as the trees are moving out, the forests which were empty all these nights will be full of trees by the morning.

It is important to note here that the trees are actually not moving. The poet is imagining the movement of the trees.

Stanza 2

All night the roots work
to disengage themselves from the cracks
in the veranda floor.
The leaves strain toward the glass
small twigs stiff with exertion
long-cramped boughs shuffling under the roof
like newly discharged patients
half-dazed, moving to the clinic doors.

Explanation In these lines, the poet says that it seems like the trees work silently in the night in order to get free from the boundaries of the house. The roots of the trees work all night to free themselves through the cracks on the veranda floor.

The leaves of the trees try very hard to put a lot of pressure on the window glass so that they could break it and go outside. The small twigs have become very hard due to applying too much pressure to free themselves.

The larger branches of the trees have shrunk and had bent because of being inside the walls and under the roof, where they cannot grow much. Now, the larger branches of the trees try to move outside slowly. While doing so, they look like newly discharged patients, who are half-shocked on coming out into the outside world.

Stanza 3

I sit inside, doors open to the veranda
writing long letters
in which I scarcely mention the departure of
the forest from the house.
The night is fresh, the whole moon shines in
a sky still open the smell of leaves and lichen
still reaches like a voice into the rooms.

Explanation The speaker, who could be the poet herself, sits in her house. The doors of her house open to the veranda. The poet is writing long letters in which she hardly mentions the departure of trees from the house.

The poet says that the night is fresh and the whole moon is shining in the open sky. The smell of leaves and lichen reaches the poet like a voice coming from the rooms of the house.

Stanza 4

My head is full of whispers
which tomorrow will be silent.
Listen. The glass is breaking.
The trees are stumbling forward
into the night. Winds rush to meet them.
The moon is broken like a mirror,
its pieces flash now in the crown
of the tallest oak.

Explanation The speaker listens to the sounds coming from the leaves and lichens on the trees. These sounds will not be present on the next day as the trees will have moved out into the forest in the night. The poet can hear the glass breaking. As the glass breaks, the trees hurry to go outside. As the trees go in the open, it seems that the wind is rushing or moving fast towards them to meet them.

After going out into the forest, the tall trees stand straight in the forest. Their branches cover the Moon due to which it looks like a broken mirror. The broken pieces of the Moon seem like a crown of the tallest oak tree.

Poetic Devices Used in the Poem

Simile When comparison is made between two words using 'like' or 'as'.

- Like newly discharged patients.
- Still reaches like a voice into the rooms.
- The moon is broken like a mirror.

Imagery Imagery means to use figurative language to represent objects, actions and ideas in such a way that it appeals to our physical senses.

- Its pieces flash now in the crown of the tallest oak.

Personification When human characteristics are attributed to inanimate things.

- "Sun bury its feet in shadow."
- "Leaves strain toward the glass."

Word Meaning

Word	Meaning
Stanza 1	
Bury	covered so that it is not visible
Stanza 2	
Disengage	get free
Strain	make a lot of effort
Twigs	branches
Stiff	hard
Exertion	pressure
Cramped	shrunk
Boughs	larger branches of a tree
Shuffling	slow dragging motion without lifting feet, changing place
Half-dazed	half- shocked/ half asleep
Stanza 3	
Scarcely	hardly
Lichen	crusty patches on tree trunks
Stanza 4	
Stumbling	falling over
Flash	shine
Crown	topmost point
Oak	the name of a tree

NCERT FOLDER

NCERT Exercise Questions

THINKING ABOUT THE POEM

(NCERT PAGE 78-79)

Q.1 **(i) Find, in the first Stanza, three things that cannot happen in a treeless forest.**

(ii) What picture do these words create in your mind: "... sun bury its feet in shadow..."? What could the poet mean by the sun's 'feet'?

Ans. (i) The three things that cannot happen in a treeless forest, as mentioned in first Stanza are

(a) No birds can sit on trees.

(b) No insect can hide in trees.

(c) Sunlight cannot be covered under the shadow of the trees.

(ii) The picture that these words create in our minds is that if there are no trees, the rays of the Sun fall directly to the ground. If there is a forest with trees, then the Sun rays are covered by the shadow of the trees.

The Sun's 'feet' refers to the rays of the Sun or Sunlight that fall on the Earth.

Q.2 **(i) Where are the trees in the poem? What do their roots, their leaves and their twigs do?**

(ii) What does the poet compare their branches to?

Ans. (i) In the poem, the trees are in the poet's house.

- The roots of the trees work all night to release themselves from the cracks in the veranda floor.
- The leaves try very hard to move towards the window glass and put a lot of pressure on it so that it breaks and they can free themselves.
- The small twigs (branches) have become very hard due to applying a lot of pressure to gain freedom.

(ii) The poet compares the branches to newly discharged patients from a clinic. The larger branches of the trees become cramped (bent) because of being inside the walls and under the roof as they cannot move. When they get free, they quickly move outside due to which they fall on each other.

While doing so, they look half-shocked and weak like the patients, who wait for a long time to get out from a clinic.

Q.3 **(i) How does the poet describe the Moon: (a) at the beginning of the third Stanza and (b) at its end? What causes this change?**

(ii) What happens to the house when the trees move out of it?

(iii) Why do you think the poet does not mention "the departure of the forest from the house" in her letters?

Could it be that we are often silent about important happenings that are so unexpected that they embarrass us? Think about this again when you answer the next set of questions.

Ans. (i) (a) At the beginning of the third Stanza, the poet says that the whole Moon is shining in the open sky.

(b) At the end of the poem, the poet describes that the Moon breaks into pieces like a broken mirror and seems like a crown on the top of the tallest oak tree.

The cause of this change is that as the trees move outside, their branches cover some parts of the Moon due to which it can be seen only in parts. This is why it seems that the Moon has broken into pieces.

(ii) When the trees move out of the house, the glass on the windows will break. In addition, the house will go completely silent as the smell of the leaves and lichens, which was coming from the rooms like a voice, will no longer be smelt or heard.

(iii) The poet makes no mention of 'the departure of the forest from the house' in her letters probably because she is both puzzled (shocked) and embarrassed at the sudden happening. She did not expect the forest to move out of the house one day.

Or The poet makes no mention of 'the departure of the forest from the house' in her letters because it is a part of human nature to remain quite or ignore important matters of life. Even after knowing the importance of trees, human beings cut it for decorative purposes.

The unexpected movement led the poet to the realisation of the natural habitat of trees, i.e. forests. Thus, she is embarrassed.

Q.4 **(i) Does the poem present a conflict between man and nature? Compare it with '*A Tiger in the Zoo*'. Is the poet suggesting that plants and trees, used for 'interior decoration' in cities while forests are cut down, are 'imprisoned' and need to 'break out'?**

Ans. Yes, the poem 'The Trees' presents a conflict between man and nature. According to the poem, man is responsible for the degradation of nature. He uses nature for his own benefit without thinking of its consequences.

Not only trees but man is also endangering animals. The poem 'A Tiger in a Zoo' by Leslie Norris also presents a conflict between man and nature. In this poem, a tiger who should have been living free is caged.

Both plants and animals have come under the mercy of man who has no value for them. Man has not only enslaved animals but also imprisoned the trees and plants within the walls of his house. He cuts forests and uses trees as ornaments/ decoration for his house. As a result, the trees revolt.

The poem 'The Trees', thus, presents the need of trees to break out of the enclosed spaces and live in their natural habitats i.e. forests.

(ii) On the other hand, Adrienne Rich has been known to use trees as a metaphor for human beings; this is a recurrent image in her poetry. What new meanings emerge from the poem if you take its trees to be symbolic of this particular meaning?

Or **'The Trees' is symbolic poem and Adrienne Rich has used trees as a metaphor for human beings. What do they symbolise? Explain.** **CBSE 2024**

Ans. When considering Adrienne Rich's tendency to use trees as a metaphor for human beings in her poetry, the poem takes on a new layer of meaning. Rich is using the trees to subtly talk about the existence of women. They feel trapped inside the household (or society) with others controlling their actions and decisions. Women are exploited for their gifts to the extent that they lose their individuality.

Through this poem, Rich is calling out for women to break their shackles and grow organically (naturally) like the trees in a forest. Thus, they will be able to break the glass ceiling and grow into their potentials.

Q.5 **Read the poem 'On Killing a Tree' by Gieve Patel (Beehive–Class IX NCERT). Compare and contrast it with the poem you have just read.**

Ans. 'On Killing a Tree' by Gieve Patel and 'The Trees' by Adrienne Rich both explore the theme of trees, but in different ways.

Patel's poem presents a practical approach to the act of killing a tree. He uses vivid imagery to describe the process while highlighting the resilience and tenacity of the tree in the face of destruction.

On the other hand, Rich employs a more symbolical approach. She tackles the problem of deforestation by talking about the imprisonment of the natural world in glass cages of green houses. She also uses trees as a metaphor for women and challenges traditional gender roles and societal expectations.

While Patel focuses on destruction, Rich focuses on emancipation and regeneration.

REVIEW EXERCISE
Including Competency Based Questions

Part – I

Multiple Choice Questions

1. Who has been personified in the line 'no sun bury its feet in shadow'?

(a) Sun (b) Feet
(c) Shadow (d) None of these

Ans. (a) Sun

2. What reaches like a voice into the rooms?

(a) Noise of the roots (b) Shuffling of the branches
(c) Smell of leaves and lichens (d) Light of the moon

Ans. (c) Smell of leaves and lichens

3. "All night the roots work to <u>disengage</u> themselves from the cracks in the veranda floor" – what does the underlined word mean in the poem 'The Trees'?

(a) Free (b) Stop interacting
(c) Stop communicating (d) Getting busy

Ans. (a) Free

4. What has the poet skipped mentioning in her letter in the poem 'The Trees'?

(a) The departure of the forest from the house
(b) The decorative plants

(c) The sight of full Moon
(d) All of the above

Ans. (a) The departure of the forest from the house

5. What kind of 'whispers' are talked about in the following lines of the poem 'The Trees'? – 'My head is full of whispers'

(a) The breaking of glass
(b) The breaking of Moon
(c) The whisper of the small twigs
(d) The whisper of leaves leaving the house

Ans. (d) The whisper of leaves leaving the house

6. Identify the literary device used in 'The moon is broken like a mirror,'

(a) Metaphor (b) Simile
(c) Alliteration (d) Imagery

Ans. (b) Simile

7. The pieces of the Moon can be seen in the crown of ....

(a) Apple tree (b) Hemlak tree
(c) Oak tree (d) Walnut tree

Ans. (c) Oak tree

8. What are the trees symbolic of in the poem 'The Trees'?

(a) Nature (b) Women
(c) Plants (d) Positivity

Ans. (b) Women

9. The poem 'The Trees' is about the plants ....

(a) which grow in abundance
(b) which bring good luck
(c) which grow in houses for beautification
(d) which bring prosperity

Ans. (c) which grow in houses for beautification

10. As per the poem 'The Trees', what has man done with nature?

(a) Taken undue advantage
(b) Confined it to the four walls
(c) Destroyed it completely
(d) Burnt the forests

Ans. (b) Confined it to the four walls

11. What does the poet try to convey in her poem 'The Trees'?

(a) Like human beings trees need freedom too
(b) Grow more trees
(c) Uproot trees and plant them indoors
(d) The trees are made for indoor beautification

Ans. (a) Like human beings trees need freedom too

12. Select the appropriate option to complete the sentence, according to the extract.

The idea of a forest that has been 'empty all these days' is ....

(a) unnatural (b) scary
(c) magical (d) legendary

Ans. (a) unnatural

Extract Based Questions

1. Read the following extract carefully and answer the questions that follow.

The trees inside are moving out into the forest,
the forest that was empty all these days
where no bird could sit
no insect hide
no sun bury its feet in shadow
the forest that was empty all these nights
will be full of trees by morning. **CBSE SQP 2023**

(i) Complete the sentence appropriately.

It is clear that personification is the poetic device used for 'No sun bury its feet....' because .... (Clue: explain how personification applies here)

Ans. the Sun is attributed the human trait of having feet

(ii) The poet has used a poetic device in the given lines. What effect does she wish to create by its use?

...no bird could sit
no insect hide
no sun...

(a) Emphasis (b) Comparison
(c) Rhyme (d) Humour

Ans. (a) Emphasis

(iii) State whether the following statement is True or False. The extract uses trees as a symbol for conservative people.

Ans. False

(iv) How does the use of enjambment impact this extract?

Ans. The use of emjabment in the poem creates momentum. As there is no pause or end, when we move from one line to another, we feel the pressure that is felt by the trees in trying to break free from the confinement.

2. Read the following extract carefully and answer the questions that follow.

All night the roots work
to disengage themselves from the cracks
in the veranda floor.
The leaves strain toward the glass small
twigs stiff with exertion

long-cramped boughs shuffling under the roof
like newly discharged patients
half-dazed, moving
to the clinic doors.

(i) What does the poet compare the larger branches to? Competency Based

Ans. The poet compares the larger branches with patients who have been recently discharged and are leaving the clinic doors.

(ii) What struggle do the trees go through to free themselves from the boundaries?

Ans. Every part of the trees works to get itself free. The roots struggle to break free from the cracks of the veranda floor while the leaves put pressure on the window glass to break it. The large branches try to break open the roof to get out of the house.

(iii) The poet thinks that the trees .... night.

(a) work to free themselves from the boundaries of the house at
(b) grow underground slowly to take over the house during the
(c) spread their roots to beyond the boundaries to surround the house during the
(d) All of the above

Ans. (a) work to free themselves from the boundaries of the house at

(iv) What do roots work upon all night?

Ans. Roots work to free themselves from the cracks in the veranda floor.

3. Read the following extract carefully and answer the questions that follow.

My head is full of whispers
which tomorrow will be silent.
Listen. The glass is breaking.
The trees are stumbling forward
into the night. Winds rush to meet them.
The moon is broken like a mirror,
its pieces flash now in the crown
of the tallest oak.

(i) Whose whispers are mentioned here?

Ans. Whispers of trees are mentioned here.

(ii) Study the following statements.

1. The glass is breaking.
2. The moon is broken like a mirror.
3. Tomorrow will be filled with celebrations.

(a) 1 is right but 2 is wrong.
(b) 3 is right but 1 and 2 are wrong.
(c) 1 and 2 are right but 3 is wrong.
(d) 3 is wrong and only 2 is right.

Ans. (c) 1 and 2 are right but 3 is wrong.

(iii) Which poetic device has been used in the line 'The Moon is broken like a mirror'?

(a) Metaphor (b) Alliteration
(c) Simile (d) Personification

Ans. (c) Simile

(iv) Why are the trees stumbling forward?

Ans. The trees are stumbling forward because they have grown too big and can't be contained.

Part – II

Short Answer Type Questions

1. Why are the trees moving outside?

Ans. The trees are moving outside because they want to set themselves free from the walls that humans have put around them. They belong to the forest and that's why they are making efforts to go there.

2. What changes would the departure of the trees from the house bring to the forest?

Or **What happens to the house when trees move out of it? Comment.** CBSE 2025

Ans. The departure of the trees from the house to the forest would result in the birds sitting on their branches again, insects hiding in them and the Sun hiding its rays in the trees' shadows. The empty forest will become full of trees and there will be a balance in nature.

3. Why are the trees described in the first Stanza not useful for birds or insects?

Ans. The trees described in the first Stanza are not useful for birds or insects because they are decorative plants. Such ornamental plants/trees are kept in the house in the form of sculptures, paintings or picture. Therefore, they do not serve nature. Birds cannot sit on their branches and insects cannot hide in them.

4. What efforts do the trees make to get free?

Or **Describe the struggle of the roots, leaves, small twigs and long boughs to free themselves and break open the artificial barriers created by man.** Competency Based

Ans. In the poem, the trees and its roots, leaves, small twigs and long boughs put in a lot of efforts to break the artificial barriers created by man. The roots of the tree struggle all night to break free from the cracks of the veranda floor.

The leaves exert (put) a lot of pressure on the window glass to break them and the small twigs have become hard due to applying a lot of pressure to free themselves. The boughs (large branches) of the trees have shrunk and bent due to being inside the walls and under the roof. They are also trying to break open the roof and come out of the house.

5. What are the whispers that fill the head of the poet?

Ans. The whispers that fill the head of the poet are of the smell of the leaves and lichen that reaches her like voices into the rooms of the house. These voices/ whispers represent the silent struggle of the trees to free themselves from man. Trees are now struggling/ revolting to move to the forests, i.e. their natural habitat.

6. How is the night when the forests depart from the house? What are the changes that the poet expects to take place during the night/by the morning? Competency Based

Ans. When the forests depart from the house, the night outside is fresh. The sky is clear with the whole Moon shining brightly. The poet expects that during the night the trees will move out of the house. So, by the morning, the trees will cover the forests that were treeless.

7. In the poem 'The Trees', the poet compares the trees to 'newly discharged patients'. Highlight any two reasons for the same.

Ans. The poet compares the trees with newly discharged patients who look half-dazed (half-slept) while going towards the door of the clinic because the trees are weak. They have been struggling since long to get freedom from the four walls of the house. They could not grow fully there as they did not get proper nutrition. Further, when they get out, they feel relieved to finally leave the place they didn't want to be in, similar to hospital patients.

8. The process of 'moving out' was tedious for the trees. Support the statement with reference to the poem. CBSE Question Bank 2021

***Or* Change never comes easy. Justify the quote in the context of the poem 'The Trees'**

Ans. It is true that the process of 'moving out' was tedious for the trees. The poet says that the roots worked for the whole night to separate themselves from the veranda floor. The leaves tried hard to reach the window of glass so that they could go outside. Even the small stems of the trees put much of their effort in order to set themselves free.

9. The poet uses trees as a symbol for women breaking patriarchal notions. Do you agree? Why/Why not?

Ans. Yes, I think that the poet uses the trees as a symbol for women breaking patriarchal notions. In a male dominated society, women are cramped into houses like trees. Their natural freedom is lost under the shackles of the restrictions and limitation that oppress them. The poet now feels that it is high time that they escape the setup.

10. The poem ends on a note of victory. Justify with reference to the literal and symbolic meaning. CBSE Question Bank 2021

Ans. The poem 'The Trees' ends with the note of victory for both trees and women. Trees have escaped and entered their natural habitat after a lot of struggle. Similarly, the poet is sure that the women will also taste freedom after this struggle.

11. Analyse the symbolic meaning of the forest in the poem. How does it contrast with the home, and what does this reveal about the speaker's aspirations?

Ans. The forest symbolises freedom and the unknown, contrasting with the home, which represents safety and constraints. This contrast reveals the speaker's aspirations for growth beyond familiar boundaries. The forest invites exploration, suggesting a desire to break free from limitations and embrace new experiences, reflecting a search for identity.

12. How does Rich's use of personification affect the reader's understanding of the trees and their desires? What impact does this have on the theme of autonomy?

Ans. Rich personifies the trees, giving them desires and voices, which helps readers connect to the poem emotionally. This portrayal emphasises their longing for freedom, highlighting the theme of autonomy. By making trees relatable, Rich encourages us to reflect on our own desires for independence and self-determination in life.

13. What message or insight does Rich convey about change and transformation through 'The Trees'?

Ans. Through 'The Trees', Adrienne Rich conveys that change and transformation are natural, inevitable, and necessary for growth and liberation. The poem illustrates the trees breaking free from the confines of a human-made structure, symbolising a return to their authentic state. This act of liberation reflects broader themes of breaking away from restrictions and reclaiming one's true essence. Rich emphasises that while change can be disruptive, it also brings renewal and vitality. The trees' movement back to the forest signifies a powerful and natural resurgence, suggesting that embracing change, though challenging, leads to a more genuine and harmonious existence. This insight encourages respect for natural processes and the resilience inherent in all life forms.

14. What is the significance of the breaking glass in the context of the poem?

Ans. The breaking glass signifies the trees' final liberation from confinement, symbolising a decisive, dramatic break from their restraints. It marks the transition from stagnation to freedom, emphasising the powerful, transformative act of reclaiming their natural space and the inevitable, forceful nature of change.

15. How does the poet use the contrast between night and day to enhance the theme of transformation?

Ans. The poet contrasts night and day to underscore the dynamic transformation process. Night symbolises a period of confinement and stagnation, while the day's arrival represents the dawn of change and liberation. This juxtaposition enhances the theme of transformation by highlighting the shift from darkness to light, from restriction to freedom.

16. What role does the setting play in unfolding the poem's events?

Ans. The setting plays a crucial role in unfolding the events of 'The Trees' by Adrienne Rich, emphasising the transition from confinement to freedom. The initial indoor setting, with trees constrained by the veranda floor and glass, symbolises restriction and unnatural order. This confined space reflects an oppressive environment, both for the trees and metaphorically for the human experience. As the poem progresses, the setting shifts to the open night, a place of liberation and natural order. The fresh night air, shining moon, and the smell of leaves and lichen contrast sharply with the indoor confinement, highlighting the vitality and renewal of returning to nature. The breaking glass and rushing winds further dramatise this transition, underscoring the power and inevitability of nature reclaiming its space.

17. How does the speaker's perspective change throughout the poem? Competency Based

Ans. The speaker's perspective in Adrienne Rich's 'The Trees' evolves from passive observation to a deeper awareness of the trees' departure. Initially, the speaker is inside, detached, writing letters that scarcely mention the significant event occurring. This indicates a sense of normalcy or denial about the impending change. As the poem progresses, the speaker becomes more attuned to the natural world, noting the fresh night, the shining moon, and the smell of leaves and lichen. The breaking glass and stumbling trees shift the speaker's perspective to one of realisation and witness to the dramatic transformation. The final imagery of the broken moon's pieces flashing in the tree crowns signifies a profound acknowledgement of the trees' powerful and liberating movement.

18. How does the imagery of the trees' movement from the house to the forest, in 'Trees', reflect broader themes of liberation and growth in human experiences? CBSE SQP 2024

Ans. The imagery of the trees' movement from the house to the forest reflects broader themes. The breaking free of trees from the constraints of the house is symbolic of desire for freedom and autonomy. The movement of trees towards the forest embodies the journey towards self-discovery and possibility. It, thus, highlights themes of liberation and growth in human experiences.

Long Answer Type Questions

1. The trees in the poem stretch out their branches, break barriers and struggle hard to move out in the open in their natural environment. Analyse the efforts that one puts in to break away captivity and strive for freedom.

Ans. A lot of efforts are put in to break away from captivity and to enjoy freedom. For anyone, freedom is much more important than any kind of comfort, growth or development. Even if we have all the riches in the world but no freedom, we do not really have anything. Freedom is essential for all living beings be it man, a bird or trees. All beings strive for freedom and are happiest when free.

Any kind of compromise against freedom, then, is met with struggle. In the poem, 'The Trees', the poet Adrienne Rich presents the intensity of the efforts put in by the trees to break away from the bondage of man.

All parts of a tree, be it roots, leaves, small twigs and its long boughs, stretch out to the maximum to break away from the enclosed walls of the house. They struggle hard to move out of the house into the open-natural environment, to their natural habitat, i.e. forests.

Similar efforts are put by man and all other living species. One can look at the freedom struggle of countries all around the world. Not only do they do everything within their limits but people also give their lives for freedom. Therefore, one can say that freedom is gained after a lot of efforts.

2. A conflict between man and nature is depicted in this poem. Man is disregarding the natural growth of plants and trees. In total confinement, nature also rebels against civilisation and becomes destructive. Elaborate with reference to 'The Trees'.

Ans. In the conflict between man and nature, man has caused much harm to nature. With civilisation, man has learnt to acquire a lot of material goods but has forgotten the importance of nature. He has cut down large forests and done several other such acts in its pursuit of progress. Man judges nature to be weak. However, nature is powerful. It rebels/struggles against man and destroys what man has created.

The poem, 'The Trees', presents this powerful revolt of nature against man. In the poem, the trees destroy the house. The window glass is broken and the floor of the veranda is cracked. The house that is decorated by man using the trees is destroyed by the same trees.

Man must understand that, no matter how powerful he is, he can never overpower nature. The real power lies with nature. Any attempt to control or confine nature, will end in failure. Nature will revolt and will destroy everything to teach man his limits. It will strike back at man and remind him that, by spoiling nature, man is inviting a threat to his peaceful existence.

3. What message does Adrienne Rich want to convey through the poem, 'The Trees'? **CBSE 2020**

Ans. **The Trees**

In the poem 'The Trees' by Adrienne Rich, the poet conveys a message of renewal, liberation, and resilience. Through the imagery of trees growing and reclaiming space, Rich reflects on themes of personal and collective growth, resistance, and the reclaiming of power.

The poem presents the trees as symbolic of life's capacity for renewal and strength. They are portrayed as breaking free from the constraints of their environment, bursting through the boundaries, and reclaiming what is theirs. This action represents a struggle for freedom and the will to thrive despite obstacles.

Rich's trees also serve as metaphors for the human spirit or societal conditions, indicating the potential for transformation. The speaker of the poem seems to suggest that just as trees reclaim their space and grow despite human interference, humans too can reclaim their agency, rebuild, and find strength amidst adversity.

In a broader sense, 'The Trees' can be interpreted as a call for personal and social awakening. Rich might be emphasising that, like trees, individuals or societies need to grow, break free from past limitations, and reclaim their potential for growth and renewal. The poem carries a message of hope, renewal, and the importance of resilience in the face of hardship.

4. The poem 'The Trees' appears to be about trees, environment, deforestation and afforestation. On a deeper level we discover that Adrienne Rich is expressing her concerned about women and their emancipation. Elaborate with reference to the poem. **CBSE Question Bank 2021**

Ans. 'The Trees' is a short symbolic poem focusing on the movement of trees that are initially indoors but seeking to escape to freedom in the forest. The trees represent nature but also the nature of being - womanhood in particular. 'The Trees', then, is an extended metaphor since the trees are indeed people, specifically females who are in need of healing.

Trees normally make up the forest but until now it's been empty for many days and nights. This is symbolic of women being left in the dark for too long not knowing their true identities and where they belong. Thus, there is a struggle for this identity and a new forest is formed. This new forest will take shape very quickly, pointing towards a sort of change in identity, a collective identity for women.

5. How does the symbolism of the moon evolve throughout the poem?

Ans. In 'The Trees' by Adrienne Rich, the moon's symbolism change throughout the poem. Its full presence in the beginning casts a fresh light on the night's events, while its breaking into pieces in the end reflects the dramatic transformation. This imagery enhances the atmosphere of dynamic change, movement and the breaking of old confines to embrace newfound freedom.

Initially, the moon is described as shining fully in an open sky, symbolising clarity, constancy and a witness to the events unfolding. As the trees depart, the moon's presence highlights the freshness and renewal of the night. However, as the climax of the trees' liberation approaches, the moon's image shifts dramatically. It is described as breaking 'like a mirror', signifying a profound disruption and transformation. The shards of the broken moon flashing in the crowns of the trees symbolise the scattering of old forms and the emergence of a new reality. This evolution highlights the theme of radical change and the power of nature's resurgence.

6. Describe the imagery used to convey the movement of the trees.

Ans. Adrienne Rich uses vivid and dynamic imagery to convey the movement of the trees in 'Trees'. The roots 'disengage themselves from the cracks in the veranda floor', illustrating a slow but determined escape from confinement. Leaves 'strain toward the glass' and 'small twigs stiff with exertion' depict the effort and struggle of breaking free. The boughs are described as 'long-cramped', moving like 'newly discharged patients half-dazed', highlighting a return to life and freedom. The breaking glass and stumbling trees create a sense of urgency and force, while the rushing winds meeting the trees evoke a dramatic, almost triumphant departure. The moon breaking 'like a mirror' and its pieces flashing in the tree crowns further enhance the sense of transformation and liberation.

7. You have been chosen to address a student gathering from the neighbourhood schools, to peak on the resilience of human spirit required to transcend discrimination. Prepare the speech draft in not more than 120 words, with reference to the commonality of themes in 'Nelson Mandela: Long Walk to Freedom' and 'The Trees' by Adrienne Rich.

You may begin this way

Good morning everyone, Today, I'd like to discuss two pieces of literature that offer a powerful insight into the resilience of the human spirit required to transcend discrimination.

You may end this way

To conclude, I'd like to say that ... Thank you **CBSE SQP 2023**

Ans. Good morning everyone, Today, I'd like to discuss two pieces of literature that offer a powerful insight into the resilience of the human spirit required to transcend discrimination. They are 'Nelson Mandela: Long Walk to Freedom (excerpt)' and Adrienne Rich's 'The Trees'. Both Mandela's excerpt and Rich's poem address the issue of discrimination. Mandela speaks of how his own experiences of discrimination made him more determined to fight against it. He emphasises the need to move beyond the divides created by race, gender and class.

Similarly, Rich's poem acknowledges the discrimination faced by trees, which are often overlooked and undervalued. She argues that these trees deserve to be recognised and appreciated, just as all living beings should be.

Despite the challenges faced, both Mandela's excerpt and Rich's poem showcase the resilience of the human spirit. Mandela's perseverance and unwavering determination to fight against discrimination, even in the face of great adversity, inspires us to do the same. Rich's poem also speaks to the resilience of nature, which continues to thrive even in the face of human neglect and disregard.

To conclude, I'd like to say that the common themes are prevalent in both these pieces of literature and they remind us of the strength of the human spirit and the importance of standing up for what we believe in, even when faced with obstacles.

Thank you

ASSESSMENT EXERCISE

Extract Based Questions

Read the following extract carefully and answer the questions that follow.

The trees inside are moving out into the forest,
the forest that was empty all these days
where no bird could sit no insect hide
no sun bury its feet in shadow

(i) Why was the forest empty?

(a) Due to wild animals (b) Absence of other creatures
(c) Cutting down of trees (d) Due to fire

(ii) Which things can not happen in a treeless forest?

(iii) What happens to Sun in absence of trees?

(iv) Select whether the following statement is True or False.

Birds have no place to hide since the trees have moved out of the forest.

Short Answer (SA) Type Questions

1. What happens to the Sun when the trees move out?
2. Do you think the poet is happy about the trees moving out of her house? **Competency Based**
3. How is the image of moon crucial to the poem?
4. The poet does not mention the departure of trees. Why?

Long Answer (LA) Type Questions

1. Do you think that trees are right in asserting their freedom and breaking the boundaries of the house? Is it important? Why?
2. Justify how trees can be a metaphor for women.
3. Do you think that the poem employs the use of senses? If yes, justify.

Fog

by Carl Sandburg

CHAPTER 8

Introduction The following poem 'Fog' has been written by Carl Sandburg. The poet compares on the natural phenomenon of 'fog' to the silent movement of a cat. Through carefully chosen words Sandburg paints a vivid portrait of fog as a silent, shape-shifting force that covers the entire city. 'Fog's rich imagery turns a simple concept into a memorable poem.

Stanzawise Explanation

The fog comes
on little cat feet.
It sits looking
over harbour and city
on silent haunches
and then moves on.

Explanation The poet says that the fog comes silently like a cat that comes on its little feet. Further, just like a cat sits silently by folding her knees and looks around the nearby places and things, the fog also sits over the harbour and the city covering everything. Then, after sometime just like the cat moves on silently, the fog also disappears from the harbour and the city quietly.

Poetic Devices Used in the Poem

- **Analogy** Metaphor/Personification Comparison of fog to a cat
- **Rhyme Scheme** No rhyme. The poem is in free verse.
- **Imagery** The poet creates a clear image of fog covering the harbour and the city.

Word Meaning

Word	Meaning
Harbour	port (a place where the ships load and unload goods)
On silent haunches	sitting with knees bent

NCERT FOLDER

NCERT Exercise Questions

THINKING ABOUT THE POEM (NCERT PAGE 93)

Q.1 (a) What does Sandburg think the fog is like?

(b) How does the fog come?

(c) What does 'it' in the third line refer to?

(d) Does the poet actually say that the fog is like a cat? Find three things that tell us that the fog is like a cat.

Ans. (a) Sandburg (the poet) thinks that the fog is like a cat.

(b) The fog comes silently like a cat on its small feet.

(c) 'It' in the third line refers to fog.

(d) The poet does not actually say that the fog is like a cat but he uses the metaphor of a cat for comparison.

Three things that tell us that the fog is like a cat are

(*i*) It comes silently in the same manner like a cat comes on its small feet.

(*ii*) Lines 3, 4 and 5 of the poem compare the fog with a cat that sits by folding its knees and looks around the nearby places silently.

(*iii*) In the last line, the fog moves on quietly just like a cat.

Q.2 You know that a metaphor compares two things by transferring a feature of one thing to the other.

(a) Find metaphors for the following words and complete the table below. Also try to say how they are alike. The first is done for you.

Storm	Tiger	Pounces over the fields, growls
Train		
Fire		
School		
Home		

Ans.

Storm	Tiger	Pounces over the fields, growls
Train	Snake	Long rope like body
Fire	Sun	Symbol of power
School	Temple	Teaches moral values, virtues
Home	Shelter	Safety, warmth

(b) Think about a storm. Try to visualise the force of the storm, hear the sound of the storm, feel the power of the storm and the sudden calm that happens afterwards. Write a poem about the storm comparing it with an animal.

Ans. For self-attempt

Q.3 Does this poem have a rhyme scheme? Poetry that does not have an obvious rhythm or rhyme is called 'free verse'.

Ans. This poem does not have a rhyme scheme as the lines in the poem do not end with similar sounding words. In this poem, there is no pattern of similarity in the sounds of the ending words of any of the lines. The method of such a poem is called free verse.

REVIEW EXERCISE

Including Competency Based Questions

Part – I

Multiple Choice Questions

1. How does the fog arrive and depart?

(a) By announcing its arrival
(b) Silently
(c) Loudly
(d) Both (a) and (c)

Ans. (b) Silently

2. What is the rhyme scheme of the poem?

(a) ababab (b) aababa
(c) aabaab (d) No rhyme scheme

Ans. (d) No rhyme scheme

3. Which scenic beauty is very well captured in the poem 'Fog'?

(a) A day in the winters
(b) The moment when the fog comes over
(c) The snow clad mountains
(d) The river stream

Ans. (b) The moment when the fog comes over

4. How does the poet give a strong image of the fog in the poem 'Fog'?

(a) Through a beautiful painting
(b) Through soulful lines

(c) Through a metaphorical cat
(d) All of the above

Ans. (c) Through a metaphorical cat

5. How do cats behave when they are stalking, as in the poem 'Fog'?
(a) They walk silently on their tiny, silent feet
(b) They make weird noises
(c) They pounce at you
(d) They look here and there

Ans. (a) They walk silently on their tiny, silent feet

6. Why do you think the poet compares the fog to a cat in the poem 'Fog'?
(a) They both look soft and fluffy
(b) Both fog and cat look cute
(c) Like a cat, the fog slips and slides in silently
(d) All of the above

Ans. (c) Like a cat, the fog slips and slides in silently

7. What idea does the poet introduce in the poem 'Fog'?
(a) Fog is an alive entity (b) Fog is as cuddly as a cat
(c) Fog is soft (d) Fog is a silent creature

Ans. (a) Fog is an alive entity

8. Why do you think fog is a free verse poem?
(a) It has only six lines
(b) It has no regular rhyme scheme
(c) It is divided in two paragraphs
(d) Both (a) and (b)

Ans. (b) It has no regular rhyme scheme

9. 'It sits looking over the harbour', what does the word 'harbour' mean in the poem 'Fog'?
(a) Place where people go for picnics
(b) Place by the sea
(c) River bank
(d) Place where ships load and unload

Ans. (d) Place where ships load and unload

10. What does the fog do in the end in the poem 'Fog'?
(a) Moves on (b) Continues being there
(c) Becomes more thick (d) All of these

Ans. (a) Moves on

11. Which figure of speech is prominent in the poem 'Fog'?
(a) Simile (b) Metaphor
(c) Alliteration (d) Onomatopoeia

Ans. (b) Metaphor

12. How does the poem 'Fog' represent nature?
(a) In various descriptions
(b) In its artificial surroundings
(c) In its raw and natural side
(d) None of the above

Ans. (c) In its raw and natural side

Extract Based Questions

1. Read the following extract carefully and answer the questions that follow.

The fog comes
on little cat feet.
It sits looking
over harbour and city
on silent haunches
and then moves on.

CBSE Question Bank 2021 Modified

(i) Choose the option with qualities of the cat that Carl Sandburg applies to the fog?
1. Cats are independent animals, they don't follow rules, they slip and slide in and out of our lives as they please.
2. Cats are distrustful of strangers and can be jealous and moody.
3. Cats are stealthy, moving in slow motion at times and they appear to be moving in a mysterious fashion.
4. Cats often communicate with a combination of a distinctive sound and body language.
5. Cats like to move on at their own pace and before you know it, they've disappeared.

Ans. 1, 3 and 5

(ii) Which one/s of the following applies to the given lines?

1.	Personification is a literary device where you give an animal, object or natural phenomenon, qualities or abilities that only a human can have.	2.	Transferred epithet a literary device when an adjective usually used to describe one thing is transferred to another.
3.	Imagery is the language used by poets, and writers to create visual representation of ideas in the minds of the readers.	4.	Oxymoron is a figure of speech in which contradictory terms appear side by side.

(a) 1 and 4 (b) 2 and 3
(c) Only 1 (d) Only 3

Ans. (d) Only 3

(iii) Choose the statement that does not list movement of the fog.

A. It stole in on us like a foot-pad Somewhere out of the sea and air... –E.J. Pratt

B. The fog it tricks the eye The wonder of the veil of white Under the clear blue sky. –K.C. Cox

Ans. Statement (B) is not correct.

(iv) What has the poet used as a extended metaphor in the poem?

Ans. Poet has used cat as the extended metaphor in the poem.

2. Read the following extract carefully and answer the questions that follow.

The fog comes
on little cat feet.
It sits looking
over harbour and city
on silent haunches
and then moves on.

(i) How is dual imagery used in the poem 'Fog'? Choose the correct option.

(a) Cats are stealthy, moving in slow motion at times. They can fix themselves onto an object or creature, seemingly in a trance.

(b) Cats like to move on at their own pace-at their leisure.

(c) This poem captures a little of this feline mystery – thick white fog slowly turning into a cat, cat morphing back into the fog.

(d) Cats have the habit of finding a place which gives them an overview of a landscape or territory.

Ans. (c) This poem captures a little of this feline mystery – thick white fog slowly turning into a cat, cat morphing back into the fog.

(ii) What is fog doing?

Ans. Fog is sitting silently and watching over the harbour and city.

(iii) Comment, in detail, on the significance of the closing phrase of the poem- 'moves on'.

Ans. The phrase 'moves on' is crucial to depict the mysterious quality of the fog. It comes and leaves suddenly without being noticed by anyone.

(iv) Complete the following analogy on the basis of the above extract.

Snake : Reptile :: Cat : ....

Ans. Feline

3. Read the following extract carefully and answer the questions that follow.

The fog comes
on little cat feet.
It sits looking
over harbour and city
on silent haunches
and then moves on.

CBSE Additional SQP 2023

(i) In what way does the language used in this poem challenge traditional ideas of what poetry should be?

Ans. The language used in this poem is simple. It creates a vivid picture in the reader's mind to set a powerful and suggestive mood.

This challenges the traditional idea of poetry having complex rhyme schemes and metaphors.

(ii) What is the significance of the use of the word 'little' to describe the fog in the poem and how does this word choice contribute to the overall mood and tone of the poem? Answer in about 40 words. **Competency Based**

Ans. The word 'little' used to describe the fog in the poem suggests the subtle and quiet nature of the fog. The word 'little' also evokes a sense of innocence and vulnerability, as if the fog is a harmless creature moving through the city.

This contributes to the overall mood and tone of the poem, which is calm and peaceful, with a touch of mystery.

(iii) Complete the sentence with the appropriate option.

The lines from the poem tell us that the city is ....

(a) hilly
(b) coastal
(c) industrial
(d) under-developed

Ans. (b) coastal

(iv) Identify the type of imagery used in the lines of the poem.

Ans. Visual and animal imagery has been used in the given lines. It allows the reader to visualise the fog and creates a sense of atmosphere in the poem.

Part - II

Short Answer Type Questions

1. How does the poet compare fog to a cat?

Ans. The poet compares the fog to a cat because of similarity in their movements. The silent steps of a cat and the way it sits by folding its knees are both very similar to the way fog comes and surrounds the city and harbour and looks over it.

2. The poem 'Fog' states/presents fog, as full of opposite forces. Do you agree? Justify your answer.

Ans. Yes, I agree that the poem 'fog' presents fog as full of opposite forces. In the poem, fog is conceived to come and go silently like a cat. In contrast to this secretive nature, fog is also overpowering. It spreads over to the harbour and looks very carefully at the whole cityscape and moves on after some time.

3. Stealth is an important aspect of fog. State any two instances from the poem 'Fog' that suggest the same. CBSE Question Bank 2021

Ans. Stealth is an important characteristic of fog. In the poem, it is compared to a stealthy cat which silently comes and sits. It looks over the harbour and again leaves very silently.

4. Highlight any two characteristics of fog from its description in the poem and justify your choice of characteristics briefly.

Ans. The fog is a silent and mysterious thing. It enters a city without any warning or sign and leaves just as silently. We, as readers, are not aware of its creation or the reason for its leaving.

5. Is the fog portrayed as a resident of the city or as an outsider? Support your answer with two such references from the poem 'Fog'.

Ans. The fog is portrayed as an outsider who is looking over the city. It comes silently and mysteriously and leaves without doing anything other than observing.

6. Would you describe the role of the fog as active or passive? Support your answer with reference to the poem 'Fog'. Competency Based

Ans. The fog plays the role of an passive participant in the poem. It is a silent spectator and observer who does not do anything except observing the city and the harbour.

7. Why does the poet use the phrase 'silent haunches'? Substantiate your answer with reference to the poem 'Fog'.

Ans. By using the phrase 'silent haunches', the poet reminds us of the cat-like quality of the fog. Just like a cat which silently comes and sits on her hind legs, the fog comes and rests for a while without any noise and leaves as silently.

8. What does 'Fog' tell us about the speaker's relationship with nature? Support your answer with an example from the text. CBSE Additional SQP 2022

Ans. The poem 'Fog' tells us that the poet/speaker is observant and attentive to his surroundings. As a result, he could see similarities between living beings and the different aspects of the nature. For fog, he feels that it is like a cat. So, he compares little cat feet to the fog to make it more endearing and relatable to the audience. Just as the fog comes, stays and leaves silently, so does the cat.

9. Interpret how nature is a living entity as characterised by Carl Sandburg in his poem. CBSE 2024 C

Ans. In his poem 'Fog', Carl Sandburg personifies nature as a living entity by describing fog with human-like qualities such as the ability to think, act and move purposefully. The fog 'comes on little cat feet' and 'moves on'. It 'sits' on its 'silent haunches'. It appears suddenly and silently, like a cat. This vivid and cohesive portrayal enhances the reader's understanding by conveying the fog's quiet, subtle movements and observational, transient nature. It adds depth to the poem, pointing our that even the mundane details of the natural world that people take for granted are mysterious and beautiful.

10. How does the poem create a sense of quietness and mystery?

Ans. The poem creates a sense of quietness and mystery by comparing the fog to a cat, using phrases like 'little cat feet' and 'silent haunches'. The fog's stealthy arrival, silent observation, and gentle departure evoke a calm, elusive atmosphere, enhancing the mysterious quality of its presence.

Long Answer Type Questions

1. Difficulties come but they do not stay forever. They come and go. Comment on this statement by referring to the poem 'Fog'. Competency Based

Ans. In the poem 'Fog', the poet presents the natural phenomenon of fog as a temporary visitor. It comes like a cat, looks/spreads over the harbour and city and soon, leaves the place. In other words, it leaves as quietly as it comes. It does not stay at a place and trouble anyone permanently.

Difficulties are also similar to fog. Just like fog, difficulties are temporary. They come in life but do not stay forever. They come and go like fog.

Difficulties leave people hopeless and shattered. Often people give up and lose all their confidence in difficult situations. It takes a lot of courage to face problems and solve them. In such a scenario, one must remember the inherent temporary nature of difficulties. One need not be hopeless or lose courage but rather think of it as fog which will disappear soon.

2. Nature has many wonders that people take for granted and never pay attention towards it. How is the poem 'Fog' different from this perspective?

Ans. Nature has many wonders and beauties. It is full of mysterious and fascinating sceneries and phenomenon. However, man has taken it for granted. They never pay any attention to it.

The poet of the poem 'Fog', Carl Sandburg, differs in this perspective. He is a poet who is amazed at the wonders of the beautiful nature. He takes utmost pleasure in nature and its phenomenon. One such natural phenomenon that captures his attention is fog. He is so amazed by fog that he not only wrote about it but also thought of its resemblance with other things. On close attention, he found the fog similar to a cat.

He even describes this resemblance (the way a cat moves and sits) in his poem 'fog'. The fact that such a resemblance was found by the poet shows how

connected he is to nature that others have taken for granted. The poem, then, acts as a motivation for people who do not pay any attention to nature to find interesting similarities in everyday life.

3. What effect does the short structure of the poem 'Fog' have on its meaning? **CBSE 2023**

Or **In what ways does the poem 'Fog' reflect the nature of fog through its structure and language? Provide specific examples from the text to support your analysis.**

Ans. The poem 'Fog' reflects the nature of fog through its concise structure and simple language. The brevity of the poem, consisting of only six lines, mirrors the transient and elusive nature of fog, which appears and disappears quickly. The line breaks to create a slow, deliberate pace, mimicking the fog's gradual movement. Phrases like 'on little cat feet' and 'silent haunches' use minimal but vivid imagery to convey the fog's quiet and stealthy presence. The short lines and simple structure reflect the fog's quiet, discreet arrival and departure, making the poem feel like a quick, passing moment. The brevity leaves a lingering impression, like a fog that momentarily shrouds a landscape before disappearing.

The poem's sparse, unembellished language reflects the fog's simplicity and subtlety, avoiding complex descriptions to capture the essence of fog with directness and clarity. This minimalist approach effectively encapsulates the fog's fleeting, gentle presence over the harbour and city.

4. Examine the role of nature in the poems 'The Dust of Snow' and 'Fog' **CBSE 2025**

Ans. In 'Dust of Snow' and 'Fog', Robert Frost explores nature's profound influence on human emotions and perceptions. In 'Dust of Snow', a simple moment-snow falling from a hemlock tree-shifts the speaker's mood from negative to positive, showing how nature's smallest gestures can have a healing effect. The snow, often associated with purity and calm, offers the speaker a moment of peace and renewal. In 'Fog', the fog is described as a mysterious, almost living entity, moving silently like a cat over the city and harbour. This creates an atmosphere of stillness and reflection, showing nature's ability to transform the environment and change how we see the world. Through both poems, Frost emphasises that nature, whether in small moments or mysterious forces, can deeply affect our emotions and outlook on life.

ASSESSMENT EXERCISE

Extract Based Questions

Read the following extract carefully and answer the questions that follow.

The fog comes
on little cat feet.
It sits looking
over harbour and city
on silent haunches
and then moves on.

(i) Why poet has compared fog with cat?
   (a) Both walk or enter silently
   (b) Both are unpredictable
   (c) Both are independent
   (d) All of the above

(ii) What sits looking over horbour and city?

(iii) What kind of atmoshphere is reated in the extract?

(iv) Complete the sentence appropriately.
It is clear that personification is the poetic device used in the line 'It sits looking over' because ....
(Clue: explain how personification applies here)

Short Answer (SA) Type Questions

1. On what grounds does the poet compare the fog to a cat?

2. Highlight any two characteristics of fog from its description in the poem and justify your choice of characteristics briefly.

Long Answer (LA) Type Questions

1. With what other things does the fog can be compared to? Give reasons for your comparison.

2. What image does the poet give to the fog in the poem? What similarities do you find between the fog and that image. **Competency Based**

The Tale of Custard the Dragon

by Ogden Nash

Introduction 'The Tale of Custard the Dragon' has been written by Ogden Nash. It is a funny poem (ballad) that tells the story of a girl named Belinda and her four pets the kitten, mouse, dog and dragon. The central character in the story is Belinda's pet dragon, Custard who is described as a coward. However, when a real danger comes, all the pets run away except Custard. Custard shows courage and bravery at the right moment and saves everyone's life.

Stanzawise Explanation

Stanza 1

Belinda lived in a little white house,
With a little black kitten and a little grey mouse,
And a little yellow dog and a little red wagon,
And a realio, trulio, little pet dragon.

Explanation Belinda lived in a little white house with her four pets – a little black kitten, a little grey mouse, a little yellow dog and a little dragon. She also had a little red wagon. In the last line of the stanza, 'realio' and 'trulio' are used by the poet as an expression for the little dragon meaning 'really' and 'truly, respectively.

Stanza 2

Now the name of the little black kitten was Ink,
And the little grey mouse, she called him Blink,
And the little yellow dog was sharp as Mustard,
But the dragon was a coward, and she called him Custard.

Explanation The name of the little black kitten was Ink and the name of the little grey mouse was Blink. The name of the little dog was Mustard because its colour was sharp and yellow as mustard. The dragon was a coward and Belinda called him Custard.

Stanza 3

Custard the dragon had big sharp teeth,
And spikes on top of him and scales underneath,
Mouth like a fireplace, chimney for a nose,
And realio, trulio, daggers on his toes.

Explanation Custard, the dragon, had big sharp teeth, spikes on his top and scales on his stomach. His mouth had been compared to a fireplace because it had been assumed by the poet that dragons release fire from their mouth. His nose was compared to a chimney from which smoke came out. His toes were so pointed and sharp that they could cut anything like a dagger.

Stanza 4

Belinda was as brave as a barrel full of bears,
And Ink and Blink chased lions down the stairs,
Mustard was as brave as a tiger in a rage,
But Custard cried for a nice safe cage.

Explanation In these lines, the poet compares the bravery of all the characters of the poem.
Belinda's bravery has been compared to the bravery of a group of bears. Ink and Blink, despite being so small in size, had the power to chase away lions down the stairs. Mustard's bravery has been compared with that of an angry tiger. However, Custard was completely opposite to all of them. He was a coward who always demanded a safe cage.

Stanza 5

Belinda tickled him, she tickled him unmerciful,
Ink, Blink and Mustard, they rudely called him Percival,

They all sat laughing in the little red wagon
At the realio, trulio, cowardly dragon.

Explanation Belinda used to tickle Custard cruelly. Ink, Blink and Mustard made fun of Custard by comparing him to Percival. Percival was one of the best knights of King Arthur's court who was known for his courage and bravery. All of them sat together in the little red wagon and made fun of Custard. They laughed at his cowardice.

Stanza 6

Belinda giggled till she shook the house,
And Blink said Weeck!, which is giggling for a mouse,
Ink and Mustard rudely asked his age,
When Custard cried for a nice safe cage.

Explanation Belinda laughed a lot at the dragon. She laughed so hard that it seemed that the house was shaking due to her laughter. Blink, the mouse, used to laugh and make a sound of 'Weeck'. Ink and Mustard rudely asked the dragon's age to make fun of him. All the while, Custard asked for a nice safe cage for himself.

Stanza 7

Suddenly, suddenly they heard a nasty sound,
And Mustard growled, and they all looked around.
Meowch! cried Ink, and Ooh! cried Belinda,
For there was a pirate, climbing in the winda.

Explanation While all of them were busy making fun of the dragon, they heard an unpleasant sound from the house. Mustard, the dog started growling and they all looked around. Ink cried 'Meow' and Belinda cried 'Ooh' as they saw a pirate climbing the window of the house.

Stanza 8

Pistol in his left hand, pistol in his right,
And he held in his teeth a cutlass bright,
His beard was black, one leg was wood;
It was clear that the pirate meant no good.

Explanation The appearance of the pirate seemed very dangerous. He was carrying pistols in both hands and a small sword between his teeth. He had a black beard and one of his legs was made of wood. His looks made it very clear to the housemates that the pirate meant to harm the people and pets living there.

Stanza 9

Belinda paled, and she cried, Help! Help!
But Mustard fled with a terrified yelp,
Ink trickled down to the bottom of the household,
And little mouse Blink strategically mouseholed.

Explanation Belinda became pale with fear after seeing the pirate and cried for help. All her brave pets could not help her and everyone ran away from there. Mustard made a huge cry and ran away. Ink ran down towards the bottom of the house and Blink very smartly ran into his hole.

Stanza 10

But up jumped Custard, snorting like an engine,
Clashed his tail like irons in a dungeon,
With a clatter and a clank and a jangling squirm
He went at the pirate like a robin at a worm.

Explanation When everyone ran away on seeing the pirate, it was the cowardly dragon, Custard, who came to rescue Belinda and fought the pirate bravely.

He jumped in front of the pirate and made a loud and angry sound through his nose. The sound was one that is made by an engine. He started to move his tail powerfully producing a sound like that of iron or metals striking in a dungeon (prison). With all these dangerous sounds, he followed the pirate like a bird follows a worm.

Stanza 11

The pirate gaped at Belinda's dragon,
And gulped some grog from his pocket flagon,
He fired two bullets but they didn't hit,
And Custard gobbled him, every bit.

Explanation The pirate was shocked by the dragon's reaction. He stared at Belinda's dragon with his mouth open. He drank some wine from a container that he carried in his pocket. The pirate, then, took out his pistol and fired two bullets at Custard. However, he failed to hit him. Finally, Custard swallowed the pirate.

Stanza 12

Belinda embraced him, Mustard licked him,
No one mourned for his pirate victim
Ink and Blink in glee did gyrate
Around the dragon that ate the pirate.

Explanation Everyone celebrated the death of the pirate. Belinda hugged Custard and Mustard licked him affectionally.

No one felt sorrow for the pirate's death. Ink and Blink started dancing in joy around the dragon who had eaten the pirate.

Stanza 13

But presently up spoke little dog Mustard,
I'd have been twice as brave if I hadn't been flustered.

And up spoke Ink and up spoke Blink,
We'd have been three times as brave, we think,
And Custard said, I quite agree
That everybody is braver than me

Explanation The incident clarified who was a coward and who was brave. Mustard said that he would have been twice as brave as Custard if he had not been nervous. After this, Ink and Blink said that they would have been thrice as brave as the Custard. Custard agreed and said that everybody there was braver than him.

Stanza 14-15

Belinda still lives in her little white house,
with her little black kitten and her little grey mouse,
And her little yellow dog and her little red wagon,
And her realio, trulio little pet dragon.
Belinda is as brave as a barrel full of bears,
And Ink and Blink chase lions down the stairs,
Mustard is as brave as a tiger in a rage,
But Custard keeps crying for a nice safe cage.

Explanation Stanza 14 and 15 are an almost repetition of Stanza 1 and 4. There is only one difference that Stanza 1 and 4 present the condition of the housemates in the past and Stanza 14 and 15 present their condition after the pirate incident.

The situation has not changed at all. Everything has gone back to normal with Belinda and her three 'brave' pets making fun of the "cowardly", pet dragon.

Poetic Devices Used in the Poem

Simile When comparison is made between two things using 'like' and 'as'.

- Mouth like a fireplace
- Sharp as Mustard
- Belinda as a brave as a barrel full of bears
- Snorting like an engine, etc.

Repetition When a phrase/line is repeated to emphasise something.

- a little
- a realio, trulio
- Suddenly, suddenly they heard
- she cried Help! Help!
- But Custard cried for a nice safe cage.

Metaphor When comparison is made between two different things without the use of 'like' and 'as'

- Nose for a Chimney

Alliteration Repetition of the initial consonant sound in the same line.

- And he held in his teeth

Onomatopoeia When a word is used to describe a sound

- Weeck
- Meowch

Rhyme Scheme

Every stanza of the poem has the rhyme scheme aabb except Stanza 13. The rhyme scheme of Stanza 13 is aabbcc.

Word Meaning

Word	Meaning
Stanza 1	
Wagon	a carriage, a cart
Realio	really (used in the poem for effect)
Trulio	truly (used in the poem for effect)
Stanza 2	
Sharp	intelligent
Coward	someone who is not brave and avoids danger, difficulty or pain
Stanza 3	
Spikes	a thin pointed structures on the body
Scales	small hard flat pieces of skin on the bodies of animals

Word	Meaning
Fireplace	the place where fire is burnt to keep the house warm
Chimney	a long pipe that opens on the roof to let out the smoke released from the fireplace
Dagger	small sword
Stanza 4	
Barrel	drum (usually used for keeping liquids)
Rage	anger
Stanza 5	
Tickle	to touch (a body part) lightly to cause laughter
Unmercitul	cruel
Percival	a warrior in king Arthur's court

Word	Meaning
Rudely	not in a civil manner or mannerlessly
Stanza 6	
Giggling	laughing
Stanza 7	
Nasty	unpleasant
Growled	the sound of growling as made by animals
Pirate	dacoit, robber
Winda	window
Stanza 8	
Cutlass	a small sword with a slightly curved blade
Stanza 9	
Paled	became pale yellow due to fear
Fled	ran
Yelp	cry
Trickled	stepped down
Strategically	cleverly
Mouseholed	holes made by a mouse (it is not a word but has been made into a word to fit the rhyming scheme)
Stanza 10	
Snorting	huge sound made through nose
Clashed	striked

Word	Meaning
Dungeon	an underground prison
Clatter and a clank and a jangling	sounds of two metals striking
Squirm	to move in a twisted manner
Robin	a bird
Stanza 11	
Gaped	stared with mouth wide open
Gulped	swallowed
Grog	wine
Flagon	a container made of silver in which drink is stored
Gobbled	swallowed
Stanza 12	
Embrace	to hug
Licked	to touch with tongue
Mourned	to grieve
Glee	happiness
Gyrate	make circular movements
Stanza 13	
Flustered	got nervous

NCERT FOLDER

NCERT Exercise Questions

THINKING ABOUT THE POEM
(NCERT PAGE 110)

Q.1 Who are the characters in this poem? List them with their pet names.

Ans. There are six characters in the poem. These include Belinda and her four pets and a pirate.

Her pets are

(i) A little black kitten, Ink

(ii) A little grey mouse, Blink

(iii) A yellow dog, Mustard

(iv) A dragon, Custard

Q.2 Why did Custard cry for a nice safe cage? Why was the dragon called 'cowardly dragon'?

Or **Why does Custard long for a nice safe cage?** **CBSE 2025**

Ans. Custard cried for an nice safe cage because he was a 'coward' who wanted peace and safety.

He was called a 'cowardly dragon' because apart from him, all other pets were described as very brave. Belinda was as brave as a big group of bears, Ink and Blink could chase lions and Mustard was like an angry tiger.

Compared to all of them, the dragon demanded a nice safe cage, so it was called 'cowardly dragon'.

Q.3 "Belinda tickled him, she tickled him unmerciful..." Why?

Ans. Belinda tickles her pet dragon, Custard quite cruelly. She did so because she wanted to excite Custard as he was a lazy dragon. In addition, it amused her. She along with her other pets laughed at the dragon's weakness and cowardice.

Q.4 The poet has employed many poetic devices in the poem. For example "Clashed his tail like iron in a dungeon" — the poetic device here is a simile. Can you, with your partner, list some more such poetic devices used in the poem?

Ans. In the poem, 'The Tale of Custard, the Dragon', the poet has used a lot of poetic devices.

Following are some of the devices used

(i) **Simile** Mouth like a fireplace.

(ii) **Repetition** The repetitive use of the word 'little' in Stanza 1.

(iii) **Onomatopoeia** Use of sound words such as 'weeck' and 'meowch'.

(iv) **Metaphor** Use of comparison such as 'Nose for a Chimney'.

Q.5 **Read Stanza three again to know how the poet describes the appearance of the dragon.**

Or **What did Custard look like?** **CBSE 2023**

Or **How would you describe Custard, the Dragon?** **CBSE 2022 Term II**

Or **Describe Custard the Dragon.** **CBSE 2022 Term II**

Ans. Stanza three of the poem 'The Tale of Custard the Dragon' describes the physical appearance of the dragon. Custard, the dragon has big sharp teeth. He has spikes on top and scales underneath him. His mouth is like a fireplace and his nose is like a chimney. He had pointed and sharp toes that looked like daggers.

Q.6 **Can you find out the rhyme scheme of two or three stanzas of the poem?**

Ans. The rhyme scheme of the poem is 'aabb'.

Q.7 **Writers use words to give us a picture or image without actually saying what they mean. Can you trace some images used in the poem?**

Ans. Writers always use phrases and words that do not tell us directly what they mean but always give us an indication of the meaning. Such words or phrases are used to trigger our own imagination in painting the picture that they mean. Use of such images in the poem are 'mouth like a fireplace', 'chimney for a nose', 'brave as a barrel full of bears', 'brave as a tiger in a rage', 'went at the pirate like a robin at a worm', etc.

Q.8 **Do you find 'The Tale of Custard the Dragon' to be a serious or a light-hearted poem? Give reasons to support your answer.**

Or **'The Tale of Custard the Dragon' is a humorous ballad. How does Ogden Nash create humour and entertainment in the poem.** **CBSE 2024**

Ans. 'The Tale of Custard the Dragon' is a very light hearted funny poem that is meant to be enjoyed by everyone. The fixed rhyme scheme and the use of wrong spelling to maintain it, makes it easy and enjoyable to read. Even the names of the pets are rhyming and evokes laughter.

The description of Belinda and her pets makes the poem entertaining. Belinda's bravery is described as equal to a group of bears. The smallest of her pets, her kitten Ink and mouse Blink have been shown so brave that they can scare a lion.

The dog Mustard is like an angry tiger. However, the biggest of them all, the dragon is nice and cowardly. He is always crying for a safe cage. In addition, the reactions of these characters to the dangerous pirate, also makes it funny.

Q.9 **This poem, in ballad form, tells a story. Have you come across any such modern song or lyric that tells a story? If you know one tell it to the class. Collect such songs as a project.**

Ans. Do it yourself.

REVIEW EXERCISE

Including Competency Based Questions

Part – I

Multiple Choice Questions

1. **'The Tale of Custard the Dragon' poem narrating a story in short stanzas is called a/ an ....**

(a) free verse (b) ballad (c) lyric (d) epic

Ans. (b) ballad

2. **Identify the poetic device used in the line "And the little yellow dog was sharp as Mustard."**

(a) Oxymoron (b) Metaphor
(c) Assonance (d) Simile

Ans. (d) Simile

3. **........... was sarcastically compared to the brave knight, Percival.**

(a) Ink (b) Blink (c) Belinda (d) Custard

Ans. (d) Custard

4. **A cage means captivity. Why is Custard inclined to remain in a cage despite what it symbolises? This is so because he viewed it as a** **CBSE Question Bank 2021**

1. sanctuary
2. guardhouse
3. cubicle
4. refuge
5. booth

(a) 1, 2 and 4
(b) 1 and 4
(c) 3, 4 and 5
(d) 3 and 5

Ans. (b) 1 and 4

5. **What is the theme of the poem 'The Tale of Custard the Dragon'?**

1. Appearance vs reality 2. Hypocrisy

3. Courage 4. Jealousy

(a) Only 4 (b) 2 and 3

(c) 1, 2 and 4 (d) All of these

Ans. (d) All of these

6. **"And he held in his teeth a cutlass bright." What is a cutlass?**

(a) A short sword with a curved blade

(b) A big hammer

(c) A short axe

(d) A very sharp bladed saw

Ans. (a) A short sword with a curved blade

7. **'He went at the pirate like a robin at a worm.' Why has this comparison been used here? Just like the robin catches the worm,** CBSE Question Bank 2021

(a) Custard attacked the pirate after careful observation

(b) Custard attacked the pirate without delay

(c) Custard attacked the pirate valourously

(d) Custard attacked the pirate stealthily

Ans. (b) Custard attacked the pirate without delay

8. **"The pirate gaped at Belinda's dragon" means that**

(a) the pirate was looking at the dragon

(b) the pirate was shocked to see such a big dragon

(c) the pirate got scared on seeing the dragon

(d) None of the above

Ans. (b) the pirate was shocked to see such a big dragon

9. **What did the pirate do to prepare himself for the fight?**

(a) Gulped some liquor (b) Had some breath

(c) Shouted a war cry (d) Made up his mind

Ans. (a) Gulped some liquor

10. **"Belinda is as brave as <u>a barrel full of bears</u>" what does the underlined phrase mean?**

(a) A person without fear of what may happen

(b) A barrel which contains bears inside

(c) A group of bears

(d) None of the above

Ans. (a) A person without fear of what may happen

11. **Which of these can be concluded about Ink, Blink and Mustard after reading 'The Tale of Custard the Dragon'?** Competency Based

(a) They were boastful creatures

(b) They were courageous warriors

(c) They were obedient towards Belinda

(d) They were kidnappers sent by the pirate

Ans. (a) They were boastful creatures

12. **... And Ink and Blink <u>chased lions down the stairs</u>**

What does the underlined phrase from 'The Tale of Custard the Dragon' convey about Ink and Blink? Competency Based

(a) How fast they were (b) How loyal they were

(c) How large they were (d) How brave they were

Ans. (d) How brave they were

13. **'The Tale of Custard the Dragon' is a fantasy ballad.**

Which of these options supports the above statement? Competency Based

(a) That Belinda has a pet dragon

(b) That everyone mocked custard

(c) That the pirate was loaded with weapons

(d) That Mustard vanishes at the sight of danger

Ans. (a) That Belinda has a pet dragon

14. **Re-arrange the following events as they occur in the poem 'The Tale of the Custard Dragon'.** Competency Based

(i) Belinda's house is attacked by a Pirate.

(ii) Belinda and the animals make fun of Custard.

(iii) The animals are frightened beyond their wits.

(iv) Mustard justifies why he was unable to be brave.

(a) (ii), (iv), (iii), (i)

(b) (i), (ii), (iv), (iii)

(c) (iii), (iv), (i), (ii)

(d) (ii), (i), (iii), (iv)

Ans. (d) (ii), (i), (iii), (iv)

Extract Based Questions

1. **Read the following extract carefully and answer the questions that follow.**

Now the name of the little black kitten was Ink,
And the little gray mouse, she called her Blink,
And the little yellow dog was sharp as Mustard,
But the dragon was a coward, and she called him
Custard.

(i) How did the poet describe Custard? Answer in one word.

Ans. Timid

(ii) What were kitten and the mouse called by Belinda?

Ans. The kitten and the mouse were called Ink and Blink, respectively.

(iii) Complete the following analogy on the basis of the above extract.

Arrival : Departure :: .... : Brave

Ans. Coward

(iv) Select the option that applies the same rhyme scheme as the given extract.

(a) It is an ancient Mariner,
And he stoppeth one of three.
By thy long beard and glittering eye,
Now wherefore stopp'st thou me?

(b) Twenty odd years have turned to air;
Now she's the girl I didn't dare
Approach, ask out, much less declare
My love to, mired in young despair.

(c) There is ruin and decay
In the House on the Hill:
They are all gone away,
There is nothing more to say

(d) "I cannot go to school today,"
Said little Peggy Ann McKay.
"I have the measles and the mumps,"
A gash, a rash and purple bumps.

Ans. (d)

2. Read the following extract carefully and answer the questions that follow.

Belinda was as brave as a barrel full of bears,
And Ink and Blink chased lions down the stairs,
Mustard was as brave as a tiger in a rage,
But Custard cried for a nice safe cage.

(i) How brave were the kitten and the mouse?

Ans. The kitten and the mouse were so brave that they could chase wild animals.

(ii) How did Mustard show his bravery?

Ans. Mustard showed his bravery by getting angry like a tiger.

(iii) Why did Custard cry for a nice safe cage? Did this demand change by the end of the poem? Give reasons.

Ans. Custard was a coward and so, he cried for the safety of a nice cage.

No, this demand didn't change by the end of the poem. Despite proving that he was braver than everyone else when he killed and ate the pirate, Custard didn't change in his demand. He still wanted his nice safe cage.

(iv) The poet has used a poetic device in the given line. The effect that he wishes to create by its use is ....

"Belinda was as brave as a barrel full of bears"

(a) Contrast (b) Emphasis
(c) Comparison (d) Humour

Ans. (c) Comparison

3. Read the following extract carefully and answer the questions that follow.

Pistol in his left hand, pistol in his right,
And he held in his teeth a cutlass bright,
His beard was black, one leg was wood;
It was clear that the pirate meant no good.

(i) How many pistols was the pirate carrying?

Ans. The pirate was carrying two pistols.

(ii) How does the poet describe his beard?

(a) It was off-white
(b) Black
(c) Mustard
(d) Very long beard

Ans. (b) Black

(iii) How did the pirate appear? Why

Ans. The pirate appeared frightening. This was so because he was carrying pistols and a sword. He had a black beard and one of his legs was made of wood. It seemed that he had come to harm Belinda and her pets.

(iv) Select the option that applies the same rhyme scheme as the given extract.

(a) The tree that never had to fight
For sun and sky and air and light,
But stood out in the open plain
And always got its share of rain,

(b) Row, row, row the boat
Gently down the stream.
Merrily, merrily, merrily, merrily,
Life is but a dream.

(c) O my Luve is like a red, red rose
That's newly sprung in June;
O my Luve is like the melody
That's sweetly played in tune.

(d) "Heed not the folk who sing or say
In sonnet sad or sermon chill",
"Alas, alack, and well-a-day,
This round world's but a bitter pill".

Ans. (a)

4. Read the following extract carefully and answer the questions that follow.

"Ink trickled down to the bottom of the household,
And little mouse Blink strategically mouseholed. But up jumped Custard, snorting like an engine, Clashed his tail like irons in a dungeon, With a clatter and a clank and a jangling squirm, He went at the pirate like a robin at a worm."

(i) Which option supports the ideas in the extract?

(a) Fear makes strangers of people who would be friends

(b) If you're brave enough to start, you're strong enough to finish

(c) You get in life what you have the courage to ask for

(d) All of the above

Ans. (b) If you're brave enough to start, you're strong enough to finish

(ii) What is the poet's purpose of using onomatopoeic words in the extract?

Ans. The poet's purpose of using such words is to emphasise on the might and boldness of Custard.

(iii) Mention what the poet wants to convey through these lines.

Ans. The given lines show that the animal, who was considered by all to be a coward, was actually braver than them. While the rest of Belinda's pets cower in fear at the sight of the pirate, it is Custard the cowardly dragon that attacks him and saves everyone. This shows that the poet wants to convey that whether someone is truly brave or not can only be discovered in the face of real danger.

(iv) The extract mentions 'irons' in dungeons. According to this extract, irons refers to ....

Ans. iron chains holding the prisoners captive

5. Read the following extract carefully and answer the questions that follow.

Belinda paled, and she cried Help ! Help !
But Mustard fled with a terrified yelp,
Ink trickled down to the bottom of the household,
And little mouse Blink strategically mouseholed.

CBSE 2024 C

(i) Which animal came out as a real hero in this situation?

Ans. Custard came out as a real hero in this situation.

(ii) 'Help! Help! is an example of

(a) personification (b) alliteration

(c) simile (d) repetition

Ans. repetition

(iii) The phrase 'trickled down' means ....

(a) stepped down quickly

(b) ran away fearfully

(c) tricked mercilessly

(d) moved down slowly

Ans. (d) moved down slowly

(iv) How did Belinda react in the face of crisis?

Ans. Belinda reacts to a crisis by becoming pale with fear, crying for help and being terrified.

Or **CBSE SQP 2024**

(i) Examine the portrayal of Blink in the given lines.

Ans. Blink's retreat is portrayed as a calculated and swift movement to safety. The imagery of Blink 'strategically' making the mousehole suggests a quick and calculated response to the perceived danger. This further highlights Blink's instinctual survival skills in the face of adversity.

(ii) Complete the following suitably.

The word 'paled' implies that Belinda ....

Ans. recognised that she was in a threatening situation

(iii) What kind of picture is painted by the poet through the line, 'Ink trickled down to the bottom of the household'?

Ans. In this context, the picture painted by the poet is that of a slow descent, with Ink trying to avoid drawing attention to itself and seeking safety in a cautious and inconspicuous manner.

(iv) What kind of atmosphere is created through these lines?

1. Urgency 2. Apprehension 3. Uncertainty
4. Mystery 5. Aggression

Select the correct option

(a) 1 and 4 (b) Only 2

(c) 1, 2 and 3 (d) 4 and 5

Ans. (c) 1, 2 and 3

6. Read the following extract carefully and answer the questions that follow.

Belinda embraced him, Mustard licked him,
No one mourned for his pirate victim
Ink and Blink in glee did gyrate
Around the dragon that ate the pirate.

(i) Who is called a victim here?

Ans. The pirate is called a vicitim here.

(ii) Study the following statements.

1. Belinda embraced Blink

2. Custard was a brave dragon

3. Ink was licking Custard

(a) 1 is right 2 is wrong

(b) 2 is right 3 is wrong

(c) 3 is right 1 is wrong

(d) 3 is right 2 is wrong

Ans. (b) 2 is right 3 is wrong

(iii) Who has written the above lines?

Ans. Ogden Nash has written the above lines.

(iv) Whom did Belinda embrace?

Ans. Belinda embraced the dragon.

Or CBSE 2023

(i) Mustard was happily licking the ....

Ans. dragon, Custard, for saving all of them from the dangerous pirate

(ii) Belinda embraced Custard

1. Out of shock
2. Out of helplessness
3. Out of happiness
4. Out of gratitude

Choose the correct option.

(a) 1 and 4 (b) Only 3
(c) 2 and 3 (d) 3 and 4

Ans. (d) 3 and 4

(iii) Why were Ink and Blink happy? Competency Based

Ans. Ink and Blink were happy to be out of danger. They were in harm's way when the pirate had come. As a result, they had hidden themselves in the house. However, when the dragon had eaten the pirate, they were very happy to be saved.

(iv) Complete the analogy and choose the word from the extract that means the opposite of the given word.

Day : Night :: Steady : ....

Ans. Gyrate

Part – II

Short Answer Type Questions

1. Where did Belinda live and with whom?

Ans. Belinda lived in a little white house with her four pets and a red wagon. She had a black kitten named Ink, a grey mouse named Blink, a yellow dog named Mustard and a coward dragon named Custard.

2. Did Custard match his physical appearance?

Ans. No, Custard did not match his appearance, as he looked dangerous but actually was a coward. He always cried for a nice and safe cage, while everyone laughed at him for his cowardice.

3. Describe the bravery of everyone in the house.

Ans. In the poem, everyone in the house except the dragon was brave. Belinda was as brave as a barrel full of bears. Ink and Blink were brave enough to chase lions away. Even Mustard was as brave as an angry tiger. It was only Custard, who was a coward.

4. Why was Custard, the dragon, teased as Percival?

Ans. Custard, the dragon is teased as Percival by Ink, Blink and Mustard for his timidity. They teased him as Percival because unlike Custard, he was a courageous and brave knight of King Arthur. Custard, in contrast, was meek and always cried for a nice safe cage.

5. What did everyone do when the pirate came?

Or **Belinda and other animals have been described as brave. But on seeing the pirate they behaved in a cowardly way. How did they react?** CBSE 2024

Ans. When the pirate came, Belinda cried for help and became pale with fear.

Mustard ran away with a terrified cry and Ink hid himself at the bottom of the house, while Blink disappeared in his hole.

It was only Custard who showed the courage and jumped in front of the pirate to fight him.

6. How did Custard face the pirate?

Or **How did Custard prove 'the cowardly dragon' tag to be untrue?** CBSE 2022 Term II

Or **Describe how Custard the Dragon fights the pirate.** CBSE 2023

Ans. When the pirate came in Belinda's house, all of her pets, except Custard, hid themselves. Custard jumped infront of the pirate to fight him. He even clashed his tail.

During this fight, the pirate shot two bullets at him but missed the aim. Finally, Custard ate him and left no trace of him.

7. How did everyone react after Custard ate the pirate?

Or **How did the other pets celebrate Custard getting rid of the pirate?** CBSE 2023

Ans. After Custard ate the pirate, there was joy all around the house. No one mourned for the pirate and everyone was grateful to the dragon.

Belinda hugged Custard while Mustard licked him. Ink and Blink started dancing around Custard.

8. How did the other three pets boast of their bravery?

Ans. When the pirate had been killed by the dragon Custard, all other pets of Belinda started making excuses for their cowardice. Mustard said that if he had not been nervous he would have been twice as brave as Custard. Ink and Blink boasted that they would have been thrice as brave as Custard.

9. Were Belinda and her pets grateful to Custard for killing the pirate? How did Custard react to their reactions? **Competency Based**

Ans. Yes, Belinda and her pets were grateful to Custard for killing the pirate, but it was only temporary.

Soon after expressing gratitude, Mustard, Ink and Blink started giving excuses for their cowardice and things went back to normal as it was before the pirate incident.

Custard, the dragon, reacted in a humble manner and accepted that all other pets were braver than him.

10. Was everyone really as brave as they claimed?

Ans. Belinda and her three pets, excluding Custard, were very proud of their bravery but they were not really brave. It was only Custard, who had the courage to face the pirate and fight him. So, among all, only Custard was brave.

11. Custard humbly accepts that other animals are braver than him. Give a reason to support your stance that humility is a virtue worth possessing. **Competency Based**

Ans. Custard humbly accepts that other animals are braver than him because humility is a virtue worth possessing. Humility helps us in not placing too much importance to our achievements. It also allows us to accept our vulnerabilities.

12. The usage of words like 'realio trulio' creates a wonderful poetic effect. How? **CBSE Question Bank 2021**

Or **Read the lines given below from the poem 'The Tale of Custard the Dragon'. What effect do the words 'realio, trulio' have on the poem?**

"Custard the dragon had big sharp teeth,
And spikes on top of him and scales underneath,
Mouth like a fireplace, cheminey for a nose,
And realio, trulio, daggers on his toes".

Competency Based

Ans. The words 'realio', 'trulio' create a wonderful poetic effect by making the poem interesting to read. In reality, there are no such words as 'realio' and 'trulio'. They actually mean 'really' and 'truly', respectively. The inclusion and repitition of these words give a rhythmic and melodic effect to the poem.

13. Why is it fair to say that Custard could be the 'poster-boy' for the belief that the real nature of a person is revealed in times of the greatest difficulty?

Ans. Custard could be the perfect poster-boy for the belief that the real nature of a person is revealed in times of the greatest difficulty. This is because Custard showed his true courageous nature when he fought fiercely with the pirate. He was considered as cowardly by his house mates before this incident.

14. Give one reason why 'The Tale of Custard the Dragon' is more a fable than a ballad.

Or **How does the poem 'The Tale of Custard The Dragon' differ from the traditional ballad?** **CBSE 2023**

Ans. 'The Tale of Custard the Dragon' is more a fable than a ballad because just like a fable it contains animals as characters and gives a strong moral message. On the other hand, a ballad is a narrative verse that can either be heroic or very silly.

15. Custard was not treated properly by Belinda and his fellow animals.

Justify the above statement in 20-30 words with an example from 'The Tale of Custard the Dragon'. **Competency Based**

Ans. It is true that Custard was not treated properly by Belinda and his fellow animals. They used to make fun of him by comparing him to a courgeous warrior named Percival. They used to mock Custard's cowardice and Belinda used to tickle him a lot. Belinda and his fellow animals used to laugh at Custard so hard that even the house seemed the shake with them.

16. How does Custard subvert the traditional hero archetype? What commentary does this provide on conventional notions of heroism?

Ans. Custard challenges the archetype of the traditional hero by being scared at first but he ultimately saves the day. This suggests that heroism isn't just about being strong and brave; it can also mean overcoming personal fears and stepping up when it matters most.

17. What kind of picture is painted by the poet through the line, "Ink trickled down to the bottom of the household"? **CBSE SQP 2024**

Ans. The line serves to establish the difference between the external commands directed at Amanda and her internal imaginative escapes. This also highlights the contrast between Amanda's reality and her desires. This aids in the reader's understanding of her struggle between sticking to the expectations and seeking freedom through imagination.

Long Answer Type Questions

1. The dragon, Custard was considered a coward. The humble dragon proved his bravery in adversity. Analyse that certain qualities like bravery and courage are situational and spontaneous. Express your views with reference to the poem, 'The Tale of Custard, the Dragon'.

Ans. It is true that bravery and courage are situational and spontaneous. This fact has been aptly conveyed in the poem 'The Tale of Custard the Dragon', wherein the dragon was considered a coward. He was laughed at for crying for a nice safe cage. He never boasted of his bravery and courage, unlike Belinda and her other pets do.

Everyone else, including Belinda, Ink, Blink and Mustard claim to be brave. They even made fun of Custard's cowardice. However, when the time to show their courage came, none of them could face the danger. They hid themselves in some corner of the house.

It was only Custard who dared to face the frightening pirate. He not only fought the pirate but also ate him up.

It was a dangerous situation to which Custard spontaneously responded. His courage and bravery came out in a threatening situation. Hence, it is true that qualities like courage and bravery are situational and spontaneous.

2. Do you think that one should be made fun of because of their preferences and choices in life? Explain in the context of Custard, the dragon.

Ans. According to me, one should never make fun of anyone on the basis of their lifestyle and their choices. One must always remember that choices and preference can depend on unexplainable factors.

In the poem 'The Tale of Custard the Dragon', Custard makes one such choice of wishing for a 'nice safe cage'. He prefers comfort and safety. However, Belinda and her other pets always laugh at him. They think of him as a coward for choosing to stay in a safe cage and make fun of him. Custard, the dragon, soon proved that his choice of comfort doesn't make him a coward. Infact, instead of all the 'brave' pets of Belinda, it was Custard who fought the pirate. It was Custard who showed courage to face the pirate and kill him.

Therefore, one must never judge anyone for their choices. Appearances may be deceptive. Just like the dragon who appeared to be a coward but was actually courageous, another person might also be different from what we assume about them based on their preferences.

3. A ballad includes the telling of a tale as well as a surprise ending. Using evidence from the poem, explain how these features are included in 'The Tale of Custard the Dragon'. CBSE SQP 2022 Term II

Ans. 'The Tale of Custard the Dragon' by Ogden Nash exhibits several characteristics of a ballad, despite having a modern and amusing twist. The poem tells a story about a dragon named Custard and his surprising behaviour in the face of danger. Like traditional ballads, it has a clear narrative structure with a beginning, middle, and end. The use of simple language with rhyming words is consistent with the ballad tradition of using straightforward language. Nash employs a regular rhyme scheme and rhythm, contributing to the poems musicality, just like traditional ballads. The use of repitition, particularly in the refrain 'Cowardly Custard!' adds emphasis and rhythm. The incorporation of dialogue and the overall storytelling nature of the poem reflect the ballads influence. Hence, 'The Tale of Custard the Dragon' captures the essence of ballads by combining narrative structure simplicity of language, rhythmic qualities, and emotional resonances in a delightful and memorable way.

4. How does Ogden Nash's 'The Tale of Custard the Dragon', challenge the notion that individuals should conform to societal expectations? CBSE Additional SQP 2023-24

Ans. Ogden Nash's 'The Tale of Custard the Dragon' challenges the notion that individuals should conform to societal expectation. The poem presents Belinda as a brave and independent female character. She is described as brave as a barrel full of bears, a trait that is stereotypically associated with masculinity. In contrast, the male characters (Ink, Blink, Mustard) are portrayed as weaker and less courageous.

The actions of Ink, Blink, Mustard seem motivated by fear of social judgement and ridicule, of being perceived as weak while Custard is unafraid of crying for a nice safe cage. Normally, dragons are associated with characteristics such as brave, fierce, powerful and cunning. But none of these characteristics can be associated with Custard. He is not fierce, powerful, or cunning.

Thus, the poem promotes the idea that everyone has unique talents and abilities and they should be encouraged to pursue their passions and strengths, at their pace, rather than conforming to societal expectations or stereotypes.

5. Describe the pirate's appearance and intentions.

Ans. The pirate in 'The Tale of Custard the Dragon' is depicted as a menacing figure with distinct physical features and nefarious intentions. He has a black beard, one wooden leg, and brandished pistols in both hands, with a dagger clenched between his teeth. This description evokes the stereotypical image of a pirate from folklore and literature. The pirate's intentions are malicious, as indicated by his aggressive actions of climbing into Belinda's house armed with weapons. His purpose is to cause harm, as evidenced by his attempt to intimidate Belinda and her pets and his firing of bullets in their direction. The pirate is a classic antagonist, embodying danger and chaos in the narrative.

ASSESSMENT EXERCISE

Extract Based Questions

Read the following extract carefully and answer the questions that follow.

But up jumped Custard, snorting like an engine,
Clashed his tail like irons in a dungeon,
With a clatter and a clank and a jangling squirm
He went at the pirate like a robin at a worm.

(i) Select the appropriate option to complete the sentence, according to the extract.
The fact that coward went at the pirate, attacking him, proves his ....

(ii) Which figure of speech is used in line 3rd of the Stanza?
(a) Alliteration (b) Simile
(c) Onomatopoeia (d) Metaphor

(iii) Why is custard, the dragon, compared to a robin?

(iv) State whether the following statement is True or False:
Custard fought the pirate and was defeated.

Short Answer (SA) Type Questions

1. Why is the poem 'The Tale of Custard the Dragon' called a ballad?
2. What is the true nature of Custard, the dragon?
3. Describe the pirate who comes through the window.
4. What character trait of Custard is revealed when he accepts that other animals are braver than him?

Long Answer (LA) Type Questions

1. What does bravery mean to you? Who is a real brave heart? Elaborate with reference to 'The Tale of Custard the Dragon'.
2. Imagery and Personification are used abundantly in 'The Tale of Custard the Dragon'.
State one evidence each for their usage and analyse the author's purpose behind it in 100-120 words.
Competency Based

For Anne Gregory

by William Butler Yeats

CHAPTER 10

Introduction The poem 'For Anne Gregory' has been written by a famous Irish poet W.B. Yeats. It is about the perception of love by different people. The poem is in the form of a dialogue between two people-Anne Gregory and another person, whose identity has not been made clear by the poet.

The poem shows the true nature of humans as they are always carried away by the outer beauty and never pay attention to the true nature of a person. Only God can love a person for their inner beauty and not for their physical beauty.

Stanzawise Explanation

Stanza 1

"Never shall a young man,
Thrown into despair
By those great honey-coloured
Ramparts at your ear,
Love you for yourself alone
And not your yellow hair."

Explanation In these lines, the speaker (most probably the poet) says to Anne that her beautiful honey-coloured hair can make any young man fall hopelessly in love with her. This love is not for Anne but for her beautiful yellow hair.

Anne's honey-coloured hair around her ears have been compared to walls, which prevent anyone from looking inside her soul. This beauty can capture any man's attention in such a way that he may never be able to look into Anne's inner beauty or character. Thus, no man can love Anne for her inner beauty.

Stanza 2

"But I can get a hair-dye
And set such colour there,
Brown, or black, or carrot,
That young men in despair
May love me for myself alone
And not my yellow hair."

Explanation In these lines, Anne replies to the speaker. Anne says that she can get her hair-dyed and change the colour of her hair into brown or black or the red colour of a carrot. She believes that such an act will make the young men love her for herself or her inner beauty and not for her outward appearance.

Anne wants to convey that what is visible from the outside is very artificial. It is changeable and thus, is not important or true.

Stanza 3

"I heard an old religious man
But yesternight declare
That he had found a text to prove
That only God, my dear,
Could love you for yourself alone
And not your yellow hair."

Explanation In these lines, the speaker mentions an old religious man who had announced last night that he had found a religious text. It is written in this text that only God is capable of looking beyond the external beauty of a person.

Here, the speaker means that humans do not have the capacity and understanding to look inside the soul of a person. Humans are always attracted towards the outer beauty. They never care to know the person behind the beautiful appearance. Therefore, the speaker finally tells Anne that only God can love her for her inner qualities and not for her yellow hair.

Poetic Devices Used in the Poem

Metaphor A device which compares two things or qualities which are unlike
- honey-coloured ramparts

Alliteration Repetition of initial consonant sounds in the same line
- And not your yellow hair

Rhyme Scheme abcbdb

Word Meaning

Word	Meaning
Stanza 1	
Despair	a miserable condition or hopelessness
Ramparts	protecting wall around a fort, here it is used for Anne's honey-coloured hair around her ears
Stanza 2	
Hair dye	a natural or synthetic substance used to change the colour of a person's hair
Stanza 3	
Yesternight	last night
Declare	to announce

NCERT FOLDER

NCERT Exercise Questions

THINKING ABOUT THE POEM (NCERT PAGE 119)

Q.1 What does the young man mean by "great honey-coloured /Ramparts at your ear?" Why does he say that young men are "thrown into despair" by them?

Ans. The lines "great honey-coloured/Ramparts at your ear" describe the physical attributes of Anne Gregory, particularly her hair, which is likened to the colour of honey. Anne's hair have been called a rampart meaning a wall. It is called so because her hair acts as a wall as they prevent young men from looking beyond Anne's physical beauty and into her soul. According to the speaker, young men are thrown into despair as her hair is so attractive and pretty that they, hopelessly fall in love with her. They love her for her yellow hair and not for her nature or personality.

Q.2 What colour is the young woman's hair? What does she say she can change it to? Why would she want to do so?

Ans. Anne's hair is yellow like the colour of honey. Anne says that she can dye her hair and change it to black, brown, carrot or any other colour she wants. She says so to show that the outer beauty is changeable and is not permanent or real.

Anne wants young men to look into her soul and love her for her inner beauty. In order to do so, she needs to show them the artificiality of her external beauty.

Q.3 Objects have qualities which make them desirable to others. Can you think of some objects (a car, a phone, a dress...) and say what qualities make one object more desirable than another? Imagine you were trying to sell an object: what qualities would you emphasise?

Ans. People desire objects because of their qualities that suit their need. In the things we consume or the goods we use such as a car, a phone, a dress, etc., physical qualities matter the most. Before buying anything, it is always considered that the object is durable and looks pretty.

If I were to sell a dress, I would select the one that is very appealing to the eye and comfortable for the body. Then, I would emphasise on the durability of the dress so that the customer feels that he/she is spending his/her money at the right place and on the right thing.

Q.4 What about people? Do we love others because we like their qualities, whether physical or mental? Or is it possible to love someone "for themselves alone"? Are some people 'more lovable' than others? Discuss this question in pairs or in groups, considering points like the following.

(i) A parent or caregiver's love for a newborn baby, for a mentally or physically challenged child, for a clever child or a prodigy

(ii) The public's love for a film star, a sportsperson, a politician, or a social worker.

(iii) Your love for a friend, or brother or sister.

(iv) Your love for a pet, and the pet's love for you.

Ans. The students should attempt this question on their own.

Q.5 **You have perhaps concluded that people are not objects to be valued for their qualities or riches rather than for themselves. But elsewhere Yeats asks the question: How can we separate the dancer from the dance? Is it possible to separate 'the person himself or herself' from how the person looks, sounds, walks and so on? Think of how you or a friend or member of your family has changed over the years. Has your relationship also changed? In what way?**

Ans. The students should attempt this question on their own.

REVIEW EXERCISE

Including Competency Based Questions

Part – I

Multiple Choice Questions

1. In the poem 'For Anne Gregory' ....

(a) Anne's qualities are depicted
(b) the poet praises physical outlook of a person
(c) love between a man and a woman is presented
(d) God's loving ability

Ans. (c) love between a man and a woman is presented

2. 'Thrown into despair' from the poem 'For Anne Gregory' means ....

(a) confused in love (b) betrayed in love
(c) disappointed in love (d) being selfish in love

Ans. (c) disappointed in love

3. Identify the literary device used in the line 'and set such colour there' from the poem 'For Anne Gregory'.

(a) Oxymoron (b) Alliteration
(c) Assonance (d) None of these

Ans. (b) Alliteration

4. Who can love us for who we are and not for how we look?

(a) Poet (b) Young men
(c) God (d) None of these

Ans. (c) God

5. What does the girl think she can do to get rid of lovers?

(a) Cut her hair (b) Dye her hair
(c) Cover her hair (d) All of these

Ans. (b) Dye her hair

6. What does the girl want?

(a) To be loved for herself
(b) To be loved for her hair
(c) To be loved for her appearance
(d) To be loved for her riches

Ans. (a) To be loved for herself

7. What is the poet's advice to young men in regard to love, as in the poem 'For Anne Gregory'?

(a) Fall in love with a lady's soul
(b) Fall in love after judging a lady's own merit
(c) Fall in love with a lady who has a pure heart
(d) All of the above

Ans. (d) All of the above

8. What does the poet feel about Anne in the poem 'For Anne Gregory'?

(a) No one will love her for who she is
(b) Everyone will fall for her nature
(c) No one can ever love her
(d) None of the above

Ans. (a) No one will love her for who she is

9. How did the religious man prove that only God can loves us for ourselves?

(a) Through a text in some religious book
(b) By meeting God
(c) Because he believed so
(d) Through a practical experiment

Ans. (a) Through a text in some religious book

10. What is the theme of the poem 'For Anne Gregory'?

1. The idea of outer beauty
2. The concept of spiritual beauty
3. Human nature
4. Human love
5. Love of God

Options

(a) 1, 2 and 3 (b) 2,3, 4 and 6
(c) 1, 4, 5 and 6 (d) All of these

Ans. (d) All of these

11. What is the rhyming scheme of the poem 'For Anne Gregory'?

(a) abcdab (b) abcbdb (c) abbcbb (d) abcbab

Ans. (b) abcbdb

12. What is the tone of the poem 'For Anne Gregory'?

(a) Soft and casual
(b) Harsh and rude
(c) Full of love
(d) Sad and gloomy

Ans. (a) Soft and casual

13. What is the central idea of the poem 'For Anne Gregory'?

(a) True love involves both inner and outer beauty.
(b) True love exists regardless of physical appearance.
(c) We must love each other for what we are.
(d) All of the above

Ans. (d) All of the above

14. What could be the philosophical meaning of the poem 'For Anne Gregory'? Competency Based

(a) We do not need human beings to love us but only God. We should be in god's shelter throughout our lives.
(b) This poem may have been written by Yeats for his lover who has rejected him. He is imagining a conversation with her.
(c) This is a conversation between the mind or soul and the body. The mind is telling the body that the body will only be loved for its external beauty as man cannot understand the beauty of the soul.
(d) Both (a) and (b)

Ans. (c) This is a conversation between the mind or soul and the body. The mind is telling the body that the body will only be loved for its external beauty as man cannot understand the beauty of the soul.

Extract Based Questions

1. Read the following extract carefully and answer the questions that follow.

Never shall a young man,
Thrown into despair
By those great honey-coloured
Ramparts at your ear,
Love you for yourself alone
And not your yellow hair.

(i) Select the option that applies the same rhyme scheme as the given extract.

(a)
I have lost my turtledove:
Isn't that her gentle coo?
I will go and find my bae.
Here you mourn your mated boo;
Oh, God-I am mourning now:
I have lost my love too.

(b)
Salute her, with long fingers
Caress her freezing hair
Sip, Goblin, from the very lips
The Lover - hovered - o'er
Unworthy, that a thought so mean
Accost a Theme - so - fair

(c)
And our poor fancy-play
For them is wasted skill:
There is nothing more to say.
There is ruin and decay
In the House on the Hill:
They are all gone away,

(d)
They are all gone away,
The House is shut and still,
There is nothing more to say.
Through broken walls and grey
The winds blow bleak and shrill:
They are all gone away.

Ans. (a)

(ii) What does the poet want to convey through the word 'despair' in the line – 'Never shall a young man, thrown into despair'? Answer in not more that 5 words.

Ans. Love leads to hopelessness

(iii) Comment on the poet's purpose behind these lines.

Ans. The poet presents the idea that Anne's honey-coloured hair can make any man fall in love with her. His love, however, is not for her but for her hair. The poet says that Anne's beautiful hair is like a wall that prohibits a person from looking into her soul. Thus, no man can see her inner beauty and fall in love with her. The poet's purpose, thus, is to show that humans are always carried away by outer beauty and never pay attention to a person's true nature.

(iv) What is the poetic device used in the following lines?

... great honey coloured/Ramparts at your ear'

Ans. The poetic device used in the given lines is metaphor.

2. Read the following extract carefully and answer the questions that follow.

"But I can get a hair-dye
And set such colour there,
Brown, or black, or carrot,
That young men in despair
May love me for myself alone
And not my yellow hair." CBSE SQP 2023

(i) What is the poet's tone in the extract?

Ans. The poet is agitated at Anne's belief that changing her hair colour would make men love her for herself. The poet is also argumentative when he keeps his belief infront of Anne.

(ii) Complete the analogy about the speaker's hair.

Yellow : Blonde :: ...... : Carrot.

Ans. Red/Orange

(iii) Identify the reason for the speaker's need to colour her hair, as per the extract.

(a) Her control over what makes her look beautiful.
(b) Her desire to be loved for inner beauty.
(c) Her need to change people's perception about beauty.
(d) Her conviction that she is beautiful inside.

Ans. (b) Her desire to be loved for inner beauty.

(iv) What causes the young men to 'despair', according to the extract?

Ans. Being hopelessly in love and the uncertainty in it causes the young men to 'despair'.

3. Read the following extract carefully and answer the questions that follow.

"I heard an old religious man
But yesternight declare
That he had found a text to prove
That only God, my dear,
Could love you for yourself alone
And not your yellow hair."

(i) Fill in the blank.
The above stanza strongly defines the idea of .... .

Ans. external beauty

(ii) Choose the phrase that best represents 'love you for yourself alone'.

(a) Unconditional love (b) Unseemly love
(c) Unrequited love (d) Understated love

Ans. (a) Unconditional love

(iii) Where did the religious man find that God loves everyone selflessly? **Competency Based**

Ans. The religious man found it in a religious text that God loves everyone selflessly.

(iv) What did the speaker of the above lines hear?

Ans. The speaker of the above lines heard that only God can love everyone for their inner beauty.

Part – II

Short Answer Type Questions

1. Between whom does the conversation in the poem takes place? What does the first speaker say to the second speaker? **Competency Based**

Ans. The poem 'For Anne Gregory' is a conversation between Anne Gregory and another speaker whose identity is not disclosed by the poet. However, we assume that it is the poet himself.

The first speaker (probably the poet) tells the second speaker (Anne) that young men would love her for her outer beauty, i.e. her beautiful yellow hair. They will not love her for herself or her inner beauty.

2. Why would young men never love Anne Gregory for 'herself alone'?

Ans. Young men would never love Anne Gregory for 'herself alone' because they are attracted to her external beauty.

Her outward appearance, i.e. her yellow hair is so beautiful and attractive that no man can ignore it and pay attention to her inner beauty or soul.

3. What did the old religious man declare? What did he want to prove?

Ans. The old religious man declared to the poet that he had found a text the previous night. In this text, it is written that only God is capable of looking beyond external beauty.

Humans are always attracted towards the physical appearance of a person and are not capable of looking beyond external beauty.

The old man wants to prove that only God can love a person for his inner beauty.

4. The advice given by elders is crucial to young lives. Explain in the context of the poem 'For Anne Gregory'.

Ans. The statement "the advice given by elders is crucial to young lives" holds true for the poem 'For Anne Gregory'. Anne had decided to change her hair colour so that somebody would love her for herself alone. However, the speaker informs her of an elder's advice that only God will love her for herself.

This advice of an elder is crucial for the younger generation as it helps them understand life.

5. The 'yellow hair' is a symbol in the poem. Briefly support the statement with reference to the poem 'For Anne Gregory'. **CBSE Question Bank 2021**

Ans. The yellow hair possessed by Anne Gregory is a symbol of the physical beauty which tempts people to only focus on the physical aspect of things. In the poem, it distracts the men so much so that they love Anne Gregory for her physical beauty and not internal beauty.

6. The poet in the poem 'For Anne Gregory' conveys beauty as temporary. Explain with reference to the poem. CBSE 2023

Ans. It is true that the poet in the poem 'For Anne Gregory' conveys beauty as temporary. The poet opines that external appearance and beauty are illusory in nature and do not stand the test of time. External beauty can be changed just like the honey coloured hair can be dyed to any colour.

7. In the poem for Anne Gregory, Anne Gregory's suggestion to dye her hair serves two main purposes. What are these? CBSE Additional SQP 2023

Present your response this way : One purpose is .... Another purpose is ....

Ans. One purpose is to gain genuine love by proposing that she can change her hair colour to make young men love her for her inner self, not just her yellow hair. Another purpose is to prove her point to the speaker who initially expressed doubt that anyone would love her for anything other than her external beauty.

8. How does the speaker's perception of Anne's beauty evolve throughout the poem, and what does this transformation suggest about the nature of attraction?

Ans. The speaker initially admires Anne's physical beauty, focusing on her hair and face. As the poem progresses, he shifts to valuing her inner qualities. This transformation suggests that true attraction goes beyond superficial appearances, emphasising the importance of deeper emotional connections.

9. What is the significance of the poem's closing lines? How do they encapsulate the overall message regarding beauty and its transience?

Ans. The closing lines emphasise the idea that beauty is fleeting and ultimately superficial. They encapsulate the poem's message by illustrating how real value lies in inner qualities, urging readers to appreciate deeper connections rather than being entranced by transient appearances.

10. How does the speaker propose distinguishing genuine love from superficial attraction in the poem?

Ans. The speaker suggests that by altering external features, such as changing the colour of the hair, it may be possible to test whether a person loves Anne Gregory for herself alone, regardless of her physical appearance. This implies a desire to discern authentic, unconditional love from superficial infatuation.

11. What is the central idea of the poem 'For Anne Gregory'?

Ans. The central idea of the poem 'For Anne Gregory' by William Butler Yeats revolves around love and the challenge of distinguishing genuine love from superficial attraction based on physical characteristics. The speaker expresses concern that individuals may be drawn to someone, in this case, Anne Gregory, not for their true self but for external features, such as their hair colour. The poem explores the complexness of love, addressing the superficiality that can influence romantic feelings and the speaker's yearning for a deeper, more authentic connection. Introducing the religious man's perspective adds a spiritual dimension, suggesting that only divine love, represented by God, can truly appreciate and love an individual for their intrinsic qualities rather than external attributes.

12. How does the poem's title relate to its content and message?

Ans. The poem's title, 'For Anne Gregory', directly connects to its content and message by signalling that it is explicitly addressed to Anne Gregory and revolves around her experiences. By naming the poem after Anne, Yeats personalises the exploration of love and superficiality, making it more intimate and relatable. The title emphasises Anne's central role in the poem and suggests that its insights and reflections are directed towards her. Furthermore, it sets the stage for examining Anne's struggle with being loved for her true self rather than superficial qualities like her yellow hair. Thus, the title is a thematic anchor, highlighting the poem's focus on Anne's journey and the broader themes of love and authenticity.

Long Answer Type Questions

1. The poet in the poem 'For Anne Gregory' conveys that we should give importance to the inner beauty and not the physical appearance. Elaborate with reference to the poem.

Or Physical beauty is not permanent, but the beauty of character or internal beauty is permanent. Justify on the basis of your reading of 'For Anne Gregory'. CBSE 2023

Ans. In the poem 'For Anne Gregory', a conversation between Anne Gregory and another speaker, most probably the poet, takes place. The poet through this conversation conveys that we should give importance to the inner beauty and not the physical appearance. He tells Anne Gregory that many young men fall in love with her because of her beautiful hair. They do not love her for her inner qualities.

To such a statement, Anne replies that she would change the colour of her hair so that men would love her for her personality and inner beauty. This reply along with the poet's assertion that only God loves one for one's inner beauty, presents the poet's message clearly. The poet believes that outward appearances are artificial and hence, are not true. Thus, man must prefer internal beauty over physical appearance.

2. God does not love a person for his/her outer appearance but for the person himself. Elaborate.

Ans. God does not love any person for his/her outer appearance and richness. It is human beings who pay attention to material things. Unlike God, they prefer to see only outward beauty. They prefer things that appear pretty from outside and never look for what lies inside. In the poem 'For Anne Gregory', the poet highlights this preference of man.

He informs Anne Gregory that men (many young men) love her only for her beautiful yellow hair. They do not see her true nature or personality. The poet further points that it is only God who can avoid external beauty and look beyond it. He even mentions a text that proves it as truth. For the poet, outward appearances are temporary as it fades away and thus, is not true. The truth for him is clear that God does not love a person for his/her outer appearance, he loves him for his inner qualities.

3. Do we love people because we like their appearances or we are fascinated by their physical appearance? How does Anne Gregory want to be loved? Is her wish fulfilled?

Ans. It is completely right to say that we love people because of their external appearance and not for their good qualities or nature. The world today is full of show where people have become objects. Their value is judged through their physical beauty or how they look. People are loved because they look beautiful.

In the poem 'For Anne Gregory', the poet asserts that Anne is loved for her beautiful yellow hair and not for her personality. However, Anne Gregory does not want to be loved for her beauty. She is ready to get her hair dyed to show the artificiality of her outward appearance. She wants to be loved for herself.

Anne's wish does not get fulfilled. The poet tells her that it is only God who would love her for her internal qualities. Humans will go on being tempted by her beautiful yellow hair.

4. The theme of 'For Anne Gregory' by W.B. Yeats revolves around the superficiality of love based on physical appearance and the contrast between earthly love and divine or spiritual love. Comment.

Ans. The theme of 'For Anne Gregory' by W.B. Yeats revolves around the superficiality of love based on physical appearance and the contrast between earthly love and divine or spiritual love.

Superficial Nature of Love The poem explores the idea that individuals are often attracted to external qualities, such as physical beauty, rather than appreciating the inner qualities of a person. The speaker suggests that a young man may be enamoured by Anne Gregory's 'yellow hair' and may not love her for who she is. The consideration of changing the hair color with dye is a metaphor for altering external attributes to test the sincerity of love.

Search for Authentic Love The speaker is grappling with the desire for authentic, unconditional love. By contemplating changing physical features, the speaker questions whether someone could love the person inside rather than external appearances. This reflects a deeper longing for genuine connections that go beyond the superficial.

Spiritual Love The poem introduces a religious element in the third stanza, suggesting that only God can love someone purely for who they are, independent of physical attributes. This adds a spiritual dimension to the theme, highlighting that true, selfless love may be unattainable in human relationships and is reserved for a divine realm.

Contrast Between Mortal and Divine Love The distinction between the mortal (human) and divine (God's) capacity for love highlights the limitations of earthly relationships. It raises questions about the nature of love and whether true, unconditional love can exist among humans or if it is a quality reserved for a higher, spiritual plane.

5. The idea of beauty is a one-dimensional cultural conception or one that has been created by human beings themselves. Comment on the statement with reference to the conventional ideas of beauty viz-a-viz the poet's central idea of the poem 'For Anne Gregory'. **CBSE 2024 C**

Ans. The concept of beauty, particularly as portrayed in literature and cultural discourse, is a one-dimensional construct shaped by societal norms and expectations. Generally, beauty has been ascribed to physical attributes such as symmetry, youth, grace and other traits often glorified in art, media and popular discourse. In 'For Anne Gregory', the poet engages with these conventional ideas of beauty by delving into the deeper layers of what it means to be beautiful.

The poem unfolds as a dialogue where Anne Gregory, represented as a young woman, is preoccupied with the notion that her beauty will secure her romantic prospects. She reveals the societal pressure placed upon women to conform to certain standards of aesthetic appeal, highlighting the one-dimensional viewpoint that beauty is synonymous with desirability in romantic relationships.

In contrast, the speaker suggests that true beauty transcends physical attributes. In the poem, he proposes that any love or attraction based solely on appearance is inherently superficial and transient.

This assertion invites a deeper consideration of what constitutes genuine beauty-one that includes qualities such as character, intellect and emotional richness. Outer beauty is momentary, diminishes or fades with time making the idea of judging by appearance misleading or deceptive. Further, it points that since God looks at your internal beauty, he accepts you unconditionally.

Thus, Auden emphasises the notion that beauty is not merely a fixed attribute but rather a multifaceted experience shaped by individual perceptions and emotions.

6. Both the texts, 'For Anne Gregory' and 'The Sermon at Benares', grapple with the idea that external attributes are fleeting and subject to decay. Examine the similarities. **CBSE SQP 2024**

Ans. Both 'Anne Gregory' and 'The Sermon at Benares' confront the short-lived nature of external attributes. In the poem, the speaker's shifting perception of Anne's beauty, from cherishing her hair and face to valuing her inner qualities, highlights the transient nature of physical appearance.

Similarly, in 'The Sermon at Benares', the Buddha's teachings emphasise the inevitability of death and the impermanence of life, urging listeners to recognise the fleeting nature of existence. Both texts suggest that external attributes, whether beauty or life itself, are fleeting and subject to decay, prompting contemplation of deeper truths beyond the surface. This highlights the significance of internal beauty and internal aspects of human self.

ASSESSMENT EXERCISE

Extract Based Questions

Read the following extract carefully and answer the questions that follow.

"But I can get a hair-dye
And set such colour there,
That young men in despair
Brown, or black, or carrot,
May love me for myself alone
And not my yellow hair."

(i) Which of the following tones is being used by the author in the above extract?

1. Reflective
2. Irritated
3. Quarrelsome
4. Insulting
5. Commanding

(ii) What does Anne want in reality?

(a) Someone who loves her for her real self
(b) Avoid people who are drawn to her outer beauty
(c) To live alone
(d) To find a suitable life partner

(iii) What colour is Anne's hair?

(iv) Complete the following analogy about the men in the above extract.

Hope : Despair :: Old : ....

Short Answer (SA) Type Questions

1. What did the old religious man find in the text?
2. Does the love that Anne gets from young men make her happy? Justify your answer.
3. Why are young men not able to look at Anne's internal beauty?

Long Answer (LA) Type Question

1. Do you think that the love felt for someone's physical appearance is not pure and true? Write your answer reflecting on the poem 'For Anne Gregory'.

Competency Based

Section C : Literature
Textbook : Footprints Without Feet *(Supplementary)*

A Triumph of Surgery

by James Herriot

'A Triumph of Surgery' by James Herriot is a story about a pampered dog Tricki and how he recovers from his illness. Tricki is overfed by his rich owner and falls ill. He is, then, taken by the author for treatment. The story presents Tricki's journey to recovery without any actual surgery.

Tricki Looks Ill

When Dr. James was driving, he saw Mrs. Pumphrey and Tricki walking down the street. As he stopped his car, he was shocked to see that Tricki had become very fat like a sausage. His eyes were red and his tongue was hanging out. It looked like Tricki lacked energy and was ill. So, Dr. James enquired about Tricki's health from Mrs. Pumphrey.

Dr. James Enquires about Tricki

Mrs. Pumphrey explained to Dr. James that Tricki was looking weak and ill. She felt that he was suffering from malnutrition. So, she had been giving him some extra food (malt, cod-liver oil and horlicks) between his main meals. Hearing this, Dr. James asked Mrs. Pumphrey whether she had cut down the sweet things from Tricki's diet. Mrs. Pumphrey replied that she had tried but failed as Tricki used to love cream cakes and chocolates.

Dr. James knew that Tricki was greedy and had not refused any food given to him. So, he further asked if Tricki had been exercising. To this, Mrs. Pumphrey answered that Tricki only walked with her and did not play games like ring-throwing which he played earlier.

Dr. James Advice

After knowing about Tricki's condition and his routine, Dr. James seriously informed Mrs. Pumphrey that if she would not reduce his food and increase his exercise, her dog would fall ill. He also advised her to strictly follow the prescribed diet. Mrs. Pumphrey confessed that it would be very difficult for her. However, she agreed to try and walked off with Tricki.

Dr. James looked at Tricki and knew that Tricki was pampered. So, he also knew that he would receive a call about Tricki's health from Mrs. Pumphrey soon.

Dr. James Receives the Expected Call

After a few days, Mrs. Pumphrey called and informed Dr. James about Tricki's health. She told him that Tricki was not eating anything and had been vomiting. She, further, informed him that her dog spent all his time lying on a rug and did not do anything.

Dr. James knew that the only way to cure Tricki was to get him out of the house for some time. He suggested Mrs. Pumphrey to hospitalise Tricki for a fortnight for his proper treatment.

Tricki's Farewell

Dr. James' suggestion broke Mrs. Pumphrey's heart but, she allowed him to take Tricki along with him to his clinic. Dr. James carried Tricki, who was wrapped in a blanket, to his car. The maids started to put together things that Tricki would need during hospitalisation. These included his beds (day and night), cushions, toys, bowls, coats, etc.

Dr. James started to drive off as he knew that his car could not carry so many things. As he drove off, he noticed in the mirror that everybody was in tears.

Tricki's Stay and Recovery

When Dr. James reached his clinic, all other dogs surrounded him. Tricki looked at them and as he was put down, he laid motionless on the carpet. Many other dogs in the hospital sniffed him, found him uninterested and went off. Tricki was put on a water diet for first two days. At the end of the second day, Tricki started to show some interest in his surroundings. On the third day, he made a low sound when he heard other dogs. On that day, as Dr. James opened the door, Tricki went out to the greyhound (a dog) and his friends in the garden. He followed the dogs wherever they went.

Later that day, when food was served and all dogs had eaten their food, Tricki came near the bowls and licked some of them. Next day, a different bowl was placed for Tricki.

Tricki's Recovery

Tricki recovered at a very fast pace. No medicine had been given to Tricki for his treatment. However, he had started running all day long and enjoyed with other dogs. He played with other dogs and became a part of the pack of dogs at the hospital. He not only fought with them for food but also chased rats with them at night.

Mrs. Pumphrey's Concern

As Tricki was recovering, Mrs. Pumphrey used to phone the vet's clinic several times in a day as she was keen to know about Tricky's recovery. Dr. James did not pay much attention to her questions about Tricki's comforts, but he assured her that Tricki was out of danger.

Hearing that Tricki's health was improving, Mrs. Pumphrey started sending food items, like eggs, wine and brandy for Tricki. Since this was not required for Tricki's diet, the vet and his partner consumed those items themselves. They ate eggs in the morning, drank wine in the afternoon and brandy at night.

Everybody was so happy with the unusual delicious food that they wanted to keep Tricki as a permanent guest.

Tricki Goes Home

Dr. James knew that Mrs. Pumphrey loved Tricki very much so he called and informed her that Tricki was fit and could go home. Mrs. Pumphrey reached the surgery within half an hour and enquired about Tricki's actual condition.

Dr. James informed her that Tricki was fine and went to get Tricki from the garden. Tricki had become healthy and strong in his two weeks stay at the clinic.

As soon as the dog saw his owner, he jumped into her lap and started licking her face. Mrs. Pumphrey was very happy at finding Tricki as excited as he used to be. She thanked Dr. James Herriot and called the treatment 'A triumph of surgery'.

Word Meaning

Word	Meaning
pampered	spoilt
mistress	owner
bloated	full of food or gas and therefore bigger than normal in a way that is unpleasant and uncomfortable
rheumy	watery
lolled	to hang out loosely
hastened	to say or do things quickly without delay
malt	grain, usually left in water for a period of time and then dried, used for making beer, whisky etc
relent	to agree upon something after refusing
severe	serious
wrung	joined
regime	schedule
dropping	bending

Word	Meaning
harness	a rope tied around an animal's neck to control its movements
tottering	to walk or move with weak unsteady steps
distraught	extremely worried
fortnight	A period of 2 weeks
pine	cry
firm	strict
wailings	loud cries
roused	woken up
swooned	to become unconscious
despairing	the feeling of having lost all hope
gasping	taking short breaths of air
whimper	a low weak cry a person or an animal makes when hurt, frightened or sad

Word	Meaning
slopped	to make liquid or food come out of a container in an untidy way
scrimmages	rough or confused struggle
tramped on	stepped on
squashed	crushed
hovered	stayed
convalescing	recovering from an illness, to spend time getting your health and strength back after an illness

Word	Meaning
reverently	leisurely
sustained by	followed by
compelled	forced to
gleaming	shining
clasped	joined
trembled	shook
lithe	flexible (moving or bending easily in a way that is elegant)

NCERT FOLDER

NCERT Intext and Exercise Questions

READ AND FIND OUT (NCERT PAGE 1)

Q.1 Why is Mrs. Pumphrey worried about Tricki?

Ans. Mrs. Pumphrey is worried about Tricki because she feels that he is suffering from a serious health issue such as malnutrition as he has become dull and seems to have no energy.

Q.2 What does she do to help him? Is she wise in this?

Ans. To help Tricki in improving his condition, Mrs. Pumphrey started giving him extra food like malt, cod-liver oil and horlicks, in between his main meals. She also continued to give him sweets like cream cakes and chocolates.

She was not wise in doing so because overfeeding Tricki was worsening his condition instead of improving it. It made him very fat and lazy.

Q.3 Who does 'I' refer to in this story?

Ans. 'I' refers to the narrator, Dr. James Herriot, a veterinary doctor who guides Mrs. Pumphrey in taking care of her dog, Tricki.

READ AND FIND OUT (NCERT PAGE 3)

Q.1 Is the narrator as rich as Tricki's mistress?

Ans. No, the narrator is not as rich as Tricki's mistress, Mrs. Pumphery. We can say so because the narrator seems fascinated by how much Mrs. Pumphrey spends on the well-being and maintenance of her pet. He is unusually surprised by the enriching items she sends for Tricki as he cannot afford them for himself.

Q.2 How does he treat the dog?

Ans. James Herriot treats Tricki just like he would treat an overweight and lazy dog. He cuts down his food and keeps him under strict observation for the initial days at the hospital. He gradually increases Tricki's food and sets him free for physical activities to improve his health.

Q.3 Why is he tempted to keep Tricki on as a permanent guest?

Or

Why is Dr. Herriot tempted to keep Tricki on as a permanent guest? **CBSE 2023**

Ans. James Herriot is tempted to keep Tricki on as a permanent guest because of the good food and wine he is enjoying in Tricki's name. He does not want to lose the luxurious inflow of fresh eggs, wine and brandy that Tricki's mistress, Mrs. Pumphrey, sends for her dog.

Q.4 Why does Mrs. Pumphrey think the dog's recovery is 'a triumph of surgery'? **CBSE 2025**

Ans. Mrs. Pumphrey thinks that Tricki's recovery is 'a triumph of surgery' because according to her, his illness was very serious. She was of the opinion that there were very few chances of Tricki's improvement and he needed immediate medical attention. Thus, Tricki's revival was a great achievement.

THINK ABOUT IT (NCERT PAGE 6)

Q.1 What kind of a person do you think the narrator, a veterinary surgeon, is? Would you say he is tactful as well as full of common sense?

Ans. The narrator, a veterinary surgeon, is a capable and wise doctor. He handles Tricki properly which shows that he is sincere about his profession. He does not operate upon the dog unnecessarily and cures him by changing his diet and activities.

He is a tactful person as he knew exactly how to convince Mrs. Pumphrey to hospitalise Tricki for a surgery. His decision to inform Mrs. Pumphrey to take Tricki home supports his sensibilities even though he was tempted to keep Tricki as a permanent guest.

Q.2 Do you think Tricki was happy to go home? What do you think will happen now?

Ans. Yes, I think Tricki was happy to go back home as he really loved his mistress and the comfort of his lavish life. He didn't have any friends at home like in the hospital but he was excited at the sight of Mrs. Pumphrey.

I think that Mrs. Pumphrey will now be careful about Tricki's diet and health. She may also give him exercise daily as prescribed by the veterinary doctor earlier.

Q.3 Do you think it is a real-life episode or mere fiction? Or is it a mixture of both?

Ans. The story seems to be a mixture of both. It is possible for rich people to overfeed their pets due to love. It is also not unusual for them to maintain a big wardrobe for them either.

However, it is unlikely for a veterinary doctor to go out of the way in order to save an animal. It is also unusual for anyone to consume food which is given in the name of a pet's health.

TALK ABOUT IT (NCERT PAGE 7)

Q.1 This episode describes the silly behaviour of a rich woman who is foolishly indulgent, perhaps because she is lonely. Do you think such people are merely silly or can their actions cause harm to others?

Ans. Mrs. Pumphreys's silly behaviour of being foolishly indulgent with her dog Tricki, most probably rises out of her loneliness. She treats Tricki like a child. She not only dresses him up according to the weather but also pampers him.

Such actions of Mrs. Pumphrey are not only silly, but also cause harm to others. Because of her over pampering, Tricki's condition gets worsened and he needs to be hospitalised to be kept away from her.

Q.2 Do you think there are also parents like Mrs. Pumphrey?

Ans. Yes, I think there are some parents like Mrs. Pumphrey who spoil their children by over-pampering them. They overfeed their children/pets despite being aware of its harmful effects on their health. They regret only when things get worse.

Q.3 What would you have done if you were

(i) a member of the staff in Mrs. Pumphrey's household.

(ii) a neighbour?

What would your life have been like, in general?

Ans. (i) If I were a member of the staff in Mrs. Pumphrey's household, I would have not followed her command to feed Tricki blindly. Infact, I would have fed him according to the vet's advice. I would have also skipped sending the unnecessary stuff like toys, cushions, etc, to the hospital. My life would have been a very busy one as I would have had to take care of the household chores and meet Tricki's demands on time.

(ii) If I were Mrs. Pumphrey's neighbour, I would have advised her to consult a vet and follow his advice strictly keeping in mind Tricki's deteriorating health. I would have also been supportive in their hard time when Tricki was hospitalised. My life as Mrs. Pumphrey's neighbour would have been full of surprises and gifts as Mrs. Pumphrey was a loving lady.

Q.4 What would you have done if you were in the narrator's place?

Ans. If I were in the narrator's place, I would have treated Tricki with a similar amount of compassion and love. I would have been equally caring towards Tricki as Dr. James Herriot. I would have just been a little more serious while advising Mrs. Pumphrey to put Tricki on a strict diet knowing her way of showing love. I would have also not consumed Tricki's share of eggs, wine and brandy sent by Mrs. Pumphrey.

REVIEW EXERCISE

Including Competency Based Questions

Part - I

Multiple Choice Questions

1. Initially, Dr. Herriot described Tricki as hugely fat and compared him to a ....

(a) bloated sausage (b) hamburger
(c) pizza (d) doughnut

Ans. (a) bloated sausage

2. Mrs. Pumphrey thought that Tricki was suffering from

(a) stomach ache (b) lung infection
(c) eye infection (d) malnutrition

Ans. (d) malnutrition

3. "And did you cut down on the sweet things that I told you?"
The above statement was spoken by

(a) Mrs. Pumphrey (b) Hodgkin
(c) Mrs. Pumphrey's maid (d) Dr. Herriot

Ans. (d) Dr. Herriot

4. According to the narrator, Tricki's only fault was ....

(a) laziness (b) hyperactiveness
(c) grumpiness (d) greed

Ans. (d) greed

5. Arrange the sequence of events in the correct order in the context of 'Triumph of Surgery'.

1. Tricki is hospitalised
2. Dr. Herriot meets Tricki and his mistress on the way
3. Dr. Herriot advises Tricki's mistress to reduce his diet
4. Tricki's mistress calls Dr. Herriot

(a) 1, 2, 3, 4 (b) 4, 3, 2, 1
(c) 2, 4, 3, 1 (d) 2, 3, 4, 1

Ans. (d) 2, 3, 4, 1

6. What were the symptoms of Tricki before he was admitted to the hospital?

1. He would eat only once a day
2. He would not eat anything
3. He would eat only his favourite dishes
4. He had bouts of vomiting

(a) 1 and 4 (b) 2 and 4 (c) 3 and 4 (d) 1 and 3

Ans. (b) 2 and 4

7. What might the atmosphere of the household when Tricki was taken to the hospital signify?

(a) Mrs. Pumphrey's status in society reflected in Tricki's lifestyle
(b) The staff's love for Tricki matched that of Mrs. Pumphrey
(c) The grand life of comforts and luxuries that Tricki enjoyed
(d) Mrs. Pumphrey's indulgence and anxiety acted upon by the staff

Ans. (b) The staff's love for Tricki matched that of Mrs. Pumphrey

8. ....maids rushed in and out bringing his day bed, his night bed, favourite cushions, toys and rubber rings, breakfast bowl, lunch bowl, supper bowl.

Mr. Herriot gives the above description in the story 'A Triumph of Surgery' to show how ....

(a) spoilt and pampered Tricki was
(b) difficult it was to keep Tricki healthy
(c) privileged and rich Mrs. Pumphrey was
(d) important Mrs. Pumphrey was as a client

Ans. (a) spoilt and pampered Tricki was

9. The narrator describes Tricki as a 'pathetic little animal'. The use of the word 'pathetic' indicates that the narrator

(a) was very fond of Tricki
(b) thought Tricki was contemptible
(c) pitied Tricki's condition
(d) believed Tricki's health was deteriorating

Ans. (c) pitied Tricki's condition

10. What type of questions did Dr. Herriot avoid when Tricki was hospitalised?

(a) Whether Tricki was out of danger
(b) Whether Triki's cushions were being formed regularly
(c) Whether Tricki had worn the correct coat according to the weather
(d) Both (b) and (c)

Ans. (d) Both (b) and (c)

11. What did Mrs. Pumphrey bring at first when Tricki was hospitalised?

(a) Two dozen stale eggs (b) Two dozen fresh eggs
(c) Four dozen fresh eggs (d) Three dozen stale eggs

Ans. (b) Two dozen fresh eggs

12. It was a temptation to keep Tricki on as a permanent guest,...
Why did Mr. Herriot not give in to the temptation to keep Tricki at the surgery in 'A Triumph of Surgery'?

(a) He could not afford to take care of Tricki
(b) He felt Tricki would be unhappy at the surgery
(c) He knew Mrs. Pumphrey was miserable without Tricki
(d) He continued feasting on items Mrs. Pumphrey sent for Tricki

Ans. (c) He knew Mrs. Pumphrey was miserable without Tricki

13. Which of the following statements are correct in reference to the story 'A Triumph of Surgery'?

(i) Tricki, the dog, had become extremely thin and fit after his stay at the hospital
(ii) Mrs. Pumphrey did not feed Tricki properly before and hence, sent eggs for him at the hospital
(iii) The other dogs at the hospital befriended Tricki after he got better
(iv) Mrs. Pumphrey brought the other dogs home along with Tricki
(v) Dr. Herriot didn't let Tricki consume any eggs and wine that was sent by Mrs. Pumphrey

(a) (i) and (iv) (b) (iii) and (v)
(c) (ii), (iii) and (iv) (d) (i) and (v)

Ans. (b) (iii) and (v)

14. For Tricky's Present condition

(A) Both Mrs. Pumphrey and Tricky are to blame.
(B) Only Tricky is to blame. **CBSE SQP 2021 Term 1**

(a) (A) is right and (B) is wrong
(b) (B) is right and (A) is wrong
(c) Both (A) and (B) are right
(d) Both (A) and (B) are wrong

Ans. (a) (A) is right and (B) is wrong

15. What does the exclamation, 'This is a triumph of surgery' by Mrs. Pumphrey, mean? **CBSE 2021 Term 1**

(a) The surgery was successful
(b) The mistress could take back her pet
(c) The doctor was a great veterinarian
(d) The planned venture was fruitful

Ans. (d) The planned venture was fruitful

16. Read the statements given below and choose the correct option.

Statement 1 Tricki was loved by Dr. Herriot's team for the dog was lovable.

Statement 2 Mrs. Pumphrey was in awe of the activeness of her dog.

(a) Statement 1 is true but Statement 2 is false
(b) Statement 2 is true but Statement 1 is false
(c) Both the statements are true
(d) Both the statements are false

Ans. (b) Statement 2 is true but Statement 1 is false

Extract Based Questions

1. Read the following extract carefully and answer the questions that follow.

I was really worried about Tricki this time. I had pulled up my car when I saw him in the street with his mistress and I was shocked at his appearance. He had become hugely fat, like a heated sausage with a leg at each corner. His eyes bloodshot and rheumy, stared straight ahead and his tongue lolled from his jaws.

(i) State the present condition of Tricki.

Ans. Tricki had become very fat with red eyes and tongue out.

(ii) The statement that is true according to the passage is

(a) The narrator was a surgeon
(b) The narrator was worried for Tricki
(c) Tricki's mistress had been keeping him on a diet
(d) Tricki looked like he was suffering from malnutrition

Ans. (b) The narrator was worried for Tricki

(iii) Tricki had become very fat, looking like a sausage with a leg at each corner. Elaborate on the events that had let up to this situation.

Ans. When the doctor saw Tricki in such an unhealthy state, he enquired Mrs. Pumphrey about what led to it. She told him that Tricki looked so dull and weak that he gave him extra food between meals. Further, she tried to cut down on sweets, as suggested by the doctor, but failed because Tricki loved them.

(iv) Fill in the blank with the correct phrase/word from the bracket.

I had .... (to stop/to wait) my car when I saw him.

Ans. to stop

2. Read the following extract carefully and answer the questions that follow.

The expected call came within a few days. Mrs. Pumphrey was distraught. Tricki would eat nothing. Refused even his favourite dishes; and besides, he had bouts of vomiting. He spent all his time lying on a rug, panting. Didn't want to go for walks, didn't want to do anything.

I had made my plans in advance. The only way was to get Tricki out of the house for a period. I suggested that he be hospitalised for about a fortnight to be kept under observation. **CBSE 2024**

(i) Which of the following is not a reason why Mr. Herriot thinks Tricki needs to be taken out of the house for a period? **Competency Based**

(a) He wanted to keep Tricki away from Mrs. Pumphrey
(b) He wanted to keep Tricki under observation
(c) He wanted to do an experiment on Tricki
(d) He wanted to improve Tricki's health

Ans. (c) He wanted to do an experiment on Tricki

(ii) What was the main reason for Mrs. Pumphrey to be distraught? Answer in about 40 words.

Ans. Mrs. Pumphrey was worried and distraught because Tricki, her beloved dog, would not eat anything. It even refused to eat its favourite dishes and had bouts of vomiting. He was laying on his rug while breathing heavily. Further, he refused to do anything.

(iii) State True or False.

When Mr. Herriot says, "I had made my plans in advance" — what he actually means is, he had already seen this trauma coming foor Tricki.

Ans. True

(iv) Which of the following best describes Mrs. Pumphery?

(a) Unkind and inconsiderate
(b) Impractical but compassionate
(c) Anxious and ambitious
(d) Fearful but confident

Ans. (b) Impractical but compassionate

3. Read the following extract carefully and answer the questions that follow.

I marched out to the car carrying the little dog wrapped in a blanket.

The entire staff was roused and maids rushed in and out bringing his day bed, his night bed, favourite cushions, toys and rubber rings, breakfast bowl, lunch bowl, supper bowl.

(i) Complete the sentence appropriately.
In the above extract, 'his' refers to

Ans. Tricki

(ii) The staff was carrying out his things because

(a) he was getting hospitalised
(b) he was going to the park
(c) he was going to the mall
(d) he was going on a trip

Ans. (a) he was getting hospitalised.

(iii) Who carried the little dog wrapped in a blanket? Why?

Ans. Dr. James Herriot carried the little dog wrapped in a blanket. He did so because he needed to separate the dog from his owner for some time to treat Tricki's inactivity and greed for food.

(iv) Complete the analogy by selecting the suitable word from the text.
Right : Wrong :: Partial : ....

Ans. Entire

4. Read the following extract carefully and answer the questions that follow.

As I moved off, Mrs. Pumphrey, with a despairing cry, threw an armful of the little coats through the window. I looked in the mirror before I turned the corner of the drive, everybody was in tears. Out on the road, I glanced down at the pathetic little animal gasping on the seat by my side.

I patted the head and Tricki made a brave effort to wag his tail.

(i) Why was Tricki sent to the hospital?

(a) Because Tricki refused to eat anything
(b) Because Mrs. Pumphrey was worried about Tricki's health
(c) Because Tricki had bouts of vomiting
(d) All of the above

Ans. (d) All of the above

(ii) The extract uses the phrase 'with a despairing cry'. Which of the following expressions is incorrect with respect to the word 'despairing'?

(a) Thought (b) Times (c) Expression (d) Month

Ans. (d) Month

(iii) Tricki is called 'pathetic little animal'. Do you agree?

Ans. Yes, Tricki is a pathetic little animal whose owner pampered and over-fed him. As a result, he had become fat and lazy. He also got ill and Dr. James had to separate him from his mistress.

(iv) Why was everybody in tears?

Ans. Everybody was in tears because Tricki was being hospitalised.

5. **Read the following extract carefully and answer the questions that follow.**

He discovered the joys of being bowled over, tramped on and squashed every few minutes. He became an accepted member of the gang, an unlikely, silky little object among the shaggy crew, fighting like a tiger for his share at mealtimes and hunting rats in the old henhouse at night. He had never had such a time in his life. All the while, Mrs. Pumphrey hovered anxiously in the background, ringing a dozen times a day for the latest bulletins. **CBSE Question Bank 2021 Modified**

(i) **Why does the narrator describe being 'tramped on and squashed' as joys?**

(a) To suggest the irony about the strange ways of dogs.

(b) To mention the simple pleasures of canine life.

(c) To compare it to Tricki's earlier play-time at the house.

(d) To direct attention towards Tricki's successful recovery.

Ans. (b) To mention the simple pleasures of canine life.

(ii) **Pick the option that reveals Tricki's characteristics in the context of "fighting like a tiger for his share at mealtimes and hunting rats in the old henhouse at night."**

1. Selfish
2. Happy
3. Greedy
4. Confident
5. Sturdy
6. Cruel

Ans. Happy, Confident and Sturdy

(iii) **What does the phrase 'ringing a dozen times for the latest bulletins' mean?**

Ans. The phrase means that Mrs. Pumphrey used to call the narrator several times in a day to ask the latest news about Tricki.

(iv) **What does the reference to Tricki as a 'silky little object' signify?**

Ans. The reference to Tricki as a 'silky little object' signifies that Tricki had lived a life of luxury unlike other dogs at the clinic.

6. **Read the following extract carefully and answer the questions that follow.**

The word 'convalescing' seemed to do something to Mrs. Pumphrey. She started to bring round fresh eggs, two dozen at a time, to build up Tricki's strength. For a happy period my partners and I had two eggs each for break fast, but when the bottles of wine began to arrive, the real possibilities of the situation began to dawn on the household.

(i) **State any one inference about Mrs. Pumphrey from the given extract.**

Ans. It can be inferred from the given extract that Mrs. Pumphrey was very attached to her dog, Tricki. She loved him a lot, which is why she became very worried when he fell sick.

(ii) **State True or False.**

None of the terms (a) - (d) can be applied to the statement - She started to bring round fresh eggs, two dozen at a time, to build up Tricki's strength.

(a) A hypothesis - a proposed explanation for a phenomenon

(b) An assumption - something that is taken for granted or assumed to be true

(c) A hyperbole - exaggerated statements or claims not meant to be taken literally

(d) A premise - a proposition that forms the basis of an argument

Ans. True, the given statement is not a hypothesis, an assumption, a hyperbole or a premise.

(iii) **Mrs. Pumphrey reaction to the word 'convalescing' proved to be beneficial for the narrator. Elaborate with reference to the extract.** **Competency Based**

Ans. Her immediate reaction to hearing the word 'convalescing' was to send more food for him to build strength. This food and later, wine and brandy were also consumed by the vet and his partners. Thus, they benefitted from having Tricki in their clinic and were tempted to keep him permanently.

(iv) **Which phrase would correctly substitute 'convalescing' in the given sentence from the extract?**

The word 'convalescing' seemed to do something to Mrs. Pumphrey.

Ans. getting better

Part - II

Short Answer Type Questions

1. **Why was Dr. Herriot really worried about Tricki?**

Or **Why was Mr. Herriot shocked at Tricki's appearence?** **CBSE 2023**

Ans. Dr. Herriot was really worried about Tricki's health. When he saw the dog with his mistress, Mrs. Pumphrey, he was shocked at his appearence.

The dog had become hugely fat. His eyes were red and his tongue was hanging out. Such a miserable condition of the dog really worried the surgeon.

2. What 'extra' did Mrs. Pumphrey start to give Tricki and why?

Ans. Mrs. Pumphrey thought that Tricki was suffering from malnutrition as he was weak and dull. So, she started to give him extra food like cod-liver oil and malt between the main meals and horlicks after dinner to make him sleep. She also gave him cream cakes and chocolates.

3. What was the only fault of Tricki as diagnosed by Dr. Herriot? Why did he say so?

Or **What was the major flaw in Tricki?** CBSE 2020

Ans. Dr. Herriot diagnosed that the only fault of Tricki for his health condition was his greed for food.
The surgeon says so because he knew that the pampering of Tricki's owner, Mrs. Pumphrey created problems for the dog.

4. "You must harden your heart and help him in a strict diet." Why does Mr. Herriot suggest this to Mrs. Pumphrey? Competency Based

Ans. Mr. Herriot suggested Mrs. Pumphrey to be strict with Tricki because he knew about Mrs. Pumphrey's love for her pet. The surgeon is aware that even though she tries to follow the diet prescribed for Tricki, she would be unable to refuse anything. Her love and care had harmed her dog and thus, Dr. Herriot suggests Mrs. Pumphrey to reduce his diet.

5. What was Mr. Herriot's strict advice? Did Mrs. Pumphrey agree to his advice? CBSE 2023

Ans. Mr. Herriot's strict advice was to cut down all the extra food that Mrs. Pumphrey gave to Tricki and to make him exercise. Mrs. Pumphrey agreed to follow the advice. However, she accepted that it is very difficult for her to do so because Tricki looked ill to her.

6. What excuses did Mrs. Pumphrey make about Dr. Herriot's advice? CBSE 2023

Ans. Dr. Herriot's advice was to cut down on the sweet things and to make Tricki do plenty of exercise. However, Mrs. Pumphrey thought Tricki was weak. So, she gave him cream cakes and chocolates.

7. What made James Herriot expect a call from Mrs. Pumphrey?

Ans. James Herriot's encounter with Mrs. Pumphrey and Tricki's condition made him expect a call for help.
He was sure that the extra diet and no physical activity would soon put Tricki's health in danger.

8. How did Mrs. Pumphrey and her servants behave when Tricki was being taken away to the surgery?

Ans. Mrs. Pumphrey started crying upon realising that Tricki was being taken away to the surgery. All the servants were woken up. They rushed in and out carrying all the things that Tricki would need after hospitalisation. These things included beds, cushions, toys, bowls, coats, etc.

9. How can you say that it was hard for Mrs. Pumphrey to part with her doting pet?

Ans. It was hard for Mrs. Pumphrey to part with her doting pet because Tricki was like her child. She loved him very much and would do everything to please her dog.
So, when the surgeon suggested its hospitalisation, it was a terrible and tearful moment for her. However, she agreed for the betterment of her pet.

10. How do you know that Tricki had an affluent life? How did Mrs. Pumphrey treat Tricki? CBSE 2023

Ans. We know that Tricki had an affluent life because he was a loved and pampered pet of a wealthy owner,
Mrs. Pumphrey. Mrs. Pumphrey made sure that her pet had everything he may need or require. He not only had a complete wardrobe of coats but also separate bowls for food. He also had many toys, cushions and rubber rings. All these luxury items show that he lived a well-off life.

11. What kind of treatment was given to Tricki? Did it help in his recovery?

Or **" I think I know a cure for you." What was the 'cure' given to Tricki?** Competency Based

Ans. Tricki was given a non-medicinal treatment.
His diet was changed according to his body's response to it. He was kept on water for the first two days and then, his diet was gradually increased.

Yes, this treatment did help Tricki as it built up energy in him and transformed him into an energetic dog in just a fortnight.

12. Do you think Tricki was enjoying his stay at the hospital?

Ans. Yes, Tricki was definitely enjoying his stay at the hospital.
He had befriended the gang of hairy household dogs.
He had found a new joy in being bowled over (pushed), trampled on and squashed. He had also become very energetic. He used to play and run all day long with the dogs. He was having a great time.

13. Briefly describe Herriot's days of content.

Or **What was the impact of the goodies that came for Tricki during his convalescence, on the household?** CBSE Additional SQP 2023

Ans. The impact of the goodies that came for Tricki during his convalescence was that the people in the household enjoyed a period of indulgence and luxurious living.
The household members, including the doctor and his partners, enjoyed the extra eggs, wine, and brandy.
It added a sense of festivity to their daily routines, with

lunch becoming a ceremonial occasion and evenings by the fire becoming more enjoyable.

14. Why is Mrs. Pumphrey responsible for Tricki's condition? CBSE 2020

Ans. Mrs. Pumphrey was responsible for Tricki's condition because of her overindulgent behaviour. She did not cut down on Tricki's food and did not provide him with proper exercises, even after Tricki's doctor's advice. Instead, she used to feed him extra food as she felt that Tricki was suffering from malnutrition. As a result, Tricki's condition deteriorated.

15. "Tricki's only fault was greed", says the narrator. What might be Mrs. Pumphrey's 'only fault'? CBSE Question Bank 2021

Ans Mrs. Pumphrey's only fault was her affluence and over caring nature. She had provided luxurious things to Tricki that replaced his actual needs and made him ill and obese.

16. Was Tricki suffering from any ailment in reality? If not, then what made him inactive and lethargic?

Ans. No, Tricki was not suffering from any ailment. What made him inactive and lethargic was his greed for food and the love of his mistress that spoilt his health to such an extent. He was being overfed everyday and that made him fat and lazy.

17. What do you think would happen to Tricki after he went back to Mrs. Pumphrey? CBSE Question Bank 2021

Ans. I think that Tricki would again be over-pampered by Mrs. Pumphrey. He might develop the same health issues gradually because Mrs. Pumphrey was not aware of the actual treatment given to him.

18. Do you think the narrator's decision to not reveal the actual treatment to Mrs. Pumphrey was unprofessional? Justify your stance.

Ans. I think the narrator's decision of not revealing the actual treatment was not unprofessional. Mr. Herriot knew that Mrs. Pumphrey would never allow him to keep the dog on fasting which was the only and natural treatment to save the dog.

19. 'Privilege often confuses actual needs for perceived ones.' Evaluate this statement with reference to Mrs. Pumphrey. CBSE Question Bank 2021

Ans. Everyone knows that animals do not need silk clothes, playful toys, and various utensils to stay happy. But Mrs. Pumphrey had provided these privileges to an animal. Being a pet to a rich lady, these luxuries replaced the dog's actual needs and made him ill and dull.

20. Dr. Herriot knew his patients as well as their owners really well. Discuss. CBSE SQP 2023

Ans. It is true to say that Dr. Herriot knew his patients and their owners pretty well. We can say so because his worry for Tricki and the knowledge that Tricki was greedy displays that he knew the dog really well. Further, Dr. Herriot could also understand Mrs. Pumphrey's love and care for her dog. So, he never became rude or angry at her.

21. According to a popular quote— where there is no struggle, there is no strength. In what way is this quote relevant to the events of the story? Competency Based

Ans. The given quote is quite relevant to the events of the story. The beginning of the story proved that Tricki was dull because he did not struggle to digest his food. In the later part of the lesson, Dr. Herriot helped the dog to regain his strength by involving him in regular exercise and food regime. Food without exercise can lead to disease and discomfort for everyone.

22. The story, A Triumph of Surgery is a powerful example of the importance of saying "no". Explain.

Ans. It is true to say that 'A Triumph of Surgery' is a powerful example of the importance of saying 'no'. In the story, the dog Tricki suffers from obesity and laziness because his owner, Mrs. Pumphrey could not refuse to give food to her beloved pet. She not only feeds him sweets but also does not take him out for much exercise. As a result, Tricki needs to be hospitalised for treatment.
The story, thus, highlights the fact that sometimes, the best way to help someone is to say no and steer them towards a better path, even if it may be uncomfortable or unpopular at the moment.

Long Answer Type Questions

1. Excess of everything is bad. Comment in the wake of Mrs. Pumphrey's love for Tricki.

Or Mrs. Pumphrey, the overindulgent and caring mistress of Tricki, pampers her pet dog like a spoiled child. Comment. CBSE 2020

Based on 'A Triumph of Surgery', state how Mrs. Pumphrey did more harm than good to Tricki? CBSE Additional Paper 2023

Ans. It is true that excess of everything is bad. It does more harm than good. This fact has aptly been justified in the story 'A Triumph of Surgery' wherein Mrs. Pumphrey, a rich lady overpampers her dog, Tricki. She wants Tricki to live as luxuriously as her. To make sure that her dog lives a lavish life, she not only makes sure that Tricki has everything but also fulfils his greed. Her love and care for Tricki makes her overfeed him. She feeds him extra food in between his main meals and does not reduce sweets like cream cakes and chocolates.

In her love for Tricki, she never realised that Tricki was a greedy dog and her over-caring nature would harm him. Even though the surgeon prescribes her a diet for Tricki, she was not able to follow it. Consequently, Tricki's condition gets worse. He becomes lazy, inactive and very fat.

Tricki's excessive diet spoilt his health to such an extent that he had to be hospitalised. Mrs. Pumphrey's fondness and care for Tricki leads her to provide excess food for her dog, even in the hospital. This shows that excess of everything can be harmful.

2. Dr. James Herriot was a competent veterinary surgeon. His practical approach and common sense helped in the rapid recovery of Tricki. Comment.

***Or* Pen down incidences in support of values one should inculcate from Dr.James Herriot.**

Ans. Dr. James Herriot was a capable veterinary surgeon who treated Tricki. He was a compassionate doctor and a wise as well as sympathetic human being. He showed his capabilities almost immediately when he advised Mrs. Pumphrey to put Tricki on a strict diet after understanding his symptoms.

Dr. Herriot was also an understanding and tactful person as he knew exactly how to free Tricki from the spoiling love of Mrs. Pumphrey. He does not operate upon the dog unnecessarily and adopted a practical approach to treat him. His method worked and soon Tricki was transformed into an energetic dog.

Dr. James was a caring and polite individual as he successfully tackles Mrs. Pumphrey's anxiety about Tricki's recovery patiently. Dr. Herriot was not only a sincere doctor but was also a good-natured man. He knew that the things sent by Mrs. Pumphrey could not be given to Tricki. So, without hurting her feelings, he kept the food items and consumed them on his own. Hence, one can inculcate the habits and characteristics of Dr. James Herriot as he was an animal lover and knew that over pampering could make any animal idle and dull. He loved his profession and treated his patient with due care and attention.

3. Do you think parents like Mrs. Pumphrey exist? If yes, is it a good thing to pamper children? Why or why not?

Ans. Yes, parents like Mrs. Pumphrey definitely exist. Such people spoil their children by making sure that all their demands are met. They not only feed them junk food but also spoil their social habits in the name of giving them love and care.

This kind of behaviour is very harmful for children. Such overprotective parental behaviour also hinders their growth as adults. In fact, it develops greed and dependency in them. They become stubborn and do not learn to value anything. For them, hard work is a myth as they get everything easily.

Over pampered children often fail to face the hardships of life later, as for them life has been simple. So, pampering children in moderation is healthy, but excess of it is harmful. It is not just bad for humans but also for animals, as we see in the story 'A Triumph of Surgery'.

4. Imagine that Mrs. Pumphrey from 'A Triumph of Surgery,' reflects upon her behaviour, learns from her mistakes, and writes a diary entry about the consequences of overindulgence. Write this diary entry as Mrs. Pumphrey in about 120 words.

Ans. 22nd May, 20XX, Friday 10:00 p.m.

Today, I had a dreadful realisation. I love my dear Tricki but I fear that that love has caused me to excessively indulge and pamper my dear pet. The sight of him, bloated and unhealthy, broke my heart.

I believed that showering him with treats and rich delicacies was a sign of care and would make him feel better. But instead, I was causing him more harm than good.

Thank goodness for Mr. Herriot. He aptly deduced that the reason for Tricki's decline in health was my lack of strict boundaries with Tricki. He advised me to cut down Tricki's food, make him exercise and provide a strict diet. When he noticed that I was not following his advice, he took Tricki away from me to take care of him. During Tricki's absence, I began to reflect upon my actions. I was still deeply worried about Tricki though, so I sent indulgent gifts to Mr. Herriot.

Old habits die hard, but I will try my best to be a better caretaker for Tricki now that he is back home. It brought me great joy to see Tricki transform into a healthy and happy dog after his stay with Mr. Herriot.

5. Evaluate how James Herriot's characterisation contributes significantly to the overarching theme of responsible pet ownership and animal welfare. CBSE SQP 2024

Ans. James Herriot's characterisation as a compassionate yet firm veterinary surgeon contributes significantly to the overarching theme of responsible pet ownership and animal welfare. Herriot's compassion towards animals is evident throughout the narrative. He genuinely cares about Tricki's well-being and is willing to go the extra mile to ensure the dog receives the care and attention it needs. This compassion is reflected in his interactions with Mrs. Pumphrey, where he patiently educates her about proper pet care and advocates for Tricki's health.

Herriot's firmness highlights his commitment to advocating for the best interests of the animals under his care. Despite Mrs. Pumphrey's initial reluctance to acknowledge Tricki's health issues, Herriot remains steadfast in his recommendations for dietary and lifestyle changes. His firm yet compassionate demeanour shows the importance of setting boundaries and making tough decisions for the well-being of pets. This aspect of Herriot's characterisation reinforces the theme of responsible pet ownership by emphasising the need for owners to prioritise their pets' health and welfare above personal indulgence.

ASSESSMENT EXERCISE

Extract Based Questions

Read the following extract carefully and answer the questions that follow.

It was a temptation to keep Tricki on as a permanent guest, but I knew Mrs. Pumphrey was suffering and after a fortnight, felt compelled to phone and tell her that the little dog had recovered and was awaiting collection.

(i) Why was it a temptation to keep Tricki as a permanent guest?

(a) Because Tricki's owner was not worried.

(b) Because Dr. Herriot and his partner did not want to loose the treat.

(c) Because Tricki's owner was sending eggs and bottles of wine for Tricki.

(d) Both (b) and (c)

(ii) Why was Mrs. Pumphrey suffering? Is it justified?

(iii) Fill in the blank appropriately.
Tricki was .... (loved/cared for) at Dr. Herriot's clinic.

(iv) What was informed to Mrs. Pumphrey on phone?

Short Answer (SA) Type Questions

1. Do you think Mrs. Pumphrey should have changed her way of caring for Tricki? Why or why not?
2. How did Mrs. Pumphrey show her concern for Tricki when he was at the surgery?
3. The title 'A Triumph of Surgery' is misleading. Do you agree? Justify.

Long Answer (LA) Type Questions

1. Relishing the eggs, wine and brandy that Mrs. Pumphrey sent for Tricki was not right on the part of Dr. James Herriot. It portrays him as a greedy and materialistic man. Do you agree? Give reasons in support of your answer. Also state the values you can draw from his character. **Competency Based**
2. Tricki was more than a dog. He was more like a member of the Pumphrey family. Elaborate.

The Thief's Story

by Ruskin Bond

CHAPTER SUMMARY The story 'The Thief's Story' by Ruskin Bond highlights how kindness, compassion and trust can change even criminals. In the story, a 15 year old thief named Hari Singh, undergoes a change when he meets Anil, a 25 year old writer. Anil's unspoken words and kind gestures leave a very positive impact on Hari Singh's life. He realised the importance of education and became a better man under Anil's company.

Hari Singh (The Narrator) Approaches Anil

The narrator, Hari met Anil when he was a 15 years old thief. Hari was an experienced thief. However, he had not been able to steal from anyone for some time. Hari approached Anil while he was watching a wrestling match. Anil was a tall, thin, easy going and simple type of man. So, Hari thought that Anil could be an easy target for him to rob.

Hari used some flattering words to gain Anil's confidence and soon, they started conversing. He lied to Anil that his name was Hari Singh. Hari had to change his name every month to hide himself from police and his previous employers. After this introduction, they talked about wrestlers and then, Anil walked away.

Hari Follows Anil

When Anil started to walk away, Hari followed him and told him that he wanted to work for him. To this, Anil expressed his inability to pay Hari. Then, Hari questioned Anil if he could feed him. Anil told Hari that he would employ him only if Hari knew how to cook. Hari lied that he knew how to cook and was employed.

Anil Brings Hari to his Room

Anil took Hari to his room which was located over Jumna Sweet Shop. He also told Hari that he could sleep in the balcony. That night Anil gave the food cooked by Hari to a stray dog because it tasted very bad.

Anil had realised that Hari didn't know how to cook. So, he asked Hari to leave but Hari stayed there and looked at Anil with his most appealing smile. Anil patted Hari's head and told him that he would teach him how to cook.

Anil Teaches Hari to Read and Write

Apart from cooking, Anil also taught Hari to write his name. He also promised to teach Hari how to write whole sentences and to add numbers. Hari was happy and grateful for getting educated as he knew that he could do anything once he could write like an educated man.

Hari enjoyed working for Anil. He made tea in the morning and later, would go to buy the day's supplies. He would also make a profit of a rupee which he knew Anil did not mind.

Anil's Work

Anil had no regular income. He made money by writing articles for the magazines. Sometimes, he would have enough money to celebrate and sometimes, he had to borrow money.

Hari Gained Anil's Trust

One evening, Anil came back with a bundle of currency notes which he had earned by selling his book to a publisher. At night, Anil put the money under his mattress and Hari noticed it. Hari had been working for Anil for almost a month and had gained his trust. Anil had given the key of the room to Hari.

For Hari, this was the opportunity to rob Anil. However, it was a difficult task because he was a careless man and sometimes careless men didn't even notice that they had been robbed. Somehow, Hari ignored these thoughts and decided to rob Anil that night.

Hari Robbed Anil

At night, Hari thought about his plan and carefully came near the bed when Anil was asleep. He slid his hand under the mattress and took out the money quietly. He, then, quickly got out of the room and ran away. He had secured the money with the string of his pyjama.

He was running towards the railway station to catch 10.30 Express to Lucknow as he had planned. When he counted the money, he was happy to find 600 rupees.

Hari didn't Board the Train

Hari reached the station just when the train was moving out. He did not buy any ticket and directly went to the platform. Hari could have jumped to get into one of the carriages but he did not catch the train. Instead, he stood alone on the platform. He did not know where to go as he had no friends except Anil whom he knew very well.

Hari's Confused Feelings

Hari decided to leave the station and thought about how Anil would feel when he would come to know about the theft. Hari had observed many people and found how different people react to being robbed. He knew that greedy people show fear, rich people show anger and poor people show acceptance. However, Anil would show sadness as his trust was broken.

Soon, Hari reached the maidan (ground). It was November and it had started raining. Hari was wet due to rain. So, he went to the bazaar and sat down under the clock tower. It was 12 o'clock and Hari thought about Anil. He knew that Anil would have given him 2 or 3 rupees to go watch a movie. Anil would have also taught him how to write complete sentences.

Importance of Education

In the excitement of theft, Hari had forgotten that apart from giving him some money, Anil also educated him. He realised that education would have made him into a big, clever and respected man. He understood that it was easy to steal but it was difficult to be respected like Anil.

So, Hari decided to go back to Anil. He went back into the room and cautiously put back the wet currency notes under the mattress and went to sleep.

Anil Reacted Normally in the Morning

Hari woke up late in the morning. He found that Anil had already prepared tea. Anil gave a fifty rupee note to Hari which was still wet. He told Hari that he had earned some money a day before and now, he would be able to pay him regularly. He also told Hari that they would start writing sentences from that day. Hari felt that Anil knew about the theft but he didn't say anything to him about it.

Word Meaning

Word	Meaning
lean	Thin in a healthy and attractive way
easy-going	relaxed and open-minded
of late	recently
get into … confidence	win the young man's trust
flattery	insincere praise
put me off	distracted me
modestly	humbly
ahead of	undetected
grunting	a short sound indicating anger or pain
appealing	attractive
to be off	to go away
hung around	did not leave
fits and starts	irregularly

Word	Meaning
cheque	payment for work done
queer	strange, unusual or not expected
tuck	to keep under something
crept	moved in a quiet, careful way to avoid being noticed
unlined	showing no sign of worry or anxiety
startled	shocked
fifties	50 rupee notes
dashed	ran
deserted	isolated
damp	wet
undetected	unnoticed
heart sank	felt disappointed and discouraged
spirits rose	mood became happy

NCERT FOLDER

NCERT Intext and Exercise Questions

READ AND FIND OUT (NCERT PAGE 8)

Q.1 Who does 'I' refer to in this story?

Ans. 'I' refers to Hari Singh, the narrator of the story. He is a 15 year old experienced thief.

Q.2 What is he "a fairly successful hand" at?

Ans. He is 'a fairly successful hand' at stealing which means that he is an experienced thief. He is so clean and cautious in his work that he robs people without being caught.

Q.3 What does he get from Anil in return for his work?

Ans. In return of Hari Singh's work, Anil gives him food and a place to live.

READ AND FIND OUT (NCERT PAGE 10)

Q.1 How does the thief think Anil will react to the theft?

Ans. According to Hari, Anil would be sad not because of the loss of money but because of the loss of trust he had in Hari.

Q.2 What does he say about the different reactions of people when they are robbed?

***Or* What does the thief say about the different reactions of the people when they are robbed?** **CBSE 2023**

Ans. Hari's experience at theft had made him aware of the differences in reactions of people when they're robbed. According to him, a greedy man shows fear, a rich man shows anger and a poor man shows acceptance.

Q.3 Does Anil realise that he has been robbed?

Ans. Yes, Anil realises that he has been robbed. He would have noticed it because all the notes that he kept were wet the next morning. He also knew that it had rained the previous night so he must have known that somebody had taken the notes out.

THINK ABOUT IT (NCERT PAGE 13)

Q.1 What are Hari Singh's reactions at the prospect of receiving an education? Do they change overtime?

(*Hint*: Compare, for example, the thought: "I knew that once I could write like an educated man there would be no limit to what I could achieve" with these later thoughts: 'Whole sentences, I knew, could one day bring me more than a few hundred rupees. It was a simple matter to steal- and sometimes just as simple to be caught. But to be a really big man, a clever and respected man, was something else.") What makes him return to Anil?

Ans. Hari was very happy and grateful when he learned to write his name. He was very excited when Anil promised to teach him to write whole sentences as well. He knew that being an educated man will add to his abilities and he could achieve unlimited material success.

No, Hari's reactions did not change overtime. He was always excited at the idea of getting educated. However, initally Hari was excited at the possibilities education would bring to him. Later, Hari's excitement was related to the respect, reputation and possibilities that would come to him once he was educated. The realisation to receive education and earn respect compelled him to return the money to Anil.

Q.2 Why does Anil not hand the thief over to the police? Do you think most people would have done so? In what ways is Anil different from such employers?

***Or* Why does Anil not hand over Hari Singh to the police?** **CBSE 2020, 2023**

***Or* According to a popular quote– "Kindness is stronger than iron bars." Anil did not hand the thief over to the police. In what way did Anil's act of wisdom and forgiveness transform Hari Singh?** **CBSE 2025**

Ans. Anil does not handover Hari to the police on theft charges. Even though he knew about the theft, he did not even mention it in front of Hari. This was so because Anil knew that Hari had realised his mistake and the importance of education in life. Anil wanted Hari to become a literate man and lead a respectful life.

Unlike Anil, most people would have beaten up Hari or would have handed him to the police for stealing the money.

Anil is different from other such employers because he is very understanding. Hari's return gave him the hope of a change in the thief. Anil wishes to reform the young thief through love and sympathy.

TALK ABOUT IT (NCERT PAGE 13)

Q.1 Do you think people like Anil and Hari Singh are found only in fiction, or are there such people in real life?

Ans. People like Anil and Hari Singh are found only in fiction and not in real life. Unlike Anil, most people would have either beaten up the thief or would have handed him to the police. People like Anil are rarely found in today's world.

Anil was a kind and considerate person who was concerned about Hari's education and future. Hari was a thief whose heart changes after realising the importance of education for his future. In the present world, such people are only found in imaginary stories or novels.

Q.2 Do you think it is a significant detail in the story that Anil is a struggling writer? Does this explain his behaviour in any way?

Or **Examine how Anil's identity as a writer could have contributed to his understanding of Hari Singh?**

CBSE Additional SQP 2024

Ans. Yes, it is a significant detail that Anil is a struggling writer. He had no regular source of income. Consequently, he used to spend according to the amount of money he had. When he had money he would celebrate and when he didn't have money, he borrowed it. This fact somewhere explains the kindness and sympathy with which he treats Hari. His condition is to some extent similar to Hari. Just like Hari, he also struggles to get proper meals. He understands Hari's condition and thus, helps Hari.

Q.3 Have you met anyone like Hari Singh? Can you think and imagine the circumstances that can turn a 15 year old boy into a thief?

Ans. No, I haven't met anyone like Hari Singh. But I am sure about the existence of such people who win someone's confidence and then, cheat that person.

Hari Singh is a 15 year old boy who had been a thief since long. There can be many reasons for him to enter such a profession. It can be due to poverty or illiteracy. He may have been an orphan who had never been to school and thus had become a thief.

Q.4 Where is the story set? (You can get clues from the names of the persons and places mentioned in it). Which language or languages are spoken in these places? Do you think the characters in the story spoke to each other in English?

Ans. The story is set somewhere in Uttar Pradesh near Lucknow. We can say so because the story mentions that there is a railway station for Express train to Lucknow. The presence of sweet shops and bazaars also indicate it to be a decent-sized town. Hindi is mostly spoken in these places.

No, the characters in the story do not speak to each other in English. They probably spoke in Hindi.

REVIEW EXERCISE

Including Competency Based Questions

Part - I

Multiple Choice Questions

1. Anil looked easy-going, kind and simple to the narrator.

Which of the given characteristics would not fit in with this description?

(a) Compassionate (b) Suave
(c) Uncomplicated (d) Carefree

Ans. (b) Suave

2. What was the name of the shop above which Anil lived?

(a) Laddu Sweet Shop
(b) Ganga Sweet Shop
(c) Jumna Sweet Shop
(d) Jogi Sweet Shop

Ans. (c) Jumna Sweet Shop

3. In 'The Thief's Story', it states, 'I knew that once I could write like an educated man there would be no limit to what I could achieve." What inference can be made about the narrator based on this statement? **Competency Based**

(a) He values education and knows it will take him far
(b) He is a better thief and will continue making his life that way
(c) He does not value his relationship with Anil
(d) Anil feel obligated to teach the narrator

Ans. (a) He values education and knows it will take him far

4. Anil made money 'by fits and starts' means that he **CBSE SQP 2021 Term 1**

(a) deemed it fit to start investing money
(b) started earning money in the recent past
(c) received money intermittently
(d) put his money to use frequently

Ans. (c) received money intermittently

5. It was quite pleasant working for Anil as CBSE 2021 Term 1

(a) he was quite rich
(b) he never complained
(c) he was a very simple person
(d) he could be easily fooled

Ans. (c) he was a very simple person

6. Anil's carelessness made stealing from him .... for Hari Singh. CBSE SQP 2021 Term 1

(a) uninteresting
(b) difficult
(c) systematic
(d) predictable

Ans. (a) Anil's carelessness made stealing from him uninteresting for Hari Singh

7. Where did Hari Singh go to after stealing money from Anil?

(a) To maidan
(b) To clock tower
(c) To the station
(d) To the bus stop

Ans. (c) To the station

8. The thief was grateful to Anil in many ways. Out of these, the greatest one was

(a) giving him a job and teaching him
(b) giving him money
(c) watching wrestling match with him
(d) talking to him

Ans. (a) giving him a job and teaching him

9. "I made some money yesterday. Now you'll be paid regularly." Who said this to whom?

(a) Anil to Hari Singh
(b) Hari Singh to Anil
(c) Kusable to Max
(d) Hack driver to the lawyer

Ans. (a) Anil to Hari Singh

10. Which of the following feeling is suggested by the narrator while returning the money to Anil?

(a) Beauty is in the eye of the beholder
(b) Home is where the heart is
(c) Knowledge is power
(d) It is more rewarding to work hard for what you have than take from others

Ans. (d) It is more rewarding to work hard for what you have than take from others

11. What evidence best supports the inference that Anil knew the narrator took his money?

(a) "I hurried back to the room feeling nervous."
(b) "But when I took the note, I saw it was still wet from the night's rain."
(c) "In the morning he would probably have given me two or three rupees to go to the cinema, but now I had it all."
(d) "I smiled at Anil in my most appealing way."

Ans. (b) "But when I took the note, I saw it was still wet from the night's rain."

12. Based on your understanding of Anil in 'The Thief's Story', choose the option that synchronises with his thinking.

(a) So what if I don't have much money? Giving it to that person is important as they could do with a helping hand.
(b) I better learn how to protect my money. I think I'm being looted.
(c) I earn money with such tremendous effort. Where does it all go?
(d) When I become rich, I can begin to help friends then. Right now, I will spend only on myself.

Ans. (a) So what if I don't have much money? Giving it to that person is important as they could do with a helping hand.

13. What would you have done with Hari Singh if you were in place of Anil?

1. You would have forgiven him.
2. You would have called the police for stealing money.
3. You would be teaching him.

(a) 1 and 2
(b) Only 1
(c) 1 and 3
(d) Only 3

Ans. (c) 1 and 3

14. How did the narrator's feelings towards Anil develop the theme of the chapter 'The Thief's Story'?

(a) Anil trusts the narrator at the beginning of the story and the narrator feel so comfortable with Anil that he never steals his money.
(b) At the beginning of the story, the narrator steals from Anil immediately. After that, he never earns his trust back, which leads the narrator to continue to steal.
(c) The narrator befriends Anil at the beginning of the story and when the narrator tries to steal from Anil, the narrator is caught.
(d) At the beginning of the story, the narrator wants to steal from Anil. As the story continues, the narrator earns the trust of Anil, which leads him to feel guilty about stealing his money.

Ans. (d) At the beginning of the story, the narrator wants to steal from Anil. As the story continues, the narrator earns the trust of Anil, which leads him to feel guilty about stealing his money.

15. Given below are the virtues for Anil. Choose the correct option.

1. Friendly
2. Kind
3. Helpless
4. Cheater

(a) 1 and 2
(b) 3 and 4
(c) 1, 2 and 4
(d) 2, 3 and 4

Ans. (a) 1 and 2

16. What is the crux of the story 'The Thief's Story'?

(a) You may be wealthy through being dishonest, but you will not really happy

(b) You may be wealthy by cheating others

(c) Education is important in life

(d) Stealing is necessary for living

Ans. (a) You may be wealthy through being dishonest, but you will not really happy

Extract Based Questions

1. Read the following extract carefully and answer the questions that follow.

I was still a thief when I met Anil. And though only 15, I was an experienced and fairly successful hand. Anil was watching a wrestling match when I approached him. He was about 25, a tall, lean fellow, and he looked easy-going, kind and simple enough for my purpose. I hadn't had much luck of late and thought I might be able to get into the young man's confidence.

''You look a bit of a wrestler yourself,'' I said. A little flattery helps in making friends.

''So do you,'' he replied, which put me off for a moment because at that time I was rather thin.

''Well,'' I said modestly, ''I do wrestle a bit.''

''What's your name?''

''Hari Singh,'' I lied. I took a new name every month. That kept me ahead of the police and my former employers.

(i) Complete the sentence on the basis of the given extract.

I might be able to get into the young man's confidence. Based on the line above, we can say that Hari wanted to ....

Ans. gain Anil's trust to exploit him

(ii) Which of these about the narrator can not be inferred from the extract?

(a) He was a lean fellow.

(b) He was fond of wrestling.

(c) He was good at making friends.

(d) He had ways to avoid being arrested.

Ans. (b) He was fond of wrestling.

(iii) On the basis of the given extract, how would you judge the Hari? **Competency Based**

Ans. The given extract tells us that Hari was a smart and intelligent boy who had no one to support him. He did not have any family and thus, started stealing to earn his livelihood.

(iv) He was about 25 — a tall, lean fellow — and he looked easy-going, kind and simple enough for my purpose. How does this observation impact Hari?

Ans. This observation helps Hari decide that Anil was the perfect target for him.

2. Read the following extract carefully and answer the questions that follow.

Anil was watching a wrestling match when I approached him. He was about 25– a tall, lean fellow – and he looked easy-going, kind and simple enough for my purpose. I hadn't had much luck of late and thought I might be able to get into the young man's confidence.

'You look a bit of a wrestler yourself," I said. A little flattery helps in making friends. **CBSE Question Bank 2021 Modified**

(i) 'I might be able to get into the young man's confidence.'

Choose the option that does not display what the statement means.

(a) He wanted to win his trust.

(b) He wanted him to share his thoughts without caution.

(c) He wanted him to feel comfortable revealing more details about himself.

Ans. (c) He wanted him to feel comfortable revealing more details about himself.

(ii) The narrator judges a person and then, decides to rob him/her. Do you agree? Justify.

Ans. It is true to say that the narrator judges a person and then, decides to rob him/her. The narrator, Hari Singh, is an experienced thief. So, he knows that he needs to select the person who he is going to rob. He, first, observes Anil and finds him to be an easy target to rob. Then only, he moves ahead to rob Anil.

(iii) Based on the line, "A little flattery helps in making friends.", choose the option that displays the quote closest in meaning.

(a) Imitation is the best form of flattery, people generally understand that my comedy is not intended to hurt anybody.

(b) I know imitation is the highest form of flattery, but stealing one's identity is totally different.

(c) One may define flattery as a base companionship which is most advantageous to the flatterer.

Ans. The phrase 'A little flattery helps in making friends' indicates that flattery is a base companionship which is most advantageous to the flatterer.

(iv) What does the 'I hadn't had much luck of late' means that the boy hadn't?

Ans. 'I hadn't had much luck of late' means that the boy hadn't been successful in duping people lately.

3. Read the following extract carefully and answer the questions that follow.

I followed casually.

"Hello again," he said.

I gave him my most appealing smile. "I want to work for you," I said.

"But I can't pay you."

I thought that over for a minute. Perhaps I had misjudged my man. I asked, "Can you feed me?"

"Can you cook?"

"I can cook," I lied again.

"If you can cook, then maybe I can feed you."

He took me to his room over the Jumna Sweet Shop and told me I could sleep on the balcony.

But the meal I cooked that night must have been terrible because Anil gave it to a stray dog and told me to be off. But I just hung around, smiling in my most appealing way, and he couldn't help laughing.

CBSE SQP 2021 Term 1 Modified

(i) Identify Hari Singh's intention behind the deceiving smile.

Ans. Hari's appealing smile showed his intention of deceiving Anil.

(ii) List Anil's characteristics, as revealed in the extract.

Ans. The given extract reveals that Anil was not a judgemental man. He was kind and naive enough to not question Hari's intention of following him and asking him for work.

(iii) Select the most appropriate option based on (1) and (2).

1. Anil gave his meal to a stray dog.

2. Hari Singh did not know how to cook.

(a) 2 is true and 1 is false.
(b) 2 is the result for 1.
(c) 2 is the cause for 1.
(d) 2 is false and 1 is true.

Ans. (c) 2 is the cause for 1.

(iv) 'Hari knew that his lie was caught'. Do you agree? Justify. **Competency Based**

Ans. Yes, I agree that Hari knew of his lie being caught. Hari initially told Anil that he could cook but the meal he made was not edible Anil had to feed it to the stray dag. When Anil told him to leave, he knew that his lie had been caught.

4. Read the following extract carefully and answer the questions that follow.

When the train had gone, I found myself standing alone on the deserted platform. I had no idea where to spend the night. I had no friends.

(i) The speaker was standing alone on the platform because

(a) he wanted to be left alone.
(b) he has reached the wrong station.
(c) the train had just left.
(d) the train had got cancelled.

Ans. (c) the train had just left.

(ii) Why did the speaker not have any friends?

Ans. The speaker does not have any friends because he thought that friends were more trouble than help.

(iii) Select the option that correctly captures the usage of the word 'deserted' in the above extract.

(a) The coastal resorts are deserted in winter.
(b) She deserted the stage for army.
(c) He deserted his friends in time of great need.
(d) The officer deserted to the enemy.

Ans. (a) The coastal resorts are deserted in winter.

(iv) Why was the platform deserted?

Ans. The platform was deserted because it was midnight and most of the people were sleeping. Further, those who had been travelling had boarded the train that had left.

5. Read the following extract carefully and answer the questions that follow.

There was a fifty rupees note between his fingers. My heart sank. I thought I had been discovered."I made some money yesterday," he explained. "Now you'll be paid regularly."My spirits rose. But when I took the note, I saw it was still wet from the night's rain. "Today, we'll start writing sentences," he said. He knew. But neither his lips nor his eyes showed anything.

(i) State True or False.

None of the terms (a) - (d) can be applied to the statement - "Today, we'll start writing sentences," he said. He knew

(a) A hypothesis - a proposed explanation for a phenomenon
(b) An assumption - something that is assumed to be true without proof or taken for granted
(c) A hyperbole - exaggerated statements or claims not meant to be taken literally
(d) A premise - a proposition that forms the basis of an argument

Ans. False; An assumption

(ii) What did Anil do on knowing about Hari's guilt?

Ans. Even after knowing about Hari Singh's theft, Anil did nothing to harm Hari. In fact, Anil gave a 50 rupee note to Hari and reminded him what he was going to teach him.

(iii) Why did Hari Singh feel guilty?

Ans. Hari Singh felt guilty because even though Anil trusted him, helped him and educated him, he stole Anil's money. By doing this, he also broke Anil's trust.

(iv) Fill in the blank appropriately.

The phrase 'my heart sank' means ....

Ans. sudden dismay.

6. Read the following extract carefully and answer the questions that follow.

My spirits rose. But when I took the note, I saw it was still wet from the night's rain. "Today we'll start writing sentences", he said, He knew. But neither his lips nor his eyes showed anything. I smiled at Anil in my most appealing way. And the smile came by itself, without any effort.

(i) State True or False.

None of the terms (a) - (d) can be applied to the statement - And the smile came by itself, without any effort.

(a) A hypothesis - a proposed explanation for a phenomenon

(b) An assumption - something that is assumed to be true without proof or taken for granted

(c) A hyperbole - exaggerated statements or claims not meant to be taken literally

(d) A statement - a definite or clear expression of something in speech or writing

Ans. False; A statement

(ii) Which word in the extract means the same as the underlined word/phrase?

My <u>hopes</u> regarding the incident were positive.

Ans. spirits

(iii) Hari realised Anil knew but neither his lips nor his eyes showed anything. Elaborate on the reason behind this with reference to the extract.

Ans. Hari realised Anil knew that he had robbed Anil last night but he didn't disclose his knowledge because Hari's changed decision gave him hope. Hari returned the money and this made Anil believe in his character.

(iv) What did Anil's lips and eyes not show?

Ans. Anil's lips and eyes did not show that he knew about Hari Singh's robbery.

Part - II

Short Answer Type Questions

1. What strategy did the narrator initially employ to gain Anil's trust, and did it prove effective?

Ans. The narrator employs flattery and lies, pretending admiration for Anil's demeanour and skills. Despite initial suspicion, the narrator's persistent appeal and charming demeanour eventually win Anil over, demonstrating the effectiveness of manipulation in gaining trust. Anil's eventual trust facilitated the narrator's opportunity for personal gain.

2. 'Anil walked away. I followed casually.' Why do you think the narrator followed Anil?

Ans. The narrator's purpose of robbing Anil had just begun and the narrator knew that he had to gain Anil's trust to be able to rob him. So, he followed Anil to look for an opportunity that may help him give shape to his plans.

3. What did Anil and Hari agree upon to be the mode of payment?

Ans. When Anil expressed his inability to pay Hari, he questioned Anil if he could feed him. Anil told Hari that he could feed him only if he knew how to cook. Therefore, food and a place to live were agreed upon as the mode of payment to Hari to work for Anil.

4. Did Hari like working for Anil? Give reasons in support of your answer.

Ans. Yes, Hari liked working for Anil. He made tea in the morning and would go to buy day's supplies. He would also make a profit of a rupee by his work. Apart from the work, he was also grateful for getting educated by Anil.

5. "The greedy man showed fear; the rich man showed" anger; the poor man showed acceptance. With reference to the above line from 'The Thief's Story explain why different people react differently when their money is stolen. Answer in 40-50 words. Competency Based

Ans. The greedy man is always in want more money, so the thought of losing money scares him. The rich man has worked hard to earn his money, and is naturally angry when it is stolen. The poor man is used to being treated unfairly and has accepted loss as a part of his life.

6. Why was it difficult for Hari to rob Anil?

Ans. It was difficult for Hari to rob Anil because Anil was the most trusting person Hari had ever met. He was really simple and kind. Hari knew that loss of money would not affect Anil but the loss of trust would surely make him sad.

7. How did Hari Singh justify to himself his stealing Anil's money? CBSE 2023

Ans. Hari Singh justified stealing Anil's money to himself by stating that stealing was his habit and he had not stolen anything for a long time. Further, he adds that Anil would waste his money on his friends. He also states that Anil had not paid him, so him robbing Anil is acceptable.

8. Was Anil from 'The Thief's Story' good at managing his money properly? Justify your answer. Competency Based

Ans. No, Anil in the story does not manage his money properly. He earns irregularly and has phases wherein he has to borrow money from his friends. The times when he has money, he wastes it on his friends. He does not save any money for the time he would not be able to earn.

9. In 'The Thief's Story', why did Hari believe that friends were more trouble than help? State your opinion with one reason. Competency Based

Ans. Hari believed that friends were more trouble than help because as a criminal he would need to hide his whereabouts and his identity. If any friend knew him, police would get an opportunity to look for him and arrest him. Hence, he believed that having no friends was better for his trade of stealing.

10. Was Hari Singh successful in robbing Anil? Was Anil the only one who was robbed or did Hari also rob himself of something?

Ans. Yes, Hari Singh was successful in robbing Anil. However, Anil was not the only one who was robbed at that time. Hari had robbed himself as well. He had lost the chance of receiving education and being literate.

Hari had robbed Anil monetarily but he had also robbed himself of the chance for a better and brighter future, which was much more valuable.

11. What made Hari Singh go back to Anil's house? CBSE 2020

Ans. Hari Singh decided to go back to Anil's house because he realised the importance of the education he was receiving from Anil. He knew that learning how to write and being a literate person would open doors to many opportunities.

He was sure that he would then be able to earn more than a few hundred rupees he had in hand at that time.

12. How was the morning after the night of the theft?

Ans. The morning after the night of the theft was just like a normal one except for the fact that Hari woke up late and Anil had made tea for him.

Anil gave a fifty-rupee-note to Hari and told him that he would now be paid regularly. Hari felt that Anil knew about the theft but he didn't show anything.

13. How do you think Anil may have come to know about the theft?

Ans. Anil may have come to know about the theft because of the wetness of the notes. He was a kind but wise man. It wouldn't have been difficult for Anil to make out the series of events that would have taken place in the night.

14. Had Anil really forgiven Hari Singh? Support your answer with evidence.

Or **According to you, why didn't Anil confront Hari about stealing his money in 'The Thief's story'.** Competency Based

Ans. Yes, Anil had forgiven Hari Singh. It is evident because Anil handed over to Hari a fifty-rupee-note as soon as Hari woke up. Though he knew that Hari had robbed the money at first, his subsequent actions gave him hope of change in Hari's character.

15. How was Hari Singh's 'appealing smile' at the end different from his similar smiles on earlier occasions?

Ans. Hari Singh's 'appealing smile' at the end is different from his similar smiles on earlier occasions. Earlier, his smiles were fake and artificial. They were full of flattery that aimed to fulfill his goal. But in the end, his smile was real; it was natural and appealing.

16. What was the thought behind using appealing smiles frequently on Anil? CBSE Question Bank 2021

Ans. One can attract others through the right gestures and facial expressions. The narrator wanted to appear honest and trustable in front of Anil, hence, he used appealing smiles frequently on him to win over his trust.

17. Why did Hari Singh smile in his most appealing smile toward the end of the story? CBSE 2023

Ans. Hari Singh smiled in his most appealing way towards the end in a natural manner because it came from the innermost corner of his heart. It was spontaneous and real unlike the previous artifical ones.

18. While asking for the job, Hari Singh desplays his most appealing smile. This smile in crucial to the story and maker a few more appearence. Explain why and how this smile is a calculated one. CBSE 2024 C

Ans. The first smile given by Hari is the most appealing smile he could display. This smile makes a few more appearances in the story. All of these smiles serve a very specific purpose showing Hari's intentions. All smiles except for the last smile are calculated and shows Hari's immoral intentions of theft. Hence, whenever, we see Hari smiling it is because he is planning something that could possible harm someone.

19. How did Anil help the narrator improve his practical and educational skills?

Ans. Anil taught the narrator cooking skills and promised further education, demonstrating patience and kindness. He provided opportunities for practical learning through daily tasks and initiated educational sessions to improve the narrator's literacy and numeracy. Anil's support and guidance were instrumental in enhancing the narrator's life's practical and academic aspects.

20. How did the narrator's perception of Anil change throughout the story, and what did he ultimately learn from their relationship?

Ans. The narrator's perception of Anil evolved from seeing him as an easy target to appreciating his kindness and generosity. Through their relationship, the narrator learns the value of trust, honesty and genuine human connection. He realised the importance of integrity and the impact of one's actions on others.

Long Answer Type Questions

1. Money can't make a man as much as education can. Elucidate the statement with reference to 'The Thief's Story'.

Ans. The statement "money can't make a man as much as education can" stands true in almost all the aspects of life. Money may buy us all the luxuries and fulfill our needs but it cannot buy us knowledge, civilised thinking, skills and abilities to achieve our dreams. Education lays the platform for all to act upon our goals according to our abilities. It enables us to keep up with the fast moving world and opens up opportunities we did not know exist.

Money, on the other hand, can assist us to a certain level. It can buy us a plan but education gives us the knowledge of its execution.

In the story 'The Thief's Story', Hari Singh — a young thief realises the importance of education. He meets a struggling writer Anil who allows him to work for him. Anil teaches Hari to write. Hari who had befriended Anil to rob him of money, returns because he understands that education will make him a big, clever and a respected man. He accepts that with education, he would be able to earn much more than what he had robbed.

2. Hari Singh didn't board the express and returned to Anil. It shows that everyone has some conscience that they do not put in practice. Elaborate with reference to 'The Thief's Story'. **Competency Based**

Ans. Everyone has an inner conscience that tells them about right or wrong. It fills one with guilt when one does something wrong and delights one when something right happens. In the story 'The Thief's Story', the narrator's/Hari's conscience is pricked as he robs the honest and kind man, Anil. He works for Anil with the purpose of looking for an opportunity to rob him. However, during his stay with him he not only learns about love, sympathy and trust but also understands the importance of education.

Even though Anil knows that Hari keeps one rupee as profit from his daily routines, he never asks Hari for it and teaches him to write. When Hari robs Anil, he states that it is difficult for him to rob Anil but it is much difficult for him to run away after robbing Anil.

He has a guilty conscience. He does not want to hurt Anil and wants to change himself. This does not only force him to return the money but also makes him want to get educated.

The inner conscience which came forward in Hari had been dormant (hidden) before he had stolen Anil's money. Just like Hari did not put it into practice, many people ignore it. It is the circumstances that awaken the inner conscience and put it into practice.

3. Education, love and sympathy can transform even a thief. How is it true in the case of Hari Singh? **CBSE 2020**

Or **Trust and compassion can reform a person. Justify this statement in the light of the lesson 'The Thief's Story'.** **CBSE 2023**

Ans. A man is essentially a product of the circumstances and the environment that he lives in. Hari Singh was a boy of just fifteen but was an experience thief who had a fairly successful hand in his profession. It was his circumstances that led him into such a profession which he retained even while he lived with Anil. He went to live with Anil with a purpose of robbing him and was even successful in doing so.

However, Anil was not a fool. He knew about Hari's act of theft but did not hand over Hari to the police. It was his care, love and sympathy that affected Hari so much so that he could not run away after robbing Anil. Anil's compassion and kind-heartedness brought about a change in Hari.

Further, Anil taught Hari how to read and write. The prospect of education created a deep impression on Hari's mind. He realised that with education, he would not only be able to earn money but will also become a respected man.

Hence, it is true that education, love and sympathy can transform even a thief like Hari Singh.

4. **Education means different things to different people. Evaluate how it impacted the young thief in the story.** **CBSE Question Bank 2021**

Ans. It is true that education means different things to different people. The young boy had come after Anil with the sole purpose to cheat him. When Anil taught him to add numbers he realised that education could make a big difference in his life. Now, he had understood that to become a big, clever and respectable man, he must be educated. He felt that he could achieve anything if he learned to read and write whole sentences. Later when he was thinking to flee with the stolen money, his mind was struck again with the importance of education. Besides, the nice behaviour and trust of his employer had transformed a thief's heart and he returned and put the money back. This way it can be said that education had a makeover effect on the thief, Hari Singh.

5. **Fiction writers prefer creating grey characters rather than black and white. Analyse this in detail, with reference to both the characters of 'The Thief's Story'.** **CBSE SQP 2023**

Ans The two characters in the story 'The Thief's Story' are neither completely wrong (black) nor completely right (white). On one hand, there is the thief, Hari Singh, who has fooled many victims and even the police. He was never ashamed of stealing and lying. He even continued this with Anil. However, the negativity in his character didn't last long. He changed owing to Anil's love and his strong trust in him.

On the other hand, there is Anil who is a helpful, simple and trusting man. He forgave Hari Singh even after knowing he was a thief. His knowledge even stopped him from saying anything about the theft. Simultaneously, his actions prove that he is casual about money as he ignored what Hari Singh was doing. He knew that it was not right but he never took any steps to stop him.

Thus, it can be said that neither of them was a black or white character. They can be categorised as grey characters. Both of them have their own vices and virtues. Because of this, they are redeemed as people who need improvements. Their presence confuses the readers as they cannot decide how to categorise Hari and Anil.

6. **A character arc is the transformation or development of a character throughout a story and refers to the changes a character undergoes as a result of their experiences, challenges, and interactions with other characters.**

In the light of the above information, trace the character arc of the thief in Ruskin Bond's 'The Thief's Story', in about 120 words. **CBSE 2023**

Ans. The thief's character arc in the story shows a transformation from a career criminal to a person who learns to trust and work hard for a living. At the beginning of the story, the thief is portrayed as an experienced criminal who is focused on escaping the law. He is initially attracted to Anil because he believes he can exploit the young man's trusting nature and rob him. As a criminal, he is solely focused on his own personal gain and uses his skills as a thief to achieve this.

As the story progresses, the thief begins to develop a friendship with Anil, who teaches him how to cook, write and read. As a result, a transformation starts. This transformation of the thief's character reaches a climax when he is presented with an opportunity to steal money from Anil. He is even successful in doing so. However, soon he considers the consequences of his actions. Although the thief has not completely abandoned his criminal ways, the fact that he hesitated to jump on the train to escape with the stolen money shows that he has developed a moral conscience. The story implies that the thief has realised that a life of crime is not fulfilling and he needs to change. He realises that this change will come with education which Anil can provide him.

7. **Hari Singh says — "He knew it but neither his lips nor his eyes showed anything." Anil successfully addressed the situation by not addressing it all. Elaborate based on your reading of 'The Thief's Story'.** **CBSE 2024**

Ans. Anil's reaction to the theft committed by Hari Singh, truly reflects his strength of character and wisdom. Anil chooses not to confront Hari directly, assuming a confrontation would lead Hari back onto the path of thievery and deceit due to guilt and fear. Instead, Anil provides Hari with an opportunity to confess and make amends by giving the same drenched note that Hari had stolen and then, secretly returned.

This approach reaffirms Anil's trust in Hari, making him more remorseful of his actions. Instead of pushing him further into his life of crime, Anil provides an opportunity for repentance and reformation. Anil creates an environment of trust and teaches Hari the values of honesty, care and responsibility, showing that they are more valuable than easy money.

ASSESSMENT EXERCISE

Extract Based Questions

Read the following extract carefully and answer the questions that follow.

He also taught me to write my name and said he would soon teach me to write whole sentences and to add numbers. I was grateful. I knew that once I could write like an educated man there would be no limit to what I could achieve.

(i) **State True or False.**

None of the terms (a) - (d) can be applied to the statement - I knew that once I could write like an educated man there would be no limit to what I could achieve.

(a) A hypothesis - a proposed explanation for a phenomenon

(b) An assumption - something that is assumed to be true without proof or taken for granted

(c) A hyperbole - exaggerated statements or claims not meant to be taken literally

(d) A premise - a proposition that forms the basis of an argument

(ii) What did Hari do for a living? Why was he grateful for education?

Elaborate with reference to the extract.

(iii) The dominant tone of the extract is

(a) hopeful (b) regretful (c) nostalgic (d) joyful

(iv) State the reason that the narrator was grateful.

Short Answer (SA) Type Questions

1. Describe Hari Singh's life with Anil.
2. What different shortcomings of Hari Singh did Anil ignore?
3. "Anil could see a hope for change in Hari". Justify.

Long Answer (LA) Type Questions

1. "But neither his lips nor his eyes showed anything". Anil did not show that he knew about the theft. What kind of a person do you think Anil was? Also throw light on the virtues you learn from his character.
2. "But I just hung around, smiling in my most appealing way, and he couldn't help laughing."
   Do you think that Anil was fooled by Hari's appealing smile? Why/Why not? Give reasons for your answer.
3. Imagine that Anil from 'The Thief's Story' recounts the sequence of events of the night. Hari stole the money and ran away. When Hari came back and returned the money, he feels a sense of relief, pride and guilt. Write a diary entry as Anil expressing his feelings in about 120 words. **Competency Based**

The Midnight Visitor

by Robert Arthur

CHAPTER SUMMARY

'The Midnight Visitor' by Robert Arthur is a story about two smart secret agents who try to outsmart each other. Ausable, a secret agent, is expecting to receive a very important report. Another secret agent, Max also wants to get the report and so, threatens Ausable. However, Ausable traps him with his convincing stories and eliminates Max using his presence of mind.

Fowler Meets Ausable, a Secret Agent

Fowler, a young writer had come to meet a secret agent, Ausable in a room at the top floor of a French hotel. Ausable was a secret agent but he did not look like one at all. He was fat and spoke French and German with an American accent. Fowler was disappointed to see Ausable as he could not find any characteristics of a secret agent in Ausable as he had read.

Fowler had imagined Ausable to be a mysterious figure with a crack of pistols and drugs in wine. Instead, he met a fat man in an unromantic location. Ausable guessed Fowler's disappointment. He, then, told Fowler that soon he would receive a very important report that could change the course of history.

Another Secret Agent Max

When both Ausable and Fowler entered Ausable's hotel room and switched on the light, they saw a man pointing a small automatic pistol towards them. This man was Max, another secret agent. Ausable was surprised to see Max in France as according to the information he had, Max was suppossed to be in Berlin.

Max's Mission

Max was thin but not very tall. He appeared crafty and cunning. He clearly told Ausable the purpose of being in his room. He wanted to take away the highly confidential reports about some new missiles that Ausable would get that night.

Ausable Talks about the Balcony

Ausable sat on the armchair and complained about the balcony that was attached to his room. He told Fowler that this was the second time that someone used the balcony to secretly enter his room.

Max, then, clarified that he did not enter the room through the balcony. He had entered with the help of a pass key. Ausable explained to Fowler that it was actually not his balcony but the balcony of the next apartment. He, further, told him that his room and the next apartment were earlier a larger unit. Now, the unit had been divided but the balcony still existed. The management had done nothing to block the balcony.

Waiting for the Report

Max began to talk about the arrival of the report. He told Fowler to sit down and that the report would arrive in half an hour. Ausable corrected him and told him that he was supposed to get the report at 12:30. Ausable wanted to know how Max came to know about the report but Max asked Ausable how his people had got that report.

Max's Attempt to Escape

Suddenly, there was a knock at the door. Ausable informed Max that it was the police whom he had called for extra protection. This information made Max nervous. As the knocking was repeated loudly, Max angrily threatened Ausable to ask the police to go away or he would shoot him. However, Ausable told Max that the door was unlocked and police would shoot him. The knocking at the door became louder and someone shouted Ausable's name.

Max decided to wait in the balcony until the police went away. He climbed the window sill and jumped out of it. His high-pitched scream was heard as the door was opened.

An Unexpected Twist

The door of the room was opened and a waiter came in with drinks. Fowler was shocked. He wanted to know where the police was and how Max would get arrested. Ausable informed him that there was no police and it was only the waiter, Henry, with the drinks he had ordered. Fowler was still worried that Max would return with a pistol but Ausable reassured him that Max wouldn't return because there was no balcony and Max had jumped to his death as the room was on the sixth floor.

Word Meaning

Word	Meaning
musty	smelling of mould/ fungus
gloomy	cheerless
let down	disappointed
romantic adventure	exciting event
accent	a distinctive way in which people in a particular area, country or social group pronounce words
passably	just well enough to be understood
wheezily	with a whistling sound
espionage	spying
envisioned	imagined
sloppy	(here) carelessly dressed
slipped	passed secretly
prosaic	routine/ordinary
chuckled	laughed quietly without opening the mouth
disillusioned	disappointed
take cheer	be happy
affect the course of history	change the way things happened or will happen
drama	excitement
authentic thrill	a real feeling of excitement
wheezed	spoke breathing noisily and heavily
start	shock

Word	Meaning
slender	gracefully thin
crafty, pointed countenance	cunning look
menacing	dangerous
missiles	weapons directed by remote control or automatically
raise the devil	make a strong protest
grimly	seriously
nuisance	causing annoyance
pressing blackly	showing total darkness
inflection	change of tone
passkey	duplicate key
glanced	looked
block it off	close it
stiffly	straight and like a statue
check on	meet
backed swiftly	went back quickly
take my chances	to do something that involves risks
shrilly	piercingly/in a high pitch
deftly	neatly and skilfully
uncorked	removed the top cover
white-faced	pale from fear

NCERT FOLDER

NCERT Intext and Exercise Questions

READ AND FIND OUT (NCERT PAGE 14)

Q.1 How is Ausable different from other secret agents? **CBSE 2020**

Ans. Ausable is different from other secret agents in several ways. He was extremely fat. Inspite of living in Paris for over twenty years, he spoke French and German with difficulty and had an American accent. Instead of getting messages passed secretly to him by beautiful girls, he got only a routine telephone call for making an appointment.

Q.2 Who is Fowler and what is his first authentic thrill of the day?

Ans. Fowler is a writer and he had come to meet Ausable in order to get some material for his writings. His first authentic thrill of the day came when he saw a man in Ausable's room pointing a pistol towards Ausable and himself.

READ AND FIND OUT (NCERT PAGE 15)

Q.3 How has Max got in?

Ans. Max had gotten into the room by using a pass key or master key.

Q.4 How does Ausable say he got in?

Ans. Ausable said that Max had got into the room through the balcony.

THINK ABOUT IT (NCERT PAGE 18)

Q.1 "Ausable did not fit any description of a secret agent Fowler had ever read." What do secret agents in books and films look like, in your opinion? Discuss in groups or in class some stories or movies featuring spies, detectives and secret agents, and compare their appearance with that of Ausable in this story. (You may mention characters from fiction in languages other than English.

In English fiction you may have come across Sherlock Holmes, Hercule Poirot, or Miss Marple. Have you watched any movies featuring James Bond?)

Ans. Secret agents in fiction are projected like the ideal man, 'Tall, dark and handsome'. They are usually well-built and keep beautiful women for company. They would smoke a pipe (like Sherlock Holmes) or a cigar and execute death-defying stunts (like James Bond). Movies based on James Bond show hi-tech gadgets which assist the detective in countering villains. However, there are some exceptions to this appearance of a secret agent.

A character named Feluda was created by Satyajit Ray, the famous Bengali filmmaker. Feluda was a tall athletic figure who relied on his superb analytical ability and observation skills.

(Students can discuss about more detective or secret agent figures)

Q.2 How does Ausable manage to make Max believe that there is a balcony attached to his room? Look back at his detailed description of it. What makes it a convincing story?

Or **Describe Ausable's fabricated tale regarding the balcony.** **CBSE 2025**

Ans. Ausable makes Max believe that a balcony is attached to his room by providing a detailed and plausible explanation. He mentions that the room used to be part of a larger unit with a living room with a balcony. Ausable explains that someone could access the balcony from the neighbouring apartment and then enter his room through the window.

This story is convincing because it incorporates specific details about the layout of the building and uses real-life scenarios, such as shared balconies in apartment buildings, to support Ausable's claim. Ausable's frustration with the management for not blocking off the balcony adds authenticity to his account, making it seem more believable to Max.

Q.3 Looking back at the story, when do you think Ausable thought up his plan for getting rid of Max? Do you think he had worked out his plan in detail right from the beginning? Or did he make up a plan taking advantage of events as they happened?

Ans. No, I don't think that Ausable had worked out his plan in detail from the very beginning. Infact, the plan was spontaneous. Ausable, essentially, took advantage of events as they happened.

Ausable made up a story of the balcony outside the room and as there was a knock at the door, he told Max that it would be the police. He knew that all this information would make Max desperate and restless. As a result, Max would take a wrong decision and lose his life.

TALK ABOUT IT (NCERT PAGE 18 AND 19)

Q.1 In this story, Ausable shows great 'presence of mind', or the ability to think quickly and act calmly and wisely, in a situation of danger and surprise. Give examples from your own experience, or narrate a story, which shows someone's presence of mind.

Ans. In the story 'The Midnight Visitor', Ausable shows great presence of mind or the ability to think quickly, and act calmly and wisely in a situation or danger.

Such a similar presence of mind is shown by Gerrard in the story/play 'If I Were You'. When Gerrard is held hostage by a criminal, he not only treats him as a guest but also traps him with his confidence.

Gerrard convinces the criminal that he is also a criminal. He tells him to run away through the exit door which is actually a cupboard. The criminal believes Gerrard and gets trapped in the cupboard while Gerrard calls the police. Thus, it is his presence of mind that helps him get out of a difficult situation.

Q.2 Discuss what you would do in the situations described below. Remember that presence of mind comes out of a state of mental preparedness. If you have thought about possible problems or dangers, and about how to act in such situations, you have a better chance of dealing with such situations if they do arise.

(i) A small fire starts in your kitchen.

(ii) A child starts to choke on a piece of food.

(iii) An electrical appliance starts to hiss and gives out sparks.

(iv) A bicycle knocks down a pedestrian.

(v) It rains continuously for more than twenty-four hours.

(vi) A member of your family does not return home at the usual or expected time.

You may suggest other such situations.

Ans. (i) If a small fire starts in my kitchen, I would first look for its source. If it is due to an electrical problem, a blanket should be put over the fire to shut out the air. If the fire is not due to an electrical problem, water can be thrown on it. If it is due to a short-circuit, electricity must be disconnected immediately before taking any other action.

(ii) When a child starts to choke on a piece of food, the child's back must be thumped slowly until the piece of food stuck in the child's mouth is vomited out. However, in case it continues, the child should be given trained medical aid immediately.

(iii) When an electrical appliance starts to hiss and gives out sparks, the electricity supply to the appliance should be immediately disconnected. If it is plugged into a socket, the plug must be removed from the socket. Later on, the appliance should be repaired by an authorised person.

(iv) If a bicycle knocks down a pedestrian, first aid should be given to the injured person at once. Public help may also be asked, if necessary. Depending on the seriousness of the injury, the affected person may be shifted to a hospital.

(v) Flooding may be caused by a heavy downpour. So, all necessary precautions for saving various possessions should be taken. Preventive acts and awareness acts would become central.

(vi) A family member not returning home at the usual time should be enquired for at the place he or she was expected to visit. If he or she was with friends, these friends or the friends' families should be contacted. If there is no result from these enquiries, as a last resort (last option), the local police may be informed.

REVIEW EXERCISE

Including Competency Based Questions

Part - I

Multiple Choice Questions

1. Why does Ausable refer to Fowler as 'my young friend'? Competency Based

(a) To make a sarcastic comment about Fowler's childishness

(b) To remind Fowler that young people are usually cheerful

(c) To reassure Fowler that they are indeed friends

(d) To highlight how naive and innocent Fowler is

Ans. (d) To highlight how naive and innocent Fowler is

2. Following sentence is given in the story 'The Midnight Visitor': 'Someday soon that paper may well affect the course of history.' Choose the option that correctly paraphrases the given sentence.

(a) In the near future, this document might probably have an effect on the development of history.

(b) In the past, this document might probably had an affect on the development of history.

(c) In the present, this document may probably have an affect on the development of future.

(d) None of the above

Ans. (a) In the near future, this document might probably have an effect on the development of history.

3. "In that thought is drama, is there not?" Which of these would be the most suitable response from Fowler if Ausable is successful in helping him 'take cheer'? Competency Based

(a) No, there is no drama in a mere piece of paper.

(b) 'Now I am intrigued; please tell me more about it.'

(c) Yes, we should take action to mark our names in history.'

(d) Is it? I am very disappointed that I came all the way for this.'

Ans. (b) 'Now I am intrigued; please tell me more about it.'

4. What was Fowler's 'first thrill of the day'?

(a) Meeting Ausable.

(b) Sight of a man with automatic pistol.

(c) Seeing a very important paper.

(d) None of the above.

Ans. (b) Sight of a man with automatic pistol.

5. See the options given below and choose the correct option in the context of 'The Midnight Visitor'.

1. Setting : Room in a French Hotel.

2. Plot : Disillusionment and realisation of a journalist on the deceptive nature of a detective.

3. Characters : Ausable, Henry, Fowler, Max.

4. Climax : Max assuming a balcony under Ausable's window jumps to his death.

(a) Only 1 (b) 1 and 3

(c) 2 and 4 (d) All of these

Ans. (d) All of these

6. Read the given statements and choose the correct answer.

(A) Ausable already had a plan to eliminate Max.

(B) Max had not anticipated Ausable's trick.

(a) A is true B is false (b) A is false B is true

(c) Both are true (d) Both are false

Ans. (b) A is false B is true

7. How did Fowler feel at the end of the story?

(a) Disappointed (b) Thrilled

(c) Sad (d) Unhappy

Ans. (b) Thrilled

8. What is the theme of the story 'The Midnight Visitor'?

(a) Wisdom is more powerful than any weapon.

(b) Never judge a person by his appearance.

(c) First impressions could be misleading.

(d) He who laughs last, laughs longest.

Ans. (a) Wisdom is more powerful than any weapon.

Extract Based Questions

1. Read the following extract carefully and answer the questions that follow.

Ausable did not fit any description of a secret agent Fowler had ever read. Following him down the musty corridor of the gloomy French hotel where Ausable had a room, Fowler felt let down. It was a small room, on the sixth and top floor, and scarcely a setting for a romantic adventure. Ausable was, for one thing, fat. Very fat. And then there was his accent. Though he spoke French and

German passably, he had never altogether lost the American accent he had brought to Paris from Boston twenty years ago. "You are disappointed," Ausable said wheezily over his shoulder.

(i) Which of the following can be associated with Ausable?

(a) Breaking stereotypes (b) Badass Villian
(c) Moral Hero (d) Spectacular leader

Ans. (a) Breaking stereotypes

(ii) State any one reference about a secret agent from the given extract.

Ans. It can be inferred from the extract that a secret agent is expected to be fit and suave.

(iii) Where was Ausable's room?

Ans. Ausable's room was on the sixth and top floor of the hotel.

(iv) Why was Fowler disappointed by Ausable when he met him?

Ans. Fowler was disappointed by Ausable when he met him because he didn't have the personality of a spy. He was fat and had an accent. Furthermore, he did not look mysterious or dangerous at all.

2. Read the following extract carefully and answer the questions that follow.

Ausable did not fit any description of a secret agent, Fowler had ever read. Following him down the musty corridor of the gloomy French hotel where Ausable had a room, Fowler felt let down. It was a small room, on the sixth and top floor, and scarcely a setting for a romantic adventure. Ausable was, for one thing, fat. Very fat. And then there was his accent. Though he spoke French and German passably, he had never altogether lost the American accent he had brought to Paris from Boston twenty years ago. "You are disappointed", Ausable said wheezily over his shoulder. "You were told that I was a secret agent, a spy, dealing in espionage and danger. You wished to meet me because you are a writer, young and romantic. You envisioned mysterious figures in the night, the crack of pistols, drugs in the wine."

CBSE Additional SQP 2023

(i) Which of these describes how Fowler felt at the beginning of the extract?

(a) His heart sank.
(b) He was shaken up.
(c) His stomach was in knots.
(d) He was at the end of his rope.

Ans. (a) His heart sank.

(ii) State one observation about Ausable based on the way he handled Fowler's disappointment with him.

Competency Based

Ans. Ausable's reaction on seeing Fowler's disappointment shows that he was perceptive and observant as he noticed Fowler's disappointment as well as the cause of it. Moreover, Ausable was confident. He didn't feel the need to apologise for disappointing Fowler. He accepted his disappointment without judgement. He was experienced enough in his field to understand that the reality of being a spy differs from, the perceptions of it.

(iii) How did the atmosphere of the French hotel influence Fowler's mood? Answer in 40 words.

Competency Based

Ans. The French hotel is described as 'gloomy', 'musty' and 'small'. This sombre atmosphere of the hotel added to Fowler's feeling of disappointment. He expected a grand atmosphere of mystery and danger, and was disappointed by the reality of the situation.

(iv) Which of these means the same as 'romantic' in the line below?

It was a small room, on the sixth and top floor, and scarcely a setting for a romantic adventure.

Ans. exciting

3. Read the following extract carefully and answer the questions that follow.

"Instead, you have spent a dull evening in a French music hall with a sloppy fat man who, instead of having messages slipped into his hand by dark-eyed beauties, gets only a prosaic telephone call making an appointment in his room. You have been bored!". The fat man chuckled to himself as he unlocked the door of his room and stood aside to let his frustrated guest enter. "You are disillusioned," Ausable told him. "But take cheer, my young friend. Presently you will see a paper, a quite important paper for which several men and women have risked their lives, come to me. Some day soon that paper may well affect the course of history. In that thought is in drama, is there not?"

Competency Based

(i) Which of these describes what Ausable is doing in the extract?

(a) He is relating to Fowler and attempting to change his view.
(b) He is justifiying his appearance to Fowler as that of a real spy.
(c) He is summarising events to help Fowler make sense of them.
(d) He is shaming himself so that Fowler's disappointment reduces.

Ans. (d) He is shaming himself so that Fowler's disappointment reduces.

(ii) What does being disillusioned mean?

Ans. Being disillusioned means to be disappointed at something being different from what one had expected it to be.

(iii) According to the extract, which elements are expected to be present in the life of a spy?

(a) Attractive women who deliver information.
(b) Discreet phone calls from other famous spies.
(c) Dramatic events that involve guns and action.
(d) An athletic body that moves in an agile manner.

Ans. According to the passage, the elements mentioned in a, c and d are to be present in the life of a spy.

(iv) Complete the sentence appropriately.

But take cheer my young friend the author means

Ans. be happy or not be disappointed

4. Read the following extract carefully and answer the questions that follow.

And as the light came on, Fowler had his first authentic thrill of the day. For halfway across the room, a small automatic pistol in his hand, stood a man.

Ausable blinked a few times.

(i) The 'man' referred to in the extract is

(a) the gatekeeper (b) the pantry boy
(c) Max (d) the hotel manager

Ans. (c) Max

(ii) Read the given statements and choose the correct statement.

(A) Fowler was excited to see pistol in Max's hand.

(B) The room belonged to Ausable.

Ans. (B) is right

(iii) How did Ausable react on seeing the 'man'? Give reasons for such a reaction.

Ans. Ausable was shocked to see 'the man', another secret agent, Max. This was so because according to the information provided to him, Max should be in Berlin.

(iv) Given an antonym of 'authentic'.

Ans. Fake

5. Read the following extract carefully and answer the questions that follow.

Max was slender, a little less than tall, with features that suggested slightly the crafty, pointed countenance of a fox. There was about him — aside from the gun — nothing especially menacing. "The report," he murmured. "The report that is being brought to you tonight concerning some new missiles. I thought I would take it from you. It will be safer in my hands than in yours." Ausable moved to an armchair and sat down heavily. "I'm going to raise the devil with the management this time, and you can bet on it," he said grimly. "This is the second time in a month that somebody has got into my room through that nuisance of a balcony!"

(i) State the reason why owning a gun gave a menacing impression to Max's character.

Ans. Owning a gun gave a menacing impression to Max's character because a gun has a threatening implication.

(ii) Which word can replace 'sat down heavily' in the sentence —'Ausable moved to an armchair and sat down heavily'?

Ans. Flumped

(iii) State True or False.

None of the terms (a) - (d) can be applied to the statement - It will be safer in my hands than in yours.

(a) A hypothesis - a proposed explanation for a phenomenon
(b) An assumption - something that is taken for granted or assumed to be true
(c) A hyperbole - exaggerated statements or claims not meant to be taken literally
(d) A premise - a proposition that forms the basis of an argument

Ans. False; An assumption

(iv) Max wouldn't appear menacing if not for the gun. Elaborate with reference to the extract.

Ans. Max was slender, a little less than tall, with features that suggested a crafty, pointed countenance of a fox. His appearance wasn't especially menacing except for the gun.

Part - II

Short Answer Type Questions

1. 'Stereotypes are often misleading'. Elaborate on the given quote in the context of 'The Midnight Visitor'. CBSE Question Bank 2021

Ans. It is true that stereotypes are often misleading. When Fowler came to meet Ausable, he had expected a smart looking active man who would deal with pistols, wine and dark eyed beauties. However, the reality was far from it. Ausable was a fat and sloppy man with an accent.

2. Did Fowler find the episode with Max thrilling or disappointing ? Give reasons for your answer.

Ans. Fowler must have found the episode with Max to be very thrilling. He was earlier disappointed to see Ausable but was very surprised at the tactful nature of the secret agent. His purpose of getting to know how Ausable reacts in different situations was fulfilled.

3. Why had Fowler wanted to meet Ausable? Is the meeting successful? Give reasons for your answer.

Or **What could be a reason for Fowler to visit Ausable in 'The Midnight Visitor'?** Competency Based

Ans. Fowler was a writer who wanted to meet Ausable, a secret agent, most probably to get material for his writings. He wanted to know how Ausable tackled different dangerous situations.

Yes, his meeting with Ausable is successful as he comes across a dangerous situation when Max, another secret agent came to take an important document from Ausable.

4. Describe Ausable's reaction after finding Max in his room.

Ans. Initially, when Ausable saw Max in his room he got a shock but he remained calm. Max also had a pistol with him, so Ausable didn't try anything disputable. He just kept himself calm and fooled Max by using his brain to invent stories.

5. Why did Ausable frame the story of the balcony? CBSE 2023

Or **Examine the wilty strategy used by Ausable in emerging as a super spy.** CBSE 2025

Ans. Ausable framed the story of the balcony to save himself and Fowler from the rival secret agent, Max. The rival would have been able to get the important report about the new missiles if Ausable had not created this story.

6. Why did Max's face turn black with anger? What did he want Ausable to do?

Ans. Max's face turned black with anger because he felt that his plan of extracting the important document from Ausable was in danger. He knew his plan could fail due to the knocking on the door, which Ausable identified as the police. He wanted Ausable to send the police away.

7. How did Ausable get rid of Max without using a weapon? CBSE 2023

Or **What story did Ausable cook up regarding the arrival of the police? How did it affect Max?** CBSE 2025

Ans. Ausable used his quick thinking, wit and creativity to get rid of Max. When he found Max waiting for him in his room, he made a story of a balcony under his window. He convinced Max about the balcony. Thus, when someone knocked at the door, Max fearing it to be the police, jumped out of the window and died.

8. Who actually had knocked at the door of Ausable's room? Why did he come there?

Ans. The waiter (Henry) in the hotel where Ausable stayed knocked at the door of Ausable's room. He had brought the drinks which Ausable had ordered when Fowler arrived at the hotel.

He came there because he was doing his duty of serving a customer of his hotel.

9. Describe Max as a secret agent. CBSE 2023

Ans. Max was a secret agent and an enemy of Ausable. He was thin but not very tall. He appeared clever and cunning like a fox. (Fowler comes across him in Ausable's room when he saw Max. Max had come to take the important report about new missiles. However, he is deceived by Ausable who made him jump out of his window.)

10. "Ausable shows great presence of mind in a situation of danger and surprise." Do you agree with this statement? If yes, why? Competency Based

Ans. Yes, I agree with this statement. Ausable showed great presence of mind when Max pointed a gun at him as he entered the hotel room with Fowler. He remained calm and cool and started inventing stories as required to fool Max into jumping to his death.

11. Who was Henry? What role did he play in Ausable's plan? CBSE 2024

Or **Henry unintentionally saved Ausable's life. Briefly comment.** CBSE Question Bank 2021

Ans. Henry was the waiter of the hotel in which Ausable lived. He helped Ausable unintentionally by coming on time and by not telling from outside the door that he had brought the drink he ordered. As a result, Max believed Ausable and jumped out of the window to his death.

12. Fowler's day took a one-eighty degree turn by the end of the evening. Examine the statement with reference to 'The Midnight Visitor'.

Ans. It is true that Fowler's day took a one-eighty degree turn by the end of the evening. He, as a young and romantic writer, wanted to interview the famous Ausable. However, he got a first hand experience of the dangerous situations faced by the detective.

13. Ausable was always one step ahead of everyone. Highlight any two instances from 'The Midnight Visitor' when this holds true.

Ans. It is true that Ausable was always one step ahead of everyone. There are various episodes in the story that show this. We see this as he outwitted Max and made him fall to his death. He had ordered a drink and had the waiter knocking just in time to trick Max into believing it was the police at door.

14. Max was unprepared for his mission. Discuss with reference to the chapter 'The Midnight Visitor'. **CBSE Question Bank 2021**

Ans. It can be truly said that Max was unprepared for his mission. Even though Max was a clever man with a gun in his hand, he did not prepare himself to match the cleverness of Ausable. He does not make sure that he knows the place where Ausable was staying and thus, was easily convinced about the balcony. As a result, he fell to his death.

15. 'Attack is the secret of defence.' Justify the statement in case of Ausable.

Ans. In the case of Ausable, attack is the secret of defence. He decided to use his brain and attack his opposition Max instead of defending himself. He does not take out his gun or attempt to fight Max. He uses his mind and creates a story that will ultimately led to Max's death. His story of the balcony is an attack that he makes on Max.

16. State one likely reason the writer of 'The Midnight Visitor' chose to characterise Ausable as short and fat. **CBSE SQP 2023**

Ans. The writer of 'The Midnight Visitor' chose to characterise Ausable as short and fat because the writer wanted to draw the readers' attention to his wittiness and strong mental ability. He wanted the readers to realise that intelligence did not need an attractive physical appearance.

17. State any one way in which Ausable or Max from 'The Midnight Visitor' are different from the usual portrayal of spies in movies and books. Why do you think the author has portrayed the characters in this way? Answer in 40-50 words. **Competency Based**

Or **Comment on the writer's likely choice to create an unconventional spy character like Ausable in 'The Midnight Visitor'.** **CBSE Additional SQP 2023**

Ans. In the story, Ausable is shown to be a fat and sloppy man which stands in a stark contrast to the image of a spy shown. One would expect to be fitter or muscular, as if they are ready for action at any moment. I think the author has done this to make the story look more real as compared to glamorous films that are not very realistic.

18. The various elements of Robert Arthur's writing style work together to create a sense of tension, uncertainty and suspense, well-suited to the mystery and suspense genre of the story, 'The Midnight Visitor'. Comment, with reference to any one element.

Ans. The author employs various elements of writing style to create a sense of tension, uncertainty and suspense, well-suited to the story's mystery and suspense genre. The conversation between Ausable and Max is filled with half-truths which heightens the story's sense of mystery. The reader is left wondering about Max's true motives and intentions, which adds to the sense of uncertainty and tension in the story. Further, the author carefully builds the tension throughout the story, gradually revealing new information and plot twists that keep the reader guessing and on edge.

19. What makes Ausable a good spy? Explain one quality with close reference to the story. **Competency Based**

Ans. We can say that Ausable is a good spy because he shows a great presence of mind. He is witty, creative and manipulative. He remains calm and composed in the time of crisis. We can say so because he not only makes up the story of the balcony but also uses the happenings of the day to his advantage. As a result of his quick thinking, he is able to get rid of Max.

20. How does the story's resolution challenge the reader's assumptions?

Ans. The story's resolution challenges the reader's assumptions by revealing that critical elements, such as the balcony and the police presence, were illusions crafted by Ausable. This twist forces readers to reevaluate their understanding of the story, demonstrating the deceptive nature of appearances and the protagonist's strategic cunning.

Long Answer Type Questions

1. Ausable was a clever secret agent. Do you agree with the statement? Justify your answer.

Ans. Yes, I agree with the statement that Ausable was a clever secret agent. Initially when Fowler met him, Ausable did not look at all like a conventional secret agent. He was fat and had an American accent. He was unlike the usual secret agents. However, just like spies and secret agents he was very sharp and active.

He saved himself as well as Fowler from a dangerous situation by using his intelligence. He cleverly created two stories, one about the balcony outside the window of his room and the other about calling the police for extra protection.

In the face of eminent danger, he remained calm and composed. His composture also saved the important documents from going into the wrong hands of Max.

Ausable's intelligence fooled Max into believing a false story and made him jump out of the window. His presence of mind, tactfulness and calmness, all point towards his cleverness and wisdom.

2. Why did Max scream shrilly when he dropped to the balcony?

Ans. In the story, 'The Midnight Visitor', Max screamed shrilly when he dropped to the balcony because the balcony did not exist at all. It was just a piece of Ausable's imagination.

Ausable had created the story of the balcony to save himself, Fowler and the important papers from reaching to wrong hands. He befooled Max into believing that his balcony exists. His brief description to his guest Fowler regarding the presence of the balcony and his complaints regarding the hotel management convinced Max into believing that there was a balcony just outside the window of Ausable's room.

Therefore, when Ausable creates another story of the police, Max tried to jump onto the non-existent balcony without looking. As the room was on sixth floor, Max fell from it unexpectedly and must have died by falling from such a height. His scream was then a result of this unexpected fall.

3. A calm mind can help you tackle the direct stress. Elaborate with reference to 'The Midnight Visitor'.

Ans. It is true to say that of a calm mind can help us tackle the direct stress easily. When we face difficult situations, we are always told to stay calm, cool and focussed.

If we panic, it hampers our thinking ability and we are unable to take proper decisions. Our minds don't work properly and we lose hope.

In the story 'The Midnight Visitor', Ausable, the secret agent remains calm. This calmness and composure saves not only him and Fowler but also the important papers. It also enables him to create two imaginary stories that led him to outwit (deceive) Max. If he had panicked and done something fishy, then Max would have probably killed him and his guest Fowler. But, Ausable kept his mind cool and deceived Max into believing his story. Consequently, Max fell to his death.

Just like Ausable, we also need to calm our nerves and cool our mind in times of difficulty. If we keep our mind cool and focussed, we can find ways to get out of a dangerous situation.

4. Max was a cunning spy but his carelessness and foolishness proved fatal for him. Do you agree that it were these characteristics that led to his downfall? **Competency Based**

Or **Though Max was very cunning, still he was but 'a little spy' before Ausable. Explain.**

Ans. Yes, I agree that carelessness and foolishness led to the downfall of Max. Though Max was a cunning secret agent, he was indeed careless and foolish. He was overconfident and proud which failed his mission. As a clever spy, Max was sent on an important mission of procuring a vital document on the new missiles from his rival, Ausable. But, he was deceived.

Max's pride and foolishness led to his downfall. He, in his carelessness, did not take any pains to inspect the hotel as well as Ausable's room in advance.

Consequently, when Ausable tells him about a balcony outside his window and the police knocking at the door, Max believes him without any doubt. He trusted his rival blindly without any thoughts and as a result, failed himself as well as his mission.

Unlike him, Ausable's calmness and presence of mind saved him, his guest Fowler and the important papers he was about to receive.

He set up a successful trap by putting up very little efforts. Max foolishly fell into this trap. This carelessness and foolishness rendered him to be a little spy before Ausable and also cost him his life.

5. Describe the twist in the plot in 'The Midnight Visitor'. Analyse how Fowler's opinion of Ausable must have undergone a change after the plot twist.

Ans. The story 'The Midnight Visitor' contains two twists that change the direction of the story. The first one is the knock on the hotel room door. According to Ausable, it should be a policeman but in reality it was a waiter who had been asked to bring up drinks. The second one is that the room did not have an attached balcony, as described by Ausable.

So, when Max stepped out, he was injured since he landed on the hard ground below instead of a balcony. The sudden shifts in the story lead to a change in Fowler's impression of Ausable. When Fowler met Ausable, he was nothing like the typical spy that Fowler had seen in the movies and novels. The day had been an ordinary one rather than one full of car chases and gun-slinging criminals.

However, at the end, Ausable's interaction with Max and how he outwits him really impressed Fowler. He realised that first impressions could be wrong and appearances can be deceptive. Ausable outwits Max with his intelligence by telling a believable story to create a trap. Thus, while Fowler was initially disappointed and unimpressed by Ausable, his opinion is most likely to have changed to one of respect and awe after Ausable was able to outwit Max.

6. The non-existent balcony plays a crucial role in 'The Midnight Visitor'. How? Examine the witty strategy used by Ausable in emerging as a super spy. **CBSE 2024 C**

Ans. In The Midnight Visitor by Robert Arthur, the non-existent balcony, which Ausable claims to overlook from his window, serves as a crucial plot device. It stands as a representation of both illusion and deception, two vital components of a spy's toolkit. When confronted by Max, Ausable strategically invokes the idea of the balcony and misdirects Max's attention, creating the illusion that there is an escape route and a potential danger that could disrupt Max's plans. This critical moment highlights Ausable's brilliance in turning a seemingly trivial detail into a life-saving diversion.

Ausable's ability to conjure the image of the balcony showcases his resourcefulness. As a spy, he employs keen observation and a deep understanding of human psychology. By invoking the nonexistent balcony, he persuades Max to second-guess himself, realising the uncertainty and danger that a possible escape route could entail. In doing so, Ausable not only escapes his imminent threat but also reshapes the power dynamics of their confrontation.

In conclusion, 'The Midnight Visitor' masterfully weaves together themes of intellect, deception, and survival, with the non-existent balcony playing a crucial role in Ausable's emergence as a super spy. By deftly manipulating perceptions and creating illusions, Ausable showcases the power of wits over weapons, reinforcing the notion that the mind is indeed a formidable weapon in the high-stakes world of espionage.

ASSESSMENT EXERCISE

Extract Based Questions

Read the following extract carefully and answer the questions that follow.

Who is that? Who is at the door?
Flower jumped at the sudden knocking at the door.
Ausable just smiled. "That will be the police," he said.

(i) State True or False.

None of the terms (a)-(d) below can be applied to the question.

That will be the police.

(a) A hypothesis-a proposed explanation for a phenomenon.

(b) An assumption-something that is taken for granted or assumed to be true without proof.

(c) A theory-a well-substantiated explanation for a natural phenomenon

(d) A premise-a proposition that forms the basis of an argument.

(ii) Why did Ausable smile? What does it tell us about Ausable?

(iii) The sudden knocking at the door made Fowler and Max feel ....

(iv) Complete the analogy by selecting the sutable word from the text.

Slow : Slowly :: .... : Suddenly

Short Answer (SA) Type Questions

1. Why was Fowler with Ausable when they entered the hotel room?
2. What surprise waited for Ausable and Fowler when they entered the flat?
3. Why was the balcony a nuisance to Ausable ?
4. What reason did Ausable give Max for calling the police to the hotel room?
5. What role did the waiter bringing the drinks play in this whole drama?
6. How did Ausable make sure that Max did not know what was outside the window?

Long Answer (LA) Type Questions

1. Sometimes, appearances can be deceptive. Elaborate with reference to 'The Midnight Visitor'.
2. Presence of mind and intelligence are more powerful than a gun. How far is it true in the case of Ausable, the secret agent?
3. Can you think of the reasons why the author had shown Ausable as different? Justify your answer.

A Question of Trust

by Victor Canning

The story is about Horace Danby, 'a good, honest citizen'. Horace robbed a safe every year to finance his hobby of reading rare and expensive books. The story describes his last attempt wherein he was caught by the police due to a pretty young lady who claims to be owner of the house.

Horace Danby

Horace Danby had a good reputation in society. He was a good and an honest citizen who was about fifty years old. He was unmarried and lived with a housekeeper who took care of his health. He suffered from attacks of hay-fever (an allergy) in summer. Horace Danby was a successful lock-maker and had two helpers. However, he was not a completely honest man.

Horace was an unusual thief because of his hobby. He loved collecting rare and expensive books. So, he robbed a safe every year and secretly bought the books through an agent. However, fifteen years ago, he was sent to prison for the first time and had to work in the prison library.

Horace Plans a Robbery

Horace had planned a robbery at Shotover Grange. He was sure that just like his earlier robberies, this one would also be successful even though he could slightly feel the hay fever in his nose. He had carefully studied the rooms, electric wiring, the path and the garden of Shotover Grange for two weeks. He knew that the family had gone to London and that the servants living there were going for a movie.

Horace knew that there were about fifteen thousand pounds' worth of jewels in the Grange safe. If he sold them one by one, he would get approximately 5000 in money. This would help him buy three very interesting books in the sale in autumn.

Horace Enters the House

As the servants left the house, Horace came out from behind the garden wall carrying a bag full of the required tools. Horace had seen that the housekeeper hang the key to the kitchen door. Horace wore his gloves, took the key and entered the house. He saw a small dog lying in the kitchen but Horace silenced it. Horace knew that he only needed to say the dog's real name with love to silence it.

The Target Safe

Horace knew that the safe was in the drawing room behind a poor painting. He had read a detailed description of the house and seen its picture in a magazine article which made his job easy. He also knew that the safe was connected to a poorly built burglar alarm. Horace knew that he had four hours to complete his robbery. So, after arranging his tools, he went to cut its wire.

Horace Finds it Difficult to Work

A bowl of flowers was kept on the table. Because of the flowers, Horace started sneezing. As a result, he found it difficult to work. So, he covered his face with a handkerchief.

Horace Met a Young and Pretty Lady

Suddenly, Horace heard a voice asking him about the reason for sneezing. Not realising that someone had caught him, he answered hay fever. The voice suggested him to get a cure for his disease and find out which particular plant was causing him allergy. The voice added that Horace could be heard from the top of the house.

The voice was quiet, kind and firm. As Horace looked at the source of the voice, he noticed a woman standing in the doorway. She was young, pretty and was dressed in red.

The Lady of the House

As Sherry was rubbing against the lady, she told it to calm down. She, then, added that she came back in time but had not expected to meet a burglar in her house.

Horace was shocked but he also had some hope because the lady seemed to be amused at meeting him. He thought that he might avoid trouble if he treated her in the right way. So, he told the lady that he hadn't expected to meet any one from the family of the owner of the Shotover Grange.

Hearing this, the lady asked him what he was going to do now. Horace told the lady that first he thought to run away. But when the lady threatened Horace to call the police, he said that he would cut the telephone wire and leave her helpless. When the lady asked him if he was going to hurt her, Horace replied that he only wanted to frighten her.

Horace Doesn't Want to Go to Prison

Horace told the lady to forget the incident and to let him go. However, the lady refused. She told Horace that he was planning to rob her. If she let him go, he would rob someone else. To this, Horace told the lady that he does not commit theft for any evil purpose. He stole from the rich for a very good reason. He also added that he does not want to go to prison.

Horace begged her to let him go and even promised that he would never steal again. To persuade her, Horace takes off his gloves to help the lady to light her cigarette.

Lady's Condition For Horace's Freedom

After realising that Horace did not want to go the prison the lady put forward a condition for Horace's freedom. She told him that she had promised her husband to take the jewels to the bank. However, she forgot and kept the jewels in her safe. She wanted to wear them at a party but had forgotten the combination of numbers to open the safe. So, she needed him to open the safe. Horace agreed to this condition. Within an hour, Horace opened the safe, giving the jewels to the lady and went away.

Horace Got Arrested

Two days after the incident, Horace planned to rob again to satisfy his hobby. However, he couldn't do so because by noon, a policeman had arrested him for a robbery at Shotover Grange. He was told that his fingerprints were found all over the safe as he had opened the safe without his gloves.

Horace's Trust was Broken

Horace told the police that the lady of the house had told him to open the safe. However, the real owner of the house was a sixty years old lady with grey hair and sharp tongue. She claimed that Horace's story was nonsense. Horace realised that the pretty young woman was also a thief who had manipulated him and used his skill to steal the jewels. Horrace, then, became an assistant librarian in prison. He often thought about the clever lady who tricked him and broke the honour among thieves.

Word Meaning

Word	Meaning
housekeeper	person looking after the domestic work in a house
hay fever	disease affecting the nose and throat caused by allergy to pollen or dust
served	spent
sentence	punishment
safe	a strong locked box used for storing valuable items
Grange	a large house in the countryside with farm building attached to it
stirred	started to wake up

Word	Meaning
tickle	itching
make him happy	keep him satisfied
burglar alarm	alarm to warn about thieves
hindering	delaying
one with firmness in it	having determination
get you	arrest you
desperate	without any hope
mended	repaired
look for	steal from/rob

NCERT FOLDER

NCERT Intext and Exercise Questions

READ AND FIND OUT (NCERT PAGE 20)

Q.1 What does Horace Danby like to collect?

Ans. Horace Danby likes to collect rare and expensive books.

Q.2 Why does he steal every year?

Ans. He steals every year so that he could buy the rare and expensive books that he loved to collect.

READ AND FIND OUT (NCERT PAGE 22)

Q.1 Who is speaking to Horace Danby?

Ans. A lady standing in the doorway is speaking to Horace Danby.

Q.2 Who is the real culprit in the story?

Ans. The real culprit in the story was the woman in the red dress who pretended to be a member of the family living at Shotover Grange. She tricked Horace Danby into believing her and cleverly took away all the jewels that were kept in the safe.

THINK ABOUT IT (NCERT PAGE 25)

Q.1 Did you begin to suspect, before the end of the story, that the lady was not the person Horace Danby took her to be? If so, at what point did you realise this and how?

Ans. Yes, we begin to suspect before the end of the story that the lady was not the person Horace Danby took her to be. Our suspicion begin when she stays calm upon seeing an intruder in her home. Moreover, she did not call the police and instead, asked Horace to take out all the jewels from the safe. Besides, it seemed highly unlikely that she would forget the number to open the safe. Therefore, it was evident, before the story ended that the lady was not the person who she claimed to be.

Q.2 What are the subtle ways in which the lady manages to deceive Horace Danby into thinking she is the lady of the house? Why doesn't Horace suspect that something is wrong?

Ans. The lady's confident walk, her familiarity with the dog Sherry, her act of touching up her make-up and the ease with which she picks a cigarette from the right place are enough to deceive Horace into thinking that she was the lady of the house.

Further, she engages Horace in conversation, and appears friendly and non-threatening, putting him at ease. Horace doesn't suspect something is wrong because he is focused on carrying out his robbery and is eager to please the lady to secure his release. He is also preoccupied with avoiding detection and doesn't question her authority or presence in the house.

Q.3 "Horace Danby was good and respectable - but not completely honest". Why do you think this description is apt for Horace? Why can't he be categorised as a typical thief?

Ans. Horace Danby was good and respectable but not completely honest is an apt description for Horace. He was a respectable lock-maker who had a good reputation in the society. However, Horace was also an unusual thief. He had a hobby of collecting rare and expensive books which he fulfilled by robbing a safe every year. Thus, he was not a completely honest man. Horace cannot be categorised as a typical thief because he was not a regular offender. He robbed once a year and only took what was required.

Q.4 Horace Danby was a meticulous planner but still he faltered. Where did he go wrong and why?

Ans. It is true that Horace Danby was a meticulous planner but he had faltered in the robbery he was carrying out in Shotover Grange.

This failure was because of the lady in red who deceived and tricked Horace into believing that she was the lady of the house. Horace, who had carefully planned the robbery, did not care to get any information about the housemates. Consequently, he blindly believed that the lady in red was the lady of the house. So, when she suddenly appeared, Horace carelessly opened the safe without his gloves.

TALK ABOUT IT (NCERT PAGE 25)

Q.1 Do you think Horace Danby was unfairly punished, or that he deserved what he got?

Ans. I think Horace Danby deserved what he got. A crime is a crime, no matter if it is committed for your own benefit or for somebody else's benefit.

Q.2 Do intentions justify actions? Would you, like Horace Danby, do something wrong if you thought your ends justified the means? Do you think that there are situations in which it is excusable to act less than honestly?

Ans. 'Ends do not justify means' is a very old and time tested saying. To reach one's own profitable or good end one should never harm others.

No, unlike Horace Danby, I would never do something wrong if the end justified the means.

(The last part of the question must be discussed among students)

REVIEW EXERCISE

Including Competency Based Questions

Part I

Multiple Choice Questions

1. Horace had served his sentence in prison ....

(a) 20 years ago (b) 5 years ago
(c) 15 years ago (d) 20 years ago

Ans. (c) 15 years ago

2. Which of the following can you associate with Horace Danby?

1. Stole Paintings **2. Book Lover**
3. Good Citizen **4. Assistant Librarian**

(a) 1, 2 and 3 (b) 2, 3 and 4
(c) 2 and 3 (d) None of these

Ans. (b) 2, 3 and 4

3. Why do you think Horace had to serve his first prison sentence?

(a) He stole a rare and an expensive book.
(b) He stole a safe to buy books.
(c) He stole a painting.
(d) He was caught red-handed while selling locks.

Ans. (b) He stole a safe to buy books.

4. Where did the housekeeper hang the keys?

(a) At the kitchen door (b) At the keyboard
(c) Behind the door (d) None of these

Ans. (a) At the kitchen door

5. Where had the servants at Shotover Grange gone that afternoon?

(a) To their homes (b) To the market
(c) To the park (d) To the cinema

Ans. (d) To the cinema

6. How many hours did Horace have before the servants return?

(a) One hour (b) Two hours
(c) Five hours (d) Four hours

Ans. (d) Four hours

7. Why was it not much difficult for Horace to open the safe at Shotover Grange?

(a) He was an expert in opening safe.
(b) He had lived with locks and safes all his life.
(c) He knew the numbers to open the safe.
(d) None of the above.

Ans. (b) He had lived with locks and safes all his life.

8. Arrange in order the steps followed by Horace Danby to enter the Shotover Grange.

1. He opened the door
2. He cut the wire of burglar alarm
3. He took the key
4. He put on a pair of gloves
5. He talked to Sherry

(a) 3, 2, 4, 5, 1 (b) 2, 3, 1, 4, 5
(c) 5, 4, 3, 2, 1 (d) 4, 3, 1, 5, 2

Ans. (d) 4, 3, 1, 5, 2

9. The 'lady of the house' made a promise to her husband that ....

(a) she would wear the jewels in the party
(b) she would take the jewels to the bank
(c) she would return the jewels to her husband
(d) she would not the safe in his absence

Ans. (b) she would take the jewels to the bank

10. How would you assess Horace for opening safe for the lady in red?

(a) A wrong deed done with good intention cannot make it right
(b) He was honest and innocent
(c) He should not have been arrested
(d) He did the right thing to save his life

Ans. (a) A wrong deed done with good intention cannot make it right

11. In the chapter 'A Question of Trust', Horace was arrested on the basis of the ....

(a) lady in red's confession
(b) fingerprints left on the safe
(c) owner of the house complaint
(d) None of the above

Ans. (b) fingerprints left on the safe

12. What was the lady in red gifted with?

(a) Rare personality (b) Full of confidence
(c) Smart and intelligent (d) All of these

Ans. (d) All of these

13. What is the theme of the story 'A Question of Trust'?

(a) We should not trust anyone.
(b) Overconfidence leads to failure.

(c) A lady in red can be fool anyone.
(d) Wear your gloves while working.

Ans. (a) We should not trust anyone.

14. It is said that you must set a thief to catch a thief. But it is also said that there is honour among thieves. Which saying does the story 'A Question of Trust' illustrate?

(a) You must set a thief to catch a thief
(b) Honour among thieves
(c) Both (a) and (b)
(d) None of the above

Ans. (b) Honour among thieves

Extract Based Questions

1. Read the following extract carefully and answer the questions that follow.

So he robbed a safe every year. Each year he planned carefully just what he would do, stole enough to last for twelve months and secretly bought the books he loved through an agent.

(i) Why did 'he' rob only one safe every year?

Ans. He robbed only one safe a year because the money that he stole lasted 12 months and was enough to satisfy his hobby.

(ii) Which of the following best describes 'he'?

(a) Bad and dishonest
(b) Very good and honest
(c) Good, respectable and completely honest
(d) Good, respectable but not completely honest

Ans. (d) Good, respectable but not completely honest

(iii) Complete the analogy by selecting the suitable word from the text.
Beginning : End :: First : ....

Ans. Last

(iv) What did 'he' plan carefully every year? How?

Ans. 'He' carefully planned his robbery every year. He studied the houses carefully to the last detail so that he can steal as efficiently as possible.

2. Read the following extract carefully and answer the questions that follow.

A small dog was lying in the kitchen. It stirred, made a noise and moved its tail in a friendly way.

"All right, Sherry" Horace said as he passed. All you had to do to keep dogs quiet was to call them by their right names, and show them love.

(i) How did he manage to handle the dog?

(a) By beating him (b) By calling him
(c) By showing him love (d) Both (b) and (c)

Ans. (d) Both (b) and (c)

(ii) .... in the passage means the same as 'cordial'.

Ans. Friendly

(iii) What is the meaning of 'stirred'?

Ans. The meaning of 'stirred' is to move or cause something to move slightly.

(iv) What is the name of the dog mentioned in the above extract? Where is it?

Ans. Sherry is the name of the dog mentioned in the given extract. It was sleeping in its house.

3. Read the following extract carefully and answer the questions that follow.

How foolish people are when they own valuable things, Horace thought. A magazine article had described this house, giving a plan of all the rooms and a picture of this room. The writer had even mentioned that the painting hid a safe! But Horace found that the flowers were hindering him in his work. He buried his face in his handkerchief. Then he heard a voice say from the doorway, "What is it? A cold or hay fever?" Before he could think, Horace said, "Hay fever," and found himself sneezing again. The voice went on, "You can cure it with a special treatment, you know, if you find out just what plant gives you the disease. I think you'd better see a doctor, if you're serious about your work. I heard you from the top of the house just now."

(i) When Horace was trying to work, who/what interferred him in his work?

Ans. The flowers in the room were giving him a sudden allergy which resulted in Horace's work being interferred with.

(ii) Which magazine could have published the article mentioned in the given extract?

(a) Paws and Claws
(b) Outdoors and Landscaping
(c) Interiors
(d) None of the above

Ans. (c) Interiors

(iii) Before he could think, Horace said, "Hay fever". How would you judge the nature of the response?

Ans. The response given by Horace is spontaneous. Horace is so engrossed in his task that he does not pay attention to that fact that there is someone else present in the Grange. So, when he is asked a question, he gives an automatic response.

(iv) Identify the sentence which can be an example of sarcasm from the extract.

Ans. The following sentence in the extract is an example of sarcasm

"I think you'd better see a doctor, if you're serious about your work."

4. Read the following extract carefully and answer the questions that follow.

But he never got the chance to begin his plan. By noon a policeman had arrested him for the jewel robbery at Shotover Grange. His fingerprints, for he had opened the safe without gloves, were all over the room, and no one believed him when he said that the wife of the owner of the house had asked him to open the safe for her. The wife herself, a gray-haired, sharp-tongued woman of sixty, said that the story was nonsense. Horace is now the assistant librarian in the prison. He often thinks of the charming, clever young lady who was in the same profession as he was, and who tricked him. He gets very angry when anyone talks about 'honour among thieves'.

CBSE Question Bank 2021

(i) Based on the extract, choose what you think are the main feelings Horace probably has, for the young lady who tricked him, when he thinks about her?

(a) Anger and blame
(b) Admiration and respect
(c) Respect and gratitude
(d) Anger and vengeance

Ans. (b) Admiration and respect

(ii) Who was the wife of the owner of Shotover Grange? Was she the same person Horace had met when he broke into the Shotover Grange?

Ans. The wife of the owner of Shotover Grange was a gray-haired woman of sixty years who had a sharp tongued.

No, she was not the same person as the lady he had met that day was a charming and clever young lady.

(iii) Which evidence was found at Shotover Grange that proved Horace guilty of theft?

Ans. Horace's fingerprints were found all over the safe as he opened it without gloves, which proved him guilty of theft.

(iv) 'Honour among thieves' is an example of a/an .... (idiom/foreign word)

Ans. idiom

Part II

Short Answer Type Questions

1. Give a brief description of Horace Danby.

Ans. Horace Danby was a good and respectable man. He was a 50-year-old bachelor who lived with a caretaker. He was a successful locksmith with two helpers. He was a healthy man who sometimes suffered from attacks of hay fever.

Horace Danby, however, was also a thief who robbed to satisfy his love of collecting rare and expensive books.

2. What was the passion of Horace Danby and how did he satisfy it?

Or **What was Horace Danby's hobby? How did he manage to fulfill it?**

Ans. Horace Danby's hobby and passion was to collect rare and expensive books. To fulfill it or to satisfy this passion, he used to rob a safe every year and then, brought the books secretly through an agent.

3. How did Danby prepare for the robbery at Shotover Grange?

Or **How did Horace Danby plan his robberies?**

Or **Why was Horace Danby sure that his robbery at Shotover Grange would be a successful one?**

Or **Horace Danby was a typical thief. Describe how he planned his work.** **CBSE 2024**

Ans. Horace Danby always planned his robberies meticulously. He prepared for the robbery at Shotover Grange by studying the house, its rooms, the electric wiring, paths and garden. He knew that the family was in London. He also knew that the servants were going out to watch a movie that afternoon.

Further, he knew the location of the safe and that it could be opened only through a specific code inaddition, he also read that the safe had a poorly built burglar alarm attached to it.

4. Describe the safe at Shotover Grange.

Or **Where was the safe at Shotover Grange? What was there inside it? What did Horace expect to get if he sold them one by one?**

Ans. The safe at Shotover Grange was kept in the drawing room behind a poor painting. The safe had jewels worth about 15000 pounds kept in it. Because of his careful planning, Horace Danby was sure that his robbery at Shotover Grange would be a successful one. Horace expected to get at least 5000 pounds if he sold the jewels one by one.

5. Whom did Horace Danby see in the kitchen? How did they greet each other? What tact did Horace apply there?

Ans. Horace Danby saw the family dog, Sherry, in the kitchen. The dog greeted Horace by stirring, making a noise and wagging its tail in a friendly way.
Horace greeted the dog by tactfully calming it down, calling it by its name and showing love to it.

6. What did Horace Danby wonder about for a moment? What did he think and decide?

Ans. On seeing the poor painting in front of the safe, Horace Danby wondered for a moment whether to collect pictures instead of books. But then, he thought that books were better in a small house like his, as paintings took up too much space in the room.

7. How did flowers hinder Horace in his work?

Ans. Flowers hindered Horace in his work because he suffered from the attack of hay fever, a disorder affecting the nose and throat, caused by an allergy to pollen or dust. Due to this problem, whenever he came close to flowers, he began to sneeze and could be caught.

8. When and why did the woman in red say, "Society must be protected from men like you". Doesn't it sound ironical?

Or **"Society must be protected from men like you." Comment on the irony of the given quote.** **CBSE Question Bank 2021**

Ans. When Horace asked the woman in red to forget the incident and let him go, she told him that if she lets him go, he would rob someone else.

Society, then, must be protected from men like him, i.e. robbers. The statement is ironical as she herself was a thief who decieved Horace and robbed the house.

9. What are the subtle ways in which the lady manages to deceive Horace Danby into thinking she is the mistress of the house? **Competency Based**

Ans. The subtle ways in which the lady manages to deceive Horace Danby into thinking she is the mistress of the house are her grace, charm, comfort level, knowledge, persistence, way of talking confidently and familiarity with the household.

10. Did the lady in red keep her promise? Give reasons for your answer.

Ans. Yes, the lady in red kept her promise for two days after the incident as everything went normally for Horace. Horace was arrested because the owners of the house had found the broken safe with Horace's fingerprints on it. Hence, it can be said that the lady in red did not call the police as promised.

11. The woman posing as house owner's wife had laid out a careful plan to dupe Horace Danby. Cite any two instances from the text that suggest the same. **CBSE Question Bank 2021**

Ans. It is true that the woman posing as the house owner's wife had laid out a careful plan to dupe Horace Danby. The woman spoke to Horace Danby in an authoritative tone to open the safe as she had forgotten the password. In another instance, she further promised him that she would not report to the police about this theft if the jewels are taken out for her by him.

12. In the chapter 'A Question of Trust', Horace Danby's final arrest was a blessing in disguise. Comment briefly.

Ans. Horace Danby's final arrest was a blessing in disguise because after his arrest, he became the assistant librarian in the prison. He, further, fulfilled his desire of reading books.

13. 'A Question of Trust' is a story about the robbery of the robber. Expound.

Or **"Horace Danby is a thief who was cheated by another thief." Justify.** **CBSE 2024**

Ans. It is true that 'A Question of Trust' is a story about the robbery of the robber. The story essentially is about Horace Danby, a book robber who meticulously plans a robbery at Shotover Grange. But he himself is robbed of his respect and freedom when another robber tricks and deceives him into robbing the place for him.

14. What does the phrase 'honour among thieves' mean? Why does Horace get angry at this phrase? **CBSE 2023**

Ans. The phrase 'honour among thieves' means that thieves would never cheat each other in their deeds. Horace gets angry at this phrase because he got cheated by another thief while he was in the midst of his planned robbery.

15. How did Horace feel about the prospect of going to prison?

Ans. Horace felt terrified at the prospect of going to prison, as he despised the idea of being incarcerated and losing his freedom. He pleaded with the woman to spare him from imprisonment, expressing genuine fear and desperation to avoid the consequences of his criminal actions.

16. How did Horace feel about 'honour among thieves' after his experience?

Ans. Horace felt angry and disillusioned about the notion of 'honour among thieves' after his experience. He realised that others in the criminal world did not share his ideals of honesty and respectability, leading him to resent the false sense of camaraderie or morality that this concept implied.

Long Answer Type Questions

1. Horace was clever but the lady in red was cleverer. Do you agree with this statement? Justify your answer.

Or **"The lady in red was a more professional thief than Horace Danby." Elaborate .**

Ans. Yes, it is true that Horace was clever but the lady in red was cleverer than him. The lady in red was a more professional thief than Horace Danby. Horace Danby is a meticulous planner who had carefully planned the robbery. He had all the information he needed to carry out his plans. He not only had read a detailed description of the house but also knew that the servants were going for a movie.

Even while robbing he wore gloves and was careful not to leave any fingerprints. However, all his planning falls short with the presence of the lady in red.

The lady in red also knew everything about the house. However, her presence of mind gave her an upper hand in the robbery. The charm and confidence with which she carries herself in front of Horace make him believe that she is the owner of the house. She exploited Horace's fear of being discovered very skillfully and ensured that Horace's fingerprints were left on the site. She even robbed the safe without Horace knowing her real identity.

She not only tricked Horace Danby but also left him to be blamed for the robbery.

2. Do you think that there are certain situations in which you can be excused for acting dishonestly? Elaborate with reference to 'A Question of Trust'. **Competency Based**

Ans. Yes, there are situations in which we can be excused for acting dishonestly. If something wrong is done unintentionally, it may be excused or pardoned with minimal punishment. However, it cannot be excused if it is carried out with the knowledge of the action being wrong. In the story, 'A Question of Trust', Horace Danby intentionally robs the rich people.

He robs to satisfy his love for collecting rare and expensive books which might be considered to be done with good intention. However, it is not justified.

Horace Danby was considered to be a good and a respected person. He had a good reputation in society even though he was thief. This intentions may not be harmful for anyone yet, it cannot be pardoned at all. A crime always remains a crime and the guilty must always be punished. I think that there are certain situations in which one can be excused for acting dishonestly. Such situations must help others as well as oneself and in any case, must not be harmful for anyone.

3. Horace was a successful thief because he carefully planned his robberies. Should we call him a successful thief and still appreciate his work? Why or why not?

Ans. Yes, Horace is a successful thief as he carefully planned his robberies and completes them well. As a thief, he had never been caught expect for once. Horace's last robbery at Shotover Grange was very carefully planned. Before carrying out his plans, he had made sure to carefully study the infrastructure of the house for two weeks. He had briefly looked at the electrical wiring, the path and the gardens of the house.

Horace cleverly entered the house and made sure to wear gloves so that no fingerprints were left. He had even studied the schedules of the people in the house. All the meticulous planning does make him a successful thief.

However, we cannot appreciate his work. The wealth that he had gathered was a result of his robberies. It did not belong to him. By stealing other people's valuables, he may have become successful but he can never stop to be a thief/criminal. He may be efficient but should not be appreciated.

4. 'Honour among thieves' is considered a popular quote. Examine 'A Question of Trust' as a story woven around this code. **CBSE SQP 2023**

Ans. It is commonly believed that thieves don't betray or double cross each other. Rather they may even help each other. This goes hand-in-hand with the protagonist of 'A Question of Trust', Horace Danby was careful whenever he conducted a theft once a year. He prepared for his thefts so well that it would have been impossible for him to be ever caught. In the story, then, his only fault was trusting the lady in red blindly. He failed to anticipate the skills of the lady in red who fooled him to commit a theft herself.

The lady in red did not follow the code of honour that normally exists between two thieves even though she herself was a thief. Infact, she made a fool of him and incriminated him for a theft that she profitted from. Thus, Horace ended up going to prison for the second time in his life. He felt very betrayed by a fellow thief.

ASSESSMENT EXERCISE

Extract Based Questions

Read the following extract carefully and answer the questions that follow.

The voice went on, "You can cure it with a special treatment, you know, if you find out just what plant gives you the disease. I think you'd better see a doctor, if you're serious about your work."

(i) Whose voice is referred to in the above extract?

(a) The old lady who pretended to be a member of the household

(b) The young lady who pretended to be a servant of the household

(c) The young lady who pretended to be a member of the household

(d) The young man who pretended to be a member of the household

(ii) What was the first thought that came to Horace's mind as soon as he saw the woman ?

(iii) What is the tone of the voice in the above extract?

(iv) Complete the analogy by selecting the suitable word from the text.

Waist : Waste :: .... : Sea

Short Answer (SA) Type Questions

1. Why was it not difficult for Horace to open the safe?
2. Why can't Horace Danby be categorised as a typical thief?
3. "Horace Danby was good and respectable but not completely honest." Is this an apt description of Horace? If yes, why?
4. How did the lady use Horace Danby's fear to her advantage?
5. How did Horace help the 'landlady'?

Long Answer (LA) Type Questions

1. What impression do you form of the 'landlady' that Horace meets?
2. Do you think Horace Danby was unfairly punished or that he deserved what he got? Do you think that honesty in wrong acts is not desirable? **Competency Based**

Footprints Without Feet

by HG Wells

The story is an extract from the novel titled 'The Invisible Man'. It centres around a brilliant scientist, Griffin who had discovered how to make himself invisible. The story narrates certain episodes of how Griffin had misused his discovery for his own benefit.

Boys See Footprints on a Street

Two boys on a street in London were surprised to see fresh muddy footprints of bare feet on the steps of a house. As they were still gazing (looking carefully), fresh footmark appeared. This fascinated the boys as they couldn't find the person making them and so, they followed the footmarks. However, the footprints soon disappeared.

Mystery of the Footprints

The footprints had been made by Griffin, a crazy and strange scientist who had discovered how to make his body invisible or transparent. He had conducted many experiments to prove that the human body could become invisible. Finally, he swallowed some drugs that made his body transparent and solid like glass.

Griffin : A Lawless Scientist

Griffin was a great scientist but a lawless person. His landlord did not like him and tried to evict (throw out) him from the house. So, Griffin set fire to his landlord's house.

To escape from this situation, Griffin removed his clothes and became invisible. Later, he became a homeless wanderer in London without any clothes and money.

Hidden in a Big London Store

Griffin managed to escape from the observation of the two keen boys. As it was mid-winter and the weather was bitterly cold in London, Griffin decided to slip into a big London store for warmth. When the store closed at night, Griffin wore some warm clothes, shoes, an overcoat and a hat. Thus, he became a visible person.

He ate cold meat and drank some coffee from the kitchen of the store. He even had some sweets and wine from the grocery store and then, went to sleep on a pile of quilts.

Griffin is Invisible Again

When Griffin woke up next morning, the shop assistants had already arrived at the shop. On being seen, Griffin panicked and started running. As he was being chased, he again took off his newly found clothes. Consequently, he again became invisible and had to remain naked in the chilly winter.

Griffin at a Theatrical Company

Griffin decided to try the goods of a theatrical company. So, he reached Drury Lane and entered a shop that sold theatrical items. A little later, he came out wearing bandages, dark glasses, a false nose, big bushy whiskers and a large hat. Then, he attacked the shopkeeper and robbed his money.

Griffin Arrived at Iping Village

After robbing the shopkeeper, Griffin left London and took a train to the village of Iping. Here, he booked two rooms in a local inn. Griffin's presence at the inn and his appearance was a topic of gossip for all villagers. The owner's wife, Mrs. Hall tried to be friendly with Griffin, However, Griffin told her that he had an accident and did not want to be disturbed. Mrs. Hall excused his strange behaviour and anger as he had paid her in advance.

Burglary at Clergyman's House

Soon, the money that Griffin had stolen from theatrical company was finished. As a result, Griffin had to tell Mrs. Hall that he was expecting to receive some money very soon. So, he robbed the clergyman's house.

Very early in the morning, the clergyman and his wife were disturbed by some sounds. They heard the chink of money being taken away from the drawer. The clergyman silently opened the door and warned the thief to surrender. However, he was shocked to find that nobody was there but the money was missing.

Furniture Showed Strange Behaviour

On the same day, when Mrs. Hall found Griffin's room open, with his bandages and clothes lying around, she and her husband entered the room. Suddenly, Mrs. Hall heard a sniff and the hat near the bedpost was thrown on her face. Then, the bedroom chair was thrown at her legs. Both the landlord and his wife were pushed out of the room. Mrs. Hall felt that the furniture was haunted by spirits as she could not see anybody there.

Griffin is Suspected

Mrs. Hall blamed Griffin for the strange events while the neighbours blamed witchcraft. Soon, the news of burglary at clergyman's house was spread. Most people in the village felt that the strange scientist was involved in it because he paid his due rent, whereas earlier he was not able to do so. As a result, the village police constable Mr. Jaffers was called.

Griffin becomes Invisible

However, before Mr. Jaffers arrived Mrs. Hall went to Griffin and enquired what he had been doing with her chair in the room. She also enquired him how he came out of an empty room and entered a locked room.

Griffin became very angry and decided to show her everything. He threw off his bandages, spectacles, whiskers and his nose. People who had gathered were horrified to see the headless man.

Griffin Escapes from Iping

When constable Jaffers had arrived, he was surprised to know that he had to arrest a man without a head. Yet, he tried to catch him. Griffin removed all that he was wearing to become invisible.

The constable was trying to catch a man he couldn't see. Some people tried to help Jaffers but were hit by a blow they could not see. Soon, Jaffers was knocked unconscious and Griffin ran away.

Word Meaning

Word	Meaning
started	jumped
imprints	marks due to pressure
progressing	moving
impressions	footmarks
fainter	reduced/lighter
bewildered	puzzled
rare drugs	chemicals/medicines not easily available
eject	remove
by no means	not yet
pile	objects positioned one on top of another
stock	items
callously	unfeelingly
set all tongues wagging	to do something that people will talk or guess about your private life
eccentric	strange
clergyman	Christian priest

Word	Meaning
chink	high pitched ringing sound
poker	metal rod
flung open	suddenly opened
sniff	sound made by nose drawing in air
bedpost	an upright support of a bed
dashed	struck
springing	jumping
foremost	first
slam	quickly close
hysterics	a wildly emotional reaction
witchcraft	the practice of magic, especially for evil purposes
quick-tempered	losing temper quickly
warrant	official authorisation
blows	powerful hits with the hands
knocked	to hit forcefully and cause to move or fall

NCERT FOLDER

NCERT Intext and Exercise Questions

READ AND FIND OUT (NCERT PAGE 26)

Q.1 How did the invisible man first become visible?

Ans. The invisible man first became visible after he had stepped on mud which made his footprints visible on the steps of a house in London. These footprints were noticed by two boys who followed them till they disappeared.

Q.2 Why was he wandering the streets?

Ans. He was wandering down the streets because he had set his landlord's house on fire to take his revenge for trying to evict him. As a result, he had nowhere to go.

READ AND FIND OUT (NCERT PAGE 28)

Q.1 Why did Mrs. Hall find the scientist (the new guest) eccentric? CBSE 2020

Ans. Mrs. Hall found the scientist eccentric because of his strange behaviour. When she tried to be friendly with him, he rejected her by telling her that he had come there for peace and did not want to be disturbed in his work.

Q.2 What curious episode occurs in the study?

Or **Describe the curious episode which took place in a clergyman's study.** CBSE 2020

Ans. A curious episode occured in the study of the clergyman's house. One very early morning, the clergyman and his wife heard noises coming from their study. They heard the sound of money being taken. However, when they entered the study, nobody could be found but the money was stolen.

Q.3 What other extraordinary things happen at the inn?

Ans. Many extraordinary things happened at the inn with Mrs. Hall and her husband. One day, early in the morning, they found the scientist's door to be open and went inside, while there was nobody in the room.

Suddenly, Mrs. Hall heard a sniff. Soon, a hat kept on the bedpost was thrown on her face. Then, a chair was thrown at her legs and it pushed both Mrs. Hall and his husband out of the room. This made Mrs. Hall think that the furniture was haunted.

THINK ABOUT IT (NCERT PAGE 31)

Q.1 "Griffin was rather a lawless person." Comment.

Ans. Griffin was a brilliant scientist but he was a lawless person. After becoming invisible because of his experiment, he not only set his landlord's house on fire but also robbed a theatrical shop in London. Later in Iping, he robbed the clergyman and also hit the villagers including Mrs. Hall, her husband and constable Jaffers.

Q.2 How would you assess Griffin as a scientist?

Ans. Griffin was a brilliant scientist. His great capabilities come forward when he continuously conducts experiments to prove that the human body can become invisible. After a lot of efforts, he proves so by making himself invisible. However, his greatness is reduced because of his lawless actions. This discovery could have been used to benefit the society but is used only by him for his own benefit.

TALK ABOUT IT (NCERT PAGE 31)

Q.1 Would you like to become invisible? What advantages and disadvantages do you foresee, if you did?

Ans. Yes, I would like to become invisible for some time. Becoming invisible can be an exciting idea for many people. Invisibility can have many advantages and disadvantages. For a child, invisibility may mean a licence for all kinds of pranks without getting caught. Like a Hindi movie, invisibility can help you beat all the villains and get rid of them. Once you become invisible, nobody would notice you.

However, the sadness of isolation will take over the excitement of being invisible. You will have no friend. You will tend to behave like the eccentric scientist in the story 'Footprints Without Feet'.

REVIEW EXERCISE

Including Competency Based Questions

Part - I

Multiple Choice Questions

1. The two boys started in surprise at the fresh muddy imprints of a pair of bare feet. What was a barefooted man doing on the steps of a house, in the middle of London? And where was the man? Why does the author begin 'Footprints Without Feet' with these questions? Competency Based

(a) To seek answers to the queries
(b) To spark curiosity about the story
(c) To show a lack of knowledge about the plot
(d) To highlight the unusual reaction of the characters

Ans. (b) To spark curiosity about the story

2. As they gazed, a remarkable sight met their eyes. Who is referred to as 'they' in given sentence in context with 'Footprints Without Feet'?

(a) Staff of the big London store
(b) Two boys
(c) Clergyman and his wife
(d) Griffin and his friends

Ans. (b) Two boys

3. Select the option that completes the given sentence correctly.
The boys who followed Griffin in 'Footprints Without Feet' .... and .... CBSE Additional SQP 2021

1. had found Griffin's laboratory
2. were curious about the footprints
3. knew who the footprints belonged to
4. had almost discovered Griffin's secret
5. had been looking for Griffin for quite some time

(a) 1 and 5 (b) 2 and 3
(c) 2 and 4 (d) 3 and 5

Ans. (c) 2 and 4

4. Identify the option that aptly describes Griffin. CBSE SQP Term 1 2021

(a) Greedy, yet kind
(b) Proud and honourable
(c) Considerate and selfless
(d) Brilliant but lawless

Ans. (d) Brilliant but lawless

5. Griffin became a homeless wanderer because he **CBSE Term 1 2021**

(a) was an eccentric scientist
(b) was very greedy
(c) had to go without clothes
(d) had set fire to his landlord's house

Ans. (d) had set fire to his landlord's house

6. Why was it a bad time for Griffin to wander about in London?

(a) It was mid-winter (b) He did not have clothes
(c) He wanted to be alone (d) Both (a) and (c)

Ans. (a) It was mid-winter

7. Read the given statements and choose the correct answer.

(A) Griffin stole clothes from the store.
(B) Griffin was a revengeful man.

(a) (A) is right (B) is wrong (b) (A) is wrong (B) is right
(c) Both are right (d) Both are wrong

Ans. (c) Both are right

8. Why does the author state "he became a fully dressed and a visible person"?

1. **Because the protagonist was feeling cold**
2. **Because the protagonist was a beggar**
3. **Because the protagonist was invisible**
4. **Because people are finally noticing him**
5. **Because the protagonist was blind**

Select the correct option.

(a) 1 and 4 (b) 2 and 3
(c) Only 3 (d) 2, 4 and 5

Ans. (c) Only 3

9. What was the centre of the theatrical world as mentioned in the story 'Footprints Without Feet'?

(a) Big London store (b) Iping Inn
(c) Drury Lane (d) None of these

Ans. (c) Drury Lane

10. Griffin wore bandages to outline his ....

(a) face (b) nose
(c) mouth (d) hairs

Ans. (a) face

11. Where did Griffin go to avoid the crowded London?

(a) Inn (b) Village of Iping
(c) Big London store (d) Drury Lane

Ans. (b) Village of Iping

12. How did Mrs. Hall find the scientist when she first met him?

(a) Strange (b) Curious
(c) Idiotic (d) Polite

Ans. (a) Strange

13. Which option best describes Mrs. Hall from 'Footprints Without Feet'? **Competency Based**

(a) Hospitable but firm
(b) Scared and superstitious
(c) Accommodating but curious
(d) Opportunistic and insensitive

Ans. (a) Hospitable but firm

14. Why did the people start talking about the stranger's arrival? **CBSE Additional SQP 2021**

1. **Because he was mostly quiet**
2. **Because he was mean to people**
3. **Because he was enjoying the snow**
4. **Because he paid the inn charges in cash**
5. **Because he was dressed in a strange manner**

Select the correct option.

(a) 1 and 5 (b) 2 and 3 (c) 3, 4 and 5 (d) Only 4

Ans. (a) 1 and 5

15. In the story 'Footprints Without Feet', Mrs. Hall agreed to provide accommodation to Griffin because he had .... **CBSE Additional SQP 2021**

(a) expressed that her inn was perfect for his experiments
(b) a bad temper and she was scared of him
(c) agreed to not disturb her peace of mind
(d) made some payment to her in advance

Ans. (d) made some payment to her in advance

16. Why did clergyman and his wife creep downstairs?

(a) To drink water
(b) As they were awakened by Mrs. Hall
(c) As they received a call from Mrs. Hall
(d) As they heard some noise coming from their room

Ans. (d) As they heard some noise coming from their room

17. Mrs. Hall felt the room was haunted by spirits because ....

(a) she could see evil spirits
(b) she heard strange noise
(c) uncanny things happened there
(d) the door slammed shut

Ans. (c) uncanny things happened there

18. How did Mr. Jaffers feel when he saw Griffin for the first time?

(a) Happy (b) Surprised (c) Upset (d) Irritated

Ans. (b) Surprised

19. In 'Footprints Without Feet' Griffin's invisibility causes .... among the people around him. **Competency Based**

1. **jealousy and hatred**
2. **crime and bloodshed**

3. awe and amazement
4. chaos and destruction

(a) 1 and 2 (b) 2 and 3
(c) 3 and 4 (d) 4 and 1

Ans. (c) 3 and 4

20. What is the theme of the story 'Footprints Without Feet'?

(a) One should not misuse science
(b) A brilliant scientist can turn into a lawless person
(c) One can do anything after becoming invisible
(d) Both (a) and (b)

Ans. (a) One should not misuse science

Extract Based Questions

1. Read the following extract carefully and answer the questions that follow.

The two boys started in surprise at the fresh muddy imprints of a pair of bare feet. What was a barefooted man doing on the steps of a house in the middle of London? And where was the man?
As they gazed, a remarkable sight met, their eyes. A fresh footmark appeared from nowhere!
Further footprints followed, one after another, descending the steps and progressing down the street. The boys followed, fascinated, until the muddy impressions became fainter and at last disappeared altogether. **CBSE 2023, CBSE Question Bank Modified**

(i) Why were the boys surprised to see a barefooted man in London?

Ans. The boys were surprised to see a barefooted man in London because while new and fresh footmarks were appearing on a steps of a house, they could not see the person making them. Further, no one would walk barefoot in London.

(ii) Fill in the blank.
All of the given words can fill the given statement. According to the extract the boys were .... when they saw the footmark.

Ans. curious

(iii) How can the boys reaction best be described?

Ans. The boys reaction can best be described as captivated and interested.

(iv) Pick the option that best describes how the boys are feeling based on the extract.

(a) Enchanted, curious, puzzled
(b) Captivated, curious, puzzled
(c) Repulsed, curious, captivated
(d) Enchanted, repulsed, curious

Ans. (b) Captivated, curious, puzzled

2. Read the following extract carefully and answer the questions that follow.

He escaped easily enough from the boys who followed his footprints in London. But his adventures were by no means over. He had chosen a bad time of the year to wander about London without clothes. It was mid-winter. The air was bitterly cold and he could not do without clothes. Instead of walking about the streets, he decided to slip into a big London store for warmth. **CBSE 2021 Term 1 Modified**

(i) It was mid-winter. The given statement is ....

(a) a fact - a thing that is known or proved to be true
(b) an assumption - something that is taken for granted or assumed to be true
(c) a hyperbole - exaggerated statements or claims not meant to be taken literally
(d) a premise - a proposition that forms the basis of an argument

Ans. (a) a fact- a thing that is known or proved to be true.

(ii) State the reason why could escape from the boys.

Ans. He could escape from the boys because he went along a street where there was no mud.

(iii) Mention what happened that day after the invisible man slipped into a big London store.

Ans. After the invisible man slipped into a big London store for warmth, he waited for the closing time. As soon as the door was shut, he clothed and fed himself without thinking of expense. He then went to sleep on a pile of quilts.

(iv) The phrase 'slip into' means the same as

Ans. enter quietly

3. Read the following extract carefully and answer the questions that follow.

Brilliant scientist though he was, Griffin was rather a lawless person. His landlord disliked him and tried to eject him. In revenge Griffin set fire to the house, to get away without being seen he had to remove his clothes. Thus, it was that he became a homeless wanderer, without clothes, without money and quite invisible – until he happened to step in some mud and left footprints as he walked!

(i) How can you say that Griffin was a brilliant scientist?

Ans. It can be said that Griffin was a brilliant scientist as he carried out various experiments to prove that human body could become invisible.

(ii) State True or False.

None of the terms (a) - (d) can be applied to the statement - His landlord disliked him and tried to eject him.

(a) A hypothesis - a proposed explanation for a phenomenon
(b) An assumption - something that is taken for granted or assumed to be true
(c) A hyperbole - exaggerated statements or claims not meant to be taken literally
(d) A premise - a proposition that forms the basis of an argument

Ans. True

(iii) State the reasons why he was wandering on the streets?

Ans. He was wandering on the streets because he had set fire to his landlord's house.

(iv) Which phrase would correctly substitute 'a lawless' in the given sentence from the extract?

Brilliant scientist though he was, Griffin was rather a lawless person.

Ans. an anarchic

4. Read the following extract carefully and answer the questions that follow.

The arrival of a stranger at an inn in winter was in any case an unusual event. A stranger of such uncommon appearance set all tongues wagging. Mrs. Hall, the landlord's wife, made every effort to be friendly. But Griffin had no desire to talk and told her, "My reason for coming to Iping is a desire for solitude. I do not wish to be disturbed in my work. Besides, an accident has affected my face." Satisfied that her guest was an eccentric scientist and in view of the fact that he had paid her in advance, Mrs. Hall was prepared to excuse his strange habits and irritable temper. But the stolen money did not last long and presently Griffin had to admit that he had no more ready cash. He pretended, however, that he was expecting a cheque to arrive at any moment.

CBSE Additional SQP 2022

(i) In which of these does 'ready' have the same meaning as used in the extract?

(a) Griffin didn't believe that he was ready to speak before the audience
(b) The landlord usually got the rooms ready before any guests arrived
(c) Mrs. Hall said there was a ready supply of food at the hotel
(d) The stranger was getting ready to take on new challenges

Ans. (c) Mrs. Hall said there was a ready supply of food at the hotel

(ii) Complete the analogy by selecting a suitable word from the text.

Arrival : Exit :: .... : Company

Ans. Solitude

(iii) Which of the given statements is false for the inn?

(a) Its location was remote.
(b) Its customers were mainly locals.
(c) It was a popular tourist destination.
(d) It required rent to be paid in advance.

Ans. (c) It was a popular tourist destination.

(iv) Mrs. Hall was prepared to ignore Griffin's rudeness and weird behaviour. State two reasons why this was so.

Competency Based

Ans. Mrs. Hall was prepared to ignore Griffin's rudeness and weird behaviour because she had accepted that Griffin was a strange scientist. Moreover, Griffin has already paid his rent in advance. So, Mrs. Hall had no problem with her new guest.

5. Read the following extract carefully and answer the questions that follow.

As she and her husband turned away in terror, the extraordinary chair pushed them both out of the room and then appeared to slam and lock the door after them. Mrs. Hall almost fell down the stairs in hysterics. She was convinced that the room was haunted by spirits and that the stranger had somehow caused these to enter into her furniture.

"My poor mother used to sit in that chair," she moaned! To think it should rise up against me now! The feeling among the neighbours was that the trouble was caused by witchcraft."

CBSE Question Bank 2021 Modified

(i) In two words, state how Mrs. Hall must be feeling at the moment described in the extract.

Ans. Stunned and agitated

(ii) Pick the options that displays a cause -> effect relationship.

(a) pushed and locked out -> hysterical
(b) rising of the chair -> moaning
(c) troubled neighbours -> witchcraft
(d) stranger -> haunted spirits

Ans. (a) pushed and locked out -> hysterical

(iii) The neighbours thought it was 'witchcraft'. What does this tell us about the neighbours?

Ans. When Mrs. Hall recounted the incident of how the chair that her mother used, had pushed her husband and her out of the room, the neighbours thought that the reason must be witchcraft. This tells us that the neighbours were rather superstitious.

(iv) Complete the sentence appropriately.

Mrs. Hall felt that the room was haunted by spirits because ....

Ans. strange things happened there

Part - II

Short Answer Type Questions

1. Why were the two boys in London surprised and fascinated?

Or What made the boys follow Griffin? CBSE 2020

Ans. The two boys in London were surprised and fascinated by the fresh muddy footprints they saw at the steps of a house. When they followed the footprints (Griffin), they were shocked to see that footprints were appearing but there was no man around the place.

2. Why did Griffin decide to slip into a big London store?

Ans. Griffin decided to slip into a big London store to get warm. It was mid-winter season and the weather was chilly. Hence, it became difficult for him to wander around without clothes in London.

3. How did Griffin find himself invisible but naked in the chill January air for the second time?

Ans. Griffin found himself invisible but naked in the chill January air for the second time when two attendants of the London store discovered him hiding in their store and tried to chase him. Hence, in order to protect himself, he threw away all his clothes and became invisible again.

4. What did Griffin do in the shop of a theatrical company?

Ans. In the shop of a theatrical company, the invisible Griffin dressed himself to become visible. He wore bandages, sunglasses, whiskers and a fake nose. Further to avoid being seen, he attacked the shopkeeper and robbed all the money that he could find.

5. Why did the landlady, Mrs. Hall try to be friendly and prepared to excuse Griffin's irritable habits?

Ans. Mrs. Hall, the landlady of the inn where Griffin had booked his rooms was glad to get an unexpected guest in the winter season. She tried to be friendly with her guest to make him comfortable but Griffin ignored her.

He plainly told her that he did not want to be disturbed. Such a behaviour was excused by Mrs. Hall because Griffin had paid her in advance.

6. What happened when Mr. and Mrs. Hall entered the stranger's room? CBSE 2023

Ans. When Mr. and Mrs. Hall entered the stranger's room, they found that the bed was cold and all his bandages were lying around. Suddenly, Mrs. Hall heard a sniff and the hat on the bedpost was thrown into her face. Then, the bedroom chair was thrown at them and the Halls were pushed outside the room. As a result, Mr. and Mrs. Hall were very scared.

7. The neighbours suspected Griffin of burglary. State why this was or was not justified. CBSE Question Bank 2021

Ans. The neighbours suspected Griffin of burglary because he had produced some ready cash the next day after having accepted that he did not have any money with him. Their suspicion was justified.

8. How did the visible man become invisible? What did he do then?

Ans. The visible man became invisible because of his quick temper. He got furious at the constant questioning of Mrs. Hall. Consequently, he took off all the things he was wearing on his forehead to become a man without a head. Soon, constable Jaffers came to arrest him. So, he took off all the clothes he was wearing to become completely invisible. He knocked Mr. Jaffers unconscious and escaped.

9. What do you think would have happened if Griffin was caught by Jaffers and the latter hadn't become unconscious? Competency Based

Ans. If Griffin was caught by Jaffers and the latter hadn't become unconscious, then first Griffin would have been taken to jail. Later, as his case of invisibility would come forward, he would have become subject to experiments that would uncover the secret behind his invisibility and further remove his invisibility.

10. Griffin's had shaken himself free and no one knew where to lay hands on him.

In 20-30 words, give one example from 'Footprints Without Feet' to describe the price Griffin had to pay for his freedom. Competency Based

Ans. Griffin's invisibility came at a great price to him. Although he could do all he wanted, he had to stay naked in the cold winter. Further, he became a criminal and could have been caught if he had not been invisible. The London shop assistants, the Clergyman and even Mr. Jaffers would have caught him for his crimes.

11. Scientists contribute to make the world a better place. Griffin is an antithesis to this statement. Justify. Competency Based

Ans. Griffin was a brilliant scientist but he was an antithesis to the fact that scientists contribute to make the world a better place. This is so because he uses his mind for making a good drug which could make anyone invisible but he used the drug unethically and immorally.

He looted stores and showed violent behaviour after being invisible which takes away his credibility (honour and respect).

12. Do you find the story based on being invisible a mere figment of one's imagination or a phenomenon that is plausible? Elaborate with your opinion. CBSE Question Bank 2021

Ans. I find the story based on being invisible to be a story based on a mere figment of one's imagination. I think that the possibility of that being a reality would be very miniscule, even though I do not think that it is impossible.

13. State any two features that make 'Footprints Without Feet' an adventure story. Competency Based

Ans. 'Footprints without Feet' is an adventurous story because it narrates the thrilling experience of the scientist named Griffin. In the story, there is a hero villain, a scientist who takes risks and becomes invisible. Then, he participates in many illegal and criminal activities and escapes from it. Thus, the chapter is a action driven story with a farfetched aspect of invisibility which makes it adventurous.

14. Do you think Griffin is a brilliant scientist who degenerated into a lawless person? Compare him as a scientist and a human being. CBSE 2024 C

Ans. Griffin is truly a brilliant scientist who degenerated into a lawless person. As a brilliant scientist, he discovered the scientific formula to make a human body invisible. However, his experiment made him a lawless person who robbed people, set his landlord's house on fire, threw a chair at Mr. and Mrs. Hall, among other things. Griffin abused his intelligence, became a criminal who had no respect for humanity.

Long Answer Type Questions

1. Describe the landlord's and his wife's experience with the strange scientist.

Ans. The landlord and his wife had a very strange experience with the eccentric scientist. Once in an early morning, both of them were shocked to find the door of the scientist's room to be open. They knew that their guest did not like being disturbed and would normally keep the room locked. So, they looked inside only to find that nobody was present in the room. As they entered the room to investigate it, they found that the bed was cold, and the clothes and bandages that their guest regularly wore were lying about in the room.

Suddenly, Mrs. Hall heard a sniff and soon the hat on the bedpost was thrown at her face. Then, the chair was thrown at her legs and it pushed Mrs. Hall and her husband out of the room. The door was automatically shut and was locked.

These shocking turn of events made Mrs. Hall hysterical. She almost fell down the stairs. She thought that her furniture was haunted and that the strange scientist was to be blamed for it.

2. "Griffin's unlawful activities devalue his scientific discovery." Comment.

Or **Griffin was a lawless person eventhough he was brilliant scientist. Discuss.** CBSE 2025

Or **Was Griffin a true scientist inspite of his great discovery? Didn't he misuse his discovery for his petty gains and thefts rather than for the welfare of humanity?**

Or **Griffin's great discovery did not make him a popular and respectable person. Explain with instances from the text. Was he a disaster for himself and for society?** Competency Based

Or **Discoveries of science can be used for the welfare of mankind as well as for its destruction. How is this applicable to Griffin's scientifc discovery? Explain giving examples from the text.** CBSE 2020

Or **Did Griffin from 'Footprints Without Feet' follow the saying 'with great power comes great responsibility? Justify your answer in 120 words.** CBSE Additional SQP 2023

Or **Griffin's brilliance as a man of science fades before his darker traits. Give reasons from the text to support your answer.** CBSE 2024

Ans. Griffin was a brilliant and a competent scientist. He discovered that the human body could become invisible and transparent as a result of long and constant experimentation. However, he was a lawless person. He misused his invisibility only for his personal gains. He committed thefts and beat innocent people for his own benefits.

Griffin did not understand that his power brought him great responsibility. His great discovery could have made him popular and respectable. It would have earned him fame and respect. However, instead of being responsible, Griffin degenerated himself into a criminal. He became a disaster for himself as well as his society. He lacked respect for humanity and as a consequence, became a homeless wanderer without any clothes or money.

As a result, Griffin's great discovery is reduced to nothing. His greatness and brilliance was lost with his criminal activities which not only included thefts but also included material damage. His condition was such that he had to wander without clothes in the middle of winter. In other words, instead of any popularity and respect, his great discovery brought him disrepute and dishonour.

3. How did Griffin's invisibility come to his help whenever he found himself in trouble? CBSE 2020

Ans. Griffin was once a brilliant scientist who had worked hard to discover a drug (medicine) that could make a human body invisible and transparent. However, instead of using it for the welfare of the society, Griffin used his experiment to help him to commit petty crimes, thefts and burglaries. He became a lawless person hitting, beating and robbing innocent people. His invisibility only came to help whenever he caught himself in trouble or was in the danger of being caught and arrested.

The first time when his invisibility helped Griffin was when he laid asleep fully dressed on a pile of quilts in the big London store. When the employees of the store saw him, he panicked and ran away. When he was chased, he threw away all his clothes and save himself as he had become completely invisible. Griffin's invisibility helped him rob not only a theater costume shop but also a clergyman in village Iping. Finally, when the village constable Jaffers came to arrest him, Griffin again became invisible. He, then, not only made the constable unconsicious but also hit all those people who came to his help.

4. If somehow you discovered how to become invisible, how would you use that opportunity?

Ans. If I discovered how to become invisible, I would use the opportunity to punish all those people who cause trouble to others for their own selfish motives. I would catch them and hand them over to the police without letting them know that I was behind them. I will also help the law-enforcing agencies when they conduct raids on criminal hideouts as I will be able to move in the open without fear of being seen. This will help the people of the country to become more law-abiding citizens.

We all should also realise that if we are bestowed with a power, we have to follow some duties and fulfill some responsibilities towards our society, our nation and the world. We all have to use those powers in other's welfare. A misuse of power can make us devil, while its proper and good use will definitely make us an angel or superhero in other's eyes. So, it is up to us to choose the right path.

5. Based on your reading of the textual cue given below, write a conversation between the two characters – Mrs. Hall and Griffin.

"Mrs. Hall, the landlord's wife made every effort to be friendly, but Griffin had no desire to talk." CBSE Additional SQP 2023

Ans. **Mrs. Hall** It is such a pleasure to have you as my guest, Mr.......

Griffin Never mind my name, Madam. I guess I have made my payment in advance and you should not bother me any further.

Mrs. Hall Well, yes of course. Thanks a lot for the payment. I was just wondering if you would need any help with something since you seem to be in a terrible state, these bandages and all.

Griffin Oh, no! All is fine with me. No concern required at all. Now, if you may please leave me to do my important work for which I sought solitude in this village on the outskirts of the city.

Mrs. Hall Sure. It's fine with me. Still, I mean in case you ever need any assistance, feel free to call me...

Griffin Madam, stop being overindulgent. I can manage all my needs. Please leave and close the door behind you.

6. A character arc is the transformation or development of a character throughout a story and refers to the changes a character undergoes as a result of his/her experience, challenges and interactions with other characters.

In light of the above information, trace the character arc of Griffin in H. G. Well's 'Footprints Without Feet'.

Ans. It is true to say that a character arc is the transformation or development of a character throughout a story and refers to the changes a character undergoes as a result of his/her experiences, challenges and interactions with other characters.

In H.G. Wells' story 'Footprints Without Feet,' the character Griffin undergoes a significant character arc that showcases his transformation and development throughout the narrative. Griffin is introduced as a mysterious and invisible man who is struggling with the consequences of his scientific experiment that rendered him unseen.

As the story progresses, Griffin's character arc can be traced through various stages.

Introduction of Griffin At the beginning of the story, Griffin is portrayed as a reclusive and secretive scientist who has successfully turned himself invisible.

Quest for Reversing Invisibility Griffin's initial motivation revolves around finding a way to reverse his invisibility and regain his visible form. This quest drives his actions and interactions with other characters in the story, as he seeks a solution to his predicament.

Transformation into a Villain As Griffin struggles to find a cure for his invisibility, he becomes increasingly desperate and resorts to unethical means to achieve his goals.

Conflict with Society Griffin's transformation into a villain leads to conflicts with society, as his actions become more destructive and harmful. He becomes a threat to those around him.

Overall, Griffin's character arc in 'Footprints Without Feet' highlights the complexities of human nature and the consequences of unchecked ambition and power.

Through his transformation from a curious scientist to a dangerous figure, Griffin serves as a cautionary tale about the dangers of losing oneself in pursuit of one's desires.

8. Evaluate how Griffin's character is shaped by a combination of personal ambition, the unintended consequences of his scientific pursuits, and the reactions of the society he faces. **CBSE SQP 2024**

Ans. Griffin's character is a combination of personal ambition, the unintended consequences of his scientific pursuits, and the reactions of the society he faces. Griffin is deeply motivated by his desire to achieve scientific breakthroughs and willingly isolates himself to focus on his experiments, indicating a prioritisation of personal goals over social or ethical considerations.

The state of invisibility, however, leads to paranoia and a disconnection from human relationships which alters his perception and interaction with the world. Society's initial reaction is a mix of curiosity and fear, which quickly shifts to hostility as Griffin's actions become more desperate and harmful. The lack of understanding from others about his condition and needs deepens his resentment and estrangement, fuelling his hostile behaviour.

ASSESSMENT EXERCISE

Extract Based Questions

Read the following extracts carefully and answer the questions that follow.

1. He pretended, however, that he was expecting a cheque to arrive at any moment.
Shortly afterwards a curious episode occured. Very early in the morning a clergyman and his wife were awakened by noises in the study. Creeping downstairs, they heard the chink of money being taken from the clergyman's desk.

(i) Why did he pretend that he would get money soon?

(ii) 'The curious episode' referred to here is
(a) a ghostly appearance at Mrs. Hall's guest house
(b) an invisible face of Griffin
(c) a theft by an unknown force
(d) All of the above

(iii) Complete the sentence appropriately.
The episode occured at ....

(iv) Complete the analogy by selecting the suitable word from the text.
Brayed : Braid :: Check : ....

2. The feeling among the neighbours was that the trouble was caused by witchcraft. But witchcraft or not, when news of the burglary at the clergyman's home became known, the strange scientist was strongly suspected of having had a hand in it. Suspicion grew even stronger when he suddenly produced some ready cash, though he had admitted not long before that he had no money.

(i) How did the neighbours connect the burglary with the strange scientist?

(ii) State True of False.
None of the terms (a)-(b) can be applied to the statement—
The feeling among the neighbours was that the trouble was caused by witchcraft.
(a) A hypothesis—a proposed explanation for a phenomenon
(b) An assumption—something that is taken for granted or assumed to be true without proof
(c) A premise – a proposition that forms the basis of an argument
(d) A theory – a well-substantiated explanation for a natural phenomenon

(iii) Complete the sentence appropriately.
The scientists had said that he didn't have money not long before ....

(iv) What does the phrase 'having a hand' mean in the above abstract?

Short Answer (SA) Type Questions

1. What did the clergyman of Iping do after he found his money missing?
2. What did the London boys follow and why were they fascinated?
3. Why did Mrs. Hall feel that something was seriously wrong with the scientist who was staying at her inn?
4. What experiments did Griffin carry out? What was the final result of those experiments?
5. Why was the strange scientist strongly suspected of having a hand in the burglary at the clergyman's home?

Long Answer (LA) Type Questions

1. "The scientist was a man of irritable temper." Comment.
2. One must be a law-abiding citizen of the country. Griffin lacked this value in his character. How did it make him an undesirable person? **Competency Based**

The Making of a Scientist

by Robert W Peterson

The chapter 'The Making of a Scientist' is about the great scientist Richard H Ebright. Ebright became a successful scientist after he discovered how cells can read DNA. The story covers Ebright's scientific mind since his childhood. In doing so, it points out the skills that are important for anyone to be successful.

Richard's Success of Young Age

The story of Richard's success began when he was twenty two years old. An article written by Richard H Ebright and his college roommate was published in an important scientific journal named 'Proceedings of the National Academy of Science'. The article was important as it explained the theory of how cells work. It become more special because it was the first time that an important journal published the work of college students.

Richard's journey to his scientific success began with butterflies.

Richard's Childhood

Richard was the only child of his parents. They lived in Pennsylvania, USA. As Richard had no one to play football or baseball with, he developed the habit of collecting things such as rocks, fossils and coins. As a young boy, Richard also collected butterflies. Further, he took interest in astronomy and also loved to gaze at the stars all night.

Richard's Mother : His True Companion

Richard lost his father when he was in third grade so his mother was his only companion. His mother encouraged his interest in learning. She took him on trips and bought him telescopes, microscopes, cameras, mounting materials and many other equipments. She also supported him in his hobbies and invited his friends to play with him. She helped him learn about new things at a young age and he earned top grades in his school.

Richard Reads 'The Travels of Monarch X' Book

Richard was deeply interested in butterflies since his early childhood. When he was in second grade, he had collected all of the 25 species of butterflies found around his hometown. His interest would have ended but his mother gifted him the book 'The Travels of Monarch X.' The book described the migrating patterns of monarch butterflies to Central America and opened up a new world of science for Richard.

Tagging Butterflies for Research

At the end of the book, Richard found an invitation for studying the migration of butterflies. Readers were told to tag butterflies for research by Dr. Frederick A Urquhart of University of Toronto, Canada. Soon, Richard started tagging monarch butterflies. Anyone who found the butterflies were asked to send the tag to Dr. Urquhart. The butterfly collecting season in his area lasted for six weeks in late summer. It was difficult to chase them one by one. So, Richard took a decision to raise a stock of butterflies. He would catch a female monarch and take her eggs.

He studied their development from egg to caterpillar to pupa and to an adult butterfly. Then, he would tag their wings and free them. Richard raised thousands of butterflies in the basement of his home. However, soon he started losing interest in butterflies since it was tedious and did not give much result.

Richard's Entry in the County Science Fair

Richard was in seventh grade when he realised what true science is. He displayed his slides of frogs at the county science fair but did not win any award. He realised the winners in the fair had tried to do real experiments. He decided that next year, he would also do a real experiment.

Richard's Eighth Grade Project

For his next project, he wrote to Dr. Urquhart for ideas and received many suggestions. Soon, Richard achieved his first success. In Richard's eighth grade project, he had tried to find the cause of a viral disease that kills monarch caterpillars. Richard thought that the disease might be carried by a beetle. He tried raising caterpillars in presence of beetles but failed. However, he won a prize in the county fair.

Richard's Next Project on Viceroy Butterflies

Richard's next project was testing the theory that viceroy butterflies copy monarch butterflies. Viceroy butterflies do so to protect themselves from birds as birds don't like to eat monarchs while they like to eat viceroys. He also found that a bird starling would only eat monarch butterflies and not ordinary bird food.

This project was placed first in the zoology division and third in overall county science fair.

Richard's Discovery of a Hormone

In his second year of high school, Richard discovered an unknown insect hormone which also led to his new theory on the life of cells. By this project, his purpose was to know the reason behind the twelve tiny gold spots on monarch's pupa.

Richard along with another science student built a device which showed that the spots were producing a hormone necessary for the butterfly's full development. This project won Richard first place in the county science fair. He also got entry into the International Science and Engineering Fair. There, he won third place for zoology and also got a chance to work at the entomology laboratory of the Walter Reed Army Institute of Research during summer.

Richard Continues his Research on Monarch Pupa

When Richard was a high school junior, he continued his advanced research on the monarch's pupa. Later in his senior year, he grew cells from monarch's wing in a culture. He showed that the cells would develop into normal butterfly wings scales only when they were fed by the hormones produced by the gold spots. This project won the first place for zoology at the International Fair. As a result, Richard spent the summer after graduation doing further work at the army laboratory and at the laboratory of the US Department of Agriculture.

Richard's Study of Cell and DNA

Richard joined Harvard University after summer. While studying at Harvard, Ebright went back to the laboratory of the Department of Agriculture and did more work on the hormone from the gold spots. Using the laboratory's complex instruments, he was able to identify the hormone's chemical structure.

After one and a half years, as a junior, Ebright got the idea of his new theory about cell life while looking at the X-ray photos of chemical structure of a hormone. He believed that his study could tell how the cell can read the blueprint of its DNA (It is the substance in the nucleus of a cell that controls heredity).

Richard and his college roommate James R. Wong worked all night constructing the plastic models of molecules to show how it could happen. Later, they together wrote a paper explaining their theory.

Highest Honours in Harvard

Richard graduated with the highest honours and second position in a class of 1510 students. He became a graduate student researcher at Harvard Medical school and started experimenting to prove his new theory. His theory may create new ways to prevent some types of cancer and other diseases.

Richard: An All Rounder

Richard was not just a scientist. He was an all rounder. He was a champion debater and a public speaker. He was a good canoeist and an outdoor person too. He was also a great photographer.

In his high school, he was a part of the Debating and the Model United Nations Clubs. There, he met Richard A Weiherer, his social studies professor whom he admired a lot.

Richard: A True Scientist

Mr. Weiherer (Ebright's teacher) praised Richard for his hard work. He also praised Richard's healthy competitiveness which was just for the sake of doing his best. Richard had all the qualities that made him a true scientist. He had a first rate mind, curiosity and a will to win for all the right reasons.

Word Meaning

Word	Meaning
scout	a member of the scout association
journal	a newspaper or magazine that deals with a particular subject
making the big leagues	becoming part of a successful or important group
kindergarten	school for small children
astronomer	a scientific observer of stars and planets
determination	firmness of purpose
eager	strongly wanting to do or have something
star-gazing	looking at the stars
variegated	having patches, stripes or marks of different colours
crescent	a shape that is curved, wide at its center and pointed at its two ends like a crescent moon
species	a group of animals or plants that are similar and can produce young animals or plants
fritillary	a butterfly with orange- brown wings that are chequered with black
monarch and viceroy	types of butterflies found in North America
tedious	boring and too slow or long
adhesive	able to stick fast to a surface or object; sticky

Word	Meaning
chase	to hurry after someone or something in order to catch him/her or it
stack	large number
starling	a dark brown or black bird that is common in Europe and the US
zoology	the branch of science that involves the study of animals and animal behaviour
ornamental	showy, decorative
entomology	a branch of science that deals with the study of insects
culture	the growing of cells in a specially prepared nutrient medium
scales	small, thin, horny or bony plates
eureka	a cry of joy when one discovers something
blueprint	a design plan
hormone	a natural substance that is produced in the body and that influences the way in which body grows or develops
pupa	an insect that is in the stage of development between larva and adult
canoeist	person paddling a canoe
exhibits	things
sake	for the purpose of

NCERT FOLDER

NCERT Intext and Exercise Questions

READ AND FIND OUT (NCERT PAGE 32)

Q.1 How did a book become a turning point in Richard Ebright's life?

Ans. The book 'The Travels of Monarch X' became a turning point in Richard Ebright's life as after reading it, he became interested in studying the migration of butterflies. The book inspired him to pursue his curiosity, leading to his later discoveries and success as a scientist.

Q.2 How did his mother help him?

How did Ebright's mother help him become a scientist? CBSE 2023

How did Ebright's mother help him in becoming a scientist? CBSE 2020

Or **What role did Ebright's mother play in his success?** CBSE 2022 Term II

Or **"A parent should try to be a companion to a child". Explain with reference to Richard's mother.** CBSE 2022 Term II

Ans. Richard Ebright's mother helped him in becoming a scientist by encouraging his interest in learning. She took him on trips and bought scientific equipment for him. She spent all her time in setting up challenges for him. This helped Richard learn a lot. She presented him the book 'The Travels of Monarch X', the book that changed Richard's life forever.

READ AND FIND OUT (NCERT PAGE 34)

Q.1 What lesson does Ebright learn when he does not win anything at a science fair? **CBSE 2023**

Ans. When Ebright entered the county science fair, he learnt what science was all about. He learnt that science was not a neat and tidy display of tissues on a slide. It was about the real experiments that were performed to get some real results.

Q.2 What experiments and projects did he then undertake?

Ans. Richard Ebright undertook many projects and experiments. His first project was to prove that a beetle carries a viral disease that kills monarch caterpillars.

Then, he tried to prove that viceroy butterflies copy monarchs. Later, he studied the twelve golden spots on monarch pupa and discovered a new hormone. Further, he found out how cells read their DNA.

Q.3 What are the qualities that go into the making of a scientist?

Ans. The three essential qualities that make a scientist are a first-rate mind, the presence of curiosity and the will to do the best and win.

THINK ABOUT IT (NCERT PAGE 38)

Q.1 How can one become a scientist, an economist, a historian ...? Does it simply involve reading many books on the subject? Does it involve observing, thinking and doing experiments?

Ans. Reading books and being aware of the technical terminology is important for becoming a scientist, an economist and a historian. However, it is not enough to make one successful. Apart from the knowledge gained from books, one must be able to think independently while analysing everything around properly to be successful in one's profession.

Yes, one also requires a keen interest in observing, thinking and doing experiments and gain as much practical knowledge as possible to be successful in their fields.

Q.2 You must have read about cells and DNA in your science books. Discuss Richard Ebright's work in the light of what you have studied. If you get an opportunity to work like Richard Ebright on projects and experiments, which field would you like to work on and why?

Ans. For self-attempt.

TALK ABOUT IT (NCERT PAGE 38)

Q.1 Children everywhere wonder about the world around them. The questions they ask are the beginning of scientific inquiry. Given below are some questions that children in India have asked Prof Yash Pal and Dr Rahul Pal as reported in their book, *Discovered Questions*. (published by NCERT in 2006).

(i) What is DNA fingerprinting? What are its uses?

(ii) How do honeybees identify their own honeycombs?

(iii) Why does rain fall in drops?

Can you answer these questions? You will find Prof Yash Pal's and Dr Rahul's answers (as given in *Discovered Questions*) on Page 75.

Ans. (i) DNA fingerprinting is a forensic technique used to identify individuals by the characteristics of their DNA. It is used in parentage testing. It is also used in criminal investigation to identify a person or to place him at the scene of crime.

(ii) Honeybees have signalling chemicals. They leave trails for fellow honeybees so that they can reach their honeycomb.

(iii) Rainfalls in drops as the only solid thing in the air are dust particles. Water vapour uses it as a centre of attraction when it becomes too heavy. Water vapour condenses on the dust particle as a drop and falls on Earth.

REVIEW EXERCISE

Including Competency Based Questions

Part I

Multiple Choice Questions

1. Richard Ebright published his cell theory in ....

(a) Proceedings of the National Academy of Science
(b) Proceedings of the National Academe Sciences
(c) Minutes of the National Academy of Science
(d) Minutes of the International Journal of Science

Ans. (a) Proceedings of the National Academy of Science

2. Why could Richard not play football or baseball?

(a) Because he didn't know how to play.
(b) Because he didn't want to play.
(c) Because his mother didn't allow him to play.
(d) Because he had nobody to team up with.

Ans. (d) Because he had nobody to team up with.

3. "I was his only companion until he started school." Who said this in the context of 'The Making of a Scientist'? Competency Based

(a) Richard E. Bright (b) Richard's mother
(c) Dr. Urquhart (d) James R. Wong

Ans. (b) Richard's mother

4. Among the butterflies that Ebright captured in his hometown, which were not a part of the list?

(a) Bog Copper (b) Red Admiral
(c) Pearl Crescent (d) Olympia

Ans. (b) Red Admiral

5. The book 'The Travels of Monarch X' told how monarch butterflies migrate to ....

(a) Northern America (b) Canada
(c) Central America (d) Pennsylvania

Ans. (c) Central America

6. Which of these best summarises Ebright's reaction to losing at the county science fair in th eseventh grade? Competency Based

(a) He felt discouraged but was happy about his efforts.
(b) He felt dejected but was motivated to do better next time.
(c) He felt defeated but accepted that other were better than him.
(d) He felt hapeless but became aggressive about winning next time.

Ans. (b) He felt dejected but was motivated to do better next time.

7. Which experiments did Richard continue as a high school junior?

(a) Experiments on Cells
(b) Experiments on DNA
(c) Experiments on Monarch pupa
(d) Experiments on Viceroy butterflies

Ans. (c) Experiments on Monarch pupa

8. Which project won Ebright first prize in the county fair?

(a) Device that showed the golden spots on monarch were producing a hormone necessary for the butterfly's full development.
(b) How the cell can read the blueprint of its DNA.
(c) Discovery of unknown insect hormone and the structure of the hormone.
(d) All of the above

Ans. (a) Device that showed the golden spots on monarch were producing a hormone necessary for the butterfly's full development.

9. Which entomology lab did Richard get the opportunity to work at?

(a) Walter Reed Army Institute of Research
(b) Model United Nations Club
(c) Army Laboratory
(d) US Department of Agriculture

Ans. (a) Walter Reed Army Institute of Research

10. Select the correct option for (i) and (ii). Competency Based

(i) Richard's mother motivated him and his scientific curiosity.

(ii) Richard was a graduate from Harvard Medical School.

(a) (i) is the result of (ii)
(b) (i) and (ii) are independent of each other
(c) (ii) is the result of (i)
(d) (i) is true (ii) is false

Ans. (b) Statements (i) and (ii) are independent of each other.

11. Which other qualities than being a scientist did Richard possess?

(i) Debater **(ii) Photographer**
(iii) Public Speaker **(iv) Cannoeist**

(a) (i), (ii) and (iii) (b) (ii), (iii) and (iv)
(c) (i), (iii) and (iv) (d) (i), (ii), (iii) and (iv)

Ans. (d) (i), (ii), (iii) and (iv)

12. Who was Richard's Social Studies teacher?

(a) Mr. Weiherer (b) Dr. Urquhart
(c) James R. Wong (d) None of these

Ans. (a) Mr. Weiherer

13. Mr. Weiherer said, "For the right reasons he wants to be the best."
What did he mean by the given statement?

A. Richard was not interested in winning prizes.
B. Richard did not want to win the first prize for the sake of winning.
C. Richard wanted to do his best job for the welfare of people.

(a) Only A (b) A and B
(c) B and C (d) None of these

Ans. (c) B and C

Extract Based Questions

1. Read the following extract carefully and answer the questions that follow.

Then in the seventh grade he got a hint of what real science is when he entered a county science fair-and lost. "It was really a sad feeling to sit there and not get anything while everybody else had won something," Ebright said. His entry was slides of frog tissues, which he showed under a microscope. He realised the winners had tried to do real experiments, not simply make a neat display.

Already the competitive spirit that drives Richard Ebright was appearing. "I knew that for the next year's fair I would have to do a Meal experiment, he said "The subject I knew most about was the insect work I'd been doing in the past several years."

Competency Board

(i) Which of these could be one of the winners' projects for the county science fair?

(a) A diagram of human cheek cells under a microscope
(b) A model of the water cycle with miniature water bodies
(c) A study on mint leaves that shows how light affects its growth
(d) A summary of past research on how caterpillars become butterflies

Ans. (b) A model of the water cycle with miniature water bodies

(ii) Why does the author quote Ebright at several points in the extract? Competency Based

Ans. The author quotes Ebright at several points in the extract to show the authenticity of his text and to support the statement he is making about the scientist.

(iii) What changed for Ebright after he lost in the County Science fair? Competency Based

Ans. After losing at the County Science Fair, Ebright realised that true science was not about successfully doing an experiment but performing an experiment.

(iv) Fill in the blank.

Then in the seventh grade he got a hint of what (true/practical) science is........... .

Ans. True

2. Read the following extract carefully and answer the questions that follow.

The question he tried to answer was simple: What is the purpose of the twelve tiny gold spots on a monarch pupa?

"Everyone assumed the spots were just ornamental," Ebright said. "But Dr Urquhart didn't believe it."

To find the answer, Ebright and another excellent science student first had to build a device that showed that the spots were producing a hormone necessary for the butterfly's full development. This project won Ebright first place in the county fair and entry into the International Science and Engineering Fair. There he won third place for zoology. He also got a chance to work during the summer at the entomology laboratory of the Walter Reed Army Institute of Research.

CBSE Additional SQP 2023

(i) State any one inference about Dr Urquhart from the given context: Competency Based

Everyone assumed the spots were just ornamental," Ebright said.

"But Dr Urquhart didn't believe it."

Ans. It can be inferred from the given lines that Dr. Urquhart was a scientist who questioned existing assumptions.

(ii) State True or False.

None of the terms (a) - (d) below, can be applied to the question - What is the purpose of the twelve tiny gold spots on a monarch pupa?

(a) A hypothesis - a proposed explanation for a phenomenon
(b) An assumption - something that is taken for granted or assumed to be true without proof
(c) A premise - a proposition that forms the basis of an argument
(d) A theory - a well-substantiated explanation for a natural phenomenon

Ans. True

(iii) Ebright's approach towards finding the purpose of the gold spots on a monarch pupa was highly effective. Elaborate in about 40 words, with reference to the extract.

Ans. Ebright's approach towards finding the purpose of the gold spots on a monarch pupa was highly effective. By building a device that showed that the spots were producing a hormone necessary for the butterfly's full development, he was able to provide evidence that contradicted the prevailing assumption that the spots were purely ornamental. This earned him recognition in science fairs and provided him with opportunities to work at research laboratories.

(iv) Which phrase would correctly substitute 'a chance', in the given sentence from the extract.

He also got a chance to work during the summer at the entomology laboratory of the Walter Reed Army Institute of Research.

Ans. The phrase 'an opportunity' would correctly substitute 'a chance' in the given sentence.

3. Read the following extract carefully and answer the questions that follow.

When he saw those photos, Ebright didn't shout, 'Eureka!' or even, 'I've got it!' But he believed that, along with his findings about insect hormones, the photos gave him the answer to one of biology's puzzles: how the cell can 'read' the blueprint of its DNA. DNA is the substance in the nucleus of a cell that controls heredity. It determines the form and function of the cell. Thus, DNA is the blueprint for life. Ebright and his college roommate, James R Wong, worked all that night drawing pictures and constructing plastic models of molecules to show how it could happen. Together they later wrote the paper that explained the theory.

(i) Ebright was perhaps expected to shout 'Eureka!' because he had

(a) realised that he needed a partner to work with to finalise his findings.
(b) discovered something new and 'Eureka!' was a cry to announce it.
(c) worked hard and was relieved at nearing the end of his project.
(d) given shape to the teachings of his teachers by choosing this field of science.

Ans. (b) discovered something new and 'Eureka!' was a cry to announce it.

(ii) Complete the sentence appropriately.

The article is important because it was first published in ....

Ans. Proceedings of the National Academy of Science.

(iii) What did Ebright do all night with his partner?

Ans. Ebright along with his roommate James R Wong worked all night drawing pictures and constructing models to show DNA is the blueprint of life.

(iv) Which biology's puzzle was going to be answered with the help of his findings?

Ans. The biology's puzzle: how the cell can read the blueprint of its DNA could be answered with the help of his findings.

4. Read the following extract carefully and answer the questions that follow.

Ebright and his college roommate, James R Wong, worked all that night drawing pictures and constructing plastic models of molecules to show how it could happen. Together they later wrote the paper that explained the theory.

Surprising no one who knew him, Richard Ebright graduated from Harvard with highest honours, second in his class of 1510.

(i) What does 'it' here refer to?

(a) Theory on monarch's pupa
(b) Theory on golden spot hormone
(c) Theory on how cells read DNA
(d) All of the above

Ans. (c) Theory on how cells read DNA

(ii) Complete the sentence appropriately.

.... and .... wrote the scientific paper to explain the theory.

Ans. Ebright, James R Wong

(iii) Why was no one surprised at Ebrights graduation? Competency Based

Ans. No one was surprised at Ebrights graduation because everyone knew Ebright would do so.

(iv) Complete the analogy by selecting the suitable word from the text.

Hole : Whole :: Rote : ....

Ans. Wrote

5. **Read the following extract carefully and answer the questions that follow.**

"Richard would always give that extra effort," Mr. Weiherer said. What pleased me was, here was this person who put in three or four hours at night doing debate research besides doing all his research with butterflies and his other interests.

'Richard was competitive,' Mr. Weiherer continued, 'but not in a bad sense'. He explained, "Richard wasn't interested in winning for winning's sake or winning to get a prize. Rather, he was winning because he wanted to do the best job he could. For the right reasons, he wants to be the best."

(i) **Why did Mr. Weiherer call Richard a true winner?**

(a) Because he wasn't interested in wining.
(b) Because he wanted to give his best.
(c) Because he wanted to win a prize.
(d) Both (a) and (b).

Ans. (d) Both (a) and (b).

(ii) **Complete the sentence appropriately Mr. Weiherer thought that Richard was a hard-worker because ....**

Ans. with his research, he also put time in debate research.

(iii) **'Put in' here means ....**

Ans. time taken in doing some work.

(iv) **Who was Mr. Weiherer? What did he think about Richard?**

Ans. Mr. Weiherer was Ebright's Social Studies teacher. He thought that Richard was a sincere and dedicated child.

Part II

Short Answer Type Questions

1. **What rare achievement did Richard manage at the age of twenty-two?**

Ans. Richard had a rare achievement at the age of twenty-two. He wrote an article with his friend about a theory of how cells work. The article was published in the scientific journal 'Proceedings of the National Academy of Science.' It was the first time that this journal had ever published the work of college students.

2. **Richard became a collector at an early age. How?**

Ans. Richard was the only child of his parents. He had no company at home to play with. So, he started collecting things in his spare time. He would collect coins, fossils, rocks and butterflies as a hobby. In this way, Richard became a collector at an early age.

3. **Do you think Richard's mother was too indulgent when she bought him things like cameras, telescopes, microscopes? Give two reasons to support your answer.** CBSE Question Bank 2021

Ans. I don't think that Richard's mother was too indulgent when she bought him things like cameras, telescopes, etc. due to the following reasons

- She knew that Richard was highly curious and had a bright mind.
- He wanted to learn things. Thus, Richard's mother was justified in providing him the appropriate equipment to help him in the process.

4. **Hobbies play a very important role in one's life. Elaborate this with reference to 'The Making of a Scientist'.**

Ans. It is true that hobbies play a very important role in one's life. It was Richard Ebright's hobbies that led him into the field of science. His hobbies were encouraged by his mother who always motivated him to learn new things. Further, it is because of his hobbies that he became a curious all rounder, always ready to participate in things that he loved to do.

5. **Who was Dr. Frederick A Urquhart? Why did Richard Ebright look to him for fresh ideas?**

Ans. Dr. Frederick A Urquhart was a scientist and teacher at the University of Toronto, Canada. He was conducting a research on butterfly migrations. Ebright sent him many tagged butterflies for his research work. Richard also requested him for fresh ideas and suggestions because he needed to perform a practical experiment at the County Science Fair.

6. **Why did Richard Ebright raise a flock of butterflies?**

Ans. Richard Ebright was interested in researching the Monarch butterfly's migratory patterns. Ebright discovered that raising a flock of butterflies in captivity would be a more efficient way to study already existing butterflies. This was so because the butterfly catching season only lasted six weeks which would make his endeavour inefficient.

7. **Why did Richard lose interest in tagging butterflies?** CBSE 2020

Ans. Richard raised thousands of butterflies, tagged them and released them to study their migration. However, soon, he lost interest because only two of his tagged butterflies were recaptured and they had travelled only seventy-five miles.

8. Which project did Richard undertake in the eighth grade?

Ans. In the eighth grade, Richard undertook the project to find the cause of a viral disease that had killed monarch caterpillars. He thought that a beetle might carry the virus. So, he raised caterpillars in the presence of beetles.

9. Why do viceroy butterflies copy the monarch butterflies?

Ans. Birds eat viceroy butterflies because they taste good to them, whereas monarch butterflies do not taste good to the birds. So, the viceroys try to copy the monarchs to protect themselves from the birds.

10. Richard's project on the purpose of the twelve tiny gold spots on a monarch pupa was highly valuable in two ways. List the two ways. Competency Based

Ans. Richard's project on the purpose of the twelve tiny gold spots on a monarch pupa was highly valuable in the following two ways

(i) First, he discovered a hormone that was necessary for the growth of the pupa

(ii) Second, he got a chance to work at a famous laboratory as he won the first prize in the county fair and entry into the International Science and Engineering Fair.

11. In addition to science, what were the other interests of Richard?

Ans. Apart from science, Richard was a good debater and a public speaker as well as a canoeist and an outdoor person. He also loved photography and liked to collect different kinds of things and butterflies.

12. Mr. Weiherer pays a glowing tribute to Richard. What did he say?

What opinion did Mr. Weiherer, Ebright's social science teacher have about him? CBSE 2023

Ans. Mr. Weiherer was Ebright's social studies teacher and the advisor to the clubs that Richard Ebright had joined. He praised him for his brilliant mind, his curiosity and a will to win for the right reason. He also admired Richard for his spirit to do his best all the time.

13. What are the essential qualities for becoming a scientist, according to Ebright's teacher? CBSE 2022 Term II

Ans. According to Ebright's teacher, the essential qualities of becoming a scientist are to have a first rate mind, scientific curiosity and a will to win for the right reasons. In addition to that, a person should have the zeal to excel for the sake of doing the best job.

14. Suggest two ways through which you feel scientific temperament can be developed in a child. CBSE Question Bank 2021

Ans. Scientific temperament is all about questioning. It can be developed in a child in the following ways

- By encouraging him/her to ask questions rather than making him/her accept something blindly.
- Logical thinking is another way to develop scientific temperament in children.

15. Validate the importance of small, fun learning tasks towards successful careers, in the context of Richard Ebright in 'The Making of Scientist'. CBSE Additional SQP 2023

Ans. By reading about Richard Ebright in 'The Making of a Scientist', the readers can understand the importance of small, fun learning tasks because even though he started collecting and breeding butterflies just for fun, he later became curious about the gold spots. This fun activity finally helped him build a career as a well renowned scientist, after being able to discover a theory of cell structure and later DNA.

16. What is common about the role that Dr. Urquhart and Mr. Weiherer played in Richard Ebright's life? Describe any one commonality with evidence from the text 'The Making of a Scientist' in 20-30 words. Competency Based

Ans. Both Dr. Urquhart and Mr. Weiherer play an important role in Richard Ebright's life. Both of them gave direction to Richard in his projects. They provided him with ideas and mentored him in the way he required. They supported his interests and helped him achieve excellence.

17. "Richie was my whole life after his father died." said Richard's mother. Describe Richard Ebright's relationship with his mother. CBSE 2024

Ans. Richard Ebright was in third grade when his father died. Since then, Richard became the sole focus of his mother's life. His mother was her only friend till he started school her mother used to find things for him to do not physical work but stuff to learn. She used to take him on trips and bought him microscope, telescope, camera and mounting material. It was his mother's focus and attention to his hobbies that Richard became a successful scientist. Thus, the relationship between Richard and his mother were based on trust, love, friendship and companionship.

18. Justify the opinion that Ebright's ealy successes were essential for his later achievements in science. CBSE SQP 2024

Ans. Ebright's early successes were essential for his later achievements in science as these wins motivate him, validate his talent, and open up opportunities for growth. These steps instilled confidence in his abilities, affirmed his passion for science, and cultivated a competitive spirit that drove him to excel further in his scientific pursuits. Thus, they shape his trajectory as a successful scientist.

Long Answer Type Questions

1. Richard's mother had a great influence on him. Discuss.

Or **Discuss the role of Ebright's mother in making him a scientist.**

Or **What was the role of Ebright's mother in his life?** **CBSE 2025**

Ans. Richard's mother played a huge role in making him a great scientist. Ebright was a single child. After his father died, his mother made him the focus of her life. She would buy him all kinds of microscopes, telescopes and other equipments. After dinner, she gave him problems to solve. This helped Richard to learn a lot.

Richard's mother always tried to give him work that required no physical labour but those which enhanced his learning skill. It was his mother who got him the book 'The Travels of Monarch X'. This book opened the world of science for Richard. She also wrote to Dr. Urquhart to guide her son. The scientist helped Richard and guided him. Thus, his mother shaped him into an extraordinary scientist.

2. Give a brief character sketch of Ebright's mother. **CBSE 2020**

Ans. Richard H Ebright's mother was a gentle and kind lady who encouraged and inspired Ebright's interest in learning. It was she who laid the foundation of his success as a scientist.

After her husband's death, her son, who was studying in the third grade, became her life. She encouraged her son's keen interest in learning. She understood that her son had a curious and a bright mind.

She recognised her son's scientific temper, so she made sure that her son had everything that he needed. She took him on trips and bought him telescopes, microscopes, cameras, mounting material and all other equipments.

She was his only companion before Richard started going to school. When Richard's school started it was she who encouraged him to make friends. She would invite his friends to their house and she would sit with him at night. Even when Richard did not have any work to do, his mother made sure that she found something to engage her son. It was she who got him the book 'The Travels of Monarch X' and opened the world of science for him.

She knew that her son had a passion and did all things possible to fulfill them. This support, guidance, care and concern of Ebright's mother made him into the prodigal and successful scientist.

3. How did Ebright use determination and preservance to achieve his aim of becoming a scientist? **CBSE 2019**

Ans. Beginning in the Kindergarten, Ebright collected butterflies with the same determination that marked all his activities. In the second grade, he had collected all 25 species of butterflies found around his hometown. Due to his determination to study butterflies, he raised a flock of butterflies.

In his school years, he experimented with various projects. His experiments included raising caterpillars with beetles to find out the viral disease that kills the monarch caterpillars, the theory that viceroy butterfly copy monarchs and the experiment with monarch pupa to study the significance of the gold spots on monarchs.

During subsequent years, he went on to complete a number of research projects and graduated from Harvard with highest honours, second in his class of 1510 students. Ebright went on to become a graduate student researcher at Harvard Medical School. There, he began doing experiments to test his theory how the cell can read the blueprint of its DNA. Thus, Richard Ebright's determination and preservance made him a famous scientist.

4. "Success is failure turned inside out". Prove the above statement with instances from the journey taken by Richard Ebright from losing at the science fair to winning at the international fair.

Ans. Success is a result of failure. It never comes straight or directly. It takes a journey through failure which motivates an individual to move to the path of success.

Similar thing happened with Richard Ebright as well. Although he had a keen interest in science and earned top grades in school, he was just like a normal kid. He faced failures just like everyone else. However, every failure strengthened his will to succeed.

When he was in the seventh grade, Richard had participated in a county science fair with his slide of frog tissues but he did not win. This saddened him. He soon realised his mistake and became determined to win the next year. He requested Dr. Urquhart for suggestions and worked on them. His hardwork finally paid off.

The next year when he participated in the county science fair, he won a prize. This prize further motivated him to further his studies. He extended his projects from studying Monarch butterflies to find how cells read their DNA. Thus, for Ebright, we can say that success is failure turned inside out.

5. Richard Ebright displayed a well-rounded personality. Do you agree? Elucidate in the context of the given text.

Ans. Richard Ebright displayed a well-rounded personality from his childhood. His genius was obvious by the time he was in second grade. He not only collected butterflies but also collected rocks, fossils and coins. He had managed to collect all the twenty-five species of butterflies that were found in his hometown and had classified them.

Science was not his only passion. He was an active member of his school's debating club and Model United Nations Clubs and was also an effective debator and public speaker. He was an enthusiastic canoeist and an all-round outdoor person with a keen interest in photography. Because of his interest and hobbies, it was simple for him to devote time and energy to many other interests. He was a champion, not because of his desire to win for the sake of winnings but for attempting to do his best. All of these qualities make him a well-rounded personality.

6. How important is curiosity to scientific exploration and discovery? Justify your answer with examples from the text 'The Making of a Scientist'. **CBSE Additional SQP 2023**

Ans. Curiosity is extremely important to scientific exploration and discovery. It is curiosity that leads a person to question things around them, which in turn could help them stumble onto new discoveries. It was Ebright's curiosity that led him to collect items such as butterflies, fossils and coins. His desire to explore and constantly learn served as the foundation for his future scientific pursuits.

It was curiosity that led Ebright to investigate different aspects of butterflies for his school projects. Since he was curious to understand the cause of the viral disease that killed monarch butterflies, that was what he studied. While in high school, Ebright was curious about the purpose of the twelve gold spots found on a monarch pupa. This drove him to conduct more research on the topic, which indirectly led to his new theory on the life of cells.

ASSESSMENT EXERCISE

Extract Based Questions

Read the following extract carefully and answer the questions that follow.

So he did and did he ever! Beginning in Kindergarden, Ebright collected butterflies with the same determination that has marked all his activities. He also collected rocks, fossils and coins. He became an eager astronomer, too. Sometimes star-gazing all night.

(i) What does the writer mean by 'so he did and did he ever!'?

(ii) The extract uses the phrase, 'marked all his activities'. Which of the following expressions is correct with respect to the word 'marked'?

(a) Accent

(b) Improvement

(c) Time

(d) Ways

(iii) Complete the analogy by selecting the suitable word from the text.

Gleam : Shine :: Keen: ....

(iv) What more did he collect besides butterflies?

Short Answer (SA) Type Questions

1. Richard showed that he was not an average boy in second grade. How?

2. What was heart-warming about the competitive spirit in Richard?

3. How did Ebright excite the world of science at the age of twenty-two?

4. Why couldn't Richard Ebright play baseball during his childhood days?

Long Answer (LA) Type Questions

1. What did Ebright realise when he did not win any prize in the county science fair?

2. Although Richard does not win anything at the science fair, it was a stepping stone for his success. In the light of the above statement, give your comments whether competitions are for the sake of winning or to give your best at your work.

3. The proverb 'Where there is a will, there is a way' fits Richard Ebright as he had the will to become a scientist although he was not having adequate resources. Then how did he become a successful scientist? Briefly outline how he found the way. **Competency Based**

The Necklace

by Guy De Maupassant

CHAPTER SUMMARY 'The Necklace' is a story that revolves around a middle class lady named Matilda Loisel. It depicts how Matilda's desire for wealth and luxuries lead to her ruin. In the story, Matilda loses a diamond necklace that she had borrowed from her good friend. In order to replace the necklace, Matilda and her husband had to leave the life of the little luxury that they had. Through the story, we learn to accept our circumstances and life as it is.

Matilda Loisel and her Unhappiness

Matilda Loisel was a pretty married lady who had high ambitions. She wished to be wealthy and dreamt of a marvellous life. However, she was born into a family of clerks and was married to a clerk, M Loisel who worked in the office of Board of Education.

Matilda believed that she was born for a life of luxury. She always used to dream of elegant dinners, fine crockery, beautiful frocks and delicious dishes. However, her reality was poverty and this made her miserable as well as unhappy. She was always dissatisfied with her life and envied (was jealous of) her rich friend.

M Loisel Brought an Invitation

One evening Matilda's husband, M Loisel, returned from his office with a large envelope. The envelope consisted an invitation to a ball at the Minister's residence. M Loisel thought that his wife would be happy to read the invitation but Matilda threw the invite away in anger.

When her husband informed Matilda of his intention, she told him that she did not have a fancy dress to wear to the ball. She even refused her husband's idea of a dress she had and asked him to give the invite to a colleague.

New Dress was Bought

After realising Matilda's distress, her husband told her that she could buy a new dress. He asked her how much money she would need. Matilda thought for a while and asked for 400 francs as she knew if she asked for more money, her husband would refuse.

M Liosel gave her the money. He had saved 400 francs to buy a gun to join his friends when they went to shoot larks on Sunday.

Matilda was Still Unhappy

Matilda bought a new dress but she was still unhappy. When her husband asked about the reason of her unhappiness, Matilda told him that she did not have any jewellery to wear with her dress. Her husband suggested natural flowers.

However, Matilda was not convinced and replied that she would look shabby among the rich women. Finally, her husband advised her that she should go to Mme Forestier, her rich friend to borrow her jewellery.

Matilda Got Necklace from Mme Forestier

Next day, Matilda went to her friend's house. She told Mme Forestier her problem. So, Mme Forestier brought her jewel case and asked Matilda to make her choice. Matilda tried various pieces of jewellery but ultimately decided to borrow a diamond necklace.

Matilda at the Night of Ball

The night of the ball arrived and Matilda looked very beautiful. Everyone liked her and she was the centre of attraction. She danced with great enthusiasm and happiness. While her husband sat with some other men. The Loisels decided to go home at 4 am in the morning. Matilda quickly wore her old cloak and hurriedly went into the street where no one would see her.

The Loisels could not find any carriage in the street. So, they walked for some distance towards the river. Finally, they found a carriage that took them home.

The Necklace was Lost

When Matilda returned home and was changing her dress, she wanted to have a final view of herself before the mirror. Suddenly, she noticed that the necklace was not around her neck. She cried out and informed her husband about the same.

Her husband searched for the necklace everywhere they went last night. He went to the police and the cab offices. He also put an advertisement in the newspapers offering a reward but the necklace was not found. So, he advised his wife to write a letter to her friend telling her that the clasp of the necklace was broken and she needed some time to get the necklace repaired.

Matilda Replaces the Necklace

At last, Matilda and her husband decided to replace the necklace. They searched for a similar necklace everywhere and found it in a shop at Palais Royal.

The necklace cost them 36000 Francs. Her husband gave his 18000 francs which his father had left for him. He also took loans of the remaining amount and purchased a diamond necklace. Finally, Matilda returned the necklace to her friend.

Life of Poverty

After replacing the necklace, Matilda and her husband lived in poverty. They sent away the maid, changed their lodgings and rented some rooms in an attic. Matilda had to do all the household work. She started dressing simply and even went to get her grocery.

Her husband worked day and night. He spent his evening putting the books of some merchants and did some copying at night. Finally after ten years, they were able to pay off their debt.

Matilda had Changed

After ten years, Matilda had changed. She had became an old, strong and hard woman. Her hair was messy, her skirts were uneven, her hands were red and she spoke in a loud tone. She also often wondered of the life she would have lived if she had not lost the necklace.

The Truth of Necklace Revealed

One Sunday while Matilda was walking in the Champs-Elysees, she saw Mme Forestier. She was looking charming and beautiful as she had looked ten years before.

Matilda was hesitant but decided to tell Mme Forestier about her necklace. Initially, Mme Forestier did not recognise her. However, upon introduction, she was shocked.

When she got to know about Matilda's misery and her necklace, she was even more surprised. She told Matilda, that the necklace she had replaced was fake and cost around only 500 francs.

Word Meaning

Word	Meaning
petty	of lesser rank or importance
incessantly	continuously
tureen	a deep bowl with a cover used for serving soup
exquisite	finely made
despair	a complete loss of hope
elated	to be extremely joyful
spitefully	hurtfully
stammered	to speak with difficulty
stupefied	shocked
dismay	disappointed
vexation	anger
reflected	thought
pale	almost ill
adorn	decorate
humiliating	insulting
trembled	shook
ecstatic	very happy and excited
embraced	hugged
salon	a room used for entertaining guests
modest	not expensive

Word	Meaning
cloak	a sleeveless garment that hangs loosely from shoulders
detained	stopped
descended	came down
hailing	calling
cast down	upset
clashed	contrasted
bewilderment	confusion
chaplet	a string of (diamonds)
usurer	money lender
frigid	cold/strict
lodging	house
attic	a space or room inside the roof a building
crude	very simple
sou	a French coin of low value
perceived	noticed, spotted
personage	name
astonishment	shocked
stopped short	was surprised
perceive	realise
false	artificial

NCERT FOLDER

NCERT Intext and Exercise Questions

READ AND FIND OUT (NCERT PAGE 39)

Q.1 What kind of a person is Mme Loisel and why is she always unhappy?

Ans. Mme Loisel is a pretty young woman who always wants more. Despite having a good husband and a modest home, she is unhappy with her life. She dreams of a wealthy life with beautiful clothes and jewellery. Her unhappiness comes from her desire for luxury and her belief that she deserves more than what she has. She feels discontent because she doesn't appreciate what she already has.

Q.2 What kind of a person is her husband?

Ans. Matilda's husband, M Loisel is an ordinary clerk in the office of the Board of Education. He is a loving and caring husband who wanted to make his wife happy.

READ AND FIND OUT (NCERT PAGE 41)

Q.1 What fresh problem now disturbs Mme Loisel?

Ans. A fresh problem that disturbs Mme Loisel is that she does not have a beautiful jewel to go with her dress that she was supposed to wear at the ball. So, she asks her husband to pass on the invitation to someone else.

Q.2 How is the problem solved?

Ans. Matilda Loisel's husband, M Loisel solved Matilda's problem. First, he suggested her to wear fresh flowers. Then, he advised her to borrow jewels from her rich friend, Mme Forestier. Thus, the problem is solved as Mme Forestier lends her a beautiful diamond necklace.

READ AND FIND OUT (NCERT PAGE 42)

Q.1 What do M and Mme Loisel do next?

Ans. The Loisels did everything to find the necklace. M. Loisel went back and searched for the lost necklace. Then, he went to the police and to the cab offices. They also put out an advertisement in the newspapers and offered a reward to anyone who finds the necklace. However, all their efforts went in vain.

Q.2 How do they replace the necklace?

Ans. After all other efforts fail, the Liosel's decided to buy a new identical necklace to replace the lost one. M Loisel gave eighteen thousand Francs that his father had left for him and took a loan for the rest. Then, the couple managed to buy the new necklace for thirty six thousand francs and returned it to Mme Forestier.

THINK ABOUT IT (NCERT PAGE 46)

Q.1 The course of the Loisels' life changed due to the necklace. Comment.

Ans. It is true that the necklace changed the course of the Loisels' life. It took the Loisels ten years to pay back the money they had borrowed to buy the necklace.

Everything changed for the Loisels in the ten years. They had to move to the poorest quarters of the city. With no maids or assistance, Matilda had to cook, clean, mend, sew and bargain with the grocer and butcher to save every sou (a French coin of low value) just for their mere survival. The husband had to work in the evening and night to pay their debt.

Q.2 What was the cause of Matilda's ruin? How could she have avoided it?

Ans. The cause of Matilda's ruin was her over ambitiousness and dissatisfaction from life. She was an extremely beautiful girl who expected too much from life. However, she was married to an ordinary man who could not provide her with all the materialistic luxuries.

She could have avoided it if she had told the fact to her friend that she had lost the necklace. By hiding the reality, she ruined her life.

Moreover, she should have been satisfied with what she had instead of imitating rich people.

Q.3 What would have happened to Matilda if she had confessed to her friend that she had lost her necklace?

Ans. If Matilda had confessed to her friend that she had lost her necklace, she might have been in lesser trouble than what she faced after having replaced the necklace. Her friend would have been angry with her and most probably would have asked Matilda to replace it. She would have given her the details from where she bought the necklace and how much it had cost her. As a result, Matilda would have known that the jewels in the necklace were not real diamonds. It would have cost her a far lesser amount to replace it. Thus, Matilda would have saved herself and her husband from all the trouble they went through.

Q.4 If you were caught in a situation like this, how would you have dealt with it?

Ans. If I was caught in such a situation, I would have let the truth out and then, faced the consequences. Honesty would have been the way out for me.

TALK ABOUT IT (NCERT PAGE 46)

Q.1 The characters in this story speak in English. Do you think this is their language? What clues are there in the story about the language its characters must be speaking in?

Ans. Though the characters speak in English, it does not seem to be their language. Maupassant (the author) wrote the story in French and it was translated into English.

The text has enough words in French to prove it otherwise. First, the very names of characters like Mme Loisel, Mme Forestier and the Minister's name George Ramponneau indicate their French origin.

Furthermore, the words for currency like 'Franc' and 'Sou' show the same. In addition, the shop's location at 'Palais- Royal' and 'Champs-Elysees' also point out the French history of the characters and the story.

Q.2 Honesty is the best policy.

Ans. Honesty is definitely the best policy. Falsehood and hypocrisy seem very attractive and rewarding at first. However, the path they tread on leads to nothing but misery, evil and utter gloom. Honesty, on the contrary, seems to be a difficult choice in pursuit of material happiness. Yet, it is the only choice for a life of contentment, peace and everlasting happiness.

Q.3 We should be content with what life gives us.

Ans. One must learn to live within one's means and be content with what one has. Life is a great mystery. For some, it is all riches, comfort, name and fame while for others, it is nothing but sheer hunger, poverty, anguish and an everyday quest for bare survival.

One may try to improve one's life by honest means but eventually must be at peace with what one manages to have.

REVIEW EXERCISE

Including Competency Based Questions

Multiple Choice Questions

1. Where did Loisel used to work?

(a) Board of Education
(b) Board of Public Instruction
(c) Ministry of Public Instruction
(d) Ministry of Education

Ans. (a) Board of Education

2. Matilda was .... regarding the invite.

(a) doubtful (b) stressed (c) confused (d) dejected

Ans. (d) dejected

3. Identify the option that aptly describes M. Loisel.

(a) Greedy yet kind
(b) Considerate and selfless
(c) Proud and honourable
(d) Brilliant but lawless

Ans. (b) Considerate and selfless

4. Why did Matilda need the jewels?

(a) To go to a party of rich people
(b) For a photoshoot
(c) To get a replica made
(d) for wearing them at home

Ans. (a) To go to a party of rich people

5. What did Matilda's husband suggest regarding the jewellery? Competency Based

(a) That she does not wear any jewellery.
(b) That she should go out and buy a piece of beautiful jewellery.
(c) That she should wear what she has.
(d) That she should borrow jewels from her rich friend.

Ans. (d) That she should borrow jewels from her rich friend.

6. Which of the following sentences tell us that Matilda greatly desired the necklace?

1. **Her heart began to beat with uncontrolled desire.**
2. **Her hands trembled as she took it. She fastened it around her neck and stood lost in ecstasy.**
3. **Then she asked anxiously, hesitating, "Would you lend me this, just this?**
4. **She threw her arms around her friend's neck embraced her with passion, then went away with her treasure.** Competency Based

(a) Only 1 (b) 2 and 4
(c) 3 and 4 (d) All of these

Ans. (d) All of these

7. Where did Loisel sleep when his wife was enjoying the party?

(a) At his own house (b) At the venue of the party
(c) In a little salon (d) Outside in a carriage

Ans. (c) In a little salon

8. Select the correct option for (i) and (ii). Competency Based

(i) Loisels suffered for ten long years to repay the rent.

(ii) Mme Loisel was regretting her decision of borrowing the necklace.

(a) (i) is true (ii) is false
(b) (ii) is true (i) is false
(c) Both (i) and (ii) are false
(d) (ii) furthers the meaning of (i)

Ans. (d) (ii) furthers the meaning of (i)

9. Where did Matilda find her friend, Mme Forestier after ten years of sufferings?

(a) Drury Lane (b) On the street
(c) At minister's ball (d) Champs-Elysees

Ans. (d) Champ-Elysees

10. How do you think Mme Loisel feel when she got to that the necklace she borrowed was fake? Choose the correct option. Competency Based

(i) Mme Forestier cheated with me!
(ii) I should have told the truth to Mme Forestier.
(iii) She should have told me that the necklace was fake.
(iv) How stupid I am! I wasted ten years of my life because of that fake necklace!

(a) (i) and (ii) (b) (i), (ii) and (iv)
(c) (ii), (iii) and (iv) (d) All of the above

Ans. (c) (ii), (iii) and (iv)

Extract Based Questions

1. **Read the following extract carefully and answer the questions that follow.**

"She suffered incessantly, feeling herself born for all delicacies and luxuries.

She suffered from the poverty of her apartment, the shabby walls and the worn chairs. All these things tortured and angered her.

When she seated herself for dinner opposite her husband who uncovered the tureen with a delighted air, saying, "Oh! the good potpie! I know nothing better than that...," she would think of elegant dinners of shining silver; she thought of the exquisite food served in marvellous dishes. She had neither frocks nor jewels, nothing. And she loved only those things. She had a rich friend, a schoolmate at the convent, who she did not like to visit- she suffered so much when she returned.

She wept for whole days from despair and disappointment. **CBSE Question Bank 2021 Modified**

(i) Choose the option that list the set of statements that are not true according to the given extract.

1. **Matilda was very pleased with her life.**
2. **Matilda envied her friend for being well-off.**
3. **M Loisel didn't appreciate what Matilda cooked.**
4. **Matilda despised the fact that she lived a life of poverty.**
5. **Matilda never felt troubled, though she desired a luxurious life.**
6. **Matilda thought of grand dinners and silverware sitting at the dinner table.**
7. **Matilda felt depressed after visiting her friend.**

(a) 1, 3, 6 (b) 3, 5, 7
(c) 1, 3, 5 (d) 2, 4, 7

Ans. (c) Statements 1,3 and 5 are not true.

(ii) Why didn't 'she' like to visit her rich friend? What do you think she feels? **Competency Based**

Ans. 'She' did not like to visit her rich friend because it reminded of her poverty. She felt jealous of her rich friend and sad for herself.

(iii) The extract uses the phrase 'elegant dinners'. Which of the following expressions is incorrect with respect to the word 'elegant'?

1. **Furnishings**
2. **Wave**
3. **College**
4. **Interiors**

Ans. Option (3)

(iv) Which characteristic was displayed by M Loisel in the extract.

Ans. M Loisel, Matilda's husband, was contented with what he had.

2. **Read the following extract carefully and answer the questions that follow.**

He was silent, stupefied, in dismay, at the sight of his wife weeping. He stammered, "What is the matter? What is the matter?" By a violent effort, she had controlled her vexation and responded in a calm voice, wiping her moist cheeks, "Nothing. Only I have no dress and consequently I cannot go to this affair. Give your card to some colleague whose wife is better fitted out than I." He was grieved, but answered, "Let us see, Matilda. How much would a suitable costume cost, something that would serve for other occasions, something very simple?" She reflected for some seconds thinking of a sum that she could ask for without refusal and a frightened exclamation from the economical clerk. **CBSE 2025**

(i) What can we infer about Matilda's emotions and financial situation based on her reaction and response to the affair?

Ans. Matilda feels discontent and frustrated with her modest life. She yearns for luxury and elegance but lacks the financial means to fulfill her desires. Her reaction indicates that she is deeply affected by her social standing and wishes to appear wealthier than she actually is.

(ii) Which of the following is NOT a reason for Matilda's distress in the extract?

(a) She has no suitable dress for the affair.
(b) She is upset about her husband's reaction.
(c) She is worried about the cost of a suitable costume.
(d) The card did not bear her name.

Ans. (d) The card did not bear her name.

(iii) What did Matilda suggest that her husband do with the card?

Ans. Matilda indirectly suggested that her husband should provide her with a new dress so she could attend the event looking elegant. She likely implied that they should spend money on an appropriate outfit for the occasion.

(iv) In the given extract, what does the term 'economic clerk' imply?

Ans. The term 'economic clerk' implies that Matilda's husband is a modest government employee with a limited income. It highlights their financial constraints and his practical, budget-conscious nature.

3. **Read the following extract carefully and answer the questions that follow.**

She was not convinced. 'No', she replied, "there is nothing more humiliating than to have a shabby air in the midst of rich women."

Then her husband cried out, "How stupid we are! Go and find your friend Madame Forestier and ask her to lend you her jewels."

She uttered a cry of joy. 'It is true!' she said. "I had not thought of that."

(i) **Why did she need the jewels?**

(a) To go to a party of rich people

(b) For a photoshoot

(c) To get a replica made

(d) For wearing them at home

Ans. (a) To go to a party of rich people

(ii) **Complete the analogy by selecting the suitable word from the text.**

Tempest : Storm :: Scruffy : .... (Shabby/Stupid)

Ans. Shabby

(iii) **At what was Matilda not convinced and What does Matilda's husband suggest her?** **Competency Based**

Ans. Matilda was not convinced at wearing natural flowers to the party of the rich people. She thought that wearing flowers would make her look shabby which was quite humiliating for her. Upon further thinking, Matilda's husband suggested her that she should borrow jewels from her rich friend Mme forestier.

(iv) **Complete the following appropriately.**

Matilda can be called .... (vain/selfish)

Ans. vain

Short Answer Type Questions

1. **Why was Mme Loisel always unhappy?** **CBSE 2020**

Ans. Mme Loisel was always unhappy because she felt that she was, by mistake, born in the family of clerks. She believed that she was born for all the delicacies and luxuries in life.

She always dreamt of a luxurious life filled with elegant dresses, jewellery, exquisite foods served in silver dining. She felt tortured and angered with her present living conditions and suffered incessantly.

2. **Why do you think M. Loisel was a loving husband?**

Ans. M. Loisel was a loving husband as he cared about his wife's emotions. He looked after all needs and desires of his wife. He made her buy a new dress for the party. When his wife lost her diamond necklace, he did not lose his cool and helped her in returning the necklace by replacing it with a diamond necklace. He helped in repaying the debt by working in the evenings and night to earn extra money.

3. **Why did Matilda throw the invitation spitefully?**

Ans. Matilda was simply displeased when her husband showed her the invitation. She felt humiliated and threw the invitation spitefully, as she had nothing beautiful enough to wear at the ball.

4. **Do you think Mme Loisel had an enjoyable evening at the ball? Give reasons for your answer.**

Ans. Mme Loisel was the centre of attention at the ball. Her beauty, her grace, her joy and the gorgeous smile attracted everyone. She danced happily. Hence, she had a successful enjoyable evening at the ball.

5. **Why did Matilda leave the ball in a hurry ? What does it show about her character?**

Ans. Matilda left the ball in a hurry because she did not want to be seen with the ordinary wrap that she carried. She believed that the poor looks of her wrap contrasted with the elegance of the other ladies, who were wrapping themselves in rich furs.

This shows that she only wanted to keep up the appearance just to flatter her pride, without being in touch with the real truth of her life.

6. **Describe Mme Loisel after ten years.**

Ans. Ten years of poverty and hardship stole away Matilda's youth and beauty. She became a strong and hard woman, who was poorly dressed with untidy hair and rough hands. Her skirts were awry (uneven) and she spoke in a loud voice. She had become a commoner who had to do all things by herself.

7. **Why was Matilda's friend astonished to see her at the end of the story?**

or **Why did Jeanne (Mme Forestier) not recognise her friend, Matilda?**

Ans. Jeanne Forestier, Matilda's friend, could not recognise her at the end of the story. She was astonished to see that Matilda looked like an old and worn out poor woman. She was no longer her former beautiful and joyous self. She had lost her charm and was living an unfortunate life.

8. **Mme Loisel now knew the horrible life of necessity. Do you think Mme Loisel accepted this change willingly? Give two reasons in support of your answer.** **Competency Based**

Ans. Yes, I think Mme Loisel accepted this change willingly due to the following reasons

(i) She understood that in order to pay the debt, she would have to cut down on her luxuries.

(ii) She learned the work of kitchen, washed the clothes, brought up the water from the street and sent away the maid to help save money to pay off the debt.

9. Mention two things you would have done, other than what M Loisel did, to help resolve the problem of the lost necklace. CBSE Question Bank 2021

Ans. The two things I would have done to help resolve the problem of the lost necklace are

(i) I would have told Mme Forestier the truth about what happened and asked for her forgiveness.

(ii) I would also have promised her to replace the necklace as soon as possible.

10. How did the necklace change the life of the Loisels? CBSE 2022 Term II

Ans. The Loisels life changed after replacing the lost necklace with a new one, as the couple had to repay all the money that they had borrowed to buy the new necklace. They had to live life in hardship because of the situation brought up by the incident. They sent away the maid and changed their lodgings. Mrs. Loisel had to do all the household chores to survive then.

11. How did Matilda's belief that she was 'an error of destiny' result in a lifetime of sorrow for her? CBSE Additional SQP 2022

Ans. An 'error of destiny' is the belief that one is meant for a different type of life and does not have control over one's life, or is unable to correct the circumstances of one's life. Matilda was born and married into a poor family but she desired a life of luxury. Her desire to look luxurious in an event made her borrow a necklace from a friend. However, Matilda ended up losing it.

As a result, she and her husband spent the next ten years trying to repay the debt, which put them through greater hardship. Hence, the little luxury that she had was taken away from her and she had to lead a life of sorrow.

12. How does 'The Necklace' teach a moral lesson on the importance of contentment?

Ans. The story 'The Necklace' teaches a powerful moral lesson on the importance of finding contentment in what one already has. Matilda's desire for social status and material possessions led to her own downfall and a decade of hardship. Had Matilda simply been grateful and content with all that she had, she could have avoided a lot of pain.

13. How does the writer's use of the literary device-a twist in the tale- towards the story's end, impact the narrative of 'The Necklace'? CBSE Additional SQP 2023

Ans. The writer uses irony to point out a twist in the tale. The twist at the end of the story revealed the true value of the necklace. This emphasises the emptiness that lies in the pursuit of material wealth that Matilda had been after all throughout the story.

14. 'The Necklace' is a lesson in discontent and unreasonable materialism. Discuss the protagonist's greatest failing. CBSE 2024 C

Or **Considering 'The Necklace' as a tale of dissatisfaction and excessive materialism, analyse Matilda's primary flaw.** CBSE 2025

Ans. 'The Necklace' is a lesson in discontent and unreasonable materialism. It presents that we should be happy with what we have through Matilda, a young lady who believed that objects/money have the power to change life. She believed that she was meant to be happy, admired and envied. She had a sense of entitlement for all luxurious things. As a result, she remained discontent and disgruntled all the time.

15. What psychological impact did the ten years of hardship and poverty have on Matilda and her husband? Competency Based

Ans. The ten years of hardship and poverty had a deep psychological impact on both Matilda and her husband. Matilda, who once dreamed of a glamorous life, became worn out and lost her beauty due to the hard work and constant worry. She felt frustrated and bitter as she had to sacrifice her hopes for luxury. Her husband, on the other hand, grew more tired and less happy. He worked tirelessly to repay the debt, losing his carefree nature. Both of them became more serious and weary, showing how the burden of debt and poverty can change a person's spirit. The loss of the necklace and the years of struggle it caused forever affected their lives.

16. How does Matilda's reaction to losing the necklace contradict her husband's response, and what does this tell us about their relationship? Competency Based

Ans. Matilda reacts to losing the necklace with panic and anxiety, fearing the shame of telling her friend the truth. She immediately thinks of replacing the necklace without considering simpler solutions. Her husband, on the other hand, is calm and practical. He suggests searching for the necklace and even offers to take on the financial burden without hesitation. The contrast in their responses highlights their different personalities. Matilda's emotional and impulsive nature contrasts her husband's more sensible and caring approach. Their relationship shows a lack of communication and mutual understanding. This difference in priorities leads to a strained, difficult life for both.

17. How does Matilda's desire for material wealth drive the plot of 'The Necklace'? **CBSE SQP 2024**

Ans. Matilda's desire for material wealth leads her to borrow a necklace from her friend Mme. Forestier to appear wealthy at a party. She loses the necklace and along with her husband, she embarks on a desperate journey to replace it. This incident ultimately leads to their financial ruin. Her desire for material wealth sets off a chain of events that shape the plot of the narrative.

Long Answer Type Questions

1. Mme Loisel's disposition invites her doom. Elucidate/elaborate with reference to the text. **CBSE 2023**

Or **Matilda wanted to live a life above her status. How did this desire of her's led to her sufferings?**

Or **Matilda realised that one little act of negligence can lead to total ruin. What do you learn from this and how would you move on in life?** **CBSE 2022 Term II**

Or **Matilda was very proud of her beauty and charm and this led to her downfall. Elaborate.** **CBSE 2020**

Ans. Mme Loisel belonged to a family of clerks but wanted to live a life above her status. She and her husband lived on small income, enough for meeting the basic needs but not to fulfill aspirations. However, she is so caught up in her dreams of wealth and pleasure that she was out of touch with the truths of her real life.

In order to keep up appearances and just to flatter her pride, she spent four hundred francs on a dress. She also went on to borrow a necklace from her friend. All of this was just to impress the wealthy and the rich with her beauty and glamour. No doubt, her pride was flattered when her wish of fine dining and wearing expensive dresses and jewels was satisfied. However, it came at a great price.

Unfortunately, the necklace was lost and the couple had to cough up their entire inheritance and borrow as well to replace it. Repayment of the debt took away the next ten years of their youth. They lived in utter poverty and had to work very hard to repay the loan.

If Matilda had accepted her reality and remained happy with what she had, she would not have suffered so badly. Therefore, one can say that it was her disposition that led her to doom.

2. What changes occurred in Matilda's lifestyle after she had lost the necklace? **CBSE 2020**

Ans. When Matilda lost the necklace she borrowed from Mme Forestier, she bought a new diamond necklace on loan.

The repayment of debt changed Matilda's life drastically. The Loisels became poor, they had to send away their maid and changed their lodgings to a room in an attic. Matilda learnt the household chores. She learned to do the dishes, and wash the soiled linens, clothes and dishcloths.

She had to walk to the street to bring up the water. She had to dress like an ordinary woman and had to go to grocerer, butcher and fruit seller all by herself keeping in mind to save each and every penny she could. Her husband also worked in the evenings. He used to put the books of some merchants in order and at night, he did copying at five sous a page. This miserable life lasted for ten years to repay the debt.

3. Mme Forestier proved to be a true friend. Elucidate. **CBSE 2020**

Ans. Mme Forestier, a true friend of Mme Loisel, plays a very vital role in the story. As a friend to Matilda, we find her to be really genuine.

She helps Matilda in the hour of her need. When Mme Loisel needed to borrow jewels, she turned to Mme Forestier and Mme Forestier does not refuse. Displaying her generosity, she opens up the entire case of her jewels for Matilda to choose from. Also, she was considerate when the Loisel's delayed the return of the necklace. At the end of the story, she concludes the entire narrative.

Mme Forestier reveals to Matilda that her necklace was just a fake. She is not at all worried in the light of the fact that she may have to return the necklace. It shows her honesty. She was a true friend who feels bad for Matilda at her unnecessary suffering.

4. Do you think the story is aptly titled? Justify your answer.

Ans. The whole narrative of the story 'The Necklace' revolves around a young woman Matilda, who in her foolish pride borrows a necklace inviting misery and sorrow for herself as well as for her husband. The 'necklace' was lost and the Loisels fall into a tremendous debt. They spend the next ten years of their life in paying debt for the replacement of the lost necklace.

Their entire life moves around impoverished everyday saga of misery and hunger. Thus, the necklace, in fact, changes the very course of their life. Further, it is against the back drop of the necklace that Matilda's pride and dishonesty are highlighted. At the same time, the necklace serves a twist at the end as it turns out to be a fake one. Hence, the story is most aptly titled because the necklace is, in fact, the leading character of this ironic tale of desire, doom and tragedy.

5. Read the following quote.

"We are too involved in materialistic things, and they don't satisfy us. The loving relationships we have, the universe around us, we take these things for granted."
- Mitch Albom

Matilda was never satisfied with her life and desired more. The given quote reflects her character. Justify.
CBSE Question Bank 2021

Or **As a reader, do you sympathise with Matilda? Give reasons from the text to support your answer.**
CBSE 2022 Term II

Ans. Mitch Albom righty says that we are too involved in materialistic things, and they don't satisfy us. The loving relationships we have, the universe around us, we take these things for granted. In the present day world, relationships, love and acre have lost their charm and humans have started focusing on luxuries and possession. This is reflected in Matilda Liosel who was never satisfied with her life and desired more.

Despite having a mediocre lifestyle, Matilda was always full of complaints. She always longed for luxuries in life. Her desire for more led her on the path of debt wherein it took her 10 years to pay it off.

As a result, we cannot sympathise with Matilda. She was greedy, discontented and materialistic. She had a high opinion of herself. She demanded a lot from life and when she did not get it, she became unhappy. In her desires, Matilda became insensitive to her husband. She constantly complained marrying a petty clerk and made her life miserable with unending demands.

She does not care that her husband gave his 400 franc savings for her dress. Even then, she remains unhappy with her situation and remains in self-pity. Later when she loses the necklace and had to live a poor life, she could not accept her reality and burst at her friend Mms Forestier, blaming her for the misfortune that she has been facing.

6. Imagine that M. Loisel, from *The Necklace* by Guy de Maupassant, writes a diary entry, exploring the theme of class and social status, and the nature of social mobility, in the context of his own experience.
Write this diary entry as M. Loisel, in about 120 words.
CBSE Additional SQP 2023

Ans. Thursday, 22nd May, 20XX 9:30 p.m.

Dear diary

It's been tough the past few years for my wife, Matilda and me. As I reflect on our experience, I can't help but think about the broader societal issues that have contributed to our predicament.

It's clear to me now that our society is structured in a way that makes upward mobility difficult, if not impossible.

The rich get richer, while the rest of us struggle to make ends meet. We live in a world where social status is determined by the amount of wealth one possesses, rather than by one's character or virtues. This narrow view of success has led many people, including Matilda, to pursue material possessions at the expense of their own happiness.

The loss of the borrowed necklace was a painful lesson for both of us. It reminded us that the pursuit of social status and upward mobility can be a trap, leading people to sacrifice their happiness and well-being in the pursuit of an unattainable dream.

M Loisel

7. What is the significance of the necklace being a fake? How does this irony affect the story's message about materialism and pride?

Ans. The fake necklace adds an important twist to the story. Matilda believes it is a valuable piece of jewellery and borrows it to appear wealthy. She works hard for ten years to replace it, only to learn that the necklace is not real. The irony highlights how Matilda's obsession with material things and her desire for status led her to make poor decisions.

The necklace's true worth shows how easily outward appearances can mislead people. The story teaches that valuing material possessions over inner qualities and true happiness can lead to unnecessary suffering. It shows the dangers of pride and how seeking external approval can cause more harm than good.

8. How does the twist at the end of the story alter our understanding of the characters' struggles and sacrifices?

Ans. The twist at the end of 'The Necklace' completely changes how we see the characters' struggles. After ten years of hard work and sacrifice, Matilda and her husband learn that the necklace is a fake, worth far less than they had paid to replace it. Thus, all their suffering was for nothing.

The revelation shows that their sacrifices were based on a lie, which makes their struggle seem even more tragic. Matilda's years of poverty could have been avoided if she had known the truth. The twist teaches us about vanity's dangers, honesty's importance, and how pride can lead to unnecessary hardship.

ASSESSMENT EXERCISE

Extract Based Questions

Read the following extracts carefully and answer the questions that follow.

1. 'No, I am Matilda Loisel'.

Her friend uttered a cry of astonishment, 'Oh! My poor Matilda! How you have changed!'

''Yes, I have had some hard days since I saw you; and some miserable ones - and all because of you ...''

(i) Why was Matilda's friend was shocked?

1. On seeing Matilda working as a maid
2. On seeing Matilda's rough looks
3. On seeing the change in Matilda
4. On seeingher pleasing appearance
5. On seeing her robbed

Select the correct option.

(a) Only 3
(b) 4 and 5
(c) 1 and 2
(d) 1, 2 and 3

(ii) Why did Matilda say that her friend is responsible for the 'hard days'?

(iii) Complete the analogy by selecting the suitable word from the text.

Which : Witch :: .... : Eye

(iv) Why did Matilda have 'some hard days'?

2. The husband worked evenings, putting the books of some merchants in order, and nights he often did copying at five sous a page. And this life lasted for ten years. At the end of ten years, they had restored all.

Mme Loisel seemed old now. She had become a strong, hard woman, the crude woman of the poor household. Her hair badly dressed, her skirts awry, her hands red, she spoke in a loud tone, and washed the floors with large pails of water. But sometimes, when her husband was at the office, she would seat herself before the window, and think of that evening party of former times, of that ball where she was so beautiful and so flattered.

(i) ''At the end of ten years, they had restored all.'' What did they restore after ten years?

(a) The debt of when they had to replace the diamond necklace.
(b) Their former glory and respect.
(c) Their old house and the maid.
(d) Mme Loisel's dream of living a luxurious life.

(ii) How did Mme Loisel change drastically?

(iii) State any one inference about M. Loisel from the given context :

The husband worked evenings, putting the books of some merchants in order, and nights he often did copying at five sous a page.

(iv) What would Mme Loisel often wonder about?

Short Answer (SA) Type Questions

1. Describe Matilda's feelings and thoughts as she returned the box of the necklace to her friend.

2. The story has a surprise ending. Discuss.

3. Do you agree Matilda is more sinned against than sinning?

Long Answer (LA) Type Questions

1. What efforts did Matilda and her husband make to look for the best necklace?

2. Matilda's craving for a bubble reputation was the cause of her ruin. Draw a conclusion as to how she could have avoided the misfortune that dawned upon her.

3. Matilda's over ambitiousness was the cause of her destruction. Justify.

Bholi

by KA Abbas

The story 'Bholi' is about a simple and innocent girl named Sulekha and how education transforms her. Sulekha is called Bholi by everyone and is neglected by everyone around her. However, with education, Sulekha gains the power to fight for her rights. She gains confidence and self respect. Consequently, she stands against the evil dowry system.

Bholi as a Child

Bholi's real name was Sulekha but since her childhood everyone called her Bholi. She was the fourth daughter out of the seven children of Ramlal, Numberdar of the village. When Bholi was 10 months old, she had fallen off the cot which had damaged some part of her brain. Since then, she remained a backward child.

Further, when she was two years old, she suffered from an attack of small pox and her entire body was disfigured by deep black pock-marks. She learned to speak at the age of five and stammered while speaking. So, children used to make fun of her. As a result, Bholi talked very less.

Bholi's Family

Bholi's father was a rich farmer who sent his three sons to the city for studies. The eldest daughter Radha was already married whereas the second daughter Mangla's marriage was also settled. All of them, were good looking and healthy girls. Ramlal was worried only about Bholi as she was neither beautiful nor intelligent.

Bholi Goes to School

Bholi was seven years old when Mangla was married and a primary school opened in their village. A Tehsildar had come to inaugurate the school. He advised Ramlal to send his daughters to school to set an example for others. Ramlal could not deny him. His wife objected that no one would marry the girls if they would go to school. However, she felt that Bholi was ugly and nobody would marry her. So, they decided to send Bholi to school.

Bholi Prepares for School

Next day, Bholi's father held her hand and told her that he would take Bholi to school. Bholi got scared. She remembered how her cow Lakshmi was sold and felt that something similar was going to happen to her. Then, she was made to wear new clothes. She was given a bath and her hair was oiled. This treatment made Bholi realise that she was going someplace that was better than her home.

At school, Ramlal left Bholi with the headmistress which scared Bholi. Inside the school, there were several rooms wherein girls were sitting, reading from books or writing on slates. The headmistress, asked Bholi to sit down in a corner in one of the classrooms. Bholi did not know anything about the school but she was happy to find many girls of her own age there. The lady teacher who was in the class was saying something to the girls but Bholi could understand nothing.

Bholi's First Day at School

Bholi was attracted to the colourful pictures on the wall. She was much impressed by the realistic pictures of birds and animals. The teacher asked her name. Bholi couldn't speak, stammered and then, started crying.

After the class was over, the teacher went to Bholi. She called her lovingly and encouraged her to tell her name. This time, Bholi tried to speak her name and was successful. The teacher told Bholi to come to school everyday.

The Teacher Gives her a Book

The teacher gave her a book with pictures of dog, cat, goat, etc. The teacher told her that she would be able to read like everyone else and then, no one would laugh at her. Bholi was happy as the teacher encouraged her and gave her hope of a new life.

Progress of Village

Many years passed, the village progressed and converted into a small town. The primary school became a high school. There were now a cinema under a tin shed and a cotton ginning mill. The mail train also began to stop at their railway station.

Bholi's Marriage Proposal

One night after dinner, Ramlal and his wife were talking about a marriage proposal for Bholi. Bishamber was a forty five or fifty years old lame widower. He was a grocer and had grown up children from his first wife. Bishamber was rich and had not demanded any dowry. Ramlal was not very happy with this proposal but his wife believed that it was the best marriage proposal for Bholi.

She told Ramlal that since Bishamber was from another village, he didn't know about Bholi's pockmarks and lack of sense. So, they fixed her marriage with Bishamber. Bholi listened to everything silently from her cot.

Wedding Procession

On the day of the wedding, Bishamber came as a bridegroom with his friends and family with a lot of pomp and show. Ramlal was very happy to see Bholi getting married with great pomp.

Soon, it was time for Bholi to come out. Bholi came out in a red coloured silk saree and sat near the sacred fire. When it was time for the garland ceremony, Bishamber saw Bholi's face.

On seeing her pock-marks, Bishamber asked for a dowry of five thousand rupees and threatened to leave without marrying Bholi, if the money is not given.

Ramlal pleaded to him and put his turban at his feet. He requested Bishamber to take 2000 rupees. However, Bishamber did not agree and at last, Ramlal had to bring the amount of 5,000 rupees.

Bholi Stops the Marriage

After receiving the money, Bishamber again took the garland to put around Bholi's neck. However, this time Bholi was not shy.

She was looking at Bishamber with hatred. As Bishamber was putting the garland, Bholi stopped Bishamber and threw the garland into the fire. She got up and threw away the veil. Then, she addressed her family, who were shocked to hear her speak confidently. She told her father that she would not marry Bishamber and asked him to take the money back.

Bholi's refusal angered Bishamber and he shouted at her. Bholi told her father that she was marrying Bishamber for them but she would not marry the greedy and evil man. Bholi even replied angrily to an old lady of her village.

The Courageous Bholi

When Bishamber and everyone went away, Ramlal felt ashamed and sorrowful. He asked Bholi what she would do with her future. Bholi told him that she would not marry and would take care of her parents in their old age. She also told them that she would teach at the school just like her teacher.

Sulekha's teacher who was watching all this drama approved Bholi's decision. She smiled at her with satisfaction just like an artist who is satisfied after completing a masterpiece.

Word Meaning

Word	Meaning
backward	mentally disabled
pock-marks	marks on the skin left by the small-pox disease
mimicked	copy the behaviour or speech of other people in order to make fun of them
stammered	to speak with many pauses or repetitions because of having a speech problem
disfigured	spoiled or damaged
revenue	the income that a government receives regularly, or an amount representing such income
matted (of hair)	tangled into a thick mass
squatted	sat on their heeds
scurried	to move quickly with short steps
soothing	having a gently calming effect
blossomed a tree or plant	to produce flowers

Word	Meaning
heart was throbbing	heart was beating much harder and faster than usual due to excitement
witless	very foolish or stupid
grocer	one who sells food and household goods
prompted	to cause (someone) to do something
poised	not moving but ready to move
humiliate	to make someone feel very ashamed or foolish
muttered	to speak quietly so that it is difficult for other people to hear what you say.
triumphant	victorious
prospective	likely to be or become something specified in the future
like a streak of lightening	very quickly
contempt	a strong feeling of disregard for someone
thunderstruck	extremely surprised or shocked
contemplating	thinking deeply or carefully about something

NCERT FOLDER

NCERT Intext and Exercise Questions

READ AND FIND OUT (NCERT PAGE 47)

Q.1 Why is Bholi's father worried about her?

Ans. Bholi's father, Ramlal was worried for Bholi because she was an ugly and dumb girl. She had pockmarks on her face and stammered while speaking which might become a hurdle in her marriage.

Q.2 For what unusual reason is Bholi sent to school?

Ans. Bholi was sent to school because when the primary school opened in their village the Tehsildar advised her father to send his daughter to the school as an example for the villagers. After talking with his wife, it was decided that if the ugly Bholi went to school, it would not harm the marriage prospects of their other daughters.

READ AND FIND OUT (NCERT PAGE 48)

Q.1 Does Bholi enjoy her first day at school?

Ans. Initially, Bholi was scared to go to school. She cried and sat in the corner of her classroom. However, she was fascinated by the colourful pictures on the walls which were very realistic. Therefore, Bholi was not completely afraid in the school and did enjoy some part of it.

Q.2 Does she find her teacher to be different from the people at home?

Ans. Yes, Bholi found her teacher to be different from the people at home. At home, she was neglected and no one paid attention to her. She never bathed nor were her clothes washed. She was criticised and everyone made fun of her.
In contrast, her teacher was entirely different. She was kind, soft and affectionate. She encouraged her and filled her with a hope of new life.

READ AND FIND OUT (NCERT PAGE 51)

Q.1 Why do Bholi's parents accept Bishamber's marriage proposal?

Ans. Bholi's parents accepted Bishamber's marriage proposal as he was a prosperous grocer and had not asked for any dowry.

Q.2 Why does the marriage not take place?

Or **Why did Bholi not marry Bishamber?** **CBSE 2020**

Ans. At the time of the marriage, Bishamber asked for a dowry of five thousand rupees because he saw Bholi's pock-marked face. Ramlal had no choice but to pay. However, Bholi refused to marry such a greedy man.

THINK ABOUT IT (NCERT PAGE 55)

Q.1 Bholi had many apprehensions about going to school. What made her feel that she was going to a better place than her home?

Ans. Bholi had many apprehensions about going to school because the day she was going to school she was forced by her parents to dress nicely. She was bathed and her hair were oiled. She was even given a clean dress to wear. The special way in which everyone treated her made her feel that she was going to a better place.

Q.2 How did Bholi's teacher play an important role in changing the course of her life?

Ans. It is true to say that Bholi's teacher played an important role in changing the course of her life. Bholi used to stammer and was afraid to speak when she attended school in the beginning. Her teacher treated her kindly and encouraged her to have confidence. She taught Bholi to read and write and made her an independent girl who was aware of her rights. It was because of her teacher's guidance that Bholi developed her personality. Thus, with her kindness, love and affection, she changed Bholi's life.

Q.3 Why did Bholi at first agree to an unequal match? Why did she later reject the marriage? What does this tell about her?

Ans. Bholi agreed to the unequal match at first to fulfil her parents' wishes. Later on, she rejected the marriage when the bridegroom asked for dowry. This tells us that Bholi was not a timid and dumb girl. She was aware of her rights. She also knew how to fight for her own dignity and feared no one.

Q.4 Bholi's real name is Sulekha. We are told this right at the beginning. But only in the last but one paragraph of the story is Bholi called Sulekha again. Why do you think she is called Sulekha at that point in the story?

Ans. The word 'Bholi' means a simpleton. Throughout the story, she had been a simpleton who hardly expressed her opinion on any matter. The word Sulekha means 'a person with a beautiful sense of letters'. In this story, this word has a larger meaning of being a literate, intelligent and mature individual. After her education, Bholi had really changed and turned into Sulekha. So, the use of, 'Sulekha' at the time of the marriage is her announcement to the world that she is no more a Bholi, but is a Sulekha.

TALK ABOUT IT (NCERT PAGE 55)

Q.1 Bholi's teacher helped her overcome social barriers by encouraging and motivating her. How do you think you can contribute towards changing the social attitudes illustrated in this story ?

Ans. There are many ways in which we can contribute towards changing the social attributes that place women and differently abled into the inferior category. They are

- We can contribute by saying no to taking or giving dowry.
- We must not discriminate between a boy and a girl. Both should be given equal rights and opportunities to grow.
- We must also learn to respect those who are differently -abled and treat them equally.

Q.2 Should girls be aware of their rights and assert them? Should girls and boys have the same rights, duties and privileges? What are some of the ways in which society treats them differently? When we speak of 'Human rights', do we differentiate between girl's rights and boy's rights?

Ans. Yes, girls should be aware of their rights and duties. Further, both the girls and boys should have the same rights, duties and privileges.

However, in our society there is a differentiation between a girl's and a boy's rights. Although equal in the eyes of law, our society treats boys as superior and girls as inferior. Parents spend more on a boy's education than that of a girl. A girl is just trained to be a wife and mother. Boys also have special privileges in matters of food, career or freedom.

Q.3 Do you think the characters in the story were speaking to each other in English? If not, in which language were they speaking? (You can get clues from the names of the persons and the non-English words used in the story.)

Ans. No, we do not thinks that the characters in the story were speaking to each other in English. They spoke in Hindi. Several words like '*numberdar*', '*tehsildar sahib*', 'izzat' and 'pitaji' are words of Hindi. Even the names of characters like 'Ramlal' and 'Bholi' are in Hindi.

REVIEW EXERCISE

Including Competency Based Questions

Multiple Choice Questions

1. What do you understand by the word 'simpleton' as used in the chapter to describe Bholi?

(a) Simple (b) Foolish
(c) Basic (d) None of these

Ans. (b) Foolish

2. Why did Bholi talk very little?

(a) She stammered
(b) Other kids mimicked her and made fun of her stammering
(c) She was an introvert
(d) None of the above

Ans. (b) Other kids mimicked her and made fun of her stammering

3. How was Bholi treated in the family?

(a) She was not given new clothes
(b) None cared to wash her clothes
(c) None cared to comb her hair
(d) All of the above

Ans. (d) All of the above

4. What was the name of the cow that Bholi had?

(a) Lakshmi (b) Gayatri
(c) Ganga (d) Gayya

Ans. (a) Lakshmi

5. "What's the matter with you, you fool? I am only taking you to school." Who said this to whom?

(a) Tehsildar to Ramlal (b) Teacher to Bholi
(c) Ramlal to Bholi (d) Head-mistress to Bholi

Ans. (c) Ramlal to Bholi

6. Whose paintings did she see on the classroom wall?

(a) Cow (b) Goat
(c) Parrot (d) All of these

Ans. (d) All of these

7. What do you think how Bholi used to feel about herself before she started to going to school?

(i) Nobody loves me.
(ii) I'm a burden on my family.
(iii) I am of no good to anyone.
(iv) I wish I could speak and look like other children of my age.

(a) (i) and (ii) (b) (ii) and (iv)
(c) (iii) and (iv) (d) All of these

Ans. (d) All of these

8. Why did the garland remain poised in Bishamber's hands?

(a) On seeing pock-marks on Bholi's face
(b) He was shocked to see Bholi
(c) On hearing Bholi's stammering
(d) On seeing veil over bride's face

Ans. (a) On seeing pock-marks on Bholi's face

9. Ramlal went and placed his turban at Bishamber's feet. Here 'his turban' represents ....

(a) a piece of cloth (b) his honour
(c) his money (d) None of these

Ans. (b) 'his honour'

10. How did Bholi react when Bishamber was about to place garland round her neck?

(a) She happily accepted the garland.
(b) She flung the garland into sacred fire.
(c) She stood up and threw away her veil.
(d) Both (b) and (c)

Ans. (d) Both (b) and (c)

11. Choose the option that gives the most appropriate response to the statement made by the speaker. Ramlal was more concerned about his izzat than Bholi's life.

(a) I think Ramlal and his wife were right at their point.
(b) I think Bholi took the right decision by calling off the marriage.
(c) I think Bholi should not have called off the wedding.
(d) I think Bholi should not have said a word.

Ans. (b) I think Bholi took the right decision by calling off the marriage.

12. Choose the correct option for (i) and (ii).

(i) Everyone was shocked on hearing Bholi at the time of her wedding.
(ii) Bholi spoke without any stammering.

(a) (i) is true (ii) is false
(b) (ii) is true (i) is false
(c) (i) is the result of (ii)
(d) Both (i) and (ii) are false

Ans. (c) (i) is the result of (ii)

Extract Based Questions

1. Read the following extract carefully and answer the questions that follow.

They were good-looking, healthy girls and it was not difficult to find bridegrooms for them. But Ramlal was worried about Bholi.

(i) Who are 'they' in the extract?

Ans. Radha, Mangla and Champa are 'they' in the extract.

(ii) Complete the sentence appropriately.

Bholi was neither .... nor ....

Ans. good-looking, intelligent

(iii) Study the statements given below and identify the correct statement.

(A) Ramlal had four daughters

(B) Bholi was not liked by anyone in her family?

(a) (A) is wrong (B) is right
(b) (A) is right (B) is wrong
(c) Both are wrong
(d) Both are right

Ans. (d) Both are right

(iv) Why was Ramlal worried about Bholi?

Ans. Ramlal was worried about Bholi because she was an ugly and a dumb girl.

2. Read the following extract carefully and answer the questions that follow.

"What's the matter with you, you fool? Shouted Ramlal. "I am only taking you to school." Then he told his wife, "Let her wear some decent clothes today or else what will the teachers and the other school girls think of us when they see her?

New clothes had never been made for Bholi. The old dresses of her sisters were passed on to her. No one cared to mend or wash her clothes. But today she was lucky to receive a clean dress which had shrunk after many washings and no longer fitted Champa. She was even bathed and oil was rubbed into her dry and matted hair. Only then did she believe that she was being taken to a place better than her home! When they reached the school, the children were already in their classrooms. **CBSE Question Bank 2021 Modified**

(i) Pick the option that best describes how Bholi felt at the end of her first day in school.

(a) lost and scared
(b) calm and peaceful
(c) elated and peaceful
(d) hopeful and elated

Ans. (d) hopeful and elated.

(ii) The phrase 'passed on' is similar to ....

Ans. hand-me down which means wearing someone's old clothes.

(iii) Why was Bholi's hair matted?

Ans. Bholi's hair was matted because it was never oiled or combed. She was a neglected child in the family. She didn't get the luxury of someone caring for her or washing her clothes. Bholi had been left without care for so long that her hair was matted.

(iv) Why did Ramlal call Bholi a fool?

Ans. Ramlal called Bholi a fool because Bholi shouted in fear and pulled her hand away.

3. And suddenly Bholi noticed that the teacher was standing by her side, smiling at her. "What's your name, little one?"

"Bh-Bho-Bho" She could stammer no further than that.

Then she began to cry and tears flowed from her eyes in a helpless flood. She kept her head down as she sat in her corner, not daring to look up at the girls who, she knew, were still laughing at her. When the school bell rang, all the girls scurried out of the classroom, but Bholi dared not leave her corner. Her head still lowered, she kept on sobbing.

"Bholi"

The teacher's voice was so soft and soothing! In all her life she had never been called like that. It touched her heart. **CBSE SQP 2024**

(i) What is the tone the teacher is unlikely to have used in the line, "What's your name, little one?"

(a) Reassuring (b) comforting
(c) Settling (d) Calming

Ans. (c) Settling

(ii) How does the author's use of Bholi's perspective help build the narrative in the extract?

Ans. The author's use of Bholi's perspective in the extract helps readers to look directly into Bholi's thoughts, emotions and experiences.
By experiencing the vents through Bholi's eyes, it becomes easy to understand the depth of Bholi's vulnerability. This allows the author to convey the impact of the teacher's kindness in contrast with her classmates' laughter more effectively. It enhances the reader's engagement with the narrative.

(iii) Fill in the blank with the correct word from the bracket.

The word 'flood' in the line '...tears flowed from her eyes in a helpless flood.' Indicates that Bholi was crying .... (uncontrollably / unintentionally).

Ans. uncontrollably

(iv) How does the teacher's comforting demeanour contrast with the behaviour of the other girls in the classroom?

Ans. The teacher's behaviour is gentle towards Bholi. She approaches her with kindness and understanding, which offers a supportive presence for her. The other girls display insensitivity by laughing at Bholi stammering.

4. Read the following extract carefully and answer the questions that follow.

He came with a big party of relations with him for the wedding. A brass-band playing a popular tune from an Indian film headed the procession, with the bridegroom riding a decorated horse. Ramlal was overjoyed to see such pomp and splendor. He had never dreamt that his.

(i) The given extract depicts an Indian wedding about to happen. Whose wedding is it? Does the wedding take place? Elaborate with reference to the extract.

Ans. It was the day of Bholi's wedding to Bishambher. No, the wedding didn't take place. As soon as Bishambher saw Bholi's face, he threatened to not marry her if not given a dowry of ₹ 5000. Ramlal pleaded to him and arranged the money but seeing all this, Bholi refused to marry Bishamber.

(ii) What had Ramlal never dreamt?

Ans. Ramlal had never dreamt that his fourth daughter would have such a grand wedding.

(iii) State True or False.

None of the terms (a) - (d) can be applied to the statement - He came with a big party of relations with him for the wedding.

(a) A hypothesis - a proposed explanation for a phenomenon

(b) An assumption - something that is assumed to be true without proof or taken for granted

(c) A hyperbole - exaggerated statements or claims not meant to be taken literally

(d) A statement - a definite or clear expression of something in speech or writing

Ans. False; A statement

(iv) Which phrase would correctly substitute 'splendor' in the given sentence from the extract?

Ramlal was overjoyed to see such pomp and splendor.

Ans. magnificent appearance

5. Read the following extract carefully and answer the questions that follow.

"Ramlal stood rooted to the ground, his head bowed low with the weight of grief and shame. The flames of the sacred fire slowly died down. Everyone was gone. Ramlal turned to Bholi and said, "But what about you, no one will ever marry you now. What shall we do with you?"

And Sulekha said in a voice that was calm and steady. "Don't you worry, Pitaji! In your old age I will serve you and Mother and I will teach in the same school where I learnt so much. Isn't that right, Ma'am?" The teacher had all along stood in a corner, watching the drama. "Yes, Bholi, of course," she replied. And in her smiling eyes was the light of a deep satisfaction that an artist feels when contemplating the completion of her masterpiece."

(i) State the reason Bholi had refused to get married.

Ans. Bholi refused to get married as the bridegroom had been greedy and was disrespectful.

(ii) State True or False.

None of the terms (a) - (d) can be applied to the statement - What shall we do with you?

(a) A hypothesis - a proposed explanation for a phenomenon

(b) An assumption - something that is taken for granted or assumed to be true

(c) A hyperbole - exaggerated statements or claims not meant to be taken literally

(d) A premise - a proposition that forms the basis of an argument

Ans. True

(iii) Why did the teacher stand in one corner watching the drama? Answer in about 40 words.

Competency Based

Ans. The teacher was standing in one corner watching the drama because she had faith in Bholi standing up for herself.

(iv) Why did Ramlal stand rooted to the ground?

Ans. Ramlal stood rooted to the ground because he was in a state of shock.

Short Answer Type Questions

1. Why is Sulekha called 'Bholi'?

Ans. Sulekha is called 'Bholi' because she is a simpleton who had suffered some brain damage after falling off a cot when she was ten months old. As a result, she is slow in learning things and also stammered while speaking.

2. Ramlal was worried about Bholi as she didn't have good looks. Counter the belief that it's important for a girl to be good looking and give a reason for the same. CBSE Question Bank 2021

Ans. The belief that it's important for a girl to be good looking, is wrong. It is not good looks that bring a person comfortable and prosperous life. It is a person's good behaviour, intelligence, pure heart and courage that ensures that he/she lives a happy life. Good looks doesn't stay forever, whether in a boy or a girl, it's a person's virtues that stay forever and thus, are more important.

3. How did you feel when you read about Bholi being ignored and ill-treated by her parents as a child?

Ans. I fell terribly sorrowful when I read about Bholi being ignored and ill-treated by her parents for no fault of her own. All the problems faced by Bholi were not caused by her, they were accidents and mishaps. In this case, her parents' behaviour was not justified.

4. What filled Bholi, a dumb cow, with a new hope in her?

Or **Bholi's heart was overflowing with a 'new hope and a new life'. What does the phrase 'a new hope and a new life' mean to Bholi ?** CBSE 2020

Or **Bholi's heart was brimming with "fresh optimism and a renewed existence". What significance does the expression 'a new hope and a new life' hold for Bholi?**

Ans. Bholi's heart was overflowing with 'a new hope and a new life'. This means that the new hope which came into Bholi's life was the hope of education. When Bholi went to school, her teacher showed her the path of a new life through education.

She assured Bholi that she would be able to speak without a stammer and that she would be the most learned person in the village and no one would laugh at her instead they would respect her.

5. What objections does Ramlal have to Bishamber's proposal?

Ans. Ramlal was not very happy with Bishamber's proposal. He did not like the fact that Bishamber was of his age. He had a limp (lameness, difficulty in walking) and his children from his first wife were quite grown up.

6. What kind of mother was Ramlal's wife?

Ans. Ramlal's wife (Bholi's mother) was a traditional housewife who believed that daughters should not be educated as it would be difficult to find grooms for them. She neglected Bholi as she was ugly and dumb, and wanted to get rid of her by marrying her off to just anyone.

7. How would you have reacted if you were one of the guests witnessing Bholi's wedding when she refused to marry Bishamber Nath? Competency Based

Ans. I would have been very proud that Bholi took a stand for herself. It is important for us to understand that no one can humiliate a person like this just because they are not good looking. I would definitely praise Bholi for being so brave.

8. Do you think Bholi's father would have agreed to the match if her mother hadn't insisted upon it? Why/why not? CBSE Question Bank 2021

Ans. I think Bholi's father would have agreed to the match even if her mother didn't insist upon it. It is clear that he was thinking about it as he had been worried about her looks when her sister was getting married. He had already thought that because of her looks and lower intelligence, the chances of Bholi's marriage will be very less.

9. Bholi was believed to be a dumb cow? What turned her into a fearless, bold and confident girl?

Ans. It is true to say that Bholi was believed to be a dumb cow. However, she is not really so as an adult. Education made Bholi aware of her rights and gave her a voice to fight against wrongs. It gave her the confidence to be bold and fearless.

10. The Tehsildar was an agent of change in Bholi's life. Justify. CBSE Additional SQP 2022

Ans. It is true to say that the Tehsildar changed Bholi's life as he was the one who convinced her father to send her to school. Bholi's mother did not want to send her to school, but her father could not disobey the Tehsildar and was forced to admit Bholi in school. Going to school turned out to be the biggest blessing of Bholi's life. Education gave Bholi the confidence to challenge societal norms, and protest against evil practices like dowry and an unequal marriage. As an educated person, Bholi knew her worth in society.

11. Do you think Bholi could have confidently refused to marry Bishamber if she wasn't educated? Give reasons. CBSE 2024

Ans. No, I do not think that Bholi would not have had the confidence to refuse the marriage to Bishamber without her education. The story suggests that education gave her voice and courage as Bholi was previously teased and belittled for her stammer. Education empowered Bholi, enabling her to recognise her self-worth and stand against the unfair treatment of being sold off to a greedy and uncaring man.

The knowledge and belief that she had a future as a school teacher allowed her to reject the marriage confidently.

Long Answer Type Questions

1. Bholi is a child different from others. This difference makes her an object of neglect and laughter. Elaborate.

Ans. Bholi was a child different from others. She suffered from a weak mind due to her accident (falling from the cot) when she was ten months old. She also started to a stammer while speaking. Then, she became ugly due to the pock-marks on her face and body on contracting the smallpox disease. All these made her family and other children treat her badly, resulting in her becoming an introvert.

To help such children face the world bravely, we must treat them with love and affection and encourage them to join the mainstream society. We must not mock their disabilities, instead we should give them hope that they can be as good as the other children by motivating and uplifting them.

Since every child is special, proper guidance and support should be given to boost up their morals and encourge them to do good in their lives. There are a lot of children like Bholi in our society who need utmost care and affection. We must help them to improve their lives to excel in their future.

2. How did Bholi's teacher help her to overcome her fear of school and become a confident girl? CBSE 2020

Or **The credit of Bholi's transformation to Sulekha goes to her teacher. Elaborate with reference to the text.** CBSE 2022 Term II

Ans. It is true to say that the credit of Bholi's transformation to Sulekha goes to her teacher. Bholi was a meek girl. She had pockmarks all over her body. She was a slow learner and used to stammer while speaking.

When Bholi was sent to school for the first time, she did not know anything about the school. On reaching school, she sat down in the corner of her class. When the teacher asked her name, she stammered and could not tell her name. All the girls laughed at her and Bholi felt ashamed. After school got over, the teacher came to Bholi and again asked her name. Bholi, with much stammering finally spoke and told her name.

The teacher boosted her confidence by appreciating her effort. She assured Bholi that with time, she would be able to speak confidently. The teacher started by giving her a picture book and then promised to help her in reading, writing and learning other big books.

Her kind attitude towards Bholi, her affection and encouragement motivated Bholi to overcome the fear of school and become a confident girl.

3. What do you know about Bishamber Nath? Why did Bholi refuse to marry him? CBSE 2020

Ans. Bishamber Nath was a well-to-do prosperous grocer who was of the same age as Bholi's father. He was a widower who had a shop and a house of his own along with a big bank balance. With grown up children from his first wife, Bishamber decided to get married again and agreed to the proposal of marrying Bholi.

On the day of the marriage, Bishamber came to the venue with his friends and family. He entered the venue with much pomp and show.

At the time of the ceremony, Bholi entered the venue and her veil was slipped. Initially, Bishamber had not asked for any dowry but after looking at Bholi's pock-marked face, he asked Bholi's father to give ₹ 5000 as dowry. Ramlal, Bholi's father started crying and bought out ₹ 5000. Satisfied with the dowry, Bishamber proceeded with the ceremony but Bholi refused to marry him. She told her father that she would not marry a greedy man such as Bishamber. She would rather take care of her parents in their old age.

4. Bholi choose a dignified life of service rather than surrendering herself to a greedy old man for the rest of her life. Education provides the required stimulus to overcome one's personal barriers.

Explain the role of education in shaping the life of a child with respect to the lesson 'Bholi'. CBSE 2012

Or **How did education change Bholi's personality?** CBSE 2020

Or **After reading the story 'Bholi', you find her to be 'a role-model' for village girls. Discuss.** CBSE 2022 Term II

Or **How does education play a transformative role in Bholi's life?** CBSE SQP 2023

Or **Bholi manages to break out of her shell and metamorphosize from an underconfident girl to a bold woman, who brimmed with confidence. Analyse the impact of education on her life. How does the story of self transformation give us hope and encourage us to never compromise in our self respect and dignity** CBSE 2024 C

Ans. Education brought about a huge change in Bholi's personality. Bholi was a backward child. As a kid, she was a meek girl who had pockmarks all over her body and used to stammer. She could not speak until she was 5 years old. Because of these reasons, she was a neglected child of her family. No one cared for her and she lost all the confidence in herself. When her father was forced to send one of his daughters to school for education, Bholi was the first option. In the school, Bholi bloomed. The teacher treated her with love and care which she had never experienced before. She encouraged the little girl and guided her into becoming strong-minded.

Bholi learned to read, write and speak without stammering. As a result, she became confident and independent while being aware of her rights. She learnt to fight against what she thought was wrong. It was because of her education that she could speak up against the groom and refused to marry a greedy man.

The now independent Bholi told her parents that she would teach at the school and take care of her parents in their old age. This Bholi stands in sharp contrast to the old weak Bholi, all because of her education. Thus, she is a role-model for village girls.

5. After reading Bholi's story you decide to write a blog on the importance of educating the girl child and how it empowers her. Write that blog expressing your views. CBSE Question Bank 2021

Or **Imagine you are Bholi and you have been invited to give a speech on the importance of girl education. Write the speech on 'Girl Education and Empowerment'.** CBSE 2022 Term II

Ans. 'Girl Education and Empowerment'

Right to Education is one of the Fundamental Rights as recognised by our Constitution. And yet, in many parts of our country, girls are not sent to school by their parents.

For the longest time, education has been treated as 'privilege' which only the boy child deserved because people thought girls should only focus on household chores and taking care of their family. And, because of this lack of education, they have been ill-treated.

Thus, it's imperative that we educate the girls. It will help them understand what is good for them and will also empower them to stand and fight for their rights. It will stop the mistreatment as it has done for many. Education can also help them become independent, thus, helping them become more confident and self-dependent rather than depending on their family.

Once a girl becomes confident and independent, she can be truly safe and happy.

6. Destiny had been cruel to Bholi yet she made a place for herself in a conservative society. Discuss. CBSE 2023

Ans. Bholi was a weak and timid person. She was an ignored child. Her parents treated her like a burden. She was neglected, ill-treated and considered a dumb cow by her family. She was sent to school as her parents thought she would not be able to get a match of marriage with her slow brain and pockmarked ugly face. This was a twist of fate for her.

At the school, Bholi met an encouraging teacher who instilled in her traits of self-confidence, self-respect and courage. Bholi's transformation comes to light when she refuses to marry Bishamber in front of everyone. She was confident in her refusal and even called Bishamber a greedy, mean and heartless fellow. Bholi, then, decided to become a school teacher and serve her parents in their old age. Thus, with the help of her school teacher, Bholi changed her future and made it better. She transformed from a timid, dumb cow into a bold, courageous, confident and self-respecting person and in this way, overcame her cruel destiny.

7. "Put the fear out of your heart and you will be able to speak like anyone else." These words of encouragement from the teacher highlight that change of social attitude and encouragement can help a child like Bholi to become confident and face the world bravely. With reference to the story 'Bholi' write how the social attitude towards Bholi made her an introvert. What should be done to help such children to face the world bravely? CBSE 2023

Ans. The given words of encouragement from the teacher are crucial to understand that Bholi undergoes a major character development because of it. Bholi, since her childhood, has been bullied and mocked for her disfigured face and pock-marks. No one cared for her and her family even ignored her. As a result, Bholi lacked love and care. She talked very little and grew fearful of new surroundings. We can see her fear when she is taken to the new school and left there. This changed when the teacher came into Bholi's life. The teacher talked to Bholi affectionately and in a friendly manner. She assured Bholi that if she put the fear out of her heart, she would be able to speak like anyone else. It was a difficult task but years of efforts transformed Bholi's personality completely. This can be seen when Bholi refused to marry a greedy man who was trying to exploit her father due to her looks.

Hence, it is true that a change of social attitude and encouragement can help a child like Bholi become confident and face the world bravely.

Children like Bholi are special. They need to be constantly encouraged by the parents, teachers and even by the other relations. They must be taught to fight back against their handicaps rather than accept it as fate.

8. Imagine that Bholi writes a diary entry, exploring the themes of 'Girl Child' and 'Impact of Education', in the context of her own experiences. Write a dairy entry, as Bholi. CBSE 2024

Ans. 11th May, 20XX 9:00 p.m.

Dear Diary

Today was an interesting day. I was supposed to get married but did not. I refused to marry such a greedy old man just to please everyone.

As a girl, one is supposed to be sincere, obedient and submissive but why. This is the norm of our society. If you have a girl child, educated her on how to run a household and be a good wife. daughter, mother, etc. They are not educated to be independent and live life on her own terms. Education in general is not given to many even today.

Look at me. Today, you will find me to be a self-assured and independent young lady. However, it was the polar opposite when I started school. I was terrified, reliant, illiterate, and stammering because I was never cared for. My school on the other hand, assisted me in becoming educated, and my teacher assisted me in revealing my secret confidence.

Education can be used as a weapon. Through education, you might discover your hidden talents and abilities, empowering you to face your fears. A self-assured person can tell the difference between right and wrong. You should think twice about embracing the prejudices that society has imposed on us. I was able to summon the courage to refuse to marry a self-centered man who had humiliated my parents as a result of my education. Today, I can make as much as my brother and help my elderly parents financially. Finally, I'd like to emphasise the importance of self-education and demonstrating your true worth to the world.

Sulekha/Bholi

ASSESSMENT EXERCISE

Extract Based Questions

Read the following extract carefully and answer the questions that follow.

On Bishamber's greedy face appeared a triumphant smile. He had gambled and won.

(i) Why was there triumphant simile on Bishamber's face ?

(ii) What gamble did he play?

(a) of demanding 5000 rupees to marry Bholi

(b) of demanding 2000 rupees to marry Bholi

(c) of demanding 1000 rupees to marry Bholi

(d) of demanding 3000 rupees to marry Bholi

(iii) Complete the sentence appropriately.

Bholi was Ramdas ....(third/fourth) daughter.

(iv) Complete the analogy by selecting the suitable word from the text.

Nail : Sail :: Needy : ....

Short Answer (SA) Type Questions

1. How can we change social attitude towards people who are different?
2. Why did Ramlal not send all his daughters to school?
3. Why did Bishamber demand dowry at the time of marriage although he had not done so when the marriage was fixed?
4. What was the role of the teacher in changing Bholi's attitude to life?

Long Answer (LA) Type Questions

1. Sending Bholi to school was a 'blessing in disguise'. Do you agree? Support your answer on the basis of the text.
2. The story, 'Bholi', throws light on some social evils being practised in our society. Bholi took a stand and succeeded in overcoming the social barriers. What can you contribute to change the social attitudes illustrated in the story? CBSE 2014
3. Education is always a great asset in the life of a woman. How did Bholi an educated girl, face the challenges posed by Bishamber's greed? CBSE 2023

The Book that Saved the Earth

by Claire Boiko

'The Book that Saved the Earth' by Claire Boiko is set in the twenty-fifth century. It is a humorous tale of how a book of nursery rhymes saves Earth from an invasion by Martians.

Scene - I

The first scene of the play belongs to the twenty-fifth century in the Museum of Ancient History on the planet Earth. The focus is on the historian who is sitting on a table with a projector on it.

Historian talks about a Book that Saved the Earth

The historian tells the audience that twentieth century was called the Era of books. Books contained information about everything. Books taught people how to, when to, where to and why to. They were used to illustrate, educate and decorate. One of the strangest thing a book did was that it saved the Earth. The historian, then, tells them that a book saved the Earth from the Martian invasion in 2040. The historian shows the audience the invasion.

Think-Tank and Noodle

Think-Tank is seated on a raised box with arms folded. He has a huge, egg-shaped head and he is wearing a long robe decorated with stars and circles. His apprentice, Noodle is standing beside him at a switch-board. Think-Tank is the commander-in-chief and the ruler of Mars. He is being praised with proper salutation by his apprentice Noodle.

Think-Tank Calls for the Invasion

Think-Tank informs Noodle that he will invade the ridiculous planet called Earth. He wants to communicate with the manned space probe to the planet Earth. Then, he consults his speaking mirror if he is the most intellectually gifted being in the whole land. An off-stage voice tells him that he is the most intellectually gifted being. Think-Tank scolds the mirror for being slow. Then, he moves proudly and says that Martians are much more attractive than Earthlings who have very small heads.

Scene - II

The scene shifts to Mars space control in the Centerville Public Library. The people (Martians) present in the space probe are Captain Omega, Sergeant Oop and Lieutenant Iota. They are confused and puzzled. They are not familiar with books and do not understand them.

Communication with Space Probe

Think-Tank and Noodle make a voice contact with the space probe. Captain Omega informs that they have reached Earth and are taking shelter in a square place (library).

They do not have any idea about their location. Iota thinks that the place must be some kind of a storage barn as it has two thousand peculiar items (books).

Guesses made by Martians about the Books

The people (Martians) in the space probe got confused about the strange items, all of them start making guesses about the books. Sergeant Oop thinks that the books are hats. Think-Tank calls them sandwiches and orders the crew to eat them. When Oop eats it, he finds it tasteless.

Just then, the wise Noodle gently suggests that they may be devices of communication. So, Think-Tank asks the probe team to listen to them. However, Oop, Iota and Omega do not hear anything.

Noodle, then, very politely suggests that the Earthlings watch them. So, all the three Martians of the space probe sit to read them. Omega picks up the book 'Mother Goose' while Iota and Oop sit with him. However, even now they cannot read the books. So, they come to a conclusion that the printed lines and pictures must be some kind of code.

Think-Tank Commands the Team to Take Vitamins

Noodle, now, tells Think Tank that their chemical department had given them some vitamins to increase their intelligence. So, Think-Tank ordered the probe team to eat the vitamins given to them to read the code. They follow him and are able to read the book. The lines are about Mistress Mary and her garden of cockle shells and silver bells.

Mighty Think-Tank is Alarmed

As captain Omega read the rhyme, Think-Tank thinks that the Earthlings are very advanced. They have discovered how to combine agriculture and mining. They can grow cockle shells and silver. They have taught their domesticated animals musical culture and space techniques.

He thinks that the Earthlings are about to send cows for an invasion to the moon. He is, further, terrified when he sees the picture of the fallen Humpty-Dumpty. He thinks it to be his picture. He declares that the Earthlings have seen him and they are planning to capture Mars Central Control as well as him.

Think-Tank Calls Off the Invasion

Thinking that the Earthlings are planning to capture him, Think-Tank cancels the invasion. He orders Noodle to prepare a space capsule for him to escape. He asks his probe to leave. He orders his fleet to escape to the star Alpha Centauri and evacuate the entire planet of Mars.

Martians and Earthlings are Friends

The Historian reveals that it was 'Mother Goose', a book of rhymes, that saved the Earth. Mars and Earth are now friends. Noodle succeeded Think-Tank and became the head of Mars. Earthlings have even set up a library in their capital city of Marsopolis. However, Martians can never gather the courage to read the 'Mother Goose' book again.

Word Meaning

Word	Meaning
easel	a wooden frame to support a blackboard or picture
zulus	an ethnic group of people belonging to South Africa
apprentice	trainee
peevishly	feeling or showing irritation
intellectually	possessing or showing intellect

Word	Meaning
riffling	turning pages of a book quickly and casually
crew	group of people who operate a ship, aircraft etc
barn	large farm building used for storing hay/grain
haberdashery	shop which sells clothing, small articles of dress, pins, cotton, etc.

NCERT FOLDER

NCERT Intext and Exercise Questions

READ AND FIND OUT (NCERT PAGE 56)

Q.1 Why was the twentieth-century called the 'Era of the Book'?

Or **20th century is referred to as the 'Era of the Book'. Comment briefly.**

Ans. The twentieth century was called the 'Era of the Book' because there were books for everything, from ant-eaters to Zulus. Books taught people what to do, how to do, when to do and why to do.

Q.2 Who tried to invade the Earth in the twenty-first century?

Ans. The Martians tried to invade the Earth in the twenty-first century.

READ AND FIND OUT (NCERT PAGE 58)

Q.1 What guesses are made by Think-Tank about the books found on Earth?

Ans. Think-Tank guessed that the books were sandwiches that the Earthlings loved to eat. He made another guess that the books were some communication device used by Earthlings. Later on, he thought that the books were meant for watching.

THINK ABOUT IT (NCERT PAGE 67)

Q.1 Noodle avoids offending Think-Tank but at the same time he corrects his mistakes. How does he manage to do that?

Ans. Noodle avoids offending Think-Tank while correcting his mistakes by presenting his own thoughts. To do so, he refers to his thoughts as points of no particular importance. Whenever he had to say something contrary to what Think-Tank had said, he would do this. In this way, he would correct Think-Tank's errors without making Think-Tank feel that he was being corrected.

Q.2 If you were in Noodle's place, how would you handle Think-Tank's mistakes?

Ans. If I were in his place, I would have done the same. I would have politely and gently suggested the corrections.

Q.3 Do you think books are being replaced by the electronic media? Can we do away with books altogether?

Ans. Yes, these days, online reading has replaced traditional books to a large extent. Internet, facebook, twitter etc. have decreased interest in reading. However, books cannot be totally replaced. Books can never go out of life although they may exist in a different form.

Q.4 Why are books referred to as a man's best companion? Which is your favourite book and why? Write a paragraph about that book.

Ans. A book is a man's best companion because it is always there and never leaves us alone. It is there with us even when everyone else is gone. Books guide us, instruct us, make us laugh, inform us, inspire us and are always true to us.

My favourite book is Peter Pan, a fairy tale. I love the character of Peter as he lives in fantasies. He is a child who never wants to grow up and so, he never does. He enjoys thrills and adventures, and even takes the kids from Earth on a merry adventure, The book shows that one can remain a child at heart forever. The sense of wonder, innocence, purity and joy, and a capacity to dream can stay in the human heart forever.

TALK ABOUT IT (NCERT PAGE 68)

Q.1 In what ways does Think-Tank misinterpret innocent nursery rhymes as threats to the Martians? Can you think of any incidents where you misinterpreted a word or an action? How did you resolve the misunderstanding?

Or **How did Think — Tank interpret the following nursery rhyme?**

"How does your garden grow with cockle shells and silver bells?" **CBSE 2024**

Ans. Think-Tank wrongly interpreted the nursery rhymes as threats to the Martians. The words like 'shell' and 'silver' makes Think-Tank think that humans grew them in farms. Then, there is a line about 'cow' and 'moon'. This makes him think that the Earthlings are launching an interplanetary attack of millions of cows. Also, the picture of Humpty-Dumpty and the rhyme of 'great fall' make Think-Tank think that humans were about to invade Mars and capture him.

Yes, I had a similar misunderstanding with a friend. However, I was fortunate as I got to know the actual truth just in time. I did not believe what I had heard earlier.

REVIEW EXERCISE

Including Competency Based Questions

Part - I

Multiple Choice Questions

1. 'You haven't heard about the Martian invasion of ....?'

(a) 2010 (b) 2020 (c) 2040 (d) 2050

Ans. (c) 2040

2. Which century is named the Era of the Book, according to the Historian in the story 'The Book that Saved the Earth'? Competency Based

(a) Twentieth century (b) Twenty-first century
(c) Twenty-second century (d) None of these

Ans. (a) Twentieth century

3. How did Think-Tank refer to Earth?

(a) Earth ball (b) Primitive ball of mud
(c) A planet (d) None of these

Ans. (b) Primitive ball of mud

4. When did Think-Tank want to invade the Earth?

(a) Before dinner (b) Before breakfast
(c) In the evening (d) Before lunch

Ans. (d) Before lunch

5. Where on Earth did Think-Tank's team arrive for invasion?

(a) Model Library (b) Centerville Public Library
(c) A Square Place (d) A Clock Tower

Ans. (b) Centerville Public Library

6. Choose the option that explains what Think-Tank meant by saying- Elementary, my dear Omega.

(a) 'It's simple general knowledge, Omega.'
(b) 'It's something that a primary school person won't understand, Omega.'
(c) 'It's quite obviously deducible, Omega'
(d) 'It's a little more than complicated, Omega.'

Ans. (c) 'It's quite obviously deducible, Omega'

7. How did Omega describe the codes appeared in the books?

(a) Little lines
(b) Squiggles and dots
(c) Thousands of them alongside the pictures
(d) All of the above

Ans. (d) All of the above

8. What did Oop and Think-Tank infer from the picture of Humpty Dumpty? Competency Based

(a) Think-Tank's balloon brain
(b) Earthians are after Think-Tank
(c) Earthians have seen Think Tank
(d) All of the above

Ans. (d) All of the above

9. After how many years of Martial invasion, did the Earthlings resume contact with Martians?

(a) 50 centuries (b) 50 years
(c) 500 years (d) 1000 years

Ans. (c) 500 years

10. What is the theme of the story 'The Book that Saved the Earth'? Competency Based

(a) Half-fed knowledge is always dangerous
(b) Arrogance leads to one's downfall
(c) Intelligent people can rule the planet
(d) Earthlings are more developed than Martians

Ans. (a) Half-fed knowledge is always dangerous

Extract Based Questions

1. Read the following extract carefully and answer the questions that follow.

Think-Tank That's better Noodle, I wish to be placed in communication with our manned space probe to that ridiculous little planet we are going to put under our generous rulership. What to they call it, again?

Noodle Earth, your Intelligence.

Think-Tank Earth – of course. You see how insignificant the place is? But first something important My mirror I wish to consult my mirror. CBSE 2023

(i) Think-Tank wants to communicate with the ....

(a) people of Earth
(b) scientists on Earth
(c) environmentalists on Earth
(d) Martians on Earth

Ans. (d) Martians on Earth

(ii) Complete the analogy by selecting the suitable word from the passage.

Read : Learn :: Explore : ....

Ans. Probe

(iii) What does Think-Tank want to do? Is he successful and why/why not?

Ans. Think-Tanks wants to rule over the Earth. No, he is not successful in his project as he misinterprets nursery rhymes and thinks that the Earthlings want to capture him and Mars.

(iv) Fill in the blank with one word only.

Think-Tank is a .... of the Martian team.

Ans. Commander-in-chief

2. Read the following extract carefully and answer the questions that follow.

THINK-TANK Mirror, mirror, in my hand. Who is the most fantastically intellectually gifted being in the land?

OFFSTAGE VOICE (after a pause) You, sir.

THINK -TANK (smacking mirror) Quicker. Answer quicker next time. I hate a slow mirror. (He admires himself in the mirror.) Ah, there I am. Are we Martians not a handsome race? So much more attractive than those ugly Earthlings with their tiny heads. Noodle, you keep on exercising your mind, and someday you'll have a balloon brain just like mine.

NOODLE Oh, I hope so, Mighty Think-Tank. I hope so.

THINK -TANK Now, contact the space probe. I want to invade that primitive ball of mud called Earth before lunch.

NOODLE It shall be done, sir. (He adjusts levers on switchboard. Electronic buzzes and beeps are heard as the curtains open.) **CBSE Additional SQP 2023**

(i) What does Think-Tank's interaction with the mirror reveal about his attitude towards intelligence and appearance? Answer in 30-40 words. **Competency Based**

Ans. Think-Tank's interaction with the mirror reflects his extreme arrogance. He seeks confirmation of his intellectual superiority and places high value on physical appearance. His contempt for Earthlings and admiration for Martian aesthetics show a superiority complex rooted in intelligence and appearance.

(ii) State whether True or False.

Noodle's hopeful response to Think-Tank's comment lends an insight into the rich heritage and culture of the Martian society. **CBSE Additional SQP 2023-24**

Ans. False. Noodle's hopeful response to Think-Tank's comment suggests more about the influence of Think-Tank's mindset on Martian society rather than providing insight into the richness of Martian heritage and culture. It highlights a culture that idealises intellectual arrogance rather than showcasing the depth of Martian cultural values.

(iii) Select the appropriate option to fill the blank.

The desire to conquer a 'primitive ball of mud' reflects a .... mindset.

(a) diplomatic
(b) colonial
(c) conciliatory
(d) democratic

Ans. (b) colonial

(iv) The playwright's decision to put certain content in brackets serves the purpose of ....

Ans. providing stage directions intended for the actors, directors, or production team rather than the audience.

3. Read the following extract carefully and answer the questions that follow.

OOP I haven't a clue. I've been to seven galaxies, but I've never seen anything like this. Maybe they're hats. (He opens a book and puts it on his head.) Say, maybe this is a haberdashery! OMEGA: (bowing low) Perhaps the Great and Mighty Think-Tank will give us the benefit of his thought on the matter. THINK-TANK: Elementary, my dear Omega. Hold one of the items up so that I may view it closely. (Omega holds a book on the palm of her hand.) Yes, yes, I understand now. Since Earth creatures are always eating, the place in which you find yourselves is undoubtedly a crude refre- shment stand.

OMEGA (To Iota and Oop) He says we're in a refreshment stand. OOP: Well, the Earthlings certainly have a strange diet. **CBSE Question Bank 2021 Modified**

(i) Choose the option that associates the person to a haberdashery.

(a) Jagdeep is a primary school teacher who teaches English.
(b) Tanishq is a tailor who makes garments for men only.
(c) Falguni is a chemist who manufactures her own medicine.
(d) Asma is an engineer who works on designing space stations.

Ans. (b) Tanishq is a tailor who makes garments for men only.

(ii) Earth inhabitants are Earthlings and those from Mars are Martians, what are the inhabitants of Venus addressed as in most sci-fi stories?

Ans. The inhabitants of Venus are addressed as Venusians in most sci-fi stories.

(iii) Complete the sentence appropriately.
The quality of being crude has been allotted to the refreshment stand because ....

Ans. it produces food that is unrefined and unprocessed in nature.

(iv) Why did Omega bow low before Think-Tank?

Ans. Omega bowed low before Think-Tank as a mark of respect and recognition of supremacy.

4. Read the following extract carefully and answer the questions that follow.

Omega Well, Oop?

Iota Well, Oop? (Oop coughs. Omega and Iota pound him on the back).

Think-Tank Was it not delicious, sergeant

Oop (saluting) That is correct, sir. It was not delicious. I don't know how the Earthlings can get those sandwiches down without water. They're dry as Martian dust.

Noodle Sir, Great and Mighty Think-Tank. I beg your pardon, but an insignificant bit of data floated into my mind about those sandwiches.

Think-Tank It can't be worth much, but go ahead. Give us your trifling bit of data.

(i) Why did Oop cough?

Ans. Oop coughed because he had difficulty in swallowing the sandwich

(ii) Select the option that correctly captures the usage of the word 'pound' in the above extract.

(a) There are one hundred pence in a pound.
(b) Ann's baby weighed eight and a half pounds at birth.
(c) He got frustrated and started to pound the piano keys.
(d) One pound is approximately equal to 454 grams.

Ans. (c) He got frustrated and started to pound the piano keys.

(iii) Complete the sentence appropriately.

That 'trifling bit of data' that floated into Noodle's mind is that ....

Ans. the sandwiches were communication devices

(iv) How are Oop's and Noodle's attitude towards Think-Tank? **Competency Based**

Ans. Oop is sergeant in rank and thus, salutes Think-Tank. He also speaks with utmost respect when he speaks to Think-Tank.
Noodle is also lower in rank to Think-Tank and always speaks with respect, lowering his opinions as insignificant.

5. Read the following extract carefully and answer the questions that follow.

Omega Listen to them?

Iota and Oop (to each other, puzzle) Listen to them?

Think-Tank Do you have marbles in your ears? I said, listen to them. (Martians bow very low).

Omega It shall be done, sir. (They each take two books from the case, and hold them to their ears, listening intently).

Iota (whispering to Omega) Do you hear anything?

Omega (whispering back) Nothing. Do you hear anything, Oop?

Oop (loudly) Not a thing! (Omega and Iota jump in fright.)

Omega and Iota Sh-h-h! (They listen intently again).

Think-Tank Well? Well? Report to me. What do you hear?

Omega Nothing, sir. Perhaps we are not on the correct frequency.

Iota Nothing, sir. Perhaps the Earthlings have sharper ears than we do.

Oop I don't hear a thing. Maybe these sandwiches don't make sounds.

(i) Who does 'them' in the extract refer to? Where are they?

Ans. 'Them' in the extract refers to books. They are at Centerville Public Library

(ii) Read the given statements and choose the correct answer. **Competency Based**

(A) Martians thought of books as sandwiches.

(B) Think Tank suggested to hear those 'sandwiches'.

(a) (A) is right (B) is wrong
(b) (A) is wrong (B) is right
(c) Both are wrong
(d) Both the statements are right

Ans. (d) Both the statements are right.

(iii) The word 'puzzled' in the extract means ....

Ans. confused

(iv) Who made the next guess about what the sandwiches actually were?

Ans. Noodle made the next guess about what the sandwiches actually were.

6. Read the following extract carefully and answer the questions that follow.

OMEGA It shall be done, Sir. Remove vitamins. (Crew takes vitamins from boxes on their belts.) Present vitamins.

(They hold vitamins out in front of them, stiffly.) Swallow vitamins. (They pop the vitamins into their mouths and gulp simultaneously. They open their eyes wide, their heads shake and they put their hands to their foreheads.)

THINK-TANK Excellent. Now, decipher that code.

ALL It shall be done, Sir. (They frown over the book, turning pages.)

OMEGA (Brightly) Aha!

IOTA (Brightly) Oho!

OOP (Bursting into laughter) Ha, ha, ha.

THINK-TANK What does it say? Tell me this instant. Transcribe, Omega. **CBSE SQP 2023**

(i) According to the extract, what did THINK-TANK most likely want OMEGA to do when he said 'Transcribe...'?

1. Read aloud 2. Translate
3. Make notes 4. Interpret
5. Record reactions

Ans. 2 and 4

(ii) Complete the analogy by selecting the suitable word from the text.

Frown: Smile :: Gloomily : ....

Ans. Brightly

(iii) Select the option that displays the reason why all crew members were asked to have vitamins. In order to

(a) boost their physical energies
(b) adapt to their circumstances.
(c) quickly turn all the pages
(d) accomplish a specific task

Ans. (d) accomplish a specific task

(iv) The playwright places certain words and sentences in brackets in the given extract. List any ways these benefits both the director and actors. **Competency Based**

1. .... 2. ....

Ans. Two ways in which the playwrights bracketed words/phrases benefit both the director and the actors are

1. Helping them in gaining clarity about the emotions and gestures important during the performance
2. Helps in understanding stage setting and movements.

Part - II

Short Answer Type Questions

1. Describe Think-Tank in your own words.

Ans. Think-Tank was the ruler of the planet Mars. His head is huge and egg-shaped. He wears a robe decorated with stars and circles. He considered himself very mighty and was very proud of his intelligence.

2. What is Think-Tank proud of? How do you know?

Ans. Think-Tank was proud of his intelligence and might. He always tried to prove himself as the most intelligent Martian, as seen in his self-praise and boastful habits. One such incidence is how he liked to be addressed by Noodle as 'Great and Mighty'.

3. What difficulty do the crew of the space probe face on Earth?

Ans. The space probe landed in a public library. The crew in the probe was shocked because the place looked very strange to them as they had no idea of what the books were. They thought the library to be some kind of storage area. They were confused as they were not familiar with books.

4. Why do the space probe crew take vitamins?

Ans. Think-Tank wanted the probe crew to find out what was in the books. So, the probe crew took vitamins to increase their intelligence. As a result, they were able to read the books after taking those vitamins.

5. Describe briefly how the Martians reach upon the correct application of the book. **CBSE Question Bank 2021**

Ans. Initially, when Martians found the books in the library, they took them to be sandwiches or a communication device. Later, when they realised the real use of books, they were asked to take certain vitamins. This helped them reach upon the correct application of books.

6. Give any two reasons for Oop's breaking into laughter on reading the first nursery rhyme.

Ans. Oop's breaking into laughter on reading the first nursery rhyme indicates that the vitamins had worked such that Oop was able to understand the meaning behind the nursery rhymes. Further, because Oop could understand the rhymes literally, he found the images depicted to be humorous.

7. What is Think-Tank's interpretation of words like 'shells', 'silver bells' and 'garden' from the nursery rhyme? What is its impact? **Competency Based**

Ans. Think-Tank interprets the given words to mean that the Earthlings grew shells and silver in their gardens. The impact of this was that he cancelled the invasion of Earth as he felt that Earth was more advanced than Mars.

8. Think-Tank thinks that Earthlings are after him. What is the reason?

Or **Think- Tank assumes that the Earthlings are after him. Give any two reasons for the same.**

Ans Think-Tank assumes that the Earthlings are after him after listening to the books of the nursery rhymes wherein he sees himself in Humpty Dumpty. Further, when the poems were read, the incorrect interpretations made by him makes him think that the Earthlings were planning to invade Mars and capture him.

9. How did one old book of nursery rhymes save the Earth from a Martian invasion?

Or **How did a book change Think-Tank's opinion about the Earthlings?**

Ans. The invasion of the Earth was stopped because the Martian Commander-in-Chief misinterpreted the rhyme "Humpty Dumpty had a great fall." Think Tank interpreted the word 'shells', 'silver' and 'garden' to be representative of superior weapons. Further, he saw an image of Humpty, which looked like him, and thought that the Earthling were planning to capture Mars Central Control and him. He ordered the invasion fleet to evacuate the entire planet of Mars.

10. Mention any two points of differences between Earthlings and Martians in the 20th century.

Ans. Earthlings and Martians were different in the 20th century. Earthlings produced books and had a library which the Martians did not have anything as such. Further, their languages were also different. We know this because the Martians had to take a pill to understand the language of the Earthlings.

11. Martians were never able to bring themselves to read the book Mother Goose. Discuss why the Historian said so. **CBSE Question Bank 2021**

Ans. Martians were never able to bring themselves to read the book Mother Goose. Historians said so because it was this nursery rhyme which made the Martian leader Think Tank believe that the Earthlings would attack them and capture Mars.

12. Based on 'The Book that Saved the Earth', state how jumping to conclusions had an unintended consequence for the Martians. **CBSE Additional SQP 2022**

Ans. It is true to say that jumping to conclusion had an unintended consequence for the Martians. Think-Tank had planned a Martian invasion of Earth based on the assumption that the Martians were a more advanced race than the Earthlings. However, due to his incorrect interpretation of some nursery rhymes, the Martians had to hurriedly leave Earth and evacuate Mars.

13. How does 'The Book that Saved the Earth' include elements of satirical science fiction? **CBSE SQP 2024**

Or **The play 'The Book that Saved the Earth' uses humour and misunderstandings between the Martians and Earthlings to explore the thems of perception and cultural differences. Comment.** **CBSE 2025**

Ans. 'The Book that Saved the Earth' protrudes exaggerated portrayal of Martian characters and the interactions with Earth culture. The play gives a humorous critique of human behaviour and social standards by presenting Martians as arrogant and intellectually superior beings who misunderstand basic Earth concepts.

Long Answer Type Questions

1. Noodle hails Think-Tank as the most powerful and intelligent creature in the whole universe. Do you agree? Write your opinion of Think-Tank citing instances from the given text. **Competency Based**

Ans. Noodle is a trainee under Think-Tank. He bows before him and hails his ruler as the most powerful and intelligent creature in the universe. However, Think-Tank is not really intelligent. He misinterprets the nursery rhymes completely. 'Silver', 'shells' and 'garden' for him mean that the Earthlings are growing metals in gardens.

Think-Tank thinks books to be sandwiches and wants the crew to eat them. When the nursery rhyme which says, 'Humpty-Dumpty had a great fall' is read out to him, he is terrified and plans his escape from Mars.

Thus, Think-Tank is nothing more than a show off and a pompous fool.

2. Compare and contrast the characters of Noodle and Think-Tank.

Or **Compare and contrast the characters of Great and Mighty, Think-Tank and Noodles.** **CBSE 2020**

Ans. Noodle and Think-Tank have contrasting characters. Think-Tank is the ruler of the planet Mars, who likes to be called the 'Great and the Mighty'. He is an egotistical and proud person who believes that he is the smartest of all being. However, he is wrong about everything. He likes to pass on other's ideas as his own. He is a coward who simply boasts about his power.

Noodle, his apprentice on the other hand, is very clever and wise. He corrects the mistakes of Think-Tank very gently. He never takes credit for his ideas but offers them to the ruler very gently. Think-Tank makes them his own.

When Noodle succeeds Think-Tank and becomes the head of Mars, he becomes friend with Earthlings. While Think-Tank was afraid of Earthlings, Noodle allows Earthlings to set up a library there. So, both Noodle and Think-Tank are different from each other.

3. The play 'The Book that Saved the Earth' conveys the message that misunderstanding of cultural differences between various races can cause confusion and conflict. Based on your reading of the play, write how such confusion and conflicts can be checked so that peace and harmony is maintained.

Or **How did the people on the Earth help the Martian people? How did this effort help the people on both the planets?** **CBSE 2020**

Or **'The Book that Saved the Earth' communicates the idea that misinterpretation of cultural disparties among different groups can leads to misunderstandings and disputes. From the play, discuss methods to prevent such confusion and conflicts, ensuring the preservation of peace and harmony.** **CBSE 2025**

Ans. Mars and Earth are two different planets in our Solar System. Hence, it is a fact that the people belonging to both the planets will have different lives, lifestyles, cultures, languages, etc. Therefore, any attempt at communication will lead to confusion and conflict between the cultures.

In the chapter 'The Book that Saved the Earth', such a difference creates a lot of animosity (considering someone as enemy) between the two planets. Consequently the leader/ruler of Mars, i.e. Think-Tank decides to attack Earth. Think-Tank's plan, however, fails as he does not understand many things that his team finds on the planet.

To ensure that such conflict and confusion are checked so that peace and harmony are maintained, wise people should be sent out to deal with other cultures. This step was taken by Noodle when he became the ruler. As a result of his action, the people of Earth helped the Martians in understanding their culture.

Martians were taught how to read and a library was set up for them. This effort to understand each other spreads awareness and enables people to others and their cultures.

4. A satire is when a person, idea, or institution is criticised by highlighting their faults and weaknesses using humour. Describe how 'The Book that Saved the Earth' can be considered a satire with supporting examples from the text. **CBSE Additional SQP 2023**

Ans. A satire is when a person, idea, or institution is criticised by highlighting their faults and weaknesses using humour. Considering this definition, 'The Book that Saved the Earth' can be considered as satire because it uses humour and exaggeration to criticise and mock the Martians' intelligence. The Martians misinterpret Earth's books, especially the nursery rhymes. This creates a satirical commentary on cultural misunderstandings and the dangers of jumping to conclusions.

In the end, it was a simple book of nursery rhymes that became the key to saving the Earth from the invasion by an alien military force, creating an ironic and satirical twist to the story. Think-Tank's intelligence is described in exaggerated terms as the 'most powerful and intelligent creature in the whole universe'. He is even described as having a large 'balloon brain'. This is an example of satire and mockery as Think-Tank is shown to be more pompous than intelligent.

ASSESSMENT EXERCISE

Extract Based Questions

Read the following extract carefully and answer the question that follow.

Oop : Ha, ha, ha. Imagine that. Pretty maids growing in a garden.

Think-Tank (alarmed) Stop! This is no time for levity. Don't you realise the seriousness of this discovery? The Earthlings have discovered how to combine agriculture and mining. They can actually grow crops of rare metals such as silver and cockle shells. They can grow high explosives, too. Noodle, contact our invasion fleet.

Noodle They are ready to go down and take over Earth, sir.

Think-Tank Tell them to hold. Tell them new information has come to us about Earth. Iota, transcribe.

Iota Yes, sir. (She reads very gravely.)

(i) Complete the analogy by selecting the suitable word from the text.

Opaque : Transparent :: Seriousness : ....

(ii) How did Oop interpret the meaning of the poem read to him?

(a) Literally (b) Figuratively
(c) Accurately (d) Quickly

(iii) Oop used to consider earthlings as .... before this incident happened.

(iv) What was the title of the book from where the poems were read?

Short Answer (SA) Type Questions

1. What does Oop think about those 'sandwiches'?
2. Think-Tank thinks Earthlings have reached a high level of civilisation. Why does he think so?
3. Why do the Martians decide to evacuate Mars? Where do they go?

Long Answer (LA) Type Questions

1. Half knowledge leads to disaster. Explain this with reference to the play 'The Book that Saved the Earth'.
2. Pride has a fall. Justify this statement with reference to 'The Book that Saved the Earth.'
3. Imagine that Noodle, from 'The Book that Saved the Earth', writers a diary entry, recounting the time he, under the command of Think-Tank sent a team to Earth to invade the Earth. Explain how it all turned out and the inference drawn from the experience. Write this diary entry as Noodle in about 120 words. **Competency Based**

Assessment of Speaking and Listening Skills

CBSE has clearly outlined the significance of Speaking and Listening Skills as a part of co-scholastic areas of achievement by every learner and also stressed the clear integration of Assessment of Speaking and Listening Skills as a part of the curriculum.

As good communication skills raise the self-esteem of a student, CBSE essentially desires that the students acquire proficiency in it by the time they leave school. In the present day global markets, speaking and listening are considered to be the essential skills of real life. So it has been felt for a long time that CBSE must focus on assessing speaking and listening skills for qualification in examination.

Considering this, CBSE has proposed to give 5% weightage to the Assessment of Speaking and Listening Skills from 2017-18 onwards. Therefore, the Assessment of Speaking and Listening Skills will be done formally at the term-end examination. Schools may conduct ASL themselves as per the guidelines provided by the CBSE.

The overall purpose of the test is to help improve and standardise students' communicative skills. Thus, in keeping with the international standards, the CBSE has put this assessment in place.

Listening Skills

The **Listening Comprehension** section tests the student's ability to listen for basic interpersonal, instructional and academic purposes. A number of sub-skills need to be developed in the everyday classroom transaction. Given below are some of the sub-skills of listening which need to be assessed.

(i) Listening for specific information
(ii) Listening for general understanding
(iii) Predictive listening
(iv) Inferential listening
(v) Listening for pleasure
(vi) Intensive listening
(vii) Evaluative listening

Role of Examiner

Here the Examiner is assigned the job of assessing a candidate's performance in any of the skills that is to be assessed.

It is extremely important to keep in mind the factors listed below as they can significantly influence the expected outcome of the Listening Test.

- Size of the room
- Seating arrangement
- Acoustics of the room
- Equipment used
- Quality of the recording of the listening input
- Quality of the oral rendering of the listening input (in case it is to be read aloud by the Examiner), in terms of volume, clarity, enunciation, intonation, pace etc.

Test Administration *For the Examiner (Teacher)*

- Select the time and date of the assessment.
- Plan the seating arrangement in advance.
- Decide exactly as to how much time is to be reserved for instructions or any possible interaction regarding clarifications, etc and for the actual test.
- Make the announcement giving general instructions directed to the candidates before the recording is played or before the reading of the text.
- Adhere strictly to the time specified for each of the three phases of the Test (Pre-listening, While listening and Post-listening)
- The general instructions given below should be followed while conducting the test.

The Listening Assessment

The Listening Assessment comprises of a variety of tasks. These tasks are graded according to the length of the task and the difficulty level. Schools may download the sample tasks and reorganise them into two parts - transcripts and the marking scheme for the examiner and the worksheets for the students on which students will write answers.

General Instructions for Students

You are not allowed to ask questions or interrupt the Examiner at any point.

- You are being tested on your Listening Skills.
- You will hear a set of recordings of the Listening Input or listen to a reading of the Listening Input.
- Each of the recordings will be played twice. In case there is an oral rendering of the Listening Input, it shall take place twice.
- You are required to answer a set of questions based on each of the Listening Inputs.
- The assessment consists of 4 sections.
- You are required to attempt all 4 sections of the assessment.
- Familiarise yourself with the questions on the worksheet. It will help you to answer them later on.
- After you have listened to the input, you will be given specified minutes to answer the questions on your worksheet.
- You may answer the questions on your worksheet while listening.
- Do not interact/comment until you have moved out of the examination room.

PRACTICE ASSIGNMENT

Instructions

1. There are ten questions in this test.
2. Answer the questions as you listen to the transcripts.
3. You will listen to four short extracts. As you listen to each one, answer the questions.

TASK 1

Through the given QR code or link you will hear to the news reports about some incidents happening worldwide. Read the sentences below then listen to the news and write the correct answer for the given questions. You will hear to the recording twice.

TO LISTEN THIS TRANSCRIPT

Link https://goo.gl/fLXnyk OR **Scan the Code**

Transcript

1. **Kathmandu, May 14** Thirteen Indians were among the 15 people killed when their 20-seater aircraft slammed into a cliff in Western Nepal, less than seven months after 10 Indian tourists were killed in an air accident. Six people miraculously survived the crash.
2. E-mailing has enabled us to communicate messages to one another at a very fast pace. However, there are times when we have to post important letters and documents by surface or air mail. The postal department is very slow.
3. City dwellers often depend on cars, buses or metros to travel from one place to another. Bicycles used to be a popular mode of travel once. I think we need to popularise them once again if we need to tackle the pollution problem.
4. 'The Mars Rover, Curiosity, landed on the Martian surface to begin a two-year mission, seeking evidence that the Red Planet once hosted ingredients for life'. NASA said.

   Mission controllers at the Jet Propulsion Laboratory near Los Angeles burst into applause and cheered as they received signals relayed by a Mars orbiter confirming that the Rover had survived a make-or-break descent and touched down within its landing zone.
5. A V-chip has been developed. In addition to spelling out the age-based ratings, letters will be displayed to warn parents if a show contains violence or other objectionable content. A group of major networks and producers have agreed to go along with the system, but NBC will not.

Questions

1. What is the news report about?

(a) There was an explosion before the crash.
(b) The crash was a consequence of collision with a cliff.
(c) There have been several air crashes in the recent past.
(d) Indians always die in the air crashes in and around Nepal.

Answer ______

2. **After listening to the comment by an officer to his colleague, what option do you think the speaker would not opt for?**

(a) E-mail (b) Air mail (c) Postal department (d) Surface mail

Answer [ ]

3. **Now listen to an environment activist who is talking to one of his friends. The speaker advocates the use of ....**

(a) cars (b) buses (c) bicycles (d) metros

Answer [ ]

4. **What is the news report about?**

(a) Invention of Curiosity
(b) Landing of Curiosity
(c) Happiness at the Jet Propulsion Laboratory
(d) Possibility of life on Mars

Answer [ ]

5. **What does the V-chip do?**

(a) It allows the cable company to monitor what TV programmes you watch.
(b) It turns your TV into a "virtual reality" computer.
(c) It allows parents to block out certain programmes, so their children cannot watch them.
(d) It reduces the use of the remote control device.

Answer [ ]

TASK 2

Through the given QR code or link you will hear a talk about the tigers and wildlife tourism. Read the statements below, then listen to the text (talk) and answer the questions given below. You will hear the talk twice.

TO LISTEN THIS TRANSCRIPT

Link https://goo.gl/KAWXWj OR **Scan the Code**

Transcript

Tigers are being loved to death. Tourists desperate for a glimpse of a tiger are damaging the habitat and harassing tigers. This by no means decides that tiger tourism or wildlife tourism is a bad thing. Wildlife tourism has a lot of advantages. Wildlife tourism helps people of the area who get employment in tourism. In this way, wildlife is valued, rather than poached or encroached upon.

Wildlife also inspires the people who see it. For many, a dramatic view of one of the world's great beasts—a tiger, a leopard, a whale—is a life-changing experience. Such a sighting makes people aware of the fragility of the planet and the folly of our short-term thinking. Above all, it prompts people to step back from our traditional chauvinism. Wildlife tourism is similarly equivocal. When carried out with wisdom and responsibility, it is the best possible news for the creatures and the people of the area and for the people doing the touring. Wildlife tourism can sometimes, with the best of intentions, be stupid, greedy and destructive.

An adjustment of practice in India's wildlife tourism is a good thing. It is not tourists that are killing off tigers : it is, above all, the world's ever-increasing human population, and its incontinent need for room to live in.

Questions

1. State whether the following statements are True or False.

(a) People's fascination with the tigers is causing them harm.

(b) Wildlife tourism should be banned.

(c) Tiger tourists are destroying their living places.

2. Fill in the blanks with a word or phrase.

(a) Wildlife tourism helps in ....

(b) .... and .... behaviour is expected from tourists who go for wildlife sightings.

TASK 3

Through the given QR code or link you will hear a lecture about libraries. Read the questions below, then listen to the extracts and choose the correct option from a, b or c to complete the statements in each questions. You will hear the recording twice.

TO LISTEN THIS TRANSCRIPT

Link https://goo.gl/LGrbVH OR **Scan the Code**

Transcript

Libraries It has been a great pleasure to be here this evening and to hear all the things that have been said about libraries in general, and the librarians, without whom the libraries would be of little use. What libraries mean is fairly obvious to all of us, especially to those who are here this evening. We know that without libraries, we cannot have educated people who will carry out their jobs successfully. But as I sat here I was worried about the fact that there are so many places in the world that have no libraries and that have no way of getting books. A lack of money for the books and the librarians is a problem in some places, but I wonder if the biggest problem is really that no one is interested in reading anymore?

Young students often go straight to the internet for readymade notes on a subject. They no longer want to go to libraries to do their own research. Although many students will use the library when they have an examination to study for; once the exams are over, they never return. Even reading books for fun and relaxation is no longer popular amongst the young. A young man, I interviewed recently admitted that he could not name a single book by an Indian author that he had read recently. Demand for non-fiction increases every year, particularly career-oriented books. Students want just to pass an examination and get a job; they no longer have time to read stories.

The more I have thought about the problem, the more I have felt that we do not use all our opportunities to develop an interest in books. Today everything in which people are interested, the radio, the movies - all of these - should, if properly used, stimulate reading. For instance, if there is a remarkably good film 'The Life of Pasteur', I think it should be used by teachers to create an interest in the life of that person. So, in studying Pasteur's achievements and the people around him, students can then use their libraries to read more about the lives of great and famous people. I am sure that if we put our minds to it, there are a great many ways in which we can use the electronic media, films and the internet to stimulate an interest in books and reading. Maybe then our young people will visit libraries more often.

Questions

1. The speaker thinks that librarians ....

(a) are very important for libraries

(b) fulfil many functions in a library

(c) are more useful today than previously

2. The speaker says that libraries have an obvious effect on ....

(a) schools (b) cities (c) business

3. According to the speaker, there are not enough libraries in the world because ....

(a) it is hard to build libraries in some areas
(b) libraries are very expensive
(c) there is a lack of interest in books

4. According to the speaker, students are using libraries less because the internet ....

(a) makes research easier for them
(b) has more up-to-date information
(c) give them answers to exam questions

5. Today, students do not read books because they have no ....

(a) interest (b) money to buy books (c) motivation

6. The speaker says that the demand for fiction books is ....

(a) decreasing with young audiences
(b) being replaced by exam books
(c) focused on non-Indian authors

7. The speaker believes that film and radio can ....

(a) be a good alternative to reading
(b) encourage people to read more
(c) teach us about famous people

8. What example does the speaker give of a way to increase interest in reading?

(a) Good books (b) Famous people (c) Historical films

9. The speaker feels that it is possible to encourage interest in reading if ....

(a) we spend more time on the internet
(b) we think about how to use electronic media
(c) we visit the library more often

10. Young people can use the library more if they ....

(a) stop buying books
(b) take interest in electronic media, films and internet
(c) have an access to it

TASK 4

Through the given QR code or link you will hear 5 short extracts of friends talking about the significance of sports and games in their life. Read the statements below, then listen to the extracts and match each statement A–G to each Friend 1–5. There are two statements you do not need. You will hear the recording twice.

TO LISTEN THIS TRANSCRIPT

Link https://goo.gl/1LJw1E OR **Scan the Code**

Transcript

Friend 1 Friends, we should play sports and games regularly, because I believe that they are the most important source of entertainment. We enjoy and please ourselves when we play sports and games.

Friend 2 For me the best use of sports is earning a livelihood. These days the people who play games and sports not only earn a lot of money but also are given a great deal of money as prizes. Therefore, I strongly believe that playing games and sports is a very good way of earning a comfortable income.

Friend 3 Sports and games are very good way of keeping good health. All those who play games regularly remain healthy for a longer time. So, if we really wanted to be healthy, we must regularly play outdoor games of our choice.

Friend 4 Dear friends, I believe that we should play games to keep ourselves occupied. If we regularly play sports and games we keep ourselves busy in constructive work.

Friend 5 Sports and games make us both mentally and physically strong to face the challenges of life. The discipline and practice of games and sports give us enough strength to bear the harsh realities of life.

Questions

Which of the following statements are true?

A. Sports and games keep you in good health.
B. Playing sports gives you a feeling of entertainment.
C. Sports and games make you intelligent.
D. Sports are a good source of earning money.
E. Sports make you strong to face challenges.
F. Sports make you grow tall and attractive.
G. Playing sports is a good way to avoid bad company.

TASK 5

Through the given QR code or link you will hear an interview with veterinarian Dr Mohit Sharma on the importance of keeping pets. Read the sentences below, then listen to the conversation and choose A, B or C for each sentence. You will hear the recording twice.

TO LISTEN THIS TRANSCRIPT

Link https://goo.gl/97WvUC OR **Scan the Code**

Transcript

Interviewer You are a great advocate of keeping pets. Would you like to tell our listeners something about them?

Dr Sharma Pets make great friends for everyone in the family because they are a great source of love and friendship. Pets are playful beings in the house as they keep everyone, young and old, happy.

Interviewer That's really true, but do you think that pets also help people make friends.

Dr Sharma Having a pet at home, you often need to go out for walks every day. Initially you may not like it, but over a few days you'll begin to love the routine.

Interviewer What is the impact of the pets on people's moods?

Dr Sharma Oh yes! Pets really boost your mood. Playing with the pet, can increase the brain activity and enhance pleasure and tranquility.

Interviewer Do pets help in inculcating educational values?

Dr Sharma Yes, they do and that's true! With pets, children also learn basic lessons on building a strong character like loyalty and trust.

Interviewer What is the impact of pets on their owner's fitness levels?

Dr Sharma Having a pet at home you are on your toes at all times. Pets make you more agile in the house, they expect you to play with them, be concerned for them.

Interviewer Don't you think that it is very stressful having to care for a pet?

Dr Sharma No. not at all. In fact people with pets have lower blood pressure and stress levels as compared to the people without pets.

Questions

1. Pets make great friends because they are

A. very attractive B. great achievers C. good companions

2. Pets help you make new friends as they make you

A. appear more beautiful B. go out for a walk C. change your attitude

3. Pets boost your mood because

A. playing with pets makes you feel fresh. B. they help you pass time

C. they love you so much

4. Pets inculcate educational values because

A. they are very valuable and precious B. they make you study more and more

C. they enable you develop habits of daily care

5. Pets help you remain fit because

A. they make you to eat less food B. they make you go to the gym

C. they make you more active

6. Pets help you in being in good health because

A. your blood pressure is maintained B. you don't have to visit your doctor

C. you care about your pet a lot

Answers

Task 1

1. (b) The crash was a consequence of collision with a cliff **2.** (c) Postal department

3. (c) bicycles **4.** (b) Landing of Curiosity

5. (c) It allows parents to block out certain programmes, so their children cannot watch them.

Task 2

1. (a) True (b) False (c) True

2. (a) employing people/generating employment (b) Wise; responsible

Task 3

1. (a) are very important for libraries **2.** (c) business

3. (c) there is a lack of interest in books **4.** (a) makes research easier for them

5. (a) interest **6.** (a) decreasing with young audiences

7. (b) encourage people to read more **8.** (c) Historical films

9. (b) we think about how to use electronic media

10. (b) take interest in electronic media, films and internet

Task 4

Friend	Statement
1	B
2	D
3	A
4	G
5	E

Task 5

1. C **2.** B **3.** A **4.** C **5.** C **6.** A

Speaking Skills

Speaking skill has acquired a very important place as a communication skill. Like listening skill, a number of sub-skills of speaking need to be consciously developed among students. Some of the sub-skills which can be assessed are as follow

- Speaking intelligibly using appropriate word stress, sentence stress and intonation patterns.
- Narrating incidents and events, real or imaginary in a logical sequence.
- Presenting oral reports or summaries; making announcements clearly and confidently.
- Expressing and arguing a point of view clearly and effectively.
- Taking active part in group discussions, showing ability to express agreement or disagreement, summarising ideas, eliciting the views of others and presenting own ideas.
- Expressing and responding to personal feelings, opinions and attitudes.
- Participating in spontaneous spoken discourse in familiar social situations.

General Instructions

1. The total administration time for the speaking assessment is approximately 10-12 min.
2. The speaking assessment will be conducted for two students at a time.
3. There will be a single teacher to function as the examiner.
4. The examiner should be a qualified English teacher.

Role of Examiner

- The examiner should ensure that the room is quiet and has good acoustics.
- The tone, manner and body language of the examiner should be relaxed, encouraging and pleasant. Care should be taken to make the candidates feel at ease.
- Students must not be discouraged from making a fresh start in case they are unable to do so at the first attempt.
- The examiner needs to be flexible, sympathetic and reassuring in her/his demeanour.
- The examiner should also be a proficient user of the language in order to conduct the speaking assessment successfully. For example, the examiner should be skilled in elicitation techniques, so that questions such as... "Explain how"/"Why"..."Tell me what you think of" .... may be asked. Yes/ No questions should generally be avoided.
- Ideally, the examiner should award marks after the candidates have left the examination room. If necessary, notes can be made discreetly to be used later in the scoring, so that it does not make the candidates unduly tense and self-conscious.

The Speaking Assessment is divided into three stages

Stage 1 General Introduction

The aim of this introductory task is to put the candidate at ease through some general, open-ended questions, thereby creating a space for the candidate to respond with personal feelings and opinions. Simple warm up questions based on the candidate's name, place of residence, leisure preferences etc are asked.

Stage 2 Topic Presentation

This can take the form of PowerPoint/ OHP presentations, book reviews, debates, speech etc. The focus of this task is to assess a candidate's ability to sustain a straightforward, subjectwise description, mapped out in a fluent and cohesive style.

In this section, the examiner gives each candidate the choice to pick up a Role Card or a Cue Card with a topic written on it. The candidates are given 1 minute to prepare. The examiner should be ready with sheets of paper and a pencil. Candidates may organise their thoughts and ideas. Prior to the day of the speaking assessment, as an assistance to students to prepare for the presentations, the teacher can give a choice of 20 to 30 topics in class to students so that they can prepare presentations based on the topics and organise their ideas. Similar topics can be given in the actual; assessment.

Students are not allowed to write full length answers. They may jot down points only in the sheets given by the examiner. Therefore, a pencil and sheet of paper should be provided on the table. Students are not allowed to carry pen, paper or mobile phone to the examination room. After a minute for making notes, each student will be given 2 minutes each to present his/ her ideas. In case a student is unable to speak during/ for the allotted time, the Examiner may ask some rounding off questions.

Stage 3 Problem Solving (Pair Interaction)

The third section of the test is for 3 minutes. Both students are given a verbal or visual stimulus and asked to respond to it. Both the students are given a total of 3 minutes to interact. Both of them will talk together. After 2 minutes the examiner can ask questions based on their discussion.

Closing

The closing is for 1 minute duration only. In case a student has not been able to speak or has been unable to speak owing to nervousness, the dominance of the second candidate or any other factor, then the examiner may use the 1 minute to give a fresh opportunity to that student.

CBSE Assessment of Speaking and Listening (ASL) **Descriptors for Assessment of Speaking**

Interactive Competence	5	4	3	2	1
Task Management	Contributions are highly effective and fulfil the task. Can fulfil the communicative functions of the level with spontaneity.	Contributions are effective and fulfil the task. Can fulfil the communicative functions of the level.	Contributions are adequate and fulfil the task. Can fulfil functions of the level but may not do so consistently.	Contributions are limited and there is some attempt at the task which is not fulfilled and/or may be repetitive.	There is almost no contribution and/or contributions may not be related to the task.
Initiation and Turn-taking	Is prompt to initiate discussions on the themes/ functions at the given level appropriately. Contributes spontaneously to keep the interaction going; takes turns appropriately.	Is easily able to initiate discussions on the themes/ functions at the given level appropriately. Contributes effectively to keep the interaction going and takes turns appropriately.	Is able to initiate discussions on the themes/ functions at the given level. Makes an effort to keep the interaction going; takes turns.	Struggles to initiate discussions on the themes/functions at the given level. Makes little effort to keep the interaction going;	Does not initiate discussions. Makes no effort to keep the interaction going.
Appropriacy and Relevance	Speaks with a clear sense of purpose and audience in both formal and informal situations. Contributions are always appropriate to the context/ situation.	Speaks with a fair sense of purpose and audience in both formal and informal situations. May be less confident in normal situations.	Speaks with an awareness of purpose and audience may not adapt register effectively. Contributions are appropriate to the context/ situation.	Has unclear sense of purpose and may be unable to adapt register. Contributions may be unconnected to the context/ situation.	Has hardly any sense of purpose and cannot adapt to register.

Fluency	5	4	3	2	1
Cohesion and Coherence Speed of Delivery	Presents information in a logical sequence of linked utterances with a clear connection between ideas, arguments and statements. Uses a range of cohesive devices. Speak fluently with minimal hesitation. Intelligible speed of delivery.	Presents information in a logical sequence of linked utterances with a connection between ideas, arguments and statements. Uses with ease some cohesive devices. Speaks fluently with some hesitation. Intelligible speed of delivery.	Presents information generally in a logical order but overall progression may not always be clear. Uses a range of cohesive devices but some over/under use. Coherence may be affected by hesitancy or rephrasing. Intelligible speed of delivery.	Presents information but without clear progression. Uses limited cohesive devices repetitively. Severe hesitation may impede communication. Speed of delivery impedes understanding.	Presents information with no progression and/or little control of organisational features. May use only isolated words and phrases.
Pronunciation	**5**	**4**	**3**	**2**	**1**
Pronunciation, Stress and Intonation	Has clear, natural pronunciation that can be easily understood by the listener. Varies stress and intonation in keeping with the task, content and meaning.	Has pronunciation that can be easily understood by the listener. Varies stress and intonation in keeping with the task, content and meaning.	Is intelligible though there are examples of some mispronunciation. Tries to speak, varying stress and intonation according to task, content and meaning.	Is not always intelligible and the listener may have to ask for repetition from time to time. Flat intonation and/or inappropriate stress for the task, content or meaning	Is not intelligible.
Language	**5**	**4**	**3**	**2**	**1**
Accuracy	Uses a range of grammatical patterns with accuracy, including some complex forms. Makes only negligible errors.	Uses a range of grammatical patterns with accuracy, including few complex forms and makes only noticeable errors.	There may be some mistakes which affect meaning but there is an attempt to correct most of these mistakes.	There are mistakes which affect meaning but there is hardly an attempt to correct these mistakes.	Communicates with fragments of words and structures but does not manage to bridge the gaps or correct his/her mistakes.
Range	Uses an expressive and appropriate range of structures, words and phrases on topics appropriate to the level and to deliver an effective message.	Uses an expressive and appropriate range of words and phrases on topics appropriate to the level. These may be repetitive.	Can use the language of the level but is repetitive. May search for words with the risk of the message becoming weaker.	Uses basic, simple words and phrases for the level. There may be an effort to find suitable words, which may hamper the message.	Uses simple, isolated words for the level. There is little effort to find words.

AN OVERVIEW OF SPEAKING TEST

STAGE 1

1. Introduction (1 min)

Section Time	Procedure
10 secs	Examiner Hello, please sit down. My name is X. What's your name? *(to Candidate A)* And what's your name? *(to Candidate B)* So your names are *(name and serial number A)* and *(name and serial number B)*.
25 secs	*(Candidate A)*, tell me something about *(e.g. where you live)*. Candidate A responds.
25 secs	*(Candidate B)*, tell me something about *(e.g. your school)*. Candidate B responds.

STAGE 2

2. Topic Presentation (4 min)

Section Time	Procedure
5 secs	Examiner Now *(Candidate A)*, you are going to tell us about your topic. When you have finished, *(Candidate B)* will ask you a question and then I will ask you some more questions. Would you like to begin please?
1 minute	Candidate A speaks.
15 secs	Examiner Thank you. *(Candidate B)* can you ask *(Candidate A)* a question please? Candidate B asks question; Candidate A responds.
40 secs	Examiner asks 2 or 3 follow-up questions as appropriate from the topic prompt list Stage 2 example follow-up questions How often do you .... ? Why? When you .... do you .... ? Why do think .... is important?
5 secs	Examiner Thank you. Now *(Candidate B)*, you are going to tell us about your topic. When you have finished, *(Candidate A)* will ask you a question and then I will ask you some more questions. Would you like to begin please?
1 minute	Candidate B speaks.
15 secs	Examiner Thank you. *(Candidate B)* can you ask (Candidate A) a question please? Candidate A asks question; Candidate B responds.
40 secs	Examiner asks 2 or 3 follow-up questions as appropriate from the topic prompt list.

3. Problem Solving (3 min)

Section time	Procedure
25 secs	Examiner Thank you. Now let's go to the next task. I'm going to give you a card which has information about a problem. I'd like you to read the information and then discuss together how you are going to solve the problem. You have 2 minutes to do this. Here is your problem. Stage 3 sample problem solving card *Your classmates have not been keeping the school tidy. After lessons there is litter in the classrooms and in the halls.* *With your partner, discuss this problem and decide what you can do to make the school a nicer, cleaner place for everyone.* Candidates read card (20 secs) then asked to start speaking.
2 mins	Candidates discuss the problem and a solution.
35 secs	Examiner OK, can you stop now please. Option A (for candidates who have reached a solution). Thank you. (Move straight on to a question) Option B (for candidates who have not reached a solution). Can you agree on a solution ? What is it? Candidates explain. Then examiner asks 1 or 2 follow up questions as appropriate from the list of problem solving prompts. Stage 3 example follow-up questions • Do you think your (solution) will be effective enough? Why?/Why not? • What role do you think .... plays in this problem? Why? • .... sounds interesting. Could you tell me more about that/this? Please stop here. That's the end of the test. Thank you and goodbye.

PRACTICE ASSIGNMENT

Instructions

1. The speaking test will be conducted for two students at a time.
2. Students should not have pen, paper, mobile, etc.
3. The teacher will act as the Examiner (who is involved in a conversation) as well as an assessor who will also give marks to the candidates.

STAGE 1

1. General Introduction (1 min)

The Examiner makes the students feel comfortable.

Examiner	Hello! Good morning, I am .... May I know your name please?
Student A	My name is ..../ I am ....
Examiner	And yours? *(Looking at student B)*
Student B	....
Examiner	Where do you live? *(To student B)*
Student B	....
Examiner	How about you? *(To student A)*
Student A	....
Examiner	What do you do in your leisure? *(To student A)*
Student A	....
Examiner	And what do you do in your free time? *(To student B)*
Student B	....
Examiner	What hobby would you like to cultivate? *(To student A)*
Student A	....
Examiner	How about you? *(To student B)*
Student B	....

STAGE 2

2. Presentation (5 min) In this part of the test, teacher will give 1 min to prepare and 2 min each to both students to present

The oral examiner can frame any input; the following two frames are suggested

1. **To student B** Describe something that you own and you value tremendously. You have 1 min to prepare and 2 min to present.
   - Where did you get it from?
   - How long have you had it?
   - What do you use it for?
   - Why is it so important for you?

   If the student is not able to speak at length, the teacher could ask rounding off questions.
   - Did you buy it/ was it a gift?
   - Would it be easy to replace it?
   - Is it valuable in term of money?

2. **To student A** You will be given 1 minute to prepare based on your most memorable journey and you will have 2 minutes to describe your journey. (Each student is given 2 minutes to present.)

For Student A

- Where did you travel to?
- What was the highlight of your visit? (monument/ temple/park/relatives)
- Which place would you like to visit next?
- Why are such journeys relaxing?

If the student is not able to speak at length the teacher could ask rounding off questions

- Was it a trip organised by the school?
- Did you go with the family?
- Was it a place you had never seen before?
- What fascinated you?

Ask student B to ask a question.

To student A (Repeat)

Qualities that I Value in a Friend

For Student B

- Qualities I like in a friend?
- How many of these qualities do I have?
- Why do I consider these qualities important?
- What is that one quality that I would like to inculcate?

If the student is not able to speak at length, the teacher could ask rounding off questions

- Do you have a lot of friends?
- Why do your friends care for you?
- Why did you pick on them?

Ask student A to ask a question.

Changing Role of Women

- Varied jobs
- Financial security
- Working mothers
- Economic/social independence

If the student is not able to speak at length, the teacher could ask rounding off questions.

- Do women in your family work outside the house?
- Do you appreciate women working? Why?
- Do you think the advantages outweigh the disadvantages?

STAGE 3

3 Problem Solving (3 min)

(a) **Teacher to both students A and B**

Look at the visual carefully. Talk together for 2 mins.

Students are given 1 min to think and prepare. And then they respond to the visual/ verbal stimulus.

1. Child Marriage

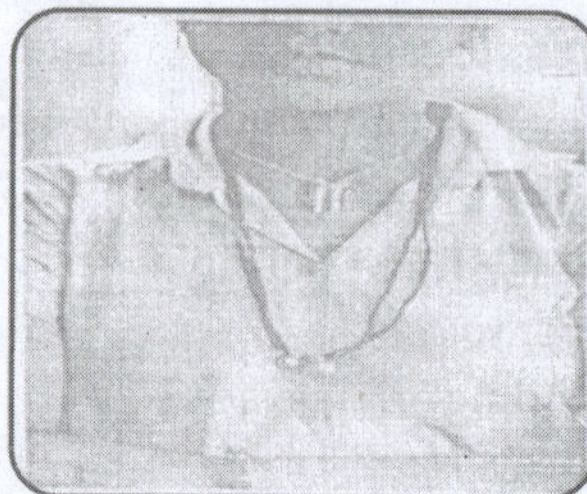

2. Growing Obesity

Verbal Stimulus

3. **How do you imagine life in cities in the future?**

The examiner can give the following hints

- Work
- Leisure/Entertainment
- Travel

4. **What responsibilities do you think individuals have towards the environment?**

The examiner can give the following hints

- Lifestyle
- Shopping
- Finance

CLOSING (1 min)

Thank you very much. That was the end of your test. The examiner retrieves the pencil and paper.

Suggested Topics for Presentation

1. Violent Computer Games Should be Banned
2. My Choice of a Career
3. E-learning
4. Demonetisation
5. Gender Discrimination
6. Peer Pressure—Harmful or Beneficial
7. Beauty Pageants Just a Way of Objectifying Women
8. Bullying
9. Problem of Child Abuse
10. Honour Killings in India
11. Beggary Business
12. Drug Abuse
13. Extreme Sports—The Risks and the Thrill
14. Uniforms are Better
15. Animal Dissection Should be Banned
16. Should Juveniles be Tried as Adults?
17. Are Social Networking Sites doing us Any Good? or Are They Just a Sophisticated Way of Stalking People?
18. Are Security Cameras an Invasion of Privacy?
19. News Channels have Turned into Entertainment Channels
20. Caste System has Completely Ruined Us

Suggested Questions for Problem Solving Task

1. Some of your classmates persuade you to watch a movie after school hours. However, your parents have instructed you to come straight home after school hours. Now you are worried that the other students will laugh at you if you tell them the truth. With your partner, discuss what you should do in the situation.
2. The drinking water taps on the ground floor of your school building are not working properly. Water is always found to be leaking from one tap or the other. With your partner, discuss this problem and decide what you can do to reduce the wastage of water.
3. Some of the senior boys are often seen bullying their juniors. It has caused fear among the students and they perform the tasks given to them out of terror. With your partner, discuss what could be done to help them.

CBSE Examination Paper 2025

English Language and Literature

Time : 3 hrs	M.M. : 80

General Instructions

Read the instructions very carefully and strictly follow them.

1 This question paper comprises 11 questions. All questions are compulsory.

2 This question paper contains THREE sections.

- Section A : Reading Skills
- Section B : Grammar and Creative Writing Skills
- Section C : Literature

3 Attempt questions based on specific instructions for each part.

Set - I

Section – A (Reading Skills) **(20 Marks)**

1. Read the following text. **(10)**

1. Education for Sustainable Development (ESD) is now high on the international agenda and ESD is seen as a way to encourage greater sustainable consumption and production, (to counter the effects of climate change, address threats to biodiversity and provide more effective disaster risk reduction. Education for Sustainable Development is seen by UN as a lifelong process from early childhood to higher and adult education and goes beyond formal education. As values, lifestyles and attitudes are established from an early age, the role of education is of particular importance for children! (ESD has often been associated with curriculum projects linked with recycling, energy and water conservation; pollution reduction and sustainable consumption all developed to contribute towards achieving a more sustainable future.

2. Research from developmental psychology, longitudinal studies, social-cultural analysis, and neuroscience have all shown that it is in the early years that children have the greatest capacity to learn, and it is in these years that many of our fundamental attitudes and values are first put into place. Children are already investigating issues related to recycling, energy conservation, waste disposal and changes in their local environment. ESD in Early Childhood Care and Education (ECCE) is of great significance. The development of ESD and ECCE requires more than just curriculum development. It provides the possibility of a transformational reconstruction.

3. UNICEF reports show that children under the age of eight represent the highest percentage of affected population in today's global emergencies. A UNESCO survey has shown that the ministries of education, environment and sustainable development in 97 UN member states identify poverty as the highest priority area to be addressed in achieving sustainable development. In fact, reductions in poverty and inequality are widely recognised as the priority in efforts to create a more sustainable world. At a global level, millions of children start school carrying the handicap that comes with the experience of malnutrition, ill-health and poverty. Yet, equitable access to high-quality pre-school programmes remain a problem in both rich and poor countries. Sustainable development projects that enable rapid progress in maternal health, child nutrition and survival already exist, even in some of the world's poorest countries. Linking health and education agenda has been recognised as extremely important.

Answer the following questions, based on the passage above.

(i) **Complete the following with a suitable explanation with reference to Paragraph 1.** **(2)**

ESD is now high on the international agenda because ....

(ii) **Based on the given passage, how does UN view ESD as a lifelong process? What are the critical areas of emphasis? (Paragraph 1)** **(2)**

(iii) **List two curriculum projects that ESD (Education for Sustainable Development) has been linked with. (Paragraph 1)** **(1)**

(iv) **Complete the following suitably.** **(1)**

Many of our fundamental attitudes and values are put into plan in the early years as .... (Paragraph 2)

(v) **Substitute the underlined word with the correct word from Paragraph 2.** **(1)**

ESD in Early Childhood Care and Education provides the possibility of <u>transformational</u> reconstruction.

(a) positive change (b) power to reform (c) negative impact (d) creative

(vi) **What do UNICEF reports reveal about the vulnerability of children under the age of eight during global emergencies? (Paragraph 3)** **(1)**

(a) UNICEF reports highlight the resilience of children under the age of eight during global emergencies.
(b) UNICEF reports indicate that children under the age of eight are rarely affected by global emergencies.
(c) UNICEF reports show that children under the age of eight represent the highest percentage of affected population in global emergencies.
(d) UNICEF reports suggest that children under the age of eight are primarily responsible for responding to global emergencies.

(vii) **What remains a problem in both rich and poor countries? What has been recognised as crucial? (Paragraph 3)** **(1)**

(viii) **Complete the sentence with the correct response.** **(1)**

The writer's tone in the passage is ....

2. Read the following text. **(10)**

1. Electric Vehicles (EV) market is growing rapidly all over the world. In India also the EV market has gained significant momentum. It has grown more after the implementation of FAME (Faster Adoption and Manufacture of Hybrid and Electric Vehicles) scheme in 2015 by Ministry of Heavy Industry and Public Enterprises.
2. Electric vehicles are solutions to be independent and free from imported energy resources. Electric cars can bring a major change to India in becoming self-sustainable. EV could also be the alternative to decrease carbon dioxide gas. Carbon dioxide from automobiles is one of the causes of air pollution.
3. An EV can be used for flexible load, for standardising the grid with substantial share of fluctuating renewable energy generation. EV emits 30-80% less greenhouse gas when compared with Internal Combustion Engine (ICE) vehicle. EVs do not consume any energy when it is stationary as compared to ICE vehicles where fuel in consumed when it is idle. EV is recognised as promising alternatives to vehicles and will potentially replace ICE vehicles in the near future.
4. The electric vehicles have low emissions, high efficiency and smooth operation. The energy consumption and emissions for plug in hybrid electric vehicles found that compared to gasoline vehicles there is 37.5% less energy consumption and 35% less greenhouse gas emissions.

The government have started financial policies to encourage EV adoption; however, decision-makers have to plan a long-term perspective to get them implemented efficiently.

Answer the following questions, based on the passage above.

(i) **What does the phrase 'gained significant momentum' in Paragraph 1 tell us about the impact of EV market?** **(1)**

(a) It is momentarily important (b) It has developed very quickly
(c) It has gained profit (d) It has to develop a significant market

(ii) **Select the option that is true for the Assertion and Reason given below.** **(1)**

Assertion (A) Electric vehicles can bring a major change to India.

Reason (R) It can bring India to becoming self-sustainable.

(a) Both (A) and (R) are true, and (R) is the correct explanation of (A).
(b) Both (A) and (R) are true, but (R) is not the correct explanation of (A).

(c) (A) is true, but (R) is false.

(d) (A) is false, but (R) is true.

(iii) Give two benefits of using electric vehicles over internal combustion engine vehicles. **(2)**

(iv) With reference to the passage, the word 'idle' in Paragraph 3 most nearly means .... **(1)**

(v) How do electric vehicles contribute to diminishing a country's reliance on imported energy? **(1)**

(vi) Read the given prompt and select the correct option in the brackets to fill in the blank. **(1)**

EV could be the alternative to .... (enhance/reduce) the carbon dioxide gas emission.

(vii) Give evidence from the passage to show that government is encouraging the use of Electric Vehicles. **(1)**

(viii) Complete the sentence suitably. **(1)**

The result of the implementation of FAME (Faster Adoption and Manufacture of Electric vehicles) is ....

(ix) Complete the following with a suitable reason. **(1)**

The long-term perspective by decision-makers is to ensure ....

Section – B (Grammar) **(20 Marks)**

3. Complete ANY TEN of twelve of the following tasks, as directed. **(10)**

(i) Complete the newspaper report by using the correct form of the verb given in the bracket. **(1)**

He was a renowned business person. He .... (purchase) a house in the city last year.

(ii) Fill in the blank by choosing the correct option to complete the concluding part of an article on 'Exploitation of Children'. **(1)**

It ...... (may/should/could) be our concerted effort not to employ children in industries and to save them from any kind of exploitation.

(iii) Read the given line and identify the error. Also provide with the correct word. **(1)**

Mobile phones has become an integral part of life.

Error	Correction

(iv) Take a look at the conversation between two friends Riya and Simran discussing a book that one of them has recently read. **(1)**

Riya The book really caught my attention. It's called 'Eternal Echoes'.

Simran Sounds interesting! I'll definitely add it to my reading list. Thanks for the recommendation!

Select the correct option to complete the reporting of the above dialogue.

Riya told Simran about the book called Eternal Echoes that had captured her interest. Simran, in response, expressed that it .... and mentioned that she would consider reading it.

(a) sound interesting
(b) sounded interesting
(c) will be interesting
(d) was found to be interesting

(v) Select the option that identifies the error and supplies the correction for the line given below. **(1)**

He usually ate breakfast before he goes to school.

Options	Error	Correction
(a)	Usually	always
(b)	ate	eats
(c)	before	after
(d)	goes	went

(vi) Report the dialogue between a teacher and a student by completing the sentence. **(1)**

Teacher Good morning! Today, we're going to learn about the importance of trees. They play a vital role in our ecosystem. Can you think of any other reasons?

Student I pledge to plant some trees this weekend.

The student understood the importance of trees and added that be ....

(vii) Identify the error and supply correction for the given sentence talking about importance of a 'Sound Sleep'. **(1)**

Sleep is important in maintain one's health and well being.

Use the given format for your response

Error	Correction

(viii) Complete the given narrative, by filling the blank with the correct option. **(1)**

When they began to play it .... to rain.

(a) start (b) started (c) starts (d) having started

(ix) Fill in the blank choosing the most appropriate option. **(1)**

The teacher distributed a piece of paper to .... student.

(a) few (b) all (c) many (d) each

(x) Fill in the blank by choosing the correct option, to complete the line given below. **(1)**

Oral hygiene .... be inculcated in children early in life. (should, would).

(xi) Complete the given sentence by selecting the correct option. **(1)**

The information given here........... to all the produces in this section.

(a) apply (b) applied (c) is applied (d) applies

(xii) Identify the error and supply correction for the following sentence. **(1)**

Be the changes you want to see in the world.

Use the given format for your response.

Error	Correction

Creative Writing Skills **(10 Marks)**

Note: All details presented in the questions are imaginary and created for assessment purpose.

4. Attempt ANY ONE from (A) and (B) given below. **(5)**

(A) You are Sonia Sonu, residing at 67/98 Malkaganj, Sonepat. Compose a letter in about 120 words to the Head Librarian of your child's school drawing attention to the poor library facilities. Give suggestions on how things can be improved to inculcate reading habits among children.

Or

(B) As Sharmila Sahani, a conscientious resident of 25/22, Rajpur. Fatehabad, you have recently come across numerous newspaper articles featuring tragic incidents where lives have been lost due to reckless driving and not following the traffic rules. Write a letter to the editor of a national daily, shedding light on this issue and give suggestions on what can be done.

5. Attempt ANY ONE from (A) and (B) given below. **(5)**

(A) Today, many projects in India are being initiated and implemented with the aim of transforming India into a digitally empowered society and economy.

Digital India Programme

IT-Jobs

E-governance

E-Kranti Electronic Delivery of Services

Broadband for all - Urban and Rural

Information for all

Write an analytical paragraph of 100-120 words based on the given information.

Or

(B) Read the given details of the different activities that interest children in the age group of 14-17 years.

- Dance, music, art
- Outdoor sports like cricket, hockey, basketball, soccer, tennis
- Computer games
- Net surfing
- Social media

Analyse the details and write an analytical paragraph in about 120 words about the suitability of the given activities. Focus on factors like interest, physical, mental and emotional development, personality development and suitability.

Section – C (Literature Textbook) (40 Marks)

6. Read the given extracts and answer the questions for ANY ONE of the two given. **(5)**

(A) "Paper has more patience than people. I thought of this saying on one of those days when I was feeling a little depressed and was sitting at home with my chin in my hands, bored and listless, wondering whether to stay in or go out. I finally stayed where I was, brooding: Yes, paper does have more patience, and since I'm not planning to let anyone else read this stiff backed notebook grandly referred to as a 'diary', unless I should ever find a real friend, it probably won't make a bit of difference." *(From the Diary of Anne Frank)*

(i) In light of the excerpt, what can we infer about the speaker's emotional state? **(1)**

(ii) The narrator enhances the narrative technique of the extract by using **(2)**

(a) descriptive language (b) literary allusions (c) humour (d) reflective

(iii) Fill in the blank with the correct word from the bracket. **(1)**

The narrator doesn't plan to let anyone read her diary as she doesn't have any real .... *(friend/incidents)*

(iv) Why does the narrator say that 'paper has more patience than people'? **(1)**

Or

(B) "He was silent, stupefied, in dismay, at the sight of his wife weeping. He stammered, "What is the matter? What is the matter?" By a violent effort, she had controlled her vexation and responded in a calm voice, wiping her moist cheeks, "Nothing. Only I have no dress and consequently I cannot go to this affair. Give your card to some colleague whose wife is better fitted out than I." He was grieved, but answered, "Let us see, Matilda. How much would a suitable costume cost, something that would serve for their occasions, something very simple?" She reflected for some seconds thinking of a sum that could ask for without bringing with it an immediate refusal and a frightened exclamation from the economical clerk." *(The Necklace)*

(i) **What can we infer about Matilda's emotions and financial situation based on her husband's reaction and her response to not having a dress for the affair?** **(2)**

(ii) **Which of the following is not a reason for Matilda's distress in the extract?** **(1)**

(a) She has no suitable dress for the affair.
(b) She is upset about her husband's reaction.
(c) She is worried about the cost of a suitable costume.
(d) The card did not bear her name.

(iii) **What did Matilda suggest that her husband do with the card?** **(1)**

(iv) **In the given extract what does the term 'economic clerk' imply?** **(1)**

7. Read the given extracts and answer the questions for ANY ONE of the two given. **(5)**

(A) Belinda giggled till she shook the house,
And Blink said Weeck! Which is giggling for a mouse,
Ink and Mustard rudely asked his age,
When Custard cried for a nice safe cage.
Suddenly, suddenly they heard a nasty sound,
And Mustard growled, and they all looked around.

(The Tale of Custard the Dragon)

(i) **What inference can be drawn from the repetition of 'suddenly, suddenly' in the above extract?** **(1)**

(a) The scene shook the house
(b) It highlights the swift assault
(c) It emphasises that an unexpected noise was heard
(d) It directs our notice to Mustard's growling

(ii) **Despite its symbolism of captivity, what leads Custard to have a preference for staying in a cage?** **(2)**

(iii) **Select the option that applies the same rhyme scheme as the lines of the first four lines of the given extract.** **(1)**

(a) Through the telescope she saw a star
which she thought was very far
She stretched her hand
and felt the crumple of the sand.

(b) Through the telescope she saw a star
She stretched her hand
As it was very far
But felt the crumble of the sand.

(c) Through the telescope she saw a star
Which she thought was very far
Her hand she stretched a far
But felt the crumble of the sand.

(d) Through the telescope she saw a star
Which she thought was very far
Her hand she stretched a far
But felt the crumble of the sand.

(iv) **In the given extract.** **(1)**

The difference between the other animals and Custard is that Custard behaves like a .... (coward/dragon).

Or

(B) I sit inside, doors open to the veranda writing long letters in which I scarcely mention the departure of the forest from the house. The night is fresh, the whole moon shines in a sky still open .... *(The Trees)*

(i) What atmosphere or mood is created by the language and imagery used in the above lines? (2)

(ii) Choose the option that correctly pairs the two different meanings implied by the use of 'open' twice in the extract. (1)

(a) Entry point - vastness
(b) Sharing a common space - great view
(c) Allowing access and vision - expanse of space
(d) Advantage - obstacles ahead

(iii) From the provided extract, what is conspicuously absent from she long letters the speaker is writing while they sit indoors with the doors open to the veranda? (1)

(iv) How does the poet describe the night? (1)

1. Dark   2. Frightening   3. Dense   4. Fresh   5. Bright

Select the correct option.

(a) 1 and 5   (b) Only 3   (c) 4 and 5   (d) 2 and 4

8. Answer ANY FOUR of the following five questions, in about 30-40 words each. (4 × 3 = 12)

(i) Every creature possesses a unique characteristic that defines it, and this trait is closely linked to its nature. This concept is beautifully illustrated in the poem 'How to Tell Wild Animals'. Elucidate.

(ii) Pranjal seemed to have a different level of enthusiasm compared to Rajvir when they both saw the tree plantation. Justify. (Glimpses of India)

(iii) In the poem 'Dust of Snow', the 'Hemlock Tree' and the 'Crow' hold specific meanings. Elaborate on how these symbols are utilised within the context of the poem.

(iv) In what manner did Lencho's cornfield suffer damage? Did he hold any expectations of receiving assistance? (A Letter to God)

(v) Engaging in discussions and disputes rarely leads to problem resolution. Support the statement with evidence from the text. (The Proposal)

9. Answer ANY TWO of the following three questions, in about 40-50 words each. (2 × 3 = 6)

(i) Bholi's heart was brimming with 'fresh optimism and a renewed existence'. What significance does the expression 'a new hope and a new life' hold for Bholi?

(ii) Lunch transformed into a significant ceremonial event for Mr. Herriot and his associates. Do you agree? Explain with reference to 'A Triumph of Surgery'.

(iii) Describe Ausable's fabricated tale regarding the balcony. (The Midnight Visitor)

10. Answer ANY ONE of the following two questions, in about 100-120 words. (1 × 6 = 6)

(A) Explore the theme of loss as it is depicted in both 'The Ball Poem' and 'The Sermon at Benaras', highlighting the evitable nature of this aspect in life?

(B) Analyse the similarities and differences between the young seagull from 'Two stories about flying' and Lencho from 'A Letter to God', and provide a rationale for the significant role faith plays in challenging and adverse situations in life.

11. Answer ANY ONE of the following two questions, in about 100-120 words. (1 × 6 = 6)

(A) Evaluate Griffin's character as a brilliant scientist and a lawless person. (Footprints without Feet)

(B) Half-baked knowledge is always dangerous. Rushing to conclusions without going deep into the details of things always leads to uninvited chaos and disasters. Explain the above mentioned statements in the light of Think-Tank's interpretation of the rhymes in the book 'Mother Goose'. (The Book that Saved the Earth)

SET-II

(Only Uncommon Questions from Set - I)

Section-B **(20 Marks)**

Creative Writing Skills **(10)**

Note: All details presented in the questions are imaginary and created for assessment purpose.

4. Attempt ANY ONE from (A) and (B) given below. **(5)**

(a) You are Raashi / Rahul of Simargarh, Himachal Pradesh. Write a letter in about 100-120 words to the Municipal Commissioner of the city drawing attention to the unattended condition of the public parks in your town. They are poorly maintained with garbage strewn and pools of stagnant water. Give suggestions on how the parks can be maintained.

Or

(b) You are Bela / Baloo of Palanpuri. You recently visited a 'craft mela'. You were delighted to see the diversity of handicrafts, handlooms and cultural fabric of India. However, you were dismayed that not many people were there to encourage the artisans. Write a letter to the editor in 100-120 words, expressing your views on the situation and the need to support indigenous art and craft.

9. Answer ANY TWO of the following three questions, in about 40-50 words. **(2 × 3 = 6)**

(i) Books play a significant role in shaping the personality of a person. In what way did a book cause a significant shift in Richard Ebright's life? (The Making of a Scientist)

(ii) Bholi's sent to school for an uncommon reason, leading to a distinctive twist, in her story. Elucidate.

(iii) Fowler's disappointment arose when he laid eyes on Ausable. Rationalise the statement. (The Midnight Visitor)

10. Answer ANY ONE of the following two questions, in about 100-120 words. **(1 × 6 = 6)**

(i) The inherent instinct for freedom is a fundamental trait in all living creatures. Justify this statement with reference to 'Mijbil the Otter' and 'A Tiger in the Zoo'.

(ii) Both 'Nelson Mandela: Long Walk to Freedom' by Nelson Mandela and 'The Trees' by Adrienne Rich explore themes of transformation, Liberation and the power to change. Examine the commonality of themes in both the works.

11. Answer ANY ONE of the following two questions, in about 100-120 words. **(1 × 6 = 6)**

(i) Griffin was a lawless person even though he was a brilliant scientist. Discuss. (Footprints without Feet)

(ii) 'The Book that Saved the Earth' communicates the idea that misinterpretation of cultural disparities among different groups can lead to us understandings and disputes. From the play, discuss methods to prevent such confusion and conflicts, ensuring the preservation of peace and harmony. (The Book that Saved the Earth)

SET-III

(Only Uncommon Questions from Set I & II)

Section-B

(20 Marks)

Creative Writing Skills

(10)

Note: All details presented in the questions are imaginary and created for assessment purpose.

4. Attempt ANY ONE from (A) and (B) given below. **(5)**

(A) In recent weeks, there have been several incidents of theft in your area, and despite reaching out to the local law enforcement authorities, there has been no improvement in the situation. Write a 100-120 words letter to the editor of a local newspaper, highlighting this issue and urging higher authorities to take action. You are Jyoti / Arvind residing at 54/47, Lohia Apartments, Nagpur.

Or

(B) You are Shivani Dube of B-3, Indira Nagar, Kota. You have recently relocated to the city and are taken aback by the condition of roads in the city. There are huge pot holes and no traffic lights, nor pedestrian crossings. At peak hours there is chaos at the intersections. Write a letter in 100-120 words to the Municipal Commissioner expressing your views and urging him to take action.

9. Answer ANY TWO of the following three questions, in about 40-50 words each. **$(2 \times 3 = 6)$**

(i) Why was Bholi frightened to go to school? (Bholi)

(ii) Why did Mrs. Pumphrey think the dogs recovery is a triumph of surgery? (A Triumph of Surgery)

(iii) What story did Ausable cook up regarding the arrival of the police? How did it affect Max? (The Midnight Visitor)

10. Answer ANY ONE of the following two questions, in about 100-120 words. **$(1 \times 6 = 6)$**

(i) Robert Frost's view of nature changes when he talks about it positively in 'Dust of Snow', but negatively in 'Fire and Ice'. Justify the statement.

(ii) Compare and contrast the role of faith between the young seagull from the 'Two Stories about Flying' and Lencho from 'A Letter to God'.

11. Answer ANY ONE of the following two questions in about 100-120 words. **$(1 \times 6 = 6)$**

(i) Discuss Griffin as a brilliant scientist who degenerates into a lawless and homeless wanderer? (Footprints without Feet)

(ii) How does Valli's journey to the city serve as her initiation into understanding the profound mysteries of life and death, and how does her inquisitive nature shape her perceptions as she encounters these aspects of human existence? (Madam Rides the Bus)

Answers

1. (i) it encourages greater sustainable consumption and production, counters the effects of climate change, addresses threats to biodiversity, and provides more effective disaster risk reduction.
   (ii) The UN views ESD as a lifelong process that extends from early childhood to higher and adult education, going beyond formal education. The critical areas of emphasis include fostering values, lifestyles, and attitudes from an early age to promote sustainability.
   (iii) Two curriculum projects that ESD has been linked with are
   (a) Recycling
   (b) Energy and water conservation
   (iv) research from psychology, social-cultural analysis, and neuroscience shows that young children have the greatest capacity to learn during this stage.
   (v) (d) creative
   (vi) (c) UNICEF reports show that children under the age of eight represent the highest percentage of affected population in global emergencies.
   (vii) A problem in both rich and poor countries is equitable access to high-quality preschool programmes. It has been recognised as crucial is linking health and education agendas to ensure sustainable development.
   (viii) informative and persuasive

2. (i) (b) It has developed very quickly
   (ii) (a) Both the (A) and (R) are true, and (R) is the correct explanation of (A).
   (iii) Two benefits of using EV over internal combustion engine vehicles are
   (a) EVs emit 30-80% less greenhouse gases compared to ICE vehicles.
   (b) EVs do not consume fuel when stationary, unlike ICE vehicles that continue to burn fuel even when idle.
   (iv) not in use/stationary
   (v) EVs reduce the dependence on fossil fuels, which are majorly imported. They utilise renewable energy sources such as solar and wind power, promoting energy independence.
   (vi) reduce
   (vii) Evidence from the passage showing the government is encouraging the use of EVs
   - The government introduced financial policies to promote EV adoption.
   - The FAME scheme was implemented in 2015 to support the faster adoption of hybrid and electric vehicles.

   (viii) the significant growth of EV market leading to increased adoption and manufacturing of electric vehicles
   (ix) the efficient implementation of EV policies for sustainable development and widespread EV adoption

3. (i) purchased (ii) should
   (iii)

Error	Correction
has	have

   (iv) (b) sounded interesting
   (v) (b)

Error	Correction
ate	eats

   (vi) pledged to plant some trees that weekend
   (vii)

Error	Correction
maintain	maintaining

   (viii) (b) started (ix) (d) each
   (x) should (xi) (d) applies
   (xii)

Error	Correction
changes	change

4. (A) 67/98 Malka Ganj
   Delhi

   26th April, 20XX

   The Head Librarian
   Gitanjali Public School
   Delhi

   Subject Improvement of Library Facilities

   Sir/Madam

   I am writing to bring to your attention the poor condition of the school library, which is hindering students' reading habits. The library lacks a sufficient collection of books, and many existing books are outdated or in poor condition. Additionally, the reading space is inadequate, and there is a shortage of comfortable seating arrangements.

   To improve the situation, I suggest updating the book collection with a variety of genres, including fiction, non-fiction, and educational material.

Organising reading competitions, interactive storytelling sessions, and a dedicated reading hour can also encourage students to develop a love for books.

I sincerely request you to take the necessary steps to enhance the library facilities. This will greatly benefit students and help inculcate reading habits.

Thank you for your time and consideration.

Yours sincerely

Sonia

Or (B) 25/22, Rajpur

Fatehabad

19th February, 20XX

The Editor

Hindustan Times

New Delhi

Subject Rising Concerns Over Reckless Driving and Traffic Violations

Sir/Madam

Through the columns of your esteemed newspaper, I wish to draw attention to the alarming increase in reckless driving and non-adherence to traffic rules. Recent reports of fatal accidents due to overspeeding, signal violations, and drunk driving are deeply concerning. Lives are being lost due to negligence, and urgent action is needed.

Strict enforcement of traffic rules, installation of more speed cameras, and harsher penalties for offenders can help curb this issue. Additionally, awareness campaigns should be launched in schools and colleges to educate young drivers about responsible driving. The government must also improve road infrastructure and ensure proper lighting and signage.

I hope this issue receives the attention it deserves, leading to safer roads for all.

Yours sincerely

Sharmila Sahani

5. (A) India is rapidly advancing towards becoming a digitally empowered society and economy through various initiatives. The Digital India Programme is at the forefront of this transformation, aiming to improve IT infrastructure and increase digital literacy. One of the key aspects of this programme is the creation of IT jobs, which has significantly boosted employment opportunities in the technology sector. E-Governance has made government services more accessible and efficient, reducing paperwork and increasing transparency. The E-Kranti initiative focuses on delivering electronic services in areas like healthcare, education, and financial inclusion. Another crucial step is ensuring broadband connectivity for all, both in urban and rural areas, bridging the digital divide. Additionally, the initiative information for all ensures that citizens have easy access to government data and services, promoting transparency and inclusivity. These digital initiatives have strengthened India's economy and improved the quality of life for its citizens. With continuous advancements, India is moving towards a more connected and digitally empowered future.

Or (B) Adolescents aged 14-17 engage in a variety of activities that contribute to their overall development. Creative pursuits like dance, music, and art enhance self-expression, emotional well-being, and cognitive abilities. Outdoor sports such as cricket, hockey, basketball, soccer, and tennis promote physical fitness, teamwork, and discipline, fostering both mental and emotional resilience. Computer games can improve problem-solving skills and hand-eye coordination but may lead to excessive screen time if not regulated. Net surfing and social media provide access to information and social interaction, aiding personality development. However, they can also pose risks like distraction and reduced physical activity. Balancing these activities is essential for holistic growth, ensuring that adolescents develop their interests while maintaining their physical, mental, and emotional well-being.

6. (A) (i) The speaker, Anne Frank, is feeling lonely, bored, and slightly depressed. She lacks a close friend to confide in and finds comfort in writing in her diary, which she believes is more patient and understanding than people.

(ii) (d) reflective

(iii) friend

(iv) Anne says 'paper has more patience than people' because writing allows her to express herself freely without fear of judgement or interruption. Unlike people, who may not always listen or understand, paper patiently absorbs all her thoughts, providing her comfort in times of loneliness.

(B) (i) Matilda feels frustrated, insecure, and disheartened about her modest lifestyle. She believes she deserves luxury but is financially constrained. Her husband's reaction shows that they live a modest, middle-class life, where even buying a dress requires careful budgeting.

(ii) (d) The card did not bear her name.

(iii) She suggested that he give the invitation to a colleague whose wife is better dressed for such occasions, implying she would rather not attend than go in a simple dress.

(iv) It implies that Matilda's husband is a modest, thrifty government employee who carefully manages finances and avoids unnecessary expenses.

7. (A) (i) (c) It emphasises that an unexpected noise was heard

(ii) Custard prefers staying in a cage because he is timid and fearful. Unlike traditional dragons, he lacks courage and feels safer in a confined space where he is protected from threats.

(iii) (a) (iv) coward

(B) (i) The mood created is one of loneliness and quiet contemplation. The speaker is indoors, writing long letters, seemingly detached from the changes happening outside. The imagery of the 'fresh night' and the 'whole moon shining in a still sky' adds to the sense of calmness, yet there is also a feeling of separation from nature.

(ii) (c) Allowing access and vision - expanse of space

(iii) The letters scarcely mention the departure of the forest from the house, meaning they do not acknowledge the trees moving out, which symbolises deforestation or a loss of nature. This suggests a disconnect between human activities and the natural world.

(iv) (c) 4 and 5

8. (i) In 'How to Tell Wild Animals', Carolyn Wells humorously highlights the unique traits of various wild animals. Each creature is described through its distinctive features and behaviour, such as the lion's roar, the tiger's ferocity, and the leopard's quick attacks, making identification entertaining and vivid.

(ii) Pranjol, being a native of Assam, was already familiar with tea plantations, so he showed less excitement than Rajvir. In contrast, Rajvir was highly enthusiastic, as it was his first visit, and he was eager to learn about tea cultivation.

(iii) In 'Dust of Snow', Robert Frost uses the crow and hemlock tree as symbols of gloom and negativity. However, the falling snow from the crow's movement unexpectedly uplifts the poet's mood, showing that even dark, unpleasant things can bring positivity and change.

(iv) Lencho's cornfield was destroyed by a severe hailstorm, leaving his family without food. Despite the devastation, he firmly believed in God's help and wrote a letter requesting financial aid, showing his unshakable faith in divine assistance.

(v) In 'The Proposal,' Lomov, Natalya, and Chubukov engage in endless arguments over petty issues like land ownership and dogs. Instead of resolving problems, their disputes escalate, showing that arguments create unnecessary tension rather than leading to solutions.

9. (i) For Bholi, 'a new hope and a new life' signifies her transformation from a timid, neglected girl to a confident and self-respecting woman. Education empowers her to reject societal norms, refuse a dowry-driven marriage, and take control of her life, embracing a future of dignity and independence.

(ii) Yes, lunch became a significant event for Mr. Herriot and his associates as goodies that came for Tricki during his convalescence was that the people in the household enjoyed a period of indulgence and luxurious living. The household members, including the doctor and his partners, enjoyed the extra eggs, wine, and brandy. It added a sense of festivity to their daily routines, with lunch becoming a ceremonial occasion and evenings by the fire becoming more enjoyable.

(iii) Ausable tricked Max by inventing a story about a balcony outside his window, claiming that police frequently used it for security checks. Panicked and desperate, Max tried to escape through the imaginary balcony, only to fall to his death, proving Ausable's cleverness and quick thinking.

10. (i) Both 'The Ball Poem' by John Berryman and 'The Sermon at Benares' highlight the inevitability of loss in life. In 'The Ball Poem', the young boy loses his ball, symbolising the loss of innocence and childhood, teaching him that loss is a part of growing up. Similarly, in 'The Sermon at Benares', Gautama Buddha explains that death and suffering are inevitable and that one must accept them with detachment. He tells us that loss of irreparable things brings grief and sorrow but as wise people we must learn to stay calm and accept the loss while understanding tht we might lose things we love, even we once loved. Both texts emphasise that grief is a natural process, and one must learn to cope with loss rather than cling to what is gone.

(ii) The young seagull in 'Two Stories About Flying' hesitates to fly out of fear, but eventually takes the leap when he is pushed by hunger. Similarly, Lencho, in 'A Letter to God', faces adversity when his crops are destroyed, but he does not lose hope and places absolute faith in divine help. The key difference is that the seagull's faith in his instincts is forced upon him, while Lencho's faith in God is unwavering. Both stories highlight that faith gives strength in difficult times, helping individuals overcome challenges with courage and belief.

11. (i) Griffin, in 'Footprints Without Feet', is portrayed as a genius scientist who discovers the formula for invisibility. His brilliance is evident in his groundbreaking invention, but his lack of morality turns him into a lawless person. Instead of using his knowledge for good, he misuses it to commit theft, arson, and violence. He assaults innocent people, steals from shops, and terrifies villagers. His unchecked arrogance and unethical choices ultimately lead to his downfall. Thus, while Griffin's intelligence is remarkable, his lack of responsibility and criminal mindset prove that science without ethics is dangerous.

(ii) In 'The Book that Saved the Earth', Think-Tank, the leader of Martians, misinterprets nursery rhymes from Mother Goose due to his half-baked knowledge. When he reads about 'eating' words, he wrongly assumes that humans consume books for intelligence. Similarly, simple rhymes about cows and Humpty Dumpty make him believe that Earth's inhabitants are dangerous beings preparing for war. His hasty and uninformed conclusions lead him to abort the invasion of Earth out of fear. This highlights how shallow understanding and jumping to conclusions can cause unnecessary chaos and confusion, reinforcing that true wisdom comes from thorough learning and rational thinking.

Set II

4. (A) For answer refer to page no. 63 question no 6.

Or (B) 86, Star Apartment
Palanpuri

17th March, 20XX

The Editor
The Hindu
Palanpuri

Subject Need to Support Indigenous Art and Craft

Sir/Madam

Through the columns of your esteemed paper, I would like to draw the attention of media person to the role that they can play in promoting diversity of handi crafts, handlooms and cultural fabric of India.

I recently visited a craft mela and was mesmerised by the rich diversity of Indian handicrafts, handlooms, and cultural heritage. Each artifact reflected the skill and dedication of artisans who have kept these traditions alive for generations. However, it was disheartening to see the lack of visitors, leaving these talented craftsmen struggling for recognition and livelihood.

Indigenous art and craft form the soul of our heritage and deserve active promotion. The government and society must step forward to encourage artisans through awareness, fair pricing, and better market opportunities. Without support, these art forms may fade into oblivion. I urge readers to appreciate and promote our traditional crafts.

Yours sincerely
Bela

9. (i) A book, 'The Travels of Monarch X', caused a significant shift in Richard Ebright's life by igniting his fascination with Monarch butterflies. This sparked his passion for science, leading him to conduct groundbreaking research, shaping his career as a biologist and influencing his future achievements.

(ii) For answer refer to page no. 469 Question 2 (Read and Find Out Page 47).

(iii) Fowler's disappointment arose when he laid eyes on Ausable because when he came to meet Ausable, he had expected a smart looking active man who would deal with pistols, wine and dark eyed beauties. However, the reality was far from it. Ausable was a fat and sloppy man with an American accent.

10. (i) The inherent instinct for freedom is evident in both 'Mijbil the Otter' and 'A Tiger in the Zoo'. In 'Mijbil the Otter', Mijbil demonstrates a natural desire for freedom, reveling in the joy of playing and swimming in open spaces. His behaviour starkly contrasts with captivity, where he feels confined. Similarly, in 'A Tiger in the Zoo', the tiger's longing for freedom is clear as it paces restlessly in its cage, showing signs of frustration. Both animals, though tamed, reveal a strong, instinctive need for freedom, emphasising that the desire for liberty is a fundamental trait shared by all living creatures, whether wild or domesticated.

(ii) Both 'Nelson Mandela: Long Walk to Freedom' by Nelson Mandela and 'Trees' by Adrienne Rich explore themes of transformation, liberation, and the power to change. In Long Walk to Freedom, Mandela's journey symbolises the struggle for freedom and the transformative power of resilience in the fight against apartheid. Similarly, in Trees, Adrienne Rich uses the metaphor of a tree to symbolise personal growth and liberation, depicting how the tree's roots represent strength and the freedom to flourish. Both works highlight the importance of inner strength and transformation, showing how both individuals and nature can overcome hardships and emerge liberated, symbolising hope and change.

11. (i) For answer refer to page no. 442 Question no. 2
(ii) For answer refer to page no. 486 Question no. 3

Set III

4. (A) Jyoti/Arvind
54/47, Lohia Apartments
Nagpur

17th March, 20XX

The Editor
The Times

Subject Rising Thefts and Lack of Action by Authorities

Sir/Madam

Through the columns of your esteemed paper, I would like to draw the attention of concerned authority to the increasing incidents of theft in our area. In recent weeks, several houses in Lohia Apartments and nearby localities have been targeted. Despite multiple complaints to local law enforcement, no concrete action has been taken, leaving residents anxious and vulnerable.

The lack of police patrolling and delayed response have emboldened miscreants. We urge higher authorities to intervene immediately by increasing security measures and ensuring stricter law enforcement. The safety of citizens should be a top priority. I hope this issue receives the attention it deserves before the situation worsens.

Yours sincerely
Jyoti

(B) B-3, Indira Nagar
Kota
17th March, 20XX

The Municipal Commissioner
Municipal Corporation, Kota

Subject Urgent Need for Road Repairs and Traffic Management

Sir/Madam

This is to inform you that I, Shivani Dube recently relocated to Kota and was shocked by the poor condition of the city's roads. Huge potholes make driving hazardous, while the absence of traffic lights and pedestrian crossings leads to chaos, especially during peak hours. The situation at major intersections is alarming, with frequent traffic jams and near-accidents.

It is crucial to address these issues immediately by repairing roads, installing traffic signals, and ensuring proper pedestrian crossings. A well-maintained traffic system is essential for public safety and smooth commuting. I urge you to take prompt action before the situation worsens.

Yours sincerely
Shivani Dube

9. (i) Bholi was frightened to go to school because she had a speech impairment, and she was afraid that the other children would make fun of her. She also felt insecure about her appearance, as she was often called 'the dumb girl' by others.
(ii) For answer refer to page no. 392 Question no. 4.
(iii) For answer refer to page no. 421 Question no. 7.

10. (i) In 'Dust of Snow', Robert Frost presents nature positively. The falling snow helps the speaker change his negative mood, symbolising how nature can uplift and heal. The small act of falling of snow from a tree transforms the speaker's mood, showing nature as a source of comfort and renewal.

In contrast, in 'Fire and Ice', Frost portrays nature in a more destructive way. The poem reflects on how the elements-fire and ice-can symbolise the destructive forces of desire and hate. While nature is still powerful, it is shown here as something that can bring destruction rather than peace. Thus, Frost's view of nature shifts from healing and positive in 'Dust of Snow' to destructive in 'Fire and Ice'.

(ii) In 'Two Stories About Flying' and 'A Letter to God', faith plays an important role but in different ways. The young seagull in 'Two Stories About Flying' lacks faith in its ability to fly at first, but when it takes a leap of faith and trusts in its own strength, it learns to fly. In contrast, Lencho in 'A Letter to God' has faith in God to provide for him after a storm destroys his crops. He believes that God will send him money, and when he receives only part of it, he still trusts that God will help him. While the seagull's faith is in itself, Lencho's faith is in divine intervention.

11. (i) For answer refer to page no. 442 Question no. 4.
(ii) In 'Madam Rides the Bus', Valli's journey to the city marks her initiation into the deeper realities of life and death. Driven by her curiosity and desire for independence, she takes the bold step of traveling alone to the city, eager to experience the world beyond her village. As she observes the bustling city, Valli's inquisitive nature leads her to marvel at the new sights and sounds. However, her encounter with a dead cow on the road introduces her to the harsh reality of death. This moment marks a turning point, where she begins to understand the fragility of life. Valli's curiosity shapes her perceptions, helping her grasp the mysteries of human existence.

Sample Question Paper 1 (Solved)

A Highly Simulated Sample Question Paper for CBSE Class X

English Language and Literature

Time : 3 hrs	M.M. : 80

General Instructions

1 This question paper comprises 11 questions, All questions are compulsory.

2 The question paper contains three sections

Section A : Reading Skills

Section B : Grammar and Creative Writing Skills

Section C : Literature

3 Attempt questions based on specific instructions for each part.

Section – A (Reading Skills) (20 Marks)

1. Read the following passage carefully. **(10)**

1. Peer pressure is a phenomenon wherein we tend to get influenced by the lifestyle and the ways of thinking of our peers. Peer pressure can prove beneficial but it is most often observed to have negative effects.
2. The thought, behaviour and taste in fashion, music, television and other walks of life of the masses are often seen to have a deep impact on society. We tend to get influenced by the lifestyle of our peer group. The changing ways of life of our peers often force us to change our ways of looking at life and leading it. It's a human tendency to do what the crowd does. Few have the courage to resist peer pressure and be their own selves rather than being one among the lot.
3. Peer pressure is bound to affect most of us both positively and negatively. The distinction between positive and negative peer pressure lies in a thoughtful analysis of the views of the masses. Following your peers blindly leaves a negative impact on your life while an analytical approach to looking at peer behaviour can help you act positively.
4. Peer pressure is not always bad. It can help you analyse yourself and contemplate your ways of life. Some of the practices that the masses follow may actually teach you the way of living. You may be able to change yourself for the better. Looking at what others do, can help you bring about a positive change in your way of thinking. If you can pick selectively, peer pressure can actually result in a positive change in your way of life.
5. Teenage is that phase of life when you are exposed to the world outside. These are the years when you spend most of your time with your friends. Teenage is the phase of beginning to become independent in life; the years of forming your ideals and principles, the years that shape your personality and the years that introduce you to your own self. As adolescents you often spend most of your daily time with friends and owing to this, you tend to imitate your friends. The people around you are bound to influence you. However the effect of the influences of the masses is greater during your teen years. Parents have a vital role to play during this phase of your life.
6. Parents and teachers need to be careful while dealing with teenagers, as they are most susceptible to succumbing to peer pressure during these years of their life. Teenage individuals need to be taught to distinguish between the good and the bad, the right and the wrong and should be taught to be thoughtful in life.

7. A strong support from family, an ability to differentiate between the positive and the negative and a skill to choose friends from among peers this three-pronged strategy is the best way to keep away from negative peer pressure.

Based on your understanding of the passage, answer the following questions.

1. **What does the writer project with reference to the following?** **(1)**

   Parents and teachers need to be careful while dealing with teenagers, as they are most susceptible to succumbing to peer pressure during these years of their life.

2. **Complete the sentence appropriately.** **(1)**

   Changing ways of life of our peers can affect us because ....

   (a) it forces us to change the ways in which we live our lives

   (b) it forces us to change our social circle

3. **The writer mentions *The people around you are bound to influence you.* (Paragraph 5)** **(2)**

   Mention one reason from the passage that supports the above statement. (40 words)

4. ***The writer says Teenage is that phase of life when you are exposed to the world outside.*** **(1)**

   Identify the words that correctly state the meaning of the term 'exposed' as used in the passage.

(i) Visible	(ii) Vulnerable	(iii) Public
(iv) Introduce	(v) Reveal	(vi) Displayed

5. **State whether the following statement is True or False with reference to the given extract.** **(1)**

   By 'the way of living' the writer means our behaviour towards others, our views, ideas, and preferences.

6. **Select the option that corresponds to the following relation below.** **(1)**

   Peer pressure can prove beneficial but it is most often observed to have negative effects.

   (a) Beginnings and ends are easier to remember than middles.

   (b) Sleep is good for memory but too much sleep can also be linked to health problems.

   (c) Food tastes better when someone else makes it.

   (d) Some people enjoy seeing anger in others.

7. **Justify the following in about 40 words.** **(2)**

   Parents and teachers need to be careful while dealing with teenagers, as they are most susceptible to succumbing to peer pressure during these years of their life.

8. **Which of the following the reason for the effect of peer pressure in teenage years.** **(1)**

   (a) Teen years are always unmanageable.

   (b) Teenagers spend more time with their peers and friends.

   (c) Teenagers spend more time with their parents and old people.

   (d) It is impossible to convince them.

2. Read the following passage carefully. **(10)**

1. India is home to an estimated 10% of the global Snow Leopard population spread across five Himalayan states of Jammu and Kashmir, Himachal Pradesh, Uttarakhand, Sikkim and Arunachal Pradesh which is only 5% of the available global habitat for the animal.
2. Project Snow Leopard was introduced in India by the Project Snow Leopard Committee instituted by the Ministry of Environment and Forests, Government of India, in the year 2009 to safeguard and conserve India's unique natural heritage of high-altitude wildlife populations and their habitats by promoting conservation through participatory policies and actions.
3. Project Tiger and Project Elephant are prevalent in India with the former introduced in 1973 garnering worldwide attention.

4. The Snow Leopard usually occurs at an altitude of >2700m above sea level and is the apex predator in the Himalayan Region along with the Tibetan Wolf. The project is not only to protect the Snow Leopard but as with Project Tiger, it is considered an umbrella species and with its protection, comes the protection of other species and the habitat of which they are all a part.
5. Top 3 National Parks in India where the Snow Leopard can likely be seen
   (i) Kibber Wildlife Sanctuary - Himachal Pradesh
   (ii) Ulley Valley - Ladakh
   (iii) Hemis National Park - Himachal Pradesh

6. The reasons for the introduction of Project Snow Leopard are as follows.
   (i) High altitudes of India > 3000m including the Himalayan and Trans-Himalayan biogeographic zones support a unique wildlife assemblage of global conservation.
   (ii) There has been relatively less attention on the region from the viewpoint of wildlife conservation.
   (iii) The region represents a vast rangeland system supporting important traditional pastoral economies and lifestyles.
   (iv) The region provides essential ecosystem services and harbours river systems vital for the nation's food security.
   (v) India has ratified international agreements promoting the conservation of high-altitude wildlife species such as the snow leopard.
   (vi) The region is important for the country's national security as well as international relations.
   (vii) The high-altitude wildlife in India today faces a variety of threats.
   (viii) The existing high-altitude protected areas in India require considerable strengthening.
   (ix) Wildlife Management in the region needs to be made participatory.

Based on your understanding of the passage, answer the following questions.

1. Which of the following is true about the passage? **(1)**
   (a) Wildlife Management in the region need not be made participatory.
   (b) High altitudes of India > 3000m including the Himalayan and Trans-Himalayan biogeographic zones support a unique wildlife assemblage of global conservation.
   (c) Project Tiger and Project Elephant are prevalent in India with the latter introduced in 1973 garnering worldwide attention.
   (d) Project Snow Leopard was introduced in India by the Project Snow Leopard Committee instituted by the Ministry of Science and Technology.

2. **Select the option that is true for the assertion and reason given below.** **(1)**

Assertion (A) The project promotes conservation through participatory policies and actions.

Reason (R) The project has been successful in its endeavour.

(a) Both the (A) and (R) are true, and (R) is the correct explanation of (A).

(b) Both the (A) and (R) are true, but (R) is not the correct explanation of (A).

(c) (A) is true, but (R) is false.

(d) (A) is false, but (R) is true.

3. **Infer the meaning of the phrase 'umbrella species' from the passage.** **(1)**

4. **Project Tiger and Project Elephant are prevalent in India with the former introduced in 1973. What has the former gathered?** **(1)**

5. **Fill in the blanks with the appropriate option from those given in brackets, based on your understanding of Paragraph 4.** **(1)**

The '.................' (Snow Leopards/Arctic Fox) which usually occur at an altitude of >2700m, are the apex predators in the Himalayan Region.

6. **List any two reasons for the introduction of Project Snow Leopard in high altitudes.** **(2)**

1. .... **2. ....**

7. **Complete the following analogy correctly with a word/phrase from the passage.** **(1)**

Population in India : 400-600 : : Population in world : ....

8. **Complete the sentence with a suitable reason.** **(1)**

Project Snow Leopard was a necessity in the Indian conservation journey because ....

9. **List any one reason why Project Snow Leopard was introduced in India.** **(2)**

Section – B (Grammar) **(20 Marks)**

3. Attempt any *ten* of twelve of the following questions. **(10)**

(i) Fill in the blank by choosing the correct option to complete the sentence. **(1)**

When we hear commentary on the radio we easily .... what is happening at a particular moment.

(a) visualise (b) visualised (c) visualising (d) will visualise

(ii) Identify the error in the following sentence. **(1)**

India and Antarctica are once part of the same landmass.

Use the given format for your response.

Error	Correction

(iii) Mahi and her mother had a conversation about honesty. Report the reply of Mahi's mother. **(1)**

Mahi Honesty doesn't always lead to good results.

Mother Honesty is the best policy.

(iv) Fill in the blank by using the correct form of the word, for the given portion of the letter. **(1)**

Respected Sir/Ma'am

I am Drishya, a member of NGO Prada. I .... (am writing/writes/wrote) to you to bring to your notice the increasing effect of air pollution in our neighbourhood and in the surrounding area.

(v) **Report Rahul's question to Saba.** **(1)**

Rahul Do you know that Ranjit met with an accident and is in hospital ?

(vi) **Select the option that identifies the error and supplies the correction for the following line. He had no accuse for attacking that old man.** **(1)**

Options	Error	Correction
(a)	had	has
(b)	accuse	excuse
(c)	for	to
(d)	attacking	attack

(vii) **Read the conversation between the teacher and the student. Complete the sentence by reporting the student's reply correctly.** **(1)**

Teacher For how many hours do you study at home, Rakesh?

Rakesh I cannot study for more than half an hour.

The teacher, asked Rakesh about the number of hours he studied, to which, Rakesh informed .... for more than half an hour.

(a) that he could not study (b) that he cannot study (c) that he will not study (d) that he always studies

(viii) **Identify the error in the following advertisement of a school.** **(1)**

MM School
New Delhi, Delhi
We go beyond our textbooks because knowledge know no bounds.

Use the given format for your response.

Error	Correction

(ix) **Complete the narration of the dialogue between Ajay and his classmate Mohan.** **(1)**

Ajay Do you want to play with us?

Mohan Yes, but I have been too late.

Ajay asked Mohan if he wanted to play with them. Mohan replied to him positively and told him that he ....

(x) **Complete the given sentence by filling in the blank with the correct option.** **(1)**

He's been working all day long. He .... to be very tired.

(a) should (b) would (c) could (d) might

(xi) **Select the correct option to fill in the blank for the given line, from a health article.** **(1)**

Americans .... get the new Omicron-specific COVID-19 vaccine before Halloween to boost their immunity levels ahead of a potential infection surge this winter.

(a) should (b) must (c) ought to (d) will

(xii) **Report the dialogues to complete the paragraphs that follow.** **(1)**

Mother You seem so tired. Take some rest.

Suraj I can't even think of relaxing. I have lots of homework to do.

Mother You should not take so much of stress.

Suraj Don't worry. Please give me a hot cup of tea.

Mother said to Suraj that he seemed so tired and advised him to take rest. Suraj replied that ....The mother advised him not to take so much of stress. Suraj told his mother not to worry and requested her to give him a hot cup of tea.

Creative Writing Skills (10 Marks)

Note : All details presented in the questions are imaginary and created for assessment purpose.

4. Attempt any *one* from (A) and (B) given below. (5)

A. There has been a spate of chain and mobile snatching incidents in your locality. Masked youths come on motorbikes, commit the crime and run away without being caught or traced causing a lot of insecurity and fear among the residents. Write a letter in 100-120 words to the editor of a local newspaper drawing attention of the concerned authorities to the problem. You are Shweta Kapoor, Secretary, RWA Anand Niketan, Agra.

Or **B. You live in a room in college which you can share with another student. However, there are many problems with this arrangement and you find it very difficult to work. Write a letter to the accommodation officer at the college explaining the situation and requesting an earliest redressal. (100-120 words)**

5. Attempt any *one* from (A) and (B) given below. (5)

A. The bar chart shows the scores of teams A, B and C over four different seasons. Write an analytical paragraph on the given data in about 100-120 words.

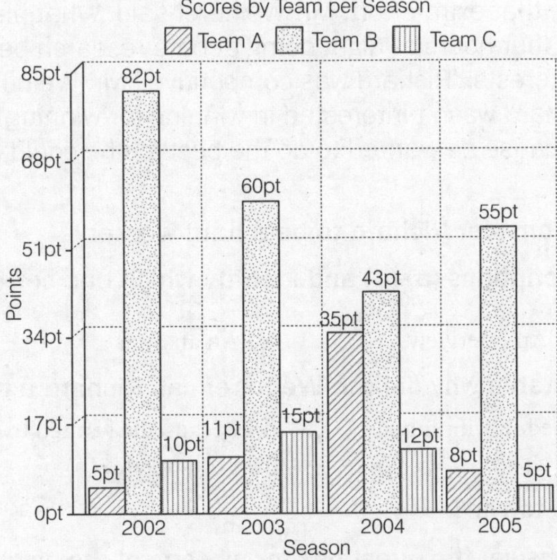

Or **B. The table illustrates the proportion of monthly household income five European countries spend on food and drink, housing, clothing and entertainment. Using the given data, write an analytical paragraph in 100-120 words.**

Proportion of Household Income of Five European Countries Spend on Food and Drink, Housing, Clothing and Entertainment

	Food and drink	Housing	Clothing	Entertainment
France	25%	31%	7%	13%
Germany	22%	33%	15%	19%
UK	27%	37%	11%	11%
Turkey	36%	20%	12%	10%
Spain	31%	18%	8%	15%

Section – C (Literature Textbook) (40 Marks)

6. Read the given extracts and answer the questions for any *one* of the given two, (A) or (B). **(5)**

A. That day had come about through the unimaginable sacrifices of thousands of my people, people whose suffering and courage can never be counted or repaid. I felt that day, as I have on so many other days, that I was simply the sum of all those African patriots who had gone before me. That long and noble line ended and now began again with me. I was pained that I was not able to thank them and that they were not able to see what their sacrifices had wrought. (Nelson Mandela : Long Walk to Freedom)

(i) Fill in the blank with the correct word from the bracket. **(1)**

The given lines forms a part of .... (report/speech).

(ii) A few of the speaker's qualities are being through his words in the above lines. Elaborate in about 40 words with reference to the extract. **(2)**

(iii) Which phrase would correctly substitute 'the unimaginable' in the given sentence from the extract? **(1)**

That day had come about through the unimaginable sacrifices of thousands of my people, people whose suffering and courage can never be counted or repaid.

(iv) That long and noble line ended and now began again with me. 'The' noble line refer to **(1)**

(a) Africans (b) Racists (c) African patriots (d) Mandela's family

Or

B. "Richard would always give that extra effort, Mr. Weiherer said. What pleased me was, here was this person who put in three or four hours at night doing debate research besides doing all his research with butterflies and his other interests. 'Richard was competitive,' Mr. Weiherer continued, 'but not in a bad sense'. He explained, "Richard wasn't interested in winning for winning's sake or winning to get a prize. Rather, he was winning because he wanted to do the best job he could. For the right reasons, he wants to be the best." (The Making of a Scientist)

(i) Why did Mr. Weiherer consider Richard to be a hard worker? **(1)**

(ii) Read the following descriptions (a)-(d) and identify which one correctly corresponds to the extract. **(1)**

(a) A review (b) An interview (c) An analysis (d) A comment

(iii) Select the option that states why did mr. Weiherer call Richard a true winner. **(1)**

(a) Because he wasn't interested in winning. (b) Because he wanted to give his best.
(c) Because he wanted to win a prize. (d) Both (a) and (b)

(iv) Why was Richard trying to win? **(2)**

7. Read the given extracts and answer the questions for any *one* of the given two, (A) or (B). **(5)**

A. Has given my heart
A change of mood
And saved some part
Of a day I had rued. (Dust of Snow)

(i) Comment on why the poet says that he had 'saved some part of a day I had rued'. **(2)**

(ii) Fill in the blank appropriately.

.... had changed the poet's mood. **(1)**

(iii) How has mood of the poet changed? **(1)**

(iv) Select the option that applies the same rhyme scheme as the lines of the given extract. (1)

A. This bird so small and sweet
She doesn't know how to tweet.
So small so joyful.
Her life is full of innocence.

B. Perched on a branch green
This bird so sweet and lean,
Sings aloud in a voice sweet,
Chirp, chirp, tweet, tweet.

C. This bird sings without a care,
sweet Perched on a branch green,
A song with the world to share,
With its feelings so keen.

D. Her voice a melody.
Calls us to rejoice and dance
The Clamour surrounding her
Is something we wish for.

Or

B. He hears the last voice at night
The patrolling cars
And stares with his brilliant eyes
At the brilliant stars.

(A Tiger in the Zoo)

(i) Who is 'he' in the given lines? Why is he staring at the stars? Answer in about 40 words. (2)

(ii) Fill in the blank appropriately.

The tiger's eyes shine like stars because he is .... (1)

(iii) Which is the purpose of patrolling cars that the animal sees? (1)

(iv) Identify poetic device the used in the given lines. (1)

1. Personification **2. Repetition** **3. Imagery** **4. Oxymoron** **5. Irony**

(a) 1, 2 and 3 (b) 2, 3 and 4 (c) 3, 4 and 5 (d) 1, 4 and 5

8. Answer any *four* of the following questions in 40-50 words each. (4 × 3 = 12)

(i) According to the poet, what do 'Fire and Ice' represent? Do you agree with him? (3)

(ii) What tells you that Anne loved her grandmother? (From the Diary of Anne Frank) (3)

(iii) Describe the magnificent views of the tea estate with reference to the lesson, 'Tea from Assam'. (Glimpses of India) (3)

(iv) Summarise what happened when Maxwell decided to transport Mijbil to England by air? (Mijbil the Otter) (3)

(v) What did the baker do first once he reached a house? (A Baker from Goa) (3)

9. Answer any *two* of the following questions in 40-50 words each. (2 × 3 = 6)

(i) How did Matilda come to know about the reality of the diamond necklace? (The Necklace)

(ii) What other interests, besides science, did Richard Ebright pursue? What opinion did Mr. Weiherer, his social studies teacher, have about Ebright? (The Making of a Scientist)

(iii) Why did Bholi not want to go to school? (Bholi)

10. Answer any *one* of the following questions in 100-120 words. **(1 × 6 = 6)**

A. Imagine that Nelson Mandela read 'Fire and Ice'. As Mandela, write a diary entry associating the impact of the troubled history of South Africa with the idea expressed in the poem.

You may begin like this.

10th May, 1994, Tuesday 10 p.m.

Today, when I am the President of South Africa, I can't help recalling Robert Frost's 'Fire and Ice'

Or

B. Valli posed herself to be very confident when the conductor offered her help to ride the bus. Later on she felt shy when all laughed at her.

What does this tell you about Valli's character? What do we learn from her character?

11. Answer any *one* of the following question in 100-120 words. **(1 × 6 = 6)**

A. Do you think that over-pampering by Mrs. Pumphrey was the main reason for Tricki's ailment? Explain.

Or

B. Bholi's teacher is one of the minor but the most important character in the lesson titled Bholi. Justify.

Answers

1.
1. Caution
2. (a) it forces us to change the ways in which we lead our lives
3. The writers states that the people around us have a deep influence on us because according to him it is a human tendency to follow our peers. Thus, we cannot resists the tastes of our peers and are influenced by them.
4. (ii) Vulnerable and (iv) Introduce
5. True
6. (b) Sleep is good for memory but too much sleep can also be linked to health problems.
7. As adolescents often spend most of their daily time with friends they tend to imitate and copy them blindly parents and teachers, being experienced, can prevent teenagers and adolscents from following wrong and dangerous trends and attitudes. Thus, they are to be careful while dealing with teenagers.
8. (b) Teenagers spend more time with their peers and friends.

2.
1. (a) Wildlife Management in the region need not be made participatory. 3. 'Umbrella species' refers to such species whose protection will ensure the protection of other species.
2. (b) Both the (A) and (R) are true, but (R) is not the correct explanation of (A).
3. 'Umbrella species' refers to such species whose protection will ensure the protection of other species.
4. The former, i.e. Project Tiger, has gathered worldwide attention, thus shifting the focus on wildlife conservation.
5. Snow Leopards
6. (i) High altitudes of India > 3000m including the Himalayan and Trans-Himalayan biogeographic zones support a unique wildlife assemblage of global conservation.
   (ii) There has been relatively less attention on the region from the viewpoint of wildlife conservation.
7. 4500-7500
8. many of the Indian states are home to this species.
9. Project Snow Leopard was introduced in India by the Project Snow Leopard Committee instituted by the Ministry of Environment and Forests, Government of India, in the year 2009 to safeguard and conserve India's unique natural heritage of high-altitude wildlife populations and their habitats by promoting conservation through participatory policies and actions.

3. (i) (a) visualise

(ii)

Error	Correction
are	were

(iii) Mahi's mother said to her that honesty is the best policy.

(iv) am writing

(v) Rahul asked Saba if he knew that Ranjit had met with an accident and was hospitalised.

(vi) (b)

Error	Correction
accused	excuse

(vii) (a) that he could not study

(viii)

Error	Correction
know	knows

(ix) had been too late

(x) (a) should

(xi) (a) should

(xii) he couldn't even think of relaxing as he has lots of homework to do

4. A. Anand Niketan
Agra

16th March, 20XX

The Editor
The Heritage
Agra

Subject Increasing Incidents of Mobile and Chain Snatching

Sir/Ma'am

Through the columns of your esteemed daily, I want to draw the attention of the concerned authorities towards the rise in cases of mobile and chain snatching in Anand Niketan area of Agra. The residents of the locality are frequently becoming the victims of mobile and chain snatchers. Masked youth come on motorbikes, commit the crime and run away without being caught or traced.

Repeated complaints have been lodged by the victims but to no avail. The officials just give assurance but nothing has been done so far to control the situation. It has caused a lot of insecurity and fear among the residents. The absence of law and order in the town has been making the culprits bolder. Hence, we need to make sure that the area is safe for one and all. Constant vigilance and stricter punishment can help reduce the crime.

I hope this letter would make the concerned authorities aware and the situation will be very soon under control.

Thanking you

Yours sincerely
Shweta Kapoor
(Secretary, RWA)

Or B. Hostel Number XX
Dehradun

10th August, 20XX

Accommodation Officer
ABC University
Dehradun

Subject Problems with roommate

Sir/Ma'am

This is to bring to your kind notice that I, Aisha Khurana, live in room F-202, which is shared with another student. I am writing this letter to notify you of my concerns about my current roommate, who is making my stay in the college hostel difficult. I am having unavoidable and unmanageable problems due to her activities and those are impacting my study badly.

My previous housemate was rational, extremely cooperative and inclined to studies. However, my present roommate is a completely opposite. She is always throwing parties in the room without any prior information. She also plays loud music in the late hours. She is two years senior to me and I cannot protest her irrational behaviours due to which my studies are being hampered.

My semester final is approaching and I would like you to shift either me or my roommate to another room. I do not mind the room type as long as it is quiet and favourable for studies.

Thanking you

Yours faithfully
Aisha Khurana

5. A. The given bar chart shows the scores of three teams, A, B and C in four consecutive seasons of a game. It is evident from the chart that Team B scored far higher than the other two teams over the seasons, though their score decreased as a whole over the period. In 2002, the score of Team B far exceeded that of the other two teams, standing at 82 points compared to only 10 for Team C and 5 for Team A. Over the next two years, the points for Team B decreased, dropping to 43 by 2004. However, they still remained above the points for the other teams. In contrast, though team A and C's points were lower, they were rising. Team A's points had increased by 600% from 2002 to reach 35 points by 2004, nearly equal to Team B. Team C, meanwhile had managed only a small increase over this time. In the final year, Team B remained ahead of the others as their points increased again to 55, while Team A and C saw their point scores reverse and drop to 8 and 5, respectively.

Or

B. The table shows the amount of household income that five countries in Europe spend per month on four items. Overall, it is evident that all five countries spend the majority of their income on food and drink, and housing but much less on clothing and entertainment. Housing is the largest expenditure item for France, Germany and the UK, with all of them spending around one-third of their income on this, at 31%, 33% and 37%, respectively. In contrast, they spend around a quarter on food and drink. However, this pattern is reversed for Turkey and Spain, wherein people spend around a fifth of their income on housing but approximately one-third on food and drink. All five countries spend much less on the remaining two items. For clothing, France and Spain spend less than 10%, while the other three countries spend around the same amount, ranging between 11% and 15%. At 19%, Germany spends the most on entertainment, whereas UK and Turkey spend approximately half this amount, with France and Spain's spending between those other three countries.

6. A. (i) (c) Speech

(ii) The speaker, Nelson Mandela, appears compassionate and empathetic towards the cause of the freedom fighters. He is also very humble about his actions and achievements. He knows the struggles his countrymen had faced and is dedicated towards making his nation a safe place for everyone.

(iii) the inconceivable

(iv) (c) African patriots

Or

B. (i) Mr. Weiherer considered Richard to be a hard worker because he put in three or four hours at night doing debate research besides doing all his research with butterflies and his other interests.

(ii) (d) A comment (iii) (d) Both (a) and (b)

(iv) Richard was not interested in winning for winning's sake or winning to get a prize. Rather, he was winning because he wanted to do the best job he could.

7. A. (i) The poet's day had been rather gloomy, dull and hopeless. He had a feeling that the whole day would go waste. However, the falling of fine dust of snow on him suddenly changes his mood. It cheered his depressed spirits. He felt as if he had saved some part of the day.

(ii) Falling of snow

(iii) The poet's mood has changed from sadness to happiness.

(iv) (c)

Or

B. (i) 'He' is a tiger who is caged in a zoo. He is staring at the stars with hope that one day he will be free of his cage and with sadness that he is still locked up in a cage.

(ii) hopeful

(iii) The purpose of patrolling cars is to check for any problems and to make sure that all animals are sleeping peacefully.

(iv) (a) 1, 2 and 3

8. (i) According to the poet 'fire' represents 'desire' and 'ice' represents 'hatred'. I agree with the poet as both have the capability of destroying life. Desire like fire spreads and hatred fills one's whole life with poison ultimately leading to death and destruction.

(ii) Anne's statement that no one could understand her intensity of love for her grandma tells that she loved her grandmother a lot. Moreover, the touching gesture of lighting one candle for her grandmother during Anne's birthday is also a touching reminder of her love for her grandmother.

(iii) Assam has the largest concentration of tea plantations in the world. Hence, the view of the tea estates of Assam is truly majestic. One can see large groups of women with bamboo baskets on their backs, who pluck the newly sprouted tea leaves from the plants and store them in the baskets.

(iv) When Maxwell decided to transport Mijbil to England, Mijbil was kept into a box. He tore off the box and wounded himself. Then, Mijbil disappeared down the aircraft, terrorising the other passengers. After that, he settled on Maxwell's knee and was no further inconvenience to others.

(v) Once the baker reached a house, he would first greet the lady of the house by saying 'Good Morning'. He would then place the basket on the vertical bamboo and deliver the loaves to the servant.

9. (i) After many years one day, Matilda met Madame Forestier who was surprised to see the change in Matilda. Matilda told her that it was all due to her necklace. Then, Madame Forestier told Matilda that her necklace was false and cheap. That is how Matilda came to know the reality of the diamond necklace.

(ii) Other than science, Richard Ebright was interested in collecting rocks, coins and fossils and was also interested in star-grazing and astronomy. He was also a good debater, canoeist and expert photographer. Mr. Weiherer felt that Richard not only was interested in his experiments but also kept his mind open for other things and put in that extra effort to attain success.

(iii) Bholi did not want to go to school because she did not know anything about school. She became frightened as their old cow, Lakshmi had been brought out of the house and sold away. She felt that something similar was going to happen to her.

10. A. Tuesday, 10th May, 1994 10 p.m.

Dear Diary

Today, when I am the President of South Africa, I can't help recalling Robert Frost's 'Fire and Ice'.

My countrymen faced oppression and adversities caused by both desire and hatred. We have been the victims of such cruelty and torture that even thinking about it terrifies me. The people of South Africa spent fifty years in the struggle against discrimination based on the colour of skin.

Today, when we have gained freedom, it is like our world has gained life. Till now we were not alive because our freedom had been snatched away from us. I agree with Robert Frost's view that both Fire and Ice can destroy the world.

However, I feel that ice is stronger than fire, hatred can cause much more destruction as compared to greed. Yet,

I don't hope any destruction for anyone because I know that the world can be saved with love and peace.

Nelson

Or

B. Valli posed to be very confident in front of the conductor when he offered her help to ride the bus. This shows her confidence, intelligence and careful nature. However, when everybody laughed at her, she felt shy. This shows that even though she was confident, she was innocent too. Being aware of that fact that she was travelling for the first time, she was taking every precaution not to be fooled by anybody.

Although she should not have travelled alone, it was wise on her part to behave confidently. Sometimes, situations arise when a child has to travel or live alone. In such a situation, it is necessary for children to get training in order to be self-confident. She teaches us to be confident, compassionate and sympathetic towards others.

11. A. It is true to say that over-pampering by Mrs. Pumphrey was the main reason behind Tricki's ailment. She fed him thrice a day or even more with fatty foods such as chocolates, creamcakes etc. All this over-feeding made Tricki inactive, fat, unhealthy and listless. He indulged in no physical activity at all. Whenever he became slow, he was given more to eat. This led to his serious ailment.

In our attempt to show our love, we sometimes tend to cause more harm than good. The same thing happened with Mrs. Pumphrey. She had a great fondness for the dog and hence, overfed him. She forgot that excess of everything is bad and made him sick by overfeeding him. If she had not overfed Tricki, he would have been a healthy and an active pet. In addition, he would not have been hospitalised. Thus, it is because of the over-pampering by Mrs. Pumphrey that Tricki was suffering from a serious ailment.

Or

B. Bholi's teacher is one of the minor but the most important characters in the lesson titled Bholi. She is a generous lady who has a good heart and a wise mind. We first come across her on the first day of Bholi's school. Unlike everyone else that Bholi had come across, she treated Bholi with kindness, love and compassion. She patiently helped Bholi and encourages her to learn. She is a warm hearted lady who gave the deserved attention to the little girl.

The presence of such a kind teacher affected Bholi deeply. She gained interest in learning and thus proved her teacher to be true by becoming one of the most educated person in her village. It was because of her teacher that Bholi could understand her rights and become confident as well as bold enough to raise her voice against any injustice.

Sample Question Paper 2 (Solved)

A Highly Simulated Sample Question Paper for CBSE Class X

English Language and Literature

Time : 3 hrs	M.M. : 80

General Instructions

1 This question paper comprises 11 questions, All questions are compulsory.

2 The question paper contains three sections

Section A : Reading Skills

Section B : Grammar and Creative Writing Skills

Section C : Literature

3 Attempt questions based on specific instructions for each part .

Section – A (Reading Skills) (20 Marks)

1. Read the following passage carefully. **(10)**

1. Even international students whose first language is English can find themselves struggling to understand an alien academic culture. The problems are very familiar. Students' first problem is often with listening skills. They may feel nervous about this and it is certainly a steep learning curve. They need a structured listening experience, for instance how to pick out the main ideas. They also need help with academic reading – how to approach an article or book, how to skim, read and make notes.
2. However, while a student's confidence in listening skills grows, it is in the area of academic writing where more serious cultural differences become apparent. Much of British education is based on essay writing, but this may be a demanding task for students from other cultures. Suddenly, they are faced with the need to express their own ideas, develop their opinions and evaluate different issues, all in polished English. For some, the concept of originating this kind of written discourse can prove problematic and they may find themselves scoring low marks because of plagiarism or reproducing someone else's ideas. In Britain, plagiarism is regarded as academic theft, though this is not always the case in other countries. Students are expected to do research in a library before tackling an assignment and simply regurgitating lecture notes is also not acceptable.
3. The best way to overcome these hurdles is to be prepared. The first step is to take a test to assess the English language skills needed to cope with the issues of academic culture.
4. If an accredited test indicates that a student's language skills are not sufficient to embark on a university degree, the next step is to consider pre-sessional courses, generally at the university where the student will take a degree. These can last from three weeks to an academic year, so it is wise for students to be realistic about their needs. It is generally accepted that approximately 200 hours of study are needed to improve on one bad score on some tests. Some of the new universities that formed from polytechnics in 1992 are experimenting with new styles of pre-sessional and foundation courses. Elspeth Jones, Director of the Centre for Language Study at Leeds Metropolitan University explains, "Our courses are monthly and so students from parts of the world with a different academic year can enrol at any time."
5. She feels that language training in new universities is generally more flexible than in older institutions. "Universities like ours can take students with lower language test grades and can put them through a programme that will bring them up to the required standard, though we cannot guarantee how long it will take."

Based on your understanding of the passage, answer the following questions.

1. **What does the writer project with reference to the following?** **(1)**

   Much of British education is based on essay writing, but this may be a demanding task for students from other cultures.

2. **Complete the sentence appropriately.**
   Essay writing is a demanding task because .... **(1)**
   (a) one needs to develop ideas and evaluate issues in polished English
   (b) one needs to research in the library

3. **What according to the author causes international students to score low marks? State any one reason in about 40 words.** **(2)**

4. **Identify the words/phrases that incorrectly state the meaning of 'accredited' as used in the passage.** **(1)**
   (a) Officially recognised or authorised
   (b) To give an appointment

5. **State whether the following statement is True or False with reference to the given extract.**
   British education is primarily based on playground activities. **(1)**

6. **What does academic writing include?** **(1)**
   (a) How to approach an article
   (b) How to read a work
   (c) How to make notes
   (d) All of these

7. **Based on your reading of the text, list any 1 benefit of pre-sessional courses in about 40 words.** **(2)**

8. **Which of the following will be the most appropriate title for the passage?** **(1)**
   (a) Overcoming Language Hurdles
   (b) Language Training
   (c) British English- Ways to Cope
   (d) Emergence of New Kinds of Courses

2. Read the following passage carefully. **(10)**

1. Right from literacy, accessibility to schools and household expenditure on education, the rural-urban gap remains significant. There is a digital divide, too, with just 4% of rural households having access to computers as compared to 23% in urban areas. These and other trends on a rural-urban gap in education are revealed in the details of a survey conducted by the National Statistical Office (NSO).
2. The report on 'Household Social Consumption: Education' surveyed 1.13 lakh households spread across over 8,000 villages and 6,000 urban blocks between July 2017 and June 2018. The study involved 1.52 lakh students across different levels of study.
3. On accessibility, while 92.7% of the rural households have a primary school within 1 km as compared to 87.2% in urban areas, the situation gets skewed as only 38% of the rural households have access to secondary school as compared to 70% in the urban areas on similar parameters.
4. While accessibility to a neighbourhood school at the primary level is not an issue in rural areas, the gross attendance ratio is also satisfactory with nearly 100% of boys and girls in rural as well as urban areas attending classes. However, in sync with reduced accessibility, there is a gap at the secondary level between rural and urban settings. The all-Indian literacy rate among persons aged 7 years and above is 77.7%. However, for the same age group, rural literacy is 73.5% and for urban areas, it is, 87.7%.
5. The digital divide between rural and urban households is stark with just 4% of the rural population having access to computers. The report highlighted that while only 15% surveyed population in the rural cluster has internet access, 42% of the students in the urban areas have access to the internet.
6. At the school level while the majority of the urban households had shown a preference for private schools, it's the opposite for rural households. The report highlights that 76.1% of the rural children are attending a primary and middle school run by the government, while only 38% of the urban children attend government schools. However, for graduate and above studies, 49.7% of rural students are attending classes in government institutions as compared to 41% of their urban counterparts in government institutions.

Based on your understanding of the passage, answer the following questions.

1. **Based on your understanding of the passage, choose the option that lists the factors that indicate the rural-urban gap.** **(1)**

   (a) Right to literacy (b) Accessibility to schools (c) Employment opportunities (d) All of these

2. **Select the option that is true for the assertion and reason given below.** **(1)**

   Assertion (A) The rural-urban gap is a result of imbalanced household expenditure.

   Reason (R) Digital divide is a direct part of rural-urban divide.

   (a) Both the (A) and (R) are true, and (R) is the correct explanation of (A).
   (b) Both the (A) and reason are true, but (R) is not the correct explanation of (A).
   (c) (A) is true, but (R) is false.
   (d) (A) is false, but (R) is true.

3. **What did the survey conducted by the NSO cover?** **(1)**

4. **What data shows that the rural-urban gap is visible at the secondary level of education?** **(2)**

5. **Fill in the blanks with the appropriate option from those given in the brackets, based on your understanding of passage.** **(1)**

   Rural areas have .... (more/less) primary schools .... (within/without) a km as compared to that in urban areas.

6. **In which aspect is the condition of education in the urban and rural households equal?** **(1)**

7. **Complete the analogy correctly with a word/phrase from the passage.** **(1)**

   Illiteracy : Literacy : : .... : Urban

8. **Fill in the blank by selecting the correct option.** **(1)**

   The majority of urban households show preference to ....

9. **What did the 'Household Social Consumption: Education' survey found out?** **(1)**

Section – B (Grammar) **(20 Marks)**

3. **Complete any *ten* of twelve of the following questions, as directed.** **(10)**

   (i) Fill in the blanks by choosing the correct option to complete the online update. **(1)**

   The coronavirus lockdown .... us to live our lives, not just plan to live them.

   (a) has taught (b) had taught (c) will teach (d) teach

   (ii) Identify the error and supply the correction in the sentence. **(1)**

   "No person ought smoke in any public place provided that in a hotel having thirty rooms provision for a smoking area may be made."

   Sameer The bacteria is very small, that's why you can't see the diagram.

   Use the given format for your response.

Error	Correction

(iii) Chetan asked Sneha about her work from home. Report Chetan's question. (1)

Do you work from home?

(iv) Fill in the blank by using the correct form of the word in the bracket, for the given portion of the letter. (1)

Subject Request for approval

Dear Mr. Green

I am .... (send) this request for your approval of our marketing proposal for our next project. The team and I have created a detailed plan that I've attached to this email.

(v) Report the dialogue between Garima and Karan, by completing the sentence. (1)

Garima So, after a decade in the industry, are you truly 'satisfied'?

Karan I love the film industry. It has its flaws though.

Garima asked Karan if after a decade in the industry ....

(vi) Select the option that identifies the error and supplies the correction for the following line.

When the girls on the team got to the hotel, they dropped off her luggage. (1)

Option No.	Error	Correction
(a)	girls	girl
(b)	her	their
(c)	the	a
(d)	team	teams

(vii) Complete the given narrative by filling in the blank with the correct option. (1)

He .... down the road, towards the harbour and the dead end, the industrial buildings laid low by the unexpected weight of late summer Sun.

(a) looked (b) looking (c) looks (d) was looking

(viii) Identify the error in the given sentence taken from a report online. (1)

The percentage of employees who called in sick and the number of employees who left their jobs within 2 years is reflective of the level of job satisfaction.

Error	Correction

(ix) Select the correct option to complete the narration of the dialogue given below. (1)

Doctor How do you feel now?

Patient Slightly better.

Doctor Did you take the medicines regularly?

Patient Yes.

The doctor asked the patient how he felt then. The patient replied he felt slightly better. When the doctor asked him if .... the medicines regularly, he replied in affirmation.

(x) Fill in the blank by choosing the correct option, to complete the notice written on the road. (1)

You .... follow the traffic rules.

(a) should (b) shall (c) must (d) can

(xi) Read the conversation between the Biology teacher and Sameer. (1)

Biology Teacher I instructed you to draw the diagram of bacteria. Why did you submit a blank sheet?

Sameer The bacteria is very small, that's why you can't see the diagram.

Select the option to complete the reporting of the above dialogue.

The biology teacher asked Sameer why he had submitted a blank sheet. Sameer calmly expalined that .... but it was too small to see.

(a) he had drawn the diagram
(b) he could not draw the diagram
(c) he was drawing the diagram
(d) he will draw the digaram

(xii) Report the dialogue. **(1)**

Mother Rita, finish your food.

Mother told Rita ....

Creative Writing Skills **(10 Marks)**

Note : All details presented in the questions are imaginary and created for assessment purpose.

4. Attempt any *one* from (A) and (B) given below. **(5)**

A. You have recently had an ear surgery and are on rest period. Some construction work had started by your neighbour while you were away. The noise from the work is loud and it disturbs you. You had tried to tell them to postpone the work for sometime but with no avail. Write to the housing president regarding the situation. You are Akshat/Akshara. (100-120 words).

Or **B. You want to spend a week-long holiday at Shimla in the month of October. You have decided to stay at Hotel Snow View. Write a letter in 100-120 words to the manager to book a room. Mention the dates, facilities in the room, food, sightseeing facilities, etc. you will need. You are Amar/ Amrita Maheshwari of M-114, Lake Road, Karnal.**

5. Attempt any *one* from (A) and (B) given below. **(5)**

A. The chart shows Indian students travelling to foreign destination for further studies to selected destinations between 2014 and 2017. Write an analytical paragraph on the given data in about 100-120 words.

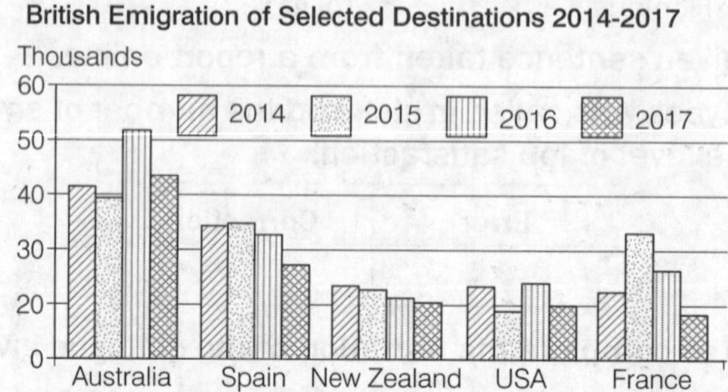

Or **B. The graph below shows how people buy music. Analyse the given data and write an analytical paragraph in 100-120 words.**

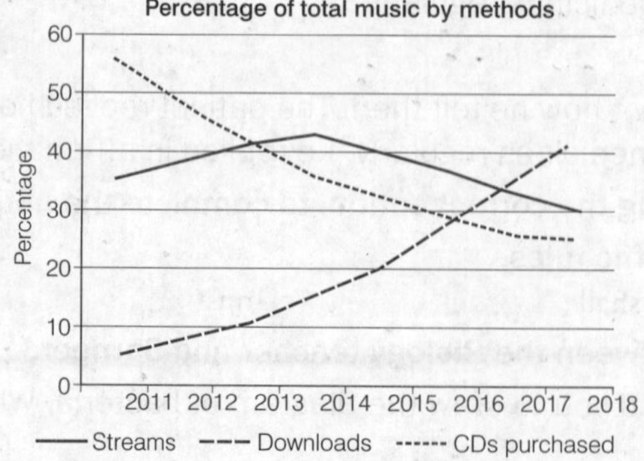

Section – C (Literature Textbook) **(40 Marks)**

6. Read the given extracts and answer the questions for any *one* of the given two, (A) or (B). **(5)**

A. All through the night, Lencho thought only of his one hope: the help of God, whose eyes, as he had been instructed, see everything, even what is deep in one's conscience. Lencho was an ox of a man, working like an animal in the fields, but still he knew how to write. (A Letter to God)

(i) How is Lencho feeling when he remembers God?

(a) Holy (b) Desperate (c) Shallow (d) Angry

(ii) 'He knew how to write.' What is the significance of this line? **(2)**

(iii) Fill in the blank with a word from the bracket. **(1)**

Lencho was a .... (lazy/diligent) farmer and a deeply religious man.

(iv) Mention the only hope that Lencho had. **(1)**

Or

B. LOMOV Hear me out, I implore you! The peasants of your father's grandfather, as I have already had the honour of explaining to you, used to bake bricks for my aunt's grandmother. Now my aunt's grandmother, wishing to make them a present.

NATALYA I can't make head or tail of all this about aunts and grandfathers and grandmothers. The Meadows are ours, that's all.

LOMOV Minc.

NATALYA Ours! You can go on proving it for two days on end, you can go and put on fifteen dress jackets, but I tell you they're ours, ours, ours! I don't want anything of yours and I don't want to give anything of mine. So there! (The Proposal)

(i) Read the following descriptions (a)-(c) and identify which one correctly corresponds to the extract. **(1)**

(a) An argument is an exchange of diverging or opposite views, typically a heated or angry one.

(b) A soliloquy is a speech given by a character alone on stage, which reveals their innermost thoughts and feelings to the audience.

(c) An aside is a brief comment or remark made by a character directly to the audience, which is not intended to be heard by other characters on stage.

(d) A propaganda wherein the speakers try others to accep their point.

(ii) What was Natalya adamant about? What effect did this have on Lomov? Answer in about 40 words. **(2)**

(iii) Which word from the extract is an antonym of 'aristocrat'? **(1)**

(iv) What did Lomov forget in the midst of the argument? **(1)**

7. Read the given extracts and answer the questions for any *one* of the given two, (A) or (B). **(1)**

A. Belinda embraced him, Mustard licked him,
No one mourned for his pirate victim.
Ink and Blink in glee did gyrate
Around the dragon that ate the pirate.

(The Tale of Custard the Dragon)

(i) Why did no one mourn the dragon's pirate victim? **(1)**

(ii) Fill in the blank. **(1)**

.... does not indicate the happiness felt by everyone.

(iii) **Why did Belinda embrace her pet? Answer in about 40 words.** **(2)**

(iv) **What is the rhymxe scheme of the given lines?** **(1)**

(a) aabb (b) abcc (c) abab (d) abca

Or

B.

Don't eat that chocolate Amanda!
Remember your acne, Amanda!
Will you please look at me when
I'm speaking to you, Amanda!

(Amanda!)

(i) The speaker is so worried about acne. What does it show? **(1)**

(ii) Complete the sentence appropriately. **(1)**

Amanda is not looking at the speaker because she is ....

(a) daydreaming (b) painting
(c) singing (d) sleeping

(iii) Why is Amanda not looking at the speaker? Answer in about 40 words. **(2)**

(iv) Identify the poetic device used in the poem and discuss its importance? **(1)**

8. Answer any *four* of the following questions in 40-50 words each. **(4 × 3 = 12)**

(i) What does Anne Frank write about her family in her diary? (From the Diary of Anne Frank)

(ii) What did the Buddha do after he had attained enlightenment? Why? (The Sermon of Benares)

(iii) Write the message given by the poet of the poem 'Fire and Ice'.

(iv) Assess Anne's views on external beauty? (For Anne Gregory)

(v) Describe Coorg's weather. When is it most pleasant for the tourist to visit Coorg? (Coorg)

9. Answer any *two* of the following questions in 40-50 words each. **(2 × 3 = 6)**

(i) What was Loisel's reaction to his wife's desire for a new dress? (The Necklace)

(ii) What was Fowler's perception about a secret agent? (The Midnight Visitor)

(iii) What was Tricki's ailment? How did it worry Mrs. Pumphrey? (A Trumph of Surgery)

10. Answer any *one* of the following questions in 100-120 words. **(1 × 6 = 6)**

A. "The narrator knew that he could not fly up due to storm and lack of fuel but still he continued." What do you gather about the narrator from the above lines?

Or

B. Do you think Chubukov is a good father? Justify your opinion based on your reading of the text.

11. Answer any *one* of the following questions in 100-120 words. **(1 × 6 = 6)**

A. "She suffered incessantly, feeling herself born for all delicacies and luxuries. She suffered from the poverty of her apartment, the shabby walls and the worn chairs. All these things tortured and angered her."

It was Mme Loisel's disposition that invites her doom. Comment.

Or

B. "Money can't make a man as much as education can." Elaborate the line with reference to 'The Thief's Story'.

Answers

1. 1. Concern
2. Both (a) and (b) one needs to develop ideas and evaluate issues in polished English and one needs to research in the library
3. British education is focused on essay writing. International students who are not accustomed to essay writing then find it difficult to assess, create and formulate their ideas and opinions. They plagiarise thus, end up scoring low marks.
4. (a) Officially recognised or authorised
5. False
6. (d) All of these
7. Pre-sessional courses assess and prepare the students who find difficulty in their ongoing courses. They equip them with the necessary skills needed for their course.
8. (b) Language Training

2. 1. (d) All of these
2. (d) (A) is false, but (R) is truc.
3. The survey covered over 8,000 rural and 6,000 urban households.
4. The facts that, only 38% households of in rural areas have access to secondary schools and more than 70% of households in urban areas have access to secondary schools, shows that the rural-urban gap is visible at the secondary level of education.
5. more, within
6. The condition of education in the urban and rural households equal on the accessibility of primary schools.
7. Rural
8. private schools
9. 'Household Social Consumption: Education' Survey found out that there is a stark divide in the secondary education received by children vis-a-vis rural-urban divide.

3. (i) (a) has taught

(ii)

Error	Correction
Ought	Shall

(iii) He asked me if I worked from home.

(iv) sending

(v) he was truly 'satisfied'. Karan told her that he loved the film industry although it had its flaws.

(vi) (b)

Error	Correction
her	their

(vii) (a) looked

(viii)

Error	Correction
is	are

(ix) (a) he had taken

(x) (a) should

(xi) (a) he had drawn the digaram

(xii) to finish her food

4. A. B-35, Anna Complex
Kerala
23rd March, 20XX
The Housing President
Anna Complex
Kerala
Subject Problems with the neighbour.
Sir/Madam
This is to inform you that I, Akshat, am a resident of B-35 Anna Complex. I have written this letter to tell you about the uncomfortable and sometimes unbearable noise which keeps coming from the ongoing construction work at my neighbour's house.
At other situation, the construction work would have not been as much an issue of problem. However, this time, my situation is such that it cannot be ignored. I recently had an ear surgery which required me to take rest and be away from noise.
The noise of their construction work is very loud and is hampering my recovery. I had tried to tell them to postpone their construction till my recovery time but they refused to cooperate.
Therefore, I would like to request you to interfere in the matter and ask them to postpone the construction work till 15th April so that I can recover properly.
Thanking You
Yours faithfully
Akshat

Or

B. M-114
Lake Road
Karnal
Haryana
14th August, 20XX

The Manager
Hotel Snow View
Shimla

Subject Enquiry about facilities at Hotel Snow View

Sir/Ma'am

This is in reference to an e-advertisement that I saw on the internet. I have written this mail regarding to stay at your hotel. I am coming to Shimla for a week. For the same, I shall be grateful if you could book a room for me from 10th October, 20XX to 17th October, 20XX. I would also appreciate if the room is sun – facing and has a good overview of the place. My food preference is vegetarian and I would love to go for sightseeing every day, if you could arrange a car for me at reasonable rates.

I am sure my stay would be made comfortable and memorable. Please let me know the total cost, including the transport charges.

Looking forward to an early reply!

Thanking you

Yours faithfully

Amar/Amrita Maheshwari

5. A. Brain drain is not a new concept. Every year during the times of admissions, thousands of students leave the country to pursue higher education in foreign nationalities. The bar chart shows the number of Indian students who emigrated to five destinations over the period 2014 to 2017. It is evident from the chart that throughout the period, the most popular place to move to was Australia. Emigration to Australia stood at just over 40,000 people in 2014, which was approximately 6,000 higher than for Spain and twice as high as the other three countries. Apart from a jump to around 52,000 in 2016, it remained around this level throughout the period. The next most popular country to move to was Spain, though its popularity declined over the time frame to finish at below 30,000 in 2017. Despite this, the figure was still higher than for the remaining three countries. Approximately 20,000 people emigrated to New Zealand each year, while the USA fluctuated between 20-25,000 people over the period. Although the number of visitors to France spiked to nearly 35,000 in 2015, it was the country that was the least popular to emigrate to at the end of the period, at just under 20,000 people. The number however, still remains in thousands.

Or

B. In this busy and crowded world, music has become an agency for us to be happy and relaxed. Its importance is very well depicted by the new music and new applications for music streaming being introduced everyday. The given graph illustrates the trends in music buying habits between 2011 and 2018. The data presents three different methods of buying music: streaming, downloading and buying CDs. Overall, both downloads and physical sales of music have steadily declined. The latter has slumped since 2011, while the downturn for the former began in 2014. However, there has been a sharp rise in people streaming music since 2013. In 2011, the majority of music sales were of CDs, at 55% of all sales. In contrast, streaming was not common at all. Also, although people had started to download music, it only represented 35% of sales. As sales of CDs began to fall, the era of downloads began. Downloading soon overtook physical sales in mid-2013. During the same period, with newer technology streaming doubled to 10% and started to grow more dramatically.

6. A. (i) (b) Desperate

(ii) The given line indicates that Lencho was educated and that he was going to write a letter to God.

(iii) diligent

(iv) God was the only hope Lencho had.

Or

B. (i) (a) An argument is an exchange of diverging or opposite views, typically a heated or angry one.

(ii) Natalya was adamant that Oxen Meadows was hers. This not only irritated Lomov as he believed in his right on the Meadows but also aggravated and excited him to the point of having a verbal fight.

(iii) Peasant

(iv) Lomov forgot about marriage proposal for Natalya in the midst of the argument.

7. A. (i) No one mourned the dragon's pirate victim because he came with the intention of hurting them and the dragon saved them all.

(ii) Mourned

(iii) Belinda embraced Custard, her pet, because he saved everyone's life from the pirate.

(iv) (b) abcc

Or

B. (i) It shows importance is given to physical beauty.

(ii) (a) daydreaming

(iii) Amanda is not looking at the speaker because she is lost in her thoughts and is thus not paying attention to the instructions.

(iv) The poetic device used in the poem is refrain. The repetition of 'Amanda!' serves to emphasise the speaker's frustration with the listener.

8. (i) Anne Frank writes that she has very lovely and caring family. Her parents and her elder sister love her a lot. There are about thirty people nearby her whom she can call her friends. She has loving aunts and a good home but she wants to have a true friend with whom she can share feelings and thoughts.

(ii) Buddha attained enlightenment after meditating for seven days under a big tree. As he got wisdom under that tree, he called it the Bodhi Tree. He decided to share his understandings and preachings with people so that he can make them free from their sorrows.

(iii) The message that the poet is trying to give through 'Fire and Ice' is that nothing in this world is eternal. The poet first concludes that the world must end in fire after considering his personal experience with desire and passion, the emotions of fire. However, at the same time, ice or hatred can also bring total destruction to this world. We should thus, not forget this supreme reality and keep ourselves away from all selfish matters.

(iv) Anne does not believe in external beauty and wants to be loved for herself. She says that her beautiful hair that attract so many men can be changed and coloured differently. This shows that Anne thinks that external beauty is not important as it is changeable.

(v) Coorg receives heavy rainfall during monsoon.The weather of Coorg is pleasant for tourists during months from September to March. At this time, the smell of coffee is spread all around.

9. (i) The Loisels had been invited to a party at the Minister's residence. When Matilda told her husband that she wanted a new dress to wear, first of all he asked her to wear whatever she possessed. When she got angry and refused to go to the party at all, he finally agreed to let her buy a new dress.

(ii) Fowler had a romantic perception about a secret agent. He used to think that a secret agent should be tall and handsome. He should deal with a dangerous situation. His life should be full of thrill and action. He should receive messages from mysterious beautiful woman and be surrounded by mysterious figures.

(iii) Mrs Pumphrey gave Tricki little extra between meals, i.e. malt, cod-liver oil, etc. He was not given any physical exercise. This was the reason for Tricki's ailment. It made Mrs Pumphrey so much worried that she had to call the veterinary surgeon, Dr Herriot for his treatment.

10. A. The narrator of the chapter 'The Black Aeroplane' was stuck in a situation wherein even though his plane did not have enough fuel, he did not lose hope. He knew that he could not fly up nor he could fly around the clouds due to the paucity of fuel. Yet, he decided to take a risk and entered his plane into the clouds because he wanted to visit his family at breakfast. This shows him to be a courageous and a family loving person. Even though he knew that it was risky to enter the cloud, he did so to save his fuel.

However, his decision could have landed him in deep trouble if the pilot of the strange black aeroplane had not helped him to safety. So, at the control tower he specifically went to thank the person who helped him out of a difficult situation. This shows him to be a grateful person too.

Or

B. No, I do not believe that Chubkov is a good father. The following points justify my opinion.

(i) He says to Natalya "Go, there's a merchant come for his goods". This line indicates that he considers his daughter to be a commodity to be sold off in an economically good deal.

(ii) He further laments that it is 'a burden to be the father of a grown-up daughter'. This dialogue suggests a misogynistic worldview.

(iii) Even though there are plenty of evidences to suggest that Lomov is physically ill and on the verge of dying. Chubukov still marries off his daughter to Lomov. He does so to uphold his prestige in society but doesn't pause to think about the consequences of marrying his daughter to an unhealthy man who may soon die.

(iv) When Lomov falls unconscious and everyone assumes that he is dead, Chubukov laments

Lomov's death; not because he is sad of Lomov's dying, but because it' had'nt mean that his daughter would not be able to marry anymore. Then, he dramatically asks for a pistol or a knife so that he may kill himself instead of living with the burden of an unwed daughter.

11. A. It is truly said that Mme Loisel herself invited her doom. Mme Loisel belongs to a family of clerks. Her existence is quite average. They live on meager income, enough for basic needs, but not to fulfill her aspirations. Mme Loisel is so caught up with her dreams of wealth and pleasure that she is out of touch with the truths of her real life. In order to keep up appearances just to flatter her pride, she spends four hundred francs on a gorgeous dress. Still not contented, she goes on borrowing a necklace from her friend. All of this is just to impress the wealthy and the rich with her beauty and glamour. At the party, her pride is flattered and her wish of fine dining, expensive dresses and jewels is satisfied. However, her satisfaction comes at a great price. Unfortunately, the necklace was lost and the couple had to give up their entire inheritance and borrow as well to replace it. It took the Loisel's 10 years to repay the debt. In those ten years, they lived a life of poverty and hardship. She lost the little luxury that she had. If Mme Loisel been satisfied with what she had, she might have lived a better life with her husband.

Or

B. 'Money cannot make a man as much as education can' holds absolutely true. However, one focuses more on money as it can buy all the luxuries and needs of life. Yet, it is not enough to buy knowledge, civilised thinking, skills and abilities. Education allows one to keep up with the fast moving world and lays platform for all to work upon one's goals. The importance of education is aptly proven in the story 'The Thief's Story' wherein a thief pretends to be Hari Singh to rob a kind and an honest fellow Anil. Anil, who is a struggling writer slowly starts educating Hari Singh while the latter is waiting for the right opportunity to rob Anil. After stealing the money, Hari plans to go away forever but cannot as he desires a life of respect which he could get if he stays under Anil. He prioritises being literate over a certain amount of money. His decision to go back to Anil driven by the realisation that Anil could change the course of Hari's life by educating him. Hari realises that he could earn a respectable living if he is properly educated Thus, education will always be above money.

Sample Question Paper 3 (Unsolved)

A Highly Simulated Sample Question Paper for CBSE Class X

English Language and Literature

Time : 3 hrs M.M. : 80

General Instructions

1 This question paper comprises 11 questions, All questions are compulsory.

2 The question paper contains three sections

Section A : Reading Skills

Section B : Grammar and Creative Writing Skills

Section C : Literature

3 Attempt questions based on specific instructions for each part.

Section – A (Reading Skills) (20 Marks)

1. Read the following passage carefully. **(10)**

1. Corruption, terrorism, communalism, greed for power and wealth and the list of ailments that affect modern society continues. More than half the population of India is below the age group of 25 and the future of the country will only be bright if youngsters are equipped to deal with these ailments.
2. A child is a storehouse of potential and it is essential to nurture and develop these attributes from a very young age. Since they spend much of their time in school, the curriculum in school should be such that it enables children to understand, care and practise ethical values like respect, justice and civic sense. Education should aim to develop a sense of rights and duties as well as moral values like honesty, responsibility and respect for others.
3. Moral education should be directed towards enhancing a child's ability to critically analyse situations, make decisions, empathise with people and work in cooperation towards a common goal.
4. As a means of direct instruction to students, schools are very influential in the character development of a child and the methods of education affect the development of morally upright citizens who can bring about a much-needed change in the country.
5. The youth of today have to face many problems like drug abuse, violent behaviour and family issues. If they are not taught morals, they would fail to differentiate between good and bad values. Hence, they would be incapable of dealing with different types of issues.
   A sound moral base would help a child make the right decisions, especially in an era where the youth is increasingly coming under the negative influence of the media.
6. Schools in India have introduced moral education as part of their curriculum because they realise that morally sound citizens are the need of the hour. Since most children look up to their teachers as role models, it is most appropriate that they be the facilitators of moral values.
7. Thus, schools should focus more on the personality development of children since it is one of the most important responsibilities of a school. Schools should take the initiative to mould children into better human beings so that they can make the world a better place to live in.

Based on your understanding of the passage, answer the following questions.

1. **State a solution to the given problem.** **(1)**
   Incapable of differentiating between good and bad, children would be unable to deal with everyday issues.
2. **Complete the sentence appropriately.** **(1)**
   According to the given passage, schools are integral in ....
   (a) making child moral and responsible (b) making a child future ready
3. **Why is it important to inculcate moral values since childhood?** **(2)**
4. **The passage includes some words that are similar in meaning to each other. From the sets (a) - (e) below, identify two sets of antonyms.** **(1)**
   (a) Corruption and terrorism (b) Affect and equipped
   (c) Nurture and develop (d) Youth and youngsters
   (e) Behaviour and values
5. **State whether the following statement is True or False.** **(1)**
   More than half the population of India is above the age group of 25 years.
6. **Select the option that conveys the message, "Morally sound citizens are the need of the hour."** **(1)**
   (a) Government should take major decisions about spreading moral education.
   (b) Better human beings can make the world a better place to live in.
   (c) Developing moral qualities is the only way to solve these social issues.
   (d) Moral citizens can only be possible by giving moral education to the mass population.
7. **Which moral values are important for children to learn?** **(2)**
8. **What kind of problems are being faced by today's youth?** **(1)**
   (a) Drug abuse (b) Family issues (c) Violent behaviour (d) All of these

2. Read the following passage carefully. **(10)**

1. Through the Sustainable Development Goal (SDG), the countries of the world have resolved to achieve universal access to safe drinking water and adequate sanitation and hygiene for all by 2030. The aim is to ensure the consumption of safe drinking water and practice safe sanitation and hygiene, resulting in lower exposure to a contaminated environment, resulting in lower morbidity and mortality, especially amongst children.
2. The Swachh Bharat Mission was launched by the Government of India on 2nd October, 2014 to achieve the vision of 'Swachh Bharat' by 2nd October, 2019. The Swachh Bharat Mission Gramin-SBM (G) endeavours to accelerate rural sanitation coverage, reduce open defecation and improve the management of solid and liquid wastes in rural areas. The implementation of SBM (G) is the responsibility of the Ministry of Drinking Water and Sanitation (MDWS). The MDWS, while issuing guidelines for Open Defecation Free (ODF) verification stressed on "safe technology option which aimed at no contamination of surface soil, groundwater or surface water; excreta management inaccessible to flies or animals; no human handling of fresh excreta and freedom from odour and unsightly condition". Over the past 4 years, over 92 million new households have received access to household toilets and by the end of the SBM (G) programme, all 16.5 million rural households will have such access. However, the issue is of usage and thus, the goal is to create ODF communities and villages, with no one defecating in the open.
3. The status of ODF villages published on the website of MDWS indicates that as of 01.04.2019, over 99% of rural HHs in India have toilet access. The declared ODF villages at all India level accounted for 556,824 spreading over 247,723 Gram Panchayats, 6,031 Blocks and 616 Districts.
4. UNICEF in India accords high priority to the provision of safe sanitation and water services to people in rural areas and has over the past many years aided through catalytic technical support to MDWS, the Government of India and 15 state governments in the implementation of the various sanitation programmes and since 2014, specifically to the SBM (G). With the progress of the SBM (G) and the declaration of ODF communities, there is an emerging question on whether the campaign to eliminate open defecation and create ODF communities is resulting in a decrease in faecal contamination in the environment.

Based on your understanding of the passage, answer the following questions.

1. **Which of the following is not an aim of the Sustainable Development Goal?** **(1)**
   (a) Safe drinking water (b) Adequate hygiene
   (c) Safe Sanitation (d) Primary education
2. **Select the option that is true for the assertion and reason given below.** **(1)**
   Assertion (A) The focus of SDGs is to provide safe drinking water for all.
   Reason (R) Sanitation, hygiene and water conservation are intimately related.
   (a) Both the (A) and (R) are true, and (R) is the correct explanation of (A).
   (b) Both the (A) and (R) are true, but (R) is not the correct explanation of (A).
   (c) (A) is true, but (R) is false.
   (d) (A) is false, but (R) is true.
3. **According to the passage, who is responsible for the progress of the Swachh Bharat Mission?** **(1)**
4. **Infer one reason for the following.** **(1)**
   The government is successful in providing access to toilets to over 99% of rural households.
5. **Fill in the blank by selecting the correct option.** **(1)**
   The purpose of the launch of Swachh Bharat Mission (G) was to ....
   Choose the correct option.
   (a) accelerate rural sanitation coverage
   (b) increase open defecation
   (c) improve management of solid and liquid wastes in urban areas
6. **What does the writer mean by the following.** **(1)**
   "Over the past 4 years, over 92 million new households have received access to household toilets."
7. **Complete the following analogy.** **(1)**
   Swachh Bharat Mission : 2019 :: ....: 2030
8. **Fill in the blank.** **(1)**
   The passage provides data that proves that ....
9. **What is the aim of the SDGs? Answer in reference to the above passage.** **(2)**

Section – B (Grammar) (20 Marks)

3. **Complete any *ten* of twelve of the following questions, as directed.** **(10)**

   (i) Fill in the blank by using the correct form of the word in the bracket, for the given portion of the letter. **(1)**

   Subject Complaint against misbehaviour

   Dear Sir

   This is to respectfully submit that I .... (write) this letter with extreme pain and disgust against the misbehaviour of the government officials in the office.

   (ii) Identify the error in the given sentence and supply the correction. **(1)**

   After using the computer for a long time, looking into a distance for about five minutes relaxed the eyes.

   Use the given format for your response.

Error	Correction

(iii) Shreya shared some information, with Sneha, about the location of post office. Report Shreya's question. **(1)**

Shreya said, "Do you know where the nearest post office is?"

(iv) Fill in the blank by choosing the correct option to complete an online update. **(1)**

The constellation they .... (were/are) going to observe is clearly visible from here.

(v) Report the following conversation. **(1)**

Divya I am planning to buy a car.

Arti Which car do you intend to buy?

Divya I intend to buy the latest model of any popular company.

Divya told Arti that .... Then Arti asked her which car she intended to buy. Divya said that she intended to buy the latest model of any popular company.

(vi) Select the option that identifies the error and supplies the correction for the following line. Today, the number of people who enjoys winter sports is bigger than that of twenty years ago. **(1)**

Option	Error	Correction
A	the	a
B	people	The people
C	enjoys	enjoy
D	is	are

(vii) Complete the given narrative by filling in the blank with the correct option. **(1)**

.... Frank in Toronto?

(a) Did you meet (b) Have you met (c) Were you meeting (d) Will you met

(viii) Identify the error and supply the correction in the sentence. **(1)**

Ananya I will want to order a big pineapple cake for my birthday.

Use the given format for your response.

Error	Correction

(ix) Report the dialogue between Neha and Namita by completing the sentence. **(1)**

Neha I'm really looking forward to the class picnic tomorrow.

Namita Yes, after a long time we will be meeting our friends and teachers.

Neha told Namita that she was really, the next day looking forward to the class picnic. Namita agreed that after a long time ....

(x) Select the correct option to fill in the blank in the given line. **(1)**

He .... wake up early in the morning and go to work.

(a) would (b) will (c) must (d) shall

(xi) Fill in the blank by choosing the correct option to complete the given statement. **(1)**

She .... become the youngest pro soccer player ever.

(a) will (b) may (c) should (d) shall

(xii) Report the given dialogue to complete the paragraph that follows. **(1)**

Swara Hey, Ruchi! How are you? Did you enjoy during the holidays?

Ruchi Yes, I had a lot of fun with my family. We all went to Kerala for ten days and it was an amazing experience.

Swara exclaimed as she met Ruchi and asked her how she was. Further, she asked ....

Creative Writing Skills **(10 Marks)**

Note : All details presented in the questions are imaginary and created for assessment purpose.

4. Attempt any *one* from (A) and (B) given below. **(5)**

A. You recently had your computer fixed at a local computer store; however, you are not pleased with the service you received. Write a letter to the store manager describing your situation by explaining why you are dissatisfied.

Or

B. You are Nitin/Nita of Class X of Army Public Shool, Delhi Cantt. You are among many children of your school who want to have the facility of a good canteen in your school. Write a letter to your school describing the current situation and requesting him to open a good canteen so that students can get good hygiene food in school.

5. Attempt any *one* from (A) and (B) given below. **(5)**

A. Write a paragraph in 100-120 words based on the clue given below.

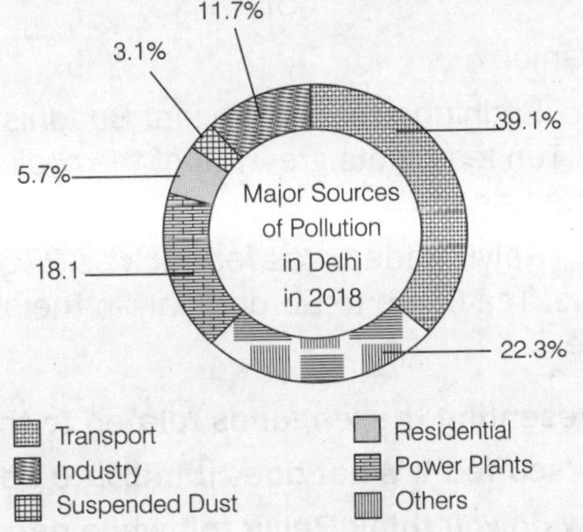

Or

B. Write a paragraph based on the graph that follows (100-120 words).

TRACKING LOCUSTS, OVER THE YEARS

UPSURGE YEARS

Year	Swarm Incursions	'Plague' Years
1964	4	1812-1821
1984	167	1843-1844
1973	6	1863-1867
1974	6	1869-1873
1975	19	1876-1881
1976	2	1889-1891
1978	20	1900-1907
1983	26	1912-1920
1986	3	1926-1930
1989	15	1940-1946
1993	172	1949-1955
1997	4	1959-1962
2019	1500	
2020*	27	

Section – C (Literature Textbook) **(40 Marks)**

6. Read the given extracts and answer the questions for any *one* of the given two, (A) or (B). (5)

A. "Another aeroplane? Up there in this storm? No other aeroplanes were flying tonight. Yours was the only one I could see on the radar". So who helped me to arrive there safely without a compass or a radio and without any more fuel in my tanks? Who was the pilot on the strange black aeroplane, flying in the storm, without lights? (Two Stories About Flying)

(i) What is 'I' feeling in the given lines? (1)

(a) Gloom (b) Relief (c) Confused (d) Agitated

(ii) Why did the narrator desire to meet the pilot of the black aeroplane? Was he able to meet the pilot? (1)

(iii) Which phrase would correctly substitute 'the strange' in the above extract? (2)

(iv) Fill in the blank appropriately. (1)

The other aeroplane had the narrator's .... (mentor/imagination).

Or

B. "Tell me another!" scoffed Pranjol.

"We have an Indian legend too. Bodhidharma, an ancient Buddhist ascetic, cut off his eyelids because he felt sleepy during meditations. Ten tea plants grew out of the eyelids. The leaves of these plants when put in hot water and drunk, banished sleep."

"Tea was first drunk in China," Rajvir added, "as far back as 2700 B.C.! In fact, words such as tea, chai and chini are from the Chinese. Tea came to Europe only in the sixteenth century and was drunk more as medicine than as beverage."

(Tea From Assam)

(i) What is the purpose of presenting the lengends related to the tea. (1)

(ii) Why do you think Pranjol 'scoffed'? What does it indicate about his views on legends? (2)

(iii) Based on this extract, how do you think Rajvir felt while narrating? (1)

(a) (i) excited (ii) agitated (b) (i) hysterical (ii) nervous

(c) (i) nervous (ii) agitated (d) (i) enthusiastic (ii) passionate

(iv) Which word would correctly substitute 'a person luho follows severe self discipline'? (1)

7. Read the given extracts and answer the questions for any *one* of the given two, (A) or (B). (5)

A.

Pistol in his left hand, pistol in his night,
And he held in his teeth a cutlass bright,
His beard was black, one leg was wood
It was clear that he meant no good.

(The Tale of Custard the Dragon)

(i) What does the phrase 'Meant no good' in the extract mean? (2)

(ii) What is 'he' likely to say? (1)

(iii) The poet is likely to .... (threaten/save) Belinda? (1)

(iv) Select the option with the same rhyme scheme as the lines above. (1)

(a) He won
she done
It weighs tone
what you've done?

(b) I live in peace
As I wear fleece
I live in green.
Afraid to be seen

(c) Love live laugh
I can call you duff
You are not what you seem
I want to eat ice cream.

(d) None of the above

Or

B. He should be lurking in shadow,
Sliding through long grass
Near the water hole
Where plump deer pass.

(A Tiger in the Zoo)

(i) What will the tiger do near the water hole? (1)

(ii) Complete the following suitably.

The poet wants that the tiger should be .... (1)

(iii) What does the fact that the tiger is near the water hole from where a deer would pass tell us? (2)

(iv) Identify the poetic device(s) used in the lines above. (1)

1. Alliteration **2. Imagery** **3. Repetition** **4. Irony**

(a) 1 and 2 (b) 3 and 4 (c) 2 and 3 (d) 2 and 4

8. Answer any *four* of the following questions in 40-50 words each. **(4 × 3 = 12)**

(i) Mention any two things that the narrator experienced when he was surrounded by clouds in the lesson, 'The Black Aeroplane'. (Two Stories about Flying)

(ii) Why didn't Valli want to make friends with the elderly woman? (Madam Rides the Bus)

(iii) How is the Coorgi tradition of courage and bravery recognised in Modern India? (Coorg)

(iv) Does Amanda's mother have a nagging behaviour? Justify your Answer. (Amanda!)

(v) Write down the two different views about the end of the world with reference to the poem 'Fire and Ice'.

9. Answer any *two* of the following questions in 40-50 words each. **(2 × 3 = 6)**

(i) Why did Mrs. Hall accept Griffin as a guest despite his strange behaviour? (Footprints without Feet)

(ii) What conditions did Anil put forward before appointing Hari Singh as a servant? (Thief's Story)

(iii) Bholi's heart was overflowing with a 'new hope and a new life'. What does the phrase 'a new hope and a new life' mean to Bholi? (Bholi)

10. Answer any *one* of the following questions in 100-120 words each. **(1 × 6 = 6)**

A. Robert Frost's poems 'Dust of Snow' and 'Fire and Ice' presents the dual qualities of nature. Explain.

Or

B. The principle 'forgive and forget' works to maintain cordial relations with people. Do you think Anton Chekhov gives this message in 'The Proposal'?

11. Answer any *one* of the following question in 100-120 words each. **(1 × 6 = 6)**

A. "Everyone must be given a chance to reform." How did Anil worked upon these values and succeeded. (Thief's Story)

Or

B. Bholi's real name is Sulekha. We are told this in the beginning. But only in the last paragraph of the story is Bholi called Sulekha again. Why do you think she is called Sulekha at the last point in the story? (Bholi)

Sample Question Paper 4 (Unsolved)

A Highly Simulated Sample Question Paper for CBSE Class X

English Language and Literature

Time : 3 hrs M.M. : 80

General Instructions

1 This question paper comprises 11 questions, All questions are compulsory.
2 The question paper contains three sections
 Section A : Reading Skills
 Section B : Grammar and Creative Writing Skills
 Section C : Literature
3 Attempt questions based on specific instructions for each Part .

Section – A (Reading Skills) (20 Marks)

1. Read the following passage carefully. **(10)**

1. The conquest of happiness has meant different facts to different generations. Our forefathers took pride in scholarship, a spirit of sacrifice and solicitude for the welfare of others. Gone are those days. Today we live only for ourselves. We are jealous of the advancement of our neighbours. We end up tense and unhappy.
2. The term 'happy' has a variety of meanings. It stands for the lucky, fortunate, content, glad or apt. Happiness lies within the mind of the individual. No amount of external wealth may be helpful in making him happy.
3. Our forefathers had life styles, very much different from those we have today. Their life was based mainly on the concept of 'Simple living and high thinking.' People were satisfied with whatever they obtained after working hard. Excessive material wealth did not mean much for them. They aimed at deriving mental satisfaction and enrichment from whatever they did.
4. The structural framework of our forefathers' families was different from those of ours. They lived in a cohesive joint family structure where they were happier than we. They cared for each other. The siblings grew up with their cousins. The bond of love which they share cannot be easily found in the nuclear family of the day. The family provided an emotional cushioning effect against tension and stress. However, in the nuclear family, we are detached from the feelings towards our kith and kin. At times even the cousins do not recognise one another, when they happen to be self-centered. Disputes in the family may lead to divisions. This may finally destroy the family psyche.
5. The joint family system provided a proper environment for the child to grow up. The value of respect, tolerance, responsibility, integrity, etc. were internalised in the child. In the long run, they became better human beings, compared to those in the present generation. Our forefathers felt happiest if their children became 'honest' human beings. But today we are happy only if we attain our coveted material ends. We are ready to resort to any means to attain that end. Our philosophy of life has turned out totally Machiavellian.
6. Our forefathers had a vision to make India the best. To attain their ambitions, they were ready to make all sorts of personal sacrifices. Their happiness lay in that of the millions of Indian brothers and sisters. On the other hand, today people are ready to migrate to the West, to enjoy a comfortable life. They run away from the evils of the Indian society without trying to remedy them. Often they become successful in foreign lands. But in the process, they become alienated from their motherland. The nostalgic feeling of their childhood and the relationship they left lingered on, which cannot make them happy. Distance from their ailing parents is a

worrying factor and keeps them perturbed. It is not easy for them to return, as their children will not be able to adjust to the Indian environment and the way of life. Thus, in our generation, tradition and modernity have intermingled to form our special system.

Based on your understanding of the passage, answer the following questions.

1. **What does the writer project with reference to the following?** **(1)**

   Our forefathers had a vision to make India the best.

2. **Complete the sentence appropriately.** **(1)**

   According to the writer, people are ready to migrate to the West because ....

3. **According to the passage, state two aspects which bring out the difference between lives of our forefathers and today's generation. Answer in about 40 words.** **(2)**

4. **Choose the option which suggests the following meaning. "We are jealous of the advancement of our neighbours".** **(1)**

   (a) Frog in the well (b) Crab in the barrel (c) Green with envy (d) Evil eye

5. **State whether the following statement is True or False.** **(1)**

   The intermingle of modernity and tradition is shown by the joint family system.

6. **What concept was our forefathers' life based upon?** **(1)**

   (a) Simple living and high thinking. (b) Satisfied with whatever they obtained after working hard.

   (c) Excessive material wealth did not mean much for them. (d) All of the above

7. **How does the joint family system make a child a good human being? Answer in about 40 words.** **(2)**

8. **The passage includes some words that are opposites of each other. Form the given sets, identify two sets of antonyms.** **(1)**

   (a) external and outer (b) joint and detach (c) lucky and fortunate (d) individual and personal

   (e) division and cohesion

2. Read the following passage carefully. **(10)**

1. The emergence of novel COVID-19 epidemic has been spreading in India which brought the sudden lockdown situation in the country. After government execution of lockdown with different stages, beings rapidly change their pattern of living. The affection of such controls affected entertainment with several entities. Many productions of entertainment programs get stopped that results the broadcast of new programs and several episodes has been stationary till the unlocked. To avoid the forfeiture in revenue, production houses used the concept of minimax programming that belongs to repeated telecast of running or evergreen programs. "Their current success may seem as an aberration at first glance. Doordarshan itself has replayed its old shows in the past too and these have always gone unnoticed," says Shailesh Kapoor, founder and CEO at Ormax Media. Meanwhile, the condition of movie theatre is much similar to other entertainment substances that have been closed and unable to perceive the entertainment.

2. Under such circumstances, web series enable to emphasis the audiences with its own concept of 'anywhere-anytime' where audience can watch and interact with programs with their convenience and of personal medium. Web series are developing a new breed for new content providers, who produce fresh content for digital audiences. Spreading the Internet access in rural and urban areas is much responsible for increasing of audience of web series in digital platform. Since, the revolution of 4G in India, OTT (Over-The-Top) platform such as Hotstar, Netflix, Amazon Prime video, ALTBalaji are delivering the content like web series, movies, TV serials, sports and news with different languages to the user (audience) with a boundless quality. A study revealed that 95% youth (age between 18 and 25) have admitted to watching web series in a metro city like Mumbai and approximately 81% audiences are watching in online manner by using OTT platform where in 42% of audiences watching web series on a daily basis, by using OTT high rate.

3. In a study, certain responses were collected on watching habits of web series between before and after lockdown. It was clear that approximately 15% of rise was seen in audiences during lockdown. Audiences showed their interest more towards web series. In the same study, another interpretation showed the meaning of free time to watch web series during lockdown. Before lockdown, 'all day' users of web series were quite low to approximately 4% but during lockdown, an increase of users approximately 36% was seen in category.

Based on your understanding of the passage, answer the following questions.

1. Select the chart that appropriately represents the trend in the audience of watching web series. **(1)**

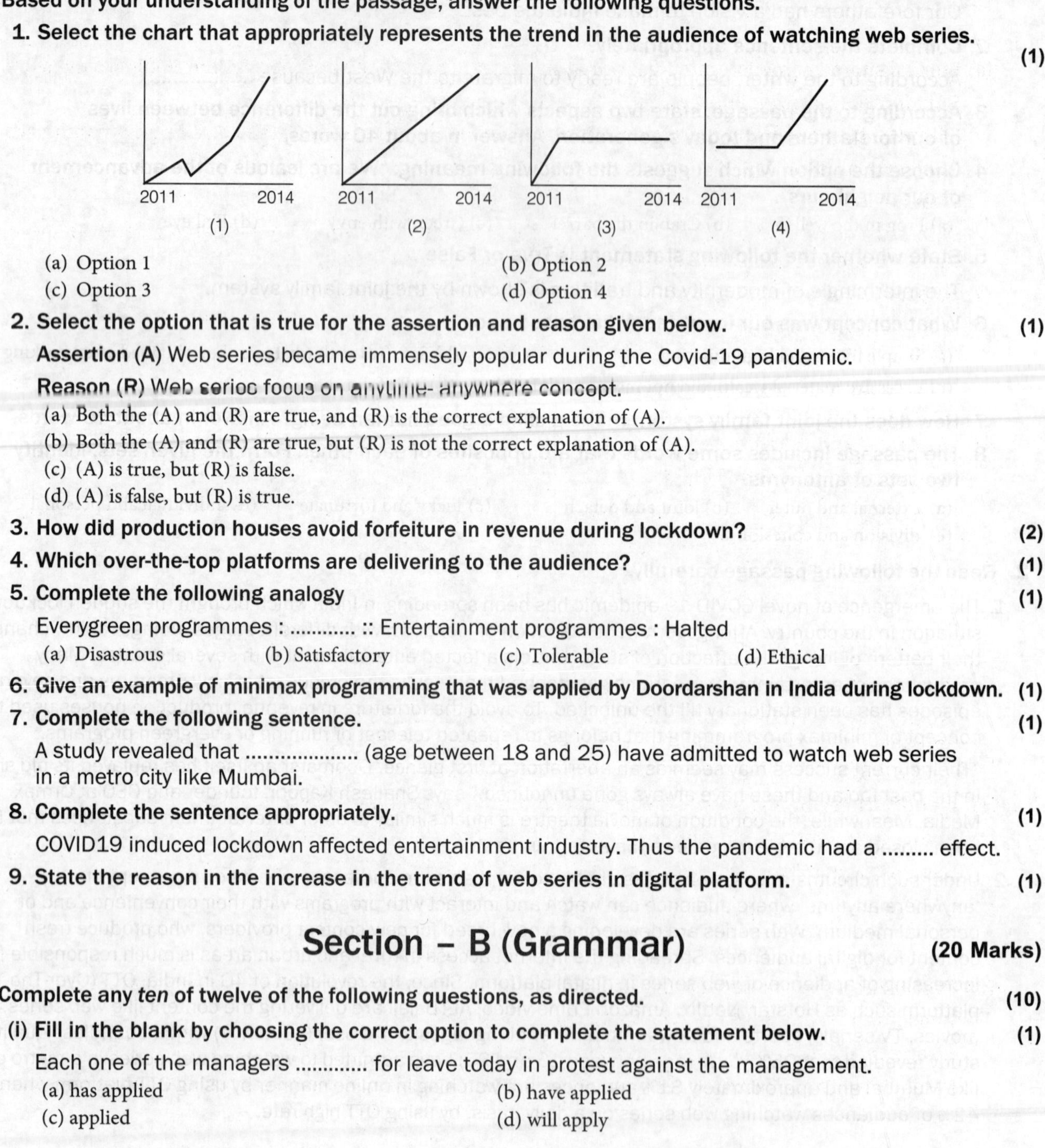

(a) Option 1
(b) Option 2
(c) Option 3
(d) Option 4

2. Select the option that is true for the assertion and reason given below. **(1)**

Assertion (A) Web series became immensely popular during the Covid-19 pandemic.

Reason (R) Web series focus on anytime- anywhere concept.

(a) Both the (A) and (R) are true, and (R) is the correct explanation of (A).
(b) Both the (A) and (R) are true, but (R) is not the correct explanation of (A).
(c) (A) is true, but (R) is false.
(d) (A) is false, but (R) is true.

3. How did production houses avoid forfeiture in revenue during lockdown? **(2)**

4. Which over-the-top platforms are delivering to the audience? **(1)**

5. Complete the following analogy **(1)**

Everygreen programmes : .... :: Entertainment programmes : Halted

(a) Disastrous (b) Satisfactory (c) Tolerable (d) Ethical

6. Give an example of minimax programming that was applied by Doordarshan in India during lockdown. **(1)**

7. Complete the following sentence. **(1)**

A study revealed that .... (age between 18 and 25) have admitted to watch web series in a metro city like Mumbai.

8. Complete the sentence appropriately. **(1)**

COVID19 induced lockdown affected entertainment industry. Thus the pandemic had a .... effect.

9. State the reason in the increase in the trend of web series in digital platform. **(1)**

Section – B (Grammar) (20 Marks)

3. Complete any *ten* of twelve of the following questions, as directed. **(10)**

(i) Fill in the blank by choosing the correct option to complete the statement below. **(1)**

Each one of the managers .... for leave today in protest against the management.

(a) has applied
(b) have applied
(c) applied
(d) will apply

(ii) Identify the error in the given sentence and supply the correction. **(1)**

The researchers stressed that the need of the hour is to increasing awareness among people to reduce ecological pollution.

Use the given format for your response.

Error	Correction

(iii) Sunidhi shared some information, with Amit, about the exam the next day. Report Sunidhi's question. **(1)**

Sunidhi said, "Do you know when the final term exam begins"?

(iv) Fill in the blank by using the correct form of the word in the bracket, for the given portion of the letter. **(1)**

Subject Complaint against open potholes

Dear Sir

With extreme trouble and pain I .... (beg) to draw your attention through this letter to the rampant open pot-holes in our locality; Shastri Nagar, New Delhi.

(v) Select the correct option to complete the narration of the dialogue. **(1)**

Manu Where are you going?

Annu I am going to the market. Do you want anything?

Manu asked Annu where she was going. Annu replied .... and further asked Manu whether she wanted anything.

(vi) Select the option that identifies the error and supplies the correction for the following line. **(1)**

My uncle and guardian want me to start my own business.

Option	Error	Correction
(a)	guardian	my guardian
(b)	want	wants
(c)	start	started
(d)	business	a business

(vii) Complete the given narrative by filling in the blank with the correct option. **(1)**

When I reached the station I did not stop at the ticket office but .... straight to the platform.

(a) dashed
(b) dash
(c) did dash
(d) dashing

(viii) Identify the error and supply the correction for the following. **(1)**

Anand said Renu that he didn't know what Gayathri was doing those days.

Use the given format for your response.

Error	Correction

(ix) Report the dialogue between the policeman and stranger by completing the sentence. **(1)**

Policeman "Who are you? Where do you come from?"

Stranger "I am a common man, lost in the crowds."

In response to the query about himself and his whereabouts, the stranger replied to the policeman that ....

(x) **Select the correct option to fill in the blank for the given line.** **(1)**

We .... only hope that everything turns out well.

(a) must (b) could (c) can (d) need

(xi) **Fill in the blank by choosing the correct option to complete the given statement.** **(1)**

Many .... admit doing so. For those who do, there was no need for guilt.

(a) will not (b) may not (c) shouldn't (d) shall not

(xii) **Report the dialogues to complete the paragraph that follows.** **(1)**

Himanshu The landlord has come. Take out the money you have set aside.

Himanshu told his wife that the landlord had come, she should take out ....

Creative Writing Skills **(10 Marks)**

Note : All details presented in the questions are imaginary and created for assessment purpose.

4. **Attempt any *one* from (A) and (B) given below.** **(5)**

A. Your friend has sent you a letter 2 weeks ago by registered post. It had some important documents in it. Till date you have not received the letter. Write a letter to the Post Master of your local post office explaining the situation. (100-120 words)

Or

B. Write a letter to the Station House Officer of your area explaining him/her the situation about the non-following of social distancing rules in the Gramin Seva mini-buses that are running in your area alerting him about the grave consequences to the passengers due to the ongoing COVID-19 pandemic. (100-120 words)

5. **Attempt any *one* from (A) and (B) given below.** **(5)**

A. Write a paragraph in 100-120 words based on the following clue.

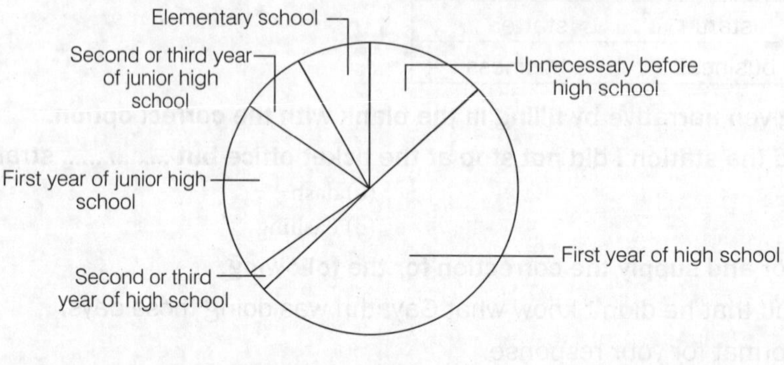

Or

B. The given graph shows the data collected regarding the sale of different kind of books to understand which category is popular amongst teenagers. Using this data, write an analytical paragraph in 100-120 words.

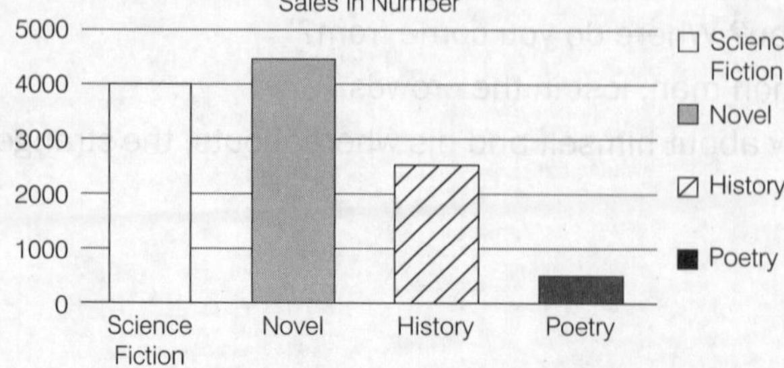

Section – C (Literature Textbook) (40 Marks)

6. Read the given extracts and answer the questions for any *one* of the given two, (A) or (B). (5)

A. Ausable did not fit any description of a secret agent Fowler had ever read. Following him down the musty corridor of the gloomy French hotel where Ausable had a room, Fowler felt let down. It was a small room, on the sixth and top floor, and scarcely a setting for a romantic adventure. Ausable was, for one thing, fat. Very fat. And then there was his accent. Though he spoke French and German passably, he had never altogether lost the American accent he had brought to Paris from Boston twenty years ago. "You are disappointed," Ausable said wheezily over his shoulder. "You were told that I was a secret agent, a spy, dealing in espionage and danger. You wished to meet me because you are a writer, young and romantic. You envisioned mysterious figures in the night, the crack of pistols, drugs in the wine." ?

(The Midnight Visitor)

(i) Which of these describes how Fowler felt at the beginning of the extract? (1)

(a) His heart sank (b) He was shaken up
(c) His stomach was in knots (d) He was at the end of his rope

(ii) State one observation about Ausable based on the way he handled Fowler's disappointment with him. (1)

(iii) How did the atmosphere of the French hotel influence Fowler's mood? Answer in 40 words. (2)

(iv) Fill in the blank appropriately. (1)

It was a small room, on the sixth and top floor, and scarcely a setting for a .... (exclting/ romantic) adventure.

Or

B. He just felt a bit dizzy. Then he flapped his wings once and he soared upwards. 'Ga, ga, ga, Ga, ga, ga, Gaw-col-ah,' his mother swooped past him, her wings making a loud noise. He answered her with another scream. Then, his father flew over him screaming. He saw his two brothers and his sister flying around him curveting and banking and soaring and diving. Then he completely forgot that he had not always been able to fly and commended himself to dive and soar and curve, shrieking shrilly.

(Two Stories about Flying)

(i) How would you describe the screams of the seagulls in the given extract? (1)

(ii) Why did the young sea gull feel dizzy? Answer in about 40 words. (2)

(iii) What does the line "he completely forgot that he had not always been able to fly" imply? (1)

(a) Great confidence the young sea gull had in his skills.
(b) Naturalness of the act of flying for the young sea gull.
(c) Satisfaction and joy of flying together as a family.
(d) Desire of the young sea gull to leave his fears behind.

(iv) Which literary device is used in the phrase 'shrieking shrilly'? (1)

7. Read the given extracts and answer the questions for any *one* of the given two, (A) or (B). (5)

A.

But if I had to perish twice,
I think I know enough of hate
To say that for destruction ice
Is also great
And would suffice.

(Fire and Ice)

(i) What does the poet preach in the extract through symbols 'fire and ice'? **(1)**

(ii) What is the poet's tone in the extract? **(1)**

(a) Appreciative (b) Celebratory (c) Sarcastic (d) Gloomy

(iii) Comment on the poet's use of imagery in these lines. **(2)**

(iv) Fill in the blanks appropriately.

The poet .... (supports/refutes) destruction by fire.

Or

B.

What is the boy now, who lost his ball,
What, what is he to do? I saw it go
Merrily bouncing, down the street and then
Merrily over – there it is in the water!

(The Ball Poem)

(i) What is the significance of the ball in the poem? **(1)**

(ii) Fill in the blank appropriately. **(1)**

The dash in the fourth lines of the stanza conveys ....

(iii) What happens to the boy who has lost the ball? What is the poet's reaction to the boy's state? Answer in about 40 words. **(2)**

(a) sudden interruption (b) familiarity (c) excitement (d) outburst of emotions

(iv) Identify and discuss the poet's use of metaphor in the poem 'The Ball Poem'. **(1)**

8. Answer any *four* of the following questions in 40-50 words each. **(4 × 3 = 12)**

(i) Comment on the relationship Anne had with her grandmother. (Anne Frame)

(ii) Describe the strange things that the pilot noticed about the 'Black Aeroplane'. (Two stories about Flying)

(iii) Describe Oxen Meadows. How were they a source of quarrel between Lomov's and Natalya's family? (The Proposal)

(iv) What did the Otter look like? (Mijbil the Otter)

(v) Why does the tiger express his rage quietly? (A Tiger in the Zoo)

9. Answer any *two* of the following questions in 40-50 words each. **(2 × 3 = 6)**

(i) What did the thief mean when he said "It is easy to rob a greedy man ..... but, it is difficult to rob a careless man ...."?

(ii) What would have happened to Matilda if she had confessed to her friend that she had lost her necklace?

(iii) Why does the landlord's wife think that Griffin was an 'eccentric scientist'?

10. Answer any *one* of the following question in 100-120 words each. **(1 × 6 = 6)**

A. "India is not a nation, nor a country. It is a subcontinent of nationalities." Comment with reference to your understanding of the stories given in 'Glimpses of India'.

Or

B. "Loss and suffering are eternal truths. One must accept it as a part of life". Reflect your views on this statement with reference to 'The Sermon at Benaras' and 'The Ball Poem'.

11. Answer any *one* of the following question in 100-120 words. **(1 × 6 = 6)**

A. "Where there is a will, there is a way." Elaborate in context of the story 'The Making of a Scientist'.

Or

B. Education means different things to different people. Evaluate how it impacted the young thief and Bholi. (Bholi)

Sample Question Paper 5 (Unsolved)

A Highly Simulated Sample Question Paper for CBSE Class X

English Language and Literature

Time : 3 hrs	M.M. : 80

General Instructions

1 This question paper comprises 11 questions, All questions are compulsory.

2 The question paper contains three sections

Section A : Reading Skills

Section B : Grammar and Creative Writing Skills

Section C : Literature

3 Attempt questions based on specific instructions for each part.

Section – A (Reading Skills) (20 Marks)

1. Read the following passage carefully. **(10)**

1. Parents are changing the plots of classic fairy tales when reading them aloud because of violence and political incorrectness. Traditional fables such as 'Little Red Riding Hood', 'The Ginger Bread Man' and 'The Three Little Pigs' were deemed the worst offenders, with parents linking some of their endings to horror films.
2. The poll which was commissioned by Music Magpie included 2000 parents and revealed that one in four took creative liberties when sharing fairytales with their children to suit their beliefs and ideologies. Meanwhile, another 16% confessed to banning them altogether.
3. While these classic tales might seem playful and innocent on the surface, a closer look at the plot, lines and characters reveals some problematic traits. For example, in 'Little Red Riding Hood', 'The child is eaten alive by a wolf, only to be saved by a hunter who cuts her out of the animal's stomach with an axe'. 'The Three Little Pigs' also reaches a rather gory conclusion with the pigs murdering a wolf and eating it. Lest we forget 'The Ginger Bread Man', whose protagonist is also eaten by a fox. It is an ending that's hard for parents to swallow, with one of them labelling it as 'too cruel' in the survey.
4. However, a deeper analysis of some of the nation's most popular tales unveiled even further issues with regard to political correctness. One in four parents found it inappropriate that 'Cindrella has to do all of the cleanings in her home while another 25% argued that 'sleeping beauty' poses a consent issue, given that prince charming kisses the princess while she is asleep. Meanwhile, 27% believe that 'Pinocchio' encourages children to tell lies while one in four claims that 'The Ugly Duckling' in which an abused duckling is only accepted by society after he has grown into a swan, advocates body shaming.
5. Some of these stories have been around for generations. 'But times have changed and there are elements to these classics which for some don't really fit into society as they once did. We all agree that stories play a vital role in the growth and development of children. The books they read and the characters they get to know can become like friends. Reading stories also helps children with their confidence levels, coping with emotions and language learning.
6. So stories are a great way to learn in a natural way as there is no teaching involved in it. The learners learn from simply reading the story. The choice of stories must be judicious.

Based on your understanding of the passage, answer the following questions.

1. **According to the passage, what is the problem with the classics?** **(2)**
2. **Complete the sentence appropriately.** **(1)**
   An appropriate reason that makes a tale not worth story-telling is ....
3. **What does the writer project with reference to the following?** **(1)**
   The choice of stories must be judicious (Paragraph 6)
4. **From the sets below, identify two sets of synonyms.** **(1)**
   (a) Violence and assault (b) Unvieled and vieled (c) Charming and repellent (d) Analysis and examination
   (e) Inappropriate and appropriate
5. **State whether the following statement is True or False.** **(1)**
   A closer look at the plot, lines and characters reveals some problematic traits.' Mention any two examples to support the statement.
6. **According to the writer, what kind of 'liberty' are the parents taking?** **(1)**
   (a) To change the characters (b) To change the story to suit their ideology
   (c) To ignore many parts of the story (d) To understand the story through different themes
7. **What kind of liberties are modern-day parents taking?** **(2)**
8. **Select the option that corresponds to the following relation.** **(1)**
   While these classic tales might seem playful and innocent on the surface, a closer look at the plot, lines and characters reveal some problematic traits.
   (a) Junk food may seem to be more palatable and energy-giving for a brief moment, but is unhealthy for the body in the long run.
   (b) Books that are not bound well will lose paper eventually.
   (c) We all must take care of our health lest we may fall ill.
   (d) Listening to music is not only therapeutic but also changes one's mood.

2. Read the following passage carefully. **(10)**

1. The automobile industry in India is the world's fourth-largest. India was the world's fourth-largest manufacturer of cars and the seventh-largest manufacturer of commercial vehicles in 2019. The Indian automotive industry (including component manufacturing) is expected to reach 16.16-18.18 trillion (US $ 251.4-282.8 billion) by 2026. The industry attracted Foreign Direct Investment (FDI) worth US $ 24.21 billion from April 2000 to March 2020 according to the data released by the Department for Promotion of Industry and Internal Trade (DPIIT).
2. Two-wheelers and passenger vehicles dominate the domestic Indian auto market. Passenger car sales are dominated by small and mid-sized cars. Two-wheelers and passenger cars accounted for 80.8 per cent and 12.9 per cent market share, respectively, accounting for a combined sale of over 21.55 million vehicles in FY20. The CAGR during FYI 6-FY20 is 1.29 per cent.
3. The government aims to develop India as global manufacturing and Research and Development (R and D) hub. It has set-up National Automotive Testing and R and D Infrastructure Project (NATRiP) centres as well as National Automotive Board to act as a facilitator between the government and the industry. Under (NATRiP), five testing and research centres have been established in the country since 2015. NATRiPs proposal for "Grant-In-Aid for test facility infrastructure for Electric Vehicle (EV) performance certification from NATRiP Implementation Society" under FAME (Faster Adoption and Manufacturing of (Hybrid) and Electric Vehicles in India) scheme was approved by Project Implementation and Sanctioning Committee (PISC) on 3rd January, 2019.
4. The Indian Government has also set-up an ambitious target of having only EVs sold in the country. The Ministry of Heavy Industries, Government of India, has shortlisted 11 cities in the country for the introduction of EVs in their public transport system under the FAME scheme. The first phase of the scheme was extended to March 2019 while in February 2019, the government approved the FAME II scheme with a fund requirement of ₹ 10,000 crore (US $ 1.39 billion) for FY20-22. Under Union Budget 2019-20, government announced providing an additional income tax deduction of Z 1.5 lakh (US $ 2146) on the interest paid on the loans taken to purchase EVs.

5. EV sales, excluding e-rickshaws, in India witnessed a growth of 20 per cent and reached 1.56 lakh units in FY20 driven by two-wheelers. The Government of India expects the automobile sector to attract US $ 8-10 billion in local and foreign investment by 2023.

Based on your understanding of the passage, answer the following questions.

1. **Based on your understanding of the passage, choose the option that lists the initiatives taken by the government to promote the automobile industry.** **(1)**
   (a) Established NATRiP and a NAB.
   (b) Set up 6 testing and research centres.
   (c) Introduction of EVs in their private transport.
   (d) Increase in tax on loans for EVs.
2. **Select the option that is true for the assertion and reason given below.** **(1)**
   Assertion (A) EVs are growing exponentially in India.
   Reason (R) The Indian government has launched the FAME mission to support EVs.
   (a) Both the (A) and (R) are true, and (R) is the correct explanation of (A).
   (b) Both the (A) and (R) are true, but (R) is not the correct explanation of (A).
   (c) (A) is true, but (R) is false.
   (d) (A) is false, but (R) is true.
3. **What does the Indian Government want to establish?** **(1)**
4. **What was the NATRiP's proposal?** **(1)**
5. **Complete the following sentence.** **(1)**
   Para 4 focuses on the ambitious target of having ....
6. **What does the Department for Promotion of Industry and Internal Trade highlight?** **(1)**
7. **Complete the following analogy.** **(1)**
   FAME Scheme : .... :: Fourth Largest automobile industry of the world : India
8. **Select the appropriate option to fill in the blanks.** **(1)**
   We can infer that the Department for .... of Industry and Internal Trade highlights that India has received a considerable amount from ....
9. **Which field does the government of India want to grow?.** **(2)**

Section – B (Grammar) **(20 Marks)**

3. Complete any *ten* of twelve of the following questions, as directed. **(10)**

(i) Fill in the blank by choosing the correct option to complete the given statement. **(1)**

She told me that she .... English fluently and was very happy.

(a) could speak (b) could have spoken (c) can speak (d) will speak

(ii) Identify the error in the given sentence and supply the correction. **(1)**

Shilpa Can I borrow your English textbook?

Use the given format for your response.

Error	Correction

(iii) I shared some information, with Jasmine, about my father. Report Jasmine's question. **(1)**

"Does your father always come home late?"

(iv) **Fill in the blank by using the correct form of the word in the bracket to complete the sentence.** **(1)**

They .... (live) in an apartment right now because they can't find a cheap house.

(v) **Complete the narration of the dialogue.** **(1)**

Jenny I haven't brought it because I had gone to my uncle's house with my parents, so I forgot to keep it.

Susan asked Jenny .... Jenny said that she hadn't brought it as she had gone to her uncle's house with her parents so she had forgotten to keep it.

(vi) **Select the option that identifies the error and supplies the correction for the following line. According to tradition, Gautama Buddha sat in meditation in the Bodhi tree in Bodhgaya.** **(1)**

Option	Error	Correction
A	sat	sit
B	tradition	traditions
C	in	under
D	In	At

(vii) **I want to buy a soft drink. Can you lend me .... Euro?** **(1)**

(a) an (b) the (c) any (d) a

(viii) **Identify the error in the given sentence and supply the correction.** **(1)**

Buying a life insurance policy help to ensure your children have some security.

Use the given format for your response.

Error	Correction

(ix) **Report the dialogue between Sanjay and Madan to complete the sentence.** **(1)**

Sanjay I am surprised to see you here in Delhi. When did you come?

Madan I came here yesterday. I have been offered a job here.

Sanjay told Madan that he was surprised to see him there in Delhi and asked when he had come. Madan replied that he had come there the previous day and added that ....

(x) **Complete the given narrative by filling in the blank with the correct option.** **(1)**

No one even noticed when I got home. The .... the big game on TV.

(a) had all been watching (b) have all watched (c) had all watched (d) were all watching

(xi) **Fill in the blank by using the correct form of the word in the bracket, for the given portion of the letter.** **(1)**

Subject Repair of the road in Cheran Nagar

Dear Sir

I would like to bring to your notice that the people in and around Cheran Nagar .... difficulties in travelling back and forth because of the bad condition of the roads there.

(a) facing (b) face (c) face (d) will face

(xii) **Report the dialogues to complete the paragraph given below.** **(1)**

Customer Why is the meal so sour?

Waiter Nobody has complained for five days sir, about the meal.

One day a customer was taking dinner in a hotel. He asked the waiter why the meal was so sour. The waiter told him ....

Creative Writing Skills **(10 Marks)**

Note : All details presented in the questions are imaginary and created for assessment purpose.

4. Attempt any *one* from (A) and (B) given below. (5)

A. You are studying for a qualification and you would like some time off from your work to complete it. Write a letter to your manager explaining your situation. You are Ambika. (100-120 words)

Or

B. You recently went shopping at the local supermarket. When you got home and noticed your bill, you found that you had been charged for items you did not purchase. Write a letter to the supermarket manager explaining what has happened. Tell the manager how you feel about the error and what you would like him/her to do about it. (100-120 words)

5. Attempt any *one* from (A) and (B) given below. (5)

A. Given below is a graph illustrating behaviour of people while streaming shows on various sites such as Netflix, Amazon Prime, etc. Write an analytical paragraph on the binging habits of people in about 100-120 words.

Or

B. The following bar chart shows the different modes of transport used to travel to and from work in one city in 1980, 2010 and 2018.Using the given data, write analytical paragraph in 100-120 words.

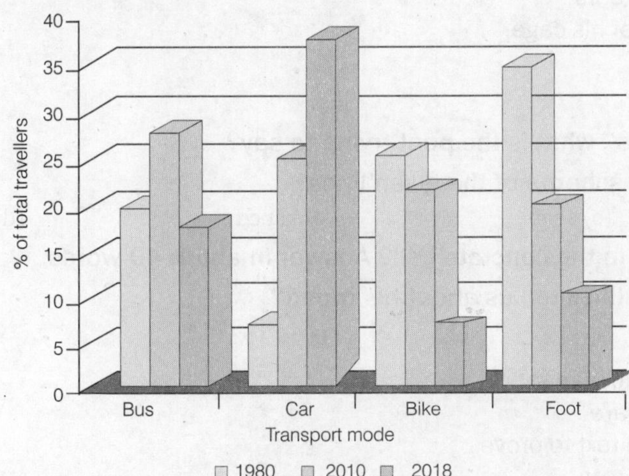

Section – C (Literature Textbook) (40 Marks)

6. Read the given extracts and answer the questions for any *one* of the given two, (A) or (B). **(5)**

A. On the day of the inauguration, I was overwhelmed with a sense of history. In the first decade of the twentieth century, a few years after the bitter Anglo-Boer war and before my own birth, the white skinned peoples of South Africa patched up their differences and erected a system of racial domination against the dark-skinned peoples of their own land. The structure they created formed the basis of one of the harshest, most inhumane, societies the world has ever known.

(Nelson Mandela: Long Walk to Freedom)

(i) The tone of the information about apartheid can be called **(1)**

(a) angry (b) gloomy (c) factual (d) nostalgic

(ii) Why did the speaker call that structure 'one of the harshest and the most inhumane'? Answer in about 40 words. **(2)**

(iii) Which phrase would correctly substitute 'pre-eminence'? **(1)**

(iv) Fill in the blank appropriately. **(1)**

The inauguration was a celebration of South Africa's .... (first autocratic government/democracy).

Or

B. He waited a moment in surprise, wondering why she did not come nearer and then, maddened by hunger, he dived at the fish. With a loud scream he fell outwards and downwards into space. Then a monstrous terror seized him and his heart stood still. He could hear nothing. But it only lasted a minute. The next moment he felt his wings spread outwards.

(Two Stories about Flying)

(i) How had the Seagull been feeling in the given extract? **(1)**

(ii) Why did his mother stop midway while giving him the fish? **(2)**

(iii) Which one of the following best describes the tone of the given extract? **(1)**

(a) Persuasive (b) Nostalgic (c) Terrified (d) Cautionary

(iv) What does The phrase 'his wings spread outwards' means? **(1)**

7. Read the given extracts and answer the questions for any *one* of the given two, (A) or (B). **(5)**

A. But he's locked in a concrete cell,
His strength behind bars,
Stalking the length of his cage,
Ignoring visitors.

(A Tiger in the Zoo)

(i) By 'ignoring visitors', what is the poet trying to say? **(1)**

(ii) What is the rhyme scheme of the given lines? **(1)**

(a) aabb (b) abab (c) abcd (d) abcc

(iii) Why is 'he' locked in the concrete cell? Answer in about 40 words. **(2)**

(iv) What do the given lines tell us about his mood? **(1)**

Or

B. "I heard an old religious man
But yesternight declare
That he had found a text to prove
That only God, my dear,
Could love you for yourself alone
And not your yellow hair."

(For Anne Gregory)

(i) The above stanza strongly defines an idea. What idea is it? **(1)**

(ii) Complete the sentence appropriately.

The above stanza strongly defines the idea of .... **(1)**

(a) beauty (b) religion (c) physicality (d) enmity

(iii) Comment on the poet's use of language in these lines. **(2)**

(iv) Where did the religious man find that God loves everyone selflessly? **(1)**

8. Answer any *four* of the following questions in 40-50 words each. **(4 × 3 = 12)**

(i) Why was the writer happy when he decided to fly in the night? (The Black Aeroplane)

(ii) How do you usually understand the idea of 'selfishness'? Do you agree that Kisa Gotami was being 'Selfish in her grief'? (The Sermon of Benares)

(iii) What is the underlying message for us in our hectic life with reference to the poem? (Dust of Snow)

(iv) Why is baking called a profitable profession? (A Baker from Goa)

(v) What guesses did the Londoners make about what Mij was? (Mijbil the Otter)

9. Answer any *two* of the following questions in 40-50 words each. **(2 × 3 = 6)**

(i) Hari Singh did not catch the train deliberately while he could catch it easily. Why?

(ii) Why Bholi didn't want to go to school? How did her fear disappear after she had gone to school?

(iii) What was the achievement that Richard Ebright managed at the age of twenty two?

10. Answer any *one* of the following question in 100-120 words. **(1 × 6 = 6)**

A. "Diary of A Young Girl" in some parts throws light on teacher-student relationship, class atmosphere and discipline. Discuss with reference to the story 'From the Dairy of Anne Frank'.

Or

B. 'The Black Aeroplane' and Poem 'Fog' both can be called mysterious. Do you agree? Give reasons for your answer.

11. Answer any *one* of the following question in 100-120 words. **(1 × 6 = 6)**

A. Bholi's real name is Sulekha. We are told this right at the beginning. But only in the last one paragraph of the story Bholi is called Sulekha again. Why do you think she is called Sulekha at the last point in the story?

Or

B. Curiosity and motivation are the basic foundation for becoming a successful scientist. In addition to it what are the other values required in becoming a successful scientist. What do you learn from the character of Richard? Elaborate with reference to the lesson 'The Making of a Scientist'.